1947	1948	1949	1950	1951	1952	1953	1954	1955	1956	1957	1958	1959	1960	1961
$165.4	$178.3	$181.2	$195.0	$209.8	$219.8	$232.6	$238.0	$257.0	$270.0	$284.8	$293.0	$313.5	$328.5	$339.0
31.5	43.1	33.0	50.0	56.3	49.9	50.0	48.9	63.8	64.4	66.6	54.9	72.7	72.4	69.6
28.4	34.5	40.2	39.0	60.5	76.0	82.8	75.3	75.6	79.0	86.2	92.6	97.2	99.7	108.7
9.0	3.5	3.8	.6	2.4	1.3	−.4	.9	1.1	2.9	4.9	1.2	-0.8	2.9	4.0
234.3	259.4	258.1	284.6	327.0	347.0	365.4	363.1	397.5	419.2	442.5	441.7	482.7	503.4	521.3
13.0	15.5	17.3	19.1	22.0	24.0	26.5	28.8	32.0	34.4	36.9	37.9	41.0	43.2	45.2
221.3	244.0	240.8	265.5	307.0	323.0	338.9	334.3	365.5	384.8	405.6	403.8	441.7	460.2	476.1
23.1	20.5	24.1	23.6	27.7	30.8	33.3	32.5	35.3	34.0	39.1	37.7	41.2	44.7	45.9
198.2	223.5	216.7	241.9	279.3	292.2	305.6	301.8	330.2	350.8	366.5	366.1	400.5	415.5	430.2
5.7	5.2	5.7	6.9	8.2	8.6	8.7	9.9	10.0	12.6	14.6	15.1	17.6	20.6	21.8
11.3	12.5	10.4	17.9	22.4	19.5	20.2	17.2	21.8	21.2	21.1	18.2	23.2	22.4	22.8
5.8	11.0	10.4	8.6	9.5	9.3	7.9	6.7	10.1	8.6	8.2	6.1	10.8	8.6	8.8
16.2	15.8	17.0	19.9	17.5	18.2	10.4	21.6	22.9	24.5	27.9	32.3	35.0	36.9	39.9
191.6	210.4	208.3	228.5	256.7	273.1	288.3	289.8	310.2	332.9	350.6	359.0	383.9	400.8	416.7
21.5	21.1	18.6	20.8	29.2	34.4	35.8	32.9	35.8	40.0	42.7	42.5	46.8	51.4	51.8
170.1	189.3	189.7	207.7	227.5	238.7	252.5	256.9	274.4	292.9	307.9	316.5	337.1	349.4	364.9
165.4	178.3	181.2	195.0	209.8	219.8	332.6	238.0	256.9	269.9	284.8	293.0	313.5	328.5	339.0
4.7	11.0	8.5	12.6	17.7	18.9	19.8	18.9	17.5	23.0	23.0	23.5	23.6	20.9	25.9
282.3	293.1	292.7	318.1	341.8	353.5	369.0	363.1	392.7	400.9	408.6	401.3	428.6	440.2	447.9

SOURCES: **Survey of Current Business, Federal Reserve Bulletin, Economic Report of the President, Economic Indicators.**

1947	1948	1949	1950	1951	1952	1953	1954	1955	1956	1957	1958	1959	1960	1961
95.5	102.8	101.8	102.8	111.0	113.5	114.4	114.8	114.5	116.2	120.2	123.5	124.6	126.5	127.8
100	104	97	112	120	124	134	125	139	143	143	134	159	164	165
113.6	111.6	111.2	117.7	124.5	129.0	130.6	134.5	138.2	139.7	138.6	144.1	144.9	143.8	148.5
2.3	2.3	3.7	3.4	2.1	1.9	1.9	3.6	2.9	2.8	2.9	4.7	3.8	3.9	4.8
3.9	3.8	5.9	5.3	3.3	3.1	2.9	5.6	4.4	4.2	4.3	6.8	5.5	5.6	6.7
11.6	14.4	17.3	21.4	22.6	27.5	31.4	32.5	38.8	42.3	44.8	45.0	51.3	55.8	56.9

1947	1948	1949	1950	1951	1952	1953	1954	1955	1956	1957	1958	1959	1960	1961

ECONOMICS: PRINCIPLES, PROBLEMS, AND POLICIES

CAMPBELL R. McCONNELL

Professor of Economics, University of Nebraska

McGRAW-HILL BOOK COMPANY, INC.

ECONOMICS: PRINCIPLES, PROBLEMS, AND POLICIES

Second Edition

NEW YORK ● SAN FRANCISCO ● TORONTO ● LONDON

TO MARILYN

ECONOMICS: PRINCIPLES, PROBLEMS, AND POLICIES

Library of Congress Catalog Card Number: 62–21115

II

44856

PREFACE

This revision of *Economics* is prompted by the gracious and widespread reception accorded the first edition and by the numerous changes in the economic milieu which have occurred in the last three years.

The purpose of this book is to introduce the beginning economics student to the principles essential to an understanding of fundamental economic problems and the policy alternatives society may utilize to contend with these problems. It is hoped that the ability to reason accurately and objectively about economic matters and the development of a lasting interest in economics will be two valuable by-products of this basic objective.

The present revision is substantial in terms of subject matter and presentation. In particular, two new chapters have been added: Chapter 19 on the problems and policies associated with American economic growth and Chapter 36 on the crucial social imbalance controversy. Several other chapters, for example, Chapters 7 and 35, have been substantially reduced in length. Rewriting for greater clarity and for the growing importance of new concepts, institutions, and trends has been extensive.

In terms of content I feel this text embraces a number of departures in content and organization which distinguish it from other books in the field.

1. The principles course usually fails to provide students with a comprehensive and meaningful definition of economics. To remedy this shortcoming one complete chapter (Chapter 2) is devoted to a careful statement and development of the economizing problem and an exploration of its implications. The foundation thereby provided should be helpful in putting the many particular subject areas of economics into proper perspective.

2. There is a rather apparent intellectual lag among economists in their discussions of the economic functions of government. Government is an integral and increasingly important component of modern capitalism. Its economic role, therefore, should not be treated piecemeal or as an afterthought. This text attempts to overcome these difficulties by introducing the economic functions of government early and according them systematic treatment in philosophical (Chapter 6), factual (Chapter 9), and controversial (Chapter 36) terms. A special effort is made to explode a number of popular myths which surround the operation of government in the economic sphere.

3. This volume puts considerable emphasis upon the crucial topic of economic growth.

Chapter 18 develops a conceptual framework for analyzing economic growth and applies this framework in explaining the growth record of the American economy. Chapter 19 deals with a number of problems associated with the growth of our economy and suggests appropriate policies. Chapter 39 employs the conceptual framework of Chapter 18 in treating the obstacles to economic growth that plague the underdeveloped countries. An important segment of Chapter 40 concerns the growth record of Soviet Russia's controlled economy. Beyond this it will be found that the chapters on price theory pay special attention to the implications that the various market structures have for technological progress.

4. It is understandable that the elusiveness of general equilibrium analysis eminently qualifies this topic for omission at the principles level. The result, however, is a grievous shortcoming of most introductory courses. A sincere effort is made in this book to remedy this deficiency. Specifically, an entire chapter (Chapter 5) is devoted to the notion of the price system, and the nature and significance of general equilibrium analysis is explicitly outlined (Chapter 31).

5. This volume forgoes the presentation of necessarily sketchy descriptions of a number of alternative economic systems in favor of a detailed discussion of the Soviet economy and the challenge it poses for the "free world." I feel this emphasis upon the Soviet system is more vital, more timely, and decidedly more interesting to students.

6. I have purposely given considerable attention to microeconomics in general and to the theory of the firm in particular. There are several reasons for this emphasis. In the first place, the concepts of microeconomics are difficult for most beginning students. Short expositions usually compound these difficulties by raising more questions than they answer. Second, a majority of economists now agree that we possess the fiscal and monetary tools necessary for the maintenance of full employment. This tends to shift the economic spotlight back to the question of resource allocation and ultimately to the operation of the price system. Finally, I have coupled analysis of the various

market structures with a discussion of the social implications of each. The impact of each market arrangement upon price and output levels, resource allocation, and the rate of technological advance is carefully assessed.

7. Chapter 31 is rather unique, I believe, in that it provides a concise statement of both the accomplishments and the shortcomings of American capitalism.

8. Another differentiating feature of this text is the treatment of the social imbalance question in Chapter 36. The objective here is to offer a balanced treatment of what may be the most important domestic economic issue of our times.

9. In the over-all selection of topics, considerable care has been exercised to include only those which have significant bearing upon the twin problems of full employment and allocative efficiency.

In terms of organization, this book has been written with the conviction that the basic prerequisite of an understandable economics text is the logical arrangement and clear exposition of subject matter. This concern with organization is most evident in Part 1, which centers upon the step-by-step development of a comprehensive and realistic picture of American capitalism. This coherent group of introductory chapters is substituted for the traditional smattering of more-or-less unrelated background topics that ordinarily introduce the student to the study of economics.

Throughout this volume the exposition of each particular topic and concept is directly related to the level of difficulty which in my experience the average student is likely to encounter. It is for this reason that national income accounting, microeconomics, and to a lesser degree, employment theory are purposely accorded comprehensive and careful treatments. Simplicity in these instances is correlated with comprehensiveness, not brevity. Furthermore, my experience suggests that in the treatment of each basic topic—employment theory, money and banking, international economics, and so forth—it is highly desirable to couple analysis and policy. A three-step development of basic analytical tools is employed: (1) verbal description and illustration, (2) numerical examples, and (3) graphic presentation based upon these numerical illustrations.

The material is organized around seven basic topics: (1) an introduction to American capitalism; (2) national income, employment, and fiscal policy; (3) money and monetary policy; (4) American economic growth; (5) economics of the firm and resource allocation; (6) current domestic economic problems; and (7) international economics, the underdeveloped countries, and the Soviet economic challenge.

Part 1 is designed to introduce the method and subject matter of economics and to develop the ideological framework and the factual characteristics of American capitalism. This group of chapters develops in an orderly fashion the overall picture of how our economy operates. After an introduction to the methodology of economics in Chapter 1, an entire chapter is devoted to defining and explaining the economizing problem. Chapters 3 to 5 develop the capitalistic ideology and the notion of the most fundamental institution of capitalism—the price system. Early emphasis upon the price system is designed to provide the necessary orientation for the detailed treatment of pricing found in Part 5 and to contribute to an understanding of the national income analysis of Part 2 and, more specifically, the topics of inflation and deflation. Chapter 6 introduces government as a basic economic component of modern capitalism; government's economic functions are systematically explained and evaluated. Upon this superstructure of a mixed public-private economy Chapters 7 to 9 add the factual information concerning the household, business, and government aggregates of the economy, thereby making our mixed capitalism model much more realistic.

Part 2 treats national income analysis and fiscal policy. Chapter 10 on national income accounting reflects my conviction that this difficult topic merits detailed treatment. Chapter 11 employs the national income measures in describing the last four decades of American business cycle experience. This I feel is an important undertaking for college sophomores who, fortunately, have grown up amidst the virtually unabated prosperity of the last twenty years. The next three chapters are devoted to neo-Keynesian employment theory and fiscal policy.

Part 3 emphasizes the balance sheet approach to money and banking. This approach seems most in accord with the goal of providing the student with an analytical tool needed in reasoning through, as opposed to memorizing, the economic impact of the various basic banking transactions. Just as fiscal policy is linked directly to income theory in Part 2, monetary policy immediately follows the discussion of money and banking. The first half of the book is completed with Part 4 on American economic growth and problems related thereto.

For reasons already noted the treatment of pricing and resource allocation in Part 5 is purposely detailed. Throughout Chapters 24 to 27 emphasis is placed upon the social implications of the various market structures. What is the significance of each market structure for price and output levels, resource allocation, and technological progress? Emphasis in the discussion of distribution—Chapters 28 to 30—is generally in accord with the relative quantitative importance of the various market shares in our economy. I have not belabored the analysis of interest, rent, and profits where, it seems to me, economic analysis leaves much to be desired. Chapter 31 provides a very simple verbal discussion of general equilibrium and a summary evaluation of the operation of American capitalism.

Part 6 deals with the domestic economic problems of monopoly, the farm problem, labor relations and collective bargaining, the economics of inequality and insecurity, and social balance. In each of these chapters an attempt has been made to (1) describe the historical and factual background of the problem, (2) analyze its causes and effects, (3) explore government policy, and (4) offer a thought-provoking discussion of public policy alternatives.

The first two chapters of Part 7 survey international trade and finance. Chapter 39 explores the very crucial problems surrounding the efforts of the underdeveloped countries to achieve economic growth. Finally, Chapter 40 offers a relatively comprehensive discussion of the Soviet economy, its accomplishments, and the economic challenge it poses for the West.

End-of-chapter summaries provide a concise, pointed recapitulation of each chapter. Much thought has gone into the end-of-chapter questions. Though purposely intermixed, these questions are of three general types. Some are designed to highlight the main points of each chapter. Others are "open-end" discussion or thought questions. Wherever pertinent, numerical problems which require the student to derive and manipulate key concepts and relationships are employed. Numerical problems are stressed in those chapters dealing with national income accounting and analysis, money and banking, and price theory. The bibliographical references at the end of each chapter are designed to provide both breadth and depth for the ambitious student. Yet care has been taken to see that these references are not beyond the grasp of the average college sophomore. Students will find the *Study Guide to accompany McConnell: Economics* by Prof. Robert C. Bingham an invaluable supplement to the text.

This second edition of *Economics* is accompanied by a book of supplementary materials, *Economic Issues: Readings and Cases* which Professor Bingham and I have prepared. We are sufficiently immodest to feel that it embodies some distinctive features which make it a highly usable supplement for this or any other standard principles of economics textbook.

Though economics instructors are in general agreement as to the basic content of a principles of economics course, there are considerable differences of opinion as to what particular arrangement of material is best. The structure of this book is designed to provide considerable organizational flexibility. And I am happy to report that a number of users of the first edition have informed me that they accomplished substantial rearrangements of chapters with little sacrifice of continuity. Though I have chosen to move from macro- to microeconomics, there is no reason why the introductory material of Part 1 cannot be followed immediately by the microanalysis of Part 5. Similarly, in my judgment money and banking can best be taught after, rather than before, national income analysis. Those who disagree will encounter no problems by preceding Chapter 10 with Chapters 15, 16, and 17. Furthermore, some instructors will prefer to intersperse the microeconomics of Part 5 with the problems chapters of Part 6. This is easily accomplished. Chapter 33 on the farm problem may follow Chapter 24 on pure competition; Chapter 32 on monopoly may follow Chapters 25 to 27 on imperfect competition. Chapter 34 on labor unions and collective bargaining may either precede or follow Chapter 29 on wages, and Chapter 35 on income inequality may follow Chapters 29 and 30 on the distributive shares of national income.

Finally, those interested in the one-semester course will be able to discern several possible groups of chapters that will be appropriate to such a course. The one-semester course which emphasizes macroeconomics will obviously center upon those chapters contained in Parts 1, 2, 3, and 4. The one-semester course stressing microeconomics will embody Parts 1, 5, and 6. A tentative outline for a one-semester course introducing both macro- and microeconomics is provided.

This endeavor has benefited greatly from the advice and counsel of many teachers and students. Let me first restate my debt to the reviewers of the original manuscript: L. S. Van Scoyoc of Bowling Green State University, John Auten of Rice Institute, J. J. Kaufman of Pennsylvania State University, Raymond W. Ritland of Auburn University, and Howell E. Jones of Bethany College. I owe a special debt to Prof. Arthur M. Okun of Yale University who contributed much to both the content and organization of this text. Also, I have unashamedly exploited the brainpower of a number of present and former University of Nebraska colleagues: Robert C. Bingham, Wallace C. Peterson, Clemens B. Thoman, and Harry M. Trebing. Many users of the first edition were kind enough to offer me their counsel and criticism: in particular I must mention Professors Clayton Hall and Fred Picard of Ohio University, David G. Brown of the University of North Carolina, and Carl Stern of Randolph-Macon. As tradition demands, I accept sole responsibility for all errors of omission and commission.

Campbell R. McConnell

CONTENTS

Part 1. An Introduction to American Capitalism

Chapter 1

THE NATURE AND METHOD OF ECONOMICS

Why study economics?
How should we go about it?   Descriptive economics   Economic theory   Policy economics
Pitfalls to straight thinking   Terminology   Bias and preconceptions   Fallacy of composition   Prosperity and depression   Cause and effect   Effect of expectations   Intentions versus realizations   Logical explanations and social practice   Economic quackery.

Chapter 2

AN INTRODUCTION TO THE ECONOMIZING PROBLEM

The foundation of economics   Unlimited wants   Scarce resources
Economics defined   Full employment and full production   Production possibilities table   Production possibilities curve   Law of increasing costs
Some modifications   Unemployment and underemployment   A growing economy
Economizing: Five Fundamental Questions   What is to be produced   Organizing production   Distributing output   Level of resource use   Flexibility
The "isms"

Chapter 3

PURE CAPITALISM AND THE CIRCULAR FLOW OF WEALTH

Capitalist ideology   Private property   Freedom of enterprise and choice   Role of self-interest   Competition   Markets and prices   Limited government
Other characteristics   Extensive use of capital goods   Specialization   Use of money
Circular flow of wealth   Circular flow model of the economy   Limitations of the circular flow model

Government spending and private investment   Pressure groups and inflation
Cost-push inflation   Long-run deficits
The public debt   Growth and ownership of the public debt   Public versus private
debt   War finance and the public debt   Quantitative importance of the public debt
Problems posed by a large public debt   Advantages of a public debt

Part 3. Money, Monetary Policy, and Economic Stability

Chapter 15

The functions of money
Money in American capitalism   Coins   Paper money   Demand deposits
Near-monies and bank and Treasury holdings
What "backs" the money supply?
Institutional framework of the American banking system   Need for centralization
Structure of the Federal Reserve System   Functions of the Federal Reserve System

Chapter 16

The balance sheet of a commercial bank
A single commercial bank in a banking system   Formation of a commercial bank
Money-creating transactions of a commercial bank   Profits and liquidity
A monopoly bank
The commercial banking system as a whole   The banking system's lending potential
Some modifications

Chapter 17

Objective of monetary policy
Consolidated balance sheet of the Federal Reserve banks   Assets   Liabilities
Mechanisms of monetary policy   General, quantitative controls   Selective, qualitative
controls and moral suasion   Techniques of monetary control and their relative
effectiveness
Combining fiscal and monetary policies   Treasury expenditures   Treasury tax receipts
Deficit financing and the money supply   Retiring public debt and the money supply
Treasury gold purchases and sales   Treasury purchases of gold   Treasury sales of
gold
Fiscal policy, gold transactions, and monetary policy
How effective is monetary policy?   The case for monetary policy   The case against
monetary policy

Price and output determination   Monopoly demand and administered prices   Cost data   Equating marginal revenue and marginal cost   Misconceptions concerning monopoly pricing   Possible restraints upon profit maximization
Economic effects   Price, output, and resource allocation   Income distribution Technological advance

Wages in particular labor markets Competitive model   Monopsony model   Some
union models   Bilateral monopoly model   Do unions raise real wages?
Wage differentials Noncompeting groups   Equalizing differences   Market
imperfections
Effect of wage changes on employment Single firm or industry   Economy as a whole

Chapter 30

Chapter 31

Part 6. Current Domestic Economic Problems

Chapter 32

Chapter 33

International disequilibrium
Restoring international equilibrium   Freely flexible exchange rates   The gold
standard   Exchange controls

Chapter 38

Chapter 39

Chapter 40

SUGGESTED OUTLINE FOR A ONE-SEMESTER COURSE

PART 1

AN INTRODUCTION TO AMERICAN CAPITALISM

Chapter 1

THE NATURE AND METHOD
OF ECONOMICS

MAN, UNFORTUNATE CREATURE, is plagued with wants. He wants, among other things, love, social recognition, and the material necessities and comforts of life. Man's striving to improve his material well-being, to "make a living," is the concern of economics. More specifically, economics is the study of man's behavior in producing, exchanging, and consuming the material goods and services he wants. Most of us think of economics in terms of specific problems—balancing the household budget, labor disputes, farm surpluses, taxes, debt, inflation, unemployment. Although limited, this thinking is not incorrect. These specific problems are fragments or signs of the larger problem of man's attempt to satisfy his material wants.

It is tempting to seek out immediately answers and solutions to specific problems of current interest. But this would be precipitate; certain preliminary matters must be discussed first. In particular, we must know the answers to these questions: (1) *Why* should we study economics? (2) *How* should we study economics—what are the proper procedures? (3) What specific problems, limitations, and pitfalls might we encounter in studying economics? These topics will occupy our attention in this introductory chapter.

WHY STUDY ECONOMICS?

The answer to this question is threefold: (1) There is the matter of seeking knowledge for the sake of knowledge. We live in a complex physical and social environment—we ought to be curious about the nature of it. Economics helps us to comprehend that environment. (2) A basic understanding of economics is essential if we are to be well-informed citizens. Many of the specific problems of the day have important economic aspects, and we, in a democracy, who comprise that society make the ultimate decisions in meeting those problems. Intelligence at the polls therefore requires that we have a working knowledge of economics. (3) Economics is of practical value in business. An understanding of the over-all operation of the economic system puts the businessman in a better position to formulate his policies. For example, if he understands the causes and consequences of inflation, he is better equipped during inflationary periods to make intelligent decisions concerning his enterprise than he might be otherwise. Indeed, more and more economists are appearing on the payrolls of large corporations. Their job? To gather and interpret economic information upon which rational business decisions can be made.

3

This last reason for studying economics must be interpreted with care. Economics is an academic, not a vocational, subject. Unlike accounting, advertising, corporation finance, and salesmanship, economics is not a how-to-make-money area of study.[1] A knowledge of economics may be helpful in running a business, but this is not its primary objective. In economics, problems are examined from the social, not from the individual, point of view. The production, exchange, and consumption of goods and services are discussed from the viewpoint of society as a whole, not from the standpoint of one businessman's bankbook. Thus economics will prove of little direct value in helping us to sell used cars or insurance.

HOW SHOULD WE GO ABOUT IT?

What do economists do? What are their goals? What procedures do they employ? The title of this volume—*Economics: Principles, Problems, and Policies*—contains a thumbnail answer to the first two questions. Economists are concerned with the derivation of economic *principles* which are useful in the formulation of *policies* designed to solve economic *problems*. The procedure employed by the economist is that summarized in Figure 1-1. The economist must first ascertain and gather the facts which are relevant to consideration of a specific economic problem. This aspect of his job is sometimes called "descriptive economics." The economist then puts his collection of facts in order and summarizes them by "distilling out" a principle, that is, by generalizing about the way individuals and institutions actually behave. Deriving principles from facts is called "economic theory," or "economic analysis." Finally, the general knowledge of economic behavior which economic principles provide can then be used in formulating policies, that is, remedies or solutions, for correcting or avoiding the problem under scrutiny. This final aspect of the field is sometimes called "applied economics" or "policy economics."

[1] An economist has been defined as an individual with a Phi Beta Kappa key on one end of his watch chain and with no watch on the other.

Still using Figure 1-1 as a point of reference, let us now examine this three-step procedure in more detail.

Descriptive economics

All sciences are empirical. All sciences are based upon facts, that is, upon observable and verifiable behavior of certain data or subject matter. In the physical sciences the factual data are inorganic. As a social science, economics is concerned with the behavior of individuals and institutions engaged in the production, exchange, and consumption of goods and services.

The first major step, then, in investigating a given problem or a specific segment of the economy is to gather the facts. This can be an infinitely complex task. The world of reality is cluttered with a myriad of interrelated facts. The economist therefore must use discretion in fact gathering. He must distinguish economic from noneconomic facts and then determine which economic facts are relevant and which are irrelevant for the specific problem under consideration. But even when this sorting process has been completed, the relevant economic facts may appear diverse and unrelated.

Economic theory

A conglomeration of facts is relatively useless; mere description is not enough. To be meaningful, facts must be systematically arranged, interpreted, and generalized upon. This is the task of economic theory or analysis. Principles and theories—the end result of economic analysis—bring order and meaning to a number of facts by tying these facts together, putting them in correct relationship to one another, and generalizing upon them. "Theories without facts may be barren, but facts without theories are meaningless."[2]

The interplay between the levels of fact and theory is more complex than Figure 1-1 indi-

[2] Kenneth E. Boulding, *Economic Analysis*, 3d ed. (New York: Harper & Row, Publishers, 1955), p. 5.

cates. Principles and theories are meaningful statements drawn from facts, but facts, in turn, serve as a constant check on the validity of principles already established. Facts—how individuals and institutions actually behave in producing, exchanging, and consuming goods and services—change with time. Consumers and business firms do not behave in exactly the same way every year. This makes it essential that economists continuously check existing principles and theories against the changing economic environment. The history of economic ideas is strewn with once-valid generalizations about economic behavior which were rendered obsolete by the changing course of events. For example, principles which were meaningful and accurate in the embryonic capitalism which sprang forth in England some two centuries ago may be completely outmoded in terms of the environment of modern American capitalism.

Terminology. A word on terminology is essential at this juncture. Economists talk about "laws," "principles," "theories," and "models." These terms all mean essentially the same thing: generalizations, or statements of regularity, concerning the economic behavior of individuals and institutions. The term "economic law" is a bit misleading because it implies a high degree of exactness, universal application, and even moral rightness. So to a lesser degree does the term "principle." And some people incorrectly associate the term "theory" with idle pipe dreams and ivory-tower hallucinations, divorced from the facts and realities of the world. The term "model" has much to commend it. A model is a simplified picture of reality, an abstract generalization of how the relevant data actually behave. In this book these four terms will be used synonymously. The choice of terms in labeling any particular generalization will be governed by custom or convenience here. Hence, the relationship between the price of a product and the quantity consumers purchase will be called the "law" of demand, rather than the theory or principle of demand, because it is customary to so designate it.

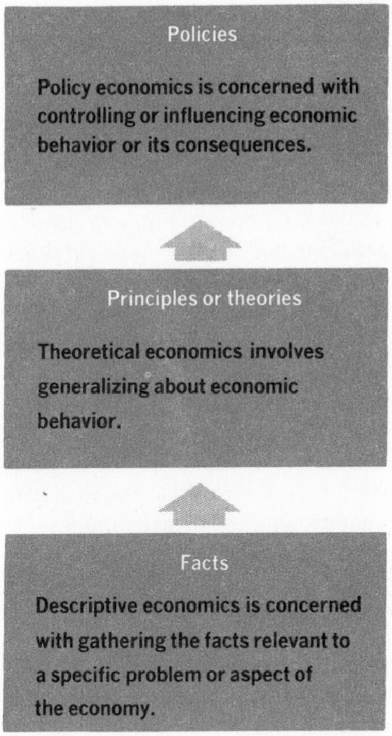

Policies

Policy economics is concerned with controlling or influencing economic behavior or its consequences.

Principles or theories

Theoretical economics involves generalizing about economic behavior.

Facts

Descriptive economics is concerned with gathering the facts relevant to a specific problem or aspect of the economy.

FIGURE 1-1. THE RELATIONSHIP BETWEEN FACTS, PRINCIPLES, AND POLICIES IN ECONOMICS.
In studying any problem or segment of the economy the economist must first gather the relevant facts. These facts must then be systematically arranged, interpreted, and generalized upon. These generalizations are useful, not only in explaining economic behavior but also in predicting and therefore controlling future events.

These comments on terminology raise two points which merit further consideration: first, economic principles (laws, theories, or models) are *generalizations,* and second, they are *abstractions.*

Generalizations. Economic principles are generalizations and, as such, subject to exceptions and to quantitatively imprecise statement. Economic facts are usually diverse; some individuals and institutions act one way and some another. Hence, economic principles are frequently stated in terms of averages or statistical probabilities. For example, when economists say that the average household earns an income of $5,720 per year, they are making a generalization. It is recognized that some households earn much more and a good many others much less. Yet this generalization, properly handled and interpreted, can be very meaningful and useful. Or an economist may conclude that 95 per cent of the time—95 chances out of 100—consumers will increase their purchases of a product when its price falls. Five per cent of the consumers constitute an exception to the general rule.

The main reason for the inexactness of economic principles is the fact that the economist cannot conduct controlled experiments—he does not have a laboratory in which he can create simplified and controlled conditions. The laboratory of the social sciences is the real world, where the specific aspects of human behavior we wish to examine cannot be readily isolated from the social and cultural milieu. The chemist can "make other things equal" in his controlled experiments; the economist cannot.

Unable to make other things equal in their analysis, economists do the next best thing: they *assume* other things are equal in isolating certain data for analysis. To illustrate: in analyzing the relationship between the price of product X and the amount of X purchased, economists assume that of all the factors influencing the amount of X purchased, only its price varies. To cut the problem down to size, they must assume that all other factors which might influence the amount of X purchased are unchanged or "equal." In this way economists can isolate the relationship between price and quantity demanded from all sorts of real-world complications. However, in applying the resulting generalization—consumers buy more of X at a low price than they do at a high price—to a real-world situation, exceptions may be encountered. Why? Because other things are not often equal in the real world. For example, an increase in incomes—another consideration which, in addition to a price change, will

cause the amount of X purchased to alter—may complicate the application of the general conclusion about the relationship between the price of X and the amount of X purchased. The economist may find that, although the price of X has risen, the quantity demanded has *increased* contrary to his generalization. This does not mean that the generalization is invalid, but rather that peculiar circumstances—higher incomes—have entered this particular application of the principle to upset its accuracy. This is merely an exception to the rule, and in economics such exceptions may be rather frequent. Economics is admittedly an inexact science.

Abstractions. Economic principles, or theories, are necessarily abstractions. They do not have the full bloom of reality. The very process of sorting out noneconomic and irrelevant facts in the fact-gathering process involves abstracting from reality. Unfortunately, the abstractness of economic theory prompts the uninformed to identify theory as something which is impractical and unrealistic. This is nonsense! As a matter of fact, economic theories are practical for the simple reason that they are abstractions. The level of reality is too complex to be very meaningful. Economists theorize in order to give meaning to a maze of facts which would otherwise be confusing and useless and to put facts into a more usable, practical form. Thus to generalize is to abstract; generalization for this purpose is practical, and therefore so is abstraction. An economic theory is a model—a simplified picture or map—of some segment of the economy. This enables us to better understand reality because it avoids the details of reality. Finally, theories—*good* theories—are grounded on facts and therefore are realistic. Theories which do not fit the facts are simply not good theories.

Graphic expression. Theories, or models, can be expressed in many ways. For example, the physicist and chemist illustrate their theories by building Tinker-Toy arrangements of multicolored wooden balls that represent protons, neutrons, and so forth, held in proper relationship to one another by wires or sticks. Economists are not so lucky as to have theories that lend themselves to such tangible demonstrations. Economic models must take the form of verbal description, numerical tables, simple equations, or graphs. The last are particularly helpful and will be used with some frequency throughout this book. Most of the principles we shall encounter will explain the relationship between just two sets of economic facts, for example, the relationship between the price of a specific product and the quantity of it which consumers buy. Simple two-dimensional graphs are a convenient and clear way of summarizing and manipulating these relationships.

As shown in Figure 1-2, graphs are drawn on squared paper divided into four quarters, or quadrants, by a horizontal axis and a vertical axis which intersect at right angles. The point of intersection is called the *origin*. Each axis has a scale of numerical values. On the vertical axis all values above the origin are positive, and all values below are negative. On the horizontal axis, values to the right of the origin are positive; those to the left are negative. The point of intersection, that is, the origin, designates zero. Though the vertical and horizontal scales in Figure 1-2 measure the same numerical values, this need not be the case. Each unit on the vertical axis may measure $1, while the same distance on the horizontal axis denotes 1,000 bushels of corn.

In elementary economics we are virtually always concerned with the relationship be-

FIGURE 1-2. ECONOMIC PRINCIPLES CAN BE EXPRESSED GRAPHICALLY.
Two-dimensional graphs are a convenient way of presenting and manipulating relationships between data. The relationship between two sets of economic data whose numerical values are positive is shown in the upper right quadrant of the chart.

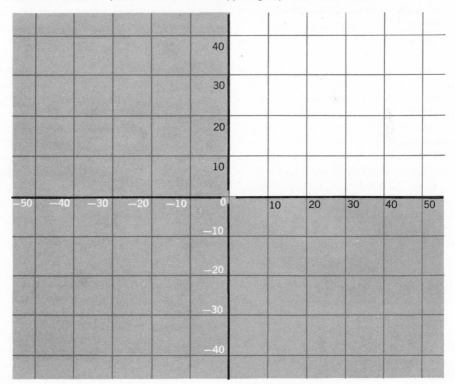

tween two sets of economic facts whose values are positive. Hence, we are concerned with the upper right-hand quarter of the chart where both scales measure positive values.

Now let us explore an example or two to illustrate the construction and interpretation of graphs. Suppose detailed factual investigation reveals that the relationship between the price of corn per bushel and the amount farmers are willing to produce and offer for sale per year is as shown in Table 1-1.

How can this be shown graphically? Simply by putting the two sets of facts—product price and quantity supplied—on the two axes of the chart and locating the five price-quantity-supplied combinations shown in Table 1-1. Convention or convenience dictates which set of facts goes on the vertical axis and which on the horizontal axis. By convention, economists put "price" on the vertical and "quantity" on the horizontal axis as indicated in Figure 1-3. The five price-quantity combinations are plotted on the chart by drawing perpendiculars from the appropriate points on the two axes. For example, in plotting the $5–12,000-bushel combination, perpendiculars must be drawn across from the vertical (price) axis at $5 and up from the horizontal (quantity-supplied) axis at 12,000 bushels. Their point of intersection locates the $5–12,000-bushel combination on the graph. The same procedure locates the other four price-quantity combinations. If it is assumed that the same general relationship between price and quantity supplied will prevail at all points between the five graphed, a line or curve

can be drawn to connect these points. In this instance the two sets of data are *directly related;* that is, price and quantity supplied move in the same direction. As price increases, the quantity supplied increases. As price declines, so does the quantity supplied. When two sets of data are directly related, they will always graph as an upsloping line or curve such as SS in Figure 1-3.

Now suppose that fact gathering reveals that the price of corn and the quantity which consumers will buy per year are related in the manner shown in Table 1-2. These data indicate that consumers will demand more corn when its price is low than they will when the price is high; that is, price and quantity are *inversely related.* If price increases, the amount purchased will decline. If price declines, the quantity purchased will increase. An inverse relationship will always graph as a downsloping line, or curve, such as *DD* in Figure 1-4.

Dangers of models. When properly constructed and interpreted, economic models are invaluable tools. But we must be aware of certain potential dangers in deriving and applying these models.

1. The fundamental danger in constructing an economic model or principle is that the economist might fail to distinguish correctly between relevant and irrelevant facts. If the economist "boils out" some relevant facts, the resulting principle may be a disjointed, misleading, and, at best, incomplete analytical tool. A related difficulty stems from the possibility that an overzealous economist might

TABLE 1-1. THE QUANTITIES OF CORN FARMERS WILL SUPPLY AT VARIOUS PRICES

Price per bushel	Bushels of corn supplied at this price
$5	12,000
4	10,000
3	7,000
2	4,000
1	1,000

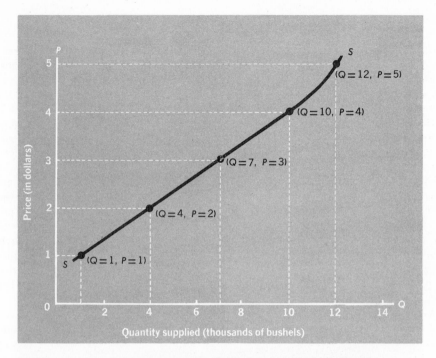

FIGURE 1-3. RELATIONSHIP BETWEEN PRICE AND QUANTITY SUPPLIED.
Two sets of economic data which are directly related, such as price and quantity
supplied, graph as an upsloping curve (SS).

abstract from too many facts and construct a
model which is hyperabstract and truly out of
touch with reality.

2. In applying economic models, we must
always recognize them for what they are—
useful first approximations. It is easy, but dangerous, to slip into the practice of becoming

so enthusiastic about logical clarity that we
forget such models are simply rough outlines of
reality. There may be many omissions between
a simplified economic model and reality.

3. We must be on guard in applying economic models so as not to impute any ethical or
moral qualities to them. Economic models are

**TABLE 1-2. THE QUANTITIES OF CORN CONSUMERS WILL
PURCHASE AT VARIOUS PRICES**

Price per bushel	Bushels of corn demanded at this price
$5	2,000
4	4,000
3	7,000
2	11,000
1	16,000

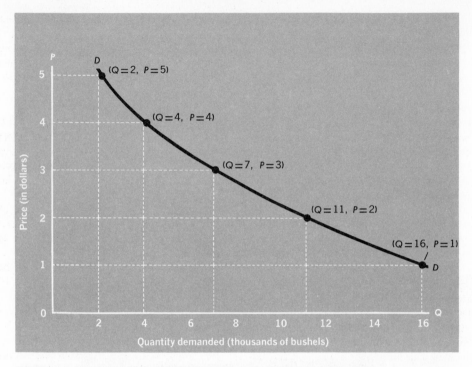

FIGURE 1-4. RELATIONSHIP BETWEEN PRICE AND QUANTITY DEMANDED.
Two sets of economic data which are inversely related, such as price and quantity
demanded, graph as a downsloping curve (*DD*).

the analytical tools of the economist, and, as such, they are ethically neutral. Because they are constructed of facts, economic models afford general statements about "what is," not indications of what "ought to be." Figure 1-3 does not tell us that farmers *should* supply more corn at higher prices than at lower prices, but rather that they *actually do*. Economic models are not tin gods to be worshiped as an end in themselves, or as a compendium of ethically desirable results. Instead, they should be recognized for what they are—a means to an end, a summary of factual data.

Policy economics

Of what value are economic principles? The answer is twofold. There is first the matter of explanation for explanation's sake—economic principles help to explain to us why certain events occur the way they do. Through economic principles we can comprehend why prices change, how surpluses and shortages of products arise, what causes depression and unemployment, and so forth. Our curiosity concerning these and similar phenomena can be satisfied through the development of economic principles to serve as tools for the understanding of reality.

Apart from pure explanation, economic principles can also be extremely valuable as predictive devices, and prediction is the prerequisite of control. If an undesirable event can be predicted by the application of an economic principle, then that event can be influenced or controlled.

If we cannot control an event, we gain from prediction invaluable time to prepare for adjusting to its consequences. Ability to predict a rainstorm does not give us control over the weather, but it does permit us to prepare for it by carrying a raincoat and umbrella.

Values. It is evident that value judgments —opinions as to what is desirable or undesirable—come into the picture at this juncture. Descriptive economics and economic theory are both concerned with facts; the former immediately and the latter once removed. Policy economics necessarily entails value judgments as to the desirability of certain events. When operating at this level, economists are no longer functioning as scientists, but rather as policy makers. They are dealing not only with facts, but also with values.

An example or two will help at this point. Our previously noted principle of consumer behavior is the basis for one illustration: "Consumers generally buy more of a product at a low price than they do at a high price." Suppose a clothing merchant finds that he is greatly overstocked with summer clothing at a time when shipments of fall and winter clothing are due. The merchant has the problem of ridding himself of his undesired surplus stock of summer wear. Our principle of consumer behavior helps the merchant to solve this problem by predicting for him how consumers will react to price changes. In particular, the principle predicts that the merchant will be able to increase his sales and "move" the surplus by lowering prices. The merchant, formulating his price policies accordingly, "runs a sale." The surplus disappears.

A second example, of greater consequence to the economy as a whole, involves the fundamental principle that, within certain limits, there is a direct relationship between total spending and the level of employment in the economy. "If total spending increases (decreases), then the volume of employment will rise (fall)." This principle can be invaluable to government in determining its economic policies. For example, if government economists note that available statistics indicate an actual slackening of total expenditures, the principle will permit them to predict the undesirable consequence of unemployment. Aware of this anticipated result, public officials are now in a position to set in motion certain government policies designed to bolster total spending and head off expected unemployment. In short, we must be able to predict in order to strengthen control. Economic principles help make prediction possible.

Economic goals of American capitalism. It is important at this point that we note and reflect upon a number of economic goals or values which are widely, though not universally, accepted in our society. These goals may be briefly listed as follows:

1. Economic growth. The production of more and better goods and services, or more simply stated, a higher standard of living, is desired.

2. Full employment. Suitable jobs should be available for all who are willing and able to work.

3. Price stability. Sizable upswings or downswings in the general price level, that is, inflation and deflation, should be avoided.

4. Economic freedom. Businessman, workers, and consumers should enjoy a high degree of freedom in their economic activities.

5. An equitable distribution of income. No groups of citizens should face stark poverty while others wallow in luxury.

6. Economic security. Provision should be made for those who are chronically ill, disabled, handicapped, aged, or otherwise dependent.

Now this list of widely accepted goals provides the basis for several significant points. First, note that this or any other statement of basic economic goals inevitably entails problems of interpretation. What are "sizable" changes in the price level? What is a "high degree" of economic freedom? What is an "equitable" distribution of income? While most of us might accept the above goals as generally stated, we might also disagree very substantially as to their specific meanings and hence as to the types of policies needed to attain these goals. It is noteworthy that, although goals 1 to 3 are subject to reasonably accurate measurement, the inability to quantify goals 4 to 6 undoubtedly contributes to any controversy over their specific meaning.

Second, certain of these goals are complementary in that to the extent one goal is achieved, some other goal or goals will also tend to be realized. For example, the achieving of full employment (goal 2) obviously means the elimination of unemployment, a basic cause of low incomes (goal 5) and economic insecurity (goal 6). Furthermore, considering goals 1 and 5, it is generally agreed that the sociopolitical tensions which may accompany a highly unequal distribution of income are tempered to the extent that all incomes are rising absolutely as a result of economic growth.

Third, some goals may be conflicting or mutually exclusive. Currently a number of highly regarded economists argue that those forces which further the attainment of economic growth and full employment may be the very same forces which cause inflation. That is, to some degree goals 1 and 2 may conflict with goal 3. Other economists are reluctantly concluding that to some extent economic growth and full employment (goals 1 and 2) may conflict with economic freedom (goal 4). It is felt that the expanding role of government which rapid growth and continuous full employment require will inevitably impinge upon the free choices of businessmen, workers, and consumers.

This leads us to a fourth point: when basic goals do conflict, society is forced to develop a system of priorities for the objectives it seeks. To illustrate: if full employment and price stability are to some extent mutually exclusive, that is, full employment entails some inflation and price stability entails some unemployment, society must decide upon the relative importance of these two goals. Suppose the relevant choice is between, say, a 3 per cent annual increase in the price level accompanied by full employment on the one hand, and a perfectly stable price level with 5 per cent of the labor force unemployed on the other. Which is the better choice? Or how about a compromise goal in the form of, say, a 1 per cent increase in the price level each year with 3 per cent of the labor force out of work? There is obviously ample room for disagreement here.

There would admittedly be disagreement among individuals in our society as to the priorities to be assigned these six goals or, for that matter, as to whether this is a "correct" list in the first place. Now, finally, we must keep in mind that other societies can, and do, have substantially different goals. Soviet society—or perhaps more accurately the Soviet state—puts relatively greater emphasis upon goals 1 and 2 and, our experts tell us, do a better job of achieving these goals than we do (Chapter 40). A good part of the explanation of the success of the Soviet Union in achieving rapid growth and full employment is that they attach a much lower priority than we do to other goals. In particular, Soviet disregard for economic freedom allows the use of policies for achieving full employment and rapid growth which would be completely unacceptable in our society. In short, other societies assign different weights or priorities to various goals, and these differing priorities may permit these other societies to do a better job in achieving certain of these objectives.

Formulating economic policy. It is one thing to talk of broad economic goals. It is quite another to create policies designed to achieve these goals. Let us look briefly at some of the essential steps involved in the formulation of economic policy; the problems which policy formulation involves will become evident.

The first step in policy formulation is to make a clear statement of objectives or goals. This is essential if we want our policy recommendations to be something more than a shot in the dark. Next, we must state all alternative solutions to the problem at hand and, in so far as possible, analyze their probable effects on the economy. This entails clear-cut recognition of the political feasibility, the economic impact, and the costs (economic and otherwise) which various solutions or programs might entail. In practice, this problem is frequently one of determining the proper blend of several more or less distinct programs, each of which makes some definite contribution toward resolving the problem under consideration. Finally, we would be shirking our obligations to future generations if we did not look back on our experiences with a given program after applying it. Were the results other than our understanding of the economy led us to antic-ipate? If so, how and why did the program go astray? To see more clearly what is involved, let us apply these three steps to solving the problem of unemployment.

1. We must define our objective. Exactly what do we have in mind when we go about the task of setting up a program designed to give us "full employment"? Do we mean that unem-ployment is zero; that is, that everyone be-tween, say, eighteen and sixty-five years of age has a job? Or do we mean that everyone who *wants* to work has a job? Should we allow for some "normal" unemployment caused by peo-ple voluntarily changing jobs or by the "decay-ing" of certain industries? Are there any related objectives, such as price stability, which should be given high priority along with the basic ob-jective of full employment? If so, we are then faced with the additional problem of assigning priorities to these two objectives, which we have seen may be conflicting. What is the most desirable balance between the goals of full em-ployment and price stability?

2. We must formulate a program for achiev-ing our objective. Having determined what our objective is—for example, "near full employ-ment with relatively stable prices" [3]—we must tackle the knotty problem of formulating and analyzing possible alternative programs to at-tain this goal. Fortunately, knowledge from past experience—frequently gained through the cumbersome and painful process of trial and error—gives the policy maker a starting point. In this instance, experience and eco-nomic analysis have taught us that certain governmental taxation and expenditure policies have apparently helped to alleviate or prevent unemployment; appropriate management of the economy's money supply through the exer-cise of certain governmental controls over the banking system has also helped. On the other hand, some other countries have put great reliance on more direct governmental control of the operation of the economy.

The questions then are these: What are the relative merits and demerits of the various

alternative programs which might be invoked? What specific policy, or combination of poli-cies, is most appropriate in light of the given unemployment situation which we assume the economy faces? These queries imply that, to come up with an acceptable solution, we must somehow judge, mostly on the basis of past ex-perience, the advantages and costs of the vari-ous programs. What about the political feasibility of each? Direct and detailed governmental controls—for example, government manipula-tion of wages and prices—*may* do the job. But the chances of political enactment of controls may be nil. What of the rapidity with which the various programs can be put into effect? How long must we wait for results? What of the economic and human costs involved? Spe-cifically, are we sacrificing economic progress or freedom of choice in achieving full employ-ment? All these questions are of basic impor-tance in formulating "the best" policy.

3. We must record and appraise the per-formance of alternative economic policies when applied to specific historical situations. If we are currently witnessing a siege of unemploy-ment and have encountered it in the past, there is reason to believe that we may face a similar problem in the future. Common sense tells us to keep an accurate record of the rela-tive effectiveness, the costs, the shortcomings, and the problems of application entailed by the use of each policy. Current policies can be im-proved upon for future application only when we have an accurate understanding of their relative merits and shortcomings. Usually even "the best" economic policies leave room for improvement. Furthermore, caution is required at this point: in a dynamic economy such as ours, reasoning by historical analogy may have limited value or even be dangerous. The past is of limited use as a guide to the future.

Restated, the three points of emphasis in policy formulation are: (1) Differences in social and economic objectives can enter into the process of creating economic policy at many different points, thereby making the task of actually creating policy an exceedingly difficult one. (2) There is frequently no single remedy for a given economic problem. Choosing be-

---

[3] In order to be realistic, basic policy objectives are frequently stated in such a qualified form.

tween alternative policy measures is a basic job facing the economist as a policy maker. (3) The improvement of economic policy demands after-the-fact evaluation of applied policies.

To these points, a final reminder might be added: Because our economy is a dynamic, changing organism, one must not expect clear-cut, once-and-for-all answers to basic economic problems, but rather short-run adjustments which may rapidly become obsolete. Policy making is a never-ending task. What is correct policy today may be rendered inappropriate tomorrow by a rapidly changing economic environment.

PITFALLS TO STRAIGHT THINKING

Our discussion of the economist's procedure has, up to this point, skirted some of the problems and pitfalls frequently encountered in deriving and applying economic principles. Some of these difficulties—for example, problems of terminology and bias—are almost self-evident. Indeed, they are so obvious that we tend to overlook them, which makes explicit comment imperative. Other difficulties, particularly those which take the form of logical pitfalls, are rather complex and most conducive to faulty economic reasoning.

Terminology

It is extremely important in studying any science to understand its terminology, but this is particularly so in the social sciences. There are three specific reasons why a clear, objective grasp of relevant terms will prove to be half the battle in understanding many aspects of economics:

1. The economic terminology to which we are exposed in newspapers and popular magazines is sometimes emotionally loaded. The writer—or more frequently the particular interest group he represents—may have a cause to further or an ax to grind, and his terms will be slanted to solicit the support of the reader. Hence, we may find a governmental irrigation project in the Great Plains region called "creeping socialism" by its opponents and "intelligent

democratic planning" by its proponents. We must be prepared, therefore, to discount such terminology in achieving objectivity in the understanding of important economic issues.

2. It is embarrassing to admit that economists are often guilty of dual terminology— the unfortunate practice of using two or more labels to designate the same thing. In part, this is a matter of historical accident. It is also the result of economic inquirers discovering that two different theories or explanations are actually the same. The dual labels persist after the theories have been merged. For example, the terms "economic resources," "productive services," and "factors of production" have identical meanings. Similarly, in probing the causes of depression, we hear some authorities laying the blame at the door of "underconsumption," while others cite "oversaving" as the villain. The beginner who is not familiar with the definitions of these terms may envision a basic conflict of views. Actually, "oversaving" and "underconsumption," properly defined, refer essentially to the same phenomena.

3. It is important to keep in mind that no scientist is obligated to use common-sense or man-in-the-street definitions of his terms. He may find it convenient and essential to define his terms in such a way that they are clearly at odds with the definitions held by laymen in everyday speech. So long as the economist is explicit and consistent in his definitions, he is on safe ground. A couple of examples may be of value. The term "investment" to John Q. Citizen is associated with the buying of bonds and stocks in the securities market. How often have we heard someone talking of investing in General Motors stock or government bonds? But to the economist, "investment" means the purchase of real capital assets such as machinery and equipment, or the construction of a new wing on a factory building, not the purely financial transaction of swapping cash or part of a bank balance for a neatly engraved piece of paper. As a matter of fact, we shall discover in Chapter 10 that what the layman calls "investment" is a swapping of assets or a form of saving, as the economist sees it. Again, in Chapter 15, our definition of "money" is likely

to be at odds with typical, man-in-the-street interpretations. Other examples will present themselves as we go along.

Bias and preconceptions

The beginning student in chemistry or physics traditionally knows little or nothing about the subject matter of these fields at the outset. He starts from scratch with a blank, but supposedly clear, mind. Not so in the social sciences in general or in economics in particular. For a variety of reasons the budding economist ordinarily launches into his field of study with a bundle of preconceptions about the operation of our economy and its component parts. Such issues as the farm problem, the public debt, the legitimate functions of labor unions, big business versus competition, the nature and operation of our tax system, and the like are everyday topics of conversation. Unless we live in a void, most of us have some *preconceived notions* on these issues. Unfortunately, all too often these preconceptions are flatly wrong or, at best, partially true; in other cases they are hopelessly biased. Thus as neophyte economists—in contrast to physicists or chemists—we start at a disadvantage in our search for truth, and our task in learning economics is doubled: we must recognize and "unlearn" misguided preconceptions, and we must supplant these inaccuracies with valid concepts and generalizations.

These observations contain an urgent plea for objectivity in studying economics. Economic principles can become a vice rather than a valuable analytical tool if, in using them, we are obsessed with a point of view. By approaching them from the angle or viewpoint of, say, management or labor, we jeopardize much of the value these principles hold for us. Dissociating ourselves from any particular viewpoint —whether that of the workingman, the businessman, or the farmer—will pay us dividends, because such associations can imperceptibly undermine our reason and hopelessly color our conclusions. Objectivity is an obvious prerequisite to the successful pursuit of scientific truth. This objectivity is most likely to be achieved when a *social point of view* is em-braced. "How does this policy or action affect the economy (society) as a whole and *all* its relevant parts?" is a question much superior to "How does this policy or action affect me as a businessman or laborer?" We must keep an open mind in pursuing economic knowledge.

Fallacy of composition

Many of the false preconceptions people have about economics are attributable to the fallacy of composition. This fallacy contends that "what is true for the individual or part is necessarily also true for the group or whole." This is a logical fallacy; it is not correct. The validity of a particular generalization for an individual or part does not necessarily ensure its accuracy for the group or whole.

A noneconomic example may help: You are watching a football game on a sunny autumn afternoon. The home team executes an outstanding play. In the general excitement, you leap to your feet to get a better view. *Generalization:* "If you, *an individual,* stand, then your view of the game is improved." But does this also hold true for the group—for everyone watching the game? Certainly not! If everyone stands to watch the play, everyone—including you—is likely to have the same or even a worse view than he had when seated!

Now an illustration from economics: An *individual* farmer who is fortunate enough to realize a bumper crop is likely to find that his resulting income is larger than usual. This is a correct generalization. Does it apply to farmers as a *group?* Possibly not, for the simple reason that to the individual farmer, crop prices will not be influenced (reduced) by this bumper crop, because each farmer is producing a negligible fraction of the total farm output. But to farmers as a group, prices vary inversely with total output.[4] Thus, as all farmers realize bumper crops, the total supply of farm products rises, thereby depressing prices. If price declines overbalance the unusually large output, farm incomes *fall.*

Consider now a final illustration which we

[4] This assumes there is no government price fixing.

shall explain in Chapter 16: An individual commercial bank can safely make loans to borrowers in an amount equal to the bank's excess reserves, or the amount of funds the bank has deposited in the Federal Reserve Bank in excess of the amount specifically required by law. Yet the commercial banking *system*—all commercial banks *taken as a group*—is able to lend by a multiple of its excess reserves. Again, what holds true for the individual or part need not hold true for the group or whole. It should be fairly obvious that dogmatic statements proclaiming that "what is good for business (or labor or the farmer) is good for the economy as a whole" should be examined in a most critical manner before being accepted as gospel.

In a sense, these comments on the fallacy of composition boil down to this: There are two essentially different levels of analysis at which the economist may derive laws concerning economic behavior. The level of *macroeconomics* is concerned either with the economy as a whole or with the basic subdivisions or aggregates—such as "government," "households," and "businesses"—which comprise the economy. An aggregate is a collection of specific economic units which are treated *as if* they were one unit. Thus, we might find it convenient to lump together the 56 million households in our economy and treat them as if they were one huge unit. In dealing with aggregates, macroeconomics is concerned with obtaining an overview, or general outline, of the structure of the economy and the relationships between the major aggregates which comprise the economy. No attention is given to the specific units which make up the various aggregates. It is not surprising, then, to find that macroeconomics entails discussions of such magnitudes as *total* output, the *total* level of employment, *total* income, *total* expenditures, the *general* level of prices, and so forth in analyzing various economic problems. The problems of unemployment and inflation, by the way, are the primary topics of macroeconomics. In short, macroeconomics examines the forest, not the trees. It gives us a bird's-eye view of the economy.

On the other hand, *microeconomics* is concerned with *specific* economic units and a *de-*tailed consideration of the behavior of these individual units. When operating at this level of analysis, the economist figuratively puts an economic unit, or very small segment of the economy, under the microscope to observe the details of its operation. Here we talk in terms of an individual industry, firm, or household and concentrate upon such magnitudes as the output of a *specific* product, the number of workers employed by a single firm, the revenue or income of a particular firm or household, the expenditures of a given firm or family, the price of a particular product, and so forth. In microeconomics we examine the trees, not the forest. Microeconomics is useful in achieving a worm's-eye view of some very specific component of our economic system.

The basic point is this: the fallacy of composition reminds us that *generalizations which are valid at one of these levels of analysis may or may not be valid at the other.*

Prosperity and depression

Closely related to the fallacy of composition is the fact that notions or ideas which are valid during prosperity may be invalid during depression, or vice versa. Some economic principles rest upon a specific presupposition concerning the phase of the business cycle; a given principle's validity may depend upon the existence of good times or bad times. For example, the economist deems thrift or saving as economically beneficial and therefore desirable during periods of prosperity involving sharp inflation. Why? Because, as we shall discover, a high level of saving will tend to reduce inflationary pressure. Yet during periods of depression, the economist is equally correct in generalizing to the effect that saving is an economic vice, the reason being that too much saving is the immediate cause of unemployment or depression.

Cause and effect

The discovery of cause and effect relationships is an important and difficult part of any science. The absence of controlled experimentation adds significantly to the woes of the social scientist in isolating such cause-effect relationships. It is therefore exceedingly important to warn against grasping at straws in constructing cause-effect sequences. In particular, beware of the "after this, therefore because of this" fallacy—the incorrect notion that simply because one event precedes another, the first is necessarily the cause of the second.

A classic example clearly indicates the fallacy inherent in such reasoning. Suppose that early each spring the medicine man of a native tribe performs his ritual by cavorting around the village in a green costume. A week or so later the trees and grass turn green. Can we safely conclude that event A, the medicine man's gyrations, has caused event B, the landscape's turning green? Most certainly not. "One who had many times seen a rabbit pursued by a dog, and had never seen rabbits and dogs otherwise, would think the rabbit the cause of the dog."

Assume that a sizable tax increase is put into effect by the government. Suppose, too, that employment increases noticeably a short time thereafter. Can we generalize that the tax boost caused the increase in employment? As Chapter 13 will reveal, a tax increase, as such, is usually conducive to a drop in employment. Hence any cause-effect conclusion in this case would be premature indeed. In this case, unemployment would fall *despite*—not because of—the tax increase. Another example: many people believe that the stock market crash of 1929 caused the Great Depression of the 1930s. Although there is an element of accuracy in this statement, it is basically incorrect. The stock market crash itself was a *result* of certain more fundamental forces within the economy which precipitated the Depression.

In short, cause-and-effect relationships are typically not self-evident in economics; the economist must look carefully before he leaps to the conclusion that event A caused event B. Certainly the simple fact that A preceded B is not sufficient to warrant any such conclusion.

Effect of expectations

The anticipations, or expectations, of consumers and businesses are frequently of great importance in economics. This is so because the widespread anticipation of an event can prompt behavior which may cause the expected event to become a reality. For example, if consumers are suspicious that inflation lies on the economic horizon, they may increase their current levels of spending to "beat" expected higher prices. But increased consumer outlays are likely to cause the anticipated inflation to materialize. Such was the case at the start of the Korean War. Conversely, if the economy expects a siege of unemployment, its natural reaction is to retrench on spending. Building a nest egg of savings seems to be a logical means of financing ourselves through an anticipated economic slump. But increasing savings means less spending, and this is likely to cause expected unemployment to become a reality. Similarly, if speculators expect the price of a stock to dip, they will attempt to sell that stock before the decline occurs. The resulting increased offerings of that stock relative to the demand for it will then cause the value of that stock to nosedive.

In short, what people think will happen has a vital influence upon what actually does occur in the economy.

Intentions versus realizations

It is also important to recognize that what consumers or business firms attempt or intend to do may be considerably at odds with what they are actually able to accomplish or realize. In our own experience we may plan to wage a campaign of hard work and frugality each summer vacation in order to provide adequate finances for school expenses, but at summer's end we find we have managed to save considerably less than we had originally planned. Events can drastically alter plans. As a matter of fact, the very attempt to achieve a given goal may create certain circumstances which prevent the attainment of that objective. For example, we shall find in Chapter 13 that if the economy attempts to achieve too high a rate of saving, unemployment will result. Unemployment means lower incomes, and this in turn undermines the ability to save. The attempt to save too much may create a situation in which the economy can actually save little or nothing at all. Plans on the one hand and accomplishments on the other may be very different things.

Logical explanations and social practice

Economics is concerned with both describing and explaining human behavior. Explanations in economics, however, occasionally fall short of logical standards. Thus, some explanations in the following chapters will not be "logical" but will, nevertheless, expound the actual operation of our economic units in terms of current social or business practice. For example, we might construct a more logical system of practices and regulations under which our monetary and banking system could operate than those currently employed. It would be misleading, however, to devote our efforts to an understanding of such a logical masterpiece, since it is out of touch with reality. Of course, our system might be of great value as a guide to reform. Or we might later question the logic of classifying the construction of private residential housing as investment goods rather than as consumer goods. After all, housing is generally bought by individual consumers just as automobiles, bread, and shoes are purchased. Yet, for good reasons of their own, government statisticians classify private housing as an investment good. For us to learn it otherwise—despite the apparent logic of the situation—would be flatly incorrect. In short, we will occasionally find ourselves relying upon that's-the-way-it-is explanations in which logic is subservient to business or social practice.

Economic quackery

A final general warning. The field of economics is, and always has been, a fertile ground for quacks and charlatans. While few feel capable of offering aid and advice to the nuclear physicist or research chemist, a great many people envision themselves as unrecognized geniuses in economics and politics. The world abounds with self-styled economists who stand ready to cure the world's ills with seemingly simple changes in the structure, legal framework, or ideology of our economy. Some half-baked schemes are frequently appealing in their directness and simplicity, and the task of undermining such schemes is not easy. The ideas of the quack chemist or physicist can be taken to the laboratory and quickly tested for validity. But no clear-cut testing ground is available for rapidly exposing the remedies of economic quacks.

The economist's job is made even more difficult by the fact that hard scraping and manipulating will uncover statistics that "prove" just about any point desired! Thus, quack schemes often achieve considerable popular support before they are exposed and relegated to the scrap heap as nonsense or half-truths.

We would be foolish to accept medical advice for the treatment of cancer from our milkman or corner grocer. We would be silly if we let an automobile mechanic advise us on dental work. We should be equally hesitant to accept the economic analyses and remedies offered by untrained but highly vocal amateurs. Let us remember that answers to major economic problems are rarely self-evident or clear-cut. If they were, the given problem would in all likelihood have been solved and forgotten long ago. The best answers to complex economic problems rarely present themselves in terms of blacks and whites, but rather as varying shades of gray. Easy answers do not often go hand in hand with complex questions.

SUMMARY

1. Economics is studied for several reasons: (*a*) economics provides valuable knowledge concerning man's social environment and his behavior; (*b*) it equips a democratic citizenry to render fundamental decisions intelligently; (*c*) although not a vocational discipline, economics may provide the businessman with valuable information.

2. Economics is based upon facts concerning the activities of individuals and institutions in producing, exchanging, and consuming goods and services. The task of descriptive economics is the gathering of those economic facts which are relevant to a particular problem or specific segment of the economy.

3. These facts are then studied, arranged, and generalized upon. The resulting generalizations are called "principles," "theories," or "models." The derivation of these principles is the task of economic theory.

4. Economic principles have several noteworthy characteristics. First, they are generalizations and, as such, are subject to exceptions and elude quantitatively precise statement. Further, economic principles are models of reality and are hence abstract; their usefulness depends upon this abstraction. Finally, economic principles often can be conveniently expressed on two-dimensional graphs.

5. In deriving and applying principles, the economist must (a) not omit any relevant facts, (b) recognize that principles are simplified models of reality, and (c) take care not to impute any moral qualities to these principles.

6. Economic principles are particularly valuable as predictive devices; they are the bases for the formulation of economic policy designed to solve problems and control undesirable events. The formulation of economic policy requires (a) a clear understanding of policy objectives, (b) the statement and evaluation of all relevant policy alternatives, and (c) an evaluation of policies after their application for the future improvement of policy.

7. Economic growth, full employment, price stability, economic freedom, equity in the distribution of income, and economic security are all widely accepted economic goals in our society. Some of these goals are complementary; others are mutually exclusive.

8. There are numerous pitfalls in studying economics which the beginner may encounter. Some of the more important chuckholes strewn along the road to economic understanding are (a) terminological difficulties, (b) biases and erroneous preconceptions, (c) the fallacy of composition, (d) the fact that the validity of some economic ideas may depend upon the stage of the business cycle, (e) the difficulty of establishing clear cause-effect relationships, (f) the fact that expectations may influence actual events, (g) the fact that intentions and accomplishments may be at odds, (h) possible discrepancies between logic and social practice and, finally, (i) the ever-present threat of economic quackery.

QUESTIONS AND STUDY SUGGESTIONS

1. "The trouble with economics is that it is not practical. It has too much to say about theory and not enough to say about facts." Critically evaluate.

2. Define descriptive economics, economic theory, and policy economics, and explain the relationships among the three.

3. Analyze and explain the following quotation: [5]

"Facts are seldom simple and usually complicated; theoretical analysis is needed to unravel the complications and interpret the facts before we can understand them . . . the opposition of facts and theory is a false one; the true relationship is complementary. We cannot in practice consider a fact without relating it to other facts, and the relation is a theory. Facts by themselves are dumb; before they will tell us anything we have to arrange them, and the arrangement is a theory. Theory is simply the unavoidable arrangement and interpretation of facts, which gives us generalizations on which we can argue and act, in the place of a mass of disjointed particulars."

[5] Henry Clay, *Economics for the General Reader* (New York: The Macmillan Company, 1925), pp. 10–11.

4. "As is the case with other sciences, economics is not content with merely descriptive knowledge. Economics tries to discern general patterns of uniformity in human behavior." Explain.

5. Of what significance is the fact that economics is not a laboratory science? What problems may be involved in deriving and applying economic principles?

6. "Like all scientific laws, economic laws are established in order to make successful prediction of the outcome of human actions." [6] Explain.

7. "Abstraction . . . is the inevitable price of generality . . . indeed abstraction and generality are virtually synonyms." [7] Explain.

8. To what extent would you accept the six economic goals stated and described in this chapter? What priorities would you assign to them? It has been said that we seek simply four goals: progress, stability, justice, and freedom. Is this list of goals compatible with that given in the chapter?

9. "In comparison with the free economy, the Russian system shows elements of decided strength. Its power to . . . carry out plans without opposition gives it an advantage that may overcome grave handicaps in other respects. If we reject this system, as we most decidedly do, we must found our rejection on our attachment to freedom, not on economic grounds. . . . We want freedom, and we are willing to pay an economic price for it, by sacrificing the larger output that we might have in a forced draft economy." [8] Interpret and explain. Do you agree with this view?

10. Explain and give an illustration of (a) the fallacy of composition and (b) the "after this, therefore because of this" fallacy. Why are cause-and-effect relationships difficult to isolate in the social sciences? Distinguish clearly between macroeconomics and microeconomics.

11. "Economists should never be popular; men who afflict the comfortable serve equally those who comfort the afflicted and one cannot suppose that American capitalism would long prosper without the critics its leaders find such a profound source of annoyance." [9] Interpret and evaluate.

12. Briefly explain the use of graphs as a means of presenting economic principles. What is an inverse relationship? How does it graph? What is a direct relationship? How does it graph? Graph and explain the relationships one would expect to find between (a) the number of inches of rainfall per month and the sale of umbrellas, (b) the amount of tuition and the level of enrollment at a university, and (c) the size of a university's athletic scholarships and the number of games won by its football team. In each case cite and explain how considerations other than those specifically mentioned might upset the expected relationship.

SELECTED REFERENCES

Boulding, Kenneth E., *Economic Analysis,* 3d ed. (New York: Harper & Row, Publishers, 1955), chap. 1.

[6] Oskar Lange, "The Scope and Method of Economics," *Review of Economic Studies,* vol. 13, 1945–1946, p. 20.

[7] George J. Stigler, *The Theory of Price* (New York: The Macmillan Company, 1947), p. 10.

[8] Henry C. Wallich, *The Cost of Freedom* (New York: Harper & Row, Publishers, 1960), p. 48.

[9] John Kenneth Galbraith, *American Capitalism,* rev. ed. (Boston: Houghton Mifflin Company, 1956), p. 49.

Keynes, J. N., *The Scope and Method of Political Economy*, 4th ed. (New York: The Macmillan Company, 1930).

Lange, Oskar, "The Scope and Method of Economics," *Review of Economic Studies*, vol. 13, 1945–1946, pp. 19–32, reprinted in A. P. Hess, R. E. Gallman, J. P. Rice, and C. Stern, *Outside Readings in Economics*, 1st ed. (New York: Thomas Y. Crowell Company, 1951), pp. 1–20.

Stigler, George J., *The Theory of Price* (New York: The Macmillan Company, 1947), chap. 1.

Warner, Aaron W., and Victor R. Fuchs, *Concepts and Cases in Economic Analysis* (New York: Harcourt, Brace & World, Inc., 1958), chap. 1.

Chapter 2

AN INTRODUCTION TO THE

ECONOMIZING PROBLEM

THE PRIMARY OBJECTIVE of this chapter is to introduce and explore certain fundamental considerations which constitute the foundation of economic science.

But we must be more specific. We shall first seek to introduce a more sophisticated definition of economics. No longer can we content ourselves with the mere statement that economics is concerned with man's behavior in making a living, or that economics has to do with the production, exchange, and consumption of goods and services. These accurate, but not particularly revealing, facts concerning the nature of economics must give way to a comprehensive understanding of the economizing problem. To this end, the sophisticated definition of economics will be illustrated, extended, and modified by the use of so-called production possibilities tables.

We shall then restate and discuss the economizing problem in terms of certain practical questions which every economy, regardless of its institutional and ideological characteristics, must face.

Finally, we shall survey briefly the different ways in which institutionally and ideologically diverse economies go about solving the economizing problem.

THE FOUNDATION OF ECONOMICS

Two fundamental facts provide a foundation for the field of economics. It is imperative that we carefully state and fully understand these two facts, since everything that follows in our study of economics depends directly or indirectly upon them. The first fact is this: *human material wants are virtually unlimited or insatiable.* Secondly: *economic resources are limited or scarce.*

Unlimited wants

Let us systematically examine and explain these two facts in the order stated. In the first statement, precisely what do we mean by "human material wants"? We mean simply the desires we have to obtain and use various *goods* and *services* which give us pleasure or satisfaction.[1] An amazingly wide range of products fills the bill in this respect: houses, automobiles, tooth paste, pencils, onions, sweaters, and the like. In short, innumerable products which we

[1] This leaves a variety of wants—recognition, status, love, and so forth—for the other social sciences to worry about.

sometimes classify as *necessities* (food, shelter, clothing) and *luxuries* (perfumes, yachts, mink coats) are all capable of satisfying human wants. Needless to say, that which is a luxury to Smith may be a necessity to Jones, and what is a commonplace necessity today may have been a luxury a few short years ago.

But services may satisfy our wants as much as tangible products. A repair job on our car, the removal of our appendix, a haircut, and even legal advice have in common with goods the fact that they satisfy human wants. As a matter of fact, on reflecting, we realize that we buy many goods, for example, automobiles and washing machines, for the services they render. The differences between goods and services are often less than they seem to be at first.

As a group, these human wants are, for practical purposes, *insatiable,* or *unlimited.*[2] This means simply that human wants for goods and services are incapable of being completely satisfied. A simple experiment will help to verify this point: suppose we are asked to list those goods and services we want but do not now possess. If we take time to ponder our unfilled material wants, chances are our list will be impressive. And over a period of time, our wants seem to multiply so that, as we fill some of the wants on the list, at the same time we add new ones. Human wants, like rabbits, have a high reproduction rate. This is particularly so in the United States where the relatively rapid introduction of new products whets our appetites and extensive advertising tries to persuade us that we need countless items we might not otherwise consider buying. Not too many years ago, the desire for television, air conditioners, stereophonic phonographs, and tubeless

tires was non-existent. Furthermore, we cannot stop with simple satisfaction: upon acquiring a lowly Ford or Chevrolet, we become interested in owning a Cadillac, an Imperial, a Lincoln. And the business tycoon who acquires a summer home in the Colorado Rockies becomes vaguely aware of the fact that a winter home in Florida would add immeasurably to his happiness.

In short, we may say that at any point in time humans have innumerable unfulfilled material wants. Some of these wants—food, clothing, shelter—have biological roots. But some are also influenced by the conventions and customs of society: the specific kinds of food, clothing, and shelter we seek are frequently determined by the general social and cultural environment in which we live. Over time, wants change and multiply, abetted by the development of new products and by extensive advertising and sales promotion.

Finally—although we may be getting ahead of ourselves—let us emphatically add that the over-all end or objective of all economic activity is the attempt to satisfy these diverse human material wants. In other words, all man's activities in the production and exchange of goods and services are directed toward trying to fulfill the wants of consumers. Consumption is the ultimate goal of economic activity.

Scarce resources

Consider now the second fundamental fact: *economic resources are limited or scarce.* What do we mean by "economic resources"? In general, we are referring to all the natural, human, and man-made resources that go into the production of goods and services. This obviously covers a lot of ground: factory and farm buildings and all sorts of equipment, tools, and machinery used in the production of manufactured goods and agricultural products; a variety of transportation and communication facilities; innumerable types of labor; and, last but not least, land and mineral resources of all kinds. There is an apparent need for a simplified

---

[2] It should be mentioned in passing that the fallacy of composition is relevant here. Our wants for a *particular* good or service can obviously be satisfied; that is, over a short period of time we can get sufficient amounts of tooth paste, beer, or Ivy League suits. Certainly one appendicitis operation is par for the course. But goods *in general* are another story. Here we do not, and cannot, get enough. We shall have more to say about the satisfying of wants for specific goods in a later chapter.

classification of such resources which we shall meet with the following categories of resources: (1) *property* resources—land or raw materials and capital; (2) *human* resources—labor and entrepreneurial ability.

What does the economist mean by *land?* Much more than the layman. Land refers to all natural resources—all "free gifts of nature" which are usable in the productive process. Such resources as arable land, forests, mineral and oil deposits, and water resources come under this general classification. What about *capital?* Capital, or investment goods, has a variety of meanings attached to it. The one that is correct for our purposes refers to all manmade aids to production, that is, all tools, machinery, equipment, and factory, storage, transportation, and distribution facilities used in producing goods and services and getting them to the ultimate consumer.[3] We should note especially that the term "capital" as here defined does not refer to money. True, businessmen and economists often talk of "money capital," referring to money which is available for use in the purchase of machinery, equipment, and other productive facilities. But money, as such, produces nothing; hence, it is not to be considered as an economic resource.

Labor is a broad term which the economist uses in referring to all man's physical and mental talents employed in producing goods and services (with the exception of a special set of human talents—entrepreneurial ability—which, because of their special significance in a capitalistic economy, we choose to consider separately). Thus the services of both the lowly ditchdigger or gandy dancer and the skilled chemical engineer or nuclear physicist fall under the general heading of labor.

Finally, what can be said about this special human resource which we label *entrepreneurial ability* or, more simply, *enterprise?* We shall give the term a specific meaning by assigning four related functions to the entrepreneur. (1) The entrepreneur takes the initiative in

[3] We shall see in Chapter 10 that inventories of processed materials, or finished goods, in the hands of producers are also considered to be capital.

combining the resources of land, capital, and labor in the production of a good or service. Both a spark plug and a catalyst, the entrepreneur is at once the driving force behind production and the agent that combines the other resources in what he hopes will be a profitable venture. (2) He has the chore of making basic business-policy decisions, that is, those nonroutine decisions which set the course of a business enterprise. (3) The entrepreneur is an innovator—he is the one who attempts to introduce on a commercial basis new products, new productive techniques, or even new forms of business organization. (4) The entrepreneur is obviously a risk bearer. This is apparent from a close examination of his other three functions. The entrepreneur in a capitalistic system has no guarantee that he will make a profit. The reward for his time, efforts, and abilities may be attractive profits or immediate losses and eventual bankruptcy. In short, the entrepreneur risks not only his time, effort, and business reputation, but his invested funds and those of his associates or stockholders.

We shall see shortly how these resources are provided for business institutions in exchange for money income. The income received from supplying property resources—raw materials and capital equipment—is called *rental* and *interest income.* The income accruing to those who supply labor is called simply *wages* and includes salaries and various wage and salary supplements in the form of bonuses, commissions, royalties, and so forth. Entrepreneurial income is called *profits,* which, of course, may be a negative figure, that is, losses.

These four broad categories of economic resources, or *factors of production* as they are often called, leave room for debate when it comes to classifying specific resources. For example, suppose you receive a dividend on some General Motors stock which you may be fortunate enough to own. Is this an interest return for the capital equipment which the company was able to buy with the money you provided in buying GM stock? Or is this return a profit which compensates you for the risks involved in purchasing corporate stock? What about the earnings of a one-man general store where the owner is both the entrepreneur and the labor force? Are his earnings to be considered as wages or profit income? The answer to both queries is, "Some of each." The important point is this: although we might quibble about classifying a given flow of income as wages, rent, interest, or profits, all income can be listed without too much arbitrariness under one of these general headings.

All economic resources, or factors of production, have one fundamental characteristic in common: *economic resources are scarce or limited in supply.* Without a doubt, our economy possesses extremely large amounts of arable land, mineral deposits, capital equipment, and labor. These are, however, not infinitely large supplies; they have limits. A civilian labor force of 71 or 72 million workers may seem extremely large, but it is not an infinite amount. World War II, for example, reminded us of just how scarce labor actually is. Critical shortages of semiskilled and skilled labor constituted a formidable obstacle in the production of vitally needed armaments. Much the same can be said for the other factors in production.

One additional point: these economic resources—land, labor, capital, and entrepreneurial ability—are obviously the *means* by which we produce goods and services in trying to satisfy human wants. Consumption, we recall, is the fundamental objective of economic activity. We are now pointing out that the means of attaining the goal of consumption are our available supplies of various economic resources. And these resources, though abundant in the absolute sense, are scarce in relation to the demand for them in the production of goods and services.

ECONOMICS DEFINED

Recalling that wants are unlimited and resources are scarce, economics can be defined as *the social science concerned with the problem of using or administering scarce resources (the means of producing) so as to attain the greatest or maximum fulfillment of our unlimited wants (the goal of producing).* Economics is concerned with "doing the best with what we have." If our wants are virtually unlimited and our resources are scarce, we cannot conceivably satisfy all our human wants. The next best thing is to achieve the greatest possible satisfaction of our wants. Economics is without a doubt a science of efficiency—efficiency in the use of scarce resources.

Precisely what is meant by *efficiency* as economists use the term? It means something akin to, but not identical with, the term "efficiency" as used in engineering. The mechanical engineer tells us that a steam locomotive is only "60 per cent efficient" because a large part—some 40 per cent—of the energy in its fuel is not transformed into useful power but is wasted through friction and heat loss. The maximum output of usable power is not derived from the inputs of fuel.

Economic efficiency is also concerned with *inputs* and *outputs.* Specifically, it is concerned with the relationship between the units of scarce resources which are put into the process of production and the resulting output of some wanted product; economic efficiency has to do with inputs of scarce resources and outputs of useful products.

Full employment and full production

Economic efficiency is achieved when unemployment is avoided. Unemployment, however, may assume two different forms. On the one hand, a worker is clearly unemployed when he is involuntarily out of work. This is the man who is standing in a relief line or a bread line or waiting to pick up his unemployment compensation check. This is a case of *apparent unemployment* or simply *unemployment;* the worker obviously has no job connection. On the other hand, a worker may have a job but still be in a sense "unemployed." For example, a worker who is harvesting wheat by hand or cutting a lawn with a pair of scissors is "partially unemployed." In this case, however, it is a matter of *disguised unemployment* or, more simply, *underemployment.* The worker has a job but simply is not being employed efficiently.

The *un*employed worker who has no job and the *under*employed worker who has a job but is producing in a highly inefficient manner differ more in degree than in kind. Both entail the relatively inefficient use of resources. The point is this: there are two major aspects of economic efficiency. On the one hand, there is the *full-employment* problem—the problem of providing jobs for all who are able and willing to work. On the other hand, there is the closely related *full-production* or resource-allocation problem—the problem of using employed resources in the most efficient manner. These two facets of economic efficiency are of such importance as to merit further comment.

Eliminating unemployment. Economic efficiency requires, first, that available resources are actually utilized in the production of goods and services rather than allowed to lie idle. An unused locomotive is of zero efficiency. The same can be said for unemployed resources. Unutilized resources—both human and property—obviously mean waste and inefficiency. Unemployment is the height of economic inefficiency: when society fails to put its available resources into the productive process, it obviously realizes no output at all.

Note that we specify that all *available* resources should be employed. Each society has certain established customs and practices which determine what particular resources are available for employment. For example, legislation and custom provide that children and the very aged should not be employed. Also, we should not employ all our farmland every year; it is desirable for productivity to allow land to lie fallow periodically. Furthermore, society wants to avoid complete utilization and rapid exhaustion of particularly scarce resources in order to conserve them as long as possible. In short, society wants to employ only those resources that are available for employment and whose current employment is desirable.

In a capitalistic economy we shall discover that it is the volume of total spending which determines the level at which resources are employed. If buyers are willing and able to spend in large amounts in satisfying their wants,

entrepreneurs will respond by employing large amounts of resources in producing goods and services to fulfill these wants. Conversely, a meager volume of spending will mean unemployment. Part 2 of this book is devoted to a detailed analysis of this particular aspect of the problem of economic efficiency.

Eliminating underemployment. But the full employment of available resources is not sufficient for the achieving of economic efficiency. Society also seeks full production: resources must be used in the production of goods and services most wanted by consumers, and the production of such goods must be carried out with the best available productive techniques.

Resources must be allocated among the various possible employments so that those products most wanted by society are produced in large amounts, and, conversely, those not so highly desired are produced in small quantities or not at all. To allow resources to remain idle and to employ resources in the production of goods and services society does not want differ only in degree. Current employment of resources to produce spats, buggy whips, and stagecoaches would obviously involve the inefficient use of resources. The useful, or *wanted*, production resulting from resources put into these lines of endeavor is very low. The power generated by a steam locomotive is useful only when employed in the transportation of loads. The employment of resources is only useful to society when this employment results in the production of goods and services which consumers want.

There is a second aspect to achieving full production—the question of getting the maximum amount of a useful good produced with a given input of resources. We refer here to the important problem of choosing the best technique for producing a wanted product. An economy might fully employ its resources and direct these resources toward the production of those goods most wanted by society, but it might at the same time be economically inefficient, because it fails to use the best productive techniques available to it. A very simple example will make this clear. Other things being equal, a given volume of resources will produce more wheat when crop rotation is employed as a technique of production. To plant the same acres to wheat year after year will wear out the soil and eventually result in a relatively small output. By employing the same amounts of land, capital, labor, and entrepreneurial resources and by practicing the technique of crop rotation, a larger output of wheat can be realized.

In Part 5 of this book we explore the full-production or resource-allocation aspect of economic efficiency. We shall find that it is the composition of total spending—along with such considerations as the level of technological knowledge, the relative abundance of the various resources, and the structure of industry—which determines the degree to which a capitalistic economy realizes full production from its available resources.

Production possibilities table

The nature of the economizing problem can be brought into even clearer focus by the use of a production possibilities table.[4] This ingenious device reveals the core of the economizing problem: a full-employment, full-production economy cannot have an unlimited output of goods and services.

Let us make several specific assumptions to set the stage for our illustration. (1) Let us assume that the economy is operating at full employment and achieving full production. Neither *un*employment nor *under*employment exists. (2) Let us assume that the available supplies of the factors of production are fixed. But, of course, they can be shifted or reallocated, within limits, between different uses; for example, a common laborer can work on a farm, on an automobile assembly line, or in a munitions factory. (3) Let us assume that the technological state of the arts is constant; that is, technology does not change during the course of our analysis. The second and third assump-

[4] Paul A. Samuelson, *Economics,* 5th ed. (New York: McGraw-Hill Book Company, Inc., 1961), pp. 19–24.

tions are another way of saying that we are looking at our economy at some specific point in time, or over a very short period of time. Over a relatively long period it would clearly be unrealistic to rule out technological advances and the possibility that resource supplies might vary. In short, we assume full employment and full production, fixed resources, and a fixed technology.

To simplify our illustration further, let us suppose that our economy is producing just two products—for example, drill presses and bread—instead of the innumerable goods and services actually produced. Bread is symbolic of *consumer goods,* that is, those goods and services which directly satisfy our wants; drill presses are symbolic of *capital goods,* that is, those goods which satisfy our wants *indirectly* by permitting more efficient production of consumer goods. Now is it not evident from the assumptions we have made that our economy is faced with a very fundamental choice? Our total supplies of resources are limited. Thus the total amounts of drill presses and bread that our economy is capable of producing are limited. Limited resources mean a limited output. A choice must be made as to what quantities of each product society wants produced. Since resources are limited in supply and fully employed, any increase in the production of drill presses will necessitate the shifting of resources away from the production of bread. And the reverse holds true: if we choose to step up the production of bread, needed resources must come at the expense of drill-press production. Society cannot have its cake and eat it, too. This is the essence of the economizing problem.

Let us generalize by noting in Table 2-1 some of the alternative combinations of drill presses and bread which our economy might conceivably choose. Though the data in this and ensuing tables are hypothetical, the points illustrated are of tremendous practical significance. At alternative A our economy would be devoting all its resources to the production of drill presses, that is, capital goods. At alternative E, all our resources would be devoted to the production of bread, that is, consumer goods. Both these alternatives are clearly un-

TABLE 2-1. PRODUCTION POSSIBILITIES OF BREAD AND
DRILL PRESSES WITH FULL EMPLOYMENT, 1963

Type of product	Production alternatives				
	A	B	C	D	E
Bread (in hundred thousands)	0	1	2	3	4
Drill presses (in thousands)	10	9	7	4	0

realistic extremes: any economy typically strikes a balance in dividing its total output between capital and consumer goods. As we move from alternative A to E, we step up the production of consumer goods (bread). How? By shifting resources away from capital goods production. Remembering that consumer goods directly satisfy our wants, any movement toward alternative E looks tempting. In making this move, society increases the current satisfaction of its wants. But there is a cost involved. This shift of resources catches up with society over time as its stock of capital goods dwindles—or at least ceases to expand at the current rate—with the result that the efficiency of future production is impaired. In short, in moving from alternative A toward E, society is in effect choosing "more now" at the expense of "much more later." In moving from E toward A, society is choosing to forgo current satisfaction of wants. This sacrifice of current consumption frees resources which can now be used in stepping up the production of capital goods. By building up its stock of capital in this way, society can anticipate more efficient production and, therefore, greater consumption in the future. The important point is this: *at any point in time, a full-employment, full-production economy must sacrifice some of product X to obtain more of product Y.* The basic fact that economic resources are scarce prohibits such an economy from having more of both X and Y.

Production possibilities curve

To insure our understanding the production possibilities table, let us view this data graphically. We employ a simple two-dimensional

graph, putting the output of drill presses on the vertical axis and the output of bread on the horizontal axis, as in Figure 2-1. The process of plotting the production possibilities data of Table 2-1 is evident. We simply want to locate those points on the graph which designate alternatives A through E. To find each of these points, we draw perpendiculars from the appropriate points on the two axes. Alternative C, for example, is found by drawing perpendiculars from 2 on the horizontal axis and 7 on the vertical axis. Their point of intersection determines alternative C. Having done this for all five alternatives, we can then draw a curve connecting these points. This is done on the implicit assumption that the relationship between the output of bread and drill presses reflected in the five alternatives will also prevail at all intermediate points. The resulting curve is called the "production possibilities," or "transformation,"[5] curve.

It is interesting to compare the production possibility choices made by the United States and by Soviet Russia in recent years. Russia, as we know, got a very late start in its industrialization. It remained a relatively underdeveloped country until well into the twentieth century. Then, shortly after the revolution in 1917, Russian leaders, attempting to make up for lost time, embarked on a series of Five-year Plans designed to bring about Russian industrialization overnight. To a very considerable extent

[5] Why "transformation"? Because in moving from one alternative to another, say from B to C, we are in effect transforming drill presses into bread by shifting resources from the production of the former to the production of the latter.

the Russians have been successful in their program of industrialization. But, aside from immeasurable and much-publicized noneconomic costs, there has been inherent in this program a great economic cost—a retarded and relatively low standard of living for consumers. Russian consumers have had to tighten their belts to free resources for use in the industrialization programs. This is not to say that Soviet Russia has been wrong in emphasizing industrialization; any answer to this question is more a matter of moral values than of fact. We are noting that the remarkable accumulation of capital goods achieved by Russia in recent years has necessarily involved the use of resources which otherwise could have provided more consumer goods and a higher standard of living for today's Soviet citizenry.

In contrast, the United States is one of those nations which have long enjoyed the Industrial Revolution. With a relatively large stock of capital equipment currently available, the United States finds itself in the very enviable position of being able to provide currently a high standard of living for its consumers, because it is not pressed to devote an overwhelming amount of resources to capital goods production.

Law of increasing costs

Implicit in Table 2-1 and Figure 2-1 is another important economic principle which must not escape us. The alert reader has probably noted that, in moving from alternative A to alternative E, the sacrifice of drill presses involved in getting each additional 100,000 units of bread increases. Hence, in moving from A to B, just 1 unit of drill presses is sacrificed for 1 more unit of bread; but going from B to C involves the sacrifice of 2 units of drill presses for 1 more of bread; then 3 of drill presses for 1 of bread; and finally 4 for 1. Why does the sacrifice of drill presses increase as we get more bread? The answer to this query is rather complex. But, simply stated, it amounts to this: *economic resources are not completely adaptable to alternative uses.* As we attempt to step up bread production, resources which are less and less adaptable to agriculture must be in-

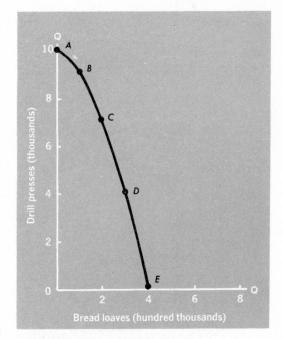

FIGURE 2-1. THE PRODUCTION POSSIBILITIES CURVE.
The production possibilities curve is concave in relation to the origin because of the law of increasing costs; economic resources are not completely adaptable as between alternative uses.

duced, or "pushed," into that line of production. If we start at A and move to B, we can first pick resources whose productivity of bread is greatest in relation to their productivity of drill presses. But as we move from B to C, C to D, and so forth, those resources which are highly productive of bread become increasingly scarce. To get more bread, resources whose productivity in drill presses is great in relation to their productivity in bread will be needed. It will obviously take more and more of such resources—and hence an increasingly great sacrifice of drill presses—to achieve a given increase of 1 unit in the production of bread. This lack of flexibility, or adaptability, on the part of resources and the resulting increase in the sacrifice of one good that must be made in the acquisition of more and more units of another

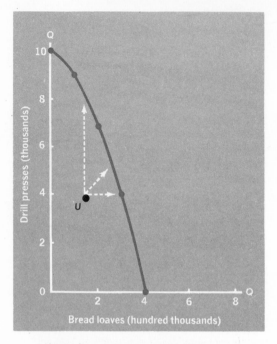

FIGURE 2-2. UNEMPLOYMENT AND THE PRODUCTION POSSIBILITIES CURVE.
Any point inside the production possibilities curve, such as *U*, indicates unemployment or underemployment. By moving towards full employment and full production, the economy can produce more of either or both of the two products, as the arrows indicate.

good is sometimes termed the *law of increasing costs,* costs in this case being stated as sacrifices of goods and not in terms of dollars and cents. The student should (1) verify that the law of increasing costs also holds true in moving from alternative *E* to alternative *A* and (2) explain how the shape (concave in relation to the origin) of the production possibilities curve in Figure 2-1 reflects this law.

SOME MODIFICATIONS

It is of signal importance that we understand what happens when the three assumptions underlying the preceding explanation are released.

Unemployment and underemployment

The first assumption was that our economy is characterized by full employment and full production. How would our analysis and conclusions be altered if idle resources were available or if employed resources were used inefficiently? With full employment and full production, our five alternatives represent a series of maximum outputs; that is, they illustrate what combinations of drill presses and bread might be produced when the economy is operating at its full capacity. With *un*employment or *under*employment, the economy would obviously be producing less at each alternative.

Graphically, a situation of unemployment or underemployment can be illustrated by a point *inside* the original production possibilities curve which has been reproduced in Figure 2-2. Point *U* is such a point. Here the economy is obviously falling short of the various maximum combinations of bread and drill presses reflected by all the points *on* the production possibilities curve. The dotted arrows on Figure 2-2 indicate three of the possible paths back to full employment and full production. A movement toward full employment and full production will obviously entail a greater output of one or both products. And there are points *outside* the production possibilities curve which will be superior to any point on the curve, but such points are unobtainable, given the current supplies of resources and technology. The production barrier of full employment prohibits the production of any combination of capital and consumer goods lying outside the production possibilities curve.

It is interesting to note that in beginning to produce war goods for World War II the United States found itself with considerable unemployment. Hence, our economy was able to accomplish the production of an almost unbelievably large quantity of war goods and at the same time increase the volume of consumer goods output.[6] The Russians, on the other hand, en-

[6] There did occur, however, rather acute shortages of specific types of consumer goods.

tered World War II at almost capacity production; that is, they were operating close to full employment. Therefore, their military preparations entailed a considerable shifting of resources from the production of civilian goods and a concomitant drop in the standard of living.[7]

A growing economy

What happens to the production possibilities curve when we drop the remaining assumptions that the quantity and quality of resources and technology are fixed? The answer is: the production possibilities curve will shift to the right; that is, the total output of the economy will expand or grow.

Expanding resource supplies. Now let us drop the simplifying assumption that our total supplies of land, labor, capital, and entrepreneurial ability are fixed. Common sense tells us that over a period of time the rapidly growing population which we have in the United States will bring about significant increases in the supplies of labor and entrepreneurial ability.[8] Historically, our stock of capital has increased at a remarkable, though unsteady, rate. And although we are depleting some of our oil and mineral deposits, new sources are constantly being discovered. The drainage of swamps and

[7] Needless to say, it is sheer folly to leap to the conclusion that this contrast illustrates the desirability of unemployment at the outbreak of hostilities!

[8] This is not to say that population growth as such is always desirable. In Chapter 39 we shall discover that overpopulation is a constant drag upon the living standards of underdeveloped countries.

the development of irrigation programs add to our supply of arable land. Assuming continuous full employment and full production, the net result of these increased supplies of the factors of production will be the ability to produce more of both drill presses and bread. Thus in, say, 1983, the production possibilities of Table 2-1 may be obsolete, having given way to those shown in Table 2-2. Note that the greater abundance of resources results in a greater output of one or both products at each alternative; economic growth has occurred.

Technological advance. Our final simplifying assumption was that technology was constant. Simple observation tells us that technology has progressed with amazing rapidity over a long period of time. What does an advancing technology entail? New and better goods and improved ways of producing these goods. For the moment, let us think of technological advance as entailing simply improvements in capital facilities—more efficient machinery and equipment. How does such technological advance alter our earlier discussion of the economizing problem? In this way: technological advance, by improving productive efficiency, allows society to produce more goods with a fixed amount of resources. Or, alternatively, it permits us to produce the same amount of goods with a smaller amount of resources. Like increases in resource supplies, technological advance produces more drill presses and more bread.

What happens to the production possibility curve of Figure 2-2 when the supplies of resources increase or an improvement in technology occurs? The curve shifts outward and to the right as illustrated by the brown curve in Figure

TABLE 2-2. HYPOTHETICAL PRODUCTION POSSIBILITIES OF BREAD AND DRILL PRESSES WITH FULL EMPLOYMENT, 1983

Type of product	Production alternatives				
	A'	B'	C'	D'	E'
Bread (in hundred thousands)	0	2	4	6	8
Drill presses (in thousands)	14	12	9	5	0

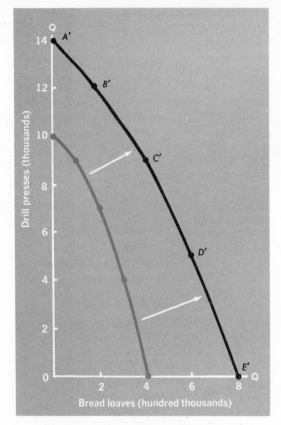

FIGURE 2-3. ECONOMIC GROWTH AND THE PRODUCTION POSSIBILITIES CURVE. The expanding resource supplies and technological advances which characterize a growing economy move the production possibilities curve outward and to the right. This permits the economy to enjoy larger quantities of both types of goods.

2-3. Increases in resource supplies and technological advances permit us to enjoy a greater output of both bread and drill presses; the economy's productive potential has grown. But note this important point: such a favorable shift in the production possibilities curve does not guarantee that the economy will operate at a point on that new curve. The economy might fail to realize its new potentialities. Some 71 million jobs will give us full employment at the

present time, but ten years from now our labor force, because of a growing population, will be much larger, and 71 million jobs will not be sufficient to give us full employment. In short, the production possibilities curve may shift, but the economy may fail to produce at a point on that curve. On Figure 2-2 the student should pencil in two new production possibility curves: one to show the situation where a better technique for producing drill presses has been developed, the technology for producing bread being unchanged, and the other to illustrate an improved technology for bread, the technology for producing drill presses being constant.

Present choices and future curve location. You may have anticipated this important point in the foregoing paragraphs: *an economy's current choice of position on its production possibilities curve is a basic determinant of the future location of that curve.* To illustrate this notion let us designate the two axes of the production possibilities curve as "goods for the future" and "goods for the present" as in Figure 2-4a and b. By "goods for the future" we refer to such things as capital goods, research and education, preventive medicine, and so forth, which obviously tend to increase the quantity and quality of property resources, enlarge the stock of technological information, and improve the quality of human resources. By "goods for the present" we mean pure consumer goods in the form of foodstuffs, clothing, transistor radios, automobiles, power mowers, and so forth.

Now suppose there are two economies, Alphania and Betania, which at the moment are identical in every respect, except that Alphania's current (1963) choice of position on its production possibilities curve strongly favors "present goods" as opposed to "future goods." The black dot in Figure 2-4a indicates this choice. Betania, on the other hand, renders a current (1963) choice which stresses large amounts of "future goods" and lesser amounts of "present goods" (Figure 2-4b). Now, all other things being the same, we can expect the future (1983) production possibilities curve of Betania to be further to the right than that of Alphania. That is, by currently choosing an

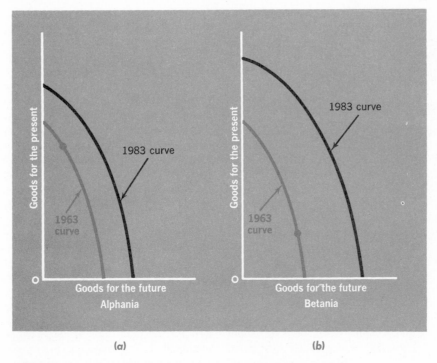

(a)   *(b)*

FIGURE 2-4. AN ECONOMY'S PRESENT CHOICE OF POSITION ON ITS PRODUCTION POSSIBILITIES CURVE HELPS DETERMINE THE CURVE'S FUTURE LOCATION.
A current choice favoring "present goods," as rendered by Alphania in (a), will cause a modest rightward shift of the curve. A current choice favoring "future goods," as rendered by Betania in (b), will result in a greater rightward shift of the curve.

output which is more conducive to technological advance and to increases in the quantity and quality of property and human resources, Betania will tend to achieve greater economic growth than will Alphania, whose current choice of output puts less emphasis upon those goods and services which cause the production possibilities curve to shift rightward.

It is this sort of analysis, incidentally, which helps explain why the total output of the Soviet Union is expanding each year at a rate which is 2 or 3 times as great as that of the United States (7 to 8 per cent for the U.S.S.R. as compared to 2½ to 3 per cent for the U.S.A.). The Soviet economy has been "plowing back" a larger proportion of its current output as goods for the future than has that of the United States.

Relatively greater Soviet emphasis upon goods for the future also helps explain why the Soviet standard of living is currently so very low relative to the United States and, in particular, why automobiles and television sets are so scarce and housing so remarkably poor.

ECONOMIZING: FIVE FUNDAMENTAL QUESTIONS

In order to provide a broad understanding of the essence of the economizing problem, the preceding discussion is pitched at a fairly abstract level. Let us now be more practical and examine some of the specific questions or problems that *any economic system* must answer in attempting to use its scarce resources to achieve the maximum satisfaction of consumer wants. Basically, there are Five Fundamental Questions which any economy must answer in attempting to achieve and maintain efficiency in the use of its scarce resources.

What is to be produced

Society must somehow decide what collection of goods and services will most fully satisfy its wants. This decision concerning the composition of total output must be consistent with the production possibilities currently facing the economy. Choosing a combination of capital and consumer goods lying *inside* the production possibilities curve entails economic inefficiency in the form of unemployment. Seeking a combination *outside* the current production possibilities curve is unrealistic; society is obviously setting its sights on an unattainable target.

Actually, the basic question of determining what is to be produced can be divided into two closely related subquestions: First, what goods and services are to be produced? Second, in what quantities does society want these goods produced?

Consider the first subquestion: What goods and services should be produced? Answering this entails, in effect, the setting up of a list of goods and services which society deems important enough to produce. How should society apportion its scarce resources among those products which it is capable of producing? Should our list include bread? Drill presses? Fords? Cadillacs? Color television? High-buttoned shoes? Mink coats? Buggy whips? Football stadia? ICBMs? Society must somehow decide what items to include in—and what items to exclude from—the list of goods that are to be produced.

But this decision is only half the battle. Once society has decided what to produce, somehow it must then assign proper weights to each of the items on the list. Without asking how this decision has been reached, suppose society has decided that bread, drill presses, Fords, and football stadia are the items from the above list which it actually wants to produce. The

fact that resources are scarce tells us that society cannot produce unlimited amounts of the goods on this list. Must society not decide *how many* loaves of bread, *how many* drill presses, *how many* Fords, and *how many* football stadia it wants in its total output? Society must not only decide the relative amounts of capital and consumer goods to be produced—the question posed on our production possibilities illustrations—but it must also determine the specific quantities of each type of capital goods and each type of consumer goods that will best fulfill society's material wants. Even in relatively primitive economies these decisions can become complex.

Remember, too, that in deciding the relative amounts of capital and consumer goods to be produced, society is of necessity weighing the relative merits of future, as opposed to current, want fulfillment. More resources devoted to technological research and to the expansion of the economy's capital facilities means less available for the production of goods for current consumption. The choice here is between more now or much more later. By cutting back on research and on the expansion of our productive facilities, society can produce a greater current output. But sacrificing some current consumption in order to free resources for research and capital expansion will mean an expanded output in the future.

These two subquestions—what goods shall we produce? in what quantities?—have been considered in a very simplified way in our analysis of the production possibilities tables. We solved—or dodged!—the first by assuming the economy had somehow decided to produce only bread and drill presses.

The answer to the second question entails society's choosing which one of the five alternatives—A, B, C, D, or E— yields the highest level of satisfaction. Thus the perennial question of consumer goods versus capital goods is part of the larger question of deciding the specific composition of the total output. In a wartime or mobilization situation, the question of civilian versus war goods falls under the same general heading.

Organizing production

Hand in glove with our decision as to the composition of total output is another query: *How should this total output be produced?* This major question can also be broken into parts. (1) How does society steer resources into industries producing goods that we want produced and, conversely, keep resources away from industries producing goods wanted in very small amounts or not at all? (2) What firms in the various industries are to do the producing, and how are they to obtain the needed resources? (3) What is the most efficient combination of resources for each firm to use in producing a given level of output? More subtly, what is the best technology to use in production? All these questions center upon the goal of achieving full production from society's available resources.

A reminder: although the question of organizing production is spelled out here in terms of an industrially advanced economy, similar questions would be pertinent for a primitive or underdeveloped economy.

Distributing output

The third basic decision comes close to home: *How is society to divide or ration the total output among the various economic units which comprise our economic system?* How should the total output of consumer goods be shared by the various households in our economy? Similarly, how should any additions to our stock of capital equipment included in our total output be apportioned to the various industries and the individual firms in those industries? What part of total output—if any—should be given over to government? In short, the question of how the total output is to be distributed among households, businesses, and government must somehow be answered by society. Obviously, these questions involve not only economics but also politics and ethics.

Two less obvious but highly important problems are lurking in the background of this discussion. One is that of determining the level of resource use; the other is that of providing for economic flexibility. Both demand careful attention.

Level of resource use

Society is obligated to determine the degree to which its economic resources are to be utilized. This decision is more complex than it first appears. Two related subquestions are involved: (1) To what degree is society *willing* to utilize its human and property resources? (2) To what extent is society actually *able* to employ its resources? Let us briefly explore these subquestions in the order stated.

A society which seeks to maximize the immediate fulfillment of its material wants must be willing to utilize its human and property resources to a very high degree. For human resources this means that both men and women must enter the labor force at an early age, retire at a very old age, and work long hours with few holidays and vacations in the intervening span of years. This obviously means little leisure. In all economies the decision as to how the time at the disposal of human resources is to be divided between production and leisure is influenced by sociocultural factors. The mores and customs of society are important in determining what percentage of the population is to work, the number of work hours, and, as a matter of fact, the intensity of labor.

The problem of resource conservation is primary in discussing the willingness of society to utilize its property resources currently. The nature of this decision can best be envisioned in terms of nonrenewable natural resources such as petroleum, natural gas, and a host of mineral deposits. The rapid exploitation of these resources currently makes for a high output now but at the same time lessens the ability of the economy to produce in the future. A lower current rate of utilization will spread more evenly over time the output of goods and services whose production is dependent upon these resources.

Having determined the level of resource utilization which it desires, society must then achieve that level of resource use. Society must avoid the involuntary idleness of its human and property resources. Involuntary idleness is the height of economic inefficiency. To be efficient, any economic system must somehow provide for high and stable levels of employment. We shall discover in Part 2 of this book that one of the basic defects of modern capitalism lies in the fact that it does not guarantee economic stability—full employment accompanied by a stable level of prices. Unemployment—actual or potential—is generally recognized as the greatest domestic problem which American capitalism currently faces. Inflation can be an equally potent adversary.

In a primitive Robinson Crusoe economy there is no problem of achieving full employment. The consumer and the producer are one and the same. Thus the producer, if he so desires, can spend all his waking hours in an effort to fulfill his material wants. Though we cannot pause at this point for lengthy explanations, it must be emphasized that the problem of achieving full employment is not so simple a task in such modern industrial societies as American capitalism. Here producers and consumers—sellers and buyers—have different identities, and their decision making is linked only imperfectly by the use of money in buying and selling both goods and resources. Hence, although consumers on the one hand and producers on the other both desire full employment, their nonidentity raises the possibility that inconsistencies in their spending and producing decisions may lead to unemployment. If the spending of buyers is deficient in amount, producers will not find it advantageous to employ all the economy's available resources. Why hire resources to produce goods that no one will buy? Conversely, too much spending may result in price inflation. In between lies some specific level of spending that will give the economy full employment with relatively stable prices. The point is this: nothing guarantees that an industrially advanced economy—particularly a capitalistic economy—will operate at a point on its production possibilities curve. Finally, it is also worth noting that an economy with an expanding population and labor force must provide more and more jobs each year to sustain full employment; the *status quo* with respect to the level of employment is not enough in a growing economy.

Flexibility

To achieve and maintain efficiency, the economy must be flexible and adaptable to change. Modern economies are far from static, unchanging things. Indeed, their basic feature is *change*. What changes? Several things: consumer tastes, the supplies of resources, and technology. Why does our basic objective of efficiency in the use of scarce resources demand that the economy be adaptable to such changes? Because a changing technology, changes in consumer tastes, and variations in resource supplies imply significant reallocations of our resources in order to preserve efficiency in their use. The collection of goods and services which maximizes consumer satisfactions today will fail to do so tomorrow if consumer wants have changed in the meantime. The collection of goods and services which pleased our parents in the 1920s will simply not be acceptable to us in the 1960s. Put more bluntly, we would not be particularly happy if today's output provided for large quantities of buggy whips, high-buttoned shoes, and mustache cups at the expense of stereophonic phonographs, transistor radios, and ballpoint pens. Similarly, changing resource supplies and the development of improved techniques of production will call for changes in the combinations of resources used in the production of given products if efficiency is to be maintained.

And, needless to say, flexibility is a basic prerequisite of such sudden economic transformations as those entailed by the shift from peace to war and, for that matter, from war to peace. Gigantic and sudden reallocations of our resources are necessary in such emergency situations.

We should keep constantly in mind that scarcity of economic resources lurks behind all five of these Fundamental Questions and their component parts; the Five Questions are merely a breakdown of the basic economizing problem of scarce resources and unlimited wants. Also, the apparent interrelatedness of these questions is almost self-evident, as we shall see in the following chapters, where we shall attempt to describe in detail how a capitalistic economy answers these questions. Indeed, it is difficult to treat the Five Questions independently of one another—they demand simultaneous treatment.

THE "ISMS"

If we lived in an isolated, one-man economy —a Robinson Crusoe economy—the answers we would provide to our imposing list of questions would be relatively simple. But when millions of diverse economic units exist, seeking somewhat different objectives and promoting different means for attaining these objectives, no simple answers to these queries present themselves. How is society to strike a mutually acceptable balance between the business tycoon's demand for a Cadillac, the Negro's demand for improved housing, the school child's demand for bubble gum and roller skates, and the housewife's demand for an automatic washer? Certainly no simple answer can be expected. And, to complicate matters, we know that answers which are acceptable today may not be acceptable tomorrow. The preferences of economic units change over time, and so do productive techniques, supplies of resources, and standards of equity in distributing output. In short, there are no final, once-and-for-all answers of a universal nature to the questions which comprise the economizing problem.

The previous discussion mentions at several points that any and all economic systems must answer the Five Fundamental Questions. As a matter of fact, *economic systems differ from one another because they see fit to answer these questions in different ways.* The feudal system of the Middle Ages answered these questions in terms of a strict social hierarchy in which one's contributions to producing and one's share of society's output were closely prescribed by tradition and custom.

Even modern economies differ immensely in terms of their economic objectives (what they want produced) and in their means of attaining those goals. Generally speaking, a survey of modern economic systems will promote the conclusion that there are two fundamentally different philosophies concerning the means of achieving the best answers to the Five Fundamental Questions. At one extreme, emphasis is put upon the freedom of individual economic units to make those choices which they feel are most appropriate in terms of their own specific objectives. The other extreme philosophizes that the sum of free economic choices by individual economic units is unlikely to result in efficiency in the use of scarce resources; hence, some omnipotent authoritarian power is needed in answering the Five Questions. The former philosophy crudely describes the core of *pure, or laissez-faire, capitalism;* the latter, the basic tenet of authoritarian socialism, or *communism.* Between these two hypothetical extremes can be arrayed an infinite number of variations and compromises. There is, strictly speaking, an unlimited number of ways of attempting to achieve maximum satisfaction from a society's scarce resources.

Table 2-3 summarizes the fundamental assumptions, institutional characteristics, and basic methods employed in achieving efficiency in the use of resources which are associated with pure capitalism, communism, and an intermediate hybrid—liberal socialism. While students of comparative economic systems might quibble a bit about these descriptions, all would agree with the basic point emphasized by the table. And that point is: there are no unique or universally accepted answers to the Five Fundamental Questions. Various societies, having different cultural and historical backgrounds, different mores and customs, and contrasting ideological frameworks—not to mention resources which differ both quantitatively and qualitatively—supply significantly different answers to the Five Questions. Russia, the United States, Great Britain, and Pakistan, for example, are all—in terms of their accepted goals, ideology, technologies, resources, and culture—attempting to achieve efficiency in the use of their respective resources. The best method for answering the Five Questions in one economy may be completely inappropriate for another economic system.

TABLE 2-3. THE "ISMS" AND THE ECONOMIZING PROBLEM

Economic system	Underlying assumption	Institutional characteristics	Method of solving economizing problem
Pure, or laissez-faire, capitalism	Each economic unit decides what choices and policies are best for it; such choices will prove to be in the social interest.	Private ownership of resources and business institutions; freedom of choice for consumers, resource suppliers, and enterprisers	Emphasis upon a system of free, competitive markets—virtually no governmental planning or control
Liberal, or democratic, socialism	Some governmental intervention is needed to improve upon the choices and policies of individual economic units.	Mixture of public and private ownership and public and private decision making	Mixture of loose governmental planning and regulation of basic industry; reliance on system of markets and prices in other segments of economy
Communism, or authoritarian socialism	The state is in the best position to know what choices and policies are beneficial for the economy as a whole and for its component parts.	Public ownership and control of the bulk of industry and agriculture; severe restriction of individual choices when in conflict with state-determined objectives	Governmental plans as established by central planning authority; heavy reliance on government directives; some reliance on a price system to implement the plans

The ensuing four chapters undertake to explain how the so-called *mixed capitalism* of the United States, which stands at some intermediate position between pure capitalism and liberal socialism in Table 2-3, goes about deciding the objectives of the economy, how production is to be organized, and how output is to be distributed. Chapter 3 discusses the institutional framework of capitalism and provides a very general picture of the operation of pure, or laissez-faire, capitalism. Chapter 4 explains the mechanics of supply and demand as price- and output-determining forces. The role of markets and prices in answering the Five Fundamental Questions is the topic of Chapter 5. Government is brought into the picture in Chapter 6, enlarging our picture of pure capitalism to one of mixed capitalism.

SUMMARY

1. The science of economics centers upon two basic facts: first, human material wants are virtually unlimited; second, economic resources are scarce.

2. Economic resources may be classified as property resources—materials and capital—or as human resources—labor and entrepreneurial ability.

3. Economics is concerned with the problem of administering scarce resources in the production of goods and services for the fulfillment of the material wants of society. Both the full employment and the full production of available resources are essential if this administration is to be efficient.

4. At any point in time a full-employment, full-production economy must sacrifice the output of some types of goods and services to achieve increased production of others.

5. Over time, technological advance and increases in the quantity and quality of human and property resources permit the economy to produce more of all goods and services. Society's choice as to the composition of current output is a determinant of the future location of the production possibilities curve.

6. Any economy faces Five Fundamental Questions in attempting to use its scarce resources to achieve the maximum fulfillment of its mate-rial wants. They are: (a) What goods and services do we want to produce and in what specific amounts? (b) How is production to be organized in getting these goods and services produced? (c) How will this output of goods and services be distributed among the various economic units which comprise the economic system? (d) What must an economy do to obtain and maintain the full employment of its available resources? (e) How does an economy provide the internal flexibility or adaptability required to maintain efficiency in the use of its resources?

7. The various economic systems of the world differ in their ideologies and their approaches in answering the Five Fundamental Questions.

QUESTIONS AND STUDY SUGGESTIONS

1. "Economics is the study of the principles governing the allocation of scarce means among competing ends when the objective of the allocation is to maximize the attainment of the ends."[9] Explain. Why is the problem of unemployment a part of the subject matter of economics?

2. "Wants aren't insatiable. I can prove it. I get all the coffee I want to drink every morning at breakfast." Critically analyze.

3. "Goods and services are scarce because resources are scarce." Explain.

4. What are the major functions of the entrepreneur?

5. "Economics is concerned with two problems. One has to do with achieving full employment of the economy's available resources. The other has to do with allocating employed resources among various possible uses. Both aspects emphasize efficiency in the use of resources." Explain.

6. The following is a production possibilities table for war goods and civilian goods:

Type of product	Production alternatives				
	A	B	C	D	E
Automobiles (in millions)	0	2	4	6	8
Guided missiles (in thousands)	30	27	21	12	0

a. Show these production possibilities data graphically. What do the points on the curve indicate? How does the curve reflect the law of increasing costs? Explain.

b. Label point G inside the curve. What does it indicate? Label point H outside the curve. What does this point indicate? What must occur before the economy can attain the level of production indicated by point H?

[9] George J. Stigler, *The Theory of Price* (New York: The Macmillan Company, 1947), p. 12.

c. Upon what assumptions is the production possibilities curve based? Be specific. What happens when each of these assumptions is released?

d. Suppose improvement occurs in the technology of producing guided missiles but not in the production of automobiles. Draw the new production possibilities curve. Now assume that a technological advance occurs in producing automobiles but not in producing guided missiles. Draw the new production possibilities curve. Finally, draw a production possibilities curve which reflects technological improvements in the production of both products.

7. "The present choice of position on the production possibilities curve is a major factor in economic growth." Explain.

8. State and thoroughly discuss the Five Fundamental Questions which all economies face. Why must an economy be adaptable to change in order to maintain efficiency in the use of scarce resources? Contrast the means by which pure capitalism, democratic socialism, and communism attempt to answer the Five Questions.

9. "Economics is . . . neither capitalist nor socialist: it applies to every society. Economics would disappear only in a world so rich that no wants were unfulfilled for lack of resources. Such a world is not imminent and may be impossible, for time is always limited." [10] Carefully evaluate and explain these statements. Do you agree that conceptually time is an economic resource?

SELECTED REFERENCES

Due, John F., and Robert W. Clower, *Intermediate Economic Analysis*, 4th ed. (Homewood, Ill.: Richard D. Irwin, Inc., 1961), chap. 1.

Galbraith, John K., *American Capitalism*, rev. ed. (Boston: Houghton Mifflin Company, 1956), chap. 2.

Heilbroner, Robert L., *The Making of Economic Society* (Englewood Cliffs, N.J.: Prentice-Hall, Inc., 1962), chap. 1.

Heilbroner, Robert L., *The Worldly Philosophers*, rev. ed. (New York: Simon and Schuster, Inc., 1961), chap. 2.

Knight, Frank H., "Social Economic Organization," in Ralph C. Epstein and Arthur D. Butler (eds.), *Selections in Economics* (Buffalo: Economica Books, 1958), chap. 2.

[10] Joseph P. McKenna, *Intermediate Economic Theory* (New York: The Dryden Press, Inc., 1958), p. 2.

Chapter 3

PURE CAPITALISM AND THE
CIRCULAR FLOW OF WEALTH

THE TASK of the present chapter is to describe the capitalist ideology and to explain how pure, or laissez-faire, capitalism operates. Strictly speaking, pure capitalism has never existed and probably never will. Why, then, do we bother to consider the operation of such an economy? Because it gives us a workable *first approximation* of how modern American capitalism functions, and approximations, when properly handled, can be very useful. In other words, pure capitalism constitutes a simplified point of reference which we shall then modify and adjust to correspond more closely to the reality of American capitalism.

In explaining the operation of pure capitalism, we shall discuss (1) the institutional framework and basic assumptions which comprise the capitalist ideology; (2) certain institutions and practices common to all modern economies; (3) capitalism and the circular flow of wealth; (4) how product and resource prices are determined; and (5) the market system and the allocating of economic resources. The first three topics constitute the present chapter; the latter two, Chapters 4 and 5, respectively.

CAPITALIST IDEOLOGY

Unfortunately, there is no neat and universally accepted definition of capitalism to aid us in our present task. We are therefore required to examine in some detail the basic tenets of capitalism to acquire a comprehensive understanding of what pure capitalism entails. In short, the framework of capitalism embodies the following institutions and assumptions: (1) private property, (2) freedom of enterprise and choice, (3) self-interest as the dominant motive, (4) competition, (5) reliance upon the price system, and (6) a limited role for government. Let us explore these characteristics to ensure our understanding them.

Private property

Under a capitalistic system, the means of production—that is, scarce resources—are owned by private individuals and private institutions as opposed to government. Private property, coupled with the freedom to negotiate binding legal contracts, permits private persons or businesses to obtain, control, employ, and dispose of economic resources as they see fit. The institution of private property is sustained over time by the *right of inheritance*, that is, by the right of a property owner to designate the recipient of his property at the time of death.

Needless to say, there are broad legal limits to this right of private ownership. For example, the use of one's resources for the production of narcotics is prohibited by legislation. Nor is public ownership nonexistent. Even in pure capitalism, recognition is given to the fact that public ownership of certain "natural monopolies" may be essential to the achievement of efficiency in the use of resources of the economy.

Freedom of enterprise and choice

Closely related to private ownership of property is freedom of enterprise and choice. Capitalism charges its component parts with the responsibility of making certain choices which are registered and made effective through the free markets of the economy.

Freedom of enterprise means that under pure capitalism private business enterprises are free to obtain economic resources, to organize these resources in the production of a product of the firm's own choosing, and to sell this product in the markets of their choice. No artificial obstacles or restrictions imposed by government or other producers block an entrepreneur's choice to enter or leave a particular industry.

Freedom of choice means that owners of property resources and money capital can employ or dispose of these resources as they see fit. It also means that laborers are free to enter any of those lines of work for which they are mentally and physically qualified. Finally, it means that consumers are at liberty, within the limits of their money incomes, to buy that collection of goods and services which they feel is most appropriate in satisfying their wants. Freedom of consumer choice may well be the most profound of these freedoms. The consumer is in a particularly strategic position in a capitalistic economy; in a sense, the consumer is sovereign. The range of free choices for suppliers of human and property resources is circumscribed by the choices of consumers. The consumer ultimately decides what the capitalistic economy should produce, and resource suppliers must make their free choices within the boundaries thereby delineated. Resource suppliers and businesses are not really "free" to produce goods and services which consumers do not desire.

Again, broad legal limitations prevail in the expression of all these free choices.

Role of self-interest

Since capitalism is individualistic, it is not surprising to find that the primary driving force of such an economy is the promotion of one's self-interest. When we say that self-interest is the basic motive under which economic units act and react, we simply mean that each economic unit attempts to do what is best for itself. Hence, entrepreneurs aim at the maximization of their firms' profits. They seek the greatest differential between their revenues—what they get from the sale of their products—and their costs of production—what they must pay for the resources used in production.

Other things being equal, owners of property resources attempt to achieve the highest price obtainable from the rent or sale of these resources. Given the amount and irksomeness of the effort involved, those who supply human resources will also attempt to obtain the highest possible incomes from their employment. Consumers, in purchasing a given product, will seek to obtain it at the lowest price. In short, capitalism presumes self-interest as the fundamental *modus operandi* for the various economic units as they express their free choices. The motive of self-interest gives direction and consistency to what might otherwise be an extremely chaotic economy.

While the seeking of maximum monetary returns is the sparkplug of capitalism, there is ample room for losses to be encountered. Capitalism is a profit system, but it is also a loss system. This is particularly relevant in so far as the entrepreneur is concerned. The freedom of individual businesses to use the resources which they possess or can command entails risk taking.

A final reminder: although self-interest is the basic motive underlying the functioning of capitalism, there are again exceptions to the rule. It is true that businesses and individuals do not always act in their own self-interest. Altruistic motives are part of the makeup of economic units. Yet self-interest is the best single statement of how economic units actually behave.

Competition

Freedom of choice exercised in terms of promoting one's own monetary returns provides the basis for competition, or economic rivalry, as a fundamental feature of capitalism. Competition, as economists see it, entails (1) the presence of large numbers of independently acting buyers and sellers operating in the market for any particular product or resource and (2) the freedom of buyers and sellers to enter or leave particular markets. Let us briefly explore these two related aspects of competition:

1. The essence of competition is the widespread diffusion of economic power among the individual units—businesses and households—which comprise the economy. In particular, when a large number of buyers and sellers are present in a market, no one buyer or seller will be able to demand or offer a quantity of the product sufficiently large to noticeably influence its price. Let us examine this statement in terms of the selling or supply side of the product market.

We have all observed that, when a product becomes unusually scarce, its price will skyrocket. (We recall, for example, that during World War II, shortages of sugar, gasoline, automobiles, and cigarettes entailed sharply rising prices on these items.) Thus, if a single producer, or small group of producers acting together, can somehow control or restrict the total supply of a product, he can raise its price to his own advantage. By controlling supply, the producer can "rig the market" on his own behalf. Now the essence of competition is that there are so many sellers that each, because he is contributing an almost negligible fraction of the total supply, has virtually no control over the supply or, therefore, over the product price.

For example, suppose there are 10,000 farmers each of whom is supplying 100 bushels of corn in the Kansas City grain market at some particular time when the price of corn happens to be $2 per bushel. Could a single farmer, who happens to be dissatisfied with the existing price, cause an artificial scarcity of corn and thereby boost the price above $2? The answer is obviously "No." Farmer Jones, by restricting his output from 100 to 75 bushels, exerts virtually no effect upon the total supply of corn. In fact, he only reduces total supply from 1,000,000 to 999,975 bushels. This obviously is not much of a shortage! Supply is virtually unchanged and, therefore, the $2 price persists. In brief, competition means that each seller is providing a drop in the bucket of total supply. The individual seller can make no noticeable dent in total supply; hence, he cannot *as an individual producer*[1] manipulate product price. This is what is meant when it is pointed out that an individual competitive seller is "at the mercy of the market."

The same rationale applies to the demand side of the market. Buyers are plentiful and act independently. Thus no single buyer can manipulate the market to his advantage.

The important point is this: the widespread diffusion of economic power which competition involves controls the use and limits the potential abuse of that power. Economic rivalry prevents economic units from wreaking havoc on one another as they attempt to further their self-interests. Competition imposes limits upon expressions of self-interest by buyers and sellers. Competition is a basic regulatory force in capitalism.

2. Competition also assumes that it is a simple matter for producers to enter (or leave) a particular industry; there are no artificial legal or institutional obstacles to prohibit the expansion (or contraction) of specific industries. This aspect of competition is prerequisite to the flexibility which is essential if an economy is to remain efficient over time. Freedom of entry is necessary if the economy is to adjust appropriately to changes in consumer tastes, technology, or resource supplies. This matter will receive detailed treatment in Chapter 5.

[1] Of course, if a number of farmers simultaneously restricted their production, then the resulting change in total supply could no longer be ignored, and price would be expected to rise.

Markets and prices

Private property, freedom of choice, and self-interest—all subject to the regulatory force of competition—set the stage for what is perhaps the basic feature of the capitalistic system. *Capitalism is a market economy.* The decisions rendered by the buyers and sellers of products and resources are made effective through a system of markets. The preferences of sellers and buyers are registered on the supply and demand sides of various markets, and the outcome of these choices is a system of product and resource prices. These prices are guideposts upon which resource owners, entrepreneurs, and consumers make and revise their free choices in furthering their self-interests. Just as competition is the controlling mechanism, so a system of markets and prices is a basic organizing force. The price system is an elaborate communications system through which innumerable individual free choices are recorded, summarized, and balanced against one another. Those who obey the dictates of the price system are rewarded; those who ignore it are penalized by the system. Through this communications system, society renders its decisions concerning what the economy should produce, how production can be efficiently organized, and how the fruits of productive endeavor are to be distributed among the individual economic units which comprise capitalism.

Not only is the price system the mechanism through which society renders decisions concerning how it allocates its resources and distributes the resulting output, but it is through the price system that these decisions are implemented and carried out. However, a word of caution: economic systems based upon the ideologies of socialism and communism also depend upon price systems, but not to the same degree nor in the same way as does pure capitalism. The socialistic and communistic societies use markets and prices merely to implement the decisions rendered wholly or in part by a central planning authority. In capitalism, the price system functions both as a device for rendering innumerable choices of free individuals and businesses and as a mechanism for implementing or carrying out these decisions.

The two chapters that follow analyze the mechanics and the operation of a capitalistic price system.

Limited government

A competitive capitalist economy is thought to be conducive to a high degree of efficiency in the use or allocation of its resources. Hence, there is allegedly little real need for governmental intervention in the operation of such an economy beyond its aforementioned role of imposing broad legal limits upon the exercise of individual choices and the use of private property. The historical development of the concept of pure capitalism as a self-regulating and self-adjusting type of economy precludes any significant economic role for government. As we will see shortly, capitalism in practice has not been self-regulating to the degree economists once supposed. But for the moment, at least, our analysis will exclude government. Chapter 6 will elaborate the functions of government in present-day mixed capitalism.

OTHER CHARACTERISTICS

Private property, freedom of enterprise and choice, self-interest as a motivating force, competition, and reliance on a price system are all institutions and assumptions which are more or less exclusively associated with pure capitalism. In addition, there are certain institutions and practices which are characteristic of all modern economies. They are (1) the use of an advanced technology, (2) specialization according to the principle of comparative advantage, and (3) the use of money. Specialization and the use of an advanced technology are prerequisites to the efficient employment of any economy's resources. The use of money is a permissive characteristic which allows society more easily to practice and reap the benefits of specialization and the employment of advanced productive techniques.

Extensive use of capital goods

All modern economies—whether they approximate the capitalist, socialist, or communist ideology—are based upon an advanced technology and the extensive use of capital goods. Under pure capitalism it is competition, coupled with freedom of choice and the desire to further one's self-interest, which provides the means for achieving a rapid rate of technological advance. The capitalistic framework is felt to be highly effective in harnessing incentives to develop new products and improved techniques of production. Why? Because the monetary rewards derived therefrom accrue directly to the innovator. Pure capitalism therefore presupposes the extensive use and rapid development of complex capital goods: tools, machinery, large-scale factories, and storage, transportation, and marketing facilities.

Why are the existence of an advanced technology and the extensive use of capital goods important? Because the most direct method of producing a product is usually the least efficient.[2] Even Robinson Crusoe avoided the inefficiencies of direct production in favor of "roundabout production." It would be ridiculous for a farmer—even a backyard farmer—to go at production with his bare hands. Obviously, it pays huge dividends in terms of a more efficient and, therefore, a more abundant output to fashion tools of production, that is, capital equipment, to aid in the productive process. The best way of getting water out of a well is not to dive in after it!

But there is a catch involved. As we recall our discussion of the production possibilities curve and the basic nature of the economizing problem, it is evident that, with full employment and full production, resources must be diverted from the production of consumer goods in order to be used in the production of capital goods. We must currently tighten our belts as consumers to free resources for the production of capital goods which will increase productive efficiency and permit us to have a greater output of consumer goods at some future date. In short, in adding to the stock of capital, consumers must accept less now to get more later. The Russian Five-year Plans, aimed at an accelerated build-up of the country's capital facilities, provide an excellent illustration of this point. As noted earlier, the Soviet citizenry has paid for this overnight mechanization of industry in terms of a standard of living below that which would have otherwise prevailed.

Specialization

The extent to which society relies upon specialization is astounding. The vast majority of consumers produce virtually none of the goods and services they consume and, conversely, consume little or nothing of what they produce. The hammer-shop laborer who spends his life stamping out parts for jet engines may never consume an airplane trip. The assembly-line worker who devotes eight hours a day to the installation of windows in Chevrolets may not own a car, or if he does, it may be a Ford. Few households seriously consider any extensive production of their own food, shelter, and clothing. Many a farmer sells his milk to the local creamery and then buys oleomargarine at the Podunk general store. Society learned long ago that self-sufficiency breeds inefficiency. The Jack-of-all-trades may be a very colorful individual, but he is certainly lacking in efficiency.

In what specific ways might human specialization—the division of labor—enhance productive efficiency? First, specialization permits individuals to take advantage of existing differences in their abilities and skills. If caveman A is strong, swift afoot, and accurate with a spear, and caveman B is weak and slow, but patient, then this distribution of talents can be most efficiently utilized by making A a hunter and B a fisherman. Second, even if the abilities of A and B are identical, specialization may prove to be advantageous. Why? Because by

---

[2] Remember that consumer goods satisfy wants directly, while capital goods do so indirectly through the more efficient production of consumer goods.

devoting all his time to a single task, the doer is more likely to develop the appropriate skills and to discover improved techniques than when apportioning his time among a number of diverse tasks. One learns to be a good hunter by hunting! Finally, specialization—devoting all of one's time to, say, a single task—obviously avoids the loss of time which is entailed in shifting from one job to another. For all these reasons the division of labor results in greater productive efficiency in the use of human resources.

Specialization also is desirable on a regional basis. Oranges could be grown in Nebraska, but because of the unsuitability of the land, rainfall, and temperature, the costs involved would be exceedingly high. Florida could probably achieve some success in the production of wheat, but, for similar reasons, such production would be found to be a relatively costly business. As a result, Nebraskans produce those products—wheat in particular—for which their resources are best adapted, and Floridians do the same, producing oranges and other citrus fruits. In so doing, both produce a surplus. Nebraska produces far more wheat than its inhabitants can consume, and Florida produces great excesses of oranges. Then, very sensibly, Nebraskans and Floridians swap some of their surpluses. Specialization permits each area to put its best foot forward, that is, to turn out those goods which its resources can most efficiently produce. In this way both Nebraska and Florida can enjoy a larger amount of both wheat and oranges than would otherwise be the case. In short, human and geographical specialization are both essential in achieving efficiency in the use of resources.

These simple illustrations make very plausible the contention that specialization is economically desirable because it results in more efficient production. Indeed, the point is almost self-explanatory. But, because the concept of specialization is so vital to an understanding of the production and exchange processes of modern economies, let us tackle a couple of more exacting illustrations of the gains which accrue from specialization. Our examples will be simplified to make the principles involved as clear as possible.

Absolute advantage. Suppose there are two equally skilled farmers, Anderson and Brooks. They each own, say, 6-acre farms, and each devotes the same total amount of time to farming. There is just one difference: their farmland is not of equal quality and fertility. We shall assume, to start with, that if Anderson devoted one-third of his time and land to the production of wheat and two-thirds to corn, he could produce 30 bushels of wheat and 10 bushels of corn. If Brooks devoted one-third of his time and land to the production of wheat and two-thirds to corn, his output would be 20 bushels of each product. We summarize this hypothetical data in Table 3-1, noting in parenthesis the fraction of land and total working time each farmer devotes to the production of each crop.

Anderson obviously has an *absolute advantage* in producing wheat; by devoting one-third of his time and land to wheat Anderson can produce a larger absolute amount of wheat —30 as compared with 20 bushels—than Brooks can by using the same amount of time and land. But Brooks has an absolute advantage when it comes to producing corn. Since the two farmers are equally skilled and devote the same amounts of time and land to the production of each good, the different absolute outputs tell us that Anderson's land is better suited to the production of wheat than Brooks's and, conversely, Brooks's land is better suited to corn than is Anderson's.

Should the farmers specialize? Yes, they most certainly should, because both stand to benefit. Anderson should devote full time and all his land to wheat, the product which his land produces most efficiently. Similarly, Brooks should use all his time and land to produce corn. If they do this, the data in Table 3-1 change to the data given in Table 3-2. The 1s in parentheses show that Anderson devotes full time and all his land to wheat and that Brooks does the same with respect to corn.

Comparing the totals of Tables 3-1 and 3-2, it is immediately evident that the two farmers taken together have the same total amount of corn and 40 bushels more wheat than they realized when *not* specializing. Supposing Brooks exchanges 10 bushels of corn for 40 bushels of Anderson's wheat; Anderson will

TABLE 3-1. NONSPECIALIZED PRODUCTION OF WHEAT
AND CORN

	Wheat, bushels	Corn, bushels
Anderson	30 (⅓)	10 (⅔)
Brooks	20 (½)	20 (⅔)
Total	50	30

then have 50 bushels of wheat and 10 bushels of corn. Brooks will have 40 bushels of wheat and 20 of corn. This is shown in Table 3-3.

Comparing Table 3-3 with 3-1, we note that both Brooks and Anderson have the same a-mount of corn they could have produced by not specializing and 20 bushels more of wheat a-piece. Clearly, both farmers have benefited by specializing according to absolute advantage and by trading some of their specialties. *Specialization is apparently an excellent method for allocating scarce resources so as to get the greatest total output from them.* This is obvious from our simple example: the same total inputs, or resources, result in a greater total output when used under conditions of specialization.

Comparative advantage. Strange as it may first seem, specialized production also results in the more efficient employment of resources and therefore in a greater output when one farmer, say Anderson, has an absolute advantage in the production of both corn and wheat. Table 3-4 illustrates such a situation. In this example, we assume that Anderson's land is better suited to the production of both crops than is Brooks's. Hence, as both farmers devote one-third of

their time and land to wheat and two-thirds to corn, Anderson will outproduce Brooks in both cases. Yet Anderson's absolute advantage in corn exceeds that in wheat. Anderson can outproduce Brooks in corn 2 to 1, but only 3 to 2 when it comes to wheat.

Economists say that an individual has a *relative*, or *comparative*, *advantage* in that product in which (1) his absolute advantage is greater (in the case of Anderson) or (2) his absolute *disadvantage* is less (in the case of Brooks). Anderson has an absolute advantage in both products, but that absolute advantage is relatively or comparatively greater in corn than in wheat. Hence, Anderson may be said to have a comparative advantage in corn. Brooks, on the other hand, is at an absolute disadvantage in the production of both goods; however, that absolute disadvantage is relatively less in wheat than in corn. Hence, Brooks is said to have a comparative advantage—though absolute disadvantage!—in wheat.

Now common sense does not tell us that Anderson and Brooks will benefit from specialization; this conclusion must await the completion of our illustration. But common sense does suggest that, if specialization is to occur, it should be based upon comparative advantage.

TABLE 3-2. SPECIALIZED PRODUCTION OF WHEAT AND
CORN ACCORDING TO ABSOLUTE ADVANTAGE

	Wheat, bushels	Corn, bushels
Anderson	90 (1)	0
Brooks	0	30 (1)
Total	90	30

TABLE 3-3. THE DISTRIBUTION OF WHEAT AND CORN
AFTER EXCHANGE

	Wheat, bushels	Corn, bushels
Anderson	50	10
Brooks	40	20
Total	90	30

That is, Anderson should devote full time and all his land to corn, where he has the greater absolute advantage, and Brooks to wheat, where he faces the lesser absolute disadvantage. Specialization in this way changes the data of Table 3-4 in the manner indicated in Table 3-5.

By comparing Table 3-5 with 3-4, we discover that specialization according to *comparative advantage* results in the same total output of corn and a greater output of wheat. In this case, the gain resulting from specialization is 10 bushels of wheat. Specialization according to comparative advantage has obviously improved the allocation of resources; more output has resulted from the same volume of resource inputs.

Terms of trade. Using our example of comparative advantage, let us now look at the trade which is likely to result between the two farmers. What will be the *terms of trade* between Anderson and Brooks; that is, at what rate will they exchange corn and wheat? We can safely say that Anderson will accept nothing *less than* 30 bushels of wheat for giving up 10 bushels of his corn. Why? Because, as a comparison of Tables 3-4 and 3-5 indicates, by not specializ-

ing in wheat but by devoting one-third of his time to it, Anderson could produce 30 bushels of wheat himself. And this would cut his corn production by only 10 bushels. Brooks, on the other hand, will certainly not give *more than* 40 bushels of wheat for 10 bushels of corn. How do we know? Because Table 3-4 tells us that Brooks, by devoting two-thirds of his time to corn production, could produce by himself 10 bushels of corn at a sacrifice of 40 units of wheat. In brief, the terms of trade must be 1 bushel of corn equals 3 bushels or more of wheat, or Anderson will not trade; the terms of trade must be 1 bushel of corn equals 4 bushels or less of wheat, or Brooks will not trade. Having established the upper and lower limits of the terms of trade, let us suppose that the two agrarians, being equally shrewd bargainers, settle on a rate of 1 bushel of corn equals 3½ bushels of wheat. Now, if Brooks swaps 35 bushels of his wheat for 10 bushels of Anderson's corn, then Brooks and Anderson will have on hand the amounts of the two products shown in Table 3-6.

Comparison with Table 3-4 clearly shows that specialization and trade based upon comparative advantage have netted Anderson and

TABLE 3-4. NONSPECIALIZED PRODUCTION OF WHEAT
AND CORN

	Wheat, bushels	Corn, bushels
Anderson	30 (½)	20 (⅔)
Brooks	20 (½)	10 (⅔)
Total	50	30

TABLE 3-5. SPECIALIZED PRODUCTION OF WHEAT AND
CORN ACCORDING TO COMPARATIVE ADVANTAGE

	Wheat, bushels	Corn, bushels
Anderson	0	30 (1)
Brooks	60 (1)	0
Total	60	30

Brooks each an extra 5 bushels of wheat and the same amounts of corn they would have realized by not specializing. The total gain from specializing is obviously 10 bushels of wheat.

It should be emphasized that specialization and an advanced technology go hand in hand. Specialization and technological advance reinforce one another. Anderson and Brooks are more likely to discover better techniques for producing corn and wheat when specializing than they would if each divided his energies between the two products. Specialization encourages technological advance, and technological advance in turn stimulates greater specialization.

One final word: serious reflection on this matter of geographical and human specialization reveals certain drawbacks. For example, the monotony and drudgery of specialized work are well known. Brooks, for example, might be reluctant to produce only wheat, because this is much more tedious than dividing his efforts between wheat and corn. And imagine the boredom of our previously mentioned assembly-line worker who is still putting windows in Chevrolets. Second, specialization and mutual interdependence vary directly with one another. The less each of us produces for himself, the more we are dependent upon the output of others. The less wheat produced in Florida, the greater is that state's dependence upon Nebraska wheat. Specialization obviously makes Brooks dependent upon Anderson for corn and Anderson dependent upon Brooks for wheat. For the economy as a whole, it is not surprising to discover what profoundly serious consequences may stem from a transportation strike or, on a more localized basis, from the breakdown of an assembly line. A third problem centers upon the exchanging of the surpluses which specialization entails. An examination of this problem leads us into a discussion of the use of money in the economy.

Use of money

Virtually all economies, advanced or primitive, are money-using. In these economies, money performs a variety of functions, two of which are vital to our present analysis. Money is, first, a medium of exchange and, second, a standard of value. For completeness, we note a third function: money is a store of value.

TABLE 3-6. THE DISTRIBUTION OF WHEAT AND CORN
AFTER EXCHANGE

	Wheat, bushels	Corn, bushels
Anderson	35	20
Brooks	25	10
Total	60	30

As a medium of exchange. In our Anderson-Brooks example it was necessary for Brooks to trade 35 bushels of wheat for 10 bushels of Anderson's corn if both farmers were to share in the fruits of specialization. If trade were prohibited for some reason, the benefits of specializing according to comparative advantage might be lost to society. Why? Because consumers want a wide variety of products and, in the absence of trade, would tend to devote their human and material resources to many diverse types of production. If exchange could not occur or was very inconvenient to transact, Anderson and Brooks would be forced to be more self-sufficient. Hence, each would produce both wheat and corn. Each would therefore fail to put his best foot forward, and the advantages of specialization would not be realized. *In short, a convenient means of exchanging goods is a prerequisite of specialization.*

Now exchange can, and sometimes does, occur on the basis of bartering, that is, swapping goods for goods. A moment ago we assumed that Brooks bartered wheat for some of Anderson's corn. But bartering as a means of exchange can pose serious problems for the economy. Specifically, exchange by barter requires a *coincidence of wants* between the two transactors. In our example, we assumed that Brooks had excess wheat to trade and that he wanted to obtain corn. And we assumed Anderson had excess corn to swap and that he wanted to acquire wheat. So exchange occurred. But if this coincidence of wants did not exist, trade would be stymied. Let us pose such a problem.

Suppose Brooks does not want any of Anderson's corn but is interested in buying vegetables from Johnson, a third farmer. Ironically enough, Johnson wants Anderson's corn but not Brooks's wheat. And, to complicate matters, we shall say that Anderson wants some of Brooks's wheat but none of Johnson's vegetables. It seems complicated, but it all boils down to the situation shown in Figure 3-1.

In no case do we find a coincidence of wants. Trade by barter would be difficult. To overcome such a stalemate, modern economies use *money*, which is simply a convenient social invention for facilitating the exchange of goods and services. Historically, cattle, cigarettes, shells, stones, pieces of metal, and many other diverse commodities have been used, with varying degrees of success, as a medium for facilitating exchange. But to be money, an item needs to pass only one test: *it must be generally acceptable by buyers and sellers in exchange.* Money is socially defined; whatever society accepts as a medium of exchange is money. Most modern economies, for reasons made clear in Chapter 15, find it convenient to use pieces of paper as money. We shall assume that this is the case with the Brooks-Anderson-Johnson economy; they use pieces of paper which they call "dollars" as money. Can the use of paper dollars as a medium of exchange overcome the stalemate shown in Figure 3-1?

Obviously it can, with trade occurring in this way:

1. Anderson can exchange money for some of Brooks's wheat.

2. Brooks can take the money realized from the sale of wheat and exchange it for some of Johnson's vegetables.

3. Johnson can then exchange the money received from his sale of vegetables for some of Anderson's surplus corn.

These transactions are shown by the arrows in Figure 3-2.

The willingness to accept paper money (or any other kind of money, for that matter) as a medium of exchange has permitted a three-way trade which allows each farmer to specialize in one product and obtain the other product(s) he desires, despite a noncoincidence of wants. Barter, resting as it does upon a coincidence of wants, would have impeded this exchange and in so doing would have induced the three farmers to become nonspecialists. Of course, the efficiencies of specialization would then have been lost to the Brooks-Anderson-Johnson economy. Strange as it may first seem, two exchanges—surplus product for money and then money for a wanted product —are simpler than the product-for-product exchange which bartering entails! Indeed, in this example, product-for-product exchange would not be likely to occur at all.

A legitimate question is: Why are Brooks,

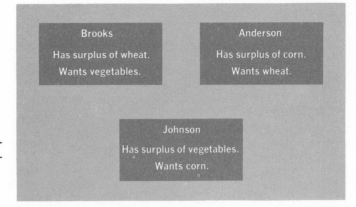

Brooks

Has surplus of wheat.

Wants vegetables.

Anderson

Has surplus of corn.

Wants wheat.

Johnson

Has surplus of vegetables.

Wants corn.

FIGURE 3-1. THE NONCOINCIDENCE OF WANTS. Trade by barter would be inconvenient or even blocked by a noncoincidence of wants.

Johnson, and Anderson willing to accept pieces of paper for those goods they have worked so hard to produce? For the simple reason that they are confident this paper money will be acceptable in exchange for the goods they desire. That is, Brooks is willing to give up wheat for Anderson's paper money because he knows that Johnson will be willing to accept these pieces of paper in exchange for vegetables. And Johnson will accept the paper money because he is confident that Anderson will accept it in exchange for wheat! Why? Because Brooks in turn will accept it! We must remember that whatever is generally acceptable by society as a medium of exchange is money. So long as transactors are willing to accept an item as payment in exchange, that item is money. Money is money because people accept it as such. This is true in all economies, regardless of ideological leanings.

As a standard of value. The use of money alleviates two other related problems which would plague transactors in a barter economy. Obviously, under a system of barter, prices would have to be stated in terms of other products. This would result, first of all, in a great many individual product prices. Such a multitude of prices would be difficult to remember, and this would be an obstacle to exchange. Furthermore, prices stated in terms of other products are hard to compare. This makes it difficult to recognize readily the relative worth of various products and impedes the making of

rational decisions concerning the production and consumption of goods. Let us explore these two problems in some detail.

Even if the Brooks-Anderson-Johnson economy had a coincidence of wants, trade by barter would be hampered by the large number of prices the transactors would have to keep in mind. Since there are three products, and the price of any one can be measured in terms of each of the other two, there is a total of six prices for the transactors to keep in mind. We shall suppose that the actual values of the three products in exchange are such that 1 bushel of corn *equals* 2 bushels of wheat *equals* 4 bushels of vegetables. From this information, six prices can be derived:

1. The price of corn in terms of wheat:

   1 bushel of corn = 2 bushels of wheat

2. The price of corn in terms of vegetables:

   1 bushel of corn = 4 bushels of vegetables

3. The price of wheat in terms of corn:

   1 bushel of wheat = ½ bushel of corn

4. The price of wheat in terms of vegetables:

   1 bushel of wheat = 2 bushels of vegetables

5. The price of vegetables in terms of corn:

   1 bushel of vegetables = ¼ bushel of corn

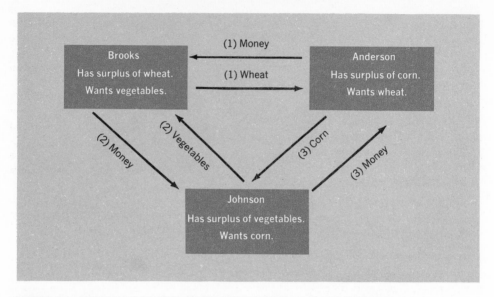

FIGURE 3-2. MONEY FACILITATES TRADE WHERE WANTS DO NOT COINCIDE.
By the use of money as a medium of exchange, trade can be accomplished, as
indicated by the arrows, despite a noncoincidence of wants. By facilitating exchange,
the use of money permits an economy to realize the efficiencies of specialization.

6. The price of vegetables in terms of wheat:

   1 bushel of vegetables = ½ bushel of wheat

This looks very confusing. In a modern economy, wherein consumers purchase thousands of different products, the difficulty would be compounded, because the number of prices to remember would be astronomical. Indeed, this is the very point we want to recognize. Stating the price of each product in terms of all other available products results in *too many noncomparable prices* to be readily remembered. Exchange would be very tedious under such circumstances.

To alleviate this problem of too many prices, modern economies use the monetary unit, be it pesos, pounds sterling, rubles, or dollars, as a common denominator or standard of value. In so doing, all prices are simply stated in terms of the monetary unit. This drastically reduces the number of prices one must remember. For example, if the price of corn in the market happens to be $4 per bushel,[3] we can easily re-

state the relative worth of all other products in terms of dollars. Since transactors are willing to swap 1 bushel of corn for 2 bushels of wheat, a bushel of wheat must be worth $2. And, since 1 bushel of corn trades for 4 bushels of vegetables, a bushel of vegetables must be worth just $1. Now there are only three prices, instead of six, to remember: (1) 1 bushel of corn equals $4, (2) 1 bushel of wheat equals $2, and (3) 1 bushel of vegetables equals $1.

Secondly, aside from the larger number of prices involved, it is apparent that prices stated in terms of other products are difficult to compare, because there is no common denominator. Looking at the six barter prices shown above, can we readily state the relative worth of 7½ bushels of corn or 3⅓ bushels of vegetables? Certainly not. It is as if we were suddenly asked to compare the fractions ⅔₁₈ and ⅝₄ and to indicate which is the larger. It is sad but true

[3] We shall see in the next chapter that it is the supply of, and the demand for, a product in the market that will determine its money price.

that most of us would have to think a moment before answering, because the two fractions are not immediately comparable. However, by stating the two fractions in terms of a common denominator—that is, by changing $\frac{2}{18}$ to $\frac{6}{54}$ —we can make a ready comparison and easily see that $\frac{2}{18}$ is obviously larger than $\frac{5}{54}$.

So it is with prices. A common denominator —stating all prices in terms of the monetary unit—permits a quick and direct comparison of the relative worth of different goods and services. Since 1 bushel of corn is worth $4, we can quickly determine that 7½ bushels are worth $30. And, most important of all, by stating all prices in terms of the monetary unit, the relative, per unit worth of various products is immediately evident. Needless to say, this greatly simplifies the choices of consumers as they attempt to obtain, with the limited number of dollars at their disposal, that collection of goods which will give them maximum satisfaction of their wants. The same holds true for businessmen as they attempt to acquire the least costly combination of resources to produce a given commodity. Money prices provide a simple, clear-cut, and extremely handy index for comparing the relative worth of heterogeneous goods which are very difficult to compare in terms of one another.

We shall quickly glance at a final example that stresses the importance of money as a medium of exchange and standard of value. Let us imagine a Detroit laborer producing crankshafts for Oldsmobiles. At the end of the week, instead of receiving a brightly colored piece of paper endorsed by the company comptroller, or a few pieces of paper neatly engraved in green and black, the laborer receives from the company paymaster four Oldsmobile crankshafts. Inconvenient as this is, and with no desire to hoard crankshafts, the laborer ventures into the Detroit business district, intent upon spending his hard-earned income on a basket of food, a suit of clothes, a baseball game, a haircut, and, in anticipation of a late return, a box of candy to pacify his wife. Needless to say, he is faced with some inconvenient and time-consuming trading, and he might not be able to negotiate any exchanges at all. Find-

ing a clothing merchant who has a suit which meets his approval and who happens to be in the market for an Oldsmobile crankshaft is a formidable task. And, even if he locates a barber in need of a crankshaft, how is the barber going to make change for the laborer's haircut? Finally, is the laborer starting out to buy the really best combination of goods and services? After all, there is no convenient means in a barter economy for evaluating the relative worth of suits, ball games, haircuts, and baskets of food—the economic value of these heterogeneous goods cannot be readily compared. For these reasons all modern economies are money-using economies.

As a store of value. Money performs one other basic function in all economies: it is a convenient means of storing wealth. If an income receiver does not want to exercise currently all his dollar claims against the output of society, he may hoard or store some of these claims for future use. The holder of money simply has a stock of generalized purchasing power which he can spend over time in acquiring wanted goods and services. The income receiver might choose to store wealth in the form of money to prepare himself for such emergencies as sickness, accident, or unemployment, or to provide a ready source of funds with which to take advantage of unexpected bargain purchases. Or he might hoard money to provide for retirement or the education of his family or to permit the making of large purchases which exceed a single pay check.

This, then, is the ideology of pure capitalism, the institutions peculiar to it, and the institutions it shares in common with alternative economic systems.

CIRCULAR FLOW OF WEALTH

Our discussion has pointed out the role of markets and prices as a mechanism for the tabulation and communication of the decisions of individual economic units. In pure capitalism, the free decisions of businesses and households concerning what the economy should produce, how production should be organized, and how total output should be distributed are rendered effective through a system of markets and prices. Also, the convenience of money prices as a device for comparing the relative worth of heterogeneous products and resources has been stressed.

The next logical step in this discussion is to examine in some detail the nature of markets and prices. The remainder of this chapter is devoted to a general overview of the market system of pure capitalism for the purpose of pinpointing the two basic types of markets of pure capitalism and noting the character of the transactions which occur therein. In Chapter 4 a rather detailed examination of how specific prices are actually determined in pure capitalism is presented. Then Chapter 5 provides a more rigorous discussion of how pure capitalism goes about answering the Five Fundamental Questions through the workings of the price system.

Circular flow model of the economy

How does pure capitalism work? Several answers can be offered, depending upon the amount of detail one desires.

Real flows. In a barter economy households, which directly or indirectly (through their own-ership of business corporations) own all economic resources, supply these resources to businesses as is shown in the upper loop of Figure 3-3. (Let us for the moment think of businesses simply as organizational charts, that is, institutions on paper apart from the capital, raw materials, labor, and entrepreneurial ability which breathe life into them and make them "going concerns.") Businesses, of course, will want resources, because these are the means by which goods and services are produced. In return for making their resources available for use by businesses, households will receive payments in kind; that is, they will be paid in terms of the goods and services they have helped produce. This flow of payments is shown in the lower loop of Figure 3-3. Of course, households, being paid in terms of crankshafts, shoes, doughnuts, and so forth will face some difficult exchange problems in swapping goods for goods with one another in seeking to satisfy their various wants. In any event this simple picture of the economy does accurately locate the main "real" flows, that is, the flow of resources and the flow of goods and services which occur in a capitalistic economy.

Money flows. To circumvent problems of inconvenience in bartering, all modern economies are money-using economies. How does our circular flow picture change as we progress from a barter to a monetary economy? The fact that

FIGURE 3-3. THE OPERATION OF A BARTER ECONOMY.
In a nonmonetary, or barter, economy households supply their economic resources (upper loop) and receive finished goods and services (lower loop) in return.

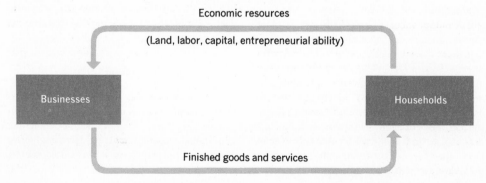

Economic resources

(Land, labor, capital, entrepreneurial ability)

Businesses

Households

Finished goods and services

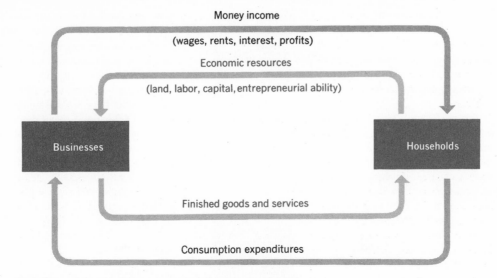

FIGURE 3-4. THE OPERATION OF A MONETARY ECONOMY.
In a money-using economy households exchange their economic resources for money income (upper loop) which can then be spent on finished goods and services (lower loop).

money is a medium of exchange suggests that money is used as a go-between to facilitate the exchanges of resources and products which occur between businesses and households. In Figure 3-4, the upper loop shows a counterclockwise flow of resources accompanied by a clockwise flow of money payments of income in the form of wages, rent, interest, and profits. These income payments are made in the acquisition of resources and are looked upon as costs to the business firms making them. Note, incidentally, that in economics we treat profits —the expense involved in retaining the firm's supply of entrepreneurial ability—as a cost of production.

But money income received from the sale of resources does not, as such, have real value. Consumers cannot eat or wear coins and paper money. Households will want to obtain a share of the fruits of production by spending their money incomes. Indeed, money income received by a household for the resources it supplies constitutes dollar claims against the total output it helped produce. Households exercise these claims by spending their money incomes —all their incomes, let us assume—on the goods

and services of their choice. The clockwise flow of consumption expenditures and the counterclockwise flow of goods and services shown in the lower loop of Figure 3-4 reflect the exchange of income for products. From the viewpoint of businesses, the flow of consumption expenditures coming from households is receipts or revenue.

In other words, in a monetary economy, households, as resource owners, sell their resources to businesses and, as consumers, spend the money income received therefrom in buying goods and services. Businesses must buy resources in order to produce goods and services; their finished products are then sold to households in exchange for consumption expenditures or, as businesses view it, receipts. The net result is a counterclockwise, real flow of economic resources and finished goods and services and a clockwise, money flow of income and consumption expenditures. These flows are simultaneous and repetitive.

Real flows, money flows, and markets. Figure 3-5 adds a final step to our circular flow picture. The cost-income and resource flows of the

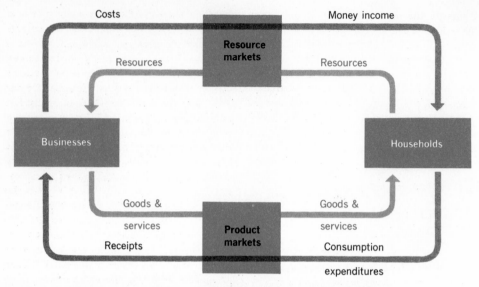

FIGURE 3-5. RESOURCE AND PRODUCT MARKETS IN A MONETARY ECONOMY.
The prices paid for the use of land, labor, capital, and entrepreneurial ability
are determined in the resource market shown in the upper loop. Businesses are on
the demand side and households on the supply side of this market. The prices
of finished goods and services are determined in the product market located in the
lower loop. Households are on the demand side and businesses on the supply side of
this market.

upper loop and the goods-expenditure flows of
the lower loop of Figure 3-4 pass through markets where money is exchanged for resources
and for goods and services. In the upper loop
of Figure 3-5, income payments and resources
flow through resource markets. Here households
supply resources at certain existing market
prices and receive money income in return
from businesses that buy or demand these resources. Obviously, the amount of money income flowing through the resource markets and
into the hands of households will depend upon
the quantities of the various resources supplied
by households and the prices at which they are
sold. Similarly, in the lower loop, consumer expenditures and goods and services pass through
product markets. The size of these consumption
flows will depend upon the quantities of the
various goods and services purchased and the
prices at which they sell. In other words, there
are two basic types of markets in a capitalistic

economy—resource markets and product markets. Businesses are on the buying or *demand*
side of the resource markets, and households,
as resource owners and suppliers, are on the
selling or *supply* side. In the product market,
these positions are reversed; households, as
consumers, are on the buying or demand side,
and businesses are on the selling or supply side.
Each group of economic units both buys and
sells. It is the basic objective of Chapter 4 to
discover how product demand decisions of
households and product supply decisions of
businesses determine the prices at which, and
the quantities in which, products are exchanged.
Similarly, we shall seek to find how the supply
decisions of households and the demand decisions of businesses determine the prices of resources and the quantities exchanged.

Note that the specter of scarcity haunts
these transactions. Because households have
only limited amounts of resources to supply to

businesses, the money incomes of consumers will be limited. This means that each consumer's income will go only so far. A limited number of dollars obviously will not permit the purchase of all the goods and services which the consumer might like to buy. The consumer is handicapped by limited money income; he necessarily operates under a *budget restraint.* Similarly, because resources are scarce, the output of finished goods and services is also necessarily limited. Scarcity permeates our entire discussion.

Limitations of the circular flow model

There are certain noteworthy shortcomings and omissions inherent in the circular flow overview of the workings of pure capitalism: (1) This simple model ignores the transactions which occur within the business and household sectors of the economy. The sale of processed materials to manufacturers, parts to fabricators, and finished products to wholesalers and then to retailers is all ignored. So it is also with transactions occurring within the household sector. This is not a crucial defect, however. At this stage of our discussion, these intrabusiness and intrahousehold transactions are not vital to our understanding of how pure capitalism operates. (2) We must acknowledge that the circular flow model does not reflect the myriad of facts and details about specific households, specific businesses, and specific resource and product markets. Indeed, the main virtue of the circular flow model is that it lays bare the fundamental operations of pure capitalism without ensnaring the viewer in a maze of details. We do not intend to deny the importance of details—they are vital in analyzing specific problems. But that is not our current objective. We seek here a view of the whole forest; the examination of specific trees will come later. (3) The circular flow model makes no mention of the economic role of government. The reason? The institutions of pure capitalism would allegedly give rise to a self-contained, self-regulating economy in which government's role would be minor. In Chapter 6 the circular flow will be modified to

reflect the economic functions of government in the mixed capitalism which now characterizes the American economy. (4) This model assumes that households spend exactly all their money income and that, therefore, the flows of income and expenditure are constant in volume. In real terms this means that the levels of output and employment are constant. In other words, our model assumes that money functions only as a medium of exchange and as a standard of value; were we to assume that households used money also as a store of value, variations in the expenditure and income flows, and hence in the real flows of resources and output, could and would occur. In Part 2 of this book we shall take such variations into account. (5) Our discussion of the circular flow assumes the existence of certain resource and product prices, but it does not explain how resource and product prices are actually determined. This is the task to which we turn in the ensuing chapter: How are resource and product prices determined in a purely capitalistic economy?

SUMMARY

1. The capitalistic system is characterized by the private ownership of resources and the freedom of individuals to engage in the economic activities of their choice as a means for advancing their material well-being. Self-interest is the driving force of such an economy and competition functions as a regulatory or control mechanism. Capitalistic production is not organized in terms of a government plan but rather features the price system as a means of organizing and making effective the myriad of individual decisions which determine what is produced, the methods of production, and the sharing of output. Indeed, government plays a minor and relatively passive role.

2. Specialization according to the principle of comparative advantage and an advanced technology based on the extensive use of capital goods are features common to all modern economies.

3. Functioning as a medium of exchange, money circumvents the problems entailed in

bartering and thereby permits greater specialization. As a standard of value, money reduces the number of prices in the economy and permits a ready comparison of the values of heterogeneous products and resources. Money is also a store of value, that is, a convenient form in which to accumulate wealth.

4. An overview of the operation of the capitalistic system can be gained through the circular flow of wealth. This simplified model locates the product and resource markets and presents the major income-expenditure flows and resource-output flows which constitute the life blood of the capitalistic economy.

QUESTIONS AND STUDY SUGGESTIONS

1. "Capitalism may be characterized as an automatic self-regulating system motivated by the self-interest of individuals and regulated by competition." [4] Explain and evaluate.

2. Explain how the price system is a means of communicating and implementing decisions concerning the allocation of the economy's resources.

3. What advantages result from "roundabout" production? What problem is involved in increasing a full-employment, full-production economy's stock of capital goods? Illustrate this problem in terms of the production possibilities curve. Does an economy with unemployed resources face the same problem?

4. What are the advantages of specialization in the use of human and material resources? Be specific.

5. Dr. Johnson is an outstanding administrator. He is also an excellent teacher, better than anyone else on the staff. Yet the university employs Johnson as dean of his college rather than as a teacher. Explain in terms of the principle of comparative advantage how the university's choice might entail the most efficient use of its labor resources.

6. The following table shows the amounts of apples and oranges which Adams and Bingham, two equally skilled agrarians, can produce on their farms when each devotes one-third of his time to producing apples, and two-thirds to producing oranges.

	Apples, bushels	Oranges, bushels
Adams	40 (⅓)	30 (⅔)
Bingham	30 (⅓)	15 (⅔)
Total	70	45

a. According to the principle of comparative advantage, should these two farmers specialize? If so, what product should each produce?

b. What will be the total production of apples and oranges when the two farmers are specializing? What is the resulting gain in output?

c. What will be the limits of the terms of trade? At what rate would you estimate that Adams and Bingham would trade their surplus products?

[4] Howard R. Bowen, *Toward Social Economy* (New York: Holt, Rinehart and Winston, Inc., 1948), p. 249.

d. Can you conclude from this illustration that specialization according to comparative advantage results in the more efficient use of the economy's resources? Explain.

7. What problems does barter entail? Be precise.

8. "Money is a medium of exchange and a standard of value." Explain and give illustrations.

9. "Money is the only commodity that is good for nothing but to be gotten rid of. It will not feed you, clothe you, shelter you, or amuse you unless you spend or invest it. It imparts value only in parting." [5] Explain this statement.

10. Describe the operation of pure capitalism as portrayed by the circular flow of wealth. Emphasize the fact of scarcity throughout your discussion.

SELECTED REFERENCES

Bowen, Howard R., *Toward Social Economy* (New York: Holt, Rinehart and Winston, Inc., 1948), chaps. 1–5.

Ebenstein, William, *Today's Isms,* 3d ed. (Englewood Cliffs, N.J.: Prentice-Hall, Inc., 1961), chap. 3.

Heilbroner, Robert L., *The Making of Economic Society* (Englewood Cliffs, N.J.: Prentice-Hall, Inc., 1962), chaps. 2–4.

Loucks, William N., *Comparative Economic Systems,* 6th ed. (New York: Harper & Brothers, 1961), chap. 2.

[5] "Creeping Inflation," *Business Review,* Federal Reserve Bank of Philadelphia, August, 1957, p. 3.

Chapter 4

THE MECHANICS OF INDIVIDUAL PRICES:

DEMAND AND SUPPLY

THE MUCH-SIMPLIFIED ANALYSIS of the operation of pure capitalism presented at the conclusion of Chapter 3 assumed that resources and goods and services sell for certain given prices. This permitted us to sidestep the fundamental question to which we now turn: How are prices "set," or determined, in pure capitalism? The answer is easy to state but a bit more difficult to understand. In short, prices are determined in the product market by the interaction of the supply decisions of competing businesses and the demand decisions of competing households. In the resource market, the demand decisions of competing businesses coupled with the supply decisions of competing households determine prices. Our immediate objective is to verify these answers. In doing so we shall concentrate on the product market, then shift our attention later in the chapter to the resource market. The immediate task is to explain the mechanics of prices. How does the interaction of demand and supply decisions set product and resource prices?

DEMAND

The term demand has a very definite meaning to the economist. *Demand is defined as a schedule which shows the various amounts of a product which a consumer is willing and able*

to purchase at each specific price in a set of possible prices during some specified period of time. Demand simply portrays a series of alternative possibilities which can be set down in tabular form. As our definition of demand indicates, we usually view demand from the vantage point of price; that is, we read demand as showing the amounts consumers will buy at various possible prices. It is equally correct and sometimes more meaningful to view demand from the reference point of quantity. That is, instead of asking what quantities can be sold at various prices, we can ask what prices can be got from consumers for various quantities of a good. Table 4-1 is a hypothetical demand schedule for a single consumer who is purchasing bushels of corn.

This tabular portrayal of demand reflects the relationship between the price of corn and the quantity that our mythical consumer would be willing and able to purchase at each of these prices. Note that we say willing and *able*, because willingness alone is not effective in the market. I may be willing to buy a Cadillac, but if this willingness is not backed by the ability to buy, that is, the necessary dollars, it will not be effective and, therefore, not reflected in the

[1] In adjusting this definition to the resource market, simply substitute the word "resource" for "product" and "business" for "consumer."

60 *Demand - schedule showing various amts of a prod which a consumer is willing & able to purchase at each specific price*

as price falls, quantity demanded increases

TABLE 4-1. AN INDIVIDUAL BUYER'S DEMAND FOR CORN (hypothetical data)

Price per bushel	Quantity demanded per week at each price
$5	10
4	20
3	35
2	55
1	80

market. In Table 4-1, if the price of corn in the market happened to be $5 per bushel, then our consumer would be willing and able to buy 10 bushels per week; if it were $4, then 20 bushels per week, and so forth.

The demand schedule in and of itself does not tell us which of the five possible prices will actually exist in the corn market. As we have already said, this depends on demand *and supply.* Demand, then, is simply a tabular statement of a buyer's plans, or intentions, with respect to the purchase of a product.

Note that to be meaningful the quantities demanded at each price must relate to some specific time period—a day, a week, a month, and so forth. To say that "a consumer will buy 10 bushels of corn at $5 per bushel" is vague and meaningless. To say that "a consumer will buy 10 bushels of corn *per week* at $5 per bushel" is clear and very meaningful.

Law of demand

A fundamental characteristic of demand is this: as price falls, the corresponding quantity demanded rises or, alternatively, as price increases, the corresponding quantity demanded falls. In short, there is an *inverse* relationship between price and quantity demanded. Economists have labeled this inverse relationship the *law of demand.* Upon what foundation does this law rest? There are many levels on which the case can be argued, but it is sufficient for our purposes to rest the case on common sense and simple observation.[2] People ordinarily do

buy more of a given product at a low price than they do at a high price. To the consumer price is an obstacle which deters him from buying. The higher this obstacle, the less of a product he will buy; the lower the price obstacle, the more he will buy. In other words, a high price discourages the consumer from buying and a low price encourages him to buy. The simple fact that businessmen have sales is concrete evidence of their belief in the law of demand. Bargain, or sales, days are based on the law of demand.

The law of demand can also be explained in terms of the substitutability of products for one another. There are usually (but not always) a number of reasonably good substitutes for any particular product. Hence, an increase in the price of this product will make consumers substitute other products for it. A decline in the price of the given product will induce consumers to substitute it for other products. To be more specific, if the price of butter goes up, consumers substitute oleomargarine and therefore purchase less butter at the higher price. If the price of butter declines, consumers substitute butter for oleomargarine, thereby purchasing more butter at the lower price.

The demand curve

This inverse relationship between product price and quantity demanded can be presented on a simple two-dimensional graph measuring

[2] Common sense and simple observation will give way to a more sophisticated explanation in Chapter 22.

inverse relationship between price and

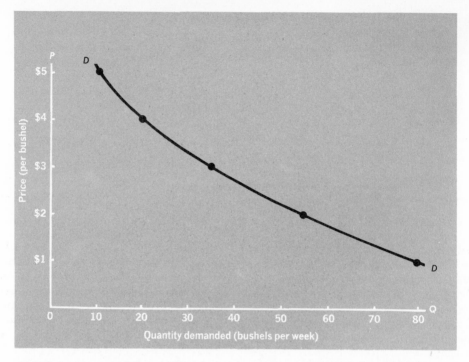

FIGURE 4-1. AN INDIVIDUAL BUYER'S DEMAND CURVE FOR CORN.
An individual's demand schedule graphs as a downsloping curve such as *DD*, because price and quantity demanded are inversely related. Specifically, the law of demand generalizes that consumers will buy more of a product as its price declines.

quantity demanded on the horizontal axis and price on the vertical axis.[3] From Chapter 1, we recall that the process involved is simply that of locating on the graph those five price-quantity possibilities shown in Table 4-1. We do this by drawing perpendiculars from the appropriate points on the two axes. Thus in plotting the "$5-price–10-quantity-demanded" possibility, a perpendicular must be drawn from the horizontal (quantity) axis at 10 to meet a perpendicular drawn from the vertical (price) axis at $5. If this is done for all five possibilities, the result is a series of points as shown in Figure 4-1. Each of these points represents a specific

[3] Putting price on the vertical axis and quantity demanded on the horizontal axis is a matter of convention; we do it for the same reason the mathematician makes X the unknown quantity in his equations.

price and the corresponding quantity which the consumer will choose to purchase at that price. Now, assuming the same inverse relationship between price and quantity demanded at all points between the ones graphed, we can generalize on the inverse relationship between price and quantity demanded by drawing a curve to represent *all* price–quantity-demanded possibilities within the limits shown on the graph. The resulting curve is called a *demand curve* and is labeled *DD* in Figure 4-1. It slopes downward and to the right because the relationship it portrays between price and quantity demanded is inverse. The law of demand—people buy more at a low price than they do at a high price—is reflected in the downward slope of the demand curve.

What is the advantage of graphing our demand schedule? After all, Table 4-1 and Figure

TABLE 4-2. MARKET DEMAND FOR CORN, THREE BUYERS

Price per bushel	Quantity demanded, first buyer	+	Quantity demanded, second buyer	+	Quantity demanded, third buyer	=	Total quantity demanded per week
$5	10	+	12	+	8	=	30
4	20	+	23	+	17	=	60
3	35	+	39	+	26	=	100
2	55	+	60	+	39	=	154
1	80	+	87	+	54	=	221

4-1 contain exactly the same data and reflect the same relationship between price and quantity demanded. The advantage of graphing is that it permits us to represent clearly a given relationship—in this case the law of demand—in a much simpler way than we could if we were forced to rely upon verbal and tabular presentation. A single curve on a graph, if understood, is simpler to state *and to manipulate* than tables and lengthy verbal presentations would be. Graphs are invaluable tools in economic analysis, as has been previously indicated. They permit simple expression and handling of oft-times complex relationships.

Individual and market demand

Until now we have been dealing in terms of just one consumer. The assumption of competition makes us consider a situation in which a large number of buyers are in the market. The transition from an *individual* to a *market* demand schedule can be accomplished by the simple process of summing the quantities demanded by each consumer at the various possible prices. If there were just three buyers in the market, as is shown in Table 4-2, it would be a simple chore to determine the total quantities demanded at each price. Figure 4-2 shows the same summing procedure graphically, using only the $3 price to illustrate the adding-up process.

Competition, of course, entails many more than three buyers of a product. So—to avoid a lengthy addition process—let us suppose there are 200 buyers of corn in the market, each of whom chooses to buy the same amount at each of the various prices as our original consumer does. Thus, we can determine market demand by multiplying the quantity demanded data of Table 4-1 by 200, as in Table 4-3.

Curve D_1 in Figure 4-3 indicates this market demand curve for the 200 buyers.

Determinants of demand

What causes the demand schedule, for example, D_1 in Figure 4-3, to be in the exact position indicated? Why isn't the total demand curve for corn located at some position to the left or right of D_1? The answer is that, in selecting any specific demand curve from the many demand curves that might exist, we are assuming that those factors which determine or "locate" consumer demand are of a given magnitude. In other words, the selection of a fixed demand schedule involves the assumption that the determinants of consumer demand are fixed or constant.

What are the determinants of market demand? The basic ones are: (1) the tastes or preferences of consumers, (2) the money incomes of consumers, (3) the prices of other related goods, (4) consumer expectations with respect to future prices and incomes, and (5) the number of consumers in the market. The

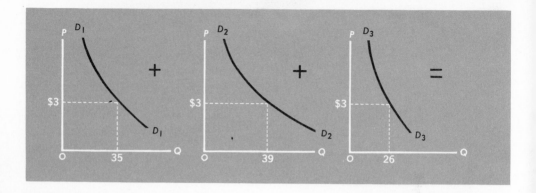

presentation of a given demand schedule, such as columns 1 and 4 of Table 4-3, or a single stationary demand curve, such as D_1 in Figure 4-3, is based on the supposition that these determinants are fixed or constant.

Changes in demand

What happens if one or more of the determinants of demand should change? The answer is obvious: a change in one or more of the determinants will change the demand schedule data in Table 4-3 and therefore the location of the demand curve in Figure 4-3. Such a change in the demand schedule data, or, graphically, a shift in the location of the demand curve, is designated as a *change in demand*.

Let us examine those changes in the five determinants which would bring about an *increase*

in demand, that is, a situation in which consumers would be willing and able to buy more of a product at each possible price. An increase in demand may stem from any one or more of the following changes in the determinants: (1) an intensification of consumer preferences for the particular product, possibly prompted by advertising or a change in fashions; (2) an increase in consumer incomes which permits the consumer to buy more of this product, and possibly of other products, too, at each possible price; (3) a rise in the price of substitute goods which now makes this particular product a "better buy" in the eyes of the consumer; (4) consumer expectation of higher prices, which prompts the consumer to buy now in order to "beat" the anticipated price rise, and expectation of higher incomes, which may induce the consumer to be less tight-fisted in his current

TABLE 4-3. MARKET DEMAND FOR CORN, 200 BUYERS

(1) Price per bushel	(2) Quantity demanded per week, single buyer		(3) Number of buyers in the market		(4) Total quantity demanded per week
$5	10	×	200	=	2,000
4	20	×	200	=	4,000
3	35	×	200	=	7,000
2	55	×	200	=	11,000
1	80	×	200	=	16,000

change in determinants of demand will change demand schedule, and location of demand curve

R This is change in demand as opposed to change in quantity demanded

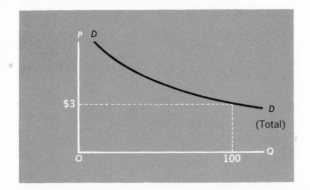

FIGURE 4-2. THE MARKET DEMAND CURVE IS THE SUM OF THE INDIVIDUAL DEMAND CURVES.
Graphically the market demand curve (D total) is found by summing horizontally the individual demand curves (D_1, D_2, and D_3) of all consumers in the market.

spending; and (5) an increase in the number of buyers in the market, which may reflect a population increase or a widening of the market. The result of such changes? Consumers are now willing and able to buy more of this particular product at each possible price than is reflected in column 4 of Table 4-3. In Figure 4-3 this is reflected in a shift of the demand curve to the right; for example, from D_1 to D_2.

A *decrease in demand* puts the shoe on the other foot. Consumers are now willing and able to buy *less* of this particular product at each possible price. Graphically this entails a shift in the demand curve to the left, for example, from D_1 to D_3 in Figure 4-3. The reader should carefully review the determinants of demand and decide what specific changes would cause a decrease in demand.

Changes in the quantity demanded

A *change in demand* must not be confused with a *change in the quantity demanded*. We have noted that a change in demand refers to a shift in the entire demand curve either to the right (an increase in demand) or to the left (a decrease in demand). The consumer's state of mind concerning his purchases of this product has been altered. The cause: a change in one or more of the determinants of demand. As used by economists, the term "demand" refers to a schedule or curve; therefore a change in demand must mean that the entire schedule

has changed or that the curve has shifted its position.

In contrast, a change in the quantity demanded designates the movement from one point to another point—from one price-quantity combination to another—on a fixed demand curve. The cause of a change in the quantity demanded is a change in the price of the product under consideration. In Table 4-3 a decline in the price of corn from $5 to $4 will increase the quantity of corn demanded from 2,000 to 4,000 bushels.

Figure 4-3 is helpful in making the distinction between a change in demand and a change in the quantity demanded. The shift of the demand curve D_1 to either D_2 or D_3 entails changes in demand. But the movement from point *a* to point *b* on curve D_1 is a change in the quantity demanded.

The reader should decide whether a change in demand or a change in the quantity demanded is involved in each of the following illustrations: (1) consumer incomes rise, with the result that more jewelry is purchased; (2) a barber raises the price of haircuts and finds that his volume of business declines; (3) the price of Fords goes up, and, as a consequence, the sales of Chevrolets increase.

SUPPLY

Supply may be defined as *a schedule which shows the various amounts of a product which a producer is willing and able to produce and make available for sale in the market at each*

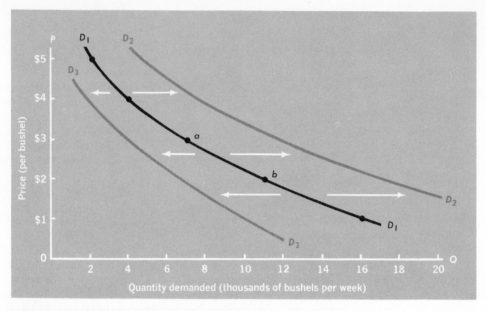

FIGURE 4-3. CHANGES IN THE DEMAND FOR CORN.
A change in one or more of the determinants of demand—consumer tastes, money
incomes, the prices of other goods, consumer expectations, or the number of buyers
in the market—will cause a change in demand. An increase in demand shifts the demand curve to the right as from D_1D_1 to D_2D_2. A decrease in demand is shown
graphically as a movement of the demand curve to the left as from D_1D_1 to D_3D_3.
A change in the quantity demanded involves a movement, caused by a change in the
price of the product under consideration, from one point to another—as from a to b—
on a fixed demand curve.

*specific price in a set of possible prices during
some specified time period.*[4] This schedule portrays a series of alternative possibilities, such as
those shown in Table 4-4 for a single producer.
Let us just suppose that our producer, in this
case, is a farmer producing corn, the demand
for which we have just considered. Our definition of supply indicates that supply is usually
viewed from the vantage point of price. That
is, we read supply as showing the amounts producers will offer at various possible prices. It is
more useful and quite correct in some instances

[4] In talking of the resource market, our definition
of supply reads: a schedule which shows the various
amounts of a resource which its owners are willing to
supply in the market at each possible price in a series
of prices during some period of time.

to view supply from the reference point of
quantity. Instead of asking what quantities will
be offered at various prices, we can ask what
prices will be required to induce producers to
offer various quantities of a good.

Law of supply

It will be immediately noted that Table 4-4
shows a *direct* relationship between price and
quantity supplied. As price rises, the corresponding quantity supplied rises; as price falls,
the quantity supplied also falls. This particular
relationship is called the *law of supply.* It simply tells us that producers are willing to produce and offer for sale more of their product
at a high price than they are at a low price.

TABLE 4-4. AN INDIVIDUAL PRODUCER'S SUPPLY OF CORN (hypothetical data)

Price per bushel	Quantity supplied per week at each price
$5	60
4	50
3	35
2	20
1	5

Why? This again is basically a common-sense matter.

Price, we recall, is a deterrent from the consumer's standpoint. The obstacle of a high price means that the consumer, being on the paying end of this price, will buy a relatively small amount of the product; the lower the price obstacle, the more the consumer will buy. The supplier, on the other hand, is on the receiving end of product price. To him, price is an inducement or incentive to produce and sell a product. The higher the price of the product, the greater the incentive to produce and offer it in the market.

It is important to note that the idea of a supply schedule or curve is based upon the assumption that individual sellers take product price as given, that is, they have no power to put price tags on their product. It does not make sense to ask how a seller will react to various prices if he is able to manipulate those prices himself. It does not make sense to ask someone how he will react to an event or set of data which he himself can control. It is like asking ourselves how we will respond to our own invitation to attend Saturday's football game.

You will also remember that the law of demand was explainable on the basis of product substitution. When the price of product X rises, consumers tend to substitute other goods for it, therefore buying less of X. When the price of X declines, consumers buy more of X, substituting it for other products. The direct relationship between price and quantity supplied can also be explained on the basis of substituta-

bility. In many instances the resources and productive techniques used by a supplier are readily adaptable to a variety of products. For example, a farmer's land and capital may be of about equal efficiency in producing corn, wheat, soy beans, milo, and so forth. As the market price of one of these products—say, wheat—rises, the farmer will shift his resources from the other commodities to wheat. Why? Because it pays him to produce more wheat when price goes up.

A simple example may help at this point. Suppose a farmer has just 2 acres of land. He finds from experience that these 2 acres are equally prolific in the production of both corn and wheat. Specifically, he has found that each acre is capable of producing *either* 20 bushels of wheat *or* 20 bushels of corn. Suppose, too, that no matter how our farmer decides to apportion his 2 acres between wheat and corn, his total costs of production are always the same —say $25. To begin, let us say that the price of wheat is $1 per bushel and that of corn is $2 per bushel. The farmer will obviously plant all his land to corn, producing 40 bushels. Total revenue will be $80 (= 40 × $2) and profits will be $55 (= $80 − $25). The output of wheat, the crop in which we are particularly interested, will be zero. To plant any wheat at a price of $1 per bushel will necessarily result in profits of less than $55. But what if the market price of wheat rises to $3, while the price of corn remains at $2? It would now be profitable for the farmer to shift all his resources to wheat, that is, to substitute wheat for corn pro-

TABLE 4-5. MARKET SUPPLY OF CORN, 200 PRODUCERS

(1) Price per bushel	(2) Quantity supplied per week, single producer		(3) Number of sellers in the market		(4) Total quantity supplied per week
$5	60	×	200	=	12,000
4	50	×	200	=	10,000
3	35	×	200	=	7,000
2	20	×	200	=	4,000
1	5	×	200	=	1,000

duction. By doing so, his total revenue will be increased to $120 (40 × $3) and his profits to $95 (= $120 − $25). Although this example is greatly simplified, the basic point is clear: it is profitable to substitute the production of relatively high-priced for the production of relatively low-priced goods by shifting resources accordingly. Given the $2 price of corn, no wheat will be produced when its price is $1 per bushel, but 40 bushels will be forthcoming when its price is $3. Product substitution explains this direct relationship between the price of wheat and the quantity supplied.

In practice, this substitution may be more complex and time-consuming than our illustration implies: very different products whose production requires radically different methods and resources may be involved. The process may well necessitate the shifting of resources between different producers. The basic conclusion, however, still holds true.

The supply curve

As in the case of demand, it is convenient to present graphically the concept of supply. Our axes in Figure 4-4 are the same as those in Figure 4-3, except for the obvious change of "quantity demanded" to "quantity supplied." The graphing procedure is the same as that previously explained, but of course the quantity data and relationship involved are different. The market supply data graphed in Figure 4-4 as S_1 are shown in Table 4-5, which assumes there are 200 suppliers in the market having the same supply schedules as the producer previously portrayed in Table 4-4.

Determinants of supply

The determinants of demand have been noted and discussed. Changes in consumer tastes, consumer incomes, the prices of related goods, consumer expectations, and the number of buyers in the market will all cause the demand for a particular product to shift.

A similar set of considerations determines the location of a supply curve. The basic determinants of supply are: (1) the technique of production, (2) resource prices, (3) prices of other goods, (4) price expectations, and (5) the number of sellers in the market. A change in any one or more of these determinants will cause the supply curve for a product to shift to either the right or the left. A shift to the right, from S_1 to S_2 in Figure 4-4, designates an *increase in supply:* producers are now offering more of the product at each possible price. A shift to the left, S_1 to S_3 in Figure 4-4, indicates a *decrease in supply:* suppliers are offering less at each price.

Changes in supply

The first two determinants of supply—technology and resource prices—are the two components of production costs. And the relation-

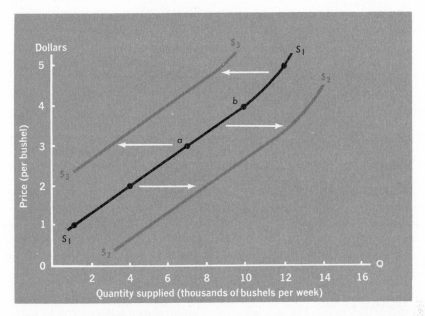

FIGURE 4-4. CHANGES IN THE SUPPLY OF CORN.
A change in one or more of the determinants of supply—productive techniques, resource prices, the prices of other goods, price expectations, or the number of sellers
in the market—will cause a change in supply. An increase in supply shifts the supply
curve to the right as from S_1S_1 to S_2S_2. A decrease in supply is shown graphically as
a movement of the curve to the left as from S_1S_1 to S_3S_3. A change in the quantity
supplied involves a movement, caused by a change in the price of the product under
consideration, from one point to another—as from a to b—on a fixed supply curve.

ship between production costs and supply is an
intimate one. (As a matter of fact, in Chapter 24
we will find that cost and supply data are synonymous.) For our present purposes, it is sufficient to note that anything which serves to
lower production costs, that is, a technological
improvement or a decline in resource prices,
will increase supply. With lower costs, businessmen will find that it is profitable to offer a larger
amount of the product at each possible price.
An increase in the price of resources (a deterioration of technology being unlikely) will cause
a decrease in supply; that is, the supply curve
will shift to the left.

Changes in the prices of other goods can also
shift the supply curve for a product. A decline
in the price of corn may cause a farmer to produce and offer more wheat at each possible
price. Conversely, a rise in the price of corn may

make farmers less willing to produce and offer
wheat in the market.

Expectations concerning the future price of
a product can also affect a producer's current
willingness to supply that product. It is difficult,
however, to generalize concerning the way the
expectation of, say, higher prices will affect the
present supply curve of a product. Farmers
might withhold some of their current wheat
harvest from the market, anticipating a higher
wheat price in the future. This will cause a decrease in the current supply of wheat. On the
other hand, in many types of manufacturing,
expected price increases may induce firms to
expand production immediately, causing supply
to increase.

Finally, given the scale of operations of each
firm, the larger the number of suppliers, the
greater will be market supply. As more firms

enter an industry, the supply curve will shift to the right. The smaller the number of firms in an industry, the less the market supply will be. This means that as firms leave an industry, the supply curve will shift to the left.

Changes in quantity supplied

The distinction between a *change in supply* and a *change in the quantity supplied* parallels that between a change in demand and a change in the quantity demanded. A change in supply is involved when the entire supply curve shifts. An increase in supply shifts the curve to the right; a decrease in supply shifts it to the left. The cause of a change in supply is a change in one or more of the determinants of supply. The term "supply" is used by economists to refer to a schedule or curve. A change in supply therefore must mean that the entire schedule has changed or that the curve has shifted.

A change in the quantity supplied, on the other hand, refers to the movement from one point to another point on a stable supply curve. The cause of such a movement is a change in the price of the specific product under consideration. In Table 4-5 a decline in the price of corn from $5 to $4 decreases the quantity of corn supplied from 12,000 to 10,000 bushels.

Shifting the supply curve from S_1 to S_2 or S_3 in Figure 4-4 obviously entails changes in supply. The movement from point *a* to point *b* on S_1, however, is merely a change in the quantity supplied.

The reader should determine which of the following involves a change in supply and which entails a change in the quantity supplied: (1) because production costs decline, producers sell more automobiles; (2) the price of wheat declines, causing the number of bushels of corn sold per month to increase; (3) fewer oranges are offered for sale because their price has decreased in retail markets.

SUPPLY AND DEMAND: MARKET EQUILIBRIUM

We are now in a position to put the concepts of supply and demand together to see how the interaction of the buying decisions of households

and the selling decisions of producers will determine the price of a product and the quantity which is actually bought and sold in the market. In Table 4-6 columns 1 and 2 reproduce the market supply schedule for corn (from Table 4-5) and columns 2 and 3 the market demand schedule for corn (from Table 4-3). Note that in column 2 we are using a common set of prices. We assume competition—the presence of a large number of buyers and sellers.

Now the question to be faced is this: Of the five[5] possible prices at which corn might sell in this market, which will actually prevail as the market price for corn? Let us derive our answer through the simple process of trial and error. For no particular reason, we shall start with an examination of $5. Could this be the prevailing market price for corn? The answer is "No," for the simple reason that producers are willing to produce and supply to the market some 12,000 bushels of corn at this price while buyers, on the other hand, are only willing to take 2,000 bushels off the market at this price. In other words, the relatively high price of $5 encourages farmers to produce a great deal of corn, but that same high price discourages consumers from taking the product off the market. Other products appear as "better buys" when corn is high-priced. The result in this case is a 10,000-bushel *surplus* of corn in the market. This surplus, shown in column 4, is simply the excess of quantity supplied over quantity demanded at the price of $5.

Could a price of $5—even if it existed temporarily in the corn market—persist over a period of time? Certainly not. The very large surplus of corn would prompt competing sellers to bid down the price in order to encourage buyers to take this surplus off their hands. Suppose price gravitates down to $4. Now the situation has changed considerably. The lower price has encouraged buyers to take more of this product off the market and, at the same time, has induced farmers to use a smaller amount of resources in producing corn. The surplus, as a result, has diminished to 6,000 bushels. Because a surplus still exists, competition among sellers will once again bid down

[5] Of course, there are many possible prices; our simple example shows only five of them.

TABLE 4-6. MARKET SUPPLY AND DEMAND FOR CORN

(1) Total quantity supplied per week	(2) Price per bushel	(3) Total quantity demanded per week	(4) Surplus (+) or shortage (−) (arrows indicate effect on price)
12,000	$5	2,000	+10,000 ↓
10,000	4	4,000	+ 6,000 ↓
7,000	3	7,000	
4,000	2	11,000	− 7,000 ↑
1,000	1	16,000	−15,000 ↑

the price of corn. We can conclude then that prices of $5 and $4 will be unstable, because they are "too high." The market price for corn must be something less than $4.

To avoid letting the cat out of the bag before we have a full appreciation of how supply and demand determine product price, let us now jump to the other end of our price column and examine $1 as the possible market price for corn. It is evident that at this price, quantity demanded is in excess of quantity supplied by 15,000 units. This relatively low price discourages farmers from devoting their resources to corn production; the same low price encourages consumers to attempt to buy more corn than would otherwise be the case. Corn is a "good buy" when its price is relatively low. In short, there is a 15,000-bushel *shortage* of corn. Can this price of $1 persist as the market price? No. Competition among buyers will bid up the price to something greater than $1. In other words, at a price of $1, many consumers who are willing and able to buy at this price will obviously be left out in the cold. Many potential consumers, in order to ensure that they will not have to do without, will express a willingness to pay some price in excess of $1 to ensure getting some of the available corn. Suppose this competitive bidding up of price by buyers boosts the price of corn to $2. This higher price obviously has reduced, but not eliminated, the shortage of corn. For $2, farmers are willing to

devote more resources to corn production, and some buyers who were willing to pay $1 for a bushel of corn will choose not to buy corn at a price of $2, deciding to use their incomes to buy other products or maybe to save more of their incomes. But a shortage of 7,000 bushels still exists at a price of $2. We can conclude that competitive bidding among buyers will push market price to some figure greater than $2.

By trial and error we have eliminated every price but $3. So let us now examine it. At a price of $3, *and only at this price*, the quantity which farmers are willing to produce and supply in the market is identical with the amount consumers are willing to buy. As a result, there is neither a shortage nor a surplus of corn at this price. We have already seen that a surplus causes price to decline and a shortage causes price to rise. With neither a shortage nor a surplus at $3, there is no reason for the actual price of corn to move away from this price. The economist calls this price the *equilibrium price*, equilibrium meaning "in balance" or "at rest." At $3, quantity supplied and quantity demanded are in balance; hence, $3 is the only stable price of corn under the supply and demand conditions shown in Table 4-6. Or, stated differently, the price of corn will be established where the supply decisions of producers and the demand decisions of buyers are mutually consistent. Such decisions are consistent with one another only at a price of $3. At any higher

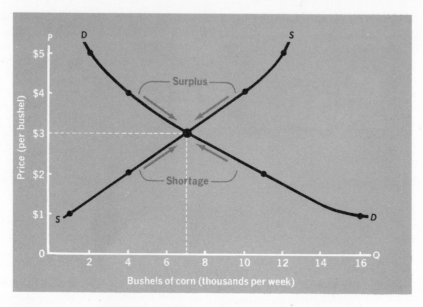

FIGURE 4-5. THE EQUILIBRIUM PRICE AND QUANTITY FOR CORN AS
DETERMINED BY MARKET DEMAND AND SUPPLY.
The intersection of the downsloping demand curve D and the upsloping supply curve
S indicates the equilibrium price and quantity, $3 and 7,000 bushels in this instance.
The shortages of corn which would exist at below-equilibrium prices drive price up and
in so doing increase the quantity supplied and reduce the quantity demanded until
equilibrium is achieved. The surpluses which above-equilibrium prices would entail
push price down and thereby increase the quantity demanded and reduce the quantity
supplied until equilibrium is achieved.

price, suppliers want to sell more than consumers want to buy; at any lower price, consumers want to buy more than producers are willing
to offer for sale. Discrepancies between supply
and demand intentions of sellers and buyers,
respectively, will prompt price changes which
subsequently will bring these two sets of plans
into accord with one another.

A graphic analysis of supply and demand
should yield the same conclusions. Figure 4-5
puts the market supply and market demand
curves for corn on the same graph, the horizontal axis now reflecting both quantity demanded
and quantity supplied. A close examination of
this diagram clearly indicates that at any price
above the equilibrium price of $3, quantity
supplied will exceed quantity demanded. This
surplus will cause a competitive bidding
down of price by sellers eager to relieve themselves of their surplus. The falling price will

cause less corn to be offered and will simultaneously encourage consumers to buy more. Any
price below the equilibrium price will entail a
shortage; that is, quantity demanded will exceed quantity supplied. Competitive bidding
by buyers will push the price up toward the
equilibrium level. And this rising price will simultaneously bring forth a greater supply from
producers and ration buyers out of the market,
thereby causing the shortage to vanish. Graphically, the intersection of the supply curve and
the demand curve for the product will indicate
the equilibrium point.

Rationing function of prices

The ability of the competitive forces of supply and demand to establish a price where
supply and demand decisions are synchronized
is sometimes called the _rationing function_ of

prices. In this case, the equilibrium price of $3 clears the market, leaving no burdensome surplus for the seller and no inconvenient shortage for the potential buyers. The composite of freely made individual buying and selling decisions sets this price which clears the market. In effect, the market mechanism of supply and demand says this: any buyer who is willing and able to pay $3 for a bushel of corn will be able to acquire one; those who are not, will not. Similarly, any seller who is willing and able to produce bushels of corn and offer them for sale at a price of $3 will be able to do so successfully; those who are not, will not. Were it not for competitive prices automatically bringing supply and demand decisions into consistency with one another, some type of administrative control by government would be necessary to avoid or control the shortages or surpluses which might otherwise occur. We shall see in a later chapter some of the administrative problems involved when government steps into the picture and establishes a legal price higher or lower than the equilibrium price. Such supported prices and ceiling prices rob the price mechanism of its rationing ability, thereby making it necessary for government to assume responsibility for balancing quantity demanded and quantity supplied. The important point is that free, competitive prices automatically synchronize buying and selling decisions and "clear the market"; this is the rationing function of prices.

Changes in supply and demand

It was noted earlier that demand might change because of fluctuations in consumer tastes or incomes, changes in consumer expectations, or variations in the prices of substitute goods. On the other hand, supply might vary in response to changes in technology or in resource prices. Our analysis would be incomplete if we did not stop to consider the effect of changes in supply and demand upon equilibrium price.

To keep our thinking on the straight-and-narrow, let us first analyze the effects of a change in demand, assuming that supply is conveniently constant. Suppose now that demand

increases, as shown in Figure 4-6a. What is the effect upon price? Noting that the new intersection of the supply and demand curves is at a higher point on both the price and quantity axes, we can conclude that an increase in demand, other things (supply) being equal, will have a *price-increasing effect* and a *quantity-increasing effect*. (The value of graphic analysis now begins to become apparent; we need not fumble with figures in determining the effect on price and quantity but only compare the new with the old point of intersection on the graph.) A decrease in demand, as illustrated in Figure 4-6b, reveals *price-decreasing* and *quantity-decreasing effects*. Price falls and quantity also declines. In brief, we find a direct relationship between a change in demand and the resulting changes in equilibrium price and quantity.

Let us reverse the procedure and analyze the effect of a change in supply on price, assuming that demand is constant. If supply increases, as in Figure 4-6c, the new intersection of supply and demand is obviously at a lower price. Equilibrium price falls; equilibrium quantity, however, increases. If supply decreases, on the other hand, this will tend to increase product price. Figure 4-6d illustrates this situation. Here price increases but quantity declines. In short, an increase in supply has a *price-decreasing* and a *quantity-increasing effect*. A decrease in supply has a *price-increasing* and a *quantity-decreasing effect. There is an inverse relationship between a change in supply and the resulting change in equilibrium price, but the relationship between a change in supply and the resulting change in equilibrium quantity is direct.

Obviously, a host of more complex cases might arise, involving changes in both supply and demand. Two cases are possible when it is supposed that supply and demand change in *opposite directions*. Assume first that supply increases and demand decreases. What effect does this have upon equilibrium price? This example couples two price-decreasing effects, and the net result will be a price fall greater than that which would result from either change taken in isolation. How about equilibrium quantity? Here the effects of the changes in supply and demand are opposed: the increase in sup-

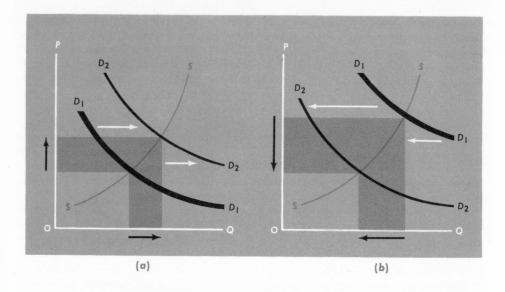

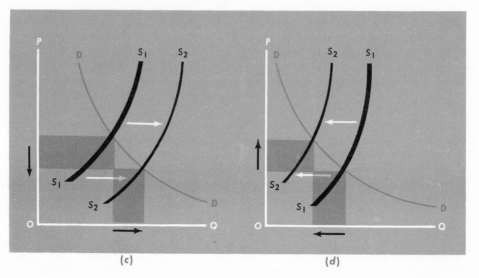

FIGURE 4-6. CHANGES IN DEMAND AND SUPPLY AND THE EFFECTS ON PRICE AND QUANTITY.

The increase in demand of (a) and the decrease in demand of (b) indicate a direct relationship between a change in demand and the resulting changes in equilibrium price and quantity. The increase in supply of (c) and the decrease in supply of (d) show an inverse relationship between a change in supply and the resulting change in equilibrium price, but a direct relationship between a change in supply and the accompanying change in equilibrium quantity.

ply tends to increase equilibrium quantity, but the decrease in demand tends to reduce the equilibrium quantity. The direction of the change in quantity depends upon the relative sizes of the changes in supply and demand. The second possibility is for supply to decrease and demand to increase. Two price-increasing effects are involved here. We can predict an increase in equilibrium price greater than that caused by either change taken separately. The effect upon equilibrium quantity is again indeterminate, depending upon the relative size of the changes in supply and demand. If the decrease in supply is relatively larger than the increase in demand, the equilibrium quantity will be less than it was initially. But if the decrease in supply is relatively smaller than the increase in demand, the equilibrium quantity will increase as a result of these changes. The reader should trace through these two cases graphically to verify for himself the conclusions we have outlined.

What if supply and demand change in the *same direction?* Suppose first that supply and demand both increase. What is the effect upon equilibrium price? It depends. Here we must compare two conflicting effects upon price—the price-decreasing effect of the increase in supply and the price-increasing effect of the increase in demand. If the increase in supply is of greater magnitude than the increase in demand, the net effect will be for equilibrium price to decrease. If the opposite holds true, equilibrium price will increase. The effect upon equilibrium quantity is certain: increases in supply and in demand both have quantity-increasing effects. This means that equilibrium quantity will increase by an amount greater than that which either change would have entailed in isolation. In the second place, a decrease in both supply and demand can be subjected to similar analysis. If the decrease in supply is greater than the decrease in demand, equilibrium price will rise. If the reverse holds true, equilibrium price will fall. Because decreases in supply and demand both have quantity-decreasing effects, it can be predicted with certainty that equilibrium quantity will be less than that which prevailed initially.

Incidentally, the possibility that supply and demand will both change in a given period of time is not particularly unlikely. As a matter of fact, a single event might simultaneously affect both supply and demand. For example, a technological improvement in cheese production might lower both the supply of and the demand for fluid milk.

Needless to say, special cases might arise where a decrease in demand and a decrease in supply, on the one hand, and an increase in demand and an increase in supply, on the other, cancel out. In both these cases, the net effect upon equilibrium price will be zero; price will not change. The reader should again work out these more complex cases in terms of supply and demand curves to verify all these results.

The resource market

What about the shape of the supply and demand curves in the resource market? As in the product market, resource supply curves are typically upsloping, and resource demand curves are typically downsloping, Why?

Resource supply curves generally slope upward, that is, they reflect a *direct* relationship between resource price and quantity supplied, because it is in their own interests for resource owners to supply more of a particular resource at a high price than at a low price. High income payments in a particular occupation or industry encourage households to supply more of their human and property resources. Low income payments discourage resource owners from supplying resources in this particular occupation or industry and, as a matter of fact, encourage them to supply their resources elsewhere.[6]

[6] There are important exceptions to the rule of an upsloping supply curve in the resource market. For example, for a time higher wage rates may induce workers to toil longer hours. But beyond some point still higher wage rates may provide workers with an income large enough for them to afford to work fewer hours and still enjoy a comfortable standard of living. Where this situation is pertinent, the supply curve will bend backward, as shown in the labor supply curve on the next page. In ensuing chapters, we ignore those exceptions in favor of the general case.

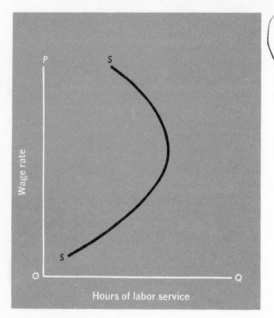

On the demand side, businesses, in trying to minimize production costs, shy away from the purchase of relatively high-priced resources and, conversely, prefer to use relatively low-priced resources when possible. Entrepreneurs will find it profitable to substitute low- for high-priced resources. More of a particular resource will be demanded at a low price than at a high price. The result? A downsloping demand curve for the various resources.

In short, just as the supply decisions of businesses and the demand decisions of consumers determine prices in the product market, so the supply decisions of households and demand decisions of businesses set prices in the resource market.

SUMMARY

1. Demand refers to a schedule which summarizes the willingness of buyers to purchase a given product during a specific time period at each of the various prices at which it might be sold. According to the law of demand, consumers will ordinarily buy more of a product at a low price than they will at a high price.

Therefore, the relationship between price and quantity demanded is inverse; demand graphs as a downsloping curve.

2. Changes in one or more of the basic determinants of demand—consumer tastes, the money incomes of consumers, the prices of other goods, consumer expectations, and the number of buyers in the market—will cause the market demand curve to shift. A shift to the right is an increase in demand; a shift to the left, a decrease in demand. A change in demand is to be distinguished from a change in the quantity demanded, the latter involving the movement from one point to another point on a fixed demand curve because of a change in the price of the product under consideration.

3. Supply is a schedule showing the amounts of a product which producers would be willing to offer in the market during a given time period at each possible price at which the commodity might be sold. The law of supply says that producers will offer more of a product at a higher price than they will at a low price. As a result, the relationship between price and quantity supplied is a direct one, and the supply curve is upsloping.

4. A change in productive techniques, resource prices, the prices of other goods, price expectations, or the number of sellers in the market will cause the supply curve of a product to shift. A shift to the right is an increase in supply; a shift to the left, a decrease in supply. In contrast, a change in the price of a given product will result in a change in the quantity supplied, that is, a movement from one point to another on a given supply curve.

5. Under competition, the interaction of market demand and market supply will adjust price to that point at which the quantity demanded and the quantity supplied are equal. This is the equilibrium price. The corresponding quantity is the equilibrium quantity. Equilibrium price and equilibrium quantity will change in response to a change in demand or supply.

6. The ability of market forces to synchronize selling and buying decisions so as to eliminate potential surpluses or shortages is sometimes termed the "rationing function of prices."

7. A change in either demand or supply will cause equilibrium price and quantity to change. There is a direct relationship between a change in demand and the resulting changes in equilibrium price and quantity. Though the relation-ship between a change in supply and the resulting change in equilibrium price is inverse, the relationship between a change in supply and equilibrium quantity is direct.

8. The concepts of supply and demand are also applicable to the resource market.

QUESTIONS AND STUDY SUGGESTIONS

1. Define demand. Explain the law of demand. Why does a demand curve slope downward? What are the determinants of demand? What happens to the demand curve when each of these determinants changes? Distinguish between a change in demand and a change in the quantity demanded, noting the cause(s) of each.

2. Define supply. Explain the law of supply. Why does the supply curve slope upward? What are the determinants of supply? What happens to the supply curve when each of these determinants changes? Distinguish between a change in supply and a change in the quantity supplied, noting the cause(s) of each.

3. Suppose the total demand for wheat and the total supply of wheat per month in the Kansas City grain market are as follows:

Thousands of bushels demanded	Price per bushel	Thousands of bushels supplied	Surplus (+) or shortage (−)
90	$1.70	70	
85	1.80	72	
80	1.90	73	
75	2.00	75	
70	2.10	77	
65	2.20	79	
60	2.30	81	
55	2.40	83	

a. What will be the market or equilibrium price? What is the equilibrium quantity? Using the surplus-shortage column, explain why your answers are correct.

b. Using the above data, graph the demand for wheat and the supply of wheat. Be sure to label the axes of your graph correctly. Label equilibrium price "P" and equilibrium quantity "Q."

c. Why will $1.80 not be the equilibrium price in this market? Why not $2.30?

d. Now suppose that the government establishes a ceiling price of, say, $1.90 for wheat. Explain carefully the effects of this ceiling price. Demonstrate your answer graphically. What might prompt government to establish a ceiling price?

e. Assume now that the government establishes a supported price of, say, $2.20 for wheat. Explain carefully the effects of this supported price. Demonstrate your answer graphically. What might prompt the government to establish this price support?

f. "Legally fixed prices strip the price mechanism of its rationing function." Explain this statement in terms of your answers to 3*d* and 3*e*.

4. What effect will each of the following have upon the demand for product B?

a. Product B becomes more fashionable.

b. Consumer incomes decline.

c. The price of product C, a good substitute for B, goes down.

d. Consumers anticipate declining prices and falling incomes.

e. There is a rapid upsurge in population growth.

5. What effect will each of the following have upon the supply of product B?

a. A technological advance in the methods of producing B.

b. A decline in the number of firms in industry B.

c. An increase in the prices of resources required in the production of B.

d. The expectation that the equilibrium price of B will be lower in the future than it is currently.

e. A decline in the price of product A, a good whose production requires substantially the same techniques and resources as does the production of B.

6. "In the corn market, demand often exceeds supply and supply sometimes exceeds demand." "The price of corn rises and falls in response to changes in supply and demand." In which of these two statements are the terms "supply" and "demand" used correctly? Explain.

7. "Surpluses drive prices up; shortages drive them down." Do you agree?

8. How will each of the following changes in demand and/or supply affect equilibrium price and equilibrium quantity in a competitive market; that is, do price and quantity *rise, fall, remain unchanged,* or are the answers *indeterminate,* depending upon the magnitudes of the shifts in supply and demand? You should rely on a supply and demand diagram in verifying your answers.

a. Supply falls and demand remains constant.

b. Demand falls and supply remains constant.

c. Supply rises and demand is constant.

d. Demand rises and supply rises.

e. Demand rises and supply is constant.

f. Supply rises and demand falls.

g. Demand rises and supply falls.

h. Demand falls and supply falls.

9. "Prices are the automatic regulator that tend to keep production and consumption in line with each other." Explain.

SELECTED REFERENCES

Boulding, Kenneth E., *Economic Analysis,* 3d ed. (New York: Harper & Row, Publishers, 1955), chaps. 4 and 5.

Henderson, Hubert, *Supply and Demand* (Chicago: University of Chicago Press, 1958), chap. 2.

Warner, Aaron W., and Victor R. Fuchs, *Concepts and Cases in Economic Analysis* (New York: Harcourt, Brace & World, Inc., 1958), pp. 41–62, 79–82, and 94–115.

Chapter 5

THE FIVE FUNDAMENTAL QUESTIONS
AND THE PRICE SYSTEM

WE SAW in Chapter 3 that the capitalist ideology makes clear the importance of freedom of enterprise and choice. Consumers are at liberty to buy what they choose; businesses, to produce and sell what they choose; and resource suppliers, to make their property and human resources available in whatever occupations they choose. Upon reflection, we might wonder why such an economy does not collapse in complete chaos. If consumers want bread, businesses choose to produce automobiles, and resource suppliers want to offer their services in manufacturing shoes, it would seem that production would be deadlocked because of the obvious inconsistency of these free choices.

Fortunately, two other features of capitalism—a system of markets and prices and the force of competition—provide the coordinating and organizing mechanisms which overcome the potential chaos posed by freedom of enterprise and choice. The competitive price system is both a mechanism for communicating the decisions of consumers, producers, and resource suppliers to one another and for synchronizing those decisions toward consistent production objectives.

Armed with an understanding of individual markets and prices gained from Chapter 4, we are now in a position to analyze the operation of the price system.[1] More specifically, our objectives in the present chapter are twofold. (1) We want to understand precisely how the price system operates as a mechanism for communicating and coordinating individual free choices. (2) We seek to evaluate the operation of a market economy, that is, an economy which operates through a system of prices. In other words, how does the price system answer the Five Fundamental Questions, and how satisfactory are these answers? To make our task a bit more manageable, we shall dodge the question of the level of resource use at this point. In Part 2 of this book, we shall discover that the price system functions imperfectly in providing for the full employment of available resources. The reasons for this shortcoming of the price system and the remedies that are available will there receive detailed treatment.

In the present chapter, our concern will be with how the price system (1) determines what is to be produced, (2) organizes production, (3) distributes total output, and (4) adapts itself to change.

---

[1] Our discussion in this chapter is necessarily simplified. Part 5 presents a more rigorous, more sophisticated description of the price system and its operation.

80

FRAMEWORK OF THE PRICE SYSTEM

If we could suddenly "freeze" a purely capitalist economy at some point in time, here is what we would find:

1. Households, as consumers, have a variety of material wants. For all practical purposes, these wants are unlimited. Possessing a limited money income derived from the sale of limited amounts of resources at their disposal, each household seeks to purchase that combination of goods and services which will give it the greatest satisfaction. These various consumer wants in effect are tallied on the demand side of the product market. The demand schedule or curve for each product communicates to producers how much competing consumers would purchase of that product at various prices. The demand curve for each product is downsloping, because consumers find it to their advantage to substitute low-priced for high-priced products. Because of the large number of consumers buying each product, no one influences actual product prices.

2. Competing business institutions stand on the supply side of the product market. Their goal is to maximize profits. In so doing, they must decide what product will be most profitable to produce, in what quantity it will be most profitable to produce it, and what combination of resources will produce the desired output at the least cost. For the business sector as a whole, these decisions, which in effect indicate the willingness of businesses to produce and offer various products, are reflected in product supply curves. These supply curves are upsloping, indicating that, other things being equal, businesses will profit by substituting the production of high-priced for the production of low-priced goods. Together with the product demand curves which mirror consumer preferences, these supply curves will establish an equilibrium price for all those products which consumers might want and which businesses might be willing to supply.

3. Businesses require resources in accomplishing production. As we noted in Chapter 4, businesses will minimize their costs and, other things being equal, maximize their profits by substituting low-priced resources for high-priced resources; this means that resource demand curves will be downsloping. These resource demand curves will communicate to resource suppliers how much of each resource businesses will be willing to employ at various possible resource prices.

4. Finally, households as resource suppliers offer the land, labor, capital, and entrepreneurial talents which they own to businesses. The decisions of competing resource suppliers are reflected in resource supply curves. These curves are generally upsloping, reflecting the fact that households seek the greatest return from the sale of their resources. The upsloping nature of these curves implies that households not only want, but within limits are able, to shift resources from low-paying to high-paying lines of employment.

In brief, the product demand intentions of households and the product supply decisions of businesses will determine a series of product prices. Similarly, the resource demand decisions of businesses and the resource supply decisions of households will establish a series of resource prices.

ECONOMIC CHOICES, SCARCITY, AND SUBSTITUTABILITY

It is evident that our picture of the price system merely envisions a series of interrelated choices on the part of households as consumers and resource suppliers and businesses as producers and resource users. These choices are based upon the fact of scarcity and influenced by considerations of substitutability.

Society is faced with the problem of making economic choices because resources are scarce. If resources were infinitely abundant in relation to the demand for them, the economizing problem would dissolve in a sea of affluency. Consumers would not have to choose between various products; abundance would make it possible for every consumer to have any type and any amount of goods and services he desired. The same would be true for businesses in the using of resources to carry on production.

But, unfortunately, this describes economic utopia, not economic reality; in real life, resources, and therefore products, are relatively scarce. Hence, consumers with money incomes limited by their sales of scarce resources are forced to choose between relatively scarce commodities. And businesses, possessing limited money receipts from the sale of relatively scarce products, must choose between scarce resources in carrying on their productive efforts. Indeed, the presence of the basic theme of scarcity in our picture of the price system is mirrored in the very fact that products and resources have price tags on them! Only when something is scarce in relation to the demand for it will it command a price in the market.

How does substitutability come into the picture? Within limits, both resources and products are versatile. Consumer wants can usually be satisfied with various goods. The want for a trip from New York to Chicago can be satisfied by purchasing a car, a train ticket, a plane ticket, or a bus ticket. Hunger can be satisfied by a wide variety of foods—a bowl of rice, a hamburger, or a sirloin steak. And so it is with producing specific products. Resources, within limits dictated by technology, are substitutable for one another. Various resource combinations can be employed in the production of most products. The nature of both the supply and demand choices in a market economy are strongly influenced by substitutability. The demand curve for a product is downsloping because consumers will substitute other products for any particular product whose price happens to rise. And producers tend to substitute alternative resources for that resource whose price rises. Upsloping product and resource supply curves also imply substitutability. Producers tend to substitute high-priced for low-priced products in formulating their production intentions. And resource suppliers shift their human and property resources from low-paying to high-paying employments.

This, of course, is not to say that substitutability is perfect. It obviously is not. A bowl of rice is not a perfect substitute for a sirloin steak. Yet within limits the possibility of substitution exists in both the product and resource market. Indeed, if substitutability did

not exist, businesses would have no choices to make in hiring resources to produce specific goods. And if resources were not versatile, households would have no choices to make in supplying them. Similarly, if various products were not substitutable, households would have no problem of choice in spending their incomes.

Thus we may say that economic choices must be rendered because resources, and therefore products, are scarce. The particular choices rendered by businesses and households depend upon (1) the prices of resources and products as indicators of relative scarcities and (2) the possibilities of substituting between resources, on the one hand, and products, on the other.

The interrelationship between scarcity and substitution is even more intimate than we have suggested. For example, if a product becomes particularly scarce, its price as an index of its relative scarcity will rise. This will signal buyers to substitute other products for the now higher-priced product. This substitution will rechannel consumer purchases away from this particularly scarce product toward others less scarce. Substitution eases this particularly acute scarcity by, in effect, transferring consumer purchases to other substitutable products. Through substitutability, society alters its choices so as to use less of particularly scarce products and resources and more of less scarce ones. By substituting, society conserves most on those products and resources which are most scarce.

OPERATION OF THE PRICE SYSTEM

Now with this point-in-time picture of the price system before us and with the significance of scarcity and substitutability in the making of economic choices clearly in mind, let us examine in some detail the manner in which the competitive price system would answer the Fundamental Questions.

Determining what is to be produced

Given the product and resource prices established by competing buyers and sellers in both the product and resource markets, how would a purely capitalistic economy decide the types and quantities of goods to be produced? Remembering that businesses are motivated to seek profits and avoid losses, we can generalize that those goods and services which can be produced at a profit will be produced and those whose production entails a loss will not. And what determines profits or the lack of them? Two things: (1) the total receipts which a firm gets from selling a product and (2) the total costs of producing it. Both total receipts and total costs are price-times-quantity figures. Total receipts are found by multiplying product price by the amount of the product sold. Total costs are found by multiplying the price of each resource used by the amount employed and summing the costs of each.

To say that those products which can be produced profitably will be produced and those which cannot will not is only an accurate generalization if the meaning of economic costs is clearly understood. In order to grasp the full meaning of costs, let us once again think of businesses as simply organizational charts, that is, businesses "on paper," distinct and apart from the capital, raw materials, labor, and entrepreneurial ability which make them going concerns. In order to become actual producing concerns, these "on paper" businesses must secure all four types of resources. The payments which must be made to secure and retain the needed amounts of these resources are *economic costs*. The per unit size of these costs will be determined by supply and demand conditions in the resource market. Now the point to note is that, like land, labor, and capital, entrepreneurial ability is a scarce resource and therefore has a price tag on it. Costs therefore must include not only wage and salary payments to labor and interest and rental payments for capital and land, but also payments to the businessman or entrepreneur for any routine labor services, capital, or land he owns and supplies in the operation of his own enterprise. The cost payment for these contributions by the entrepreneur is called a *normal profit*. Hence, a product will be produced only when total receipts are large enough to pay wage, interest, rental, and normal profit costs. Now if total receipts from the sale of a product more

than cover all production costs, including a normal profit, the remainder will accrue to the entrepreneur as the risk taker and organizing force in the going concern. This return above costs is called a *pure, or economic, profit*. It is not an economic cost, because it need not be realized in order for the business to acquire and retain entrepreneurial ability.

A few hypothetical examples will explain more concretely how the price system determines what is to be produced. Suppose that the most favorable relationship between total revenue and total cost in producing product X occurs when the firm's output is 15 units. Assume, too, that the best combination of resources to use in producing 15 units of X entails 2 units of labor, 3 units of land, 1 of capital, and 1 of entrepreneurial ability, selling at prices of $2, $1, $3, and $3 respectively. Finally, suppose that the 15 units of X which these resources produce can be sold for $1 per unit. Will firms enter into the production of product X? Yes, they will. A firm producing product X under these conditions will be able to pay wage, rent, interest, and normal profit costs of $13 $[= (2 \times \$2) + (3 \times \$1) + (1 \times \$3) + (1 \times \$3)]$. The difference between total revenue of $15 and total costs of $13 will be an economic profit of $2.

This economic profit is evidence that industry X is a prosperous one. Such an industry will tend to expand as new firms, attracted by these above-normal profits, are created or shift from other less profitable industries. But the entry of new firms will be a self-limiting process. As new firms enter industry X, the market supply of X will increase relative to the market demand. This will lower the market price of X to the end that economic profits will in time disappear. The market supply and demand situation prevailing when economic profits become zero will determine the total amount of X produced.

But what if the initial market situation for product X were less favorable? Suppose conditions in the product market initially were such that the firm could sell the 15 units of X at a price of just 75 cents per unit. Total revenue would be $11.25 (= 15 × 75 cents). After paying wage, rental, and interest costs of $10, the firm would yield a below-normal profit of $1.25. In other words, losses of $1.75 (= $11.25 − $13) would be incurred. Certainly firms would not be attracted to this unprosperous industry. On the contrary, if these losses persisted, entrepreneurs would seek the normal or economic profits offered by more prosperous industries. This means that existing firms in industry X would in time go out of business entirely or migrate to other industries where normal or better profits prevail. However, as this happens, the market supply of X will fall relative to the market demand, thereby raising product price to the end that losses will in time disappear. Industry X will then stabilize itself in size. The market supply and demand situation that prevails at that point where economic profits are zero will determine the total output of product X.

The important role of consumer demand in determining the types and quantities of goods produced must be emphasized. Consumers, unrestrained by government and possessing money incomes from the sale of resources, spend their dollars upon those goods which they are most willing and able to buy. These expenditures are in effect "dollar votes" by which consumers register their wants through the demand side of the product market. If these votes are great enough to provide a normal profit, businesses will produce that product. An increase in consumer demand, that is, an increase in the dollar votes cast for a product, will mean economic profits for the industry producing it. These profits will signal the expansion of that industry and increases in the output of the product. A decrease in consumer demand, that is, fewer votes cast for the product, will result in losses and, in time, contraction of the adversely affected industry. As firms leave the industry, the output of the product declines. In short, the dollar votes of consumers play a key role in determining what products profit-seeking businesses will produce. As noted in Chapter 3, the capitalistic system is sometimes said to be characterized by *consumer sovereignty*, because of the strategic role of consumers in determining the types and quantities of goods produced.

From the viewpoint of businesses, we now see that firms are not really "free" to produce what they wish. The demand decisions of consumers, by making the production of some products profitable and others not, restrict the choice of businesses in deciding what to produce. Businesses must synchronize their production choices with consumer choices or face the penalty of losses and eventual bankruptcy.

Much the same holds true with respect to resource suppliers. In seeking to maximize the returns from the sale of their human and property resources, resource suppliers are prompted by the price system to make their choices in accord with consumer demands. If those firms which produce goods wanted by consumers can operate profitably, then only those firms will demand resources. Resource suppliers will not be "free" to allocate their resources to the production of goods consumers do not value very highly. The reason? There will be no firms producing such products, because consumer demand is not sufficient to make it profitable to do so. In short, consumers register their preferences on the demand side of the product market, and producers and resource suppliers respond appropriately in seeking to further their own self-interests. The price system communicates the wants of consumers to business and resource suppliers and elicits appropriate responses.

Organizing production

How is production to be organized in a market economy? This fundamental question, we recall, is comprised of three subquestions: (1) How should resources be allocated among specific industries? (2) What specific firms should do the producing in each industry? (3) What combination of resources—what technology—should each firm employ?

The preceding section has answered the first subquestion. The price system steers resources to those industries whose products consumers want badly enough to make their production profitable. It simultaneously deprives unprofitable industries of scarce resources. If all firms had sufficient time to enter prosperous industries and to leave unprosperous industries, the output of each industry would be large enough for the firms to just make normal profits. If total industry output at this point happens to be 1,500 units and the most profitable output for each firm is 15 units as in our previous example, the industry will obviously be comprised of 100 competing firms.

The second and third subquestions are closely intertwined. In a competitive market economy, the firms which do the producing are those which are willing and able to employ the economically most efficient technique of production. And what determines the most efficient technique? Economic efficiency depends upon (1) available technology, that is, the alternative combinations of resources or inputs which will produce the desired output, and (2) the prices at which the needed resources can be obtained. The combination of resources which is most efficient economically depends not only upon the physical or engineering data provided by available technology but also upon the relative worth of the required resources as measured by their market prices. Thus, a technique which requires just a few physical inputs of resources to produce a given output may be highly *inefficient* economically if the required resources are valued very highly in the market. In other words, economic efficiency entails getting a given output of product with the smallest input of scarce resources, when both output and resource inputs are measured in dollars-and-cents terms. In short, that combination of resources which will pro-

duce $15 worth of product X at the lowest possible money cost is the most efficient.

Table 5-1 will help illustrate these points. Suppose there are three different techniques by which the desired $15 worth of product X can be produced. These techniques and the prices of the required resources are shown in Table 5-1. By multiplying the quantities of the various resources required by the resource prices in each of the three techniques, the total cost of producing $15 worth of X by each technique can be determined. It can be concluded that technique No. 2 is economically the most efficient of the three, for the simple reason that it is the least costly way of producing $15 worth of X. Technique No. 2 permits society to obtain $15 worth of output by using up a smaller amount of resources—$13 worth— than would be used up by the two alternative techniques. Technique No. 2 is the most efficient, because it gives society $15 worth of output for an input of $13 worth of resources; the alternative techniques entail an input of $15 worth of resources for the same amount of output.

But what guarantees that technique No. 2 will actually be used? After all, techniques No. 1 and No. 3 entail a normal profit and thereby will permit firms to survive at least for the moment by using either of these two techniques. The answer to this question is twofold. (1) Technique No. 2 allows the user an economic profit of $2. And firms, seeking to further their own interests, can be expected to employ techniques which

TABLE 5-1. TECHNIQUES FOR PRODUCING $15 WORTH OF PRODUCT X*

Resource	Technique No. 1	Technique No. 2	Technique No. 3	Price per unit of resource
Labor	4	2	1	$2
Land	1	3	4	1
Capital	1	1	2	3
Entrepreneurial ability	1	1	1	3
Total cost of $15 worth of X	$15	$13	$15	

*Hypothetical data.

permit them to realize the greatest profits. Firms will *want* to use the most efficient technique, because it yields the greatest profit. (2) Competition will literally *force* firms to use the most efficient technique. The firm that fails to employ the least costly method of production will find that other existing firms or new firms coming into the industry will adopt the least costly technique. This leads to an increase in supply and hence to a reduction in the price of X. This will turn the normal profit of the inefficient firm into losses unless it switches to the most efficient technique. The competitive price system makes the adoption of the most efficient production techniques a condition of survival.

We must emphasize that a change in either technology or resource prices may cause the firm to shift from the technology now employed. For example, if the price of labor falls to 50 cents, technique No. 1 will be superior to technique No. 2. That is, businesses will find that they can lower their costs by shifting to a technology which involves the use of more of that resource whose price has fallen. This shift in techniques illustrates why resource demand curves are downsloping. In this case, a decline in the price of labor prompts businesses to shift to a technique employing more labor and less land. The reader should verify that a new technique involving 1 unit of labor, 4 of land, 1 of capital, and 1 of entrepreneurial ability will be preferable to all three techniques given in Table 5-1, assuming the resource prices given in the table.

products? The size of his money income. And money income in turn depends upon the types and quantities of the various property and human resources which the income receiver supplies and the prices which they command in the resource market. Thus, resource prices play a key role in determining the size of each household's claim against the total output of society. Within the limits of a consumer's money income, his willingness to pay the equilibrium price for X determines whether or not some of this product is distributed to him. And this willingness to buy X will depend upon his preference for X in comparison with available close substitutes for X and their relative prices. Thus, product prices play a key role in determining the expenditure patterns of consumers.

We should emphasize that there is nothing particularly ethical about the price system as a mechanism for distributing the output of pure capitalism. Those households which manage to accumulate large amounts of property resources by inheritance, through their business acumen, or by crook will receive large incomes and thus command large shares of the economy's total output. Others which offer only labor resources valued low by the price system will receive meager money incomes and small portions of total output. The price system is impersonal, and if money incomes are very unequally distributed, a very unequal distribution of the fruits of production will follow. Chapter 7 and later Chapter 35 will have more to say on the question of income inequality.

Distributing total output

The price system enters the picture in two ways in solving the problem of distributing total output. Generally speaking, any given product will be distributed to consumers on the basis of their ability and willingness to pay the existing market price for it. If the price of X is $1 per unit, those buyers who are able and willing to pay that price will get a unit of this product; those who are not, will not. This, we recall, is the rationing function of equilibrium prices.

What determines a consumer's ability to pay the equilibrium price for X and other available

Providing for flexibility

In order to ensure efficiency in the administration of its resources over a period of time, an economy must be flexible. It must be readily adaptable to changes in certain basic data upon which the operation of the economy is predicated. In particular, efficient production assumes that the economy is producing those products which are desired or wanted by society, that is, by consumers. The first question then is this: Can the price system of pure capitalism negotiate adjustments appropriate to specified changes in consumer tastes? But there is another aspect to the question of flexibility: it is highly desirable for an economy to be not only permissive of, and adaptable to, changes but also to be conducive to those changes which will lead to greater affluence and a higher standard of living. Technological advance and the accumulation of capital are the primary means to a higher standard of living. The second query then is this: Is the price system conducive to rapid technological advance and the extensive accumulation of capital equipment?

Is the price system adaptable to change? Let us suppose a change occurs in consumer tastes. Specifically, let us say that consumers decide they want more shoes and fewer shirts than the economy is currently providing. Will the price system communicate this change to businesses and resource suppliers and prompt appropriate adjustments?

The assumed change in consumers' tastes will be communicated to producers through an increase in the demand for shoes and a decline in the demand for shirts. This means that shoe prices will rise and shirt prices will fall. Now, assuming firms in both industries are enjoying precisely normal profits prior to these changes in consumer demand, higher shoe prices will mean economic profits for the shoe industry, and lower shirt prices will entail losses for the shirt industry. Self-interest guarantees that competitors will enter the prosperous shoe industry. Losses will in time force firms to leave the depressed shirt industry. As a matter of fact, some firms leaving the shirt industry might enter the shoe industry. But in all probability, most firms entering the shoe industry will be newly created, and those leaving the shirt industry will become permanently defunct.

In any event, the prosperous shoe industry will expand, and the unprosperous shirt industry will contract. But these adjustments, we recall, are both self-limiting. The expansion of the shoe industry will continue only to the point at which the resulting increase in the market supply of shoes brings shoe prices back down to a level at which normal profits again prevail. Similarly, contraction in the shirt industry will persist until the accompanying decline in the

market supply of shirts brings shirt prices up to a level at which the remaining firms can receive a normal profit. The crucial point to note is that these adjustments in the business sector are completely appropriate to the assumed changes in consumer tastes. Society, that is, consumers, wants more shoes and fewer shirts, and that is precisely what it is getting as the shoe industry expands and the shirt industry contracts.

But this analysis proceeds on the assumption that resource suppliers are agreeable to these adjustments. Will the price system prompt resource suppliers to reallocate their human and property resources from the shirt to the shoe industry, thereby permitting the output of shoes to expand at the expense of shirt production? The answer is "Yes."

The economic profits which initially follow the increase in demand for shoes will not only provide that industry with the inducement to expand but will also give it the added receipts with which to obtain the resources essential to its growth. Higher shoe prices will permit firms in that industry to pay higher prices for resources, thereby drawing resources from what are now less urgent, alternative employments. Willingness and ability to employ more resources in the shoe industry will be communicated back into the resource market through an increase in the demand for resources. Substantially the reverse occurs in the adversely affected shirt industry. The losses which the decline in consumer demand initially entails will cause a decline in the demand for resources in that industry. Workers and other resources released from the contracting shirt industry can now find employment in the expanding shoe industry. As a matter of fact, the increased demand for resources in the shoe industry will mean higher resource prices in that industry than those being paid in the shirt industry, where declines in resource demand have lowered resource prices. The resulting differential in resource prices will provide the incentive for resource owners to further their self-interests by reallocating their resources from the shirt to the shoe industry. And this, of course, is the precise shift needed to permit the shoe industry to expand and the shirt industry to contract.

The ability of the price system to communicate changes in such basic data as consumer tastes and to elicit appropriate responses from both businesses and resource suppliers is sometimes called the *directing* or *guiding function* of prices. By affecting product prices and profits, changes in consumer tastes direct the expansion of some industries and the contraction of others. These adjustments carry through to the resource market as expanding industries demand more resources and contracting industries demand less. The resulting changes in resource prices guide resources from the contracting to the expanding industries. In the absence of a price system, some administrative agency, presumably a governmental planning board, would have to undertake the task of directing business institutions and resources into specific lines of production.

Analysis similar to that outlined above would indicate that the price system would adjust appropriately to similar fundamental changes, for example, to changes in technology and changes in the relative supplies of various resources.

Is the price system conducive to change? Adjusting to given changes is one thing; inducing changes, particularly desirable changes, is something else again. Is the competitive price system congenial to technological improvements and capital accumulation, the interrelated changes which lead to greater productivity and a higher level of material well-being for society? This is not an easy question to answer. We state our reply at this point without stopping for qualifications and modifications.

The ideology of pure capitalism, with its emphasis upon the competitive price system, is a fertile environment for technological advance. Competition provides the *opportunity* for entrepreneurs to introduce new techniques and new products, unimpeded by the artificial barriers which a noncompetitive environment might entail. The competitive price system also furnishes the *incentive* for technological advance. The introduction of cost-cutting techniques provides the innovating firm with a temporary advantage over its rivals. Lower production costs mean economic profits for the pioneering firm. By passing a part of its cost reduction on to the consumer through a lower product price, the innovating firm can achieve a sizable increase in sales and lucrative economic profits at the expense of rival firms. And, remember, because the monetary rewards of the successful introduction of a new technique will accrue to the innovating firm, the price system will be very effective in harnessing individual incentives in the cause of technological advance.

Looking at technological advance from the social point of view, we should note that the innovating firm's economic profits will be a temporary phenomenon. Other firms can also adopt the new cost-reducing technique. Indeed, as we have seen, they will be forced to do so. Why? Because by price cutting, the innovating firm will turn the once-normal profits of its competitors into losses. This is of considerable significance: it is in this fashion that the competitive price system communicates the technological improvements of one firm to all other firms in that industry. Rivals must follow the lead of the most progressive firm or suffer the immediate penalty of losses and the eventual pain of bankruptcy.

We should note that the lower product price which the technological advance permits will cause the innovating industry to expand. This expansion may be the result of existing firms expanding their rates of output or of new firms entering the industry under the lure of the economic profits initially created by a technological advance. This expansion, that is, the diversion of resources from nonprogressive to progressive industries, is as it should be. Sustained efficiency in the use of scarce resources demands that resources be continually reallocated from industries whose productive techniques are relatively less efficient to those whose techniques are relatively more efficient.

But technological advance typically entails the use of increased amounts of capital goods. Can the price system provide the capital goods upon which technological advance relies? More specifically, can the entrepreneur as an innovator command through the price system the resources necessary to produce the machinery and equipment upon which technological advance depends?

Obviously, he can. If society registers dollar

votes for capital goods, the product market and resource market will adjust to these votes by producing capital goods. In other words, the price system acknowledges dollar voting for both consumer and capital goods. Indeed, the relative sizes of these two types of dollar voting determine how a market economy will divide its total output between consumer goods, which satisfy wants directly, and capital goods, which satisfy wants indirectly through the more efficient production of consumer goods.

But who will register votes for capital goods? First, the entrepreneur as a receiver of profit income can be expected to apportion a part of his income to the accumulation of capital goods. By so doing he can achieve an even greater profit income in the future if his innovation proves successful. Furthermore, by paying a rate of interest, entrepreneurs can borrow portions of the incomes of other households and use these borrowed funds in casting dollar votes for the production of more capital goods.

In practice, the process of technological advance and capital accumulation is much more complex than envisioned here. Chapter 12 will picture the major determinants of capital accumulation and discuss in more detail the relationship between technological advance and the purchase of capital goods. The important point for present purposes is that the market economy embodies the opportunity and incentive for technological advance and the means for providing the capital goods which such advance typically presumes.

Competition, control, and the "invisible hand"

Though the price system is the organizing mechanism of pure capitalism, it is essential to recognize the role of competition as the mechanism of control in such an economy. The market mechanism of supply and demand communicates the wants of consumers (society) to businesses and through businesses to resource suppliers. It is competition, however, which forces businesses and resource suppliers to make appropriate responses. To illustrate: the impact of an increase in consumer demand for some product will raise that good's price above the

wage, rent, interest, and normal profit costs of production. The resulting economic profits in effect are a signal to producers that society wants more of the product. It is competition— in particular, the ability of new firms to enter the industry—that simultaneously brings an expansion of output and a lowering of price back to a level just consistent with production costs. However, if the industry was not competitive, but dominated by, say, one huge firm which was able to prohibit the entry of potential competitors, then that firm could enjoy economic profits by preventing the expansion of the industry.

But competition does more than guarantee responses appropriate to the wishes of society. It is competition which forces firms to adopt the most efficient productive techniques. In a competitive market, the failure of some firms to use the least costly production technique means eventual elimination by other competing firms who do employ the most efficient methods of production. Finally, we have seen that competition provides an environment conducive to technological advance.

A very remarkable aspect of the operation and the adjustments of a competitive price system is that a curious and important identity is involved—the identity of private and social interests. That is, firms and resource suppliers, seeking to further their own self-interest and operating within the framework of a highly competitive market system, will simultaneously, as though guided by an "invisible hand," [2] promote the public or social interest. For example, we have seen that, given a competitive environment, business firms use the least costly combination of resources in producing a given output because it is in their self-interest to do so. To act otherwise would be to forgo profits or even to risk bankruptcy over a period of time. But at the same time it is obviously also in the social interest to use scarce resources in the least costly, that is, most efficient, manner. To do otherwise would be to produce a given output at a greater cost or sacrifice of alternative

[2] Adam Smith, *The Wealth of Nations* (New York: Modern Library, Inc., originally published in 1776), p. 423.

goods than is really necessary. Furthermore, in our more-shoes–fewer-shirts illustration, it is self-interest, awakened and guided by the competitive price system, which induces the very responses appropriate to the assumed change in society's wants. Businesses seeking to make higher profits and to avoid losses, on the one hand, and resource suppliers pursuing greater monetary rewards, on the other, negotiate the very changes in the allocation of resources and therefore the composition of output which society now demands. The force of competition, in other words, controls or guides the self-interest motive in such a way that it automatically, and quite unintentionally, furthers the best interests of society.

AN EVALUATION OF THE PRICE SYSTEM

Is the price system the best means of deciding how total output is to be determined, how production of that output should be organized, and how total output should be distributed? This is a complex question; any complete answer necessarily leaps the boundary of facts and enters the realm of values. This means there is no scientific answer to the query. The very fact that there exist many competing ways of allocating scarce resources is ample evidence of disagreement as to the effectiveness of the price system.

The case for the price system

1. The basic economic argument for the price system is that it leads to an efficient allocation of resources. The competitive price system, it is argued, guides resources into the production of those goods and services most wanted by consumers. It forces the use of the most efficient techniques in organizing resources for production, and it is conducive to the development and adoption of new and more efficient production techniques. In short, proponents of the price system argue that the "invisible hand" will in effect harness self-interest so as to provide society with the greatest output of wanted goods from its available resources. This, then, suggests the maximum economic efficiency.

2. The major noneconomic argument for the price system is its great emphasis upon personal freedom. The price system permits—indeed, it thrives upon—freedom of enterprise and choice. Entrepreneurs and workers are not herded from industry to industry to meet the production targets established by some omnipotent governmental agency. On the contrary, they are free to further their own self-interests, subject, of course, to the rewards and penalties imposed by the price system itself.

The case against the price system

The case against the price system is somewhat more complex. Critics of the market economy base their position on the following points:

1. They argue that capitalistic ideology is conducive to the demise of its main controlling mechanism—competition. The alleged weakening of competition as a control mechanism comes from two basic sources.

On the one hand, though desirable from the social point of view, competition is most irksome to the individual producer subject to its rigors. It is allegedly inherent in the free, individualistic environment of the capitalistic system that the profit-seeking entrepreneur will attempt to break free of the restraining force of competition in trying to better his position. Combination, conspiracy, cutthroat competition, and sheer productive efficiency are all means to the end of reducing competition and escaping its regulatory powers.

On the other hand, the very technological advance which the price system fosters has contributed to the decline of competition. Modern technology typically requires (1) the use of extremely large quantities of real capital, (2) large markets, (3) a complex, centralized, and closely integrated management, and (4) large and reliable sources of raw materials. Such an operation implies the need for producers who are large-scale not only in the absolute sense but also in relation to the size of the market. In other words, the achievement of maximum productive efficiency through the employment of the best available technology often requires the existence of a small number of large firms rather than a large number of small ones.

To the degree that competition declines, the price system will be weakened as a mechanism for efficiently allocating resources. Producers and resource suppliers will be less subject to the will of consumers; the sovereignty of producers and resource suppliers will then challenge and weaken the sovereignty of consumers. The "invisible hand" identity of private and social interest will begin to lose its grip.

2. Critics also challenge the assertion that the price system provides the goods most wanted by society. This criticism has several roots. First, to the extent that a weakening of competition, as discussed above, lessens consumer sovereignty, the price system becomes less proficient in allocating resources in precise accord with the wishes of consumers.

Second, critical socialists contend that the price system allows the more efficient, or more cunning, entrepreneurs to accumulate vast amounts of property resources, the accumulation process being extended through time by the right of inheritance. This, in addition to differences in the amount and quality of human resources supplied by various households, causes a highly unequal distribution of money incomes in a market economy. The result is that families differ greatly in their ability to express their wants in the market. The wealthy have more dollar votes than the poor. Hence, it is concluded that the price system allocates resources to the production of frivolous luxury goods for the rich at the expense of the output of necessities for the poor. A country that

. . . spends money on champagne before it has provided milk for its babies is a badly managed, silly, vain, stupid, ignorant nation. . . . The only way in which such a nation can make itself wealthy and prosperous is by good housekeeping: that is by providing for its wants in order of their importance, and allowing no money to be wasted on whims and luxuries until the necessities have been thoroughly served.[3]

In the third place, critics point out that the price system sometimes fails to register all the costs and benefits associated with the produc-

tion of certain goods and services. That is, consumer demand only embodies the satisfactions which accrue to individual consumers who purchase goods and services; it does not reflect the fact that the purchase of such services as polio shots and chest X rays yields widespread benefits or satisfactions to the community (society) as a whole. Similarly, the supply decisions of producers hinge upon the costs which they must bear and do not reflect certain costs associated with production which might accrue to society as a whole. The smoke, smog, and pollution of rivers which have characterized the production of certain industries illustrate such costs. The point is this: where demand and supply do not accurately reflect all the benefits and all the costs of production, the price system cannot be expected to bring about an allocation of resources which best satisfies the wants of society.

A final argument is this: the price system only tabulates individual wants. There are many wants involving goods and services which cannot be financed by individuals as such. For example, such goods and services as public education, highways, and national defense cannot be purchased in desired amounts by households on an individual basis. They can only be consumed economically on a social, or collective, basis. The price system, it is argued, is incapable of registering such social, or collective, wants.

3. The price system has also been criticized for its failure to adjust rapidly to drastic changes in society's production objectives. There is allegedly a persistent time lag between society's production targets and the actual pattern of resource allocation provided by the price system. Even in a highly competitive market economy, the occupational and geographic mobility of human resources will be far from perfect.

[3] George Bernard Shaw, *The Intelligent Woman's Guide to Socialism and Capitalism* (New York: Brentano's, 1928), pp. 50–55. It should be noted that this criticism is not as scientific as it might first appear. The argument presumes that every consumer has a capacity equal to that of every other consumer for enjoying goods, a presumption which cannot be proved (or disproved). Used by permission of the Public Trustee and the Society of Authors.

Laborers are hesitant to sever social ties and move to a strange community to take a new job. Such a move may also be costly, particularly if the worker must equip himself with new skills. And property resources are usually reallocated through the price system with even less rapidity. In other words, the economy may be plagued with certain declining, or "sick," industries. This is the case with agriculture in the United States. For a variety of complex reasons (to be discussed in a later chapter), agriculture has declined significantly in its relative importance to the economy. This decline calls for an exodus of resources to expanding industries, an exodus which in practice has simply not been fast enough. The result? Too many resources engaged in the production of farm commodities whose relative importance to consumers has declined and not enough resources engaged in the production of antibiotics, synthetic fibers, and plastics.

In particular, critics contend that the price system is incapable of adjusting with rapidity and certainty to the dramatic alteration in production goals which war entails. The price system can make appropriate adjustments in time to modest shifts in the pattern of society's wants. It is not capable of rapidly reallocating its resources from civilian to war goods production in that critical situation in which time is the most important resource of all. The same general argument, of course, applies to somewhat less drastic changes in production goals caused by such considerations as the disruption of international trade due to, say, political considerations, or the sudden and unanticipated introduction of a particularly significant technological advance.

4. Finally, as we noted at the beginning of this chapter, the price system is widely recognized as an imperfect mechanism for providing the continuous, full employment of the economy's resources.

Which of these two positions is correct? To a degree both are. The several criticisms of the market economy are reasonably accurate and certainly too serious to ignore. On the other hand, we cannot judge an issue by the number of arguments pro and con. The basic economic argument for the price system—it tends to provide an efficient allocation of resources—is not easily undermined. In practice, the price system is—or at least can be—reasonably efficient.

Relevance, realism, and the price system

Does the price system of American capitalism function in the same fashion as the price system discussed in this chapter? In principle, yes; in detail, no. Our discussion of the price system provides us with a working model—a first approximation—of the actual price system of American capitalism. Our analysis presents a much-simplified, yet useful, picture of the real thing.

Specifically, the basic differences between the price system as pictured in this chapter and the actual price system of American capitalism are two in number:

1. In many product and resource markets, competition clearly has been supplanted by a few giant business corporations and huge labor unions. Competition is simply not as vigorous in practice as our discussion of the price system presumed. This means that the decisions of business and resource suppliers are less than perfectly synchronized with those of consumers and that changes in the production goals of society are less precisely communicated throughout the economy. Giant business and labor groups in American capitalism have the power to resist the dictates of consumer sovereignty and, as a matter of fact, will usually find it personally advantageous to do so.

2. Another major difference between our model price system and the market system of American capitalism lies in the economic role of government in the latter. In contrast with the passive, limited government envisioned in the ideology of pure capitalism, the government of American capitalism is an active and integral component of the economy. In particular, the economy of the United States has taken cognizance of the elements of truth which permeate the noted criticisms of the price system.

Through government, society has taken steps to correct these shortcomings. Hence, government pursues policies designed, not only to preserve and bolster competition, but also to adjust certain inequities fostered by the price system, to speed on occasion the reallocation of resources, and to help maintain full employment. It is with these and related economic functions of government that the ensuing chapter is concerned.

Is our analysis of the price system realistic? Does it provide a workable description of the price system of American capitalism? A scholar[4] has recently provided a meaningful reply to these questions:

For all the new quality of twentieth-century industrial society, the great principles of self-interest and competition, however watered down or hedged about, still provide basic rules of behavior which no economic organization can afford to disregard entirely . . . the laws of the market can be discerned . . . if we look beneath the surface.

SUMMARY

1. In a market economy, the interacting decisions of competing buyers and sellers will determine a system of product and resource prices at any given point in time.

2. The relative scarcity of economic resources makes the operation of any economy a matter of choosing between alternatives. At any point in time, these choices depend upon the relative scarcity of resources and products. Over time, the degree to which these choices are altered as product and resource prices change depends upon the willingness and ability of consumers to make substitutions among products and the willingness and ability of producers to make substitutions among resources. Substitutability tends to relieve particular scarcities of resources and products.

3. Those products whose production and sale yield total receipts sufficient to cover all costs,

[4] Robert L. Heilbroner, *The Worldly Philosophers*, rev. ed. (New York: Simon and Schuster, Inc., 1961), p. 44.

including a normal profit, will be produced. Those whose production will not yield a normal profit will not be produced.

4. Economic profits designate an industry as prosperous and signal its expansion. Losses mean an industry is unprosperous and result in a contraction of that industry. Industrial expansion and contraction are self-limiting processes. As expansion increases market supply relative to market demand, the price of a product falls to the point where all economic profits disappear. As contraction decreases market supply relative to market demand, the resulting increase in product price eliminates losses and makes the industry normally profitable once again.

5. Consumer sovereignty dominates a competitive market economy. The penalty of losses and lure of profits force both business and resource suppliers to channel their efforts in accordance with the wants of consumers.

6. Competition forces firms to use the least costly and therefore economically the most efficient productive techniques.

7. The price system plays a dual role in distributing total output among individual households. The prices commanded by the quantities and types of resources supplied by each household will determine the number of dollar claims against the economy's output each household receives. Given consumer tastes, product prices are of fundamental importance in determining consumer expenditure patterns. Within the limits of each household's money income, consumer preferences and the relative prices of products determine the distribution of total output.

8. The competitive price system can communicate changes in consumer tastes to resource suppliers and entrepreneurs, thereby prompting appropriate adjustments in the allocation of the economy's resources. The competitive price system also provides an environment conducive to technological advance and capital accumulation.

9. Competition, the primary mechanism of control in the market economy, will foster an

identity of private and social interests; as though directed by an "invisible hand," competition harnesses the self-interest motives of businesses and resource suppliers so as to simultaneously further the social interest.

10. The basic virtue of the price system is its continuing emphasis upon efficiency. It produces what consumers want through the use of the most efficient techniques. Operation and adjustments of the price system are automatic in the sense that they are the result of individual, decentralized decisions of government.

11. Criticisms of the price system are several: (*a*) the controlling mechanism, competition, tends to weaken over time; (*b*) inherent income inequalities, inability to register collective wants, and the exclusion of certain costs and satisfactions from supply and demand prevent the price system from producing that collection of goods most wanted by society; (*c*) the price system reallocates resources too slowly during war and similar emergencies; (*d*) the competitive price system does not guarantee continued full employment.

12. The price system of American capitalism differs from the competitive price system in that the former is characterized by (*a*) giant corporations and unions in certain product and resource markets and (*b*) government intervention in the economy to correct the major defects of the price system. Yet the competitive price system does provide a working model whereby we can understand the price system of American capitalism.

QUESTIONS AND STUDY SUGGESTIONS

1. Describe in detail how the price system answers the Five Fundamental Questions.

2. Why must economic choices be made? How do scarcity and substitutability influence the rendering of economic choices? Be specific.

3. "The capitalistic system is a profit and loss economy." Carefully analyze and explain the significance of this statement.

4. Define and explain the significance of "dollar voting," "consumer sovereignty," and the "invisible hand."

5. What is the directing or guiding function of the competitive price system? Contrast the guiding function with the rationing function discussed in Chapter 4.

6. "Production methods which are inferior in the engineering sense may be the most efficient methods in the economic sense." Explain.

7. Evaluate and explain the following statements:

a. "The most important feature of capitalism is the absence of a central economic plan."

b. "Competition is the indispensable disciplinarian of the market economy."

8. "The beautiful consequence of the market is that it is its own guardian. If output prices or certain kinds of remuneration stray away from their socially ordained levels, forces are set into motion to bring them back to the fold. It is a curious paradox which thus ensues: the market, which is the acme of individual economic freedom, is the strictest taskmaster of all. One may appeal the ruling of a planning board or win the dispensation of a minister; but there is no appeal, no dispensation, from the anonymous pressures of the market mechanism. Economic freedom is thus more illusory than at first appears. One can do as one pleases in the market. But if one pleases to do what the market disapproves, the price of individual freedom is economic ruination." [5] Explain fully the meaning and significance of this quotation.

9. Assume that a business firm finds that its profits will be at a maximum when it produces $40 worth of product A. Suppose also that each of the three techniques shown in the following table will produce the desired output.

Resource	Technique No. 1	Technique No. 2	Technique No. 3	Price per unit of resource
Labor	5	2	3	$3
Land	2	4	2	4
Capital	2	4	5	2
Entrepreneurial ability	4	2	4	2

a. Given the resource prices shown above, which technique will the firm choose? Why?

b. Assume now that a new technique, technique No. 4, is developed. It entails the use of 2 units of labor, 2 of land, 6 of capital, and 3 of entrepreneurial ability. Given the resource prices in the table, will the firm adopt the new technique? Explain your answer.

c. Suppose now that the price of labor falls to $1.50 per unit, all other resource prices being unchanged. What technique will the producer now choose? Explain.

d. "The price system causes the economy to conserve most in the use of those resources which are particularly scarce in supply. Resources which are scarcest relative to the demand for them have the highest prices. As a result, producers use these resources as sparingly as is possible." Evaluate this statement. Does your answer to question 9c bear out this contention? Explain.

10. "Soviet industrialization has taken place against the background of an abundance of manpower. . . . It was therefore economically sensible for them to use labor lavishly, substituting it whenever possible for capital goods, and bringing in more workers whenever it was possible by doing so to squeeze a bit more output out of existing enterprises. The result of such a policy was to make output per worker low, but it was still the correct thing to do in the light of the abundance of labor." [6] Interpret and explain in terms of Table 5-1. Output per Soviet worker is considerably lower than output per American worker. Does this necessarily mean that the Soviet economy is inefficient and wasteful as compared to the United States' economy? Explain.

11. What are the major criticisms of the price system? Carefully evaluate these criticisms.

[5] Robert L. Heilbroner, *The Worldly Philosophers*, rev. ed. (New York: Simon and Schuster, Inc., 1961), p. 42.

[6] Robert W. Campbell, "Problems of United States–Soviet Economic Comparisons," in Joint Economic Committee, *Comparisons of the United States and Soviet Economics* (Washington: Government Printing Office, 1960), p. 26.

SELECTED REFERENCES

Boulding, Kenneth E., *Economic Analysis*, 3d ed. (New York: Harper & Row, Publishers, 1955), chap. 9.

Buckingham, Walter S., Jr., *Theoretical Economic Systems* (New York: The Ronald Press Company, 1958), chaps. 2–4.

Harlan, H. C. (ed.), *Readings in Economics and Politics* (New York: Oxford University Press, 1961), readings III-7 and V-1.

Heilbroner, Robert L., *The Worldly Philosophers*, rev. ed. (New York: Simon and Schuster, Inc., 1961), chap. 3.

Oxenfeldt, Alfred R., *Economic Systems in Action*, rev. ed. (New York: Holt, Rinehart and Winston, Inc., 1957), pp. 6–38.

Radford, R. A., "The Economic Organization of a POW Camp," *Economica*, November, 1945, pp. 189–201.

Slichter, Sumner H., "Free Private Enterprise," in P. A. Samuelson, R. L. Bishop, and J. R. Coleman (eds.), *Readings in Economics*, 3d ed. (New York: McGraw-Hill Book Company, Inc., 1958), chap. 6.

Chapter 6

MIXED CAPITALISM AND THE ECONOMIC

FUNCTIONS OF GOVERNMENT

WE NOW BEGIN the move from our abstract working model of pure capitalism to a discussion of American capitalism. In so doing we inject a significant dose of reality into our analysis.

In the preceding chapter we analyzed in some detail the operation of a purely capitalistic economy, with our discussion taking the form of an abstraction or model. Pure capitalism, as described in Chapter 5, has never existed and, without a doubt, never will. The value of our discussion of pure capitalism lies in the fact that it indicated the manner in which a price-directed, or *market*, economy would function and revealed that consumer sovereignty would direct the operation of such an economy in answering the Five Fundamental Questions. The price system is the mechanism through which the decisions of consumers are communicated to producers and resource suppliers, who respond by allocating their efforts and resources into those lines of production most desired by consumers. In effect, the expenditures of consumers constitute dollar votes which competing businesses and competing resource suppliers must heed. Competition, as the primary regulating force in the market economy, guarantees that the economy's resources will be mobilized in accordance with consumer wants. The whip of competition prompts producers,

through the reward of profits and the penalty of losses, to produce in accordance with consumer desires. Such are the main characteristics of a market economy.

At the other extreme, it is a simple matter to sketch a model of a governmentally directed or planned economy. Here the Five Fundamental Questions would be answered through decisions rendered by public officials. In such a society, government would set the production goals for the economy, goals which might or might not reflect accurately the wishes of the citizenry. Incorporating these objectives in a master economic plan, government would then direct the actions of businesses and households toward the fulfillment of the plan. Governmentally determined goals would replace free consumer choice in setting society's output targets, and government directives would supplant the competitive price system as a mechanism for guiding resources into the various alternative lines of production. Such are the bare bones of a planned economy.

All real-life economies combine characteristics of the market economy model and the planned economy model. All present-day economies are "mixed"; government and the price system share the function of answering the Five Fundamental Questions. Yet the various economies of the world differ drastically in the par-

97

ticular blend of government direction and market direction which they embody. The economy of Soviet Russia, the topic of the final chapter of this book, leans heavily toward the planned economy model. Here the price system plays a role clearly secondary to that of government. American capitalism, on the other hand, is predominantly a market economy. Yet the economic functions of government—Federal, state, and local—are of very considerable significance. In American capitalism a number of strategic economic decisions are rendered, not by individuals as such, but collectively through government. A rough indicator of the relative importance of the market and government in American capitalism is the fact that in peacetime about four-fifths of the total output of the economy is provided by the market system, the remaining one-fifth being produced under the sponsorship of government. In short, the economy of the United States can be accurately described as _mixed capitalism_. Our economy holds _generally_ to the capitalist ideology outlined in Chapter 3 and relies primarily upon the price system, the rudiments and functioning of which were outlined in Chapters 4 and 5. Government, however, in a variety of significant ways, assists and modifies the functioning of the price system.

ECONOMIC FUNCTIONS OF GOVERNMENT

The economic functions of government are many, and they are varied. As a matter of fact, the economic role of government is so broad in scope that it is virtually impossible to establish an exclusive list of its economic functions. We shall employ the following breakdown of government's economic activities as a pattern for our discussion, recognizing that some overlapping is unavoidable.

First, some of the economic functions of government are designed to strengthen and facilitate the operation of the price system. The two major activities of government in this area are:

1. Providing the legal foundation and a social environment conducive to the effective operation of the price system

2. Maintaining competition

Through a second group of functions, government supplements and modifies the operation of the price system. There are four major functions of government here. They involve:

1. Providing a minimum standard of living for all households in the economy

2. Adjusting the composition of total output to account for social costs and revenues

3. Providing society with social goods and services

4. Controlling unemployment and inflation caused by the business cycle

Our immediate objective is simply that of seeing how government affects the character and operation of the economy. More specifically, we want to know how the economic functions of government affect (1) the level at which the economy is employing its available resources and (2) the efficiency with which the economy allocates its employed resources among alternative employments. In short, we want to discover the role of government in the achievement of full employment and full production. We also seek a basic understanding of the methods or techniques by which government affects employment and resource allocation.

But a word of warning: it is exceedingly difficult to trace the effect of specific governmental functions upon resource allocation and the level of employment. In some instances the impact of government activity upon resource allocation and employment is muted, indirect, and decidedly nebulous. Yet—with rare exceptions—there is little doubt that all six basic economic functions of government do influence both employment and resource allocation in some fashion and to some degree. To facilitate our discussion, we shall generalize that the first five functions of government have their greatest impact upon the allocation of resources. In some cases the intended objective is the reallocation of scarce resources; in others, the resulting reallocation is more or less incidental to some other goal. The final function—offsetting the business cycle—is obviously aimed at influencing the level of employment in the economy. Discussion of this sixth function is deferred until Part 2 of this book where we shall analyze it in detail. In this chapter our attention will be focused upon those governmental activities which either draw resources from private to public uses or cause resources to be shifted among alternative private uses. Any discussion of government's explicit efforts to influence the level of employment is avoided in this chapter by the simple expedient of assuming full employment.

Legal and social framework for the price system

Government assumes the task of providing the legal framework and certain basic services prerequisite to the effective operation of a market economy. The necessary legal framework involves such things as providing for the legal status of business enterprises, defining the rights of private ownership, and providing for the enforcement of contracts. Government also establishes legal "rules of the game" to govern the relationships of businesses, resource suppliers, and consumers with one another. Through legislation, government is enabled to referee economic relationships, detect foul play, and exercise authority in imposing appropriate penalties. The basic services provided by government include the use of police powers to maintain internal order, provision of a system of standards for measuring the weight and quality of products, and establishment of a monetary system to facilitate the exchange of goods and services.

The Pure Food and Drug Act of 1906 and its various amendments provide an excellent example of how government has strengthened the operation of the price system. This act sets rules of conduct to govern producers in their relationships with consumers. It prohibits the sale of adulterated and misbranded foods and drugs, requires the net weights of products to be specified on their containers, establishes quality standards which must be stated on the labels of canned foods, and prohibits fraudulent claims on patent-medicine labels. These measures all prevent fraudulent activities on the part of producers and, simultaneously, increase the public's confidence in the integrity

of the price system. In later chapters we shall discuss similar legislation pertaining to labor-management relations and the relations of business firms to one another.

How is resource allocation affected by this type of government activity? Resource allocation will be altered and, in general, improved upon. Supplying a medium of exchange, ensuring the quality of products, defining ownership rights, and enforcing contracts tend to increase the volume of exchange. This widens markets and permits greater specialization in the use of both property and human resources. Such specialization, we saw in Chapter 3, means a more efficient allocation of resources.

Maintaining competition

Competition is the basic regulatory mechanism in a capitalistic economy. It is the force which subjects producers and resource suppliers to the dictates of consumer sovereignty. With competition it is the supply and demand decisions of many sellers and buyers which determine market prices. This means that individual producers and resource suppliers can only adjust to the wishes of consumers as tabulated and communicated by the price system. Profits and survival await the competitive producers who obey the price system; losses and eventual bankruptcy are the lot of those who deviate from it. With competition, consumers are the boss, the market is their agent, and businesses their servant.

The growth of monopoly drastically alters this situation. What is monopoly? Broadly defined, it is the situation wherein the number of sellers becomes small enough for each seller to influence total supply and therefore the price of the commodity being sold. What is its significance? Simply this: when monopoly supplants competition, sellers can influence, or "rig," the market in terms of their own self-interests. Through their ability to influence total supply, monopolists can create artificial shortages of products and thereby enjoy higher prices and, very frequently, persistent economic profits. This is obviously in direct conflict with the interests of consumers. Monopolists are not regulated by the will of society as competitive sellers are. Producer sovereignty supplants consumer sovereignty to the degree that monopoly supplants competition. The result is that resources are allocated in terms of the profit-seeking interests of monopolistic sellers rather than in terms of the wants of society (consumers) as a whole. In short, monopoly tends to cause a misallocation of economic resources. In later chapters we shall have more to say about the growth and characteristics of monopoly, and public policy toward business monopoly will be explored in considerable detail. The important points for present purposes are these: (1) monopoly impairs the efficiency with which the price system allocates resources and (2) government assumes responsibility for retarding monopoly or, where its growth is inevitable, for preventing undue abuse of monopoly power through some form of social regulation.

Even if the legal foundation of capitalistic institutions is assured and competition is maintained, there will still be a need for certain additional economic functions on the part of government. *The market economy at its best has certain biases and shortcomings which compel government to supplement and modify its operation.*

Minimum standard of living

The price system is an impersonal mechanism. In particular, it follows no code of ethics in determining the manner in which total output is distributed. Households owning resources which are very productive in turning out goods and services highly valued by society will realize large money incomes. But some households possess resources that are relatively unproductive or capable only of producing goods and services society does not value very highly. Worse yet, the aged, the physically and mentally handicapped, the widowed, and the unemployed are unable to earn any income at all through the price system. In short, the price system entails considerable inequality in the distribution of money income and therefore in the distribution of total output among individual households.

To remedy this situation, government has assumed the responsibility of providing a minimum standard of living for its citizenry. This responsibility is reflected in a variety of policies and programs. *Public assistance programs* provide emergency relief to the destitute, aid to the dependent and handicapped, unemployment compensation to the unemployed. These programs provide income for households which would otherwise have little or no income. They achieve this goal by altering the income distribution which the price system provides. Other programs involve *direct market intervention,* in which the government alters income distribution by modifying the prices established by the forces of supply and demand. Price supports for farmers and minimum wage legislation both involve government price fixing designed to aid those whose incomes would otherwise be niggardly. Furthermore, the *taxation and expenditure* programs of government have a Robin Hood effect upon the economy: taxes bear down relatively more on the rich than on the poor, and many government expenditures of these tax revenues are for goods and services the benefits of which accrue primarily to the poor. Free public schools, public libraries, free public medical and legal services are cases in point.

All these programs and policies will be discussed at some length in a later chapter. The question we now ask is this: How will these modifications in the distribution of income affect the structure of society's product demands and, therefore, the allocation of resources? The answer is most evident in the case of public assistance programs. These programs are financed through taxes levied upon households and businesses as a whole. These taxes cause consumers to pare the least essential items from their budgets and businesses to reduce the size of their dividend payments and their levels of investment spending. The receivers of the various public assistance payments, being on the lowest rung of the income ladder, will assumedly spend this income on bare necessities. The net result? The structure of consumer demand and ultimately the allocation of resources will be altered. Fewer resources will be allocated to the production of Buicks, fur coats, jewelry, entertainment, and the construction of capital facilities and more to the production of basic foodstuffs and clothing.

Adjusting output for social costs and revenues

The price system of pure capitalism operates in response to decisions made by *individual* consumers and *individual* business firms. In deciding what is to be produced and not produced, the price system reacts to the summation of individual wants or satisfactions. And the specific amounts of various goods produced will depend upon the costs which individual firms must bear in acquiring the resources necessary for production. The production of certain goods and services, however, may entail satisfactions and costs which accrue not to individual consumers and individual firms but rather to society as a whole. The price system contains a bias: it does not take into account certain social benefits and social costs which the production of specific goods may entail.

Social costs. Under competition, supply and demand will set product price at a level that will cover the costs—including a normal profit paid to the entrepreneur—of obtaining the economic resources needed in producing a particular commodity. These costs, which are determined in the resource market, are sometimes called *private costs.* They are costs which private business concerns *must* bear if they are to continue to obtain resources.

But the productive process may sometimes entail certain other costs which are not necessarily incorporated in the price system. These costs do not entail the direct depletion or using up of specific resources, but result rather in the over-all debasement of the environment in which the production of a commodity occurs. Some examples will clarify this point. Occasionally a firm may avoid the expense of properly disposing of its waste materials by polluting nearby lakes or rivers with such wastes, thereby destroying the beauty and recreational value of these lakes and rivers. Or heavy indus-

try may spew smoke and dust on an otherwise serene residential area rather than foot the cost of smoke- and dust-abatement equipment. Or production may entail unpleasant odors or the risk of explosions. In each case the guilty firms are shifting a portion of those costs, which legitimately they should be expected to bear, onto society as a whole. The costs which private industry shifts to society are called *social costs.*

How do social costs affect output and, therefore, the allocation of economic resources? By pushing some of their costs onto the community, firms find that their total costs of production are lower than would otherwise be the case. With lower costs, the producer will be in a position to produce a greater output of his product at each possible price (see Chapter 4). This greater supply, given consumer demand, means a lower price and a larger output of this product than would otherwise result. In other words, more of such goods are produced and sold than would be the case where *all costs* are borne directly by the producer. A greater output of these products occurs than a more accurate accounting of all costs—both private and social—would entail. In brief, a loophole in the price system—that is, the possibility of a firm's or industry's shifting some of its costs to society as a whole—creates a bias in favor of greater production of those products in which significant social costs are involved. Economic resources are misallocated accordingly; too many resources will be used in the production of those products which entail substantial social costs.

Recouping social costs. What can government do to correct this shortcoming of the price system? Two courses of action are plausible. Looking at our initial example, the first and most direct step is to legislate against the pollution of rivers and lakes, smoke and dust hazards, and so on. This forces the guilty firms to bear all costs connected with the production of the given product. Because costs are now higher, supply will fall. This causes a rise in price, curtailed consumption of the product, and a reallocation of resources from the guilty firms or industries to alternative uses. A second and more indirect policy would be for government—specifically the local government of the community bearing the social costs—to levy special taxes sufficient to cover the social costs. If the community must suffer the costs entailed in clearing its polluted rivers and lakes or suffer the inconvenience of having them polluted, the community is justified in recouping these costs from the guilty party. In effect, through a special tax, government attempts to shove back onto those offending firms the costs which private industry has sought to avoid. With the added tax costs the producers will now have to demand a higher price at each possible level of output. This means a decline in supply relative to demand. As a result, price rises and sales decline. Resources will then be freed from these firms for other uses. The net result will be an improved allocation of resources—an allocation more consistent with the *total* costs of production. The tax will tend to correct the bias in the price system which arises when significant social costs are present. Similarly, smoke and dust hazards necessitate more frequent painting of houses, added medical costs, higher laundry bills, and so forth. Risks of explosion add to insurance premiums in the community. Once again special tax levies may help recoup these costs for the community.

Social revenues. But the reverse of this situation may also arise. In a competitive economy, goods are produced on the basis of *individual* wants. If the wants of many individual consumers are very intense for a particular product, producers will find it profitable to supply society with a large volume of that commodity. The number of individual consumers who want a product and the intensity with which they desire it depends upon the satisfactions, benefits, or "revenues" [1] which private consumers get from the particular product. The operation of the price system is thus geared to *private revenues,* or private benfits. This is so because goods and services in a purely capitalistic sys-

tem are bought almost exclusively by private consumers acting as individuals. *As a result, the price system may overlook certain widespread benefits or revenues which accrue to the community as a whole when individuals consume certain goods and services.* Such benefits are called *social revenues.* For example, chest X rays and polio immunization shots result in direct private benefits to the immediate consumer. But an early diagnosis of tuberculosis and the prevention of a contagious disease yield widespread benefits or revenues to the entire community. And these social revenues are significant. The price system of a purely capitalistic system has no way of responding to such social revenues. Why? Because pure capitalism is an individualistic economy which reacts only to the private revenues or satisfactions of individual consumers. Here, then, is another bias or shortcoming in the price system of pure capitalism—it does not take into account the total benefits or revenues accruing from the production of a product but only those benefits received directly and immediately by individual buyers.

Compensating for social revenues. How does this bias affect the allocation of resources in the economy? If our goal is to achieve the greatest satisfaction of wants, that is, the maximum amount of benefits or revenues *for the economy as a whole,* society should obviously allocate more resources to the production of those goods and services which entail significant social revenues than the price system provides.

Assuming that the social revenues involved are not inordinately large as compared with private revenues, government can encourage the production of such goods by subsidizing their output. This subsidy may assume a variety of forms—an outright bounty to the producer for each unit of output, favorable tax treatment, free use of government materials and facilities, and so forth. Regardless of its form, the subsidy will encourage firms to produce more of such products than would otherwise be the case, which, in turn, means a greater allocation of resources to their production. Government subsidization of the polio im-

[1] "Revenue" in this case is not a dollars-and-cents magnitude but rather a subjective concept. The revenue to which we refer in this case is the pleasure which consumers get from particular products.

munization program is a case in point. In short, subsidies can be used to stimulate the output and consumption of those products from which the social revenues are too significant for society to ignore.

Social goods and services

There are certain types of goods and services which are produced in grossly insufficient amounts, or possibly not at all, in an economy that relies entirely upon the price system in answering the Five Fundamental Questions. Such products are called *social* or *collective goods.* If society is to obtain social goods in desired amounts, their production must be sponsored, or directly carried on, by government. It is important at the outset to contrast social goods with the *individual,* or *private,* goods which are produced by private enterprises through the price system.

Private goods and social goods. The bulk of the goods and services which we consume—for example, loaves of bread, shoes, Fords, transistor radios, suits, oranges, and so forth—are private goods. These goods have the following basic characteristics: (1) They are *divisible.* Private goods can be produced in units sufficiently small for individual households to purchase them directly through the price system from private industry. (2) The satisfactions, benefits, or "revenues" from the consumption of private goods are limited almost exclusively to the individual who purchases them.

As a result of these characteristics—product divisibility and the virtual absence of social revenues—private goods are purchased on a purely voluntary basis by consumers out of their private incomes. The specific amounts of private goods consumed depend upon such considerations as the preferences or tastes of households, the size of money incomes, and the relative prices of the various private goods.

Social goods and services—national defense, highways, education, police and fire protection, and so forth—differ from private goods in one or both of the following ways: (1) Social goods are *indivisible.* They come in such large units

that they cannot be readily purchased by individual households or, therefore, profitably produced through the initiative of private industry. (2) Social goods, because of their bulk and nature, typically yield large and widespread benefits or satisfactions to the community and society as a whole. In other words, social goods entail very great and widely apportioned social revenues.

Because of the widespread nature of the social revenues which social goods entail, there is no way of accurately measuring and charging each member of society for the benefits he gets from a particular social good or service. Because of the size of these social revenues, it is impossible to rely upon subsidization as a technique for stimulating greater production of these goods and services. As a consequence, *the production of social goods is sponsored, and sometimes directly undertaken, by government. This production is generally financed through taxes levied upon society as a whole.*

Social goods are purchased through the government on the basis of group, or collective, choices in contrast to private goods, which are purchased from private enterprises on the basis of individual choices. More specifically, the types and quantities of the various social goods produced are determined in a democracy by political means, that is, by voting. The quantities of the various social goods consumed are a matter of public policy.[2] These group decisions, made in the political arena, supplement the individual choices of households and businesses in answering the Five Fundamental Questions.

It should be very evident by now that the primary goal of government in supplying social goods and services is to reallocate resources. Social goods have characteristics which virtually

[2] There are obvious differences between *dollar voting,* which dictates output in the private sector of the economy, and *political voting,* which determines output in the public sector. The rich man has many more votes to cast in the private sector than does the poor man. In the public sector, each—at least in theory— has an equal say. Furthermore, the children who cast their meager votes for bubble gum and comic books in the private sector are banned by virtue of their age from the registering of social choices.

preclude their production by private industry through the price system. Because social goods and services are recognized by society as being a desirable and essential segment of the economy's total output, it is safe to conclude that the price system, by virtue of its failure to provide sufficient resources for their production, misallocates economic resources. A basic economic function of government is the correction of this misallocation. Government must reflect and render effective the group wants of society which by their very nature are incapable of fulfillment through the price system as such.

Goods necessary for war and national defense are perhaps the most outstanding example of social goods. No one, short of a pacifist, would question the desirability of assigning a portion of the economy's resources for the production of those goods and services necessary for its defense or the successful completion of a war. The goods and services involved come in tremendously large and extremely expensive units. Each modern aircraft, missile, and atomic submarine will bear a price tag involving millions of dollars. The benefits from the production of these goods are obviously widespread, accruing to the entire citizenry. And these widely dispersed social revenues are impossible to gauge on an individual-to-individual basis. Hence, if war goods are to be produced, governmental action will be necessary.

Allocating resources to social goods production. Precisely how are resources reallocated from the production of private goods to the production of social goods? In a full-employment economy, government is faced with the task of freeing resources from private employment to make them available for the production of social goods. During peacetime, the best means of releasing resources from private uses is to reduce private demand for them. This is accomplished by levying taxes on businesses and households, thereby diverting some of their incomes—some of their potential purchasing power—out of the income-expenditure streams. With lower incomes, businesses and households will be forced to curtail their investment and consumption spending. *In short, taxes tend to diminish private demand for goods and serv-*

ices, which in turn prompts a drop in the private demand for resources. By diverting purchasing power from private spenders to government, taxes free resources from private uses. Government expenditure of the tax proceeds can then reabsorb these resources by providing social goods and services. For example, corporation and personal income taxes release resources from the production of investment goods—drill presses, boxcars, warehouses—and consumer goods—food, clothing, perfumes, and television sets. Government expenditures tend to reabsorb these resources in the production of guided missiles, munitions, jet aircraft, and new schools and highways. Government purposely reallocates resources to bring about significant changes in the composition of the economy's total output. In this instance, government interferes with both the resource and product markets; government alters the money incomes of resource suppliers and changes the structure of product demand.

It should be noted that in a few instances government attempts to finance the production of a few social goods and services by levying taxes directly upon that particular group which seems to receive the bulk of the benefits from the social goods. State highway finance is a case in point. State tax receipts from levies on gasoline and motor vehicles are typically earmarked for the construction and repair of highways. Yet even in this instance many of the benefits of a network of highways and streets obviously accrue to individuals and groups other than the immediate users. And in the case of most social goods and services, the dispersion of benefits is more diverse than with highways. Consequently, it is not surprising to find that in levying taxes, government rarely makes any attempt to collect taxes in terms of social revenues received.

Controlling unemployment and inflation

The final—and in many respects the most important—function of government is to provide for economic stability. Government has assumed a considerable degree of responsibility for providing a full-employment level of resource utilization in American capitalism. This responsibility is discussed in detail in Part 2 of this book.

EVALUATING THE ECONOMIC ROLE OF GOVERNMENT

Thus far we have been content to state the major economic functions of government and to assess the over-all impact of their successful performance upon the economy. There now arises a series of related questions which must be faced in any attempt to evaluate the economic role of government:

1. Is it desirable for government to perform the stated six functions?

2. How successful is government in performing its economic functions?

3. Is government playing too great a role in our economy?

Don't expect clear-cut answers to these queries. Indeed, there are none. Government's economic role is extremely difficult to evaluate. There are no simple quantitative standards by which the scope and quality of government's performance can be assessed. And, as a matter of fact, the above questions necessarily exceed the boundaries of economic science and plunge us into the larger realms of political theory and philosophy. Nevertheless, discussion of the issues involved may turn up some worthwhile insights and explode a few of the more popular misconceptions about the economic functions of government. In this way each of us may be in a more strategic position to formulate intelligent opinions on these questions.[3]

Desirability of government's economic functions

Should government perform the six economic functions we have just discussed? All things considered, there is rather startling agreement that these functions entail tasks which legitimately

[3] The ambitious student will do well to compare the philosophies of government presented in Francis M. Bator, *The Question of Government Spending* (New York: Harper & Row, Publishers, 1960), and Henry C. Wallich, *The Cost of Freedom* (New York: Harper & Row, Publishers, 1960).

accrue to government. True, there is a small minority within the United States which espouses the philosophy that that government is best which governs least. At the other extreme, there are those who look upon an expansion of the functions of government as a panacea for any and all the ills of society. Though these groups are highly vocal, it must be emphasized that they are minorities. The vast majority of people are in fairly close agreement that government has an obligation in each of the six areas outlined and discussed in this chapter. This is not to deny that there is much controversy about specific actions of government. This controversy, however, is not so much concerned with whether or not government should perform the six functions as it is with how far these functions should be pursued. Few question the desirability of government's providing education, highways, and similar social goods. On the other hand, governmental action to provide electric power and housing are very controversial borderline cases. Are these social goods? To what degree should government provide them? Furthermore, the nebulous nature of social revenues and social costs makes it very difficult to correct the resulting biases in the price system with any great degree of precision. This does not mean that the public disapproves of government action in this area; instead it only proves that the six functions are difficult to delineate and apply in specific cases. In short, the controversy surrounding the economic functions of government is more concerned with the application of these functions in specific instances than with the over-all desirability of government's performing in these six areas. On the latter point there is general, though not unanimous, agreement.

Beyond these general comments, three more specific points are worth remembering:

1. The economic role of government in American capitalism is not a phenomenon of recent vintage. With the exception of the sixth function—offsetting the business cycle—government has performed all the functions discussed to a greater or lesser degree throughout American economic history.

2. The actions of a democratic government mirror the will of society with considerable ac-

curacy. This point is so obvious as to be frequently overlooked: a democratic government does essentially what the citizenry wants it to do.

Government, in the United States, is not an independent entity; it does not possess a will of its own; it is not animated by purposes that are alien to the desires of its citizens. The American government is a creature of the American people; it responds to the pressures that they bring to bear upon it; its policies and its programs, wise or unwise, find their origin in organized demand and depend for their survival upon popular sufferance. . . . It [government] intervenes only when it is forced to intervene. It acts reluctantly, deliberately, and tardily, in response to overwhelming pressures. Criticism of public intervention is criticism, not of dictatorship, but of the results of the democratic process.[4]

3. It must be emphasized that on economic grounds the sole test of the desirability of government's economic functions is the effect which their performance has upon the level of resource use and the efficiency with which resources are allocated. And we have seen that in each of the six functions discussed in this chapter government is aiming at a higher level of resource use or an improved allocation of employed resources by strengthening or modifying the operation of the price system. Now this is not to say that the standard of efficient resource use is the only criterion by which government activity is to be appraised. Nor is it to imply that the task of evaluation by any standard is an easy task. But it certainly does imply that each individual action by government in the economic sphere should be evaluated seperately for its effect upon the degree of efficiency in resource use in estimating its *economic* desirability. The actions of government must not be condoned or condemned per se, that is, adjudged good or bad simply because they are performed by government.

4 Clair Wilcox, *Public Policies Toward Business*, rev. ed. (Homewood, Ill.: Richard D. Irwin, Inc., 1960), pp. 8–9.

Effectiveness

Assuming some agreement as to the proper economic functions of government, a second question becomes relevant. How successful is government in performing these functions? How effective is government in its efforts to strengthen the price system and to correct its shortcomings?

Again there is no simple answer. Though the over-all goals of full employment and improved resource allocation may be commendable, it is of course possible that government has been relatively ineffective in attaining these goals. Whether or not government is actually successful in promoting these ends depends on (1) the ability of government to recognize resource misallocations and unemployment, (2) government's ability to ascertain, and its willingness to legislate, effective remedial programs, and (3) government's capacity to administer such programs. This is a tall order. There is ample room for errors in fact, judgment, and administration in the performance of government's economic functions. Indeed, the basic difficulties in policy formulation have already been cited (Chapter 1). It is not too surprising that on occasion government has grossly misjudged the economic problems of society, failing to correct shortcomings of the price system as a result of inappropriate action or inaction. And government has sometimes failed to act decisively and rapidly in remedying well-recognized defects in the economy's operation. Then, too, there is persistent evidence that governmental agencies are bureaucratic, plagued by red tape and at times by wasteful administration. Worst of all, the interests of society as a whole have sometimes been neglected by government in promoting the ends of pressure groups or in the interest of political expediency.

But the effectiveness of government's performance is not without substantial defenses. At worst one can take the position that it is preferable to have government correct the defects of the price system in an imperfect or partial manner than not at all. After all, the private sector of the economy falls short of 100 per cent efficiency; do we have the right to expect complete efficiency in the public sector? At best it can be argued that the historical record shows that government on balance has clearly played a positive role in fostering the smooth operation of American capitalism.

Beyond these general observations each of us must establish his own opinion as to the effectiveness of government. Here are a few guideposts that may be of some assistance in reaching an intelligent opinion:

Noncomparable performance standards. When attempting to gauge the efficiency of government's economic activities, it is usually not appropriate to use the performance standards of the private sector. In particular, beware of dogmatic comparisons of governmentally operated or controlled enterprises and privately owned and operated businesses. Why? Because they are horses of different colors. It is like trying to compare the quality of an apple with that of an orange, or of a jazz band with the New York Philharmonic. They are different propositions and not subject to simple, clear-cut comparisons. Two considerations go far to explain the absence of a common standard for comparing the efficiency of the private and public sectors of American capitalism:

On the one hand, the objective of private businesses is profits, while that of government enterprise is "service to society," or "promotion of the general welfare." Government and private enterprise are not seeking identical goals; therefore, they are not to be compared by the same standard of success. Now, admittedly, there is room for considerable overlapping in seeking profits and in serving society. As a group, business enterprises in producing innumerable goods and services undoubtedly perform a great service to the economy. Yet, in the final analysis, the immediate targets of government economic activities and private enterprise are essentially different. Businesses as a matter of necessity are seeking profits. And it is basically by their ability to do so that their success is judged. The economic activities of government, on the other hand, are judged by numerous standards, virtually all of which are somewhat subjective and therefore less precise quantitatively than a profit and loss statement. For example, there is no simple and accurate measure of the success of our national defense, public education, and highway construction programs. Rather there are many vague and diverse methods of evaluation. Unfortunately, it is ordinarily easy to find a standard to confirm one's bias or prejudgment of any given government program. In any event, the lack of a single, quantitatively precise measure of the success of governmental activities goes far to explain the endless debate over government spending and tax policies. The major point is obvious: it is hardly fair to take the standard of success for private industry, that is, net profits, and apply it as a criterion for judging the success or efficiency of government's economic activities. Put more concretely, let us not label our postal system as "inefficient" or "unsuccessful" simply because it fails to show a profit for the year's operations.

A second reason for avoiding the use of performance standards for the private sector of the economy in gauging the efficiency of government lies in the fact that the fallacy of composition may negate such comparisons. For example, it is tempting to take time-honored notions as to the propriety of private debt and apply them without qualification to public debt. The evils of the fallacy of composition must be kept clearly in mind to warn us that notions and principles which are accurate when applied to the debts of *individual* households or *individual* businesses may not be valid when applied to the aggregate of government. This point will be pursued at some length in Chapter 14.

Fallacy of limited decisions. In evaluating the economic performance of government, critics are prone to invoke what we shall call the *fallacy of limited decisions.* These critics implicitly assume that during any particular period of time there is a limited, or fixed, number of decisions to be made in connection with the operation of the economy. Hence, if government makes more of these decisions in performing its stated functions, the private sector of the economy will necessarily have fewer "free" decisions or choices to make. For example, critics argue that by making decisions to provide electric power, government will frighten off private businesses and private investors in this area of production. The net effectiveness of government in providing electric power, it is concluded, is very low when this discouragement of private production is taken into account.

Some serious reflection will reveal the fallacy which may plague such reasoning. The vast majority of the social goods and services provided by government are of such a nature that private businesses would simply not consider their production without government sponsorship. Highway construction and the manufacture of war goods are simply not undertaken by private enterprises on their own initiative. As a matter of fact, it can be plausibly argued that the range of free choice is *extended* by government sponsorship of the production of such social goods as highways, national defense, and education; these goods and services would simply not be available for consumer choice in the absence of government provision. Note, too, that in providing most social goods, government does not typically undertake production itself but rather purchases these goods through private enterprise. When government makes the decision to build an interstate highway, private concerns are given the responsibility for making a myriad of specific decisions and choices in connection with the carrying out of this decision. Furthermore, government decisions which break up the monopolistic control of either product or resource markets may allow new firms and resource suppliers to enter these markets and significantly increase the number of economic decisions rendered in them.

Finally, it should be noted that during a depression the number of choices made by private businesses and households is greatly restricted. Why? Because production has been slowed and incomes drastically curtailed. The businessman has fewer choices to make concerning, for example, the types of products and combinations of resources he may use. Indeed, some firms will be temporarily closed down

and making no decisions at all. The consumer has fewer decisions to make in disposing of his income, because his income is now very small or conceivably nonexistent. Now if government, by increased participation and intervention in the economy, can correct or even alleviate a depression, the number of decisions and choices open to both businesses and consumers will increase. That is, government, by making more decisions concerning the operation of the economy, might restore prosperity, permitting the number of private decisions to increase also. Hence, the number of private and public decisions made in the operation of the economy may, *within limits*, vary in the same direction. A larger number of governmental decisions may or may not mean a smaller number of private decisions.

Remoteness of government transactions. The economic services of government seem vague and remote to the individual, because he does not acquire these services through specific purchases. This becomes clear upon contrasting purchases from private enterprise and purchases of social goods and services through government.

When John Doe buys a pair of shoes, he is party to an immediate and clear-cut this-for-that transaction. He hands over a part of his purchasing power—say, $15—to a shoe retailer and receives directly a product of his choosing in return. The buyer obviously regards the benefits he will receive from the shoes as worth the $15 expenditure, or he would simply not choose to make this transaction. Purchasing from a private enterprise is a voluntary and clear-cut bit of economic behavior. The consumer knows how much he is spending and precisely what he gets in return for his money.

This is not generally true of purchases which consumers make through government. Even though goods and services provided by government are received and paid for by consumers in general, there is no explicit this-for-that exchange. Hence, government transactions typically appear nebulous and decidedly out of focus to the typical taxpayer. National defense provides an excellent example. There is no doubt that the benefits of our national defense program which accrue to individuals and businesses in our economy are very great. Yet it is impossible to judge *how much* benefit from our military strength is enjoyed by individual households and business firms. Public education is another good example. The benefits of a public school system are received directly by students, semidirectly by the students' parents and families, and indirectly by the community and nation as a whole. In this case, those who pay the tax costs of the education—that is, the adult population of the community—are clearly receiving no explicit, clear-cut good or service in return. No this-for-that transaction occurs.

This vagueness between consumer expenditures in the form of taxes paid to government and benefits received results in many an uninformed taxpayer's feeling perfectly justified in griping about high taxes while simultaneously demanding better highways, more adequate police and fire protection, and an ever-improving educational system for his sons and daughters! We want the benefits of government's economic activities but are typically reluctant to foot the bill.

The point we are driving at is this: we must be careful not to write off government spending on goods and services as unproductive or wasteful just because no clear-cut this-for-that transaction is involved. Indeed, if a this-for-that relationship between spending and benefits received were present, government might not have to assume responsibility for providing the particular good or service. If it were feasible for individuals to consume national defense and education economically, in sufficient amounts and on a this-for-that basis, government would not have the chore of providing these goods and services. In short, government transactions may be every bit as beneficial or productive as the more direct this-for-that transactions characteristic of the private sector of the economy. Don't let the indirect, remote nature of government purchases cause you to prejudge such purchases as wasteful or unproductive.

Government spending and "economy." Finally in evaluating the economic role of government, one should be wary of the now-popular myth that "economy in government" and "reduced government spending" are synonymous. As we are well aware from reading Chapter 2, economy is concerned with the efficient allocation of resources. Indiscriminate cutbacks in government spending on high-priority social goods and services *may* free resources for less essential low-priority private goods and services. The most efficient allocation of resources between social and private goods is vague at best. But this does not excuse us from tripping on the fallacy that providing less social goods and more private goods necessarily entails a more efficient allocation of resources. It may or it may not. Each economic action on the part of government should be weighed on its own merits. Will the particular action result in a more efficient use of society's resources than now prevails? Is government in a better position to carry out this activity than private industry? Beware of catchall rules which flatly approve or condemn any and all economic functions of government.

A concluding point should be emphasized: this series of comments is not designed to stack the deck in favor of government intervention and participation in the functioning of the economy. On the contrary, its purpose is to caution us against the widespread preconception that, by definition, the economic activities of government are "bad" and those of the private sector "good." It is easy and often convenient to accept the popular prejudice that the economic activities of government are "operation rathole," that is, that government activities are inherently less efficient and less productive than private economic activities. Such is not the case. Each instance concerning the appropriateness of public or private responsibility must be carefully judged on its own merits.

Is government's economic role too large?

Precisely how large is government's role in American capitalism? Unfortunately, there is no simple way of measuring quantitatively the many diverse functions of government. Probably the best single indicator of government's economic role is its expenditure on goods and services expressed as a percentage of the economy's total output. Columns 3 and 4 of Table 6-1 suggest that government's role has expanded not only in absolute but also in relative terms. Note, however, that this growth has been somewhat sporadic. Government—Federal, state, and local combined—now accounts for about one-fifth of the total output of American capitalism. How is this long-run expansion of government's economic activities to be explained? Causal factors are undoubtedly many, but two seem to be of paramount importance. On the one hand, war shifts the production target of the economy drastically in the direction of more social goods and less civilian goods. Note the upsurge of government purchases during World War II when in 1944 almost one-half

of total output was taken by government. A lesser expansion of government spending accompanied the Korean War. The current cold war necessitates unusually high levels of military spending, keeping government's share of total output considerably above that of four or five decades ago.

A second factor has also contributed to the relative growth of government in the economy: as the incomes of American consumers have risen historically, the pattern of consumer wants has altered in the direction of relatively more social goods and relatively less private goods. The members of a relatively poor economy must take their entire incomes in the form of the most urgently needed commodities: food, shelter, and clothing—all private goods provided by the private sector of the economy through the

TABLE 6-1. GOVERNMENT PURCHASES AS A PERCENTAGE OF TOTAL OUTPUT, SELECTED YEARS, 1902–1961

(1) Year	*(2)* Total output (in billions)	*(3)* Government purchases of goods and services (in billions)	*(4)* Government purchases as a percentage of total output, or (3) ÷ (2)
1902	$ 20.7	$ 1.6	7.6
1913	40.1	3.0	7.4
1922	68.4	9.0	13.1
1929	104.4	8.5	8.1
1933	56.0	8.0	14.3
1936	82.7	11.8	14.3
1939	91.1	13.3	14.6
1941	125.8	24.8	19.7
1944	211.4	96.5	45.7
1947	234.3	28.4	12.1
1951	329.0	60.5	18.4
1954	363.1	75.3	20.7
1958	441.7	92.6	21.0
1961	521.3	108.7	20.8

SOURCES: Figures for 1902, 1913, and 1922 are from Arnold M. Soloway, "The Growth of Government over the Past Fifty Years: An Analytical Review," in Joint Economic Committee, "Federal Expenditure Policy for Economic Growth and Stability" (Washington: Government Printing Office, 1957), p. 58; figures for the remaining years, from the "Survey of Current Business."

price system. But after these basic wants have been largely fulfilled, the growing wealth of society permits it to turn its attention more and more to the satisfaction of somewhat less urgent, but nevertheless important, wants. Many of the wants in this second category entail social goods and services: education, streets and highways, police and fire protection. These goods, produced in minimal amounts in a poor economy, are demanded and provided in increasing amounts as the wealth of the society increases. As a matter of fact, the increasing complexity of a growing economy necessitates, and, indeed, economic growth itself depends upon, the provision of these social goods and services. The result is a tendency for government to play an increasingly important role in the economy as a provider of these social commodities and services.

A word of warning: although Table 6-1 correctly portrays American capitalism as becoming more and more a mixed public-private economy, we must emphasize that government's role as an owner and operator of business enterprises has not expanded to any significant degree. The job of producing government's increased purchases of social goods and services still lies primarily within the realm of private enterprise. Government sponsors and handles the financing of highways, schools, and war goods, but their actual production is carried on by private enterprises. Roughly one-half the government's purchases are for goods and services produced by private, profit-guided producers. Production actually undertaken by government itself is relatively small, and its relative growth has been very modest. Consumers now buy relatively less goods directly from private enterprises but more goods indirectly from private enterprises through government. Private enterprise has expanded more or less proportionately with the total output of the economy.

The tendency for a growing economy to want the production of social goods and services to increase in proportion to the output of private goods and services does not, of course, rule out the possibility that government's role has expanded at a rate faster than is justified

by this generalization. Does government provide too many goods and services at the present time?

There are some who emphatically argue that government's economic role has been grossly overextended. Yet simple observation yields some startling evidence to the contrary. There is glaring evidence of a serious "social imbalance" in the total output of American capitalism. In many instances the production of private goods has seriously outstripped the production of social goods. This generalization has been backed by a multitude of disturbing, hard-to-ignore examples. Children, underequipped with such social goods and services as schools, parks, playgrounds, and police protection, are grossly overequipped with such private goods as toys, clothing, and television sets. The most eloquent critic of this social imbalance summarizes the problem thus:[5]

The family which takes its mauve and cerise, air-conditioned, power-steered, and power-braked automobile out for a tour passes through cities that are badly paved, made hideous by litter, blighted buildings, billboards, and posts for wires that should long since have been put underground. . . . They picnic on exquisitely packaged food from a portable icebox by a polluted stream and go on to spend the night at a park which is a menace to public health and morals. Just before dozing off on an air mattress, beneath a nylon tent, amid the stench of decaying refuse, they may reflect vaguely on the curious unevenness of their blessings. Is this, indeed, the American genius?

The social imbalance thesis is sufficiently important to merit detailed discussion—pro and con—in Chapter 36.

SUMMARY

1. The American economy can be described as mixed capitalism. It is primarily a market econ-

[5] John Kenneth Galbraith, *The Affluent Society* (Boston: Houghton Mifflin Company, 1958), p. 253. The final section of this chapter draws heavily upon chaps. 18, 19, and 22 of Professor Galbraith's brilliant but disturbing book.

omy, yet government influences the operation of the price system in a variety of ways.

2. The basic economic functions of government entail (*a*) providing a legal and social framework appropriate to the effective operation of the price system, (*b*) maintaining competition, (*c*) providing a minimum standard of living for all the citizenry, (*d*) adjusting total output to allow for social costs and social revenues, (*e*) providing for the production of social goods and services, and (*f*) controlling the business cycle. These functions are designed to assist the private sector of the economy in achieving full employment and full production.

3. The economic role of government is difficult to evaluate. Society generally condones government activity in the six areas outlined above. However, there is considerable disagreement concerning the extent to which government should pursue these functions and whether specific governmental actions fall within the scope of these six functions. In evaluating the economic role of government, we should remember that (*a*) for the most part the current economic functions of government are not a recent development, (*b*) a democratic government generally mirrors the will of society, and

(*c*) the sole economic test of the desirability of governmental action is its effect upon the employment and allocation of resources.

4. Several guideposts are helpful in attempting to gauge the effectiveness of government in carrying out its economic functions: (*a*) there is no common standard for measuring the performances of the public and private sectors of the economy; (*b*) the fallacy of limited decisions may prejudice one's thinking in evaluating the effectiveness of government in the economic sphere; (*c*) the fact that the economic transactions of government lack the immediacy and clarity of their private counterparts incorrectly implies that government is unproductive and inefficient in fulfilling its economic functions; (*d*) minimal government spending and "economy" are not to be identified.

5. As measured by its purchases, government's economic role has increased historically in both absolute and relative terms. War and the more than proportionate increase in the demand for social goods which rising incomes entail help explain this growth. Simple observation suggests that American capitalism is probably more abundantly supplied with private goods than it is with social goods.

QUESTIONS AND STUDY SUGGESTIONS

1. What are the salient features of a market economy? Of a planned economy? Why is the American economy called "mixed capitalism"?

2. Enumerate and briefly discuss the main economic functions of government.

3. Distinguish clearly between (*a*) social goods and private goods; (*b*) private revenues (benefits) and costs and social revenues and costs. Give illustrations of each. How should government modify the operation of the price system to allow for social goods and to take into account the presence of social costs and revenues? Emphasize the impact of governmental action upon the allocation of resources.

4. What difficulties arise in attempting to assess the economic role of government? Be specific.

5. Carefully evaluate this statement: "The public, as a general rule . . . gets less production in return for a dollar spent by government than from a dollar spent by private enterprise." [6]

[6] National Association of Manufacturers, *The American Individual Enterprise System* (New York: McGraw-Hill Book Company, Inc., 1946), p. 952.

6. "The conclusion seems inescapable that pure capitalism . . . would be subject to grave deficiencies and inconsistencies. Such a system would have little chance of survival" [7] Do you agree? Why?

7. "It is conceivable that the federal government can contribute materially to economic stability and greater efficiency in the use of resources without interfering in the details of business and personal life." Do you agree? Explain.

8. "The admitted functions of government embrace a much wider field than can be easily included within the ring fence of a restrictive definition . . . it is hardly possible to find any ground of justification common to them all, except the comprehensive one of general expediency; nor to limit the interference of government by any universal rule, save the simple and vague one that it should never be admitted but when the case of expediency is strong." [8] Carefully evaluate this statement. Contrast its philosophy with that evidenced in question 5.

9. "Plan or no plan? Everyone believes in planning in the literal sense of the word: and, for that matter, everyone believes that national governments should execute some plans for economic life. No one favors bad planning. Plan or no plan is no choice at all; the pertinent questions turn on particular techniques: Who shall plan, for what purposes, in what conditions, and by what devices? Free market or regulation? Again, this issue is badly posed. Both institutions are indispensable." [9] Interpret and evaluate this quotation. What do you feel are the virtues, if any, of government planning? How does the price system "plan"? Explain.

SELECTED REFERENCES

Bator, Francis M., *The Question of Government Spending* (New York: Harper & Row, Publishers, 1960).

Due, John F., *Government Finance,* rev. ed. (Homewood, Ill.: Richard D. Irwin, Inc., 1959), chaps. 1, 2, and 26.

Galbraith, John Kenneth, *The Affluent Society* (Boston: Houghton Mifflin Company, 1958), chaps. 18, 19, and 22.

Joint Economic Committee, *Federal Expenditure Policy for Economic Growth and Stability* (Washington: Government Printing Office, 1957), particularly the papers submitted by Arnold M. Soloway, Solomon Barkin, Walter W. Heller, and Procter Thomson.

Morris, Bruce R., *Problems of American Economic Growth* (New York: Oxford University Press, 1961), chap. 8.

Wallich, Henry C., *The Cost of Freedom* (New York: Harper & Row, Publishers, 1960), particularly chap. 2.

Wilcox, Clair, *Public Policies Toward Business,* rev. ed. (Homewood, Ill.: Richard D. Irwin, Inc., 1960), chaps. 1, 2, and 32.

[7] Howard R. Bowen, *Toward Social Economy* (New York: Holt, Rinehart and Winston, Inc., 1948), p. 321.

[8] John Stuart Mill, *Principles of Political Economy* (New York: D. Appleton & Company, Inc., 1878), vol. II, p. 392.

[9] Robert A. Dahl and Charles E. Lindblom, *Politics, Economics and Welfare* (New York: Harper & Row, Publishers, 1953), p. 5.

Chapter 7

THE FACTS OF AMERICAN CAPITALISM:

HOUSEHOLDS

THIS CHAPTER and the ensuing two are designed to put meat on our bareboned model of mixed capitalism. We have discussed the three major aggregates of mixed capitalism—business, households, and government—on a very general and somewhat abstract basis. We must now add color to our crude sketch of mixed capitalism by painting in the factual characteristics of these three major transactors as they function in our American brand of mixed capitalism. In short, we must breathe reality into our abstract model of capitalism by adding "the facts" of American economic life. The present chapter contributes factual information pertinent to households. The following two chapters do the same for the business and government sectors of the economy. In each case the discussion will focus upon the source of the sector's income or receipts and the manner in which it disposes of that income.

The household sector of American capitalism is currently composed of some 54 million families. These households play a dual role: they are the ultimate suppliers of all economic resources and simultaneously the major spending group in the economy. Hence, we shall consider households, first, as income receivers and, second, as spenders.

HOUSEHOLDS AS INCOME RECEIVERS

Two preliminary points merit emphasis before we begin an examination of American households as income receivers. First of all, at this juncture our concern is with the factual, not the ethical, aspects of household incomes. In this chapter we answer the factual question "How *is* income actually distributed among the households of American capitalism?" We defer until a later chapter the controversial ethical question "How *should* income be distributed in American capitalism?" A second and related point is that the present chapter is not directly concerned with the many programs and policies (mentioned in Chapter 6) whereby government modifies the distribution of income. Though we shall of necessity note the flow of certain types of household income to and from government, our primary goal is not a discussion or evaluation of the impact of government upon the flow of income to, and the flow of expenditures from, the household segment of the economy. Again this is a task assigned to a subsequent chapter.

There are two related approaches to studying the facts of income distribution. The *functional distribution* of income is concerned with

114

the manner in which society's total money income is divided among wages, rents, interest, and profits. Here total income is distributed according to the function performed by the income receiver. Wages are paid to labor, rents and interest compensate property resources, and profits flow to the owners of corporations and unincorporated businesses. The *personal distribution* of income has to do with the way in which the total money income of society is apportioned among individual households. A basic understanding of both the functional and the personal distribution of income is essential to understanding the role of households in American capitalism.

Functional distribution of income

The distributive shares of the national income for 1961 were as follows:

	Billions of dollars	Per cent of total
Wages and salaries...	$302.9	70
Proprietors' income	49.6	11
Corporate profits.....	46.2	11
Interest...........	20.0	5
Rents.............	11.5	3
National income...	$430.2	100

Figure 7-1 illustrates the changes that have taken place in the *absolute size* of these shares since 1929. Changes in the *relative shares* of the national income since 1929 are shown in Figure 7-2. Certain generalizations are evident from an examination of this data:

1. It is clear from Figure 7-1 that all the shares of national income tend to expand during prosperity and to decline during depression. *In absolute terms,* none of the major income-receiving classes benefit from bad times. Thus the drastic decline in national income ushered in by the Great Depression of the 1930s affected all income groups adversely. On the other hand, the war-born prosperity of the early 1940s and the postwar boom significantly boosted the incomes of all groups.

2. In terms of the *relative* shares of national income, the outstanding fact shown in Figure 7-2 is the remarkable stability of the share going to labor. With rare exceptions, labor's share of the national income over the last three decades has hovered two or three percentage points on either side of 65 per cent.

3. In contrast to the relative stability of labor's share, corporate profits have proved to be highly unstable over the years. In 1929 corporate profits accounted for about 12 per cent of the national income but became a negative figure (losses) during 1932 and 1933. Even since the beginning of World War II, corporate profits have fluctuated rather violently in both absolute and percentage terms. Specifically, corporate profits have varied from 10 to 15 per cent of the national income in the last two decades.

4. Proprietors' incomes—that is, the incomes of doctors, lawyers, small businessmen, shopkeepers, farmers, and other unincorporated enterprises—have fluctuated between 12 and 20 per cent of the national income. As Figure 7-2 indicates, the percentage of national income going to this group has been declining somewhat since the close of World War II. No doubt depressed farm incomes have played a major role in this decline.

5. The relatively small shares of national income accruing to rent and interest receivers are worth mentioning. Figure 7-2 shows that on the eve of the Great Depression of the 1930s, interest receivers were getting about 7 per cent of the national income; during the Depression this share ranged upward as high as 12 per cent. Since 1940, interest has declined rather steadily and it now comprises about 5 per cent of the national income. Several factors help explain this decline in the relative importance of interest incomes. First, interest payments are fixed obligations. In view of the very large increases in the absolute size of the national income which have occurred in the last two decades, the fairly stable dollar payments of interest have measured less and less in relative terms.

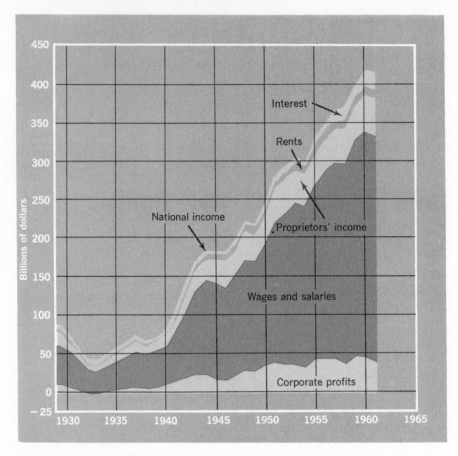

FIGURE 7-1. THE FUNCTIONAL DISTRIBUTION OF NATIONAL INCOME IN BILLIONS OF DOLLARS, 1929 TO 1961.
All national income shares decrease absolutely during depression and increase absolutely during periods of prosperity and growth. Wages and salaries constitute the largest component of the national income. (U.S. Department of Commerce.)

Second, private debt simply did not expand by very significant amounts between 1929 and the end of World War II, and only interest on private debt is included in the national income. Finally, over the three decades in question, the long-run trend has been toward the decline of interest rates. Government policy has been instrumental in bringing about this decline. The decline in rental income has been comparable. In 1929 rental income was just under 7 per cent

of the national income. Since the mid-thirties, rents have fluctuated between 3 and 4 per cent of national income.

Personal distribution of income

Why is the personal distribution of money income important in understanding the operation of American capitalism? What impact does the distribution of money income among households have upon the operation of the economy? The manner in which income is distributed among families affects both the *size* and the *composition* of output.

1. The personal distribution of income is a major determinant of how society divides its total money income between consumption and saving. We will discover in Chapters 12 and 13 that this division is of utmost significance in determining the levels of output and employment in the economy. Consumption, being a form of spending, induces production and employment. Saving, defined by economists as that part of current income which is not spent, does not account for production and employment. It follows that a distribution of income which results in a large volume of saving in relation to consumption *may* be conducive to declining levels of production and employment. On the other hand, a distribution which entails a very small volume of saving in relation to consump-

tion will promote high levels of production and employment.

2. The personal distribution of money income goes a long way toward determining the pattern of consumer spending in the economy. A highly unequal distribution of income among individual households results in an expenditure pattern much different from that which a more nearly equal distribution would entail. Generally speaking, the more unequal the distribution of a given total money income, the greater will be the demand for and the output of luxury goods. Businesses, as we have seen, usually find it to their advantage to adjust their outputs to consumer demands. As a consequence, the economy's product mix is largely geared to the composition of consumer expenditures. And in turn, the economy's product mix obviously determines the manner in which scarce resources are allocated.

To repeat, the personal distribution of income

FIGURE 7-2. THE FUNCTIONAL DISTRIBUTION OF NATIONAL INCOME IN PERCENTAGES, 1929 TO 1961.
In relative terms the share of national income going to labor has been remarkably stable over time. Corporate profits have been very unstable, and interest and rental incomes have tended to decline. (U.S. Department of Commerce.)

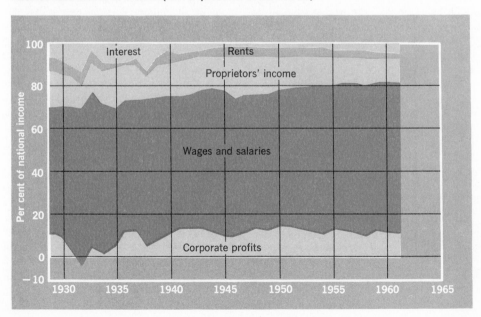

has direct and significant consequences for the two major aspects of economic science: (1) the level of resource use and (2) the allocation of resources among alternative uses.

Determinants of a household's income. What determines the amount of money income received by an individual household in, say, a year? Common sense tells us that (1) the quantities of the various human and property resources which a household is able and willing to supply to businesses, (2) the prices which these resources command in the resource market, and (3) the actual level of employment of these resources are the immediate determinants of a household's money income. For the majority of American households, labor service is the only resource supplied. Thus by taking, for example, 2,000 hours of labor service at a wage rate of $2 per hour, total money income for the year is found to be $4,000. But the third determinant poses a possible qualification: though the household may be willing and able to supply 2,000 hours of labor service per year, there is no guarantee that businesses will purchase that amount. Money income depends on the extent to which businesses are willing to employ available supplies of resources. If businesses are only able to use profitably 1,500 of the hours offered, the worker's money income will obviously decline accordingly.

In capitalistic economies, money income is roughly based upon the contribution which a household's resources make to the total production of the economy. Households earn money incomes which are generally in accord with the value of their contributions to total output. If the resources in a household's possession are capable of efficiently producing goods which consumers want, the income earned will be high; if not, it will be low. The prices established by the forces of supply and demand in the resource market roughly gauge the relative worth or "productivity" of the various resources. If a business enterprise pays $2 an hour for unskilled labor and $4 per hour for highly skilled labor, it implies that the skilled labor is twice as productive as unskilled labor. If the market places a high value on the contri-

butions of a resource to production, the supplying household receives a large income. If the market puts a low value on a resource's contribution, the supplying household's income tends to be low.

We shall see later that this productivity principle of income distribution is accurate only in a very general sense. There are many qualifications to this principle, qualifications stemming from the tax and expenditure policies of government, the economy's legislative framework, and a host of institutional forces which have varying impacts on the demand for and the supply of resources. Yet the principle is a useful first approximation.

Personal distribution of income in American capitalism. How is money income actually distributed among households in our economy? The answer, in brief, is that there exists considerable inequality in the personal distribution of income. Column 2 of Table 7-1 indicates the percentage of all households falling in each of the seven income classes shown in column 1. Column 3 reflects the percentage of total personal income—that is, income before personal taxes—received by all the households falling in each of the seven income classes. Hence, columns 1 to 3 tell us that in 1961 about 12 per cent of all consumer units—that is, families and unattached individuals—received an annual income before taxes of less than $2,000 and that the income received by this 12 per cent was only about 2 per cent of the total personal income received that year. Furthermore, 19 per cent of all families and individuals received an annual income between $2,000 and $3,999, the portion of personal income accruing to this group being about 8 per cent. Columns 4 and 5 simply cumulate the data of columns 2 and 3, respectively. Thus we find in column 4 that 31 per cent of all consumer units received an annual before-tax income of less than $4,000, and in column 5 that the income received by this 31 per cent was only 10 per cent of total personal income. At the other extreme, only 6 per cent of the consumer units receive annual incomes of $15,000 or more, but this group gets about 23 per cent of

TABLE 7-1. THE DISTRIBUTION OF PERSONAL INCOME BY CONSUMER UNITS, 1961

(1) Personal income classes*	(2) Per cent of all consumer units in this class	(3) Per cent of total personal income received by consumers in this class	(4) Per cent of all consumer units in this class and all lower classes	(5) Per cent of income received by this class and all lower classes
Under $2,000	12	2	12	2
$2,000–$3,999	19	8	31	10
$4,000–$5,999	22	16	53	26
$6,000–$7,999	19	18	72	44
$8,000–$9,999	11	14	83	58
$10,000–$14,999	11	19	94	77
$15,000 and over	6	23	100	100
	100	100		

*Average (median) income: $5,720.
SOURCE: "Survey of Current Business," April, 1962.

the total personal income. The richest 6 per cent of the population gets over two times as much income as does the poorest 31 per cent. In brief, the American income pyramid has an exceedingly wide base and a high, but narrow, peak. Note, too, that the average (median) income in 1961 was $5,720—a rather modest figure by American standards.

Reasons for income inequality. Generally speaking, differences in (1) native abilities, (2) training, education, and opportunities to advance, (3) property ownership, (4) ability to exert market power, and (5) the arbitrary and unequal distribution of unemployment, accidents, illness, and similar misfortunes are the major sources of income inequality.

Native abilities. Nature has been very arbitrary in apportioning mental, physical, and aesthetic talents. Some individuals have had the good fortune to inherit the exceptional mental qualities essential to entering the relatively high-paying fields of medicine, dentistry, and law. Others, rated as "dull normals" and "mentally retarded," are assigned to the most menial and low-paying occupations or

are incapable of earning income at all. Some are blessed with the physical capacity and coordination to become highly paid professional athletes. The clumsy and frail must settle for much less. Some have the aesthetic qualities prerequisite to becoming great artists or musicians. Others could not carry a tune in a basket or paint a discernible likeness if their lives depended upon it. In brief, native talents put some individuals in a position to make contributions to total output which command very high incomes. Others are in much less fortunate circumstances.

Training, education, and opportunities to advance. Despite high-sounding claims to the contrary, opportunities to develop latent talents and to acquire new abilities are not equally available to all. Discrimination on the basis of race, religion, and sex block many paths to self-betterment. Similarly, the inability to finance extended periods of training and the virtual closing of certain occupational doors by unions or professional associations are equally effective obstacles. Thus, even if everyone were blessed with identical physical and mental talents, income inequality would still result because of the fact that opportunities to develop and employ those talents are not equally available.

Property ownership. The ownership of property resources, and hence the receipt of property incomes, is very unequal. The vast majority of households own little or no property resources, while the remaining few supply very great quantities of machinery, real estate, farmland, and so forth. Basically, property incomes account for the position of those households at the very pinnacle of the income pyramid. The right of inheritance and the fact that "wealth begets wealth" reinforce the role played by unequal ownership of property resources in determining income inequality.

Ability to exert market power. Ability to "rig the market" on one's own behalf is undoubtedly a major factor in accounting for income inequality. Certain unions and professional groups have adopted policies which limit the supplies of their productive services, thereby boosting the incomes of those "on the inside." Exorbitant initiation fees, prolonged apprenticeship periods, flat refusal to accept new members, or the setting of unrealistic standards of performance are well-known and frequently employed tactics for manipulating the market on the behalf of a particular group. The same holds true in the product market: profit receivers in particular stand to benefit when their firm develops some degree of monopoly power. More will be said of this in later chapters.

Unequal distribution of misfortune. Many of the households are at the base of the income pyramid as a result of economic misfortune. A host of economic hazards in such forms as prolonged illness, serious accident, death of the family breadwinner, or unemployment may plunge a family into relative poverty. The burden of such misfortunes is borne very unevenly by the population and hence contributes to the degree of income inequality.

Miscellaneous factors. There are obviously other important forces which play a part in explaining income inequality. Luck, chance, and "being in the right place at the right time" have all caused individuals to stumble into fortunes. Discovering oil on a run-down farm, meeting the right press agent, or making a favorable impression on the boss's daughter have accounted for many high incomes. Nor can personal contacts and political influence be discounted as means of attaining the higher income brackets.

Interstate and international income comparisons. In contrast with foreign nations, there can be little doubt as to the superior position of the average American income receiver. Table 39-1 indicates that the American per capita income is the highest in the world, very considerably higher than that of many of the so-called "underdeveloped" nations. Figure 7-3 indicates that geographic differences in incomes are also significant within the United States. Note the low per capita incomes in the Southern states.

HOUSEHOLDS AS SPENDERS

Having discussed households as income receivers, let us now examine the other side of the coin by viewing households as disposers of income. In doing so, we must first understand the difference between income earned and income received by households.

Income earned versus income received

In viewing the functional distribution of income, we talked in terms of the national income. This is a measure of the total income _earned_ by households in any given year for the property and human resources they supply to business firms. Now, in shifting our discussion to households as disposers of income, we are immediately concerned with the actual amount of income _received_ by households. Income received in any year is called "personal income." But why should national income (income earned) and personal income (income received) differ? There are two reasons:

On the one hand, not all income earned by households is actually received as income. Specifically, there are three portions of the income earned by households which households do not receive. (1) The contributions of both

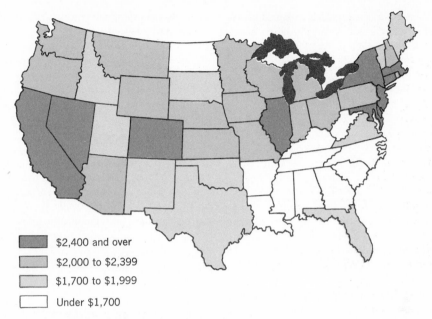

$2,400 and over

$2,000 to $2,399

$1,700 to $1,999

Under $1,700

FIGURE 7-3. PER CAPITA PERSONAL INCOME BY STATES, 1961.
There are considerable regional differences in per capita incomes in the United States.
(U. S. Department of Commerce.)

employers and employees to the social security program flow to government. (2) So does a part of corporate profits in the form of corporate income taxes. (3) Lastly, another chunk of corporate income will typically be retained in the business sector as undistributed corporate profits or, more simply, as business saving. In other words, social security contributions, corporate income taxes, and undistributed corporate profits are three parts of income earned by households as resource suppliers which are not actually received and available for disposition by households.[1]

On the other hand, we noted in Chapter 6 that government transfers income among households. These money transfers, called simply "transfer payments," take the form of relief and welfare payments, social security payments, veterans' benefits, and so forth. They represent income which is received but not currently earned.

In short, we here acknowledge a discrepancy between the national income earned by households as resource suppliers and the per-

sonal income actually received by them and therefore available for their disbursement as spenders. To make the adjustment between national and personal income, one must subtract out those three portions of national income which are not received (social security contributions, corporate income taxes, and undistributed corporate profits) and add in income received though not earned (transfer payments).

Disposing of personal income

How, then, do households dispose of the personal income which they receive? In general terms the answer is simple: a part is given to government in the form of personal taxes, and the remainder is divided between personal

[1] Two additional points by way of explanation: (1) corporate income is earned by households through their ownership of corporations; (2) withheld personal income taxes are not actually received by households either; we shall, however, treat these as a disbursement of personal income.

consumption expenditures and personal saving. Specifically, here is the way in which households disposed of their personal income in 1961:

	Billions of dollars	Per cent of total
Personal taxes.......	$ 51.9	13
Personal consumption expenditures......	339.0	81
Personal saving......	25.8	6
Personal income...	$416.7	100

Figures 7-4 and 7-5 show the absolute and relative importance of personal taxes, consumption expenditures, and personal saving over the last three decades. We note immediately that in absolute terms all three components move with personal income. But let us examine each of these components separately.

Personal taxes

Personal taxes, of which the Federal personal income tax is the major component, have risen sharply in both absolute and relative terms since 1941. In 1929, households paid $2.6 billion, or about 3 per cent of their $85.8 billion personal income, in personal taxes. In 1961, $51.9 billion, or about 13 per cent of that year's $416.7 billion personal income, flowed to government as personal taxes. World War II and the need to finance vast expenditures on war goods in the postwar era constitute the major explanatory factors.

The income received by households after personal taxes have been paid is called "disposable income." Remembering that economists define saving as "not spending," households have just two choices with their incomes after taxes—to spend or to save.

Personal consumption expenditures

Figures 7-4 and 7-5 clearly show that the bulk of personal income flows from income receivers back into the business sector of the economy as personal consumption expenditures.

But note that, although consumption has been increasing by large absolute amounts in recent years, it has declined in relative terms. The tendency for personal income to increase even more sharply than personal consumption expenditures has permitted this to be the case. As with personal taxes and personal saving, the amount of consumption which occurs depends upon the business cycle. The bad times of the thirties caused all three to contract. Yet, as Figure 7-5 shows, consumption actually increased in relative terms during the Depression. For example, during the Depression years of 1932 and 1933, households spent over 98 per cent of their personal income on consumer goods. Currently, households are spending over five times as much as they were during the depth of the Great Depression, but this still only amounts to about 81 per cent of personal income.

Since the size and composition of the economy's total output depend to a very considerable extent upon the size and composition of the flow of consumer spending, it is imperative that we examine how households divide their expenditures among the various goods and services competing for their dollars. Consumer expenditures may be classified in several ways. For example, classification is made on the basis of service or product and, in turn, by the durability of the products involved. Thus the Department of Commerce classifies consumer spending as (1) expenditures on nondurables, (2) expenditures on durables, and (3) expenditures on services. If a product generally has an expected life of one year or more, it is called a "durable good"; if its life is less than one year, it is labeled "nondurable." Automobiles, refrigerators, washing machines, television sets, and most furniture are good examples of consumer durables. Most food and clothing items are nondurables. Services, of course, refer to the services which lawyers, barbers, mechanics, and so forth provide to consumers.

Statistics show that of the $339.0 billion spent by consumers in 1961, $155.5 billion was for nondurables, $42.2 billion for durables, and $141.2 billion for services. This threefold breakdown is of considerable importance, because it reminds us that a good many con-

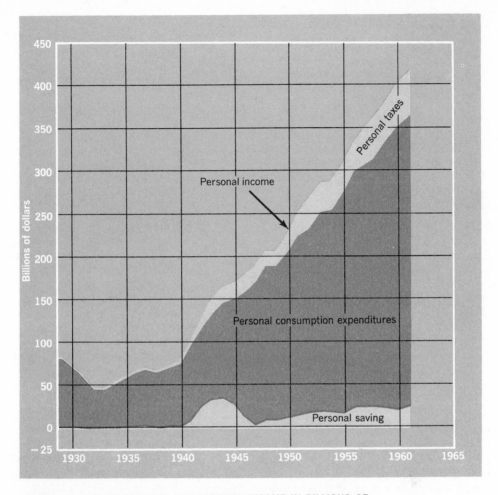

FIGURE 7-4. THE DISPOSITION OF PERSONAL INCOME IN BILLIONS OF DOLLARS, 1929 TO 1961.
Consumption expenditures, personal tax payments, and personal saving have all increased as personal income has expanded. Increases in personal saving during the early 1940s reflect wartime scarcities of consumer goods and high money incomes.
(U. S. Department of Commerce.)

sumer outlays are discretionary or postponable. During good times, durable, or "hard," goods are typically traded in or scrapped before they become utterly useless. This is ordinarily the case with automobiles and most major household appliances. But if bad times threaten or begin to materialize, consumers may forgo expenditures on durables, choosing to put up with an old model car and outdated household appliances. When depression threatens, the desire to conserve dollars for the nondurable necessities of food and clothing may cause a radical shrinkage of expenditures on durables. Much the same is true of many services. True, one cannot postpone an operation for acute appendicitis. But education, dental work, and a wide variety of less pressing services can be deferred or, if necessary, forgone entirely. In

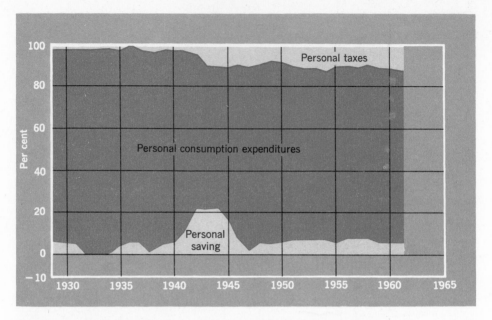

FIGURE 7-5. THE DISPOSITION OF PERSONAL INCOME IN PERCENTAGES, 1929 TO 1961.
Currently personal consumption expenditures account for about 81 per cent of personal income, personal taxes for 13 per cent, and personal saving for 6 per cent. (U. S. Department of Commerce.)

brief, the durable goods and services segments of personal consumption expenditures are subject to considerably more variation over time than are expenditures on nondurables. Like saving, many types of spending on durables and services are expendable during an economic crisis. Figure 7-6 provides us with a more detailed look at the composition of personal consumption expenditures.

Personal saving: current flows versus accumulations

Those portions of current household incomes which are paid as taxes and consumed will remain within the income-expenditure streams of the economy, flowing in this case to government and businesses. However, saving—that part of the current income which is neither paid in taxes nor consumed—presents a different picture. In effect, households channel their

current saving out of the income-expenditure streams and accumulate or stock this unspent income in various forms of financial assets. This means, of course, that "saving" is a slippery term. On one hand, it can refer to that portion of current (this year's) income which is not paid out in taxes or in the purchase of consumer goods but rather flows into bank accounts, insurance policies, bonds and stocks, and other financial assets which represent accumulated savings. On the other hand, the term "saving" is also used in referring to the present size of these financial assets which have been accumulated or stocked over a long period of years. Saving, in brief, can refer to a current flow of income into financial assets or to the accumulated size of such assets. In our discussion, we shall reserve the term "savings" (plural) for designating the accumulation or stock of financial assets held by households. The term "saving" (singular) will designate the

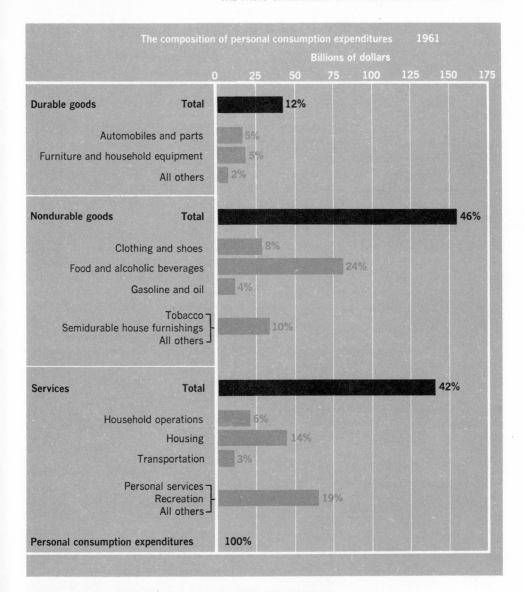

FIGURE 7-6. THE COMPOSITION OF PERSONAL CONSUMPTION EXPENDITURES, 1961.
Households currently spend about 46 per cent of their personal incomes on nondurable goods, 12 per cent on durables, and 42 per cent on services. (U.S. Department of Commerce.)

portion of current income which flows into, or is added to, this accumulation.[2] Occasionally we shall talk of "accumulated savings" or "the stock of savings," on the one hand, and "cur-

[2] The choice of terms is fairly obvious. "Saving," a verb, designates a current action. "Savings," a noun, signifies an object, in this case an accumulated stock of liquid assets.

rent saving" or "the flow of saving," on the other, to remind us of the savings-saving distinction.

At the end of 1960 individuals held some $382 billion of savings in the form of savings accounts, postal savings, shares in savings and loan associations, United States savings bonds, and so forth. The $25.8 billion of personal saving which occurred during 1961 obviously increased this volume of accumulated savings.[3]

Much of this accumulation of savings resulted from peculiar economic circumstances which accompanied World War II. (1) Many consumer durable goods—particularly such items as automobiles, refrigerators, washing machines, gas ranges, and so forth—were simply not available. In a sense, households had no choice but to save. (2) Wartime prosperity boosted money incomes to all-time highs. Households were in a better position to take advantage of the luxury of saving than they had ever been. (3) Strong patriotic appeals were made to encourage saving in an effort to hold down the level of total spending and therefore reduce the strong inflationary pressures which wartime production had forced on the economy. Postwar prosperity has also aided households in adding to their accumulated savings, but the war years were the big ones for savers.

Why do households want to save? After all, it is ultimately goods and services which satisfy consumer wants, not the pieces of paper which we call checkbooks, savings account books, and bonds. The reasons for saving are many and diverse, but they center around *security* and *speculation*. Households save to provide a nest egg for unforeseen contingencies—sickness, accident, unemployment—for retirement from the work force, or simply for the over-all financial security of one's family. On the other hand, saving might well occur for speculation. One might channel a part of his income to the pur-

chase of securities, speculating as to increases in their monetary value. Or, a household might accumulate funds in bank accounts or as idle dollars in a sugar bowl, speculating as to a change in the purchasing power of those dollars.

The desire or willingness to save, however, is not enough. This willingness must be accompanied by the *ability* to save. And, as we shall discover later (Table 12-1), the ability to save depends basically upon the size of one's income. If income is very low, households may *dissave,* that is, they may consume in excess of their disposable incomes. They manage this by borrowing and by digging into savings which they may have accumulated in years when their incomes were higher. However, both saving and consumption vary directly with income; as households get more disposable income, they divide it between saving and consumption. Actually, the bulk of the personal saving that occurs in our economy is done by those households in the $50,000, $100,000, or higher income brackets. It is estimated that the top 5 per cent of the income receivers account for two-thirds of all personal saving in the United States. The top 10 per cent account for virtually all personal saving.[4]

SUMMARY

1. All three sectors of the economy—households, businesses, and government—receive and spend income. Much can be learned concerning the actual operation of American capitalism by analyzing the sources and uses of the income received by each sector.

2. In so far as the functional distribution of income is concerned, wages and salaries or labor income currently account for about 70 per cent of the national income. Corporate profits account for 11 per cent, proprietors' income for 11 per cent, and interest and rental income for 5 per cent and 3 per cent of national income, respectively.

[3] From National Industrial Conference Board, *The Economic Almanac, 1962* (New York, 1962), p. 405. The $382 billion personal savings figure is undoubtedly an understatement because it excludes currency and checking accounts.

[4] Simon Kuznets, "Economic Growth and Income Inequality," *American Economic Review,* March, 1955, p. 7.

3. The personal distribution of income is rather unequal in the United States. Differences in native abilities, training and education, property ownership, the ability to exert market power, and a host of other factors explain this inequality. Considerable regional differences in incomes also exist within the United States.

4. The manner in which personal income is distributed among individual households is a determinant of both the level and the composition of total output.

5. Households divide their personal incomes among personal taxes, personal consumption expenditures, and personal saving. Currently about 13 per cent of personal income is paid to government as personal taxes, 81 per cent is spent on consumer goods, and the remaining 6 per cent is saved.

6. Since World War II, personal taxes have risen sharply in both absolute and relative terms. The waging of World War II and the need for large armament expenditures in the postwar era have been the major causal factors underlying this upsurge.

7. In relative terms, personal consumption expenditures increase during bad times and decline during good times. However, in absolute terms consumption varies directly with the level of incomes. Expenditures on durables and the purchase of some services are more postponable than expenditures on nondurables. Since saving can be forgone entirely and indefinitely, personal consumption expenditures tend to be more stable over time than is personal saving.

8. Personal saving, defined as income which is not spent on consumer goods or in paying taxes, is directly related to the level of incomes. War-born prosperity, war-caused shortages of consumer goods, and postwar prosperity have teamed to permit a very sizable accumulation of savings by households.

9. As income rises, both consumption and saving tend to increase.

QUESTIONS AND STUDY SUGGESTIONS

1. Distinguish between the personal distribution of income and the functional distribution of income.

2. What changes have taken place in the absolute and relative size of the major shares of national income? What accounts for these changes? How do you account for the relative stability of labor's share?

3. What implications does the personal distribution of income have for the size and composition of the economy's total output? For resource allocation? Explain.

4. Comment upon the degree of inequality of income distribution in the United States. What factors account for this inequality?

5. What happens to the volumes of consumption and saving as disposable income rises? What is "dissaving"? When is dissaving most likely to occur?

6. Distinguish between consumer durable goods and consumer nondurables. Give examples of each. Why is the demand for durables less stable than that for nondurables?

7. Define and distinguish between national income, personal income, and disposable income.

8. "Poverty [in America] is not an economic malady so much as it is a social disgrace." [5] Interpret and explain. Do you agree?

[5] Robert L. Heilbroner, *The Worldly Philosophers* (New York: Simon and Schuster, Inc., 1953), p. 283.

9. What changes have taken place in the absolute and relative size of personal taxes, personal consumption expenditures, and personal saving over the last three decades? Be specific.

10. Distinguish between saving as a "flow" and as a "stock." How did World War II increase the volume of personal savings?

11. "If we want capitalism, we must also accept inequality of income distribution." Evaluate and explain.

12. "The economist can criticize the inequality of income distribution on the grounds that it eliminates the possibility of satisfying wants in order of their importance." [6] Do you agree?

13. "The trouble with income inequality is that it sets the stage for political inequality. In politics, money talks. An unequal distribution of income can therefore be an obstacle to the effective functioning of a democracy." [7] Evaluate and explain.

SELECTED REFERENCES

Cochrane, W. W., and C. S. Bell, *The Economics of Consumption* (New York: McGraw-Hill Book Company, Inc., 1956), particularly chaps. 4 and 11–13.

Grey, Arthur L., Jr., and John E. Elliott (eds.), *Economic Issues and Policies* (Boston: Houghton Mifflin Company, 1961), readings 46, 47, 49, and 50.

Hicks, J. R., A. G. Hart, and J. W. Ford, *The Social Framework of the American Economy*, 2d ed. (New York: Oxford University Press, 1955), chap. 17.

Katona, George, *The Powerful Consumer* (New York: McGraw-Hill Book Company, Inc., 1960).

Survey of Current Business, April, 1962, pp. 9–16.

[6] George N. Halm, *Economic Systems: A Comparative Analysis*, rev. ed. (New York: Holt, Rinehart and Winston, Inc., 1960), p. 53.

[7] Robert A. Dahl and Charles E. Lindblom, *Politics, Economics, and Welfare* (New York: Harper & Row, Publishers, 1953), p. 139.

Chapter 8

THE FACTS OF AMERICAN CAPITALISM:

BUSINESSES

PRIVATE BUSINESSES constitute the second major aggregate of American capitalism. This chapter is a factual description of the business segment of the economy. More specifically, the goals of our discussion are threefold: (1) The major characteristics of the business population will be explored. Emphasis here will be upon the diversity and fluidity of the business population, the various legal forms which private enterprises may assume, and the major industrial classifications. (2) The development of "big business" which has accompanied the development of the American economy will be explored in terms of the causes, the means, and the effects of this growth. (3) The dual role of businesses as producers and employers will be analyzed in terms of a single firm and then in terms of businesses as a group.

THE BUSINESS POPULATION

To avoid any possible confusion, we preface our discussion of the business population with some comments concerning terminology. In particular, one must distinguish between a plant, a firm, and an industry. A *plant* is a physical unit of production; it is a physical establishment in the form of a factory, farm, mine, retail or wholesale store, or warehouse which performs one or more specific functions in the fabrication and distribution of goods and services. A business *firm*, on the other hand, is the business organization which owns and operates these plants. While most firms operate only one plant, many firms own and operate a number of plants. For example, without exception, each of the large steel firms of our economy—United States Steel, Bethlehem Steel, Republic Steel, and so forth—owns ore and coal mines, limestone quarries, coke ovens, blast furnaces, rolling mills, forge shops, foundries, and, in some cases, fabricating shops. The large chain stores in the retail grocery field are composed of hundreds or, in some instances, thousands of plants. In brief, a firm may be comprised of many plants at the same stage of production or at many different stages of production. Economists call the former "horizontal" combinations and the latter "vertical" combinations.

An *industry* is a group of firms producing identical, or at least similar, products. Though an apparently simple concept, industries are usually difficult to identify in practice. For example, how are we to identify the automobile industry? The simplest answer is "All firms producing automobiles." But automobiles are heterogeneous products. While Cadillacs and Buicks are similar products, and Buicks and Fords are similar, and Fords and Ramblers

129

are similar, and Ramblers and Volkswagens are similar, it is clear that Volkswagens and Cadillacs are very dissimilar. At least most buyers think so. And what about trucks? Certainly small pickup trucks are similar in some respects to station wagons. Is it better to speak of the motor vehicle industry rather than of the automobile industry? This matter of delineating an industry becomes all the more complex when it is recognized that most enterprises are multiproduct firms. American automobile manufacturers are also responsible for such diverse products as diesel locomotives, buses, refrigerators, guided missiles, and air conditioners. We pose these questions, not with a view to resolving them, but merely to note that industry classifications are rarely clear-cut and always somewhat arbitrary.

Diversity and fluidity

If we were able to stand back and achieve a broad overview of the business sector of American capitalism, we would be amazed by the phenomenal diversity of its approximately 11 million component firms. Indeed, no two business enterprises are exactly alike. At one extreme, you would be impressed by a giant corporation such as General Motors, which in 1961 owned total assets of $8.3 billion, employed 553,000 people, and realized annual sales of over $11 billion. At the other end of the scale you could not help being amazed by the extremely large number of "shoestring" enterprises in the form of corner groceries, neighborhood beaneries, and small specialty shops with gross sales of less than $50 per day, and maybe one or two employees and some relatively worthless showcases or counters as their only real capital assets.

The American business population is also very fluid. "Here today, gone tomorrow" is a fitting slogan for the business population of American capitalism. New firms are constantly entering and old firms leaving the business population. For example, in 1960 some 443,000 new business enterprises were launched, and about 386,000 existing firms failed in the same period. Because these figures

are based on a much narrower definition of the business population than the one we have adopted, they are undoubtedly on the conservative side. Average age of all operating firms? About seven years.[1] Although the lion's share of the failures is among the "shoestring" enterprises, it is not uncommon for firms of significant size to slip into the sea of bankruptcy. Some interpret such statistics with alarm. All things considered, however, it is amazing that so many of the small "shoestring" enterprises which are started every year survive and thrive as well as they do. It should be noted, too, that change also characterizes the types of commodities produced by businesses, the productive techniques employed, the organization and structure of the firms, and the composition of the various industries.

Legal forms of business enterprises

The very diverse nature of the business population makes it imperative that we do some classifying. There are many bases for classifying business firms—legal structure, type of product, and size are common criteria. We shall use all three of these, in varying degrees.

The present emphasis, however, is upon the basic legal forms which businesses might assume: (1) sole proprietorship, (2) partnership, and (3) the corporation. Let us define and outline the advantages and disadvantages associated with each.

Sole proprietorship. A sole proprietorship is simply an individual in business for himself. It is typically "a one-man show." The proprietor owns or obtains the materials and capital equipment used in the operation of his business and personally supervises its operation. Responsibility for the efficient co-ordination of the re-

[1] The statistics noted are based on a business population of about 4.7 million firms. Our definition of the business population totals about 11 million firms, because we have chosen to include as a part of the business sector farmers and professional people who are in business for themselves. Data from the *Economic Report of the President,* January, 1962, p. 287.

sources he owns or can command rests directly upon the proprietor's shoulders.

Obviously, this extremely simple type of business organization has certain distinct advantages:

1. A sole proprietorship is very easy to organize—there is virtually no legal red tape or expense. The businessman simply acquires the needed facilities and is "in business."

2. The proprietor is his own boss. He has complete freedom of action, and since his own profit income depends upon his enterprise's success, there is a strong and immediate incentive to manage wisely. Furthermore, since the proprietor is sole owner, problems of disagreement and dissension among owners cannot arise.

This looks very rugged and individualistic. And it is, but the disadvantages of the sole proprietorship are great:

1. With rare exceptions, the financial resources of a sole proprietorship are insufficient to permit the firm to grow into a large-scale enterprise. Specifically, finances are usually limited to what the proprietor has in his bank account and to what he is able to borrow. Since the mortality rate is very great for proprietorships, commercial banks are not overly eager to extend much credit to them.

2. Being in complete control of an enterprise forces the proprietor to carry out all basic management functions. The proprietor must be a Jack-of-all-trades. He must make all basic decisions concerning, for example, buying, selling, and the acquisition and maintenance of personnel, not to mention the technical aspects which might be involved in producing, advertising, and distributing his product. In short, the potential benefits of specialization in management are usually inaccessible to the typical small-scale proprietorship.

3. Most important of all, the proprietor is subject to *unlimited liability*. This means that an individual in business for himself risks not only the assets of his firm but also his personal assets. Should the assets of an unsuccessful proprietorship be insufficient to satisfy the claims of creditors, those creditors can file claims against the proprietor's personal prop-

erty. The stakes are high in so far as individual proprietorships are concerned.

Partnership. The partnership form of business organization is more or less a natural outgrowth of the sole proprietorship. As a matter of fact, partnerships were developed in an attempt to overcome some of the major shortcomings of proprietorships. A partnership is almost self-defining. It is a form of business organization wherein two or more individuals agree to own and operate a business. Usually they pool their financial resources and their business know-how. Similarly, they share the risks and the profits or losses which may accrue to them. There are innumerable variations. In some cases all partners are active in the functioning of the enterprise; in others, one or more partners may be "silent"—that is, they contribute their finances but do not actively participate in the management of the firm.

What are the advantages of a partnership arrangement?

1. Like the sole proprietorship, it is easy to organize. Although a written agreement is almost invariably involved, legal red tape is not great.

2. Greater specialization in management is made possible, because there are more participants. Managerial functions can be apportioned among the partners in terms of their abilities and training, with increased efficiency as the potential result.

3. Again, because there are several participants, the odds are that the financial resources of a partnership will be less limited than those of a sole proprietorship. Partners can pool their money capital and are usually somewhat better risks in the eyes of bankers.

But the disadvantages cannot be minimized. The partnership does less to overcome the shortcomings of the proprietorship than first appears and, indeed, raises some new potential problems which the sole proprietorship does not entail.

1. Whenever there are several people participating in management, this division of authority can lead to inconsistent, divided policies or to inaction when action is required. Worse

yet, partners may flatly disagree on basic policy. For all these reasons, management in a partnership may be very unwieldy and cumbersome.

2. The finances of partnerships are still limited, although generally superior to that of a sole proprietorship. The financial resources of three or four partners may be such as to restrict severely the potential growth of an enterprise.

3. The continuity of a partnership is very precarious. The withdrawal or death of a partner generally entails the dissolution and complete reorganization of the firm. Needless to say, this may severely disrupt the firm's operations.

4. Finally, unlimited liability plagues a partnership, just as it does a proprietorship. As a matter of fact, each partner is now liable for all business debts incurred, not only as a result of his own management decisions but also as a consequence of the actions of any other partner. A wealthy partner risks all his riches on the prudence of his partners.

Corporation. Corporations are legal entities, distinct and separate from the individuals who own them. As such, these governmentally created "legal persons" can acquire resources, own assets, produce and sell products, incur debts, extend credit, sue and be sued, and carry on all those functions which any other type of enterprise performs.

The advantages of the corporate form of business enterprise have catapulted this type of firm into a dominant position in modern American capitalism.

1. The corporation is by far the most effective form of business organization for raising money capital. The corporation features new methods of finance—the selling of stocks and bonds—which allow the firm to tap the savings of untold thousands of households. Through the securities market, corporations can pool the financial resources of extremely large numbers of people.[2] Furthermore, corporations ordinarily have easier access to bank credit than do other types of business organization. This is the case not only because corporations are better risks but also because they are more likely to provide banks with profitable accounts.

2. Corporations have the distinct advantage of *limited liability.* The owners (stockholders) of a corporation risk only what they paid for the stock purchased. Their personal assets are not at stake if the corporation founders on the rocks of bankruptcy. Creditors can sue the corporation as a legal person, but not the owners of that corporation as individuals. Once again, this eases the corporation's task in acquiring money capital.

3. As a legal entity, the corporation has a life independent of its owners and, for that matter, of its individual officials. Proprietorships are subject to sudden and unpredictable demise, but, legally at least, corporations are immortal. The transfer of corporate ownership through the sale of stock does not disrupt this continuity which the corporation boasts. In short, corporations have a certain permanence which is lacking in other forms of business organization. This permanence is conducive to long-range planning and growth.

4. Corporations, because of their strategic position in acquiring money capital, typically have the ability to secure more specialized, and therefore more efficient, management than can proprietorships and partnerships.

5. Last but not least is the possible tax advantage which incorporation may entail for an enterprise whose net profits are sizable. As we shall find in Chapter 9, the maximum 52 per cent marginal tax rate facing a corporation is preferable to the maximum 91 per cent marginal rate of the personal income tax.

These advantages are of tremendous significance and clearly override any accompanying

[2] Financing by the sale of securities also has decided advantages from the viewpoint of the purchasers of these securities. First, households can now participate in enterprise and share the expected monetary reward therefrom without having to assume an active part in management. And, in addition, an individual can spread his risks by buying the securities of a variety of corporations. Finally, it is easy for the holder of corporate securities to dispose of his holdings. Organized stock exchanges facilitate the transfer of securities among buyers and sellers. Needless to say, this increases the willingness of savers to buy corporate securities.

disadvantages. Yet the drawbacks of the corporate form of organization merit mentioning.

1. There is some red tape and legal expense in obtaining a corporate charter.

2. Corporate charters usually specify the corporation's field of operation, thus making the corporation seem less flexible than other forms in its business activities. In practice, however, these restrictions have tended to be very broad and, in some cases, are flatly ignored, rendering this particular shortcoming more apparent than real.

3. From the social point of view, it must be noted that the corporate form of enterprise lends itself to certain abuses. Because the corporation is a legal entity, unscrupulous businessmen sometimes can avoid personal responsibility for questionable business activities by adopting the corporate form of enterprise. And, despite legislation to the contrary, the corporate form of organization has been a cornerstone for the issue and sale of worthless securities. Note, however, that these are potential abuses of the corporate form, not inherent defects.

4. A further possible disadvantage of corporations has to do with the taxation of corporate income. Briefly, that part of corporate income which is paid out as dividends to stockholders is taxed twice—once as a part of corporate profits and again as a part of the stockholder's personal incomes. We have already noted above that this disadvantage is offset by the fact that the maximum tax rates on corporate enterprises are less than those which may apply to unincorporated firms.

5. In the sole proprietorship and partnership forms, those who own the real and financial assets of the firm also manage or control those assets.[3] Most observers agree that this is as it should be. But in larger corporations, where the ownership of common stock is widely diffused over thousands or tens of thousands of stockholders, a fundamental cleavage between ownership and control will arise. This divorce of corporate ownership and control is intriguing, because, in theory at least, corporations are organized democratically. Each share of

[3] The silent-partner arrangement is the exception.

common stock has one vote in electing the firm's board of directors, which has ultimate authority for the operation of the enterprise. The more common stock you own, the more votes you have in selecting the corporation's officials.

How, then, do ownership and control come to be separated? The roots of the cleavage lie in the lethargy of the typical stockholder. Most stockholders simply do not exercise their voting rights or, if they do, merely sign these rights over by proxy to the corporation's present officers. And why not? The average stockholder knows nothing about the efficiency with which "his" corporation is being managed. So long as his dividends are regular and comparable in size to those received by the other members of his golf foursome who also hold common stock in various concerns, he is not troubled by the question of efficient management. And, after all, since the typical stockholder may only own 10 of 150,000 shares of common stock outstanding, his vote "really doesn't make a bit of difference"!

Not voting, or the automatic signing over of one's proxy to current corporate officials, has the effect of making those officials self-perpetuating. True, there are exceptions. Yet the New York Central Railroad and the New Haven Railroad management turnovers of 1953–1954 and the less successful Montgomery Ward battle are hardly indicative of a trend.

The separation of ownership and control is of no fundamental consequence so long as the actions of the control (management) group and the wishes of the ownership (stockholder) group are in accord. The catch lies in the fact that the interests of the two groups are not always identical. For example, management, seeking the power and prestige which accompanies control over a *large* enterprise, may favor unprofitable expansion of the firm's operations, or a conflict of interest can easily develop with respect to current dividend policies. What portion of corporate earnings after taxes should be paid out as dividends, and what amount should be retained by the firm as undistributed profits? More obviously, corporation officials may vote themselves large salaries, pensions, bonuses, and so forth, out of corporate earnings which might otherwise be used for increased dividend payments.

But let us not go overboard. Most of the time, management and stockholder interests coincide. And, although abuses have occurred and undoubtedly will continue to occur, there can be little question that productive efficiency is greater under the present system than would be the case if large numbers of stockholders had an immediate hand in formulating basic corporate policy decisions. In short, the divorce of ownership and control which characterizes large corporations is permissive of certain abuses by the control group, but these abuses are not an inherent defect of the corporate form of enterprise.

To incorporate or not to incorporate?

Which legal form of enterprise—proprietorship, or corporation—is best? Probably the basic determinant of the legal form of enterprise is the amount of funds which a given line of production requires. For example, the corner magazine stand or the small curio or gift shop will have very modest money capital requirements. The only fixed assets which tie up some money capital are a few relatively inexpensive display counters. And the volume of business is so small that the need for "working capital" (funds which bridge the gap between costs and sales receipts) is also minimal. Why go to the cost and trouble of incorporating such a firm when the primary advantage of incorporating—the accessibility of large amounts of money capital through the sale of securities —is actually of little relevance? In contrast, modern technology and a much larger dollar volume of business make incorporation imperative in many lines of production. For example, in most branches of manufacturing—automobiles, steel, fabricated metal products, electrical equipment, household appliances, and so forth—very substantial money requirements for investment in fixed assets and for working capital are involved. The typical manufacturing concern in the United States may have $15,000 to $20,000 worth of capital equipment *per*

worker! Given these circumstances, there is little choice. To exist is to incorporate. In brief, the best legal form of business enterprise varies from industry to industry and the primary determinant of legal form is the money capital requirement of the particular industry.

Actually the American business population is distributed among the three legal forms in the manner indicated in Table 8-1. It is strikingly clear that the proprietorship form is numerically dominant. Yet corporations, though small in number, are frequently large in size and scale of operations. In fact, corporations account for approximately 60 per cent of the output of private enterprises.

Industrial distribution of the business population

What do the 11 million firms which comprise the business sector of our economy produce? Table 8-2 measures in several different ways the significance of the various industry classifications. Columns 2 and 3 indicate the numerical distribution of the business population among the various industries. Columns 4 and 5 show in both absolute and relative terms the portion of the national income originating in the various industries. Columns 6 and 7 indicate the absolute and relative amounts of employment provided by each industry. Several points in Table 8-2 are noteworthy:

1. The relatively small number of firms in manufacturing account for about one-third of national income and total employment. These figures correctly suggest that American capitalism is a highly industrialized economy, characterized by gigantic business corporations in its manufacturing industries.

2. The wholesale and retail industries and the service industries (hotels, motels, personal services, and so forth) are heavily populated with firms and are simultaneously very important sources of employment and incomes in the economy.

3. Note, too, the large number of firms engaged in agriculture but the relative insignificance of agriculture as a provider of incomes and jobs.

4. Table 8-2 reminds us that not all of the

TABLE 8-1. THE BUSINESS POPULATION BY FORM OF LEGAL ORGANIZATION, 1962

Form	Number of firms	Per cent of total
Sole proprietorships*	8,800,000	82
Partnerships	954,000	9
Corporations	990,000	9
Total	10,744,000	100

*Includes farmers and professional people in business for themselves.
SOURCE: Department of Commerce data and author's estimates.

economy's income and employment originates in private domestic enterprises. Government and foreign enterprises account for about 14 per cent of the economy's national income and employ about 16 per cent of the labor force.

BIG BUSINESS IN AMERICAN CAPITALISM

To a very significant extent, American capitalism is a "big business" economy. A good many of our major industries are dominated by

TABLE 8-2. INDUSTRY CLASSES: NUMBER OF FIRMS, NATIONAL INCOME ORIGINATING, AND EMPLOYMENT PROVIDED*

(1) Industry	(2) (3) Number of private businesses		(4) (5) National income originating		(6) (7) Full-time workers employed	
	Thousands of firms	Per cent of total	Billions	Per cent	Thousands	Per cent
Agriculture, forestry, and fisheries	4,700	50	$ 17.2	4	2,615	5
Mining	43	1	5.5	1	637	1
Construction	479	5	22.5	5	2,291	4
Manufacturing	324	4	121.5	29	16,363	29
Wholesale and retail trade	2,334	24	68.6	17	11,285	20
Finance, insurance, and real estate	405	4	42.3	10	2,744	5
Transportation, communications, and public utilities	210	2	34.4	8	3,863	7
Services	893	10	50.0	12	7,507	13
Government			52.5	13	9,045	16
Rest of world			2.3	1		
Total	9,338	100	$417.1	100	56,350	100

*Columns 2 and 3 are for 1961; 4 and 5 for 1960; 6 and 7 for January, 1962.
SOURCE: Department of Commerce, Treasury Department, and "Economic Almanac, 1962."

corporate giants which enjoy assets and annual sales revenues calculated in billions of dollars, employ hundreds of thousands of workers, have a hundred thousand or more stockholders, and earn annual profits after taxes running into hundreds of millions of dollars. The previously noted fact that corporations, although constituting only 9 per cent of the business population, produce 60 per cent of the economy's total output hints at the existence of large corporate producers. The major questions to be faced in connection with the existence of big businesses in American capitalism are these: (1) To what degree does big business prevail in the American economy? (2) Why have businesses sought "bigness"; that is, what are the incentives for a firm to grow? (3) By what means have big businesses evolved? (4) What dangers, if any, are posed by the existence of giant business firms?

Extent of bigness

To what degree does big business prevail in the American economy? Unfortunately, there exists no simple index to measure the economic power concentrated in the hands of big business enterprises. Indeed, there is a host of conceptual and statistical problems involved in deriving and interpreting statistics on big business.[4] Nevertheless, available statistics rather clearly portray the important role played by these corporate giants and the extent to which they dominate various industries. Table 8-3 gives us a general idea of the degree of business concentration in certain major industries. A recent government report presents a thumbnail summary of "bigness" in American capitalism by pointing out that

. . . in 1947 the 113 largest manufacturing corporations, with assets in excess of $100,000,-000 each, owned $16,093,000,000 of net capital

assets (property, plant, and equipment), or 46 per cent of the total for all manufacturing, both corporate and noncorporate.[5]

Economists disagree as to whether concentration of economic power is on the increase. In some industries it evidently is, while in others concentration seems to be on the wane. The over-all picture is blurred. If concentration is increasing, the pace is apparently not rapid enough to be clearly discernible.

Incentives for bigness

What motivates businesses to grow? The incentives are complex and to some extent overlapping.

1. The desire to achieve greater _productive efficiency_ has undoubtedly played a role in the growth of big business. Large firms are frequently in a better position to realize "mass-production economies" than are their small-scale brethren. Yet it seems that the production economies of many mergers are nil. Indeed, some consolidations have probably resulted in operating inefficiencies because of the complicated management problems posed in attempting to co-ordinate a cumbersome industrial giant.[6]

2. The search for _power and prestige_ by business leaders has been a factor in the growth of big business. Being the largest employer, or controlling the largest quantity of real capital assets, in a given industry carries a certain amount of prestige that is generally recognized and much sought for in the business world.

3. _Security and assurance of long-run survival_ have been factors in the growth of big business. Combination is often effected to "diversify the product line" of a firm as a safeguard against seasonal and cyclical fluctuations in business activity. Diversification also affords some measure of protection against the risk of

[4] Because most large firms produce a variety of products, the already noted conceptual problem of clearly defining various industries arises. Statistical problems center around the question of choosing an appropriate measure of "bigness," or industrial concentration.

[5] Federal Trade Commission, _The Concentration of Productive Facilities_ (Washington: 1950), p. 14.

[6] See in particular Joe S. Bain, "Economies of Scale, Concentration, and the Condition of Entry in Twenty Manufacturing Industries," _American Economic Review_, March, 1954, pp. 15–39.

TABLE 8-3. CONCENTRATION IN SELECTED MANUFACTURING INDUSTRIES, 1954

Industry	Industry output produced by first four firms, per cent
Primary aluminum	100
Passenger cars	98
Linoleum	94
Electric lamps (bulbs)	93
Gypsum products	89
Telephone and telegraph equipment	89
Locomotives and parts	89
Steam engines and turbines	85
Cigarettes	82
Tin cans and tinware	80
Synthetic fibers	79
Tires and inner tubes	78
Typewriters	78
Sewing machines	76
Phonograph records	69
Tractors	67
Distilled liquor	63

SOURCE: United States Senate Committee on the Judiciary, Subcommittee on Antitrust and Monopoly, "Concentration in American Industry" (Washington: Government Printing Office, 1957).

unfavorable changes in consumer tastes. A multiproduct firm, by not putting all its eggs in one basket, is in a better position to survive the fickleness of consumers. And, of course, the goal of long-run survival prompts firms to branch out into newly developed industries where the prospects of future growth seem to be good. Similarly, combination may serve to ensure a firm of steady and continuing supplies of raw materials, semifinished goods, and product parts.

4. The seeking of greater financial rewards has been the dominant factor in the growth of big business. One aspect of this profit seeking has to do with the windfall gains, or promoter's profits, resulting from the immediate combi-

nation of several corporations. But of greater significance in the long pull is the enhancement of prospective profits through the demise of competition which combination typically entails.

How big businesses have developed

Generally speaking, there are two methods by which small firms grow to be industrial giants. The first is internal growth; the second is combination. The two means are not mutually exclusive. Many a corporate colossus has freely employed both techniques in achieving growth.

Internal growth. In a relatively few cases, gigantic business enterprises have developed through the reinvestment of the firm's earnings and the acquisition of additional funds for expansion by floating new issues of securities. The Ford Motor Company and Alcoa (Aluminum Company of America) are good examples of big businesses which have relied mainly upon internal growth to attain their present positions. However, the vast majority of firms which we presently classify as "big business" have practiced some form of combination to achieve positions of dominance in their respective industries.

Combination. A most obvious means of concentrating economic power is to merge with competing firms. A *merger* occurs when one operating corporation acquires the stock of one or more other corporations and then dissolves the acquired firms, making them a part of the first corporation. *Consolidation* is a closely related means of combination. A consolidation occurs when a new corporation is formed for the expressed purpose of taking over two or more existing firms. In both cases a group of formerly independent producers are, in effect, molded into one larger enterprise. The merger movement was strong during the 1925–1929 era, had a strong resurgence in the 1940–1947 period, and has continued at a rapid rate in the postwar years.

Historically, one of the earliest techniques for combining business enterprises is the *trust.* Under a trust arrangement, formerly independent firms turn over their stock—that is, their shares of ownership—to a group of trustees. Former stockholders receive in return "trust certificates" on which dividends are paid when profits are sufficient and the trustees so inclined. But now the power to control the member firms resides in the trust as holders of the stock of all member concerns. The 1880s were the heyday of the trusts. The Standard Oil, tobacco, and sugar trusts are (in)famous milestones in American economic history. But with the passage of the Sherman Antitrust Act in 1890, business combination shifted ground to an ingenious new technique: the holding company.

A *holding company* is a corporation, the objective of which is to obtain, or "hold," enough shares of stock in other corporations to control them. In a good many cases it is a purely financial enterprise and produces no goods itself. The amazing feature of the holding company is its ability to bring about a maximum amount of combination and control with a minimum expenditure for stock. This is facilitated by the fact that of the various securities issued by a corporation—common stock, preferred stock, and bonds—only common stock ordinarily entails the right to vote for a corporation's directors.

To illustrate, let us suppose there are ten operating concerns in an industry and that each has the following capitalization:

Common stock	$ 2,000,000
Preferred stock	4,000,000
Bonds	4,000,000
Total	$10,000,000

At most, one would need something slightly in excess of half of each firm's common stock to control it. With ten firms—each of which can be controlled through ownership of half, that is, $1 million of its common (voting) stock—a total of $10 million (1 million times 10) would be required to purchase the common stock needed to control the entire ten-firm industry. By forming a holding company with, say, the same capitalization as that of one of the ten operating firms shown above, the needed $10 million can be acquired. Furthermore, in order to control the holding company itself, one needs to own at most something slightly in excess of $1 million, that is, one-half its common stock. In short, $1 million will control the holding company which supplied the $10 million of its capitalization to gain control of ten competing firms. The capitalization of these firms is $100 million.

Two final considerations make the potentialities of the holding company more startling. On the one hand, very typically an operating concern will have total assets whose value is three or four times the value of its capitalization. Thus, in our example, the ownership of $1 million worth of stock may permit control of ten firms whose capitalization is $100 million but whose total assets are $300 or $400 million. That is to say, $1 million controls $300 or $400 million worth of assets. Secondly, our illustration assumes that it takes 50 per cent of a firm's common stock to control. Because of the lethargy of most stockholders, 10 or 15 per cent of a company's stock is often sufficient for control. Our illustration, therefore, is not an exaggeration.

Should big business be feared?

This is a knotty question, permitting honest differences of opinion. Two basic schools of thought exist on this issue. We summarize these views here and defer a detailed analysis to subsequent chapters.

One school of thought holds that big business is a natural and necessary outgrowth of a progressive industrial economy. In particular, it is argued that modern technology requires (1) the use of extremely large quantities of real capital, (2) wide markets, (3) a complex, closely integrated management, and (4) large and reliable sources of raw materials. Such an operation implies the need for large-scale producers. In short, the achievement of maximum productive efficiency through the employment of the best available technology often presupposes the concentration of economic power. Efficient production is only attainable when business units are large.

Equally competent observers view the situation much differently. Though efficiency may require "bigness" up to a point, it is argued that many American businesses have grown far beyond the size necessary for the achievement of maximum productive efficiency. Indeed, it is pointed out that some industrial giants are inefficient because they are too large; bureaucratic red tape has made them inflexible and unresponsive to fundamental changes in the economy. Furthermore, it is contended that bigness and monopoly power frequently go together. When this is the case, big businesses

entail all the potential evils of monopoly power. This power may even be of a cumulative character: big business employers prompt the growth of big labor unions, and the relations between the two may demand public control and therefore the growth of big government. All this implies fundamental changes in the capitalist ideology.

THE DUAL ROLE OF BUSINESSES

Businesses, as well as households, play a dual role in American capitalism. On the one hand, businesses are the main fountainhead of the economy's total output of goods and services; over 85 per cent of total output is produced and sold by private enterprises (see Table 8-2). On the other hand, in accomplishing this production, businesses purchase or hire the bulk of the economy's available supplies of resources. In so doing, businesses provide employment and, therefore, wage, rent, interest, and profit incomes to resource suppliers. In brief, businesses produce and sell goods and in so doing acquire money receipts. These money receipts in turn are used to pay the costs of employing the resources necessary in the productive process, not to mention tax revenues. Like the household sector, businesses receive and disburse money flows.

Income statement: a single firm

The nature of these flows can best be visualized through the income or profit and loss statement of an individual firm. An income statement is simply an accounting statement which shows the sources of a firm's income or receipts and the manner in which these receipts are allocated or disbursed during any given year. More specifically, an income statement shows how much a firm gets in receipts from its sales of goods and services and how these receipts are apportioned among various production costs and profits. The statement balances, because profits (or losses) are the difference between receipts and costs. Table 8-4 presents a simplified income statement for a manufacturing firm. We assume that this con-

TABLE 8-4. THE INCOME STATEMENT: A SINGLE FIRM

Allocations			Receipts		
(1) Wages and salaries		$ 35,000	(8) Sales of output...........		$100,000
(2) Materials		25,000	(a) To Firm A....	$40,000	
(3) Interest.......................		8,000	(b) To Firm B....	60,000	
(4) Rents.........................		4,000			
(5) Depreciation....................		1,000			
(6) Taxes.........................		15,000			
(a) Payroll taxes	$ 3,000				
(b) Indirect business taxes (sales taxes, excises, etc.)	2,000				
(c) Corporate profits taxes	10,000				
(7) Corporate profits (after taxes)		12,000			
(a) Dividends	$ 8,000				
(b) Undistributed profits ...	4,000				
		$100,000			$100,000

cern is a corporation which realizes all its receipts from the sale of a single product to wholesale Firms A and B. Sales receipts (net of discounts and rebates) are $100,000.

How are these receipts apportioned between costs and profits? The left side of Table 8-4 provides the answer. Sizable payments for wages and salaries, materials provided by other firms, and interest and rental payments for the use of property resources are typical costs. Item 5, depreciation, requires some explanation. Most resources—labor services and materials, for example—are used up in the accounting period in which they are purchased. Here the firm's monetary outlays coincide with the use of the particular resource.

Capital equipment is a different story, however. A building or piece of machinery may last for many years, even though the actual payment for that machinery may occur entirely in the year of purchase. For example, suppose a $10,000 machine is purchased by a firm in 1963. Its estimated life is ten years. Now, if the entire $10,000 cost of this machine was figured in the income statement for 1963, that

year's profits would be grossly understated. Indeed, sizable losses might be incurred. Then, in ensuing years, while the machine is actually being used up, profits would be overstated. The machinery would be contributing to output and therefore to receipts but would entail no cost to the firm. To avoid such arbitrary effects of durable machinery and building purchases upon annual profits and losses, accountants estimate that portion of the value of the machine which will be used up in each year of its estimated ten-year life. This amount, called a "depreciation charge," is then apportioned more or less evenly over the ten-year period. In this way a more accurate picture of annual profits is achieved. Thus, although the actual disbursement for machinery may be made in one year, annual depreciation charges adjust the firm's profits as if the equipment costs occurred evenly over the lifetime of the machinery. In short, the depreciation charge is merely a bookkeeping entry which makes for a more accurate estimate of profits over a period of time.

Table 8-4 also indicates the importance of

taxes as a cost of doing business. A corporation will be faced first with payroll taxes which are contributions made in the financing of the social security programs. Sales and excise taxes are other important expenses. Such taxes are listed as "indirect business taxes," because they are not levied directly upon the firm as such but rather upon the product which the firm produces. Corporate income taxes are levied directly upon the net taxable profits of the corporation. What remains, corporate profits after taxes, is typically divided among dividends paid out to stockholders and undistributed corporate profits or business saving.

Income statement: the business sector

Table 8-5 is a consolidated income statement for the entire business sector of American capitalism for 1961. This is merely a gigantic income statement for all the business firms which comprise the business sector of our economy. In most respects, it is similar to the income statement for a single firm.

The importance of the consolidated income statement for the business sector is that it provides us with a picture of the size and composition of the total output provided by the major producing sector of the economy.[7] The receipts side of this consolidated statement tells us that the business sector produced approximately $445 billion worth of goods and services in 1961. The breakdown of these sales indicates in a general way the composition of this output. Some $318 billion, or 71 per cent of the business sector's production, was in the form of consumer goods; $70 billion, or 16 per cent, in the form of capital goods (machinery, equipment, and buildings) which firms produced and sold to one another; and $57 billion, or 13 per cent, took the form of social goods and services (mostly armaments) sold to government.

It should be emphasized that the consolidated income statement leaves out most interbusiness

[7] For simplicity's sake, we assume that there is no change in inventories to cause a discrepancy between the volume of production and the volume of sales in any given year.

TABLE 8-5. THE INCOME STATEMENT: THE BUSINESS SECTOR, 1961*

Allocations			Receipts		
(1) Wages and salaries		$215	(8) Sales of output		$445
(2) Interest		13	(a) To consumers	$318	
(3) Rents		12	(b) To other businesses	70†	
(4) Depreciation		45	(c) To government	57	
(5) Taxes		89			
(a) Payroll taxes	$18				
(b) Indirect business taxes	48				
(c) Corporate income taxes	22				
(6) Corporate profits (after taxes)		23			
(a) Dividends	$15				
(b) Undistributed profits	8				
(7) Proprietors' income		48			
		$445			$445

* In billions of dollars.
† Includes foreign sales.
SOURCE: Calculated from "Survey of Current Business," July, 1962.

transactions. As a matter of fact, all transactions between business, except those where the buying firm is the actual user or consumer of the product, are concealed by the consolidated income statement. This is as it should be if we seek an accurate picture of the size and composition of the business sector's yearly output. The inclusion of "intermediate" transactions between businesses would lead to an exaggeration of the business sector's output. A simple illustration will make this evident. There are likely to be several stages of production in turning out a finished product. In producing a suit, the rancher sells wool to a mill for $10, the mill sells woolen textiles to a manufacturer for $20, the manufacturer sells the finished suit to a wholesaler for $40, the wholesaler sells it to a retailer for $50, and the retailer sells it to you as a consumer for, say, $70. To include all these transactions would tell us that $190 (= $10 + $20 + $40 + $50 + $70) worth of production has occurred in making a suit. But this is nonsense! Only $70 worth of production has occurred. Why? Because the intermediate transactions leading up to the final sale of the product to the consumer are covered, or included in, the $70 selling price. The value of the raw wool, the value of the processing done at the mill, the value of the handling and distributional services performed by the wholesaler and retailer are all included in the $70. To count these intermediate transactions separately would be to exaggerate grossly the output of the business sector. However, we do include sales between businesses when the buying firm is the ultimate user of the product. The production of capital goods, that is, machinery and equipment, by some firms for use by other firms is as much a part of the year's production as is the production of shoes and soap flakes for consumers and of highways and schools for government. To omit these final sales of capital goods would be to understate the year's production.

On the disbursement side of the picture, we see how the businesses allocate their total receipts. In Table 8-5, items 1, 2, 3, 6a, and 7—item 7 added in acknowledging that the business sector is composed of both incorporated and nonincorporated businesses—are payments for resources supplied by households. These items, totaling $303 billion, are income payments from the viewpoint of households. Item 4, depreciation, is a bookkeeping adjustment to give us a more accurate picture of business profits. Tax items 5a, 5b, and 5c, totaling $89 billion, flow to government. Item 6b is that part of business profits which is retained in the business sector; it constitutes business saving. Percentagewise, about 68 per cent of business receipts flow as wage, rent, interest, and profit payments to households. Taxes account for about 20 per cent. The remaining 12 per cent is business saving and depreciation.

The reader will probably have noted that the allocation for materials has been dropped in moving from the single firm's income statement to the consolidated statement for the business sector. The reason again has to do with "intermediate" transactions. For the *individual* firm, relationships with other firms from which it buys materials are important, and such purchases must be listed as disbursements or allocations. But for businesses *as a group*, these transactions are self-canceling; payments from one firm to another in the purchase of materials offset one another. The allocation of $25,000 for materials by Firm X is offset by $25,000 of receipts flowing to Firm Y, the seller of the materials. In other words, the consolidated income statement eliminates or cancels the expenditures and receipts which occur between firms in the business sector and shows only the relationship of the business sector to the household and governmental sectors of the economy. Note that all the allocations shown in Table 8-5 flow to the household sector as income payments, to the governmental sector as taxes, or simply stay in the business sector as undistributed receipts.

SUMMARY

1. The business population of American capitalism is both heterogeneous and fluid.

2. Sole proprietorships, partnerships, and corporations are the major legal forms which business enterprises may assume. Though proprietorships dominate numerically, the bulk of total output is produced by corporations. Corporations have grown to their position of dominance in the business sector because they are (a) characterized by limited liability and (b) in a superior position to acquire money capital for expansion.

3. Manufacturing accounts for a larger percentage of national income and employment in American capitalism than does any other industrial classification. The wholesale, retail, and service industries are also major sources of income and employment.

4. Many basic industries in our economy are dominated by a small number of large corporations. Major incentives underlying the growth of these big businesses are: (a) the desire to achieve greater productive efficiency, (b) the search for power and prestige by business leaders, (c) security and the assurance of a long-run survival, and (d) the pursuit of greater financial rewards.

5. Big businesses have developed by means of internal growth and by combination. Mergers, consolidations, trusts, and holding companies are some of the more common techniques of business combination.

6. Economists disagree on the desirability of big businesses. One view holds that big businesses are essential for achieving efficient production. Others contend that many American businesses have grown far beyond the size essential for efficiency in production and have acquired considerable monopoly power as a result of size.

7. The business sector produces about 90 per cent of the economy's total output. Currently about 70 per cent of this output is consumer goods, and the remainder is divided about equally among capital goods for the business sector itself and social goods and services for government. Over two-thirds of total business receipts is paid out to households as income for resources which the latter supply to businesses. Taxes, business savings, and depreciation account for the remainder.

QUESTIONS AND STUDY SUGGESTIONS

1. Distinguish clearly between a plant, a firm, and an industry. Why is an "industry" difficult to define in practice?

2. What are the major legal forms of business organization? Briefly state the advantages and disadvantages of each. How do you account for the dominant role of corporations in our economy? Distinguish between bonds and stocks.

3. Explain and evaluate the separation of ownership and control which characterizes the corporate form of business enterprise. Explain the following statement: "In the economic realm . . . [a] situation prevails that runs counter to the basic concept of democracy: corporation managers wield far-reaching power over stockholders and employees, and they constantly make decisions affecting the public interest, without any clearly defined responsibility to the public. Whereas in a capitalist democracy political policies are arrived at through processes of consent that begin at the bottom and end at the top, in corporate business economic policies are made from the top and passed on to the bottom." [8]

4. What are the major industries in American capitalism in terms of (a) the number of firms in operation and (b) the amount of income and employment provided?

5. By what means have big businesses developed in the United States? What factors have motivated this growth? What are the pros and cons of big business?

[8] William Ebenstein, *Today's Isms*, 3d ed. (Englewood Cliffs, N.J.: Prentice-Hall, Inc., 1961), p. 166.

6. What is an income statement? Of what value is a consolidated income statement for the business sector? Why does the consolidated income statement exclude all interbusiness transactions except the sale of capital goods to their ultimate users? Why is this desirable?

7. Explain and evaluate the following statements:

a. "It is the consumer, and the consumer alone, who casts the vote that determines how big any company should be."

b. "The very nature of modern industrial society requires labor, government, and businesses to be 'big' and their bigness renders impossible the functioning of the older, small-scale, simpler, and more flexible capitalist system." [9]

c. "The legal form which an enterprise assumes is dictated primarily by the financial requirements of its particular line of production."

SELECTED REFERENCES

Bain, Joe S., *Industrial Organization* (New York: John Wiley & Sons, Inc., 1959), chaps. 3 and 4.

Boulding, Kenneth E., *Economic Analysis,* 3d ed. (New York: Harper & Row, Publishers, 1955), chaps. 23 and 24.

Buckingham, Walter S., Jr., *Theoretical Economic Systems* (New York: The Ronald Press Company, 1958), chaps. 7 and 8.

Federal Trade Commission, *The Concentration of Productive Facilities* (1950).

Golob, Eugene O., *The Isms* (New York: Harper & Row, Publishers, 1954), chap. 3.

Levin, Harvey J., (ed.), *Business Organization and Public Policy* (New York: Holt, Rinehart and Winston, Inc., 1958), chaps. 4–17.

Robertson, Dennis, and Stanley Dennison, *The Control of Industry* (Welwyn, England: James Nisbet and Company, Ltd., 1960), chaps. 1–8.

[9] Eugene O. Golob, *The Isms* (New York: Harper & Row, Publishers, 1954), p. 53.

Chapter 9

THE FACTS OF AMERICAN CAPITALISM:

GOVERNMENT

CURRENT FACTS characterizing the private sectors of the economy were discussed in Chapters 7 and 8. A factual look at the governmental or public sector of American capitalism is the basic task of the present chapter. The controversy surrounding the scope of government's economic role (see Chapter 6) makes it particularly important that the facts of government be clearly understood and placed in proper perspective.

DUAL ROLE OF GOVERNMENT

Although, as Chapter 6 revealed, there are many ways in which government affects economic life, it is through taxation and expenditures that the functions of government are most directly felt. Indeed, changes in the size and composition of government spending and the volume of tax revenues reflect with a fair degree of accuracy any changes in the size and character of government's role in the economy. It is with the public sector's role as a transactor, that is, as a receiver and disposer of "income," that this chapter is concerned.

One point must be emphasized at the outset. There is a significant difference between the transactions of the private and public sectors of the economy: the former are voluntary, and the latter compulsory. The receipts and expenditures of households and

businesses are the result of voluntary decisions by those two aggregates in buying and selling goods and resources. Government tax revenues are the result of compulsory levies: households and businesses have no choice but to pay taxes. To a lesser degree, this compulsion appears on the expenditure side of government's transactions. While no one is compelled to use governmentally sponsored highways, libraries, or health clinics, all physically and mentally capable children who are within stated age brackets must consume public education or its equivalent.

GROWTH OF GOVERNMENT TAX REVENUES AND EXPENDITURES

Our comments in this and the succeeding section are concerned with all units of Federal, state, and local government combined. Following this, we shall take a more detailed look at the taxation and expenditure features of each of the three levels of government.[1] Then, finally, we shall analyze the controversial prob-

[1] The statistics used in this chapter in discussing Federal, state, and local finance are not from the same sources; thus, the total government budget picture presented in Table 9-1 is not equal to the sum of the Federal, state, and local budgets shown in Tables 9-2 to 9-4.

145

lem of apportioning the tax burden in the economy.

Figures 9-1 and 9-2 make clear the growing importance of the public sector of the economy by summarizing the long-term *absolute* growth in government spending and taxation. But this is not all: government's role as a transactor has also expanded significantly in *relative* terms. In 1929 government expenditures claimed only about 8 per cent of total output. By 1939 this figure had expanded to 15 per cent. At the peak of the war effort in 1943–1944, government expenditures had expanded to 45 per cent of total output. In the

FIGURE 9-1. FEDERAL, STATE, AND LOCAL EXPENDITURES, 1902–1960.
Government expenditures have grown both absolutely and as a percentage of total output. Hot and cold wars, population growth, more and better social goods, and inflation are some of the more important factors underlying this growth. U.S. Bureau of the Census, "Governmental Finances in the United States, 1902–1957" (March, 1959) and "Government Finances in 1960" (September, 1961).]

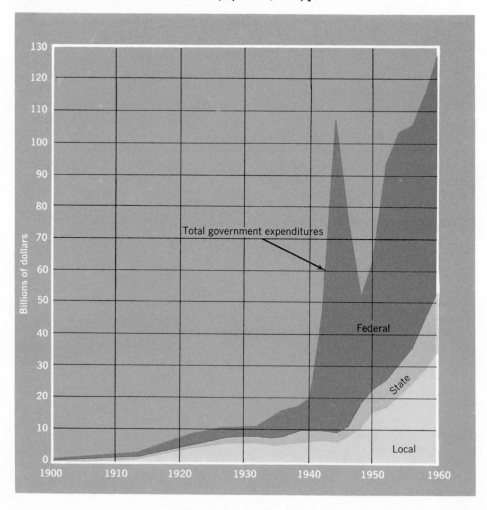

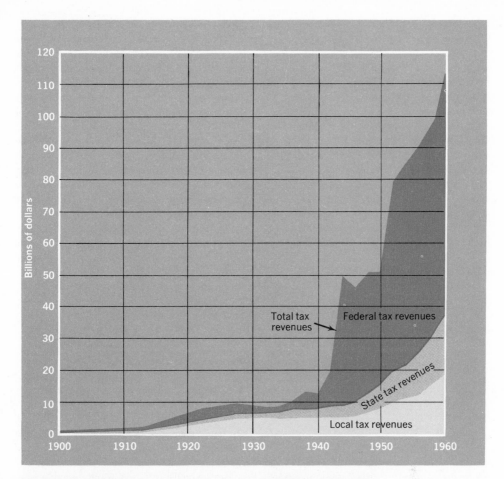

FIGURE 9-2. FEDERAL, STATE, AND LOCAL TAX REVENUES, 1902–1960.
Government tax collections have also increased significantly over time, roughly
matching the increases in government spending. [U.S. Bureau of the Census, "Governmental Finances in the United States, 1902–1957" (March, 1959) and "Government
Finances in 1960" (September, 1961).]

uneasy peace of the postwar era, government
expenditures have varied from 20 to 25 per
cent of total output (see Table 6-1). The 20 per
cent of total output purchased by government
in 1960 was largely financed by an average tax
bill of $628 presented to every man, woman,
and child in the United States!

The spectacular growth in government
spending and, consequently, tax collections has
a multiplicity of causes. As noted in Chapter 6,

root causes center around the desire of the
citizenry to correct or alleviate the instability,
inefficiency, and inequities which the price
system of pure capitalism may foster. But
more immediate causes are also abundant:
(1) Hot and cold wars have sustained Federal
expenditures at peak levels since 1940. War
and national defense are the major causes of
the phenomenal growth in government spending and taxing over the last two decades.

(2) With population increases, more people require services from the various levels of government. (3) The public has demanded more and better social goods and services to "match" the rising standard of living provided in the private sector of the economy. For example, we need better roads to accommodate more and better cars. (4) Inflation—generally rising prices—has forced government to spend larger and larger sums for given quantities of products. And this list is by no means complete.

As with the business and household sectors of the economy, the receipt and expenditure of income need not match in any particular year or period of years. Surpluses and deficits—the latter in particular—are not at all uncommon in so far as public finance is concerned. Figures 9-1 and 9-2 tell us, however, that tax collections have *generally* followed the trend of government spending. The major exception was the deficit financing which occurred during World War II.

CURRENT BUDGET OF THE PUBLIC SECTOR

In 1961 the total spending and taxing activities of all units of government—Federal, state, and local combined—stacked up somewhat as in Table 9-1.

Because tax receipts of $143.7 billion fell short of government expenditures of $150.2 billion, government units as a group incurred a deficit of about $6.5 billion in 1961.

The immediate task is that of taking a more detailed look at the major classifications of tax receipts and expenditures shown in Table 9-1. This will be a first step in the direction of our major goal of examining contrasting taxation and expenditures at each of the three levels of government. Let us first discuss the major tax classifications listed in Table 9-1.

1. *Personal taxes* consist mainly of personal income taxes levied against the incomes of households and unincorporated businesses but also include inheritance (gift and death) taxes and taxes levied against the personal property of households.

2. *Indirect business taxes* consist primarily of sales and excise taxes, customs duties on imported goods, and business property taxes. These taxes are collected from corporations and unincorporated businesses.

3. *Corporate income taxes* are self-defining. They are taxes levied by government against the net earnings of incorporated businesses.

4. *Payroll taxes,* or social security contributions, represent the compulsory payments made by employees and employers in conjunction with the existing social security program.

On the expenditures side of the picture:

1. *Government purchases of goods and services* are almost self-explanatory. Purchases of goods run the gamut from paper clips and typewriter ribbons to school buildings and jet fighters. The list of products purchased by government is long and varied. In some cases, the

TABLE 9-1. TAX RECEIPTS AND EXPENDITURES OF THE GOVERNMENT SECTOR, 1961

Tax receipts	Billions of dollars	Per cent of total	Expenditures	Billions of dollars	Per cent of total
Personal taxes	$ 51.9	36	Purchases of goods		
Indirect business taxes ...	47.1	33	and services	$108.7	72
Corporate income taxes ..	22.8	16	Transfer payments	41.5	28
Payroll taxes	21.9	15	Total expenditures	$150.2	100
Total tax receipts	143.7	100			
Add deficit	6.5				
Total receipts	150.2				

SOURCE: Department of Commerce data. Because of rounding, figures may not add up to totals.

goods purchased by government clearly overlap the range of products purchased by households and private business firms, for example, paper clips, automobiles, and foodstuffs. In other cases, the products purchased are uniquely social goods, for example, hand grenades, atomic submarines, superhighways, and space capsules.

Government also obtains services from businesses and, in some cases, directly from the household sector of the economy. Government expenditures in this case flow to scientists, statisticians, clerical employees, teachers, firemen and policemen, servicemen, and a myriad of government officials.

2. *Transfer payments* are money expenditures for which government currently receives no products or services in return. Most government "welfare" expenditures fall in this classification, for example, social security payments to the aged, unemployment compensation, relief payments, and aid to the handicapped. A few transfer payments, called "subsidies," go to businesses, for example, certain payments to farmers under the current agricultural program. Because transfer payments rechannel tax revenues back to households and businesses, these payments in effect are "negative taxes."

There is a noteworthy difference between transfer payments and government purchases of goods and services. Through government spending on goods, society reallocates resources from private to social goods consumption. Through transfers, government changes the composition of the output of private goods. If government taxes $10, we can expect purchases of private goods and services to decline by roughly that amount. In purchasing social goods and services with this $10 worth of tax revenue, government is in effect negotiating a substitution of social for private goods. Transfer payments are different: instead of increasing social goods at the expense of private goods, transfers merely tend to "rearrange" private consumption. Though $10 in tax revenues will reduce the private goods consumption of taxpayers by about that amount, households to whom this $10 is transferred can be expected

to increase their expenditures on private goods by about $10. But in all probability, the recipients will purchase somewhat different goods than the taxpayers. Hence, transfers alter the composition of private goods production.

FEDERAL, STATE, AND LOCAL FINANCE

With this very general breakdown of government disbursements and tax receipts in mind, we are now in a position to examine taxation and expenditures at each level of government—Federal, state, and local.

But first a brief comment concerning the relative economic significance of the three levels of government. Figure 9-1 reflects the long-term growth in Federal, state, and local spending. Figure 9-2 presents similar data on the taxation side of the picture. Although the last two decades have witnessed significant increases in expenditures and tax revenues at all three levels of government, the relatively greater upsurge in the role of the Federal government is clear. As previously noted, war and defense expenditures are the major component in the remarkable growth in Federal spending and taxing which has occurred since 1940.

Federal finance

Now for a more detailed look at Federal tax revenues and expenditures. What types of goods and services does the Federal government purchase? And from what sources are taxes collected to finance these outlays? The Federal "receipts-expenditures," or budget statement, shown in Table 9-2 tells the story for 1961.

Federal expenditures. Even a cursory glance at the Federal budget makes painfully clear the economic costs of mobilization and war. The first four categories of spending are the result of past wars, the present cold war, and the desire to head off future wars.

National security expenditures include outlays (1) to maintain and equip the armed services, (2) to provide military aid to our allies, (3) to support our atomic energy pro-

TABLE 9-2. THE FEDERAL BUDGET FOR 1961

Tax receipts	Billions of dollars	Per cent of total	Expenditures	Billions of dollars	Per cent of total
Personal income taxes	47.8	46	National security.........	50.7	50
Corporate income taxes ...	21.0	20	Veterans' services	6.0	6
Payroll taxes	18.4	18	Interest on public debt	6.6	6
Excise taxes	14.1	14	International affairs and		
Estate and gift taxes	2.0	2	finance	2.4	2
Total	103.3	100	Health, education, wel-		
Less tax refunds	−4.9		fare	23.4	23
Total tax receipts	98.4		Agriculture and agri-		
Add deficit	3.8		cultural resources	4.2	4
Total receipts	102.1		Natural resources	1.7	2
			Commerce and housing ...	5.1	5
			General government	2.7	3
			Total expenditures	102.1	100

SOURCE: Department of Commerce data. Because of rounding, figures may not add up to totals.

gram, (4) to stockpile strategic materials, and (5) to finance armament research. National security outlays account for about 50 per cent of total Federal expenditures. But even this gigantic outlay belies the economic costs of wars and military preparedness. The next three types of spending are also closely associated with mobilization and war. *Veterans' services* —which include GI Bill payments, medical care, disability pay, and pensions to veterans and their dependents—obviously are expenditures resulting from the two World Wars and the Korean War. And, since the bulk of the Federal debt of some $296 billion was incurred in financing World War II, the annual payment of *interest on the public debt* also must be considered as a war-born outlay. Finally, *international affairs and finance* involve expenditures for the economic and technological development of foreign countries and the costs of administering our foreign affairs. In part, these outlays stem from altruistic motives. But a selfish reason dominates: these expenditures are designed to keep foreign countries from turning to communism. As a group, these four

expenditure categories account for about $66 billion, or about 65 per cent of total Federal outlays. War and military preparedness carry extremely high price tags.

A word of explanation about the nondefense expenditures which comprise the remaining 35 per cent of the Federal government's expenditures. *Health, education, and welfare* include public assistance to the needy and disabled and Federal aid to education. Expenditures for *agriculture and agricultural resources* are outlays to farmers under current price-support programs; also included, however, are expenditures for rural electrification, farm credit, and soil conservation programs. *Natural resource* outlays are for flood control, the development of water resources, reclamation, and multiple-purpose projects. Expenditures for the development and conservation of forest, mineral, wildlife, and recreational resources are also included. *Commerce and housing* entail expenditures for highway construction, subsidies to air and water transportation, and outlays for public housing and community development programs. *General government* expenditures are basically those made in connection with the financing of the legislative, executive, and judicial branches of government.

Federal receipts. The receipts side of Table 9-2 makes it clear that the Federal government relies on a variety of taxes for revenue. It is equally evident that the *personal income tax* and the *corporate income tax* are the basic revenue getters. About 46 cents of each dollar of gross tax revenue collected by the Federal government is in the form of personal incomes taxes. Another 20 cents of each dollar collected is accounted for by the corporate income tax. The remaining 34 cents comes primarily from payroll and excise taxes. What is the nature of these major sources of Federal revenue?

Personal income tax. The personal income tax is a tax levied on the incomes of households and unincorporated businesses after certain deductions and exemptions have been taken into account.[2] The basic characteristic of this tax is that progressive tax rates are applied to taxable income. The larger your taxable income, the higher the *rate* at which that income is taxed. As the personal income tax is applied in the United States, these higher and higher rates apply to the *increments* of income earned and not to total income. For example, a family of four in 1961 would pay no income tax if its income was about $2,700[3] or less, because its taxable income would be zero. Assuming no additional deductions or exemptions, the next $4,000 of income earned would be taxed at a rate of 20 per cent. Thus, our family of four, earning a $6,700 income, would pay about $800 (20

per cent of $4,000) in personal income taxes. The next $4,000 chunk of income would be taxed at a higher rate, 22 per cent. In other words, a family of four earning $10,700 would pay $1,680 in personal income taxes—nothing on the first $2,700, $800 on the next $4,000, and $880 on the next $4,000. Should you be fortunate enough to earn a taxable income of say $40,000 per year, you would encounter a tax rate of 56 per cent on any additional income. And, at the extreme, those who pull down a taxable income in excess of $400,000 per year will find the Federal income tax claiming 91 per cent of each dollar earned in excess of $400,000. *Note:* You can never be worse off by making an extra dollar. At least 9 cents of it will be yours.

It is important to note that, although the *marginal tax rate*—the percentage of each *additional* chunk of income received which is paid in taxes—goes up sharply as income increases, the effective or *average tax rate*—the rate of tax paid on one's *total* income—is usually considerably less. Our mythical family, for example, encounters a marginal tax rate of 20 per cent on each dollar of income earned between $2,700 and $6,700, but the average rate of taxation is only about 12 per cent ($800 divided by $6,700). However, as income rises, the marginal tax rates rise so sharply that even the average tax rate, though less than the marginal tax rate, comes to be large. Using the extreme example, a family receiving a taxable income of $400,000 per year will encounter the peak *marginal* tax rate of 91 per cent. The family's Federal income tax bill would be about $314,000, making the *average* tax rate about 78 per cent.

In all fairness it must be noted that the Federal income tax has a bark worse than its bite. There are numerous provisions in Federal income tax legislation which provide ample opportunity for legally avoiding tax payment. First, capital gains and losses, that is, changes in the value of real and paper assets, are accorded more favorable treatment from the taxpayer's point of view than earned income. Second, the income earned from state and municipal bonds is exempt from the personal in-

---

[2] The major deductions and exemptions from gross income in determining taxable income are (1) business costs and expenses incurred in earning income, (2) gifts to charitable institutions, (3) interest payments, (4) most other tax payments, and (5) a $600 exemption for the taxpayer and each of his dependents.

[3] Four exemptions of $600 each plus a flat 10 per cent blanket deduction of $270 total just short of $2,700.

come tax. Third, an individual whose earnings stem from participation in the ownership or operation of a corporation may be able to leave a substantial share of his profits or salary in the corporation, thereby not realizing it as personal income. In this way, he can increase his wealth and, at the same time, avoid the personal income tax through the lower rates which apply to corporate income. Or, the undertaking of risky ventures—drilling for oil is a case in point—puts you in line for very favorable tax treatment on any resulting earnings. Any tax accountant or lawyer who is worth his salt can point out numerous other means of legally avoiding income tax payments. As a net result, it is doubtful that those who fall in the higher tax brackets—where the average tax rate is, say, 75 or 80 per cent—actually pay at a rate in excess of 50 per cent.

During World War II, the withholding system of collecting the Federal income tax was installed. Under this system, the employer deducts an employee's income taxes from his paycheck and forwards them to the Treasury. Although this method of payment puts the government in the position of a preferred creditor, there are distinct advantages in the withholding system for both the government and the taxpayer. From the government's point of view (1) income tax evasion is reduced, (2) tax receipts are more closely attuned to changes in tax rates and size of incomes, and (3) the tax is generally easier to administer. From the taxpayer's point of view, the system in effect puts his income tax bill on the installment plan and makes it somewhat less burdensome to pay.

Corporate income tax. The corporate income tax, the Federal government's second major source of revenue, has a relatively simple structure. Any corporation whose annual net earnings are under $25,000 is taxed at a rate of 30 per cent. For corporations earning in excess of $25,000, the rate on all dollars earned above the $25,000 mark is 52 per cent. For example, a corporation realizing a net annual income of $50,000 would pay $20,500 in corporate income taxes—$7,500 (30 per cent of the first

$25,000) plus $13,000 (52 per cent of the remaining $25,000). Intermittently, the corporate income tax has been supplemented with an *excess profits tax.* This was the case during the two World Wars and the Korean War. During the Korean War, for example, excess profits, in addition to being taxed at the existing corporate income tax rates, were also taxed an extra 30 per cent. Thus, if the corporation mentioned above had the last $10,000 of its $50,000 of net profits classified as "excess," [4] its total tax payment would be $23,500, that is, $7,500 (30 per cent of the first $25,000) plus $13,000 (52 per cent of the remaining $25,000) plus $3,000 (30 per cent of the $10,000 classified as excess profits).

The corporate income tax entails a highly controversial problem—"double taxation." That particular part of the income stream which takes the form of dividends is taxed twice, while other forms of income are taxed but once. All corporate net income is first taxed under the corporate income tax as described above. In addition, that portion of corporate earnings which flows to stockholders is taxed for a second time as personal income. This double taxation of dividends is felt by many economists to be a glaring inequity in the present structure of income taxes. The inequity, however, is at least partially offset by the fact that retained corporate earnings are not subject to tax rates higher than 52 per cent.

Sales and excise taxes. Commodity or consumption taxes may take the form of sales taxes or excise taxes. The difference between the two is basically one of degree. Sales taxes fall on a wide range of products while excises are taxes on a small, select list of commodities.

The Federal government does not levy a general sales tax; sales taxes are the bread and butter of most state governments. But as Table 9-2 indicates, the Federal government does collect excise taxes. In 1961, of the $14.1 billion collected in excise taxes, $3.3 billion and $2.0 billion were from the taxation of alcoholic bev-

---

[4] Excess profits were defined in terms of earnings in "normal" years, or as a percentage of the corporation's invested capital.

erages and tobacco, respectively. The remaining $8.8 billion was derived from taxes on a wide variety of other products—cosmetics, tires, sugar, automobiles, jewelry, transportation, certain types of entertainment, gas and oil, cameras, radios, television sets, playing cards, and so forth.

Payroll and other taxes. Social Security contributions, or payroll taxes, are the premiums paid on the compulsory insurance plans provided for by existing social security legislation. These taxes are paid by both employers and employees. For the most part, these funds flow into insurance trust funds held by the Federal government.

Table 9-2 also shows limited amounts of funds flowing to government as gift and estate taxes and as the result of the sales of various licenses and permits. Conspicuous by its absence is the property tax. This tax is not employed by the Federal government but, as we shall see shortly, it is the basic source of tax revenue for local units of government.

State and local finance

State and local governments employ essentially the same types of taxes as are imposed by the Federal government. However, the relative importance of the various taxes and tax rates differs greatly. In particular, while the Federal government finances itself largely through personal and corporate income taxation, state and local governments rely heavily upon sales and property taxes respectively. And although there is considerable overlapping in the types of expenditures made by the three levels of government, national defense and related outlays account for the majority of Federal expenditures, while education, highways, and public welfare lead at state and local levels.

State expenditures and receipts. Table 9-3 gives us an over-all view of state finances. Note that the basic sources of tax revenue at the state level are sales and excise taxes which account for about 58 per cent of all state tax revenues.

State personal income taxes, which entail much more modest rates than those employed by the Federal government, run a poor second. Taxes on corporate income, property, inheritances, and a variety of licenses and permits comprise the remainder of state tax revenue. On the expenditure side of the picture, the major outlays of state governments are for (1) highway maintenance and construction and (2) education.

It is important to note that the budget statement shown in Table 9-3 tells us little about the finances of individual states. The figures in Table 9-3 are aggregates and therefore conceal information about component parts. Individual states vary tremendously in the types of taxes employed. Thus, although sales and personal income taxes are the major sources of revenue for all state governments combined, fifteen states have no general sales tax and seventeen do not use the personal income tax. Furthermore, great variations in the size of tax receipts and disbursements exist among the states.

Local expenditures and receipts. The receipts and expenditures shown in Table 9-4 are for all units of local government. This includes counties, municipalities, townships, and school districts. One major source of revenue and a single basic use of revenue stand out: the bulk of the revenue received by local government comes from property taxation; the bulk of local revenue is spent for education. Other less important sources of funds and types of disbursements are self-explanatory.

Intergovernmental grants. The budget summaries shown in Tables 9-3 and 9-4 do not show intergovernmental grants which flow (1) from Federal to state and local governments and (2) from state to local governments. These grants have become increasingly large over the years and are currently of very considerable significance. For example, in 1960 the Federal government made grants of $7.0 billion to state and local governments—$6.4 billion to the states and $0.6 billion directly to local units of government. In the same year, state government made grants of about $9.3 billion to local units of government. Local governments

TABLE 9-3. CONSOLIDATED BUDGETS OF ALL STATE GOVERNMENTS FOR 1960

Tax receipts	Billions of dollars	Per cent of total	Expenditures	Billions of dollars	Per cent of total
Sales, excise, and			Highways	6.1	34
gross receipts taxes	10.5	58	Education	3.6	20
Personal income taxes ...	2.2	12	Public welfare	2.2	12
Corporate income taxes ...	1.2	7	Health, hospitals	1.9	11
Property taxes	0.6	4	Police and general		
Death and gift taxes	0.4	2	government	0.9	5
Others, licenses, and			Natural resources	0.8	4
permits	3.1	17	Interest on debt	0.5	3
Total tax receipts	18.0	100	Others	1.9	11
			Total expenditures	17.9	100

SOURCE: Bureau of the Census, "Summary of Government Finances in 1960," September, 1961. Because of rounding, figures may not add up to totals.

were thus on the receiving end of $9.9 billion in grants from Federal and state governments.

The rationale underlying these grants is not too difficult to find. Federal grants to states are designed to help equalize income differentials among them. In effect, a portion of personal and corporate income tax revenues paid by wealthier states is paid out in grants which accrue primarily to the poorer states (see Figure 7-3). Much the same holds true for state-to-

local grants. The wealthier portions of a state may pay taxes which are apportioned out in favor of less fortunate areas in that state. Very often, though not always, this means that a state draws much of its tax revenues from the industrial metropolitan areas and favors depressed rural areas in its program of grants to local governments.

In short, Federal grants in some small measure equalize the incomes of the states, and

TABLE 9-4. CONSOLIDATED BUDGET OF ALL LOCAL GOVERNMENTS FOR 1960

Tax receipts	Billions of dollars	Per cent of total	Expenditures	Billions of dollars	Per cent of total
Property taxes	15.8	87	Education	15.2	45
Sales and excises	1.3	7	Police, fire, and gen-		
Personal and corporate			eral government	4.1	12
income taxes	0.3	2	Highways	3.4	10
Others, licenses, and			Public welfare	2.2	6
permits	0.7	4	Health and hospitals	1.9	6
Total tax receipts	18.1	100	Interest on debt	1.1	3
			Others	6.0	18
			Total expenditures	33.9	100

SOURCE: Bureau of the Census, "Summary of Governmental Finances in 1960," September, 1961. Because of rounding, figures may not add up to totals.

state grants in turn help to equalize the incomes of local governmental units. The existence of these grants also means that there is considerable financial dependency of state governments upon the Federal government and even greater dependence of local upon state governments.

A final important point: Table 9-4 suggests a very large deficit for local governments—specifically a deficit of some $15.8 billion ($33.9 minus $18.1 billion). However, nontax revenues —$9.9 billion in Federal and state grants plus some $4.3 billion in sales receipts from municipally owned utilities, liquor stores, and a variety of other sources—virtually eliminate this deficit.

APPORTIONING THE TAX BURDEN

The very nature of social goods and services (see Chapter 6) makes it exceedingly difficult to measure precisely the manner in which their benefits are apportioned among individuals and institutions in the economy. It is virtually impossible to determine accurately the amount by which John Doe benefits from military installations, a network of highways, a public school system, and local police and fire protection.

The situation is a bit different on the taxation side of the picture. Statistical studies reveal rather clearly the manner in which the over-all tax burden is apportioned. Needless to say, this is a question which affects each of us in a very vital way. Although the average citizen is concerned with the overall level of taxes, chances are he is even more interested in exactly how the tax burden is allocated among individual taxpayers.

Benefits received versus ability to pay

Two basic philosophies as to how the economy's tax burden should be apportioned are evident in American capitalism:

The *benefits received principle* of taxation asserts that households and businesses should purchase the goods and services of government

in basically the same manner in which other commodities are bought. It is reasoned that those who benefit most from government-supplied goods or services should pay the taxes necessary for their financing. Some social goods are financed essentially on the basis of the benefits principle. For example, gasoline taxes are typically earmarked for the financing of highway construction and repairs. Those who benefit from good roads pay the cost of those roads. At the local level of government, special assessments for the paving of streets and sidewalks and for the installation of street lights are levied upon those specific homeowners who directly benefit from these improvements. Difficulties immediately arise, however, when an accurate and widespread application of the benefits principle is considered.

1. How does one go about determining the benefits which individual households and businesses receive from national defense, education, and police and fire protection? The remoteness of government transactions (see Chapter 6) makes such a determination virtually impossible. Even in the case of highway finance, it is obvious, on second thought, that individual car owners benefit in different degrees from the existence of good roads. And those who do not own cars also benefit. Businesses certainly benefit greatly from any widening of their markets which good roads will encourage.

2. The shortcomings of the benefits principle become even more apparent when certain government welfare programs are considered. Relief payments and payments to the physically handicapped would be self-defeating if they were financed on the benefits principle. It would be ridiculous to think of taxing unemployed workers to finance the unemployment compensation payments which they receive. In short, government activities designed to redistribute income preclude the use of the benefits principle in their financing.

The *ability-to-pay principle* of taxation stands in sharp contrast to the benefits principle. Ability-to-pay taxation rests on the idea that the tax burden should be geared directly to one's financial position. As the ability-to-pay principle has come to be applied in the United States, it contends that individuals and businesses with larger incomes should pay more taxes —both absolutely and relatively—than those with more modest incomes.

What is the rationale of ability-to-pay taxation? Proponents argue that each additional dollar of income received by a household will yield smaller and smaller amounts of satisfaction. It is argued that the first dollars of income received by a household in any period of time will be spent upon basic high-urgency goods. Successive dollars of income will go for less urgent goods and finally for trivial goods and services. This means that a dollar taken through taxes from a poor man who has few dollars constitutes a greater sacrifice on his part than does a dollar taken by taxes from the rich man who has many dollars. Hence, to balance the sacrifices which taxes impose on income receivers, it is contended that taxes should be apportioned according to the amount of income one receives.

This is appealing, but problems of application exist here, too. In particular, there arises the question of how much more in taxes should the rich man pay than the poor man? We might agree that the household earning $10,000 per year has a greater ability to pay taxes than does the household receiving a paltry $3,000. But this does not tell us *how much more* ability to pay the first family has compared with the second. There is no scientific way of measuring one's ability to pay taxes. Thus, in practice, the answer hinges upon guesswork, the tax views of the political party in power, expediency, and the urgency with which government needs revenue. As we shall discover in a few moments, the tax structure of our economy is somewhat more in tune with the ability-to-pay principle than with the benefits received principle.

Progressive, proportional, and regressive taxes

Any discussion of the ability-to-pay and the benefits received principles of taxation leads ultimately to the question of tax rates and the manner in which tax rates change as the size of the tax base—that is, the value of that which is being taxed—increases. Taxes are ordinarily classified as being progressive, proportional, or regressive.

1. A tax is *progressive* if its rate *increases* as the tax base increases. Such a tax claims not only a larger absolute amount, but also a larger fraction or percentage of the tax base as the base increases.

2. A *regressive* tax is one whose rate *declines* as the tax base increases. Such a tax takes a smaller and smaller proportion of the tax base as the base increases. A regressive tax may or may not take a larger absolute amount of the tax base as the base expands.

3. A tax is *proportional* when its rate *remains the same*, regardless of the size of the tax base.

Let us illustrate in terms of an income tax. Here taxable income is obviously the tax base. Suppose the tax rates are such that everyone pays 10 per cent of his income in taxes, regardless of the size of his income. This would obviously be a proportional income tax. But suppose the rate structure is such that the household with an annual taxable income of less than $1,000 pays 5 per cent in income taxes, the household realizing an income of $1,000 to $2,000 pays 10 per cent, $2,000 to $3,000 pays 15 per cent, and so forth.[5] This, as we have already explained, would obviously be a *progressive* income tax. The final case is where the rates decline as taxable income rises: you pay 15 per cent if you earn less than $1,000, 10 per cent on $1,000 to $2,000, 5 per cent on $2,000 to $3,000, and so forth. This is a *regressive* income tax. Generally speaking, progressive taxes are those which bear down most heavily on the rich; regressive taxes are those which hit the poor hardest.

But there is a hidden difficulty in attempting to label taxes as progressive, regressive, or proportional. And that is the problem of choosing an appropriate tax base. As illustrated above, there is no real difficulty when you are dealing with the income tax: taxable income is your

---

[5] We refer here to average or effective tax rates, not to marginal tax rates.

only choice. But with a sales tax, for example, it is a different story. *At first glance, it would seem that a sales tax of, say 3 per cent, is proportional. And it is, if you choose expenditures on taxable items as the tax base.* With this base you will pay 3 per cent, or 3 cents, on a $1 purchase and 3 per cent, or $30, on a $1,000 purchase.

Yet all taxes ultimately come out of someone's total income. So maybe income is a more appropriate base to use than the value of a consumer's purchases. For example, suppose that Smith has an income of $3,000 and spends all of it. Jones, on the other hand, earns an income of $6,000 and spends $4,000, or two-thirds of it. Now, assuming a 3 per cent sales tax applies to each dollar spent by these two individuals, Smith will obviously pay $90 (3 per cent of $3,000) worth of sales taxes and Jones will pay $120 (3 per cent of $4,000). Using expenditures as a base, the sales tax is obviously proportional; both Smith and Jones are paying 3 per cent of their total expenditures as sales taxes. But the picture changes when income is substituted for expenditures as a tax base. While *all* Smith's $3,000 income is subject to the sales tax, only two-thirds of Jones's $6,000 income is taxed. Jones in effect avoids sales taxation on $2,000 of his income by saving rather than spending that amount. As a result, Smith pays $90, or 3 per cent, of his $3,000 income as sales taxes, but Jones pays $120, or just 2 per cent, of his $6,000 income as sales taxes. *Using income rather than expenditures as a tax base, the sales tax turns out to be a regressive tax.* It is regressive because a larger portion of the poor man's income is exposed to the tax than is the case with a rich man. The latter avoids the tax on the part of his income that he saves.

Shifting and incidence of taxes

Suppose society has decided how it wants the current tax burden to be apportioned among specific households and businesses. Now a complicating factor arises. Taxes do not always stick where the government puts them. Some taxes can be *shifted* among various parties in the economy. It is therefore necessary to locate as best we can the final resting place or *incidence* of the major types of taxes.

Personal income tax. The incidence of the personal income tax generally falls on the individual upon whom the tax is levied; little chance exists for shifting. There is one possible exception worthy of note. Unions might regard personal income taxes as part of the cost of living and, as a result, bargain for higher wages. If they are successful, they may shift a portion of the tax from workers to employers. Generally, however, we can conclude that the individual upon whom the tax is initially levied bears the burden of the personal income tax. The same ordinarily holds true of inheritance taxes.

Corporate income tax. The incidence of the corporate income tax is much less certain. The traditional view has it that a firm which is currently charging the profit-maximizing price and producing the profit-maximizing output will have no reason to change price or output when a corporate income tax is imposed. That price-and-output combination which yields the greatest profit before the tax will still be the most profitable after government takes a fixed percentage of the firm's profits in the form of income taxes. According to this view, the company's stockholders must bear the incidence of the tax in the form of lower dividends. On the other hand, in recent years many economists have argued that the corporate income tax is shifted in part to consumers through higher prices and to resource suppliers through lower prices. In modern industry, where a small number of firms may control a market, producers may not be in the profit-maximizing position initially. The reason? By fully exploiting their market position currently, monopolistic firms might elicit adverse public opinion and governmental censure. Hence, they may await such events as the imposition of taxes, increases in tax rates, or wage increases by unions to provide adequate excuse for price increases with less fear of public criticism. When this actually occurs, a portion of the corporate income tax may be shifted to consumers through higher prices.

Both positions are plausible. Indeed, the incidence of the corporate income tax may well be shared by stockholders and the firm's customers and resource suppliers. The consensus seems to be that stockholders bear most of the tax.

Sales and excise taxes. Sales and excise taxes are the "hidden taxes" of our economy. They are hidden because such taxes are typically shifted by producers to consumers through higher product prices. There may be some difference in the shiftability of sales taxes and excises, however. Because a sales tax covers a much wider range of products than an excise, there is little chance for consumers to resist the price boosts which sales taxes entail by reallocating their expenditures to untaxed products.

Excises, however, fall on a relatively short, select list of goods. This means that the possibility of consumers turning to substitute goods and services is greater. For example, an excise tax on theater tickets which does not apply to other types of entertainment might be difficult to pass on to consumers via price increases. Why? Because price boosts might result in considerable substituting of alternative types of entertainment by consumers. From the seller's point of view, the higher price will cause such a marked decline in sales that he will be better off to bear all, or a large portion of, the excise rather than the sharp decline in sales. With many excises, however, modest price increases have little or no effect on sales. Excises on gasoline, cigarettes, and alcoholic beverages are cases in point. Here there are few good substitute products to which consumers can turn as prices rise. For these commodities, the seller is in a better position to shift the tax.

In general, it is safe to say that the bulk, if not the entire amount, of a sales or excise tax will generally be shifted to the consumer through higher product prices.

Property taxes. Many property taxes are borne by the property owner for the simple reason that there is no other party to whom they can be shifted. This is typically true in the case of taxes on land, personal property, and owner-occupied residences. For example, even when land is sold, the property tax is not likely to be shifted. The buyer will tend to discount the value of the land to allow for the future taxes which he will be required to pay on it, and this will be reflected in the price he is willing to offer for the land.

Taxes on rented and business property are a different story. Taxes on rented property can be, and usually are, shifted wholly or in part from the owner to the tenant by the simple process of boosting rents. Business property taxes are treated as a business cost and therefore are taken into account in establishing product price; thus such taxes are ordinarily shifted to the firm's customers.

Table 9-5 summarizes this discussion of the shifting and incidence of taxes.

Progressiveness of the American tax structure

As we have seen, the Federal, state, and local governments of the United States employ a variety of taxes. Using income as the tax base, we have concluded that some of these taxes—the personal and corporate income taxes and inheritance taxes—are progressive while others—sales taxes, excises, and property taxes—are for the most part regressive. What is the total picture? Is our tax system as a whole progressive or regressive? The most recent estimates—and these figures must be estimates because of the uncertainty of tax incidence—are shown in Table 9-6.

Employing family income as the tax base, column 2 of this table tells us the percentage of income taken by Federal taxes in each of the seven income classes. For example, those receiving an annual income of less than $2,000 pay 15.7 per cent of their income in Federal taxes. Those earning $4,000 to $5,999 pay 15.9 per cent, and so forth. Column 3 presents the same information for all state and local taxes. Finally, column 4 sums the two preceding columns and shows the percentage of income taken in Federal, state, and local taxes combined from each of the listed income groups. The bottom figures tell us that Federal

TABLE 9-5. THE PROBABLE INCIDENCE OF TAXES

Type of tax	*Probable incidence*
Personal income tax	The household or individual upon which it is levied
Corporate income tax	Disagreement. Most economists feel the firm on which it is levied bears the incidence; others conclude the tax is passed, wholly or in part, to consumers
Sales and excise taxes	With exceptions, on consumers who buy the taxed products
Property taxes	Owners in the case of land and owner-occupied residences; tenants in the case of rented property; consumers in the case of business property

taxes take 19.2 per cent, and state and local taxes 8.2 per cent of all incomes. All taxes combined take over one-fourth of total personal income.

Column 4, of course, is the vital one. Note that slight regressivity is found in the "under $2,000" income class and that rather significant progressivity is evidenced in the very high "$15,000 and over" income class. But the basic conclusion is that *the tax burden is roughly*

proportional to income over the entire $2,000 to $14,999 income range—a range which includes approximately 80 per cent of all families. The often heard lamentations as to the highly progressive character of our tax structure are simply not accurate in so far as the bulk of American income receivers are concerned. So far as most income receivers are concerned, the progressivity which exists in Federal taxation (column 2), dominated by

TABLE 9-6. ESTIMATED TAX RATES BY INCOME LEVELS, 1958
(taxes as a percentage of income)

(1) *Family income level*	*(2)* *Federal* *taxes*	*(3)* *State and* *local taxes*	*(4)* *All taxes, or* *(2) + (3)*
Under $2,000	15.7%	12.6%	28.3%
$2,000–$3,999	15.9	10.4	26.3
$4,000–$5,999	16.4	9.5	25.9
$6,000–$7,999	17.2	8.5	25.7
$8,000–$9,999	16.2	7.8	23.9
$10,000–$14,999	17.2	6.9	24.0
$15,000 and over	29.8	6.1	35.9
All income classes	19.2	8.2	27.4

SOURCE: George A. Bishop, "The Tax Burden by Income Class, 1958," "National Tax Journal," March, 1961, table 6, p. 54.

personal and corporate income taxation, is very substantially offset by the regressivity of state and local taxes (column 3), wherein sales and property taxes prevail.

SUMMARY

1. Like households and businesses, government is simultaneously a receiver and spender of income.

2. Historically, government tax receipts and expenditures have grown rapidly both in absolute amounts and relative to the size of the national income. This growth has been particularly marked over the last two decades.

3. Federal expenditures and tax revenues are much greater than those of state and local governments. The twin evils of mobilization and war have been the basic forces underlying the tremendous growth in Federal expenditures and tax collections.

4. About two-thirds of all Federal spending is for national defense and related programs. Personal and corporate income taxes combined account for two-thirds of the Federal government's tax revenue.

5. Approximately 58 per cent of all state revenue is derived from sales and excise taxes. The construction and maintenance of highways is the major state expenditure, accounting for 34 per cent of the total.

6. At the local level of government, property taxes provide about 87 per cent of total tax revenue. Education absorbs almost 45 per cent of local expenditures.

7. Intergovernmental grants generally contribute to income equality between states and between local units of government. But at the same time, these grants enhance the financial dependence of state and local governments.

8. The ability-to-pay principle of taxation is more evident in the American tax structure than is the benefits received philosophy.

9. Taxes on personal and corporate incomes and inheritance taxes are progressive. General sales, excise, and property taxes tend to be regressive.

10. Sales and excise taxes are likely to be shifted; personal income taxes are not. There is disagreement as to whether or not corporate income taxes are shifted. The incidence of property taxes depends primarily upon whether or not the property is owner- or tenant-occupied.

11. Over the income range which includes the bulk of American households, the over-all tax structure is roughly proportional.

QUESTIONS AND STUDY SUGGESTIONS

1. Describe the over-all changes in government expenditures and taxes which have occurred during the last three decades. How do you account for these changes? Why have Federal tax collections and expenditures grown relative to those of state and local governments? Why might it be significant to distinguish between "transfer payments" and "government purchases of goods and services" in evaluating the growth of government expenditures and the impact of this spending upon resource allocation?

2. What is the most important source of revenue and the major type of expenditure at the Federal level? At the state level? At the local level?

3. Briefly describe the mechanics of the Federal personal income and corporate income taxes. Explain why the average or effective personal income tax rate is less than the marginal tax rate.

4. What are the effects of intergovernmental grants?

5. Distinguish clearly between the benefits received and the ability-to-pay principles of taxation. Which philosophy is more evident in our present tax structure? Justify your answer. To which principle of taxation do you subscribe? Why?

6. Precisely what is meant by a progressive tax? A regressive tax? A proportional tax?

7. Comment upon the progressivity or regressivity of each of the following taxes: (*a*) the Federal personal income tax; (*b*) a 3 per cent state general sales tax; (*c*) a Federal excise tax on playing cards; (*d*) a municipal property tax on real estate; (*e*) the Federal corporate income tax.

8. What is likely to be the incidence of each of the taxes mentioned in question 7? Be as specific as you can.

9. "With expenditures as a base, the sales tax is proportional. But when income is substituted as the base, this tax is regressive." Explain. Which base do you feel is more appropriate?

10. Comment upon the over-all progressivity of the American tax structure.

11. Explain and evaluate each of the following statements:

a. "Any system of public finance should be conceived simply with a view to the maximum social advantage in the long run, and it follows that any tax system . . . should be conceived with the same object."

b. "No tax on income can be a just tax unless it leaves individuals in the same relative condition in which it found them."

c. "Because there is no sure definition of the limits to progression, no firm basis of its 'reasonable' use, no protection against its unconscionable abuse, those who uphold the system as a revenue device are playing into the hands of the group that would use progressive taxation as the means of destroying private capitalism and ushering in the collectivist state."

d. "Even tho it be an open question whether all inequality in wealth and income be unjust, such great degrees of inequality as the modern world shows are regarded as not consonant with canons of justice. Very rich persons should be called to pay taxes not only in proportion to their incomes but more than in proportion."

SELECTED REFERENCES

Due, John F., *Government Finance*, rev. ed. (Homewood, Ill.: Richard D. Irwin, Inc., 1959), particularly chaps. 3, 5, and 6.

Poole, Kenyon E., *Public Finance and Economic Welfare* (New York: Holt, Rinehart and Winston, Inc., 1956), particularly chaps. 1–3, 5, and 6.

Rolph, Earl R., and George F. Break, *Public Finance* (New York: The Ronald Press Company, 1961), chaps. 1–3.

Smith, Dan Throop, *Federal Tax Reform* (New York: McGraw-Hill Book Company, Inc., 1961), particularly chap. 1.

Taylor, Philip E., *The Economics of Public Finance*, 3d ed. (New York: The Macmillan Company, 1961), chaps. 1, 3, 13, and 24.

PART 2

NATIONAL INCOME,
EMPLOYMENT,
AND FISCAL POLICY

TABLE 10-1. COMPARING HETEROGENEOUS OUTPUTS BY USING MONEY PRICES

Year	Annual outputs	Market value of this output
1	3 oranges and 2 apples	3 at 2 cents + 2 at 3 cents = 12 cents
2	2 oranges and 3 apples	2 at 2 cents + 3 at 3 cents = 13 cents

Fortunately, national income accountants have been able to resolve this difficulty: they deflate GNP for rising prices and inflate it when prices are falling. These adjustments give us a picture of GNP for various years *as if* prices and the value of the dollar were constant.

Inflating and deflating

Some examples will help us understand how GNP figures are adjusted for price changes. First, an exceedingly simple example: assume our economy produces only one good, product X, and in the amounts indicated in Table 10-2 for years 1, 2, and 3. An examination of columns 1 and 2 tells us that the *money* GNP for years 2 and 3 as shown in column 4 greatly overstates the increases in *real* output occurring in those two years. That is, the monetary measure of production (money GNP) does not accurately indicate the actual changes which have occurred in physical output (real GNP). A considerable portion of the sharp increase in

money GNP in years 2 and 3 is due to the drastic inflation shown in column 2, the remainder being due to the changes in physical output shown in column 1. Both increases in physical output and price increases are reflected in the money GNP.

Now the situation facing our social accountants is this: In gathering statistics from the financial reports of businesses and deriving GNP for years 1, 2, and 3, governmental accountants come up with the figures for money GNP shown in column 4. They will not know directly to what extent changes in price and quantity of output have accounted for the given changes in money GNP. Social accountants will not have before them the data of columns 1 and 2, but only the data of column 4. Being resourceful individuals, they attempt to adjust the money GNP figure for price changes. They do this by deriving a general price index which estimates over-all changes in the price level. By expressing this index as a decimal and dividing it into money GNP, one can obtain real GNP. In our example, wherein we

TABLE 10-2. DEFLATING MONEY GNP

Year	(1) Units of output	(2) Price of X	(3) Price index, per cent	(4) Unadjusted, or money, GNP	(5) Adjusted, or real, GNP
1	5	$10	100	$ 50	$50 (= $ 50 ÷ 1.00)
2	7	20	200	140	70 (= 140 ÷ 2.00)
3	8	25	250	200	80 (= 200 ÷ 2.50)
4					
5					

are dealing with only one product, a simple single price index number is all that is required. Such a price index is nothing more than a *percentage comparison from a fixed point of reference.* This point of reference, or benchmark, is called the *base year.* By comparing prices in previous and ensuing years with prices in the base year, we can tell how much prices have increased or decreased *relative to* what they were in the base year. Suppose product X sells for $10 in year 1, $20 in year 2, and $25 in year 3. Selecting year 1 as the base year, we can express the prices of product X in years 2 and 3 relative to X's price in year 1 through the formula

$$\text{Price index} = \frac{\text{price in any given year}}{\text{price in base year}} \times 100$$

We multiply the price comparison by 100 in order to express it as a percentage. Using year 2 as the given year we find that

$$\text{Price index} = \frac{\$20}{\$10} \times 100 = 200 \text{ per cent}$$

and for year 3,

$$\text{Price index} = \frac{\$25}{\$10} \times 100 = 250 \text{ per cent}$$

For year 1 the index must be 100 per cent since the given year and the base year are identical. In this case,

$$\text{Price index} = \frac{\$10}{\$10} \times 100 = 100 \text{ per cent}$$

These index numbers simply tell us that the price of product X in the year 2 was 200 per cent of what it was in year 1 and in year 3 it was 250 per cent of year 1's price. There are several ways in which the index numbers of column 3 can be used to deflate the inflated money GNP figures of column 4. As already noted, *the simplest and most direct method of deflating is to express these index numbers as hundredths, that is, in decimal form, and divide them into the corresponding money GNP.*[2]

[2] This yields the same result as the more complex procedure of dividing the money GNPs by the corresponding index number and multiplying the quotient by 100.

Column 5 shows the results. These real GNP figures measure the value of total output in years 1, 2, and 3 as if the price of product X had been constant at $10 throughout the three-year period. Real GNP thus shows the market value of each year's output measured in terms of constant dollars, that is, dollars which have the same value, or purchasing power, as in the base year. Real GNP is clearly superior to money GNP as an indicator of the economy's productive performance over a period of time.

To ensure his understanding of the deflating process, the reader is urged to add years 4 and 5 to Table 10-2, assuming that output was 10 and price $30 in year 4, and 11 and $28 in year 5. Second, it is recommended that you rework the entire deflating procedure using year 3 as the base year. You will find, by the way, that in this case you must inflate some of the money GNP data, just as we have deflated it in our examples.

Table 10-3 provides us with a much more realistic illustration of the inflating and deflating process. Here we are taking actual money GNP figures for selected years and adjusting them with an index of the general price level to obtain real GNP. Note that the base year is 1954. Because the long-run trend has been for the price level to rise, the problem is one of *inflating* the pre-1954 figures. This upward revision of money GNP acknowledges that prices were lower in years prior to 1954 and, as a result, money GNP figures understated the real output of those years. Column 4 indicates what GNP would have been in all these selected years if the 1954 price level had prevailed. However, the rising price level has caused the money GNP figures for the post-1954 years to overstate real output; hence, these figures must be *deflated* as in column 4 in order for us to gauge what GNP would have been in 1958 and 1961 if 1954 prices had actually prevailed. In short, while the money GNP figures reflect both output and price changes, the real GNP figures allow us to make a better estimate of changes in real output, because the real GNP figures, in effect, hold the price level constant. The reader should trace through the computations involved in deriving the real GNP fig-

TABLE 10-3. ADJUSTING GNP FOR CHANGES IN THE PRICE LEVEL
(selected years, in billions of dollars)

(1) Year	(2) Money, or unadjusted, GNP	(3) Price level index,* per cent (1954 = 100)	(4) Real, or adjusted, GNP, 1954 dollars
1929	$104.4	57.4	181.8
1933	56.0	44.2	126.6
1937	90.8	49.5	
1941	125.8	52.9	238.1
1945	213.6	68.0	314.1
1949	258.1	88.2	
1951	329.0	96.2	341.8
1954	363.1	100.0	363.1
1958	441.7	110.7	
1961	521.3	116.2	448.8

* Department of Commerce implicit price deflators.
SOURCE: Department of Commerce, "Survey of Current Business," July 1959 and February 1962.

ures given in Table 10-3 and also determine real GNP for years 1937, 1949, and 1958, for which the figures have been purposely omitted.

Double counting

To measure total output accurately all goods and services produced in any given year must be counted once, but not more than once. Most products go through a series of production stages before reaching a market. As a result parts or components of most products are bought and sold many times. Hence, to avoid counting several times the parts of products that are sold and resold, GNP only includes the market value of final goods and ignores transactions involving intermediate goods.

What do we mean by *final goods?* Goods and services which are being purchased for final use and not for resale or further processing or manufacturing. Transactions involving *intermediate goods*, on the other hand, refer to purchases of goods and services for further processing and manufacturing or for resale. The

sale of final goods is included and the sale of intermediate goods is excluded from GNP. Why? Because the value of final goods includes all the intermediate transactions involved in their production. The inclusion of intermediate transactions would involve double counting and an exaggerated estimate of GNP.

An example will clarify this point. Suppose there are five stages of production in getting a Hart Schaffner & Marx suit manufactured and into the hands of a consumer who, of course, is the ultimate or final user. As Table 10-4 indicates, Firm A, a sheep ranch, provides $15 worth of wool to Firm B, a wool processor. Firm A pays out the $15 it receives in wages, rents, interest, and profits. Firm B processes the wool and sells it to Firm C, a suit manufacturer, for $25. What does Firm B do with this $25? As noted, $15 goes to Firm A, and the remaining $10 is used by B to pay wages, rents, interest, and profits for the resources needed in processing the wool. And so it goes. The manufacturer sells the suit to Firm D, a clothing wholesaler, who in turn sells it to

TABLE 10-4. VALUE ADDED IN A FIVE-STAGE PRODUCTIVE PROCESS

(1) Stage of production	(2) Sales value of materials or product	(3) Value added
Firm A, sheep ranch	$15	$15
Firm B, wool processor	25	10
Firm C, suit manufacturer	45	20
Firm D, clothing wholesaler	55	10
Firm E, retail clothier	70	15
		$70
Consumer, the final user		

Firm E, a retailer, and then, finally, it is bought for $70 by a consumer, the final user of the product. At each stage, the difference between what a firm has paid for the product and what it receives for its sale is paid out as wages, rent, interest, and profits for the resources used by that firm in helping to produce and distribute the suit.

The basic question is this: How much should we include in GNP in accounting for the production of this suit? Just $70, the value of the final product! Why? Because this figure includes all the intermediate transactions leading up to the product's final sale. It would be a gross exaggeration to sum all the intermediate sales figures and the final sales value of the product in column 2 and add the entire amount, $210, to GNP. This would be a serious case of double counting, that is, counting the final product and the sale and resale of its various parts in the multistage productive process.

There is an alternative means of determining the $70 figure which is to be included in GNP. And this is by the *value added* method, that is, by summing the value added to the total worth of the product at each step in the productive process. Column 3 summarizes this procedure. Note that this measures the total income derived from the production and sale of the suit. As you might expect, it is easier for the national income accountants to be careful to count only final goods than to pursue the value added method of deriving GNP.

GNP excludes nonproductive transactions

GNP attempts to measure the annual production of the economy. In so doing, the many nonproductive transactions which occur each year must be carefully excluded. Nonproductive transactions are of two major types: (1) purely financial transactions and (2) second-hand sales.

Purely financial transactions in turn are of three general types: public transfer payments, private transfer payments, and the buying and selling of securities. We have already mentioned public transfer payments (Chapter 9). These are the social security payments, relief payments, and veterans' payments which government makes to particular households. These payments are in effect gifts; recipients make no contribution to current production in return for them. Thus, to include them in GNP would be to overstate this year's production. Private transfer payments, for example, a university student's monthly subsidy from home or an occasional gift from a wealthy relative, do not entail production but simply the transfer of funds from one private individual to another. *Security transactions,* that is, the buying and selling of stocks and bonds, are also excluded from GNP. Stock market transactions simply involve the swapping of paper assets. As such, these transactions do not directly involve current production. It should be noted, however, that by getting money from the hands of savers into the hands of spenders, some of these security transactions may indirectly give rise to spending which does account for output.

The reason for excluding secondhand sales from GNP is fairly obvious: such sales either reflect no *current* production, or they involve double counting. For example, suppose you sell your 1960 Ford to a neighbor. This transaction would be excluded in determining GNP because no current production is involved. The inclusion of the sales of goods produced some years ago in this year's GNP would be an exaggeration of this year's output. Similarly, if you purchased a brand new Ford and resold it a week later to your neighbor, we would still want to exclude the resale transaction from the current GNP. Why? Because when you originally bought the new car, its value was included in GNP. To include its resale value would be to count it twice.

GNP is not an ideal measure

GNP is a reasonably accurate and extremely useful measure of national economic well-being. Nevertheless, despite adjustments for price level changes and the careful exclusion of intermediate and nonproductive transactions, it must be recognized that GNP is not an ideal measure of economic welfare. There are several reasons for this:

1 *Nonmarket transactions.* There are certain productive transactions which do not appear in the market. Hence, GNP as a measure of the market value of output fails to include these productive transactions. Standard examples include the productive services of the housewife, the efforts of the carpenter who re-

pairs his own home, or the erudite professor who writes a scholarly but nonremunerative article. Such transactions are not reflected in the profit and loss statements of business firms and therefore escape the national income accountants. However, some very important nonmarket transactions, such as that portion of a farmer's output which the farmer consumes himself, are estimated by national income accountants.

2 *Leisure.* Over a long period of years leisure has increased very significantly. The current average work week is less than forty hours, while as late as the 1920s a sixty-five or seventy-hour work week was not uncommon in many industries. Increased leisure has added immeasurably to our well-being. Yet our system of social accounting does not directly take cognizance of this. Nor do the accounts reflect the satisfaction—the "psychic income" —which one might derive from his work.

3 *Improved product quality.* GNP is a quantitative rather than a qualitative measure. It does not accurately reflect improvements in the quality of products. This is a shortcoming: quality improvement obviously affects economic well-being every bit as much as does quantity of goods.

4 *The composition and distribution of output.* Changes in the composition and the allocation of total output among specific households may influence economic welfare. We have already encountered the view that the composition of total output is every bit as important as its magnitude. GNP reflects only the size of output and does not tell us anything about whether this collection of goods is "right" for society. And although there is anything but unanimity on this question, many economists feel that a more equal distribution of total output would increase national economic well-being. If these economists are correct, a future trend toward a more nearly equal distribution of GNP would enhance the economic welfare of society. A less nearly equal future distribution will have the reverse effect. In short, GNP measures the size of total output, but does not reflect changes in the composition and distribution of output which might also affect the economic well-being of society.

5. Per capita output. For many purposes the most meaningful measure of economic well-being is per capita output. Because GNP is a measure of total output, it may conceal or misrepresent changes in the standard of living of individual households in the economy. For example, GNP may rise significantly, but if population is also growing rapidly, the per capita standard of living may be relatively constant or may even be declining.

Two sides to GNP

Recognizing the characteristics and the shortcomings of GNP as a measure of output, we now raise this question: How can the market value of any unit of output—or for that matter total output—be measured? How can we measure, for example, the market value of a cashmere sweater?

In two ways: First, we can simply look at how much a consumer, as the final user, spends in obtaining it. Second, we can add up all the wage, rental, interest, and profit incomes created in the production of the sweater. This is simply the value added approach we spoke of above. These are, indeed, two ways of looking at the same thing. What is spent on a product is received as income by those who contributed to its production. Indeed, the circular flow model previously discussed is based upon this notion. If $20 is spent on the sweater, that is necessarily the total amount of income derived from its production. This equality of the expenditure for a product and the income derived from its production is guaranteed, because profit income serves as a balancing item. Profit—or loss—is the income which remains after wage, rent, and interest incomes have been paid by the producer. If the wage, rent, and interest incomes which the firm must pay in getting the sweater produced are less than the $20 expenditure for the sweater, the difference will be the firm's profits.[3] Conversely, if

wage, rent, and interest incomes exceed $20, then profits will be negative, that is, losses will be realized, to balance the expenditure on the product and the income derived from its production.

The same line of reasoning is also valid for the output of the economy as a whole. There are two different ways of looking at GNP: One is to look at GNP as the sum of all the expenditures involved in taking that total output off the market. This is called the *output,* or *expenditures, approach.* The other is to look at it in terms of the income derived or created from the production of the GNP. This is called the *earnings,* or *income,* or *allocations, approach* to the determination of GNP. A closer analysis of these two approaches will reveal that they amount to this: *GNP can be determined either by adding up all that is spent on this year's total output or by summing up all the incomes derived from the production of this year's output.* Putting this in the form of a simple equation we can say that

$$\left. \begin{array}{l} \text{The amount spent} \\ \text{on this year's total} \\ \text{output} \end{array} \right\} = \left\{ \begin{array}{l} \text{the money income} \\ \text{derived from the} \\ \text{production of this} \\ \text{year's output} \end{array} \right.$$

As a matter of fact, this is more than an equation: it is an identity. Buying—that is, spending money—and selling—that is, receiving money income—are actually two aspects of the same transaction. Buying and selling are two sides of the same shield. *What is spent on a product is income to those who have contributed their human and property resources in getting that product produced and to market.*

For the economy as a whole we can expand the above identity to read as in Table 10-5. This summary statement simply tells us that all final goods produced in the American economy are purchased either by the three domestic sectors, households, government, and businesses, or by foreign nations. It also shows us that the total receipts which businesses acquire from the sale of total output are allocated

---

[3] The term "profits" is used here in the accounting sense so as to include both normal profits and economic profits as defined in Part 1.

TABLE 10-5. THE INCOME AND OUTPUT APPROACHES TO GNP

Output, or expenditures, approach		*Income, or allocations, approach*
Consumption expenditures by households plus Government purchases of goods and services plus Investment expenditures by business plus Expenditures by foreigners	= GNP =	Wages plus Rents plus Interest plus Profits plus Nonincome charges or allocations

among the various resource suppliers as wage, rent, interest, and profit income. Later we shall explain two additional nonincome allocations of total receipts. Using this summary as a point of reference, let us point out in some detail the meaning and significance of the various types of expenditures and the incomes derived therefrom.

THE EXPENDITURES APPROACH TO GNP

To determine GNP through the expenditures approach one must add up all types of spending on finished or final goods and services. But our national income accountants have much more sophisticated terms for the different types of spending than the ones we have employed in Table 10-5. We must therefore familiarize ourselves with these terms and their meanings.

Personal consumption expenditures (C)

What we have simply called "consumption expenditures by households" is "personal consumption expenditures" to the national income accountants. It entails expenditures by households on durable consumer goods (automobiles, refrigerators, gas ranges, and so forth), nondurable consumer goods (bread, milk, beer, cigarettes, shirts, tooth paste), and consumer expenditures for services (of lawyers, doctors, mechanics, barbers). We shall use the letter "C" to designate the total of these expenditures.

Government purchases of goods and services (G)

This classification of expenditures includes all governmental spending, Federal, state, and local, on the finished products of businesses and all direct purchases of resources—labor, in particular—by government. It excludes, however, all government transfer payments, because such expenditures, as previously noted, do not reflect any current production but merely transfer governmental receipts to certain specific households.

Gross private domestic investment (I_g)

This seemingly complicated term refers to all investment spending by American business firms. What is included as investment spending? Basically three things: (1) all final purchases of machinery, equipment, and tools by business enterprises; (2) all construction; and (3) changes in inventories. This obviously entails more than we have imputed to the term "investment" thus far. Hence, we must explain why each of these three items is included under the general heading of gross private domestic investment.

The reason for inclusion of the first group of items is apparent. This is simply a restatement of our original definition of investment spending as the purchase of tools, machinery, and equipment. The second item—all construction— merits some explanation. It is clear that the building of a new factory, warehouse, or grain elevator is a form of investment. But why include residential construction as investment rather than consumption? The reason is this: apartment buildings are clearly investment goods because, like factories and grain elevators, they are income-earning assets. Other residential units which are rented are for the same reason investment goods. Finally, owner-occupied houses are classified as investment goods because they could be rented out to yield a money income return, even though the owner does not choose to do so. For these reasons all residential construction is considered as investment.

Inventory changes and investment. Remembering that GNP is designed to measure total current output, we must certainly make an effort to include in GNP any products which are produced *but not sold* this year. In short, if it is to be an accurate measure of total output, GNP must include the market value of any additions to inventories which accrue during the year. Were we to exclude an increase in inventories, GNP would understate the current year's total output. If businessmen have more goods on their shelves and in their warehouses at the end of the year than they had at the start, the economy has produced more than it has consumed during this particular year. This increase in inventories obviously must be added to GNP as a measure of *current* production.

What about a decline in inventories? This must be subtracted in figuring GNP, because in such a situation the economy sells a total output which exceeds current production, the difference being reflected in an inventory reduction. Some of the GNP taken off the market this year reflects not current production but rather a drawing down of inventories which were on hand at the beginning of this year. And the inventories on hand at the start of any year's production represent the production of previous years. Consequently, a decline in inventories in any given year means that the economy has consumed more than it has produced in that year; that is, society has consumed all of this year's output plus some of the inventories inherited from previous years' production. Remembering that GNP is a measure of the current year's output, we must omit any consumption of past production, that is, any drawing down of inventories, in determining GNP.

Actual versus planned investment. At the risk of getting ahead of ourselves, it is to be emphasized that changes in inventories are a basic cause of "actual," or "realized," investment's getting out of kilter with the investment "plans," or "intentions," of businessmen. Business firms have more or less complete control over their intentions to buy machinery and equipment or to construct a new building or warehouse. Hence, whether or not a firm's intentions to buy new equipment are realized is a matter which lies immediately at the discretion of the firm itself. Not so with inventories. A businessman cannot control his volume of sales. Thus, if sales are unexpectedly low, a firm or industry might end the year with much larger inventories than was intended or desired. Actual investment exceeds intended investment. Or the opposite might occur: because of an unexpectedly high volume of sales, the firm finds at the end of the year that its inventories are lower than planned. In this case, intended investment exceeds actual investment. We shall have much more to say about the differences between intentions and realizations in ensuing chapters. The important point to keep in mind at this juncture is that intentions, or plans, on the one hand, and what is actually accomplished, on the other, may be much different. The national income accounts are measures of what *has* happened; hence, gross private domestic investment is a measure of *actual* investment.

Noninvestment transactions. We have discussed what investment is; it is equally important to emphasize what investment is not. Specifically, investment does not refer to the transfer of paper assets or secondhand tangible assets. The buying of stocks and bonds is excluded from the economist's definition of investment, because such purchases merely transfer the ownership of existing assets. The same holds true of the resale of existing assets. Investment is the construction or manufacture of *new* capital assets. It is the creation of such earning assets that gives rise to jobs and income, not the exchange of claims to existing capital goods.

We have now broadened our concepts of investment and investment goods to include purchases of machinery and equipment, all construction, and changes in inventories. Now let us focus our attention on the three modifiers, "gross," "private," and "domestic," which national income accountants see fit to use in describing investment. The second and third terms simply tell us that we are talking about spending by private business enterprises as opposed to governmental (public) agencies and that the firms involved are American—as opposed to foreign—firms.

Gross versus net investment. The term "gross," however, cannot be disposed of so easily. *Gross private domestic investment* includes the production of all investment goods—those which are to replace the machinery and equipment used up in the current year's production plus any net additions to the economy's stock of capital. In short, gross investment includes both replacement and added investment. On the other hand, we reserve the term *net private domestic investment* to refer only to the added investment which has occurred in the current year. A simple example will make the distinction clear. In 1961 our economy produced about $70 billion worth of capital goods. However, in the process of producing the GNP in 1961 the economy used up some $45 billion worth of machinery and equipment. As a result, our economy added $25 (or $70

minus $45) billion to its stock of capital in 1961. Therefore, *gross* investment was $70 billion in 1961, but *net* investment was only $25 billion. The difference between the two is the value of the capital used up or depreciated in the production of 1961's GNP.

Net investment and economic growth. The relationship between gross investment and depreciation provides a good indicator of whether or not our economy is expanding, static, or declining. Figure 10-1 illustrates these three cases. When gross investment exceeds depreciation, as in Figure 10-1*a*, the economy is obviously expanding in the sense that its productive capacity—as measured by its stock of capital goods—is growing. More simply, net investment is a positive figure in an expanding economy. For example, as noted above, in 1961 gross investment was $70 billion, and $45 billion worth of capital goods were consumed in producing that year's GNP. This meant that our economy ended 1961 with $25 billion more capital goods than it had on hand at the start of the year. Increasing the supply of capital goods, you will recall, is a basic means of expanding the productive capacity of the economy.

A stationary or static economy reflects the situation in which gross investment and depreciation are equal. This means the economy is just standing pat; it is producing just enough capital to replace what is consumed in producing the year's output—no more or no less. In 1942, as the United States attempted to push its production of military goods into high gear, our economy approximated this situation. Resources were purposely diverted from the production of capital goods for nonessential industries, and even in essential industries resources were used sparingly for the production of capital goods. Why? Because the wartime emergency demanded astonishing amounts of finished war goods and the lion's share of our available resources was directed toward attaining that goal. Therefore, it is not surprising in 1942 that both gross investment and depreciation were approximately $10 billion. This meant that at the end of 1942 our stock of

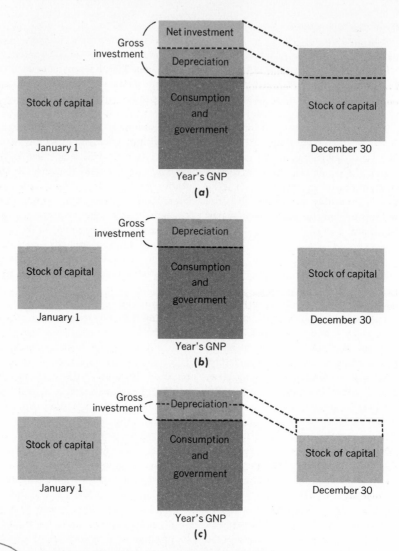

FIGURE 10-1. EXPANDING, STATIC, AND DECLINING ECONOMIES.
In an expanding economy (*a*), gross investment exceeds depreciation, which means that the economy is making a net addition to its stock of capital facilities. In a static economy (*b*), gross investment precisely replaces the capital facilities depreciated in producing the year's output, leaving the stock of capital goods unchanged. In a declining economy (*c*), gross investment is insufficient to replace the capital goods depreciated by the year's production. As a result, the economy's stock of capital declines.

capital was about the same as at the start of that year. In other words, *net* investment was about zero. Our economy was a stationary one in the sense that its productive facilities failed to

expand. Figure 10-1*b* represents the case of a static economy.

The unhappy case of a declining economy arises whenever gross investment is less than depreciation, that is, when the economy consumes more capital in a year than it manages to produce. Under such circumstances net investment will be a negative figure—the economy will be "disinvesting." Depressions foster such circumstances. During bad times, when production and employment are at a low ebb, the nation has a greater productive capacity than it is currently utilizing. Hence, there is little or no incentive to replace depreciated capital equipment, much less add to the existing stock. Depreciation is likely to outweigh gross investment, with the result that the nation's stock of capital is less at the end of the year than it was at the start. This was the case during the heart of the Great Depression. In 1933, for example, gross investment was only $1.4 billion, while the capital consumed during that year was $7.2 billion. Net disinvestment was therefore $5.8 billion. Figure 10-1c illustrates the case of a disinvesting, or declining, economy.

We shall use the symbol "I" to refer to domestic investment spending and attach the subscript "g" when referring to gross and "n" when referring to net investment.

Net foreign investment (F)

How do American international trade transactions enter into national income accounting? We can best explain it in this way: First, remember that we are trying to add up all spending in American markets which accounts for or induces the output of goods and services in the American economy. A bit of reflection will lead you to the conclusion that spending by foreigners on American goods will account for American output just as will spending by Americans. Hence, we want to add in what foreigners spend on American goods and services in determining GNP by the expenditures approach. On the other hand, what about spending by Americans on goods and services brought into American markets by foreigners? Obviously this spending induces the output of foreign goods and services. Thus, in determining the GNP for the United States by the expenditures approach we would want to subtract this type of spending from total ex-

penditures. Why? Because it accounts for no domestic production. Rather than treat these two items separately, our national income accountants simply take the difference between the two. Hence, *net foreign investment* is defined as *the amount by which foreign spending on American goods and services exceeds American spending on foreign goods and services.* For example, should foreigners buy $9 billion worth of American goods and services and Americans buy $7 billion worth of foreign goods and services in a given year, net foreign investment would be plus $2 billion. It must be emphasized that our definition of net foreign investment might result in a negative figure. If foreigners spend $10 billion on American goods and services and Americans spend $12 billion on foreign goods and services, our "excess" of foreign spending over American spending is minus $2 billion.

Although the goods and services which flow in international trade include both consumer goods and capital goods, national income accountants call the excess of exports over imports net foreign *investment*. There are two good reasons for this. First, like the domestic production of capital goods, the net exports of goods and services to foreigners, whether these be capital or consumer goods, create money income in the domestic economy without an offsetting volume of goods for domestic consumption. Net exports, like investment, create income domestically but not goods for domestic consumption. Second, like domestic production of capital goods, (positive) net foreign investment adds to the net worth of the economy. Domestic investment increases the amount of tangible assets, that is, the capital equipment, owned by the economy as a going concern. Similarly, foreign nations settle up for an excess of American exports over imports by giving American claims against foreign real assets. These claims, like an increase in domestic investment, increase the net worth of the United States economy.

The letter "F" will be used to designate net foreign investment.

The four categories of expenditures that we have discussed—personal consumption expenditures (C), gross private domestic investment (I_g), government expenditures on goods and services (G), and net foreign investment (F)—are comprehensive. They include all possible types of spending. Added together they measure the market value of the year's output; they measure GNP.

THE INCOME APPROACH TO GNP

During 1961 the total expenditures (that is, $C + I_g + G + F$) were $521.3 billion. How was this $521.3 billion allocated or distributed as income? It would be most convenient if we could say that the total expenditures upon the economy's annual output flow to households as wage, rent, interest, and profit incomes. Unfortunately, the picture is complicated somewhat by two nonincome charges against the value of total output, that is, against GNP. These are (1) a capital consumption allowance and (2) indirect business taxes.

Depreciation: capital consumption allowances

It was noted in Chapter 8 that the useful life of most capital equipment extends far beyond the year of purchase. Actual expenditures for capital goods and their productive life are not synchronized in the same accounting period. Hence, to avoid gross understatement of profit and therefore of total income in the year of purchase and overstatement of profit and of total income in succeeding years, individual businesses estimate the useful life of their capital goods and allocate the total cost of such goods more or less evenly over the life of the machinery. The annual charge which estimates the amount of capital equipment used up in each year's production is called "depreciation." Depreciation is essentially a bookkeeping entry designed to provide a more accurate statement of profit income and hence total income provided by a firm in each year.

If profits and total income for the economy as a whole are to be stated accurately, a gigantic depreciation charge for the economy as a whole must be made against the total receipts of the business sector. This depreciation charge is called a "capital consumption allowance." Why? Because that is exactly what it is—an allowance for capital goods which have been "consumed" in the process of producing this year's GNP. It is this huge depreciation charge which constitutes the previously noted difference between I_g and I_n. For present purposes, the significance of this charge lies in the fact that it designates a part of the business sector's receipts which is not available for income payments to resource suppliers. In real terms, that is, in terms of physical goods and services, the capital consumption allowance tells us in effect that a portion of this year's GNP must be set aside to replace the machinery and equipment used up in accomplishing its production. In other words, all of GNP cannot be consumed as income by society without impairing the economy's stock of productive facilities.

Indirect business taxes

The second complicating nonincome charge arises from the presence of government. Government levies certain taxes—in particular, general sales taxes, excise and business property taxes, license fees, and customs duties—which business firms treat as costs of production and therefore add to the prices of the products they sell. These taxes, as a matter of fact, are called "indirect business taxes" because sales taxes and excises are not levied directly upon the corporation, partnership, or proprietorship as such but rather upon their products or services. Businessmen, knowing the sizes of such levies, pass them on to the consumer in the form of higher prices. We can think of it in this way: A firm produces a product designed to sell at, say, $1. As we have seen, the production of this item creates an equal amount of wages, rental, interest, and profit income. But now government, in need of revenue to finance its activities, imposes a 2 per cent sales tax on all products sold at retail. The retailer simply adds this 2 per cent to the price of the product, raising its price from $1 to $1.02 and thereby shifting the burden of the sales tax to consumers.

Obviously, this 2 per cent of total receipts

which reflects the tax must be paid out to government before the remaining $1 can be paid to households as wage, rent, interest, and profit incomes. Government, in effect, is a preferred creditor. Furthermore, this flow of indirect business taxes to government is not earned income, because government contributes nothing directly to the production of the good in return for these sales tax receipts. As a matter of fact, in the case of sales and excise taxes the finished product is being handed to the consumer at the time the tax is levied. In short, we must be careful to exclude indirect business taxes when figuring the total income earned in each year by the factors of production.

Capital consumption allowances and indirect business taxes account for the nonincome allocations listed in Table 10-5. As just noted, what remains is wages, rents, interest, and profits. But for a variety of reasons national income statisticians need a more sophisticated breakdown of wages and profits than we have employed thus far in this discussion.

Wages

Specifically, wages are broken into two parts. The first we shall term *compensations to employees.* This high-sounding term includes all wages, salaries, bonuses, royalties, commissions, tips, and so forth, which flow back to labor suppliers as income. A second part of wages is *social security contributions.* This includes both the required payments made by employers and employees under our social security program.[4] We treat this part of wages separately because it flows not to households but rather to government. (We shall take payments out of our social security program into account later in this discussion.) To the businessman, social security contributions are a cost involved in obtaining

[4] As the social security program now stands, both employer and employee pay 3⅝ per cent on each dollar earned up to $4,800 per year. Self-employed individuals pay 5.4 per cent on the first $4,800 earned each year. Social security legislation provides for future increases in these payroll tax rates. The American social security system is discussed in a later chapter.

labor; such payments constitute deferred wage income to be received later by the labor supplier. From the worker's viewpoint, his contributions to social security amount to wage income earned but withheld to be received in the future during his retirement or during a siege of unemployment. The important points are these: (1) social security contributions constitute currently earned wage income but (2) are treated apart from other wages income because they flow to government instead of to households.

Rents

Rents are almost self-explanatory. They consist of income payments received by households that supply property resources.

Interest

Interest refers to money income payments which flow from private businesses to the suppliers of money capital. For reasons to be noted later, government interest payments are excluded from interest income.

Proprietors' income

What we have loosely termed "profits" is also broken into two basic accounts by national income accountants: one part is called proprietors' income or *income of unincorporated businesses* and the other *corporate profits.* The former account is largely self-defining. It refers to the profits of sole proprietorships, partnerships, and cooperatives. On the other hand, corporate profits cannot be dismissed so easily because corporate earnings may be distributed in several ways.

Corporate profits

Generally speaking, three things can be done with corporate profits: First, a part will be claimed by, and therefore flow to, government as *corporate income taxes.* Second, a part of the remaining corporate profits will be paid out to stockholders as *dividends.* Such payments flow

TABLE 10-6. THE INCOME STATEMENT FOR THE ECONOMY, 1961 (in billions of dollars)

Receipts: expenditures approach		*Allocations: income approach*	
Personal consumption expenditures		Capital consumption allowance	$ 45.2
(C)	$339.0	Indirect business taxes	45.9
Government purchases of goods and		Compensations to employees	281.1
services (G)	108.7	Social security contributions	21.8
Gross private domestic investment (I_g) ..	69.6	Rents	11.5
Net foreign investment (F)	4.0	Interest	20.0
		Proprietors' income	49.6
		Corporate income taxes	22.8
		Dividends	14.4
		Undistributed corporate profits	8.8
Gross national product	$521.3	Gross national product	$521.3

SOURCE: Department of Commerce data. Details may not add up to totals because of rounding.

to households, which, of course, are the ultimate owners of all corporations. What remains of corporate profits after both corporate income taxes and dividends have been paid is called *undistributed corporate profits*. These retained corporate earnings, along with capital consumption allowances, are invested currently or in the future in new plants and equipment, thereby increasing the real assets of the investing businesses.

Table 10-6 summarizes our detailed discussions of both the expenditure and income approaches to GNP. The reader will recognize that this is merely a gigantic income statement for the economy as a whole. The left-hand side tells us what the economy produced in 1961 and the total receipts derived from that production. The right-hand side indicates how the income derived from the production of 1961's GNP was allocated. One can determine GNP by either adding up the four types of expenditures on final goods and services or by adding up the ten categories of income which stem from that output's production. Because output and income are two sides of the same coin, the two sums will necessarily match.

OTHER SOCIAL ACCOUNTS

Our discussion thus far has centered upon GNP as a measure of the economy's annual output. However, there are certain related social accounting concepts of equal importance which can be derived from GNP. To round out our understanding of social accounting it is imperative that we trace through the process of deriving these related concepts. This procedure will also enhance our understanding of how the expenditure and income approaches to GNP dovetail one another. Our plan of attack will be to start with GNP and make a series of adjustments—additions and subtractions—necessary to the derivation of the related social accounts.

Net national product (NNP)

GNP as a measure of total output has a basic defect: it tends to give us a somewhat exaggerated picture of this year's production. Why? *Because it fails to make allowance for that part of this year's output which is necessary to replace the capital goods consumed in the year's production.*

Two examples will help make this point clear: First, suppose a farmer starts the year by planting 20 bushels of wheat, realizing a total output of 400 bushels at the end of the year. Is it correct to represent his output for the year as 400 bushels? Certainly not. He would have had 20 bushels available if he had planted nothing at all. His net output for the year is 400 minus 20, or 380 bushels. This is a more accurate measure of the production that has actually occurred this year than is 400 bushels.

Second, using hypothetical figures, suppose that on January 1, 1963, the economy had $50 billion worth of capital goods on hand. Assume also that during 1963 $20 billion worth of this equipment and machinery is used up in producing a GNP of $450 billion. Thus, on December 31, 1963, the stock of capital goods on hand stands at only $30 billion. Is it fair to say that the GNP figure of $450 billion accurately measures this year's output? No. It would be much more accurate to subtract from the year's GNP the $20 billion worth of capital goods which must be used to replace the machinery and equipment consumed in producing that GNP. This leaves a net output figure of $450 minus $20, or $430 billion.

In short, a figure for *net* output is a more accurate measure of a year's production than is *gross* output. In our system of social accounting we derive a figure for *net national product* (NNP) by subtracting the capital consumption allowance, which measures the value of the capital used up in a year's production, from GNP. Hence, in 1961

	Billions
Gross national product	$521.3
Capital consumption allowance	−45.2
Net national product	$476.1

NNP then is simply GNP adjusted for depreciation charges. It measures the total annual output which the entire economy—households, business, and governments—might consume without impairing our capacity to produce in ensuing years.

It is a simple matter, by the way, to adjust Table 10-6 from GNP to NNP. On the income side we simply strike out capital consumption allowances. The other nine allocations should add up to a NNP of $476.1 billion. On the expenditure side, one must change gross private domestic investment to net private domestic investment by subtracting replacement investment as measured by the capital consumption allowance from the former figure. In 1961, a gross investment figure of $69.6 billion less a

depreciation charge of $45.2 billion results in a net private domestic investment figure of $24.4 billion and therefore a NNP of $476.1 billion.

National income (NI)

In analyzing certain problems we are vitally interested in how much income is *earned* by resource suppliers for their contributions of land, labor, capital, and entrepreneurial ability which go into the year's net production or, alternatively stated, how much it costs society in terms of economic resources to produce this net output. The only component of NNP which does not reflect the current productive contributions of economic resources is indirect business taxes. It will be recalled that government contributes nothing to production in return for the indirect business tax revenues which it receives; government is not considered to be a factor of production. Hence, to get a measure of total wage, rent, interest, and profit incomes earned from the production of the year's output, indirect business taxes must be subtracted from NNP. The resulting figure is called the *national income.* From the viewpoint of resource suppliers it measures the incomes they have earned for their current contributions to production. From the viewpoint of businesses, national income measures factor or resource costs; national income reflects the market costs of the economic resources which have gone into the creation of this year's output. In 1961

	Billions
Net national product	$476.1
Indirect business taxes	−45.9
National income	$430.2

A glance at Table 10-6 shows that national income can also be obtained through the income approach by simply adding up all the allocations with the exception of capital consumption allowances and indirect business taxes. That is, the eight allocations of GNP which remain after the two nonincome changes have been subtracted constitute the national income.

Personal income (PI)

It was noted in Chapter 7 that income earned (national income) and income received (personal income) are likely to differ, for the simple reason that some income which is earned —social security contributions, corporate income taxes, and undistributed corporate profits —is not actually received by households and, conversely, some income which is received— transfer payments—is not currently earned. Transfer payments, you may recall, are comprised of such items as (1) old age and survivors insurance payments and unemployment compensation, both of which stem from our social security program, (2) relief payments, (3) a variety of veterans' payments, for example, GI Bill of Rights and disability payments, and (4) interest payments on the public debt.[5] Obviously, in moving from national income as a measure of income earned to personal income as an indicator of income actually received we must subtract from national income those three types of income which are earned but not received and add in income received but not currently earned. This is done as follows:

	Billions
National income (income earned)	$430.2
Social security contributions	−21.8
Corporate income taxes	−22.8
Undistributed corporate profits	−8.8
Transfer payments	+39.9
Personal income (income received)	$416.7

[5] Why include interest payments on government bonds as income *not* currently earned, particularly when interest on the bonds of private firms is included in national income as earned income? The rationale underlying the exclusion is this: war-bond sales financed the government's purchase of wartime assets, and, unlike the railroad equipment or factories purchased with the proceeds of private bond sales some ten or twenty years ago, wartime assets of 1940–1944 vintage no longer provide any current services for the economy.

Also included in transfer payments is a small amount of private transfers flowing from businesses to households in the form of pensions.

It is possible that personal income may exceed national income. For example, in 1933 personal income exceeded national income by some $7 billion. This occurred because during the Great Depression the three subtracted items were small and the added item large. Can you explain why?

Disposable income (DI)

In Chapter 7 we saw that households dispose of their personal income in three ways: First, a sizable portion flows to government in the form of *personal taxes*. Personal income taxes, personal property taxes, and inheritance taxes constitute personal taxes, the first of the three being by far the most important. What remains of personal income after personal taxes have been paid is *disposable income*. Households are free to dispose of disposable income as they see fit. Basically, the choices are two. Remembering that the economist conveniently defines personal saving as "not spending," or better, "that part of disposable income which is not spent on consumer goods," it is obvious that households divide their disposable income between personal consumption expenditures and personal saving. There are only two choices: to spend or to save. The difference between personal income and disposable income and the division of the latter are shown for 1961:

	Billions
Personal income (income received before personal taxes)	$416.7
Personal taxes	−51.8
Disposable income (income received after personal taxes)	$364.9
Personal consumption expenditures ..	−339.0
Personal saving	$ 25.9

Personal saving is a residual, that is, the amount remaining after personal taxes and personal consumption expenditures have been taken out of personal income. Remember, too, that households might dissave; they may consume in excess of their disposable incomes by drawing down on past savings or by borrowing. Such was the case in 1933 when personal saving was minus $0.6 billion.

A final comment: it is worth noting that just as GNP, NNP, and NI can be derived by adding up their component parts, so can PI and DI. DI is obviously the sum of personal saving and personal consumption expenditures. PI is the sum of personal saving, personal consumption expenditures, and personal taxes. The reader should employ the figures used in the above calculation of personal saving to verify these points.

Relationships between major social accounts

We have derived four new social accounting concepts from GNP: (1) net national product (NNP), the market value of the annual output net of capital consumption allowances, (2) national income (NI), income *earned* by the factors of production for their current contributions to production or the factor costs entailed in getting the year's total output produced, (3) personal income (PI), income *received* before personal taxes, and (4) disposable income (DI), income received less personal taxes.

The relationships among these concepts are summarized in Table 10-7.

SUMMARY

Figure 10-2 embodies a comprehensive summary and synthesis of all the social accounting measures discussed in this chapter. As a more realistic and more complex expression of the circular flow model of the economy (discussed in an earlier chapter) this figure merits careful study by the reader. Starting at the GNP rectangle in the upper left-hand corner, the expenditures side of GNP is shown to the left. For simplicity's sake, we have assumed net foreign investment to be zero. Immediately to the right of the GNP rectangle are the ten income components of GNP and then the various additions and subtractions which are needed in the derivation of NNP, NI, and PI. In the household sector we see the flow of personal taxes out of PI and the division of DI between consumption and personal saving. In the government sector the flows of revenue in the form of four basic types of taxes are denoted on the right; on the left, government disbursements take the form of purchases of goods and services and transfers. To simplify, a balanced budget is assumed in the public sector. The position

TABLE 10-7. THE RELATIONSHIPS BETWEEN GNP, NNP, NI, PI, AND DI IN 1961 (in billions of dollars)

Gross National Product (GNP)	$ 521.3
Capital consumption allowances	−45.2
Net National Product (NNP)	$ 476.1
Indirect business taxes	−45.9
National income (NI)	$ 430.2
Social security contributions	−21.8
Corporate income taxes	−22.8
Undistributed corporate profits	−8.8
Transfer payments	+39.9
Personal income (PI)	$ 416.7
Personal taxes	−51.8
Disposable income (DI)	$ 364.9
Personal consumption expenditures (C)	−339.0
Personal saving	$ 25.9

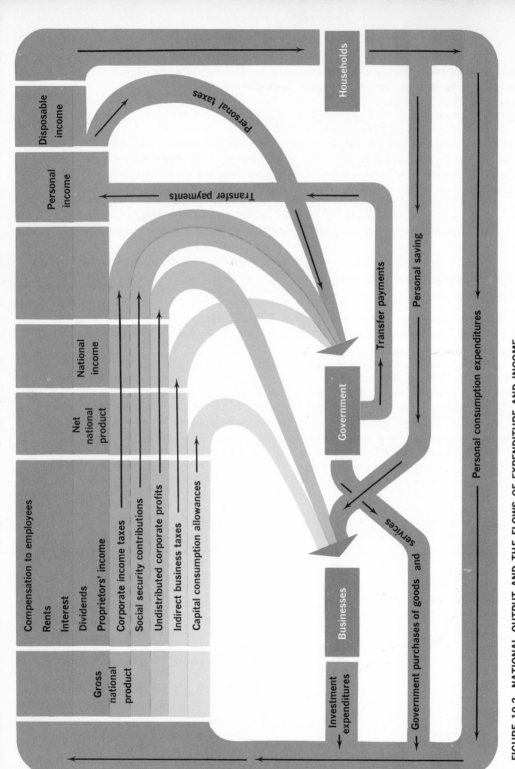

FIGURE 10-2. NATIONAL OUTPUT AND THE FLOWS OF EXPENDITURE AND INCOME.
This figure is an elaborate circular flow diagram which fits the expenditures and allocations sides of GNP to one another. The reader should trace through the income and expenditures flows, relating them to the five basic national income accounting measures.

of the business sector is such as to emphasize, on the left, investment expenditures and, on the right, the three major sources of funds for business investment.

The astute reader will note that the sum of gross business saving (capital consumption allowance and undistributed corporate profits) and personal saving is equal to business investment in Figure 10-2. This requires brief comment. How do these saving flows get spent and therefore become investment? It is not too surprising that business saving is invested; after all, the expansion of capital facilities is a basic reason underlying business saving. And, too, one can see how the portions of personal saving which are exchanged for newly issued business securities or deposited in financial institutions such as banks and then loaned out will find their way into the investment stream. Yet, given the fact that saving and investment are at least in part carried out by different groups (households and businesses) in the economy, it would seem a very extraordinary coincidence if, in any year, the total saving of the economy was precisely equal to the total of investment, as Figure 10-2 suggests is the case. Specifically, what if households should simply hoard a part of their saving, thereby making it inaccessible to possible investors? Won't this cause saving to exceed investment? The answer to this dilemma lies in the way national income accountants define investment to include changes in inventories. The circular flow diagram indicates that for every dollar's worth of current output there is created a dollar's worth of income. If a portion of this income is neither spent on consumer goods nor made available through financial institutions for investment, then obviously a part of current production will remain unsold. That is, a part of current output will be added to inventories. But we stressed in our earlier discussion of gross private domestic investment that an inventory increase is a part of investment. If consumers or other businesses fail to purchase a part of a firm's current output, that firm itself will have engaged in (unintended) investment in the form of a rise in inventories. Thus, in national income accounting total investment *must* be equal to total saving.

More will be said of the equality of investment and saving in Chapter 13.

The major virtue of Figure 10-2 is that it simultaneously portrays the expenditure and income aspects of GNP, fitting the two approaches to one another. This figure correctly indicates that these flows of expenditure and income are part of a continuous, repetitive process. Cause and effect are intermingled: expenditures give rise to income, and out of this income arise expenditures which again flow to resource owners as income, and so forth.

Finally, the following concise definitions of the most important measures of the economy's performance should be thoroughly understood in studying the diagram of Figure 10-2:

1. *Gross national product* (GNP) refers to the market value of all final goods and services produced in the economy in a given year.

2. *Net national product* (NNP) is gross national product minus capital consumption allowances (depreciation). NNP may also be found by summing personal consumption expenditures, *net private domestic investment, government purchases* of goods and services, and net foreign investment.

3. *National income* (NI) is the total income *earned* by resource suppliers for their contributions to the production of GNP National income also measures the costs of the resources used up in producing GNP. Its magnitude can be derived by subtracting indirect business taxes from NNP or by summing compensations to employees, social security contributions, rents, interest, corporate income taxes, dividends, undistributed corporate profits, and the income of unincorporated businesses.

4. *Personal income* (PI) is the total income *received* by households during a given year. PI is determined by subtracting from national income that income which is earned but not received (social security contributions, corporate income taxes, and undistributed corporate profits) and adding that income which is received but not earned (transfer payments).

5. *Disposable income* (DI) is the portion of

personal income which remains after the payment of personal taxes. Disposable income is divided between personal consumption expenditures and personal saving.

QUESTIONS AND STUDY SUGGESTIONS

1. "National income statistics are a powerful tool of economic understanding and analysis." Explain.

2. Why do national income accountants compare the market value of the total outputs in various years rather than actual physical volumes of production? Explain. What problem is posed by any comparison of the market values of various total outputs? How is this problem resolved?

3. Carefully and completely define (*a*) gross national product and (*b*) net national product. How do these measures differ?

4. What are final goods? Intermediate goods? Why do national income accountants include only final goods in measuring total output?

5. What is "double counting"? Give an example.

6. "An economy's output is its income." Do you agree? Explain.

7. What is the difference between gross private domestic investment and net private domestic investment? If you were to determine net national product through the expenditures approach, which of these two measures of investment spending would be appropriate? Explain.

8. Why are changes in inventories included as a part of investment spending? Suppose inventories declined by $1 billion during 1963. How would this affect the size of gross private domestic investment and gross national product in 1963? Explain.

9. Distinguish between an "expanding," a "static," and a "declining" economy.

10. "In 1933 net private domestic investment was minus $5.8 billion. This means in that particular year the economy produced no capital goods at all." Do you agree? Explain: "Though net investment can be positive, negative, or zero, it is quite impossible for gross investment to be less than zero."

11. Define net foreign investment. Suppose foreigners spend $7 billion on American goods and services in a given year. In the same year Americans spend $5 billion on foreign goods and services. What is net foreign investment?

12. The following is a list of national income figures for a given year. All figures are in billions. The ensuing questions will ask you to determine the major national income measures by both the expenditure and income methods. The answers derived by each approach should be the same.

Personal consumption expenditures	$245
Government transfer payments	12
Rents	14
Capital consumption allowances (depreciation)	27
Social security contributions	9
Interest	13
Proprietors' income	31
Net foreign investment	3

Dividends	$ 16
Compensations to employees	212
Indirect business taxes	18
Undistributed corporate profits	21
Personal taxes	37
Corporate income taxes	19
Government expenditures on goods and services	72
Net private domestic investment	33
Personal saving	16

a. Using the above data, determine GNP and NNP by both the expenditure and income methods.

b. Now determine NI (1) by making the required subtractions from GNP and (2) by adding up the types of income which comprise NI.

c. Make those adjustments for NI required in deriving PI. Now determine PI by adding up its various components.

d. Make the required adjustments from PI (as determined in 12c) to obtain DI. Also determine DI by adding up its component parts.

13. Given the following national income accounting data, compute (*a*) GNP, (*b*) NNP, and (*c*) NI. All figures are in billions.

Compensations to employees	$194.2
Exports of goods and services from the United States	13.4
Capital consumption allowances	11.8
Government purchases of goods and services	59.4
Indirect business taxes	12.2
Net private domestic investment	52.1
Government transfer payments	13.9
Imports of goods and services to the United States	16.5
Personal taxes	40.5
Personal consumption expenditures	219.1

14. The following table shows money GNP and an appropriate price index for a group of selected years. Compute real GNP.

Year	Money GNP, billions	Price level index, per cent (1954 = 100)	Real GNP, billions
1930	$ 91.1	55.4	
1932	56.0	44.9	
1938	85.2	48.7	
1943	192.5	64.9	
1947	234.3	83.0	
1956	419.2	104.6	
1960	504.4	114.4	

Indicate in each calculation whether you are "inflating" or "deflating" the money GNP data.

15. Which of the following are actually included in deriving this year's GNP? Explain your answer in each case.

a. Interest on an AT&T bond

b. Social security payments received by a retired factory worker

c. The services of a painter in painting his own home

d. The income of a dentist

e. The money received by Smith when he sells a 1960 Chevrolet to Jones

f. The monthly allowance which a college student receives from home

g. Rent received on a two-bedroom apartment

h. The money received by Wilson when he resells this year's model Plymouth to Wilcox

i. Interest received on government bonds

j. A two-hour decline in the length of the work week

k. The purchase of an AT&T bond

l. A $2 billion increase in business inventories

m. The purchase of ten shares of GM common stock

n. The purchase of an insurance policy

o. Wages paid to a domestic servant

p. The market value of a housewife's services

q. The purchase of a Renaissance painting by a public art museum

16. Explain: "A man diminishes the national income by marrying his cook."

SELECTED REFERENCES

Dernburg, Thomas F., and Duncan M. McDougall, *Macro-economics* (New York: McGraw-Hill Book Company, Inc., 1960), chaps. 1–5.

Department of Commerce, *Survey of Current Business*. July issues contain annual national income data.

Edey, Harold C., and Alan T. Peacock, *National Income and Social Accounting* (London: Hutchinson's University Library, 1954).

Peterson, Wallace C., *Income, Employment, and Economic Growth* (New York: W. W. Norton & Company, Inc., 1962), chaps. 2 and 3.

Ruggles, Richard, and Nancy D. Ruggles, *National Income Accounts and Income Analysis*, 2d ed. (New York: McGraw-Hill Book Company, Inc., 1956), particularly chaps. 1, 2, 6, and 7.

Chapter 11

THE BUSINESS CYCLE:

UNEMPLOYMENT AND INFLATION

THE EMPHASIS in Part 1 of this book was on full production. To facilitate our discussion of how American capitalism allocates resources, we assumed that resources would be fully employed. But actual experience indicates that American capitalism cannot take full employment for granted. Hence, in Part 2 of this book we seek to explore the problem of achieving and maintaining full employment in American capitalism.

The goals of the present chapter are essentially threefold. First, we seek to understand the meaning and significance of full employment and the immediate determinant of the level of employment. Second, the major characteristics of the business cycle are explored. Emphasis here is upon the changes in output, employment, income, and the price level which are embodied in the business cycle. Finally, the cyclical experiences of American capitalism since 1920 are surveyed to gain additional insights into the actual operation of the business cycle.

THE MEANING OF FULL EMPLOYMENT

How is "full employment" defined? When are the economy's resources fully utilized? We shall define full employment as a situation wherein everyone who is willing and able to work at prevailing wage rates and under prevailing working conditions can find a job in the line of work in which he is trained. Two facets of this definition merit comment:

1. Full employment is couched in terms of labor rather than property resources. Why? On the one hand, wages are the major component of the national income, accounting for roughly two-thirds of the total. In addition, it is easier to get a relatively precise quantitative measure of unemployment in terms of labor than it is in terms of, say, capital. It would be extremely difficult to come up with a homogeneous measure of the extent to which the economy is employing its property facilities.

2. Full employment does not mean that everyone has a job. Some people are simply not able to work. They are "too young," "too old," or handicapped either physically or mentally. These people are not unemployed; rather, they are simply not a part of the economy's available resources. Other people are able but not willing to work. The coupon clipper of the top income class is in a financial position to shun employment; the college student seeks to develop his latent talents before entering the labor force; the housewife has no time to devote to gainful employment in office or factory. Like those unable to work, these people are simply not available resources. In other words,

189

the unemployed are those who are *involuntarily idle.* They are able and willing to work but the economy provides no job opportunities for them.

In a capitalistic economy some unemployment is regarded as normal. That is, at any point in time some workers are in the process of voluntarily changing jobs and hence are temporarily unemployed. Others may be temporarily out of work because of some labor-saving technological improvement or a change in consumer tastes which has adversely affected employment in their industry. Such unemployment is looked upon as necessary—indeed, healthy—in a free, dynamic economy. It is desirable and normal that workers leave unprosperous in favor of prosperous industries. As we saw in Part 1, an efficient allocation of resources demands these shifts. Experience indicates that, on the average, such unemployment may amount to 3 to 4 per cent of the total labor force.

Because the current labor force of American capitalism is composed of some 72 million workers, an unemployment figure of 2 to 3 million is looked upon as normal. In practice, "full employment" exists today when 69 million of the economy's 72 million workers are employed.

Implications of unemployment

 The economic importance of achieving full employment is almost self-evident. The failure to utilize available resources, able and willing to be employed in the production of goods and services, is the height of economic inefficiency. The economic cost of unemployment is the unproduced goods and services which society could have enjoyed if it had managed to employ its resources fully. The economic cost of unemployment, thus measured, can be astronomical. One scholar[1] has estimated the cost of the Great Depression of the 1930s in these terms:

[1] Sherman J. Maisel, *Fluctuations, Growth, and Forecasting* (New York: John Wiley & Sons, Inc., 1957), p. 18.

A full-employment output for the 1930s would have produced $650 billion additional goods and services in terms of the 1956 price level. Such a sum would have been higher than the material cost of World War II. It would have meant roughly $5,000 more in income for each individual in the United States in that decade, or $20,000 more for the average family. If all resources had been fully employed in this manner, every family could have had a new house, several new cars, and most of the other durable goods it desired.

But unemployment is much more than an economic catastrophe; it is a social catastrophe as well. Depression means idleness. And idleness means loss of skills, loss of self-respect, a plummeting of morale, and sociopolitical unrest. The following commentaries[2] from the unemployed of the 1930s provide important insights into the noneconomic aspects of unemployment:

There is no substitute for work. . . . There is nothing I can do to keep myself efficient; odd repairs in a house are no substitute for constructional work on a steam engine.

The wife works while I look after the home. . . . Any long spell of unemployment leaves you with little to be proud of and much to be ashamed of. Our child is still too young to realize that it is her mother who works. We carefully keep her from knowing it.

These last few years since I've been out of the mills I don't seem able to take trouble, somehow; I've got no spirit for anything. But I didn't use to be like that.

My husband is a good man and he does a lot for me in the house. . . . But he is a changed

[2] Quotations cited in William H. Beveridge, *Full Employment in a Free Society* (New York: W. W. Norton & Company, Inc., 1945), pp. 243–244. The reader who wants to pursue the sociopolitical implications of prolonged unemployment will do well to consult David A. Shannon (ed.), *The Great Depression* (Englewood Cliffs, N.J.: Prentice-Hall, Inc., 1960).

man these last two years. He never complains, but I wish he would. It makes me unhappy to find him becoming quieter and quieter, when I know what he must be feeling. If I had someone to talk to about my troubles I should feel much better. . . . We quarrel far more now than we have ever done in our lives before. We would both rather be dead than go on like this.

History makes it all too clear that severe unemployment is conducive to rapid and sometimes violent social and political change. Witness the movement to the left of American political philosophy during the Depression of the 1930s. The Depression-inspired New Deal was a veritable revolution in American political and economic thinking. Witness also Hitler's ascent to power amidst a background of unemployment.

Total spending

The immediate determinant of the volume of employment is the level of total spending. In a price-directed economy such as American capitalism, businesses produce only those goods which can be sold profitably. Now obviously, if total spending is large, that is, if the demand for goods and services in general is great, businesses will be able to produce and profitably sell a large volume of goods and services. To accomplish a large volume of production, businesses will be required to employ a large volume of resources. And this means high incomes. In brief, a high level of spending will make profitable a large volume of output, and this entails a high level of employment. Conversely, a low level of total spending means that the demand for goods and services in general is depressed. This means, in turn, that the volume of output will be small; few goods and services can be sold profitably. And a small output can be produced with a small amount of resources. A low level of total spending means that resources will be involuntarily unemployed. And, finally, unemployment means low incomes.

Spending, output, employment, and demand-pull inflation

Although total spending, on the one hand, and output and employment, on the other, are directly related, this relationship is not completely rigid. When widespread unemployment prevails, a given increase in total spending will have a greater immediate impact [3] upon real output and employment than will that same increase in spending when the economy is operating near, or at, full employment. In particular, price changes loosen the link between changes in spending and the volumes of output and employment as the economy approaches full employment. Let us see exactly how this comes about:

1. Suppose initially that the economy has a large amount of unemployed resources at a time when total spending, for some reason or another, increases. In terms of specific goods, this will mean that demand has increased in relation to supply. As stated earlier, increases in the demand for specific products will have both a price-increasing and a quantity-increasing effect. During periods of substantial unemployment the price-increasing effect of an increase in demand will tend to be small and the output effect large. Why? Most obviously, there are large amounts of virtually all types of human and property resources which can be readily employed by firms *at current resource prices* to expand their outputs. Furthermore, the plants of many producers will be operating at less than their designed capacity during a period of unemployment. Hence, an expansion of output may result in a more efficient utilization of existing capital facilities. For both these reasons businesses will find that they can increase their output in response to an increase in consumer demand without any appreciable increase in their unit costs of production or, therefore, in the prices they need receive for

[3] Our present discussion is concerned only with the initial impact of a change in spending upon output and employment. Secondary effects will be brought into account in ensuing chapters.

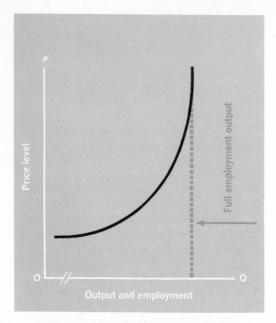

FIGURE 11-1. THE PRICE LEVEL AND THE LEVEL OF EMPLOYMENT.
The price level generally begins to rise before full employment is reached. At full employment additional spending tends to be purely inflationary.

their products. In short, during a period of widespread unemployment, an increase in demand will bring forth more or less proportionate increases in output and employment with little or no rise in prices.

2. As total spending continues to rise, however, this picture will begin to change. As production expands, supplies of unemployed resources will not vanish simultaneously. Production bottlenecks appear in the form of shortages of certain specific resources, even though unemployment is still generally widespread. As they expand output, firms will find that there are no more idle supplies of, say, skilled labor or technicians or certain metal alloys. Therefore, the prices of these fully employed resources will begin to rise as firms, anxious to partake of returning prosperity, scramble to obtain them. These price increases will mean higher costs and, in turn, that producers must

receive higher prices for their products. Labor unions will be quick to take advantage of the improved bargaining position which the decline in unemployment entails, pressing more fervently for wage increases. In addition to the developing scarcities of specific resources, costs will also rise as some firms tend to utilize their plants beyond their most efficient capacities, to man their plants with less productive workers, and to pay premium rates for overtime work. In other words, with moderate unemployment increases in the demand for products in general will have both price-increasing and output-increasing effects. Prices rise because the unit costs of producers rise.

3. When the economy reaches full employment, prices will begin to rise very sharply as total spending continues to expand. At full employment the economy encounters the production barrier of scarce resources; the economy will be operating at capacity, at a point *on* its production possibilities curve. Businessmen as a group cannot respond to increases in spending by expanding real output. This is aptly termed *demand-pull inflation* by economists: total demand in excess of society's productive capacity pulls the price level upward. Higher levels of total spending will simply bid up the prices of a fixed real output. At full employment, increases in spending will cause "pure" inflation to set in.

Figure 11-1 summarizes the relationship between the price level, on the one hand, and the levels of output and employment, on the other. The significance of the behavior of the price level as output and employment increase must be emphasized. When unemployment is great and widespread, the initial impact of an increase in total spending will be to bring forth more or less proportionate increases in output and employment. As the economy approaches full employment, however, the price level begins to rise. This means that a part of any increase in total expenditures will be dissipated in the form of higher prices, lessening its impact upon output and employment. If product X is selling at $1 per unit, a $10 increase in expenditures will induce a 10-unit increase in output. But, if the $10 increase in spending causes the price of X to rise to $2 per unit, the resulting increase in output will be just 5 units. As the economy approaches full employment, larger and larger increases in spending are required to increase real output and employment by a given amount. Once at full employment, added spending will simply pull up the price level.

The relationship expressed in Figure 11-1 is only partially reversible. That is, many product and resource prices which are flexible upwards as the economy approaches the full-employment output become relatively rigid and inflexible when declines in total spending result in reductions in output and employment. This is primarily the result of monopolistic power—the ability to influence prices—which many businesses and unions possess. Unions can usually resist wage cuts and sometimes secure modest wage boosts even though the total level of spending and therefore output and employment are falling. Monopolistic businesses are equally able to forestall reductions in product prices. Prices that go up during periods of full employment do not necessarily come down —at least all the way—when spending declines and unemployment ensues.[4] It is not surprising that the long-run trend of the price level in American capitalism has been upward. The significance of the downward inflexibility of prices will become evident in Chapter 12.

THE BUSINESS CYCLE

What is the record of American capitalism in providing for the full employment of its resources? The record is a spotty one. At times the economy has suffered from prolonged periods of underspending, the consequences of such periods being widespread unemployment, low incomes, and a depressed GNP. At other times the economy has overspent; that is, it has spent in excess of its capacity to produce.

The result has been full employment and a high GNP, on the one hand, but inflation, that is, a rising level of prices, on the other. In short, the level of economic activity has fluctuated very considerably over time. Our economy has been plagued by the business cycle—alternating periods of depression and prosperity.

The business cycle simply refers to the recurrent ups and downs in the level of economic activity which extend over a period of several years. Individual business cycles vary tremendously in detail. Yet all embody common phases which are variously labeled by different economists. Thus some economists talk of prosperity, recession, depression, and recovery as being the four phases of the business cycle. Others simply discern between the phases of expansion and contraction with upper and lower turning points to divide the two. Still other economists are content to talk merely in terms of the "upswing" and "downswing" of the business cycle.

Despite common phases, specific business cycles vary greatly. In particular, business cycles vary in duration and intensity. Measuring the interval from the peak of one prosperity phase to the peak of the next, major cyclical fluctuations average eight or nine years over-all, though some are as short as six years and others as long as twelve. Then, too, the picture is complicated by so-called minor cycles, which last an average of forty months.

Similarly, business cycles vary greatly in terms of intensity. The Great Depression of the 1930s seriously undermined the level of business activity for an entire decade. In contrast, the business declines of 1924 and 1927 were minor in both intensity and duration. Figure 11-2 provides ample historical evidence as to the existence of the business cycle and its great irregularity as to duration and intensity. It merits careful examination by the reader.

Noncyclical fluctuations in business activity

It must not be concluded that all changes in business activity are due to the business cycle. On the one hand, there are *seasonal variations* in business activity. For example, the pre-

---

[4] We shall find later that, despite the declining level of total demand which characterized the 1958 recession, the market power of unions and businesses was apparently sufficient to cause price and wage increases (so-called "cost-push" inflation).

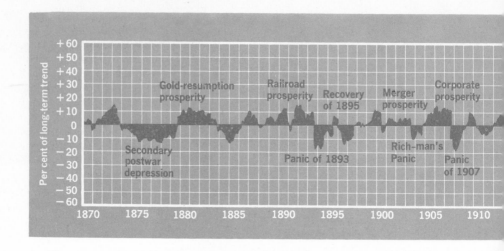

Christmas and pre-Easter buying rushes cause considerable fluctuations each year in the tempo of business activity, particularly in the retail industry. Agriculture, the automobile industry, construction—indeed, virtually all industries are subject to some degree of seasonality. These seasonal variations complicate the measurement of cyclical fluctuations in business activity. For example, an upswing in retail sales in December may or may not be evidence of a cyclical upswing in business activity. To speak with any degree of certainty one would have to compare the increase in this December's retail sales with the increase in sales which statistical records for previous Decembers indicate as being normal. If retail sales normally double in December, a tripling of sales in December, 1963, would suggest a cyclical upswing in business activity. Conversely, if retail sales for the month fall short of doubling, a cyclical downswing is implied.

Business activity is also subject to a _secular trend_. The secular trend of an economy refers to its expansion or contraction over a long period of years, for example, fifty, one hundred, or one hundred and fifty years. We simply note at this juncture that the long-run secular trend for American capitalism has entailed rather re-markable expansion, deferring detailed consideration of this growth until a later chapter. For present purposes the importance of this long-run expansion is that the business cycle entails fluctuations in business activity around a long-run growth trend. This is illustrated in Figure 11-3.

Note, too, that in Figure 11-2 cyclical fluctuations are measured as deviations from the long-run trend, a trend that has been persistently upwards. Needless to say, the long-run trend may influence the duration and intensity of particular phases of the business cycle.

The diverse impact of the business cycle

The business cycle is pervasive; it is felt in every nook and cranny of the economy. The interrelatedness of the economy allows few, if any, to escape the cold hand of depression or the fever of inflation. Periods of underspending cause the recession and depression phases of the business cycle; declining employment and production, falling incomes, and deflation are embodied in these cyclical phases. Rising levels of spending mean recovery and prosperity; expanding levels of output and employment and

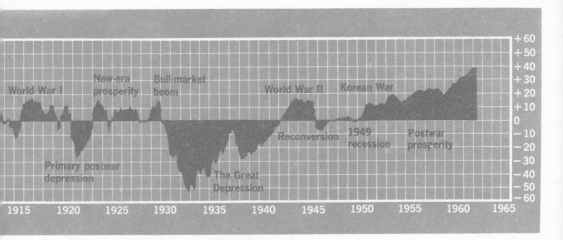

FIGURE 11-2. AMERICAN BUSINESS CYCLE EXPERIENCE.
The American economy has encountered periods of prosperity and depression. Only
minor recessions have occurred since World War II. (Cleveland Trust Company.)

rising incomes characterize these phases of the cycle. As full employment is approached, however, further increases in spending cause both output and the price level to rise. Once full employment is reached, any additional expenditures constitute "overspending." The resulting demand-pull inflation causes increases in *money* GNP, but not in *real* GNP.

These over-all effects of the business cycle conceal the fact that various individuals and various segments of the economy are affected in different ways and in different degrees by the business cycle.

Durables versus nondurables. In so far as production and employment are concerned, those industries producing capital goods and consumer durables are typically hit hardest by depression. Output and employment in nondurable consumer goods industries are less sensitive to the cycle. Industries producing heavy capital goods, farm implements, automobiles, refrigerators, gas ranges, and similar products bear the brunt of bad times. Conversely, these "hard goods" industries seem to be stimulated most by expansion.

Two facts go far to explain the vulnerability of hard goods industries to the cycle. First,

within limits the purchase of hard goods is postponable. Hence, as the economy slips into bad times, producers forestall the acquisition of more modern productive facilities. The business outlook simply does not warrant increases in the stock of capital goods. In all probability the firm's present capital facilities will still be usable. Except in bad times capital goods are usually replaced before they are completely depreciated; when depression strikes, however, businessmen will patch up their outmoded equipment and make it do. As a result, investment in capital goods will decline sharply. Chances are some firms, having excess plant capacity, will not even bother to replace all the capital which they are currently consuming. Net investment may be a negative figure.

Much the same holds true for consumer durables. When depression rolls around and the family budget must be trimmed, it is likely that plans for the purchases of durables will first feel the ax. You decide *not* to trade the old jalopy in on a new Belchfire Eight; the little woman is persuaded that she can survive the future without an electronic oven. The household retains its present high-fidelity set, deferring the purchase of stereo. And so it goes. Food and clothing—consumer nondurables—are a different

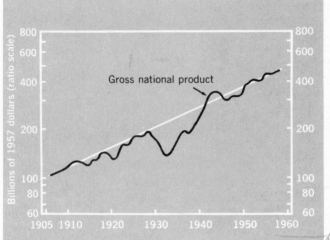

FIGURE 11-3. AMERICAN ECONOMIC GROWTH AND THE BUSINESS CYCLE.
The long-run, or secular, trend of GNP has been upward, but the level of economic activity has fluctuated around this trend. [Department of Commerce, "U.S. Income and Output" (November, 1958), p. 1, and "Survey of Current Business."]

story. A family must eat and must clothe itself. These purchases are much less postponable. True, to some extent the quantity and most certainly the quality of these purchases will decline. But not so much as is the case with durables.

There is a second reason which helps account for the very sharp declines in output and employment that the cycle brings to hard goods industries. Most industries producing capital goods and consumer durables are industries of high concentration, wherein a relatively small number of firms dominate the market. As a result, these firms are in a position to resist lowering prices by restricting supply in the face of a declining demand. This means that the impact of a fall in demand centers primarily upon production and employment. The reverse holds true in nondurable, or soft goods, industries which are of the most part highly competitive and characterized by low concentration. Price declines cannot be resisted in such industries, and the impact of a declining demand falls to a greater extent on prices than upon the levels of production. Figure 11-4 is informative on this point. It shows the percentage declines in price and quantity which occurred in ten selected industries as the economy fell from peak prosperity in 1929 to the depth of depression by 1933. Speaking very generally, high concentration industries comprise the top half of the table and low concentration industries the bottom half. Note the drastic production declines and relatively modest price declines of the high concentration industries, on the one hand, and the large price declines and relatively small output declines which took place in the low concentration industries, on the other.

Incomes and income shares. What about incomes? On an industry basis our discussion of the employment and output effects of the cycle correctly implies that those whose livelihood is linked to the production of capital goods and consumer durables are likely to encounter the greatest variations in employment and incomes.[5] Unemployment will loom larger in such industries during bad times than it will elsewhere.

In terms of national income shares, we have seen previously (Figures 7-1 and 7-2) that rent and interest payments are fairly stable over the cycle. Corporate profits, on the other hand, are subject to considerably more dramatic fluctuations than are the other shares of national income. And, while wage incomes are subject to significant fluctuation in absolute size, labor's

[5] Agriculture is a notable exception. The highly competitive nature of this industry makes agricultural incomes very sensitive to the business cycle, despite the fact that it produces nondurables.

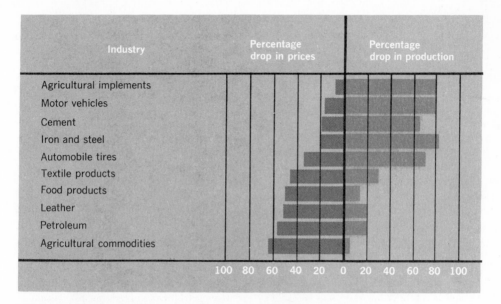

Industry	Percentage drop in prices	Percentage drop in production
Agricultural implements		
Motor vehicles		
Cement		
Iron and steel		
Automobile tires		
Textile products		
Food products		
Leather		
Petroleum		
Agricultural commodities		

100 80 60 40 20   0   20 40 60 80 100

FIGURE 11-4. RELATIVE PRICE AND PRODUCTION DECLINES IN TEN INDUSTRIES, 1929–1933.

The high-concentration industries shown in the top half of this figure were characterized by relatively small price declines and large declines in output when the economy entered the Great Depression. In the low-concentration industries of the bottom half, price declines were relatively large and production fell by relatively small amounts. [Gardiner C. Means, "Industrial Prices and Their Relative Flexibility" (Washington: Government Printing Office, 1935), p. 8.]

relative share of the national income is surprisingly stable over the cycle. During periods of expansion increases in profit incomes usually run ahead of boosts in wage incomes. Similarly, during contraction wage incomes are relatively less flexible than profits. In other words, profit incomes rise and fall more sharply than wage incomes.

INFLATION AND DEFLATION

The effects of changes in output and employment can be readily envisioned. The impact of a changing price level is a much more subtle aspect of the business cycle.

Inflation is feared by all of us, criticized by most of us, and not clearly understood by many of us. What is inflation? Why is it to be feared? *Inflation is a rising general level of prices.* This

does not mean, of course, that all prices are necessarily rising. Even during periods of acute inflation some specific prices may be relatively constant and others actually falling. Nor does inflation mean that prices rise evenly or proportionately. Indeed, one of the major sore spots of inflation lies in the fact that prices tend to rise very unevenly. Some spring upwards; others rise at a more leisurely pace; others do not rise at all. The fundamental cause of inflation has already been explored. Generally speaking, inflation results when society attempts to spend beyond its capacity to produce.

Deflation is substantially the reverse of inflation—a falling general level of prices. Once again, deflation does not mean that all prices are falling evenly. Falling prices accompany declining levels of output and employment; the cause is a deficiency of total spending.

Redistribution of income

In practice output and the level of prices typically move together. Inflation is usually associated with an expanding output (at least until full employment is achieved), and deflation is usually accompanied by a shrinking real output. But in order to isolate the effects of a changing price level upon the distribution of income, let us for the moment assume that real output is constant and at the full-employment level. Assuming the size of the pie is fixed, how does inflation affect the size of the slices going to different income receivers? At the close of our analysis we will release this simplification and modify our conclusions accordingly.

Any analysis of the redistributive impact of inflation and deflation demands that we first distinguish carefully between real and money income. *Money income* is simply the number of dollars one receives in his pay envelope. *Real income*, on the other hand, is the amount of goods and services which a consumer can obtain with his money income. A moment's reflection will make clear that one's real income depends upon (1) his money income and (2) the prices which he must pay for the goods and services he purchases.

Inflation penalizes fixed-money-income groups. With this distinction in mind it is easy to see why inflation arbitrarily penalizes people living on relatively fixed money incomes. Those households whose money incomes lag behind the rising level of product prices will find that their real incomes will deteriorate because of inflation. The purchasing power of each dollar's worth of income they receive will fall as prices rise. And, because they receive about the same number of dollars in their pay envelopes, their standard of living must decline accordingly.

Who are these people? The most obvious cases are pensioners, white-collar workers, schoolteachers, and those living on interest incomes. Some wage earners fall in this category. Those situated in declining industries or without the benefit of strong, aggressive unions may find that the price level skips ahead of their money incomes. Those employed in expanding industries and represented by vigorous unions may keep their wage incomes apace with, or ahead of, the rate of inflation.

Those living on flexible incomes will benefit from inflation. The money incomes of such households will spurt ahead of the price level, or cost of living, with the result that their real incomes are enhanced. Most businessmen and other profit receivers benefit from inflation. Product prices typically rise faster than do resource prices; that is, business receipts tend to grow at a faster rate than do costs. Thus profit incomes are likely to outdistance the rising tide of inflation.

Inflation benefits debtors at the expense of creditors. But this is not all. Inflation also redistributes income by altering the relationship between debtors and creditors. Specifically, inflation benefits debtors at the expense of creditors. Suppose you borrow $1,000 from a bank, which you are to repay in two years. If in that period of time the general level of prices were to double, the $1,000 which you repay will have only half the purchasing power of the $1,000 originally borrowed. True, if we ignore interest charges, the same number of dollars are repaid as were borrowed. But each of these dollars will now, because of inflation, buy only half as much as it did when the loan was negotiated. As prices go up, the value of the dollar comes down. Thus, because of inflation, the borrower is given "dear" dollars but pays back in "cheap" dollars.

Inflation lessens the value of savings. Inflation also casts it evil eye upon savers. As prices rise, the real value, or purchasing power, of a nest egg of liquid savings will deteriorate. Savings accounts, insurance policies, annuities, and other fixed-value paper assets which were once adequate to meet rainy-day contingencies or to provide for a comfortable retirement decline in real value during inflation. Mortgage holders and bondholders will be similarly affected. A household's accumulated claims upon the economy's output are worth less and less as prices rise. On the other hand, it should be noted that *creepy infl has expansionary affect on econo*

stock values are flexible and determined by current market conditions; hence, savings in this form will tend to increase in value with, or in some cases ahead of, the general level of prices.

Inflation arbitrarily "taxes" those who receive relatively fixed money incomes and "subsidizes" those who receive flexible money incomes. Inflation benefits debtors at the expense of creditors. Finally, inflation arbitrarily penalizes savers. It should come as no surprise that the effects of deflation are substantially the reverse. *Assuming no change in total output,* those with fixed money incomes will find their real incomes enhanced. Creditors will benefit at the expense of debtors. And savers will find that the purchasing power of their savings has grown as a result of falling prices.

Changes in prices and output

We have assumed thus far that the economy's real output is fixed at the full-employment level. As a result, the redistributive effects of inflation and deflation have been in terms of some groups gaining absolutely at the expense of others. If the size of the pie is fixed and inflation causes some groups to get larger slices, other groups must necessarily get smaller slices. This is obviously modified somewhat when inflation is accompanied by an expanding real output, as would be the case when the economy is approaching, but has not yet attained, the full-employment output. When the pie is growing, the gains which inflation brings to some will exceed the losses which it imposes upon others. In brief, although the over-all effects will be essentially the same, the redistributive impact of a given amount of inflation will tend to be less severe when inflation is accompanied by an expansion of real output.

What about deflation? Falling prices typically go along with depression and a declining total output. Hence, with a rapidly shrinking pie virtually all groups will get a smaller slice. In other words, those on relatively fixed incomes *who are able to hold their jobs* will find that their real incomes rise as a result of deflation. But these people may be few in number. Cred-

itors *who are fortunate enough to collect from debtors* will gain. But these too may be few in number. And those *who are able to hold on to their savings* as the economy backslides into depression will find the purchasing power of their savings enhanced by lower prices. But these once again may be few in number. In short, during deflation fixed-money-income receivers, creditors, and savers are not likely to be better off in an absolute sense, because in all probability total output will be falling too. But they may be "less worse off" than flexible income receivers, debtors, and nonsavers.

Creeping inflation

Virtually all economists condemn a sharply rising price level. Economists are divided, however, on the merits and demerits of mild, or "creeping" inflation, that is, a 2 or 3 per cent annual increase in the price level.

The case for creeping inflation. Despite the arbitrary redistributive effects of inflation, some competent economists[6] feel that creeping inflation may very well be desirable because of its expansionary effect upon the economy. Product prices, it is argued, tend to increase ahead of resource prices as the economy approaches full employment. This stimulates money profits and is conducive to additional investment spending, which, in turn, brings the economy closer to full employment. Furthermore, the larger stock of investment goods causes a favorable shift in the production possibilities curve, and economic growth is the result. It is concluded that only under the pressure of a high, inflation-causing level of aggregate demand does American capitalism realize full employment, capacity production, and its maximum growth potential. Mild inflation is allegedly a small price to pay for the attainment of these objectives. It is recognized that mild inflation will tread on the toes of fixed income receivers, creditors, and savers. But this redistributive impact should not

[6] See, for example, Alvin H. Hansen, *The American Economy* (New York: McGraw-Hill Book Company, Inc., 1957), pp. 45–47, and Sumner H. Slichter, "How Bad Is Inflation?" *Harper's Magazine,* August, 1952.

be overemphasized: so long as the interest rate on savings exceeds the rate of inflation (and this has generally been the case since World War II), the purchasing power of savings will increase rather than diminish. For example, the purchasing power of a $1,000 savings account will increase if the annual interest rate is, say, 4 per cent and the annual increase in the price level only 2 or 3 per cent. In any event, any arbitrary redistributive effects will be more than offset by the benefits which inflation-borne increases in output and employment will bring to the economy as a whole. More fixed income employees will have jobs, creditors will be more certain of repayment, and prosperity will permit more households to enjoy the luxury of saving. The alternatives, as these economists see it, are full employment and growth accompanied by creeping inflation *or* price stability accompanied by unemployment and the failure of the economy to realize its growth potential. The former choice, they conclude, is far superior to the latter.

The case against creeping inflation. But other competent authorities[7] take a dim view of this position. They make two major arguments against creeping inflation. First, they contend that, when compounded over the years, the redistributive impact of mild or creeping inflation can be very severe. A 3 per cent annual rise in prices will cause the price level to double in about twenty-three years. Second, it is argued that creeping inflation may readily snowball into hyper-, "galloping," inflation. And galloping inflation can precipitate depression. This second argument merits rather detailed consideration.

It is felt that, as the economy draws close to the full-employment level, individual segments of the economy will exert pressure to keep their incomes rising ahead of the creeping inflation. But this pressure will cause creeping inflation to get up and run. It happens something like this: As the cost of living rises, labor demands

[7] In recent years the monetary authorities in the United States have generally been opposed to creeping inflation. See, for example, "Creeping Inflation," *Business Review*, Federal Reserve Bank of Philadelphia, August, 1957.

and gets higher wages. Prosperity is not a good time for businessmen to risk strikes by resisting such demands. Businessmen recoup their rising labor costs by boosting the prices they charge consumers. And for good measure businesses are likely to jack prices up an extra notch or two to be sure that profit receivers keep abreast or ahead of the inflationary parade. As the cost of living skips merrily upward as a result of these price increases, labor once again has an excellent excuse to demand another round of wage increases. But this triggers another round of price increases. The net effect is a cumulative wage-price inflationary spiral. Wage and price rises feed upon each other, and creeping inflation bursts into galloping inflation. Whether increased costs "push" prices up or added spending "pulls" them up is a moot question. The important point for immediate purposes is that many economists feel that the trouble with a small dose of inflation is that it is not likely to remain small.

But, aside from capricious and disruptive effects upon the distribution of income, why is such hyperinflation to be feared? The answer is that hyperinflation can lead to a depression. As prices shoot up sharply and unevenly, normal economic relationships are disrupted. Businessmen do not know what to charge for their products. Consumers do not know what to pay. Money becomes "hot," because inflation is rapidly diminishing the purchasing power of the dollar. Prices are rising rapidly, and people come to expect them to rise further. So, rather than let their idle savings and current incomes depreciate, people are induced to "spend now" to beat anticipated price rises. Businesses do the same in buying capital goods. Action on the basis of this inflationary psychology simply intensifies the pressure on prices. In the extreme case, inflation may become so severe as to render money virtually worthless.

As inflation increases in severity, businesses may find it more profitable to hoard both materials and finished products, awaiting further price increases. But by further restricting the availability of materials and products relative to the demand for them, such action will merely tend to intensify inflationary pressures. Resource suppliers will want to be paid in kind. Creditors will hide from debtors to escape the repayment of debts with cheap money. Money will cease to do its job as a medium of exchange and a standard of value. Nor will people want to store their wealth in the form of money. The economy will literally be thrown into a state of barter. Production and exchange grind toward a halt, and the net result is economic, social, and very possibly political chaos. Hyperinflation has precipitated monetary collapse, depression, and sociopolitical disorder. The conclusion? Mild inflation is a very risky foundation for achieving healthy economic progress.

Which view is correct? It is hard to say. Both have proved accurate in specific instances. American economic history reveals that many periods of healthy economic growth have entailed mild inflation. On the other hand, other nations of the world have had mild inflation get out of control—particularly during wartime—and break into galloping inflation with disastrous results.

The inflation in Hungary exceeded all known records of the past. In August, 1946, 828 octillion (1 followed by 27 zeros) depreciated pengös equaled the value of 1 prewar pengö. The price of the American dollar reached a value of 3×10^{22} (3 followed by 22 zeros) pengös. . . . In Germany of 1923 a larger box was needed to carry money to the grocery store than to bring back the groceries bought. . . . Prices rose some 116 times in Japan, 1939 to 1948.[8]

We must settle for the conclusion that creeping inflation can be expansionary but that such inflation may expose the economy to the real risk of galloping inflation, particularly after full employment is achieved.[9]

BUSINESS CYCLES SINCE 1920

Let us now apply our rudimentary understanding of the business cycle to survey the cyclical experiences of American capitalism since 1920. Such a summary gives us many

[8] Theodore Morgan, *Income and Employment*, 2d ed. (Englewood Cliffs, N.J.: Prentice-Hall, Inc., 1952), p. 361.

[9] See question 10 at the end of this chapter.

valuable insights into both the causes and effects of economic fluctuations. The emphasis is upon variations in the different components of total spending.

If we ignore minor cycles—short recessions or inflations—the last four complete decades can be conveniently summarized as follows: the prosperity of the twenties (1922 to 1929); the Great Depression of the thirties (1929 to 1939); the prosperity and inflation of the wartime forties (1940 to 1949); and the growth and inflation of the fifties (1950 to 1959).

We shall employ Table 11-1 to substantiate our description of the 1920s. Official U.S. Department of Commerce national income statistics are available starting in 1929 and provide a factual backbone for our discussion of the ensuing three decades. These figures are presented in the inside covers of the book.

The prosperity of the twenties

Aside from a sharp but brief depression in 1921 and minor bouts with unemployment in 1924 and 1927, the 1920s were years of booming prosperity. This prosperity was reflected in an expanding GNP and in a level of unemployment which never exceeded 2 per cent of the labor force in the 1923–1929 period (see columns 3 and 4 of Table 11-1). Furthermore, this growth was cloaked in general price stability (see column 6 of Table 11-1).

The major driving force underlying this period of prosperity was a high and prolonged level of investment spending on capital equipment and construction. The following interrelated causal factors contributed to this high rate of investment:

1. ***The strong demand for capital goods.*** World War I had created a backlog of demand for investment goods. Resources simply could not be spared from the production of armaments during the war for the production of investment goods to replace or expand the nation's stock of capital. As a result, the need for capital goods to replace those worn out and rendered obsolete during the war persisted into the 1920s.

Prosperity reflected in expanding G.N.P. & level of full employment

TABLE 11-1. GNP, THE PRICE LEVEL, UNEMPLOYMENT, AND PRODUCTIVITY IN THE 1920s

(1)	(2)	(3)	(4)	(5)	(6)
Year	GNP, current dollars	Real GNP, billions of 1947 dollars	Unemployment, millions	Index of output per man-hour in manufacturing, per cent (1939 = 100)	Consumer's price index, per cent (1947–1949 = 100)
1920	$ 91.6	$102.0	0.6	48.0	85.7
1921	70.0	93.0	4.8	55.2	76.4
1922	74.3	106.6	2.9	60.5	71.6
1923	85.5	119.5	0.7	59.5	72.9
1924	85.1	119.6	2.0	63.4	73.1
1925	93.6	130.3	0.8	67.6	75.0
1926	97.8	137.1	0.5	69.5	75.6
1927	95.8	137.6	1.6	71.3	74.2
1928	98.3	139.7	1.9	75.1	73.3
1929	104.4	149.3	0.4	78.1	73.3

SOURCES: Columns 2, 3, and 6 are from The National Industrial Conference Board, "The Economic Almanac, 1958" (New York: Thomas Y. Crowell Company, 1958), pp. 71, 394. Columns 4 and 5 are from U.S. Bureau of the Census, "Historical Statistics of the United States: 1789–1945" (1949), pp. 65, 70–71.

The development of new products and industries. The spectacular rise of a group of new and important industries provided both direct and indirect stimuli to investment spending during the twenties. The development of the automobile, electric power, radio, telephone, and electric refrigerator industries all called for tremendous amounts of investment spending in these and related industries. The most notable of these vigorous new industries was the automobile industry. Widespread acceptance of the automobile—annual production increased from 2.2 million in 1920 to 5.5 million by 1929—induced tremendous expansion in the industry. Of greater importance, however, were the secondary effects which the automobile industry had upon a host of related industries. The petroleum, rubber, steel, glass, and textile industries all expanded their facilities enormously to feed parts and materials into the booming auto industry. In addition, an estimated $10 billion was spent on roads and highways during the twenties.

Expansion was almost as impressive in other new industries. The annual production of refrigerators swelled from $13.3 million in 1921 to a thumping $111.7 million by 1929. In the radio industry production soared from $13.3 million in 1923 to $253.3 million in 1929.[10]

Declining labor costs and business optimism. The development of mass production techniques and simultaneous increases in specialization sharply boosted the productivity of labor during the 1920s (see Table 11-1, column 5). Teamed with the relative ineffectiveness of labor unions in boosting wage rates during this era, these productivity increases caused labor costs per unit of output to decline. The resulting expansion of profit margins created an environment of business optimism, and this in turn was also conducive to further investment spending.

[10] All production and investment data are from D. Hamburg, *Business Cycles* (New York: The Macmillan Company, 1951), pp. 411–412.

4 *The residential housing boom.* Construction expenditures expanded considerably during the early 1920s, reaching peak levels and a plateau late in the decade. This spending was not only the result of previously cited factors—the development of new industries and highway construction—but also stemmed to a great degree from a residential housing boom.

5 *Other factors.* While the preceding factors are the major ones behind the booming twenties, a variety of other forces also played significant roles. Although monetary developments were not a prime mover in the prosperity of the 1920s, it can be said that monetary conditions were such as to permit prosperity to occur. Commercial banks were able to make money available in needed amounts and on reasonable terms. The stock market boom which accompanied the good times of the decade inflated stock prices, thereby creating conditions very favorable for business borrowing and investing.

The depletion of the nation's stock of capital during World War I, the development and growth of a number of new and important industries, productivity increases which gave rise to falling labor costs, and a high level of expenditures on construction all teamed within a favorable monetary and financial environment to result in a high and sustained level of investment spending during the twenties. The result? Prosperity and an expanding GNP. But the end of the decade brought an abrupt halt to this vigorous economic growth.

The Great Depression of the thirties

In October of 1929 the stock market collapsed, ushering in the most severe and prolonged depression of modern times. GNP plummeted from $104.4 billion in 1929 to a low of $56 billion by 1933. Unemployment rose from 1.6 million to 12.8 million in the same period (lines 5 and 23 of the table on the inside covers).

Just as a high level of investment spending was the backbone of the booming twenties, so a low and sagging level of investment was the major weight that pulled American capitalism into the economic chaos of the thirties. Gross investment spending contracted from $16.2 billion in 1929 to $1.4 billion in 1933 (line 2 of the table)—a 90 per cent decline! To a considerable degree the reasons behind this decline in investment spending have their roots in those factors which underlay the high level of investment of the booming twenties. Let us examine the more important reasons why investment declined in late 1929 and the early 1930s:

1 *Excess industrial capacity.* The new industries whose growth underscored the prosperity of the 1920s reached maturity late in that decade. The rapid expansion of these adolescent industries in the twenties occurred at a rate which could not be indefinitely maintained. The markets for these new consumer durables were becoming saturated. Hence, the rate of investment in the automobile and dependent industries began to level off and decline in the early 1930s. Much the same pattern applied to other industries whose growth had been so vigorous in the 1920s. Overexpansion in the previous decade came home to roost in the 1930s.

2 *The decline in residential construction.* The 1920s was also an era of overbuilding. The high level of construction in the 1920s was partially war-deferred construction; building occurred at a rapid rate in the 1920s to make up for the construction that was forgone during the emergency of World War I. And in part the decline in construction was due to a decline in the rate of population growth during the late twenties. In any event spending on construction began to level off as early as 1926, residential construction leading the decline. By the late twenties the construction industry had virtually collapsed.

3 *The heavy hand of debt.* Indebtedness expanded rapidly and became abnormally large as the economy burgeoned in the 1920s. This indebtedness assumed three basic forms: consumer credit, mortgage credit, and indebtedness for stock purchases. The growth of consumer credit—installment buying—had accompanied the development of the various new industries producing consumer durables in the 1920s. The building boom of the 1920s gave rise to heavy mortgage commitments on residential housing and commercial real estate.

The result of this tremendous growth in indebtedness was that by the late twenties much of the income of businesses and households was committed for the payment of interest and principal on past purchases, and hence not available for current expenditures. As expenditures declined, so did incomes and prices. And income declines prompted creditors to liquidate their debts as readily as possible. This was evidenced in a rising tide of business failures and mortgage foreclosures.

4. *The stock market crash.* The most dramatic facet of the Great Depression was the stock market crash of October, 1929. The optimism of the prosperous twenties had elevated stock market speculation to something of a national pastime. This speculation had bid up stock prices to the point where they were decidedly out of touch with reality; that is, the prices of stocks were far beyond the profit-making potentials of the issuing firms. The necessary downward adjustment came with a vengeance in 1929. It was sudden, violent, cumulative. "In that awful last week of October, 1929, the market collapsed. . . . The grim jokes of the period speak for themselves: it was said that with every share of Goldman Sachs you got a complimentary revolver, and that when you booked a hotel room the clerk inquired, 'For sleeping or jumping?' "[11] As already noted, many stock purchases had been made on credit. Speculators found themselves hopelessly in debt with only pieces of now worthless paper as reward for their efforts.

The stock market crash had significant secondary effects. Most important was the accompanying unfavorable psychological repercussions; the buoyant optimism of the 1920s gave way to a wave of crippling pessimism. In par-

[11] Robert L. Heilbroner, *The Worldly Philosophers*, rev. ed. (New York: Simon and Schuster, Inc., 1961), pp. 215–16.

ticular the crashing of stock prices created most unfavorable conditions for acquiring additional money capital for investment or for any other purpose.

5. *Shrinking of the money supply.* Closely allied with the stock market crash and the rapid contraction of indebtedness was a very sharp reduction in the money supply in the early years of the Depression. The money supply of $26.4 billion of 1929 had shrunk to $19.8 billion by 1933 (line 22 of the table on the inside covers). This shrinkage was the result of certain complex forces operating both at home and abroad. In part the shrinkage was tied to the stock market crash and its effect upon the value of bank-held assets. In part it was the result of faulty policies invoked by the monetary authorities. In part it stemmed from the very structure of the banking system—a large number of small and relatively weak banks. The important point for our purposes is that this drastic reduction in the supply of money contributed to the sharp decline in the volume of spending which characterized the early 1930s.

6. *The declining price level.* Once the contraction of the early 1930s was under way, deflation tended to reinforce that downswing in business activity. Falling product prices discouraged both consumption and investment spending. Consumers were prone to defer their purchases of durables in order to take advantage of anticipated price declines. Businessmen were discouraged from buying capital equipment for substantially the same reasons.

7. *Other considerations.* Though we have touched upon the major considerations underlying the Great Depression, many other factors also entered the picture. For example the enactment of restrictive tariffs, designed to shield domestic workers and their jobs from the rigors of international competition, backfired, dealing a death blow to the already declining volume of international trade. Rather than preserve jobs, higher tariffs only served to reduce trade and further intensify unemployment. Further-

more, drought conditions added materially to the woes of the agricultural segment of the economy in the mid-thirties. All these factors and more combined to turn the booming twenties into the stagnant thirties.

An outstanding feature of the Great Depression was its length. The economy made an abortive recovery in the mid-thirties (1933 to 1937), the "boom" of 1936 and early 1937 falling substantially short of the full-employment mark. This feeble upswing was caused by increases in both consumption and investment spending, but the very modest expansion which occurred in the latter caused the Depression to persist. The failure of investment spending to rally sufficiently has many roots. In part this was a backwash of the tremendous exploitation of investment opportunities in the residential and business construction industries during the 1920s. In part it was a carryover of the pessimistic repercussions of the stock market crash. In part investment lagged because of the failure of new investment-stimulating industries comparable to the automobile industry to appear in the thirties. In part investment may have remained depressed in the thirties because of the suspicion and hostility with which many businessmen viewed the controversial reform and recovery measures enacted by the New Deal; the economic intervention embodied in New Deal programs may well have frightened off some private investment outlays.

In retrospect it must be recognized that a portion of the blame for the length of the Great Depression is due to both government and economists. Economists simply did not have an adequate and sufficiently detailed explanation of the business cycle which could be used as a foundation for remedial government policies. True, the immediate cause—a deficiency of total spending—was recognized. But more fundamental causes were not at all evident. As a result, the New Deal was largely an experimental program which worked in a very imperfect and halfhearted way in combatting the Depression. Indeed, increases in net Federal spending were largely canceled by declines in state and local spending.

In Chapter 18 we shall note that some econ-omists came to believe in the late 1930s that the Great Depression was more than a cyclical downswing in business activity. They felt that it was the beginning of an era of persistent or "secular stagnation" in American capitalism. The dynamic, expansive forces of American capitalism were allegedly losing their force, to the end that persistent unemployment was to be the lot of the United States. With unemployment hovering close to 10 million in 1939 (line 23 of the table on the inside covers) the possibility of secular stagnation seemed to be an all-too-accurate viewpoint. But darkening war clouds in Europe were soon to resolve the persistent unemployment of the 1930s.

Prosperity and inflation of the forties

Prosperity and inflation were the economic bywords of the 1940–1949 decade. The mobilization of 1940 to 1941 and the all-out war effort of 1942 to 1945 paved the way for a vivid economic contrast with the depressed thirties. War has one great economic virtue—it creates jobs for the unemployed. But governmental expenditures in financing World War II did more than create jobs and boost output; they also gave rise to considerable inflationary pressure. Although this pressure was repressed by direct governmental controls during the war, it broke loose at the cessation of hostilities to boost the price level sharply in the postwar era. For convenience we divide this decade into the war years (1940 to 1945) and the postwar years (1946 to 1949). While prosperity was a main feature of both periods, underlying causal factors differed.

The war years *(1940 to 1945).* The root causes of prosperity in the early forties contrast vividly with those which produced good times in the twenties:

① *The upsurge of military spending.* Sharp increases in government military spending underlay the upsurge in output and employment which characterized the 1940–1945 period. As line 3 of the table on the inside covers clearly indicates, government spending boomed from a lowly $14.1 billion in 1940 to a peak of $96.5 billion by 1944. This tremendous expansion in armaments expenditures took many a worker out of the breadline and put him in the employment line of a defense plant.

2. *Rising incomes and consumer spending.* With employment and incomes rising as a result of increased government spending we should not be surprised to find that consumption spending increased during the war years. It did: the $17.9 billion consumption level of 1940 rose steadily to $121.7 billion by 1945 and was destined to increase even more sharply in the postwar years (line 1 of the table on the inside covers).

3. *The rise and forced decline of investment spending.* The role of investment spending provides an interesting contrast. Investment spurted significantly in 1940 and 1941, basically in response to the increased demand for war goods. Armament production required the use of modern, specialized capital equipment. Furthermore, both defense and civilian industries correctly anticipated future scarcities of capital goods; hence, industry stepped up the level of investment spending accordingly.

But by the end of 1941 the economy was rapidly approaching the full-employment level of production. By 1943 "overfull" employment was achieved, that is, unemployment fell below the 3 to 5 per cent normal unemployment figure (lines 23 and 24 of the table on the inside covers). As a result, further expansion in the production of war and consumer goods had to come at the expense of the production of investment goods. This is precisely what happened. The nation "lived off its stock of capital" during the 1942–1945 period. Nonessential investment spending bore the brunt of this cutback. *Net* private domestic investment was negative throughout the height of the war effort in order to free as many resources as possible for the immediate production of war goods (lines 2 and 6 of the table).

4. *Expansion of the money supply.* Monetary factors played a significant role in the wartime boom. In the six years between 1939 and 1945 the nation's supply of money almost tripled! The 1939 money supply of about $36.2

billion rose to $102.4 billion by 1945 (line 22). This expansion made possible the tremendous increase in economic activity which the war necessitated.

5. *Wartime inflationary pressures.* By 1943 the American economy had clearly hit the production barrier of full employment. But the total level of spending continued to rise, government and consumption spending leading the way. The inevitable result of spending more and more dollars on a fixed amount of goods is demand-pull inflation. And war is highly inflationary: it pours money into the pockets of civilians but fails to turn out civilian goods at a matching rate.

During the war, however, this inflationary pressure was repressed with considerable success by a bevy of government controls. Price and wage controls were aimed directly at holding the lid on inflation. At the same time tax increases and intensive warbond campaigns tried to drain off excessive purchasing power to reduce spending and thereby relieve the pressure on prices. All things considered, these programs were successful in postponing inflation until the postwar era. After the war significant increases in the general price level did occur.

The postwar years (1946 to 1949). As the war drew to a successful close, forecasts of a severe postwar depression clouded the air. Drastic declines in government military spending were expected to precipitate such a crisis. But, aside from a very mild setback in 1945 to 1946, prosperity and economic growth persisted into the postwar era. The reasons once again lay in the components of total spending. The drastic $52.4 billion *decline* in government spending which occurred between 1945 and 1946 (line 3 of the table on the inside covers) was largely offset by a $49.5 billion *increase* in private (consumption, investment, and foreign) spending (lines 1, 2, and 4). Aside from a brief recession in 1949, the levels of consumption and investment spending increased in the postwar years to the extent that rather serious inflation resulted.

1. *The investment backlog, reconversion, and the housing shortage.* The desire to re-

place capital facilities used up during the war years created a large backlog of demand for capital goods. The need to modernize existing capital facilities plus the reconversion to civilian production added to this high level of demand for investment goods. Furthermore, the chronic problem of a housing shortage had reached acute proportions during the war, with the result that the postwar era unleashed a sharp increase in residential construction activity.

2. Government and the climate for investment. In 1946 the Federal government expressed a readiness to take positive steps to correct any serious deviations from full employment. This assurance undoubtedly provided a favorable psychological climate for the resulting high level of investment.

3. Foreign investment and postwar aid. Net foreign investment also jumped sharply in the postwar era as foreign nations, flush with American loans and Marshall Plan dollars, eagerly sought American goods to aid in the reconstruction of their war-torn economies (line 4 of the table).

4. The postwar consumption boom. The lion's share of the drop in government military spending was filled by an abrupt increase in consumer spending. As line 1 of the table on the inside covers indicates, consumer spending jumped by over $25 billion between 1945 and 1946.

A host of factors contributed to the high level of consumption spending which persisted in the postwar years. First, the unavailability of consumer durables during the war meant that consumers emerged from the war with a backlog of demands for automobiles, washing machines, refrigerators, and so forth. Secondly, consumers had the means of financing a high volume of expenditures. Not only were current money incomes at record levels, but consumers had accumulated a huge volume of savings in the form of government bonds and other highly liquid assets during the war. This purchasing power was supplemented by (1) a hasty cut in personal taxes (line 15 of the table), (2) a significant increase in government transfer payments to veterans (line 13), and (3) rapid growth in the volume of consumer credit (line

25). Finally, on top of all this prices were already rising and showed little sign of falling; it seemed sensible therefore to "spend now" before further price increases occurred. All the factors were present for a consumer spending orgy. And it came to pass.

5. Postwar inflation. High levels of spending not only maintained full employment in the postwar era; it also brought rather sharp inflation. Government was able to do a fair job of repressing inflationary pressure during the war. But it was politically impossible to hold the lid on the inflationary kettle once hostilities ended. The Office of Price Administration met a sudden death in 1946. With wartime controls out of the way the field was clear for open inflation to move into the economic spotlight. Successive rounds of wage and price increases were the order of the day, and the cost of living spiraled ever upward. As a result, the consumer price index, which stood at a relatively innocent 76.9 per cent in 1945, had soared to 102.8 per cent by 1948 (line 20 of the table). This spending spree leveled off in 1949, and the result was a mild recession. But the Korean War in 1950 quickly pushed the vision of depression to one side. Specifically, the Korean hostilities bolstered both government spending and consumer spending—the former because of the need for increased military outlays and the latter because households anticipated and wanted to "beat" war-borne inflation and product shortages. As American capitalism entered the decade of the fifties, inflation was still the major economic problem of the day.

The growth and inflation of the fifties

The decade of the 1950s is not easily assessed. Generally speaking, this was a decade of over-all prosperity and mild inflation, accompanied by substantial economic growth. However, the decade was marred by recessions in 1954 and 1958, and in the 1957–1960 period unemployment was persistently in excess of the 4 per cent normal unemployment figure. The latter fact has given rise to considerable debate among economists as to whether the rate of growth in the economy's GNP is noticeably slackening. In brief, then, the 1950s were characterized by over-all prosperity, a rising price level, and significant economic growth on the one hand, and two troublesome recessions and a possible weakening of the growth rate on the other. Again the general picture is explainable in terms of the major components of total spending.

The Korean War and the 1954 recession. We have already noted that the Communist invasion of Korea in 1950 stimulated anticipatory buying by consumers and businessmen, both of whom expected shortages of goods and materials and inflated prices due to the war. This was followed in 1951 by a substantial increase in armament spending by the Federal government. The result was a buoyant, expanding economy in the 1950–1953 period. Total spending was high enough to induce substantial increases in real GNP, and in the 1951–1953 period, an unemployment rate of approximately 3 per cent of the labor force (lines 19 and 24 of the table). In fact, total spending was sufficiently strong to cause significant demand-pull inflation; the consumer's price index rose from 102.8 in 1950 to 113.5 by 1952 (line 20).

But then came a readjustment. The warborne upsurge in consumer spending was too great to be sustainable, and in 1953 and 1954 consumption expenditures leveled off. Businessmen, having geared their production to the 1951–1952 high levels of consumption, found themselves with overlarge inventories of goods. The resulting cutback in production, coupled with a gradual cutback in Federal military spending as the Korean War drew to a close, paved the way for the relatively mild "inventory recession" in 1954.

The 1955–1957 durable-goods boom. The 1954 recession might have been much more severe in duration and intensity were it not for the fact that long-term investment spending on machinery, equipment, and construction held up during this period. There were several factors at work which contributed to the stability of long-term investment: (1) technological advances and continued long-term growth in population and incomes bolstered business investment in plant and equipment; (2) population growth and governmental provision of favorable credit policies sustained the postwar demand for residential construction; (3) the expenditures of state and local governments on schools, highways, and similar social goods continued to expand steadily. These investment-stimulating factors teamed with a rapidly expanding demand for consumer durables (particularly automobiles) to make 1955 a year of vigorous economic expansion. Substantial growth in consumer credit in 1954 and 1955 (line 25) and the increased demand for furniture and appliances which accompanied the high rate of residential construction were factors in this expansion of consumer spending on durables. Real GNP surged from $363.1 to $392.7 billion between 1954 and 1955. In 1956 and 1957 expenditures for residential housing and automobiles fell rather significantly, and, despite continued strong expenditures for plant and equipment and growing expenditures by state and local governments, the economy plateaued. As a result, while prosperity was sustained in 1956 and 1957, these were years of only modest economic growth. Note (line 24 of table) that unemployment hovered at the normal unemployment mark in the entire 1955–1957 period.

The 1958 recession and recovery. Though the 1958 recession was brief—lasting less than a year—it was also the most severe of the three post-World War II recessions. Note (line 19 of table) that real GNP fell by over $7 billion between 1957 and 1958, more than in either the 1954 or 1949 recessions. Unemployment rose to 6.8 per cent of the labor force—clearly the highest figure in the post-World War II period (line 24). The basic cause of this recession was a substantial decline in business investment in machinery and equipment—a decline which was in part a reaction to the leveling of consumer spending in 1956 and 1957. In addition, the enactment of restrictive credit policies by the government in seeking to restrain the price level probably contributed to the downturn by also restraining purchases of housing and consumer durables. Furthermore, the automobile industry was simultaneously plagued by both market saturation and strong foreign competition.

Increased spending on consumer durables, an expansion of residential construction (aided by governmentally eased credit conditions), and increased government spending all underlay recovery in 1959. The increases in government spending stemmed from continually expanding state and local outlays on school and highway construction while the increases in Federal spending reflected an intensification of the cold war and, in no small measure, a reaction to Sputnik I.

1958: unemployment and cost-push inflation.
An extraordinary aspect of the 1958 recession was the fact that, despite substantial decreases in real GNP, industrial production, and employment, the price level persisted in rising (lines 19, 21, 24, and 20 of the table). This was of considerable interest and concern to economists who have traditionally envisioned inflation as a "demand-pull" phenomenon, that is, total demand in excess of that required to achieve full employment pulls up the general level of prices. Why were prices *rising* when total demand was clearly insufficient to provide for a full-employment level of output?

Though there is anything but unanimity on the point, investigation suggests that this "new inflation" was originating not from an excess of total demand, but on the supply or cost side of the market. In particular, labor unions in automobiles, steel, and several other important industries had negotiated 3-year collective-bargaining agreements in 1955 and 1956. Because they were negotiated at a time when profits were very high in these industries, the contracts were very favorable to labor and embodied automatic upward wage adjustments over the entire 3-year period. Thus, in 1958 (at a time when the economy was experiencing a short but severe recession) these previously negotiated wage increases were being put in effect. Businesses then exercised their market

power by passing these higher costs on to consumers through price increases. The result was the odd phenomenon of inflation amidst growing unemployment. More will be said of the causes and consequences of cost-push inflation in Chapter 19.

The sixties: soaring or sluggish?

Although recovery from the 1958 recession was retarded in 1959 by the longest steel strike in American history, recovery seemed to be on the horizon. Business was expanding rather rapidly amidst highly optimistic predictions that the new decade—the soaring sixties—would usher in a new golden age of affluence and an upsurge in the rate of growth in GNP. The trend of population suggested a continuous expansion of markets and rapid technological advance implied a persistently high level of investment spending. Indeed, money GNP broke the $500 billion barrier in 1960. From this optimistic position, "creeping inflation" seemed to be the only potential blemish on this encouraging picture.

But it soon became evident that such high optimism might be unwarranted. A number of economists began to cite real and potential soft spots in the economy, suggesting that the predicted "soaring sixties" might in reality prove to be the "sluggish sixties." The immediate evidence of this sluggishness was a persistently above-normal unemployment rate (line 24 of the table). Indeed, the evidence indicates that each of the three post-World War II recessions has left a larger and larger residue of unemployed workers. That is, in terms of unemployment each successive recovery has been less vigorous and less complete. Thus newspaper headlines which lamented "creeping inflation" in the 1950s were speaking of "creeping unemployment" as the 1960s began.

Several fairly evident forces seem to be contributing to this abnormally high unemployment rate. First, the labor force is now increasing at a more rapid rate; there are more new people entering the labor force to look for jobs. While the labor force grew by about 0.8 million workers per year on the average in the 1950s, the prospects are for about 1.2 million new workers per year in the 1960s. At the same time, however, automation is imposing severe limits upon the number of job opportunities in manufacturing industries; manufacturing firms are using more and more labor-saving machinery and a slightly declining number of workers to meet production requirements. In recent years goods-producing industries have been offering fewer and fewer employment opportunities. Thirdly, as Western Europe and Japan have now realized full recovery from the devastation of World War II, the United States finds itself faced with sharp competition in holding world markets. Many industries which are substantially dependent upon foreign sales have cut production and laid off workers as West German and Japanese concerns gain larger shares of world markets (Chapter 38). Finally, a number of economists have argued that in its preoccupation with correcting creeping inflation, the Federal government has invoked overly restrictive policies to the end that the goal of full employment has been sacrificed. The net result of these several factors is above-normal unemployment and a retardation of the rate of expansion of the GNP. These conflicting views on our economic prospects in the 1960s will receive further elaboration in Chapter 19.

Concluding observations

Our historical examination of the economic ups and downs of American capitalism yields several noteworthy conclusions:

1. The business cycle is clearly a complex phenomenon. In particular the factors which cause or contribute to prosperity and depression are most diverse. Though the immediate cause of the business cycle is changes in the volume of spending, we find that a host of different factors influence the course of total spending. Such diverse considerations as innovations, changes in the volume of indebtedness, productivity changes, business and consumer expectations, wars, droughts, population changes, and governmental policies at home and abroad all make for variations in total

spending and, hence, in the level of economic activity.

2. The variability of investment spending as a component of total spending is also noteworthy. A surging level of investment was the backbone of the prosperous twenties. Similarly, a declining volume of investment ushered in the prolonged depression of the thirties. Sharp increases in investment helped fill the gap left by declining governmental spending at the close of World War II. Our review of recent business cycle experience strongly suggests that the forces which contribute most to economic instability are those which bear upon the decisions of businessmen to invest.

3. Finally, our discussion suggests that within limits upswings and downswings in business activity tend to be cumulative. To illustrate: When the nation is at less than full employment, increases in, say, investment spending give rise to increases in output and employment. A higher level of employment means rising incomes, which prompt further increases in spending. Further increases in spending mean still further increases in output, employment, and incomes. The reverse interactions tend to occur as an initial decline in total spending causes the economy to backslide from a full-employment level of performance.

SUMMARY

1. Full employment exists when everyone who is willing and able to work at going wages and under prevailing working conditions can find a job in his field of endeavor. Some 3 to 4 per cent of the labor force is normally unemployed in a free and dynamic economy such as American capitalism.

2. The economic cost of unemployment consists of the goods and services which society forgoes when its resources are involuntarily idle. Unemployment is also conducive to a deterioration of national morale and to social and political unrest.

3. The level of spending determines the levels of output, employment, and incomes in Ameri-

can capitalism. Inflation becomes increasingly severe as the economy approaches full employment; an increase in total spending at full employment only serves to boost the price level. The general price level is more flexible upwards than downwards.

4. Business cycles—recurrent fluctuations in business activity of several years' duration—are a characteristic of American capitalism. These cycles vary greatly in duration and intensity. Nevertheless, four common phases—recession, depression, recovery, and prosperity—are characteristic of all. Business cycles differ from seasonal variations and the secular trend in business activity.

5. All sectors of the economy are affected by the business cycle, but in varying ways and degrees. The cycle has greater output and employment ramifications in the capital goods and durable consumer goods industries than it does in nondurable goods industries. Over the cycle, price fluctuations are greater in competitive than in monopolistic industries. Profit incomes tend to fluctuate more than do other shares of the national income.

6. Inflation—a rising general level of prices—is caused by excessive spending. Deflation is caused by a deficiency of total spending.

7. Inflation redistributes income at the expense of fixed income receivers, creditors, and savers. Deflation has substantially the reverse effects. However, changes in the real output which may accompany inflation or deflation may relieve or intensify the redistributive impact of a change in the general level of prices.

8. Economists disagree as to the effect which inflation may have upon the level of performance achieved by the economy. Some argue that mild inflation is essential in achieving full employment and maximum economic expansion. Another group feels that over time mild inflation has substantial and undesirable redistributive effects and that it is likely to precipitate hyperinflation and economic collapse.

9. During the last forty years American capitalism has encountered both stagnation and ex-

pansion. The prosperity of the 1920s is best explained in terms of a high level of investment spending. The replacement of capital goods used up during World War I, the development of a host of new industries, productivity increases, a high rate of construction activity, and a favorable monetary-financial climate all played major roles in this era of prosperity.

10. The slackening and decline of investment spending was the basic factor underlying the Great Depression of the 1930s. Many considerations contributed to this investment decline: overinvestment in capital facilities in the 1920s, the end of the building boom, a contraction of mortgage and consumer credit, the stock market crash and the subsequent failure of the monetary system, and other factors.

11. Military spending in the early 1940s returned the economy to full employment. Coupled with the increases in consumption which expanding incomes entailed, this government spending posed an inflationary threat which was repressed by direct controls during World War II.

12. In the immediate postwar years large increases in consumption, investment, and net foreign spending filled the gap created by reduced military spending. As a result, the repressed inflation of the war years blossomed into open inflation.

13. The 1950s were characterized by over-all prosperity and mild inflation, marred by recessions in 1954 and 1958 and an above-normal unemployment rate in the closing years of the decade. Cost-push inflation was an outstanding feature of the 1958 recession.

14. Whether the 1960s will be "soaring" or "sluggish" remains to be seen. While population growth and technological advance imply sustained investment spending and a prosperous economy, such factors as (*a*) an increase in the number of new labor-force entrants each year, (*b*) the limiting of job opportunities in manufacturing due to automation, (*c*) the loss of some export markets as a result of economic recovery in Western Europe and Japan, and (d) the possibility that vigorous anti-inflation policies invoked by the Federal government will restrict employment and production, may all contribute to above-normal unemployment and a retardation of the rate of growth of GNP in the sixties.

15. American business cycle experience suggests that (a) the factors which bear upon total spending and hence output, employment, and the price level are many and varied; (b) variations in investment play a crucial role in cyclical fluctuations; and (c) within limits prosperity and depression are cumulative.

QUESTIONS AND STUDY SUGGESTIONS

1. Carefully define "full employment." What is "normal unemployment"?

2. Why is unemployment an economic problem? What are the noneconomic effects of unemployment?

3. Carefully describe the relationship between total spending and the level of resource utilization. Explain the relationship between the price level and increases in total spending as the economy moves from substantial unemployment to moderate unemployment and, finally, to full employment. What is the significance of this relationship?

4. What are the major phases of the business cycle? How long do business cycles last? What are seasonal variations and secular trends in business activity? How do they complicate measurement of the business cycle?

5. Why does the business cycle affect durable goods industries more severely than industries producing nondurables? How are the various shares of the national income affected by prosperity and depression?

6. Distinguish between money income and real income. Explain how an *increase* in one's money income and a *decrease* in his real income might occur simultaneously.

7. Evaluate as accurately as you can the manner in which each of the following individuals would be affected by fairly rapid inflation:

a. A pensioned railroad worker

b. A department-store clerk

c. A UAW assembly-line worker

d. A heavily indebted farmer

e. A retired businessman whose current income is composed entirely of stock dividends

f. A widow whose income is derived entirely from interest on government bonds

g. The owner of an independent, small-town department store

8. Explain how severe inflation might lead to unemployment. Clearly distinguish between "demand-pull" and "cost-push" inflation.

9. "Inflation is a friend on the journey to full employment, but an enemy once the destination is reached." Evaluate and explain.

10. In August, 1957, William McChesney Martin, chairman of the Board of Governors of the Federal Reserve System, made the following statement before the Senate Finance Committee: "There is no validity whatever in the idea that

any inflation, once accepted, can be confined to moderate proportions. Once the assumption is made that a gradual increase in prices is to be expected, and this assumption becomes a part of everybody's expectations, keeping a rising price level under control becomes incomparably more difficult than the problem of maintaining stability when that is the clearly expressed goal of public policy. Creeping inflation is neither a rational nor a realistic alternative to stability of the general price level." Also in 1957, Alvin H. Hansen, noted Harvard economist, wrote the following comments:[12] "Periods of rapid growth have usually also been periods of moderate price increases. . . . It is not probable that we can achieve in the next twenty years anything like the growth of which we are capable, without some moderate increases in wholesale and consumer prices. . . . Thus I conclude that if in the pursuit of rigid price stability we permit, and even foster, a considerable amount of unemployment, we shall then fail to achieve the growth of which we are capable." Contrast and evaluate carefully these two points of view. To which do you subscribe?

11. A noted television comedian once defined inflation as follows: "Inflation? That means your money today won't buy as much as it would have during the depression when you didn't have any." Is his definition accurate?

12. Briefly outline the major factors which contributed to the prosperity of the 1920s. Now explain the basic considerations underlying the Great Depression of the 1930s. What relationships, if any, can you cite between the causes of the booming twenties and the depressed thirties?

13. Explain the extended period of prosperity which has been with us for the last two decades. What importance would you attach to (*a*) business and consumer expectations, (*b*) consumer credit, (*c*) changes in the supply of money, and (*d*) government policies as causal factors in this prosperity? Use the statistics presented in this chapter where applicable to substantiate your answers. Now use these data to describe our economy's performance in the late 1950s and early 1960s.

SELECTED REFERENCES

Challenge, June, 1961. A special issue on the American economy of the 1960s.

Gordon, Robert A., *Business Fluctuations,* 2d ed. (New York: Harper & Row, Publishers, 1961), particularly chaps. 8–11 and 14–16.

Haberler, Gottfried, *Prosperity and Depression* (Geneva: League of Nations, 1941), chap. 1.

Harris, Seymour E., "The Incidence of Inflation: Or Who Gets Hurts?" *Study Paper No. 7 of the Joint Economic Committee* (Washington: 1959).

Heilbroner, Robert L., *The Making of Economic Society* (Englewood Cliffs, N.J.: Prentice-Hall, Inc., 1962), chap. 6.

Maisel, Sherman J., *Fluctuations, Growth, and Forecasting* (New York: John Wiley & Sons, Inc., 1957), particularly chap. 2.

Morgan, Theodore, *Income and Employment,* 2d ed. (Englewood Cliffs, N.J.: Prentice-Hall, Inc., 1952), particularly chaps. 5 and 7.

[12] *The American Economy* (New York: McGraw-Hill Book Company, Inc., 1957), pp. 45–47.

Chapter 12

THE BACKGROUND AND ANALYTICAL TOOLS

OF EMPLOYMENT THEORY

Econom Thugs Capet capable to purchase
for unemployed Employment (Full)

THIS AND THE FOLLOWING CHAPTER are concerned with assessing the ability of a capitalistic economy to achieve the full employment of its resources. If the price system can provide for a reasonably efficient allocation of resources, what is to prevent it from providing for the full utilization of society's available resources?

More specifically, the objectives of the present chapter are threefold: In the first place, we want to understand why for many years economists thought capitalism was capable of providing for virtually uninterrupted full employment. Involved here is a discussion of the so-called classical theory of employment. Second, the shortcomings of the classical theory will be noted and analyzed. Then, finally, the tools of modern employment theory will be introduced and explained. In Chapter 13 we will employ these tools to analyze the equilibrium levels of output and employment and extend our analysis to indicate the effects of government policies upon output and employment.

Three simplifying assumptions will greatly facilitate the achievement of these stated objectives:

1. A "closed economy" will be assumed. That is, our discussion will deal only with the domestic economy, deferring the complications arising from international trade transactions until later chapters.

2. Government will be ignored throughout most of our analysis, thereby permitting us to determine whether or not laissez-faire capitalism is capable of achieving full employment. Later, as noted, we shall bring government into the picture and discuss the manner in which government can help stabilize the economy.

3. Although saving actually occurs in both the business and household sectors of the economy, we shall speak as if all saving were personal saving.[1]

One implication of the second and third assumptions is particularly noteworthy. These two assumptions permit us to treat NNP, NI, PI, and DI as being equal to one another for the simple reason that all the items which in practice distinguish them from one another are due to government (taxes and transfer pay-

---

[1] When using NNP as our measure of total output, it is accurate to assume that the bulk of the economy's saving is done by households. Table 10-7 shows personal saving at $25.9 billion and undistributed corporate profits at $8.8 billion for 1961. If GNP were employed, however, capital consumption allowances of $45.2 billion would have to be included as a part of business saving, making business saving more than twice as great as personal saving.

214

ments) and business saving (see Table 10-7). This means that we can readily shift our discussion among these various output and income measures without encountering serious complications which would otherwise arise.

Now the ground is cleared to rephrase our basic question: Is capitalism able to achieve and maintain a full-employment noninflationary total output?

THE CLASSICAL THEORY OF EMPLOYMENT

Answers to this question have varied historically. Until the Great Depression of the 1930s, most economists felt that the price system was capable of providing for the full employment of the economy's resources. It was acknowledged that now and then abnormal circumstances would arise in such forms as wars, political upheavals, droughts, speculative crises, gold rushes, and so forth, to push the economy from the path of full employment (see Figure 11-2). But when these deviations occurred, it was contended that automatic adjustments within the price system would soon restore the economy to the full-employment level of output. Those economists who espoused the view that the norm of capitalism is full employment and that deviations from that norm would be automatically self-correcting are now referred to as the classical economists.[2] Though the employment theory of this group of scholars is now rejected by the vast majority of economists (including some who earlier were leaders in this school of thought), an analysis of classical thinking will lay a firm foundation for understanding modern employment theory.

The classical theory of employment was grounded on two basic notions. First, it was argued that underspending—that is, a level of spending insufficient to purchase a full-employment output—was most unlikely to occur. Second, even if a deficiency of total spending were to arise, price-wage adjustments would

[2] Most notable among the classical economists are John Stuart Mill, F. Y. Edgeworth, Alfred Marshall, and A. C. Pigou.

occur so as to ensure that the decline in total spending would not entail declines in real output, employment, and real incomes.

Say's Law

The classical economists' denial of the possibility of underspending was based upon their faith in Say's Law. Say's Law is the disarmingly simple notion that the very act of producing goods generates an amount of income exactly equal to the value of the goods produced. That is, the production of any output would automatically provide the wherewithal to take that output off the market. Supply creates its own demand.[3] As a matter of fact, the circular flow model of the economy and national income accounting both suggest something of this sort. The income generated from the production of any level of total output would, *when spent*, be just sufficient to provide a matching total demand. Assuming that the composition of output is in accord with consumer preferences, all markets would be cleared of their output. It would seem that all businessmen need do to sell a full-employment output is to produce that output; Say's Law guarantees sufficient purchasing power for its successful disposal.

Saving: a complicating factor. However, there is one obvious omission in this simple application of Say's Law. While it is an accepted truism that output gives rise to an identical amount of money income (Chapter 10), there is no guarantee that the recipients of this income will spend it all. Some income might be saved (not spent) and therefore not reflected in product demand. Saving would constitute a break, or "leakage," in the income-expenditure flows and therefore undermine the effective operation of Say's Law. Saving is a withdrawal of funds from the income stream which will cause total expenditures to fall short of total output. If households saved a given portion of their incomes, supply would not create its own demand. Saving would cause a de-

[3] Attributed to the nineteenth-century French economist, J. B. Say.

ficiency of total expenditures. The consequences? Unsold goods, cutbacks in production, unemployment, and falling incomes. In short, supply seemingly creates its own demand only when households spend their entire incomes. If households save, a deficiency of total spending and depression will apparently result.

Saving, investment, and the interest rate. But the classical economists were reluctant to bow to those economists who suggested that such a virtuous act as saving could give rise to underspending and the calamity of depression. Instead, they argued that saving would not really result in a deficiency of total demand, because each and every dollar saved would be invested by businesses. Businessmen, after all, do not plan to sell their entire output to consumers but rather produce a considerable portion of total output in the form of capital goods for sale to one another. In other words, investment spending by businesses is a supplement or addition to the income-expenditure stream. Thus, if businesses as a group intend to invest as much as households want to save, the levels of national output and employment will remain constant. Whether or not the economy could achieve and sustain a level of spending sufficient to provide a full-employment level of output and income therefore depends upon whether businesses are willing to invest enough to offset the amount households want to save.

Now the classical economists argued that capitalism contained a very special price mechanism—the interest rate—which would guarantee an equality of saving and investment plans and therefore full employment. That is, the interest rate would see to it that dollars which leaked from the income-expenditure stream as saving would automatically reappear as dollars spent on investment goods. The rationale underlying the saving and investment equating adjustments of the interest rate was simple and, if not too carefully scrutinized, very plausible. The classical economists contended that, other things being equal, households normally prefer to consume rather than to save. The consumption of goods and services satisfies

human wants; idle dollars do not. Hence, it was reasoned that consumers would save only if someone would pay them a rate of interest as a reward for their thriftiness. The greater the interest rate, the more dollars saved; that is, the saving (supply-of-dollars) curve of households would be upsloping as in Figure 12-1. And who would be inclined to pay for the use of saving? None other than investors—businessmen who seek money capital to replace and enlarge their plants and their stocks of capital equipment. Because the interest rate is a cost to borrowing businessmen, they will be willing to borrow and invest more at low than at high interest rates. This means that the investment (demand-for-dollars) curve of businesses is downsloping as in Figure 12-1. Classical economists concluded that the money market, wherein savers supply dollars and investors demand dollars, would establish an equilibrium price for the use of money—an equilibrium interest rate—at which the quantity of dollars saved (supplied) would equal the number of dollars invested (demanded). Saving, said the classicists, does not really constitute a break in the income-expenditure stream nor a fatal flaw in Say's Law, because the money market or, more specifically, the interest rate, will guarantee that each and every dollar saved will get into the hands of investors and be spent on capital equipment. Therefore, an increase in thriftiness is not a cause for social concern, because this simply shifts the supply-of-saving curve to the right. Although saving will for a time exceed investment and cause some temporary unemployment, the surplus of saving will drive the interest rate down to a new and lower equilibrium level. And this lower interest rate will expand the volume of investment spending until it again equals the amount of saving, thereby preserving full employment. In short, changes in the interest rate would guarantee the operation of Say's Law even in an economy in which substantial saving occurs. As the classical economists saw it, the economy was analogous to a gigantic bathtub wherein the watermark measured the level of output and employment. Any leakage down the drain of saving would be returned to the tub through

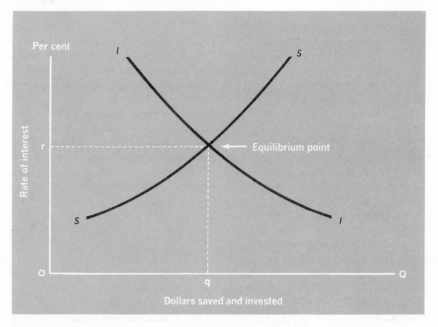

FIGURE 12-1. CLASSICAL VIEW OF THE INTEREST RATE.
The classical economists believed that the saving plans of households would be
reflected in a supply-of-dollars curve *S* and the investment plans of businesses in a
demand-for-dollars curve *I* in the money market. The equilibrium interest rate *r*, the
price paid for the use of money, would equate the amounts households and businesses
planned to save and invest, thereby guaranteeing a full-employment level of spending.

Clas mid Full employ to norm of capitalism

the spigot of investment. This had to be the
case, because the interest rate connected the
drainpipe and the spigot!

Price-wage flexibility

The classical economists bolstered their conclusion that full employment is the norm of
capitalism with a second basic argument: they
argued that the level of output which businessmen can sell depends not only upon the level
of total spending but also upon the level of
product prices. This meant that, even if the interest rate would somehow temporarily fail to
equate the amounts which households wanted
to save with the investment intentions of businesses, any resulting decline in total spending
would be offset by proportionate declines in
the price level. That is, $20 will buy four shirts

at $5, but $10 will buy the same number of
shirts if their price will only fall to $2.50.
Hence, if households somehow managed to
succeed in saving more than businesses were
willing to invest, the resulting decline in total
spending would not result in a decline in real
output, real income, and the level of employment *if* product prices declined in proportion
to the decline in expenditures.

And, according to the classical economists,
this is precisely what would happen. Competition among sellers would guarantee it! As declines in product demand became general,
competing producers would lower their prices
to dispose of accumulating surpluses. Hence,
product prices would fall. In other words, the
result of saving would be to lower prices; and
lower prices, by increasing the value of the
dollar, would permit nonsavers to obtain more

Savings will lower prices
increase value of the dollar

goods and services with their current money incomes. Saving would therefore simply lower prices, but not output and employment.

"But," ever-present skeptics asked, "doesn't this ignore the resource market? Although businesses can sustain their sales in the face of a declining demand by accepting lower product prices, won't they find it unprofitable to do so? As product prices decline, won't resource prices—particularly wage rates—have to decline significantly to permit businesses to produce *profitably* at the now lower prices?" The classical economists replied that wage rates must and would decline. General declines in product demand would be mirrored in declines in the demand for labor and other resources. The immediate result would be a surplus of labor, that is, unemployment, at the wage rate prevailing prior to these declines in the demand for labor. However, though not willing to employ all workers at the original wage rates, producers would find it profitable to employ additional workers at lower wage rates. The demand for labor, in other words, is downsloping; those workers unable to locate employment at the old higher wage rates could find jobs at the new lower wage rates.

Would workers be willing to accept lower wage rates? Competition among unemployed workers, according to the classical economists, would guarantee it. In competing for scarce jobs, idle workers would bid down wage rates until these rates (wage costs to employers) were so low that employers would once again find it profitable to hire all available workers. This would happen at the new lower equilibrium wage rate. The classical economists therefore concluded that *involuntary unemployment* was impossible. Anyone willing to work at the market-determined wage rate could readily find employment. Competition in the labor market ruled out involuntary idleness.

Classical theory and laissez-faire

Strictly speaking, each of these price system adjustments—fluctuations in the interest rate on the one hand, and price-wage flexibility on the other—seemed fully capable of maintaining full employment in a capitalistic economy. Working together, the classical economists felt, the two adjustment mechanisms made full employment a foregone conclusion. The classical economists came to embrace capitalism as a self-regulating economy wherein full employment was regarded as the norm. Capitalism was capable of "running itself." Government assistance in the operation of the economy was deemed unnecessary, nay, harmful. In an economy capable of achieving both full production and full employment, governmental interference could only be a detriment to its efficient operation.

KEYNES AND "THE NEW ECONOMICS"

One embarrassing fact persistently denied the validity of the classical theory of employment—recurring periods of prolonged unemployment and inflation. Now while one might explain a minor depression such as the brief downswings of 1924 and 1927 in terms of wars and similar external considerations, serious and prolonged downswings such as the Great Depression were not so easily rationalized. There is a remarkable inconsistency between a theory which concludes that unemployment is virtually impossible and a ten-year siege of very substantial unemployment.[4] And so various economists came to criticize both the rationale and the underlying assumptions of classical employment theory. They groped for a better, more realistic explanation of those forces which determine the level of employment.

Finally, in 1936 the renowned English economist, John Maynard Keynes, came forth with a new explanation of the level of employment in capitalistic economies. In his *General Theory*

[4] It is interesting to note that most of the classical economists stuck to their theoretical guns during the 1930s, arguing that (1) the reluctance of union and business monopolies to accept price and wage cuts, (2) misguided New Deal policies which sought to prevent price-wage declines, and (3) government policies in the area of money and banking which interfered with the operation of the interest rate prevented a quick recovery from the cyclical downswing of the early 1930s.

of *Employment, Interest, and Money*[5] Keynes virtually knocked the props out from under the classical view and, in doing so, touched off a major revolution in economic thinking on the question of unemployment. Though Keynes fathered "the new economics," many others have since refined and extended his work. In this and the following chapter we are concerned with modern employment theory as it stands today.

Modern employment theory contrasts sharply with the classical position. Its blunt conclusion is that capitalism simply does not contain any mechanisms capable of guaranteeing full employment. The economy, it is argued, might come to rest—that is, reach an equilibrium— with either considerable unemployment or severe inflation. Full employment accompanied by a relatively stable level of prices is more of an accident than a norm. Capitalism is not a self-regulating system capable of perpetual prosperity; capitalism cannot be depended upon to "run itself." Furthermore, depressions should not be associated exclusively with external forces such as wars, droughts, and similar abnormalities. Rather the causes of unemployment and inflation lie to a very considerable degree in the failure of certain fundamental economic decisions—in particular, saving and investment decisions—to be completely synchronized in a capitalistic system. Internal in addition to external forces contribute to economic instability.

Modern employment theorists back these sweeping contentions by rejecting the very mechanisms upon which the classical position is grounded—the interest rate and price-wage adjustments.

The unlinking of saving and investment plans

Modern employment theory rejects Say's Law by seriously questioning the ability of the interest rate to synchronize the saving and investment plans of households and businesses. The fact that modern capitalism is amply endowed with an elaborate money market involv-

ing innumerable banking and financial institutions does not diminish this skepticism of the interest rate as a mechanism capable of connecting the saving drain and the investment spigot. Most untenable was the classical contention that businessmen would invest more when households increased their rates of saving. After all, doesn't more saving mean less consumption? Can we really expect businessmen to expand their capital facilities as the markets for their products shrink? More generally, the modern view holds that savers and investors are essentially distinct groups that formulate their saving and investment plans for different reasons which, in each instance, are largely unrelated to the rate of interest.

1. Savers and investors are different groups. Who decides the amounts to be saved and invested in a capitalistic economy? (We continue to ignore government in our discussion.) Business organizations of all kinds and descriptions, and in particular corporations, make the vast majority of investment decisions. And who makes the saving decisions? Here the picture is a bit more cluttered. In a wealthy economy such as American capitalism, households save substantial amounts—at least when prosperity prevails (table on inside covers, line 18). It is true, of course, that business corporations also do a considerable amount of saving in the form of undistributed corporate profits. The important point is that to a significant degree saving and investment decisions are made by different groups of individuals (see footnote 1).

2. Savers and investors are differently motivated. Now the nonidentity of savers and investors would not necessarily be fatal to the classical theory if their decisions were motivated and synchronized by some common factor such as the interest rate. But this is simply not the case. Saving decisions are motivated by several considerations. Some save in order to make large purchases which exceed any single pay check; households save to make down payments on automobiles or to buy television sets and automatic washers. Some saving is simply

5 New York: Harcourt, Brace & World, Inc., 1936.

for the convenience of having a pool of liquid funds readily available to take advantage of any extraordinarily good buys which one may chance upon. Or saving may occur to provide for the future needs of an individual and his family: households save to provide for the future retirement of the family breadwinner or to expose the offspring to the rigors of a college education. Or saving may be a precautionary, rainy-day measure—a means of protecting oneself against such unpredictable events as prolonged illness and unemployment. Or saving may simply be a deeply ingrained habit that is practiced on an almost automatic basis with no specific purposes in mind.

Regardless of specific motivation, the modern view emphasizes that the amount which households desire to save is governed primarily by the level of national income, not by the rate of interest. In particular, a higher level of income will mean a high volume of both saving and consumption for households individually and as a group. When income is low, households must spend their entire incomes to achieve an acceptable standard of living; indeed, low incomes may give rise to dissaving. Higher incomes, however, permit households to increase both consumption and the level of saving. The important points are that (1) the size of the national income is much more vital as a determinant of the economy's willingness to save than is the interest rate[6] and (2) the amount households will attempt to save varies directly with national income.

Why do businesses purchase capital goods? The motivation for investment spending, as we shall discover in a few pages, is complex. The interest rate—the cost of obtaining money capital with which to invest—undoubtedly is a consideration in formulating investment plans. But the interest rate is not the most important factor. The rate of profit which businessmen expect to realize on the investment is the really crucial determinant of the amounts businessmen desire to invest. As a matter of fact, the investment plans of businesses are generally rather insensitive to changes in the interest rate. In particular, during the downswing of the business cycle, profit expectations will be so bleak that the level of investment will be low and possibly declining despite substantial reductions in the interest rates. Interest rate reductions are not likely to stimulate investment spending when increases in saving (declines in consumption) make it most sorely needed. Furthermore, if interest rates are relatively low to start with, as they typically are in industrially advanced economies, it simply is not possible for further significant declines to occur.

It is also significant that investors are not entirely dependent upon the current supply of saving in obtaining money capital. We shall find in Chapter 16 that commercial banks do not merely transfer money capital from savers to investors but rather can actually create money by granting loans. This correctly implies that businesses may attempt to invest at a rate in excess of the amount households currently desire to save.

The modern position is that saving and investment plans can be at odds and thereby result in fluctuations in total output, total income, and the volume of employment. It is largely a matter of chance that households and businesses will desire to save and invest identical amounts. Modern economists have proved themselves better plumbers than their classical predecessors by recognizing that the saving drain and the investment spigot are not connected.

The discrediting of price-wage flexibility

But what of the second aspect of the classical position—the contention that downward price-wage adjustments will eliminate the unemployment effects of a decline in total spend-

[6] Even if the interest rate were to affect significantly the desire to save, there is no guarantee that households would want to save larger amounts at higher interest rates, as the classical economists presumed. To illustrate: If the interest rate is currently 3 per cent, a household will need to save $10,000 to provide a retirement income of $300 per year. If the interest rate rises to 6 per cent and the household decides that $300 is still a satisfactory retirement income, savings can be cut from $10,000 to only $5,000. A higher interest rate may result in less, not more, saving.

ing? Modern theorists argue that, in the first place, prices and wages are in fact not flexible downward and, secondly, even if they were, it is doubtful that price-wage declines would alleviate widespread unemployment.

1. Price-wage flexibility, it is argued, simply does not exist to the degree necessary for ensuring the restoration of full employment in the face of a decline in total spending. The price system of modern capitalism is no longer a perfectly competitive one; rather it is riddled by market imperfections and circumscribed by practical and political obstacles which work against downward price-wage flexibility. To be specific, monopolistic producers, dominating many important product markets, will have both the ability and the desire to resist falling product prices as demand declines. And in the resource markets strong labor unions are equally persistent in holding the line against wage cuts. In this endeavor they are ably assisted by minimum-wage legislation, public opinion as to what are reasonable and "customary" wage rates, and practical-minded politicians who are well aware of the power of labor at the polls. In short, as a practical matter downward price-wage flexibility cannot be expected to offset the unemployment effects of a decline in total spending.

2. Furthermore, even if price-wage declines accompanied a contraction of total spending, it is doubtful that these declines would help reduce unemployment. The reason? The volume of total money demand cannot remain constant as prices and wages decline. That is, lower prices and wages necessarily mean lower money incomes, and lower money incomes in turn entail further reductions in total spending. The net result is likely to be little or no change in the depressed levels of output and employment.

The modern view points out that the classicists were tripped up in their reasoning by the fallacy of composition. Because any particular group of workers typically buy only a small amount of what they produce, the product and therefore labor demand curves of a single firm can be regarded as independent of any wage (income) changes accorded its own workers. In other words it is correct to reason

that a decline in its wage rate will move a *single firm* down its stable labor demand curve and result in more workers hired, that is, more employment. But the same reasoning, argue modern economists, is not applicable to the economy as a whole, to general wage cuts. Why? Because wages are the major source of income in the economy. Widespread wage declines will therefore result in declines in incomes and in the demand for both products and the labor used in producing them. The result is that employers will hire little additional labor (conceivably less labor) after the general wage cuts than they did before. What holds true for a single firm—a wage cut for its employees will not adversely affect labor demand —does not hold true for the economy as a whole—general wage cuts will lower money incomes and cause the demand for products and labor to decline generally.

Modern theory holds that price and wage adjustments would not cancel out the unemployment associated with a decline in expenditures for the simple reason that downward price-wage adjustments would not occur and would probably not be helpful even if they did.

THE TOOLS OF MODERN EMPLOYMENT THEORY

Our comments thus far have been directed at expounding and critically evaluating the classical theory of employment. Our conclusion is that a capitalistic economy may be subject to fluctuations in total spending and therefore in output and employment as a result of imbalances in saving and investment plans. The task now is to explain in greater detail the factors underlying the consumption-saving decisions of households and the investment decisions of businesses. More specifically, we must explore the determinants of consumption, saving, and investment and show both numerically and graphically their relationship to the output-income level of the economy. Then, having developed these tools of modern employment theory, we can use them in the next chapter in explaining how the level of employment is determined in a capitalistic society.

CONSUMPTION AND SAVING

In terms of absolute size consumption is the main component of total spending (see Figure 7-4). It is therefore of obvious importance to understand the major determinants of consumption spending. Because saving is "not spending," we simultaneously explore the determinants of saving.

Income-consumption and income-saving relationships

There are many considerations which influence the level of consumer spending. But common sense and available statistical data both suggest that the most important determinant of consumer spending is income—in particular, disposable income. And, of course, since saving is that part of disposable income which is not consumed, DI is also the basic determinant of personal saving.

National income statistics for the last three decades indicate that consumption and income are directly related. As income rises, so does consumption; as income falls, so does consumption. Figure 12-2, which plots the relationship between consumption and disposable income for the 1929–1961 period, verifies this relationship. We exclude here the war years, because the unavailability of certain consumer goods and the strong patriotic appeals to save made consumption abnormally low and saving unusually high. The straight line drawn through these points indicates the general nature of the relationship between consumption and disposable income. The white 45-degree line is added to the diagram as a point of reference. Because this line bisects the 90-degree angle formed by the vertical and horizontal axes of the graph, each point on the 45-degree line must be equidistant from the two axes. Hence, all the dots falling on the 45-degree line indicate years in which households consumed all their disposable incomes. Points lying below the line indicate years in which disposable incomes exceeded consumption, that is, saving occurred. Those several points which are slightly above the 45-degree line indicate years in which households consumed in excess of their disposable incomes, that is, dissaving occurred. The vertical distance of any dot below or above the 45-degree line measures the amount of saving or dissaving in that year.

Figure 12-2 does more than suggest a direct relationship between disposable income and consumption. The position of the straight line C, which generalizes on the income-consumption relationship, suggests that households will spend a larger portion of a small income than they will of a large income. Or, in terms of saving, the data suggests that households will save a smaller portion of a small income than they will of a large income.

Consumption schedule and saving schedule

Figure 12-2 merely shows the amounts households *actually did consume* (and save) at the various levels of DI which existed over an extended period of years. Over this period of years changes in a good many factors other than the level of DI itself undoubtedly occurred which affected the specific amounts consumed and saved at each of the DI levels. Because of the possible influence of nonincome determinants of consumption and saving, the income-consumption relationship of Figure 12-2 is not particularly useful as an analytic tool. What we need for analytical purposes is an income-consumption relationship which shows the various amounts households will *plan* or *desire to consume* at various possible DI levels over some relatively short period of time wherein it is safe to assume other nonincome determinants are constant. We need a *consumption schedule* which indicates the various amounts households as a group are willing to consume at each possible level of DI during some short period of time. The consumption schedule, you will note, is similar to the demand schedule previously discussed, which shows how much of a particular product a group of buyers intend, or plan, to buy at each of the various possible prices at which the product might sell. The demand schedule was drawn up, remember, on

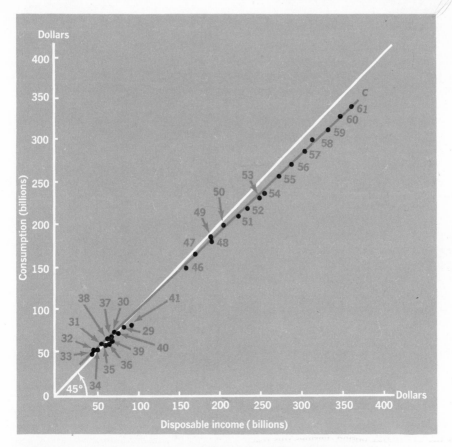

FIGURE 12-2. CONSUMPTION AND DISPOSABLE INCOME, 1929–1961.
Each dot in this figure shows disposable income and consumption expenditures in a given year. All points on the 45-degree guideline indicate the situation in which consumption and DI are equal. Thus dots falling below the 45-degree line indicate that saving has occurred; dots above indicate dissaving. The C line generalizes on the relationship between consumption and DI. It suggests that households spend a larger portion of a small income than they will of a large income. (U.S. Department of Commerce data.)

the supposition that nonprice determinants of the amount demanded were constant.

A hypothetical consumption schedule of the type we require is shown in columns 1 and 2 of Table 12-1. This schedule is plotted in Figure 12-3a. Now while this schedule is a theoretical relationship, it certainly makes sense in the absence of factual information to the contrary to draw it so it embodies the income-consumption relationships of Figure 12-2. The relationship between consumption and DI is direct, and, in addition, households supposedly will spend a *larger* proportion of a small DI than of a large DI.

It is a simple task to derive a *saving schedule.* Because disposable income equals consumption plus saving, we need only subtract consumption from disposable income to find the

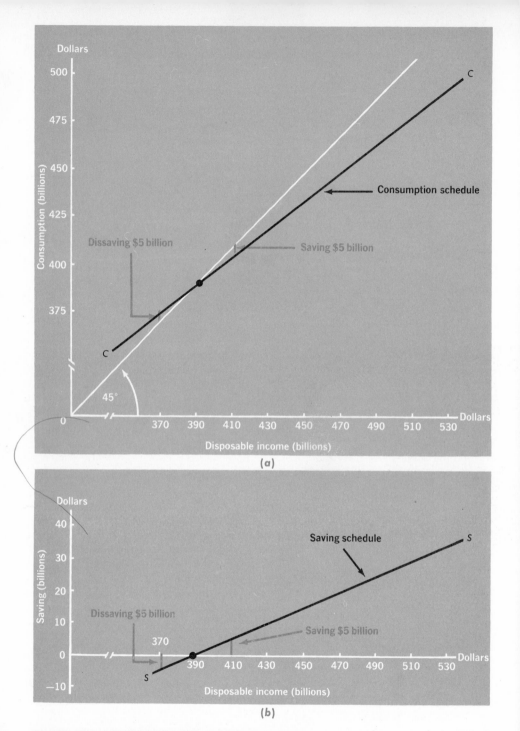

FIGURE 12-3. CONSUMPTION AND SAVING SCHEDULES.
The two parts of this figure show the income-consumption and income-saving relationships graphically. Each point on the 45-degree line in (a) indicates an equality of DI
and consumption. Therefore, because saving equals DI minus consumption, the
saving schedule in (b) is found by subtracting the consumption schedule from the 45-
degree guideline. Consumers "break even," that is, consumption equals DI (and
saving therefore equals zero), at $390 billion for this hypothetical data.

TABLE 12-1. THE CONSUMPTION AND SAVING SCHEDULES
(hypothetical data in billions)

(1) Level of output and income (NNP = DI)	(2) Consumption	(3) Saving, or (1) − (2)
$370	$375	$−5
390	390	0
410	405	5
430	420	10
450	435	15
470	450	20
490	465	25
510	480	30
530	495	35

amount saved at each level of DI. Hence, columns 1 and 3 of Table 12-1 constitute the saving schedule. This schedule is plotted in Figure 12-3b. Note that there is a direct relationship between saving and DI but that saving constitutes a *smaller* proportion of a small DI than it does of a large DI. Why? Because if households consume a smaller and smaller proportion of DI as DI goes up, they must save a larger and larger proportion.

Remembering that each point on the 45-degree line indicates an equality of DI and consumption, we see that dissaving occurs at the relatively low DI of $370 billion; that is, households consume in excess of their current incomes by drawing down accumulated savings or by borrowing. Graphically, the vertical distance the consumption schedule lies *above* the 45-degree line is equal to the vertical distance the saving schedule lies *below* the horizontal axis at the $370 billion level of output and income (see Figure 12-3a and b). In this instance these two vertical distances each measure the $5 billion of *dissaving* which occurs at the $370 billion income level. At the $390 billion income level, households "break even" by spending their entire incomes. Graphically, the consumption schedule cuts the 45-degree line, and the saving schedule cuts the horizontal axis at this income level. At all higher incomes households save a portion of their income. The vertical

distance of the consumption schedule below the 45-degree line measures this saving, as does the vertical distance of the saving schedule above the horizontal axis. For example, at the $410 billion level of income both these distances indicate $5 billion worth of saving (see Figure 12-3a and b).

Average propensities to consume and save. That fraction, or percentage, of any given total income which is consumed is called the *average propensity to consume* (APC), and that fraction of any total income which is saved is called the *average propensity to save* (APS). For example, at the $470 billion level of income in Table 12-1 the APC is 45/47 or about 96 per cent, while the APS is obviously 2/47 or about 4 per cent. By calculating the APC and APS at each of the nine levels of DI shown in Table 12-1, we find that the APC falls and the APS rises as DI increases. The fraction of total DI which is consumed declines as DI rises, and this makes it essential that the fraction of DI which is saved rises as DI rises.

Marginal propensities to consume and save. The fact that households consume a certain portion of some given total income—for example, 45/47 of a $470 billion disposable income—does not guarantee that they will consume the same proportion of any *change* in income which they might receive. The proportion, or fraction, of any change in income which is consumed is called the *marginal propensity to consume* (MPC), marginal meaning "extra." Or, alternatively stated, the MPC is the ratio of a change in consumption to the change in income which brought the consumption increase about; that is

$$\text{MPC} = \frac{\text{change in consumption}}{\text{change in income}}$$

ratio of change in consumption to change in income which brought the change in consumption about

The fraction of any change in income which is saved is called the *marginal propensity to save* (MPS). That is, MPS is the ratio of a change in saving to the change in income which brought it about:

$$\text{MPS} = \frac{\text{change in saving}}{\text{change in income}}$$

Fraction of any change in income which is saved

marginal prop to save

Thus, if disposable income is currently $470 billion and households for some reason find that their incomes rise by $20 billion, we find that they will consume $^{15}\!/_{20}$ or ¾ and save $^{5}\!/_{20}$ or ¼ of that increase in income (see Table 12-1). In other words, the MPC is ¾ or 75 per cent and the MPS is ¼ or 25 per cent. The sum of the MPC and the MPS for any given change in disposable income must always be 1. That is, consuming and saving out of extra income is an either-or proposition; that fraction of any increase in income which is not spent is, by definition, saved. Therefore the fraction consumed (MPC) plus the fraction saved (MPC) must exhaust the whole increase in income. In our example 75 per cent plus 25 per cent equals 100 per cent, or 1.

Economists are not in complete agreement as to the behavior of the MPC and MPS as income increases. For many years it was presumed that the MPC declined and the MPS increased as income increased. That is, it was felt that a smaller and smaller fraction of increases in income would be consumed and a larger and larger fraction of these increases would be saved. Many economists now feel that the MPC and MPS for the economy as a whole

are relatively constant. Statistical data such as those of Figure 12-2 support this position. We will assume the MPC and MPS to be constant not only because of this statistical evidence but also because a constant MPC, and therefore MPS, will simplify our analysis considerably. You will note that for each of the eight $20 billion income increases shown in Table 12-1, consumption increases by $15 billion, that is, by $^{15}\!/_{20}$ or ¾ of the increase in income, and saving increases by $5 billion, that is, by $^{5}\!/_{20}$ or ¼ of the increase in income. We assume the MPC and MPS to be constant at ¾ and ¼, respectively.[7]

MPC is 3/4
MPS 1/4

[7] The mathematically inclined reader will recognize that the MPC is the numerical value of the slope of the consumption schedule and the MPS is the numerical value of the slope of the saving schedule. The slope of any line can be measured by the ratio of the vertical change to the horizontal change involved in moving from one point to another point on that line. Thus, in the accompanying diagram, if the vertical

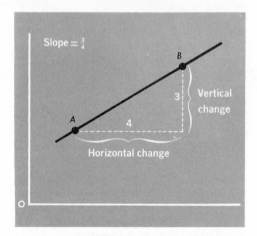

change is 15 and the horizontal change is 20, between points A and B, the slope of the line is ¾. Now it is evident in the figure that the slope of the consumption schedule between any two points is measured by the change in consumption (the vertical change) relative to the change in income (the horizontal change). And this ratio, change in consumption/change in income, is the fraction of any change in income that is spent; that is, it measures the MPC. Similar reasoning tells us that the MPS measures the slope of the saving schedule.

MPC & MPS = 1

Nonincome determinants of consumption and saving schedules

The level of disposable income is the basic determinant of the amounts households will consume and save in the same fashion that price is the basic determinant of the quantity demanded of any product. But price, you will recall, is not the sole determinant of the amount purchased of a specific product. Changes in such factors as consumer tastes, money income, and so forth, will cause consumers to alter their entire set of buying plans, or intentions, causing them to want either more or less of the specific product at each possible price and thereby shifting the location of the demand curve. Now, although income is the basic determinant of consumption spending, there are certain other determinants which might cause households as a group to consume more (and therefore save less) at each possible level of income. Some of the more important nonincome determinants of consumption and saving are (1) the stocks of liquid assets which households have on hand, (2) the stocks of durable goods consumers have on hand, (3) expectations with respect to incomes, prices, and the availability of goods, (4) the current volume of consumer credit outstanding, and (5) attitudes toward thrift.

1. Stocks of liquid assets. Generally speaking, the greater the amounts of liquid assets—private and public bonds, stocks, insurance policies, bank accounts, and so forth—owned by consumers, the greater will be their willingness to consume at each possible level of DI. The ownership of liquid assets makes households feel more secure financially and hence more willing to spend out of current disposable income. You will recall that the large volume of liquid assets accumulated by households during World War II was an important factor underlying the high level of consumption spending in the immediate postwar years.

2. Stocks of durable goods on hand. The amount which households are willing to spend at each level of income is affected by the stocks of durable goods which they currently own. If the economy has enjoyed an extended period of prosperity, consumers may find themselves well supplied with various durable goods. That is, the majority of families may own late-model cars, television sets, refrigerators, and other household appliances, all worthy of many years of future service. Hence, for a time many households will be "out of the market" for such products, with the result that consumers are willing to spend less and save more at each possible level of disposable income.

The position of consumers at the close of World War II is in sharp contrast to the situation just described. Many consumer durables all but disappeared from product markets during the war, because the resources needed in their production had been reallocated to war industries. The stock of consumer durables owned by households therefore dwindled significantly during the war. Reconversion was stimulated by a tremendous backlog of consumer demand for durable goods. This factor, along with the previously noted accumulation of liquid assets during the war, led to a high rate of spending and low level of saving in the immediate postwar period.

3. Expectations concerning incomes, prices, and product availability. Household expectations concerning future prices, money incomes, and the availability of goods may have a significant impact upon current spending and saving. Expectations of rising prices and product shortages tend to trigger more spending and less saving currently. Why? Because it is natural for consumers to seek to avoid paying higher prices or to be faced with the possibility of "doing without." Expected inflation and shortages induce people to "buy now" to escape higher future prices and bare shelves. Anticipated increases in money incomes bolster this tendency. The expectation of rising money incomes in the future tends to make consumers more footloose in their current spending.

The beginning of the Korean War affords an excellent example of how expectations can noticeably alter society's attitudes towards thrift and spending. American housewives, being shrewd and alert, remembered from the early 1940s that wars entail rising prices, shortages, and increasing money incomes. These expectations prompted a wave of consumer buying and a temporary upward shift in the consumption schedule. Ironically, this widespread attempt to "beat" inflation was doomed to failure; the sudden upsurge in spending prompted the inflation and the shortages consumers were trying to avoid!

Conversely, we can suppose that expected price declines, anticipations of shrinking incomes, and the feeling that goods will be abundantly available will induce consumers to retrench on their consumption and build up their savings.

4. The level of consumer indebtedness. The level of consumer credit can also be expected to affect the willingness of households to consume out of current income. If households are in debt to the degree that, say, 20 or 25 per cent of their current incomes are committed to installment payments on previous purchases, consumers may well be obliged to retrench on current consumption in order to reduce their indebtedness. Conversely, if consumer indebtedness is relatively low, households may consume at an unusually high rate by increasing this indebtedness.

5. General attitudes toward thrift. A final catchall item: an economy's general attitude towards frugality will help determine the amount of consumption and saving forthcoming at each possible level of DI. Attitudes toward thrift are governed as much by social and psychological considerations as they are by economic factors. If a society accepts the belief that saving is very virtuous and that "a dollar saved is a dollar earned," saving will tend to be greater and consumption less at each level of disposable income than would be the case where saving was held in lower esteem. There is some evidence to suggest that in the underdeveloped countries attitudes toward thrift are relatively weak, as most households are very anxious to consume

in order to emulate the higher living standards of the more advanced nations.

Attitudes towards thrift can be influenced by government policies. During World War II the Federal government waged intensive propaganda campaigns to encourage households to save by buying war bonds. These campaigns—coupled with the hard fact that many consumer durables were unavailable or in scant supply—were fairly successful in boosting the saving schedule and therefore in lowering the consumption schedule. Peacetime government policies may also affect the consumption and saving schedules. By committing itself to policies designed to promote full employment government may diminish the fear of unemployment and thereby weaken an important motive to save money.

Later, after government has been brought into the discussion, we shall note that changes in tax revenues and transfer payments (negative taxes) will affect both the consumption and saving schedules through their impact upon disposable income.

Change in amount consumed versus change in consumption schedule

A distinction similar to that drawn previously between a change in the quantity demanded and a change in demand is relevant in our discussion of the consumption and saving schedules. By a *change in the amount consumed* we refer to the movement from one point to another point on a given, stable consumption schedule. The sole cause of a change in the amount consumed is a change in the actual level of income. For example, in Table 12-1 the amount consumed increases from $390 to $405 billion as the result of an increase in DI from $390 to $410. Graphically this is shown as the movement from point A to point B on consumption schedule C_0 in Figure 12-4a. A change in the amount saved is similarly defined, and, as with consumption, the sole cause of a change in the quantity saved is a change in DI.

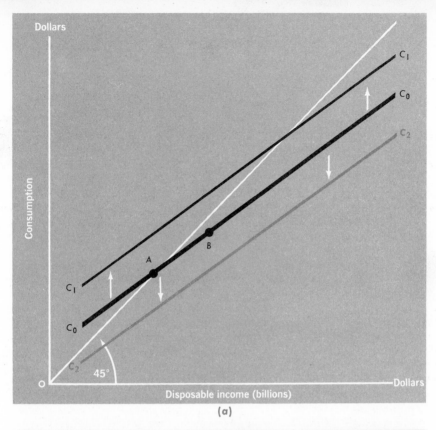

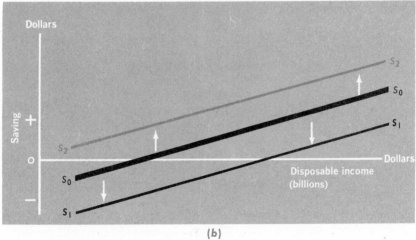

FIGURE 12-4. SHIFTS IN THE CONSUMPTION AND SAVING SCHEDULES.

A change in any one or more of the nonincome determinants will cause the consumption and saving schedules to shift. If households consume more at each level of DI, they are necessarily saving less. Graphically this means that an upshift in the consumption schedule (C_0 to C_1) entails a downshift in saving schedule (S_0 to S_1). Conversely, if households consume less at each level of DI, they are saving more. A downshift in the consumption schedule (C_0 to C_2) is reflected in an upshift of the saving schedule (S_0 to S_2).

By a *change in the consumption schedule* we obviously mean that the entire schedule, or relationship between DI and consumption, as shown in columns 1 and 2 of Table 12-1, has changed. The entire set of consumer plans, or intentions, has changed for some reason, so that households now want to consume more (save less) or consume less (save more) at each possible level of DI.

What might cause such a change in plans? The answer is a change in any one or more of the nonincome determinants of consumption and saving just discussed. For example, relatively low holdings of liquid assets, a large stock of consumer durables, expectations of falling money incomes and prices, a relatively high level of consumer indebtedness, and a high regard for thrift will all tend to depress the consumption schedule and boost the saving schedule. The opposite circumstances will tend to raise the consumption schedule and lower the saving schedule. Note in Figure 12-4a and b that, as the consumption schedule increases from C_0 to C_1, the saving schedule necessarily decreases from S_0 to S_1. If households plan to spend more at each level of DI, they necessarily desire to save less. Conversely, a drop in the consumption schedule from C_0 to C_2 means a boost in the saving schedule from S_0 to S_2. To consume less at each level of DI is to save more.

Having made all these comments about shifts in the consumption and saving schedules, we must now take note of the fact that economists believe the consumption and saving schedules to be relatively stable. This may be due to the fact that the nonincome determinants of consumption and saving are sufficient in number so that changes in them are likely to be in part self-canceling. Or this stability may stem from the fact that consumption-saving decisions are strongly governed by habit and therefore resistant to change. This is not to say, of course, that changes in the amounts consumed and saved do not occur. Though the schedules are reasonably stable, the actual level of DI can and does change, thereby causing increases and decreases in the amounts consumed and saved.

INVESTMENT

Now let us turn to the second component of private spending. What determines the rate of net investment spending? That is, what determines the amounts businesses want or plan to spend on additional machinery and equipment, new construction, and increases in inventories?

Determinants of investment: profit expectations

The simplest answer to this query is that business investment is based upon the *expected net profits* which businesses hope to realize from such spending. Note that we specify "expected" profits because the economic future is laden with uncertainty and businessmen are something less than soothsayers.

It is practically impossible to determine with any great degree of certainty the rate of profits to be realized on a machine which may be in use for fifteen or twenty years or on a factory building whose life expectancy is thirty or thirty-five years. This uncertainty is compounded by the possibility that the anticipated future life of a machine may be abruptly cut short by technological advances which render it obsolete. Note also that we specify "net" profits, that is, profits after all costs associated with the acquisition and use of the capital goods have been paid.

What are some of the more important factors which influence profit expectations? Most prominent are (1) technological advance and innovation, (2) the costs of acquiring, maintaining, and operating the proposed capital equipment, (3) the interest rate, (4) government policies, (5) the stock of capital on hand, (6) anticipated market conditions, and (7) the general state of business confidence.

1. Technological advance and innovation. Innovation—the development of new products and new techniques of production—is a major force underlying the level of investment. By putting innovating firms one jump ahead of competitors, new products frequently entail substantial profits. Realizing this, firms are anxious to invest in the capital equipment needed to produce these new products. Similarly, improved production methods mean lower costs and higher profits, and this too is conducive to a high rate of investment. In short, a rapid rate of innovation is conducive to a high level of investment, and vice versa.

2. Acquisition, maintenance, and operating costs. The initial costs of capital goods, along with the estimated costs of operating and maintaining those goods, are obviously important considerations in gauging the profitability of any particular investment. To the extent that these costs are high, expected *net* profits will be low and the level of investment will also be low. If these costs are relatively low, expected net profits and the level of investment will tend to be high. Note that the wage policies of unions affect profit expectations, because wage rates are clearly an operating cost.

3. The interest rate. The interest rate is a special type of cost involved in acquiring capital goods. Interest is a cost payment which investors must make in acquiring the money capital needed to negotiate the purchase of real capital. The higher this cost, the less the expected net profit on investment and hence the lower the level of investment. The lower the interest cost, the greater the expected profits and thus the level of investment spending. Business firms, incidentally, do not really avoid interest costs by financing investment internally, that is, by investing their own undistributed profits. By using $10,000 of its own funds to purchase real capital a firm sacrifices or forgoes the interest income which it otherwise could have earned by lending this money capital to someone else.

4. Government policies. There is little doubt that taxes affect profit expectations and the level of investment. Businessmen look to estimated profits *after taxes* in making their investment decisions. Taxes, as an added cost of doing business, tend to dampen profit expectations and retard investment spending.

The impact of government expenditures upon the profit expectations of private firms is difficult to assess. In some cases government spending, by stimulating particular firms and industries and by alleviating depressed business conditions, improves profit expectations. On the other hand, certain types of government spending—for example, the development of public power—allegedly cause the profit expectations of private power producers to deteriorate, thereby retarding investment.

5. The stock of capital goods on hand. Just as the stock of consumer goods on hand affects household consumption-saving decisions, so the stock of capital goods on hand influences expected profits from additional investment in a given industry. To the extent that a given industry is well stocked with productive facilities and inventories of finished goods, investment will be retarded in that industry. The reason is obvious: such an industry will be amply equipped to fulfill present and future market demand at prices which yield mediocre profits. If an industry has enough productive capacity or even excess productive capacity, profit expectations and further investment in that industry will not be appealing.

6. Anticipated market conditions. The future course of consumer demand is a most vital factor in determining future product prices and hence the expected profitability of particular investments. It is usually difficult to anticipate accurately the course of consumer demand—and therefore product price—over a number of future years. Yet it is clear that such factors as the size and composition of the population, the size and distribution of money incomes, alterations in consumer tastes and incomes, and the likelihood of successful competition from innovations or existing products are all relevant. Should these factors be favorable to a firm's product, then profit expectations and investment will tend to be high. If these factors are unfavorable, investment will tend to be low.

7. Business confidence and the stock market.
No one can accurately foresee the technological advances, the changes in consumer incomes and tastes, the trends in maintenance and operating costs, the changes in government policies, and so forth, which might occur in the next decade or two. The inability to foresee accurately future changes in most of the six "objective" determinants of profit expectations discussed above causes the general outlook of the business community—a "subjective" factor—to be of very considerable significance in determining net profit expectations and the rate of investment spending. If businessmen are generally confident and optimistic about the future, profit expectations and investment will tend to be high. Business pessimism about the future will lead to a low level of investment. What then determines the state of business confidence? Though this is not an easy question to answer, two factors seem to be particularly important:

First, *current business conditions* are a somewhat tangible, though not altogether logical, guide to future business conditions. If business conditions are currently good, there will be a tendency for businessmen to project these good times into expectations about the future unless there are specific reasons, as evidenced in any of or all the objective determinants of investment, to expect a change. Conversely, currently poor business conditions will be reflected in pessimism about the future among businessmen unless there is evidence to indicate an improvement.

A second factor in shaping business confidence is the *stock market.* Stock prices appear to be a fairly objective barometer of the prospective earnings of a firm or industry. After all, the securities market is in effect a sounding board for public opinion as to the future earning capacities of firms and industries. If the stocks of a certain firm or industry are trading at relatively high prices, this is a sign of public optimism as to the future of that firm or industry. Depressed stock prices indicate public pessimism; mass public opinion adjudges the future prospects of the firm or industry to be poor.

Stock prices may affect the rate of business investment in another, more immediate way. High stock prices not only bolster business optimism but also provide a favorable and ready money market for businesses; such conditions are obviously conducive to a high rate of investment in new capital facilities. On the other hand, low stock prices will not only dim business confidence but also provide an unfavorable money market for the sale of new securities. Indeed, if stock prices are relatively low, businesses may find it cheaper to acquire ownership of existing capital facilities of other firms (by buying a controlling amount of their stock) than to sell new securities and use the proceeds to invest in *new* capital facilities.

Investment and the level of income

In order to compare the investment decisions of businesses with the consumption-saving plans of households, we want to express investment plans in terms of the level of disposable income, or NNP. That is, we want to construct an *investment schedule* which shows the amounts which businessmen as a group plan or desire to invest at each of the various possible levels of income or output. Such a schedule will mirror the investment plans or intentions of businessmen in the same way the consumption and saving schedules reflect the consumption and saving plans of households.

Now common sense suggests that the relationship between investment and disposable income is such that a somewhat higher level of investment spending would be forthcoming at a high level of income than at a low level of income. A high level of income indicates a high level of business activity, and this in turn calls for increased spending on capital facilities to accommodate this activity. That is, we should expect the relationship between investment and income to resemble the data of Table 12-2 and Figure 12-5a.

On the other hand, such strategic determinants of investment as technological advances (more efficient production techniques, new products, new materials) and population growth

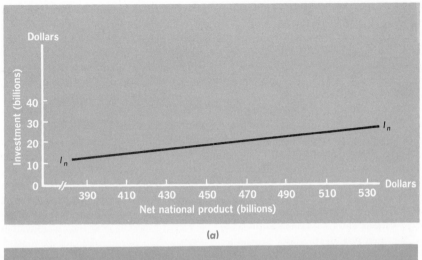

(a)

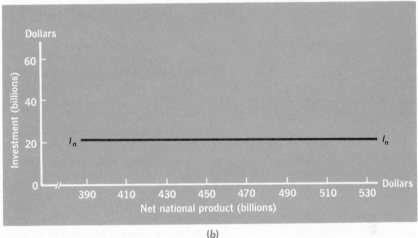

(b)

FIGURE 12-5. AN INVESTMENT SCHEDULE AND A SIMPLIFIED INVESTMENT
SCHEDULE.

In (a), which is based on Table 12-2, the relationship between investment and income
is direct, that is, a high level of income and output will induce a higher level of
spending on capital goods. Our discussion will be facilitated by employing a simplified investment schedule (b), based on Table 12-3, which assumes that the investment plans of businessmen are independent of the levels of income and output.

are more or less divorced from the level of total income over the short run. We shall simplify the income-investment relationship for the moment by supposing that the investment plans of businessmen are autonomous, or in-dependent of the level of income. That is, to simplify our analysis it will be presumed that the same amount of investment spending—say $20 billion—will be forthcoming at each and every level of income. This assumption, which we shall later release, is embodied in Table 12-3 and Figure 12-5b.

TABLE 12-2. THE INVESTMENT SCHEDULE

Level of output and income, billions	Investment, billions
$370	$10
390	12
410	14
430	16
450	18
470	20
490	22
510	24
530	26

Instability of investment spending

Investment is unstable. That is, the investment plans of businessmen as reflected in Table 12-3 and Figure 12-5b are subject to relatively frequent and irregular revisions. This means that the investment schedule shifts upward or downward suddenly and by significant amounts. What gives rise to this instability?

TABLE 12-3. SIMPLIFIED INVESTMENT SCHEDULE

Level of output and income, billions	Investment, billions
$370	$20
390	20
410	20
430	20
450	20
470	20
490	20
510	20
530	20

In the first place, the objective determinants of profit expectations—the first six items discussed above—are dynamic; they follow no regular, easily discernible pattern. Population growth can change markedly; demographers are noted for drastic revisions in their predictions of population growth. Technological advance and innovation—particularly major innovations such as the locomotive, the automobile, and atomic energy occur irregularly.

Secondly, the subjective determinant of profit expectations—business confidence—is even more capricious. Changes in the domestic political climate, changes in the status of the cold war, court decisions in strategic labor or antitrust cases, legislative actions, rumored changes in governmental policies, and a host of similar factors may set off waves of optimism or pessimism. This is all complicated by the fact that the pronouncements of leading industrialists or business groups tend to have a widespread and cumulative impact on business confidence throughout the nation. Changes in the business confidence of a strategic few may seriously alter the views of the entire business community. Dim-view lenses can replace rose-colored glasses almost overnight.

The fact that businessmen frequently gauge business confidence by stock prices is also a source of instability in investment spending. The stock market is a highly speculative thing. Many of those in the market are there not for the purpose of making long-term stock purchases, but rather to make quick profits by outguessing the rest of the market. However, because many people who are in the market are grossly ignorant of the profit potentials of the firms whose stocks they are trading, they base their own decisions to buy or sell on the basis of what others in the market are doing. Thus if the price of a given stock or of stocks in general begins to rise, uninformed individuals jump on the bandwagon and buy stocks on the assumption that *someone* must know that the future prospects for a given industry or for industry as a whole are good. The reverse happens when stock prices start to slump. This follow-the-leader tendency can greatly intensify rises or declines in stock prices. By (1) radically affecting business confidence and (2) influencing the relative attractiveness of new capital goods purchases as opposed to purchasing the ownership claims (stocks) of existing capital facilities, these upsurges and slumps in stock values can drastically affect the level of investment. You will recall our discussion of the important psychological repercussions of the stock market crash of 1929 in Chapter 11.

In short, the dynamic nature of the objective determinants of investment and the highly volatile character of business confidence contribute to considerable instability in the investment plans of businessmen. Though both may be contributing factors, the blame for fluctuations in total spending lies more at the door of investment than of consumption.

SUMMARY

1. Classical employment theory envisioned laissez-faire capitalism as being capable of providing virtually continuous full employment. This analysis was based on Say's Law and price-wage flexibility.

2. The classical economists argued that, because supply creates its own demand, general overproduction was impossible. This conclusion was held to be valid even when saving occurred, because the interest rate would automatically synchronize the saving plans of households and the investment plans of businesses.

3. Classical employment theory also held that even if temporary declines in total spending were to occur, these declines would be compensated for by downward price-wage adjustments to the end that real output, employment, and real income would not decline.

4. Modern employment theory rejects the notion that the interest rate would equate saving and investment by pointing out that savers and investors are substantially different groups who make their saving and investment decisions for different reasons—reasons which are largely unrelated to the interest rate.

5. Modern economists discredit price-wage flexibility on both practical and theoretical grounds. They argue that (*a*) union and business monopolies, minimum wage legislation, and a host of related factors have virtually eliminated the possibility of substantial price-wage reductions and (*b*) price-wage cuts will lower total income and therefore the demand for labor.

6. The basic tools of modern employment theory are the consumption, saving, and investment schedules, which show the various amounts households intend to consume and save and businesses plan to invest at the various possible income-output levels.

7. The locations of the consumption and saving schedules are determined by such factors as (*a*) the amounts of liquid assets owned by households, (*b*) the stocks of durables consumers have on hand, (*c*) expectations of future income, future prices, and product availability, (*d*) the relative size of consumer indebtedness, and (*e*) over-all attitudes toward thrift. The consumption and saving schedules are relatively stable.

8. The *average* propensities to consume and save show the proportion or fraction of any level of *total* income that is consumed and saved. The *marginal* propensities to consume and save show the proportion or fraction of any *change* in total income that is consumed or saved.

9. The immediate determinant of investment spending is net profit expectation. This expectation is influenced by such objective factors as (*a*) technological advance, (*b*) the acquisition, maintenance, and operating costs of real capital, (*c*) the interest rate, (*d*) government policies, (*e*) the stocks of capital on hand, and (*f*) anticipated market conditions. A more subjective factor—business confidence—is also of considerable importance.

10. The level of investment spending is characterized by considerable instability because of the dynamic nature of certain of the objective determinants and the extremely volatile character of business confidence.

QUESTIONS AND STUDY SUGGESTIONS

1. What is Say's Law? Explain the classical economists' conclusion that Say's Law would prevail even in an economy where substantial saving occurred. What arguments have modern economists used to undermine the classical view that Say's Law would result in sustained full employment?

2. "Unemployment can be avoided so long as businesses are willing to accept lower product prices, and workers to accept lower wage rates." Critically evaluate.

3. Define (*a*) the average propensities to consume and save and (*b*) the marginal propensities to consume and save. How do these two sets of concepts differ? Why must the sum of the MPC and the MPS equal 1?

4. What are the basic determinants of the consumption-saving schedules? Of your own level of consumption? What are the basic determinants of investment? Why is the investment schedule less stable than the consumption-saving schedules?

5. Explain precisely what relationships are shown by (*a*) the consumption schedule, (*b*) the saving schedule, and (*c*) the investment schedule.

6. Complete the following table:

Level of output and income (NNP = DI)	Consumption	Saving
$240		$ −4
260		0
280		4
300		8
320		12
340		16
360		20
380		24
400		28

a. Show the consumption and saving schedules graphically.

b. Determine the average propensity to consume and the average propensity to save for each level of income.

c. Now determine the MPC and MPS for each change in the income level.

d. Locate the "break-even" point. How is it possible for households to dissave at very low income levels?

e. If the proportion of total income which is consumed decreases and the proportion which is saved increases as income rises, explain both verbally and graphically how the MPC and MPS can be relatively constant at various levels of income.

7. Explain how each of the following will affect the consumption and saving schedules or the investment schedule:

a. A decline in the amount of government bonds which consumers are holding

b. The threat of limited, nonnuclear war in Southeast Asia, leading the public to expect future shortages of consumer durables

c. A decline in the interest rate

d. A sharp decline in stock prices

e. An increase in the rate of population growth

f. The development of a significantly cheaper method of manufacturing pig iron from ore

g. The announcement that the social security program is to be expanded in terms of both coverage and size of benefits

h. The expectation that mild inflation will persist in the next decade

8. Explain why an upshift in the consumption schedule necessarily involves an equal downshift in the saving schedule.

SELECTED REFERENCES

Chandler, Lester V., *A Preface to Economics* (New York: Harper & Row, Publishers, 1947), chap. 7.

Dillard, Dudley, *The Economics of John Maynard Keynes* (Englewood Cliffs, N. J.: Prentice-Hall, Inc., 1948), chaps. 1, 2, and 12.

Galbraith, John Kenneth, *American Capitalism,* rev. ed. (Boston: Houghton Mifflin Company, 1956), chaps. 1–6.

Hague, Douglas C., and Alfred W. Stonier, *The Essentials of Economics* (New York: Longmans, Green & Co., Inc., 1955), chaps. 8 and 9.

Heilbroner, Robert L., *The Worldly Philosophers,* rev. ed. (New York: Simon and Schuster, Inc., 1961), chap. 9.

Peterson, Wallace C., *Income, Employment, and Economic Growth* (New York: W. W. Norton & Company, Inc., 1962), chap. 4.

Sirkin, Gerald, *Introduction to Macroeconomic Theory* (Homewood, Ill.: Richard D. Irwin, Inc., 1961), chaps. 2–5.

Chapter 13

THE EQUILIBRIUM LEVELS OF OUTPUT,

EMPLOYMENT, AND INCOME

THIS CHAPTER is both a continuation and an expansion of Chapter 12. We seek, first, to use the consumption, saving, and investment schedules developed in Chapter 12 to explain the equilibrium levels of output, income, and employment. Next, changes in the equilibrium level of NNP are analyzed. Finally, we add the public sector of the economy to our discussion, assessing the impact of government spending and taxation upon the equilibrium NNP. Until government is added to our discussion, we retain the simplifying assumptions of Chapter 12 which permitted us to equate NNP and DI.

THE PRIVATE SECTOR

We now have before us all the analytical tools necessary to explain the equilibrium levels of output, employment, and income. By *equilibrium output* we refer to that level of total output which, once achieved, will be sustained. It exists where the flow of income created by the production of the output gives rise to a level of total spending sufficient to clear the product market of that output. In pursuing the important task of determining and explaining the equilibrium level of output, two closely interrelated approaches—the *aggregate demand–aggregate supply* (or $C + I_n = $ NNP)

approach and the *saving equals investment* (or $S = I_n$) approach—will be employed. Both will be discussed tabularly and graphically. For the moment we restrict our discussion of these two complementary approaches to the private sector of the economy. The public sector—government—will be added in a later section of this chapter.

Aggregate demand–aggregate supply approach

Let us first analyze the aggregate demand–aggregate supply approach in terms of simple arithmetic data. Table 13-1 merely brings together the income-consumption and income-saving data of Table 12-1 and the simplified income-investment data of Table 12-3.

This table is in many respects similar to Table 4-6, the supply and demand table for a specific product. You will recall that the demand schedule shows the amount consumers plan to purchase, and the supply schedule the amount producers plan to offer, at various prices. The equilibrium price was located at the point where the quantity demanded and the quantity supplied were equal. Barring revisions in the buying plans of consumers or the selling

238

TABLE 13-1. DETERMINATION OF THE EQUILIBRIUM LEVELS OF EMPLOYMENT, OUTPUT, AND INCOME: THE PRIVATE SECTOR

(1) Possible levels of employment, millions	(2) Aggregate supply (output and income)* (NNP = DI), billions	(3) Consumption, billions	(4) Saving, billions	(5) Investment, billions	(6) Aggregate demand (C + I_n), billions	(7) Tendency on employment, output, and incomes
40	$370	$375	$−5	$20	$395	Increase
45	390	390	0	20	410	Increase
50	410	405	5	20	425	Increase
55	430	420	10	20	440	Increase
60	450	435	15	20	455	Increase
65	470	450	20	20	470	Equilibrium
70	490	465	25	20	485	Decrease
75	510	480	30	20	500	Decrease
80	530	495	35	20	515	Decrease

* If government is ignored and it is assumed that all saving occurs in the household sector of the economy, NNP as a measure of aggregate supply is equal to NI, PI, and DI. This means that households receive a DI equal to the value of total output.

plans of producers, price and the corresponding amount exchanged would not vary from their equilibrium levels. This same general type of reasoning can be applied to *aggregate* demand and *aggregate* supply with two notable differences. First, because total output is comprised of heterogeneous goods, it is essential to state total supply in money terms rather than physical units. Second, the equilibrating factor is obviously the level of output and income rather than price.

Column 2 of Table 13-1 is in effect the total, or aggregate, supply schedule for the economy. It indicates the various possible levels of total output—that is, the various possible NNPs—which the business sector of the economy might produce. Producers are willing to offer each of these nine levels of output on the expectation that they will receive an identical amount of receipts of income from its sale. That is, the business sector will produce $370 billion worth of output, thereby incurring $370 billion worth of wage, rent, interest, and profit costs, only if

they expect that this output can be sold for $370 billion worth of receipts. Some $390 billion worth of output will be offered if businesses feel this output can be sold for $390 billion. And so it is for all the other possible levels of output.

The total, or aggregate, demand schedule is shown in column 6 of Table 13-1. It shows the total amount which will be spent at each possible output-income level. In dealing with the private sector of the economy the aggregate demand schedule simply shows the amount of consumption and net investment spending $(C + I_n)$ which will be forthcoming at each output-income level. We use net rather than gross investment because we are employing NNP rather than GNP as a measure of total output.

Now the question is this: Of the nine possible levels of NNP indicated in Table 13-1, which will be the equilibrium level? That is, which level of total output will the economy be capable of sustaining? The answer is: the equilibrium level of output is that output whose production will actually create total spending just sufficient to purchase that output. In other words, the equilibrium level of NNP is where the total quantity of goods supplied (NNP) is precisely equal to the total quantity of goods demanded $(C + I_n)$. Examination of the aggregate supply schedule of column 2 and the aggregate demand schedule of column 6 indicates that this equality exists only at the $470 billion level of NNP. This is the only level of output at which the economy is willing to spend precisely the amount necessary to take that output off the market. Here the annual rates of production and spending are in balance. There is no overproduction which results in a piling up of unsold goods and therefore cutbacks in the rate of production, nor is there an excess of total spending which draws down inventories and prompts increases in the rate of production. In short, there is no reason for businessmen to vary from this rate of production—this is therefore the equilibrium NNP.

To enhance our understanding of the meaning of the equilibrium level of NNP, let us examine other possible levels of NNP to see why they cannot be sustained. For example, at the $410 billion level of NNP businesses would find that, if they produced this output, the income created by this production would give rise to $405 billion in consumer spending. Supplemented by $20 billion of investment, the total quantity demanded $(C + I_n)$ would be $425 billion as shown in column 6. The economy obviously provides an annual rate of spending more than sufficient to purchase the current $410 billion rate of production. Because businessmen are producing at a slower rate than buyers are taking goods off the shelves, an unintended decline in business inventories will occur. Businessmen will adjust to this happy state of affairs by stepping up production. And a higher rate of output will mean more jobs and a higher level of total income. In short, if the total quantity of goods demanded exceeds the total quantity supplied, the latter will be driven upward. By making the same comparisons of NNP (column 2) and $C + I_n$ (column 6) at all other levels of

NNP below the $470 billion equilibrium level, it will be found that the economy wants to spend in excess of the level at which businesses are willing to produce. The excess of total spending at all these levels of NNP will drive NNP upward to the $470 billion level.

The reverse holds true at all levels of NNP above the $470 billion equilibrium level. That is, businesses will find that the production of these total outputs fails to generate the levels of spending needed to take them off the market. Being unable to recover the costs involved in producing these outputs, businesses will cut back on their production. To illustrate: At the $510 billion level of output businessmen will be disappointed to find that their productive efforts have not generated enough spending to permit the sale of that output. Of the $510 billion worth of income which this output creates, $480 billion is received back by businesses as consumption spending. Though supplemented by $20 billion worth of investment spending, the total quantity demanded ($500 billion) falls $10 billion short of the $510 billion quantity supplied. Inventories of goods pile up and businesses react to this unintended accumulation of unsold goods by cutting back on the rate of production. This decline in NNP will mean fewer jobs and a decline in total income. The reader should verify that deficiencies of total spending exist at all other levels of NNP in excess of the $470 billion level.

The equilibrium level of NNP exists where the total quantity supplied, measured by NNP, and the aggregate quantity demanded, $C + I_n$, are equal. Any excess of total spending over total output will drive the latter upward. Any deficiency of total spending will pull NNP downward.

The same analysis can be readily envisioned through a simple graph. In Figure 13-1 the 45-degree line indicates the aggregate supply schedule. Let us see why. Each point on the aggregate supply schedule will indicate the amounts which businessmen must expect to receive back as total spending in order to be induced to produce various possible outputs. As noted, businessmen will attempt to produce any total

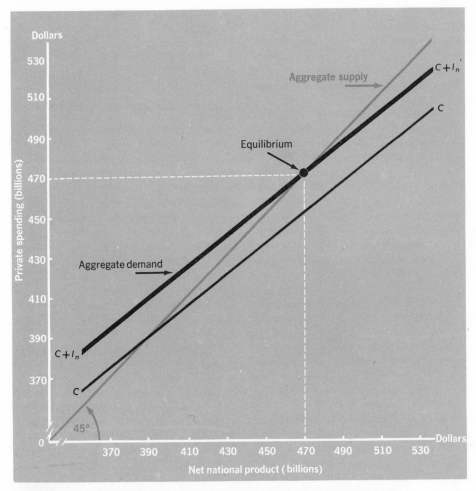

FIGURE 13-1. THE AGGREGATE DEMAND–AGGREGATE SUPPLY APPROACH TO THE EQUILIBRIUM NNP.

The aggregate supply schedule is the 45-degree line, because businesses will produce any given level of NNP only when they expect a level of total spending ($C + I_n$) just sufficient to dispose of that output. The equilibrium level of NNP is determined by the intersection of this aggregate supply schedule with the $C + I_n$, or aggregate demand, schedule. Only at this point are the production and purchasing plans of the economy consistent with one another.

output only if they expect to receive back an equal amount of total spending. That is, businessmen will offer any level of NNP only if they expect $C + I_n$ to be just sufficient to clear that output off the market. For example, businessmen will offer a $390 billion NNP only when they expect $C + I_n$ to be $390 billion. If they expected total spending to be greater or less than $390 billion, then businesses could be expected to offer an equally larger or smaller total output. Thus, a series of points—a line—equidistant from the total output (NNP) axis and the total spending $(C + I_n)$ axis will summarize the aggregate supply plans of businesses. Being equidistant from the two axes, this line is necessarily the 45-degree line. We conclude that the 45-degree line is the aggregate supply schedule. This schedule shows the various outputs which businesses will offer at each of the various levels of spending that might prevail.

To get the $C + I_n$ or aggregate demand schedule in Figure 13-1 we simply graph the consumption schedule of Figure 12-3a and add to it vertically the constant $20 billion amount from Figure 12-5b which businesses will assumedly want to invest at each possible level of NNP. More directly, we can plot the $C + I_n$ data of column 6 in Table 13-1.

The question: What is the equilibrium level of NNP? The answer: that NNP at which the aggregate quantity demanded and the aggregate quantity supplied are equal. And this must be where the aggregate supply schedule (the 45-degree line) and the aggregate demand schedule $(C + I_n)$ intersect. Because our graphed schedules are based on the data of Table 13-1, we once again find the equilibrium output to be at the $470 billion level. It is evident from Figure 13-1 that no levels of NNP above the equilibrium level are sustainable, because $C + I_n$ falls short of NNP. For example, at the $510 NNP level $C + I_n$ is only $500. Inventories of unsold goods rise to undesired levels. This unhappy state of affairs will prompt businesses to readjust their production sights downward in the direction of the $470 billion output level. Conversely, at all possible levels of NNP less than the $470 billion level, the economy desires to spend in excess of what businesses are producing. $C + I_n$ exceeds the value of the corresponding output. At the $410 billion NNP, for example, $C + I_n$ totals $425 billion. Inventories decline as the rate of spending exceeds the rate of production, prompting businessmen to raise their production sights in the direction of the $470 billion NNP. Unless there is some change in the consumption-saving plans of households or the investment plans of businesses, the $470 billion level of NNP will be sustained indefinitely.

Saving equals investment approach

The aggregate demand–aggregate supply approach to the determination of NNP has the advantage of spotlighting total spending as the immediate determinant of the levels of output, employment, and income. Though the $S = I_n$ approach is less direct, it does have the advantage of giving emphasis to the reason why $C + I_n$ and NNP are unequal at all levels of output except the equilibrium level.

The saving schedule (columns 2 and 4) and the investment schedule (columns 2 and 5) of Table 13-1 are pertinent. Our $C + I_n = $ NNP approach has just led us to conclude that all levels of NNP less than $470 billion are unstable because the corresponding $C + I_n$ exceeds these NNPs, driving them upward. A comparison of the amounts households and businesses want to save and invest at each of these below-equilibrium NNP levels explains these excesses of total spending. In particular, at each of these relatively low NNP levels businesses desire to invest more than households plan to save. For example, at the $410 billion level of NNP, households will save only $5 billion, thereby spending $405 of their $410 billion incomes. Supplemented by $20 billion of business investment, total spending $(C + I_n)$ is obviously $425 billion. Total spending exceeds NNP by $15 billion (= $425 − $410) because the amount businesses desire to invest at this level of NNP exceeds the amounts households plan to save by $15 billion. It is the fact that a very small "leakage" of saving at this relatively low income level will be more than compensated for by the relatively high level of investment spending which causes $C + I_n$ to exceed NNP and induce the latter upward.

Similarly, all levels of NNP above the $470 level are also unstable, because here NNP exceeds $C + I_n$. The reason for this insufficiency

Savings causes consumpt to fall short of NNP.

of total spending lies in the fact that at all NNP levels above $470 billion households will attempt to save in excess of the amount businesses desire to invest. That is, the saving leakage is not compensated for by the level of investment. For example, households will choose to save at the high rate of $30 billion at the $510 billion NNP. Businesses, however, will only invest $20 billion at this NNP. This $10 billion excess of saving over investment will cause total spending to fall $10 billion short of the value of total output. And this deficiency will cause NNP to decline.

Again we verify that the equilibrium NNP is at the $470 billion level. It is only at this point that the saving desires of households and the investment plans of businesses are equal. And only when businesses and households attempt to invest and save at equal rates will $C + I_n =$ NNP. Only here will the annual rates of production and spending be in balance; only here will unplanned changes in inventories be absent. One can think of it in this way: If saving were zero, consumer spending would always

be sufficient to clear the market of any given NNP; that is, consumption would equal NNP. But saving can and does occur, causing consumption to fall short of NNP. Hence, only when businesses are willing to invest at the same rate households attempt to save will the amount by which consumption falls short of NNP be precisely compensated for.

The $S = I_n$ approach to determining the equilibrium NNP can be readily demonstrated graphically. In Figure 13-2 we have merely combined the saving schedule of Figure 12-3b and the simplified investment schedule of Figure 12-5b. The numerical data for these schedules are repeated in columns 1, 4, and 5 of Table 13-1. It is evident that the equilibrium level of NNP is at $470 billion, where the saving and investment schedules intersect. Only here do households and businesses plan to save and invest at the same rates; therefore, only here will NNP and $C + I_n$ be equal. At all higher levels of NNP households will attempt to save at a rate higher than businesses are willing to invest. This causes $C + I_n$ to fall

FIGURE 13-2. THE SAVING EQUALS INVESTMENT APPROACH TO THE EQUILIBRIUM NNP.
A second approach is to view the equilibrium NNP as determined by the intersection of the saving (S) and investment (I_n) schedules. Only at the point of equilibrium will households plan to save the amount businesses want to invest. It is the consistency of these plans which causes NNP and $C + I_n$ to be equal.

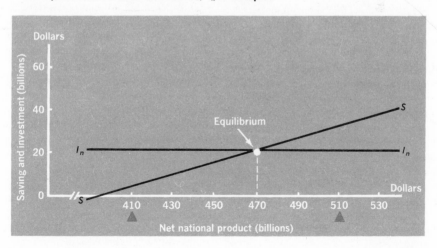

short of NNP, driving the latter downward. At the $510 billion NNP, for example, saving of $30 billion will exceed investment of $20 billion by $10 billion with the result that $C + I_n$ is $500 billion—$10 billion short of NNP. At all levels of NNP below the $470 billion equilibrium level businesses will desire to invest at a rate in excess of the amount households plan to save. The result is that $C + I_n$ exceeds NNP, driving the latter upward. To illustrate: At the $410 level of NNP the $5 billion leakage of saving is more than compensated for by the $20 billion businesses desire to invest. The result is that $C + I_n$ exceeds NNP by $15 billion, inducing businesses to produce a larger NNP.

Planned versus realized saving and investment

We must now focus our attention on an elusive but very significant distinction which has been lurking in the shadows of our analysis of the equilibrium level of output. That is the distinction between saving and investment *plans*, or intentions, and the *actual* amounts which households manage to save and businesses to invest. We have been very careful to indicate that the saving and investment schedules summarize the plans, or intentions, of consumers and businesses. These schedules tell us how much they would attempt or be inclined to save and invest at each of the various levels of output and income which might exist.

Our search for the equilibrium level of output has just revealed to us that only when the saving plans of households and the investment plans of businesses are consistent will they be accomplished or realized without further revision. Why? Because it is only at that output where saving and investment plans are consistent that the production and spending plans of the economy are consistent. More specifically, if businesses attempt to invest more than households attempt to save—as is the case at all outputs below the $470 billion equilibrium NNP—the rising level of total income that results will cause upward adjustments in the amounts households want to save. Similarly, should

households attempt to save more than businesses intend to invest—as is the case at all outputs above the $470 billion equilibrium NNP—the resulting declines in output and incomes will cause downward adjustments in the amounts households desire to save. These adjustments in income will cease only when the amount households want to save is the same amount businesses want to invest. Only at the $470 billion level of output will saving and investment plans be consistent. And only at this level of output can these plans be achieved.

In short it is essential to note that differences in saving and investment plans precipitate changes in the levels of employment, output, and income which cease only when saving and investment plans have been adjusted to a point of equality. Only at the point of equality can these plans be realized, that is, actually carried out, with no further revision. Our cause-effect chain goes something like this:

1. Differences in saving and investment plans account for differences in the production and spending plans of the economy as a whole.

2. As a result of these differences, changes are precipitated in the levels of output, employment, and income.

3. But these induced changes in output and income entail a revision of the amounts households are willing to save in the direction of an equality with the amounts businesses desire to invest.

4. At that output-income level where the rate at which households want to save and the rate at which businesses want to invest are the same, these plans can be realized without further revision.

In other words, "before the fact"—that is, before required adjustments in employment, output, and income have been completed—the rates of planned saving and planned investment may be different. But "after the fact"—that is, after the economy has adjusted to the equilibrium levels of employment, output, and income—saving and investment plans have been brought into equality by these adjustments, so these plans can then be achieved without further revision.

The distinction between *planned* saving and

investment and *actual* saving and investment is like that between the demand and supply plans of buyers and sellers concerning a specific product as reflected in their demand and supply curves, on the one hand, and the amounts of the product actually bought and sold at the equilibrium price, on the other. In a specific market the buying plans, or intentions, of consumers are summarized in a demand curve for the product; the supply plans of producers are summarized in a product supply curve. Because the buyers and sellers of the product are different groups of people, there is no apparent reason for them to reach agreement on the amount of the product to be bought and sold. Yet they do reach agreement. How? As the result of adjustments in the price of the product. At any nonequilibrium price buyers will want to consume more than producers want to offer or vice versa. The inconsistency of these purchase and sale plans will prompt price adjustments either upward or downward towards equilibrium. And at the equilibrium price the two sets of plans will be synchronized and can therefore be realized without further alteration.

The same rationale applies to saving and investment plans, the equilibrating mechanism in this case being the levels of output, income, and employment. Just as producers will plan to offer more of a particular product than consumers will plan to buy at a relatively high (above-equilibrium) price, so households will want to save more than businesses will want to invest at relatively high (above-equilibrium) levels of national output and income. Conversely, just as producers will want to offer less of a specific product than consumers will plan to buy at·a relatively low (below-equilibrium) price, so households will want to save less than businesses will plan to invest at relatively low (below-equilibrium) levels of national income. In the same fashion that above- and below-equilibrium prices will adjust downward or upward to synchronize the buying and selling plans of specific consumers and specific producers, so will the levels of output, income, and employment adjust to bring the saving and investing plans of

businesses and households into equality. When thus balanced, these plans can be carried out or realized without further revision.

Equilibrium NNP versus full-employment NNP

Too much stress cannot be placed on the fact that the $470 billion equilibrium NNP embodied in our analysis may or may not entail full employment. In Table 13-1 it will be noted that the production of a $470 billion NNP will provide 65 million jobs. If the available labor force is 70 or 75 million, this level of output will obviously entail considerable involuntary unemployment. On the other hand, the saving and investment plans of households and businesses may be such that total spending exceeds the current market value of the economy's full-employment output. This will occur where, at the full-employment NNP, businesses want to invest more than households want to save. Now once at full employment the economy obviously cannot expand its real output. But the economy can spend more and more money on a fixed amount of goods by bidding up the monetary value of those goods. More bluntly, a level of total spending in excess of the current market value of the economy's full-employment output will cause inflation. The economy's money NNP, but not its real NNP, will rise. Once the economy reaches the production barrier of full employment, the extra spending which results from businesses attempting to invest more than households want to save will cause inflation.

The important point is that because decisions to save and invest are made by substantially different groups and for substantially different reasons, there is no reason for saving and investment plans to be consistent at a level of NNP which will provide for full employment without inflation.

CHANGES IN EQUILIBRIUM NNP AND THE MULTIPLIER

Thus far we have been concerned with explaining the equilibrium levels of total output and income. But we saw in Chapter 11 that actually the NNP of American capitalism is seldom stable: rather it is characterized by long-run growth punctuated by cyclical fluctuations. Let us turn to the questions of *why* and *how* the equilibrium level of NNP fluctuates.

The equilibrium level of NNP will change in response to changes in the investment schedule or the saving-consumption schedules. Because investment spending generally is less stable than the consumption-saving schedules, we shall assume that changes in the investment schedule occur. The impact of changes in investment can be readily envisioned through Figure 13-3a and b. If technological advance, population growth, or simply business optimism enhance profit expectations, investment spending by businesses will increase by, say, $5 billion. This is indicated in Figure 13-3a as an upward shift in the aggregate demand schedule from $(C + I_n)_0$ to $(C + I_n)_1$ and in Figure 13-3b as an upward shift in the investment schedule from I_{n_0} to I_{n_1}. In each of these portrayals the result is a rise in the equilibrium NNP from $470 to $490 billion.

Conversely, a $5 billion decline in investment stemming from such considerations as high acquisition and maintenance costs on capital, a high interest rate, a low rate of technological advance, or general business pessimism will shift the investment schedule downward from I_{n_0} to I_{n_2} in Figure 13-3b and the aggregate demand schedule from $(C + I_n)_0$ to $(C + I_n)_2$ in 13-3a. In each case these shifts cause the equilibrium NNP to fall from the original $470 billion level to $450 billion. The reader should verify these conclusions in terms of Table 13-1 by substituting $25 billion and then $15 billion for the $20 billion investment figure given in the table.

When they occur, changes in the consumption-saving schedules will have similar effects. If households want to consume more (save less) at each level of NNP, the aggregate demand schedule will shift upward and the saving schedule downward in Figure 13-3a and b, respectively. In either portrayal these shifts will mean an increase in the equilibrium NNP. If households want to consume less (save more) at each possible NNP, the resulting drop in the

consumption schedule and increase in the saving schedule will in turn reduce the equilibrium NNP.

The multiplier effect

You have undoubtedly detected a curious feature of the above examples: a $5 billion change in investment spending has given rise to a $20 billion change in the output-income level. This surprising result is called the *multiplier effect*. It is based upon two seemingly innocent facts. On the one hand, the economy is characterized by repetitive, continuous flows of expenditures and income wherein the dollars spent by Smith are received as income by Jones. On the other hand, any change in income will cause both consumption and saving to vary in the same direction as, and by a fraction of, the change in income.

It follows from these two facts that an initial change in the rate of spending will cause a chain reaction which, although of diminishing importance at each successive step, will cumulate to a multiple change in NNP. The multiplier effect is illustrated numerically in Table 13-2 for a $5 billion increase in investment spending. We assume that the MPC is three-fourths; the MPS is therefore one-fourth.

The initial increase in investment generates an equal amount of wage, rent, interest, and profit income for the simple reason that spending and receiving income are two sides of the same transaction. This $5 billion income increase causes consumption to rise by $3.75 billion and saving by $1.25 billion. The $3.75 billion which is spent is received by other households as income. They in turn consume three-fourths, or $2.81 billion, of this $3.75 billion and save one-fourth, or $0.94 billion. The $2.81 billion which is consumed flows to still other households as income. Though the spending and respending effects of the initial increase in investment diminish with each successive round of spending, the cumulative increase in the output-income level will be $20 billion if the process is carried through to the last dollar.

It is no coincidence that the multiplier effect ends at the point where exactly enough saving

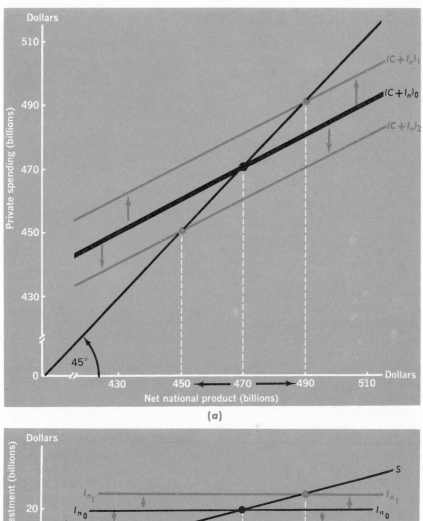

(a)

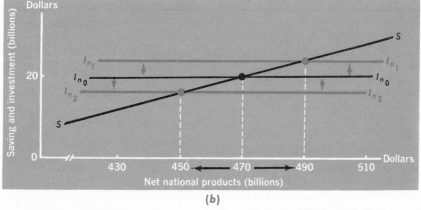

(b)

FIGURE 13-3. CHANGES IN THE EQUILIBRIUM NNP CAUSED BY SHIFTS IN (a) THE AGGREGATE DEMAND SCHEDULE AND (b) THE INVESTMENT SCHEDULE. An upshift in the aggregate demand schedule from, say, $(C + I_n)_0$ to $(C + I_n)_1$ will increase the equilibrium NNP. Conversely, a downshift in the aggregate demand schedule from, say, $(C + I_n)_0$ to $(C + I_n)_2$ will lower the equilibrium NNP. In the saving-investment figure an upshift in the investment schedule (I_{n_0} to I_{n_1}) will raise, and a downshift (I_{n_0} to I_{n_2}) will lower, the equilibrium NNP.

TABLE 13-2. THE MULTIPLIER: A TABULAR ILLUSTRATION (in billions of dollars)

	Change in income	Change in consumption (MPC = ¾)	Change in saving (MPS = ¼)
Assumed increase in investment	$ 5.00	$ 3.75	$1.25
Second round	3.75	2.81	0.94
Third round	2.81	2.11	0.70
Fourth round	2.11	1.58	0.53
Fifth round	1.58	1.19	0.39
All other rounds	4.75	3.56	1.19
Totals	$20.00	$15.00	$5.00

[handwritten: Size of MPS and multiplier are inversely related — mult equal to reciprocal of MPS]

has been generated to offset the initial $5 billion increase in investment spending. It is only then that the disequilibrium created by the investment increase will be corrected. In this case NNP and total incomes must rise by $20 billion to create $5 billion in additional saving to match the $5 billion increase in investment spending. Income must increase by four times the initial excess of investment over saving, because households save one-fourth of any increase in their incomes. In this case the multiplier—the number of times the ultimate increase in income exceeds the initial increase in investment spending—is 4.

Characteristics of multiplier. Several noteworthy characteristics of the multiplier are not sufficiently emphasized by mere illustrations of its mechanics:

1. Remember that a change in any of the components of the aggregate demand schedule will give rise to a multiplier effect. In practice, economists usually associate the multiplier with changes in investment because of the relative instability of the investment schedule as compared with the consumption schedule. But keep in mind that a shift in the consumption schedule or, as we shall see shortly, a shift in the schedule of government spending will also prompt a similar chain reaction.

2. Keep in mind too that the multiplier works in both directions. That is, a small increase in spending can give rise to a multiple increase in NNP, or a small decrease in spending can be magnified into a much larger decrease in NNP by the multiplier.

3. You may have sensed from Table 13-2 that a relationship of some sort must exist between the MPS and the size of the multiplier. There is such a relationship: the fraction of an increase in income which is saved—that is, the MPS—determines the cumulative respending effects of any initial change in I_n, G, or C, and therefore the multiplier. More specifically, the size of the MPS and the size of the multiplier are inversely related. The smaller the fraction of any change in income which is saved, the greater the respending at each round and the greater the multiplier. If the MPS is one-fourth, as in our example, the multiplier is 4. If the MPS were one-third, the multiplier would be 3. If the MPS were one-fifth, the multiplier would be 5. We can summarize these and all other possibilities by simply saying that the multiplier is equal to the reciprocal of the MPS. The reciprocal of any number is the quotient you obtain by dividing 1 by that number. In short, we can say that

$$\text{The multiplier} = \frac{1}{\text{MPS}}$$

This formula provides us with a shorthand method of determining the multiplier. All we

[handwritten: Change in any component of aggr demand schedule will give rise to multiplier effect]

need to know is the MPS (or MPC) to calculate the size of the multiplier quickly.[1]

Significance of multiplier. The significance of the multiplier is almost self-evident. A relatively small change in the investment plans of business or the consumption-saving plans of households can trigger a much larger change in the equilibrium level of NNP. The multiplier magnifies the fluctuations in business activity initiated by changes in spending. Estimates of the size of the multiplier for the United States suggest a figure of from 2 to 4.

Induced investment: the accelerator effect

For simplicity's sake we have assumed thus far that the level of investment is autonomous, that is, independent of the level of NNP. This is not entirely realistic. Common sense suggests that there will be a direct relationship between the level of NNP and the volume of investment spending. As NNP expands, so will consump-

---

[1] Since MPS + MPC = 1, it is also true that MPS = 1 − MPC. Substituting in the above formula, we can say that

$$\text{The multiplier} = \frac{1}{1 - \text{MPC}}$$

Furthermore, the importance of footnote 7 in Chapter 12 now becomes clear. There we noted that the MPS measures the slope of the saving schedule. In terms of the saving equals investment approach this means that, if the MPS is relatively large (say, one-half) and the slope of the saving schedule is therefore relatively steep (one-half), any given upward shift in investment spending will be subject to a relatively small multiplier. For example, a $5 billion increase in investment will entail a new point of intersection of the S and I_n schedules only $10 billion to the right of the original equilibrium NNP. The multiplier is only 2. But if the MPS is relatively small (say one-sixth), the slope of the saving schedule will be relatively gentle. Therefore, a $5 billion upward shift in the investment schedule will provide a new intersection point some $30 billion to the right of the original equilibrium NNP. The multiplier is 6 in this case. The reader should verify these two examples by drawing appropriate saving and investment diagrams.

tion spending, and expanding markets for consumer goods will induce the expansion of capital facilities and voluntary increases in inventories. Conversely, a decline in NNP and the accompanying shrinkage of consumer goods markets will mean excess capital facilities, inducing a decline in investment spending. In short, the investment schedule is probably somewhat upsloping as in Figure 12-5a. This tendency for changes in consumption to induce changes in investment spending is called the *accelerator effect.*

The accelerator can best be envisioned by modifying our saving equals investment diagram. Figure 13-4a shows the simplified saving equals investment diagram wherein investment spending is independent of the level of NNP. Figure 13-4b modifies this by allowing for increases in investment spending which a higher NNP will entail. In each instance the equilibrium NNP is determined where saving and investment are equal, that is, where the saving and investment schedules intersect. Now, however, equal upward shifts in the investment schedule from I_{n1} to I_{n2} caused by, say, technological advances will cause the level of NNP to increase by a larger amount in Figure 13-4b because of the induced increases in investment which occur. In Figure 13-4a the size of the increase in NNP is governed solely by the multiplier. In Figure 13-4b, however, we get a larger expansion of NNP, because the increase in consumer spending which the multiplier effect entails will induce an increase in investment spending. The increase in NNP from $470 to $490 billion is the result of the multiplier, and the further rise from $490 to $503 billion is the result of the accelerator. These conclusions can be verified numerically by (1) substituting the investment schedule of Table 12-2 in column 5 of Table 13-1, (2) assuming a $5 billion increase in this schedule, and (3) computing the point at which saving equals investment. The basic point is that the multiplier and the accelerator reinforce one another, enhancing the instability of American capitalism. The reader should verify a similar conclusion for an initial decline in the investment schedule.

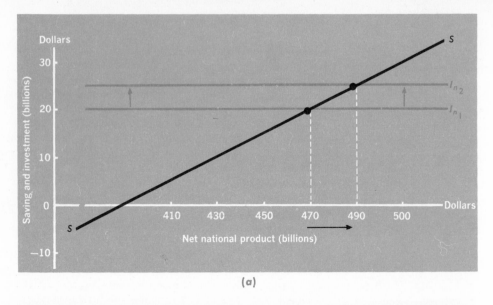

(a)

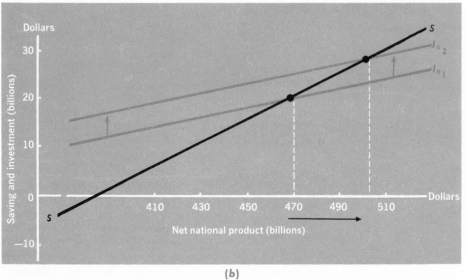

(b)

FIGURE 13-4. CHANGES IN THE EQUILIBRIUM NNP: (a) THE MULTIPLIER AND (b) THE MULTIPLIER AND ACCELERATOR.

Because of the multiplier effect, the equilibrium NNP in (a) will increase by several times the increase in investment (I_{n_1} to I_{n_2}) which causes that rise in NNP. In this case the multiplier is 4, that is, a $5 billion increase in investment spending causes the equilibrium NNP to rise by $20 billion. The multiplier also applies to declines in spending. The more realistic upsloping investment schedule in (b) reflects the fact that a higher level of NNP will induce businessmen to invest more. Under these conditions a given shift in the investment schedule (I_{n_1} to I_{n_2}) will result in a change in the equilibrium NNP which exceeds the change due to the multiplier effect. This extra change in NNP caused by induced investment is the accelerator effect.

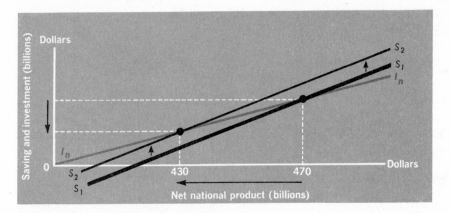

FIGURE 13-5. THE PARADOX OF THRIFT.
Unless offset by an upshift in the investment schedule, the attempt of households to save more (S_1 to S_2) will cause the equilibrium level of NNP to decline, pulling down the actual amounts saved and invested.

The paradox of thrift

You may recall from Chapter 1 that the very attempt to achieve a given objective may create certain circumstances which prevent the attainment of that goal. An upsloping investment schedule suggests such an ironic possibility: by attempting to increase its rate of saving, society may create conditions under which the amount it can *actually* save is reduced. This phenomenon is called *the paradox of thrift*.

This paradox is suggested in the saving-investment approach to NNP determination. Suppose that households, expecting a recession, try to save more in order to provide a nest egg against these anticipated bad times. This attempt to save more is reflected in an upward shift of the saving schedule from S_1 to S_2 as shown in Figure 13-5. But, if not compensated for by an increase in the investment schedule, an excess of planned saving over planned investment now exists at the original equilibrium NNP of $470. As we have seen, the multiplier and accelerator will team up to cause a relatively small increase in saving (decline in consumption) to become a much larger decline in the equilibrium NNP. In Figure 13-5 the equi-

librium NNP falls all the way back to the $430 billion level. And, because of the upsloping character of the investment schedule, this new equilibrium point entails a much smaller NNP and lower actual levels of saving and investment than existed at the original $470 billion equilibrium NNP. Even without the accelerator effect, that is, even with a simplified investment schedule, the upward shift in the saving schedule would merely lower the equilibrium NNP without affecting the actual amount households were able to save.

There is a paradox involved here in two different senses: First, by *attempting* to save more a situation is created wherein the economy is *actually* forced to save less. The attempt to save more (consume less) drives national income downward, and with smaller incomes people simply cannot afford to save as much. Second, thrift, which has always been held in high esteem in our economy, now becomes something of a social vice. From the individual point of view a penny saved may be a penny earned. But from the social point of view a penny saved is a penny not spent and therefore a decline in someone's income. The act of thrift may be virtuous from the individual's point of view but disastrous from the social point of view because of its undesirable effects upon total output and employment.

The paradox of thrift is reversible: if attempts are made to save less (consume more), increases will occur in the equilibrium NNP to the end that the economy's total income has increased to the degree that it can save more than it did previously.

PRIVATE AND PUBLIC SECTORS

Thus far we have confined our discussion to the private sector of the economy. Now we must round out our analysis of the equilibrium level of NNP by adding the public sector. To keep a potentially complex discussion as simple as possible, three simplifying assumptions are invoked. First, we continue to employ the simplified investment schedule in our analysis. Second, we will suppose that the initial impact of government spending is such that it neither depresses nor stimulates private spending. That is, government spending will not cause any upward or downward shifts in the consumption and investment schedules. Third, it will be presumed that the government's net tax revenues[2] are derived entirely from personal taxes. The significance of this is that, although DI will fall short of PI by the amount of government's tax revenues, NNP, NI, and PI will remain equal.

In our discussion of the private sector of the economy we implicitly assumed that government purchases of goods and services (G) and tax revenues (T) were both zero. Now let us suppose that G and T both increase from zero to, say, $20 billion, and note the impact of each and then the net impact of the two. As before we pursue our analysis both graphically and tabularly.

Government spending and equilibrium NNP

Suppose that government decides to purchase $20 billion worth of goods and services regardless of what the level of NNP might be.

[2] By net taxes we mean total tax revenues less negative taxes in the form of transfer payments.

By adding this amount of public spending G to the level of private spending, $C + I_n$, in Figure 13-6a, we find that the total spending schedule (public plus private) has been increased to $C + I_n + G$. That is, the aggregate demand schedule now has a third component which gives us a new and higher aggregate demand schedule. And this means a new and higher equilibrium level of NNP. In particular, the equilibrium level of NNP has increased from $470 to $550 billion. Increases in public spending, like increases in private spending, will boost the aggregate demand schedule in relation to the aggregate supply schedule and result in a higher equilibrium NNP. Note, too, that government spending is subject to the multiplier.

Figure 13-6b shows the same change in the equilibrium NNP in terms of the $S = I_n$ analysis. With G added to our discussion the equilibrium level of NNP is now determined where the amount households plan to save is offset exactly by the amount which businesses plan to invest plus the amount government desires to spend on goods and services. That is, the equilibrium NNP is determined by the intersection of the S schedule and the $I_n + G$ schedule. Note that either approach indicates the same new equilibrium NNP.

What of the effect of a decline in government spending? Obviously, a decline in G will cause the aggregate demand schedule to fall or the $G + I_n$ schedule to fall. In either case the result is a multiple *decline* in the equilibrium NNP.

Taxation and equilibrium NNP

But government also collects tax revenues. How do tax collections affect the equilibrium level of NNP? Obviously, if government increases its tax revenues from zero to $20 billion, the immediate effect will be to lower DI by $20 billion. And, because DI is comprised of consumer spending and saving, we can expect a decline in DI to lower both consumption and saving. But by how much will each decline? The MPC and the MPS hold the answer: the MPC tells us what fraction of a decline in DI

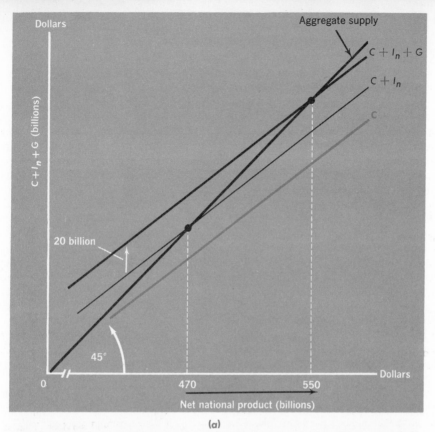

(a)

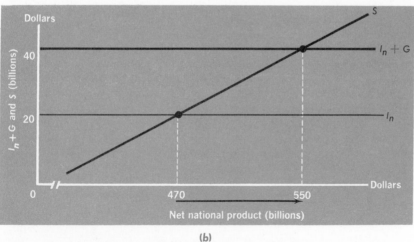

(b)

FIGURE 13-6. GOVERNMENT SPENDING AND THE EQUILIBRIUM NNP.
(a) The aggregate demand–aggregate supply approach. The addition of government expenditures G to our analysis raises the aggregate demand ($C + I_n + G$) schedule and increases the equilibrium level of NNP as would an increase in C or I_n. Note that changes in government spending are subject to the multiplier effect. (b) $S = I_n$ approach. In terms of the saving equals investment approach, government spending supplements private investment spending ($I_n + G$), increasing the equilibrium NNP.

will come at the expense of consumption, and the MPS indicates what fraction of a drop in DI will come at the expense of saving. Assuming that the MPC equals three-fourths and the MPS equals one-fourth, we can conclude that if government collects $20 billion in taxes at each possible level of NNP, the amount of consumption forthcoming at each level of NNP will drop by $15 billion (three-fourths of $20 billion), and the amount of saving at each level of NNP will fall by $5 billion (one-fourth of $20 billion).

The impact of a $20 billion increase in taxes is shown graphically in Figure 13-7a and b. In Figure 13-7a the $20 billion increase in taxes shows up as a $15 billion decline in the aggregate demand $(C + I_n + G)$ schedule. Under our simplifying assumptions this decline is solely the result of a decline in the consumption component of the aggregate demand schedule.

The equilibrium NNP shifts from $550 billion to a $490 billion level as a result of this tax-caused drop in consumption. The imposition of $20 billion in taxes has a two-fold effect in Figure 13-7b. First, the taxes reduce DI by $20 billion and, with the MPS at one-fourth, cause saving to fall by $5 billion at each level of NNP. In Figure 13-7b this is shown as a shift from S_b (saving before taxes) to S_a (saving after taxes). Then the $20 billion in taxes as such appear as a $20 billion additional leakage at each NNP level which must be added to S_a, giving us $S_a + T$. Equilibrium now exists at the $490 billion NNP where the total amount which households plan to save plus the amount of taxes government intends to collect are equal to the total amount businesses desire to invest plus the amount government plans to spend. The equilibrium condition is that $S_a + T = I_n + G$. Graphically, it is the intersection of the $S_a + T$ and the $I_n + G$ schedules which determine the equilibrium NNP.

A decline in existing taxes will cause the aggregate demand schedule to rise as a result of an upward shift in the consumption schedule or it will cause a decline in the $S_a + T$ schedule. The result in either case is a multiple *increase* in the equilibrium NNP.

Government spending and taxation

Table 13-3 shows the impact of government spending and taxation upon the equilibrium NNP in terms of simple arithmetic data. This table is merely Table 13-1 adjusted to allow for $20 billion worth of tax revenues (column 3) and $20 billion of government spending (column 8) at each possible level of NNP. The immediate effect of taxes is shown in column 4: DI falls by $20 billion. Supposing the MPC and MPS are three-fourths and one-fourth, respectively, we find in columns 5 and 6 that the amounts of consumption and saving forthcoming at each level of NNP are $15 and $5 billion less, respectively.

Thus, for example, before the imposition of taxes, where NNP equaled DI, consumption was $420 billion and saving $10 billion at the $430 billion level of NNP (Table 13-1). After taxes are added, DI of $410 billion is obviously $20 billion short of the $430 billion NNP with the result that consumption is only $405 billion and saving is $5 billion. It is in this manner that columns 4, 5, and 6 are determined. Column 7 carries over investment from Table 13-1, and column 8 adds government spending.

What is the equilibrium level of output now that taxation and government spending have been brought into the picture? The aggregate demand–aggregate supply, or $C + I_n + G = $ NNP, approach tells us to compare columns 2 and 9. It is apparent that the aggregate amounts demanded and supplied are equal only at the $490 billion NNP. At all higher levels businesses will attempt to produce in excess of what the economy, including both the private and the public sectors, plans to spend. The resulting deficiency of total spending will force these higher levels of NNP downward back to the $490 billion level. Conversely, at all levels of NNP below the $490 billion level the economy will spend at a rate in excess of NNP, inducing businesses to expand NNP. We can conclude that $490 billion is the equilibrium NNP.

Our alternative approach must and does yield the same results. With the public sector

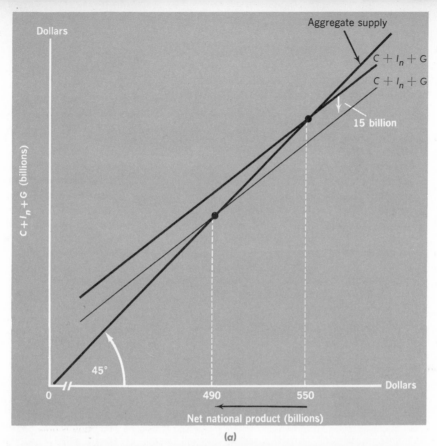

(a)

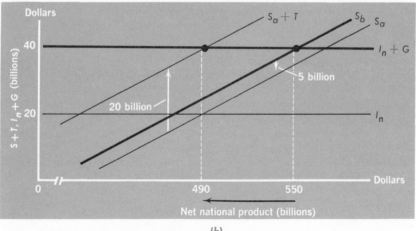

(b)

FIGURE 13-7. TAXES AND THE EQUILIBRIUM NNP.
(a) The aggregate-demand—aggregate-supply approach. If the MPC is three-fourths, the imposition of $20 billion of taxes will lower the consumption schedule by $15 billion and thereby cause a decline in the equilibrium NNP. (b) The $S = I_n$ approach. Here taxes have a twofold effect. First, with an MPS of one-fourth, the imposition of taxes of $20 billion will reduce disposable income by $20 billion and saving by $5 billion at each level of NNP. This is shown by the shift from S_b (saving before taxes) to S_a (saving after taxes). Second, the $20 billion of taxes constitute an additional $20 billion leakage at each NNP level, giving us $S_a + T$. By adding government, the equilibrium condition changes from $S = I_n$ to $S_a + T = I_n + G$.

TABLE 13-3. DETERMINATION OF THE EQUILIBRIUM LEVELS OF EMPLOYMENT, OUTPUT, AND INCOME: PRIVATE AND PUBLIC SECTORS

(1)	(2)	(3)	(4)	(5)	(6)	(7)	(8)	(9)	(10)
Possible levels of employment, millions	Possible levels of aggregate supply (NNP = NI = PI), billions	Taxes, billions	Possible levels of disposable income, billions, or (2) − (3)	Consumption, billions	Saving, billions, or (4) − (5)	Investment, billions	Government expenditures, billions	Aggregate demand (C + I_n + G), billions, or (5) + (7) + (8)	Tendency on employment, output, and income
40	$370	$20	$350	$360	$−10	$20	$20	$400	Increase
45	390	20	370	375	−5	20	20	415	Increase
50	410	20	390	390	0	20	20	430	Increase
55	430	20	410	405	5	20	20	445	Increase
60	450	20	430	420	10	20	20	460	Increase
65	470	20	450	435	15	20	20	475	Increase
70	490	20	470	450	20	20	20	490	Equilibrium
75	510	20	490	465	25	20	20	505	Decrease
80	530	20	510	480	30	20	20	520	Decrease

added to the private sector, equilibrium will prevail where $S_a + T = I_n + G$. And this is at the $490 billion level. At all lower levels you should verify that investment and government spending will more than compensate for the saving and taxation leakages, causing $C + I_n + G$ to exceed NNP and thereby induce the latter to rise. Conversely, at all levels of NNP above the $490 level, you should note that the saving and taxation leakages are not offset by investment and government spending, thus causing $C + I_n + G$ to fall short of NNP and forcing declines in NNP.

A final point: you may have detected a curious thing about our graphic and tabular illustrations. Equal changes in government spending and taxes do not leave the equilibrium level of NNP unchanged. In our examples a $20 billion increase in G and T causes the equilibrium NNP to increase from $470 to

$490 billion. Why? Because the $20 billion increase in personal taxes only reduces consumption by $15 billion, the extra $5 billion in tax revenues coming at the expense of saving. Thus the *net* effect is a $5 billion increase in total spending—the combination of a $20 billion increase in public spending and a $15 billion decline in private spending. Being subject to the multiplier, the $5 billion net increase in spending boosts NNP by $20 billion.

Fiscal policy

The rationale underlying government spending and taxation decisions—particularly at the Federal level—differ in one crucial respect from the consumption-saving and investment decisions of the private sector of the economy. The consumption-saving decisions of households and the investment decisions of businesses are based upon what each group feels to be the course of action that will best further its own self-interest. Households divide their disposable incomes between consumption and saving in the manner most satisfying to them; businesses will invest only when they feel prospective profits to be lucrative enough to justify such spending. A basic notion of modern employment theory is that the sum of these individual decisions, motivated by self-interest, need not provide for the full-employment noninflationary level of NNP. Millions of individual consumption and investment decisions, based on private self-interest, need not necessarily provide for the realization of the social goal of full employment.

Government, however, is an instrument of society as a whole, and within limits its spending and taxation decisions can be made to influence the equilibrium NNP in terms of the general welfare. Such efforts are termed "fiscal policy." In particular, a level of private spending which fails to provide for full employment can be bolstered by (1) increasing government spending, (2) lowering taxes, or (3) a combination of the two. In other words, if the budget is balanced at the outset, fiscal policy should move in the direction of a government *deficit* during a recession or depression. Conversely, a level of private spending which threatens to cause inflation, that is, a spiraling up of the monetary value of NNP, can be countered by (1) decreasing government spending, (2) increasing taxes, or (3) a combination of these two policies. Stated differently, fiscal policy calls for a government *surplus* when the economy is faced with an inflationary problem.[3]

The size of a deficit or surplus will obviously be important in determining the magnitude of its expansionary or contractionary (anti-inflationary) effects. That is, other things being the same, the larger a deficit, the greater the expansionary effect it will have upon the economy. Similarly, the larger a surplus, the greater the contractionary or deflationary effect.

[3] Minor qualification: because, as we have noted, a balanced budget is actually expansionary, a relatively small budget surplus might be slightly expansionary rather than deflationary.

Now a less obvious point is this: the absolute levels of government spending and taxation at which a deficit or surplus of a given size occurs will also influence the magnitude of the resulting expansionary or deflationary effect. Consider a government deficit. We start with just the private sector, and first add a public sector in which government expenditures are $30 billion and tax revenues are $20 billion. If the MPC is three-fourths, the net increase in total spending will be $15 billion; that is, the $30 billion increase in government spending is partially offset by the $15 billion decline in consumption which the taxes will entail. The $10 billion deficit therefore increases total spending in the economy by $15 billion. Now let us assume that government expenditures are $50 billion and taxes are $40 billion. In this instance, although we have the same $10 billion deficit as in the first case, the net increase in expenditures is $20 billion. That is, with an MPC of three-fourths, the $50 billion increase in government spending is partially offset by a $30 billion drop in consumption. We can generalize that the higher the levels of government spending and taxation at which a deficit of a given size is realized, the greater will be the expansionary effect of that deficit. The reader should verify that a similar analysis with respect to a budget surplus of a given size will reveal that the lower the levels of government spending and taxation at which a surplus of a given size is realized, the greater will be the deflationary or contractionary effect upon the economy.

The ensuing chapter is devoted to a discussion of fiscal policy and the economic and noneconomic problems which peril its application.

SUMMARY

1. The equilibrium level of NNP is that NNP at which the aggregate quantity demanded and the aggregate quantity supplied are equal or, graphically, where the $C + I_n$ line intersects the 45-degree line. At any NNP greater than the equilibrium NNP, aggregate quantity supplied will exceed the aggregate quantity demanded, resulting in unsold goods, depressed profits, and eventual declines in output, employment, and income. At any below-equilibrium NNP the aggregate quantity demanded will exceed the aggregate quantity supplied, thereby resulting in substantial profits, declining inventories, and eventual increases in NNP.

2. An alternative, complementary approach determines the equilibrium NNP at the point where the amount households plan to save and the amount businesses plan to invest are equal. This is at the point where the saving and investment schedules intersect. Any excess of planned saving over planned investment will cause a shortage of total spending, forcing NNP to fall. Any excess of planned investment over planned saving will cause an excess of total spending, inducing NNP to rise. These changes in NNP will in both cases correct the assumed discrepancies in investment and saving plans.

3. The full-employment noninflationary NNP and the equilibrium NNP need not coincide; the equilibrium level of NNP may entail considerable unemployment or be achieved only through substantial increases in money NNP.

4. Shifts in the saving-consumption schedules or in the investment schedule will cause changes in the equilibrium NNP.

5. Any given change in spending may cause the equilibrium output-income level to change by several times the amount of the initial change in spending. This phenomenon, which accompanies both increases and decreases in spending, is called the *multiplier effect*. The multiplier is equal to the reciprocal of the marginal propensity to save.

6. The *accelerator effect* is the notion that a change in income and consumption may induce an increase in investment spending. Like the multiplier, the accelerator helps magnify changes in spending into larger changes in the equilibrium NNP.

7. An upsloping investment schedule raises the possibility that an attempt by society to save more will lower NNP and thereby result in actual levels of saving and investment which are less than those which originally prevailed. This is known as the paradox of thrift.

8. Increases in government spending expand, and decreases contract, the equilibrium NNP. Conversely, increases in taxes reduce, and decreases expand, the equilibrium NNP. Appropriate fiscal policy therefore calls for increases in government spending and decreases in taxes—that is, for a budget deficit—to correct for unemployment. Decreases in government spending and increases in taxes—that is, a budget surplus—is appropriate fiscal policy for correcting inflation. The expansionary and deflationary effects of deficits and surpluses depend not only upon their size, but also upon the absolute level of government spending and taxation at which a deficit or surplus of a given size is realized.

QUESTIONS AND STUDY SUGGESTIONS

1. Explain graphically the determination of the equilibrium NNP by (*a*) the aggregate demand–aggregate supply approach and (*b*) the saving equals investment approach for the private sector of the economy. Why must these two approaches always yield the same equilibrium NNP? Now add government expenditures and then taxation, showing the impact of each upon the equilibrium NNP. Explain why equal increases in government spending and tax collections increase the equilibrium NNP.

2. Explain in detail the difference between planned saving and investment and realized saving and investment. Why is the distinction significant?

3. "The fact that households may try to save more than businesses want to invest is of no consequence, because events will in time force households and businesses to save and invest at the same rates." Critically evaluate.

4. "It is socially desirable for households to attempt to increase their rate of saving whenever a recession begins. In this way households will be able to accumulate the financial resources to pay their way through bad times." Critically evaluate.

5. What is the multiplier effect? What relationship does the MPC bear to the size of the multiplier? The MPS? What will the multiplier be when the MPS is 0, 0.4, 0.6, and 1? When the MPC is 1, ⅚, ⅔, ½, and 0? How much of a change in NNP will result if businesses increase their rate of investment by $8 billion and the MPC in the economy is four-fifths? If the MPC is two-thirds?

6. What effect will each of the changes designated in question 7 at the end of Chapter 12 have upon the equilibrium level of NNP? Explain your answer.

7. What is the accelerator effect? Of what significance is it? Explain the paradox of thrift.

8. "The expenditure-taxation decisions of government are fundamentally different from the expenditure-saving decisions of private individuals and businesses." Evaluate and explain.

9. What changes in tax collections and expenditures should the government invoke to correct for an equilibrium NNP which involves substantial unemployment? Substantial inflation?

10. Assuming the level of investment is $16 billion and independent of the level of total output, complete the following table and determine the equilibrium level of output and income which the private sector of the economy would provide.

Possible levels of employment, millions	Aggregate supply $(NNP = NI = PI = DI)$, billions	Consumption, billions	Saving, billions
40	$240	$244	
45	260	260	
50	280	276	
55	300	292	
60	320	308	
65	340	324	
70	360	340	
75	380	356	
80	400	372	

a. If this economy has a labor force of 70 million, will the equilibrium NNP provide for full employment? Explain.

b. What will happen if the available labor force is only 55 million?

c. What are the sizes of the MPC and the MPS?

d. Use the MPC and MPS concepts to explain the increase in the equilibrium NNP which will occur as the result of an increase in investment spending from $16 to $20 billion.

e. Assume investment to be at the $16 billion level once again. Now incorporate government in the above table, assuming that it plans to tax and spend $20 billion at each possible level of NNP. Assume all taxes are personal taxes and that government spending does not entail shifts in the consumption and investment schedules. Explain the change in the equilibrium NNP which the addition of government entails. More specifically, why do not equal changes in government spending and taxes leave the equilibrium level of NNP unchanged?

11. Using numerical and graphical illustrations, explain:

a. Why a $10 billion government deficit at high absolute levels of government spending and taxation will have a greater expansionary impact on the economy than will the same deficit at lower absolute levels of spending and taxation.

b. Why a $10 billion government surplus at high absolute levels of government spending and taxation will have a lesser deflationary impact on the economy than will the same surplus at lower absolute levels of spending and taxation.

SELECTED REFERENCES

Clemence, Richard V., *Income Analysis* (Reading, Mass.: Addison-Wesley Publishing Company, 1951).

Dillard, Dudley, *The Economics of John Maynard Keynes* (Englewood Cliffs, N.J.: Prentice-Hall, Inc., 1948).

Hansen, Alvin, *A Guide to Keynes* (New York: McGraw-Hill Book Company, Inc., 1953).

McKenna, Joseph P., *Aggregate Economic Analysis* (New York: The Dryden Press, Inc., 1955).

Peterson, Wallace C., *Income, Employment, and Economic Growth* (New York: W. W. Norton & Company, Inc., 1962), chaps. 5–9.

Chapter 14

FISCAL POLICY: ECONOMIC AND NONECONOMIC PROBLEMS

FISCAL POLICY REFERS to the manipulation of spending and tax revenues by the Federal government in such a way as to affect the levels of output, employment, income, and prices in the economy. As noted in Chapter 13, fiscal policy calls for increases in government spending and tax reductions during depression. The resulting deficit supplements the lagging level of total spending and helps buoy the economy towards full employment. During periods of inflation government must cut expenditures and boost taxes. The surplus which this entails means that government is diverting purchasing power from the economy and thereby relieving inflationary pressure. We will discover in Chapter 17 that government has a second stabilizing tool at its disposal—monetary policy. Through monetary policy the government manipulates the money supply and thereby the level of total spending. Fiscal policy is potentially the most important, but not the sole, stabilizing technique at government's disposal.

The size of government expenditures and tax collections is ultimately determined by Congress. Though a myriad of economic experts may advise the President, various governmental agencies, and congressional committees, the final decisions to alter expenditures and taxes are in the hands of Congress.

The present chapter has four specific objectives. First, we shall seek to understand the meaning and the significance of the Employment Act of 1946. Second, we shall explore the operation of nondiscretionary and discretionary fiscal policy. Next, some basic problems in the formulation and application of fiscal policy will be outlined. Finally, the character and significance of the large public debt to which government deficits have given rise will be discussed.

THE EMPLOYMENT ACT OF 1946

The notion that governmental fiscal actions exert an important stabilizing influence upon the economy began to gain widespread acceptance during the Depression crisis of the 1930s. As previously noted, Keynesian employment theory played a major role in emphasizing the importance of remedial fiscal measures. But it was not until 1946, when the end of hostilities re-created the specter of unemployment, that the Federal government formalized in law its area of responsibility in promoting economic stability. The Employment Act of 1946 proclaims:

The Congress hereby declares that it is the continuing policy and responsibility of the

Federal Government to use all practicable means consistent with its needs and obligations and other essential considerations of national policy, with assistance and cooperation of industry, agriculture, labor and State and local governments, to coordinate and utilize all its plans, functions, and resources for the purpose of creating and maintaining, in a manner calculated to foster and promote free competitive enterprise and the general welfare, conditions under which there will be afforded useful employment opportunities, including self-employment, for those able, willing, and seeking to work and to promote maximum employment, production, and purchasing power.

Though an apparently simple declaration of national policy, the Employment Act raises two important points: the complex meaning of full employment and the feasibility of its achievement.

Complexity and attainability of full employment

1. On the one hand, the act recognizes that full employment is a complex goal. Fiscal policy is to be enacted and applied in a manner consistent with "other essential considerations of national policy" and "in a manner calculated to foster and promote free competitive enterprise." In other words, the act recognizes explicitly and by implication that the American people seek not only full employment but also price stability, full production, an expanding real GNP, and the preservation of freedom of choice and enterprise. Certainly society wants to avoid the tragic waste of idle resources. But it also seeks to avoid the injustices which inflation and deflation entail. Further, we seek full production—the *efficient* allocation of employed resources. And all this is to be achieved without undermining the foundations of a free economy. *Full employment in the broad sense thus outlined is a very complicated, multidimensional objective.*

2. The economic goals we seek may be conflicting and to some extent mutually exclusive. For example, the line between a full-employment and an inflationary level of spending is

not a clear one. Prices typically begin to rise before full employment is achieved, and by the time full employment is attained, the resulting inflation may be considerable (see Chapter 11). Similarly, full employment and an efficient allocation of resources may conflict. Crudely put, full production means that resources should be used in producing those goods and services which society wants most. But if public works programs are necessary to achieve full employment, full production is not likely to result. Using valuable resources to produce parks, highways, and public buildings at a time when the population clamors for more food, shelter, and clothing can hardly be termed an efficient allocation of resources. On the other hand, public works programs which do entail the production of food, shelter, and clothing are in competition with private enterprise and therefore may threaten our economic freedoms.

Implications for fiscal policy

What are the implications of these two points for the enactment and application of fiscal policy?

First, the application of fiscal policy is complicated to the extent that our national economic goals are conflicting or mutually exclusive. Congress must face the knotty problem of assigning priorities to the several objectives which full employment (in the broad sense) entails. And, needless to say, a dynamic economy demands frequent reevaluations of such priorities. Furthermore, even though Congress may have established the relative importance of full employment, price stability, efficiency in the use of resources, economic growth, and economic freedom, difficult compromises will still be necessary in formulating and applying fiscal policy.

A second and more subtle implication for fiscal policy is this: full employment (in the narrow sense) is not an objective to be achieved at all costs. Severe inflation and serious incursions upon our economic freedoms may be too high a price to pay for the full employment of our available resources. Furthermore, the pursuit of full employment must not cause us to lose sight of important social and political objectives. Few of us would want economic stability if it had to be achieved through the techniques of control applied in Soviet Russia. The costs— economic and otherwise—would be too great. In brief, full employment of our available resources is not the only goal society seeks.

With these introductory points in mind, let us now turn to a discussion of nondiscretionary and discretionary fiscal policy. By *nondiscretionary fiscal policy* we refer to changes in governmental expenditures and tax revenues which are the result, not of congressional action to change existing expenditure programs, the tax structure, or tax rates, but rather of changes in the level of national income and employment. Such changes in tax revenues and expenditures are automatic in that they require no governmental action. By *discretionary fiscal policy* we mean changes in the levels of government spending and tax revenues which are the direct result of deliberate congressional action.

NONDISCRETIONARY FISCAL POLICY

To some extent appropriate changes in tax collections and government spending (more specifically, transfer payments) occur automatically as the economy moves from one phase of the business cycle to another. That is, with a given tax structure and set of tax rates, tax collections will vary directly with changes in the national income. As incomes rise, tax revenues will automatically rise; as incomes fall, tax revenues will automatically decline. These movements in tax collections are accentuated when the over-all tax structure of the economy is somewhat progressive. As incomes fall, the accompanying declines in tax receipts will be more than proportionate to the decreases in income. Conversely, as incomes rise, the resulting increase in tax collections will be more than proportionate.

To a lesser degree appropriate changes in government transfer payments also occur over the cycle apart from congressional action. During prosperity government unemployment compensation and relief payments fall, as do sub-

sidy payments to farmers. Conversely, when the economy backslides into recession, the size of these payments automatically increases.

The net effect of tax revenues moving directly with, and transfer payments varying inversely with, national income is that changes in disposable income and consumption will be less than proportionate to the changes in national income (see Table 10-7). Automatic changes in tax receipts and transfer payments partially insulate disposable income, and therefore consumption, from changes in national income. Because a decline in national income causes tax collections to decline and transfer payments to rise, disposable income will decline by less than does national income. This means in turn that consumption declines by less than would otherwise be the case, and therefore the cumulative downward movement is less than it otherwise would be. Similarly, because an increase in national income automatically causes tax receipts to rise and transfers to decline, disposable income will rise less than does national income. In turn this means that consumption will increase less than would otherwise be the case, cushioning the cumulative upward movement in national income. The reader can verify the operation of these automatic stabilizers by observing the course of personal and corporate income taxes (lines 11 and 14) and transfer payments (line 13) during the 1949, 1954, and 1958 recessions on the table inside the covers of this book. The important point is that an element of *built-in stability* is injected into our economy by these nondiscretionary changes in tax receipts and transfer payments. In technical terms, nondiscretionary fiscal policy reduces the size of the multiplier effect.

Although they have served the economy well, it must be emphasized that these automatic, or built-in, stabilizers are not sufficiently strong to offset any serious variations in the level of economic activity. Discretionary action—that is, changes in tax rates, tax structure, and expenditure programs—by Congress is required to alleviate inflation or recession of any appreciable magnitude. In particular, automatic stabilizers do not correct inflation or unemployment, but merely reduce their magnitudes and severity.

It is estimated that in the United States built-in stabilizers are currently strong enough to reduce fluctuations in national income by about one-third. In other words, a $1 billion drop in national income will cause an automatic decline in tax revenues and an automatic increase in government transfer payments to the extent that a $333 million government deficit will occur to offset partially the given decline in incomes.[1]

DISCRETIONARY FISCAL POLICY

Discretionary fiscal policy calls for congressional manipulation of the tax structure and tax rates, on the one hand, and the levels of government expenditure on the other, for the purpose of offsetting cyclical tendencies arising in the private sector of the economy. The goal of these fiscal policies is to incur deficits or surpluses—the former to cushion recession and the latter to offset inflation. Because unbalanced budgets are the core of fiscal policy, it is imperative that we explore the prevailing governmental budget philosophies prior to initiating a more specific discussion of discretionary fiscal policy.

Three budget philosophies

Generally speaking, there are three prevailing budget philosophies. The most conservative —not to say reactionary—policy is that which advocates an *annually* balanced budget. At the other extreme is *functional finance*, the most liberal view; it assigns a secondary priority to balancing the Federal budget annually or over any other time period. Standing between the two is the idea of a *cyclically* balanced budget, wherein the Federal budget is to be balanced over the course of the business cycle rather than annually.

Annually balanced budget. Until the Great Depression of the 1930s the annually balanced budget was generally accepted without question as a desirable goal of public finance. An

[1] R. A. Musgrave and M. H. Miller, "Built-in Flexibility," *American Economic Review*, March, 1948, pp. 122–128.

incorrect identification of private and public finance and widespread belief in the classical theory of employment both fostered this acceptance.

Upon examination, however, it becomes evident that an annually balanced budget rules out government fiscal activity as a countercyclical force. Worse yet, an annually balanced budget actually intensifies the business cycle. To illustrate, suppose that the economy encounters a siege of unemployment and falling incomes. As we have already noted, in such circumstances tax receipts will automatically decline. In seeking to balance its budget, government must either (1) increase tax rates, (2) reduce government expenditures, or (3) employ a combination of these two. It is obvious that all these policies are deflationary; each one further dampens rather than stimulates the level of aggregate demand.

Similarly, an annually balanced budget will also intensify inflation. As money incomes rise during the course of inflation, tax collections will automatically increase. To avoid the impending surplus, government must either (1) cut tax rates, (2) increase government expenditures, or (3) adopt a combination of both. It is clear that all three of these policies will add to inflationary pressures.

The basic conclusion, then, is evident: *an annually balanced budget is not economically neutral; the pursuit of such a policy is procyclical, not countercyclical.*

Cyclically balanced budget. The Great Depression, general acceptance of Keynesian employment theory, and the recognition that public and private finance are not comparable all contributed to the development of the idea of a cyclically balanced budget. This budget philosophy envisions government exerting a countercyclical influence and at the same time balancing its budget. In this case, however, the budget would not be balanced annually—after all, there is nothing sacred about twelve months as an accounting period—but rather over the course of the business cycle.

The rationale of this budget philosophy is simple, plausible, and appealing. To offset depression government should lower taxes and increase spending, thereby purposely incurring a deficit. During the ensuing inflationary upswing taxes would be raised and government spending slashed. The resulting surplus could then be used to retire the Federal debt incurred in financing the depression. In this way government fiscal operations would exert a positive countercyclical force, and the government could still balance its budget—not annually, but over a period of years.

A little reflection will reveal one big shortcoming of this budget philosophy which goes far to rob it of much of its luster: the upswing and downswing of the cycle may not be of equal magnitude and duration. Figure 11-2 makes this strikingly clear. In particular the very real possibility of persistent government deficits and a growing public debt arises. For example, should a long and severe depression be followed by a rather modest and brief prosperity, there would be little chance of obtaining surpluses in the good years sufficient to retire the deficits incurred in alleviating the bad years. Or the period of prosperity may be one wherein military considerations call for high levels of government spending, thereby ruling out the possibility of government's realizing a surplus. In brief, although the idea of a cyclically balanced budget looks fine on paper, there is some real question as to whether or not it is workable in practice.

Functional finance. Out of the problems associated with any application of the cyclically balanced budget has evolved the idea of functional finance. As this budget philosophy sees it, the question of a balanced budget—either annually or cyclically—is of secondary importance. The primary purpose of Federal finance is to provide for noninflationary full employment. If the attainment of this objective entails either persistent surpluses or a large and growing public debt, so be it. The problems involved in government deficits or surpluses are relatively minor compared with the extremely unsavory alternatives of prolonged depression or severe inflation. The Federal budget is first and foremost an instrument for achieving and maintaining a noninflationary full-employment level of output. Government should not hesitate to incur any deficits and surpluses required in achieving this goal. In response to those who express concern about the large Federal debt which the pursuit of functional finance might entail, proponents of this budget philosophy offer two arguments. First, they contend that the problems of a large Federal debt are not as burdensome as most people think. In particular, public debt does not involve the same problems as does private debt. Second, the government's ability to finance deficits is almost unlimited. The credit standing of the government is exceedingly good; hence the government should have no difficulty in borrowing. Furthermore, if its credit standing should somehow deteriorate, the government has the power to create money for the financing of deficits by running the printing presses.

Over the years tremendous changes have occurred in our thinking concerning public finance. Worship of a small and annually balanced budget has given way to the notion that government expenditures and taxes should be manipulated so as to compensate for any deficiency or excess of private spending in promoting full employment without inflation. Further, the budget should be balanced cyclically, or, if this is not feasible, not at all. In general the contention that government finance should be based upon "sound financial principles"—implicitly those principles which apply to private finance—has been largely supplanted by a recognition of the fact that public and private finance are so different as to be incomparable.

Need for discretionary fiscal policy

Because built-in flexibility is inadequate to cope with serious economic fluctuations, discretionary action by Congress is required. Generally speaking, there are four rather distinct facets of fiscal action. The expansionary or deflationary impact of government finance will depend upon (1) the size of the deficit or surplus incurred by government, (2) the absolute levels of government spending and taxation at which a deficit or surplus of a given size is realized, (3) the method by which a deficit is financed or a surplus disposed of, and (4) the types of taxes and expenditures employed. The first two aspects of fiscal policy require no elaborate explanation. We know that, other things being equal, the larger a deficit, the more expansionary its effect, and the larger a surplus, the greater its deflationary impact. Similarly, the higher the levels of government spending and taxation at which a deficit of a certain size is incurred, the greater will be the expansionary effect; the lower the levels of government spending and taxation at which a given surplus is realized, the greater will be the contractionary effect. The two remaining topics merit more detailed consideration.

Financing deficits and disposing of surpluses

Discretionary fiscal policy entails the intentional incurring of deficits and surpluses by the Federal government. Given the size of a deficit, its expansionary effect upon the economy will depend upon the method by which it is financed. Similarly, given the size of a surplus, its deflationary impact will depend upon its disposition.

Financing deficits: borrowing versus creating new money. One usually thinks of borrowing as the obvious means by which government can spend in excess of its receipts or income. That is, government can finance a deficit by selling bonds to the public—to households and to business firms.

Borrowing from individuals will reduce total spending to the degree that households use disposable income which would otherwise be consumed to buy government bonds. Similarly, a portion of the funds used by businesses to buy bonds might otherwise be spent on capital goods or paid out as dividend income which households then might consume. However, the purchase of government bonds is a voluntary act in so far as buyers are concerned. And it is not likely that households will greatly restrict

their standard of living, or businesses their investment plans, in order to buy government bonds.[2] The poor man simply will not be able or willing to purchase bonds, and the bond purchases of the rich man will be made mostly out of funds which otherwise would have been saved in some other form. The point is this: borrowing from the public reduces the antidepression impact of a government deficit to the extent that consumption and investment spending are reduced by the borrowing. But in all probability these declines in private spending will not be particularly great.

Government has a second basic means of financing a deficit. This method of finance is to *create new money.* In its simplest terms we can think of Congress authorizing the printing of the paper money needed to finance the deficit. By financing in this way government can avoid the depressing effects upon consumption and investment which borrowing from the public may have. Printing and spending new money permits increased government spending which does not entail direct reductions in private spending. For this reason it is a more expansionary method than borrowing in financing a deficit.

It is noteworthy that past experiences of the United States and of other nations have led the public to look upon the financing of deficits by running the printing presses with profound distrust. Government, however, accomplishes substantially the same results by borrowing from (selling bonds to) central banks. The mechanics of this process will be explored in Chapters 16 and 17.

Disposing of a surplus: debt retirement versus an idle surplus. Inflation calls for fiscal action by government which will result in a budget surplus. However, the anti-inflationary effect of this surplus depends upon what government does with it. Generally speaking, government can dispose of a surplus in one of two ways.

First, in view of the fact that the Federal

---

[2] In wartime the story is different. A strong sense of patriotism increases the likelihood of bond sales reducing the levels of consumption and investment.

government has an outstanding debt of some $296 billion, it is logical that government use a surplus to retire outstanding debt. However, the anti-inflationary impact of a surplus may be reduced somewhat by this. In retiring debt held by the general public the government transfers its surplus tax revenues into the hands of households and businesses that *might* in turn spend these funds on consumer and capital goods. But this potential increase in private spending should not be exaggerated. In all probability a sizable portion of the surplus funds received by households and businesses as their bonds mature will be used to purchase private securities rather than spent on goods and services. In brief, debt retirement will lessen the anti-inflationary impact of a surplus to the degree that holders of maturing bonds spend the surplus funds they receive. In all likelihood these increases in private spending will not be very large.

On the other hand, government can realize a greater anti-inflationary impact from its budgetary surplus by literally destroying the surplus funds or by allowing them to stand idle. An idle surplus means that the government is extracting and withholding purchasing power from the income-expenditure stream. If surplus tax revenues are not reinjected into the economy, there is no possibility of the surplus being spent. That is, there is no chance of the funds creating inflationary pressure to offset the deflationary impact of the surplus itself. Because the general public views the actual destruction of paper money as an act of considerable obscenity, a surplus will typically be held by the central banks of the economy as an idle Treasury deposit.

Types of expenditures and taxes

The expansionary impact of a deficit and the anti-inflationary significance of a surplus depend in part upon the types of taxes and expenditures employed. Unfortunately, this particular aspect of fiscal policy is clouded with inconclusive and conflicting evidence. Economists are not in agreement as to the expansionary effects of various types of government spending and

the relative deflationary effects of various taxes. Our conclusions then must be very tentative.

Purchases versus transfers. Generally speaking, there are two types of government expenditures: expenditures on goods and services and transfer payments. The former includes defense spending and what the man in the street terms "public works" projects—the building of dams, highways, parks, and public buildings. Transfer payments refer to unemployment compensation payments, subsidies to businesses, and interest on the public debt.

It is generally felt that public works expenditures are somewhat more expansionary in their effect on GNP and employment than are transfer payments. The reasons are basically twofold. First, public works spending stimulates the construction and capital goods industries, which are typically those hardest hit by depression. Second, as opposed to relief payments and subsidies, public works expenditures guarantee that government funds will be spent at least once. In contrast, the mere transfer of funds to needy families or faltering businesses through relief payments and subsidies does not directly account for any production and employment. Production is stimulated only to the extent that the recipients of these transfer payments spend them on goods and services. If the recipients of transfer payment use them to pay off existing debts or simply hoard the funds (expecting further price declines), the expansionary effect will be relatively small.

There are other advantages and shortcomings of public works spending which merit mentioning. By providing jobs, helping to maintain skills, and bolstering the morale of the labor force, public works projects seem preferable to government doles in the form of transfer payments. And, of course, very worthwhile social goods are the end result of carefully planned public works programs. On the other hand, as we shall see shortly, public works programs are typically inflexible and, too, if government is not careful in its selection of such projects, they may compete with and thereby reduce private investment. Furthermore, it can be argued that government expenditures on dams, highways, parks, and public buildings at a time when the economy needs a greater output of basic consumer goods entails a misallocation of resources.

The deflationary impacts of different taxes. What about taxes? Because they tap potential purchasing power from the income-expenditures stream, all taxes tend to be deflationary.[3] But, given the size of government's tax collections, some taxes seem to be more deflationary than others. Most economists feel that consumption taxes—excises and sales taxes—are more deflationary than are personal and corporate income taxes.[4] In other words, regressive taxation is thought to depress private spending more than does progressive taxation. It must be added, however, that this conclusion is not universally accepted. Some authorities contend that, although regressive taxation may dampen consumer spending more than does progressive taxation, heavy taxes on corporate income might entail considerable reduction in business investment. Hence, they conclude that corporate and personal income taxation causes a greater decline in consumption and investment combined than do sales and excise taxes.

PROBLEMS AND ISSUES IN FISCAL POLICY

Unfortunately, there is a great deal of difference between fiscal policy on paper and fiscal policy in practice. It is therefore imperative

[3] For two contrasting views of a possible exception to this statement the reader is referred to the articles by Colin Clark and Richard Goode in Paul A. Samuelson, Robert L. Bishop, and John R. Coleman (eds.), *Readings in Economics*, 2d ed. (New York: McGraw-Hill Book Company, Inc., 1955).

[4] Richard A. Musgrave, "The Incidence of the Tax Structure and Its Effects on Consumption," in *Federal Tax Policy for Economic Growth and Stability*, Subcommittee on Tax Policy, Joint Committee on the Economic Report (Washington: Government Printing Office, 1955), pp. 104–105.

that we examine some specific problems which may be encountered in enacting and applying appropriate fiscal policy.

Problems of timing

Several problems of timing may arise in connection with fiscal policy.

1. It is very difficult to predict accurately the future course of economic activity. Business forecasting is a very imperfect science. The result is that fiscal policy is typically put into effect only after recession or inflation is upon us. The inability to predict upswings and downswings injects a time lag between the economic illness and the fiscal medicine.

2. The expenditure aspect of fiscal policy is lacking in flexibility. In particular, expenditures on public works—the construction of dams, interstate highways, public buildings, and so forth—cannot be turned on and off like a faucet. The construction of a series of dams on a river may be an eight- or ten-year task. Expenditures for the project are clearly appropriate during periods of depression. But what if the economy shrugs off unemployment and enters a period of inflation when the project is half completed? In this embarrassing situation Congress has two choices, both of which, unfortunately, are "wrong." First, to abandon the project in order to relieve inflationary pressure would undoubtedly trigger widespread cries of "waste" and "government bungling" from taxpayers. Most vocal would be those whose incomes stand to be favorably affected by completion of the project. The other alternative is to continue the project. In this case the continuing government expenditures would serve to fan inflationary fires. The choice is not an easy one.

3. The wheels of democratic government are often slow in turning. Indeed, Congress has on occasion consumed so much time in adjusting fiscal policy that the economic situation has taken a turnabout in the interim, thereby rendering the policy action completely inappropriate. But let us now consider the more basic question as to whether Congress will initiate appropriate fiscal action at all.

Political problems

Fiscal policy is created in the political arena. Political problems may therefore arise to thwart the enactment of appropriate fiscal policy.

The basic question is this: Can Congress be depended upon to come up with appropriate fiscal medicine and in sufficient dosage to put an ailing economy back on its feet? More bluntly, will political considerations outweigh economic factors in the formation of fiscal policy? Given the general unpopularity of tax increases, can Congress be expected to increase tax rates quickly and sufficiently when severe inflation is encountered? Even if Congress quickly agrees upon needed tax increases, might its efforts founder on disagreement as to what specific types of taxes are to be raised? Can Congress reasonably be expected to reach agreement as to what specific types of expenditures should be trimmed (for example, highway construction, agricultural research, education) during inflation? It is one problem for Congress to agree on the appropriate changes in the levels of government expenditures and taxes which a given inflation or recession may require; it is an even more difficult problem to translate these over-all changes into *specific* adjustments in government expenditure programs and tax rates. More generally put, is the public willing to accept, and the politician to enact, the fiscal cures which inflation and deflation require? There is no simple answer here. But at a minimum it must be noted that the democratic political processes simply do not lend themselves to the making of such decisions quickly and smoothly. "Ineffectual or undesirable changes, or more likely, fiscal inertia, may often result from the interaction of political considerations." [5]

What does the historical record show? While it is generally agreed that the built-in stabilizers have functioned well in the post-World War II

period, the record of discretionary fiscal policy has been the subject of debate and substantial criticism. A fair share of this criticism undoubtedly stems from an imperfect functioning of the democratic political processes. A recent report to the Joint Economic Committee of Congress concludes that our postwar use of discretionary fiscal policy has been "disappointing" for several reasons: (1) except for the Korean War, government has failed to employ discretionary tax changes for countercyclical purposes; (2) the discretionary increases in government spending which have been employed during recessions have been too modest in size and too tardy in timing; and (3) primarily because of sudden and substantial changes in defense expenditures which are uncompensated for by appropriate tax adjustments, discretionary fiscal policy has on balance actually exerted a *destabilizing* influence on the economy.[6] It must be emphasized that the postwar record of fiscal policy is subject to other interpretations; some might argue that on numerous occasions Congress has clearly recognized appropriate fiscal policy and has acted with reasonable firmness and certainty. Fortunately, the postwar years have provided us with no sieges of unemployment comparable to the 1930s and no really drastic and prolonged periods of inflation to put discretionary fiscal policy to really severe tests.

State and local finance

From the viewpoint of the economy as a whole it would be desirable for the fiscal policies of all levels of government—Federal, state, and local—to be of a countercyclical nature. Unfortunately, this is not the case. State and local finance tends to reinforce, rather than alleviate, cyclical fluctuations. State and local governments do most of their spending for schools, libraries, and streets and highways during prosperity. Like households and private businesses, they cut expenditures and sometimes even retire debt during depression. The 1930s provide an excellent illustration of how

[5] Joint Economic Committee, *Staff Report on Employment, Growth, and Price Levels* (Washington: 1960), p. 209.

[6] *Ibid.*, chap. 8.

declines in state and local expenditures partially negated increases in Federal spending designed to boost the economy from the Great Depression. In the 1930–1934 period total state and local expenditures declined steadily from $8.2 billion to $6.4 billion, thereby canceling a sizable portion of the $3.6 billion increase in Federal spending which occurred in the same period.[7] At the other extreme, state and local governments have on occasion cut taxes during periods of inflationary pressure.

The reasons for the perverse nature of state and local finance are many: the weaker credit standings of state and local governments, the fact that state and local governments lack the Federal government's power to create money, the relative instability of state and local tax systems, statutory or constitutional limits on their debts, and a rather widespread belief in the alleged virtues of an annually balanced budget all contribute to the procyclical character of state and local finance.

Fiscal policy and war

Mobilization and war impose a severe limitation upon anti-inflationary fiscal policy. As noted in Chapter 9, about two-thirds of total Federal expenditures are for national defense and defense-related expenditures. Hot and cold wars make it virtually impossible to realize any substantial cuts in Federal spending as an inflation-alleviating measure.

Compensatory spending and social balance

Fiscal policy (in particular the policy of varying government spending inversely with the level of private spending) puts social goods in the position of being expendable or of a lower priority than private goods. More precisely, if the private sector of the economy is exuberant and consumption and investment are at high levels, fiscal policy will call for a cutting back of gov-

[7] Tax Foundation, *Facts and Figures on Government Finance, 1952–53* (New York: Tax Foundation, 1953), p. 51.

ernment spending as an anti-inflationary measure. If prolonged, the result might be an undue restraint of sacrifice of such vital social goods and services as education, basic technological research, and preventive medicine. In other words, the notion that public expenditures should be of a compensatory character, that is, they should be adjusted downward or upward in accordance with the exuberance or lethargy of the private sector, may not be conducive to an efficient allocation of resources between private and public goods. Stated differently, the changes in government spending which fiscal policy demands may contribute to the problem of achieving social balance—an optimum division of total output between private and public goods. This problem is accorded further discussion in Chapter 36.

Government spending and private investment

Tradition compels us to mention a longstanding argument against fiscal policy in general and government spending in particular. Some conservative business groups allege that the government spending which antidepression fiscal policy calls for is likely to hurt the incentives of private businesses to invest. If government expenditures constitute "a threat of government competition with individual enterprise" or even occur "in an atmosphere of what appears to be political hostility to individual enterprise," it is contended that the resulting declines in private investment spending might offset or more than counterbalance the increases in government spending.

Although few would deny that the "scaring off" of private investment by increasing government spending is a potential problem, it need not be a real problem at all. Government spending on projects outside the sphere of private enterprise—for example, irrigation and flood control projects, the construction of highways, parks, and recreational areas—will not interfere with the flow of private investment, but rather is likely to induce increases in private investment spending. On the other hand, public housing projects and the construction of public power facilities *may* be a different proposition. The important point is that well-planned public works programs need not undermine private investment; judicious government spending can and should be a stimulus to private investment.

Pressure groups and inflation

The attainment of full employment accompanied by relatively stable prices is complicated by the existence of strong pressure groups in the economy. In particular, the presence of big business, big labor, and the farm bloc may seriously impair the maintenance of price stability once all available resources are fully employed. Labor demands higher wages at full employment to get its "fair share" of total output. Big business, enjoying a situation of full-employment demand, shows little resistance to these demands. As a matter of fact, in an inflation-conscious economy wage increases provide an excellent excuse for businesses to increase product prices by *more than* current increases in their labor costs. The resulting jump in the cost of living will undoubtedly prompt unions to demand and achieve further wage boosts. A wage-price inflationary spiral is the result. The immediate postwar years attest to the accuracy of this brief analysis (see Chapter 11).

More will be said of pressure groups in Part 6 of this book.

Cost-push inflation

The occurrence of cost-push inflation, such as during the 1958 recession (Chapter 11), poses a serious dilemma for fiscal policy. Cost-push inflation can exert itself when total demand is somewhat deficient and unemployment is above normal. But fiscal policy is designed to restrain excess-demand inflation. In short, fiscal policy is geared to the alleviating or correcting of demand-pull inflation, but is not very relevant in dealing with inflation whose source is the cost or supply side of the market. Therefore, to the degree that cost-push inflation becomes increasingly common in our econ-omy, fiscal policy will become decreasingly effective as an anti-inflationary technique. This correctly suggests, as we shall discover in Chapter 19, that the correcting of cost-push inflation may call for new and different stabilizing techniques.

Long-run deficits

As you undoubtedly know, Federal finance has given rise over the years to a large public debt. This debt is obviously the result of sizable and rather persistent government deficits caused by two major factors. The more important was the financing of World War II. Countercyclical deficit spending during the Great Depression of the 1930s runs a poor second as a causal force.

It is imperative that we consider the present public debt and both the real and imaginary problems associated with its existence and growth.

THE PUBLIC DEBT

In reference to the public debt it has been contended that "Never have so many understood so little about so much." To a very considerable degree this statement rings true. The public debt is surrounded by awe, ignorance, and, in the extreme, outright fear. It is vital that we accurately comprehend the size, significance, and real problems associated with it. In doing so we must be particularly alert for false impressions and inappropriate analogies and comparisons.

Growth and ownership of the public debt

There is no doubt about it; the public debt is large. The Federal government's debt now stands at about $296 billion—a figure so great as to be almost beyond comprehension. The simplest comparison is to say that the debt is equal to about 57 per cent of the market value of the economy's 1961 output.

As Table 14-2 indicates, growth of the public debt has been very rapid in the last two decades. This expansion reflects the fact that *the bulk of the current Federal debt is not so much the result of depression-inspired deficit spending as it is the consequence of financing World War II.* In 1929, on the eve of the Great Depression, the public debt stood at $16.9 billion. At the end of the depressed thirties (1939) the debt had grown to $40.4 billion. The debt clearly expanded by a considerable amount as the result of deficit spending during the 1930s. But this growth is dwarfed by the almost six-fold increase during the World War II era. War, not depression-oriented fiscal policy, has been the major contributor to the debt.

Who owns the public debt? The public debt of the United States is *internally* held, that is, it is held by American citizens and American institutions. This, as we will see shortly, is of considerable importance, because the problems posed by an *externally* held debt, that is, a public debt which is held by foreign individuals, foreign institutions, for foreign governments, are different from those of an internally held debt. A breakdown of the ownership of the public debt is shown in Table 14-1.

Public versus private debt

Much misinformation concerning the public debt stems from misguided comparisons with private debt. *Public and private debt have basically distinct characteristics; hence, comparisons between the two are not particularly meaningful.*

Private debt has these two related characteristics. First, it is owed by one individual or organization to some other distinct individual or organization. A private debt is one which X owes to Y, X and Y being separate and distinct economic units. A second feature of private debt is implicit in the first: when one incurs a private debt, he obtains currency which he is likely to spend, thereby increasing his real assets or standard of living. However, the payment of interest and principal on private debt involves the transfer of assets back from the debtor to the creditor. The debtor's actual or potential standard of living is thus reduced when he pays his debt.

Public debt differs on both counts. First, the

TABLE 14-1. OWNERSHIP OF UNITED STATES GOVERNMENT SECURITIES, DECEMBER, 1961

	Billions of dollars	Per cent of total
United States government agencies and trust funds	54.5	18
Federal Reserve banks	28.9	10
Commercial banks	67.2	23
Mutual savings banks	6.1	2
Insurance companies	11.4	4
Corporations*	19.7	7
State and local governments	18.2	6
Individuals	65.7	22
Miscellaneous purchasers †	24.8	8
Total	296.5	100

* Other than commercial banks, mutual savings banks, and insurance companies.
† Savings and loan associations, dealers and brokers, foreign accounts, corporate pension funds, and nonprofit institutions.
SOURCE: "Federal Reserve Bulletin," March, 1962, p. 330.

public debt is a debt which we—American citizens and institutions—owe to ourselves. While a private debt is one between distinct economic units, a public debt is one held within a single economic unit. Strictly speaking, the public debt is owed by the United States government to those bondholding citizens and institutions listed in Table 14-1. But should the government decide to retire this debt, how would the needed funds be obtained? By collecting taxes from American citizens and institutions. Hence, the public debt is one which we owe to one another. Were the public debt externally held, that is, held by foreigners, it would be like a private debt—a debt between distinct economic units—and this owe-it-to-ourselves characteristic would not be applicable.

Second, the owe-it-to-ourselves character of the public debt tells us that, if the public debt were to be retired, there would be no direct loss of wealth for the economy as a whole. Retirement of the public debt would call for a gigantic transfer payment whereby American individuals and institutions would pay higher taxes and the government in turn would pay out those tax revenues to those same taxpaying individuals and institutions in the aggregate in redeeming the bonds which they hold. Although a redistribution of wealth would result from this gigantic financial transfer, it need not entail any immediate decline in the economy's aggregate wealth or standard of living. The repayment of an internally held public debt entails no leakage of purchasing power from the economy of the country as a whole.

These comparisons of private and public debt boil down to the fact that public debt is basically a macroeconomic concept and private debt a microeconomic concept. The fallacy of composition reminds us that different principles may govern macro- and micro- concepts. More specifically, one must be very cautious in applying the principles and practices surrounding private debt to the public debt. Much misunderstanding of the significance and burden of the public debt stems from such a misguided application.

In assessing the problems associated with a large public debt it is also noteworthy that the public debt is not suddenly going to fall due in its entirety at some specified future date and have to be retired. The public debt has been incurred over a period of time and in addition entails government securities of differing maturities. This means that the public debt comes due more or less evenly over a period of time. Hence, a relatively small fraction of the total debt falls due each month or year, not the entire $296 billion. But this is not all: the fact that a certain fraction of the public debt matures in, say, a given month does not mean that the government must necessarily cut its expenditures and boost taxes to provide funds for *retiring* this portion of the debt. (Indeed, we have seen that with depressed economic conditions this would be very unwise fiscal policy.) The immediate problem is the much more modest one of *refunding* the maturing bonds, that is, selling new bonds and using the proceeds to pay off the holders of the matured ones. Debt refunding is a less troublesome task both economically and politically than is debt retirement.

War finance and the public debt

The fact that World War II gave rise to the bulk of the present $296 billion public debt has already been emphasized. The government found that it was neither politically nor economically feasible to finance the war on a pay-as-you-go basis through taxation. Borrowing was chosen as the best alternative to supplement taxes that were considered to be at the upper limit of the economy's tolerance.

This leads us to a much-aired question: Does government borrowing as a method of finance permit the government to pass on a portion of the economic cost of a war to a future generation? The answer depends upon who buys the bonds. If internally held debt is expanded, the answer is "No." But if war entails an expansion of externally held public debt, the answer is "Yes."

Financing a war through the expansion of internally held public debt does not allow the wartime generation to dodge the economic burden of war. This is easy to see in real terms.

It is the wartime generation itself which must tighten its civilian standard of living in order to free scarce resources for the production of armaments. There is no way of sidestepping or postponing these costs. Putting the matter crudely, it was the population living during 1941 to 1946 which did without a multitude of consumer durables to permit the United States to arm itself and its allies.

In money, or financial, terms the waging of World War II increased the public debt by well over $200 billion. Is this not a financial burden for future generations to bear? For the economy as a whole, no. The making of interest and principal payments on the war-borne portion of the public debt will constitute transfers of funds from future Americans as taxpayers to future Americans as bondholders. Such a financial transfer, as we have already seen, does not entail a direct decline in the total wealth of that future generation. The fact that each American baby born in 1970 may be, say, $1,800 or $2,000 in debt at the time he enters the world is not quite as disturbing as it sounds. Each member of the 1970 baby crop will also inherit, on the average, ownership of that same amount in government bonds. The higher taxes *paid* by our grandchildren in paying interest and principal on the war-incurred public debt will be *received* by that same group of grandchildren. In short, the real economic cost of a war must be shouldered at the time the war is being fought.

There is one notable exception: the emergency of wartime production may cause a nation's stock of capital to cease to grow or to dwindle as precious resources are taken from the production of capital goods and shifted to the production of war goods. As a result, future generations inherit a smaller stock of capital goods than would otherwise be the case. This occurred in the United States during World War II (see table on inside covers, line 2). But this shifting of costs is independent of how a war is financed.

While an internally held public debt is a debt existing within an economic unit (a nation), an externally held public debt is a debt between distinct economic units (two nations). As a result, an externally held public debt has the characteristics of a private debt. Hence, a nation can ease the immediate economic burden of a war by obtaining loans from other nations and spending the proceeds on the goods and services of the lending nation. Imports thus received supplement the borrowing nation's standard of living and ease the wartime strain on its own resources. But the tables are turned when time for repayment of the loan rolls around, say, twenty years later. The borrowing nation must then make enough of its currency available to the lending nation to retire its matured bonds. The lending nation then spends these funds in acquiring a portion of the borrowing nation's GNP. In other words, the generation living at the time the bonds fall due must tighten their belts to make goods and services available for repayment of a loan incurred some twenty years earlier. A portion of the real economic cost of a war has been shifted two decades into the future by increasing a nation's externally held public debt.

Quantitative importance of the public debt

The question of the size of the public debt is a knotty one. Journalists with a bent toward sensationalism are prone to cite impressive increases in the absolute size of the public debt. The more than sixfold increase in the public debt which has occurred since 1940 is a typical focal point for such literary giants (see Table 14-2, column 2). Let us face the question of the size of the public debt as squarely as we can.

1. A historical point: over the years critics of the public debt have periodically established some crucial upper limit beyond which the debt would somehow overburden the nation and precipitate economic collapse. The exact means by which the public debt would accomplish this dastardly feat has never quite been made clear. In any event, time and time again the debt rose beyond the disaster points without resulting in economic collapse. And time and time again the critics raised their upper limits. The early crucial points of $25 billion and $50 billion have now faded into history in favor of $300 or $500 billion or $1 trillion limits. The forecast-

ers of doom have been repeatedly incorrect.

The point then is this: Historically the absolute size of the public debt has grown tremendously, but so has the strength of the economy. As a matter of fact, *some of the economy's healthiest periods of expansion and growth have occurred at times when the public debt was increasing most rapidly.* And it is easy to see why: a budget deficit means a net injection of purchasing power into the economy by government, and this, of course, has an expansionary effect upon the economy.

2. A related point: it is questionable that simple, absolute changes in the size of the public debt provide a very meaningful and accurate picture of the debt's quantitative significance. Table 14-2 is relevant. The absolute growth in the public debt shown in column 2

glosses over the fact that the wealth and productive ability of our economy have also increased tremendously over the years. It is safe to say that a wealthy nation has greater ability to incur and carry a large public debt than does a poor nation. In other words, it seems more realistic to measure changes in the public debt *in relation to* changes in the economy's GNP. Column 5 in Table 14-2 presents such data. Note that instead of the more than sixfold increase in the debt between 1940 and 1960 shown in column 2, we now find that the debt has not even come close to doubling. As a matter of fact, the *relative* size of the debt has *declined* very considerably since 1946.

3. Many economists feel that the immediate burden of the public debt is the annual interest charge that accrues as a result of the debt.

TABLE 14-2. QUANTITATIVE SIGNIFICANCE OF THE PUBLIC DEBT: THE PUBLIC DEBT AND INTEREST PAYMENTS IN RELATION TO GNP, 1910–1960

(1) Year	(2) Public debt, billions	(3) Gross national product,° billions	(4) Interest payments, billions	(5) Public debt as per cent of GNP, (2) ÷ (3)	(6) Interest payments as per cent of GNP, (4) ÷ (3)	(7) Per capita public debt
1910	$ 1.1	$ 34.6	$0.02	3%	0.06%	$ 12
1920	24.3	93.2	1.02	26	1.09	228
1930	16.2	91.1	0.70	18	0.77	132
1940	43.0	100.6	1.04	43	1.03	325
1942	72.4	159.1	1.26	46	0.79	537
1944	201.0	211.4	2.61	95	1.23	1,452
1946	269.4	209.2	4.72	129	2.26	1,905
1948	252.3	257.3	5.21	98	2.02	1,721
1950	257.4	285.1	5.75	90	2.02	1,697
1952	259.1	345.4	5.86	75	1.70	1,650
1954	271.3	361.2	6.38	75	1.77	1,670
1956	272.9	414.7	6.79	66	1.64	1,622
1958	276.3	441.7	7.61	62	1.72	1,588
1960	286.3	521.3	9.18	55	1.76	1,586

* In current dollars.
SOURCE: Department of Commerce, "Statistical Abstract of the United States" (Washington: Government Printing Office, 1961), p. 389.

The absolute size of these interest payments is shown in column 4. Interest charges as a percentage of GNP are presented in column 6. In these latter terms the burden of the debt has increased by very small amounts over the last four decades, and has actually been declining since 1946. Finally, column 7 presents growth of the public debt on a per capita basis. Here we find rapid growth through the end of World War II in 1946, but steady declines since then.

4. What about future growth? So long as the government is able to find buyers for its bonds, further expansion of the public debt is possible. And the government need not fear that there will be no takers. This assertion is supported, on the one hand, by the fact that government bonds currently sell at a premium over corporate bonds with the same interest coupon. Despite an indebtedness of some $296 billion, United States bonds are widely recognized as the safest paper asset now attainable.[8] On the other hand, the Federal Reserve banks—the central banks of our economy—can and will use their tremendous financial resources to purchase bonds not wanted by the public.

Problems posed by a large public debt

But we must be careful not to whitewash the public debt. The existence of a large public debt does pose real and potential problems. In particular a large public debt may (1) impair incentives to work and invest, (2) enhance income inequality, (3) intensify inflationary pressures, and (4) be conducive to wasteful government spending.

Incentives. Table 14-2 makes evident the fact that the present public debt necessitates an annual interest payment of over $9 billion. With no increase in the size of the debt, this annual interest charge must be paid out of tax revenues. Taxes may tend to dampen incentives to bear risk, to innovate, to invest, and to work.

[8] This is not to say that the Treasury can always sell government bonds at interest rates as low as it might like to pay.

In this way the existence of a large debt can impair economic growth.

Income inequality. In all probability the payment of interest and principal on the public debt contributes to income inequality. Aside from adverse effects upon incentives, the fact that we owe it to ourselves may largely rule out a drop in the economy's standard of living when interest or principal on the debt is paid. But it does not prevent a redistribution of income from occurring. Common sense and available statistical evidence concerning the income status of savers suggest that most government bondholders are in the middle and upper income brackets. On the other hand, under the prevailing tax structure the revenue needed to pay interest and principal on the debt would come rather evenly from all income groups (see Table 9-6). In all probability the net result of interest or principal repayment is greater income inequality. Not only is enhanced inequality felt by some to be undesirable on equity grounds, but it might also depress the consumption schedule and thereby exert a deflationary influence on the economy.

A word of caution: in weighing the possible impact of the public debt upon incentives and the personal distribution of income, two points should be kept in mind. First, the size of the annual interest charge on the debt is relatively small—about 2 per cent of the GNP. Second, the relative size of this interest charge has been fairly stable for the last fifteen years. As a matter of fact, it has declined somewhat in the postwar era.

Inflation and monetary policy. Although taxation for the payment of interest and principal on the public debt might exert a deflationary influence on the economy, the very existence of a large debt tends to be inflationary. This is so for several reasons:

1. Because they are highly liquid assets, the possession of government bonds makes consumers feel wealthier. This feeling of wealth leads to greater consumption out of their incomes. In short, the existence of a large public debt

tends to shift the consumption schedule upwards. If the economy is already at full employment, this shift will be inflationary.

2. Furthermore, government bonds can be converted into money easily and with little or no risk of loss. Government bonds, therefore, constitute a potential backlog of purchasing power which can add materially to inflationary fires. During periods of inflation it is very tempting for consumers to dig into this reserve of purchasing power in an attempt to beat rising prices. Such an attempt to beat inflation will cause more inflation. Something like this happened at the end of World War II; the inflation-causing buying spree of 1946 to 1947 was financed partly by the cashing in of bonds purchased during the war.

3. Finally, the very fact that the United States Treasury is a debtor may pose serious problems for exercising effective anti-inflationary monetary policy. We will discover in Chapter 17 that the Treasury's interest in high and stable bond prices conflicts with the monetary authorities' interest in limiting or contracting the supply of money in attempting to curb inflationary spending.

But the contention that a large public debt has an inflationary bias must be qualified. *Changes* in the size of the public debt have a much greater impact upon employment, output, and the price level than does the *absolute size* of the existing debt. Thus a $5 billion increase in the debt can be expected to exert a much greater expansionary or inflationary effect on the economy than the mere presence of an existing debt of say $296 billion.

Wasteful government spending. It is frequently argued that wasteful government expenditures tend to creep into the Federal budget when deficit financing is readily available. Politicians are motivated to screen expenditures more carefully when they are faced with the delicate problem of financing such programs out of tax increases. The fact that deficit financing gives the illusion of deferring the costs of government expenditures makes it easier for projects of questionable merit to find their way into the government's budget.

Advantages of a public debt

There is a brighter side to the public debt. Indeed, in at least three respects the existence of a large debt can be desirable.

1. Because government bonds are highly liquid and virtually risk-free securities, they make an excellent purchase for small and conservative savers.

2. It should also be noted that, although a large debt may pose inflationary problems in a full-employment economy, that same debt can cushion a cyclical downswing. That which is potentially undesirable in a full-employment economy may be very desirable in a less-than-full-employment economy. A large public debt may prove to be a kind of built-in stabilizer in so far as recessions are concerned.

3. Finally, Chapter 17 will reveal the important role which government bonds play in effectuating monetary policy. The sale and purchase of government bonds by the economy's central banks influence the money supply, the level of spending, and hence the level of economic activity.

SUMMARY

1. Government responsibility for achieving and maintaining full employment is set forth in the Employment Act of 1946. In practice the economy simultaneously seeks several related objectives—full employment, price stability, full production, and economic freedom.

2. Built-in flexibility refers to the automatic and appropriate changes in transfer payments and tax revenues which occur over the course of the business cycle. However, these nondiscretionary changes must be supplemented by discretionary fiscal action to mitigate inflation or unemployment of any severity.

3. Historically, the concept of the annually balanced budget has given ground to the cyclically balanced budget and, more recently, to the idea of functional finance.

4. The impact of discretionary fiscal policy depends upon (*a*) the size of the deficit or surplus which government incurs, (b) the absolute levels of government spending and taxation at which a deficit of surplus is incurred, (c) the manner in which the deficit is financed or the surplus disposed of, and (d) the types of taxes and expenditures employed by government.

5. Financing a government deficit through the creation of new money is more expansionary than financing the same deficit by borrowing. A surplus is more deflationary when held by government as an idle money balance than it is when used to retire outstanding public debt.

6. Generally speaking, public works expenditures are more expansionary than are transfer payments. Similarly, sales and excise taxes are generally felt to be more deflationary than are personal and corporate income taxes.

7. The enactment and application of appropriate fiscal policy are subject to certain problems and questions. Some of the most important are these: (a) Can the enactment and application of fiscal policy be better timed so as to maximize its effectiveness in heading off economic fluctuations? (b) Can the economy rely upon Congress to enact appropriate fiscal policy? (c) State and local finance generally works to intensify rather than alleviate the cycle. (d) Mobilization and war largely rule out reductions in government spending as an anti-inflationary technique. (e) Continuous fiscal restraint upon government spending during a prolonged inflationary period may contribute to social imbalance. (f) Injudicious government spending may result in a curtailment of private investment. (g) The presence of well-organized

pressure groups in the economy may increase the difficulties involved in achieving full employment without inflation. (h) Because it is designed to influence the size of aggregate demand, fiscal policy is not particularly appropriate in controlling cost-push inflation. (i) Fiscal policy may result in long-run deficits.

8. The public debt is approximately $296 billion, about one-half of the current GNP. The public debt is internally held. About 18 per cent of it is held by government agencies and in government trust funds. Central and commercial banks hold about 33 per cent; other financial and business institutions hold approximately 27 per cent. Individuals hold the remaining 22 per cent.

9. Public debt does not have the same characteristics as does private debt. The public debt (a) is owed by Americans to Americans and (b) does not entail a reduced standard of living for the economy as a whole when payment of interest or principal is made.

10. The real cost of a war or depression cannot be shifted to future generations by increasing the internally held public debt.

11. Absolute growth of the public debt is not the best measure of its quantitative significance. It is more accurate to show growth relative to changes in GNP or NI.

12. A large public debt may (a) impair incentives to innovate and invest, (b) contribute to income inequality, (c) add to inflationary pressures, and (d) be conducive to the growth of wasteful government spending.

QUESTIONS AND STUDY SUGGESTIONS

1. "Full employment must be achieved and maintained at all costs." Do you agree?

2. Distinguish between nondiscretionary and discretionary fiscal policy. How effective is built-in stability in controlling the business cycle? What suggestions would you make to improve the effectiveness of built-in flexibility?

3. Adjust the appropriate schedules in Figure 13-7a and b for the existence of built-in stability. Using these new graphs, prove that a given increase or decrease in autonomous investment will cause smaller changes in the equilibrium level of NNP with built-in flexibility than without.

4. Explain the three major budget philosophies. To which do you subscribe? Why? Why is an annually balanced budget not economically neutral?

5. What is the best method of financing a government deficit during depression? What is the best means of disposing of a surplus during inflation? Explain your answers.

6. Suppose the economy encounters a severe and prolonged period of depression. What variations in the levels of taxes and expenditures would be appropriate? What variations in the tax structure and government expenditure programs would be desirable?

7. "If the economy needs $10 billion with which to finance the expansion and improvement of its highways, it should simply print up the needed money to finance the undertaking. In this way we'll get the roads, and no one will be hurt by having to pay higher taxes." Evaluate this suggestion, first under conditions of full employment, and second under depressed conditions.

8. Briefly state and evaluate the major problems encountered in enacting and applying fiscal policy. Which do you feel are the most significant?

9. Professor Alvin H. Hansen[9] has recently endorsed the following proposals as means of strengthening our fiscal policies:

a. "We should introduce an automatic or semiautomatic system of tax-rate adjustment in the first income tax bracket, so that the rate would rise and fall according to agreed-upon criteria of employment . . . or rates of investment."

b. The rate of depreciation allowable on capital goods for tax purposes should be made countercyclical. That is, businesses should be permitted to make larger depreciation charges in calculating taxable income during a period of unemployment, but smaller depreciation charges during an inflationary boom.

c. ". . . [a special] tax on investment could be employed to choke off such unhealthy and abnormal investment spurts as that of 1955–1957."

d. ". . . advertising expenditures tend to fluctuate *with* the cycle and thus serve to intensify instability. . . . Consideration might be given to countercyclical adjustment of advertising as an allowable business expense in calculating income taxes."

e. "The public should be represented at every important collective-bargaining table."

To which of these proposals would you adhere? Why? Which would you reject? Why? Discuss any administrative problems that might arise with each proposal. Assess as best you can the political feasibility of each.

10. "No budget-balancing principle can be as important as maintaining full employment and preventing inflation." [10] Do you agree?

11. How do private and public debts differ? How does an internally held public debt differ from an externally held public debt? What would be the effects of retiring an internally held public debt?

12. "A national debt is like a debt of the left hand to the right hand." Explain.

[9] Alvin H. Hansen, *Economic Issues of the 1960's* (New York: McGraw-Hill Book Company, Inc., 1960), chap. 4.

[10] Abba P. Lerner, *The Economics of Control* (New York: The Macmillan Company, 1944), p. 319.

13. In what ways might the mere existence of a large public debt contribute to inflationary pressures? "Incurring a public debt is more inflationary than carrying an existing public debt." Do you agree?

14. Explain how a government deficit might pay for itself.

15. Distinguish clearly between refunding and retiring public debt.

16. "Rising prices cause real incomes to fall. In such circumstances all levels of government should cut taxes. This will permit the American people to maintain their standard of living." Evaluate.

SELECTED REFERENCES

Buchanan, James M., *Public Principles of Public Debt* (Homewood, Ill.: Richard D. Irwin, Inc., 1958).

Due, John F., *Government Finance,* rev. ed. (Homewood, Ill.: Richard D. Irwin, Inc., 1959), chaps. 27–31.

Hansen, Alvin H., *Economic Issues of the 1960's* (New York: McGraw-Hill Book Company, Inc., 1960), particularly chaps. 4 and 6.

Jacoby, Neil H., *Can Prosperity Be Sustained?* (New York: Holt, Rinehart and Winston, Inc., 1956), particularly chaps. 1–4.

Strayer, Paul J., *Fiscal Policy and Politics* (New York: Harper & Row, Publishers, 1958).

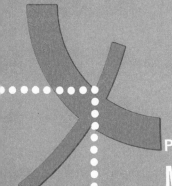

PART 3
MONEY, MONETARY POLICY, AND ECONOMIC STABILITY

Chapter 15

MONEY AND BANKING IN

AMERICAN CAPITALISM

MONEY—one of the truly great inventions of man—constitutes a most fascinating aspect of economic science.

Money bewitches people. They fret for it, and they sweat for it. They devise most ingenious ways to get it, and most ingenuous ways to get rid of it. Money is the only commodity that is good for nothing but to be gotten rid of. It will not feed you, clothe you, shelter you, or amuse you unless you spend it or invest it. It imparts value only in parting. People will do almost anything for money, and money will do almost anything for people. Money is a captivating, circulating, masquerading puzzle.[1]

Money is also one of the most crucial elements of economic science. It is much more than a passive component of the economic system—a mere tool for facilitating the economy's operation. When operating properly, the monetary system is the lifeblood of the circular flows of income and expenditure which typify all economies. A well-behaved money system is conducive to both full production and full employment. Conversely, a malfunctioning monetary system can make major contributions

[1] "Creeping Inflation," *Business Review*, Federal Reserve Bank of Philadelphia, August, 1957, p. 3.

to severe fluctuations in the economy's levels of output, employment, and prices.

In this chapter we are concerned with the nature and functions of money and the basic institutions of the American banking system. Chapter 16 looks into the methods by which individual commercial banks and the banking system as a whole can vary the money supply. In Chapter 17 we discuss how the central banks of the economy attempt to regulate the supply of money so as to promote full employment and full production.

The specific objectives of the present chapter are fourfold. We begin with a review of the functions of money. Next we designate and assess the relative importance of the various types of money used in American capitalism. Third, we pose a query: What "backs" money in the United States? Finally, the institutional structure and the basic functions of the American banking system will be described.

THE FUNCTIONS OF MONEY

What is money? Money is what money does. Anything that performs the functions of money is money. There are three functions of money; we briefly review them here (see also Chapter 3).

1. First and foremost, money is a *medium of exchange;* that is, money is usable in buying

283

and selling goods and services. As a medium of exchange, money allows society to escape the complications of barter and to thereby reap the benefits of geographic and human specialization.

2. Money is also a *standard of value*. Society finds it convenient to use the monetary unit as a yardstick for measuring the relative worth of heterogeneous goods and resources. Two related advantages are involved here. On the one hand, with a money system, the price of each product need only be stated in terms of the monetary unit rather than in terms of each of the other products for which it might be exchanged. This very substantially reduces the number of prices in the economy. On the other hand, with money prices as a common denominator of value, transactors can readily compare the relative worth of various commodities and resources. Such comparisons facilitate rational decision making. Money is also used as a standard of value for transactions involving future payments. Debt obligations of all kinds are measured in terms of money.

3. Finally, money serves as a *store of value*. Because money is the most liquid of all assets, it is a very convenient form in which to store wealth. Though it is not likely to yield monetary returns such as one gets by storing wealth in the form of real assets (property) or paper assets (stocks, bonds, and so forth), money does have the advantage of being immediately usable by a firm or a household in meeting any and all financial obligations.

MONEY IN AMERICAN CAPITALISM

Historically, such diverse items as whale's teeth, elephant tail bristles, circular stones, nails, slaves, cattle, beer, cigarettes, and pieces of metal have functioned as media of exchange. More recently, the debts of governments and of banks have been employed as money.

In so far as the United States is concerned, the money supply is comprised of only three items: (1) coins, (2) paper money, and (3) demand deposits, or checking accounts. The first two items are debts of government and governmental agencies; the third represents a debt of commercial banks. Table 15-1 shows the quantitative importance of each money item in both absolute and relative terms. Let's comment briefly on each of these components of the money supply.

Coins

Ranging from copper pennies to silver dollars, coins constitute the "small change" of our money supply. As Table 15-1 indicates, coins constitute a very small portion of our total money supply. Coins are essentially "convenience money," in that they permit us to make all kinds of very small purchases.

It is notable that all the coins in circulation in the United States are token money. This simply means that the intrinsic value—that is, the value of the bullion contained in the coin itself—is less than the face value of the coin.

TABLE 15-1. MONEY IN THE UNITED STATES, FEBRUARY, 1962

Money	Billions of dollars	Per cent of total
Coins	2.6	2
Paper money	29.6	20
Demand deposits	115.1	78
Total	147.3	100

SOURCE: "Federal Reserve Bulletin" and "Economic Indicators."

For example, a fifty-cent piece contains only about 33 cents' worth of silver bullion. This is purposely the case so as to avoid the melting down of token money for profitable sale as bullion. If a fifty-cent piece contained, say, 75 cents' worth of silver bullion, it would be highly profitable to melt these coins for sale as bullion. Despite the illegality of such a procedure, 50-cent pieces would tend to disappear from circulation. This is one of the potential defects of commodity money: its worth as a commodity may come to exceed its worth as money, causing it to cease functioning as a medium of exchange.

Paper money

Much more significant than coins, paper money constitutes about one-fifth of the economy's money supply. You have undoubtedly noticed that there are several different types of paper money currently in circulation in the United States. By far the most important are *Federal Reserve notes*. These notes, which constitute about $28 billion of the $29.6 billion worth of paper money in circulation, are issued by the Federal Reserve banks with the authorization of Congress. The remaining $1.6 billion are largely silver certificates, $1 and $5 bills issued by the Treasury in purchasing silver bullion as required by somewhat archaic legislation. Other paper money takes such minor forms as United States notes, Federal Reserve Bank notes, and treasury notes of 1890, most of which are in the process of being retired from circulation in the interest of achieving a more uniform supply of paper money. All forms of paper money other than Federal Reserve notes are sometimes called *treasury currency*. Similarly, the coin and paper money components of the money supply are frequently lumped together and simply labeled *currency*.

Demand deposits

The safety and convenience of using checks, or bank money, has made demand deposits the most important type of money in the United States. Despite the efficiency of the Post Office Department and the integrity of its employees, one would not think of stuffing, say, $4,896.47 in an envelope and dropping it in a mailbox in paying a debt; but to write and mail a check for a large sum is very commonplace. A check must be endorsed by the person cashing it; the drawer of the check subsequently receives the canceled check as an endorsed receipt attesting to the fulfillment of his obligation. Similarly, because the writing of a check requires endorsement by the drawer, the theft or loss of one's bank book is not nearly so calamitous as would be losing an identical amount of currency. It is, furthermore, simply more convenient to write a check in many cases than it is to transport and count out a large sum of currency. For all these reasons checkbook money has come to be the dominant form of money in American capitalism. Even Table 15-1 belittles the significance of bank money; it is estimated that dollarwise about 90 per cent of all transactions are carried out by the use of checks.

It might seem strange that demand deposits or checking accounts are a part of the money supply. But the reason for their inclusion is clear: checks, which are nothing more than a means for transferring the ownership of demand deposits, are generally acceptable as a medium of exchange. Furthermore, demand deposits can be immediately converted into paper money and coins on demand; demand deposits are for all practical purposes the equivalent of currency.

In short,

Money = demand deposits + currency

Currency is essentially government-created money, and demand deposits, we shall discover in Chapter 16, are bank-created money.

Near-monies and bank and Treasury holdings

Two qualifications of our definition of money must be noted.

1. The line between what we have defined as money and certain highly liquid assets called *near-monies* is a very fine one. The two

most important near-monies are time deposits, or savings accounts, and United States government bonds. Households and businesses currently hold about $85 billion worth of government bonds and own in the neighborhood of $125 billion worth of savings deposits in commercial banks, mutual savings banks, and in the postal savings system. Time deposits come very close to being money. But they must be excluded from the definition of money because they are not a medium of exchange. You cannot write checks on a savings account in making purchases or in paying debts.[2] Much the same can be said of United States government bonds: all are highly marketable and can be readily converted into currency or demand deposits with little fear of loss. As a matter of fact, your Series E bonds can be converted into currency or demand deposits at commercial banks at a stipulated price upon demand. Yet, as such, government bonds are not a medium of exchange.

Near-monies are important to our discussion for three related reasons. First, the fact that people have such highly liquid assets available affects their consuming-saving habits. Generally speaking, the greater the amount of the wealth people have in the form of near-monies, the greater is their willingness to spend out of their money incomes. Second, a sudden conversion of easily cashable near-monies into money adds significantly to the money supply and, if not offset, can pose serious problems during inflationary periods. Finally, the existence of near-monies points up the fact that the definition of money is somewhat arbitrary. In modern complex economies there is no clear-cut distinction between money and certain highly liquid assets.

2. The second qualification of our definition of money is of a somewhat technical nature. In the definition of the money supply, currency and demand deposits owned by government and by Federal Reserve or commercial banks are excluded. This exclusion is partly to avoid

overstating the money supply and partly because money in the possession of households and businesses is more relevant to the level of spending in the economy.[3]

money → checks → debts - promise to pay

WHAT "BACKS" THE MONEY SUPPLY?

The answer to this query depends upon what one means by "backs." If you are seeking an answer in terms of some precious and tangible object, such as gold or silver, the question is a bit difficult to answer. If you mean "Why do coins, pieces of finely engraved paper, and checks perform the functions of money?" a more satisfying answer can be found.

The first point to recognize is that the major components of the money supply—paper money and demand deposits—are simply debts, or promises to pay. Paper money is the debt of the Treasury and the Federal Reserve banks.[4] Paper currency is merely the circulating IOUs of the government and the central banks. Demand deposits are simply the debts of commercial banks. But these paper-money and demand-deposit debts have a special characteristic: the issuers will not give you anything tangible in exchange for these debts. Federal Reserve notes, the major component of our paper cur-

---

[2] Yet, although bankers may legally require thirty or sixty days' notice of withdrawal, time deposits are in practice immediately convertible into demand deposits or currency.

[3] A paper dollar in the hands of John Doe obviously constitutes just $1 of the money supply. But, if we were to count dollars held by banks as a part of the money supply, that same $1 would count for $2 when deposited in a commercial bank. It would count for a $1 demand deposit owned by Doe and also for $1 worth of currency resting in the bank's vault. This problem of double counting can be avoided by excluding currency resting in commercial banks (and currency redeposited in the Federal Reserve banks or other commercial banks) in determining the total money supply. The exclusion of currency held by, and demand deposits owned by, government is somewhat more arbitrary. The major reason for this exclusion is that it permits us better to gauge the money supply and rate of spending which occurs in the private sector of the economy apart from spending initiated by government policy.

[4] Federal Reserve notes in circulation are the debts or obligations of the Federal Reserve banks, and all other forms of paper money (treasury currency) are debts of the United States Treasury.

near monies ① affect consumer - savings 7HHO

Fiat money?

rency supply, boldly proclaim that "the United States of America will pay to the bearer on demand" the number of dollars stated on the note. But what form will these dollars which the government promises to pay assume? They will be in the form of other paper currency, that is, other paper promises to pay![5] The government will swap one paper $5 bill for another bearing a different serial number. That is all you can get should you ask the government to redeem some of the paper money you hold.

What of the huge supplies of gold which the government has hidden away in assorted holes in the ground? In so far as the domestic money supply is concerned, that is where the gold bullion seems destined to stay. Since 1934 American capitalism has been off the gold standard, and as a result paper money is no longer redeemable for a stipulated amount of gold bullion.[6] Paper money cannot be converted into gold but is only exchangeable for other pieces of paper money. Although of significance for international transactions, gold is actually of relatively little importance in so far as the domestic money supply is concerned. We will discover that the supply of money in circulation is only linked to the government's stock of gold bullion in a very loose and flexible manner. American capitalism has chosen to disconnect its money supply from its stock of gold bullion. What about demand deposit money? Commercial banks will only redeem these deposits for paper money. And these, we have just seen, cannot be redeemed for anything tangible.

Now don't get discouraged and tear up the $5 bill you have in your pocket. Actually, the fact that the government does not stand ready to hand you a lump of gold for every dollar

[5] The government will give you coins, if you insist, for silver certificates. But remember that the bullion value of these coins falls considerably short of their face value, so they too in part are debts.

[6] There are exceptions. Licensed buyers, for example, dentists, jewelers, and importers, may purchase gold bullion from the government. The government also stands ready to buy all gold offered to it at $35 per ounce.

you possess really is not as significant as it might first sound. *Paper money does have value, because you can exchange it for the goods and services you wish to obtain in order to satisfy your wants.* Although the government will not give you anything tangible for your $5 bill,[7] businesses and households are willing to exchange goods, services, and resources for it. Suppose you swap a $10 bill for a sweater at a clothing store. Why does the merchant accept this piece of paper in exchange for one of his products? The answer is tricky: the merchant accepts paper money because he knows that others will also be willing to accept it in exchange for goods and services. He knows that he can purchase the services of his clerks, acquire products from wholesalers, pay the rent on his store, and so forth. Each of us accepts paper money in exchange because he knows that all other households and businesses in the economy are also willing to accept it in exchange.

Government facilitates the acceptability of paper money not only by accepting it in the payment of taxes but also by having declared these circulating promises to pay as *legal tender*. This means that paper currency must be accepted in the payment of a debt or the creditor forfeits the privilege of charging interest and the right to sue the debtor for nonpayment. Put more crudely, the acceptability of paper dollars is bolstered by the fact that government says these dollars are money. The paper money in our economy is basically *fiat money*; it is money because the government says it is, not because of redeemability in terms of some precious metal. Lest we be overimpressed by the power of government, it should be noted that the fact that paper currency is generally accepted in exchange is decidedly more important than government's legal tender decree in making these pieces of paper function as money. Indeed, the government has not decreed checks to be legal tender, but they

[7] This is not entirely true. The government, of course, will accept paper money in the payment of taxes. In this case the taxpayer in effect is buying his share of the social goods and services supplied by the government.

nevertheless successfully perform the vast bulk of the economy's exchanges of goods, services, and resources.

There is just one catch to the use of paper money:[8] in order for paper money to have value, or purchasing power, in exchange, its supply must be limited in relation to the demand for it. You have probably heard or read of situations wherein a nation's currency became worthless and unacceptable in exchange. Indeed, we noted several in Chapter 11. With few exceptions these were situations where government issued so many pieces of paper currency that the value of each of these units of money was almost totally undermined. The infamous post-World War I inflation in Germany is a most notable example. In December of 1919 there were about 50 billion marks in circulation. Exactly four years later this figure had expanded to 496,585,345,900 billion marks! The result? The German mark in 1923 was worth an infinitesimal fraction of its 1919 value.[9]

Inflation, you will recall, is the consequence of society's spending beyond its capacity to produce. Other things being equal, increases in the money supply will increase total spending. Once full employment is reached and total output becomes virtually fixed, this added spending can only serve to make prices spiral up. The sweater which sold for $10 in our previous illustration may, after severe inflation, cost $100. This means that the dollar which was formerly worth one-tenth of a sweater is now worth just one one-hundredth of a sweater. The dollar's value, or purchasing power, has obviously been reduced tenfold by inflation. The value of money varies inversely with the price level.

How might inflation and the accompanying decreases in the value of the dollar affect the acceptability of paper dollars as money? Households and businesses are willing to accept paper currency as a medium of exchange so long as they know it can in turn be spent by them without any noticeable loss in its purchasing

---

[8] Or any other kind of money for that matter.

[9] Frank G. Graham, *Exchange, Prices and Production in Hyper-inflation Germany, 1920–1923* (Princeton, N.J.: Princeton University Press, 1930), p. 13.

power. But with spiraling inflation this is not the case. Runaway inflation, such as Germany faced in the early 1920s, may significantly depreciate the value of money between the time of its receipt and its expenditure. Money will be "hot" money. It is as if the government was constantly taxing away the purchasing power of dollars. Rapid depreciation of the value of the dollar may cause it to cease functioning as a medium of exchange. Businesses and households may refuse to accept paper money in exchange, because they do not want to bear the loss in its value which will occur while it is in their possession. (All this despite the fact that government says the paper currency is legal tender.) Without an acceptable medium of exchange the economy will be thrown into disorder.

Similarly, people are willing to use money as a store of value so long as there is no unreasonable deterioration in the value of those stored dollars because of inflation. And the economy can effectively employ the monetary unit as a standard of value only when its purchasing power is relatively stable. A yardstick of value which is subject to drastic shrinkage no longer permits buyers and sellers to establish clearly the terms of trade. When the value of the dollar is declining rapidly, sellers will not know what to charge and buyers will not know what to pay for the various goods and services.

Now the important point we are leading up to is this: the major "backing" of paper money is the public's confidence in the government's ability to keep the value of money reasonably stable. This entails (1) appropriate fiscal policy, as explained in Chapter 14, and (2) intelligent management of the money supply, as noted above. The acceptability of paper money depends in part upon sound management of the monetary system and the pursuit of appropriate fiscal measures by government. Businesses and households accept paper money in exchange for goods so long as they know it will command a roughly equivalent amount of goods when they in turn spend it. In our economy a blending of legislation, government policy, and social practice serves as a bulwark against any imprudent expansion of the money supply which might jeopardize its value in exchange.

What we have said with respect to paper currency also applies to demand deposit money. In this case money is the debt of the commercial banks. If you have a checking account worth $100, this simply means that your commercial bank is indebted to you for that number of dollars. You can collect this debt in one of two ways. You can go to the bank and demand paper currency for your demand deposit; this simply amounts to changing the debts you hold from bank debts to government-issued debts. Or, and this is more likely, you can "collect" the debt which the bank owes you by transferring this claim by check to someone else. For example, if you buy a $100 suit from your clothier, you can pay for it by writing a check, which transfers the bank's indebtedness from you to your clothier. The bank now owes your clothier the $100 which it previously owed to you. Why does the clothier accept this transfer of indebtedness (the check) as a medium of exchange? Because he can convert it into currency on demand or can in turn transfer the debt to others in making purchases of his choice. Thus checks, as means of tranferring bank debts, are acceptable as money because of the public's confidence in commercial banks' ability to honor these claims.

In turn, the ability of commercial banks to honor claims against them depends upon their not creating too many of these claims. We will find in a moment that a decentralized system of private, profit-seeking banks does not contain sufficient safeguards against the creation of too much check money. Hence, the American banking system has a substantial amount of governmental control to guard against the imprudent creation of check money by commercial banks.

In the United States and other advanced economies, all money is essentially the debts of government and commercial banks.

These debts efficiently perform the functions of money so long as their value, or purchasing power, is relatively stable.

The value of money is no longer rooted in carefully defined quantities of precious metals, but rather in the amount of goods and services money will purchase in the market place.

Government's responsibility in stabilizing the value of the monetary unit involves (1) the application of appropriate fiscal policies and (2) effective control over the supply of money.

A final point to ponder: the final test of any money system is the simple question "Does it work well?" The various monetary standards we hear so much about—the gold standard, bimetallism, the managed gold standard, the paper standard, and so forth—are not inherently good or inherently bad money systems. Their effectiveness depends to a very considerable degree upon the problems and circumstances faced by the particular economy involved and the competence of its monetary authorities.

INSTITUTIONAL FRAMEWORK OF THE AMERICAN BANKING SYSTEM

We have noted that the major component of the money supply, demand deposits, is created by commercial banks and that government-created money, coins and paper currency, typically comes into circulation through the commercial banks. It is essential then that we take a thorough look at the framework of the American banking system prior to a detailed analysis in Chapter 16 of how commercial banks create money.

Need for centralization

It became painfully apparent rather early in American history that, like it or not, centralization and public control were prerequisites of an efficient banking system. Congress became increasingly aware of this around the turn of the twentieth century. Decentralized banking fostered the inconvenience and confusion of a heterogeneous currency, monetary mismanagement, and an inflexible supply of money. This latter problem was particularly acute. A dynamic and growing economy demands a flexible money supply—one which will respond to the economy's varying needs. The volume of trade expands and contracts unevenly and irregularly; hence, the supply of money must be elastic in meeting the needs of the economy. "Too much" money can precipitate dangerous inflationary problems; "too little" money can stunt the economy's growth by hindering the production and exchange of goods and services. The United States and innumerable foreign countries have learned through bitter experience that a decentralized banking system is not likely to provide that particular money supply which is most conducive to the economic welfare of the economy as a whole.

An unusually acute money panic in 1907 was the straw that broke Congress' back. A National Monetary Commission was established to study the monetary and banking problems of the economy and to outline a course of action for Congress. The end result was the Federal Reserve Act of 1913.

Structure of the Federal Reserve System

The banking system which has developed under the frequently amended Federal Reserve Act is sketched in Figure 15-1. It is important that we understand the nature and functions of the various segments which comprise the banking system and the relationships which the parts bear to one another.

Board of Governors. The kingpin of our money and banking system is the Board of Governors of the Federal Reserve System. The seven members of this Board are appointed by the President with the confirmation of the Senate. Terms are long—fourteen years—and staggered so that one member is replaced every two years. The Board is staffed by appointment rather than elections in an attempt to divorce monetary policy from partisan politics. Long and staggered terms are intended to provide the Board with continuity and experienced membership.

The Board of Governors has the responsibility of exercising general supervision and control over the operation of the money and banking system of the nation. The Board's actions, which are to be in the public interest and designed to promote the general economic welfare, determine the basic policies which the commercial banking system is to follow. These basic policy decisions are made effective through the twelve Federal Reserve banks and entail the use of two sets of control techniques which are at the disposal of the Board. *Quantitative credit controls,* consisting of (1) the reserve requirement, (2) open market operations, and (3) the discount rate, are designed to negotiate those changes in the money supply which the Board deems most conducive to a stable and expanding economy. From time to time the Board invokes *selective or qualitative credit controls* to regulate the availability of certain specific types of credit, for example, consumer credit in the purchase of housing or durables and credit in buying securities in the stock market. Much of Chapter 17 will be concerned with a discussion of these two types of credit controls and the manner in which they permit the Board of Governors to influence the activities of commercial banks.

Two important bodies assist the Board of Governors in determining basic banking policy. On the one hand, the Federal Open Market Committee, comprised of the seven members of the Board plus five of the presidents of the Federal Reserve banks, sets the System's policy with respect to the purchase and sale of government bonds in the open market. These open market operations constitute the most significant technique by which the monetary authorities can affect the money supply in the economy. On the other hand, the Federal Advisory Council is comprised of twelve prominent commercial bankers, one selected annually by each of the twelve Federal Reserve banks. The Council meets periodically with the Board of Governors to voice its views on banking policy. However, as its name indicates, the Council is purely advisory; it has no policy-making powers.

The twelve Federal Reserve banks. The twelve Federal Reserve banks have three major characteristics. They are (1) central banks, (2) quasi-public banks, and (3) "bankers' banks."

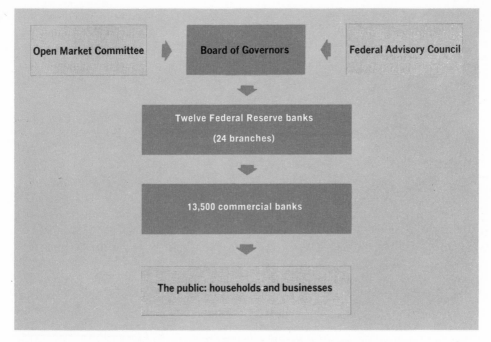

FIGURE 15-1. FRAMEWORK OF THE FEDERAL RESERVE SYSTEM AND ITS
RELATIONSHIP TO THE PUBLIC.
With the advice and counsel of the Open Market Committee and the Federal Advisory
Council, the Board of Governors makes the basic policy decisions which regulate our
money and banking systems. These decisions are made effective through the twelve
Federal Reserve banks.

1. Americans are blessed with a more or less inherent fear of centralization. As a result, the American banking system is less centralized than most of the other advanced economies of the world. As a matter of fact, the Federal Reserve Act was a compromise between exponents of centralization and advocates of decentralization. Hence, instead of creating a single central bank, the act divided the nation into twelve districts and provided for a Federal Reserve bank to function as a central bank in each of these districts. Figure 15-2 shows these twelve Federal Reserve districts. Geographic considerations were also of significance in the creation of the twelve Federal Reserve banks. It was felt that a single central bank would be unresponsive to the peculiar economic problems faced by the various regions of the econ-

omy. In any event the net result is that the twelve Federal Reserve banks comprise the central banking system of the economy. It is through these central banks that the basic policy directives of the Board of Governors are made effective. The Federal Reserve Bank of New York City is by far the most important of these central banks.

2. The twelve Federal Reserve banks are quasi-public banks. They reflect an interesting blend of private ownership and public control. The Federal Reserve banks are owned by the member banks in their districts. Upon joining the Federal Reserve System commercial banks are required to purchase shares of stock in the Federal Reserve bank in their district. But the basic policies which the Federal Reserve banks pursue are set by a public body—the Board of

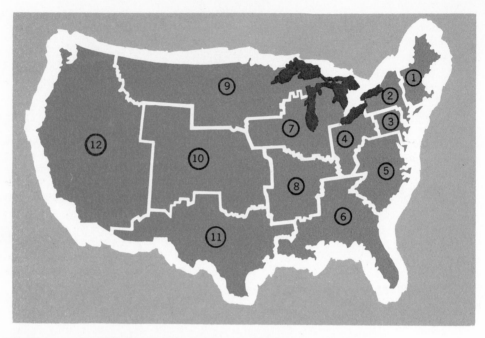

FIGURE 15-2. THE TWELVE FEDERAL RESERVE DISTRICTS.
The Federal Reserve System divides the United States into twelve districts, each of which has one central bank and in some instances one or more branches of the central bank. Hawaii and Alaska are included in the twelfth district. District central banks are located in the following cities: Boston (first), New York (second), Philadelphia (third), Cleveland (fourth), Richmond (fifth), Atlanta (sixth), Chicago (seventh), St. Louis (eighth), Minneapolis (ninth), Kansas City (tenth), Dallas (eleventh), and San Francisco (twelfth). ("Federal Reserve Bulletin.")

Governors. The central banks of American capitalism are privately owned but governmentally controlled.

The fact that the Federal Reserve banks are essentially public institutions is vitally important to an understanding of their operation. In particular it must be emphasized that the Federal Reserve banks are not motivated by profits as are private enterprises. The policies followed by the central banks are those which tend to promote the economic well-being of the economy as a whole. Hence, the activities of the Federal Reserve banks will frequently be at odds with the profit motive.[10] Furthermore, the Federal Reserve banks are not in competition with commercial banks. With rare exceptions, the Federal Reserve banks do not deal with the public, but rather with the government and the commercial banks.

3. Finally, the Federal Reserve banks are frequently called "bankers' banks." This is a shorthand way of saying that the Federal Reserve banks perform essentially the same functions for commercial banks as commercial banks perform for the public. Just as commercial banks accept the deposits of, and make loans to, the public, so the central banks accept the deposits of, and make loans to, commercial

[10] Though it is not their basic goal, the Federal Reserve banks have actually operated profitably. A part of the profits has been used to pay 6 per cent dividends to member banks on their holdings of stock; the bulk of the remaining profits has been turned over to the United States Treasury.

banks. But the Federal Reserve banks have a third function which commercial banks no longer perform: the function of issuing currency. Congress has authorized the Federal Reserve banks to put into circulation Federal Reserve notes, which constitute the bulk of the economy's paper money supply.

The commercial banks. The work horses of the American banking system are its 13,433 commercial banks. The majority of these are *state banks*, that is, private banks operating under state charters. But a good many have received their charters from the Federal government; that is, they are *national banks*. Roughly one-half of all existing commercial banks are members of the Federal Reserve System. The 4,513 national banks in our economy are required by law to join the Federal Reserve System; the remaining 8,920 state banks have the option of joining or declining to do so. As

Figure 15-3 indicates, 1,600 of the state banks have chosen to join the Federal Reserve System.

These statistics, however, tend to underestimate grossly the significance of the Federal Reserve System. Virtually all the larger commercial banks are members of the System, nonmembers being the smaller "country banks" for the most part. Thus about 85 per cent of all deposits held by the commercial banking system rest in member banks. In addition, nonmember banks can participate on a limited basis in the functioning of the Federal Reserve System. For example, nonmember banks can avail themselves of the Federal Reserve System's program for the efficient collection of checks. Nonmember banks are not entirely disassociated from the Federal Reserve System nor immune to its policy decisions.

Commercial banks, as already noted, have two basic functions. First, they hold the money

FIGURE 15-3. THE CLASSIFICATION OF COMMERCIAL BANKS, 1962.
Slightly less than half of all commercial banks are members of the Federal Reserve System. However, these member banks hold about 85 per cent of all commercial bank deposits. ("Federal Reserve Bulletin.")

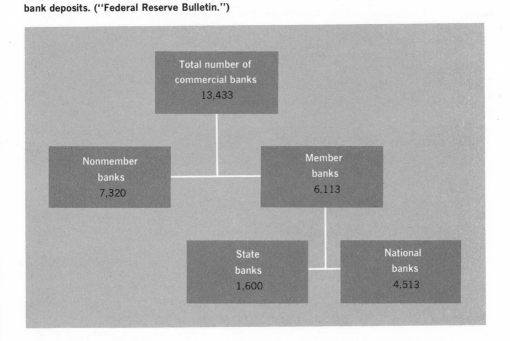

deposits of businesses and households. Second, commercial banks make loans to the public and, in so doing, increase the economy's supply of money. Detailed analysis of these functions is the main objective of Chapter 16.

Although the present analysis will be concerned only with ordinary commercial banks, it is important to recognize that the commercial banking system is thoroughly supplemented by a diverse group of specialized banking and financial institutions. For example, savings banks and savings and loan associations accept the funds of relatively small savers as time deposits and make these funds available to investors by extending mortgage loans or by purchasing marketable securities. Investment banks, on the other hand, perform the task of marketing the newly issued bonds and stocks of corporations which desire funds for capital expansion. Insurance companies accept huge volumes of savings in the form of premiums on insurance policies and annuities and use these funds, wholly or in part, to buy a variety of private, corporate, and government securities. These banking and financial institutions are merely representative; the list is by no means exhaustive.

All banking and financial institutions, including commercial banks, have one point in common: they are all dealers in credit or debt. *These individual institutions lend the savings deposited with them or acquired by them, receiving credit instruments—bonds, stocks, mortgages, or promissory notes—in return.*[11] Hence, these institutions play a significant role in the economy, functioning as *intermediaries between savers and investors.* But from the social point of view, you will recall, their operation falls short of perfection (Chapter 12). These banking and financial institutions do not provide for an exact and continuing balance of investment spending and the full-employment volume of saving. Why? Because savers and investors are essentially different groups that make their decisions in response to different motivations.

[11] Or, as is sometimes the case with insurance companies, the institution itself may invest the savings it receives.

Commercial banks, accepting both time and demand deposits and using the proceeds wholly or in part to acquire income-earning securities, also function as intermediaries between savers and investors. But commercial banks perform an additional function which other banking and financial institutions do not. That function is *to create money by extending bank credit*—that is, *by making loans*—*to businesses and households.* Other financial institutions can only *transfer* money from savers to spenders. In doing so they do not affect the total supply of money available. Commercial banks, however, can *create* demand deposit money and make it available for use by potential spenders. Banks are by no means totally dependent upon the deposits of savers in making money available to spenders. Within limits commercial banks can create the money that spenders desire. Generally speaking, it works this way: banks accept the credit of borrowing individuals and businesses (their promissory notes) and give these borrowers bank credit (demand deposits) in return. By exchanging debts that are not money (promissory notes) for debts that are money (demand deposits), commercial banks perform the unique function of increasing the money supply. In retiring bank credit commercial banks decrease the money supply. The mechanics of these transactions will be studied in some detail in the ensuing chapter. At this juncture, the basic point to recognize is this, *because of their money-creating and money-destroying abilities, commercial banks are highly strategic institutions in our economy.* Commercial banks play a particularly vital role in affecting the volume of money and, hence, the levels of spending, output, employment, and prices. Therefore, our attention is centered upon the functioning of commercial banks as opposed to the more specialized banking and financial institutions mentioned above.

Functions of the Federal Reserve System[12]

The Federal Reserve System—in particular, the twelve Federal Reserve banks and the Board of Governors—was established to achieve certain definite objectives. These goals largely stem from the defects inherent in the system of uncoordinated state and national banks which prevailed prior to the passage of the Federal Reserve Act.

Holding the deposits of member banks. Federal Reserve banks hold the deposits, or "reserves," of member banks. Private businesses and individuals find it convenient to establish checking accounts at commercial banks. These accounts are simply reserves of funds which the owner more or less regularly draws upon and occasionally replenishes. In the same manner member banks keep reserves—that is, money deposits—with the Federal Reserve bank of their district. When in need of currency, the commercial-banks can, within limits, draw upon these reserves. When in possession of surplus cash, commercial banks may deposit this extra currency in their reserves. Or, just as you may buy a bond or fulfill an obligation by drawing a check on your bank account, so may a commercial bank buy a government bond or honor some claim against itself by drawing down its reserves at the Federal Reserve bank. Much of the daily work of the Federal Reserve banks is concerned with increasing and decreasing the reserves of commercial banks as routine banking transactions occur.

Providing for the collection of checks. As previously noted, a check is merely a written order which the drawer may use in making a purchase or paying a debt. A check is collected, or "cleared," when one or more banks negotiate a transfer of part of the drawer's checking account, or demand deposit, to the demand deposit of the recipient of the check. If Jones and Smith have checking accounts in the same commercial bank and Jones gives Smith a $10 check, Smith can collect this check by taking it to the commercial bank, where his account will be increased by $10 and Jones's reduced by $10. In many cases, however, the drawer

12 For a more detailed look at the service functions of the Federal Reserve banks see Board of Governors of the Federal Reserve System, *The Federal Reserve System: Purposes and Functions,* 4th ed. (1961), chaps. 8 and 14.

and receiver of a check will be located in different towns or different states and therefore have their accounts in commercial banks far distant from one another. An important function of the Federal Reserve banks is to provide facilities for the collection of checks where the banks of the drawer and receiver are geographically remote.

Though routine, this function is important because the bulk of the exchange which occurs in our economy is transacted by the use of check money. A money system so heavily committed to the use of check money obviously needs some mechanism for the quick and cheap collection of checks, particularly if payer and payee are geographically remote from one another. A basic function of the Federal Reserve banks is to fulfill this need. At present the maximum time for collecting a check through the Federal Reserve System is three days, and the service is performed free of charge to all member banks. The mechanics of check collecting and the effect it has upon the financial position of commercial banks will be outlined in detail in the next chapter.

Supplying the economy with paper currency. It is also the responsibility of the Federal Reserve banks to supply the economy with most of its paper currency. The bulk of the economy's paper money—Federal Reserve notes— is issued directly by the central banks. As the fountainhead of the economy's paper money supply, the Federal Reserve banks function as a reservoir of cash. When the economy needs more currency, the reservoir is opened and currency spills into the economy. When the economy has more currency than it desires to hold, the excess is channeled back into the reservoir. The commercial banks act as intermediaries between the public and the Federal Reserve banks in each case. Specifically, it works something like this: During the Christmas buying rush, for example, the public wants more currency in circulation. To get this additional cash, individuals and businesses cash checks at the commercial banks. This lowers the amounts of currency resting in bank vaults. Commercial banks then turn to the bankers' banks and draw checks against their deposits (reserves) with the Federal Reserve banks to replenish their vault cash. After the Christmas rush has subsided, less currency is needed. The public deposits this extra currency in their bank accounts. As a result, commercial banks find they have an overly abundant stock of currency in their vaults. They deposit their surplus cash in the Federal Reserve banks, thereby increasing their reserves. Much more will be said of this procedure and its significance in Chapter 17.

Acting as fiscal agents for government. The Federal Reserve banks act as fiscal agents for the Federal government. As we have seen, government—the Federal government in particular—is an exceedingly big business. As such, it collects huge sums through taxation, spends equally astronomical amounts, and sells and redeems bonds. Naturally, the government wants to avail itself of banking facilities in carrying out these functions. The Federal Reserve banks function as bankers for the Federal government. The bankers' banks hold most of the Treasury's checking accounts, aid the government in collecting various tax revenues, and administer the sale and redemption of government bonds.

Supervising member banks. The Federal Reserve banks supervise the operations of member banks. A banking system stands or falls on the financial soundness of the individual commercial banks of which it is comprised. Unsound banking practices can have widespread repercussions to the point of threatening the financial structure of the entire economy. Since commercial banking is "vested with a public interest," it has been subject to government supervision.

The Federal Reserve has supervisory powers over all member commercial banks.[13] This

[13] The Federal Reserve is not alone in the task of supervision. The individual states supervise all banks which they charter. The Comptroller of the Currency supervises all national banks. Finally, the Federal Deposit Insurance Corporation has the power to supervise all banks whose deposits it insures. Hence, a member national bank which belongs to the FDIC will be subject to three supervisory agencies—the Federal Reserve, the Comptroller of the Currency, and the FDIC.

supervision usually takes the form of periodic unannounced examinations of the commercial banks. Banks which do not conform to the standards set forth by the Federal Reserve authorities may be denied the privilege of borrowing from the Federal Reserve banks, and in extreme cases the officers and directors of offending banks may be removed by the Board of Governors.

Regulating the supply of money. Finally—and most important of all—the Federal Reserve System has ultimate responsibility for regulating the supply of money. The major task of the Federal Reserve authorities is to manage the money supply in accordance with the needs of the economy as a whole. In the dynamic and expanding economy of American capitalism, this task entails making that amount of money available which is consistent with high and steadily rising levels of output and employment and a relatively constant price level. It is through the previously mentioned quantitative and qualitative credit controls that the Federal Reserve authorities attempt to manipulate the supply of money in terms of short-run stability and long-run economic growth.

In addition to being the most vital objective of the Federal Reserve System, the regulation of the money supply differs from the other Federal Reserve functions in another significant respect: while all the other functions are of a more or less routine or service nature, the goal of correctly managing the money supply entails the making of basic and unique policy decisions of a nonroutine character. Chapter 17 is concerned with Federal Reserve monetary policy and its effectiveness in achieving economic stability in a growing economy.

SUMMARY

1. Anything that functions as (*a*) a medium of exchange, (*b*) a standard of value, and (*c*) a store of value is money.

2. In the United States money is defined as demand deposits plus currency (coins and paper money) in circulation. By far the most important component of the money supply is demand deposits. Demand deposits are money because they can be spent if checks are written against them. Currency and demand deposits owned by the Treasury or by commercial or central banks are not "in circulation."

3. Money, which is essentially the debts of government and commercial banks, has value because of the goods and services which it will command in the market. Maintenance of the purchasing power of money depends to a considerable degree upon the effectiveness with which government manages the money supply and the particular set of problems and circumstances faced by the economy.

4. The American banking system is composed of (a) the Board of Governors of the Federal Reserve System, (b) the twelve Federal Reserve banks, and (c) some 13,500 commercial banks. The Board of Governors is the basic policy-making body for the entire banking system. The directives of the Board are made effective through the twelve Federal Reserve banks which are simultaneously (a) central banks, (b) quasi-public banks, and (c) bankers' banks. The commercial banks of the economy perform the tasks of accepting money deposits and making loans. In lending, commercial banks create demand deposits; these deposits are money. Commercial banks, then, are money-creating institutions.

5. The major functions of the Federal Reserve System are (a) to hold the deposits or reserves of commercial banks, (b) to provide facilities for the rapid collection of checks, (c) to supply the economy's needs for paper currency, (d) to act as fiscal agent for the Federal Government, (e) to supervise the operations of member banks, and (f) to regulate the supply of money in terms of the best interests of the economy as a whole.

QUESTIONS AND STUDY SUGGESTIONS

1. What are the three basic functions of money? Describe how drastic inflation can undermine the ability of money to perform these functions.

2. What are the disadvantages of commodity money? What are the advantages of (a) paper money and (b) check money as compared to commodity money?

3. "Money is only a bit of paper or a bit of metal that gives its owner a lawful claim to so much bread or beer or diamonds or motorcars or what not. We cannot eat money, nor drink money, nor wear money. It is the goods that money can buy that are being divided up when money is divided up." [14] Evaluate and explain.

4. Fully evaluate and explain the following statements:

a. "The invention of money is one of the great achievements of the human race, for without it the enrichment that comes from broadening trade would have been impossible."

b. "Money is whatever society says it is."

c. "When prices of everything are going up, it is not because everything is worth more, but because the dollar is worth less."

d. "It doesn't make sense: a 50¢ piece, containing 33¢ worth of silver bullion, is less valuable than a paper dollar, the paper and ink of which have negligible value."

e. "The difficult questions concerning paper (money) are . . . not about its economy, convenience or ready circulation but about the amount of the paper which

[14] George Bernard Shaw, *The Intelligent Woman's Guide to Socialism and Capitalism* (New York: Brentano's, 1928), p. 9. Used by permission of the Public Trustee and the Society of Authors.

can be wisely issued or created, and the possibilities of violent convulsions when it gets beyond bounds." [15]

5. What items constitute the money supply in American capitalism? What is the most important component of the money supply? What are near-monies? Of what significance are they? Why is the face value of a coin greater than its intrinsic value?

6. "In most modern industrial economies of the world the debts of government and of commercial banks are used as money." Explain.

7. What "backs" the money supply in the United States? Be as specific as you are able.

8. What determines the value of money? Who is responsible for maintaining the value of money? Why is it important for the money supply to be elastic, that is, capable of increasing or decreasing in size? What is meant by (a) "sound money" and (b) a "52-cent dollar"?

9. What is the major responsibility of the Board of Governors? Discuss the major characteristics of the Federal Reserve banks. Of what significance is the fact that the Federal Reserve banks are quasi-public?

10. What are the two basic functions of commercial banks? How do commercial banks differ from other financial institutions?

11. State and briefly discuss the major functions of the Federal Reserve System.

SELECTED REFERENCES

Board of Governors of the Federal Reserve System, *The Federal Reserve System: Purposes and Functions*, 4th ed. (1961), particularly chaps. 1 and 4.

Chandler, Lester V., *The Economics of Money and Banking*, 3d ed. (New York: Harper & Row, Publishers, 1959), chaps. 1, 2, and 7.

Halm, George N., *Economics of Money and Banking*, rev. ed. (Homewood, Ill.: Richard D. Irwin, Inc., 1961), chaps. 1–6 and 15–18.

Harriss, C. Lowell, *Money and Banking* (Boston: Allyn and Bacon, Inc., 1961), chaps. 1, 8, and 9.

Pritchard, Leland J., *Money and Banking* (Boston: Houghton Mifflin Company, 1958), chaps. 1–4 and 14–17.

Robertson, D. H., *Money*, 6th ed. (New York: Pitman Publishing Corporation, 1948).

[15] F. W. Taussig, *Principles of Economics*, 4th ed. (New York: The Macmillan Company, 1946), pp. 247–248.

Chapter 16

HOW BANKS CREATE MONEY

IN CHAPTER 15 we saw that the Federal Reserve banks are the primary source of the economy's paper money. However, we shall find in the present chapter that commercial banks are the fountainhead of the major component of the money system—demand deposits.

More specifically, in this chapter we want to explain and compare the money-creating abilities of (1) a single commercial bank which is part of a multibank system, (2) a monopoly bank, and (3) the commercial banking system as a whole. It will be convenient for us to seek these objectives through the commercial bank's balance sheet. An understanding of the basic items which comprise a bank's balance sheet and the manner in which various transactions change these items will provide us with a valuable analytical tool for grasping the workings of our monetary and banking systems.

THE BALANCE SHEET OF A COMMERCIAL BANK

What is a *balance sheet?* It is merely a statement of assets and claims which portrays or summarizes the financial position of a firm—in this case a commercial bank—at some specific point in time. Every balance sheet has one overriding virtue: by definition, it must balance. Why? Because each and every known *asset*, being something of economic value, will be claimed by someone. Can you think of an asset—something of monetary value—which no one claims? A balance sheet balances because assets equal claims. The claims shown on a balance sheet are divided into two groups: the claims of the owners of a firm against the firm's assets, called *net worth*, and the claims of nonowners, called *liabilities*. Thus, it can be said that a balance sheet balances because

$$\text{Assets} = \text{liabilities} + \text{net worth}$$

A balance sheet approach to our study of the money-creating ability of commercial banks is invaluable in two specific respects: On the one hand, a bank's balance sheet provides us with a convenient point of reference from which we can introduce new terms and concepts in a more or less orderly manner. On the other hand, the use of balance sheets will allow us to quantify certain strategic concepts and relationships which would defy comprehension if discussed in verbal terms alone.

A SINGLE COMMERCIAL BANK IN A BANKING SYSTEM

Our immediate goal is an understanding of the money-creating potential of a single bank which is part of a multibank banking system. How does a single commercial bank create and destroy money? What factors govern the money-creating abilities of such a bank?

299

Formation of a commercial bank

The answers to these questions demand that we understand the ins and outs of a commercial bank's balance sheet and how certain rather elementary transactions affect that balance sheet. We start with the organization of a local commercial bank.

Transaction 1: the birth of a bank. Let us

on hand and $250,000 worth of capital stock outstanding. Obviously the cash is an asset to the bank. The cash held by a bank is sometimes dubbed *vault cash* or *till money*. The outstanding shares of stock, however, constitute an equal amount of claims which the owners have against the bank's assets. That is, the shares of stock are obviously the net worth of the bank, though assets from the viewpoint of those who possess these shares. Hence, the bank's balance sheet would read as follows:

BALANCE SHEET 1: WAHOO BANK

Assets	Liabilities and net worth
Cash $250,000	Capital stock $250,000

start from scratch. Suppose some farsighted citizens of the metropolis of Wahoo, Nebraska, decide that their town is in need of a new commercial bank to provide all the banking services needed by that growing community. Assuming these enterprising individuals are able to secure a state charter for their bank, they then turn to the task of selling, say, $250,000 worth of capital stock to buyers, both in and out of the community. These financing efforts having met with success, the Merchants and Farmers Bank of Wahoo, Nebraska, now exists—at least on paper. How does the Wahoo bank's balance statement appear at its birth?

The new proprietors of the bank have sold $250,000 worth of shares of stock in the bank —some to themselves, some to other people. As a result, the bank now has $250,000 in cash

Transaction 2: becoming a going concern. The newly established board of directors must now breathe life into their infant enterprise. They must get the newborn bank off the drawing board and make it a living reality.

The first step will be to acquire property and equipment. Suppose the directors, confident of the success of their venture, purchase a building for $220,000 and some $20,000 worth of office equipment. This simple transaction merely changes the composition of the bank's assets. The bank now has $240,000 less in cash and $240,000 worth of new property assets. Using an asterisk to denote those accounts which are affected by each transaction, we find that the bank's balance sheet at the conclusion of transaction 2 appears as follows:

BALANCE SHEET 2: WAHOO BANK

Assets		Liabilities and net worth	
Cash*	$ 10,000	Capital stock $250,000	
Property*	240,000		

* Accounts affected by transaction.

Note that the balance sheet still balances, as indeed it must.

Transaction 3: accepting deposits. We have already emphasized that commercial banks have two basic functions: to accept deposits of money and to make loans. Now that our bank is in operation, let us suppose that the citizens of Wahoo decide to deposit some $100,000 in the Merchants and Farmers Bank. What happens to the bank's balance sheet?

The bank receives cash, which we have already noted is an asset to the bank. Suppose this money is placed in the bank in the form of demand deposits (checking accounts), rather than time deposits (savings accounts). These newly created demand deposits constitute claims which depositors have against the assets of the Wahoo bank. Thus the depositing of money in the bank creates a new liability account—demand deposits. The bank's balance sheet now looks like this:

Transaction 4: joining the Federal Reserve System. Being a state bank, the Merchants and Farmers Bank of Wahoo will have the option of joining or not joining the Federal Reserve System. Suppose the directors of the bank decide in favor of joining. To accomplish this, the bank must meet a very specific requirement: it must keep a *legal reserve deposit* in the Federal Reserve bank of its particular district.

This legal reserve deposit is *an amount of cash equal to a specified percentage of its own deposit liabilities which a member bank must keep on deposit with the Federal Reserve bank in its district.*[1]

The "specified percentage" is known as the *reserve ratio.* Why? Because that is exactly what it is—a ratio between the size of the deposits which the commercial bank must keep in the Federal Reserve bank and the commercial bank's own outstanding deposit liabilities. This ratio is as shown below:

BALANCE SHEET 3: WAHOO BANK

Assets		Liabilities and net worth	
Cash*	$110,000	Capital stock	$250,000
Property	240,000	Demand deposits*	100,000

* Accounts affected by transaction.

You should note that, although there is no change in the total supply of money, a change in the composition of the economy's money supply has occurred as a result of transaction 3. Bank money, or demand deposits, have *increased* by $100,000 and currency in circulation has *decreased* by $100,000. Currency held by a bank, you will recall, is not considered to be a part of the economy's money supply.

It is obvious that a withdrawal of cash will reduce the bank's demand deposit liabilities and its holdings of cash by the amount of the withdrawal. This, too, changes the composition, but not the total supply, of money.

$$\text{Reserve ratio} = \frac{\text{Commercial bank's required deposit in Federal Reserve bank}}{\text{Public's deposits in commercial bank}}$$

[1] Since 1960 banks have been permitted to count vault cash as a part of reserves. As a matter of banking practice, however, the vast bulk of bank reserves are in the form of deposits in the Federal Reserve banks. We shall simplify our discussion by supposing that our bank keeps its legal reserve *entirely* in the form of deposits in the Federal Reserve bank of its district.

Hence, if the reserve ratio were 10 per cent, our bank, having accepted $100,000 in deposits from the public, would be obligated to bundle up $10,000 and send it as a deposit, or reserve, to the Federal Reserve bank in Kansas City. If the ratio were 20 per cent, $20,000 would have to be deposited in the Federal Reserve bank. If 50 per cent, $50,000, and so forth.

How is the exact size of the reserve ratio determined? Congress has the responsibility for setting the upper and lower limits within which the ratio can vary. These legal limits differ, depending upon the size and location of commercial banks, as Table 16-1 indicates. The Board of Governors can vary the ratio at its discretion within these limits.[2] To avoid a lot of messy computations, we will suppose that the reserve ratio for all banks is 20 per cent. This is a nice round figure and is reasonably close to reality. It is to be emphasized that reserve requirements are *fractional*, that is, less than 100 per cent. This consideration will be vital in the ensuing analysis of the lending abilities of various possible banking systems.

The Wahoo bank will just be meeting the required 20 per cent ratio between its deposit in the Federal Reserve bank and its own deposit liabilities by depositing $20,000 in the

[2] State nonmember banks are required by state laws to keep reserves. These reserves usually take the form of cash and deposits in other commercial banks. Though the reserve ratio varies considerably among the states, 15 per cent is about the average.

Federal Reserve bank. To distinguish this deposit from the public's deposits in commercial banks, we will use the term *reserves* in referring to these funds which commercial banks deposit in the Federal Reserve banks.

But let us suppose that the directors of the Wahoo bank anticipate that their holdings of the public's deposits will grow in the future. Hence, instead of sending the minimum amount, $20,000, they send an extra $90,000, making a total of $110,000. In so doing, the bank will avoid the inconvenience of sending additional reserves to the Federal Reserve bank each time its own deposit liabilities increase by some small amount. And, we will see shortly that it is upon the basis of extra reserves that banks can lend and thereby earn interest income.[3]

At the completion of this transaction, the balance sheet of the Merchants and Farmers Bank will appear as on page 303.

There are several points relevant to this transaction which must still be explained:

[3] Actually, of course, the bank would not deposit all its cash in the Federal Reserve bank. However, because (1) banks as a rule only hold vault cash in the amount of 1½ or 2 per cent of their total assets and (2) vault cash can be counted as reserves (footnote 1), we shall find it expedient to assume that all the bank's cash is deposited in the Federal Reserve bank and therefore constitutes the commercial bank's total reserves. The cumbersome process of adding two assets—"cash" and "deposits in the Federal Reserve bank"—to determine "reserves" is thereby avoided.

TABLE 16-1. LEGAL RESERVE REQUIREMENTS OF MEMBER BANKS, FEBRUARY, 1962

Type of bank	Reserve ratio against demand deposits	
	Upper and lower legal limits, per cent	Actual ratio, per cent
Central reserve city banks (member banks in Chicago and New York City)	10–22	16½
Reserve city banks (member banks in medium-sized money centers)	10–22	16½
All other banks	7–14	12

SOURCE: "Federal Reserve Bulletin," March, 1962.

BALANCE SHEET 4: WAHOO BANK

Assets		Liabilities and net worth	
Cash*	$ 0	Capital stock	$250,000
Property	240,000	Demand deposits	100,000
Reserves (deposits in the Federal Reserve bank)*	110,000		

* Accounts affected by transaction.

1. A note on terminology: the amount by which the bank's actual reserves exceed its required reserves is the bank's *excess* reserves. In this case,

Actual reserves	$110,000
Required reserves	20,000
Excess reserves	$ 90,000

The only sure-fire way of computing excess reserves is to multiply the bank's demand deposit liabilities by the reserve ratio ($100,000 times 20 per cent equals $20,000) to obtain required reserves, then to subtract this figure from the actual reserves listed on the asset side of the bank's balance sheet. To ensure an understanding of this process, the reader should compute excess reserves for the bank's balance sheet as it stands at the end of transaction 4 on the assumption that the reserve ratio is (*a*) 10 per cent, (*b*) 33⅓ per cent, and (*c*) 50 per cent.

Because the ability of a commercial bank to make loans depends upon the existence of excess reserves, this concept is of vital importance in grasping the money-creating ability of the banking system.

2. What is the rationale underlying the requirement that member banks deposit a reserve in the Federal Reserve bank of their district? One might think that the basic purpose of reserves is to enhance the liquidity of a bank and thereby protect commercial bank depositors from losses; that is, it would seem that reserves constitute a ready source of funds from which commercial banks can meet large and unexpected withdrawals of cash by depositors. But this reasoning does not hold up under close scrutiny. Although historically reserves were looked upon as a source of liquidity and therefore protection for depositors, *legal,* or required, reserves cannot be used for the purpose of meeting unexpected cash withdrawals. If a banker's nightmare materialized—that is, if everyone having a demand deposit in his bank appeared on the same morning to demand his deposits in cash—the banker could not draw upon his required reserves to meet this crisis without violating the legal reserve ratio and thereby incurring the wrath and penalties of the Federal Reserve authorities. In practice, legal reserves are not an available pool of liquid funds upon which commercial banks can rely in times of emergency.[4] As a matter of fact, even if legal reserves were accessible to commercial banks, they would not be sufficient to meet a serious "run" on a bank. Why? Because, as we shall soon discover, demand deposits may be three, four, or five times as large as a bank's required reserves.

[4] This amendment must be added: as depositors withdraw cash from a commercial bank, the bank's demand deposit liabilities will obviously decline. This lowers the absolute amount of required reserves which the bank must keep, thereby freeing some of the bank's actual reserves for use in meeting cash withdrawals by depositors. To illustrate: Suppose a commercial bank has reserves of $20 and demand deposit liabilities of $100. If the legal reserve ratio is 20 per cent, all the bank's reserves are obviously required. Now, if depositors withdraw, say, $50 worth of their deposits as cash, the bank will only need $10 as required reserves to support the remaining $50 of demand deposit liabilities. Thus $10 of the bank's actual reserves of $20 are no longer required. The bank can draw upon this $10 in helping to meet the cash withdrawals of its depositors.

It is not surprising that commercial bank depositors are protected by other means. As noted in Chapter 15, periodic bank examinations are an important device for promoting prudent commercial banking practices. Furthermore, the Federal Deposit Insurance Corporation was established in 1933 to insure the deposit liabilities of member banks and qualified nonmember banks that voluntarily become members of the FDIC. At the present time about 99 per cent of all depositors have their deposits insured up to a maximum of $10,000 by the FDIC. FDIC members pay insurance premiums equal to one-twelfth of 1 per cent of their total deposits, from which the FDIC has built up a substantial insurance fund.

If the purpose of reserves is not to provide for commercial bank liquidity, then what is their function? *Control* is the answer. Legal reserves are a means by which the Board of Governors can influence the lending policies of commercial banks. The next chapter will explain in detail how the Board of Governors can invoke certain policies which either increase or decrease commercial bank reserves and thereby affect the ability of banks to grant credit. The object is to prevent banks from *over*extending or *under*extending bank credit. To the degree that they are successful in influencing the volume of commercial bank credit, the Board of Governors can help the economy avoid the business fluctuations which give rise to bank runs, bank failures, and collapse of the monetary system. It is in this indirect way—as a means of controlling commercial bank credit—that reserves protect depositors, not as a source of liquidity.

3. Let us pause to note a rather obvious accounting matter which transaction 4 entails. Specifically, *the reserve created in transaction 4 is an asset to the depositing commercial bank but a liability to the Federal Reserve bank receiving it.* To the Wahoo bank the reserve is an asset. Why? Because it is a claim which this commercial bank has against the assets of another institution—the Federal Reserve bank. To the Federal Reserve bank this reserve is a liability, that is, a claim which another institution—the Wahoo bank—has against it. Just as the demand deposit you get by depositing money in a commercial bank is an asset to you and a liability to your commercial bank, so the deposit or reserve which a commercial bank gets by depositing money in a banker's bank is an asset to the commercial bank and a liability to the Federal Reserve bank. An understanding of this relationship is necessary in pursuing transaction 5.

Transaction 5: a check is drawn against the bank. Now let us tackle a very significant and somewhat more complicated transaction. Suppose that Clem Bradshaw, a Wahoo farmer who deposited a substantial portion of the $100,000 in demand deposits which the Wahoo bank received in transaction 3, purchases $50,000 worth of farm machinery from the Ajax Farm Implement Company of Beaver Crossing, Nebraska. Bradshaw very sensibly pays for this machinery by writing a $50,000 check, against his deposit in the Wahoo bank, in favor of the Ajax company. We want to determine (1) how this check is collected or "cleared" and (2) the effect that the collection of the check has upon the balance sheets of the banks involved in the transaction.

To accomplish this, we must consider the Wahoo bank, the Beaver Crossing bank, and the Federal Reserve Bank of Kansas City.[5] Let us suppose that both the commercial banks are members of the Federal Reserve System. And to keep our illustration as clear as possible, we shall deal only with the changes which occur in those specific accounts affected by this transaction.

Let us trace this transaction in three related steps, keying the steps by letters to Figure 16-1.

a. Mr. Bradshaw gives his $50,000 check, drawn against the Wahoo bank, to the Ajax company. The Ajax company in turn deposits the check in its account with the Beaver Crossing bank. The Beaver Crossing bank increases the Ajax company's demand deposit by $50,000 when it deposits the check. (The Ajax company is now paid off.) Bradshaw is elated over his new machinery, for which he has now paid.

b. But now the Beaver Crossing bank has Bradshaw's check in its possession. This check

[5] Actually the Omaha Branch of the Federal Reserve Bank of Kansas City would handle the process of collecting this check.

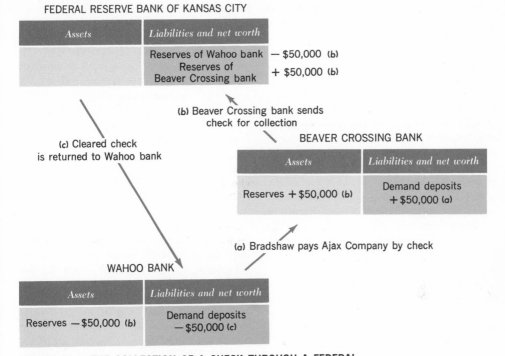

FEDERAL RESERVE BANK OF KANSAS CITY

Assets	Liabilities and net worth
	Reserves of Wahoo bank — $50,000 (b)
	Reserves of Beaver Crossing bank + $50,000 (b)

(b) Beaver Crossing bank sends check for collection

(c) Cleared check is returned to Wahoo bank

BEAVER CROSSING BANK

Assets	Liabilities and net worth
Reserves + $50,000 (b)	Demand deposits + $50,000 (a)

(a) Bradshaw pays Ajax Company by check

WAHOO BANK

Assets	Liabilities and net worth
Reserves — $50,000 (b)	Demand deposits — $50,000 (c)

FIGURE 16-1. THE COLLECTION OF A CHECK THROUGH A FEDERAL RESERVE BANK.

is simply a claim against the assets of the Wahoo bank. How will the Beaver Crossing bank collect this claim? By sending this check —along with checks drawn on other banks— to the Federal Reserve Bank of Kansas City. Here an underpaid clerk will clear, or collect, this check for the Beaver Crossing bank by increasing its reserve in the Federal Reserve bank by $50,000 and by decreasing the Wahoo bank's reserve by a like amount. The check is collected simply by making a few pen-and-ink notations to the effect that the Wahoo bank's claim against the Federal Reserve bank has been reduced by $50,000 and the Beaver Crossing bank's claim increased accordingly. Note these changes on the balance sheets.[6]

c. Finally, the cleared check is sent back to the Wahoo bank, and for the first time the Wahoo bank discovers that one of its depositors has drawn a check for $50,000 against his demand deposit. Accordingly, the Wahoo bank reduces Mr. Bradshaw's demand deposit by $50,000 and recognizes that the collection of

this check has entailed a $50,000 decline in its reserves at the Federal Reserve bank. Note that the balance statements of all three banks will still balance. The Wahoo bank will have reduced both its assets and liabilities by $50,000. The Beaver Crossing bank will have $50,000

[6] Here is an interesting sidelight: the collection of Bradshaw's check by the Beaver Crossing bank through the Federal Reserve bank involves the same type of procedure as the collection of a check between two individuals who have deposits in the same commercial bank. Suppose you and I both have checking accounts in the Wahoo bank. I owe you $10 and I pay this debt by check. You deposit the $10 check in the bank. Here a bank clerk collects the check for you by noting a "+$10" in your account and a "—$10" in my account. And that's that. The same thing happens at the Federal Reserve Bank of Kansas City when the Beaver Crossing bank clears a $50,000 check against the Wahoo bank. The banker's bank increases the Beaver Crossing bank's deposit in the Federal Reserve bank—that is, its reserve—by $50,000 and lowers the Wahoo bank's reserve by the same amount. The check is then cleared.

more in reserves and in demand deposits. The ownership of reserves at the Federal Reserve bank will have changed, but total reserves will stand the same.

The point we are making is this: *whenever a check is drawn against a bank and deposited in another bank, the collection of that check will entail a loss of both reserves and deposits by the bank upon which the check is drawn.* Conversely, if a bank receives a check drawn on another bank, the bank receiving the check will, in the process of collecting it, have its reserves and deposits increased by the amount of the check. In our example, the Wahoo bank loses $50,000 in both reserves and deposits to the Beaver Crossing bank. But there is no loss of reserves or deposits for the banking system as a whole. What one bank loses another bank gains.

Bringing all the other assets and liabilities back into the picture, the Wahoo bank's balance sheet looks like this at the end of transaction 5:

the way the Beaver Crossing bank has acquired new reserves and deposits in the present transaction.

Transaction 5 is obviously reversible. If a check drawn against another bank is deposited in the Wahoo bank, the Wahoo bank will receive both reserves and deposits equal to the amount of the check as it is collected.

Let us designate here some of the salient conclusions from the first five transactions we have analyzed:

1. When a bank accepts deposits of cash, the composition of the money supply is changed, but the total supply of money is not altered.

2. Commercial banks which are members of the Federal Reserve System are required to keep legal reserve deposits, or simply "reserves," equal to a specified percentage of their own deposit liabilities on deposit with the Federal Reserve bank of their district. The reserve ratio indicates the size of this "specified

BALANCE SHEET 5: WAHOO BANK

Assets		Liabilities and net worth	
Property	$240,000	Capital stock	$250,000
Reserves*	60,000	Demand deposits*	50,000

* Accounts affected by transaction.

The reader should verify that with a 20 per cent reserve requirement the bank's *excess* reserves now stand at $50,000.

This transaction indicates the manner in which commercial banks acquire the bulk of their reserves and deposits: from other banks through the check clearing process. While most of us in our personal dealings with banks think of demand deposits as being created by customer deposits of cash and of reserves arising as the result of the bank's redepositing some of this cash with the Federal Reserve banks, this is not actually the case. Most bank deposits and reserves are received from other banks in

percentage." Reserves are a means by which the monetary authorities can control the lending policies of commercial banks.

3. The amount by which a bank's actual reserves exceed its required reserves is called "excess reserves."

4. Commercial bank reserves are an asset to the commercial bank but a liability to the Federal Reserve bank holding them.

5. A bank which has a check drawn and collected against it will lose both reserves and deposits equal to the value of the check to the bank receiving the check.

Money-creating transactions of a commercial bank

The next two transactions are particularly crucial because they explain how a single commercial bank can literally create money by making loans to individuals and businesses and by purchasing government bonds. Though these transactions are similar in many respects, we treat them separately.

Transaction 6: granting a loan. You will recall that in addition to accepting deposits a basic function of commercial banks is the granting of loans to borrowers. What effect does com-

from the bank, the Grisley company will simply get a $50,000 increase in its demand deposit in the Wahoo bank.

In short, the Grisley company has swapped an IOU for the right to draw an additional $50,000 worth of checks against its demand deposit in the Wahoo bank. Both parties are pleased with themselves. The Wahoo bank now possesses a new asset—an interest-bearing promissory note which it happily files under the general heading of "Loans." The Grisley company, sporting a fattened demand deposit, is now in a position to expand its operations.

At the moment the loan is negotiated, the balance sheet of the Wahoo bank looks like this:

BALANCE SHEET 6a: WAHOO BANK (when loan is negotiated)

Assets		Liabilities and net worth	
Property	$240,000	Capital stock	$250,000
Reserves	60,000	Demand deposits*	100,000
Loans*	50,000		

* Accounts affected by transaction.

mercial bank lending have upon the balance sheet of a commercial bank?

Suppose that the Grisley Meat Packing Company of Wahoo decides that the time is ripe to expand its facilities. Suppose, too, that the company needs exactly $50,000—which, by some unexplained coincidence, just happens to be equal to the Wahoo bank's excess reserves —to finance this project.

The company approaches the Wahoo bank and requests a loan for this amount. The Wahoo bank is acquainted with the Grisley company's fine reputation and financial soundness and is convinced of its ability to repay the loan. So the loan is granted. The President of the Grisley company hands a promissory note—a high-class IOU—to the Wahoo bank. The Grisley company, like all other modern firms, is interested in paying its obligations by check. Hence, instead of receiving a bushel basket full of cash

All this looks innocent enough. But a closer examination of the Wahoo bank's balance statement will reveal a startling fact: *When a bank makes loans, it creates money.* The president of the Grisley company went to the bank with something which is not money—his IOU—and walked out with something that is money—a demand deposit.[7] When banks lend, they create demand deposits which are money. By extending credit the Wahoo bank has "monetized" an IOU. The Grisley company and the Wahoo bank have created and then swapped claims. The claim created by the Grisley company and given to the bank is not money; an individual's IOU is not generally acceptable as a medium of exchange. But the claim created by the bank and

[7] In transaction 3 demand deposits were created, but only by currency's going out of circulation. Hence, there was a change in the composition of the money supply but no net change in the total supply of money.

given to the Grisley company is money; checks drawn against a demand deposit are acceptable as a medium of exchange. It is through the extension of credit by commercial banks that the bulk of the money used in our economy is created.

But there are important forces which circumscribe the ability of a commercial bank to create demand deposits—that is, "bank money" —by lending. In the present case, the Wahoo bank can expect the newly created demand deposit of $50,000 to be a very active account. The Grisley company would not borrow $50,-000 at, say, 8 per cent for the sheer joy of knowing the funds were available if needed. Let us assume that the Grisley company awards a $50,000 contract to the Quickbuck Construction Company of Omaha. Quickbuck, true to its name, completes the expansion job and is rewarded with a check for $50,000 drawn by the Grisley company against its demand deposit in the Wahoo bank. The Quickbuck company, having its headquarters in Omaha, does not deposit this check back in the Wahoo bank but instead deposits it in the Fourth National Bank of Omaha. The Fourth National Bank now has a $50,000 claim against the Wahoo bank. This check is collected in the manner described in transaction 5. As a result, the Wahoo bank *loses* both reserves and deposits equal to the amount of the check; the Fourth National Bank *acquires* $50,000 of reserves and deposits. In short, assuming a check is drawn by the borrower for the entire amount of the loan ($50,-000) and given to a firm which deposits it in another bank, the Wahoo bank's balance sheet will read as follows *after the check has been cleared against it:*

You will note immediately that, after the check has been collected, the Wahoo bank is just barely meeting the legal reserve ratio of 20 per cent. The bank has *no excess reserves.* This poses an interesting question: Could the Wahoo bank have safely lent an amount greater than $50,000—an amount greater than its excess reserves—and still have met the 20 per cent reserve requirement if a check for the full amount of the loan cleared against it? The answer is "No." For example, suppose the Wahoo bank had loaned $55,000 to the Grisley company. Collection of the check against the Wahoo bank would have lowered its reserves to $5,000 (equal to $60,000 minus $55,000) and deposits would again stand at $50,000 (equal to $105,000 minus $55,000). The ratio of actual reserves to deposits would now be only $5,000/$50,000, or 10 per cent. The Wahoo bank could thus not safely have lent $55,000. By experimenting with other figures in excess of $50,000 the reader will find that the maximum amount which the Wahoo bank could safely lend at the outset of transaction 6 is $50,000. This figure is identical with the amount of excess reserves which the bank had available at the time the loan was negotiated. We can conclude that *a single commercial bank in a multibank banking system can safely lend only dollar for dollar with its excess reserves.* Why? Because when it lends, it faces the likelihood that checks for the entire amount of the loan may be drawn and cleared against the lending bank. A lending bank can anticipate the loss of reserves to other banks equal to the amount it lends.

There is a qualification to this discussion: when a bank makes a loan, some of the checks

BALANCE SHEET 6b: WAHOO BANK (after a check drawn on the loan has been collected)

Assets		*Liabilities and net worth*	
Property	$240,000	Capital stock	$250,000
Reserves*	10,000	Demand deposits*	50,000
Loans	50,000		

* Accounts affected by transaction.

drawn by the borrower *may* be redeposited back in the lending bank. To the extent that this happens, the bank is able to lend an amount greater than its excess reserves. You might try this problem: Suppose a bank with $1,000 in excess reserves knows from past experience that for every loan it negotiates, checks drawn on that loan equal to one-tenth of the value of the loan will be redeposited back in the bank. Thus, if the bank makes a $100 loan, the borrower promptly draws 10 checks for $10 each. Nine of these wind up in other banks. The tenth is redeposited by its recipient back in the lending bank. Knowing this in advance, what is the maximum amount this bank can safely lend on the basis of $1,000 of excess reserves?

Now that you are convinced that this credit-creating business can be complicated, let us accept our original conclusion that commercial banks can safely lend dollar for dollar with their excess reserves as being accurate enough for our purposes. It is a pretty good approximate statement of a single commercial bank's credit-creating potential.

If commercial banks create demand deposits —that is, money—when they make loans, it seems logical to inquire as to whether money is destroyed when the loans are repaid. The answer is "Yes." Using balance sheet 6b, let us see what happens when the Grisley company repays the $50,000 it borrowed.

To simplify we will (1) suppose that the loan is repaid not in installments but rather in one lump sum three years after the date of negotiation and (2) ignore interest charges on the loan. Repayment may take two forms. Most likely the Grisley company will write a check for $50,000 against its demand deposit, which assumedly has been fattened by extra profits resulting from the company's expanded operations. As a result the Wahoo bank's demand deposit liabilities decline by $50,000; the Grisley company has given up $50,000 worth of its claim against the bank's assets. In turn the bank will surrender the Grisley company's IOU which it has been patiently holding these many months. The bank and the company have reswapped claims. But the claim given up

by the Grisley company is money; the claim it is repurchasing—its IOU—is not. The supply of money has therefore been reduced by $50,000; that amount of demand deposits has been destroyed, unaccompanied by any increase in the money supply elsewhere in the economy. The Grisley company's IOU has been "demonetized." On the Wahoo bank's balance sheet demand deposits and loans both fall by $50,000. You will note that the decline in demand deposits increases the bank's holdings of excess reserves; this provides the basis for new loans to be made.

The second repayment alternative open to the Grisley company is to repay by cash. It would be very unlikely that the company would want to bear the risk of accumulating such a large sum of money in its safe. But even if it did, the supply of money would still decline by $50,000 when cash repayment was made. In this case, the Grisley company would repurchase its IOU by handing over $50,000 in cash to the bank. This causes loans to fall on the bank's balance sheet by $50,000 and, obviously, cash to increase by $50,000. Remember that we specifically excluded currency held by banks from the money supply on the ground that to include such cash would be double counting; it is apparent that this constitutes a $50,000 reduction in the supply of money. The Wahoo bank would probably use this additional cash either to enhance its reserves so as to permit new lending or to purchase securities.

Transaction 7: buying government securities. When a commercial bank buys government bonds[8] from individuals and business concerns, the effect is substantially the same as that of lending. New money is created. To illustrate, let us assume that the Wahoo bank's balance sheet initially stands as it did at the end of transaction 5. Now let us suppose that instead of borrowing all the needed $50,000 from the

[8] Commercial banks are restricted by law in their purchase of private securities. It is felt that banks should be restricted to the performance of recognized banking functions and not permitted to become holding companies or speculative institutions.

Wahoo bank, the Grisley company borrows just $25,000 and obtains an additional $25,000 by selling government bonds which it holds to the bank. The Wahoo bank pays for the Grisley company's IOU and the IOUs (bonds) of the government in the same way, by increasing the Grisley company's demand deposit. Demand deposit liabilities increase by $50,000, and the bank's assets of securities and loans increase by $25,000 each. Immediately after negotiating the loan and bond purchase, the Wahoo bank's balance sheet will appear as follows:

in the same way as does lending to the public. The bank accepts government bonds—which are not money—and gives the Grisley company an increase in its demand deposits—which is money. The only real difference between selling a government bond to a commercial bank and negotiating a loan is that in the first case one gives the banker a claim against someone else (the United States Treasury), and in the second case a claim against one's own assets (your IOU).

As in transaction 6, the effect of the Grisley company drawing a $50,000 check in favor of the Quickbuck company will be for the Wahoo

BALANCE SHEET 7a: WAHOO BANK (when loan is negotiated and bonds purchased)

Assets		Liabilities and net worth	
Property	$240,000	Capital stock	$250,000
Reserves	60,000	Demand deposits*	100,000
Securities*	25,000		
Loans*	25,000		

* Accounts affected by transaction.

The important point is that demand deposits, that is, the supply of money, has been increased by a total of $50,000 as it was in transaction 6. *Commercial bank bond purchases from the public increase the supply of money*

bank to lose reserves and demand deposits of $50,000 to the bank in which Quickbuck deposits the check. When the check is cleared against the Wahoo bank, its balance sheet will appear as follows:

BALANCE SHEET 7b: WAHOO BANK (after collection of check)

Assets		Liabilities and net worth	
Property	$240,000	Capital stock	$250,000
Reserves*	10,000	Demand deposits*	50,000
Securities	25,000		
Loans	25,000		

* Accounts affected by transaction.

As you must now suspect, the selling of government bonds by a commercial bank will reduce the supply of money. If the Grisley company were to repurchase $25,000 worth of securities at some future date, it would in all probability pay by check. This, of course, reduces the quantity of demand deposits or bank money. If payment were made in cash, the quantity of currency in circulation would decline, thereby reducing the supply of money. The only difference between a commercial bank selling a government bond and receiving payment on a loan is that in the former case the bank gives up a claim against the government, and in the latter a claim against a private borrower.

The impact of buying and selling government bonds upon the commercial bank's balance sheet will be explored in greater detail in Chapter 17.

Profits and liquidity

The relative importance of the various asset items on a commercial bank's balance sheet is the result of the banker's pursuit of two conflicting goals. One goal is profits. Commercial banks, like any other business, are seeking profits. To this end the bank is desirous of holding loans and securities. These two items are the major earning assets of commercial banks. On the other hand, a commercial bank must seek safety. For a bank, safety lies in liquidity —specifically such liquid assets as cash and excess reserves. Banks must be on guard for depositors transforming their demand deposits into cash. Similarly, the possibility exists that more checks will be cleared against a bank than are cleared in its favor, causing a net outflow of reserves. Bankers are thus seeking a proper balance between prudence and profits. The compromise that is achieved determines the relative size of earning assets as opposed to highly liquid assets.

A MONOPOLY BANK

We have just gauged the lending ability of a single commercial bank which is part of a multibank banking system. Our conclusion is that such a bank can only lend an amount equal to its excess reserves. This is so because a single bank faces the prospect of losing reserves equal to the demand deposits it creates by lending. The drawing of a check equal to the amount of a loan will whisk reserves and demand deposits off to the bank in which the check is deposited.

Let us now consider for a moment the lending, or money-creating, potential of a monopoly bank. Suppose that instead of some fourteen thousand commercial banks in our economy there existed just one huge commercial bank. This is admittedly very unrealistic, but there is an important lesson to be learned from studying the lending ability of such a bank. To be specific, suppose that the balance sheet of this gigantic monopoly bank were as follows:

MONOPOLY BANK OF THE UNITED STATES (in billions)

Assets		Liabilities and net worth	
Property	$ 5	Capital stock	$25
Reserves	5	Demand deposits	25
Securities	20		
Loans	20		

If the reserve ratio is 20 per cent, we find that our monopoly bank is "loaned up." It is just barely meeting its reserve requirement and consequently has no excess reserves upon which to make loans. But suppose that some citizens decide to exchange $1 billion in cash for some government bonds which the monopoly bank is willing to sell. When the public buys these bonds from the monopoly bank, the bank's holdings of securities fall to $19 billion. The monopoly bank acquires in return $1 billion in cash. Assuming the bank has on hand sufficient cash to meet the day-to-day withdrawals of people cashing checks against their deposits, the bank adds the $1 billion to its reserves. Reserves will now stand at $6 billion. As a result of this transaction, it is obvious that the bank now has $1 billion in excess reserves. On the basis of this excess reserve, by how much can the monopoly bank increase the economy's supply of money by lending?

Careful consideration of the situation reveals

of these checks *must* deposit them back in the monopoly bank. Checks drawn against the demand deposits of the monopoly bank must come directly home to roost. These checks are cleared by simply transferring the ownership of demand deposits from the drawer of the check to the recipient of the check. But the total volumes of the monopoly bank's reserves and demand deposits are unchanged when checks are drawn and used to finance purchases and sales of goods and services. With a 20 per cent reserve ratio the monopoly bank's $1 billion in excess reserves will permit a $5 billion expansion of loans from $25 to $30 billion. At the end of this transaction, the monopoly bank's balance sheet will stand as follows:

MONOPOLY BANK OF THE UNITED STATES (in billions)

Assets		Liabilities and net worth	
Property	$ 5	Capital stock	$25
Reserves*	6	Demand deposits*	30
Securities*	19		
Loans*	25		

* Accounts affected by transaction.

that on the basis of this $1 billion in excess reserves the monopoly bank can support an additional $5 billion in new loans. Why? *The monopoly bank with a 20 per cent reserve ratio can lend $5 for every $1 of excess reserves, because it has no fear of losing reserves when it lends.* Indeed, by assumption, there are no other banks to which reserves can be lost! In lending $5 billion the bank's outstanding loans will rise from $20 to $25 billion, and its demand deposits will increase from $25 to $30 billion. And remember: this $5 billion increase in demand deposits constitutes a $5 billion increase in the supply of money. Now what if the borrowers draw $5 billion worth of checks against these new deposits as they purchase various goods and services? Will the monopoly bank face the loss of reserves and deposits as did the single bank? No, because the recipients

The astute reader will recognize that the ability of the monopoly bank to lend by a multiple—five, in this case—of its excess reserves is related to the size of the reserve ratio. Suppose for the moment that the monopoly bank's reserve ratio is just 10 per cent and that at the outset its reserves are $2 billion and its outstanding demand deposits $20 billion. Again, the bank would be loaned up; it would have no excess reserves. Now the public buys $1 billion of securities and pays by cash. As before, the cash is added to reserves, giving the bank $1 billion in excess reserves. With a 10 per cent reserve ratio, how much can the monopoly bank safely lend? The answer is clear: it can lend $10 billion, thereby increasing demand deposits by $10 billion. In this case, we find that with a 10 per cent reserve ratio the monopoly bank can lend by a multiple of 10 for every dollar's worth of excess reserves it acquires.

If you are suspicious that a generalization is lurking in these two examples, you are absolutely right. A 10 per cent reserve ratio—that is, a ratio between reserves and demand deposits of 1:10—permits the monopoly bank to lend by a multiple of 10. A 20 per cent reserve ratio—that is, a 1:5 ratio between reserves and deposits—allows the monopoly bank to create new money by a multiple of 5 for each dollar's worth of excess reserves. If the ratio were 33⅓ per cent, the multiple would be 3. If 50 per cent, it would be 2. If 100 per cent, then just 1. There is obviously an inverse relationship between the size of the reserve ratio and the multiple by which the monopoly bank can lend; the smaller the reserve ratio, the greater the multiple. More specifically, our generalization is this: *the multiple by which a monopoly bank can create new money by lending is the reciprocal of the reserve ratio.* The reciprocal of any number is the quotient you obtain by dividing that number into 1. Keep in mind, however, that the ability of the monopoly bank to lend anything at all is dependent upon the existence of excess reserves. No excess reserves, no lending—regardless of the size of the multiple.

Is this process of multiple credit creation reversible? Yes, it is. Suppose the monopoly bank has $4 billion in reserves and $25 billion in outstanding demand deposits. If the reserve ratio is 20 per cent, the bank would be faced with a $1 billion deficiency in reserves. It would have to call in $5 billion in loans and extend no new credit to get its house back in order. The needed contraction in the supply of bank money is 5 times the deficiency of reserves.

In short, we can say that the monopoly bank can lend by a multiple of its excess reserves for two reasons. First, the monopoly bank, in sharp contrast to the single bank in the banking system, cannot lose reserves. When the recipients of new loans draw checks to make purchases or pay debts, these checks must be redeposited back in the monopoly bank. The

bank clears these checks by merely transferring claims against its assets—the payer's deposit is reduced and the payee's deposit increased by the amount of the check. The total volumes of demand deposits and reserves remain unchanged. Second, the monopoly bank's ability to lend by a multiple of its excess reserves hinges on the fact that the reserve ratio is fractional—that is, less than 100 per cent. A 100 per cent ratio would permit the monopoly bank to lend only dollar for dollar with its excess reserves.

THE COMMERCIAL BANKING SYSTEM AS A WHOLE

Thus far we have discovered that (1) a single bank in a banking system can safely lend dollar for dollar with its excess reserves and (2) a monopoly bank, if one existed, could lend by a multiple of its excess reserves. Now what of the lending ability of all commercial banks taken as a group? Jumping to our conclusions, we find that *the commercial banking system, like a monopoly bank, can lend by a multiple of its excess reserves. This multiple lending is accomplished despite the fact that each bank in the system can only lend dollar for dollar with its excess reserves.* The immediate task is to uncover how these seemingly paradoxical conclusions come about.

To do this it is necessary that we keep our analysis as simple as possible. Therefore, we shall rely upon three simplifying assumptions. First, suppose that the reserve ratio for all commercial banks is 20 per cent. Second, assume initially that all banks are exactly meeting this 20 per cent reserve requirement. No excess reserves exist; all banks are "loaned up." Third, we will suppose that, if any bank becomes able to increase its loans as a result of acquiring excess reserves, an amount equal to these excess reserves will be loaned to one borrower, who will write a check for the entire amount of the loan and give it to someone else, who deposits the check in another bank. This messy assumption simply means that we are assuming the worst thing possible that can happen to any lending bank—a check for the entire amount of the loan is drawn and cleared against it and in favor of another bank.

The banking system's lending potential

To get the ball rolling, suppose that someone deposits $100 in currency in Bank A. Having ample till money, Bank A adds this $100 to its reserves. Since we are recording only *changes* in the balance sheets of the various commercial banks, Bank A's balance sheet now appears as follows (a_1):

such as Bank A can only lend an amount equal to its excess reserves, we conclude that Bank A can safely lend a maximum of $80. When a loan for this amount is negotiated, Bank A's loans will increase by $80, and the borrower will get an $80 demand deposit. Let us add these figures to Bank A's balance sheet (a_2).

But now we must invoke our third assumption: the borrower draws a check for $80—the entire amount of the loan—and gives it to someone who deposits it in another bank, Bank B. As we saw in transaction 6, Bank A *loses* both reserves and deposits equal to the amount of the loan (a_3). The net result of all

BALANCE SHEET: COMMERCIAL BANK A

Assets		Liabilities and net worth	
Reserves	$+100 ($a_1$)	Demand deposits	$+100 ($a_1$)
	− 80 (a_3)		+ 80 (a_2)
Loans	+ 80 (a_2)		− 80 (a_3)

How much *excess reserves* does Bank A now have? It has acquired $100 in new reserves but in the process it has also acquired $100 in new demand deposits. This means that 20 per cent of the new reserves must be earmarked as required reserves to offset the new deposits. In short, $20 of the new reserves will be required, freeing the remaining $80 as excess reserves. Remembering that a single commercial bank

the transactions is that Bank A's reserves now stand at $20 (equal to $100 minus $80), loans at $80, and demand deposits at $100 (equal to $100 plus $80 minus $80). Note that when the dust has settled, Bank A is just meeting the 20 per cent reserve ratio.

Bank B *acquires* both the reserves and the deposits which Bank A has lost. Bank B's balance sheet looks like this (b_1):

BALANCE SHEET: COMMERCIAL BANK B

Assets		Liabilities and net worth	
Reserves	$+80 ($b_1$)	Demand deposits	$+80 ($b_1$)
	−64 (b_3)		+64 (b_2)
Loans	+64 (b_2)		−64 (b_3)

When the check is drawn and cleared, Bank A *loses* $80 in reserves and deposits and Bank B *gains* $80 in reserves and deposits. But 20 per cent, or $16, of Bank B's newly acquired

someone who deposits it in another bank (c_3).

Bank D—the bank receiving the $51.20 in reserves and deposits—now notes these changes on its balance sheet (d_1):

BALANCE SHEET: COMMERCIAL BANK D

Assets		Liabilities and net worth	
Reserves	$+51.20 ($d_1$)	Demand deposits	$+51.20 ($d_1$)
	−40.96 (d_3)		+40.96 (d_2)
Loans	+40.96 (d_2)		−40.96 (d_3)

reserves must be kept as required reserves against the new $80 in demand deposits. This means that Bank B has $64 (equal to $80 minus $16) in excess reserves. It can therefore lend $64 ($b_2$). When the borrower draws a check for the entire amount and deposits it in Bank C, the reserves and deposits of Bank B both fall by the $64 ($b_3$). As a result of these transactions, Bank B's reserves will now stand at $16 (equal to $80 minus $64), loans at $64, and demand deposits at $80 (equal to $80 plus $64 minus $64). Note that, after all this has transpired, Bank B is just meeting the 20 per cent reserve requirement.

We are off and running again. Bank C has acquired the $64 in reserves and deposits lost by Bank B. Its balance statement appears as follows (c_1):

It can now lend $40.96 ($d_2$). The borrower draws a check for the full amount and deposits it in another bank (d_3).

Now if we wanted to be particularly obnoxious, we could go ahead with this procedure by bringing Banks E, F, G, H, . . . , N into the picture. We will simply suggest that the student check through computations for Banks E, F, and G, to ensure that he has the procedure firmly in mind.

The nucleus of this analysis is summarized in Table 16-2. Data for Banks E through N are supplied so you may check your computations. Our conclusion is a rather startling one: on the basis of the $80 in excess reserves (acquired by the banking system when someone deposited $100 in Bank A), the *commercial banking system* is able to lend $400. Lo and behold, the

BALANCE SHEET: COMMERCIAL BANK C

Assets		Liabilities and net worth	
Reserves	$+64.00 ($c_1$)	Demand deposits	$+64.00 ($c_1$)
	−51.20 (c_3)		+51.20 (c_2)
Loans	+51.20 (c_2)		−51.20 (c_3)

Exactly 20 per cent, or $12.80, of this new reserve will be required, the remaining $51.20 being excess reserves. Hence, Bank C can safely lend a maximum of $51.20. Suppose it does ($c_2$). And suppose the borrower draws a check for the entire amount and gives it to

banking system is able to lend by a multiple of 5 when the reserve ratio is 20 per cent! Yet you will note that each single bank in the banking system is only lending an amount equal to its excess reserves. How do we explain these seemingly conflicting conclusions? Why is it

TABLE 16-2. EXPANSION OF THE MONEY SUPPLY BY THE COMMERCIAL BANKING SYSTEM

Bank	(1) Acquired reserves and deposits	(2) Required reserves	(3) Excess reserves, or (1) − (2)	(4) Amount which the bank can lend, = (3)
Bank A	$100.00 ($a_1$)	$20.00	$80.00	$ 80.00 (a_2)
Bank B	80.00 (a_3, b_1)	16.00	64.00	64.00 (b_2)
Bank C	64.00 (b_3, c_1)	12.80	51.20	51.20 (c_2)
Bank D	51.20 (c_3, d_1)	10.24	40.96	40.96 (d_2)
Bank E	40.96	8.19	32.77	32.77
Bank F	32.77	6.55	26.22	26.22
Bank G	26.22	5.24	20.98	20.98
Bank H	20.98	4.20	16.78	16.78
Bank I	16.78	3.36	13.42	13.42
Bank J	13.42	2.68	10.74	10.74
Bank K	10.74	2.15	8.59	8.59
Bank L	8.59	1.72	6.87	6.87
Bank M	6.87	1.37	5.50	5.50
Bank N	5.50	1.10	4.40	4.40
Other banks	21.97	4.40	17.57	17.57
Total amount loaned				$400.00

that the *banking system* can lend by a multiple of its excess reserves, but *each individual bank* can only lend dollar for dollar with its excess reserves?

The answer lies in the fact that reserves lost by a single bank are not lost to the banking system as a whole. The reserves lost by Bank A are acquired by Bank B. Those lost by B are gained by C. C loses to D, D to E, E to F, and so forth. Hence, although reserves can be and are lost by *individual* banks in the banking system, there can be no loss of reserves for the banking *system* as a whole. Remember that the monopoly bank was able to lend by a multiple of its excess reserves because it could not lose reserves. For the same reason the banking system as a whole can lend by a multiple of its excess reserves. This contrast, incidentally, is a fine illustration of why it is imperative that

we keep the fallacy of composition firmly in mind. Commercial banks *as a group* can create money by lending in a manner much different from that of the individual banks in that system.

The rationale involved in this bank money, or deposit, multiplier is not unlike that underlying the income multiplier discussed in Chapter 13. The income multiplier was based on the fact that the expenditures of one household are received as income by another; the deposit multiplier rests on the fact that the reserves and deposits lost by one bank are received by another bank. And, just as the size of the income multiplier is determined by the reciprocal of the MPS, that is, by the leakage into saving which occurs at each round of spending, so the deposit multiplier is determined by the reciprocal of the reserve ratio, that is, by the leakage into required reserves which occurs at each step of the lending process. But keep in mind that, despite the similar rationale, one of these processes has to do with creating income and the other with creating money.

The reader might experiment with these teasers in testing his understanding of multiple credit expansion by the banking system. (1) Rework the preceding analysis (at least three or four steps of it) on the assumption that the reserve ratio is 10 per cent. What is the maximum amount of money the banking system could create upon acquiring $100 in new reserves and deposits? (No, the answer is not $800!) (2) Explain how a banking system which is "loaned up" and faced with a 20 per cent reserve ratio might be forced to *reduce* its outstanding loans by $400 as a result of depositors withdrawing $100 from Bank A.

Some modifications

Our discussion of credit expansion has been conducted in a somewhat rarefied atmosphere. There are certain complications which might modify the quantitative preciseness of our analysis.

Other leakages. Aside from the leakage of required reserves at each step of the lending process, certain other leakages of money from the commercial banks might occur, thereby dampening the money-creating potential of the banking system.

1. A borrower may request that a part of his loan be paid in cash. Or the recipient of a check drawn by a borrower may present it at his bank to be redeemed partially or wholly in currency rather than added to his account. Thus, if the scoundrel who borrowed the $80 from Bank A in our illustration asked for and got $16 of it in cash and the remaining $64 as a demand deposit, Bank B would only receive $64 in new reserves (of which only $51.20 would be excess) rather than $80 (of which $64 was excess). This decline in excess reserves reduces the lending potential of the banking system accordingly. As a matter of fact, if the first

borrower had taken the entire $80 in cash and this currency remained in circulation, the multiple expansion process would have stopped then and there. But the convenience and safety of demand deposits make this unlikely.

2. As a commercial bank's loans and outstanding deposits increase, the prudent bank will increase its holdings of till money. As a bank's deposits grow, so will the day-to-day cashing of checks; hence the bank will need more till money. Thus a part—say $20—of the original $100 cash deposit which triggered our illustration might have been added to cash rather than to reserves. In this case the excess reserves of Bank A would be $60 rather than $80. Again potential credit expansion would be dampened somewhat.

3. Our analysis of the commercial banking system's ability to expand the money supply by lending is based on the supposition that commercial banks are willing to meet precisely the legal reserve requirement. In practice bankers are more prudent than this and arrange to have a "safety margin" of excess reserves to avoid the embarrassment of falling below the legal reserve ratio in the event that an unusually large amount of checks is cleared against them. Therefore, Bank A, upon receiving $100 in new cash, might choose to add $25 rather than the legal minimum of $20 to its reserves, the extra $5 serving as a buffer, or cushion, against adverse check clearings. The over-all credit expansion potential of the banking system would obviously be reduced by such additions to a bank's excess reserves.

Willingness versus ability to lend. It is only fair to emphasize that our illustration of the banking system's ability to create money rests upon the supposition that commercial banks are willing to exercise their abilities to create money by lending and that households and businesses are willing to borrow. In practice, this need not be the case. Bankers, you will recall, seek a proper balance between prudence and profits. When prosperity reigns, banks may expand credit to the maximum of their ability. Why not? Loans are interest-earning assets, and in good times there is little fear of borrowers defaulting. But if depression clouds appear on the economic horizon, bankers may hastily withdraw their invitations to borrow, seeking the safety of liquidity even if it involves the sacrifice of potential interest income. Bankers may fear the large-scale withdrawal of deposits by a panicky public and simultaneously doubt the ability of borrowers to repay. It is not too surprising that during the Great Depression of the 1930s banks had considerable excess reserves but lending was at a low ebb. Obviously, if the amount actually loaned by each commercial bank falls short of its excess reserves, the resulting multiple expansion of credit would be curtailed.

The fact that bankers may not expand the supply of money to their maximum ability is of more than passing interest. It may be a factor which contributes significantly to business fluctuations. By holding back on credit expansion as the economy begins to slip into a depression, commercial banks may further inhibit total spending and intensify that cyclical downswing. Indeed, we noted in Chapter 11 that a rapid shrinkage of the money supply contributed to the Great Depression of the 1930s. Conversely, by lending and thereby creating money to the maximum of their ability during prosperity, commercial banks may contribute to an excess of total spending and to the resulting inflationary pressures. In Chapter 17 the means by which the Board of Governors attempts to influence the lending policies of commercial banks, so that they will offset rather than enforce cyclical fluctuations, will be explored.

SUMMARY

1. Commercial banks create money—that is, demand deposits, or bank money—when they make loans. The creation of demand deposits by bank lending is the most important source of money in American capitalism.

2. The ability of a single commercial bank to create money by lending depends upon the size of its *excess* reserves. Generally speaking, a commercial bank can safely lend only an amount equal to the size of its excess reserves. It is thus limited because, in all likelihood, checks drawn by borrowers will be deposited in other banks, causing a loss of reserves and deposits to the lending bank equal to the amount it has loaned.

3. A monopoly bank would be in a position to lend by a multiple of any excess reserves which it might acquire. This is so because (*a*) a monopoly bank could not lose reserves as the result of checks drawn by borrowers and (*b*) the reserve ratio is assumed to be less than 100 per cent. The multiple by which a monopoly bank could expand the money supply through lending is found by taking the reciprocal of the reserve ratio.

4. The commercial banking system as a whole can also lend by a multiple of its excess reserves. Like the monopoly bank, the banking *system* cannot lose reserves, although individual banks can lose reserves to other banks in the system. The multiple by which the banking system can lend is, once again, the reciprocal of the reserve ratio. This multiple credit expansion process is reversible.

QUESTIONS AND STUDY SUGGESTIONS

1. Why must a balance sheet always balance? What are the major assets and claims on a commercial bank's balance sheet?

2. Explain why reserves are assets to commercial banks but liabilities to the Federal Reserve banks.

3. Why are commercial banks required to have reserves? What are excess reserves? How are they calculated? What is their significance?

4. "Whenever currency is deposited in a commercial bank, cash goes out of circulation and, as a result, the supply of money is reduced." Do you agree? Explain.

5. "When a check is drawn against Bank A and deposited in another bank, Bank A will lose reserves as the check is cleared. Yet the collection of checks entails no loss of reserves by the commercial banking system." Explain. Of what significance is this for the lending ability of the banking system?

6. "When a commercial bank makes loans, it creates money; when loans are retired, money is destroyed." Explain.

7. Explain why a single commercial bank can safely lend only an amount equal to its excess reserves but the commercial banking system can lend by a multiple of its excess reserves. Why is the multiple by which the banking system can lend equal to the reciprocal of its reserve ratio?

8. Assume that Jones deposits $500 in currency in the First National Bank. A half hour later Smith negotiates a loan for $750 at this bank. By how much and in what direction has the money supply changed? Explain.

9. Suppose the Continental Bank has the following simplified balance sheet. The reserve ratio is 20 per cent.

Assets	(1)	(2)	Liabilities and net worth	(1)	(2)
Reserves $22,000	____	____	Demand de-		
Securities 38,000	____	____	posits $100,000	____	____
Loans 40,000	____	____			

a. What is the maximum amount which this bank can safely lend? Show in column 1 how the bank's balance sheet will appear after the bank has loaned this amount.

b. By how much has the supply of money changed? Explain.

c. How will the bank's balance sheet appear after checks drawn for the entire amount of the new loans have been cleared against this bank? Show this new balance sheet in column 2.

d. Answer parts a, b, and c on the assumption that the reserve ratio is 15 per cent.

10. Suppose the National Bank of Commerce has excess reserves of $8,000 and outstanding demand deposits of $150,000. If the reserve ratio is 20 per cent, what is the size of the bank's actual reserves?

11. Suppose the Fourth National Bank has the following simplified balance sheet. The reserve ratio is 20 per cent.

Assets	(1)	(2)	Liabilities and net worth	(1)	(2)
Reserves $40,000	____	____	Demand de-		
Securities 90,000	____	____	posits $200,000	____	____
Loans 70,000	____	____			

Assume that households and businesses deposit $5,000 worth of currency in this bank and that this currency is added to the bank's reserves.

a. In column 1 show how the bank's balance sheet would appear after this transaction. Has there been a change in the supply of money as a result of these deposits?

b. How much excess reserves does this bank now have? By how much can it safely expand its loans? In column 2 show the bank's balance sheet as it appears after those loans have been made.

c. To what extent, if at all, will this lending alter the supply of money? Explain.

12. Suppose the following is a simplified consolidated balance sheet for the commercial banking system. All figures are in billions. The reserve ratio is 20 per cent.

Assets (1)		Liabilities and net worth (1)	
Reserves	$40 ____	Demand deposits	$186 ____
Securities	56 ____		
Loans	90 ____		

a. How much excess reserves does the commercial banking system have? How much can the banking system lend? Show in column 1 how the consolidated balance sheet would look after this amount has been lent.

b. Answer question 12*a* on the assumption that the reserve ratio is 15 per cent. Explain the resulting difference in the lending ability of the commercial banking system.

13. The Third National Bank has reserves of $20,000 and demand deposits of $100,000. The reserve ratio is 20 per cent. Households deposit $5,000 in currency in the bank. This $5,000 is added by the bank to its reserves. How much excess reserves does the bank now have?

14. Suppose again that the Third National Bank has reserves of $20,000 and demand deposits of $100,000. The reserve ratio remains at 20 per cent. The bank now sells $5,000 in securities to the Federal Reserve bank in its district, receiving a $5,000 increase in reserves in return. How much excess reserves does the bank now have? Why does your answer differ (yes, it does!) from the answer to question 13?

15. What are "leakages"? How might they affect the money-creating potential of the banking system? Be specific.

SELECTED REFERENCES

Chandler, Lester V., *The Economics of Money and Banking*, 3d ed. (New York: Harper & Row, Publishers, 1959), chaps. 4 and 5.

Halm, George N., *Economics of Money and Banking*, rev. ed. (Homewood, Ill.: Richard D. Irwin, Inc., 1961), chaps. 5, 13, and 14.

Kent, Raymond P., *Money and Banking*, 4th ed. (New York: Holt, Rinehart and Winston, Inc., 1961), chaps. 12–15.

Pritchard, Leland J., *Money and Banking* (Boston: Houghton Mifflin Company, 1958), chaps. 5–12.

Chapter 17

THE FEDERAL RESERVE BANKS AND

MONETARY POLICY

IN CHAPTER 16 our attention was focused upon the money-creating ability of individual banks and the commercial banking system. Our discussion ended on a disturbing note: unregulated commercial banking might contribute to cyclical fluctuations in business activity. That is, commercial banks will find it profitable to expand the supply of money during inflationary prosperity and to restrict the money supply in seeking liquidity during depression. It is the task of this chapter to see how the monetary authorities of American capitalism attempt to reverse the procyclical tendencies of the commercial banking system through a variety of control techniques.

More specifically, the goals of the present chapter are these: First, the objectives of monetary policy, the roles of participating institutions, and the route by which monetary policy affects the operation of the economy are detailed. Next, the balance sheet of the Federal Reserve banks is surveyed, because it is through these central banks that monetary policy is largely effectuated. Third, the quantitative and qualitative techniques of monetary control are analyzed in considerable detail. Then the monetary aspects of fiscal policy and of Treasury gold transactions are explained. Finally, monetary policy is evaluated as to its over-all effectiveness in restraining fluctuations in economic activity.

OBJECTIVE OF MONETARY POLICY

Before analyzing the techniques through which monetary policy is effectuated, it is essential that we clearly understand the objectives of monetary policy and locate the institutions responsible for the formulation and implementation of that policy. Certain key points made in Chapter 15 merit reemphasis at the outset of our discussion. The Board of Governors of the Federal Reserve System has the responsibility of supervising and controlling the operation of the monetary and banking systems of American capitalism. It is this Board which formulates the basic policies which the banking system follows. Because it is a public body, the decisions of the Board of Governors are made in the interests of the general economic welfare of society as a whole. The twelve Federal Reserve banks—the central banks of American capitalism—implement the policy decisions of the Board. As quasi-public banks, the Federal Reserve banks are not guided by the profit motive, but rather pursue those measures which the Board of Governors recommends.

However, to say that the Board follows policies which "promote the general economic welfare" is not enough. We must pinpoint the goal of monetary policy. It will come as no great surprise that *the objective of monetary*

321

policy is to assist the economy in achieving a full-employment noninflationary level of total output.

But precisely how does monetary policy work toward this goal? The process is complicated, but essentially it boils down to this:

1. By invoking certain control techniques the Board of Governors and the Federal Reserve banks can influence the size of the reserves—and therefore the excess reserves—of commercial banks.

2. Because excess reserves are the basis upon which commercial banks can expand the money supply by lending, any manipulations of excess reserves through the control techniques of the Board of Governors will affect the supply of money, that is, the amounts which commercial banks will be able and willing to lend at various possible interest rates.

3. Given the demand for money, changes in the supply of money will affect the cost and availability of money. That is, changes in the supply of money will affect the interest rate and the amount of credit bankers are willing to make available to borrowers.

4. Changes in the cost and availability of bank credit will in turn have an impact upon the spending decisions of society, particularly upon investment decisions, and therefore upon the levels of output, employment, income, and prices.

The cause-effect chain between monetary policy and output and employment is summarized in the outline below.

Federal monetary
policy influences
commercial bank
reserves
   which
Influences
the supply
of money
   which
Influences
the interest
rate (the cost)
and the availa-
bility of bank
credit

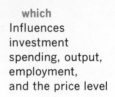

   which
Influences
investment
spending, output,
employment,
and the price level

Let us examine the operation of monetary policy through a simple example. Suppose the economy is operating somewhat short of the full-employment mark. Side-stepping troublesome complications and qualifications for the moment, we find that monetary policy would work something like this:

1. The Board of Governors would direct the Federal Reserve banks to pursue certain policies designed to increase the (excess) reserves of commercial banks.

2. Finding themselves blessed with abundant excess reserves, commercial banks are now in a position to make available a greater supply of money by granting bank credit. The banking *system* can expand the supply of money by a multiple of its excess reserves.

3. With an increase in the supply of money relative to the demand for it, interest rates will decline, and the quantity of bank credit (money) taken by borrowers will increase.

4. Low interest rates and the ready availability of bank credit will induce increases in spending. These increases in spending will be subject to the multiplier, driving the equilibrium NNP upward by a multiple of the increase in total spending.

Economists are in general agreement that the investment component of total spending is more likely to be affected by changes in the interest rate than is consumer spending. The interest rate does not seem to be a very crucial factor in determining how households divide their disposable income between consumption and saving. Indeed, it is not clear whether decreases in the interest rate will tend to increase or decrease the amount of consumption. On the one hand, a lower interest rate may induce some households, particularly those operating small businesses, to save less, because it is now cheap to finance by borrowing. On the other hand, we have noted that those who save to provide a given retirement income or to provide funds for the education of their children find that a lower interest rate will mean that a larger volume of saving will be required to earn the needed income. Then, too, the effect of higher interest rates on consumer installment buying is not great, because considerable increases or decreases in the interest rate have little impact on the size of each monthly payment; that is, the consumer is not impressed by the total interest charge but only by how much interest he must pay per month. Furthermore, any tendency for higher interest charges to diminish consumer installment buying can be largely canceled by extending the repayment period from, say, twenty-four to thirty-six months.

The impact of changing interest rates upon investment spending is greater because of the size and long-term nature of such purchases. Capital equipment, factory buildings, warehouses, and so forth, are tremendously expensive purchases. In absolute terms the interest charges on funds borrowed for these purchases will be very considerable. Similarly, the interest cost on a house purchased on a long-term contract will be very large: a ½ per cent change in the interest rate could easily amount to hundreds or even thousands of dollars on the total cost of a home. It is also important to note that changes in the interest rate may also affect investment spending by changing the relative attractiveness of capital equipment purchases and bond purchases. If the interest rate rises on bonds, then, given the profit expectations on capital good purchases, businesses will be more inclined to purchase securities than to buy capital equipment. Conversely, given profit expectations on investment spending, a fall in the interest rate makes capital purchases more attractive than bond ownership. In short, the impact of changing interest rates will be primarily upon investment spending, and through this channel upon output, employment, and the level of prices.

The above comments detail the ideal operation of an "easy money" policy. A "tight money" policy follows the same route, but the procedure is to lower commercial bank reserves, reduce the supply of money, raise the cost and lessen the availability of bank credit, and thereby curtail investment spending. Tight money should obviously be invoked when an excess of total spending is causing inflation in the economy.

So much for the objectives of monetary policy and the cause-effect chain which its application entails. We now seek an understanding of the techniques by which the Board of Governors can manipulate the size of commercial bank reserves.

CONSOLIDATED BALANCE SHEET OF THE FEDERAL RESERVE BANKS

Because monetary policy is implemented by the twelve Federal Reserve banks, it is essential to consider the nature of the balance sheet of the Federal Reserve banks. Some of the assets and liabilities found here are considerably different from those found on the balance sheet of a commercial bank. Table 17-1 is a consoli-

TABLE 17-1. TWELVE FEDERAL RESERVE BANKS' CONSOLIDATED BALANCE SHEET, FEBRUARY 28, 1962 (in billions)

Assets		Liabilities and net worth	
Cash	$ 1.0	Reserves of member banks	$16.8
Gold certificates	16.5	Treasury deposits	0.5
Securities	28.4	Federal Reserve notes (outstanding)	28.5
Loans to commercial banks	1.8	All other liabilities	6.7
All other assets	4.8		
Total	$52.5	Total	$52.5

SOURCE: "Federal Reserve Bulletin."

dated balance sheet which shows all the pertinent assets and liabilities of the twelve Federal Reserve banks as of February 28, 1962.

Assets

Cash. This is the Federal Reserve banks' holdings of Treasury currency. The Federal Reserve banks may have received this cash as a result of Treasury or commercial bank deposits.

Gold certificates. Two things should be noted about gold certificates. First, these certificates are simply warehouse receipts for the gold bullion held by the Treasury. The law requires that newly mined gold or gold coming into the United States as a result of international trade must be sold to the Treasury. The Treasury pays for such gold by drawing checks against its deposit in the Federal Reserve banks. The clearing of these checks reduces Treasury deposits in the Federal Reserve banks. To replenish these deposits the Treasury issues gold certificates—claims or warehouse receipts against the newly obtained gold—and deposits them in the Federal Reserve banks. Second, gold certificates constitute the reserves which the Federal Reserve banks must keep against certain of their liabilities. Specifically, the Federal Reserve banks must currently keep an amount of gold certificates equal to 25 per cent of the total value of its three major liabilities—reserves of member banks, Treasury deposits, and outstanding Federal Reserve notes. A glance at the balance sheet will reveal that 25 per cent of the sum of the three liabilities is $11.45 billion. The Federal Reserve banks therefore have excess reserves of $5.05 ($16.50 minus $11.45) billion.

Securities. This refers to the government bonds which the Federal Reserve banks are holding. Some of these bonds may have been purchased directly from the Treasury, but most are bought in the open market from commercial banks or the public. Although these bonds are an important source of income to the Federal Reserve banks, they are not bought and sold primarily for income. Rather they are bought and sold

(1) to influence the ability of commercial banks to create money by lending and (2) to stabilize the market for government bonds, so as to maintain public confidence in government securities and facilitate borrowing by the Treasury. We will find later that these two motives for buying and selling government securities may conflict.

Loans to commercial banks. Commercial banks occasionally borrow from the Federal Reserve banks. The IOUs which the commercial banks give to the bankers' banks in negotiating loans are listed as loans to commercial banks. From the Federal Reserve bank's point of view these IOUs are assets, that is, claims against the commercial banks that have borrowed from them. To the commercial banks these IOUs are liabilities. In borrowing, the commercial banks obtain increases in their reserves in exchange for their IOUs.

Before shifting to the liability side of the Federal Reserve banks' balance sheet, one note on terminology: "securities" and "loans to commercial banks" are sometimes called "Reserve bank credit." These two accounts represent credit which the bankers' banks have extended to (1) the government by buying government securities and (2) commercial banks by accepting their IOUs in return for increases in their reserves.

Liabilities

On the liability side we find three major items:

Reserves of member banks. We are already familiar with this account. It is an asset from the viewpoint of the member banks but a liability to the Federal Reserve banks.

Treasury deposits. Just as businesses and private individuals find it convenient and desirable to pay their obligations by check, so does the United States Treasury. It keeps deposits in the various Federal Reserve banks and draws checks on them in paying its obligations. To the Treasury such deposits are obviously assets;

to the Federal Reserve banks, liabilities. The Treasury creates and replenishes these deposits by depositing tax receipts, money borrowed from the public or the banks through the sale of bonds, gold certificates, and, less frequently, newly printed treasury currency.

Federal Reserve notes. The basic portion of our paper money supply is Federal Reserve notes. These notes are issued by the Federal Reserve banks. When in circulation, these pieces of paper money constitute circulating claims against the assets of the Federal Reserve banks and are therefore treated as liabilities. Just as your own IOU is neither an asset nor a liability to you when it is in your own possession, so Federal Reserve notes resting in the vaults of the various Federal Reserve banks are neither an asset nor a liability. Only those notes in circulation are liabilities to the bankers' banks. These notes, which come into circulation through commercial banks, are not a part of the money supply until they are in the hands of the public.

MECHANISMS OF MONETARY POLICY

With this cursory understanding of the Federal Reserve banks' balance sheet, we are now in a position to explore how the Board of Governors of the Federal Reserve System can influence the money-creating abilities of the commercial banking system. What devices can be employed at the discretion of the Board of Governors to influence commercial bank reserves?

General, quantitative controls

The general, or quantitative, controls of the monetary authorities are three in number: (1) changing the reserve ratio, (2) open market operations, and (3) changing the discount rate. These controls are general, or quantitative, in that they seek to manipulate the total quantity of bank credit. Later we shall discuss selective, or qualitative, controls which are aimed at influencing the volume of specific types of credit.

1. Changing the reserve ratio. How can the Board of Governors influence the ability of commercial banks to lend through manipulation of the legal reserve ratio? A simple example will supply a clear answer to this query. Suppose a commercial bank's balance sheet is such that reserves are $5,000 and demand deposits $20,000. If the legal reserve ratio stands at 20 per cent, the bank's *required* reserves are $4,000. Since *actual* reserves are $5,000, it is apparent that the *excess* reserves of this bank are $1,000. On the basis of this $1,000 of excess reserves we have seen that this single bank can lend $1,000, but the banking system as a whole could create a maximum of $5,000 in new bank money by lending (Table 17-2). Now what if the Board of Governors raised the legal reserve ratio from 20 to 25 per cent? Required reserves would jump from $4,000 to $5,000, shrinking excess reserves from $1,000 to zero. It is obvious that *raising the reserve ratio increases the amount of required reserves banks must keep. Either banks lose excess reserves, diminishing their ability to create money by lending, or else they find their reserves deficient and are forced to contract the money supply.* In the above case, excess reserves are transformed into required reserves and the money-creating potential of our bank is reduced from $1,000 to zero.

What if the Board of Governors announced a forthcoming increase in the legal reserve requirement to 30 per cent? The commercial bank would be faced with the embarrassing prospect of failing to meet this requirement. To protect itself against such an eventuality the bank would be forced to lower its outstanding demand deposits and at the same time to increase its reserves. To reduce its demand deposits the bank would be prone to let outstanding loans mature and be repaid without extending new credit. To increase reserves the bank might sell some of its holdings of securities, adding the proceeds to its reserves. Both courses of action will reduce the supply of money (see transactions 6 and 7, Chapter 16).

What would be the effect if the Board of Governors lowered the reserve ratio from the original 20 to 10 per cent? In this case required reserves would decline from $4,000 to $2,000,

TABLE 17-2. THE EFFECTS OF CHANGES IN THE RESERVE RATIO UPON THE LENDING ABILITY OF COMMERCIAL BANKS

(1) Legal reserve ratio, per cent	(2) Demand deposits	(3) Actual reserves	(4) Required reserves	(5) Excess reserves, or (3) − (4)	(6) Money-creating potential of single bank, = (5)	(7) Money-creating potential of banking system
10	$20,000	$5,000	$2,000	$ 3,000	$ 3,000	$ 30,000
20	20,000	5,000	4,000	1,000	1,000	5,000
25	20,000	5,000	5,000	0	0	0
30	20,000	5,000	6,000	−1,000	−1,000	−3,333

and as a result excess reserves would jump from $1,000 to $3,000. We can conclude that *lowering the reserve ratio changes required reserves to excess reserves, thereby enhancing the ability of banks to create new money by lending.* Table 17-2 summarizes all the reserve-ratio changes just discussed.

Table 17-2 reveals that a change in the reserve ratio actually affects the money-creating ability of the banking system in two ways. First, it affects the size of excess reserves. Second, it changes the multiple by which the banking system can lend. Thus, raising the reserve ratio from 10 to 20 per cent reduces the money-creating potential of the banking system from $30,000 to $5,000.

2. Open market operations. The buying and selling of government bonds by the Federal Reserve banks in the open market—that is, from or to commercial banks and the general public—also affect the excess reserves of commercial banks.

Buying securities. Suppose the Board of Governors orders the Federal Reserve banks to buy government bonds in the open market. From whom may these securities be purchased? In general, from commercial banks and the public. In either case the over-all effect is basically the same—commercial bank reserves are increased.

Let us trace through the situation in which

the Federal Reserve banks buy government bonds *from commercial banks.* This transaction is a simple one.

a. The commercial banks give up a part of their holdings of securities to the bankers' banks.

b. The Federal Reserve banks pay for these securities by increasing the reserves of the commercial banks by the amount of the purchase.

Just as the commercial bank may pay for a bond bought from a private individual by increasing the seller's demand deposit, so the bankers' bank may pay for bonds bought from commercial banks by increasing the bank's reserves. In short, the consolidated balance sheets of the commercial banks and the Federal Reserve banks will change as follows:

COMMERCIAL BANKS

Assets	Liabilities and net worth
−Securities (a) +Reserves (b)	

(a) Securities ↓   (b)+Reserves ↑

FEDERAL RESERVE BANKS

Assets	Liabilities and net worth
+Securities (a)	+Reserves of member banks (b)

The most important aspect of this transaction is that, when Federal Reserve banks purchase securities from commercial banks, the reserves —and therefore the lending ability—of the commercial banks are increased.

If the Federal Reserve banks should purchase securities *from the general public*, the effect on commercial bank reserves would be substantially the same. Suppose that the Grisley Meat Packing Company possesses some negotiable government bonds which it sells in the open market to the Federal Reserve banks. The transaction goes like this:

a. The Grisley company gives up securities to the Federal Reserve banks and gets in payment a check drawn by the Federal Reserve banks on themselves.

b. The Grisley company promptly deposits this check in its account with the Wahoo bank.

c. The Wahoo bank collects this check against the Federal Reserve banks by sending it to the Federal Reserve banks for collection. As a result the Wahoo bank receives an increase in its reserves.

In terms of the balance sheets:

Two aspects of this transaction are noteworthy. First, as with Federal Reserve purchases of securities directly from commercial banks, the reserves and lending ability of the commercial banking system have been increased. Second, in this instance the supply of money is directly increased by the central banks' purchase of government bonds aside from any expansion of the money supply which may occur as the result of the increase in commercial bank reserves.

You may detect a slight difference in the Federal Reserve banks' purchases of securities from the commercial banking system as compared with purchases from the public. Assuming all commercial banks are "loaned up" initially, Federal Reserve bond purchases will increase the actual reserves and excess reserves of the commercial banks by the entire amount of the bond purchases. Thus a $1,000 bond purchase from commercial banks would increase both the actual and excess reserves of the commercial banks by $1,000. On the other hand, Federal Reserve bank purchases of bonds from the public increase actual reserves but also increase

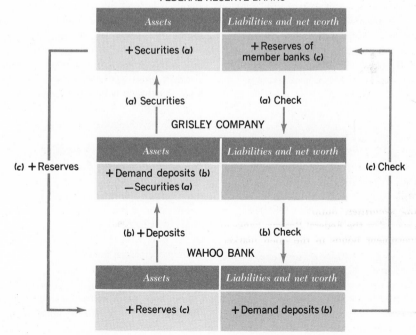

FEDERAL RESERVE BANKS

demand deposits. Thus a $1,000 bond purchase from the public would increase actual reserves of the "loaned up" banking system by $1,000; but with a 20 per cent reserve ratio the excess reserves of the banking system would only go up by $800. In the case of bond purchases from the public it is *as if* the commercial banking system had already used one-fifth or 20 per cent of its newly acquired reserves to support $1,000 worth of new demand deposit money.

However, in each transaction the basic conclusion is the same: *when the Federal Reserve banks buy securities in the open market, commercial banks' reserves will be increased.*

Selling securities. We should now be highly suspicious that Federal Reserve bank sales of government bonds will reduce commercial bank reserves. Let us confirm these suspicions.

Suppose the Federal Reserve banks sell securities in the open market *to commercial banks:*

a. The Federal Reserve banks give up securities which the commercial banks obviously acquire.

b. The commercial banks pay for these securities by drawing checks against their deposits—that is, their reserves—in the Federal Reserve banks. The Federal Reserve banks collect these checks by reducing the commercial banks' reserves accordingly.

In short, the following balance sheet changes occur:

Note specifically the reduction in commercial bank reserves.

Should the Federal Reserve banks sell securities *to the public,* the over-all effect is substantially the same. Let us put the Grisley company on the buying end of government bonds which the Federal Reserve banks are selling.

a. The Federal Reserve bank gives up government bonds to the Grisley company, the latter paying for these securities by a check drawn on the Wahoo bank.

b. The Federal Reserve banks clear this check against the Wahoo bank by reducing its reserves.

c. The Wahoo bank returns the Grisley company's check to it, reducing the company's demand deposit accordingly.

The balance sheet changes are shown at the top of the opposite page.

Note that Federal Reserve bond sales of $1,000 to the commercial banking system reduce the system's actual and excess reserves by $1,000. But a $1,000 bond sale to the public reduces excess reserves by $800 because demand deposit money is also reduced by $1,000 by the sale. In the case of bond sales to the public it is *as if* the commercial banking system had reduced its outstanding demand deposits by $1,000 to cushion the decline in excess reserves to the extent of $200.

In each of the two variations of the Federal Reserve bond sale transaction, however, the basic conclusion is the same: *when the Federal Reserve banks sell securities in the open market, commercial bank reserves are reduced.*

3. The discount rate: lending to commercial banks. The Federal Reserve banks perform essentially the same functions for commercial banks as the commercial banks perform for the public. One of these functions is the making of loans. Just as commercial banks extend credit to the public, so the bankers' banks may lend to the commercial banks.

When commercial banks borrow from Federal Reserve banks, they may turn over to the bankers' banks either IOUs drawn against themselves or the promissory notes of businesses

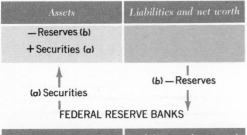

COMMERCIAL BANKS

Assets	Liabilities and net worth
—Reserves (b) + Securities (a)	

(a) Securities ↑   (b) — Reserves ↓

FEDERAL RESERVE BANKS

Assets	Liabilities and net worth
—Securities (a)	—Reserves of member banks (b)

discount rate – interest for loan

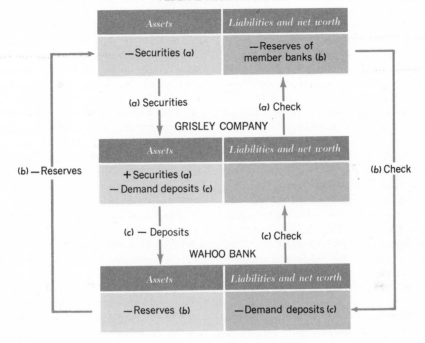

and individuals which they hold as security against loans granted to the public. Just as commercial banks charge interest on their loans, so do the Federal Reserve banks charge interest on the loans they grant to commercial banks. This interest rate is called the *discount rate,* the interest on such loans being discounted at the time the loan is negotiated, rather than collected at the time the loan is repaid.

Let us suppose commercial banks borrow from the Federal Reserve banks by drawing IOUs against themselves. These IOUs, being claims against the commercial banks, are assets to the Federal Reserve banks and appear on their balance sheet as "loans to commercial banks." To the commercial banks these IOUs are liabilities, appearing as "loans from the Federal Reserve banks" on the commercial banks' balance sheets. In payment of the loan the Federal Reserve banks will increase the reserves of the borrowing commercial banks. Since no required reserves need be kept against loans from the Federal Reserve banks, *all* new reserves acquired by borrowing from the

Federal Reserve banks would be excess reserves. These changes are reflected in the balance sheets of the commercial banks and the bankers' banks as shown below.

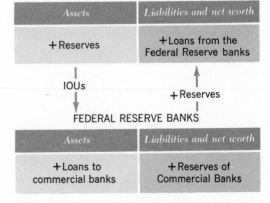

It is interesting to note that this transaction is analogous to a private person's borrowing from a commercial bank (see transaction 6, Chapter 16).

The important point, of course, is that *commercial bank borrowing from the Federal Reserve banks increases the reserves of commercial banks, thereby enhancing their ability to extend credit to the public.*

The Board of Governors of the Federal Reserve System has the power to establish and manipulate the discount rate at which commercial banks can borrow from the Federal Reserve banks. From the commercial banks' point of view, the discount rate obviously constitutes a cost entailed in acquiring reserves. Hence, a *decrease* in the discount rate encourages commercial banks to build up their reserves by borrowing. Although not obligated to do so, the Federal Reserve banks usually stand ready to extend credit to borrowing banks that can offer acceptable collateral. But if the discount rate is high, this means that commercial banks that borrow must in turn boost the interest rate at which they lend to the public to make such transactions profitable. If a commercial bank has to pay 3 per cent for the attainment of new reserves, it may have to charge 8 per cent for loans made on these new reserves to the public in order to earn an acceptable profit. Such a high rate discourages the public from increasing the money supply by borrowing from the commercial banks. Conversely, a low discount rate permits commercial banks to acquire new reserves cheaply from the Federal Reserve banks. This allows the commercial banks to lend profitably at relatively low interest rates to the public, thereby encouraging an expansion in the supply of money. Apart from these quantitative considerations, changes in the discount rate may well have significant psychological effects upon the credit policies of banks and the public. Changes in the discount rate are a very explicit means by which the Board of Governors can communicate the over-all direction of monetary policy to banks and the public.

As evidenced by the consolidated balance sheet of the Federal Reserve banks (Table 17-1), commercial banks borrow rather infrequently from the Federal Reserve banks. For this reason the discount rate is a relatively weak instrument of monetary policy.

Reserve bank credit. Early in this chapter we noted that the sum of loans to commercial banks and securities appearing on the Federal Reserve banks' balance sheet constitutes Reserve bank credit. Loans to commercial banks represent credit extended to the commercial banks, and the Federal Reserve banks' holdings of securities indicate credit granted to the government.

Obviously, when the Federal Reserve banks increase the volume of loans to commercial banks by lowering the discount rate and buy securities in the open market, Reserve bank credit increases. An expansion of Reserve bank credit increases the reserves of commercial banks and thereby enhances their ability to increase the supply of money by lending to the public. On the other hand, if the Federal Reserve banks choose to decrease loans to commercial banks by boosting the discount rate and sell securities in the open market, Reserve bank credit will decline. This decline in Reserve bank credit destroys commercial bank reserves and limits further increases in the supply of money. It may even force a contraction in the money supply. In short, *there is a direct relationship between the volume of Reserve bank credit and the size of commercial bank reserves.*

Easy money and tight money. Suppose the economy is faced with unemployment and deflation. The monetary authorities correctly decide that an increase in the supply of money is needed to stimulate the volume of spending in order to help absorb the idle resources. To induce an increase in the supply of money the Board of Governors must see to it that the excess reserves of commercial banks are expanded. What specific policies will bring this about?

1. The reserve ratio should be reduced, automatically changing required reserves into excess reserves.

2. The Board of Governors should order the Federal Reserve banks to buy securities in the open market. This will build up the size of commercial bank reserves.

3. The discount rate should be lowered to

induce commercial banks to add to their reserves by borrowing from the Federal Reserve banks. The second and third policies can be combined by simply saying that Reserve bank credit should be expanded. For obvious reasons, this set of policy decisions is called an *easy money policy.* Its purpose is to make credit easily available, so as to increase the volumes of spending and employment.

Suppose, on the other hand, an excess of spending is pushing the economy into an inflationary spiral. The Board of Governors should attempt to reduce total spending by limiting or contracting the supply of money. The key to this goal lies in reducing the reserves of commercial banks. How is this done?

1. Increasing the reserve ratio will automatically strip commercial banks of excess reserves.

2. The Federal Reserve banks should sell government bonds in the open market to tear down commercial bank reserves.

3. A boost in the discount rate will discourage commercial banks from building up their reserves by borrowing at the Federal Reserve banks. These latter two policies constitute a reduction in Reserve bank credit. This group of directives is appropriately labeled a *tight money policy.* The objective is to tighten the supply of money in order to reduce spending and inflationary pressures.

Selective, qualitative controls and moral suasion

The major techniques of monetary control are (1) changing the reserve ratio, (2) changing the discount rate, and (3) open market operations. These devices are quantitative controls; they are designed to control the quantity of bank credit generally available. But these instruments of monetary management are supplemented periodically by certain other credit controls in the form of (1) qualitative, or selective, credit controls and (2) moral suasion.

Selective credit controls. On occasion the monetary authorities have restricted certain specific types of credit:

1. *Stock market credit.* In some instances the over-all flow of money and credit in the economy has been fairly serene, and at the same time speculative stock market purchases threaten to precipitate economic difficulties. To thwart this possibility the Board of Governors has the authority to specify the *margin requirement,* or minimum percentage down payment which purchasers of stock must make. Thus a margin requirement of 70 per cent means that only 30 per cent of the purchase price of a security may be borrowed, the remaining 70 per cent being paid "cash on the barrel head." This rate will be raised when it is deemed desirable to restrict speculative stock purchases and lowered to revive a sluggish market.

2. *Consumer credit.* Congress occasionally has authorized the Board of Governors to invoke specific restraints on consumer credit. During World War II money incomes were increasing at a time when the output of civilian goods was declining because of the drastic rechanneling of resources to the production of war goods. The result was sharp inflationary pressure in certain consumer goods industries. To dampen this pressure Congress gave the Board of Governors temporary authority to specify down payments and maximum repayment periods on loans involving the purchase of real estate and a variety of consumer durables.

Moral suasion. The monetary authorities sometimes use the less tangible technique of moral suasion to influence the lending policies of commercial banks. Moral suasion simply means the employment by the monetary authorities of policy statements, public pronouncements, or outright appeals, warning that excessive expansion or contraction of bank credit might entail serious consequences for the banking system and the economy as a whole. Such pronouncements are not limited to bank credit in general; they may call for the curtailment of specific types of bank credit. For example, in attempting to relieve inflationary pressure during the Korean War in 1951, the public statements and publicity releases of the monetary authorities pleaded for the curtailment of bank lending not essential to the war effort and the general exercise of voluntary restraint by commercial bankers in creating money by lending. Private bankers' associations often aid the Federal monetary authorities in the application of moral suasion by echoing the pleas of the Board of Governors.

Techniques of monetary control and their relative effectiveness

It is generally agreed that the most important single credit control device is open market operations—the reserve ratio, the discount rate, and selective controls being of less significance. The reasons for this are somewhat complex. As things now stand, actual reserve ratios are pushing the upper limits set by Congress (see Table 16-1). This means that the anti-inflationary influence of higher reserve ratios is definitely limited in terms of future effectiveness. The obvious suggestion is that Congress raise the upper limits on the reserve ratio to permit further boosts in the actual ratio when inflation threatens. But this is more easily said than done. Further boosts in the actual reserve ratio would mean that commercial banks must keep more of their assets in reserves and therefore less as earning assets (loans and securities). This might work rather severe hardships on those banks whose profits are not particularly large.

The importance of the discount rate has not been particularly great in recent years, simply because commercial banks have not needed to borrow very extensively from the Federal Reserve banks.

But why the great importance of open market operations as such? A glance at the consolidated balance sheet for the Federal Reserve banks (Table 17-1) reveals very large holdings of government bonds ($28.4 billion), the sales of which could easily reduce commercial bank reserves from $16.8 billion to zero! Similarly, the fact that the Federal Reserve banks have large holdings of excess reserves ($5.05 billion) means that *at a maximum* commercial bank reserves could be increased through Federal Reserve bond purchases by about $20.20

billion.[1] Thus the ability of the Federal Reserve banks to affect commercial bank reserves through bond sales and purchases is potentially very great.

Note finally that the manipulation of commercial bank reserves through open market operations is accomplished at the initiative of the Federal Reserve System. By way of contrast the discount rate depends on commercial bank initiative in borrowing from the Federal Reserve banks before it can be influential as a technique of monetary policy.

COMBINING FISCAL AND MONETARY POLICIES

Monetary policy and fiscal policy are the two most important stabilization techniques which our economy possesses. It is crucial that these two techniques reinforce one another, rather than work at cross purposes. During a recession fiscal policy calls for a budget deficit, and, as we have just noted, an easy money policy would be in order. Inflation, on the other hand, should be countered with a budget surplus and a tight money policy.

Let us examine in two steps the monetary aspects of fiscal policy. We first discuss the effects of government expenditures and tax receipts upon both the actual and potential supply of money, that is, upon demand deposits and commercial bank reserves. Next the impact of various types of deficit financing and public debt retirement upon the money supply and bank reserves is examined.

[1] Remember (1) the reserves of the Federal Reserve banks are gold certificates and (2) the reserve ratio for the Federal Reserve banks is 25 per cent. This means that the multiple by which the Federal Reserve banks as a group can expand the sum of its three major liabilities for each dollar's worth of excess reserves is 4. Thus, $5.05 billion times 4 equals $20.20 billion. Unlike commercial banks, however, Federal Reserve banks do not attempt to maximize profits and therefore do not tend to acquire all the earning assets their reserves can support. The volume of their earning assets is determined by considerations of public welfare.

Treasury expenditures

How do Treasury purchases of goods and services affect the reserves of commercial banks? This question can best be answered by tracing through a specific purchase. Suppose the Treasury negotiates a contract with the Grisley company to supply meat products to several Midwestern military installations. The major components of this transaction can be analyzed as follows:

1. The Treasury buys the Grisley company's products, paying by means of a check drawn on its deposits with a Federal Reserve bank.

2. The Grisley company adds this check to its deposits with the Wahoo bank.

3. The Wahoo bank collects the check by sending it to the Federal Reserve bank, thereby receiving an increase in its reserves.

4. After the Treasury's deposits are reduced by the amount of the check, the cleared check is returned to the Treasury.

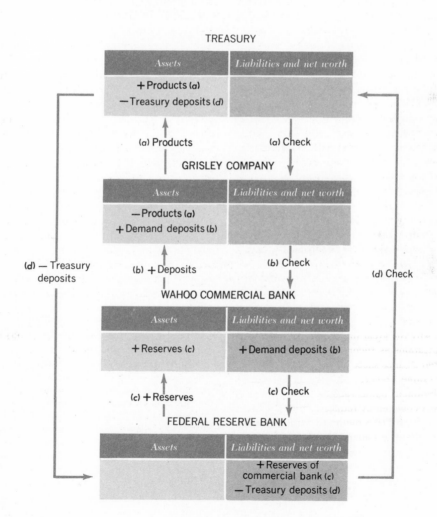

The conclusion? Treasury expenditures add to commercial banks' reserves and directly increase the supply of money.

Treasury tax receipts

The receipt of taxes by the Treasury reverses this process and thereby reduces commercial bank reserves. We see in the diagram which follows what happens when the public pays taxes to finance the social goods and services provided by government:

1. The Treasury receives tax payments in the form of checks from the public in exchange for the social goods and services provided by the government.

2. The Treasury adds these tax funds received to its deposits in the Federal Reserve banks.

3. The Federal Reserve banks clear these checks against the commercial banks upon which they are drawn by reducing the reserves of those banks.

4. The cleared checks are returned by the various commercial banks to their drawers, the

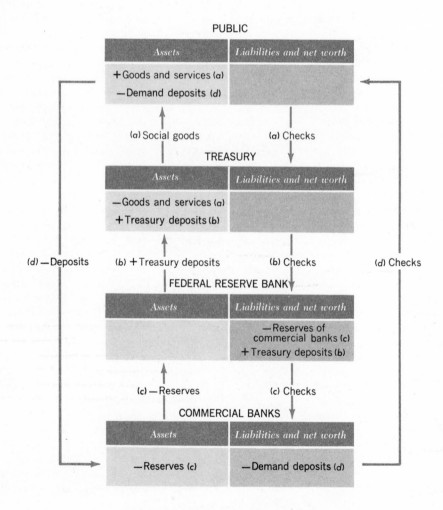

public's demand deposits being reduced accordingly.

We can conclude that the collection of taxes lowers commercial banks' reserves and directly decreases the supply of money.

Deficit financing and the money supply

Government expenditures and tax revenues are rarely in balance; deficits and surpluses frequently occur. Indeed, in Chapter 13 we stressed the appropriateness of a budget deficit during recession and a budget surplus during inflation. If government (Treasury) expenditures exceed tax receipts, one would expect the net effect of the resulting deficit to increase the supply of money and commercial bank reserves.

Actually the validity of this conclusion depends upon to whom the bonds used in financing the deficit are sold. Generally speaking, the Treasury can sell bonds to (1) the public, (2) commercial banks, and (3) the Federal Reserve banks. The effect of each type of financing upon commercial banks' reserves and the money supply differs.

Bond sales to public. Treasury sales of bonds to the public have essentially the same effect upon the money supply as does the Treasury's collection of taxes for the social goods and services it "sells" to the public. To portray bond sales to the public we need only substitute government bonds for social goods and services in the Treasury's tax receipts transaction above. (The only difference is that the sales of social goods and services lower the assets of the Treasury, and the sale of bonds— the Treasury's IOUs—increases its outstanding liabilities.) The net effect is that the Treasury transfers bonds (which are not money) to the public, and in return the Treasury gets checks in payment which, when cleared, destroy demand deposits (money) and reduce commercial bank reserves. Therefore, we can conclude that bond sales to the public directly reduce the supply of money and reduce the money-creating ability (reserves) of commercial banks in

essentially the same way as do tax collections. These declines in reserves and demand deposit money offset the increases in reserves and demand deposits arising from the deficit itself. Therefore, the *net* effect upon the money supply and commercial bank reserves of incurring a deficit *and* financing that deficit by bond sales to the public is zero.

Does this mean that the expansionary impact of the deficit has been canceled by inappropriate methods of financing it? Not at all: the deficit is still likely to be expansionary. It is reasonable to assume that people will buy government bonds with demand deposits which otherwise would have largely been idle savings; that is, government bonds are a form of savings and are not likely to be purchased at the sacrifice of consumption. The government, on the other hand, is obviously spending the proceeds of the bond sales. Thus, although a deficit financed through bond sales to the public does not increase commercial bank reserves or demand deposits, it does have an expansionary effect by turning "idle" demand deposits into "active" demand deposits; that is, demand deposits are transferred from savers to spenders.

Bond sales to commercial banks. In contrast, Treasury bond sales to commercial banks do not alter the supply of money. In this transaction the Treasury in effect gives bonds—its IOUs—to commercial banks in exchange for checks which the banks draw on themselves. The Treasury sends these checks to the Federal Reserve banks for collection; there the Treasury's deposit is increased, and the reserves of the bond-buying commercial banks are reduced. The crucial feature of this transaction is that there is no decline in demand deposits to offset the increase in demand deposits arising from the deficit itself. Therefore, the direct and immediate *net* effect upon demand deposits, and thus the money supply, of incurring a deficit *and* financing that deficit through bond sales to commercial banks is to increase demand deposits by the amount of the deficit. However, commercial banks do lose reserves when they buy government bonds, and this in effect cancels the increase in reserves entailed by the deficit itself.

Bond sales to Federal Reserve banks. Treasury bond sales to the central banks do not reduce either demand deposits or commercial bank reserves. Securities are transferred from the Treasury to the Federal Reserve banks and the central banks pay for these securities by increasing the Treasury's deposits accordingly. Hence, this type of financing does not offset at all the increases in commercial bank reserves and in the supply of money which the deficit itself entails. Therefore, the *net* effect upon the money supply and commercial bank reserves of incurring a deficit *and* financing that deficit by bond sales to the central banks is to increase both the volume of demand deposit money and commercial bank reserves by the amount of the deficit.

The expansionary effect of a budget deficit upon the supply of money and commercial bank reserves will be offset (1) wholly, (2) partially, or (3) not at all, depending upon whether the bonds are sold to (1) the public, (2) commercial banks, or (3) the Federal Reserve banks. A government deficit has the greatest expansionary effect when financed by the sale of bonds to central banks because in this instance the financing reduces neither demand deposits nor commercial bank reserves. The expansionary effect of a deficit is least when financed by bond sales to the public because this type of financing reduces both demand deposits and commercial bank reserves by the amount of the bond sales. Financing a deficit by bond sales to commercial banks stands between these other two cases: bond sales to commercial banks do not reduce demand deposits but do reduce the ability (excess reserves) of banks to create more money by lending.

Now that we are aware of these conclusions, it is not surprising to us that during the inflationary years of World War II the Treasury was most anxious to sell bonds to nonbank buyers in order to minimize the inflationary impact of the large deficits which the war necessitated. And it was reasonably successful in doing so. The public increased its government bond holdings by some $109 billion during the war, while commercial bank bond holdings increased by about $68 billion.

Retiring public debt and the money supply

Our analysis of the impact of Treasury expenditures and tax receipts suggests that a budget surplus—an excess of tax receipts over Treasury expenditures—will have both a direct and a potential contractionary effect upon the supply of money. That is, one would expect a surplus to result in a direct reduction in the volume of demand-deposit money and in a decline in commercial bank reserves.

Actually, the use of a surplus to retire public debt may offset wholly or in part the contractionary effect which the surplus itself exerts upon the money supply and commercial bank reserves. Generally speaking, the Treasury may use a surplus to retire public debt held by (1) the public, (2) commercial banks, and (3) the Federal Reserve banks.

sale of bonds to public reduces supply of money

Repurchasing bonds from public. Because the sale of bonds to the public reduces the supply of money, one would expect that the Treasury's retirement of publicly held debt would increase the supply of money. This is the case. The Treasury's repurchase of maturing bonds held by the public has the same effect on the money supply as does the Treasury's purchase of goods and services. Here we need only substitute government bonds for products in the Treasury's purchase transaction on page 333. (Note, of course, that while the purchase of goods increases the Treasury's assets, the repurchase of outstanding IOUs decreases its liabilities.) In redeeming bonds the Treasury transfers checks, drawn against its surplus tax revenues, to the public. When deposited and collected, these checks will add to the demand deposits of individuals and nonbank businesses which are cashing in their maturing bonds and will

purchase of bonds from public increases the supply of money also increase commercial bank reserves. These increases in reserves and demand deposit money offset the declines in reserves and demand deposits arising from the surplus itself. Therefore, the *net* effect on the money supply and bank reserves of incurring a surplus *and* using that surplus to retire bonds held by the public is zero.

This does not necessarily mean that the deflationary impact of a budget surplus will be negated by the use of that surplus to retire publicly held debt. It is reasonable to assume that most people who receive payment for maturing bonds will put these receipts into some other form of saving, possibly "idle" demand deposits. However, because they are compulsory, the tax collections in excess of government expenditures which provide the surplus are likely to have come at the expense of both saving and consumption. Therefore, although the use of a surplus to retire publicly held debt does not reduce commercial bank reserves or the volume of demand deposit money, it does have a contractionary impact by turning relatively "active" demand deposits into "idle" demand deposits; that is, demand deposits are to some degree transferred from spenders to savers.

Repurchasing bonds from commercial banks. What about the retirement of debt held by commercial banks? The retiring of bank-held bonds does not alter the money supply. Here the Treasury in effect buys its outstanding bonds back from commercial banks with checks drawn on its deposits in the Federal Reserve banks. The commercial banks send these checks to the Federal Reserve banks for collection. This is done by increasing the reserves of the commercial banks and reducing the Treasury's deposits by the amount of the bonds. The salient feature is that there occurs no increase in demand deposits to offset the decline in demand deposits resulting from the surplus itself. Therefore, the direct and immediate *net* effect upon the volume of demand deposit money of incurring a surplus *and* using that surplus to retire bonds held by commercial

banks is to reduce demand deposit money by the amount of the surplus. Note, however, that commercial banks do acquire additional reserves when bonds are repurchased, and this in effect cancels out the loss of reserves entailed by the surplus itself.

Repurchasing bonds from Federal Reserve banks. Treasury retirement of bonds held by the Federal Reserve banks increases neither the supply of money nor commercial bank reserves. Securities are merely transferred from the central banks to the Treasury and are paid for by reducing the Treasury's deposits with the central banks by the appropriate amount. Here there are no increases in commercial bank reserves or demand deposit money to offset at all the declines in reserves and demand deposits which the surplus itself entails. Hence, the *net* effect upon the money supply and commercial bank reserves of incurring a surplus *and* using that surplus to retire bonds held by the Federal Reserve banks is to reduce both the volume of demand deposit money and commercial bank reserves by the amount of the surplus.

The contractionary effect of a budget surplus upon the supply of money and commercial bank reserves will be offset (1) wholly, (2) partially, or (3) not at all, depending upon whether the surplus is used to retire public debt held by (1) the public, (2) commercial banks, or (3) Federal Reserve banks. A government surplus has the greatest contractionary or deflationary effect when the surplus is used to retire bonds held by the central banks because this use of the surplus increases neither demand deposits nor commercial bank reserves. The deflationary impact of a surplus is least when publicly held government bonds are retired because this use of the surplus increases both commercial bank reserves and demand deposits. Retiring bonds held by commercial banks stands in an intermediate position: repurchasing bonds from commercial banks will not increase demand deposits but will increase the reserves of banks.

TREASURY GOLD PURCHASES AND SALES

In going off the gold standard in 1934, Congress passed legislation which retired all gold coins and gold certificates from circulation in the economy. This legislation also specified that newly mined gold or gold flowing into the United States in payment for exported goods and services must be sold to the Treasury at the legally established price of $35 per ounce. In turn the Treasury will sell gold to licensed buyers: dentists, jewelers, American firms desiring to use gold in paying for the purchases of imported goods, and foreign governments that need gold to pay for goods and services purchased in international markets.

Now we are about to discover that Treasury gold purchases and sales affect the supply of money and commercial bank reserves. Furthermore, these purchases and sales are made on the basis of long-standing legislation which is *not* subject to alteration or control by the Board of Governors. Hence, Treasury gold transactions may cause changes in the supply of money and in bank reserves which are quite undesirable in so far as the objectives of our monetary authorities are concerned.

Treasury purchases of gold

The question is this: How do the Treasury's purchases of gold affect the demand deposits and reserves of commercial banks? The answer: in precisely the same way as does any other Treasury purchase. By substituting "gold" for "products" and making the Grisley company a meat exporter which has received gold bullion for its foreign sales in our Treasury purchase transaction on page 333, we find that the supply of money is directly increased, and commercial banks acquire new reserves. To the extent that the new reserves are excess, they will support a multiple expansion of the money supply by the commercial banking system as described in Chapter 16.

Treasury sales of gold

Like Treasury tax receipts, that is, Treasury "sales" of social goods and services, the effect of Treasury gold sales is to reduce directly the supply of money and, more significantly, to reduce commercial bank reserves. By substituting "gold" for "goods and services" and assuming that the public is a licensed buyer of gold in our Treasury tax receipts transaction on page 334, we can trace the exact manner in which these reductions come about. The buyer, paying the Treasury by check, gives up a demand deposit in return for gold bullion, thereby directly reducing the supply of money in the economy. The Treasury deposits this check in the Federal Reserve bank; this increases the Treasury's deposits in the Federal Reserve banks at the expense of commercial bank reserves. This loss of reserves will restrain commercial banks in creating new money and might even give rise to a multiple contraction of the money supply.

FISCAL POLICY, GOLD TRANSACTIONS, AND MONETARY POLICY

In so far as the monetary authorities are concerned, fiscal policy and gold transactions are "nondiscretionary" transactions. That is, Treasury expenditures and tax collections, on the one hand, and Treasury gold purchases and sales, on the other, are not controlled at the discretion of the Board of Governors. This is important because these nondiscretionary transactions may either facilitate or complicate monetary policy.

Because it adds to demand deposits and commercial bank reserves, a budget deficit will reinforce an easy money policy. But by the same token a deficit will conflict with a tight money policy; this is particularly so when the deficit is financed by Treasury borrowing from the central banks. On the other hand, by reducing demand deposits and bank reserves, a budget surplus will reinforce a tight money policy. But a surplus is clearly at odds with an easy money policy, particularly when the surplus is used to retire debt held by the central banks.

Similarly, by building up bank reserves and adding directly to demand deposits, net purchases of gold by the Treasury obviously reinforce an easy money policy but are an obstacle to effectuating tight money. By tearing down bank reserves and directly reducing demand deposits, net sales of gold by the Treasury obviously facilitate a tight money policy, but conflict with easy money.

HOW EFFECTIVE IS MONETARY POLICY?

Aside from these potentially troublesome nondiscretionary transactions, it would seem that monetary policy is a potent tool for achieving economic stability. Actually the effectiveness of monetary policy is a subject of heated debate.[2]

The case for monetary policy

There are those who argue that monetary policy is an effective stabilization device which has proved its worth in recent years, helping to offset, for example, the recessions of 1949 and 1954 and to restrain inflationary tendencies throughout a good portion of the 1950s. Furthermore, monetary policy enjoys a degree of flexibility which fiscal policy does not enjoy: the decisions of the Board of Governors are not subject to the time-consuming procedures which characterize congressional action nor to the time lapse which may occur between the enacting and the applying of fiscal policy. In short, it is argued that monetary policy can be altered quickly and is of considerable effectiveness in promoting economic stability.

[2] See Shelley N. Mark and Daniel M. Slate, *Economics in Action* 2d ed., (Belmont, California: Wadsworth Publishing Co., Inc., 1962), chaps. 47–51, for excellent summaries of the various views on the role and effectiveness of monetary policy in American capitalism.

The case against monetary policy

On the other hand, many respected economists now cast considerable doubt upon the effectiveness of monetary policy. Aside from the contention that the monetary authorities have made serious errors in judgment, critics of monetary policy challenge its strength as a tool for attaining economic stability. It is argued that not only are monetary actions frequently offset by outside influences, but the cause-effect chain of monetary policy itself is characterized by "loose links." Though critics of monetary policy generally discredit its effectiveness in both recession and inflation, supporting arguments are significantly different.

Weakness in fighting recession. The basic shortcoming of monetary policy during depression lies in the old saying, "You can lead a horse to water but you can't make him drink." An easy money policy can do no more than see to it that commercial banks have the ability—that is, the excess reserves—needed for making loans. It cannot guarantee, however, that loans will actually be negotiated and the supply of money increased. If the public does not want to borrow, or commercial banks, seeking liquidity, are unwilling to lend, the easy money efforts of the Board of Governors will be to little avail. An easy money policy can do no more than create excess reserves upon which loans may or may not be made.[3] During the first few years of the Great Depression an easy money policy did little to expand the supply of money and stimulate investment. Commercial banks, fearful of becoming insolvent, built up substantial excess reserves in the late 1930s to ensure their liquidity rather than risk holding the less liquid assets of loans and securities.

[3] Qualification: remember that Federal Reserve purchases of securities *from the public* directly increase the supply of money apart from any expansion of bank credit which commercial banks may make available on the basis of the reserves they acquire as the result of these bond purchases.

Shortcomings during inflation. Tight money is not subject to the same difficulty as easy money. If pursued vigorously enough, tight money can actually destroy commercial bank reserves to the point where banks are *forced* to contract the volume of loans. As tight money eliminates excess reserves, banks will be forced to allow outstanding loans to mature without making offsetting loans to other borrowers. This means a contraction in the money supply. However, tight money involves other problems which may seriously limit its effectiveness.

1. The central banks' interest in tight money may conflict with the Treasury's desire to borrow at low rates of interest. This potential problem became a troublesome reality in the years following World War II. You will recall that the Treasury relied to a very great extent upon deficit financing as a means of paying for World War II (Chapter 14). To ensure a ready market for its bonds the Treasury requested and received assurance from the Federal Reserve System that the Federal Reserve banks would stand ready to purchase any and all bonds which the public did not choose to buy at par value prices. This Federal Reserve commitment to support the market for government bonds guaranteed the Treasury a ready market in which it could borrow at low rates of interest.

A basic conflict between the Federal Reserve's commitment to buy government bonds and its responsibility to manipulate the money supply soon became very evident. World War II and the immediate postwar years brought rather sharp inflation to the American economy. The situation obviously demanded a tight money policy, the major component of which would be the *selling* of government bonds in the open market by the Federal Reserve banks. But the Federal Reserve banks were committed to *buying* government bonds in supporting the bond market. In short, the commitment to support the government bond market negated the possibility of effectuating a tight money policy. The problem was aggravated by the fact that commercial banks, which had accumulated large amounts of government bonds during World War II, became eager to sell these bonds at the attractive, supported prices and add the proceeds to reserves as a basis for lending to the public. The reason for this was simple: Private IOUs entailed a higher rate of interest than did government bonds. Furthermore, the ability of commercial banks to accumulate reserves by selling government bonds tended to strip attempts to increase the reserve ratio or the discount rate of their effectiveness as anti-inflationary techniques. The Korean War in 1950 and the increased inflationary pressures which accompanied it brought the Treasury—Federal Reserve conflict to a head. In March of 1951 the Treasury, conceding that the rigid support of government bond prices was no longer essential, released the Federal Reserve System from its earlier commitment. A new "accord" was reached, whereby the Board of Governors agreed only to maintain an "orderly market" for government bonds.

For a time the Federal Reserve banks bought government bonds for two basic reasons: (1) to control the size of commercial bank reserves and thereby the supply of money and (2) to stabilize the government bond market. These goals were found in the inflationary era of the late 1940s to be largely mutually exclusive.

2. Tight money may be of limited effectiveness in curtailing investment. As noted earlier in this chapter, it is generally agreed that tight money has little direct effect upon consumer spending. Some economists also doubt its ability to curtail investment. And for several reasons: First, the interest rate is only one of some half-dozen determinants of the level of investment spending, and it is far from the most significant. It is very possible that changes in the noninterest determinants of investment, for example, technological advance or population growth, will cause the level of investment spending to increase *despite* increases in the interest rate. Of particular importance is the fact that the rising product and stock prices which are part of inflation give rise to business optimism and a strong incentive to invest at the very time this investment will be most inflationary. Second, large monopolistic firms—

the very firms which do the bulk of the investing —are in a position to pass on any increase in interest costs to consumers in the form of higher product prices. Indeed, in many cases monopolistic firms are able to finance substantial portions of their investment programs internally and therefore will not be hindered by the unavailability of credit for investment purposes. However, tight money is likely to have a considerable impact upon smaller firms in competitive industries. This is another criticism of tight money: it discriminates against such firms.

3. *A tight money policy is not particularly appropriate in controlling cost-push inflation.* Like fiscal policy, monetary policy is designed to control inflation by restraining excess total spending. That is, an anti-inflationary monetary policy is geared to alleviate or correct demand-pull inflation. It is not very relevant in getting at the causes of inflation which might lie on the cost or supply side of the market. As a matter of fact, given the downward inflexibility of resource and product prices, the vigorous use of a tight money policy in an inflationary situation where total demand is not excessive (and possibly is deficient) might increase unemployment and retard the growth rate (Chapter 19).

Which view of monetary policy is correct? Though there is no clear-cut answer to this question, the consensus seems to be that the potential of monetary policy as a technique for economic stability is clearly less than that of fiscal policy. Monetary policy in and of itself cannot be relied upon to combat the more severe fluctuations in business activity. On the other hand, aside from human errors in judgment and a particularly unreceptive environment, monetary policy is undoubtedly an important stabilizing technique. The previously noted (Chapter 14) reluctance of Congress to use tax changes as a countercyclical device, and the political problems involved in altering government spending countercyclically, suggest that monetary policy still has a vital role to play in stabilizing the economy.

SUMMARY

1. The goal of monetary policy is full employment without inflation. The route, or cause-effect chain, through which monetary policy functions is complex: (*a*) policy decisions affect commercial bank reserves; (*b*) changes in reserves affect the supply of money; (*c*) changes in the supply of money influence the interest rate and the availability of bank credit; and (*d*) changes in the interest rate and availability of credit affect investment, the equilibrium NNP, and the price level.

2. For a consideration of monetary policy the most important assets of the Federal Reserve banks are cash, gold certificates, securities, and loans to commercial banks. The basic liabilities are the reserves of member banks, Treasury deposits, and Federal Reserve notes.

3. Table 17-3 draws together all the basic notions relevant to the application of tight and easy money policies. It therefore merits careful study.

4. A budget deficit complements an easy money policy, but is at odds with tight money. A deficit is most inflationary (expansionary) when financed by bond sales to Federal Reserve banks, somewhat less inflationary when financed by bond sales to commercial banks, and least inflationary when financed by bond sales to the public.

5. A budget surplus complements a tight money policy, but conflicts with easy money. A surplus is most deflationary (contractionary) when used to retire public debt held by Federal Reserve banks, somewhat less deflationary when used to retire debt held by commercial banks, and least deflationary when used to retire publicly held debt.

6. The effectiveness of monetary policy as a stabilizing device is much debated. The basic criticism of monetary policy as an anti-recession technique is that easy money can provide commercial banks with excess reserves but does not guarantee that loans will actually be made

TABLE 17-3. A SUMMARY OF MONETARY POLICY

I. Problem: unemployment and deflation

II. Remedy: to induce an expansion in the supply of money, and therefore spending, by reducing the cost and increasing the availability of bank credit

III. Techniques:
   A. General, quantitative controls: easy money policy
      1. Lower reserve ratio.
      2. Buy bonds in the open market.
      3. Lower discount rate.
   B. Selective, qualitative controls
      1. Lower margin requirements.
      2. Ease credit regulations on consumer durables and real estate.
      3. Use moral suasion to induce banks to lend.

IV. Possible complications:
   A. Treasury surpluses
   B. Gold outflows, Treasury sales of gold bullion

I. Problem: inflation

II. Remedy: to induce a contraction in the supply of money, and therefore spending, by increasing the cost and reducing the availability of bank credit

III. Techniques:
   A. General, quantitative controls: tight money policy
      1. Raise reserve ratio.
      2. Sell bonds in the open market.
      3. Raise discount rate.
   B. Selective, qualitative controls
      1. Raise margin requirements.
      2. Tighten credit regulations on consumer durables and real estate.
      3. Use moral suasion to encourage banks to be more selective in lending.

IV. Possible complications:
   A. Treasury deficits
   B. Gold inflows, Treasury purchases of gold bullion

on the basis of those reserves. There are several possible shortcomings of tight money: (a) The Treasury's interest in low interest rates conflicts with the higher rate of interest which tight money entails. (b) The weight of the many noninterest determinants of investment, the ability of monopolistic firms to pass increases in interest costs on to consumers through price increases, and internal financing may all weaken the ability of tight money to curtail investment spending. (c) A tight money policy is of questionable relevance in correcting cost-push inflation.

QUESTIONS AND STUDY SUGGESTIONS

1. Suppose you are a member of the Board of Governors of the Federal Reserve System. The economy is experiencing a sharp and prolonged inflationary trend. What changes in (a) the reserve ratio, (b) the discount rate, and (c) open market operations would you recommend? Explain in each case how the change you advocate would affect commercial bank reserves and influence the money supply.

2. Specify the impact of each of the following transactions upon commercial bank reserves:

a. The Federal Reserve banks purchase securities from private businesses and consumers.

b. Commercial banks borrow from the Federal Reserve banks.

c. The Board of Governors reduces the reserve ratio.

d. The Treasury sells gold bullion.

3. Evaluate the over-all effectiveness of monetary policy. Why are open market operations regarded as a more effective credit control technique than changes in the rediscount rate and the reserve ratio?

4. Briefly explain the post-World War II Federal Reserve–Treasury conflict.

5. The following are simplified consolidated balance sheets for the commercial banking system and the twelve Federal Reserve banks. In columns 1 through 5 indicate how the balance sheets would read after each of the five ensuing transactions is completed. Do not cumulate your answers; that is, analyze each transaction separately, starting in each case from the given figures. All accounts are in billions of dollars.

CONSOLIDATED BALANCE SHEET: ALL COMMERCIAL BANKS

		(1)	*(2)*	*(3)*	*(4)*	*(5)*
Assets:						
Reserves	$ 33	___	___	___	___	___
Securities	60	___	___	___	___	___
Loans	60	___	___	___	___	___
Liabilities and net worth:						
Demand deposits	$150	___	___	___	___	___
Loans from the Federal Reserve banks	3	___	___	___	___	___

CONSOLIDATED BALANCE SHEET: TWELVE FEDERAL RESERVE BANKS

		(1)	*(2)*	*(3)*	*(4)*	*(5)*
Assets:						
Gold certificates	$20	___	___	___	___	___
Securities	40	___	___	___	___	___
Loans to commercial banks	3	___	___	___	___	___
Liabilities and net worth:						
Reserves of commercial banks	$33	___	___	___	___	___
Treasury deposits	3	___	___	___	___	___
Federal Reserve notes	27	___	___	___	___	___

a. Assume foreigners ship $2 billion in gold to American exporters who have sold goods abroad. The gold, as required by law, is then sold to the United States Treasury. To replenish its deposits with the Federal Reserve banks the Treasury deposits $2 billion in gold certificates with the Federal Reserve banks. Show the new balance sheet figures in column 1.

b. Suppose a decline in the discount rate prompts commercial banks to borrow an additional $1 billion from the Federal Reserve banks. Show the new balance sheet figures in column 2.

c. The Federal Reserve banks sell $3 billion in securities to private business firms and consumers, who pay for the bonds with checks. Show the new balance sheet figures in column 3.

d. The Federal Reserve banks buy $2 billion of securities from commercial banks. Show the new balance sheet figures in column 4.

e. Suppose the Treasury, receiving $4 billion worth of checks from taxpayers, adds these checks to its deposits with the Federal Reserve banks. Show the new balance sheet figures in column 5.

f. Now review each of the above five transactions, asking yourself these three questions: (1) What change, if any, took place in the money supply as a direct and immediate result of each transaction? (2) What increase or decrease in commercial banks' reserves took place in each transaction? (3) Assuming a reserve ratio of 20 per cent, what change in the money-creating potential of the commercial banking *system* occurred as a result of each transaction?

6. Assume that the government is forced to incur a large deficit during a period of severe inflation. Under these circumstances should the Treasury attempt to sell bonds to the public, commercial banks, or central banks? Explain. Now suppose that the government realizes a very substantial surplus which it uses for debt retirement. If a minor recession is occurring, should the Treasury use the surplus to retire bonds held by the public, by commercial banks, or by central banks? Explain.

7. If the financing of a deficit through bond sales to the public leaves commercial bank reserves and demand deposits unchanged, how can a deficit be expansionary? Explain.

SELECTED REFERENCES

The American Assembly, *United States Monetary Policy* (The American Assembly, 1958).

The Board of Governors of the Federal Reserve System, *The Federal Reserve System: Purposes and Functions* (1954), particularly chaps. 1–3, 6, and 7.

Commission on Money and Credit, *Money and Credit: Their Influence on Jobs, Prices, and Growth* (Englewood Cliffs, N.J.: Prentice-Hall, Inc., 1961), particularly chap. 3.

Federal Reserve Bank of Chicago, *Workbook on Bank Deposits, Bank Reserves, and Currency* (Chicago).

Federal Reserve Bank of New York, *A Day's Work at the Federal Reserve Bank of New York,* 2d ed. (New York: 1953).

Hansen, Alvin H., *The American Economy* (New York: McGraw-Hill Book Company, Inc., 1957), particularly chaps. 3 and 4.

Harriss, C. Lowell, *Money and Banking* (Boston: Allyn and Bacon, Inc., 1961), chaps. 21–25.

Ritter, Lawrence S. (ed.), *Money and Economic Activity: Readings in Money and Banking,* 2d ed. (Boston: Houghton Mifflin Company, 1961), particularly chaps. 8–11.

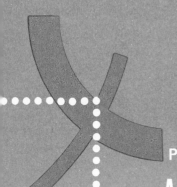

PART 4

AMERICAN ECONOMIC GROWTH: ACHIEVEMENTS, PROBLEMS, AND POLICIES

Chapter 18

AMERICAN ECONOMIC GROWTH

IN LESS THAN two hundred years our economy has grown from an industrial infant to a vigorous productive giant. The long-run growth has not occurred at a steady pace. On the contrary, it has been punctuated by periods of instability—unemployment and inflation. Parts 2 and 3 of this book have dealt with the causes and cures of short-run economic instability. The business cycle, the theory of employment, and fiscal and monetary policy have been the focal points of our analysis. The task of this chapter is to take a very long-run look at the economic growth which our economy has experienced, largely ignoring the occasional cyclical deviations from that historical trend. Our basic objective is to explain the long-run economic growth which has driven American capitalism from the clutches of poverty toward the arms of opulence. Specific objectives are several. First, we want to define economic growth, assess its significance, and note those factors which underlie it. Next we will examine the growth record of our economy. Then we turn to an analysis of those several factors which have caused economic growth to occur. Finally, the public policy aspects of economic growth are briefly noted. We defer until Chapter 19 any direct discussion of the costs and problems which rapid economic growth might entail.

DEFINING ECONOMIC GROWTH

Economic growth is a much-used and much-abused term. Indeed, it is a slippery concept.

What is economic growth? And why need we be concerned about it?

Two definitions of economic growth are commonly offered. First, economic growth may be defined in terms of the total physical output, or real income of the economy. Or, to be more sophisticated about it, economic growth refers to increases in the economy's *real* gross national product, or *real* national income. An expanding real output means that the economy is growing. A stable or declining output means that the economy is static or declining. Note that this definition hinges upon *real* and not *money* output. The production of a larger amount of goods and services signifies growth; paying a larger number of dollars for a fixed or declining quantity does not.

A second and somewhat more refined definition links economic growth to real *per capita* output. This definition correctly recognizes that the standard of living of any economy is best measured in terms of real output per person. The actual standard of living could decline in an economy if the population increased at a faster rate than the volume of real output.

Which of these definitions is best? It depends upon the specific problem with which one is dealing. If one is concerned with the question of military potential, for example, then total real output is the more appropriate measure of growth. On the other hand, per capita real income is superior for comparisons of living standards between regions or nations. Both definitions suffer from a major limitation: they

347

are material measures and do not reflect important nonmaterial considerations. The good life involves political, spiritual, and cultural as well as material objectives. Nevertheless, our definitions of economic growth will be useful because (1) our immediate concern as students of economics is with material well-being and (2) as a matter of fact a free nation which is wealthy in material things is in a strategic position to realize, if it chooses, the nonmaterial aspects of the good life.

Importance of growth

Why be concerned with economic growth? The specific reasons are numerous, but four stand out:

(1) *Economic growth means a higher standard of living.* It is obvious that an increase in per capita real output means a higher standard of living. The primary goal of the economic system is the provision of material abundance. In the long run it is an economy's growth which determines its degree of success in attaining that goal.

(2) *Economic growth is a solvent for domestic problems.* The acuteness of domestic issues—economic, social, and political—is intimately related to economic growth. Increased production and improving standards of living diminish the social and political tensions surrounding such problems as poverty, income inequality, and economic insecurity. These and other domestic problems can be managed more effectively and even largely resolved in an environment of economic growth. Conversely, the lack of growth—economic stagnation—may well cause these same problems to assume explosive proportions.

(3) *Economic growth is a source of aid to underdeveloped countries.* The specter of poverty and starvation haunts many nations of the world. The advanced nations—the United States in particular—have a tremendous moral obligation to relieve the abject poverty of less fortunate peoples. The numerous problems of the underdeveloped nations are of such vital significance that a detailed analysis is reserved for a later chapter.

(4) *Economic growth is essential in meeting the ideological challenge of Soviet Russia.* The Soviet Union not only poses a military threat to American capitalism but also has issued an explicit ideological challenge. Soviet leaders have made clear their opinion that the superiority of the communist ideology over capitalism will be proved "in the field of peaceful production." The ideological paths of many nations, particularly the underdeveloped nations, will be influenced by the course and eventual outcome of this challenge. A later chapter is devoted to a discussion of economic growth in the Soviet Union.

Ingredients of growth

What are the cornerstones of economic growth? Basically, there are six strategic ingredients in the growth of any economy. Four of these factors relate to the physical ability of an economy to grow. They are (1) the quantity and quality of its natural resources, (2) the quantity and quality of its human resources, (3) the supply or stock of capital goods, and (4) technology. These four items may be termed the *permissive factors* in economic growth. These are the physical agents of greater production. It is the availability of more and better resources, including the stock of technological knowledge, which permits an economy to produce a greater real output.

But the ability to grow and the actual realization of economic growth are two different things. The permissive factors in growth must be accompanied by two basic *implemental factors.* They are (1) the full-employment level of aggregate demand and (2) continued efficiency in the allocation of resources. To realize its productive potential a nation must provide for the full employment and full production of its available resources. The ability to expand production is not a sufficient condition for the expansion of total output; the actual utilization of available resources and the allocation of those resources in such a way as to get the maximum amount of useful goods produced are also required.

These factors can be placed in proper perspective by recalling the production possibilities curve, reproduced in Figure 18-1. This is a best performance curve in that it indicates the various *maximum* combinations of products the economy can produce, given the quantity and quality of its natural, human, and capital resources, and its stock of technological know-how. Obviously an improvement in any of the permissive factors will push the production possibilities curve to the right, as indicated by the shift from *AB* to *CD* in Figure 18-1. Increases in the quantity or quality of resources and technological advances push the curve to the right. But the implemental factors remind us that the economy need not realize its maximum productive potential; the curve may shift to the right and leave the economy behind at some level of operation *inside* the curve. In particular, an increase in the productive *potential* of the economy will not be realized if the economy fails to generate a level of aggregate demand sufficient to provide full employment and the flexibility to adjust to those changes in the allocation of resources demanded by changes in the relative supplies of resources or technological information. That is, to stay on the rightward-shifting production possibilities curve the economy must avoid *un*employment (apparent unemployment) and *under*employment (disguised unemployment).

Example: The net increase in the labor force of the United States is about one million workers per year. As such this increases the productive capacity, or potential, of the economy. But the realization of the extra output these additional workers are capable of producing presumes an appropriate increase in aggregate money demand. Furthermore, achieving the maximum additional output from this increase in the labor force presumes that these new workers will be efficiently allocated within the economy; that is, additions to the labor force should be apportioned to those industries and firms wherein the value of their contribution to total output will be greatest. It is notable that the permissive and implemental factors in growth are *not* unrelated.

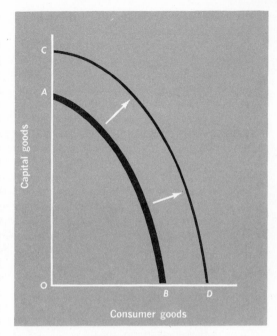

FIGURE 18-1. ECONOMIC GROWTH AND THE PRODUCTION POSSIBILITIES CURVE. Economic growth is indicated by an outward shift of the production possibilities curve as from *AB* to *CD*. Increases in the quantity and quality of resources and technological advance permit this shift; full employment and allocative efficiency are essential to its realization.

For example, unemployment tends to retard the rate of capital accumulation and may slow expenditures for research. And, conversely, a low rate of innovation and investment can be a basic cause of unemployment.

GROWTH RECORD OF AMERICAN CAPITALISM

Now let us orient our discussion of economic growth to the American economy. What level of economic growth has been achieved in American capitalism? How can this growth be explained in terms of the six ingredients or causes of growth?

Table 18-1 gives us a rough idea of economic growth in the United States over the last century as viewed through our two proposed definitions of growth. Column 2 gives us a decade-by-decade account of the economy's growth as measured by national income. Note that these figures are adjusted for price differences and, hence, reflect *real* national income. Though not steady, the upsurges of national income are rather remarkable. Except for the 1910–1930 period, *real national income has tended to double every two decades.* When the population figures of column 3 are divided into the real national income data, the result is a per capita picture of real national income. We find that, even after suitable allowance has been made for an expanding population, economic growth is impressive. *Over the last century per capita real income has more than quadrupled.*

A number of recent statistical studies esti-

mate that the growth rate of total real GNP has been about 3 to 4 per cent per year, while the annual increase in real GNP per person has been about 1½ to 2 per cent.

For at least two reasons these quantitative conclusions understate the economic growth which American capitalism has actually experienced. First, these figures do not take into account improvements in product quality. Purely quantitative data do not provide an accurate comparison between an era of crystal sets and one of stereophonic phonographs. Second, the increases in real national income and per capita national income shown in Table 18-1 were accomplished despite very sizable increases in leisure. The seventy-hour work week is a thing of the distant past. Forty hours is now the standard, with the more aggressive unions, much to the dismay of American house-

TABLE 18-1. REAL NATIONAL INCOME AND PER CAPITA NATIONAL INCOME, 1850–1961

(1) Year	(2) National income, billions of 1950 dollars	(3) Population, millions	(4) Per capita national income, 1950 dollars, or (2) ÷ (3)
1850	$ 9.4	23.2	$ 405
1860	14.4	31.4	459
1870	18.6	39.8	467
1880	25.6	50.2	510
1890	44.3	62.9	583
1900	63.3	76.0	833
1910	86.4	92.0	939
1920	94.7	105.7	896
1930	118.5	122.8	965
1940	147.0	131.7	1,116
1950	240.6	150.7	1,597
1956	296.2	168.1	1,761
1958	296.0	174.1	1,700
1961	330.9	182.7	1,811

SOURCE: Data from J. Frederic Dewhurst and Associates, "America's Needs and Resources: A New Survey" (New York: The Twentieth Century Fund, Inc., 1955), pp. 40–41, 51. Data for 1958 and 1961 calculated by the author from Department of Commerce and Census Bureau figures.

wives, whetting their appetites for a thirty-five- or thirty-hour week.

On the other hand, there are a couple of considerations which take a bit of the luster off our growth statistics. First, the United States' growth rate has been substantially less than that of a number of other industrially advanced nations. Soviet Russia, Japan, and many of the nations of Western Europe are experiencing larger annual increases in their real GNPs than we are (see Table 19-2). Second, as column 4 of Table 18-1 suggests, the growth of per capita real output has been modest in the post-World War II period. We shall discover in Chapter 19 that considerations such as these have stimulated considerable debate concerning the adequacy of our growth rate and public policies designed to accelerate our growth.

PERMISSIVE FACTORS

Now let us explain the impressive record of American capitalism in terms of the six basic ingredients of economic growth. We look first to the permissive factors, that is, to the supply side of economic growth.

Natural resources

Climate, soil, rainfall, mineral deposits, and sources of power are all important facets of any nation's natural resource base. These natural resource endowments constitute an obvious but fundamental factor in its capacity to expand, because, in contrast to the quantity and quality of labor and capital resources, the quantity and quality of a nation's natural resources are relatively fixed in supply. Note we say "relatively" fixed: within limits *available* natural resources can be increased in supply. True, given a nation's territorial limits, its mineral deposits of, for example, lead, copper, and zinc, are present only in fixed amounts. The same holds true for petroleum and natural-gas deposits. Yet the discovery and appropriation of existing deposits can add significantly to available, or usable, supplies of these resources. Similarly, arable land, pasture land, and timberland which have been exploited can frequently

be renewed by modern conservation practices. Irrigation and drainage can and have added significantly to the supply of arable land. And, as we shall soon discover, technological advancement has added significantly to available resource supplies.

For present purposes, the major question is this: Are the supplies of natural resources with which the United States is endowed sufficient to permit continued economic growth? There is no simple, unqualified answer to this question. But in so far as the majority of natural resources are concerned, the United States has been most generously endowed in terms of both quantity and quality. It is generally agreed that, with the possible exception of Soviet Russia, the United States has a larger variety and greater quantities of resources than any other nation. Actually, we are not sure of the exact quantities available—as noted, exploration and discovery continue. We are aware that known reserves of most resources insure us against scarcities in the foreseeable future.

But there is a gloomy side to the picture: the possibility of shortages and bottlenecks is also evident in so far as certain specific resources are concerned. In recent years the production and consumption of certain strategic metals— for example, lead, zinc, copper, and bauxite— indicate the need for conservation in the use of these resources. In other words, the natural resource picture is a varied and changing one. General abundance and evidence of approaching exhaustion of specific resources exist side by side. It seems fairly safe to say that the over-all resource picture at the present time is favorable to future economic growth. Bottlenecks, however, may occur in specific industries.

Alleviating scarcities. It is noteworthy that two alleviating factors have almost invariably come to the rescue when the United States has encountered serious shortages of specific raw materials.

1. Technological advance, in addition to being a basic determinant of economic growth in and of itself, has bailed American capitalism out of resource difficulties on many occasions. On the one hand, technological advance has

led to greater economy in the *use* of scarce materials. For example, the development of electroplating as a substitute for the hot-dip method of manufacturing tin plate saves 60 per cent of this scarce metal. Furthermore, technology has permitted greater efficiency in the *acquisition* of natural resources. Evidence?

Sixty years ago copper deposits of less than 3 per cent metal content would have been considered poor; now the average grade is less than one per cent. A few decades ago aluminum was so difficult to extract and so costly that it was scarcely used at all; now it ranks second only to steel in terms of metal volume. . . . The deepest oil well drilled in 1900 was about 3,000 feet; by 1950 the world's deepest well went down more than 20,000 feet—about four miles.[1]

The development of new instruments in the fields of geology, geophysics, and geochemistry —for example, magnetometers, scintillometers, and electromagnetic surveyors—are undoubtedly of great long-run significance in the discovery of new sources of raw materials. Lastly, technological advances have developed *new materials* to replace resources in particularly scarce supply. The development of plastics and synthetic rubber to supplement strategic materials during the war years provides standard and outstanding examples.

In brief, technological advance has played a key role (a) in achieving greater economy in the use of available supplies of resources, (b) in developing means for the economical recovery of known sources of raw materials, and (c) in the discovery of new, substitute materials.

2. Foreign supplies of resources can be used to supplement domestic supplies. As a matter of fact, the United States has historically changed from a world supplier to an importer of raw materials. Despite dramatic increases in the domestic *production* of most basic raw materials, simultaneous and more than proportionate increases in the domestic *consumption* of these materials have caused our economy to become a net importer of raw materials.

[1] J. Frederic Dewhurst and Associates, *America's Needs and Resources: A New Survey* (New York: The Twentieth Century Fund, Inc., 1955), p. 757.

The important point is this: foreign resources acquired through international trade can and have effectively combatted specific raw-material shortages.

In general, the natural resources of American capitalism are most abundant and serve as a solid resource base for future economic expansion. With few exceptions technological advances and the tapping of foreign supplies have overcome any serious resource bottlenecks which have threatened to jeopardize economic growth.

Conservation and the price system. A final but highly important point: the price system plays a very vital role in prompting the conservation and prudent use of our scarcest resources. For example, should a mineral resource, say, copper, come to be in particularly scarce supply in relation to the demand for it, its price will rise. This higher price has two related effects.

First, it signals manufacturers to "go easy" in the use of copper and to employ substitute materials in production where this is feasible. Stated differently, a high price for copper will tend to ration the available supply to those uses deemed most vital by society; only the manufacturers of products wanted most intensely by consumers will be able to pay the high price for copper and achieve a profit in the sale of their finished products. In addition, manufacturers who are dependent upon copper may be prompted by its high price to direct research activities toward the more efficient use of copper or the seeking of suitable substitute materials. If successful, this will tend to take pressure off the price of copper from the demand side of the market.

Second, the high price of copper induces suppliers of copper to step up production to overcome the shortage. The high price may now make possible the mining of lower-grade ores, not economically feasible at a lower price. Similarly, the high price for copper may well induce technological advances in the mining and smelting of copper. Success in such ventures will tend to reduce the price of copper from the supply side of the market. The basic point is that the price mechanism simultaneously promotes conservation in the use of particularly scarce resources and, at the same time, may induce means for alleviating such severe shortages.[2]

Human resources

The productive capacity of a nation depends not only upon the size of its labor force but also upon its quality. The size of any nation's labor force is determined primarily by the over-all size of its population. The quality of the labor force depends upon its education and training, its personal health and vigor, its morale, and its attitude towards work.

Population and the labor force. Let us first explore the *quantitative* aspect of human resources. An increase in the quantity of human resources will obviously enhance the economy's productive potential, permitting an outward shift of the production possibilities curve. Because the size of the economy's labor force[3] is obviously related directly to the size of its total population, the first question to ask is this: What long-run changes, if any, have occurred in the size of the population of the United States? Column 3 of Table 18-1 gives us the answer. A high birth rate, a declining death rate, and heavy immigration have teamed to provide the United States with a rapidly expanding population through most of its history. "During the first half of the nineteenth century, population quadrupled; it more than trebled during the last half and has doubled again since 1900."[4] There are about eight times as many Americans today as there were in 1850.

But the population has grown at varying rates. The high rates of increase of the decades prior to the 1920s began to fade in the roaring twenties and depressed thirties. The sharp

[2] See the President's Materials Policy Commission, *Resources for Freedom* (Washington: Government Printing Office, 1952), pp. 17–18.

[3] The term "labor force" is used in this instance in its broadest sense, so as to include entrepreneurs.

[4] Dewhurst, *op. cit.*, p. 49f.

population increases prior to the 1920s were accounted for in part by high immigration rates. But the 1920s saw the enactment of government policies which severely restricted this facet of population growth; in the 1930s government clamped a virtually airtight lid on the great American melting pot. Furthermore, the Great Depression of the 1930s forced many people to postpone marriage, and those who took the brave step tended to defer having children. As a result, the rate of population increase hit a new low in the 1930–1940 decade. Experts predicted a leveling off of population growth to be climaxed by a plateau or even a decline.

But much to the surprise of demographers, a combination of factors reversed this trend in the 1940s and 1950s. The war and postwar years have featured a rather startling upsurge in population growth. Prosperity is undoubtedly a partial explanation. And Uncle Sam's need for able-bodied and preferably unmarried fighting men clearly played a role. The outbreak of World War II and the creation of Selective Service caused a stream of confirmed bachelors to issue forth from the nation's better billiard parlors to embrace the holy bonds of matrimony. And, of course, in recent years significant medical advances have continued to reduce infant mortality and increase the average life span. Finally, it simply seems to have become fashionable once again to have larger families. These and a variety of other factors have all contributed to the "population explosion" of the last two decades which has brought our population to the 188 million level currently. Where will it all end? Demographers differ on this point. "Low" estimates envision a population of 231 million by 1980; "high" estimates call for 272 million.

Several conclusions can be derived from this discussion. (1) Fairly rapid population growth has been a long-run historical feature of American capitalism. (2) The population upsurge of the 1940s has transformed a declining rate of population growth into an increasing one. (3) There is little prospect that future American economic growth will be retarded by an inadequate labor supply.

Optimum population. It must be emphasized that an expanding population is not always a boon to economic growth as defined in terms of real per capita output. To explain why this is so let us assume for the moment that a nation's stock of natural resources, capital equipment, and technological information is fixed. Now suppose that the population, which is initially very small relative to these other resources, begins to expand. As more and more labor is combined with the fixed quantities of the other resources, we can expect that for a time output and therefore real income per person will rise. Why? The answer lies in increased specialization and the more efficient utilization of the nonlabor resources.

With a very small labor force there will be little opportunity for specialization; each worker will be required to divide his time among a number of tasks. But as population expands, each man can concentrate on that job for which he is best suited. As a matter of fact, by concentrating on one job workers will tend to become more proficient than when performing a variety of jobs. Furthermore, an expanding population will permit a fuller utilization of the economy's other resources—in particular its capital facilities. Modern or even somewhat archaic technology requires that capital facilities be of certain minimum size, whether output is relatively small or large. If a small quantity of labor is combined with this capital equipment, production will be relatively inefficient. Even the most modern automobile assembly line will be inefficient if it is grossly undermanned. For both these reasons output per head will rise for a time as population expands.

However, in time an opposing tendency will arise to diminish per capita output. As population continues to expand, a point will finally be reached where capital and natural resources are over-utilized. That is, each worker will be equipped with smaller and smaller amounts of materials and capital goods. This will cause output, and therefore real income per capita, to decline. In a later chapter we will find that excessively large and still expanding populations which continuously press upon the available capital and natural resources keep living standards close to the subsistence level in many of the so-called underdeveloped countries.

As Figure 18-2 suggests, if an expanding population entails an expanding real output per head up to a point and then a decline in output per person, there must be some point of maximum output and therefore real income per person. In purely economic terms the corresponding population can be regarded as of optimum size. But two points must be noted. First, our figure is hypothetical; practical problems of measurement make it virtually impossible to determine the optimum population size with any degree of accuracy. Second, increases in the nation's stocks of natural or capital resources and in its technological know-how which may accompany population growth will tend to forestall the range of increasing output per capita and forestall the range of declining output per capita. That is, an expansion of nonlabor resources will shift the point of optimum population to the right, as from L_1 to L_2 in Figure 18-2.

Quality of the labor force. Man for man the American labor force is qualitatively superior to that of any other nation in the world. The physical strength, health, education and training, and versatility of our labor force all contribute to this superiority. One eminent scholar has concluded that, if the age composition and state of health of the population of underdeveloped countries could be "Westernized," per capita incomes in these countries might rise by 20 to 30 per cent or more above existing levels.[5]

A rough indication of the improvement in the quality of the labor force is reflected in educational statistics. In 1870 only 57 per cent of the school age (five to seventeen years, inclusive) population was enrolled in elementary and secondary schools. By 1900 this figure had climbed to over 72 per cent, and by 1960 it

[5] J. J. Spengler, "The Population Obstacle to Economic Betterment," *American Economic Review, Proceedings*, May, 1951, p. 344, cited in Moses Abramovitz, "Economics of Growth," in Bernard F. Haley (ed.), *A Survey of Contemporary Economics*, vol. II (Homewood, Ill.: Richard D. Irwin, Inc., 1952), p. 138.

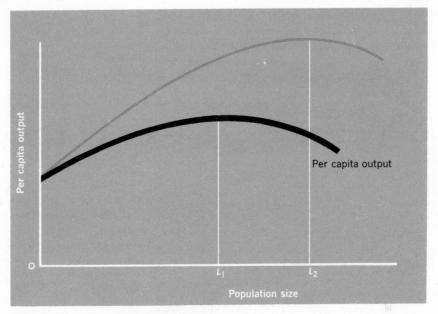

FIGURE 18-2. THE OPTIMUM POPULATION SIZE.
Given the quantity and quality of the nation's nonhuman resources, there is some
optimum population size such as L_1 at which real per capita output is at a maximum.
Increases in the quantity and quality of property resources will shift the point of optimum population size to the right, for example, from L_1 to L_2.

was approximately 94 per cent. Furthermore, the number of persons receiving college de- grees currently is almost twenty times greater than it was in 1900. The current illiteracy rate in the United States is about 2 per cent. And, of course, these statistics conceal improve- ments in the quality of education. Figure 18-3 indicates the occupational shifts which have occurred since 1870 and generally reflects an upgrading of the labor force. Note the relative decline in agriculture and the corresponding gains in professional and public services and the transportation-trade-finance occupations.

But here are some less encouraging consider- ations which tend to tarnish this glowing pic- ture. (1) Despite substantial evidence of teacher and classroom shortages, total annual expendi- tures on public education are only about 3 per cent of the GNP. (2) We apparently do a rather poor job of recruiting our best brains for col- lege; only about half of our ablest youth go on

to college. (3) Serious problems seem to be arising with respect to the composition of our labor force; workers who lose their jobs in de- clining industries generally do not have the brainpower or skills needed for reemployment in expanding industries. Although we defer any detailed discussion of these problems until Chapter 19, it should be emphasized that most authorities on economic growth feel that brain- power and the technological advances to which it gives rise are the most valuable resources of all. If this is accurate, then our economy may be failing to invest sufficient amounts in the development of its human resources.

Technological advance

Technological advance and capital formation are closely related processes. Technological ad- vance, the development and application of new products or new productive techniques, typic-

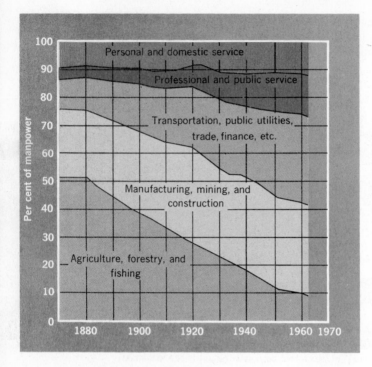

FIGURE 18-3. CHANGING INDUSTRIAL COMPOSITION OF AMERICAN MANPOWER, 1870–1962.
Long-term occupational shifts generally reflect an upgrading of the labor force. [J. Frederic Dewhurst and Associates, "America's Needs and Resources: A New Survey" (New York: The Twentieth Century Fund, Inc., 1955), p. 733. Estimates for 1962 by this author.]

ally entails investment in new machinery and equipment. The idea that there is a more efficient way to catch a rabbit than running it down led to investment in the bow and arrow. Yet in a few instances technological advance and capital accumulation are distinct. Example: modern crop rotation practices and contour plowing are ideas which contribute greatly to output, although they do not necessarily entail the use of more capital equipment. In any event we will find it rewarding to discuss technological advance and capital formation separately, recognizing that the two are usually birds of a feather.

What has been the rate of technological advance in the United States? It is very difficult to say with any real degree of precision. Simple observation recalls gas and diesel engines, conveyor belts, and assembly lines as some of the more historically profound technological advances. More recently, the lamp of technology has freed the automation jinni and with it the wonders of the electronic brains and the push-button factory. Indeed, the far-flung frontiers of technological advance are almost beyond the comprehension of the average man. Yet an examination of historical facts makes it clear that technological advance has not occurred at a balanced rate among various industries: the electronics, chemical, and metal fabrication industries, for example, have outdistanced agriculture and land transportation.

Recent empirical studies[6] suggest that technological advance is now the major factor underlying the growth record of American capitalism and that its importance is on the increase. Of the 3.5 per cent per annum increase in output which American capitalism has averaged since the early 1870s, approximately half is the result of increases in the stock of capital and in the supply of labor. Technological advance, abetted by concomitant increases in the quality of labor, accounts for the remaining half.

[6] See, in particular, Moses Abramovitz, *Resources and Output Trends in the United States Since 1870* (New York: National Bureau of Economic Research, 1956).

Research and invention. Technological advance involves both *invention*—the discovery and development of a new product or technique of production—and *innovation*—the practical application of the method, or commercial production of the product, which invention has provided.

Generally speaking, invention depends upon the quality and availability of scientific education and the provision of monetary and physical resources for basic research. We do have a rough indicator of the discovery aspect of technological advance—total research and development expenditures for the economy as a whole. Table 18-2 summarizes this data for the postwar era and provides an estimate for 1969. In absolute terms the picture to date looks very impressive, but much less so in relative terms. It is more than a bit disconcerting to find that American capitalism—the acclaimed fountainhead of technological progress—currently devotes a mere 2½ per cent of its total output to research. It is noteworthy, too, that a very substantial portion of our research expenditures originate in the public sector of the economy; private research expenditures as a per cent of GNP provide an even less impres-

sive figure. Worst of all, a significant portion of research expenditure is not for basic research but rather for applied research of an ofttimes trivial nature. It is debatable whether highly competent technicians should devote their waking hours to making Rusty Dusties the noisiest breakfast food on the market rather than to basic chemical, electronics, or space research. Brainpower is too precious a resource to squander on research of trivial importance. When political and military considerations are considered, the situation becomes more acute. As early as 1947 Soviet Russia spent as much as the United States did on research. But, because the Soviet national income was only about one-fourth that of the United States, Russia clearly devoted a relatively larger portion of her resources to the development and application of new technology.[7]

The point is this: by any reasonable absolute standard, American capitalism has done a most creditable job in achieving technological progress. Relative comparisons, however, are a bit less encouraging. For a wealthy nation the

[7] Report by the President's Scientific Research Board, *Science and Public Policy*, vol. I, August, 1947, pp. 5–6.

TABLE 18-2. SOURCES OF FUNDS FOR RESEARCH AND DEVELOPMENT IN THE UNITED STATES, 1945–1960 (in millions)

Year	*(1)* Total expenditures, or *(2) + (3) + (4)*	*(2)* Government	*(3)* Industry	*(4)* University	*(5)* Total research expenditures as a per cent of GNP
1945	$ 1,520	$ 1,070	$ 430	$ 20	0.7
1950	2,870	1,610	1,180	80	1.0
1954	5,150	2,740	2,240	170	1.4
1957	8,400	4,930	3,230	240	1.9
1959	10,990	7,050	3,660	280	2.3
1960	12,530	8,100	4,120	310	2.5
1969*	22,200	12,000	9,000	2,500	—

SOURCE: Department of Defense and National Science Foundation.
* Estimated figures for 1969 from Dexter Keezer, "American Economic Review," May, 1960, pp. 363–365.

United States may be considerably myopic in devoting resources to technological research and development.

Innovation. But the discovery of new technological knowledge is only half the battle. The commercial application of such discoveries in the production of goods is equally essential in achieving economic growth through technological advance. It is here that the size, vigor, and ability of the entrepreneurial class become all-important. Certainly other factors are vital. The costliness of financing the application of a technological improvement and its anticipated profitability undoubtedly play major roles in determining whether or not a new bit of technological know-how gets off the drawing board and is commercially applied. Yet in the long pull the most fundamental determinant of the commercial application of new technological knowledge is the character of the entrepreneur. Insight, foresight, vision, courage, adventuresomeness, the desire to make good—call it what you may, the leadership and vigor of the entrepreneurial class play the key role in determining how much new technological know-how gets out of the research department and into the assembly line. In a later section on allocative efficiency we shall note that the overall social-cultural-political environment of our economy generally has been highly receptive to the introduction of new products and new methods of production.

The future significance of technological advance—both invention and innovation—as an instrument of economic growth is visualized by a 1947 report of the President's Scientific Research Board:[8]

Throughout most of our history, the living standards of our people were raised by expanding our land areas and by bringing more and more acres under cultivation. That route has now been substantially closed for more than a generation, and we have increased our productivity through an advancing technology. The processes and machines we use in factories, the ways in which we raise and preserve

[8] *Science and Public Policy,* vol. I, p. 4.

food, all derive from theoretical discoveries in the basic sciences. The technology in which we excel and which has transformed us in some 80 years from a backward agricultural nation to a world power rests upon progress in the basic sciences. Only through research and more research can we provide the basis for an expanding economy and continued high levels of employment.

Capital formation

To a very considerable degree workers, regardless of their skills and training, are no better than the capital goods with which they are equipped. The indirect or roundabout production which capital goods affords is a basic means of enhancing productive efficiency. A nation's stock of capital goods is clearly a crucial factor in its growth potential.[9] Our American capitalism has managed to accumulate a larger stock of real capital than has any other nation of the world. Surprisingly, we are not exactly sure how much capital our economy has managed to accumulate in its lifetime. The difficulties of taking such an inventory are great; in particular, the problem of defining what is meant by "capital goods" is a difficult one.

We do know that on the average the American worker is better equipped with capital goods in his productive efforts than is the worker of any other nation. The average American worker in manufacturing is equipped with approximately $20,000 worth of capital equipment. We also know that the growth in capital facilities has been very rapid in recent years. During the war–postwar decade of the 1940s American capitalism ". . . doubled the aggregate manufacturing capacity of 1939–40 which had taken nearly three centuries to develop and build." [10] A recent estimate sets the value of America's industrial and commercial capital facilities alone at $442 billion in 1955, meas-

[9] It has recently been argued, however, that the role of capital, as opposed to human and institutional factors, in growth has been exaggerated. See Colin Clark, *Growthmanship* (London: Institute of Economic Affairs, 1961).

[10] Dewhurst, *op. cit.,* p. 813.

ured in 1929 prices. As compared to the 1869 estimate of $27 billion, this represents a sixteen-fold increase in 86 years![11]

In 1961 private businesses in the economy spent over $46 billion on capital facilities—machinery, equipment, and nonresidential construction. This means that almost 10 per cent of the economy's GNP is currently devoted to maintaining and expanding the productive facilities of private industry. Were we to add the basic "social capital" constructed by government—highways, hydroelectric dams, harbor and waterway improvements, and so forth—another $17 billion would be added to this $46 billion figure. Residential construction would involve another $21 billion.

IMPLEMENTAL FACTORS

So much for the permissive factors which expand the productive potential of the economy. Will the economy's actual performance keep pace with its expanding ability to produce? Is the economy sufficiently flexible to negotiate the continuous resource reallocations which economic growth demands?

Aggregate demand

The answers depend in part upon the level of aggregate demand. If the increased aggregate demand which the growth in real output induces is just sufficient to clear that extra output from the market, the economy's growth potential will just be realized. However, should the expansion in aggregate demand fall short of the expansion in the economy's ability to produce, society will squander a part of its enhanced productive potential through unemployment. On the other hand, if the increase in the productive ability of the economy gives rise to a surplus of added spending, inflation will accompany economic growth. In short, an expanding ability to produce does not ensure the occurrence of economic growth. The level of

[11] Simon Kuznets, *Capital in the American Economy* (New York: National Bureau of Economic Research, Inc., 1961), pp. 63–66.

aggregate demand must expand just enough to absorb that added output.

We discovered in Chapter 13 that whether or not an economy achieves full employment depends upon the interaction of its saving and investing plans. Businesses must be willing to invest an amount equal to the full-employment volume of saving if full employment is to be attained. In a static or stationary economy, that is, an economy whose permissive factors are such that its productive potential is fixed and unchanging, this is largely a matter of sustaining a constant level of investment year after year. But in a growing economy—one whose real national income is expanding—the problem is decidedly more complex. Why? Because in an expanding economy saving increases. Remember: households save a larger proportion of a large income than they do of a small income. This obviously means that if the expanding productive capacity of a growing economy is to be realized, investment spending must increase by the same amount as the full-employment level of saving.

Let us be more specific by examining a simple model. Suppose, first, that the economy is initially (in year 1) at the full-employment noninflationary level of output. Assume this entails a $500 billion NNP and a $50 billion level of investment. Suppose, secondly, that the economy is capable of expanding its total real output by 4 per cent per annum. And, finally, let us assume as in Chapter 13 that the MPS is one-fourth. Column 2 of Table 18-3 indicates that a 4 per cent rate of growth means that the economy is capable of producing $520 billion in year 2 ($500 billion plus 4 per cent of $500 billion). If businessmen attempt to utilize this increase in the economy's productive potential—that is, if businessmen produce the $520 billion NNP—will the economy spend enough to sustain this output? The answer hinges upon the rate of investment. The $20 billion increase in output and income will cause saving to increase by $5 billion (one-fourth of $20 billion). Investment spending must expand by a like amount in year 2 to compensate for this increase. Investment spending must expand from $50 to $55 billion for the growth

TABLE 18-3. INVESTMENT REQUIREMENTS IN A GROWING ECONOMY
(all figures in billions)

(1) Year	(2) Full employment NNP at 4 per cent annual growth rate	(3) Annual increase in saving	(4) Investment required to achieve full em- ployment NNP
1	$500.0	—	$50.0
2	520.0	$5.0	55.0
3	540.8	5.2	60.2
4	562.4	5.4	65.6
	etc.	etc.	etc.

potential of the economy to be realized in year 2. In year 3 the investment requirement is even greater. The economy is capable of producing an output of $540.8 billion. But the $20.8 billion increase in output and income which occurs between years 2 and 3 gives rise to $5.2 billion in additional saving. This means that investment spending must rise from an annual rate of $55 billion in year 2 to a $60.2 billion rate in year 3. And so it goes for succeeding years. The basic lesson of this simplified illustration is clear *the maintenance of a given rate of growth requires a constantly expanding volume of investment spending.* Needless to say, to increase the rate of growth requires that investment increase at an even more rapid rate.

What are American capitalism's prospects for realizing its growth potential? More specifically, will investment spending be sufficiently great to absorb the increasing volume of saving which tends to occur in an expanding full-employment economy? There are many different views on this all-important question. Here we briefly sketch the two extremes.[12]

Economic stagnation. During the prolonged depression of the thirties, many eminent economists envisioned our economy as reaching

[12] The interested reader will find A. E. Burns, A. C. Neal, and D. S. Watson, *Modern Economics*, 2d ed. (New York: Harcourt, Brace & World, Inc., 1953), chap. 43, very rewarding reading.

maturity. This maturity, it was argued, stemmed from a weakening of the basic forces underlying the incentive to invest. The result would be that planned investment would fall short of planned saving at full employment, so that there would be a chronic tendency towards unemployment and a failure of the economy to realize its growth potential.

More specifically, the stagnationist view contends that those forces which underlay the tremendous economic expansion of the nineteenth century—rapid population growth, geographic expansion, the capital-using character of technological advance, and the spirit of enterprise—are weakening in the twentieth century.

1. In the past rapid population growth gave rise to relatively cheap labor and at the same time an upsurging demand for goods and services of every kind. But this growth is now tapering off. While each decade of the 1800s brought an increase of one-fourth to one-third in the size of the American population, this rate of increase fell to about 15 per cent in the 1910s and 1920s and plummeted to about 7 per cent in the depressed thirties. This means fewer mouths to feed and fewer human beings to house and clothe. And shrinking markets dampen the incentives to purchase capital goods.

2. Furthermore, in the past geographic expansion—conquering the West—provided new,

abundant, and therefore cheap sources of raw materials and simultaneously the demand for huge quantities of investment in basic capital facilities—new roads, railways, housing, public utilities, and so forth. But now the unexplored and unexploited frontier is no more. The discovery of new sources of cheap raw materials has become increasingly rare; and the insatiable demand for basic capital goods which characterizes the opening of new territories is now largely fulfilled. Geographic maturity has lessened the number of profitable investment opportunities in the same way as has the slackening of population growth.

3. The stagnationists also argue that the scope and character of technological advance are changing in such a way that its expansive impact upon investment is weakening. On the one hand, future prospects appear dim for the future development of "great new industries" comparable to the railroads, iron and steel, electricity, and the automobile. No longer can we expect the growth of similar industries which call for tremendous investment in themselves and in a host of related industries. The automobile industry, for example, not only required large and sustained investment spending in itself, but also stimulated large-scale supplementary investment in roads and highways, petroleum, rubber, glass, and so forth. New industries do not have this explosive impact upon investment. New innovations are not so revolutionary as the automobile or electricity. And supplementary industries already exist— in many instances with excess capacity—to supply needed materials and parts.

On the other hand, the stagnationists argue that the very nature of technological advance is changing. While the great technological advances of the past were capital-consuming, more recent advances are capital-saving. For example, the development of the wireless and diesel engines has actually diminished rather than increased the need for investment in capital facilities.

4. Finally, the stagnationists believe that the closing of the frontier has weakened the spirit of enterprise in our economy. The untouched resources and unsettled lands of the West fostered a vigorous entrepreneurial spirit, char-

acterized by optimism and the willingness to undertake risky investments. The settling of the West, it is argued, has replaced this adventuresomeness with conservatism. Investors now shun the "long shots" in favor of the "sure things."

The stagnationist conclusion? The weakening of these basic expansive forces which had provided a rapid growth rate in the past will mean chronic unemployment for American capitalism in the future unless government steps in to bolster the economy through appropriate monetary and fiscal measures.

Economic expansion. Other equally eminent economists whom we shall label the "expansionists" take a more optimistic view of the economy's chances of realizing its growth potential.

Declines in the rate of population growth and the closing of the frontier are hardly recent phenomena, argue the expansionists. The rate of population growth began to decline in the mid-1800s, and the frontier was closed by 1900. If these factors are so crucial to high levels of investment and employment, why was their impact not felt until the Great Depression of the 1930s? Furthermore, other nations have adjusted to decreasing rates of population growth and have persisted in economic expansion. Conversely, some nations with large and rapidly expanding populations are poverty-stricken. More positively, the expansionists contend that investment is not rigidly linked to the number of mouths to feed and bodies to house and clothe but depends as much upon the quantity and quality of goods the population is willing and able to purchase. A higher standard of living for a slowly growing population will call for as much investment as will a relatively constant standard of living for a rapidly expanding population. In any event the fact is that the rate of population growth in the United States is not declining as it was during the depressed 1930s; on the contrary, our rate of population growth is rising. Hence, *if* population growth is a basic force underlying economic expansion, this force is currently working on the side of vigorous economic growth.

More important is the fact that the expansionists envision virtually boundless investment opportunities in the future. As we continue to probe the depths of the atomic age and stand on the threshold of the space age, it is most difficult to accept the notion that profitable investment opportunities are drying up because of a weakening of technological advance. It is much more likely that the future holds a rapid acceleration of technological advance. Witness the recent development of man-made fibers, plastics, and the many rapid advances in the electronics field. And, although the development of television, air conditioners, and food freezers may not entail the supplementary investment required by the railroads or the automobile industry, the combined impact of a large number of these less dramatic innovations cannot be minimized.

The expansionists therefore conclude that American capitalism will continue to provide investment opportunities sufficient for the achievement of an expanding full-employment level of national income. Certainly the virtually uninterrupted prosperity and growth of the 1940s and 1950s, argue the expansionists, undermine the stagnation view and support the expansionist position.

Which view is correct? We really do not know. On the one hand, reasoning by historical analogy is a dangerous business. While it is perfectly logical to interpret the Great Depression as a manifestation of stagnation, it is also possible to view it as an unfortunately severe depression arising from the unhappy, but temporary, simultaneous collapse in a variety of factors underlying investment spending. Conversely, one may interpret the booming forties and fifties as indisputable evidence of the vigor of American capitalism. But one may also ask if this growth would have been realized in the absence of extremely high and prolonged government spending stemming from World War II and the cold war. Furthermore, cause and effect are hopelessly intertwined. Depression may be the result of declining rates of population growth and technological advance; but depression also causes these rates to decline. And the same holds true of periods of

growth. An expanding economy provides the standard of living which permits early marriages and large families and an environment highly receptive to innovation. The inability to assess accurately the validity of these two views does not lessen the importance of the question to which they are addressed.

It is not surprising that this long-standing debate still rages, but in a somewhat new guise. The question now is not so much one of decay versus expansion, but rather, "Has American capitalism's rate of growth been adequate?" In Chapter 19 we shall pursue this growth rate controversy and its policy implications.

Allocative efficiency

The social environment of an economy can be every bit as significant as its physical environment in influencing economic growth. The social environment of any society must meet two requirements to facilitate economic growth. First, it must encourage those changes in products, productive techniques, and capital facilities which are vital to economic growth. Second, it must provide a suitable mechanism for negotiating with reasonable efficiency the reallocations of resources which are appropriate to the development of new products, new productive techniques, and changes in the stock of capital goods.

The social environment. Over-all the social-cultural-political environment of the United States has been very conducive to economic growth. There are several interrelated factors which comprise this favorable environment. First, as opposed to many other nations, there are virtually no social or moral taboos upon production and material progress. The free and individualistic nature of our economy has been generally conducive to the development of new products and new methods of production. Consumers are free and ordinarily willing to try new products. Indeed, American social philosophy has embraced the notion that material advance is an attainable and highly desirable economic goal. The inventor, the innovator, and the business executive are accorded high degrees of prestige and respect in American society. Second, Americans have traditionally possessed healthy attitudes towards work and risk-taking; our society has benefitted from a willing labor force and an ample supply of entrepreneurs. Third, our economy has been characterized by a stable political system wherein internal order, the right of property ownership, the legal status of enterprise, and the enforcement of contracts have been fostered. Though not subject to quantification, this bundle of characteristics has undoubtedly provided an excellent foundation for American economic growth.

The price system. Furthermore, historical observation tells us that the price system of American capitalism has performed reasonably well as a mechanism for negotiating the reallocations of resources which economic growth demands. New methods and new products call for realignments of resources. And the price system, we have seen, provides the carrot of profits and the stick of losses to induce the expansion of innovating industries and to force the contraction of those industries whose products have been rendered obsolete or less desirable by these advances. The ebb and flow of economic progress shoves old industries into oblivion and creates whole new industries to replace the old. The demise of the steam locomotive industry and the more or less simultaneous rise of the diesel locomotive industry are one of innumerable examples. The tremendous stimulus which the automobile industry gave to the steel, rubber, and petroleum industries has already been cited. The death blow which the automobile industry dealt the carriage makers is the other side of the picture.

Figure 18-3 provides a rough outline of some of the reallocations of labor which the price system has negotiated over a long period of years. Most obvious is the relative shift of labor from agricultural pursuits to other types of productive endeavor—particularly to trade, transportation, and white-collar work. Agriculture accounted for over half of the economy's employment in 1870, but only about 11 per cent in 1960. In contrast professional and pub-

lic service engaged about 3½ per cent of the economy's labor force in 1870; by 1960 this figure was about 15 per cent. These are clearly significant shifts in the allocation of manpower.

Impediments to allocative efficiency. But economic change is not an unmixed blessing. The rise of new prosperous industries and the decline of old unprosperous industries is an essential feature of economic progress, desirable from the viewpoint of society as a whole. Businesses and resource suppliers caught in declining industries are adversely affected by economic growth; they face declining incomes and the prospect of painful and costly readjustments to other expanding lines of production. It is not surprising that adversely affected groups have sought to impede the reallocations of resources essential to economic growth. Illustrations are rather numerous.

Monopolies in both product and resource markets have retarded the reallocations of resources required for economic growth. Business monopolies may find it more profitable to suppress a newly discovered product or productive technique than to have their present capital facilities rendered obsolete before they have been fully depreciated. Furthermore, remember that the expansion of prosperous industries is a self-limiting process; as new firms enter growing industries, economic profits are competed away. Therefore, firms now established in these prosperous industries may contrive monopolistic restrictions upon the entry of new firms in an effort to preserve economic profits for themselves. Some labor unions have followed similar policies, resisting new work methods which threaten to cause unemployment by making workers more productive. To illustrate: unions in the building trades have staunchly resisted the use of spray guns, fearing that workers will paint themselves out of jobs. And some unions, following restrictive membership policies, such as limiting the number of apprentices or charging high initiation fees, have created an artificial obstacle to labor mobility and have therefore limited the reallocation of human resources demanded by economic growth. Example: a growing economy typically wants more and better housing and relatively less food. This calls for fewer farmers and more carpenters, that is, a re-channeling of labor from the farm to housing projects. But the restrictive membership practices of certain building trades unions have impeded this shift.[13]

Other groups adversely affected by economic growth have been unable to resist its effects by their own tactics. Many of these have exerted political pressure for assistance, and some have received it. For example, a variety of forces (which will be detailed in a later chapter) have made agriculture a declining industry; that is, a smaller number of farmers can now produce more than enough food and fiber for the economy. This calls for a reallocation of resources from agriculture to relatively more productive uses in industry. However, public policy in the form of price supports and other subsidies have bolstered farmers' incomes and impeded the price system in reallocating farmers from agriculture to other industries where their productivity and incomes would be considerably higher. Similarly, the American watch industry has long been faced with the prospect of extinction because of the severe competition provided by foreign watches. But the American industry—manufacturers supported by the unions—has retarded this decline by seeking and getting a measure of relief from this competition through governmental enactment of higher tariffs (excise taxes) on imported watches.

These artificial impediments to growth are enforced by certain inherent resource immobilities. Apart from union and business monopolies, resources are far from perfectly mobile. The obstacles to labor mobility, for example, are many and varied. Geographic immobility stems from the reluctance of workers to break

[13] It should be emphasized that many unions have been receptive to technological advance, demanding only that (1) new machines and methods be introduced in an orderly way to facilitate the reabsorption of technologically unemployed workers and (2) the business community and society as a whole share in the costs of technological unemployment.

existing social ties, move to a new community, meet new people, and take roots. Moreover, in so far as occupational mobility is concerned, it is no easy chore to abandon one's life work at, say, middle age and assume the responsibility, costs, and inconvenience of learning a new trade. Immobility is even more evident when it comes to property resources. To use an extreme example, a wheat combine is completely immobile in the sense that it has only one use, and, price system or no price system, a combine cannot be shifted to the manufacture of automobiles or plastic toys.

But over time resource immobilities become less important. The sixty-year-old farmer who has worked the land since he was sixteen is not likely to obey the dictates of the price system to take a factory job in the city. But his son, particularly if he goes to college, will probably not go back to the farm. Instead, he is likely to seek out employment in more profitable, expanding, and therefore higher-paying industries. Many a farmer's son is now in engineering college, and if he ever comes into contact with a John Deere tractor, it will probably be on a drafting board and not in a corn field. Figure 18-3 makes it clear that decades may be involved in negotiating significant transfers in the employment of human resources.

Furthermore, even durable capital wears out in time and may not be replaced. A farm combine is useless in automobile manufacturing, but in time the combine may wear out and not be replaced. Money capital formerly flowing into farm equipment may now finance new and expanded capital facilities for the automobile industry. Hence, over the years the composition of the economy's stock of real capital changes; capital goods are in effect shifted among alternative uses.

PUBLIC POLICY

It will come as no surprise that public policy may have a very profound effect upon the growth process. Public policy affects not only the implemental factors, but also the permissive factors which underlie economic growth. Government can either tighten the reins or apply the whip to economic growth. The broad sweep of history reveals that government has actually done much to facilitate growth in the United States. Free or cheap land policies hastened westward expansion. Subsidies to railroads widened the domestic market and laid the framework for huge volumes of investment spending. Government's contributions to highway construction and communications provided a similar stimulus. More recently, we find government sharing the spotlight with private industry in financing research activity (Table 18-2). And, needless to say, the monetary and fiscal policies of government can have a crucial bearing upon the ability of the economy to achieve the level of aggregate demand required to realize fully its growth potential. In Chapter 19 we shall have occasion to outline a number of specific policies through which government might accelerate the growth rate. This is not to deny that there have been political blunders. But even from the vantage point of the present, it is fairly evident that government policies again and again have cut a clear path for economic development.

Not only does public policy affect economic growth; economic growth may also entail significant implications for the scope and character of public policies. For example, a wealthy, expanding economy can afford certain public policies—a very comprehensive social security system—which would be an intolerable burden for a less opulent society. Furthermore, as was suggested in Chapter 6, the wants of an expanding economy may change in favor of relatively larger amounts of social goods and relatively smaller amounts of private goods, implying an expanding economic role for government. Finally, growth and affluency may allow government to use certain techniques in the implementation of public policy which would be intolerable in a poorer society. To illustrate: traditionally the use of the sales tax has been strongly resisted by Congress because of its regressivity and the relatively heavy burden it imposes upon low-income families. This objec-

tion is substantially weakened, however, as economic growth causes low-income families virtually to disappear.

SUMMARY

1. Economic growth may be defined either in terms of (*a*) an expanding real national output (income) or (*b*) an expanding per capita real output (income).

2. Economic growth (*a*) provides a higher standard of living, (*b*) lessens the acuteness of domestic economic problems, (*c*) is a source of aid to less developed nations, and (*d*) is essential in meeting the Soviet economic challenge.

3. The permissive factors in economic growth are (*a*) the quantity and quality of a nation's natural resources, (*b*) the quantity and quality of its human resources, (*c*) its stock of capital facilities, and (*d*) its technology. Two implemental factors—a sufficient level of aggregate demand and allocative efficiency—are essential if the economy is to realize its growth potential.

4. In general the economy of the United States is amply endowed with natural resources. Scarcities of specific resources have been largely overcome by technological advances which have permitted the more efficient use and acquisition of such resources and the development of new substitute materials. Furthermore, in some cases abundant foreign supplies have been tapped to relieve specific scarcities. Lastly, the price system automatically tends to conserve on those resources which are most scarce.

5. Historically the American population has grown rapidly. At any point in time there is some specific optimum population which, given the nation's supplies of other resources, will provide a maximum output per person. While the education and training of the American labor force is relatively high, there is ample room for improvement.

6. Economists are assigning an increasingly crucial role to technological progress—research and innovation—in the process of economic growth. Currently the United States devotes only about 2½ per cent of its GNP to research, some of which is not of a very fundamental character.

7. In relation to other nations, American workers are very well equipped with capital facilities. However, growth in our stock of capital goods has been very irregular.

8. In a growing full-employment economy, saving tends to rise in relation to the national income. This means that a constantly increasing volume of investment spending is necessary if full employment is to be sustained. The stagnationists contend that the forces underlying investment—population growth, the frontier, the rise of great new capital-consuming industries, and the spirit of enterprise—are weakening to the end that persistent governmental fiscal and monetary actions will be required if chronic unemployment is to be avoided. On the other hand, the expansionists question the weakening of these forces and contend that technological advance may well occur at an accelerated pace in the future; therefore they conclude that investment and aggregate demand should be sufficient to sustain an expanding full-employment output.

9. The American social-cultural-political environment has been conducive to economic growth. The price system has been a reasonably efficient mechanism for negotiating those resource reallocations which economic progress invariably entails. However, impediments to reallocations do exist, particularly in the form of product and resource market monopolies and the more or less inherent immobilities of both human and property resources.

10. Public policy affects the growth process through both the permissive and the implemental factors in the growth process. In turn economic growth can influence the scope and character of public policies.

QUESTIONS AND STUDY SUGGESTIONS

1. Define economic growth. Describe the rate of growth achieved in American capitalism.

2. What difficulties are involved in measuring economic growth? Specifically, what roles do leisure and improvements in product quality play in the growth process?

3. "Economic growth entails a shifting of the production possibilities curve outward and to the right." Explain.

4. What are the major causes of economic growth? "There are both a demand and a supply side to economic growth." Explain. Why might it be important to distinguish between the "permissive" and the "implemental" factors underlying growth?

5. How do you account for the rapid increase in the rate of population growth which began in the early 1940s? "Population might increase but at the same time the labor force might shrink." Explain. Define and explain the concept of an optimum population.

6. What major occupational shifts have occurred in the allocation of labor resources? How are they to be explained?

7. "The greatest conserver of scarce natural resources is the price mechanism." Explain. In what ways has technological advance alleviated acute resource shortages? Be specific.

8. "If we want economic growth in a free society, we may have to accept a measure of instability." Evaluate.

9. "Technological advance is bound to play a more important role in economic growth in the future than it has in the past." Do you agree?

10. Explain and evaluate: "The American economy invests too much in machinery and not enough in people."

11. Why is resource mobility essential to economic growth? "Resource immobilities are less in the long run than they are in the short run." Explain.

12. What role do social, cultural, political, and institutional forces play in economic growth? Be as specific as you can.

13. The noted philosopher Alfred North Whitehead once remarked that ". . . the art of progress is to preserve order amid change and to preserve change amid order." What did he mean? Is this contention relevant for economic growth? What implications might this have for public policy? Explain.

14. "Public policy affects and is affected by economic growth." Explain and illustrate.

SELECTED REFERENCES

Abramovitz, Moses, "Economics of Growth," in Bernard F. Haley (ed.), *A Survey of Contempory Economics*, vol. II (Homewood, Ill.: Richard D. Irwin, Inc., 1952).

American Economic Review, Papers and Proceedings, May, 1956.

Committee for Economic Development, *Economic Growth in the United States: Its Past and Future* (New York: Committee for Economic Development, February, 1958).

Committee for Economic Development, *Problems of United States Economic Development* (New York: Committee for Economic Development, January, 1958).

Joint Economic Committee, *Staff Report on Employment, Growth, and Price Levels* (Washington: 1960), chaps. 1 and 2.

Morris, Bruce R., *Problems of American Economic Growth* (New York: Oxford University Press, 1961), chaps. 1–7.

Rostow, W. W., *The Stages of Economic Growth* (New York: Cambridge University Press, 1960).

Villard, Henry H., *Economic Development* (New York: Holt, Rinehart and Winston, Inc., 1959), chaps. 1–10.

Chapter 19

GROWTH IN AMERICAN CAPITALISM: COSTS, PROBLEMS, AND POLICIES

WE DISCOVERED in Chapter 18 that economic growth is a highly desirable state of affairs. Growth means a higher standard of living domestically; it is a palliative for domestic economic problems; and growth can provide the wherewithal for meeting the Soviet challenge and the acute needs of the underdeveloped nations. Other things being equal, there is no question but that rapid growth is clearly preferable to slow or modest growth. But we must now recognize that rapid economic growth is not free for the asking; nor is it a panacea for all our problems. Indeed, rapid growth may entail certain costs and may create, or contribute to, a number of economic problems.

It is the purpose of this chapter to examine some of these less pleasant facets of economic growth. First, some of the reasonably evident costs or sacrifices which the attainment of rapid growth may entail are enumerated. Second, the increasingly troublesome problem posed by the chronically depressed areas will be given rather detailed treatment. Third, the very controversial question of whether United States economic growth has been sufficiently rapid will be analyzed. Finally, we will explore the contention that the causes and character of inflation may change as an expanding economy reaches an advanced stage of growth and

study the implications of this eventuality for public policy.[1] All of this discussion is placed in the context of American capitalism. That is, we are addressing ourselves to the growth problems of an advanced economy rather than to those great obstacles faced by underdeveloped nations (Chapter 39).

THE COSTS OF ECONOMIC GROWTH

Despite the many desirable aspects of an expanding economy, it must be acknowledged that the pursuit of almost any economic objective—including rapid economic growth—entails certain costs and sacrifices. For the most part these costs, once mentioned, are sufficiently obvious to merit only brief comment. First, our production possibilities analysis of Chapter 2 reminds us that provision for the necessary research, education, capital equipment, and so forth which are so essential to rapid growth must come at the expense of current consumption. More "goods for the future" can be pro-

[1] Another problem associated with a growing, increasingly affluent economy will be deferred until Chapter 36. This is the problem of social balance—the question of whether an expanding economy tends to produce too much private goods and not enough social goods.

vided only at the cost of less "goods for the present." Second, rapid growth means an accelerated tempo of industrial life. Declines in leisure, or sacrifices of potential increases in leisure, are involved. And a higher participation rate in the labor force may be required, that is, more women, oldsters, and youngsters may be required to hold jobs. It is of interest to note that the ulcer rate is said to be extremely high among Soviet plant managers who are under great pressure from the government to fulfill or overfulfill their assigned production targets. Third, history suggests that rapid growth may be accompanied and nurtured by the wasteful exploitation of natural resources. Fourth, a growing, changing economy may be increasingly susceptible to instability. For example, the high level of total demand that is requisite to full employment and vigorous economic expansion may make it more difficult to achieve price stability. Finally, brisk growth implies rapid changes in the structure and character of the economic system; these changes may result in insecurity and unemployment for adversely affected businessmen and workers. This final point has been of increasing consequence for the United States in the postwar years and now merits detailed examination.

STRUCTURAL UNEMPLOYMENT AND DISTRESSED AREAS

In Chapter 11 we noted that the United States has encountered no serious depressions since World War II; massive unemployment has been avoided. On the other hand, postwar growth has been disrupted by three recessions (1948–1949, 1953–1954, and 1957–1958) wherein unemployment rates have been roughly double the 3 per cent "hard core" unemployment rate we have associated with "full employment" (Chapter 11). Indeed, since 1947 the average annual rate of unemployment has been about 4.5 per cent of the labor force (see Table 19-1). The addition of part-time workers who would prefer longer hours might easily add a million workers to the ranks of the unemployed and bring the above figure close to 6 per cent.

There are several less evident aspects of postwar unemployment which add to the seriousness of the situation. On the one hand, there is evidence (Table 19-1) to suggest that persistent unemployment may be on the increase. The recovery from each of the three postwar recessions seems to have been less vigorous and less complete. As Table 19-1 suggests, the postwar era may be bringing us face-to-face with a problem of "creeping unemployment." Second, unemployment seems to be of a longer duration. The portion of the unemployed who have been without work for six months or more has been on the increase. Third, only about one-half of those unemployed in years of over-all prosperity are explainable as those temporarily unemployed because of the seasonality of their industry or because they have voluntarily quit their old jobs to seek something better. In other words, about half the unemployed are clearly those who are involuntarily unemployed and who may encounter serious and prolonged difficulties in finding new jobs.

Structural unemployment

More and more economists are becoming convinced that this growing residue of unemployment is to be associated not with a deficiency of total spending, but rather with the failure of the economy to adjust fully and efficiently to certain basic changes associated with economic growth. More specifically, such factors as rapid changes in technology, shifts in the pattern of consumer demand, and the geographic relocation of industry call for substantial occupational and geographic shifts on the part of adversely affected workers if they are to be reemployed. The failure of adjustments of the required magnitude to occur has resulted in a number of chronically depressed areas—areas whose unemployment rates are substantially and persistently higher than the national average. These are very adversely affected by downswings in the national economy and recover only slowly and partially during a national economic upswing. Most of the major chronically depressed areas are in the Northeastern United States, as Figure 19-1

TABLE 19-1. UNEMPLOYMENT AND NUMBER OF MAJOR DEPRESSED AREAS, 1947 TO 1960

Year	Per cent of civilian labor force unemployed	Number of major depressed areas
1947	3.9%	*
1948	3.8	*
1949	5.9	*
1950	5.3	*
1951	3.3	15
1952	3.1	20
1953	2.9	17
1954	5.6	42
1955	4.4	33
1956	4.2	21
1957	4.3	22
1958	6.8	77
1959	5.5	54
1960	5.6	38

* Data not available.
SOURCE: Department of Labor.

FIGURE 19-1. CHRONICALLY DEPRESSED AREAS IN THE UNITED STATES.
Although minor and major areas of chronic unemployment were distributed among some twenty-two states in 1961, most of the major depressed areas are in the northeastern quarter of the United States. [Committee for Economic Development, "Distressed Areas in a Growing Economy" (New York: Committee for Economic Development, June, 1961), p. 22.]

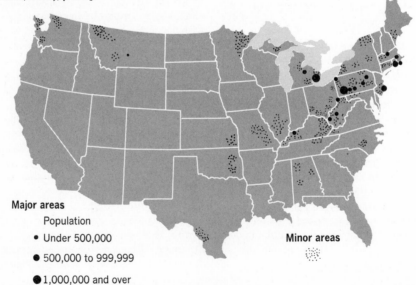

Major areas
    Population
    • Under 500,000
    ● 500,000 to 999,999
    ●1,000,000 and over

Minor areas

indicates. When smaller or minor areas of chronic unemployment are added, we find some twenty-two states are currently plagued with this problem.

Causes of structural unemployment

How did these chronically depressed areas get that way? Generally speaking, these are areas which have been highly dependent upon one or maybe two firms or industries as sources of income and employment. These firms or industries have been adversely affected, that is, they have become declining industries, because of one or more of the previously cited basic changes associated with the dynamic nature of a growing economy. Some illustrations will be helpful.[2] A number of chronically distressed areas in West Virginia, Pennsylvania, Kentucky, and southern Illinois are the result of the decline of the coal mining industry. This decline has a number of diverse causes: coal has lost out to gas and oil in home heating; technological advances in coal mining equipment have substantially reduced the need for labor; export markets for coal have dwindled because of increases in foreign trade barriers. In the cotton and wool textile manufacturing industries, firms have found it economically justified to migrate from New England and the Middle Atlantic states and relocate in North and South Carolina and Georgia, resulting in large numbers of stranded workers in the former areas. Competition from newer synthetic products and increased foreign competition have also contributed to the overall decline of the textile industry. Certain areas heavily dependent upon the manufacture and repair of railway equipment, for example, Centralia, Illinois, and Altoona, Pennsylvania, have become distressed areas largely as the result of the shift from steam to diesel engines, the persistent decline in railway passenger traffic, and inroads made on freight traffic by truck lines. Automation, changes in emphasis in government defense spending, alterations in the pat-

tern of consumer preferences as between various automobile makes and models, and the decentralization of automobile manufacturing facilities, have all contributed to chronic unemployment in Detroit and a number of other Michigan communities. It is of considerable significance that most of these chronically depressed areas are heavily populated areas. Hence, the unemployment situation—the decline in the absolute number of job opportunities—is seriously aggravated by a rapidly expanding population and labor force.

In short, the changes which characterize a growing, dynamic economy—technological changes as reflected in both products and capital equipment, changes in consumer preferences, and so forth—cause some industries and sectors of the economy to decline significantly and rapidly in importance. This has meant substantial amounts of noncyclical unemployment in adversely affected areas.

From brawn to brains

But, you might ask, won't a growing economy create enough new jobs to absorb the unemployed of the depressed areas? Shouldn't a readjustment or reallocation process such as described in Chapter 5 resolve this type of problem? The answer is that the effectiveness of the reallocation process is seriously hampered by two facts: (1) the rapidly expanding industries (electronics, plastics, antibiotics, synthetic fibers) are generally located in areas geographically distant from the distressed areas; and (2) the new jobs provided by these expanding industries typically call for more skill and training than unemployed workers in the distressed areas possess. The "men available" ads are placed by the unskilled and semiskilled, while the "help wanted" ads come from companies seeking professional people, scientists, executives, and technicians. A very remarkable change in the structure of employment opportunities is illustrated in Figure 19-2. Employment in goods-producing industries has been declining relative to employment in service industries. Absolutely the number of jobs in goods-producing industries was about the same in 1960 as in 1919, while the number of jobs in service industries has in-

[2] These examples are taken from the Committee for Economic Development, *Distressed Areas in a Growing Economy* (New York: Committee for Economic Development, June, 1961), pp. 24–28.

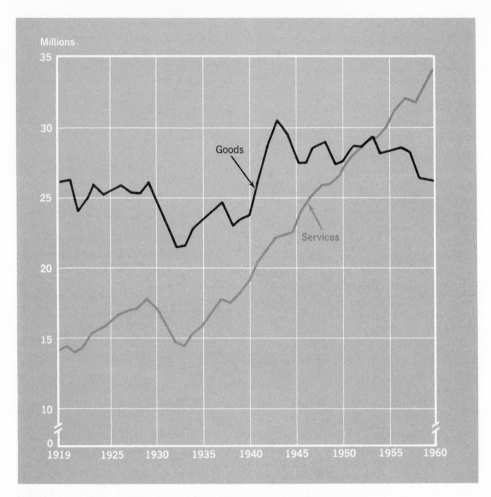

FIGURE 19-2. EMPLOYMENT IN GOODS-PRODUCING INDUSTRIES AND IN SERVICE INDUSTRIES.
In the last three decades employment has increased rather steadily in the service industries. The goods-producing industries, on the other hand, provide about the same number of jobs now as they did at the end of World War I. [Joint Economic Committee, "Staff Report on Employment, Growth, and Price Levels" (Washington: Government Printing Office, 1959), p. 174.]

creased from about 14 million in 1919 to 34 million in 1960. Figure 19-3 provides a more detailed portrayal of this phenomenon.

Why has this dramatic shift from blue-collar to white-collar labor—from brawn to brains— occurred? The answer, most simply stated, is "automation." The use of more and better capital equipment has put a ceiling on the number of material-goods–producing jobs, *despite* rapid population growth and massive government spending on military goods. Automation has permitted us to meet an expanding demand for material goods with a constant or a slightly declining number of material-goods workers. But at the same time the development and application of increasingly complex productive equipment has expanded greatly the job opportunities for all breeds of scientists, for

FIGURE 19-3. SHIFTS IN THE SIZE OF MAJOR OCCUPATIONAL GROUPS
BETWEEN 1950 AND 1960.

National requirements for higher skills have been increasing, while automation has
been replacing workers in many of the less skilled occupations. The shifts toward
higher proportions of professional, technical, and highly trained workers are expected
to continue in the 1960s. [Committee for Economic Development, "Distressed Areas
in a Growing Economy" (New York: Committee for Economic Development, June,
1961), p. 47.]

Occupational groups	Number of workers (thousands)		Percentage	
	1950	1960	Decrease	Increase
Professional, technical and kindred workers	4,910	7,566		54.1
Service workers	5,694	8,229		44.5
Managers, officials and proprietors except farm	5,018	6,960		38.7
Clerical and kindred workers	6,895	9,539		38.2
Craftsmen, foremen and kindred workers	7,783	8,342		7.2
Sales workers	3,927	4,172		6.2
Operatives and kindred workers	11,872	12,025		1.3
Laborers, except farm and mine	3,431	3,151	−8.2	
Farmers and farm laborers	6,709	4,283	−36.2	
Total	56,239	64,267		14.3

technicians, for supervisory personnel, and for high-caliber managers. Here's the nub of the structural unemployment problem: the machine-displaced blue collar workers frequently do not have the skills or education prerequisite for re-employment in most available white-collar jobs. The labor supply has failed to adjust adequately to the change in the composition or structure of labor demand.

Public policy and the distressed areas

What is the outlook for the chronically depressed areas? What remedies are appropriate?

Though it is not easy to generalize, we must frankly recognize that the outlook for many of the distressed areas is not particularly favorable. Chronic unemployment tends to create conditions which impede recovery. New industries (which, remember, seek mostly skilled, technical, and professional labor) are not likely to locate in depressed areas where manual and semiskilled labor are in surplus. Indeed, the labor force of a depressed area may deteriorate qualitatively as the younger, more capable workers move to other areas, leaving the older, less capable workers behind. A depressed regional market is obviously not an attractive place in which a consumer goods producer might locate. Furthermore, there is the bald fact that those declining areas which owe their former prosperity to now-declining extractive industries—for example, coal—may offer no locational advantages for other types of industry. There are no compelling reasons why new industries will be attracted to the hills of West Virginia as the mines afford fewer and fewer jobs. Finally, community services upon which industry depends may also seriously deteriorate as unemployment persists: bond issues and tax increases for the maintenance, much less the improving, of public utilities, school systems, streets, and so forth, are increasingly unlikely to be realized. All this makes the community less attractive to new industry.

Now what about remedies? Most obviously, over-all national prosperity helps, but does not erase, chronic unemployment. The nature of structural unemployment calls for more selective remedies. These take two general forms: (1) the relocation of unemployed workers and (2) the economic rehabilitation of the area. Or, in other words, remedies lie in moving the unemployed to new jobs in more prosperous areas or moving the new jobs (that is, new industries) into the areas of unemployment.

If the prospects for economic rehabilitation are dismal, special policies to induce a more rapid geographic outmigration of workers from the distressed areas are in order. Publicly sponsored programs to recruit and relocate the surplus labor of the chronically depressed areas through an expansion of the activities of the United States Employment Service are a frequently recommended policy. This action might be supplemented by legislation which provides for government payment of transportation and moving costs for those families willing to leave the distressed areas in favor of more prosperous regions. If area rehabilitation seems feasible, proposals such as the following might be helpful: (1) the Federal government might provide financial and technical assistance in helping local authorities evaluate their circumstances and formulate realistic redevelopment programs; (2) the Federal government might provide financial assistance to depressed municipalities and regions for the revitalization of their public facilities and services—schools, roads, water and electric utilities, and so forth—which are so essential to the attraction of new industries; (3) the Federal government in cooperation with state and local governments may make available long-term, low-interest loans to prospective employers who are willing to establish themselves in distressed areas; (4) provided minimum requirements of economic and locational efficiency can be met, the depressed areas should be given special consideration in the granting of public contracts and in the location of public facilities.

Whether the solution for a distressed area entails worker migration or area rehabilitation, vocational retraining will typically be required to match now-unemployed workers to new job opportunities (see Figure 19-3). Hence, most aid programs advocate the use of Federal funds to support vocational training. And it is often recommended that unemployed workers undergoing vocational retraining and who are not already receiving unemployment compensation payments should be extended these benefits through their retraining period. Until relocation or area rehabilitation is realized, the immediate needs of unemployed workers might be met by such measures as extending unemployment compensation benefits to those who do not qualify or who have exhausted their claims, by free distribution of government-owned food surpluses, and so forth. Advocates of the several specific aid proposals here outlined point out that the required government outlays on these programs should be large enough to work effectively toward a solution of the problem; these programs, if adopted, may be costly. But then, it is argued, the economic and social costs of unemployment are also very great.

It must be emphasized that these programs are a subject of considerable controversy. Some opponents contend that proposals designed to attract new industries into depressed areas may only interfere with the operation of market forces and thereby encourage unemployed workers to remain in areas which can never again support them at reasonable income levels. Others flatly argue that all such aid programs, by going far beyond the dictates of the Employment Act of 1946, entail an unjustified and undesirable extension of government action and the welfare state.

IS GROWTH RAPID ENOUGH?

We noted in Chapter 18 that over a long period of years the United States has achieved an enviable growth record. Yet, oddly enough, there currently exists a basic controversy concerning the adequacy of the United States' growth. There are a number of reasons for this debate. As Table 19-2 indicates, the growth rates of a number of other nations are substantially in excess of ours. Most notable and most ominous is the Soviet rate, variously estimated by Western experts at 6 to 8 per cent per year. Furthermore, in the postwar era our per capita increases in real output have been rather modest; that is, increases in total output have

TABLE 19-2. AVERAGE ANNUAL RATE OF GROWTH IN REAL
GNP IN SELECTED COUNTRIES, 1951 TO 1960*

Country	Growth rate, per cent per year
Japan	8%
West Germany	7
U.S.S.R.	7
Austria	6
Italy	6
Netherlands	5
Switzerland	5
Canada	5
France	4
Sweden	4
United Kingdom	3
United States	3

SOURCE: Committee for Economic Development and Joint Economic Committee.
* Data for Japan and Canada are for the 1950–1955 period; U.S.S.R. data are for 1955–1958.

been substantially eaten up by rapid population growth (Table 18-1). Finally, there is some evidence to support the view that American growth has been slowing in the 1950s, primarily because of higher unemployment rates and a decrease in the rate of productivity increases.[3] Though innumerable specific views exist as to the adequacy of American economic growth, there are two general positions.

Case for the affirmative

A number of highly respected economists[4] feel that our growth rate is quite adequate and that any attempt to accelerate it might do little to solve the problems we face, on the one hand, and impose intolerable costs upon our society, on the other. In more detail the rationale of this viewpoint runs something like this: Our economy is already affluent. Hence the production of more goods for domestic use is generally not a high priority goal. Internationally it is doubtful that the size and rate of growth in our GNP are particularly crucial. It is not so much the size of the GNP, but rather its composition, which determines our military position vis-a-vis the Soviet Union. After all, the Soviet military posture is roughly the equivalent of ours, although their GNP is only about 50 per cent of ours.[5] Nor is it clear that the future of the underdeveloped nations will be determined primarily by bald comparisons of U.S. and U.S.S.R. growth rates. "In short, there is little to show that the issues between us and the rest of the world will be governed predominantly by our economic successes, or that we can buy safe survival with an additional per cent or two of economic growth." [6] Of even greater long-run significance, it is argued that the policies which would be required to increase our growth rate

are politically and ideologically unacceptable. That is, more rapid growth implies in general an expanding role for government and in particular greater restraints upon consumers to free resources for investment, the direct allocation of materials and manpower to growth-oriented sectors of the economy, and wage-price controls to contain the inflation that such a high-pressure economy inevitably generates. In brief, any significant acceleration of the growth rate—from say 3 to 5 or 6 per cent—necessitates the use of techniques and controls which are incompatible with a free society. Accelerated growth can be achieved only at the cost of freedom. This, it is argued, is much too high a price to pay for a percentage point or two increase in our growth rate.

Case for the negative

Other highly regarded voices envision the situation much differently.[7] Despite our overall national wealth, there are compelling reasons why growth must be accelerated. First, the lowest 10 or 20 per cent of the income receivers in our society have yet to partake adequately of the over-all affluence of our nation. Growth will tend to raise the entire income distribution absolutely and will also enhance the ability and willingness of society to provide public assistance to these low-income groups. Second, the increasingly acute international situation demands an expanded rate of American growth. The reputation or image of our economy—indeed, of our entire society—as evaluated by underdeveloped nations is highly dependent upon our growth performance. Economic growth, rightly or wrongly, is widely accepted as an index of a nation's vitality, efficiency, and capacity for survival in the cold war. Growth rates do impress the uncommitted underdeveloped nations. Furthermore, a growing capitalism obviously has a greater capacity and probably a greater willingness to extend aid to the underdeveloped nations and to improve its own

[3] Joint Economic Committee, Staff Report on Employment, Growth, and Price Levels (Washington: 1959), chap. 3.

[4] The present discussion is based primarily upon Henry C. Wallich, The Cost of Freedom (New York: Harper & Row, Publishers, 1960).

[5] Cynics point out that the GNP of the barbarians was undoubtedly much less than that of the Romans.

[6] Wallich, op. cit., p. 158.

[7] For example, see the Joint Economic Committee, op. cit., chaps. 1–4, and Alvin H. Hansen, Economic Issues of the 1960's (New York: McGraw-Hill Book Company, Inc., 1961), particularly chap. 5.

military posture. This is so because the real output gains from an accelerated growth rate may be substantial. Example: a $500 billion GNP economy with a 2 per cent growth rate will add $10 billion to its GNP in a year; that same economy will add $25 billion if it achieves a 5 per cent rate of growth. These figures also suggest that growth helps any nation avoid a crude clash between consumer goods production, on the one hand, and capital, military, or foreign aid goods, on the other (Chapter 2).[8]

Accelerated growth is not only desirable, but it is also said to be obtainable within the present institutional-ideological framework of capitalism. Thus, after detailed analysis, the Joint Economic Committee has concluded that our economy is capable of growing at a rate of 4½ per cent per year "without changing our economic system in any fundamental way."[9] We need not embrace forced draft techniques nor accept an erosion of our freedom to achieve a significantly better growth rate than is now enjoyed.

Those who feel that past American growth is inadequate and that it can be accelerated note several policies which would promote more rapid growth and simultaneously be compatible with the institutions and ideology of a free society.

POLICIES TO ACCELERATE GROWTH

There are three policies generally recognized as crucial to the acceleration of American economic growth: (1) the achievement of continuous full employment; (2) expanded expenditures on basic scientific research; and (3) increased spending on education.

Continuous full employment

Achieving and maintaining full employment is a basic implemental factor in economic growth. Total demand must increase at a rate

[8] In Chapter 36 another point will be considered: economic growth facilitates the production of much-needed social goods and services.

[9] Joint Economic Committee, *op. cit.*, pp. xxvi and 101.

equal to the expansion of the economy's productive capacity or potential growth will not be realized. If total spending is not growing appropriately, all other efforts to raise total output will be frustrated.

The immediate impact of unemployment upon the growth rate is clear. For example, because of the 1957–1958 recession, the annual realized growth rate of the United States in the 1955–1958 period was about 0.5 per cent, short of the 3 or 3½ per cent which the United States has achieved over a long span of years and far short of the 4 or 5 per cent rate which many economists feel to be attainable without any significant changes in our institutions or economic way of life. It is notable, too, as analysis of the production possibilities curve reminds us, that to move from a position of unemployment to one of full employment entails no cost or sacrifice for society; on the contrary, it is unemployment itself which imposes the cost of foregone production upon society.

A thorough grasp of the significance of full employment for economic growth requires the understanding of two additional points. On the one hand, the movement from less-than-full employment to full employment provides a one-shot stimulus to the economy's growth rate. Thus a movement from a 6 per cent to a 3 per cent unemployment rate will stimulate the GNP and the growth rate in the year this is achieved. But now as full employment is maintained there will occur no further windfall increases in output and the rate of growth in succeeding years.

On the other hand, cyclical *unemployment* can have certain harmful "carry over" effects upon the growth rate in subsequent years of full employment through the adverse effects it might have upon the permissive factors in growth. For example, unemployment depresses investment and capital accumulation; it may give rise to a decline in the work week which is frequently demanded by organized labor as a technique to more equitably apportion the burden of unemployment; the expansion of research budgets may be slowed by recession; union resistance to technological change may stiffen, and so forth. Though it is impossible to quantify the impact of these considerations upon the growth rate, they undoubtedly can be of considerable importance.

Growth and the research revolution

We emphasized in the previous chapter that research and its end result—technological advance—are widely recognized as the most significant ingredient in economic growth.

Fundamentally, economic growth means growth in a nation's underlying ideas and skills. The immediate generator of economic growth is investment . . . but . . . investment arises from new ideas, new developments in science and technology, from education, research, innovations—new products, new processes, new resources; all of these are the real seeds of long-term economic growth.[10]

If we accept the basic role of research as a determinant of the growth rate, then it is obvious that a major policy step in accelerating economic growth is to increase expenditures upon research and development activities. But at this juncture some serious questions and problems arise.

1. Most importantly, can American capitalism generate the research expenditures needed to achieve the desired acceleration in the growth rate? It is very difficult to answer with authority. We do know that a number of forces have been operating in the postwar period to accelerate research spending—to foster a "research revolution": (a) our World War II experience demonstrated the feasibility of organizing and carrying through to completion large-scale basic research projects and also created a backlog of technological information applicable to peacetime products; (b) research and development activity has generally proven to be highly profitable; (c) 1954 revisions of our tax laws make research expenditures deductible as a current expense; and (d) research spending

tends to be cumulative, that is, "Research feeds upon itself: Discovery breeds discovery; innovation breeds innovation; and with each new discovery or innovation, the total body of scientific and technological knowledge increases." [11] Such considerations as these underlie the prediction (Table 18-3) that research and development expenditures will increase from about $12 billion in 1960 to $22 billion in 1969.

All this is impressive. But there are some less encouraging factors to consider. Absolutely, the Soviets spend somewhat more on research than we do and, with a GNP approximately half the size of ours, they spend relatively much more. And qualitatively Soviet research ranks high because more emphasis is placed upon basic or pure scientific research in contrast with greater American emphasis upon applied research and what some would classify as trivia. Thus, it is not at all clear that the quantity and quality of American research efforts will be adequate to achieve the desired acceleration of our rate of growth.

2. An advancing technology as reflected in automation is feared and resisted by groups who stand to be adversely affected. Thus, for example, organized labor does not accept with complete equanimity the widespread and rapid introduction of new labor-replacing machinery. Indeed, we have seen that the whole problem of the depressed areas is bound up with automation as it destroys unskilled and semiskilled jobs, on the one hand, while creating jobs for the skilled, the technician, and the professional person, on the other.

3. There is the knotty problem of providing the brainpower upon which research activity so heavily depends. In analyzing this problem we turn to the third policy for increasing the growth rate—devoting more resources to education.

Education: investment in human capital

Can our educational system provide the brainpower to accelerate the flow of technological advance, on the one hand, and provide better

---

[10] Leonard S. Silk, *The Research Revolution* (New York: McGraw-Hill Book Company, Inc., 1960), p. 203.

[11] *Ibid.*, pp. 162–163.

trained workers to fit the changing labor force needs of an advancing economy, on the other (Figure 19-3)? Probably the greatest social need of the United States for coming decades is getting educated people in sufficient quantity and quality. Can we do it? The numerous current appraisals of our educational needs and resources almost invariably reach pessimistic conclusions. Future demands upon the education system will be great. Our rapidly expanding population means greatly expanded enrollments. Elementary and high school enrollments, which were 25 million in 1950 and 35 million in 1959, are predicted to be about 44 million by 1965. And, despite the fact that overcrowded schools are now commonplace, it is estimated that we are currently constructing each year less than one half the extra classrooms needed to house the annual increases in enrollment. That isn't all: if the demand for a better trained work force is to be met, a larger percentage of our young people will have to receive higher education—education of increasing quality—than is now the case.

Another frequent conclusion is that we do a poor job of recruiting our best brains for higher education. Evidence: an estimated 50 per cent of our ablest young people do not go on to college primarily because of a lack of financial resources. In other words, we seriously underutilize or misallocate brainpower, our most valuable resource. In the crucial area of scientific and engineering personnel the annual number of graduates is known to be lagging seriously behind that of the U.S.S.R. Finally, at the core of our educational problems is the teacher shortage. It is estimated by the United States Office of Education that in 1960 school faculties were understaffed by 195,000 teachers. Fulfillment of the estimated need for teachers in the decade of the 1960s will require nearly 2 million college graduates—over half the total estimated 3.7 million college graduates forthcoming in that period! There are, of course, some potential alleviating factors which *may* increase the productivity of teachers: instruction by television, relieving trained teachers of routine tasks, expanding class sizes, and so forth. But, even

assuming such devices do not dilute the quality of education, there is clearly a tremendous task ahead in meeting the demands put upon the education system. Meeting these needs and simultaneously upgrading the quality of education will undoubtedly require much thought, much effort, and substantial amounts of human and property resources.[12]

Research, education, and social revenues

Although private expenditures for research and education are large and on the increase, a substantial number of economists and public officials feel that increased public support in these two crucial areas is necessary if we seek to accelerate our rate of growth. For example, a recent report of the Joint Economic Committee of Congress concludes that:

A program of Federal aid to education, designed to help the poorer school districts, is the single most important step that can be taken to raise our longrun economic growth . . . [and] . . . the Federal government must continue to exercise financial responsibility for our scientific establishment . . . the Government must make sure that sufficient scientific resources are put into basic, rather than applied, research.[13]

Can expansion of governmental activity in the areas of basic scientific research and education be justified on economic grounds? Though there are no universally accepted answers here—witness the endless and heated debate on Federal aid to education—proponents of expanded government spending in these two areas generally base their case on the grounds that basic research and education entail substantial social revenues or that they have the primary characteristics of social goods (Chapter 5).

Let us examine the area of basic scientific

---

[12] The interested student might consult Seymour E. Harris, *More Resources for Education* (New York: Harper & Row, Publishers, 1960).

[13] Joint Economic Committee, *op. cit.*, p. 31.

research. The first point to note is that basic research may entail benefits or revenues which go far beyond those realized by the sponsoring firm, that is, substantial social revenues or benefits may accrue to society as a whole. For example, provided the new knowledge is made freely available, the development of a new heat-resistant material might yield substantial benefits for, say, the electronics industry which sponsored the development, but also for a host of other industries ranging from automobiles and home appliances to our national space program. This means that, because it is geared to private benefit as measured by profitability, research activity of this type carried on by private firms will be deficient in amount. In other words, the demand for basic research facilities will understate the total benefits derivable from resulting discoveries. You will recall from Chapter 3 that the correction of such an under-allocation calls for government subsidization.

Secondly, in some instances—for example, atomic energy, space exploration, oceanography, meteorology, preventative medicine, and so forth—the required scope of the research undertaking is simply beyond the means of private enterprise. That is, research in these areas is a social good. The price system would allocate little or no resources to such projects, despite their obvious real and potential significance. Finally, resources may also be underallocated to basic research activities because of the great uncertainty as to profitability and the potentially long payoff period on successful research which may cause risk-avoiding and conservative firms to shun basic research in favor of more practical applied research undertakings.

Similar arguments can be, and have been (Chapter 5), made in justifying public support of education. All these arguments, however, do not deny the existence of legitimate disagreement as to the specific level at which public spending for research and education should be determined.

The tax-rebate growth proposal

Maintaining full employment and devoting more resources to education and research are widely accepted policy goals among those who feel that our growth rate can, and should, be accelerated. A number of more specific and more controversial programs for growth also exist, many of which are the undertakings of various interest groups. For example, as most business groups see it, the basic impediments to growth are excessive business taxation, constant and pervasive upward pressure on wage costs, and a myriad of government regulations and controls which stifle the flexibility and dynamic character of our economy. Organized labor's growth program, on the other hand, endorses greater government activity in the area of social goods—education, health, housing, urban renewal, and so forth—and argues that steadily rising real wages are requisite to the growth in consumer demand upon which full employment and economic expansion basically depend.

A number of respected economists[14] have recently offered an interesting growth proposal which merits at least brief explanation. This proposal is offered not on the assumption that it is necessarily an ideal program, but rather as a stimulus to the reader's own thinking.

The basic outline of this proposal is remarkably simple: an added system of taxes and rebates (subsidies) is to be applied to business firms in such a way as to stimulate the expansion of real GNP. More specifically, the tax-rebate proposal operates something like this: a new fixed-rate tax is to be applied to each year's percentage increase in a firm's output (as measured by value added). This is illustrated in Table 19-3, where a constant tax rate of 1 per cent (column 2) applies to all the percentage increases in a firm's output (column 1). At the same time a rebate or subsidy is imposed, the relative size of which varies directly with the percentage rate of growth in output realized by a firm (columns 1 and 3). Now the illustrative tax-rebate figures of Table 19-3 are based on the assumption that the desired or "target"

---

[14] Klaus Knorr and William J. Baumol (eds.), *What Price Economic Growth?* (Englewood Cliffs, N.J.: Prentice-Hall, Inc., 1960). Our present discussion is necessarily brief and therefore does not do justice to the proposal; nor do we pause to analyze the many possible modifications and problems associated with the proposal which are anticipated and discussed by its authors.

TABLE 19-3. NUMERICAL ILLUSTRATION OF THE TAX-REBATE GROWTH PROPOSAL

(1) Per cent increase in firm's output	(2) Per cent of output as added tax	(3) Per cent of output as rebate	(4) Net per cent of output as tax (−) or rebate (+)
0	1.0	0	−1.0
1	1.0	0.2	−0.8
2	1.0	0.4	−0.6
3	1.0	0.6	−0.4
4	1.0	0.8	−0.2
5	1.0	1.0	0
6	1.0	1.2	+0.2
7	1.0	1.4	+0.4
.	.	.	.
.	.	.	.
.	.	.	.
20	1.0	4.0	+3.0

SOURCE: Klaus Knorr and William J. Baumol (eds.)., "What Price Economic Growth?" (Englewood Cliffs, N.J.: Prentice-Hall, Inc., 1960), p. 35, with modifications by author.

rate of growth in output is 5 per cent. Thus it is obvious that firms realizing a less-than-target rate of growth will be penalized financially by this tax-rebate system because the tax obviously exceeds the rebate at all rates of increase in output which are below the 5 per cent level (column 4). On the other hand, the firm which exceeds the 5 per cent target growth rate in output will be rewarded financially for all output increases in excess of 5 per cent because at these levels the rebate or subsidy exceeds the added tax (column 4). The net result of this proposal then is to reward growth and penalize a lack of, or insufficient, growth. In the words of its authors, "The purpose of the plan . . . is to tie the earnings of a private enterprise closely to its contribution to economic growth." Expanding firms and industries would realize an added financial boost for exceeding the target growth rate. The extra financial penalty imposed by the plan on declining, static, or slow-growing firms and industries would hasten the movement of resources from these areas into the more dynamic, growing segments of the economy. In short, the tax-rebate proposal is an attempt to bolster the reward-penalty, car-rot-stick properties of the price system so as to accelerate the reallocation of resources from lagging, static segments of the economy to the dynamic, burgeoning sections and, in so doing, to increase the over-all rate of growth in total output. Indeed, the primary virtue of this proposal, aside from its potential to accelerate growth, is that it entails monetary inducements which operate through the price system. That is, the proposal allegedly circumvents any erosion of the capitalist ideology which might be entailed by more direct government controls or very substantial increases in public spending in an effort to accelerate growth. In this sense the tax-rebate proposal is complementary to increases in government spending for research and education as growth-stimulating policies.

GROWTH, UNEMPLOYMENT, AND INFLATION

Having analyzed structural unemployment and the debate over the adequacy of our growth rate, we now turn to a final growth-related problem: Have the causes and characteristics of inflation changed substantially as long-run growth has enhanced the opulence of our economy?

Traditionally, inflation has been regarded as the result of excess total demand. That is, the *demand-pull theory* of inflation states that, once the economy is operating at the full-employment level and the total output therefore becomes fixed, an excess of total demand will necessarily have the effect of pulling up the price level. Because the demand-pull theory assumes considerable flexibility of resource and product prices, changes in the composition or structure—but not the size—of total demand will leave the price level unchanged. In those sectors of the economy in which demand is increasing, prices will rise; but these increases will be offset by compensating price declines in those segments of the economy in which demand has fallen. On balance, then, a change in the structure of demand should change the *structure* of prices but yet leave the over-all price *level* constant.

Policies for dealing with demand-pull inflation are evident and familiar to us (Chapters 14 and 17). The policy goal is to eliminate the excess of total demand which is pulling the price level upward. Appropriate fiscal policy calls for tax increases and reductions in government spending, while monetary policy demands tight money.

The new inflation: two theories

The demand-pull theory of inflation is widely accepted by economists, and over the years it has provided a useful and accurate explanation of our inflationary experiences. At least, it had until the late 1950s. In the 1955–1958 period in particular, price-level–employment fluctuations occurred which were not readily explainable in terms of a simple demand-pull theory. During the 1957–58 recession, for example, economists were embarrassed to find that employment and output were *declining*, while at the same time the general price level was *rising*. Between 1956 and 1958 the consumer price index rose by over 7 points, while in the

same period the index of industrial production fell by 9 points, and unemployment jumped from 4.2 to 6.8 per cent of the labor force (see table on inside covers). Major industries, for example, automobiles and steel, found themselves with excess capacity and partially employed labor forces; yet wages and prices continued to creep upward. This oddity prompted economists to restudy in great detail the whole inflationary problem and has resulted in two possible explanations of the "new" inflation: the cost-push theory and the theory of structural inflation. Both these new explanations are closely associated with institutional changes—particularly the development of strong labor unions and monopolistic businesses—which have accompanied the process of growth in our economy.

Cost-push inflation. The cost-push theory explains inflation in the absence of full employment in this way: Unions have considerable control over wage rates, that is, they possess considerable market power. Indeed, they have so much market power that even with a moderate deficiency of total demand, some unemployment, and some excess industrial capacity, unions can demand and obtain wage increases. Large employers, faced now with increased costs but also in the possession of considerable market power, push their increased wage costs and "something extra" on to consumers by raising the prices of their products. This theory is obviously based on the presumption that both unions and businesses typically possess some significant degree of market power and therefore can within limits manipulate wages and prices independent of over-all conditions of total demand. Thus it is that we find cost-push inflation sometimes labeled "administered price" inflation or simply "seller's inflation."

Not surprisingly, management contends that wage increases initiate price increases, and therefore unions are obviously the villain, nudging wages and necessarily prices upward at a time when inflation otherwise would not occur. Labor counters by charging that the power of big businesses to adjust or administer prices results in price increases which are neither initiated nor justified by increases in wage costs.

Structural inflation.[15] A second, more recent explanation of the inflation-with-unemployment situation centers upon the effects of a change in the structure, though not the size, of total demand. Briefly stated, the rationale is based on the fact that for a number of reasons—a basic one of which is the market power of businesses and unions—prices and wages tend to be flexible upward but inflexible downward (Chapters 11 and 12). Now let us suppose that total demand is not excessive; as a matter of fact, let us assume that it is slightly deficient, resulting in, say, 5 per cent unemployment. Now a rather sharp change in the structure or composition of this total demand occurs. This structural change in demand means that prices and wages will rise in those segments of the economy experiencing an expanding demand. However, because of their downward stickiness, wages and prices will not fall, or at least will not fall by much, in those sectors of the economy witnessing a declining demand. The result is a net increase in the price and wage levels, that is, inflation will occur. Remember: this inflation arises despite the fact that there is less-than-full employment and the economy is failing to realize its growth potential.

But this is not all. Secondary effects may intensify structural inflation by transmitting wage and price rises from the increasing-demand segments of the economy to other sectors where demand might be unchanged or even falling. Suppose, for example, that one of the industries most favorably affected by our assumed change in the structure of total demand is the steel industry. The result will be a tendency for steel prices and profits to rise. But now the big steel firms are a lucrative target for the United

Steelworkers of America, which demands and receives wage increases. At this point the secondary, transmitting effects enter the picture. On the one hand, a host of industries using significant quantities of steel—including those unaffected and adversely affected by the change in the structure of total demand—find themselves faced with higher material costs. So they raise their prices to cover these cost boosts. And, as it happens, the wage increases which occur in the steel industry tend to create pressures for wage increases in other related industries such as aluminum, copper, and other fabricated metal product industries—even though these industries may be among those faced with a constant or sagging product demand. Wage rates in these related industries are traditionally patterned after wages in steel. Hence, when steel wages go up, union leaders in these related industries will be under pressure to secure comparable increases for their constituents. And, of course, the fact that the cost of living is rising provides the basis for demanding these increases. As a matter of fact, if existing collective bargaining agreements in these related or, indeed, in other unrelated industries, contain "escalator clauses," wage rates will automatically go up as the consumer's price index rises.

Oddly enough, employers in the related industries may feel obligated to grant wage increases because the severing of a traditional relationship between wages in the steel industry and the related industries may undermine worker morale and impair productivity in the latter. Firms in the related industries then recover these wage increases by raising product prices. The point is this: through these several avenues, wage and price increases originating in those sectors of the economy which are prosperous because of the favorable change in the composition of demand spill over into other sectors of the economy where the change in the structure of demand has caused unemployment and excess productive capacity. In short, a sharp change in the composition of a given level of total demand may be inflationary in both favorably and unfavorably affected seg-

[15] See Charles L. Schultze, *Recent Inflation in the United States*, Study Paper No. 1 for the Joint Economic Committee (Washington: 1959) and also Professor Schultze's "Creeping Inflation: Causes and Consequences," *Business Horizons*, Summer, 1960, pp. 65–77.

ments of the economy. This explains the paradox of inflation with unemployment; changes in the composition of demand may cause the price level to rise even though total demand is deficient and unemployment is increasing.

Now it must be emphasized that these three theories—demand-pull, cost-push, and structural inflation—are not unrelated or mutually exclusive. All three can operate simultaneously. For example, a rising level of total demand whose composition is significantly changing can cause both demand-pull and structural inflation simultaneously. And the exertion of market power may cause cost-push forces to accentuate this inflation, particularly so in those industries where unions are strong and demand most favorably affected. Thus, for example, a careful analysis of the late 1950s reveals all three types of inflationary pressure present in varying degrees.

Public policy and the new inflation

To the extent that the new inflation—cost-push and structural inflation—occurs in a growing economy, a serious public policy dilemma is posed. The reason: the new inflation can occur when total demand is deficient. And our major anti-inflationary weapons—monetary policy and fiscal policy—are designed to halt inflation by restraining total demand and forcing it into balance with the current value of the full-employment level of total output. In other words, available stabilization techniques are simply not very relevant in dealing with inflation, the source of which is not excess total demand, but rather cost-push forces and structural changes in total demand.

As a matter of fact, it is just possible that the application of a tight money policy to the new inflation might do more harm than good. Tight money, you will recall, has a *general* contractionary impact upon the economy. Now the only way tight money can be at all effective in getting at the new inflation is the indirect one of restricting the market demand for products in order to force employers to resist wage increases more vigorously. This restriction of demand, if sufficiently large, may ultimately curb the new inflation. But the accompanying costs may be great—increased unemployment and a retarded rate of economic growth. Some economists feel this sort of thing occurred during the 1957–1958 recession when cost-push and structural factors accounted for a significant share of the price-level increases. The government applied a tight money policy to an inflationary situation which tight money is simply not equipped to handle. The resulting restriction of total demand simply added to existing unemployment and slowed expansion of the GNP, but accomplished little by way of halting inflation.

New policies?

If unions and businesses possess considerable market power, and if currently available stabilization techniques cannot halt inflation except at the prohibitive cost of unemployment and impeded growth, what techniques, if any, can be invoked to halt the new inflation? This is a most difficult question which economists and public officials have been asking themselves and one another. A number of proposals have been offered, most of which embody serious questions as to their political feasibility, their effectiveness, and their impact upon our ideology and institutions. Let us briefly summarize several of them.

1. *Voluntary restraint.* One suggested approach is to have the President, the Secretary of Labor, and other respected public officials make appeals and admonitions to labor and business leaders, encouraging them to exercise self-restraint in reaching wage-price decisions. Now while the use of this form of moral suasion with respect to collective bargaining and price setting may be of some effectiveness in some situations, some observers seriously discount its over-all usefulness. The basic weakness of "creeping admonitionism," as cynics label it, is that it asks businessmen and labor leaders to abandon their primary functions—to forgo the goals of higher wages and profits. This is somewhat comparable to advising Louis Armstrong

to take up the violin or asking Bernard Baruch to quit giving advice. Effective results simply cannot be expected.

2. Reducing market power. A second avenue for attacking the new inflation embraces the rationale that, if the market power of business and labor is causing inflation, this market power must be reduced or eliminated. But how? One recommendation is to apply our antitrust laws more vigorously to big business, and possibly to unions too. Or another proposal is to prohibit unions from bargaining on a centralized, nationwide level, forcing each local union to bargain with its own immediate employer. This decentralization of union power and authority, it is hoped, will ameliorate cost-push inflation.

But serious questions can be raised about such proposals. Antitrust legislation, we shall discover (Chapter 32), has not been particularly successful in restricting the power of big business. Nor is it clear that antitrust can be applied to labor without virtually destroying unions and the institution of collective bargaining. Finally, there is little evidence to suggest that localized wage setting results in more socially acceptable wage rates than does centralized bargaining. Indeed, interlocal union rivalries, petty griefs, and less ability to realize the social consequences of its actions may all tend to make local bargaining more aggressive and potentially more inflationary than centralized bargaining.

3. Increased government participation and control. A number of observers are reluctantly coming to the conclusion that some degree of government participation in, or regulation of, wage-price determination in key industries must be invoked if the new inflation is to be controlled without depressing the level of employment and the rate of growth. A variety of techniques might be employed. For example, the Federal government might simply establish a "study group" to publicize wage and price changes. Or a factfinding board might hold hearings on proposed wage and price increases in key industries, and possibly issue a report or recommendations based thereon. Others suggest that, because major wage agreements affect the price level, and therefore the public interest, the public interest should be represented by having public officials participate in key collective bargaining negotiations. Or the government may legislate the right to suspend or delay wage or price increases which it considers to be socially undesirable, that is, highly inflationary. Finally, government, at the extreme, might simply establish public control over wages and prices in crucial industries such as steel, where the inflationary potential of substantial wage and price increases is great. These wage-price controls would be reminiscent of those exercised by the government during World War II to contain the strong inflationary pressures then existing.

These various proposals clearly entail considerable gradations in the degree of government control and participation. In particular, government participation in wage negotiations, public authority to reject proposed wage-price increases, and direct wage-price controls embody far-reaching changes in our economic way of life. Hence, many economists feel these techniques to be of a "last resort" character, to be used only if less drastic means are ineffective and if the inflationary problem becomes severe. At the same time it is important to note that many of these as yet relatively untried and unexplored means of getting at the causes of the new inflation are being accorded serious consideration by both economists and public officials.

SUMMARY

1. Though rapid economic growth is a desirable social objective, it does entail certain costs and can contribute to and create socioeconomic problems.

2. The main costs of growth include: the foregoing of current consumption; less leisure and a more rapid pace of economic life; wasteful exploitation of natural resources; enhanced short-run instability; and economic insecurity for those adversely affected by economic change.

3. Such growth-associated factors as (*a*) technological advance as reflected in the automation of production and the development of new products; (b) changes in consumer demand; and (c) the geographic relocation of industry have resulted in structural unemployment and chronically depressed areas.

4. The readjustment or reallocation process is seriously impeded in chronically depressed areas because (a) labor is relatively immobile geographically and (b) most structurally unemployed workers in, say, the coal, automobile, textile, and railway equipment industries do not have the education or skills for reemployment in such new growing industries as electronics, plastics, synthetics, and so forth.

5. Proposals of aid for depressed areas entail either or both of two approaches: (a) the geographic and occupational relocation of structurally unemployed workers and (b) the economic revitalization of depressed areas by the attraction of new industries.

6. Some respected observers feel the United States' growth rate is quite adequate and that, given the size of our GNP, little would be gained in military power or in improving the impression we make on underdeveloped nations by more rapid growth. Indeed, the policy measures necessary to the acceleration of our growth rate might seriously threaten our way of economic life. Others feel more rapid growth is vital in order to (a) take care of our low-income people; (b) more strongly illustrate the vitality and efficiency of our economy to the rest of the world; and (c) enhance our ability and willingness to increase our military strength and foreign aid programs. More rapid growth, it is argued, will strengthen, not weaken, our institutions and ideology.

7. Basic policies for accelerating United States growth include (a) the maintenance of full employment, (b) increased spending upon re-

search, and (c) expanded outlays on education. The fact that research and education entail substantial social revenues or are social goods underlies the argument that substantial public support in these areas is justified. Recently a tax-rebate plan has been proposed which would accelerate growth by penalizing slow-growing and rewarding fast-growing firms financially.

8. Although the demand-pull theory still provides the basic explanation of inflation, our unemployment-with-inflation experience of the late 1950s has caused economists to talk of a "new inflation" explainable in terms of cost-push forces and changes in the structure of total demand. The theory of cost-push inflation asserts that the market power of unions and big businesses may cause wages and prices to rise even when total demand is somewhat short of the full-employment level. The concept of structural inflation indicates that, because wages and prices are inflexible downward but flexible upward, a sharp change in the structure of total demand will cause prices to rise in demand-increasing sectors but to remain constant in demand-decreasing sectors of the economy. The resulting net increases in the price level may be reinforced by secondary effects— for example, pattern bargaining, escalator clauses, the transmission of higher material costs to other industries, and so forth.

9. Because the new inflation does not emanate from excess total demand, traditional monetary and fiscal remedies are not particularly appropriate. Policy suggestions for dealing with the new inflation include (a) inducing voluntary restraint by labor and management in wage-price determination; (b) reducing the market power of businesses and unions through vigorous antitrust action and the decentralization of collective bargaining; and (c) increased government control of, or participation in, the wage- and price-setting processes.

QUESTIONS AND STUDY SUGGESTIONS

1. Identify the costs of economic growth. Which do you feel are the most significant? To what degree, if any, are these various costs avoidable? "Growth contributes to instability and insecurity, but also provides the means to provide for those adversely affected by instability and insecurity." Comment.

2. What is structural unemployment? "There are both a demand and a supply side to the problem of chronic unemployment." Explain. How does structural unemployment differ from cyclical unemployment? What implications do these differences imply for the formulation of policies to deal with structural unemployment? Outline and evaluate the two basic policy approaches for dealing with chronic unemployment.

3. Do you feel our economy has been experiencing "creeping unemployment" in the postwar era? "The 'hard core' of unemployment can and should be substantially reduced." Do you agree? If so, formulate an appropriate program.

4. "The problem of reemploying the workers of the chronically depressed areas is, in a sense, an aspect of the law of increasing costs." Do you agree? Explain.

5. Explain the problems implied in the following two statements:

a. "The production of 6.1 million cars required 928,900 workers in 1953, but only 786,300 in 1957."

b. "In the last forty years there has been hardly any employment growth in the goods-producing sectors of the economy; by contrast in the same period the number of jobs in the service-producing sectors has more than doubled."

6. Contrast and evaluate the following two statements:

a. "Government measures to reverse or slow down such declines in employment in particular sectors of the economy are not likely to be successful and are likely to be extremely costly. . . .We should beware of becoming involved in a . . . hopeless and . . . costly program for rescuing distressed areas."[16]

b. "It does not seem fair to deny progress to a society in order to protect a few. Nor does it seem fair for society to accept all the gain at the expense of a few. Therefore, it would seem that society should find some way of caring for those who lose out by progress."[17]

To which of these views do you subscribe? Justify your answer.

7. What programs might be employed to accelerate our economic growth? Can any expansion in the role of government necessitated by these programs be justified on economic grounds? Evaluate: "The relationship between economic growth and individual liberties is such that one can be achieved only at the expense of the other."

8. Briefly analyze and evaluate:

a. ". . . human capabilities do not stay abreast of physical capital, and they do become limiting factors in economic growth."

b. ". . . we should consider creating government-sponsored productivity institutes to stimulate research for industries where increases in output appear particularly necessary."

c. ". . . under our present economic structure the social benefits of basic research

[16] National Association of Manufacturers, *Unemployment: Causes and Cures* (New York: NAM, April, 1961), pp. 8–9.

[17] Bruce R. Morris, *Problems of American Economic Growth* (New York: Oxford University Press, 1961), p. 219.

are not adequately reflected in opportunities for private profit. Indeed, there is a basic contradiction between the conditions necessary for efficient basic research— few or no constraints on the direction of research with full and free dissemination of research results—and full appropriation of the gains from sponsoring basic research in a competitive economy."[18]

d. "The best way to stimulate growth is to fight inflation. This is so for several reasons. First, inflation will undermine incentives to save and therefore limit investment. Furthermore, only with price stability is healthy, maintainable growth possible. Finally, creeping inflation inevitably accelerates to a gallop and precipitates economic collapse."

9. Discuss and compare the assumptions and operation of (a) demand-pull, (b) cost-push, and (c) structural inflation. Now explain and comment upon this statement: ". . . no one 'theory' or explanation is adequate to explain the inflation . . . since 1955. Rather, a number of varied and interrelated factors have been involved. It follows, therefore, that any public policy designed to deal with the problem must be diverse and flexible." Outline a program to deal with an inflation which occurs when 5 per cent of the labor force is unemployed.

10. "In the contemporary institutional setting of our economy, the principal effect of tight money is not to control inflation, but to create unemployment and the underutilization of capacity, and to slow down the rate of growth." Explain and evaluate.

SELECTED REFERENCES

The American Assembly, *Automation and Technological Change* (Englewood Cliffs, N.J., Prentice-Hall, Inc., 1962).

Committee for Economic Development, *Distressed Areas in a Growing Economy* (New York: Committee for Economic Development, June, 1961).

Hansen, Alvin H., *Economic Issues of the 1960's* (New York: McGraw-Hill Book Company, Inc., 1960), chaps. 1–8.

Joint Economic Committee, *Staff Report on Employment, Growth, and Price Levels* (Washington: 1960), chaps. 1–6.

Knorr, Klaus, and William J. Baumol (eds.), *What Price Economic Growth?* (Englewood Cliffs, N.J.: Prentice-Hall, Inc., 1961).

Morris, Bruce R., *Problems of American Economic Growth* (New York: Oxford University Press, 1961).

Rockefeller Brothers Fund, *The Challenge of America: Its Economic and Social Aspects* (Garden City, N. Y.: Doubleday & Company, Inc., 1958).

Schultze, Charles L., "Recent Inflation in the United States," Study Paper no. 1 for the Joint Economic Committee (Washington: 1959).

Silk, Leonard S., *The Research Revolution* (New York: McGraw-Hill Book Company, Inc., 1960).

Thorp, Willard L., and Richard E. Quandt, *The New Inflation* (New York: McGraw-Hill Book Company, Inc., 1959).

[18] Richard R. Nelson, "The Simple Economics of Basic Scientific Research," *Journal of Political Economy*, June, 1959, p. 305.

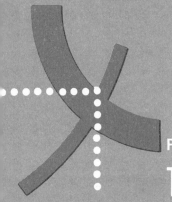

PART 5

THE ECONOMICS OF THE FIRM
AND RESOURCE ALLOCATION

Chapter 20

THE MARKET STRUCTURES OF
AMERICAN CAPITALISM

price system allocate resources
Cupet Invest

SCARCE RESOURCES and unlimited wants, you will recall, are the foundation of economic science. The efficient management of scarce resources is the social goal of all economic processes. Furthermore, there are two major facets to the problem of achieving efficient resource use. The first, which we have examined in Parts 2 and 3 and, to some degree, in Part 4 of this book, centers upon the full employment of available resources. The second aspect of the economizing problem—the one to which we now turn—has to do with allocating employed resources among alternative uses in the most efficient manner. Stated differently, Parts 2, 3, and 4 focused upon the last of the Five Fundamental Questions posed in Chapter 2: "Can the economy achieve the full employment of its available resources?" Part 5 deals with the first four questions: "Can the economy produce that output most desired by society?" "Will the production of that output be organized in the most efficient manner?" "Can the economy successfully distribute that output?" "Is the economy capable of maintaining efficiency in the use of its resources in the face of changes in the relative supplies of resources, changes in consumer tastes, and changes in technology?" All four of these questions obviously have an important bearing on the problem of achieving

and maintaining an efficient allocation of available resources.

We are well aware that one of the major characteristics of capitalistic economies is their heavy reliance upon a price system as a means for allocating resources (Chapter 5). Our major topics of discussion, then, are prices and the price system. Specifically, our basic goal in the ensuing chapters is to acquire a comprehensive understanding of the operation and relative efficiency of the *price system* in allocating resources within the framework of American capitalism. As a means to achieving this primary goal, we also seek a thorough analysis of *individual prices* under a variety of contrasting market arrangements.

Using the product market as a point of reference, the present chapter defines and describes the various market arrangements we propose to examine. In the subsequent chapters in Part 5 we review and apply our previous analysis of demand and supply, enhance our understanding of the demand side of the market, explore the production (supply) side of the market through a discussion of production costs—the major determinant of a firm's willingness to supply a given product—and examine in some detail the interaction of supply and demand under the various market arrangements described in the present chapter. Our attention will then shift to the functioning of prices in the resource market. Finally—and most important of all—the over-all operation of the price system in American capitalism is evaluated.

FOUR BASIC MARKET MODELS

There is no such thing as an "average" or "typical" industry. Detailed examination of the business sector of American capitalism reveals an almost infinite number of different market situations; no two industries are alike. At one extreme we may find a single producer completely dominating a particular market. At the other we discover thousands upon thousands— yes, even millions—of firms, each of whom supplies a minute fraction of total or market output. Between these extremes lies an almost unlimited variety of market arrangements, most of which shade into one another.

Obviously, any attempt to examine each specific industry would be an endless and impossible task. There are simply too many of them. Hence, we seek a more realistic objective —to define and discuss several basic market structures, or models. In so doing we will acquaint ourselves with the *general* way in which price and output are determined in most of the market types which characterize American capitalism.

But the use of a few market models as typifying most of American industries calls for a word or two of caution. First, the market models to be considered are necessarily abstractions. They are merely first approximations and as such do not purport to present a clear or complete picture of reality (see Chapter 1). In no case will the market models we are about to define provide a *detailed* explanation of the functioning of any specific firm. Yet they will do a reasonably good job of outlining the operation of many firms.

Furthermore, some firms and industries will not fall neatly within any of the market models we are about to outline; rather they will bear characteristics of two or more of these models.

This means that the classification of a given firm or industry might entail an element of arbitrariness. This is the same type of problem which other scientists encounter. The botanist, for example, classifies all plants under three family groups—algae and fungi (thallophytes), moss plants (bryophytes), and vascular plants (tracheophytes). Yet many forms of plant life do not neatly fit into any one of these families but rather are borderline cases. So it is with the economist in classifying industries.

Finally, it is important to recognize at the outset that the economist's definitions of the basic market models do not coincide with those typically employed by businessmen and laymen. The definitions which follow are not of common-sense vintage. "Competition," for example, has a much more precise meaning to the economist than it does to the average businessman.

Economists envision four relatively distinct market situations. These are (1) pure competition, (2) pure monopoly, (3) monopolistic competition, and (4) oligopoly. The immediate task is describing the major characteristics of each of these four market models. In doing so we will use the seller's side of the product market as a point of reference. We will see later that the same general models also are relevant for the buying side of the market.

Pure competition

A purely competitive market has several distinct characteristics which set it off from other market structures.

(1) A main feature of a purely competitive market is the presence of a large number of independently acting sellers, usually offering their products in a highly organized market.

(2) Competitive firms are producing a standardized or virtually standardized product. Given price, the consumer is indifferent as to the seller from whom he purchases. In a competitive market the products of Firms B, C, D, E, and so forth are looked upon by the buyer as perfect substitutes for that of Firm A.

(3) In a purely competitive market *individual*

firms exert no control over product price. This characteristic follows from the preceding two. Under pure competition each firm produces such a small fraction of total output that increasing or decreasing its output will have no perceptible influence upon total supply or, therefore, product price. To illustrate, assume there are 10,000 competing firms, each of which is currently producing 100 units of output. Total supply is obviously 1,000,000. Now suppose one of these 10,000 firms cuts its output to 50 units. Will this affect price? No. And the reason is clear: this restriction of output by a single firm has an almost imperceptible impact on total supply—specifically, the total quantity supplied declines from 1,000,000 to 999,950. This is obviously not enough of a change in total supply to affect product price noticeably. In short, the individual, competitive producer cannot adjust market price; he can only adjust to it.

Stated differently, pricewise the individual competitive producer is at the mercy of the market; to him product price is a given datum over which he exerts no influence. He can get the same price per unit for a large output as he can for a small output. To ask a price higher than the going market price would be futile. Consumers will not buy anything from Firm A at a price of $2.10 when his 9,999 competitors are selling an identical and therefore perfect substitute product at $2 per unit. Conversely, because Firm A can sell as much as it chooses at $2 per unit, there is no reason for it to charge some lower price, say, $1.95. Indeed, to do so would shrink its profits.

Finally, a subtle but highly important point: although the *individual* firm cannot influence product price by varying its output, all firms in a competitive industry taken *as a group* can cause market price to vary. Should all 10,000 firms cut their outputs from 100 to 50 units, the total quantity supplied will decline from 1,000,000 to 500,000 units. This is most certainly a very significant change and can be expected to boost product price considerably. In brief, the individual firm cannot influence price, but all firms as a group can. Although

product price to an individual competitive seller is fixed, that price is free to move up or down in accordance with changes in either *total* demand or *total* supply.

4. New firms are free to enter and existing firms are free to leave purely competitive industries. In particular, no significant obstacles —legal, technical, financial, or otherwise—exist to prohibit new firms from coming into being and selling their outputs in competitive markets.

5. Because purely competitive firms are producing a standardized product, there is virtually no room for *nonprice competition*, that is, competition on the basis of differences in product quality, advertising, or sales promotion. By definition each firm in a competitive market is producing an identical product. Hence, no firm has a quality edge over its rivals. Advertising by individual firms will be to no avail, because each firm's product has no distinguishing features to be advertised or promoted. Buyers will know that the products of all firms in the industry have the same features. Advertising has virtually no chance of convincing them otherwise.

What about examples? Really precise examples of pure competition are few and far between. If we neglect the government's farm program, agriculture provides us with most of the good illustrations. Thus, we find, for example, that there are literally millions of farmers producing class I corn—a product which is obviously standardized or uniform. Class I corn is class I corn! Each firm supplies such a small fraction of the total that no single farmer has any control over the market price for class I corn. He accepts the market price which exists in the highly organized market as data over which he has no influence; the individual farmer can sell as much or as little as he wants without affecting that price. He does not squander his financial resources on advertising or sales promotion. Farmer Jones knows that millions of other farmers are producing an identical product and that buyers are well aware of this. Hence, advertising would be futile, a sheer waste of time, effort, and money. The markets for wheat, cotton, barley, oats, the various types of livestock, and a good many other farm staples also fit rather well into the competitive mold we have outlined.

Pure monopoly

Now we turn to the other extreme of the spectrum. Pure monopoly provides us with the sharpest contrast to pure competition.

1. A pure, or absolute, monopolist is a one-firm industry. A single firm is the only producer of a given product; hence, the firm and the industry are synonymous.

2. It follows from this first characteristic that the monopolist's product is unique in the sense that there are no good, or close, substitutes available. From the buyer's point of view this means that he has no reasonable alternatives to which he can turn. He must buy the product from the monopolist or do without.

A question arises at this point: When are products "good" substitutes? There is no clear answer to this query. In a very broad sense all goods and services which compete for the consumer's dollar are substitutes. A down payment on a house may be a substitute for a new automobile. A two-week vacation may be a substitute for a television set. A pair of shoes may be a substitute for a new pair of slacks. A symphony concert may be a substitute for a fraternity dance. Yet in a more restricted sense of the term it is clear that some products and services simply do not have reasonably good substitutes. Candles and kerosene lamps are not good substitutes for electric lights. Other spices are poor substitutes for salt. Bus or train transportation may be a poor substitute for owning one's own automobile. To many, a symphony concert is no substitute at all for the Signa Phi Nothing formal.

In our discussion we will employ the idea of substitution in the narrower sense of the term. Hence, we can agree that, as most consumers see it, there are no good substitutes for the water piped into our homes by the municipal water works or the electric power provided by the local power company. Digging a well or importing water from a neighboring community are not realistic substitutes for running water in one's home. And few would regard candles and kerosene lighting as acceptable substitutes for electric lights. In any event your television set will not run on kerosene. Up to World War II manufacturers whose products entailed the need for a strong but lightweight metal had little choice but to purchase aluminum from Alcoa; no competing aluminum producers were in existence prior to the war.

3. We have emphasized that the individual firm operating under pure competition exercises no influence over product price. This is so because he contributes only a negligible portion of total supply. In vivid contrast the pure monopolist exercises considerable control over price. And the reason is obvious: he is responsible for, and therefore controls, the total quantity supplied. By manipulating the amount supplied he can cause product price to change. If it is to his advantage, we can expect him to use his power in this way.

4. If, by definition, a pure monopolist has no immediate competitors, there must be a reason for this lack of competition. And there is: the existence of monopoly depends upon the existence of barriers to entry. Be they economic, technological, legal, or other, certain obstacles must exist to keep new competitors from coming into the industry if monopoly is to persist. Entry is not easy under conditions of pure monopoly; on the contrary, it is blocked. More of this in Chapter 25. Barrier to entry

5. Depending upon the type of product or service involved, monopolists may or may not engage in extensive advertising and sales promotion activity. Local public utilities see no point in large expenditures for advertising; any local citizen who wants water, gas, and electric power and telephone service already knows from whom he must buy.

If pure monopolists do advertise, such advertising is likely to be of a public relations, or good-will, character rather than highly competitive, as is the advertising associated with, say, cigarettes, soap flakes, and beer. Because they have no immediate rivals, monopolists, in trying to induce more people to buy their products, need not invoke the ours-is-better-than-theirs type of advertising which plagues radio, television, and otherwise scenic highways. Rather the monopolist's pitch is likely to be

"We're really nice fellows and certainly wouldn't do anything to exploit other firms, our beloved employees, or, heaven forbid, consumers." Or the monopolist may be anxious for the public to recognize that at least 90 per cent of the firm's stock is held by destitute widows and orphans. Or, finally, the monopolist may be content simply to point out the technological progress for which the firm has been responsible.

Because pure monopoly is admittedly an extreme market model, we once again find relatively few precise illustrations. Most local public utilities are pure monopolists for the municipalities which they serve. Thus consumers either purchase their water, electricity, gas, and telephone service from the local utility or do without. Much the same may hold true of railway service in rural areas. On a nationwide basis American Telephone and Telegraph approximates a pure monopoly. Pullman Standard is the sole manufacturer of sleeping cars for the nation's railroads. Until World War II, Alcoa was a virtual monopolist in the production of most basic aluminum products; now it faces some competition from Reynolds and Kaiser. The United Shoe Machinery Company is the only manufacturer of certain equipment used in the production of shoes. IBM is the only source of certain calculating machines.

This is not to say that the pure monopolist will charge the highest price he can get for his product or service. Consumers may find it impossible to do without some amount of water and highly inconvenient to do without some quantity of electricity. But the amounts they purchase will vary inversely with price. If the prices of electricity and water were extremely high, the poor (but cheap) substitutes of kerosene lamps and digging a well would become relevant. And an extremely high price on office machines might induce firms to substitute bookkeepers for the machines.

Monopolistic competition

As its name indicates, monopolistic competition stands between the extremes of pure competition and pure monopoly. It embraces characteristics of both, but for the most part it stands closer to pure competition.

1. As is the case with pure competition, monopolistic competition entails a large number of sellers acting independently. This does not mean that there need be 1,000, 10,000, or 1,000,000 firms in the industry; 30, 40, or 100 firms of more or less equal size may prevail. The important point is that each firm produces a fairly small share of the total output.

2. In contrast to pure competition, wherein the product is standardized, product differentiation is a major characteristic of monopolistically competitive industries. Product differentiation entails not only physical differences in the products of various producers or sellers in the industry, but also differences in such factors as the location and "snob appeal" of the seller's store, the packaging of the product, the cordiality of the firm's salespeople, the effectiveness of its advertising, the availability of credit, the company's reputation for servicing, or "making good on," defective products, and so forth. The net result is that, although all firms in such an industry are producing the same general type or class of product, the particular product of each firm will have certain distinguishing features which set it off to some extent from those of other firms in the industry. In other words, the products of monopolistically competitive firms are close, but not perfect, substitutes. Just as the presence of a relatively large number of firms makes for competition, product differentiation gives rise to a measure of monopoly power. Indeed, monopolistic competition is sometimes called "the case of differentiation and large numbers."

3. Monopolistically competitive producers have a limited amount of control over product price. The control that exists depends essentially upon the degree of product differentiation and the number and proximity of competitors. The monopolistically competitive producer can raise his price modestly without having his sales fall to zero. Why? Because buyers recognize some differences between the products of various sellers. In the presence of product differentiation consumers are likely to have definite preferences for the products of specific sellers, and relatively small price increases by one firm will not cause all buyers to seek out the close substitute products of rival firms in that industry.

Generally, when the rivals of a monopolistically competitive firm are many in number and in close proximity, each firm's control over price will be less than would otherwise be the case. *Entry* 4. Entry into monopolistically competitive *easy* industries is typically easy. Nevertheless, entry may be a bit more difficult under monopolistically competitive conditions than when pure competition prevails. This is so because of product differentiation. A new firm must not only obtain the capital necessary to go into business but must also win clients away from existing firms. Securing a share of the market might entail considerable research and product development costs by the new firm to ensure that its product will have features which distinguish it from products already on the market. Similarly, considerable advertising outlays may be necessary to inform consumers of the existence of a new brand and to convince a number of them that it will be to their advantage to switch to the new product. In short, greater financial obstacles may face the potential newcomer under monopolistic competition than under pure competition.

Vigorous 5. Because products are differentiated, mo-
nonprice nopolistically competitive industries are ordi-
competition narily characterized by vigorous nonprice competition. Economic rivalry, as we have already noted, may be based not only upon price, but also upon product quality, advertising, and conditions or services associated with the sale of a product. Great emphasis is placed upon trademarks and brand names as means for convincing the consumer that the products of one's rivals are not as good substitutes for brand X as might first seem to be the case. Indeed, quality and advertising competition go hand in hand. Advertising proclaims and, if possible, magnifies real differences in product quality. While quality competition manipulates the firm's product, advertising and sales promotion attempt to manipulate the consumer.

A considerable number of industries approximate the conditions of monopolistic competition. At the manufacturing level the women's dress industry provides a good example; New York City and a few other large metropolitan areas are the locations of the large number of small manufacturers which comprise this industry. The shoe industry also has features which make it reasonably close to being monopolistically competitive. A good many types of retail trade, particularly in cities of any size, occur under conditions which approximate monopolistic competition. Most cities will contain a fairly large number of grocery stores, cleaning establishments, clothing shops, gasoline stations, restaurants, barber shops, and so forth, all of which are providing differentiated products and services.

Oligopoly

The remaining market model—oligopoly—is less precisely defined by economists than are the three market structures just discussed. Two reasons go far to explain this lack of preciseness. On the one hand, oligopoly includes a wider range of market structures than do the other three market models; in effect it embraces all the remaining market situations which do not fit the rather clearly defined market models of pure competition, monopolistic competition, and pure monopoly. On the other hand, as we will discover in a moment, oligopoly has certain characteristics which make it difficult to make hard-and-fast predictions about the behavior of oligopolistic industries.

1. The basic characteristic of oligopoly is "fewness." Oligopoly exists whenever a few firms dominate the market for a product. When we hear of the "Big Three," "Big Four," or "Big Six," we can be relatively certain that the industry is oligopolistic. This does not mean, of course, that the Big Three or Four necessarily share the total market. The dominant few may control say 70 or 80 per cent of a market, with a competitive fringe—a group of smaller firms —sharing the remainder.

When a few firms dominate a market, each of these firms will have a share of the market sufficiently large so that its actions and policies will have repercussions on the other firms. Because each firm supplies a large portion of the total industry output, actions taken by any one firm to improve its share of the market will directly and immediately affect its rivals. Hence,

Few Firms dominant

each firm must carefully weigh the expected reactions of its rivals when considering changes in product price, advertising outlays, product quality, and so forth. Such clear-cut *mutual interdependence* is peculiar to oligopoly. It is not present in pure competition or monopolistic competition because of the large numbers of firms involved. The pure monopolist has no need to worry about the reactions of rivals because he has none. Indeed, it can be said that oligopoly exists whenever the number of sellers is so few that the actions of one will have obvious and significant repercussions on the others. The firms of an oligopolistic industry are all in the same boat. If one rocks the boat, the others will be affected and in all probability will know the identity of the responsible firm and can retaliate.

2. Oligopolists may be producing virtually standardized products or differentiated products. Speaking very generally, those oligopolistic industries which are producing raw materials or semifinished goods are typically offering virtually uniform products to buyers. For example, most metal products—steel, copper, zinc, lead, and aluminum—along with cement, rayon, explosives, industrial alcohol, and some building materials, are virtually uniform goods produced in markets in which a few large firms are dominant. On the other hand, oligopolistic industries producing finished consumer goods are typically offering differentiated products to buyers. Automobiles, tires, petroleum products, soap, cigarettes, fountain pens, breakfast foods, aircraft, farm implements, plus a host of electrical appliances—refrigerators, radios, electric razors, and so forth—are produced by oligopolistic industries wherein product differentiation is considerable.[1]

3. An individual oligopolistic firm's control over price tends to be closely circumscribed by the mutual interdependence which characterizes such markets. Specifically, if a given firm lowers price, it will initially gain sales at the expense of its several rivals. However, these adversely affected rivals will have little choice

[1] Illustrations are from Joe S. Bain, *Pricing, Distribution, and Employment*, rev. ed. (New York: Holt, Rinehart and Winston, Inc., 1953), pp. 273–274, 333.

but to retaliate to recover their shrinking shares of the market; they will match or even undercut the given firm to preserve their market share. The result may be a price war and possibly losses for all firms. Conversely, if a given oligopolist increases his price, rival firms stand to gain sales and profits by adhering to their present prices. That is, a price-boosting oligopolist runs the risk of "pricing himself out of the market" to the benefit of his rivals. For both these reasons there is a strong tendency for firms in oligopolist markets not to alter their prices very frequently.

The potentially adverse effects of price warring or pricing oneself out of the market can be largely avoided by a group of oligopolistic firms through the establishment of some sort of collusive agreement by which all firms either increase or decrease their prices as a group. Under such a collusive arrangement the firms as a group can exert control over price in much the same way as can a pure monopolist.

4. Obstacles to entry are typically formidable in oligopolistic industries. The ownership of strategic patents or essential raw materials by existing firms may virtually prohibit the entry of new firms. Furthermore, the technology of heavy industry may demand that a new competitor be a large-scale producer from the outset, thus ruling out the possibility of a new firm starting on a small-scale basis and in time expanding into a significant rival for existing firms. In addition, certain advantages of being established—that is, the mere fact that existing firms are producing well-known, highly advertised products and selling them through long-established marketing outlets—may work against the successful entrance of new firms to the industry. Yet, in contrast to pure monopoly, entry is not usually blocked completely in oligopolistic industries. The relatively recent entry of Sylvania Electric into the electrical equipment industry presents a formidable rival for General Electric and Westinghouse. Kaiser's entry into the aluminum and automobile industries is also illustrative, despite very limited success in the latter field. Entry to oligopolistic industries is very difficult, but by no means impossible.

monopsony — only one buyer

monopsonistic compet present of a fairly large nr buyers

Oligopolistic industries frequently channel considerable amounts of resources into advertising and other promotional activities. But the type and amount of advertising will depend upon whether or not the firms are producing standardized or differentiated products.

Advertising competition is likely to be strong among oligopolists who are producing differentiated products. For example, each major automobile producer or cigarette manufacturer will have a large budget for convincing the consumer that his particular product is in all ways superior to those of his rivals. Such advertising is likely to be of a highly competitive ours-is-better-than-theirs nature. On the other hand, public relations advertising is the bill of fare for oligopolists who are producing virtually standardized products. United States Steel does not try to convince the public that its sheet steel is superior to that produced by Republic, Bethlehem, or any of its other rivals. Skilled buyers who purchase the raw or fabricated steel products from these firms know that any differences are negligible. Hence, advertising in such industries is to keep the company in the public's eye, to convince the public that big business is an essential cog in the American economy, and so forth.

Quality competition may be intense under oligopoly, particularly so when product differentiation prevails. The research and design departments of many oligopolistic industries are becoming increasingly important over the years. Indeed, it is through research and rapid product development that the entry of potential rivals into the industry may be thwarted.

A good many American industries fall under the heading of oligopoly. As a matter of fact, most of those industries which come to mind when we think of big business are some form or another of oligopoly. In addition to the specific examples previously mentioned, Table 8-3 contains a list of industries most of which are oligopolistic.

Imperfect competition

We shall find it convenient from time to time to distinguish between the characteristics of a purely competitive market and those of all other basic market arrangements—pure monopoly, monopolistic competition, and oligopoly. To facilitate such comparisons we shall employ "imperfect competition" as a generic term to designate all those market structures which deviate from the purely competitive market model.

THE BUYER'S SIDE OF THE MARKET

The preceding definitions of the four basic market models are couched in terms of the seller's side of the market. The same variety of market arrangements can and does exist on the buying or demand side. Here, however, the classification is almost exclusively based on the number of buyers. For example, a very large number of purchasers obviously means pure competition on the buying side of the market. *Monopsony* describes the situation in which there is only one buyer. When a few buyers dominate a market, *oligopsony* exists. *Monopsonistic competition* designates the presence of a fairly large number of buyers.

With the selling and buying sides of the market placed together as in Figure 20-1, it is easy to recognize that an almost infinite number of seller-buyer relationships can exist. A few representative examples will help underscore this point. The public utilities field is usually characterized by pure monopoly on the selling side and pure competition on the buying side. The market for raw tobacco links a large number of purely competitive tobacco farmers on the selling side with a few large buyers—American, Liggett and Myers, Lorillard, and Reynolds—dominating the demand side. Where a strong union exists, specific labor markets often approximate *bilateral monopoly*—pure monopoly on one side and pure monopsony on the other. The local union is the "seller" of labor services, and the company is the single buyer. In the "original equipment" segment of the automobile tire market we have oligopolistic buyers—General Motors, Ford, and Chrysler—linked with oligopsonistic sellers—Goodyear, Firestone, U.S. Rubber, and B. F. Goodrich. A similar arrangement exists in the market for tin plate—a few large steel companies are the sole producers, and two large tin-can manufacturers are the major buyers. And so it goes. When all

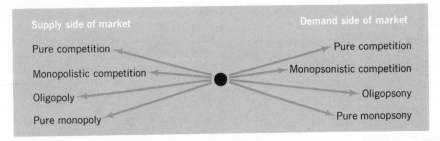

FIGURE 20-1. SOME BASIC MARKET RELATIONSHIPS.
The four basic market models are pertinent to both the selling and buying sides of markets; this suggests the existence of a very large number of selling-buying relationships.

the hybrid cases falling between the four basic market models are taken into account, it is clear that the number of possible market arrangements can be and actually is extremely large.

In short, before hastily labeling an industry as "competitive" or "monopolistic" we must be very sure that we have properly delineated the geographic boundaries of the market. The number of firms alone is not a sufficient criterion by which to gauge the competitiveness of an industry; proximity is important, too.

OTHER COMPETITIVE DIMENSIONS

It is important that we qualify and amend the foregoing definitions and explanations of the various market models in several ways.

Geographic factor

In practice the competitiveness of an industry or firm is a geographic phenomenon. That is, the degree of competition in a particular industry depends upon the size of the market. Although a given city may have seventy or eighty grocery stores, a particular supermarket in a suburban area may, for all practical purposes, be competing only with three other chain stores and one or two independent corner groceries. Similarly, commercial banking appears to be highly competitive at first glance—after all, there are over 13,000 banks in our economy providing essentially identical services. But to the farmer in Podunk Center, Iowa, borrowing from the Chase National Bank in New York City or the Bank of America in California is out of the question. In negotiating a loan Farmer Jones will look to the Podunk Center State Bank or possibly one or two of the larger banks in a nearby city.

Interindustry competition

It is important to recognize the significance of interindustry or interproduct competition. Although a few firms may be the only ones producing a specific product, they may face rather severe rivalry from other somewhat distinct products. Illustrations of such interproduct competition are numerous. The aluminum industry is a strong oligopoly with three firms—Alcoa, Reynolds, and Kaiser—dominating the market. Buyers who must use aluminum have no choice but to do business with one of these three industrial giants. However, in many cases other materials—steel, copper, and even wood or plastics—are suitable substitutes for aluminum. Hence, steel competes with aluminum in the manufacturing of many automobile parts. Aluminum and copper hotly contest the market for transmission lines. Aluminum battles both steel and wood in the construction field. Pricewise these comments add up to the fact that the control over price which the Big Three of the aluminum industry possesses is subject to limitations dictated by the prices of distinct but nevertheless competing products. Another example: The Big Two of the tin-can industry— American Can and Continental Can—dominate over 80 per cent of their market. From within the industry they face little serious competition. But from without they face the competition of glass, plastic, and paper containers.

Nonprice competition

This is a convenient juncture at which to restate a point emphasized earlier/ competition is something more than the willingness and ability to cut prices. Nonprice competition may be vigorous and important in an industry. Variations in product quality, advertising and promotional activities, and so forth are important elements of competition which may supplement or, in some cases, supplant price competition.

Technological advance

The previous explanations of the four basic market models tend to classify the various markets at some particular *point* in time. Hence, they neglect an important competitive force which only functions over a *period* of time. That competitive force is technological advance. The development of new products and new techniques of production can result in new competition for producers who previously enjoyed a considerable degree of monopoly power. Thus the leading proponent[2] of the role of technological advance as a competitive force has argued that

... in capitalist reality ... it is ... competition from the new commodity, the new technology, the new source of supply, the new type of organization (the largest-scale unit of control for instance)—competition which commands a decisive cost or quality advantage and which strikes not at the margins of the profits and the outputs of the existing firms but at their foundations and their very lives. This kind of competition is ... so ... important that it becomes a matter of comparative indifference whether

competition in the ordinary sense functions more or less promptly; the powerful lever that in the long run expands output and brings down prices is in any case made of other stuff.

... that competition of the kind we now have in mind acts not only when in being but also when it is merely an ever-present threat. It disciplines before it attacks. The businessman feels himself to be in a competitive situation even if he is alone in his field. ... In many cases, though not in all, this will in the long run enforce behavior very similar to the perfectly competitive pattern.

An example or two may help to underscore this point. For over a decade a single firm enjoyed the position of a pure monopolist in the production of rayon. Its profits, enormous by any standard, were the results of the successful competition this innovation provided for other textiles. But more recently the development of acetates, nylon, acrilon, and other "miracle fibers" has in turn provided considerable competition for rayon.[3] In a similar manner the rapid development of the dehydrated and quick-frozen food industries during World War II has permitted an intensification of the competition which paper, fiber, and plastic containers provides for the Big Two of the tin-can industry.

DETERMINANTS OF MARKET STRUCTURE

Agriculture is an almost purely competitive industry. The clothing industry fits roughly into the mold of monopolistic competition. The steel and automobile industries are obviously oligopolistic. American Telephone and Telegraph nationally, and public utilities locally, approximate pure monopolies. What forces explain the emergence of these different market structures? What factors have caused agriculture to remain highly competitive and the automobile industry, spiced in its infancy with seventy-odd producers, now to be a tight oligopoly dominated by the Big Three? Although there exists no short, easy answer to these questions, we can put our

---

[2] Joseph A. Schumpeter, *Capitalism, Socialism, and Democracy*, 3d ed. (New York: Harper & Row, Publishers, 1950), pp. 84–85.

[3] A. D. H. Kaplan, *Big Enterprise in a Competitive System* (Washington: Brookings Institution, 1954), p. 193.

fingers on some of the more important forces which historically have played significant roles in determining the competitive structures of the various American industries. Generally speaking, such factors as ① legislation and government policy, ② the policies and practices of business firms, (3) technological considerations, and (4) institutions and characteristics inherent in the capitalistic ideology go far to explain the variety of market structures which characterizes American capitalism.

Legislation and government policy

Government has promoted both monopoly and competition. By issuing *exclusive franchises* to so-called natural monopolies (for example, public utilities), government has purposely created many pure monopolies in industries which might otherwise have attained some degree of competition. Federal government commissions—the Interstate Commerce Commission, Civil Aeronautics Board, and Federal Communications Commission—play the major role in determining the degree of competition in the land and air transportation, radio, and television industries. Similarly, *patent laws* have promoted monopoly by giving innovating firms the exclusive right to manufacture a product for extended periods of time. *High tariffs* have promoted and preserved monopoly power in many domestic industries. On the other hand, there is but little doubt that the liberal Homestead Act of 1862 provided a competitive base for American agriculture. *Antitrust legislation* —the Sherman and Clayton Acts—are explicitly designed to curb the abuses of monopoly power.

We find here seemingly inconsistent government policies; but this inconsistency can be at least partly explained. Although government has pursued a generally antimonopolistic social policy, it simultaneously seeks other social objectives. One of these goals is the promotion of technological advance—an aim which patent legislation tends to promote. And in the case of public utilities, competition has simply not functioned effectively; here government has condoned and promoted monopoly, but has then provided regulatory commissions designed to prevent the abuse of this government-sponsored monopoly power.

Business policies and practices

The practices and policies pursued by various firms and industries can also be critical in determining the structure of industry. In some industries mergers, consolidations, and the development of holding companies have pushed in the direction of oligopoly or monopoly. The evolution of the corporate form of business enterprise and collusive practices between legally independent firms have played a similar role. In other industries cutthroat competition has resulted in some firms driving others from existence, thereby lowering the number of competitors in the industry. In still other instances firms have acquired ownership or control over vital raw materials so as to eliminate present rivals and destroy the possibility of new firms coming into being. These practices and developments, however, have occurred unevenly among various industries, causing some to move in the direction of monopoly and others to remain rather highly competitive.

Technology

Technology has undoubtedly become an increasingly important determinant of industrial structure. In a good many industries technology has developed to the point where the existence of large industrial giants is necessary if efficient low-cost production is to be achieved. Technology has given rise to economies of mass production which only large producers can realize. This means that, given consumer demand, efficient production necessitates the existence of a small number of large producers rather than a large number of small producers. It is thus that technological advance has "forced" the market structure of many "heavy" industries—for example, the automobile, steel, and aluminum industries—in the direction of oligopoly. Economists differ in evaluating the extent to which technological factors require bigness; we shall examine the conflicting views in greater detail in Chapter 32.

In some industries technological advance has worked towards the same end but in a somewhat different manner. Superior research on product development has permitted some firms to outgrow and often eliminate less progressive rivals. Furthermore, this tendency is frequently cumulative; by gaining a larger share of the market through its superior research a firm realizes the financial rewards that facilitate a widening of the technological advantages which it possesses over its rivals.

Capitalistic institutions

We must be reminded that the institutions of American capitalism are permissive of the concentration of economic power and the development of oligopoly and monopoly. The relatively free, individualistic economic environment of the economy is a fertile ground for the most efficient, the most courageous, the most fortunate, or the most crafty producer to conquer his rivals in an effort to free himself from the regulatory powers of competition. Freedom of contract, private property, and inheritance rights have also contributed to the concentration of economic power. And, too, the business cycle has probably abetted the tendency toward monopoly. As a recent scholar[4] puts it:

Weaklings may still fail, and disappear, especially in more difficult times. Good times make it easy to finance consolidations, and tempting for the strong company to expand and the weak to sell out. Thus, both adversity and prosperity work alike to reduce the number of firms in an industry.

SUMMARY

1. American industry is characterized by differing degrees of competition. The market models of (*a*) pure competition, (*b*) pure monopoly,

[4] John K. Galbraith, *American Capitalism*, rev. ed. (Boston: Houghton Mifflin Company, 1956), p. 35.

(*c*) monopolistic competition, and (*d*) oligopoly are classifications into which most industries can be fitted with reasonable accuracy. These market models, however, are merely first approximations of reality.

2. Table 20-1 provides a convenient summary of the major characteristics of these four market models.

3. Similar market classifications, based essentially upon numbers, are applied to the buying, or demand, side of the market.

4. The economist's definitions of the four market models focus attention upon (*a*) the number of firms, (*b*) the degree of product differentiation, and (*c*) the ease or difficulty encountered by new firms in entering the industry. However, certain other important factors which have a bearing upon the competitive nature of an industry must also be considered:

a. In practice any meaningful description of the market structure of an industry requires a proper choice of the geographic limits of the market.

b. Interindustry or interproduct competition is a significant force in many markets which might otherwise appear to be lacking in competition.

c. Nonprice competition may be an important supplement to price competition.

d. Technological advance, working as a competitive force through time, often undermines existing industries characterized by strong monopolistic elements.

5. Legislation, government policies, research and technological development, industry practices, and a variety of other factors have all played significant roles in determining the present structure of American industry.

QUESTIONS AND STUDY SUGGESTIONS

1. Under which of the four market classifications discussed in the chapter do each of the following most accurately fit: (*a*) a supermarket located in your home town; (*b*) the steel industry; (*c*) a Kansas wheat farm; (*d*) the commercial bank in which

TABLE 20-1. CHARACTERISTICS OF THE FOUR BASIC MARKET MODELS

Market model	Number of firms	Type of product	Control over price	Conditions of entry	Nonprice competition	Examples
Pure competition	A very large number	Standardized	None	Very easy, no obstacles	None	Agriculture
Monopolistic competition	Many	Differentiated	Some, but within rather narrow limits	Relatively easy	Considerable emphasis on advertising, brand names, trademarks, etc.	Retail trade, dresses, shoes
Oligopoly	Few	Standardized or differentiated	Circumscribed by mutual interdependence; considerable with collusion	Significant obstacles present	Typically a great deal, particularly with product differentiation	Steel, automobile, farm implements, meat packing, many household appliances
Pure monopoly	One	Unique; no close substitutes	Considerable	Blocked	Mostly public relations advertising	AT&T, local utilities

you or your family has an account; (e) the automobile industry. In each case justify your classification. In making your classifications, specify any assumptions you have made about the geographical limits of the various markets.

2. "Purely competitive producers have no price policy, but monopolistically competitive, oligopolistic, and purely monopolistic firms do." Explain.

3. In 1950 Crawford H. Greenewalt, president of E. I. Du Pont de Nemours & Company, made the following statements before a House committee which was studying the monopoly problem:

"The difference between three and one (firms) is very substantial. It is the difference between monopoly and no monopoly."
"Oligopoly . . . to me is meaningless, because there is either competition or there is not. If there is competition, the public interest is being served."

What differences, if any, can you detect between Mr. Greenewalt's definition of "competition" and the economist's definition of "pure competition"? Do you feel that all industries can be meaningfully categorized as competitive or not competitive? Explain your answers.

4. A single farmer is "at the mercy of the market" in that he must regard the market price for his products as being fixed. Yet agricultural prices are very flexible. Reconcile these two statements.

5. What is interindustry competition? How important is it in each of the following industries? In each case specify the competing products or industries.

a. Automobile   d. Railway
b. Cement   e. Steel
c. Coal   f. Glass container

6. What is nonprice competition? How prevalent do you think nonprice competition to be in the industries mentioned in questions 1 and 5?

7. Why doesn't a purely competitive producer advertise his product?

8. "Competition should be judged solely on the basis of the number of firms in the industry; the larger the number, the greater the competition." Critically evaluate.

9. What are some of the major forces which determine the market structure of industries? Drawing on your knowledge of American history, what is the relative significance of these forces in explaining the market structures of the following industries?

a. Automobile   e. Petroleum
b. Steel   f. Chemical
c. Agriculture   g. Tobacco
d. Television

Be as specific as you can in your answers.

10. "Technological advance has both encouraged and limited the development of monopoly." Do you agree? Explain.

SELECTED REFERENCES

Bodenhorn, Diran, *Intermediate Price Theory* (New York: McGraw-Hill Book Company, Inc., 1961), chap. 2.

Dean, Joel, *Managerial Economics* (Englewood Cliffs, N. J.: Prentice-Hall, Inc., 1951), chap. 2.

Due, John F., and Robert W. Clower, *Intermediate Economic Analysis,* 4th ed. (Homewood, Ill.: Richard D. Irwin, Inc., 1961), chap. 4.

Enke, Stephen, *Intermediate Economic Theory* (Englewood Cliffs, N.J.: Prentice-Hall, Inc., 1950), chap. 15.

Fellner, William, *Modern Economic Analysis* (New York: McGraw-Hill Book Company, Inc., 1960), chap. 17.

Hague, Douglas C., and Alfred W. Stonier, *The Essentials of Economics* (New York: Longmans, Green & Co., Inc., 1955), chaps. 1–4.

Heilbroner, Robert L., *The Making of Economic Society* (Englewood Cliffs, N.J., Prentice-Hall, Inc., 1962), chap. 5.

Weiss, Leonard W., *Economics and American Industry* (New York: John Wiley & Sons, Inc., 1961), chap. 1.

Chapter 21

DEMAND, SUPPLY, AND ELASTICITY:

SOME APPLICATIONS

IN CHAPTER 4 we familiarized ourselves with the rudiments of demand and supply analysis. In the present chapter we seek a more sophisticated understanding of demand and supply. Specifically, the tasks of this chapter are threefold. First, a brief summary of the elements of demand and supply analysis is presented. Second, we shall consider the concept of elasticity as applied to both demand and supply. Third, some specific applications of demand and supply analysis are discussed.

DEMAND, SUPPLY, AND MARKET PRICE[1]

Demand and supply both refer to schedules. The demand schedule shows the relationship between various possible prices of a product and the quantities which consumers will purchase at each of these prices (columns 1 and 2, Table 21-1). The price–quantity-demanded re-

[1] This brief review is not a substitute for Chapter 4. The student is strongly urged to reread Chapter 4 at this point.

TABLE 21-1. THE DEMAND FOR, AND SUPPLY OF, CORN

(1) Total quantity demanded per week	(2) Price per bushel	(3) Total quantity supplied per week	(4) Surplus (+) or shortage (−) (arrow indicates effect on price)
2,000	$5	12,000	+10,000↓
4,000	4	10,000	+ 6,000↓
7,000	3	7,000	0
11,000	2	4,000	− 7,000↑
16,000	1	1,000	−15,000↑

lationship thus portrayed is an inverse one. Consumers typically buy less at a high price than at a low price. This common-sense relationship is called the *law of demand*. Graphically the demand curve is downsloping (*DD* in Figure 21-1).

The supply schedule embodies the relationship between possible product prices and the quantities which producers will supply at each of those prices (columns 2 and 3, Table 21-1). The relationship between price and quantity supplied is a direct one. The *law of supply* states that producers will find it profitable to devote more resources to the production of a good when its price is high than they will when it is low. When graphed, this direct relationship results in an upsloping supply curve (SS in Figure 21-1).

The intersection of demand and supply determines the market, or equilibrium, price and quantity. Both Table 21-1 and Figure 21-1 clearly show that the demand and supply data here assumed result in an equilibrium price of

$3 and an equilibrium quantity of 7,000 units. Competition guarantees that any other price will be unstable. The surpluses which result at any above-equilibrium price will induce competing sellers to shade their prices to work off these excess stocks. The shortages which accompany below-equilibrium prices will prompt competing buyers to bid up the price, as consumers want to avoid doing without the product. At the equilibrium price the market will be cleared. The tendency of a competitive market to establish a price at which quantity demand will just equal quantity supplied is called the *rationing function* of competitive prices.

Changes in the determinants of either demand or supply can cause the demand and supply schedules (curves) to shift. Variations in consumer tastes, incomes, the prices of substitute goods, consumer expectations, and the number of buyers in the market all will account for shifts in demand. Changes in any of those factors which affect production costs will cause

FIGURE 21-1. THE EQUILIBRIUM PRICE FOR CORN AS DETERMINED BY MARKET DEMAND AND MARKET SUPPLY.

Equilibrium price and equilibrium quantity are determined by the intersection of demand *DD* and supply *SS*.

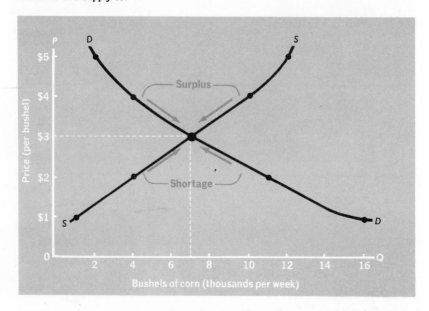

supply to shift. The relationship between a change in demand and the resulting changes in equilibrium price and quantity is a direct one. An inverse relationship exists between a change in supply and the ensuing change in price. However, the relationship between a change in supply and the ensuing change in quantity is direct.

ELASTICITY OF DEMAND

The law of demand tells us that consumers will respond to a price decline by buying more of a product. But the degree of responsiveness of consumers to a price change may vary considerably from product to product. Economists measure how responsive, or sensitive, consumers are to a change in the price of a product by the concept of *elasticity*.

The demand for some products is such that consumers are relatively responsive to price changes; price changes give rise to very considerable changes in the quantity purchased. The demand for such products is said to be *elastic*. For other products consumers are relatively unresponsive to price changes; that is, price changes result in modest changes in the amount purchased. In such cases demand is *inelastic*.

The elasticity formula

Economists measure the degree of elasticity or inelasticity by the *elasticity coefficient*, or E_d, in this formula:

$$E_d = \frac{\text{percentage change in quantity demanded}}{\text{percentage change in price}}$$

Demand is *elastic* if a given percentage change in price results in a larger percentage change in quantity demanded. Example: if a 2 per cent decline in price results in a 4 per cent increase in quantity demanded, demand is elastic. In all such cases, where demand is elastic, the elasticity coefficient will obviously be greater than 1. If a given percentage change in price is accompanied by a relatively smaller change in the quantity demanded, demand is *inelastic*. Illustration: if a 3 per cent decline in price gives rise

to a 1 per cent increase in the amount demanded, demand is inelastic. It is apparent that the elasticity coefficient will always be less than 1 when demand is inelastic. The borderline case which separates elastic and inelastic demands occurs where a percentage change in price and the accompanying percentage change in quantity demanded chance to be equal. For example, a 1 per cent drop in price causes a 1 per cent increase in the amount sold. This special case is termed *unit elasticity*, because the elasticity coefficient is exactly 1, or unity.

An annoying problem arises in applying the elasticity formula. To illustrate: in calculating the elasticity coefficient for corn for the $5–$4 price range in Table 21-2, should we use the $5–2,000 bushel price-quantity combination or the $4–4,000 bushel combination as a point of reference in calculating the percentage changes in price and quantity which the elasticity formula requires? Our choice will influence the outcome. Using the $5–2,000 bushel reference point, we find that the percentage decrease in price is 20 per cent and the percentage increase in quantity is 100 per cent. Substituting in the formula, the elasticity coefficient is 100/20 per cent, or 5. But using the $4–4,000 bushel reference point, we find that the percentage increase in price is 25 per cent and the percentage decline in quantity is 50 per cent. The elasticity coefficient is therefore 50/25 per cent, or 2. Although the formula indicates that demand is elastic in both cases, the two solutions involve a considerable difference in the degree of elasticity. In other instances—experiment, for example, with the $3–$2 price range—the formula may indicate a slightly elastic demand for one price-quantity combination and slight inelasticity of demand for the other.

Economists have reached a workable compromise to this problem by using the averages of the two prices and the two quantities under consideration for reference points. In the $5–$4 price range case the price reference is $4.50 and the quantity reference 3,000 bushels. The percentage change in price is now about 22 per cent and the percentage change in quantity about 67 per cent, giving us an elasticity coef-

TABLE 21-2. ELASTICITY OF DEMAND AS MEASURED BY THE TOTAL RECEIPTS TEST AND THE ELASTICITY COEFFICIENT

Total receipts per price x quant (handwritten)

(1) Total quantity demanded per week	(2) Price per bushel	(3) Total receipts (expenditures)	(4) Total receipts test	(5) Elasticity coefficient E_d (approximate)
2,000	$5	$10,000		
			Elastic	3.00
4,000	4	16,000		
			Elastic	2.00
7,000	3	21,000		
			Elastic	
11,000	2	22,000		
			Inelastic	0.56
16,000	1	16,000		

ficient of approximately 3. Instead of gauging elasticity at either one of the extremes of this price-quantity range, this solution estimates elasticity at the mid-point of the $5–$4 price range. In column 5 of Table 21-2 we have calculated the elasticity coefficients for the demand data of Table 21-1, using the price and quantity averages in figuring the percentage changes in price and quantity. The reader should verify these figures and calculate the elasticity coefficient which has been purposely omitted.

The total receipts test

Because total receipts is the product of price times quantity, it is also possible to test for elasticity by observing what happens to total receipts—total expenditures from the purchasers' viewpoint—when product price changes. If demand is elastic, a given percentage decline in price will be more than compensated for by a larger percentage increase in the amount sold. As a result, total receipts must rise. On the other hand, if demand is inelastic, a given percentage decline in price will give rise to a smaller percentage increase in the amount demanded, which obviously will not compensate for the price fall. Hence, total receipts will

decline. These statements are reversible. If demand is elastic, an increase in price will reduce total receipts. If demand is inelastic, an increase in price will increase total receipts. Can you explain why? Finally, if demand is of unit elasticity, a given percentage decrease (increase) in price will be exactly compensated for by an equal percentage increase (decrease) in quantity sold, leaving total receipts unchanged. Column 4 of Table 21-2 applies the total receipts test to the demand data for corn.

The alert reader may have detected two subtle but notable characteristics of elasticity from our applications of the elasticity formula and the total receipts tests. First, as Table 21-2 indicates, elasticity typically varies over the different price ranges of the same demand schedule or curve. In the case of the demand curve for corn, demand is considerably more elastic at higher prices than at low prices. This correctly suggests that, as the price of a product falls, sales will increase to the saturation point at which consumers are virtually "filled up" on the product. When this is the case, further price cuts will not induce buyers to take much more. Conversely, when prices are already relatively high, further price increases will induce buyers to seek out substitute products or do without, causing relatively sharp de-

Elasticity varies over diff price ranges (handwritten)

clines in sales. There is a tendency for most demand curves to be elastic at high prices and inelastic at low prices.

In the second place, reference to the graphic presentation of the demand for corn in Figure 21-1 correctly suggests that the graphic appearance of a demand curve is *not* a sound basis upon which to judge its elasticity. Because this demand curve has a steeper slope at relatively higher prices and a flatter slope at relatively lower prices, one is tempted to associate an inelastic demand with high prices and an elastic demand with low prices. But this is dangerous reasoning. Have we not just discovered that the elasticity formula and the total receipts test indicate that the reverse is true? The catch lies in the fact that the flatness or steepness of a demand curve is based upon absolute changes in price and quantity while elasticity has to do with relative changes in price and quantity.

Determinants of elasticity of demand

What makes the demand for any specific product elastic or inelastic? Generally speaking, the elasticity of demand for any product is greater (1) the larger the number of good substitutes available, (2) the larger the item as a part of one's total budget, and (3) where the product is regarded as a luxury item and therefore dispensable. A couple of illustrations will help.

The demand for salt tends to be highly inelastic on all three counts. There are simply no good substitutes for salt to which consumers can turn if its price rises from say 15 cents to 20 cents per pound. Furthermore, a household's expenditures on salt is such a small fraction of a family's weekly or monthly budget that the total impact of this price increase is negligible for all practical purposes. And, finally, the product is looked upon as a necessity; unsalted cooking leaves much to be desired. On the other hand, the demand for a brand X stereophonic phonograph may be relatively elastic. There are many good substitutes available in the form of competing brands of stereo, not to mention FM radios. The price of the item is large in relation to one's budget, and a given percentage change in price will have a very significant impact dollarwise upon that budget. And to most families a stereo phonograph is a luxury and therefore an expendable item in its budget.

Other factors also influence elasticity. Consumers are creatures of habit. It is only over a period of time that they alter their customary expenditure patterns in response to given price changes. Demand therefore tends to be more elastic in the long run than in the short run. Furthermore, the durability of some products has a bearing upon the elasticity of the demand for them. Few consumers actually face the choice of doing without a refrigerator or automobile. The question is rather one of repairing your old refrigerator or car or buying new ones. Repairing older durable goods is frequently a very good substitute for buying a new model. Durability therefore tends to make demand more elastic than would otherwise be the case.

In Chapter 28 we shall discover that a somewhat different group of factors determines the elasticity of demand for resources.

Some practical applications

The concept of elasticity of demand is something more than a theoretical notion designed to confuse unwary students. It is a notion of great practical significance. Some examples will make this evident.

In August of 1957 Walter Reuther, UAW president, contended that automobile manufacturers should raise wages and simultaneously cut automobile prices. Reuther, arguing that the elasticity of demand for automobiles was about 4, concluded that a price cut would help check inflation, boost the total receipts of manufacturers, and preserve or even increase the profits of producers. A spokesman for the Ford Motor Company, however, claimed that available studies suggest an elasticity of demand for automobiles in the 0.5–1.5 range. He held that price cuts would therefore shrink profits or result in losses for manufacturers. In this case the elasticity of demand for automobiles was a strategic factor in labor-management relations and wage bargaining.[2]

Another example: studies indicate that the demand for most farm products is highly inelastic. As a result, increases in the output of farm products due to a good growing season or productivity increases depress the prices of farm products and the total receipts (incomes) of farmers. For farmers the inelastic nature of the demand for their products means that a bumper crop may be a mixed blessing. For policy makers it means that higher farm incomes depend upon the restriction of farm output.

Finally, the impact of automation, that is, of rapid technological advance, upon the level of employment depends in part upon the elasticity of demand for the product being manufactured. Suppose a firm installs new laborsaving machinery, resulting in the technological unemployment of, say, five hundred workers. Suppose too that a part of the cost reduction resulting from this technological advance is passed on to consumers in the form of reduced product prices. Now the effect of this price reduction upon the firm's sales and therefore the quantity of labor it needs will obviously depend upon the elasticity of product demand. An elastic demand might increase sales to the extent that some, all, or even more than the five hundred displaced workers are reabsorbed by the firm. An inelastic demand will mean that few, if any, of the displaced workers will be reemployed, because the increase in the volume of the firm's business will be small.

These examples could be multiplied, but the main point is clear. Elasticity of demand is vitally important to businessmen, farmers, labor, and government policy makers.

Elasticity of supply

The concept of price elasticity can also be applied to supply. If producers are responsive to price changes, supply is elastic. If they are

[2] See the statement by Theodore Yntema, vice-president of finance, Ford Motor Company, before the Subcommittee on Antitrust and Monopoly of the Committee on the Judiciary, United States Senate, February 4–5, 1958.

relatively insensitive to price changes, supply is inelastic.

The elasticity formula is pertinent in determining the degree of elasticity or inelasticity of supply. The only obvious alteration is the substitution of percentage change in quantity supplied for percentage change in quantity demanded.

The main determinant of the elasticity of supply is the amount of time which a producer has to respond to a given change in product price. Generally speaking, we can expect a greater output response—and therefore greater elasticity of supply—the longer the amount of time a producer has to adjust to a given price change. Why? Because a producer's response to, say, an increase in the price of product X depends upon his ability to shift resources from the production of other products[3] to the production of X. And the shifting of resources takes time: the greater the time, the greater the resource shiftability. Hence, the greater will be the output response and the elasticity of supply.

An example may help at this point: suppose a small truck farmer brings his entire season's output of tomatoes—one truckload—to market. His supply curve will be perfectly inelastic; he will sell the truckload whether the price is high or low. Why? Because he cannot offer more tomatoes than his one truckload if the price of tomatoes should be higher than he had anticipated. Even though he might like to offer more, tomatoes simply cannot be produced overnight. It will take him another full growing season to respond to a higher-than-expected price by producing more than one truckload. Similarly, because his product is perishable, he cannot withhold it from the market. If the price is lower than he had anticipated, he will still sell the entire truckload. Costs of production, incidentally, will not be important in making this decision. Even though the price of tomatoes may fall far short of his production costs, he will nevertheless sell out to avoid a total loss through spoilage. In a very short period of time, then, our farmer's supply of tomatoes is fixed; he can offer one truckload no matter how high the price. The perishability of his product forces

[3] The prices of which assumedly remain constant.

him to sell all no matter how low the price.

In a longer period of time—say, two or three growing seasons—our farmer can make extensive adjustments to, say, an increase in the price of tomatoes. He can cultivate his tomatoes more intensively by applying more labor, capital, and fertilizer to the land planted in tomatoes. Similarly, in time he can transfer some of his land from the production of other crops to the growing of tomatoes or can even purchase additional land to be used in tomato production. Therefore, in this longer period of time we can expect a considerable change in the amount supplied in response to the assumed price increase. In Chapter 24 we shall discover that costs become an important consideration in deciding how much to offer at various prices in these longer time periods.

We have made no mention of a total receipts test for elasticity of supply. Indeed, there is none. Supply shows a direct relationship between price and the amount supplied; that is, the supply curve is upsloping. This means that, regardless of the degree of elasticity or inelasticity, price and total receipts will always move together.

APPLICATIONS OF SUPPLY AND DEMAND ANALYSIS

Supply and demand analysis and the elasticity concept will be applied repeatedly in the remainder of this book. Let us strengthen our understanding of these analytical tools and their significance by examining two important applications: (1) legal prices and (2) demand from the viewpoint of the individual firm.

Legal prices

The "facts" of the market may not always be consistent with what society feels they *ought* to be. The actual prices and quantities which are determined by supply and demand in the various markets may be in conflict with society's ethical and moral judgments as to what they should be. The free market is an impersonal mechanism which does not judge the fairness of the manner in which a product is distributed

to consumers or how equitable are the incomes which flow to resource suppliers.

Specifically, the prices of certain products and resources may be judged by society as being "too high" or "too low." Acting through government, society may attempt to bring a "proper" adjustment in such prices. Let us examine in turn the cases in which prices are felt to be unduly high and unjustly low and, in the process, explore some of the complications entailed in correcting these errant prices.

Price ceilings and shortages. With few exceptions ceiling prices in the United States have been a wartime phenomenon. Government expenditures for war goods invariably cause the general level of product prices to rise. On the other hand, government spending has varying effects upon the money incomes of households. Generally speaking, those supplying essential human and property resources will find their money incomes booming. Those offering nonessential resources may experience modest increases or, conceivably, decreases in their money incomes. The net effect of these distortions in money incomes in the midst of product price inflation is obviously an arbitrary redistribution of real incomes. Those essential resource suppliers whose money incomes race ahead of the level of product prices realize sharply increasing real incomes. Those offering nonessential resources find that the price level spurts ahead of their money incomes to the end that their real incomes are curtailed. Government imposition of ceiling prices is a means of alleviating this arbitrary redistribution of real income so that the real economic cost of the war will be more equitably distributed among the citizenry.

Let us examine the effect of a ceiling price upon a specific product—say, butter. Suppose that the war severely disrupts agriculture in allied countries, obliging the United States to provide large amounts of foodstuffs for foreign peoples and their armies. This obviously increases the demand for American butter in relation to its supply. The resulting market price, let us assume, is $1.20 per pound. The government then imposes a legal price of say 90 cents per pound. What will be the effects of this price ceiling? The rationing ability of the market mechanism will be rendered ineffective. Although the equilibrium price ($1.20) would bring quantity demanded and quantity supplied into balance, the imposition of the ceiling price will prompt producers to cut back on the rate of production and will induce consumers to step up their rate of purchase. The net result will be a persistent shortage of the product.[4]

Figure 21-2 illustrates graphically the effect of a ceiling price. Let SS and DD be the supply

[4] When a shortage exists in a free market, competition among buyers will bid up price. This induces a greater output and simultaneously rations some buyers out of the market, thereby bringing quantity demanded and quantity supplied into equality at the equilibrium price. But with an effective ceiling price it is of course illegal to bid price up to the equilibrium point.

and demand curves for butter. The equilibrium price and quantity will be P and Q respectively. If government now makes it illegal to sell butter at any price above the ceiling price of P_c, the quantity forthcoming onto the market would be only Q_s despite the fact that consumers would be willing to purchase Q_d at the ceiling price. The shortage is measured by the excess of Q_d over Q_s.

But ceiling prices pose problems for government. First, effective ceiling prices invite the development of black markets. Such illegal markets, wherein sales take place at prices above the ceiling price, can be exceedingly difficult to detect and eliminate. Second, government must undertake the job of rationing butter to consumers. Should government take no formal step to ensure a fair distribution of butter, it would probably be sold on a first-come-first-serve basis. But such unregulated shortages may

FIGURE 21-2. CEILING PRICES RESULT IN PERSISTENT SHORTAGES.
Because the imposition of a price ceiling such as P_c results in a persistent product shortage as indicated by the distance Q_sQ_d, government must undertake the job of rationing the product in order to achieve an equitable distribution.

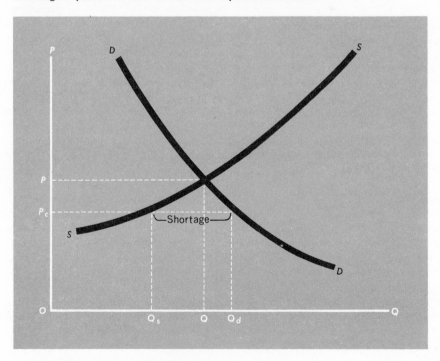

result in some consumers doing without any butter while others—those who are first in line or who manage to cultivate a friendship with the corner grocer—get as much or more than they want. An unregulated shortage may foster the very problem the ceiling price was designed to solve—the inequitable distribution of a product. To avoid a catch-as-catch-can distribution of the product government must undertake the task of fairly distributing it to consumers. This is done by issuing ration coupons to consumers on an equal basis.

Price supports and surpluses. While the imposition of price ceilings in the United States has been a wartime proposition, this has not been the case with price supports. Minimum wage legislation and the supporting of agricultural prices are the two most widely discussed examples of government price supports. Let us examine price supports as applied to a specific farm commodity.

Suppose the going market price for corn is $1 per bushel, and, as a result of this price, farmers realize extremely low incomes. Government decides to lend a helping hand by establishing a legal supported price of, say, $1.50 per bushel. What will be the effects? At any price above the equilibrium price, quantity supplied will obviously exceed quantity demanded; there will be a persistent surplus of the product. Farmers will be willing to produce and offer for sale more than private buyers are willing to purchase at the supported price. The size of this surplus will vary directly with the elasticity of demand and supply. The greater the elasticity of demand and supply, the greater the resulting surplus. As is the case with a ceiling price, the rationing ability of the free market obviously has been disrupted by the imposition of a legal price.

Figure 21-3 provides us with a graphic illustration of the effect of a supported price. Let SS and DD be the supply and demand curves for corn. Equilibrium price and quantity are obviously P and Q respectively. If government imposes a supported price of P_s, farmers will be willing to produce Q_s, but private buyers will only take Q_d off the market at that price. The surplus entailed is measured by the excess of Q_s over Q_d.

Government inherits the unsavory task of coping with the surplus which a supported price entails. There are two general approaches open to government. First, government might simply purchase and then attempt to dispose of the surplus. But this is more difficult than it sounds, as we shall discover in Chapter 33. The other alternative is for government to invoke schemes to restrict supply—that is, to shift the supply curve towards the left—in order to reduce the difference between equilibrium price and the supported price and thereby the size of the resulting surplus. In Chapter 33 we shall discuss in some detail the acreage allotment, soil bank, and conservation measures designed to take land out of cultivation which typically accompany farm price supports.

Government imposes price ceilings or price supports when hyperinflation or unusually depressed prices are working undue economic hardships on some buyers or sellers and are resulting in arbitrary windfall gains to others. But ceiling and supported prices rob the free market forces of supply and demand of their ability to bring the supply decisions of producers and the demand decisions of buyers into accord with one another. Free prices automatically ration products to buyers; legal prices do not. Therefore, government must accept the administrative problem of rationing which stems from price ceilings and the problem of buying or eliminating surpluses which price supports entail. Legal prices simply do not work unless accompanied by programs to control consumption or production.

Although legal prices involve knotty problems for government by upsetting the rationing ability of the market mechanism, one must be careful not to prejudge ceilings or supports as undesirable. Remember: legal prices are designed to correct alleged inequities which free market prices entail.

Demand from the individual firm's viewpoint

Thus far we have emphasized the concepts of demand and elasticity primarily from the buyer's point of view. But these concepts are

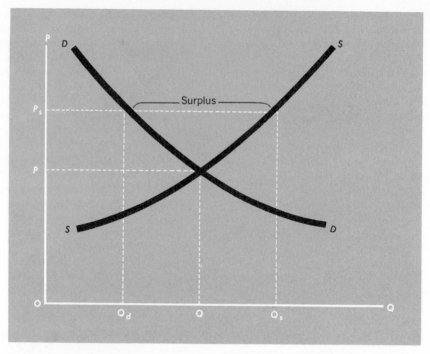

FIGURE 21-3. SUPPORTED PRICES RESULT IN PERSISTENT SURPLUSES.
A price support such as P_s gives rise to a persistent product surplus as indicated by
the distance Q_dQ_s. Government must either purchase these surpluses or take measures to eliminate them by restricting product supply.

also of vital importance from the seller's point
of view. While demand indicates price and
amount purchased from the consumer's standpoint, it simultaneously reflects revenue per
unit and sales from the seller's standpoint. We
first seek to examine the demand or average
revenue curve of an individual competitive
producer.

Demand to a purely competitive seller. You
will recall (Chapter 20) that a purely competitive market entails a very large number of producers selling a standardized product. Because
he offers a negligible fraction of total supply,
the individual competitive seller exerts no influence whatever on market price. Price is set
by the market, and the individual firm can sell
as much or as little as it chooses at that price.
Stated differently, the demand schedule is per-

fectly elastic to the individual competitive firm.

But let us digress here for a moment to voice
a word of caution. We are not saying that the
market demand curve is perfectly elastic in a
competitive market. Indeed, it is not, but rather
it is typically a downsloping curve as shown in
Figure 21-4*b*. As a matter of fact, the total demand curves for most agricultural products are
quite *in*elastic, even though agriculture is the
most competitive industry in our economy. We
are saying that the demand schedule faced by
the *individual firm* in a purely competitive industry is perfectly elastic. The distinction comes
about in this way. For the industry—that is,
for all firms producing a particular product—a
larger volume of sales can be realized only by
accepting a lower product price. All firms, acting independently but simultaneously, can and
do affect total supply and therefore market

Demand schedule also a revenue schedule

price. But not so for the individual firm. If a single producer increases or decreases his output, the outputs of all other competing firms being constant, the effect on total supply and market price is negligible. The single firm's sales schedule is therefore perfectly elastic. Figure 21-4a is illustrative. This is an instance in which the fallacy of composition is worth remembering. What is true for the group of firms (a downsloping, less than perfectly elastic demand curve), is *not* true for the individual firm (a perfectly elastic demand curve).

Columns 1 and 2 of Table 21-3 show a perfectly elastic demand curve where market price is assumed to be $131. Note that the firm cannot obtain a higher price by restricting output, nor need it lower price in order to increase its volume of sales.

Average, total, and marginal revenue to a purely competitive seller. A moment's reflection reveals that this demand schedule is simultaneously a revenue schedule. What appears in

column 1 as price per unit to the purchaser is obviously revenue per unit, or *average revenue,* to the seller. To say that a buyer must pay a price of $131 per unit for, say, 3 units is to say that the revenue per unit, or average revenue, received by the seller is $131. Price and average revenue are the same thing looked at from different points of view. $P \cdot Q = $ *total revenue*

Total revenue for each level of sales can obviously be determined by multiplying price by the corresponding quantity which the firm can sell. Multiply column 1 by column 2 and the result is column 3. In this case total receipts increase by a constant amount, $131, for each additional unit of sales. Each unit sold adds exactly its price to total revenue.

Whenever a firm is pondering a change in its output, it will be concerned with how its revenue will change as a result of that change in output. What will be the additional revenue from selling another unit of output?

Marginal revenue is the addition to total revenue, that is, the extra revenue, which re-

FIGURE 21-4. THE INDIVIDUAL COMPETITIVE FIRM'S DEMAND CURVE (a) AND DEMAND TO A COMPETITIVE INDUSTRY (b).
Industry demand is downsloping, such as *DD* in (b), that is, firms as a group must accept a lower price in order to sell a greater output. However, the product price which is determined by market demand and supply is given to the individual firm, making his demand curve *dd* perfectly elastic at that price, as shown in (a).

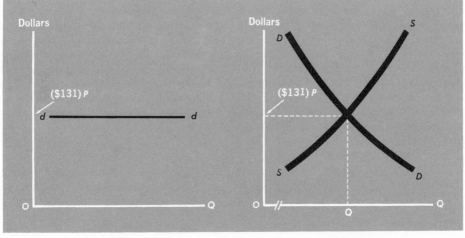

TABLE 21-3. THE DEMAND AND REVENUE SCHEDULES FOR AN INDIVIDUAL COMPETITIVE FIRM

Firm's demand or average revenue schedule		Revenue data	
(1)	(2)	(3)	(4)
Product price (average revenue)	Quantity demanded (sold)	Total revenue	Marginal revenue
$131	0	$ 0	
			$131
131	1	131	
			131
131	2	262	
			131
131	3	393	
			131
131	4	524	
			131
131	5	,655	
			131
131	6	786	
			131
131	7	917	
			131
131	8	1,048	
			131
131	9	1,179	
			131
131	10	1,310	

sults from the sale of one more unit of output. In other words, in Table 21-3 marginal revenue is simply the rate of change in total revenue. In column 3 we note that total revenue is obviously zero when zero units are being sold. The first unit of output sold increases total revenue from zero to $131. Marginal revenue— the increase in total revenue resulting from the sale of the first unit of output—is therefore $131. The second unit sold increases total revenue from $131 to $262, so marginal revenue is again $131. Indeed, you will note in column 4 that marginal revenue is a constant figure of $131. Why? Because total revenue increases at a constant rate with every extra unit sold. Under purely competitive conditions product price is constant to the individual firm;

added units therefore can be sold without lowering product price. This means that each additional unit of sales adds exactly its price— $131 in this case—to total revenue. And marginal revenue is this rate of increase in total revenue. Marginal revenue is constant under pure competition, because additional units can be sold at a constant price.

The competitive firm's demand curve and total and marginal revenue curves are shown graphically in Figure 21-5. The demand or average revenue curve is perfectly elastic. The marginal revenue curve coincides with the demand curve because the market is a purely competitive one and, as a result, product price is constant to the single firm. Each extra unit of sales increases total revenue by $131. Total revenue is a straight line up to the right. Its slope is constant—that is, it is a straight line—because marginal revenue is constant.

Let us now consider the nature of the demand and revenue schedules faced by imperfectly competitive producers, that is firms which are pure monopolies, monopolistically competitive, or oligopolistic.

Demand to an imperfectly competitive seller. Though they differ in details, the demand schedules facing imperfectly competitive firms have one basic point in common: they are downsloping. The demand curve of a pure monopolist, a monopolistically competitive producer, and an oligopolist may differ considerably in elasticity; yet all are less than perfectly elastic and therefore downsloping.

Why? An imperfectly competitive producer sells a significant percentage of the industry's total output. Therefore any decision it makes to increase or reduce its output will have a noticeable effect on total supply and therefore market price. This is most obvious in the case of the pure monopolist, where the firm and the industry are synonymous. Here the firm's output and market output are identical.

Specifically, when an imperfectly competitive producer attempts to sell more, market supply increases in relation to market demand, and price falls. As a result, the demand schedule faced by the individual firm is downsloping, that is, less than perfectly elastic. The firm must accept a lower price to achieve a larger volume of sales. Columns 1 and 2 of Table 21-4 portray this situation. Here we assume that the

FIGURE 21-5. DEMAND, MARGINAL REVENUE, AND TOTAL REVENUE OF A PURELY COMPETITIVE FIRM.

Because it can sell additional units of output at a constant price, the marginal revenue (MR) curve of a purely competitive firm coincides with its perfectly elastic demand (D) curve. The firm's total revenue (TR) curve is a straight upsloping line.

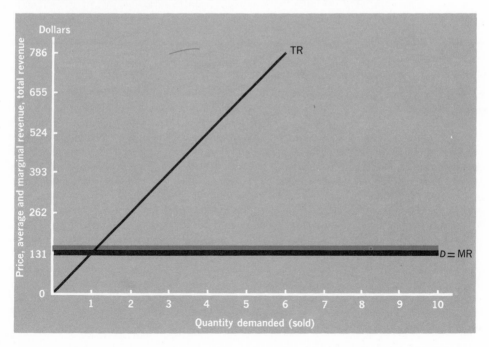

TABLE 21-4. THE DEMAND AND REVENUE SCHEDULES FOR AN INDIVIDUAL IMPERFECTLY COMPETITIVE FIRM

Firm's demand or average revenue schedule		Revenue data	
(1)	(2)	(3)	(4)
Product price (average revenue)	Quantity demanded (sold)	Total revenue	Marginal revenue
$172	0	$ 0	
			$162
162	1	162	
			142 (152 − 10)
152	2	304	
			122 (142 − 20)
142	3	426	
			102 (132 − 30)
132	4	528	
			82 (122 − 40)
122	5	610	
			62 etc.
112	6	672	
			42
102	7	714	
			22
92	8	736	
			2
82	9	738	
			−18
72	10	720	

firm must accept a $10 price cut in order to sell each succeeding unit of output.

Average, total, and marginal revenue to an imperfectly competitive seller. As for the purely competitive firm, price and average revenue are identical to the imperfectly competitive producer. Total revenue is again the product of price and the corresponding volume of sales. Note, however, that the rate of increase in total revenue is not constant, as it was under purely competitive conditions. As a matter of fact, total revenue reaches a maximum of $738 with the ninth unit sold and declines thereafter.

Under pure competition each successive unit sold adds the same amount—its price—to total revenue. Marginal revenue is constant under competition because price is constant to the individual firm. But with imperfect competition price declines as sales increase. Hence, we should expect marginal revenue to decline. It does, and as a glance at columns 1 and 4 reveals, it falls *faster* than does price. Why? The catch is this: *when an imperfectly competitive firm cuts price to increase its volume of sales, this lower price will apply not only to the extra unit sold but also to all other units of sales.* For example, when our imperfectly competitive firm is selling 1 unit at $162, total revenue is obviously $162. To increase its sales to 2 units price must be cut by $10 to $152. This new price applies not only to the extra (second) unit of sales but also to the first unit, which could have been sold at $162. In short, the second unit adds $152 (its price) less $10 (the price cut which the firm must take on the first unit), or $142, to total revenue. Similarly, to sell 3 units the firm must lower price from $152 to $142. The resulting marginal revenue will be just $122—the $142 addition to total revenue which the third unit of sales provides less $10 price cuts on the first 2 units of output. Calculations follow the marginal revenue column in Table 21-4. Note that with the tenth unit of sales marginal revenue becomes negative. Why?

Graphically the data of Table 21-4 appear as in Figure 21-6. The points of contrast with Figure 21-5 are clear. The demand, or average revenue, curve is, of course, downsloping. Total revenue increases but at an ever-declining rate. In time total revenue reaches a maximum and then actually declines. Aside from the first unit of sales, marginal revenue lies below the demand curve. The reason? Marginal revenue

is derived from total revenue and therefore reflects price declines not only on the extra unit sold but also on all prior units of output which otherwise could have been sold at a higher price.

SUMMARY

1. The present chapter extends the rudiments of demand and supply analysis developed in Chapter 4. The summarizing statements pertinent to that chapter should be reviewed at this point.

2. Elasticity of demand measures the responsiveness of consumers to price changes. If consumers are sensitive to price changes, demand is elastic. If consumers are unresponsive to price changes, demand is inelastic.

3. The price elasticity formula measures the

FIGURE 21-6. DEMAND, MARGINAL REVENUE, AND TOTAL REVENUE OF AN IMPERFECTLY COMPETITIVE FIRM.
Because it must lower price to increase its sales, the marginal revenue (MR) curve of an imperfectly competitive firm lies below its downsloping demand (D) curve. Total revenue (TR) increases at a decreasing rate, reaches a maximum, and then declines.

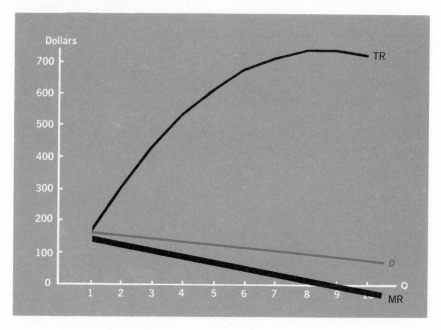

degree of elasticity or inelasticity of demand. The formula is

$$E_d = \frac{\text{percentage change in quantity demanded}}{\text{percentage change in price}}$$

The averages of the prices and quantities under consideration are used as reference points in determining the percentage changes in price and quantity. If E_d is greater than 1, demand is elastic. If E_d is less than 1, demand is inelastic. Unit elasticity is the special case in which E_d equals 1.

4. Price elasticity of demand can be determined by observing the effect of a price change upon total receipts from the sale of the product. If price and total receipts move in opposite directions, demand is elastic. If price and total receipts move in the same direction, demand is inelastic.

5. The number of available substitutes, the size of an item in one's budget, whether the product is a luxury or necessity, the time period involved, and the durability of a product are all considerations which influence elasticity of demand.

6. Elasticity varies at different price ranges on a demand curve. Furthermore, it is not safe to judge elasticity by the steepness or flatness of a demand curve on a graph.

7. The elasticity concept is also applicable to supply. Elasticity of supply depends upon the shiftability of resources between alternative employments. This shiftability in turn varies with the amount of time producers have in adjusting to a given price change.

8. Legal prices upset the rationing function of free market prices. Effective price ceilings result in persistent product shortages, and if an equitable distribution of the product is sought, government will have to ration the product to consumers. Price supports give rise to product surpluses; government must purchase these surplus products or take what measures are possible to eliminate them by imposing restrictions on their production.

9. The demand, or average revenue, curve faced by a purely competitive seller is perfectly elastic. In contrast the demand curve facing an imperfectly competitive seller is downsloping, that is, less than perfectly elastic.

10. Under pure competition product price is constant to the individual seller; therefore each extra unit of output adds exactly the same amount (its price) to total revenue. In other words, marginal revenue is constant and equal to price. Graphically, the marginal revenue curve coincides with the firm's perfectly elastic demand curve. Total revenue is a straight upsloping line.

11. The imperfectly competitive seller must lower price to sell more, and this lower price will apply to all prior units of sales. As a result marginal revenue is less than price. Graphically, the firm's marginal revenue curve lies below its demand curve. Total revenue increases at a declining rate, reaches a maximum, and finally declines.

QUESTIONS AND STUDY SUGGESTIONS

1. Answer questions 3, 4, and 8 at the end of Chapter 4.

2. In many oligopolistic industries, for example, the petroleum industry, producers justify their reluctance to lower prices by arguing that the demand of their products is inelastic. Explain.

3. How will the following changes in price affect total receipts (expenditures)—that is, will total receipts *increase, decline,* or remain *unchanged?*

    a. Price falls and demand is inelastic.

    b. Price rises and demand is elastic.

    c. Price rises and supply is elastic.

d. Price rises and supply is inelastic.

e. Price rises and demand is inelastic.

f. Price falls and demand is elastic.

g. Price falls and demand is of unit elasticity.

4. Determine the elasticity of demand and supply for the following demand and supply schedules. Use the total receipts test to check the answers given by the E_d formula.

E_s	Quantity supplied	Product price	Quantity demanded	Total receipts	E_d
____	28,000	$10	10,000	$____	____
____	22,500	9	13,000	____	____
____	17,000	8	17,000	____	____
____	15,500	7	22,000	____	____
	11,000	6	25,000	____	

5. What are the major determinants of elasticity of demand? Use these determinants in judging whether the demand for the following products is elastic or inelastic.

a. Oranges

b. Salt

c. Cigarettes

d. Chesterfield cigarettes

e. Automobiles

f. Football games

g. Gasoline

h. Diamond bracelets

i. Butter

j. This textbook

6. Why is it difficult to judge elasticity of demand or supply by simply observing the appearance of a demand or supply curve on a graph?

7. Why is it necessary for ceiling prices to be accompanied by government rationing? Price supports by surplus-purchasing or output-restricting programs? Show graphically why price ceilings entail shortages and price supports result in surpluses. What effect, if any, does the elasticity of demand and supply have upon the size of these shortages and surpluses? Explain.

8. How would you expect the elasticity of supply of product X to differ as between a situation of full employment in industry X, on the one hand, and considerable unemployment in the industry, on the other? Explain.

9. "If the demand for farm products is highly inelastic, a bumper crop may reduce farm incomes." Evaluate and illustrate graphically.

10. Suppose you are chairman of a state commission charged with the responsibility of establishing a program to raise new revenue through the use of excise taxes. Would elasticity of demand be important to you in determining those products upon which excises should be levied? Explain.

11. Use the following demand schedule to determine total and marginal revenue for each possible level of sales.

Product price	Quantity demanded	Total revenue	Marginal revenue
$2	1		
2	2		
2	3		
2	4		
2	5		
2	6		

a. What can you conclude about the structure of the industry in which this firm is operating? Explain.

b. Graph the demand, total revenue, and marginal revenue curves for this firm.

c. Why do the demand and marginal revenue curves coincide?

d. "Marginal revenue is the rate of change in total revenue." Do you agree? Explain verbally and graphically, using the above data.

12. Now determine total and marginal revenue for each level of sales for this set of data:

Product price	Quantity demanded	Total revenue	Marginal revenue
$7	0		
6	1		
5	2		
4	3		
3	4		
2	5		
1	6		

a. What can you conclude about the structure of the industry in which this firm is operating? Explain.

b. Graph the demand, total revenue, and marginal revenue curves for this firm.

c. Why does the marginal revenue curve lie below the demand curve?

SELECTED REFERENCES

Boulding, Kenneth E., *Economic Analysis*, 3d ed. (New York: Harper & Row, Publishers, 1955), chaps. 4, 5, 7, and 8.

Carter, W. Harrison, and William P. Snavely, *Intermediate Economic Analysis* (New York: McGraw-Hill Book Company, Inc., 1961), chaps. 4 and 5.

Coppock, Joseph D., *Economics of the Business Firm* (New York: McGraw-Hill Book Company, Inc., 1959), chap. 3.

Duesenberry, James S., and Lee Preston, *Cases and Problems in Economics* (Englewood Cliffs, N.J.: Prentice-Hall, Inc., 1960), chap. 3.

Warner, Aaron W., and Victor R. Fuchs, *Concepts and Cases in Economic Analysis* (New York: Harcourt, Brace & World, Inc., 1958), chap. 5 and pp. 173–182.

Chapter 22

FURTHER TOPICS IN THE THEORY

OF CONSUMER DEMAND[1]

pwd cst napr det of supf

IN CHAPTER 21 we extended our understanding of demand and supply by introducing the concept of price elasticity and by discussing some specific applications of demand and supply analysis. The present chapter is devoted to further consideration of the demand side of the market. In Chapter 23 we shall discuss production costs, which, we shall discover, are the major determinant of supply. The goal of Chapters 24 to 27 is to use our understanding of demand and supply in analyzing pricing and output decisions under the various market structures which were outlined in Chapter 20.

Now for a more detailed look at the objectives of the present chapter. First, we seek a more sophisticated explanation of the law of demand. Second, we want to understand how consumers allocate their money incomes among various goods and services. Why does a consumer buy some specific bundle of goods rather than any one of a number of other collections of goods which are available to him? Finally, we explore how changes in product prices and money income will cause a consumer to alter the collection of goods he purchases.

[1] To the instructor: this is an optional chapter which may be omitted without impairing the continuity and meaning of ensuing chapters.

TWO EXPLANATIONS OF THE LAW OF DEMAND

Thus far we have accepted the law of demand as a common-sense notion. We have simply appealed to observation in claiming an inverse relationship between price and quantity demanded. A high price usually does discourage consumers from buying; a low price typically does encourage them to buy. Now let us explore two complementary explanations of the downsloping nature of the demand curve which will back up our everyday observations.[2]

Income and substitution effects

One explanation of the law of demand says in essence that, as the price of a product de-

[2] A third explanation, based upon *indifference curves,* is in some respects more precise than the two we now discuss. The complexities of this approach, however, make it more suitable for an advanced course in economic theory. The interested reader should refer to Richard H. Leftwich, *The Price System and Resource Allocation,* rev. ed. (New York: Holt, Rinehart and Winston, Inc., 1960), chap. 5, or John F. Due and Robert W. Clower, *Intermediate Economic Analysis,* 4th ed. (Homewood, Ill.: Richard D. Irwin, Inc., 1961), chap. 5.

clines, consumers will be both *able* and *willing* to buy more of it.

As the price of steak declines, you are obviously able to buy more of it with your money income. With a constant money income of, say, $10 you can purchase 10 pounds of steak at a price of $1 per pound. But if the price of steak falls to 50 cents per pound and 10 pounds of steak are bought, then $5 per week is freed for buying more of this and other commodities. A decline in the price of steak increases the real income of the consumer. This is called the *income effect*.

But being able to buy more steak at a lower price is not a complete explanation of why you actually do buy more. As the price of steak falls—the prices of other products being unchanged—steak will become more attractive to the buyer. At 50 cents per pound it is a "better buy" than at $1 per pound. Consequently, the lower price will induce the consumer to substitute steak for some of the now less attractive items in his budget. Steak may well be substituted for pork, mutton, veal, and a variety of other foods. A lower price increases the relative attractiveness of a product and makes the consumer willing to buy more of it. This is known as the *substitution effect*.

The income and substitution effect combine to make a consumer able and willing to buy more of a specific good at a low price than at a high price.

Law of diminishing marginal utility

A second explanation centers upon the notion that, although consumer wants in general may be insatiable, wants for specific commodities can be fulfilled. In a given span of time, wherein the tastes of buyers are unchanged, consumers can get as much of specific goods and services as they want. The more of a specific product a consumer obtains, the less anxious he is to get more units of the same product. This can be most readily seen for durable goods. A consumer's want for an automobile, when he has none, may be very strong; his desire for a second car is much less intense; for a third or

fourth, very weak. Even the wealthiest of families rarely have more than a half dozen cars, despite the fact that their incomes would allow them to purchase and maintain a whole fleet of them.

Economists put forth the idea that specific consumer wants can be fulfilled with succeeding units of a commodity in the *law of diminishing marginal utility.* Let us dissect this law to see exactly what it means. A product has utility if it has the power to satisfy a want. Utility is want-satisfying power. Two characteristics of this concept must be emphasized: First, "utility" and "usefulness" are by no means synonymous. Diamond rings and paintings by Picasso may be useless in the functional sense of the term but yet be of tremendous utility to senior coeds and art connoisseurs respectively. Second—and implied in the first point—utility is a subjective notion. The utility of a specific product will vary widely from person to person. A nip of Old Tennisshoes will yield tremendous utility to the Skid Row alcoholic, but zero or negative utility to the local WCTU president.

By marginal utility we simply mean the extra utility, or satisfaction, which a consumer gets from one additional unit of a specific product. In any relatively short period of time, wherein the consumers' tastes can be assumed not to change, the marginal utility derived from successive units of a given product will decline.[3] Why? Because a consumer will eventually become saturated, or "filled up," with that particular product. The fact that marginal utility will decline as the consumer acquires additional units of a specific product is known as the *law of diminishing marginal utility.*

We have noted that utility is a subjective concept. As a result it is not susceptible to precise quantitative measurement. But for purposes of illustration, let us assume that we can measure satisfaction with units we shall call "utils." This mythical unit of satisfaction is

---

[3] For a time the marginal utility of successive units of a product may increase. A third cigarette may yield a larger amount of extra satisfaction than the first or second. But beyond some point we can expect the marginal utility of added units to decline.

merely a convenient pedagogical device which will allow us to quantify our thinking about consumer behavior. Thus in Table 22-1 we can illustrate the relationship between the quantity obtained of a product—say, product A—and the accompanying extra utility derived from each successive unit. Here we assume that the law of diminishing marginal utility sets in with the first unit of A obtained. Each successive unit yields less and less extra utility than the previous one as the consumer's want for A comes closer and closer to fulfillment. Total utility can obviously be found for any number of units of A by cumulating the marginal utility figures as indicated in Table 22-1. The third unit of A has a marginal utility of 8 utils; three units of A yield a total utility of 27 utils (10 + 9 + 8).

Now how does the law of diminishing marginal utility explain why the demand curve for a specific product is downsloping? If successive units of a good yield smaller and smaller amounts of marginal, or extra, utility, the consumer will buy additional units of a product only if its price falls. The consumer for whom this utility data is relevant may buy, say, 2 units of A at a price of $1, but because of diminishing marginal utility from additional units of A, he will decline to buy more at this price. From the seller's viewpoint diminishing marginal utility forces the producer to lower the price in order to induce buyers to take a larger quantity of the product.

THEORY OF CONSUMER BEHAVIOR

In addition to providing a basis for explaining the law of demand, the idea of diminishing marginal utility also plays a key role in explaining how a consumer should allocate his money income among the many goods and services which are available for him to buy.

Consumer choice and budget restraint

We can picture the situation of the typical consumer something like this:

1. The average consumer is a fairly rational fellow. He attempts to dispose of his money income in such a way as to derive the greatest amount of satisfaction, or utility, from it. This is not to say he is always able to achieve the maximum amount of utility from his money income; for example, inadequate knowledge of the goods available to him and the force of habit work against achieving the utility-maximizing pattern of expenditures. But we can safely assume that the typical consumer wants to get the most for his money.

2. We can suppose, too, that the average consumer has rather clear-cut preferences for various goods and services available in the market. Buyers have a pretty good idea as to how much marginal utility they will get from successive units of the various products which they might choose to purchase.

TABLE 22-1. THE LAW OF DIMINISHING MARGINAL UTILITY AS APPLIED TO PRODUCT A

Unit of product A	Marginal utility, utils	Total utility, utils
First	10	10
Second	9	19
Third	8	27
Fourth	7	34
Fifth	6	40
Sixth	4	44

3. The consumer's money income is limited in amount. Because he supplies limited amounts of human and property resources to businesses, the money income he receives will be limited. Whether the consumer finds himself at the top or bottom of the income pyramid, his income will be a finite amount. With a few exceptions —perhaps Bing Crosby and King Saud—all consumers are subject to a *budget restraint.*

4. The goods and services available to consumers have "price tags" on them. Why? Because they are scarce in relation to the demand for them, or, stated differently, their production entails the use of scarce and therefore valuable resources. In the ensuing examples we shall suppose that product prices are not affected by the amounts of specific goods which the individual consumer buys.

Obviously, if a consumer has a limited number of dollars in his pocket and the products he wants have price tags on them, the consumer will only be able to purchase a limited amount of goods. The consumer cannot buy everything he might want when each purchase exhausts a portion of his limited money income. It is precisely this obvious point which brings the economic fact of scarcity home to the individual consumer.

In making his choices, our typical consumer is in the same position as the Western prospector . . . who is restocking for his next trip into the back country and who is forced by the nature of the terrain to restrict his baggage to whatever he can carry on the back of one burro. If he takes a great deal of one item, say baked beans, he must necessarily take much less of something else, say bacon. His job is to find that collection of products which, in view of the limitations imposed on the total, will best suit his needs and tastes.[4]

In short, the consumer must make compromises; he must do some picking and choosing among alternative goods to obtain with his limited money resources the collection most satisfying to him.

[4] E. T. Weiler, *The Economic System* (New York: The Macmillan Company, 1952), p. 89.

Utility-maximizing rule

The question then boils down to this: Of all the collections of goods and services which a consumer can obtain within the limits of his budget, which specific collection will yield him the greatest utility or satisfaction? Bluntly put, the rule to be followed in maximizing his satisfactions is that *the consumer should allocate his money income so that the last dollar spent on each product purchased yields the same amount of extra utility.* We shall call this the *utility-maximizing rule.* When the consumer is "balancing his margins" in accordance with this rule, there will be no incentive for him to alter his expenditure pattern. The consumer will be in equilibrium, and, barring a change in his tastes, his income, or the prices of the various goods, he will be worse off—his total utility will decline—by any alteration in the collection of goods he is purchasing.

Now a detailed illustration to help explain the validity of the rule. For simplicity's sake we limit our discussion to just two products. Keep in mind that the analysis can readily be extended to any number of goods. Suppose that consumer Brooks is trying to decide which combination of two products—A and B—he should purchase with his limited weekly income of $10. Obviously, Brooks's preferences for these two products and their prices will be basic data determining the combination of A and B which will maximize Brooks's satisfactions. Table 22-2 summarizes Brooks's preferences for products A and B. Columns 1 and 2a show the amount of extra or marginal utility Brooks will derive from each successive unit of A. Columns 1 and 3a reflect Brooks's preferences for product B. In each case the relationship between the number of units of the product obtained and the corresponding marginal utility reflects the law of diminishing marginal utility. Diminishing marginal utility is assumed to set in with the first unit of each product purchased.

But before we can apply the utility-maximizing rule to this data, we must put the marginal utility information of columns 2a and 3a on a per-dollar-spent basis. Why? Because a con-

TABLE 22-2. THE UTILITY-MAXIMIZING COMBINATION OF PRODUCTS
A AND B OBTAINABLE WITH AN INCOME OF $10 *

(1)	(2) Product A: price = $1		(3) Product B: price = $3	
	(a)	(b)	(a)	(b)
Unit of product	Marginal utility, utils	Marginal utility per dollar (MU/price)	Marginal utility, utils	Marginal utility per dollar (MU/price)
First	10	10	24	8
Second	9	9	21	7
Third	8	8	18	6
Fourth	7	7	15	5
Fifth	6	6	9	3
Sixth	4	4	3	1

* It is assumed in this table that the amount of marginal utility received from additional units of each of the two products is independent of the quantity of the other
product. For example, the marginal utility schedule for product A is independent
of the amount of B obtained by the consumer.

sumer's choices will be influenced not only by
the extra utility which successive units of, say,
product A will yield, but also by how many
dollars (and therefore how many units of alternative good B) he must give up to obtain those
added units of A. First example: Brooks may
clearly prefer to own a Cadillac rather than a
lowly Ford; he may be twice as happy with a
Cadillac than with a Ford. Yet he may buy a
Ford because a Cadillac costs three or four
times as much as a Ford. Brooks may feel that
per dollar spent a Ford is a better buy. Second
example: in Table 22–2 you will note that the
first unit of B yields 24 units of utility while the
first unit of A yields only 10. However, B costs
$3 per unit and A only $1. This means that by
passing up the first unit of B and the 24 utils
it entails, Brooks can use the "saved" $3 to buy
3 units of A, which yield 27 utils of satisfaction.
In other words, if Brooks had just $3 to spend,
he would not spend it on B, despite the high
marginal utility of the first unit, but rather on
A. The point is this: to make the amounts of
extra utility derived from differently priced
goods comparable, marginal utility must be put

on a per-dollar-spent basis. This is done in columns 2b and 3b. These figures are obtained
simply by dividing the marginal utility data of
columns 2a and 3a by the assumed prices of A
and B—$1 and $3 respectively.

Now we have Brooks's preferences—on unit
and per dollar bases—and the price tags of
A and B before us. Brooks stands patiently with
$10 to spend on A and B. In what order should
Brooks allocate his dollars on units of A and B to
achieve the highest degree of utility within the
limits imposed by his money income? And
what specific combination of A and B will he
have obtained at the time that he exhausts
his $10?

Concentrating on columns 2b and 3b of
Table 22-2, we find that Brooks should obviously spend his first $1 on the first unit of A.
Why? Because its marginal utility per dollar of
10 utils is higher than for B. Then Brooks
should spend another $1 on the second unit of
A. The reason? The marginal utility per dollar
spent on this second unit of A (9 utils) exceeds
the marginal utility per dollar of the first unit
of B (8 utils). But now Brooks finds himself in-

different as to whether his further expenditures go for the third unit of A or the first unit of B. Both yield the same marginal utility per dollar of 8 utils. Suppose he buys both of them: Brooks now has 3 units of A and 1 of B. Note that with this combination of goods the last dollar spent on each yields the same amount of extra utility. Does this combination of A and B therefore represent the maximum amount of utility which Brooks can obtain? The answer is "No." This collection of goods only costs $6 [(3 × $1) + (1 × $3)]; Brooks has $4 of income remaining, which he can spend to achieve a still higher level of total utility.

Examining columns 2b and 3b again, we find once more that Brooks is indifferent about choosing between the next units of each. Marginal utility per dollar of the fourth unit of A and the second of B is the same—7 utils in each case. Let us again assume that Brooks purchases one more unit of each. Marginal utility per dollar is now the same for the last dollar spent on each product, and Brooks's money income of $10 is exhausted [(4 × $1) + (2 × $3)]. *The utility-maximizing combination of goods attainable by Brooks is 4 units of A and 2 of B.*[5]

It is to be emphasized that there are other combinations of A and B which are obtainable with $10. But none of these will yield a level of total utility as high as does combination 2. For example, 1 unit of A and 3 of B can be obtained for $10. However, this combination violates the utility-maximizing rule; total utility here is only 73 utils, clearly inferior to the 79 utils yielded by combination 2. Furthermore, there are other combinations of A and B, such as 5 of A and 3 of B *or* 3 of A and 1 of B, wherein the marginal utility of the last dollar spent is the same for both A and B. But such combinations are either unobtainable with Brooks' limited money income (as is 5 of A

---

[5] To simplify, we assume in this example that Brooks spends his entire income; he neither borrows nor saves. Saving can be treated as a utility-yielding commodity and incorporated in our analysis and is to be treated thus in question 4 at the end of the chapter.

and 3 of B) or fail to exhaust his money income (as does 3 of A and 1 of B) and therefore do not yield him the maximum utility attainable.

An algebraic restatement

We are now in a position to restate the utility-maximizing rule in simple algebraic terms. Our rule simply says that a consumer will maximize his satisfaction when he allocates his money income in such a way that the last dollar spent on product A, the last on product B, and so forth, yield equal amounts of additional, or marginal, utility. Now the marginal utility per dollar spent on A is indicated by MU of product A/price of A (column 2b of Table 22-2) and the marginal utility per dollar spent on B by MU of product B/price of B (column 3b of Table 22-2). Our utility-maximizing rule merely requires that these ratios be equal. That is,

$$\frac{\text{MU of product A}}{\text{price of A}} = \frac{\text{MU of product B}}{\text{price of B}}$$

and, of course, the consumer must exhaust his available income. Our tabular illustration has shown us that 4 units of A and 2 of B fulfills these conditions in that

$$7/1 = 21/3$$

and the consumer's $10 income is spent.

If the equation is not fulfilled, there will be some reallocation of the consumer's expenditures between A and B, from the low to the high marginal utility-per-dollar product, which will increase the consumer's total utility. For example, the consumer may spend his $10 on 1 of A and 3 of B. But here we find that

$$\frac{\text{MU of A: 10 utils}}{\text{price of A: \$1}} > \frac{\text{MU of B: 18 utils}}{\text{price of B: \$3}}$$

The last dollar spent on A provides 10 utils of satisfaction and the last dollar spent on B only provides 6. On a per dollar basis, units of A provide more extra satisfaction than units of B. The consumer will obviously increase his total satisfaction by purchasing more of A and less of B. As dollars are reallocated from B to A, the marginal utility from additional units of A will decline as the result of moving down the diminishing marginal utility schedule for A, and the marginal utility of B will rise as the consumer moves up the diminishing marginal utility schedule for B. At some new combination of A and B—specifically, 4 of A and 2 of B—the equality of the two ratios and therefore consumer equilibrium will be achieved. As we already know, the net gain in utility is 6 utils (79 − 73).

Now there are admittedly a number of criticisms of this theory of consumer behavior. Most obviously, we have no "utilometer" by which the consumer's preferences can be set down precisely as in Table 22-2. Nor is it easy to incorporate large, indivisible products such as houses, automobiles, pianos, or a college education in our analysis. Nevertheless, there is little doubt that the theory accurately describes the basic rationale underlying consumer behavior. In a general way the theory does explain how consumers behave. Albeit in a loose fashion, consumers do seek to maximize their satisfactions. And though the process may be crude, consumers do make marginal comparisons in allocating their limited incomes. In formulating its budget a family must choose among, say, a food freezer, a television set, and building a recreation room in the basement. And the college student must weigh the relative satisfaction to be derived from spending $10 on a Saturday-night date as opposed to a new pair of shoes or a couple of shirts. Despite its limitations, the utility-maximizing rule is a meaningful general statement of how consumers behave.

OTHER PRICES, INCOME, AND DEMAND

Our hypothetical illustration of the utility-maximizing rule makes it apparent that, given consumer tastes, there are three major economic factors which determine the specific amount of any product a consumer will buy. These factors are: (1) the price of the particular product under consideration, (2) the prices of *other* products, and (3) the money income of the consumer.

If the price of product B were to fall, for example, the marginal utility per dollar data of column 3*b* would increase. This would upset consumer equilibrium and induce the consumer to increase his purchases of B. Conversely, an increase in the price of B would reduce the marginal-utility-per-dollar data for B, causing him to purchase less of B. These adjustments, you will note, are entirely in accord with the notion of a downsloping demand curve for B. An increase in the price of B moves the consumer back up his demand curve for B; a decline in the price of B moves him down B's demand curve.

Substitute, complementary, and independent goods

But the amount of a product purchased may be affected not only by a change in its own price but also by a change in the price of some related good. The classic example: the amount of oleomargarine purchased by a consumer at a given price will depend upon the price of butter. As the price of butter rises, consumers will tend to substitute oleomargarine for butter. Conversely, as the price of butter falls, consumers will buy more butter and less oleomargarine. In general, when the price of one good and the demand for another good are directly related, the two products are *substitute*, or competing, goods. Thus it is with butter and oleomargarine, Lucky Strikes and Chesterfields, steak and hamburger, Chevrolets and Fords, and tea and coffee.

With other pairs of products, however, the situation is reversed: the price of one good and the demand for the other many be inversely related. Such products are called *complementary* goods; they "go together." For example, if the price of gasoline falls and, as a result, you drive your car more, this extra driving will increase your demand for motor oil. Gas and oil are jointly demanded; they are complements. So it is with ham and eggs, Scotch and soda, stereophonic phonographs and records, golf clubs and golf balls.

We must resist the conclusion that all pairs of products are related either as substitutes or complements. For many sets of goods a change in the price of one will have little or no effect upon the demand for the other. These are *independent* goods. Examples are butter and golf balls, potatoes and automobiles, bananas and wrist watches.

Incidentally, if products A and B in Table 22-2 were either substitute or complementary goods, the marginal utility schedule of A would depend upon the amount of B consumed and vice versa. These interrelationships would greatly complicate our application of the utility-maximizing rule but would not affect the principle itself. We have assumed that A and B are independent goods in order to avoid such difficulties.

Normal and inferior goods

A change in income will also affect the demand for various products. For most goods an increase in income gives rise to an increase in demand. Consumers typically buy more shoes, steak, stereophonic sets, and Scotch as their incomes rise. And the demand for these same products will decline in response to a decline in income. Such products, whose demand varies directly with money income, are called superior, or *normal*, goods.

Although most products are normal goods, there are a number of exceptions. Examples: as incomes rise, purchases of hamburger and oleomargarine may decline as households substitute steak and butter in their budgets. Goods whose demand varies inversely with a change in money income are called *inferior* goods.

Demand versus quantity demanded

We have noted that the equilibrium level of consumption of a specific product—say, oleomargarine—will be affected by (1) changes in the price of oleomargarine, (2) changes in the prices of substitute or complementary goods, and (3) changes in money income. Recalling our earlier distinction (Chapter 4) between a "change in demand" and a "change in the quantity demanded," the alert reader will recognize that a change in the price of oleomargarine entails a change in the quantity demanded of oleomargarine. That is, a change in the price of oleomargarine causes the consumer to move up or down his stable oleomargarine demand curve, thereby altering the quantity of oleomargarine demanded.

On the other hand, you will also recall from Chapter 4 that the prices of related goods and money income are two of the basic determinants of the location of a demand curve. Hence, changes in the prices of substitute or complementary goods and changes in money income will shift the entire demand curve for oleomargarine. Illustration: an increase in the price of substitute product butter will tend to increase, that is, shift to the right, the entire demand curve for oleomargarine. Conversely, a decline in the price of butter will cause the demand curve for oleomargarine to shift to the left. The reverse holds true for complementary goods. An increase in the price of gasoline will cause the demand curve for motor oil to shift to the left; a decline, to the right. Can you explain why? Finally, an increase in money income will shift the demand curves of normal goods to the right and the curves of inferior goods to the left.

SUMMARY

1. The law of demand can be explained on the basis of the income and substitution effects or the law of diminishing marginal utility.

2. The income effect says that a decline in the price of a product will enable the consumer to buy more of it with his fixed money income. The substitution effect points out that a lower price will make a product relatively more attractive and therefore increase the consumer's willingness to substitute it for other products.

3. The law of diminishing marginal utility states that beyond some point additional units of a specific commodity will yield ever-declining amounts of extra satisfaction to a consumer. It follows that a lower price will be needed to induce the consumer to increase his purchases of such a product.

4. The typical consumer is assumedly rational and acting on the basis of rather well-defined preferences; consumers act sensibly and know roughly the satisfaction they will derive from successive units of various products available to them. Because his income is limited and goods have prices on them, the consumer cannot purchase all the goods and services he might like to have. He should therefore select that attainable combination of goods which will maximize his utility or satisfaction.

5. The consumer's utility will be maximized when he is allocating his income so that the last dollar spent on each product purchased yields the same amount of extra satisfaction. Algebraically, the utility-maximizing rule is fulfilled when

$$\frac{\text{MU of product A}}{\text{price of A}} = \frac{\text{MU of product B}}{\text{price of B}}$$

and the consumer's income is spent. Though subject to limitations, this rule is a meaningful guide in explaining consumer behavior.

6. The equilibrium quantity demanded of any product will change as a result of a change in (*a*) its own price, (*b*) the prices of related goods, or (*c*) the consumer's money income. A change in the price of the product under consideration will entail a movement from one point to another on the demand curve for that product; changes in the prices of related goods or in money income will cause the entire demand curve for that product to shift.

7. A direct relationship between the price of one good and the demand for another suggests that those two products are substitutes. An inverse relationship indicates complementariness.

8. An increase in income increases the demand for normal goods and reduces the demand for inferior goods.

QUESTIONS AND STUDY SUGGESTIONS

1. Explain the law of demand through the income and substitution effects, using a price increase as a point of departure for your discussion.

2. Explain the law of diminishing marginal utility. Explain the law of demand in terms of diminishing marginal utility.

3. Mrs. Peterson buys loaves of bread and quarts of milk each week at prices of 20 cents and 30 cents respectively. At present she is buying these two products in amounts such that the marginal utilities from the last units purchased of the two products are 40 and 70 utils respectively. Is Mrs. Peterson currently buying the best, that is, the utility-maximizing, combination of bread and milk? If not, in what manner should she reallocate her expenditures between the two goods?

4. Schedules 1 through 4 on page 432 (table) show the marginal utility, measured in terms of utils, which Mr. Black would get by purchasing various amounts of products A, B, C, and D. Schedule 5 shows the marginal utility Black gets from saving.

Assume that the prices of A, B, C, and D are $24, $4, $6, and $18 respectively and that Black has a money income of $106.

a. What quantities of A, B, C, and D will Black purchase in maximizing his satisfactions?

b. How many dollars will Black choose to save?

c. Check your answers by substituting in the algebraic statement of the utility-maximizing rule.

5. "Nothing is more useful than water: but it will purchase scarce any thing; scarce any thing can be had in exchange for it. A diamond, on the contrary, has

Schedule 1		Schedule 2		Schedule 3		Schedule 4		Schedule 5 Number of dollars saved	
Units of A	MU	Units of B	MU	Units of C	MU	Units of D	MU		MU
1	36	1	15	1	24	1	72	1	5
2	30	2	12	2	15	2	54	2	4
3	24	3	8	3	12	3	45	3	3
4	18	4	7	4	9	4	36	4	2
5	13	5	5	5	7	5	27	5	1
6	7	6	4	6	5	6	18	6	½
7	4	7	3½	7	2	7	15	7	¼
8	2	8	3	8	1	8	12	8	⅛

scarce any value in use; but a very great quantity of other goods may frequently be had in exchange for it." [6] Explain.

6. "In the long run it may be irrational to purchase goods on the basis of habit; but in the short run habitual buying may prove to be a very sensible means of allocating income." Do you agree? Explain.

7. Explain and illustrate graphically the effect of:

a. An increase in income upon the demand curve of an inferior good

b. A drop in the price of product S upon the demand for substitute product T

c. A decline in income upon the demand curve of a normal good

d. An increase in the price of product J upon the demand for complementary good K

SELECTED REFERENCES

Bober, M. M., *Intermediate Price and Income Theory*, rev. ed. (New York: W. W. Norton & Company, Inc., 1962), chap. 3.

Enke, Stephen, *Intermediate Economic Theory* (Englewood Cliffs, N.J.: Prentice-Hall, Inc., 1950), chap. 18.

Fellner, William, *Modern Economic Analysis* (New York: McGraw-Hill Book Company, Inc., 1960), chap. 14.

Leftwich, Richard H., *The Price System and Resource Allocation*, rev. ed. (New York: Holt, Rinehart and Winston, Inc., 1960), chap. 4.

[6] Adam Smith, *The Wealth of Nations* (New York: Modern Library, Inc., originally published in 1776), p. 28.

Chapter 23

SUPPLY AND THE COSTS OF PRODUCTION

PRODUCT PRICES are determined by the interaction of the forces of demand and supply. Preceding chapters have focused our attention upon the factors underlying demand. The basic factor underlying the ability and willingness of firms to supply a product in the market is its cost of production. The production of any good requires the use of economic resources which, because of their relative scarcity, bear price tags. The amount of any product which a firm is willing to supply in the market depends upon the prices, or costs, of the resources essential to its production, on the one hand, and the price which the product will bring in the market, on the other. The present chapter is concerned with the general nature of production costs. Product prices are introduced in the following several chapters, and the supply decisions of producers are then explained.

ECONOMIC COSTS IN REAL AND MONEY TERMS

Economic costs are those payments which must be received by resource owners in order to assure that they will continue to supply them in a particular line of production. This definition goes back to the basic fact that resources are scarce and have alternative uses. First in real (physical) terms, the economist's definition of costs simply suggests that to use a resource in producing one product entails giving up some alternative product. The real cost of producing 5 units of X is the number of units of Y or Z which the resources used in X could otherwise have produced. The production possibilities curve of Chapter 2 clearly embodies this notion of costs. Note at point C in Table 2-1 that the real cost of producing 100,000 more units of bread is the 3,000-unit decrease in the production of drill presses which will necessarily be entailed. A final illustration: Suppose an assembly-line worker can be used in producing automobiles, washing machines, and refrigerators. The real cost of using this worker in producing automobiles is the contribution which he might otherwise have made in the production of washing machines and refrigerators.

When expressed in money terms, the notion of economic costs is a bit more elusive. The main reason for this is that we, like the accountant or businessman, typically think of costs as being essentially money payments, that is, cash outlays, which a firm makes to the "outsiders" who supply labor services, materials, fuel, transportation services, power, and so forth to the firm. These expenditures, or *explicit costs*, are certainly a part of the economist's definition of costs; but they are only a part. The economist would also include any nonexpenditure, or *implicit costs*, that is, the value of any resources which are owned and employed by an enterprise. The economist's reasoning is simple and

433

very pertinent: regardless of whether a resource is owned or hired by an enterprise, there is a cost involved in using that resource in a specific employment. In real terms that cost is the units of alternative products which are forgone. In money terms it is the money payment which the self-employed resource could have earned in its best alternative employments. For example, suppose Brooks operates a corner grocery as a sole proprietor. He owns his store building and supplies all his own labor and money capital. Though his enterprise has no explicit rental or wage costs, implicit rents and wages are incurred. By using his own building for a grocery, Brooks sacrifices the $200 monthly rental income which he could otherwise have earned by renting it to someone else. Similarly, by using his money capital and labor in his own enterprise, Brooks sacrifices the interest and wage incomes which he otherwise could have earned by supplying these resources in their best alternative employments. And, finally, by running his own enterprise, Brooks forgoes the earnings he could realize by supplying his management efforts in someone else's firm.

The minimum payment required to keep Brooks's money capital and his managerial talents engaged in this enterprise is sometimes called a *normal profit*. Like implicit rent or implicit wages, this normal return to the businessman for his money capital and the performing of routine managerial tasks is an implicit cost. If this minimum, or normal, return is not realized, the owner's money capital and his managerial talents will be withdrawn and reallocated to some alternative line of production.

In short, the economist includes as costs all payments—explicit and implicit, the latter including a normal profit—required to retain resources in a given line of production.

Economic, or pure, profits

Our discussion of economic costs correctly suggests that economists and accountants use the term "profits" differently. By "profits" the accountant generally means total receipts less explicit costs. But to the economist "profits" means total receipts less *all* costs (explicit and

implicit, the latter including a normal return to the businessman on his money capital and for his managerial talents). Therefore, when economists say that a firm is just covering its costs, he means that all explicit and implicit costs are being met and that the businessman is therefore receiving a return just large enough to retain his money capital and managerial talent in his present line of production. If a firm's total receipts exceed all its economic costs, any residual accrues to the businessman or entrepreneur. This residual is called an *economic*, or *pure, profit.* It is not a cost, because by definition it is a return in excess of the normal profit required to retain the money capital and managerial efforts of the businessman. In Chapter 30 we shall find that economic profits are associated with risk bearing and monopoly power.

Short run and long run

The costs which a firm or industry can achieve in producing any given output will depend upon the types of adjustment it is able to make in the amounts of the various resources it employs. The quantities employed of many resources—labor, raw materials, fuel, power, and so forth—can be varied easily and quickly. But the amounts of other resources demand more time for adjustment. For example, the capacity of a manufacturing plant, that is, the size of the factory building and the amount of machinery and equipment therein, can only be varied over a considerable period of time. In some heavy industries it may take several years to alter plant capacity.

These differences in the time necessary to vary the quantities of the various resources used in the productive process make it essential to distinguish between the short run and the long run. The *short run* refers to a period of time too short to permit an enterprise to alter its plant capacity but yet long enough to permit a change in the level at which the fixed plant is utilized. The firm's plant capacity is fixed in the short run, but output can be varied by applying larger or smaller amounts of manpower, materials, and so forth, to that plant. Existing plant capacity can be used more or less intensively in the short run.

From the viewpoint of existing firms the *long run* refers to a period of time long enough to allow these firms to change the quantities of all resources employed, including plant capacity. From the viewpoint of an industry the long run also encompasses enough time for existing firms to dissolve and leave the industry and for new firms to be created and enter the industry. While the short run is a "fixed plant" time period, the long run is a "variable plant" time period.

Some examples will make clear the distinction between the short run and the long run. If a General Motors plant were to hire an extra 100 workers or to add an entire shift of workers, these would be short-run adjustments. If the same GM plant were to add a new wing to its building and install more equipment, this would be a long-run adjustment. If Studebaker-Packard were to cease to produce automobiles, this too would be a long-run adjustment.

It is important to note that the short run and the long run are conceptual rather than specific calendar time periods. In light manufacturing industries, changes in plant capacity may be negotiated almost overnight. A small firm making men's clothing can increase its plant capacity in a few days or less simply by ordering and installing a couple of new cutting tables and several extra sewing machines. But heavy industry is a different story. It may take Ford or General Motors several years to construct a new assembly plant and to install elaborate assembly-line equipment.

We turn now to the task of analyzing production costs in the short-run, or fixed plant, period. Following this we consider costs in the long-run, or variable plant, period.

PRODUCTION COSTS IN THE SHORT RUN

A firm's costs of producing any output will depend not only upon the prices of needed resources, but also upon the quantity of resources it takes to produce that output. It is the latter aspect of costs with which we are concerned for the moment. In the short run a firm can change its output by adding variable resources to a fixed plant. Question: How does output change as more and more variable resources are added to the firm's fixed resources?

Law of diminishing returns

The answer is provided in general terms by the *law of diminishing returns*. This engineering law states that *as successive units of a variable resource (say, labor) are added to a fixed resource (capital), beyond some point the extra, or marginal, product attributable to each additional unit of the variable resource will decline.* Stated somewhat differently, if additional workers are applied to a given amount of capital equipment, as is the case in the short run, eventually output will rise less than in proportion to the increase in the number of workers employed. A couple of examples will illustrate this law.

Suppose a farmer has a fixed amount of land —say, 80 acres—which he has planted in corn. Assuming the farmer does not cultivate his cornfields at all, his yield will be, say, 40 bushels per acre. If he cultivates the land once, output may rise to 50 bushels per acre. A second cultivation may increase output to 57 bushels per acre, a third to 61, and a fourth to, say, 63. But further cultivations will add little or nothing to total output. Successive cultivations add less and less to the land's yield. If this were not the case, the world's needs for corn could be fulfilled by extremely intense cultivation of this single 80-acre plot of land. Indeed, if diminishing returns did not occur, the world could be fed out of a flowerpot.

The law of diminishing returns also holds true in nonagricultural industries. Assume a small planing mill is manufacturing unupholstered furniture. The mill has a given amount of equipment in the form of lathes, planers, saws, sanders, and so forth. If this firm hired just one or two workers, total output and production per man would be very low. These workers would have a number of different jobs to perform, and the advantages of specialization would be lost. Time would also be lost in switching from one job operation to another, and the machines would stand idle most of the time. In short, the plant would be under-manned, and production therefore would be inefficient. These difficulties would disappear as more workers were added. Equipment would be more fully utilized, and workers could now specialize on a single job. Thus as more workers are added to the initially undermanned plant, the extra or marginal product of each will tend to rise as a result of more efficient production. But this cannot go on indefinitely. As still more workers are added, problems of overcrowding will arise. Workers must wait in line to use the machinery. The extra, or marginal, product of additional workers declines because the plant is overmanned. In the extreme the continuous addition of labor to the plant would use up all standing room, and production would be brought to a standstill!

Table 23-1 illustrates the law of diminishing returns numerically. In this instance diminishing marginal product is incurred with the hire of the third worker. Total product is found by simply accumulating the extra, or marginal, product attributable to each successive worker. Total product will increase so long as marginal product is positive.

Fixed, variable, and total costs

The production data described by the law of diminishing returns must be coupled with resource prices to determine the total and per unit costs of producing various outputs. We have already emphasized that in the short run some resources—those associated with the firm's plant—are fixed. Others are variable. This correctly suggests that in the short run costs can be classified as either fixed or variable. *Fixed costs are those costs which in total do not vary with changes in output.* Fixed costs are associated with the very existence of a firm's plant and therefore must be paid even if the firm's rate of output is zero. Such costs as interest on a firm's bonded indebtedness, rental payments, a portion of depreciation on equipment and buildings, insurance premiums, the salaries of top management and key personnel, and property taxes are generally fixed costs. In column 2 of Table 23-2 we have assumed that the firm's fixed costs are $100. Note that this fixed cost figure prevails at all levels of output, including zero.

TABLE 23-1. THE LAW OF DIMINISHING RETURNS (hypothetical data)

(1) Inputs of the variable resource (labor)	(2) Extra, or marginal, product	(3) Total product
0		0
	5	
1		5
	8	
2		13
	5	
3		18
	4	
4		22
	3	
5		25
	2	
6		27

Variable costs are those costs which increase with the level of output. Variable costs include payments for labor, materials, fuel, power, transportation services, and similar variable resources. In column 3 of Table 23-2 we find that the total of variable costs changes with output, but note that the rate of increase in variable costs is not constant. As production begins, variable costs will for a time increase at a decreasing rate; this is true through the fourth unit of output. From the fifth unit on, however, variable costs increase at an increasing rate. The explanation of this behavior of variable costs lies in the law of diminishing returns. Because of increasing marginal product, smaller and smaller increases in the amounts of variable resources will be needed for a time to get successive units of output produced. This means that total variable costs will increase at a decreasing rate. But when marginal product begins to decline as diminishing returns are encountered, it will be necessary to use larger and larger additional amounts of variable resources to produce each successive unit of output. Total variable costs will therefore increase at an increasing rate.

Total cost is self-defining: it is the *sum of fixed and variable costs at each level of output.* It is shown in column 4 of Table 23-2. At zero units of output total cost is equal to the firm's

TABLE 23-2. TOTAL AND AVERAGE COST SCHEDULES FOR AN INDIVIDUAL FIRM IN THE SHORT RUN

Total cost data, per week				Average cost data, per week			
(1)	*(2)*	*(3)*	*(4)*	*(5)*	*(6)*	*(7)*	*(8)*
Total product	*Total fixed cost*	*Total variable cost*	*Total cost*	*Average fixed cost, or (2) ÷ (1)*	*Average variable cost, or (3) ÷ (1)*	*Average total cost, or (4) ÷ (1)*	*Marginal cost, or Δ(4)*
0	$100	$ 0	$ 100				
							$ 90
1	100	90	190	$100.00	$90.00	$190.00	
							80
2	100	170	270	50.00	85.00	135.00	
							70
3	100	240	340	33.33	80.00	113.33	
							60
4	100	300	400	25.00	75.00	100.00	
							70
5	100	370	470	20.00	74.00	94.00	
							80
6	100	450	550	16.67	75.00	91.67	
							90
7	100	540	640	14.29	77.14	91.43	
							110
8	100	650	750	12.50	81.23	93.73	
							130
9	100	780	880	11.11	86.67	97.78	
							150
10	100	930	1,030	10.00	93.00	103.00	

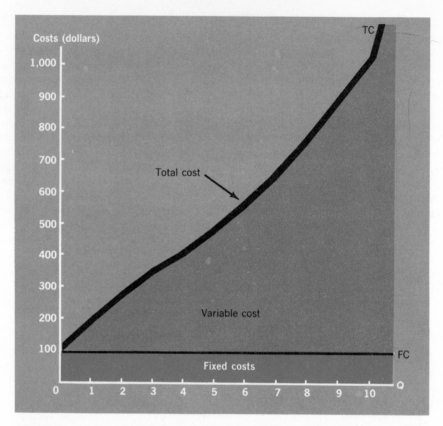

FIGURE 23-1. TOTAL COST IS THE SUM OF FIXED AND VARIABLE COSTS.
Fixed costs (FC) are independent of the level of output. Variable costs (VC) vary with output. The total cost (TC) of any output is the sum of the fixed and variable costs of that output.

fixed costs. Then for each unit of production—1 through 10—total cost varies at the same rate as does variable cost.

Figure 23-1 shows graphically the fixed, variable, and total cost data of Table 23-2.

The distinction between fixed and variable costs is of no little significance to the businessman. Variable costs are those costs which the businessman can control or alter in the short run by changing his level of production. On the other hand, fixed costs are clearly beyond the businessman's control; such costs are incurred and must be paid regardless of output level.

Per unit, or average, costs

Producers are certainly interested in their total costs, but they are equally concerned with their per unit, or average, costs. In particular, average cost data are more usable for making comparisons with product price, which is always stated on a per unit basis. Average fixed cost, average variable cost, and average total cost are shown in columns 5 to 7 of Table 23-2. It is important that we know how these unit cost figures are derived and how they vary as output changes.

Average fixed cost (AFC) is found by dividing total fixed costs by the corresponding output. AFC declines as output increases. Though total fixed costs are, by definition, independent of output, AFC will decline as output increases. As output increases, a given total fixed cost of $100 is obviously being spread over a larger and larger output. When output is just 1 unit, total fixed costs and AFC are equal at $100. But at 2 units of output, total fixed costs of $100 become $50 worth of fixed costs per unit; then $33.33, as $100 is spread over 3 units; $25, when spread over 4 units; and so forth. This is what businessmen commonly refer to

as "spreading the overhead." We find in Figure 23-2 that AFC graphs as a continually declining figure as total output is increased.

Average variable cost (AVC) is found by dividing total variable cost by the corresponding output. AVC declines initially, reaches a minimum, and then increases again. Graphically, this provides us with a U-shaped AVC curve as is shown in Figure 23-2.

Because total variable cost reflects the law of diminishing returns, so must the AVC figures, which are derived from total variable cost. Because of increasing returns it takes less and less additional variable resources to produce

FIGURE 23-2. THE AVERAGE COST CURVES.
Average total cost (ATC) is the vertical sum of average variable cost (AVC) and average fixed cost (AFC). AFC necessarily falls as a given amount of fixed costs is apportioned over a larger and larger output. AVC initially falls because of increasing physical returns but then rises because of diminishing physical returns.

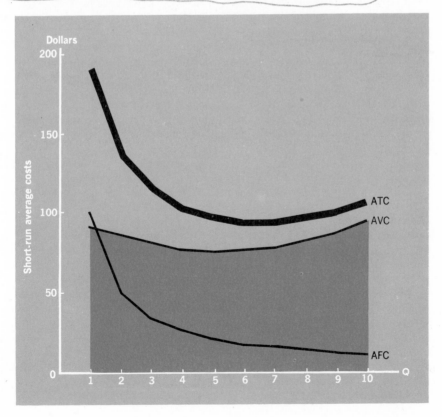

each of the first 4 units of output. As a result, variable cost per unit will decline. AVC hits a minimum with the fifth unit of output, and beyond this point AVC rises as diminishing returns necessitate the use of more and more variable resources to produce each additional unit of output. In more direct terms, at low levels of output, production will be relatively inefficient and costly, because the firm's fixed plant is undermanned. Not enough variable resources are being combined with the firm's plant; production is inefficient, and per unit variable costs are therefore relatively high. As output expands, however, greater specialization and a more complete utilization of the firm's capital equipment will make for more efficient production. As a result, variable cost per unit of output will decline. As more and more variable resources are added, some point will eventually be reached where diminishing returns are incurred. The firm's capital equipment will now be overmanned, and the resulting overcrowding and overutilization of machinery impairs efficiency. This means that AVC will increase.

Average total cost (ATC) can be found by dividing total cost by total output or, more simply, by adding AFC and AVC for each of the ten levels of output. These data are shown in column 7 of Table 23-2. Graphically, ATC is found by adding vertically the AFC and AVC curves as in Figure 23-2. Thus the vertical distance between the ATC and AVC curves reflects AFC at any output.

Marginal cost

There remains one final and very crucial cost concept—marginal cost. *Marginal cost (MC) is the extra, or additional, cost of producing one more unit of output*. MC can be determined for each additional unit of output simply by noting the change in total cost which that unit's production entails. In Table 23-2 we find that production of the first unit of output increases total cost from $100 to $190. Therefore the additional, or marginal, cost of that first unit is $90. The marginal cost of the second unit is $80 ($270 − $190); the MC of the third is $70 ($340 − $270); and so forth. MC for each of

the ten units of output is shown in column 8 of Table 23-2. MC can also be calculated from the total variable cost column. Why? Because the only difference between total cost and total variable cost is the constant amount of fixed costs. Hence, the change in total cost and change in total variable cost associated with each additional unit of output is the same.

Marginal cost is a very strategic concept, because it designates those costs over which the firm has the most direct control. More specifically, MC indicates those costs which are incurred in the production of the last unit of output and, simultaneously, the cost which can be "saved" by reducing total output by the last unit. Average cost figures do not provide this information. For example, suppose the firm is undecided as to whether it should produce 3 or 4 units of output. At 4 units of output Table 23-2 indicates that ATC is $100. But the firm does not increase its total costs by $100 by producing, nor does it "save" $100 by not producing, the fourth unit. Rather the change in costs involved here is only $60, as the MC column of Table 23-2 clearly reveals. A firm's decisions as to what output to produce are marginal decisions, that is, decisions to produce a few more or a few less units. Marginal cost reveals the change in costs which one more unit or one less unit of output entails. When coupled with marginal revenue, which we found in Chapter 21 indicates the change in revenue from one more or one less unit of output, marginal cost allows a firm to determine whether it is profitable to expand or contract its level of production. The analysis in the next four chapters centers upon these marginal calculations.

Marginal cost is shown graphically in Figure 23-3. Note that marginal cost declines sharply, reaches a minimum, and then rises rather sharply. This mirrors the fact that variable cost, and therefore total cost, increases first at a decreasing rate and then at an increasing rate (see Figure 23-1 and columns 3 and 4 of Table 23-2). This, you will recall, is in accord with the law of diminishing returns.

Furthermore, it is notable that marginal cost cuts both AVC and ATC at their minimum points. This marginal-average relationship is a

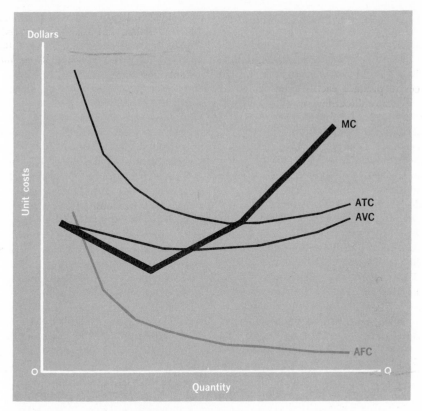

FIGURE 23-3. THE RELATIONSHIP OF MARGINAL COST TO AVERAGE TOTAL COST AND AVERAGE VARIABLE COST.

Marginal cost (MC) cuts both ATC and AVC at their minimum points. This is so because whenever the extra or marginal amount added to total cost (or variable cost) is less than the average of that cost, the average will necessarily fall. Conversely, whenever the marginal amount added to total (or variable) cost is greater than the average of total cost, the average must rise.

matter of mathematical necessity, which a common-sense illustration can make readily apparent. Suppose a baseball pitcher has allowed his opponents an average of 3 runs per game in the first three games he has pitched. Now whether his average falls or rises as a result of pitching a fourth (marginal) game will depend upon whether the additional runs he allows in that extra game are less or more than his current 3-run average. If he allows less than 3 runs —for example, 1—in the fourth game, his total runs will rise from 9 to 10, and his average will fall from 3 to 2½ (10 ÷ 4). Conversely, if he allows more than 3 runs—say, 7—in the fourth game, his total will rise from 9 to 16 and his average from 3 to 4 (16 ÷ 4). So it is with costs. When the amount added to total cost (marginal cost) is less than the average of total cost, ATC will fall. Conversely, when marginal cost exceeds ATC, ATC will rise. This means in Figure 23-3 that so long as MC lies below ATC, the latter will fall, and where MC is above ATC, ATC will rise. Therefore at the point of intersection where MC equals ATC, ATC has just ceased to fall but has not yet begun to rise. This, by definition, is the minimum point on the ATC curve. Because MC can be defined as the addition either to total cost or to total variable cost resulting from one more unit of output, this same rationale explains why MC also cuts AVC at the latter's minimum point. No such relationship exists for MC and average fixed cost, because the two are simply not related; marginal cost embodies only those costs which change with output, and fixed costs by definition are independent of output.

PRODUCTION COSTS IN THE LONG RUN

In the long run all desired resource adjustments can be negotiated by an industry and the individual firms which comprise it. The firm can alter its plant capacity; it may build a larger plant or revert to a smaller plant than that assumed in Table 23-2. The industry can also change its plant size; the long run is

an amount of time sufficient for new firms to enter or old firms to leave an industry. The impact of the entry and exodus of firms from an industry will be discussed in the next chapter; here we are concerned only with changes in plant capacity made by a single firm. And in considering these adjustments we couch our analysis in terms of ATC, making no distinction between fixed and variable costs for the obvious reason that all resources and therefore all costs are variable in the long run.

Suppose a single-plant manufacturing enterprise starts out on a small scale and then, as the result of successful operations, expands to successively larger plant sizes. What will happen to average total costs as this growth occurs? The answer is this: for a time successively larger plants will bring lower average total costs. However, eventually the building of a still larger plant will cause ATC to rise.

Figure 23-4 illustrates this situation for five possible plant sizes. ATC-1 is the average total

FIGURE 23-4. THE LONG-RUN AVERAGE COST CURVE: FIVE POSSIBLE PLANT SIZES.
The long-run average cost curve is made up of segments of the short-run cost curves (ATC-1, ATC-2, etc.) of the various-sized plants from which the firm might choose. Each point on the bumpy planning curve shows the least unit cost attainable for any output when the firm has had time to make all desired changes in its plant size.

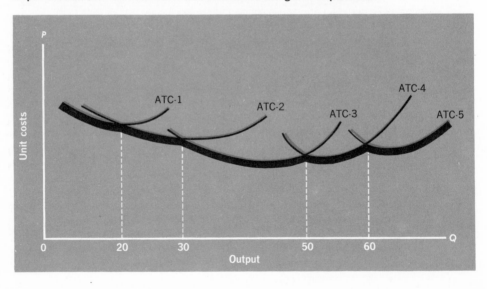

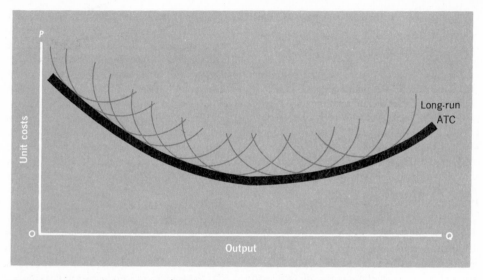

FIGURE 23-5. THE LONG-RUN AVERAGE COST CURVE: UNLIMITED NUMBER OF PLANT SIZES.
If the number of possible plant sizes is very large, the long-run average cost curve approximates a smooth curve. Economies and diseconomies of scale cause the curve to be U-shaped.

cost curve for the smallest of the five plants, and ATC-5 for the largest. The relationship of the five plant sizes to one another is clearly that stated above. Constructing a larger plant will entail lower per unit costs through plant size 3. But beyond this point a larger plant will mean a higher level of average total costs.

The dotted lines perpendicular to the output axis are crucial. They indicate those points at which the firm should change plant size in order to realize the lowest attainable per unit costs of production. To illustrate in terms of Figure 23-4: for all outputs up to 20 units the lowest per unit costs are attainable with plant size 1. However, if the firm's volume of sales expands to some level greater than 20 but less than 30 units, it can achieve lower per unit costs by constructing a larger plant—plant size 2. For any output between 30 and 50 units plant size 3 will yield the lowest per unit costs. For the 50–60-unit range of output, plant size 4 must be built to achieve the lowest unit costs. Lowest per unit costs for any output in excess of 60

units demand the construction of the still larger plant of size 5.

Tracing these adjustments, we can conclude that the long-run ATC curve for the enterprise will be comprised of segments of the short-run ATC curves for the various plant sizes which can be constructed. *The long-run ATC curve shows the least per unit cost at which any output can be produced after the firm has had time to make all appropriate adjustments in its plant size.* In Figure 23-4 the heavy, bumpy curve is the firm's long-run ATC curve or, as it is often called, the firm's planning curve. In most lines of production the choice of plant sizes is much wider than that assumed in our illustration. In fact, in many industries the number of possible plant sizes is virtually unlimited. This means that in time very small changes in the volume of output (sales) will prompt appropriate changes in the size of the plant. Graphically this means that the planning curve will be smooth rather than bumpy. Figure 23-5 is illustrative.

Economies and diseconomies of scale

We have patiently accepted the contention that for a time a larger and larger plant size will entail lower unit costs but that beyond some point successively larger plants will mean higher average total costs. Now we must explain this point. Exactly why is the long-run ATC curve U-shaped? It must be emphasized, first of all, that the law of diminishing returns is not applicable here, because it presumes that one resource is fixed in supply and, as we have seen, the long run assumes that all resources are variable. What then is our explanation? The U-shaped long-run average cost curve is explainable in terms of what economists call "economies and diseconomies" of large-scale production.

Economies of large scale. Economies of scale or, more commonly, economies of mass production, explain the downsloping part of the long-run ATC curve. As the size of a plant increases, a number of considerations will for a time give rise to lower average costs of production.

1. Increased specialization in the use of labor is feasible as a plant increases in size. The hire of more workers means that jobs can be divided and subdivided. Instead of performing five or six distinct operations in the productive process, each worker may now have just one task to perform. Workers can be used full time on those particular operations at which they have special skills. In a small plant a skilled machinist may spend half his time performing unskilled tasks. This makes for high production costs. Further, the dividing of work operations which large scale allows will give workers the opportunity to become very proficient at the specific tasks assigned them. The Jack-of-all-trades who is burdened with five or six jobs will not be likely to become very efficient in any of them. When allowed to concentrate on one task, the same worker may become highly efficient. Finally, greater specialization tends to eliminate the loss of time which accompanies the shifting of workers from one job to another.

2. Large-scale production also permits better utilization of, and greater specialization in, management. A foreman capable of handling fifteen or twenty men will be underutilized in a small plant hiring only eight or ten men. The production staff can be doubled with no increase in administrative costs. In addition, small firms will not be able to use management specialists to best advantage. In a small plant a sales specialist may be forced to divide his time between several executive functions—for example, sales, personnel, and finance. A larger scale of operations will mean that the sales expert can devote full time to supervising sales while appropriate specialists are added to perform other managerial functions. Greater efficiency and lower unit costs are the net result.

3. Small firms are often not able to utilize the most efficient productive equipment. In many lines of production the most efficient machinery is available only in very large and extremely expensive units. Furthermore, effective utilization of this equipment demands a high volume of production. This means only large-scale producers are able to afford and operate efficiently the best available equipment.

To illustrate: in the automobile industry the most efficient fabrication method entails the use of extremely elaborate assembly-line equipment. The efficient use of this equipment demands an annual output of hundreds of thousands of automobiles per year. Only very large-scale producers can afford to purchase and use this equipment efficiently. The small-scale producer is between the devil and the deep blue sea. To fabricate automobiles with the use of other equipment is inefficient and therefore costly. The alternative of purchasing the most efficient equipment and underutilizing it with a small level of output is equally inefficient and costly.

4. The large-scale producer is in a better position to utilize by-products than is a small firm. The large meat-packing plant makes glue, fertilizer, pharmaceuticals, and a host of other products from animal remnants which would be discarded by smaller producers.

All these technological considerations—greater specialization in the use of labor and management, the ability to use the most efficient equipment, and the effective utilization of by-products—will contribute to lower unit costs for the smaller producer who is able to expand his scale of operations.

A large firm may realize certain market advantages unobtainable to its smaller rivals. On the one hand, sellers of materials and parts typically offer quantity discounts to large buyers. Freight rates are also relatively lower to large shippers; less-than-carload shipments are expensive relative to carload shipments. On the other hand, large-scale producers may avail themselves of certain cost advantages in the area of finance. The cost of issuing bonds, for example, is relatively constant regardless of the size of the issue. This means that the per dollar cost of obtaining money capital will be less to the larger firm. Then, too, it has been face-tiously remarked that commercial bank credit is readily available on favorable terms only to those who can prove they do not need it! Large-scale producers are typically better able to offer such proof than are their smaller brethren.

These and other market considerations reinforce the declining unit costs which a small plant may incur upon expansion.

Diseconomies of large scale. But in time the expansion of a firm will likely give rise to diseconomies and therefore higher per unit costs.

The main factor causing diseconomies of scale has to do with certain managerial problems which typically arise as a firm becomes a large-scale producer. In a small plant a single key executive may render all the basic decisions relative to his plant's operation. Because of the firm's smallness he is close to the production line. He can therefore comprehend the various aspects of the firm's operations and digest the information fed to him by his subordinates to the end that efficient decision making is possible.

This neat picture changes, however, as a firm grows. The management echelons between the executive suite and the assembly line become many; top management is far removed from the actual production operations of the plant. It becomes impossible for one man to assemble, understand, and digest all the information essential to rational decision making in a large-

scale enterprise. Authority must be delegated to innumerable vice-presidents, second vice-presidents, and so forth. This expansion in the depth and width of management entails problems of coordination and bureaucratic red tape which can eventually impair the efficiency of a firm and lead to higher costs.

Another consideration contributing to diseconomies of scale is the rising transportation costs which large scale may bring. For example, if a food-processing plant decides to increase its scale of operations, it may be forced to buy its additional farm produce in increasingly remote areas. Similarly, the firm may have to ship its finished products to more distant markets in order to sell them.

The likelihood of a single-plant firm encountering increasing transportation costs as its scale of operations increases raises this question: Can a firm avoid diseconomies of scale by becoming a multiplant firm? Can diseconomies of scale be circumvented by establishing entirely new plants in other localities rather than expanding the size of the firm's original plant? The answer is "No." Establishing new plants may permit the firm to dodge increasing transportation costs and to forestall diseconomies of scale, but in time we can expect the problems of managerial coordination to give rise to increasing unit costs.

Significance of economies and diseconomies of scale. Economies and diseconomies of scale are something more than a plausible pipedream of economic theorists. Indeed, in most American manufacturing industries economies of scale have been of great significance. Firms which have been able to expand their scale of operations to realize the economies of mass production have survived and flourished. Those unable to achieve this expansion have found themselves in the unenviable position of high-cost producers, doomed to a marginal existence or ultimate insolvency.

Diseconomies of scale, when encountered, can be equally significant. The organizational structure of General Motors, for example, is designed to avoid managerial diseconomies which its gigantic size would otherwise entail. This industrial colossus has subdivided itself into some thirty-four operating subdivisions, each of which is basically autonomous and in some cases—for example, its five automobile producing divisions (Chevrolet, Buick, Oldsmobile, Pontiac, and Cadillac)—competing. A degree of decentralization has been sought which will allow full realization of the economies of mass production but yet will help to avoid diseconomies of scale.[1] Another example: some economists feel that U.S. Steel has declined in relative importance in the steel industry because of diseconomies of scale. One authority[2] has described U.S. Steel as

. . . a big sprawling inert giant, whose production operations were improperly coordinated; suffering from a lack of a long-run planning

[1] See Leonard W. Weiss, *Economics and American Industry* (New York: John Wiley & Sons, Inc., 1961), pp. 347–350.

[2] Statement by George Stocking, cited in Walter Adams (ed.), *The Structure of American Industry,* 3d ed. (New York: The Macmillan Company, 1961), p. 180.

agency; relying on an antiquated system of cost accounting: with an inadequate knowledge of the costs or of the relative profitability of the many thousands of items it sold; with production and cost standards generally below those considered everyday practice in other industries; with inadequate knowledge of its domestic markets and no clear appreciation of its opportunities in foreign markets; with less efficient production facilities than its rivals had; slow in introducing new processes and new products.

These comments correctly imply that economies and diseconomies of scale are a fundamental determinant of the structure of any industry. Where economies of scale are many and diseconomies are remote, the long-run ATC curve will decline over a long range of output as in Figure 23-6a. Such is the case in the automobile, aluminum, steel, and a host of other heavy industries. This means that, given consumer demand, efficient production will be achieved only with a small number of large producers. On the other hand, where economies

FIGURE 23-6. VARIOUS POSSIBLE LONG-RUN AVERAGE COST CURVES.
(a) When economies of scale are many and diseconomies remote, the ATC will fall over a wide range of production. (b) If economies of scale are few and diseconomies are quickly incurred, minimum unit costs will be encountered at a relatively low output. (c) Where economies of scale are rather rapidly exhausted and diseconomies not encountered until a considerably large scale of output has been achieved, long-run average costs will be relatively constant over a wide range of output.

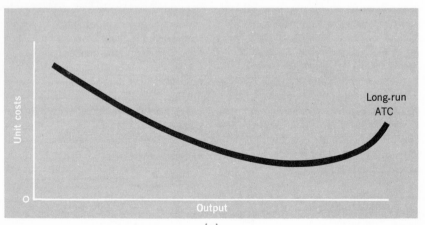

(a)

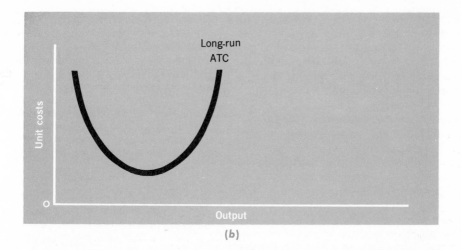

(b)

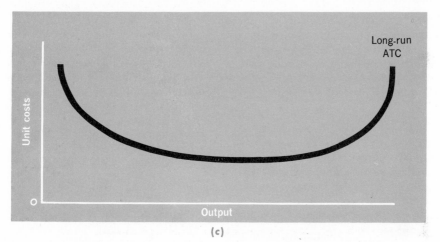

(c)

of scale are few and diseconomies quickly encountered, minimum unit costs will be achieved at a modest level of production. The long-run ATC curve for such a situation is shown in Figure 23-6b. In such industries a given level of consumer demand will support a large number of relatively small producers. Many of the retail trades and some types of farming fall into this category. So do certain types of light manufacturing, for example, the baking, clothing, and shoe industries. Fairly small firms are as efficient as, or more efficient than, large-scale producers in such industries.

In most industries we find a mixture of large and small producers operating with roughly the same degree of efficiency—the meat-pack-

ing, household-appliance, and furniture industries are representative. In such industries the long-run ATC curve may be such that there exists a wide range of output between the point at which available economies of scale are exhausted and the point at which diseconomies of scale are encountered. Or, alternatively, economies and diseconomies of scale may be largely self-canceling over an extended range of output. Figure 23-6c illustrates the situation in which average costs are relatively constant over a wide range of output.

Caution: We are not implying here that long-run unit costs are the only determinant of the structure of industry. Indeed, it was stressed in Chapter 20 that the major determinants of the competitiveness of industry are several and varied. We are saying that there is considerable evidence that cost considerations are one important force in determining the number and size of firms in a particular industry.

SUMMARY

1. Economic costs include all payments which must be received by resource owners in order to assure their continued supply in a particular line of production. This definition includes explicit costs which flow to resource suppliers who are separate from a given enterprise and also implicit costs which are the remuneration of self-owned and self-employed resources. One of the implicit cost payments is a normal profit to the businessman for the money capital and managerial efforts he provides.

2. In the short run a firm's plant capacity is fixed. The firm can use its plant more or less intensively by adding or subtracting units of variable resources, but the firm does not have sufficient time to alter its plant size.

3. The law of diminishing returns describes what happens to output as a fixed plant is used more intensively. The law states that, as successive units of a variable resource such as labor are added to a fixed plant, beyond some point the resulting marginal product associated with each additional worker will decline.

4. Because some resources are variable and others fixed, cost can be classified as variable or fixed in the short run. Fixed costs are those which are independent of the level of output. Variable costs are those which vary with output. The total cost of any output is the sum of fixed and variable costs at that output.

5. Average fixed, average variable, and average total costs are simply fixed, variable, and total cost per unit of output. Average fixed costs decline continuously as output increases,

because a fixed sum is being apportioned over a larger and larger number of units of production. Average variable costs are U-shaped, reflecting the law of diminishing returns. Average total cost is the sum of average fixed and average variable cost; it too is U-shaped.

6. Marginal cost is the extra, or additional, cost of producing one more unit of output. Graphically, marginal cost cuts ATC and AVC at their minimum points.

7. The long run is a period of time sufficiently long for a firm to vary the amounts of all resources used, including plant size. Hence, in the long run all costs are variable. The long-run ATC, or planning, curve is composed of segments of the short-run ATC curves, which represent the various plant sizes a firm is able to construct in the long run.

8. The long-run ATC curve is generally U-shaped. Economies of scale are first encountered as a small firm expands. A number of considerations—greater specialization in the use of labor and management, the ability to use the most efficient equipment, the more complete utilization of by-products, and certain market advantages—contribute to these economies of scale. Diseconomies of scale stem from the managerial complexities which accompany large-scale production and the rising transportation costs incurred as a firm buys and sells in increasingly remote locations.

9. The relative importance of economies and diseconomies of scale in an industry is often an important determinant of the structure of that industry. Generally speaking, where economies of scale extend to large levels of output, an industry tends to be comprised of a small number of large-scale producers. When economies of scale are exhausted at relatively low levels of output, there tends to be a large number of small firms in an industry.

QUESTIONS AND STUDY SUGGESTIONS

1. How do economists define costs? Distinguish between explicit and implicit costs, giving examples of each. What are the explicit and implicit costs of going to college? What are "normal profits"? Why does the economist classify normal profits as a cost? What are "economic profits"?

2. Distinguish between the short run and the long run. Which of the following are short-run and which are long-run adjustments? (*a*) General Motors builds a new assembly plant; (*b*) Acme Steel Corporation hires 200 more workers; (*c*) a farmer increases the amount of fertilizer used on his corn crop; and (*d*) an Alcoa plant adds a third shift of workers.

3. State and explain the law of diminishing returns. What bearing does this law have upon short-run costs? Be specific.

4. Distinguish between fixed and variable costs. Why can this distinction be made in the short run? "There are no fixed costs in the long run; all costs are variable." Explain.

5. Classify the following as fixed or variable costs: advertising expenditures, fuel, interest on company-issued bonds, shipping charges, payments for raw materials, real estate taxes, executive salaries, insurance premiums, wage payments, depreciation and obsolescence charges, sales taxes, and rental payments on leased office machinery.

6. Assume a firm has fixed costs of $60 and variable costs as indicated below. Complete the table. When finished, check your calculations by referring to question 3 at the end of Chapter 24.

Total product	Total fixed cost	Total variable cost	Total cost	Average fixed cost	Average variable cost	Average total cost	Marginal cost
0		$ 0					
1		45					
2		85					
3		120					
4		150					
5		185					
6		225					
7		270					
8		325					
9		390					
10		465					

a. Graph fixed cost, variable cost, and total cost. Explain how the law of diminishing returns influences the shapes of the variable cost and total cost curves.

b. Graph AFC, AVC, ATC, and MC. Explain the derivation and shape of each of these four curves and the relationships which they bear to one another. Specifically, explain in nontechnical terms why MC cuts both AVC and ATC at their minimum points.

7. What are economies and diseconomies of scale? How do they affect the shape of a firm's long-run ATC curve? What bearing may the exact shape of this curve have upon the structure of an industry?

SELECTED REFERENCES

Bain, Joe S., *Industrial Organization* (New York: John Wiley & Sons, Inc., 1959), pp. 145–169.

Bober, M. M., *Intermediate Price and Income Theory,* rev. ed. (New York: W. W. Norton & Company, Inc., 1962), chaps. 5–7.

Colberg, M. R., and W. C. Bradford, *Business Economics: Principles and Cases,* 3d ed. (Homewood, Ill.: Richard D. Irwin, Inc., 1962), chap. 4.

Dean, Joel, *Managerial Economics* (Englewood Cliffs, N.J.: Prentice-Hall, Inc., 1951), chap. 5.

Stigler, George J., *The Theory of Price* (New York: The Macmillan Company, 1947), chap. 8.

Chapter 24

PRICE AND OUTPUT DETERMINATION:

PURE COMPETITION

WE NOW HAVE at our disposal the basic tools of analysis needed to understand how product price and output are determined. These analytical tools are applicable to all four basic market models—pure competition, pure monopoly, monopolistic competition, and oligopoly. In this chapter we focus attention upon price and output determination in a purely competitive industry.

CONCEPT AND OCCURRENCE OF PURE COMPETITION

Pure competition, you will recall, presupposes that certain specific conditions are fulfilled. *1.* A purely competitive industry is comprised of a large number of independent sellers. *2.* The firms offer a standardized product. This feature rules out nonprice competition, that is, advertising, sales promotion, and so forth. *3.* No individual firm supplies enough of the product to influence its market price noticeably. *4.* In a competitive industry no artificial obstacles prevent new firms from entering or old firms from leaving the industry. Firms and the resources they employ are shiftable, or mobile.

The third characteristic is particularly important. The individual competitive firm has nothing to say about determining market price.

Because it supplies a negligible portion of total output, the competitive firm cannot influence the market price which the forces of total demand and supply have established. The competitive firm does not have a price policy, that is, the ability to adjust price. Rather the firm can merely *adjust to* the market price, which it must regard as given data determined by the market.

Pure competition is rare in practice. This does not mean, however, that an analysis of how competitive markets work is a useless and irrelevant exercise in logic. In the first place, there are a few industries which more closely approximate the competitive model than they do any other market structure. For example, much can be learned about American agriculture by understanding the functioning of competitive markets. Secondly, pure competition provides the simplest context in which to apply the revenue and cost concepts developed in previous chapters. Pure competition is a simple and meaningful starting point for any discussion of price and output determination. Finally, in the concluding section of this chapter we will discover that the operation of a purely competitive economy provides us with a standard, or norm, against which the efficiency of the real-world economy can be compared and evaluated. Though pure competition is a rela-

451

tively rare market structure in our economy, it is one of considerable analytical and some practical importance.

Our analysis of pure competition centers upon three major objectives. First, we seek an understanding of how a competitive producer adjusts to market price in the short run. Next, the nature of long-run adjustments in a competitive industry is explored. Finally, we seek to evaluate the efficiency of competitive industries from the standpoint of society as a whole.

PROFIT MAXIMIZATION IN THE SHORT RUN

In the short run the competitive firm has a fixed plant and is attempting to maximize its profits or, as the case may be, minimize its losses by adjusting its output through changes in the amounts of variable resources (materials, labor, and so forth) it employs. The economic profits it seeks are obviously the difference between total revenue and total costs. Indeed, this points out the direction of our analysis. The revenue data of Chapter 22 and the cost data of Chapter 23 must be brought together in order that the profit-maximizing output for the firm can be determined.

There are two complementary approaches to determining the level of output at which a competitive firm will realize maximum profits or minimum losses. The first involves a comparison of total revenue and total costs; the second, a comparison of marginal revenue and marginal cost. Both approaches, incidentally, can be applied not only to a purely competitive firm but also to firms operating in any of the other three basic market structures. To ensure an understanding of output determination under pure competition we will invoke both approaches, emphasizing the marginal approach. Furthermore, both hypothetical data and graphic analysis will be employed to bolster our understanding of the two approaches.

Total receipts–total cost approach

Given the market price of its product, the competitive producer is faced with three related questions: (1) Should I produce? (2) If so, what

amount? (3) What profit (or loss) will be realized?

At first glance the answer to question 1 seems obvious: "You should produce if it is profitable to do so." But the situation is a bit more complex than this. In the short run a part of the firm's total costs is variable costs, and the remainder is fixed costs. The latter will have to be paid "out of pocket" even when the firm is closed down. In the short run a firm takes a loss equal to its fixed costs when it is producing zero units of output. This means that, although there may be no level of output at which the firm can realize a profit, the firm might still produce, provided that in so doing it can realize a loss less than the fixed cost loss it will face in closing down. In other words, the correct answer to the "Should I produce?" question is this: the firm should produce in the short run if it can realize an economic profit or a loss which is less than its fixed costs.

Assuming the firm will produce, the second question becomes relevant: "How much should be produced?" The answer here is fairly obvious: In the short run the firm should produce that output at which it maximizes profits or minimizes losses.

Now let us examine three cases which will demonstrate the validity of these two generalizations and answer our third query by indicating how profits and losses can be readily calculated. In the first case the firm will maximize its profits by producing. In the second case it will minimize its losses by producing. In the third case the firm will minimize its losses by closing down. Our plan of attack is to assume given short-run cost data for all three cases and to explore the firm's production decisions when faced with three different product prices.

Profit-maximizing case. In all three cases we employ cost data with which we are already familiar. Columns 3 through 5 of Table 24-1 merely repeat the fixed, variable, and total cost data which were developed in Table 23-2. Assuming that market price is $131, we can derive total revenue for each level of output by simply multiplying output times price, as we did in Table 21-3. These data are presented in column 2. Then in column 6 the profit or loss

TABLE 24-1. THE PROFIT-MAXIMIZING OUTPUT FOR A PURELY COMPETITIVE FIRM: TOTAL REVENUE—TOTAL COST APPROACH (price = $131)

(1) Total product	(2) Total revenue	(3) Total fixed cost	(4) Total variable cost	(5) Total cost	(6) Profit (+) or loss (−), = (2) − (5)
0	$ 0	$100	$ 0	$ 100	$ − 100
1	131	100	90	190	− 59
2	262	100	170	270	− 8
3	393	100	240	340	+ 53
4	524	100	300	400	+124
5	655	100	370	470	+185
6	786	100	450	550	+236
7	917	100	540	640	+277
8	1,048	100	650	750	+298
9	1,179	100	780	880	+299
10	1,310	100	930	1,030	+280

which will be encountered at each output is found by subtracting total cost from total revenue. Now we have all the data needed to answer the three questions.

Should the firm produce? Yes, because it can realize a profit by doing so. How much? Nine units, because column 6 tells us that this is the output at which profits will be at a maximum. The size of that profit? $299.

Figure 24-1 compares total revenue and total cost graphically. Total revenue is a straight line, because under pure competition each additional unit adds the same amount—its price —to total revenue (Chapter 21). Total costs increase with output; more production requires more resources. But the rate of increase in total costs varies with the relative efficiency of the firm. For a time the rate of increase in total cost is less and less as the firm utilizes its fixed resources more efficiently. Then, after a time, total cost begins to increase at an ever-increasing rate because of the inefficiencies which accompany overutilization of the firm's plant. A break-even point occurs at about 2 units of output. And, if our data were extended beyond 10 units of output, another such point would

be incurred where total cost catches up with total revenue, as is shown in Figure 24-1. Any output within these break-even points will entail an economic profit. The maximum profit is obviously achieved where the vertical difference between total revenue and total cost is greatest. For our data this is at 9 units of output.

Loss-minimizing case. Assuming no change in costs, the firm may not be able to realize economic profits if the market yields a price considerably below $131. To illustrate: Suppose the market price is $81. As column 6 of Table 24-2 indicates, at this price all levels of output will entail losses. But the firm will not close down. Why? Because by producing the firm can realize a loss very considerably less than the fixed cost loss it will incur by closing down. Specifically, the firm will minimize its losses by producing 6 units of output. The resulting $64 loss is clearly preferable to the $100 loss which closing down will involve. Stated differently, by producing 6 units the firm earns a total revenue of $486 sufficient to pay all the firm's variable costs ($450) and also a substantial portion—$36 worth—of the firm's fixed costs.

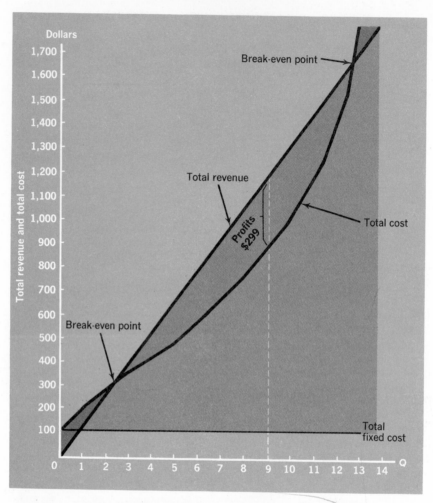

FIGURE 24-1. PROFIT MAXIMIZATION AS SHOWN BY A TOTAL-REVENUE—TOTAL-COST CHART.
A firm's profits are maximized at that output at which the vertical difference between its total revenue and total cost is at a maximum.

There are, you will note, several other outputs which entail a loss less than the firm's $100 fixed costs; but at 6 units of output the loss is minimized.

Close-down case. Assume finally that the market price is a mere $71. Given short-run costs, column 9 of Table 24-2 clearly indicates that at all levels of output losses will exceed the $100 fixed cost loss the firm will incur by closing down. Obviously, then, the firm will minimize its losses by closing down, that is, by producing zero units of output.

The reader should graph the total revenue and total cost data for the minimum loss and close-down case and verify the conclusions of each.

Marginal revenue–marginal cost approach

An alternative means for determining the amounts which a competitive firm will be willing to offer in the market at each possible price is for the firm to determine and compare the amounts that each additional unit of output will add to total revenue, on the one hand, and to total cost, on the other. That is, the firm should compare the *marginal revenue* (MR) and the *marginal cost* (MC) of each successive unit of output. Any unit whose marginal revenue exceeds its marginal cost should obviously be produced. Why? Because on each such unit the firm is gaining more in revenue from its sale than it adds to costs in getting that unit produced. The unit of output is adding to profits or, as the case may be, subtracting from losses. Similarly, if the marginal cost of a unit of output exceeds its marginal revenue, the firm should avoid producing that unit. It will add more to costs than to revenue; such a unit will not "pay its way."

In the initial stages of production, where output is relatively low, marginal revenue will usually (but not always) exceed marginal cost. It is therefore profitable to produce through this range of output. But at later stages of production, where output is relatively high, rising marginal costs will cause the reverse to be true. Marginal cost will exceed marginal revenue. Production of units of output falling in this range is obviously to be avoided in the interest of maximizing profits. Separating these two production ranges will be a unique point at which marginal revenue equals marginal cost. This point is the key to the output-determining rule: *the firm will maximize profits or minimize losses by producing at that point where marginal revenue equals marginal cost.* For convenience we shall call this profit-maximizing guide the MR = MC rule. For most sets of MR and MC data there will be no nonfractional level of output at which MR and MC are precisely equal. In such instances the firm should produce the last complete unit of output whose MR exceeds its MC.

Two features of this MR = MC rule merit comment. First, a qualification: the rule presumes that the firm will choose to produce rather than close down. Shortly we shall note that marginal revenue must be equal to or exceed average variable cost, or the firm will find it preferable to close down rather than produce the MR = MC output.

Second, it is to be emphasized that the MR = MC rule is an accurate guide to profit maximization for all firms, be they purely competitive, monopolistic, monopolistically competitive, or oligopolistic. The rule's application is not limited to the special case of pure competition. At the same time it is noteworthy that the MR = MC rule can be conveniently restated in a slightly different form when being applied to a purely competitive firm. You will recall that product price is determined by the broad market forces of supply and demand, and while the competitive firm can sell as much or as little as it chooses at that price, the firm cannot manipulate the price itself. In technical terms the demand, or sales, schedule faced by a competitive seller is perfectly elastic at the going market price. The result is that product price and marginal revenue are equal; that is, each extra unit sold adds precisely its price to total revenue (Chapter 21). Thus under pure competition—and *only* under pure competition—we may substitute price for marginal revenue in the rule, so it reads as follows: *to maximize profits or minimize losses the competitive firm should produce at that point where price equals marginal cost (P = MC).*

Now let us apply the MR = MC or, if you prefer, P = MC rule, using the same three prices employed in our total revenue—total cost approach to profit maximization.

Profit-maximizing case. Table 24-3 reproduces the unit and marginal cost data derived in Table 23-2. It is, of course, the marginal cost data of column 5 in Table 24-3 which we wish to compare with price (equal to marginal revenue) for each unit of output. Suppose first that market price, and therefore marginal revenue, is $131 as shown in column 6. What is the profit-maximizing output? It is readily seen that each and every unit of output up to and including the ninth adds more to total revenue than to total cost. That is, price, or marginal revenue, exceeds marginal cost on all of the first nine units of output. Each of these units therefore adds to the firm's profits and should obviously be produced. The tenth unit, however, will not be produced because it would add more to costs—$150—than to revenue—$131.

The level of economic profits realized by the firm can be readily calculated from the unit cost data. Multiplying price ($131) times output (9), we find total revenue to be $1,179. Total cost of about[1] $880 is found by multiplying average total cost ($97.78) by output (9). The difference of $299 is economic profits. An alternative means of calculating economic prof-

[1] In most instances the unit cost data are rounded figures. Therefore, economic profits calculated from them will typically vary by a few cents from the profits determined in the total revenue–total cost approach. We here ignore the few cents' differentials and make our answers consistent with the results of the total revenue–total cost approach.

its is to determine profit *per unit* by subtracting average total cost ($97.78) from product price ($131) and multiplying the difference (per unit profits of $33.22) by the level of output (9). The skeptical reader should calculate profits at outputs other than those indicated most profitable by the $P = MC$ rule to verify that they entail either losses or profits less than $299.

Figure 24-2 makes the comparison of price and marginal cost graphically. Here per unit economic profit is indicated by the distance *AP*. When multiplied by the profit-maximizing output, the resulting total economic profit is shown by the shaded rectangular area.

It should be noted that the firm is seeking to maximize its *total* profits, not its *per unit* profits. Per unit profits are largest at 7 units of output, where price exceeds average total cost by $39.57 ($131 minus $91.43). But by producing only 7 units the firm would be forgoing the production of additional units of output which would clearly contribute to total profits. The firm is happy to accept lower per unit profits if the resulting extra units of sales more than compensate for the lower per unit profits.

TABLE 24-2. THE PROFIT-MAXIMIZING OUTPUTS FOR A PURELY COMPETITIVE FIRM: TOTAL REVENUE—TOTAL COST APPROACH (prices = $81 and $71)

| | | Product Price = $81 | | | | | Product Price = $71 | |
| (1) | (2) | (3) | (4) | (5) | (6) | (7) | (8) | (9) |
Total product	Total revenue	Total fixed cost	Total variable cost	Total cost	Profit (+) or loss (−), = (2) − (5)	Total revenue	Total cost	Profit (+) or loss (−), = (7) − (8)
0	$ 0	$100	$ 0	$ 100	$−100	$ 0	$ 100	$−100
1	81	100	90	190	−109	71	190	−119
2	162	100	170	270	−108	142	270	−128
3	243	100	240	340	− 97	213	340	−127
4	324	100	300	400	− 76	284	400	−116
5	405	100	370	470	− 65	355	470	−115
6	486	100	450	550	− 64	426	550	−124
7	567	100	540	640	− 73	497	640	−143
8	648	100	650	750	−102	568	750	−182
9	729	100	780	880	−151	639	880	−241
10	810	100	930	1,030	−220	710	1,030	−320

TABLE 24-3. THE PROFIT-MAXIMIZING OUTPUT FOR A PURELY COMPETITIVE FIRM: MARGINAL REVENUE EQUALS MARGINAL COST APPROACH
(price = $131)

(1) Total product	(2) Average fixed cost	(3) Average variable cost	(4) Average total cost	(5) Marginal cost	(6) Price = marginal revenue
0					
				$ 90	$131
1	$100.00	$90.00	$190.00		
				80	131
2	50.00	85.00	135.00		
				70	131
3	33.33	80.00	113.33		
				60	131
4	25.00	75.00	100.00		
				70	131
5	20.00	74.00	94.00		
				80	131
6	16.67	75.00	91.67		
				90	131
7	14.29	77.14	91.43		
				110	131
8	12.50	81.23	93.73		
				130	131
9	11.11	86.67	97.78		
				150	131
10	10.00	93.00	103.00		

Loss-minimizing case. Now let us apply the same reasoning on the assumption that market price is $81 rather than $131. Should the firm produce? If so, how much? And what will the resulting profits or losses be? The answers, respectively, are: "Yes," "Six units," and "A loss of $64."

Column 6 of Table 24-4 shows the new price (equal to marginal revenue) alongside the same unit and marginal cost data presented in Table 24-3. Comparing columns 5 and 6, we find that the first unit of output adds $90 to total cost but only $81 to total revenue. One might be inclined to conclude: "Don't produce —close down!" But this would be hasty. Remember that in the very early stages of produc-

tion marginal physical returns are low, making marginal cost unusually high. The price–marginal cost relationship might improve with increased production. And it does. On the next five units—2 through 6—price exceeds marginal cost. Each of these five units adds more to revenue than to cost, more than compensating for the "loss" taken on the first unit. Beyond six units, however, MC exceeds MR. The firm should therefore produce at 6 units. In general, the profit-seeking producer should always compare price with the rising portion of his marginal cost schedule or curve.

Will production be profitable? No, it will not. At six units of output average total costs of $91.67 exceed price of $81 by $10.67 per unit.

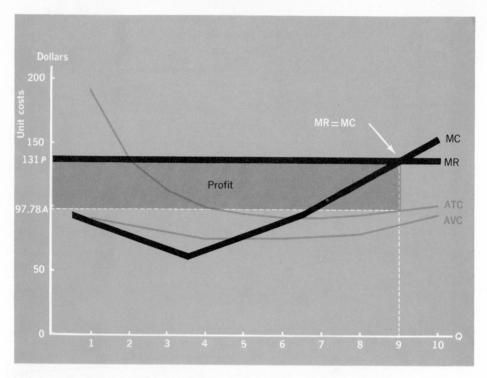

FIGURE 24-2. THE SHORT-RUN PROFIT-MAXIMIZING POSITION OF A PURELY
COMPETITIVE FIRM.
The P = MC output allows the competitive producer to maximize profits or minimize
losses. In this case price exceeds average total cost at the P = MC output of nine
units. Economic profits per unit of AP are realized; total economic profits are indicated by the shaded rectangle.

Multiply by the six units of output, and the
firm's total loss is about $64. Then why pro-
duce? Because this loss is less than the firm's
$100 worth of fixed costs—the $100 loss the
firm would incur in the short run by closing
down. Looked at differently, the firm receives
enough revenue per unit ($81) to cover its
variable costs of $75 and also provide $6 per
unit, or a total of $36, to apply against the
payment of fixed costs. Therefore, the firm's
loss is only $64 ($100 minus $36), rather than
$100.

This case is shown graphically in Figure 24-3.
Whenever price exceeds the minimum average
variable cost but falls short of average total
cost, the firm can pay a part of, but not all, its

fixed costs by producing. In this instance total
variable costs are shown by the area OVGF.
Total revenue, however, is OPEF, greater than
total variable costs by VPEG. This excess of
revenue over variable costs can be applied
against total fixed costs, represented by area
VACG.

Close-down case. Suppose now that the market
yields a price of only $71. In this case it will
pay the firm to close down, to produce nothing.
Why? Because there is no output at which the
firm can cover its average variable costs, much
less its average total cost. In other words, the
smallest loss it can realize by producing is greater

TABLE 24-4. THE PROFIT-MAXIMIZING OUTPUT FOR A PURELY COMPETITIVE FIRM: MARGINAL REVENUE EQUALS MARGINAL COST APPROACH (prices = $81 and $71)

(1) Total product	(2) Average fixed cost	(3) Average variable cost	(4) Average total cost	(5) Marginal cost	(6) $81 price = marginal revenue	(7) $71 price = marginal revenue
0						
				$ 90	$81	$71
1	$100.00	$90.00	$190.00			
				80	81	71
2	50.00	85.00	135.00			
				70	81	71
3	33.33	80.00	113.33			
				60	81	71
4	25.00	75.00	100.00			
				70	81	71
5	20.00	74.00	94.00			
				80	81	71
6	16.67	75.00	91.67			
				90	81	71
7	14.29	77.14	91.43			
				110	81	71
8	12.50	81.23	93.73			
				130	81	71
9	11.11	86.67	97.78			
				150	81	71
10	10.00	93.00	103.00			

than the $100 worth of fixed costs it will lose by closing down. The smart thing is obviously to close down. This can be verified by comparing columns 3 and 7 of Table 24-4 and can be readily visualized in Figure 24-4. Price comes closest to covering average variable costs at the $P = MC$ output of 5 units. But even here price or revenue per unit would fall short of average variable cost by $3 ($74 minus $71). By producing at the $P = MC$ output the firm would lose its $100 worth of fixed costs *plus* $15 ($3 on each of the five units) worth of variable costs, for a total loss of $115. This clearly compares unfavorably with the $100 fixed cost loss the firm would incur by choosing to close down. In short, it will obviously pay the firm to close down rather than operate at a $71 price or, for that matter, at any price less than $74.

The close-down case obligates us to modify our $P = MC$ rule for profit maximization or loss minimization. A *competitive firm will maximize profits or minimize losses in the short run by producing at that output at which $P = MC$ provided that price exceeds the minimum average variable cost figure.*

Marginal cost and the short-run supply curve. Now the astute reader will recognize that we have simply selected three different prices and asked how much the profit-seeking competitive firm, faced with certain costs, would choose to offer or supply in the market at each of these

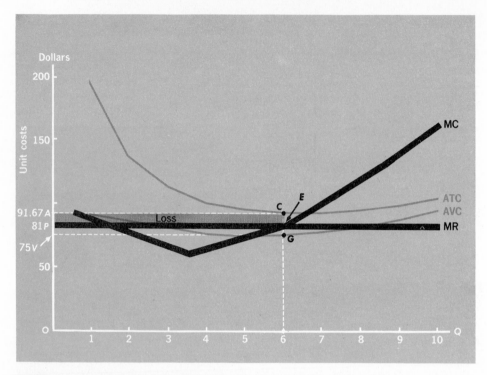

FIGURE 24-3. THE SHORT-RUN LOSS-MINIMIZING POSITION OF A PURELY COMPETITIVE FIRM.

If price exceeds the minimum AVC but is less than ATC, the P = MC output of six units will permit the firm to minimize its losses. In this instance losses are AP per unit; total losses are shown by area APEC.

prices. This information—price and corresponding quantity supplied—obviously constitutes the supply schedule for the competitive firm. Table 24-5 summarizes the supply schedule data for the three prices we have chosen—$131, $81, and $71. The reader is urged to apply the $P = MC$ rule (as modified by the close-down case) to verify the quantity supplied data for the $151, $111, $91, and $61 prices and calculate the corresponding profits or losses. The supply schedule is obviously upsloping. In this instance price must be $74 (equal to minimum average variable cost) or greater before any output is supplied. The profit-seeking firm is induced to offer more of the product as higher and higher prices are equated with the marginal cost of larger and larger outputs in the cost table.

Figure 24-5 generalizes upon our application of the $P = MC$ rule. Here we have drawn the appropriate cost curves. Then from the vertical axis we have extended a series of marginal revenue lines from some of the various possible prices which the market might set for the firm. The crucial prices are P_2 and P_4. Our close-down case reminds us that at any price *below* P_2—that price equal to the minimum average variable cost—the firm should close down and supply nothing. Actually, by producing Q_2 units of output at a price of P_2, the firm will just cover its variable costs, and its losses will be equal to its fixed costs. The firm, therefore, would be indifferent as between closing down and producing Q_2 units of output. But at any price below P_2, such as P_1, the firm will close down and supply zero units of output. P_4 is

**TABLE 24-5. THE SUPPLY SCHEDULE OF A
COMPETITIVE FIRM CONFRONTED WITH THE
COST DATA OF TABLE 24-3**

Price	Quantity supplied	Maximum profit (+) or minimum loss (−)
$151	10	
131	9	$+299
111	8	
91	7	
81	6	− 64
71	0	−100
61	0	

**FIGURE 24-4. THE SHORT-RUN CLOSE-DOWN POSITION OF A PURELY
COMPETITIVE FIRM.**
If price falls short of minimum AVC, the competitive firm will minimize its losses in
the short run by closing down. There is no level of output at which the firm can produce and realize a loss smaller than its fixed costs.

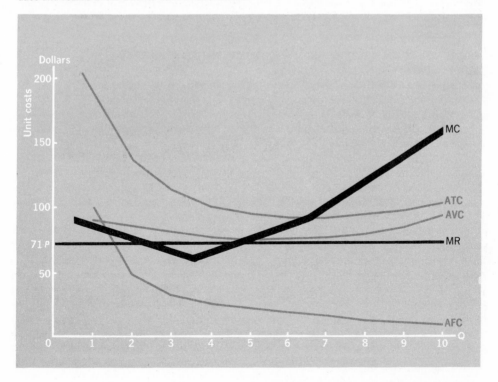

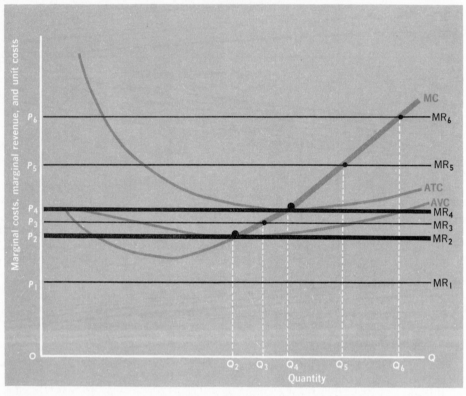

FIGURE 24-5. MARGINAL COST AND THE COMPETITIVE FIRM'S SHORT-RUN SUPPLY CURVE.
Application of the $P = $ MC rule, as modified by the close-down case, reveals that the segment of the firm's MC curve which lies above AVC is its short-run supply curve. At any price between P_2 and P_4, such as P_3, losses will be minimized by producing the $P = $ MC output. At any price above P_4, such as P_5 or P_6, profits will be maximized at the $P = $ MC output.

strategic because it is the price at which the firm will just break even by producing Q_4 units of output, as indicated by the $P = $ MC rule. Here total revenue will just cover total costs (including a normal profit). At P_3 the firm supplies Q_3 units of output and in so doing minimizes its losses. At any other price between P_2 and P_4 the firm will minimize its losses by producing to the point where $P = $ MC. At any price above P_4 the firm will maximize its economic profits by producing to the point where $P = $ MC. Thus at P_5 and P_6 the firm will realize the great-

est profits by supplying Q_5 and Q_6 units of output.

Now the basic point is this: Each of the various $P = $ MC intersection points (shown by the dots in Figure 24-5) indicates a possible product price and the corresponding quantity which the profit-seeking firm would supply at that price. These points, by definition, constitute the supply curve of the competitive firm. Because nothing would be produced at any price below the minimum average variable cost, we can conclude that *that portion of the firm's marginal cost curve which lies above its average variable cost curve is its short-run supply curve.* This is the link between production costs and supply in the short run.

Short-run competitive pricing

Let us now pause to summarize the main points we have made concerning short-run competitive pricing. Table 24-6 provides a convenient check sheet on the total revenue–total cost and MR = MC approaches to determining the competitive firm's profit-maximizing output. This table warrants careful study by the reader. In the MR = MC approach it is noteworthy that in deciding whether or not to produce, it is the comparison with price and minimum average variable cost which is all-important. Then, in determining the profit-maximizing or loss-minimizing amount to produce, it is the comparison or, better yet, the equality of *P* and MC which is crucial. Finally, in determining the actual profit or loss associated with the *P* = MC output, price and average total cost must be contrasted. A final basic conclusion implied in Table 24-6 is that that segment of the short-run marginal cost curve which lies

above the average variable cost curve is the competitive firm's short-run supply curve. This conclusion stems from the application of the *P* = MC rule and the necessary modification suggested by the close-down case.

Firm and industry: equilibrium price

Now one final wrap-up step remains. Having developed the competitive firm's short-run supply curve through the application of the *P* = MC rule, we must determine which of the various price possibilities will actually be the equilibrium price. Recalling Chapter 4, we know that in a purely competitive market equilibrium price is determined by *total, or market, supply and total demand.* To derive total supply we know that the sales schedules or curves of the individual competitive sellers must be summed. Thus in Table 24-7, columns 1 and 3 repeat the individual competitive firm's supply schedule just derived in Table 24-5. Let us now conveniently assume that there are a total of 1,000 competitive firms in this industry, each having the same total and unit costs as the single firm we have been discussing. This allows

TABLE 24-6. SUMMARY OF THE TOTAL REVENUE–TOTAL COST AND MARGINAL REVENUE–MARGINAL COST APPROACHES TO COMPETITIVE OUTPUT DETERMINATION IN THE SHORT RUN

	Total revenue–total cost approach	*Marginal revenue–marginal cost approach*
Should the firm produce?	Yes, if TR exceeds TC or if TC exceeds TR by some amount less than total fixed costs.	Yes, if price is equal to, or greater than, minimum average variable cost.
What quantity should be produced to maximize profits?	Produce where the excess of TR over TC is a maximum or where excess of TC over TR is at a minimum (and less than total fixed costs).	Produce where MR or price equals MC.
Will production result in an economic profit?	Yes, if TR exceeds TC. No, if TC exceeds TR.	Yes, if price exceeds average total cost. No, if average total cost exceeds price.

TABLE 24-7. FIRM AND MARKET SUPPLY AND MARKET DEMAND

(1) Quantity supplied, single firm	(2) Total quantity supplied, 1,000 firms	(3) Product price	(4) Total quantity demanded
10	10,000	$151	4,000
9	9,000	131	6,000
8	8,000	111	8,000
7	7,000	91	9,000
6	6,000	81	11,000
0	0	71	13,000
0	0	61	16,000

us to calculate the total or market supply schedule (columns 2 and 3) by multiplying the quantity supplied figures of the single firm (column 1) by 1,000.

Now in order to determine equilibrium price and output this total supply data must be compared with total demand data. For purposes of illustration, let us assume total demand data are as shown in columns 3 and 4 of Table 24-7. Comparing the total quantity supplied and total quantity demanded at the seven possible prices, we readily determine that the equilibrium price is $111 and that equilibrium quantity is 8,000 units for the industry and 8 units for each of the 1,000 identical firms.

Will these conditions of market supply and demand make this a prosperous or unprosperous industry? Multiplying product price ($111) by output (8), we find the total revenue of each firm to be $888. Total cost is $750, found by multiplying average total cost of $93.73 by 8 or simply by looking at column 5 of Table 24-1. The $138 difference is the economic profit of each firm. Another way of calculating economic profits is to determine *per unit* profit by subtracting average total cost ($93.73) from product price ($111) and multiplying the difference (per unit profits of $17.27) by the firm's equilibrium level of output (8). For the industry, total economic profit is obviously $138,000. This, then, is a prosperous industry.

Figure 24-6a and b shows this analysis graphically. The individual supply curves of each of the 1,000 identical firms—one of which is shown as ss in Figure 24-6a—are summed horizontally to get the total supply curve SS of Figure 24-6b. Given total demand DD, equilibrium price is found to be $111, and equilibrium quantity for the industry is 8,000 units. This equilibrium price is given and unalterable to the individual firm; that is, the typical firm's demand curve is perfectly elastic at the equilibrium price as indicated by dd. Because price is given and constant to the individual firm, the marginal revenue curve coincides with the demand curve. Price obviously exceeds average total cost at the firm's equilibrium $P = MC$ output, resulting in a situation of economic profits similar to that already portrayed in Figure 24-2.

Assuming that no changes in costs or market demand occur, these diagrams reveal a genuine equilibrium situation. There are no shortages or surpluses in the market to cause price or total quantity to change. Nor can any of the firms comprising the industry improve themselves profitwise by altering their output. Note, too, that higher unit and marginal costs, on the

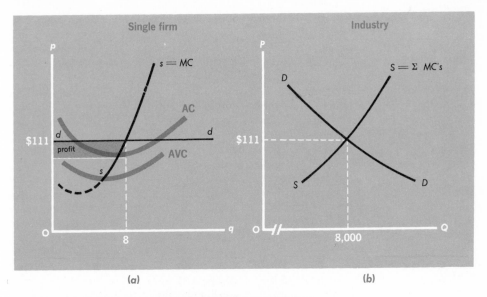

FIGURE 24-6. SHORT-RUN COMPETITIVE EQUILIBRIUM FOR A REPRESENTATIVE FIRM (a) AND THE INDUSTRY (b).
The horizontal sum of the 1,000 firms' supply (ss) curves determines the industry supply curve (SS). Given industry demand (DD), the short-run equilibrium price and output for the industry are $111 and 8,000 units. Taking the equilibrium price as given datum, the representative firm establishes its profit-maximizing output at eight units and, in this case, realizes the economic profit shown by the shaded area.

one hand, or a weaker market demand situation, on the other, could have posed a loss situation similar to Figure 24-3. The student is urged to sketch in Figure 24-6a and b how higher costs and a less favorable demand could cause a short-run equilibrium situation entailing losses.

Figure 24-6a and b brings out a final notable point. We have emphasized that product price is a given datum to the *individual* competitive firm. But at the same time the supply plans of all competitive producers *as a group* are a basic determinant of product price. If we recall the fallacy of composition, we find there is no inconsistency here. Though each firm, supplying a negligible fraction of total supply, cannot affect price, the sum of the supply curves of all the many firms in the industry constitutes the industry supply curve, and this curve does have an important bearing upon price. In short, under competition, equilibrium price is a given datum to the individual firm and simultaneously is the result of the production (supply) decisions of all firms taken as a group.

PROFIT MAXIMIZATION IN THE LONG RUN

The long run permits firms to make certain adjustments which time does not allow in the short run. In the short run there are a given number of firms in an industry, each of which has a fixed, unalterable plant. True, firms may close down in the sense that they produce zero units of output in the short run; but they do not have sufficient time to liquidate their assets and go out of business. By contrast, in the long run firms already in an industry have sufficient time either to expand or to contract their plant capacities, and, more importantly, the number of firms in the industry may either increase or decrease as new firms enter or old firms leave. We want to discover how these long-run adjustments modify our conclusions concerning short-run output and price determination.

It will facilitate our analysis greatly to make certain simplifying assumptions, none of which will impair the general validity of our conclusions.

1. We shall suppose that the only long-run adjustment is the entry and exodus of firms. Furthermore, for simplicity's sake we ignore the short-run adjustment already analyzed, which permits us to grasp more clearly the nature of long-run competitive adjustments.

2. It will also be assumed that all firms in the industry have identical cost curves. This allows us to talk in terms of an "average," or "representative," firm with the knowledge that all other firms in the industry are similarly affected by any long-run adjustments which occur.

3. We assume for the moment that the industry under discussion is a constant cost industry. This means simply that the entry and exodus of firms will not affect resource prices or, therefore, the locations of the unit cost schedules of the individual firms.

Now the job is to describe long-run competitive adjustments both verbally and through simple graphic analysis. It will be well to state in advance the basic conclusion we seek to explain: *after all long-run adjustments are completed, that is, when long-run equilibrium is achieved, product price will be exactly equal to, and production will occur at, each firm's point of minimum average total cost.* This conclusion follows from two basic facts: (a) firms seek profits and shun losses, and (b) under competition firms are free to enter and leave industries. If price exceeds average total costs, the resulting economic profits will attract new firms to the industry. But this expansion of the industry will increase product supply until price is brought back down into equality with average total cost. Conversely, if price is less than average total cost, the resulting losses will cause firms to leave the industry. As they leave, total product supply will decline, bringing price back up into equality with average total cost.

Our conclusion can best be demonstrated

and its significance evaluated by assuming that the average or representative firm in a purely competitive industry is initially in long-run equilibrium. This is shown in Figure 24-7a, where price and minimum average total cost are equal at $50. Economic profits here are zero; hence, the industry is in equilibrium or "at rest," because there is no tendency for firms to enter or leave the industry. As we know, the going market price is determined by total, or industry, demand and supply as shown by D_1D_1 and S_1S_1 in Figure 24-7b. (The market supply schedule, incidentally, is a short-run schedule; the industry's long-run supply schedule will be developed in our discussion.) By examining the quantity axes of the two graphs we note that, if all firms are identical, there must be 1,000 firms in the industry, each producing 100 units, to achieve the industry's equilibrium output of 100,000 units.

Entry of firms eliminates profits

Now our model is set up. Let us upset the serenity of this long-run equilibrium situation and trace the subsequent adjustments. Suppose that a change in consumer tastes increases product demand from D_1D_1 to D_2D_2. This favorable shift in demand obviously makes production profitable; the new price of $60 exceeds average total cost. These economic profits will lure new firms into the industry. Some of the entrants will be newly created firms; others will shift from less prosperous industries. But, as these firms enter, the market supply of the product will increase, causing product price to gravitate downward from $60 toward the original $50 level. Assuming, as we are, that the entry of new firms has no effect upon costs, economic profits will persist, and entry will therefore continue until short-run market supply has increased to S_2S_2. At this point price is again equal to minimum average total cost at $50. The economic profits caused by the boost in demand have been competed away to zero, and as a result the previous incentive for more firms to enter the industry has disappeared.

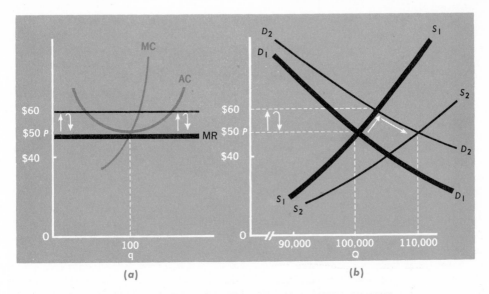

FIGURE 24-7. TEMPORARY PROFITS AND THE REESTABLISHMENT OF LONG-RUN EQUILIBRIUM IN A REPRESENTATIVE FIRM (a) AND THE INDUSTRY (b). A favorable shift in demand (D_1D_1 to D_2D_2) will upset the original equilibrium and cause economic profits. But profits will cause new firms to enter the industry, increasing supply (S_1S_1 to S_2S_2) and lowering product price until economic profits are once again zero.

Long-run equilibrium has been restored at this point.

Figure 24-7 tells us that, upon the re-establishment of long-run equilibrium, industry output is 110,000 units and that each firm in the now expanded industry is producing 100 units. We can therefore conclude that the industry is now comprised of 1,100 firms; that is, 100 new firms have entered the industry.

Exodus of firms eliminates losses

To strengthen our understanding of long-run competitive equilibrium, let us throw our analysis into reverse. In Figure 24-8a and b the heavy lines show once again the initial long-run equilibrium situation used as a point of departure in our previous analysis of how the entry of firms eliminates profits.

Now let us suppose that consumer demand falls from D_1D_1 to D_3D_3. This forces price down to $40, making production unprofitable. In time these losses will force firms to leave the industry. As capital equipment wears out and contractual obligations expire, some firms will simply toss in the sponge. As this exodus of firms proceeds, however, industry supply will decrease, moving from S_1S_1 toward S_3S_3. And as this occurs, price will begin to rise from $40 back toward $50. Assuming costs are unchanged by the exodus of firms, losses will force firms to leave the industry until supply has declined to S_3S_3, at which point price is again exactly $50, barely consistent with minimum average total cost. The exodus of firms continues until losses are eliminated and long-run equilibrium is again restored.

The reader will note from Figure 24-8a and b that total quantity supplied is now 90,000 units

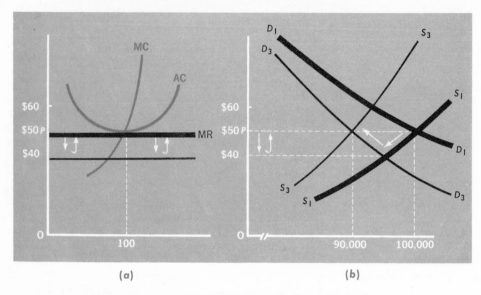

FIGURE 24-8. TEMPORARY LOSSES AND THE REESTABLISHMENT OF LONG-
RUN EQUILIBRIUM IN A REPRESENTATIVE FIRM (a) AND THE INDUSTRY (b).
An unfavorable shift in demand (D_1D_1 to D_3D_3) will upset the original equilibrium and
cause losses. But losses will cause firms to leave the industry, decreasing supply
(S_1S_1 to S_3S_3) and increasing product price until all losses have disappeared.

and each firm is producing 100 units. This
obviously means that the industry is now populated by only 900 firms rather than the original
1,000. Losses have forced 100 firms out of
business.

Our prestated conclusion has now been verified. Competition, as reflected in the entry and
exodus of firms, forces price into equality with
the minimum long-run average total cost of
production, and each firm produces at the point
of minimum long-run average total cost.

Long-run supply for a
constant-cost industry

Even though our discussion is concerned with
the long run, we have noted that the market
supply curves of Figures 24-7b and 24-8b are
short-run curves. However, our analysis itself
permits us to sketch the nature of the long-run
supply curve for this competitive industry. The
crucial factor in determining the shape of the

industry's long-run supply curve is the effect,
if any, which changes in the number of firms
in the industry will have upon the costs of the
individual firms which comprise the industry.

In the foregoing analysis of long-run competitive equilibrium we assumed the industry
under discussion was a constant-cost industry.
By definition, this means that the expansion of
the industry through the entry of new firms will
have no effect upon resource prices or, therefore, upon production costs. Graphically, the
entry of new firms does not change the position
of the long-run average cost curves of the individual firms in the industry. When will this
be the case? For the most part when the industry's demand for resources is small in relation
to the total demand for those resources. And
this is most likely to be the situation when the
industry is employing unspecialized resources
which are being demanded by many other industries. In short, when the particular industry's
demand for resources is a negligible com-

ponent of the total demand, the industry can expand without significantly affecting resource prices and costs.

What will be the nature of the long-run supply curve for a constant-cost industry? The answer is contained in our previous discussion of the long-run adjustments toward equilibrium which profits or losses will initiate. Here we assumed that the entry or exodus of firms would not affect costs. The result was that the entry or exodus of firms would alter industry output but always bring product price back to the original $50 level, where it is just consistent with the unchanging minimum average total cost of production. Specifically, we discovered that the industry would supply 90,000, 100,000, or 110,000 units of output, all at a price of $50 per unit. In technical terms the long-run supply curve of a constant-cost industry is perfectly elastic.

This is demonstrated graphically in Figure 24-9. Suppose that product demand for the industry is originally at D_1D_1, industry output is Q_1, and product price is Q_1P_1. This situation, let us suppose, is one of long-run equilibrium. Now assume that demand increases to D_2D_2, upsetting this equilibrium. The resulting economic profits will attract new firms. Because this is a constant cost industry, entry will continue, and industry output will expand until price is driven back down to the unchanged minimum average total cost level. This will be at price Q_2P_2 and output Q_2. The long-run industry supply curve SS, which connects these equilibrium points, is obviously perfectly elastic.

Long-run supply for an increasing-cost industry

But constant-cost industries are a special case. In most instances the entry of new firms will affect resource prices and therefore unit costs

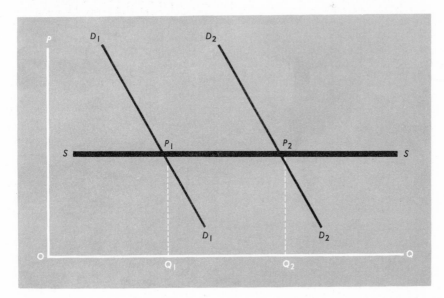

FIGURE 24-9. THE LONG-RUN SUPPLY CURVE FOR A CONSTANT-COST INDUSTRY IS PERFECTLY ELASTIC.
Because the entry of new firms does not affect resource prices or, therefore, unit costs, an increase in demand (D_1D_1 to D_2D_2) will cause an expansion in industry output (Q_1 to Q_2) but no alteration in price ($Q_1P_1 = Q_2P_2$). This means that the long-run industry supply curve (SS) will be perfectly elastic.

for the individual firms in the industry. When an industry is using a relatively large portion of some resource whose total supply is not readily increased, the entry of new firms will increase resource demand in relation to supply and boost resource prices. This is particularly so in industries which are using highly specialized resources whose initial supply is not readily augmented. The result of higher resource prices will be higher long-run average costs for firms in the industry. These higher costs, it should be noted, take the form of an upward shift in the long-run average cost curve for the representative firm.

The net result is that, when an increase in product demand causes economic profits and attracts new firms to the industry, a two-way squeeze on profits will occur to eliminate those profits. On the one hand, the entry of new firms will increase market supply and lower

product price, and, on the other, the entire average total cost curve of the representative firm will shift upward. This means that the new equilibrium price will be higher than it was originally. The industry will only produce a larger output at a higher price. Why? Because expansion of the industry has increased average total costs, and in the long run product price must cover these costs. A greater industry output will be forthcoming at a higher price, or, more technically, the industry supply curve for an increasing-cost industry will be upsloping. Instead of getting either 90,000, 100,000, or 110,000 units at the same price of $50, in an increasing-cost industry 90,000 units might be forthcoming at $50; 100,000 at $55; and 110,000 at $60. The higher price is required to induce more production because costs increase as the industry expands.

This can be seen graphically in Figure 24-10.

FIGURE 24-10. THE LONG-RUN SUPPLY CURVE FOR AN INCREASING-COST INDUSTRY IS UPSLOPING.

In an increasing-cost industry the entry of new firms in response to an increase in demand (D_1D_1 to D_2D_2) will bid up resource prices and thereby increase unit costs. As a result, an increased industry output (Q_1 to Q_2) will be forthcoming only at a higher price (Q_2P_2 is greater than Q_1P_1). The long-run industry supply curve (SS) is, therefore, upsloping.

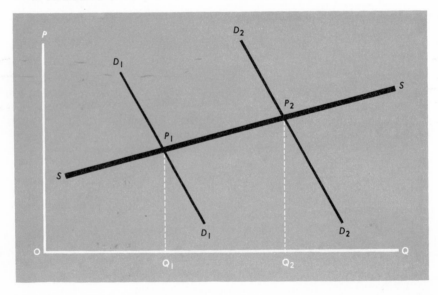

when MC>MR=PR² and a will

Original market demand, industry output, and price are D_1D_1, Q_1, and Q_1P_1 respectively. An increase in demand to D_2D_2 will upset this equilibrium and give rise to economic profits. As new firms enter, (1) industry supply will increase, driving price down and (2) resource prices will rise, causing the average total costs of production to rise. Because of these average total cost increases, the new long-run equilibrium price will be established at some level above the original price, such as Q_2P_2.

Which situation—constant or increasing costs —is characteristic of American industry? It is hard to say. Agriculture and extractive industries such as mining and lumbering are increasing-cost industries, because each utilizes a very large portion of some basic resource—farm land, mineral deposits, and timberland. Expansion will significantly affect the demand for these resources and result in higher costs. It is almost impossible to generalize with respect to manufacturing industries. In their early stages of development such industries may well be relatively constant-cost industries.[2] But as continued expansion increases the importance of these industries in resource markets, they may in time become increasing-cost industries.

AN EVALUATION OF COMPETITIVE PRICING

Whether a purely competitive industry is one of constant or increasing costs, the final long-run equilibrium position will have the same basic characteristics. As in Figure 24-11, price (and marginal revenue) will settle at the level where it is equal to minimum average cost.

[2] Under certain very special circumstances an industry may be for a time a *decreasing-cost industry*. For example, as more mines are established in a given locality, each firm's costs in pumping out water seepage may decline. With more mines pumping, the seepage into each is less, and pumping costs are therefore reduced. Furthermore, with only a few mines in an area, industry output might be so small that only relatively primitive and therefore costly transportation facilities are available. But as the number of firms and industry output expand, a railroad might build a spur into the area and thereby significantly reduce transportation costs. Under such special conditions we get a long-run supply curve which is *downsloping*.

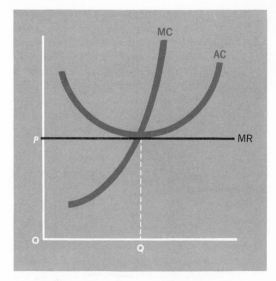

FIGURE 24-11. FOR THE COMPETITIVE FIRM IN LONG-RUN EQUILIBRIUM, $P = AC = MC$.

The equality of price and minimum average cost indicate that the firm is using the most efficient known technology and is charging the lowest price P and producing the greatest output Q consistent with its costs. The equality of price and marginal cost indicates that resources are being allocated in accordance with consumer preferences.

However, we discovered in Chapter 23 that the marginal cost curve intersects, and is therefore equal to, average cost at the point of minimum average cost. In the long-run equilibrium position "everything is equal." $P = AC = MC$. This triple equality is of more than geometric interest. It tells us that, although a competitive firm may realize economic profits or losses in the short run, it will barely break even by producing in accordance with the $P = MC$ rule in the long run. Furthermore, this triple equality suggests certain conclusions concerning the efficiency of a purely competitive economy which are of great social significance. It is to an evaluation of competitive pricing from society's point of view that we now turn.

You will recall that the overview of the price system found in Chapter 5 yielded some general conclusions with respect to the efficiency of any economy characterized by a competitive price system. Equipped now with a better understanding of costs and of price-output determination under competition, we are in a position to sharpen our understanding of the efficiency of a competitive price economy. Specifically, we want to see how our analysis of long-run competitive equilibrium implies certain highly desirable features of a competitive price system.

Efficient allocation of resources

Most economists argue that, subject to certain limitations and exceptions, a purely competitive economy will lead to the most efficient, or "ideal," allocation of resources. That is, *a competitive price economy will tend to allocate the fixed supplies of resources available to society in such a way as to maximize the satisfactions of consumers.* Actually, there are two related points which underlie this conclusion. First, it is argued that under pure competition firms will be forced to produce those goods which consumers want the most. Second, competition forces firms to use the most efficient methods in the production of these goods. To facilitate our discussion we shall examine the second point first.

1. We have just noted that in the long run competition forces firms to produce at the point of minimum average total cost of production and to charge that price which is just consistent with these costs. This is obviously a most desirable situation from the consumer's point of view. It means that firms must use the best available (least-cost) technology or they will simply not survive. And, too, it means that consumers benefit from the highest volume of production and the lowest product price which are possible under the cost conditions which currently prevail. Furthermore, the costs involved in each instance are only those costs essential in producing a product. Because products are standardized in competitive industries, there will be no selling or promotional costs

which must be added to production costs in determining product price.

2. But the competitive production of *any* collection of goods does not necessarily make for an efficient allocation of resources. Production must not only be technologically efficient, but it must also entail the "right goods," that is, the goods that consumers want the most. The competitive price system will see to it that resources are allocated so as to result in a total output whose composition best fits the preferences of consumers.

Let us see precisely how this comes about. We must first grasp the social meaning of competitive product and resource prices. The money price of any product—product X—is society's measure, or index, of the relative worth of that product at the margin. Similarly, recalling the alternative cost doctrine, the marginal cost of producing X measures the value, or relative worth, of the other goods that the resources used in the production of an extra unit of X could otherwise have produced. In short, product price measures the benefit, or satisfaction, which society gets from additional units of X, and the marginal cost of an additional unit of X measures the sacrifice, or cost to society, of other goods in using resources to produce more of X. Now, under competition the production of each product will occur up to that precise point at which price is equal to marginal cost (Figure 24-11). The profit-seeking competitor will only realize the maximum possible profit by equating price and marginal cost. To produce short of the $P = MC$ point will mean less-than-maximum profits to the individual firm and an *under*allocation of resources to this product from society's standpoint. The fact that price exceeds marginal cost indicates that society values additional units of X more highly than the alternative products which the appropriate resources could otherwise produce.

For similar reasons, the production of X should not go beyond the output at which price equals marginal cost. To do so would entail less-than-maximum profits for producers and an *over*allocation of resources to X from the standpoint of society. To produce X at some point at which marginal cost exceeds price means that resources are being used in the production of X at the sacrifice of alternative goods which society values more highly than the added units of X. In brief, *under pure competition producers will be forced to produce each commodity up to that precise point at which price and marginal cost are equated. This means that resources are efficiently allocated under competition.* Each good is produced to the point at which the value of the last unit is equal to the value of the alternative goods sacrificed by its production. To alter the production of X would necessarily reduce consumer satisfactions. To produce X beyond the $P = MC$ point would result in the sacrifice of alternative goods whose value to society exceeds that of the extra units of X. To produce X short of the $P = MC$ point would involve the sacrifice of units of X which society values more than the alternative goods resources can produce.

A further attribute of the competitive price system is its ability to negotiate appropriate adjustments in resource use as changes occur in basic data of the economy. In a competitive economy any changes in consumer tastes, resource supplies, or technology will automatically set in motion appropriate realignments of resources. For example, an increase in consumer demand for product X will increase its price. Disequilibrium will occur, in that at its present output the price of X will now exceed its marginal cost. This will create economic profits in industry X and stimulate its expansion. Its profitability will permit the industry to bid resources away from less pressing uses. Expansion in this industry will end only when the price of X is again equal to its marginal cost, that is, when the value of the last unit produced is once again equal to the value of the alternative goods society forgoes in getting that last unit of X produced. Similarly, changes in the supplies of particular resources or in the techniques pertinent to various industries will upset existing price–marginal cost equalities by either raising or lowering marginal cost. These inequalities will cause businessmen in either pursuing profits or shunning losses to reallocate resources until price once again equals marginal cost in each line of production. In so doing they

correct any inefficiencies in the allocation of resources which changing economic data may temporarily impose upon the economy.

A final appealing feature of a purely competitive economy is that the highly efficient allocation of resources which it fosters comes about because businesses and resource suppliers freely seek to further their own self-interests. That is, the "invisible hand" (Chapter 5) is at work in a competitive market system. In a competitive economy, businessmen employ resources until the extra, or marginal, costs of production equal the price of the product. This not only maximizes the profits of the individual producers but simultaneously results in a pattern of resource allocation which maximizes the satisfactions of consumers. The competitive price system organizes the private interests of producers along lines which are fully in accord with the interests of society as a whole.

Shortcomings of competitive price system

Despite these several virtues, economists acknowledge certain limitations of the price system which may impair its ability to allocate resources efficiently. Some of these criticisms have been previously noted in Chapter 6.

1. *The competitive price system does not accurately reflect the needs of consumers.* There are two major facets of this criticism. On the one hand, the price system registers and responds only to those wants which can be expressed by individuals in the market. The competitive price system therefore ignores certain important social goods and services—for example, education, highways, and national defense—which consumers need and want. On the other hand, it is also argued that the market demand for various goods does not reflect the needs of consumers very accurately, because income is unequally distributed in a competitive price economy. This uneven distribution of "dollar votes" will lead to the production of trifles for the rich and deny the most basic needs of the very poor. The price system adjusts resources in accordance with a given unequal distribution of income. Some economists

argue that the needs of society might be better served by altering the distribution of income which pure competition provides. More will be said on this point in a later chapter.

2. *The competitive price system does not accurately measure costs and revenues where social costs and social revenues are significant.* Competition forces each producer to assume only those costs which he must pay. This correctly implies that in some lines of production there are significant costs which producers can and do avoid. These avoided costs accrue to society and are aptly called *social costs.* Firms may avoid the cost of properly disposing of waste materials or of buying smoke- and dust-abatement equipment. The result is significant social costs in the form of polluted rivers, smog, and a generally debased community. Similarly, unbridled competition may cause profit-seeking firms to exploit brutally farmland, timberland, and mineral deposits through the use of the cheapest production methods. The cost to society is the permanent loss of irreproducible natural resources. On the other hand, you will recall from Chapter 6 that the consumption of certain goods and services such as chest X rays and polio shots yields widespread satisfactions, or "revenues," to society as a whole. These satisfactions are called *social revenues.*

Now the significance of social costs and social revenues for present purposes is this: the profit-seeking activities of producers will bring about an allocation of resources which is efficient from society's point of view only if marginal cost embodies *all* the costs which production entails and product price accurately reflects *all* the benefits which society gets from a good's production. Only in this case will competitive production at the $P = $ MC point balance the total sacrifices and satisfactions of society and result in an efficient allocation of resources. To the extent that price and marginal cost are not accurate indexes of sacrifices and satisfactions, that is, to the extent that social costs and revenues exist, production at the $P = $ MC point will not signify an efficient allocation of resources.

3. *The competitive price system may not always entail the use of the most efficient productive techniques or the development of improved techniques.* There are both a static or

"right now" aspect and a dynamic or "over time" aspect of this general criticism. The static aspect argues that in certain lines of production existing technology may be such that a firm must be a large-scale producer in order to realize the lowest unit costs of production. Given consumer demand, this suggests that a relatively small number of efficient, large-scale producers is needed if production is to be carried on efficiently. In other words existing mass production economies might be lost if such an industry were populated by the large number of small-scale producers which pure competition requires. This point was discussed in some detail in Chapter 23.

The dynamic aspect of this criticism concerns the willingness and ability of purely competitive firms to stimulate technological advance. The progressiveness of pure competition is debated by economists. For present purposes we simply call attention to the fact that some authorities feel that a purely competitive economy would not foster a very rapid rate of technological progress. They argue, first, that the incentive for technological advance may be weak under pure competition, because the profit rewards accruing to an innovating firm as the result of a cost-reducing technological improvement will be quickly competed away by rival firms who readily adopt the new technique. Second, the small size of the typical competitive firm raises serious questions as to whether or not such producers could finance substantial programs of organized research.

4. *The competitive price system may not provide for a sufficient range of consumer choice or for the development of new products.* This criticism, like the previous one, has both a static and a dynamic aspect. Pure competition, it is contended, entails product standardization while other market structures—for example, monopolistic competition and frequently oligopoly—entail a wide range of types, styles, and quality gradations of any product. This product differentiation widens the consumer's range of free choice and simultaneously allows his preferences to be more completely fulfilled. Similarly, critics of pure competition point out that, just as pure competition is not likely to be progressive with respect to the development

of new productive techniques, neither is this market structure conducive to the improvement of existing products or the creation of completely new ones.

The question of the progressiveness of the various market structures in terms of both productive techniques and product development will be a recurring one in the following three chapters.

SUMMARY

1. A purely competitive industry is comprised of a large number of independent firms producing a standardized product. Pure competition assumes that firms and resources are mobile as between different industries. No single firm can influence market price in a competitive industry; price, therefore, equals marginal revenue.

2. Short-run profit maximization by a competitive firm can be analyzed by comparing total revenue and total cost or through marginal analysis. A firm will maximize profits by producing that output at which total revenue exceeds total cost by greatest amount. Losses will be minimized by producing where the excess of total cost over total revenue is at a minimum and less than total fixed costs.

3. Provided price exceeds minimum average variable cost, a competitive firm will maximize profits or minimize losses by producing at that output at which price or marginal revenue is equal to marginal cost. If price is less than average variable cost, the firm will minimize its losses by closing down. If price is greater than average variable cost but less than average total cost, the firm will minimize its losses by producing the $P = MC$ output. If price exceeds average total cost, the $P = MC$ output will provide maximum economic profits for the firm.

4. Applying the $P = MC$ rule at various possible market prices leads to the conclusion that the segment of the firm's short-run marginal cost curve which lies above average variable cost is its short-run supply curve.

5. In the long run, competitive price will tend to equal the minimum average cost of production. This is so because economic profits will cause firms to enter a competitive industry until those profits have been competed away. Conversely, losses will force the exodus of firms from the industry until product price once again barely covers unit costs.

6. The long-run supply curve of a constant-cost industry is perfectly elastic. However, for an increasing-cost industry the long-run supply curve is upsloping.

7. In a purely competitive economy the profit-seeking activities of producers will result in an allocation of resources which maximizes the satisfactions of consumers. The long-run equality of price and minimum average cost indicates that competitive firms use the most efficient known technology and charge the lowest price consistent with their production costs. The equality of price and marginal cost indicates that resources will be allocated in accordance with consumer tastes. The competitive price system will reallocate resources in response to a change in consumer tastes, technology, or resource supplies so as to maintain allocative efficiency over time.

8. Economists recognize four possible deterrents to allocative efficiency in a competitive economy. (a) Income inequality and the unresponsiveness of the price system to social wants suggest that the competitive price economy does not accurately reflect the needs of consumers. (b) In allocating resources the price system does not allow for social costs and revenues. (c) A purely competitive industry may preclude the use of the best-known productive techniques and foster a slow rate of technological advance. (d) A competitive system provides neither a wide range of product choice nor an environment conducive to the development of new products.

QUESTIONS AND STUDY SUGGESTIONS

1. Strictly speaking, pure competition never has existed and probably never will. Then why study it?

2. Why is the equality of marginal revenue and marginal cost essential for profit maximization in all market structures? Explain why price can be substituted for marginal revenue in the MR = MC rule when an industry is purely competitive.

3. Assume the following unit cost data for a purely competitive producer:

Total product	Average fixed cost	Average variable cost	Average total cost	Marginal cost
0	—	—	—	
1	$60.00	$45.00	$105.00	$45
2	30.00	42.50	72.50	40
3	20.00	40.00	60.00	35
4	15.00	37.50	52.50	30
5	12.00	37.00	49.00	35
6	10.00	37.50	47.50	40
7	8.57	38.57	47.14	45
8	7.50	40.63	48.13	55
9	6.67	43.33	50.00	65
10	6.00	46.50	52.50	75

a. At a product price of $32, will this firm produce in the short run? Why, or why not? If it does produce, what will be the profit-maximizing or loss minimizing output? Explain. Specify the amount of economic profit or loss per unit of output.

b. Answer the questions of 3a on the assumption that product price is $41.

c. Answer the questions of 3a on the assumption that product price is $56.

d. ·Complete the following short-run supply schedule for the firm and indicate the profit or loss incurred at each output (columns 1 to 3).

(1) Price	(2) Quantity supplied, single firm	(3) Profit (+) or loss (−)	(4) Quantity supplied, 1,500 firms
$26			
32			
38			
41			
46			
56			
66			

e. Explain: "That segment of a competitive firm's marginal cost curve which lies above its average variable cost curve constitutes the short-run supply curve for the firm." Illustrate graphically.

f. Now assume there are 1,500 identical firms in this competitive industry; that is, there are 1,500 firms, each of which has the same cost data as shown above. Calculate the industry supply schedule (column 4).

g. Suppose the market demand data for the product are as follows:

Price	Total quantity demanded
$26	17,000
32	15,000
38	13,500
41	12,000
46	10,500
56	9,500
66	8,000

What will equilibrium price be? What will equilibrium output be for the industry? For each firm? What will profit or loss be per unit? Per firm?

4. Explain: "A competitive producer must look to average variable cost in determining whether or not to produce in the short run, to marginal cost in deciding upon the best volume of production, and to average total cost to calculate his profits or losses." Explain why a firm might produce at a loss in the short run rather than close down.

5. Using diagrams for both the industry and a representative firm, illustrate competitive long-run equilibrium. Employing these diagrams, show how (a) an increase and (b) a decrease in market demand will upset this long-run equilibrium. Trace graphically and describe verbally the adjustment processes by which long-run equilibrium is restored. Assume the industry is one of constant costs.

6. Distinguish carefully between a constant-cost and an increasing-cost industry. Answer question 5 on the assumption that the industry is one of increasing costs. Compare the long-run supply curves of a constant-cost and an increasing-cost industry.

7. Suppose a decrease in demand occurs in a competitive, increasing-cost industry. Contrast the product price and industry output which exists after all long-run adjustments are completed with those which originally prevailed.

8. In long-run equilibrium $P = AC = MC$. Of what significance for the allocation of resources is the equality of P and AC? The equality of P and MC?

9. Explain why some economists feel that an unequal distribution of income might impair the efficiency with which a competitive price system allocates resources. What other criticisms can be made of a purely competitive economy?

SELECTED REFERENCES

Bain, Joe S., *Pricing, Distribution, and Employment*, rev. ed. (New York: Holt, Rinehart and Winston, Inc., 1953), chap. 4.

Bober, M. M., *Intermediate Price and Income Theory*, rev. ed. (New York: W. W. Norton & Company, Inc., 1962), chap. 9.

Due, John F., and Robert W. Clower, *Intermediate Economic Analysis,* 4th ed. (Homewood, Ill.: Richard D. Irwin, 1961), chap. 9.

Stigler, George J., *The Theory of Price,* rev. ed. (New York: The Macmillan Company, 1952), chap. 10.

Stonier, Alfred W., and Douglas C. Hague, *A Textbook of Economic Theory,* 2d ed. (New York: Longmans Green & Co., Inc., 1957), chaps. 6 and 7.

Chapter 25

PRICE AND OUTPUT DETERMINATION:

PURE MONOPOLY

LET US now jump to the opposite end of the industry spectrum and examine the characteristics, the bases, the price-output behavior, and the social desirability of pure monopoly.

CONCEPT AND OCCURRENCE OF PURE MONOPOLY

Pure or absolute monopoly exists when a single firm is the sole producer of a product for which there are no close substitutes. By the absence of close substitutes we mean that there are no other firms producing the same product or products varying only in very minor ways from that of the monopolist. Thus there is no close substitute for the electricity or water supplied by local utilities. And, if there existed only one manufacturer of automobiles, consumers would have no reasonably good alternative to buying from the monopolistic producer. Of course, there may be competition in the broad sense that a food freezer or color television set are "substitutes" for a down payment on an automobile. But these products are clearly distinct from automobiles and do not fulfill the consumer's need for convenient local transportation. The important point is that the monopolist is the only supplier of a certain product for which there are no close substitutes available.

Defined in this way, pure monopoly is a rare phenomenon.

Yet a brief analysis of pure monopoly is important for two related reasons. First, some industries are reasonable approximations of pure monopoly. The behavior of firms with 80, 70, or even 60 per cent of a market can often be explained with considerable accuracy through the pure monopoly market model. For all practical purposes the dominant firm *is* the industry in such instances. Second, a study of pure monopoly provides us with valuable insights concerning the more realistic market structures of monopolistic competition and oligopoly, which will be discussed in Chapters 26 and 27. These two market situations combine in differing degrees the characteristics of pure competition and pure monopoly.

BARRIERS TO ENTRY

It was noted in Chapter 20 that the absence of competitors which characterizes pure monopoly is largely explainable in terms of barriers to entry, that is, considerations which prohibit additional firms from entering an industry. These barriers are also pertinent in explaining the existence of oligopoly and monopolistic competition between the market extremes of pure competition and pure monopoly. In the

479

case of pure monopoly entry barriers are sufficiently great to block completely all potential competition. Somewhat less formidable barriers permit the existence of oligopoly, that is, a few firms. Still weaker barriers permit the fairly large number of firms which characterize monopolistic competition. The virtual absence of entry barriers helps explain the very large number of competing firms which is the basis of pure competition. The important point is this: barriers to entry are pertinent not only to the extreme case of pure monopoly but also to the "partial monopolies" which are so characteristic of American capitalism.

What forms do these entry barriers assume?

Economies of scale

Modern technology is such in many industries that efficient, low-cost production can be achieved only if producers are extremely large both absolutely and in relation to the market (see Chapter 23). Where economies of scale are very significant, a firm's average cost schedule will decline over a wide range of output. Given product demand, the achieving of low unit costs and therefore low unit prices for consumers depends upon the existence of a small number of firms or, in the extreme case, only one firm. The automobile, aluminum, and steel industries are a few of many heavy industries which reflect such conditions. If three firms currently enjoy all available economies of scale and each shares roughly one-third of a market, it is easy to see why new competitors may find it extremely difficult to enter this industry. On the one hand, new firms entering the market as small-scale producers will have little or no chance to survive and expand. Why? Because as small-scale entrants they will be unable to realize the cost economies enjoyed by the existing "Big Three" and therefore will be unable to realize the profits necessary for survival and growth. New competitors in the steel and automobile industries will not come about as the result of the successful operation and expansion of small, "back-yard" producers. They simply will not be efficient enough to survive. The other option is to start out big, that is, to enter the industry as a large-scale

producer. In practice, this is virtually impossible. It is extremely unlikely that a new and untried enterprise will be able to secure the money capital needed to obtain capital facilities comparable to those accumulated by any of the Big Three in the automobile industry or, indeed, comparable to those of the Little Two. The financial obstacles in the way of starting big are so great in many cases as to be prohibitive.

Public utilities: natural monopolies

In a few industries economies of scale are particularly pronounced, and at the same time competition is impractical, inconvenient, or simply unworkable. Such industries are called *natural monopolies,* and most of the so-called public utilities— the electric and gas companies, bus and railway firms, and water and communication facilities—can be so classified. These industries are generally given exclusive franchises by government. But in return for this sole right to supply electricity, water, or bus service in a given geographic area, government reserves the right to regulate the operations of such monopolies to prevent abuses of the monopoly power it has granted.

Let us examine some illustrations. It would be exceedingly wasteful for a community to have a number of firms supplying water or electricity. Technology is such in these industries that heavy fixed costs on generators, pumping and purification equipment, water mains, and transmission lines are required. This is aggravated by the fact that capital equipment must be sufficient to meet the peak demands which occur on hot summer days when lawns are being watered and air conditioners turned on. These heavy fixed costs mean that unit costs of production decline with the number of cubic feet of water or kilowatt hours of electricity supplied by each firm. The presence of a number of water and electricity suppliers would divide the total market and reduce the sales of each competitor. Each firm would be pushed back up its declining average cost curve. Firms would underutilize their fixed plants with the result that unit cost and therefore electricity and water rates would necessarily be high. In addition, competition might prove to be highly inconvenient. For example, the presence of a half-dozen telephone companies in a municipality would entail the inconvenience of having six telephones and six telephone books—not to mention six telephone bills—to ensure communications with all other residents in the same town.

Because firms are eager to spread their fixed costs and thereby achieve lower unit costs, cutthroat price competition tends to break out when a number of firms exist in these public utilities industries. The result may be losses, the bankruptcy of weaker rivals, and the eventual merger of the survivors. The evolving pure monopoly may be anxious to recoup past losses and to profit fully by its new position of market dominance by charging exorbitant prices for its good or service.

To spare society from such disadvantageous results government will usually grant an exclusive franchise to a single firm to supply water, natural gas, electricity, telephone service, or train or bus transportation. In return government reserves the right to designate the monopolist's geographic area of operation and the prices which it may charge. The result is a regulated or government-sponsored monopoly —monopoly designed to achieve low unit costs but regulated to guarantee that consumers will benefit from these cost economies.

Ownership of essential raw materials

The institution of private property can be used by a monopoly as a means of achieving an effective obstacle to potential rivals. A firm owning or controlling a raw material which is essential in production can obviously prohibit the creation of rival firms. There are several classic examples. The Aluminum Company of America retained its monopoly position in the aluminum industry for many years by virtue of its control of all basic sources of bauxite, the major ore used in aluminum fabrication. The International Nickel Company of Canada controls approximately 90 per cent of the world's known nickel reserves. Most of the world's diamond mines are owned by the De Beers Company of South Africa. About 95 per cent of the world's molybdenum reserves are owned by the Climax Molybdenum Company.

Patents and research

By granting an inventor the exclusive right to control a product for some seventeen years, American patent laws are aimed at protecting an inventor from having his product or process usurped by rival enterprises which have not shared in the time, effort, and money outlays which have gone into its development. By the same token, however, patents may provide the inventor with a monopoly position for the life of the patent. Patent control figures prominently in the growth of many modern-day industrial giants—National Cash Register, General Motors, General Electric, du Pont, to name a few. The United Shoe Machinery Company provides a notable example of how patent control can be abused to achieve monopoly power. In this case United Shoe became the exclusive supplier of certain essential shoemaking machines through patent control. It extended its monopoly power to other types of shoemaking machinery by requiring all lessees of its patented machines to sign a "tying agreement" in which shoe manufacturers agreed also to lease all other shoemaking machinery from United Shoe. This allowed United Shoe to monopolize the market until partially effective antitrust action was taken by the government in 1955.

Research, of course, underlies the development of patentable products. Firms which gain a measure of monopoly power by their own research or by purchasing the patents of others are in a strategic position to consolidate and strengthen their market position. The profits provided by one important patent can be used to finance the research required to develop new patentable products. Monopoly power achieved through patents may well be cumulative.

Unfair competition

A firm's rivals may be eliminated and the entry of new competitors blocked by aggressive cutthroat tactics. Familiar techniques entail product disparagement, pressure on resource suppliers and banks to withhold materials and credit, the hiring away of strategic personnel, and aggressive price cutting designed to bankrupt competitors. Though many of these facets of unfair competition are now illegal or fringe upon illegality, they are of more than historical interest. For example, although Federal legislation prohibits price cutting intended to reduce competition, how is one to distinguish in practice between legitimate price competition based upon cost advantages and price competition designed to bankrupt rivals?

Economies of being established

A bit of reflection will reveal that for a variety of reasons an established, going concern has numerous advantages over new, embryonic rivals. There are good reasons why existing firms should survive and prosper, while new firms have every reason to founder and fail. Established firms which have proved themselves by their continued existence and prosperity will have relatively easy access to the capital market, on favorable terms. This advantage is not unrelated to the fact that an established concern will tend to have a relatively efficient administrative framework staffed by competent and experienced personnel. The firm's longevity will have allowed it to eliminate inappropriate policies and to have screened the dolts from its administrative ranks. It must be added that going concerns will also be in a position to expand their size and market share by internal financing.

The new concern may have great difficulties in securing needed money capital. Its personnel and policies are untried and untested; it is an industrial question mark. If funds are available to newcomers, the added risks of investing in a new concern are likely to make the terms unattractive to the firm.

In addition, an established firm will be likely to have a widely known and highly advertised product, which it sells through well-established marketing channels to long-standing customers. A new firm faces serious financial obstacles in developing and advertising a product, in establishing marketing outlets, and in building up a clientele.

Two implications

Our discussion of barriers to entry suggests two noteworthy points. First, barriers to entry are rarely complete; indeed, this is simply another way of stating our earlier point that pure monopoly is rare. While we have seen that research and technological advance may strengthen the market position of a firm, technology may also undermine existing monopoly power. Existing patent advantages may be circumvented by the development of new and distinct, yet substitutable, products. New sources of strategic raw materials may be found. It is probably not an overstatement to say that monopoly in the sense of a one-firm industry only persists over time with the sanction or aid of government.

Second, it is implied in our discussion that monopolies may be desirable or undesirable from the standpoint of economic efficiency. The public-utilities and economies-of-scale arguments suggest that market demand and technology may be such that efficient low-cost production presupposes the existence of monopoly. On the other hand, our comments upon materials ownership, patents, and unfair competition as sources of monopoly imply more undesirable connotations of business monopoly.

With these points in mind let us analyze the price-output behavior of a pure monopolist. Important insights with respect to the social desirability of monopoly will be revealed by this analysis.

PRICE AND OUTPUT DETERMINATION

Let us assume a pure monopolist who through, say, patent and materials control is able to block the entry of new firms to the market. Suppose, too, that the monopolist is unregulated; he is unhampered by the reality or the prospect of a regulatory commission. In short, we have a monopolist who is ideally situated to exploit his market fully. The pure monopolist will determine his profit-maximizing output on the basis of his cost and demand data.

Monopoly demand and administered prices

The crucial difference between a pure monopolist and a purely competitive seller lies on the demand side of the market. We recall from Chapter 24 that the purely competitive seller faces a perfectly elastic demand schedule at the market price determined by industry supply and demand. The competitive firm can sell as much or as little as it wants at the going market price. It follows that each additional unit sold will add a constant amount—its price—to the firm's total revenue. In other words, for the competitive seller marginal revenue is constant and equal to product price. But the competitive seller can do nothing about market price; it has no price policy. For better or worse, it must accept the market-determined price.

The monopolist's demand curve is much different. Because the pure monopolist *is* the industry, his demand, or sales, curve is the industry demand curve. And the industry demand curve is not perfectly elastic but rather is downsloping.[1] This is illustrated by columns 1 and 2 of Table 25-1.

There are two implications of a downsloping demand curve which must be understood. In the first place, a downsloping demand curve means that a pure monopoly can increase its sales only by charging a lower unit price for its product. *Furthermore, the fact that the mo-*

[1] Beware of this pitfall: because the individual competitive firm's demand curve is perfectly elastic, it does not follow that the monopolist's demand curve will be perfectly inelastic. Remember: even though the individual competitor regards his demand as perfectly elastic, the demand curve for a competitive *industry* is downsloping. The pure monopolist's demand curve is downsloping, but not perfectly inelastic, because here the firm *is* the industry. As with competitive industry demand, the degree of elasticity or inelasticity which characterizes the pure monopolist's demand curve depends upon those elasticity-determining factors discussed in Chapter 21.

nopolist must lower price to boost sales causes marginal revenue to be less than price (average revenue) for every level of output save the first. The reason? Price cuts will apply not only to the extra output sold but also to all other units of output which otherwise could have been sold at a higher price. Each additional unit sold will add to total revenue its price less the sum of the price cuts which must be taken on all prior units of output.[2] The marginal revenue of the second unit of output is $142 rather than its $152 price, because a $10 price cut must be taken on the first unit to increase sales from 1 to 2 units. It is this rationale which explains why the marginal revenue data of column 4 of Table 25-1 fall short of product price in column 2 for all levels of output save the first.

The second implication of a downsloping demand curve is this: in all imperfectly competitive markets in which such demand curves are relevant—that is, purely monopolistic, oligopolistic, and monopolistically competitive markets —firms have a price policy. By virtue of their ability to influence total supply, the output decisions of such firms necessarily affect product price. This is most evident, of course, in the present case of pure monopoly, where one firm controls total output. Faced with a downsloping demand curve, wherein each output is associated with some unique price, the monopolist unavoidably exercises discretion over price in deciding what volume of output to produce. The monopolist simultaneously chooses a combination of price and output. In columns 1 and 2 of Table 25-1 we find that the monopolist can sell an output of one unit only at a price of $162, an output of two units only at a price of $152, and so forth.[3]

[2] At this point it may be helpful to reread the discussion of the mechanics of this process in Chapter 21.

[3] The notion of a supply curve does not apply in a purely monopolistic (or any other imperfectly competitive) market because of the ability of the seller to control product price. A supply curve shows the amounts producers will offer at various *given* prices which may confront them in the market. But prices are not "given" to the pure monopolist; he does not respond to a fixed price, but rather sets the price himself.

TABLE 25-1. REVENUE AND COST DATA OF A PURE MONOPOLIST

	Revenue data			Cost data			
(1) Quantity of output	(2) Price (average revenue)	(3) Total revenue	(4) Mar- ginal revenue	(5) Average total cost	(6) Total cost	(7) Mar- ginal cost	(8) Profit (+) or Loss (−)
0	$172	$ 0			$ 100		$−100
			$162			$ 90	
1	162	162		$190.00	190		− 28
			142			80	
2	152	304		135.00	270		+ 34
			122			70	
3	142	426		113.33	340		+ 86
			102			60	
4	132	528		100.00	400		+128
			82			70	
5	122	610		94.00	470		+140
			62			80	
6	112	672		91.67	550		+122
			42			90	
7	102	714		91.43	640		+ 74
			22			110	
8	92	736		93.73	750		− 14
			2			130	
9	82	738		97.78	880		−142
			−18			150	
10	72	720		103.00	1,030		−310

Product prices chosen or subject to manipulation by individual producers are called administered prices. Such prices are in contrast to purely competitive prices which are "set" by the market—by the impersonal forces of supply and demand—and are therefore not subject to manipulation by individual sellers.

Caution: We shall discover in a moment that the ability to administer prices does not mean that the monopolist is completely "free" of market forces in establishing his price. Most obviously, the monopolist's downsloping demand curve means that high prices are associated with low volumes of sales and, conversely, low prices with larger outputs. The monopolist cannot "administer" his price upward without losing sales nor gain sales without charging a lower price. The question which now arises is this: What specific price-quantity combination on his demand curve will the pure monopolist choose? This depends not only upon demand and marginal revenue data but also upon costs.

Cost data

On the cost side of the picture we shall assume that, although the firm is a monopolist in the product market, it hires resources competitively and employs the same technology as our competitive firm in the preceding chapter. This permits us to use the cost data developed in Chapter 23 and applied in Chapter 24, thereby facilitating a comparison of the price-output decisions of a pure monopoly with those of a pure competitor. Columns 5 through 7 of Table 25-1 merely restate the pertinent cost concepts of Table 23-2.

Equating marginal revenue and marginal cost

A profit-seeking monopolist will employ the same rationale as a profit-seeking firm in a competitive industry. He will produce each successive unit of output so long as it adds more to his total revenue than it does to his total costs. In technical language, the firm will produce up to that output at which marginal revenue equals marginal cost.

A comparison of columns 4 and 7 in Table 25-1 indicates that the profit-maximizing output is five units; the fifth unit is the last unit of output whose marginal revenue exceeds its mar-

ginal cost. What price will the monopolist charge? His downsloping demand curve of columns 1 and 2 shows there is only one price at which five units can be sold: $122.

This same analysis is presented graphically in Figure 25-1, where the demand, marginal revenue, average total cost, and marginal cost data of Table 25-1 have been drawn. A comparison of marginal revenue and marginal cost again indicate that the profit-maximizing output is five units or, more generally, Q_m. The unique price at which Q_m can be sold is found by extending a perpendicular up from the profit-maximizing point on the output axis and then at right angles from the point at which it hits the demand curve to the vertical axis. The indicated price is P_m. By charging a price higher than P_m the monopolist must move up his demand curve, and this means that his sales will

FIGURE 25-1. THE PROFIT-MAXIMIZING POSITION OF A PURE MONOPOLIST.
The pure monopolist maximizes profits by producing the MR = MC output. In this instance profit is AP_m per unit; total profits are measured by the shaded rectangle.

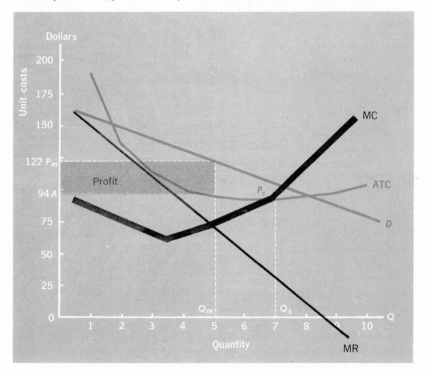

fall short of the profit-maximizing level Q_m. To charge less would involve a volume of sales in excess of the profit-maximizing output.

Columns 2 and 5 of Table 25-1 indicate that, at five units of output, product price of $122 exceeds average total cost of $94. Economic profits are therefore $28 per unit; total economic profits are then $140 (or 5 times $28). In Figure 25-1 per unit profit is indicated by the distance AP_m, and total economic profits—the shaded area—are found by multiplying this unit profit by the profit-maximizing output Q_m.

The same profit-maximizing combination of output and price can also be determined by comparing the total revenue and total costs incurred at each possible level of production. The reader should employ columns 3 and 6 of Table 25-1 to verify all the conclusions we have reached through the use of marginal revenue—marginal cost analysis. Similarly, an accurate graphing of total revenue and total cost against output will also show the greatest differential (the maximum profit) at five units of output.

Misconceptions concerning monopoly pricing

Our analysis explodes some popular fallacies concerning behavior of monopolies.

1. Because a monopolist can manipulate output and price, it is often alleged that a monopolist "will charge the highest price he can get." This is clearly a misguided assertion. There are many prices above P_m in Figure 25-1, but the monopolist shuns them for the simple reason that they entail a smaller-than-maximum profit. Total profits are the difference between total revenue and total costs, and each of these two determinants of profits depend upon quantity sold as much as upon price and unit cost.

2. The monopolist seeks maximum total profits, not maximum unit profits. In Figure 25-1 a careful comparison of the distance between average cost and price at various possible outputs indicates that per unit profits are greater at a point slightly to the left of the profit-maximizing output Q_m. This is more readily seen in Table 25-1, where unit profits are $32 at four units of output as compared to $28 at

the profit-maximizing output of five units. In this instance the monopolist is accepting a lower-than-maximum per unit profit for the simple reason that the additional sales more than compensate for the lower unit profits. A monopolist would obviously rather sell five units at a profit of $28 per unit than sell 4 units at a profit of $32 per unit.

3. It must also be emphasized that pure monopoly does not guarantee economic profits. True, the likelihood of economic profits is greater for a pure monopolist than for a purely competitive producer. The monopolist can administer his price, while the competitor cannot. And in the long run the latter is doomed by the free and easy entry of new firms to a normal profit; barriers to entry permit the monopolist to perpetuate economic profits in the long run. Of course, like the pure competitor, the monopolist cannot persistently operate at a loss. The monopolist must realize a normal profit or better in the long run or will simply not survive. However, if the demand and cost situation faced by the monopolist is less favorable than that shown in Figure 25-1, the monopolist may realize short-run losses. Despite his dominance in the market, the monopolist shown in Figure 25-2 realizes a loss in the short run by virtue of a weak demand and high costs.

Possible restraints upon profit maximization

The comments just made indicate that certain restraints are imposed upon the monopolist by the market. Cost and demand considerations set restrictions upon the monopolist's price-output behavior. Actually certain other forces may cause the monopolist to exercise restraint; these forces may cause the monopolist purposely to charge a lower price and produce a greater output than is consistent with maximum profits. Two such restraints merit comment.

In the first place, the monopolist does not enjoy anonymity; the identity of monopolistic sellers is typically well known. It follows that the monopolist who fully exploits his market position may find himself the target of public criticism. After all, in Figure 25-1 there are

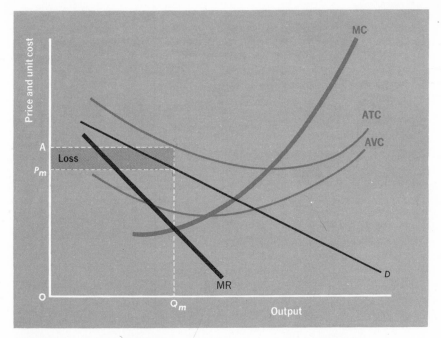

FIGURE 25-2. THE LOSS-MINIMIZING POSITION OF A PURE MONOPOLIST.
If demand *D* is weak and costs AC are high, the pure monopolist may be unable to
make a profit. He will minimize his losses in the short run by producing at that output where MR = MC. Loss per unit is AP_m and total losses are indicated by the shaded
rectangle.

many prices less than P_m which will entail outputs greater than Q_m and still yield substantial
economic profits to the monopolist. If widespread and persistent, such criticism can lead
to a loss of good will or, worse yet from the firm's
viewpoint, some form of governmental intervention—antitrust action, rate regulation, government stimulation of new competitors or, at
the extreme, nationalization of the firm. Thus,
from a very long-run standpoint it may be very
sensible for the monopolist to avoid unfavorable
comment with respect to its market behavior
even at the sacrifice of some profits.

Secondly, the monopoly may deliberately
limit its profits so as not to attract new competitors. A highly profitable monopoly may cause
potential rivals to double their efforts to overcome the monopolist's barriers. And remember:
barriers to entry are rarely insurmountable over

time. Full exploitation of a monopolist's position
in the short run may destroy that monopolistic
position in the long pull.

The importance of these "voluntary" restraints is subject to heated debate. It would be
a mistake to say that they undermine our profit-
maximizing analysis; at best they probably cause
minor deviations from the most profitable price-
output combination.

ECONOMIC EFFECTS

Let us now evaluate pure monopoly from the
standpoint of society as a whole. Our emphasis
will be upon (1) price, output, and resource
allocation, (2) the distribution of income, and
(3) economic progress, that is, technological
advance. To sharpen our analysis we ignore
any possible restraints upon the monopolist's

policies and presume that the monopolist seeks the maximum profit that his cost-revenue situation permits.

Price, output, and resource allocation

In Chapter 24 we concluded that pure competition would result in a highly efficient, or "ideal," allocation of resources. In the long run the free entry and exodus of firms would force firms to operate at the optimum rate of output where unit costs of production were at a minimum. Product price would be at the lowest level consistent with average total costs. To illustrate: in Figure 25-1 the competitive firm would sell Q_c units of output at a price of Q_cP_c. Furthermore, long-run competitive equilibrium would also entail an efficient allocation of resources, in that production would occur up to that point at which price (society's measure of a product's value) equals marginal cost (society's measure of the alternative products forgone in the production of any given commodity).

Figure 25-1 indicates that, given the same costs, a purely monopolistic firm will give much less desirable results. As we have already discovered, the pure monopolist will maximize his profits by producing an output of Q_m and charging a price of P_m. It can be readily seen that the monopolist will find it profitable to sell a smaller output and to charge a higher price than would a competitive producer. Furthermore, it is clear that, at Q_m units of output, product price is considerably greater than marginal cost. This means that society values additional units of this monopolized product higher than it does the alternative products which resources could otherwise produce. In other words, the monopolist's profit-maximizing output results in a misallocation of resources; the monopolist finds it profitable to restrict output and therefore employ fewer resources than are justified from society's standpoint.

Given identical costs, a purely monopolistic firm will find it profitable to charge a higher price, produce a smaller output, and foster an allocation of economic resources inferior to that of a purely competitive firm. These contrasting consequences are rooted in the barriers to entry which characterize monopoly.

There is one basic exception to these conclusions: the assumption that the unit costs available to the purely competitive and the purely monopolistic firm are the same does not always hold in practice. Given production techniques and therefore production costs, consumer demand may simply not be sufficient to support a large number of competing firms, each producing at an output which permits it to realize all known economies of scale. In such instances a firm must be large in relation to the market—this is, it must be monopolistic —to produce efficiently (at low unit cost). Our previous discussion of economies of scale as a barrier to entry and the desirability of establishing public utilities in certain fields is based primarily upon such cost considerations (see Chapter 23).

How important is this exception? Most economists feel that it applies for the most part only to public utilities and is therefore not significant enough to undermine our general conclusions concerning the restrictive nature of monopoly. The best available evidence (see footnote 6 in Chapter 8) suggests that the giant corporations which populate many manufacturing industries now have more monopoly power than can be justified on the grounds that these firms are merely availing themselves of existing economies of scale.

Income distribution

Business monopoly probably contributes to inequality in the distribution of income in our society. By virtue of their market power monopolists charge a higher price than would a purely competitive firm with the same costs; monopolists are in effect able to levy a "private tax" upon consumers and thereby realize substantial economic profits. These monopolistic profits, it should be noted, are not widely distributed for the simple reason that corporate stock ownership is largely concentrated in the hands of upper income groups. The owners of monopolistic enterprises thereby tend to be enriched at the expense of the rest of society.

Assuming monopoly does contribute to income inequality, is this necessarily undesirable? There is no agreement here and no scientifically correct answer will ever be found because any view necessarily entails a value judgment with respect to what one feels the distribution of income ought to be. Nevertheless, there is a rather widespread feeling in our society that the extreme degrees of income inequality to which pure monopoly frequently contributes are undesirable.

Technological advance

We have already qualified our condemnation of pure monopoly by noting that in a few instances *existing* mass production economies may be lost to an industry comprised of a large number of small, competing firms. There is also a dynamic aspect to this line of reasoning. To be specific, will competition or monopoly foster the more rapid improvement of products and productive techniques? This is fertile ground for honest differences of opinion.

Competitive firms certainly have the incentive—indeed, a market mandate—to employ the most efficient *known* productive techniques. We have seen that their very survival depends upon being efficient. But at the same time competition tends to deprive firms of economic profit—an important means and a major incentive to develop *new* products and *new* improved productive techniques. The profits of technological advance will be short-lived to the innovating competitor. An innovating firm in a competitive industry will find that its many rivals will soon duplicate or imitate any technological advance it may achieve; rivals will share the rewards but not the costs of successful technological research.

In contrast we have seen that a monopolist may persistently realize substantial economic profits. Hence, the pure monopolist will have greater financial resources for technological advance than will competitive firms. But what about the monopolist's incentives for technological advance? Here the picture is clouded.

There is one imposing argument which suggests that the monopolist's incentives to develop new products and new techniques will be weak: the absence of competitors means that there is no automatic stimulus to technological advance in a monopolized market. Because of its sheltered market position, the pure monopolist can afford to be inefficient and lethargic. The keen rivalry of a competitive market penalizes the inefficient; an inefficient monopolist does not face this penalty for the simple reason that he has no rivals. The monopolist has every reason to become satisfied with the *status quo,* to become complacent. It might well pay the monopolist to withhold or "file" technological improvements in both product and productive techniques in order to exploit existing capital equipment fully. New and improved products and techniques, it is argued, may be suppressed by monopolists to avoid any losses caused by the sudden obsolescence of existing machinery and equipment. And, even when improved techniques are belatedly introduced by monopolists, the accompanying cost reductions will accrue to the monopolist as increases in profits and only partially, if at all, to consumers in the form of lower prices and an increased output. Proponents of this view point out that in a number of industries which approximate pure monopoly—for example, steel and aluminum—the interest in research has been minimal. Such advances as have been realized have come largely from outside the industry or from the smaller firms which comprise the "competitive fringe" of the industry.

Basically there are three offsetting arguments:

1. Any gross failure to achieve some minimum level of technological advance will induce public criticism and in time government control.

2. Technological advance is a means of lowering unit costs and thereby expanding profits. And these profits will not be of a transitory nature; barriers to entry protect the monopolist from profit encroachment by rivals.

3. Research and technological advance may be one of the monopolist's barriers to entry; hence, the monopolist must persist and succeed in the area of technological advance or eventually fall prey to new competitors.

Which view is more accurate? Frankly, economists are not sure. Most economists do not envision pure monopoly as a particularly progressive market structure. At the same time they acknowledge that agriculture, the industry which most nearly fits the competitive model, has only on rare occasion provided itself with new innovations in product and method. Government research and the oligopolistic firms which produce farm equipment have provided this competitive industry with most of its improvements in products and techniques. As we shall see in Chapter 27, some respected economists seem to feel that oligopolistic industries, wherein firms are large enough to have the ability to finance research and at the same time are compelled to engage in such research because of the presence of a moderate number of rivals, may be more conducive to technological advance than any other market structure.

Now what can be offered by way of a summarizing generalization as to the economic efficiency of pure monopoly? Simply this: in a static economy, wherein economies of scale are equally accessible to purely competitive and monopolist firms, pure competition will be superior to pure monopoly in that pure competition forces use of the best-known technology and allocates resources in accordance with the wants of society. On the other hand, when economies of scale available to the monopolist are not attainable by small competitive producers, or in a dynamic context in which changes in the rate of technological advance must be considered, the economic inefficiencies of pure monopoly are not so evident.

SUMMARY

1. A pure monopolist is the sole producer of a commodity for which there are no good substitutes.

2. Barriers to entry, in the form of (*a*) economies of scale, (*b*) natural monopolies, (*c*) the ownership or control of essential raw materials, (*d*) patent ownership and research, (*e*) unfair competition, and (*f*) economies of being established, help explain the existence of pure monopoly and other imperfectly competitive market structures. Barriers to entry which are very formidable in the short run may prove to be transitory in the long run.

3. The pure monopolist's market situation differs from that of a competitive firm in that the monopolist's demand curve is downsloping. The implications of this are twofold. (*a*) The monopolist's marginal revenue curve lies below his demand curve. (*b*) Monopoly price is an administered price, that is, a price which the monopolist can manipulate through his control over output.

4. Like the competitive seller, the pure monopolist will maximize profits by equating marginal revenue and marginal cost. Barriers to entry may permit a monopolist to acquire economic profits even in the long run. It is noteworthy, however, that (*a*) the monopolist does not charge "the highest price he can get"; (*b*) the maximum total profit sought by the monopolist rarely coincides with maximum unit profits; and (*c*) high costs and a weak demand may prevent the monopolist from realizing any profit at all.

5. Given the same costs, the pure monopolist will find it more profitable to restrict output and charge a higher price than would a competitive seller. This restriction of output causes resources to be misallocated; technically, price exceeds marginal cost in monopolized markets.

6. Monopoly tends to increase income inequality.

7. Economists disagree as to how conducive pure monopoly is to technological advance. Some feel that pure monopoly is more progressive than pure competition because its ability to acquire economic profits provides for the financing of technological research. Others, however, argue that the absence of rival firms and the monopolist's desire to exploit fully his existing capital facilities weaken the monopolist's incentive to innovate.

QUESTIONS AND STUDY SUGGESTIONS

1. "No firm is completely sheltered from rivals; all firms in fact compete for the dollars of consumers. Pure monopoly, therefore, simply does not exist." Do you agree? Explain.

2. Discuss the major barriers to entry. In particular, what are "the economies of being established"? Explain how each barrier can foster monopoly or oligopoly. Which barriers, if any, do you feel give rise to monopoly that is socially justifiable?

3. Critically evaluate and explain:

a. "Because they can control product price, monopolists are always assured of profitable production by simply charging the highest price consumers will pay."

b. "The pure monopolist seeks that output which will yield the greatest per unit profit."

c. "An excess of price over marginal cost is the market's way of signaling the need for more production of a product."

d. "The more profitable a firm, the greater its monopoly power."

e. "The monopolist has a price policy; the competitive producer does not."

f. "With respect to resource allocation the interests of the seller and of society coincide in a purely competitive market but conflict in a monopolized market."

4. How does the demand curve faced by a purely monopolistic seller differ from that confronting a purely competitive firm? Why does it differ? Of what significance is the difference? Why is not the pure monopolist's demand curve perfectly inelastic? What are "administered prices"?

5. Assume a pure monopolist and a purely competitive firm have the same unit costs. Contrast the two with respect to (*a*) price, (*b*) output, (*c*) profits, (*d*) allocation of resources, and (*e*) impact upon the distribution of income. Since both monopolists and competitive firms follow the MC = MR rule in maximizing profits, how do you account for the different results?

6. What considerations might restrain a monopolist from maximizing profits? In practice, how important do you feel these restraints might be?

7. "In a sense the monopolist makes a profit for not producing; the monopolist produces profits more than he does goods." Evaluate and explain.

8. "Competition is congenial to material progress. It keeps the door open to new blood and new ideas. It communicates to all producers the improvements made by any one of them. Monopoly, as such, is not conducive to progress. The large firm may engage in research and invent new products, materials, methods and machines. But when it possesses a monopoly, it will be reluctant to make use of these inventions if they would compel it to scrap existing equipment or if it believes that their ultimate profitability is in doubt. The monopolist may introduce innovations and cut costs, but instead of moving goods by reducing prices he is prone to spend large sums on alternative methods of promoting sales. His refusal to cut prices deprives the community of any gain."[4] Carefully evaluate this widely held viewpoint. Can you offer any arguments to the contrary?

[4] Clair Wilcox, *Public Policies Toward Business* (Homewood, Ill.: Richard D. Irwin, Inc., 1955), p. 12.

9. Suppose a pure monopolist is faced with the following demand schedule and the same cost data as the competitive producer discussed in question 3 at the end of Chapter 24. Calculate marginal revenue and determine the profit-maximizing price and output for this monopolist. Verify your answer graphically.

Price	Quantity demanded	Marginal revenue
$100	1	
83	2	
71	3	
63	4	
55	5	
48	6	
42	7	
37	8	
33	9	
29	10	

SELECTED REFERENCES

Adams, Walter (ed.), *The Structure of American Industry*, 3d ed. (New York: The Macmillan Company, 1961), chap. 13.

Bain, Joe S., *Pricing, Distribution, and Employment*, rev. ed. (New York: Holt, Rinehart and Winston, Inc., 1953), chap. 5.

Bober, M. M., *Intermediate Price and Income Theory*, rev. ed. (New York: W. W. Norton & Company, Inc., 1962), chap. 10.

Due, John F., and Robert W. Clower, *Intermediate Economic Analysis*, 4th ed. (Homewood, Ill.: Richard D. Irwin, Inc., 1961), chap. 11.

Robinson, E. A. G., *Monopoly* (London: Nesbit and Company, 1941).

Schumpeter, Joseph A., *Capitalism, Socialism, and Democracy*, 3d ed. (New York: Harper & Row, Publishers, 1950), chaps. 7 and 8.

Weiss, Leonard W., *Economics and American Industry* (New York: John Wiley & Sons, Inc., 1961), chaps. 5 and 6.

Chapter 26

PRICE AND OUTPUT DETERMINATION:

MONOPOLISTIC COMPETITION

PURE COMPETITION and pure monopoly are the exception, not the rule, in American capitalism. Most market structures fall somewhere between these two extremes. In Chapter 27 we shall discuss oligopoly, a market structure which stands close to pure monopoly. In the present chapter we are concerned with monopolistic competition. Monopolistic competition correctly suggests a blending of monopoly and competition; more specifically, monopolistic competition involves a very considerable amount of competition with a small dose of monopoly power intermixed.

Our basic objectives in this chapter are (1) to define and discuss the nature and prevalence of monopolistic competition; (2) to analyze and evaluate the price-output behavior of monopolistically competitive firms; and (3) to explain and assess the role of nonprice competition, that is, competition based upon product quality and advertising, in monopolistically competitive industries.

CONCEPT AND THE OCCURRENCE OF MONOPOLISTIC COMPETITION

First of all, let us recall, and also expand upon, the definition of monopolistic competition.

Monopolistic competition refers to that market situation in which a relatively large number of small producers or suppliers are offering similar but not identical products. The contrasts afforded with pure competition are important. Monopolistic competition does not require the presence of hundreds or thousands of firms but only a fairly large number—say 25, 35, 60, or 70. Several important characteristics of monopolistic competition follow from the presence of relatively large numbers. In the first place, each firm has a relatively small percentage of the total market so that each has a very limited amount of control over market price. Then, too, the presence of a relatively large number of firms also ensures that collusion—concerted action by the firms to restrict output and rig price—is all but impossible. Finally, with a large number of firms in the industry, there is no feeling of mutual interdependence between them; that is, each firm determines its policies without considering the possible reactions of rival firms. And this is a very reasonable way to act in a market in which one's rivals are very numerous. After all, the 10 or 15 per cent increase in sales which Firm X may realize by cutting price will be spread so thinly over its 20, 40, or 60 rivals that for all practical purposes the impact upon their sales will be imperceptible. Rivals' reactions can be ignored, because the impact of one firm's actions upon each of its many rivals is so small that these rivals will have no reason to react.

Also in contrast to pure competition, a fundamental feature of monopolistic competition is *product differentiation*. Purely competitive firms produce a standardized product; monopolistically competitive producers turn out variations of a given product. Many firms produce toothpaste, but the product of each differs from its rivals in one or more respects. Indeed, it must be emphasized that product differentiation has more dimensions than are immediately apparent. "Real," or physical, differences involving functional features, materials, design, and workmanship are obviously important aspects of product differentiation. But "imaginary" differences created through advertising, packaging, and the use of trademarks and brand names can be equally significant. Finally, the conditions of sale make for differentiation; the location of a store, the courteousness of its clerks, the firm's reputation for servicing its products, and the availability of credit are all facets of product differentiation.

The significance of product differentiation is basically twofold. On the one hand, despite the presence of a relatively large number of firms, monopolistically competitive producers have limited amounts of control over the prices of their products because of differentiation. Consumers have preferences for the products of specific sellers and *within limits* will pay a higher price to satisfy those preferences. Sellers and buyers are no longer linked at random as in a purely competitive market. On the other hand, the fact that products are differentiated adds a new and complicating factor to our analysis: *nonprice competition*. Because products are differentiated, it can be supposed that products can be varied over time and that the differentiating features of each firm's product will be susceptible to advertising and other forms of sales promotion. In a monopolistically competitive market economic rivalry centers not only upon price but also upon product variation and product promotion.

Entry into monopolistically competitive industries tends to be relatively easy. The fact that monopolistically competitive producers are typically small-sized firms both absolutely and relatively suggests that economies of scale and capital requirements are few. On the other

hand, as compared to pure competition, there may be some added financial barriers posed by the need for deriving a product different from one's rivals and the obligation to advertise that product. Existing firms may hold patents on their products and copyrights on their brand names and trademarks, enhancing the difficulty and cost of successfully imitating them.

In short, monopolistic competition refers to industries comprised of a relatively large number of firms, operating noncollusively, in the production of differentiated products. Nonprice competition accompanies price competition. Ease of entry makes for competition by new firms in the long run.

It is difficult to find clear-cut illustrations of monopolistically competitive industries. Many industries which approximate monopolistic competitions also embody one or more characteristics of oligopoly. Table 26-1 contains a group of manufacturing industries which approximate monopolistic competition. Retail stores in larger cities and metropolitan areas are generally monopolistically competitive; grocery stores, gasoline stations, barber shops, dry cleaners, clothing stores, and so forth operate under conditions similar to those we have described.

PRICE AND OUTPUT DETERMINATION

Let us now analyze the price-output behavior of a monopolistically competitive firm. To facilitate this task we assume initially that the firms in the industry are producing *given* products and are engaging in a *given* amount of promotional activity. Later we shall note how product variation and advertising modify our discussion.

The firm's demand curve

Our explanation is couched in terms of Figure 26-1a. The basic feature of this diagram, which sets it off from our analyses of pure competition and pure monopoly, is the elasticity of the firm's individual demand, or sales, curve. The demand curve faced by a monopolistically competitive seller is highly, but not perfectly, elastic. It is much more elastic than the demand

TABLE 26-1. PERCENTAGE OF OUTPUT * PRODUCED BY FIRMS IN SELECTED LOW CONCENTRATION MANUFACTURING INDUSTRIES, 1954

Industry	Four largest firms	Four next largest firms	Twelve next largest firms
Upholstered furniture	17%	3%	7%
Seamless hosiery	16	7	11
Plywood	16	8	16
Paperboard boxes	16	10	15
Metal house furniture	15	9	14
Costume jewelry	13	7	10
Men's and boys' suits and coats	11	7	15
Wood furniture	8	4	8
Millinery	7	5	8
Women's suits, coats, and skirts	3	3	6

* As measured by value of shipments.
SOURCE: Senate Subcommittee on Antitrust and Monopoly, "Concentration in American Industry" (Washington: Government Printing Office, 1957), table 40, p. 133.

curve of the pure monopolist, because the monopolistically competitive seller is faced with a relatively large number of rivals producing close-substitute goods. The pure monopolist, of course, has no rivals at all. Yet, for two reasons, the monopolistically competitive seller's sales curve is not perfectly elastic as is the purely competitive producer's: (1) the monopolistically competitive firm has a smaller number of rivals, and (2) the products of these rivals are close but not perfect substitutes. Generally speaking, the precise degree of elasticity embodied in the monopolistically competitive firm's demand curve will depend upon the exact number of rivals and the degree of product differentiation. The larger the number of rivals and the weaker the product differentiation, the greater will be the elasticity of each seller's demand curve, that is, the closer the situation will be to pure competition.

The short run: profits or losses

The firm will maximize its profits or minimize its losses in the short run by producing that output designated by the intersection of mar-

ginal cost and marginal revenue for reasons with which we are now familiar. The representative firm of Figure 26-1a produces an output Q, charges a price P, and is fortunate enough to realize a total profit of the size indicated. But a less favorable cost and demand situation may exist, putting the monopolistically competitive firm in the position of realizing losses in the short run. This is illustrated in Figure 26-1b. In the short run the monopolistically competitive firm may either realize an economic profit or be faced with losses.

The long run: break-even

In the long run, however, the tendency is for monopolistically competitive firms to earn a normal profit, that is, to break even. In the short-run profits case, Figure 26-1a, we can expect the economic profits to attract new rivals, because entry is relatively easy. As new firms enter, the demand curve faced by the typical firm will fall (shift to the left) and become more elastic. Why? Because each firm has a smaller share of the total demand and now faces a larger number of close substitute products. This

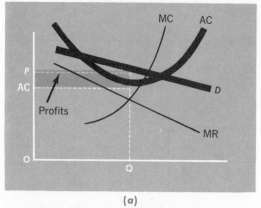

(a)

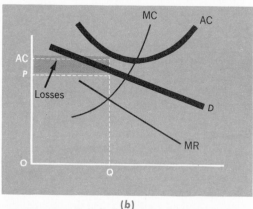

(b)

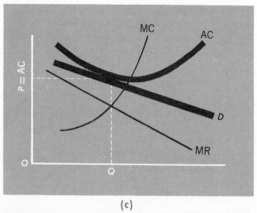

(c)

in turn tends to cause the disappearance of economic profits. When the demand curve is tangent to the average cost curve at the profit-maximizing output, as shown in Figure 26-1c, the firm is just breaking even. Output Q is the equilibrium output for the firm; as Figure 26-1c clearly indicates, any deviation from that output will entail average costs which exceed product price and, therefore, losses for the firm. Furthermore, economic profits have been competed away and there is no incentive for additional firms to enter. In the short-run losses case, Figure 26-1b, we can expect an exodus of firms to occur in the long run. Faced with fewer substitute products and blessed with an expanded share of total demand, surviving firms will find that their losses disappear and gradually give way to approximately normal profits.[1]

Note that we have been very careful in designating our long-run analysis as a statement of a tendency. The representative firm in a monopolistically competitive market *tends* to break even in the long run. There are certain complicating factors which prevent us from being more dogmatic. First, some firms may achieve a measure of product differentiation which cannot be duplicated by rivals even over a long span of time. A given gasoline station may have the only available location at the busiest intersection in town. Or a firm may hold a patent which gives it a slight and more or less permanent advantage over imitators. Such firms may realize a sliver of economic profits even in the long run. Second, remember that entry is not completely unrestricted. Because of product differentiation there are likely to be greater financial barriers to entry than other-

[1] For simplicity's sake we assume constant costs; shifts in the cost curves as firms enter or leave would complicate our discussion but not alter the conclusions.

FIGURE 26-1. MONOPOLISTICALLY COMPETITIVE FIRMS TEND TO REALIZE A NORMAL PROFIT IN THE LONG RUN.
The economic profits shown in (a) will induce new firms to enter, causing the profits to be competed away. The losses indicated in (b) will cause an exodus of firms until normal profits are restored. Thus in (c), where price just covers unit costs at the MR = MC output, the firm's long-run equilibrium position is portrayed.

wise would be the case. This again suggests that some economic profits may persist even in the long run. A third consideration may work in the opposite direction, causing losses—below-normal profits—to persist in the long run. The proprietor of a corner delicatessen persistently accepts a return less than he could earn elsewhere, because his business is a way of life to him. The suburban barber ekes out a meager existence, because cutting hair is "all he wants to do." With all things considered, however, the long-run profitless equilibrium of Figure 26-1c is probably a reasonable portrayal of reality.

WASTES OF MONOPOLISTIC COMPETITION

In contrast to pure competition, Figure 26-1c suggests that monopolistically competitive firms produce somewhat short of the most efficient (least unit cost) output; production entails higher unit costs than the minimum attainable. This in turn means a somewhat higher price than would result under pure competition. Indeed, monopolistically competitive firms must charge a higher-than-competitive price in the long run in order to manage a normal profit. Looked at differently, if each firm were able to produce at the most efficient output, a smaller number of firms could produce the same total output, and the product could be sold to consumers at a lower price. Monopolistically competitive industries tend to be overcrowded with too many firms, each of which is underutilized, that is, operating short of optimum capacity. This is typified by retail establishments, for example, the highway intersection adorned with four gleaming gasoline stations all operating far short of capacity. Underutilized plants, consumers penalized through higher-than-competitive prices for this underutilization, and producers just making a normal return in the long run—these are the so-called "wastes" of monopolistic competition.

But we must not be hypercritical of monopolistic competition. Some economists argue that in many monopolistically competitive industries the price and output results are not drastically different from those of pure competi-

tition. The highly elastic nature of each firm's demand curve guarantees that the results are nearly competitive. Furthermore, it must be kept in mind that any deviations from the purely competitive output and price may be offset by the fact that with monopolistic competition the consumer now can choose from a variety of products; he is not faced with a homogeneous commodity.

NONPRICE COMPETITION

For reasons cited above, we can conclude that the situation portrayed in Figure 26-1c may not be particularly beneficial to society. It can also be surmised that it is not very satisfying to the monopolistically competitive producer who barely captures a normal profit for his efforts. We can therefore expect monopolistically competitive producers to take steps to improve upon the long-run equilibrium position. But how can this be accomplished? The answer lies in product differentiation. Each firm has a product which is currently distinguishable in some more or less tangible way from those of his rivals. The product is assumedly subject to further variation, that is, to product development. Then, too, the emphasis of real product differences and the creation of imaginary differences may be achieved through advertising and related sales promotion. In short, the profit-realizing producer of Figure 26-1a is loath to stand by and watch new competitors encroach upon his profits by duplicating or imitating his product, copying his advertising, and matching his services to consumers. Rather he will attempt to sustain these profits and "stay ahead" of competitors through further product development and by enhancing the quantity and quality of advertising. In this way he might prevent the long-run tendency of Figure 26-1c from becoming a reality. True, product development and advertising will add to the firm's costs. But they can also be expected to increase the demand for his product. If demand increases by more than enough to compensate for developmental and promotional costs, the firm will have improved its profit position. As Figure 26-1c suggests, the firm may have little or no prospect of increasing profits by price cutting. So why not practice nonprice competition?

Product differentiation and product development

The likelihood that easy entry will promote product variety and product improvement is possibly a redeeming feature of monopolistic competition which may offset, wholly or in part, the "wastes" associated with this market structure. There are really two somewhat distinct considerations here: (1) product differentiation at a point in time and (2) product improvement over a period of time.

1. Product differentiation means that at any point in time the consumer will be offered a wide range of types, styles, brands, and quality gradations of any given product. As compared to, say, pure competition this correctly suggests possible advantages to the consumer. His range of free choice is widened, and variations and shadings of consumer tastes are more fully met by producers. But skeptics warn that product differentiation is not an unmixed blessing. Product proliferation may reach the point where the consumer becomes confused and rational choice is highly unlikely. Variety may add spice to the consumer's life, but only up to a point. Worse yet, some observers fear that the consumer, faced with a myriad of similar products, may rely upon such a dubious expedient as judging product quality by price; that is, the consumer may irrationally assume that price is an index of product quality.

2. Product competition is an important avenue of technological innovation and product betterment over a period of time. Such product development may be cumulative in two different senses. (a) A successful product improvement by one firm obligates rivals to imitate or, if they can, improve upon this firm's temporary market advantage or suffer the penalty of losses. (b) Profits realized from a successful product improvement can be used to finance further improvements. Again, however, there are notable criticisms of the product development which may occur under monopolistic competition. Critics point out that many product alterations

are more apparent than real, consisting of frivolous and superficial changes in the product which do not improve its durability, efficiency, or usefulness. A more exotic container, bright packaging, or "shuffling the chrome" are frequently the focal points for product development. It is argued, too, that particularly in the cases of durable and semidurable consumer goods, development seems to follow a pattern of "planned obsolescence," wherein firms improve their product only by that amount necessary to make the average consumer dissatisfied with last year's model.

Do the advantages of product differentiation, properly discounted, outweigh the "wastes" of monopolistic competition? It is difficult to say, short of examining specific cases, and even then concrete conclusions are difficult to come by. It is plausible to assume, though, that in the long run product changes are in accordance with consumer wants. Changes which are not appealing to the consumer will be rejected in the marketplace, and innovating firms will know from their profit and loss statements when they have miscalculated. It is important to note, too, that product improvements which appear minor and somewhat superficial over a short period of time can be very significant when compounded over a period of years. In brief, product development does tend to enhance consumer satisfactions over time, in many cases to a very substantial degree. Finally, if product differentiation and product development are subject to abuses, a part of the blame lies with the consumer himself. Consumers who are informed and who act rationally will seek out quality products at low prices; under such circumstances those firms which specialize in superficial differentiation accompanied by exorbitant prices will be duly penalized. But if consumers are poorly informed and act irrationally, producers may find that it pays to "develop" their products in the most trivial ways imaginable.

Advertising

A monopolistically competitive producer may gain at least a temporary edge on his rivals by manipulating his product. He may achieve the same result by manipulating the consumer through advertising and sales promotion. While product differentiation adapts the product to consumer demand, advertising adapts consumer demand to the product. In practice these two aspects of nonprice competition may be difficult to disentangle. Does a new and colorful method of packaging a product constitute a change in the product, or is it a means of advertising and promotion?

Though we might tentatively agree that product development is a desirable feature of monopolistic competition, the advertising which accompanies it is more difficult to evaluate. The social desirability of extensive advertising expenditures is a very controversial and clouded topic. A basic reason for this is the fact that some advertising is *informative,* that is, accurately descriptive of the qualities and prices of products, while other advertising is *competitive,* consisting of unsubstantiated ours-is-better-than-theirs exhortation. Local newspaper advertising is informative; the cigarette and soap advertisements that the television industry funnels into American living rooms are competitive.

This controversy is not an unimportant one. In recent years advertising and promotional expenditures in American capitalism have exceeded $12 billion per year. This is roughly equal to the nation's annual outlay on primary and secondary public education. Hence, if advertising is generally wasteful, any potential virtues of monopolistically competitive markets are thereby dimmed, and the need for corrective public policies is indicated.

Extreme arguments are prevalent. Some economists are prone to write off all advertising as sheer economic waste. Others—the admen themselves—manage to associate all that is just and good in American society with advertising. An accurate picture lies in the middle ground. Let us survey the basic claims for and the charges against advertising.

The case for advertising. Some of the arguments in favor of advertising follow:

1. Advertising allegedly provides the information which assists consumers in making rational choices. In a dynamic, complex economy there is an acute need for the consumer to be closely acquainted with new firms, new products, and improvements in existing products. Advertising is the medium which disperses such information.

2. Advertising supports national communications. Radio, television, magazines, and newspapers are supported wholly or in part through advertising.

3. It has been argued more recently that advertising is a stimulant to product development. Successful advertising is frequently based upon unique and advantageous features of a firm's product. Hence, a firm is obligated to improve its product to provide "sales points" for competing successfully in the advertising sphere.

4. Through successful advertising a firm can expand its production and thereby realize greater economies of scale. As shown in Figure 26-2, by shifting the firm's demand curve to the right through advertising, production will expand from, say, Q_1 to Q_2. Despite the fact that advertising outlays will shift the firm's average cost curve upwards, unit costs will nevertheless decline from, say, AC_1 to AC_2. Greater productive efficiency resulting from economies of scale more than offsets the increase in unit costs due to advertising. Consumers will therefore get the product at a lower price with advertising than they would in its absence.

5. It is also contended that advertising promotes full employment by inducing high levels of consumer spending. This is particularly crucial, it is argued, in a wealthy society such as American capitalism, where much of total production takes the form of luxury or semiluxury goods which fulfill no basic wants. One need not advertise to sell food to a hungry man, but advertising and sales promotion are essential in persuading families that they need a second car, color television, or an automatic dishwasher. Stability in an opulent society calls for want-creating activities—in particular, advertising—or high levels of production and employment will not be sustainable.

The case against advertising. Some of the arguments on the other side of the picture debunk the claims for advertising; others raise new points.

1. Critics of advertising point out that the basic objective of advertising is to persuade,

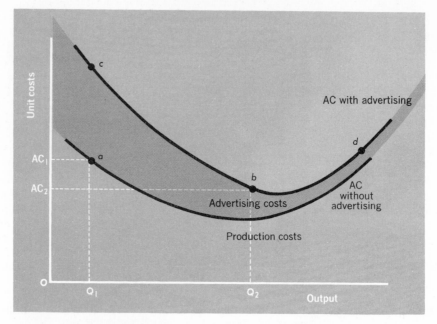

FIGURE 26-2. THE POSSIBLE EFFECTS OF ADVERTISING UPON A FIRM'S OUTPUT AND AVERAGE COSTS.
Proponents of advertising contend that resulting economies of scale will expand the firm's production from, say, *a* to *b* and lower unit costs as economies of scale are realized. Some critics argue that advertising is more likely to increase costs and leave output largely unchanged, as is suggested by the movement from *a* to *c*. Others point out that expansion realized through advertising may force diseconomies of scale upon the firm, as the movement from *a* to *d* indicates.

not to inform. Competitive advertising is based upon misleading and extravagant claims which serve to confuse and frequently insult the intelligence of the consumer, not enlighten him. Little of real value in the rendering of rational choices can be garnered from the soap and cigarette advertising which crowds our television screens and adds bulk to our slick magazines. Indeed, advertising may well persuade consumers in some cases to pay high prices for much-acclaimed but inferior products, forgoing better but unadvertised products selling at lower prices. The Pure Food and Drug and Federal Trade Commission Acts, which are aimed at protecting consumers from product misrepresentation and misleading advertising, testify as to past and present abuses by modern-day hucksters.

2. Advertising expenditures as such are relatively unproductive; they add little or nothing to the well-being of society. Advertising diverts human and property resources from other, more pressing areas. For example, lumber which is sorely needed in the production of low- and medium-priced housing is squandered on the construction of unsightly billboards. In short, advertising gives rise to a gross misallocation of resources.

In recent years the general criticism that advertising promotes a misallocation of resources has assumed a special form: advertising allegedly contributes to *social imbalance*. That is, advertising, in conjunction with a number of other considerations, has given rise to the overproduction of private goods relative to public or social goods. It is argued that advertising is peculiar to, and an integral part of, the production and sale of private goods. Gigantic advertising campaigns extoll the merits of electric canopeners, self-propelled lawnmowers, and eight-speaker stereophonic phonographs. But no similar force proclaims the virtues of social goods and services; similar persuasion does not exist to whet the consumer's appetite for better schools, improved streets and highways, increased expenditures for medical research, and so forth. The net result, it is contended, is a misallocation of resources; resources are overallocated to private goods and underallocated to public goods. Private goods are superabundant; social goods are remarkably deficient in quantity and quality. The problem of social imbalance will be pursued at length in Chapter 36.

3. Significant social costs are entailed by advertising. Billboards blot out roadside scenery and generally debase the countryside. Sound trucks disrupt suburban serenity. Of potentially greater importance are the effects which advertising support of national communications may have upon the accuracy and quality of those communications. Will a newspaper present an unprejudiced report of the labor dispute in which its major advertiser is involved? Will a television newscast conveniently ignore the fact that antitrust action has been initiated against its sponsor? Will a firm which distributes its product nationally permit the television playhouse it sponsors to present an honest and frank portrayal of the integration problem? In more general terms, it is charged that competitive advertising offends the common sense and tries the patience of society. The fact that water consumption rises enormously during television commercials adds credulity to this latter contention.

4. Critics of advertising are very dubious of the argument that advertising permits firms to expand, to achieve lower unit costs, and to offer their products at lower prices to consumers. Reasons for this doubt are several. First, it is contended that advertising tends to be self-canceling. The million-dollar advertising campaign of one cigarette manufacturer is largely offset by equally expensive campaigns waged by its rivals. Few additional people smoke cigarettes. Each firm has about the same portion of the market as it had originally. And the cost, and therefore the price, of cigarettes is higher. In Figure 26-2 self-canceling advertising may move the firm from point a to point c, not from a to b. Second, if advertising can cause a firm to realize economies of scale through growth, can it not also cause a firm to encounter diseconomies? Might not advertising shift the firm's level of output from point a to point d in Figure 26-2? Third, are there not more desirable and less costly alternative means by which a firm might expand output and achieve economies of scale? Would not product development or research on productive methods permit a firm to achieve economies of scale and at the same time avoid the upshift in its average cost schedule which advertising entails? Finally, even if a firm achieves lower unit costs through advertising, will the consumer benefit through proportionate price reductions? This point is particularly pertinent in view of the fact that the expansion of those firms whose advertising is most successful implies that less successful advertisers will fall by the wayside, causing the industry to move away from monopolistic competition and in the direction of oligopoly, wherein firms have greater control over product price.

5. Most economists are reluctant to accept advertising as an important determinant of the levels of output and employment. There has been little evidence of economic stagnation in the postwar years that would seem remediable by advertising and promotional outlays. Furthermore, the most volatile aspect of aggregate demand is not so much highly advertised consumer goods as it is little-advertised investment goods. The consensus seems to be that advertising probably affects the composition more than it does the volume of spending. And those economists who do accept the contention that advertising now has an impact upon consumer spending suggest that at some future time its effect on the level of spending may diminish to zero.

On some not distant day, the voice of each individual seller may well be lost in the collective roar of all together. Like injunctions to virtue and warnings of socialism, advertising will beat helplessly on ears that have been conditioned by previous assault to utter immunity. . . . It will be worth no one's while to speak, for since all speak none can hear.[2]

At this point an economy whose level of spending is supported by effective advertising will be plagued by serious instability. If consumer wants and consumer spending are contrived through advertising, the future failure of that contrivance could materially contribute to recession and unemployment.

At least one critic has contended that advertising expenditures are procyclical, that is, they fluctuate *with* total spending, intensifying unemployment during bad times and adding to inflationary pressures during prosperous times.[3]

6. There is evidence that in some industries advertising has become such a large part of the cost of doing business that it constitutes an important financial barrier to entry. This is generally recognized to be the case in the cigarette industry, where producers as a group may spend considerably in excess of $150 million per year on advertising and related promotional activities.

Where do these arguments and counterarguments leave us? Certainly without a clearcut conclusion. However, even though both cases are interspersed with partial truths and arguments that are valid in specific instances but not generally, we are at least in a better position to form a personal judgment upon the social worth of advertising.[4] This much can be ventured: most economists are inclined to conclude that the consumer benefits much more from nonprice competition in the form of product development than he does from advertising.

[2] John K. Galbraith, *The Affluent Society* (Boston: Houghton Mifflin Company, 1958), p. 202.

[3] Alvin H. Hansen, *Economic Issues of the 1960's* (New York: McGraw-Hill Book Company, Inc., 1960), p. 36.

[4] The student who feels compelled to pursue this controversy should compare Vance Packard, *The Hidden Persuaders* (New York: David McKay Company, Inc., 1957), and Steuart Henderson Britt, *The Spenders* (New York: McGraw-Hill Book Company, Inc., 1960).

Monopolistic competition and economic analysis

Our discussion of nonprice competition correctly infers that the equilibrium situation of a monopolistically competitive firm is actually much more complex than the previous graphic analysis indicates. Figure 26-1a, b, and c *assumes* a given product and a given level of advertising expenditures. But, alas, these we now know are not given in practice. The monopolistically competitive firm must actually juggle three variable considerations—price, product, and promotion—in seeking maximum profits. What specific variety of product, selling at what price, and supplemented by what level of promotional activity will result in the greatest level of profits attainable? This complex situation is not readily expressed in a simple, meaningful economic model. At best we can note that each possible combination of price, product, and promotion poses a different demand and cost (production plus promotion) situation for the firm, some one of which will allow him maximum profits. In practice, this optimum combination cannot be readily forecast but must be sought by the process of trial and error. And even here certain limitations may be imposed by the actions of rivals. A firm may not risk the elimination of advertising expenditures for fear his share of the market will decline sharply to the benefit of his rivals who do advertise. Similarly, patents held by rivals will rule out certain choice product variations.

DOES MONOPOLISTIC COMPETITION BREED OLIGOPOLY?

Monopolistic competition presumes a relatively large number of independently acting firms producing differentiated products in a market environment into which entry is relatively easy. Many economists feel that there are few industries in modern American capitalism in which these requirements are strictly fulfilled. Further, in those industries in which monopolistic competition does exist, certain dynamic aspects of this market situation tend to push monopolistic competition in the direction of oligopoly. Let us explain these contentions.

1. Many retail industries which outwardly fulfill the conditions of monopolistic competition are actually much more localized than they appear to be. A city may have forty or fifty grocery stores, but each store is only in direct competition with a *few* nearby rivals. Suburban stores do not compete greatly with their downtown counterparts; northside and southside grocers do not compete, and so forth. This means that, although a large number of firms exist, they are usually subdivided into smaller, *interdependent* groups.

2. Combination has caused monopolistic competition to give ground to oligopoly in some important retail industries. For example, vertical integration by large petroleum producers has pushed the oligopolistic structure of the petroleum industry forward to the retail level. Instead of thirty independent gasoline stations, we now have groups of gasoline stations affiliated with, say, four or five different brands of gasoline. Horizontal combinations in the form of chain stores at the retail level have also had the effect of reducing the number of independent firms in the areas of retail automobile supplies, groceries, and drugs. By, in effect, reducing the number of independent firms these two tendencies give rise to mutual interdependence among sellers—a basic characteristic of oligopoly.

3. Of greatest importance is the belief that nonprice competition is a dynamic facet of monopolistic competition through which such industries evolve into the less competitive market structure of oligopoly. More specifically, it is argued that product development and advertising simultaneously work to reduce the number of firms in monopolistically competitive industries and to create entry barriers which discourage their replacement by new firms. This merits some explanation.

Product differentiation and development can lead to significant entry barriers over time. This is particularly pertinent because product development is likely to be cumulative; that is, a firm which gains a temporary advantage over its rivals through a successful change in its product can employ the resulting profits to finance the research needed to widen that advantage. Temporary product advantages have a tendency to become permanent, to the end that less alert or less fortunate rivals fall by the wayside. All this is reinforced when product variations are significant enough to result in patent and copyright protection. Similarly, if the fruits of successful product variation are used to finance the development of more efficient productive techniques, the resulting economies of scale and lower unit costs provide a basis for eliminating high cost rivals and restricting the entry of new firms.

Advertising may also reduce the number of firms in a monopolistically competitive industry over a span of time. In a few instances some firms may simply "out-advertise" and thereby eliminate their rivals. On the other hand, if the advertising campaigns of monopolistically competitive rivals are largely self-canceling between firms and have little impact upon industry demand, the rising unit costs attributable to advertising may press upon price and eliminate the least efficient firms. Or possibly this price-cost squeeze will precipitate aggressive price cutting—a price war—which will have substantially the same effect. Finally, we have already noted that large advertising budgets can pose a substantial barrier to entry, thereby also undermining a basic characteristic of monopolistic competition.

If these arguments are reasonably accurate, we can conclude that the basic reasons for studying the behavior of monopolistically competitive industries are: (1) a knowledge of such industries provides important information concerning the evolution and growth of oligopoly and (2) many industries in American capitalism blend features of both monopolistic competition and oligopoly. It is with oligopolistic markets that the next chapter is concerned.

SUMMARY

1. The distinguishing features of monopolistic competition are: (*a*) there is a large enough number of firms so that each has little control over price, mutual interdependence is absent, and collusion is virtually impossible; (b) products are characterized by real and imaginary differences and by varying conditions surrounding their sale; and (c) entry to the industry is relatively easy. Many aspects of retailing, and some industries wherein economies of scale are few, approximate monopolistic competition.

2. Monopolistically competitive firms may earn economic profits or incur losses in the short run. The easy entry and exodus of firms gives rise to a long-run tendency for them to earn a normal profit.

3. The monopolistic competitor produces short of the most efficient output and therefore charges a higher-than-competitive price. However, because the firm's demand curve is highly elastic, these "wastes" of monopolistic competition should not be overemphasized.

4. Product differentiation provides a means by which monopolistically competitive firms can offset the long-run tendency for economic profits to approximate zero. Through product development and advertising, a firm may strive to increase the demand for its product more than nonprice competition increases its costs.

5. Although subject to certain dangers and problems, product differentiation affords the consumer a greater variety of products at any point in time and improved products over time. Whether these features fully compensate for the wastes of monopolistic competition is a moot question.

6. There is sharp disagreement as to the economic benefits of advertising. Proponents justify advertising on the grounds that it (a) aids consumers in exercising rational choices, (b) supports national communications, (c) speeds product development, (d) permits firms to realize economies of scale, and (e) encourages spending and a high level of employment. Critics assert that advertising (a) confuses rather than informs, (b) misallocates resources away from more urgent employments (particularly from the production of social goods), (c) involves a variety of social costs, (d) results in higher, not lower, costs and prices, (e) is not a strategic determinant of spending and employment, and (f) often constitutes a significant financial barrier to entry.

7. In practice the monopolistic competitor seeks largely through trial and error that specific combination of price, product, and promotion which will maximize his profits.

8. There is evidence to suggest that monopolistically competitive market situations tend to give way to oligopoly. Product development and advertising may well tend to eliminate existing firms and create barriers to the entry of new ones. Vertical and horizontal combination and the localized nature of retail markets have tended to undermine monopolistic competition in retailing.

QUESTIONS AND STUDY SUGGESTIONS

1. How does monopolistic competition differ from pure competition? From pure monopoly? Explain fully what product differentiation entails.

2. Compare the elasticity of the monopolistically competitive producer's demand curve with that of (a) a pure competitor and (b) a pure monopolist. Assuming identical long-run costs, compare graphically the prices and output which would result under pure competition and monopolistic competition. "Monopolistically competitive industries are characterized by too many firms, each of which produces too little." Explain.

3. "Monopolistic competition is monopoly up to the point at which consumers become willing to buy close substitute products and competitive beyond that point." Explain.

4. What is nonprice competition? "Competition in quality and in service may be quite as effective in giving the buyer more for his money as is price competition." Do you agree? Explain why monopolistically competitive firms frequently prefer nonprice to price competition.

5. Explain: "In the long run monopolistic competition leads to a monopolistic price but not to monopolistic profits."

6. Critically evaluate and explain:

a. "In monopolistically competitive industries economic profits are competed away in the long run; hence, there is no valid reason to criticize the performance and efficiency of such industries."

b. "Monopolistic competition is merely a way station on the road to oligopoly."

7. Do you agree or disagree with the following statements? Why?

a. "The amount of advertising which a firm does is likely to vary inversely with the real differences in its product."

b. "If each firm's advertising expenditures merely tend to cancel the effects of its rivals' advertising, then it is clearly irrational for these firms to maintain large advertising budgets."

8. Carefully evaluate the two views expressed in the following statements:

a. "It happens every day. Advertising builds mass demand. Production goes up— costs come down. More people can buy—more jobs are created. These are the ingredients of economic growth. Each stimulates the next in a cycle of productivity and plenty which constantly creates a better life for you."

b. "Advertising constitutes 'inverted education'—a costly effort to induce people to buy without sufficient thought and deliberation and therefore to buy things they don't need. Furthermore, advertising intensifies economic instability because advertising outlays vary directly with the level of consumer spending. Indeed, by contributing to inflation during prosperous periods, advertising may foster political pressures for the curtailment of government spending on much-needed social goods and services, thereby promoting a misallocation of resources."

Which view do you feel is the more accurate? Justify your position.

SELECTED REFERENCES

Adams, Walter (ed.), *The Structure of American Industry*, 3d ed. (New York: The Macmillan Company, 1961), chap. 2.

Bain, Joe S., *Industrial Organization* (New York: John Wiley & Sons, Inc., 1959), chap. 7.

Bober, M. M., *Intermediate Price and Income Theory*, rev. ed. (New York: W. W. Norton & Company, Inc., 1962), chap. 11.

Due, John F., and Robert W. Clower, *Intermediate Economic Analysis*, 4th ed. (Homewood, Ill.: Richard D. Irwin, Inc., 1961), chap. 10.

McKenna, Joseph P., *Intermediate Economic Theory* (New York: The Dryden Press, Inc., 1958), chap. 11.

Weiss, Leonard W., *Economics and American Industry* (New York: John Wiley & Sons, Inc., 1961), chaps. 4 and 9.

Chapter 27

PRICE AND OUTPUT DETERMINATION:

OLIGOPOLY

IN MANY of the manufacturing, mining, wholesaling, and retailing industries of American capitalism a few firms are dominant. Such industries are called *oligopolies*. It is with such industries that the present chapter is concerned. Specifically, we have four objectives. We seek first to define oligopoly, assess its occurrence, and note the reasons for its existence. The second and major goal is to survey the possible courses of price-output behavior which oligopolistic industries might follow. Third, the role of nonprice competition, that is, competition on the basis of product development and advertising, in oligopolistic industries is discussed. Finally, some comments with respect to the economic efficiency and social desirability of oligopoly are offered.

CONCEPT AND OCCURRENCE
OF OLIGOPOLY

What are the basic characteristics of oligopoly? How frequently is it encountered in American capitalism? Why has this industry structure developed?

The outstanding feature of oligopoly is "fewness." When a relatively small number of firms dominate the market for a good or service, the industry is oligopolistic. But what specifically

is meant by "a few" firms? This is necessarily vague, because the market model of oligopoly covers a great deal of ground, ranging from pure monopoly, on the one hand, to monopolistic competition, on the other. Thus oligopoly encompasses the tin-can industry, in which two firms virtually dominate an entire national market, and the situation in which, say, fifteen or twenty gasoline stations may enjoy roughly equal shares of the petroleum products market in a medium-sized town. Table 8-3 lists a large number of industries in which fewness is present in varying degrees. This table correctly suggests that the market structure of oligopoly is very common in American capitalism. And we remember from Chapter 26 that many aspects of the retail trades are characterized by oligopoly.

Rivalry between a small number of firms interjects a new and complicating factor into our discussion: *mutual interdependence*. Imagine three firms, A, B, and C, each of which has about one-third of the market for a particular product. If A cuts price, its share of the market will increase. But B and C will be directly, immediately, and adversely affected by A's price cutting. Hence, we can expect some *reaction* on the part of B and C to A's behavior: B and C may match A's price cut or even undercut A, thereby precipitating a price war. This correctly suggests that no firm in an oligopolistic industry will dare to alter its price policies without attempting to calculate the most likely reactions of its rivals. To be sure, cost and demand data are important to the oligopolist in establishing price, but to these we must add the reaction of rivals, a highly uncertain factor. The situation faced by oligopolistic producers resembles that of participants in games of strategy such as poker, bridge, or chess. There is no way of knowing beforehand the best way of playing your cards, because this depends upon the way in which other participants play theirs! Each player must pattern his actions according to the actions and expected reactions of his rivals. In recent years economists have sought to develop and apply a "theory of games" to the behavior of oligopolies.[1]

It is to be emphasized that the mutual interdependence resulting from fewness, and the consequent need for a firm to weigh the possible reactions of rivals in altering its price policy, are unique features of oligopoly. The large number of rivals which characterizes pure competition and monopolistic competition and the absence of rivals which is the earmark of pure monopoly rule out mutual interdependence in these market structures. Indeed, a good, workable definition of oligopoly is this: oligopoly exists when the number of firms in an industry is so small that each must consider the reactions of rivals in formulating its price policy.

The existence of a small number of firms correctly suggests that barriers to entry characterize oligopolistic industries. In some oligopolistic industries—for example, automobiles, agricultural machinery, and steel—technological considerations as reflected in economies of large-scale production constitute the basic barrier to entry. Many industries start out with

[1] The interested reader should consult two informative and delightful books on the subject: John D. Williams, *The Compleat Strategyst* (New York: McGraw-Hill Book Company, Inc., 1954), and John McDonald, *Strategy in Poker, Business and War* (New York: W. W. Norton & Company, Inc., 1950).

a large number of firms, but then as technology improves, each firm attempts to expand in order to achieve the lower costs which economies of scale provide. For example, estimates suggest that as many as 70 to 80 firms populated the automobile industry in its infancy. Then the introduction of mass production techniques reduced the field through failure and combination. Now the automobile industry is comprised of the Big Three and the Little Two. The existence of other oligopolies, for example, the electronics, chemical, and aluminum industries, is grounded basically upon the ownership of patents or the control of strategic raw materials. Less frequently the advantages of being established as reflected particularly in prodigious advertising outlays may present a significant financial obstacle to entry. The cigarette industry is the classic illustration.

Finally, oligopolies may produce either standardized or differentiated products. Many industrial products—steel, zinc, copper, aluminum, lead, cement, industrial alcohol, and so forth—are virtually standardized products in the physical sense and are produced under oligopolistic conditions. Of course, even here slight physical differences may exist, and the service, credit, and speed of delivery may differ between sellers, making for a measure of differentiation. But for most practical purposes these are standardized products. On the other hand, many consumer goods industries—automobiles, tires, typewriters, petroleum products, soap, cigarettes, fountain pens, and a host of electrical appliances—are differentiated oligopolies.

PRICE DETERMINATION

Now at first glance one might suspect that price-output determination similar to that of a pure monopoly would be applicable to an oligopolistic firm. The only notable difference might be that the oligopolist's sales curve would be somewhat more elastic, because he is plagued by a few close substitute goods, while the pure monopolist faces no good substitutes at all. Marginal cost and marginal revenue comparisons would then determine the profit-maximizing output and the unique price at which this output could be sold. Unfortunately, this is too simple a picture of the situation. Indeed, more and more economists are reluctantly coming to the conclusion that formal economic theory simply does not take us very far in explaining the price-output policies of oligopolies.

There are two major reasons why it is difficult to use formal economic analysis in explaining the price behavior of oligopolies.

1. The previously noted fact that oligopoly encompasses many specific market situations works against the development of a single, generalized explanation or model of how an oligopoly determines price and output. Pure competition, monopolistic competition, and pure monopoly all refer to rather clear-cut market arrangements; oligopoly does not. It includes the situation in which two or three firms dominate an entire market as well as the market in which twelve or fifteen firms compete. It includes both product differentiation and standardization. It encompasses the situations in which firms are acting in collusion and in which they are not. It embodies the situations in which barriers to entry are very strong and in which they are not quite so strong. In short, the many breeds, or strains, of oligopoly work against the development of any simple market model which provides a general explanation of oligopolistic behavior.

2. The element of mutual interdependence which fewness adds to the analysis is a most significant complication. To be specific, the inability of a firm to predict with certainty the reactions of its rivals makes it virtually impossible to estimate the demand and marginal revenue data faced by an oligopolist. And without such data firms cannot determine their profit-maximizing price and output even in theory, as we shall presently make clear.

Despite these analytical difficulties, two interrelated characteristics of oligopolistic pricing stand out. On the one hand, oligopolistic prices tend to be inflexible, or "sticky." Prices change less frequently in oligopoly than they do under pure competition, monopolistic competition, and, in some instances, pure monopoly. Figure 11-4 provides some interesting data on this point. On the other hand, when oligopolistic prices do change, firms are likely to change their prices together. There is a decided absence of price competition in most oligopolistic industries. However, when price competition does occasionally break out, it is likely to take the form of aggressive price warring.

Let us now explore several oligopolistic pricing policies to help explain these introductory comments.

"Independent action" and price inflexibility

Again suppose an oligopolistic industry comprised of just three firms, A, B, and C, each having about one-third of the total market for a differentiated product. Assume the firms are "independent" in the sense that they do not engage in collusive practices in setting prices. Suppose, too, that the going price for firm A's product is QP and its current sales are Q, as shown in Figure 27-1. Now the question is "What does the firm's demand, or sales, curve look like?" We have just noted that mutual interdependence and the uncertainty of rivals' reactions which it entails make this question difficult to answer. The location and shape of an oligopolist's demand curve depends upon how the firm's rivals will react to a price change introduced by A. There are two plausible assumptions about the reactions of A's rivals with which we might experiment.

One possibility is that firms B and C will exactly match any price change initiated by A. In this case A's demand and marginal revenue curves will look something like D_1D_1 and MR_1MR_1 in Figure 27-1. If A cuts price, its sales will increase very modestly, because its two rivals will follow suit and thereby prevent A from gaining any price advantage on them. The small increase in sales which A (and its two rivals) will realize is at the expense of other industries; A will gain no sales from B and C. If A raises the going price, its sales will fall only modestly. Why? Because B and C match its price increase, so that A does not price itself out of the market. The industry now loses some

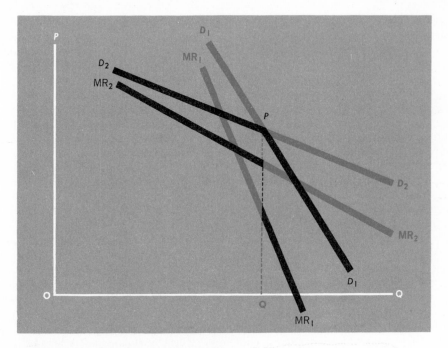

FIGURE 27-1. THE KINKED DEMAND CURVE.
The nature of an oligopolist's demand and marginal revenue curves will depend upon whether his rivals will match (D_1D_1 and MR_1MR_1) or ignore (D_2D_2 and MR_2MR_2) any price changes which he may initiate from the current price QP. In all likelihood an oligopolist's rivals will ignore a price increase but follow a price cut. This causes the oligopolist's demand curve to be kinked (as D_2PD_1) and his marginal revenue curve to have a vertical break, or gap (as black MR_2MR_1).

sales to other industries, but A loses no customers to B and C.

The other obvious possibility is that firms B and C will simply ignore any price change invoked by A. In this case the demand and marginal revenue curves faced by A will resemble D_2D_2 and MR_2MR_2 in Figure 27-1. The demand curve in this case is considerably more elastic than under the assumption that B and C will match A's price changes. The reasons are clear. If A lowers its price and its rivals do not, A will gain sales sharply at the expense of its two rivals because it will obviously be underselling them. Conversely, if A raises price and its rivals do not, A will be pricing itself out of the market and will lose many customers to B and C, which are now underselling it. Because

of product differentiation, however, A's sales do not fall to zero when it raises price; some of A's customers will pay the higher price because they have strong preferences for A's product.

Now, which is the most logical assumption for A to make as to how its rivals will react to any price change it might initiate? The answer is "some of each"! Common sense and observation of oligopolistic industries suggest that price declines will be matched as a firm's competitors act to prevent the price cutter from taking their customers, but that price increases will be ignored, because rivals of the price-increasing firm stand to gain the business lost by the price booster. In other words, the D_2P segment of the "rivals ignore" demand curve seems relevant for price increases, and the PD_1

segment of the "rivals follow" demand curve is more realistic for price cuts. It is logical, or at least a good guess, that an oligopolist's demand curve is "kinked" on the order of D_2PD_1. The curve is highly elastic above the going price but much less elastic or even inelastic below the current price. Note, too, that if it is correct to suppose that rivals will follow a price cut but ignore an increase, the marginal revenue curve of the oligopolist will also have an odd shape. It, too, will be made up of two segments —a part of the marginal revenue curve appropriate to D_1D_1 and a chunk of the marginal revenue curve appropriate to D_2D_2. Because of the sharp differences in elasticity of demand above and below the going price, there occurs a gap, or what we can treat as a vertical segment, in the marginal revenue curve. In Figure 27-1 the marginal revenue curve is shown by the two black lines connected by the dotted vertical segment, or gap.

This analysis is important in that it goes far to explain why price changes are infrequent in noncollusive oligopolistic industries. On the one hand, the kinked demand schedule gives each oligopolist good reason to believe that any change in price will be for the worse. A firm's customers will desert it in quantity if it raises price. If it lowers price, its sales at best will increase very modestly. Even if a price cut increases its total revenue somewhat, the oligopolist's costs may well increase by a more-than-offsetting amount. Should the PD_1 segment of its sales schedule be inelastic in that E_d is less than 1, the firm's profits will surely fall. A price decrease will lower the firm's total receipts, and the production of a somewhat larger output will increase total costs. Worse yet, a price cut by A may be *more than* met by B and C. That is, A's initial price cut may precipitate a price war, so that the amount sold by A may actually decline as its rival firms charge still lower prices. These are all good reasons on the demand side of the picture why noncollusive oligopolies might seek "the quiet life" and follow live-and-let-live and don't-upset-the-apple-cart price policies.

A second reason for price inflexibility under noncollusive oligopoly works from the cost side of the picture. The broken marginal revenue curve which accompanies the kinked demand curve suggests that within limits substantial cost changes will have no effect upon output and price. To be specific, any shift in marginal cost between MC_1 and MC_2 as shown in Figure 27-2 will result in no change in price or output, because the oligopolist fears a price war, on the one hand, and pricing himself out of the market, on the other.

All this is not to say that the prices of non-collusive oligopolists are completely inflexible, but rather that they are likely to change only when significant and mutually applicable cost changes occur. For example, price adjustments may await wage, tax, or interest rate increases which collective bargaining or government imposes uniformly upon the firms. Knowing its rivals are also afflicted with these cost increases, each firm boosts price with considerable certainty that each and every rival will follow suit. This shifts the entire kinked demand curve and the going price upward. The practice of linking price increases to wage or tax hikes has the further advantage of shielding oligopolies from public criticism. To many the price increase— even if in excess of cost increases—will clearly seem the fault of irresponsible unions and the insatiable appetite of government for tax revenues.

The astute reader will undoubtedly have detected a crucial shortcoming of our kinked demand analysis: it simply does not explain how the going price gets to be at PQ in the first place. Rather it merely helps to explain why oligopolists may be reluctant to deviate from any existing price which yields them a "satisfactory" or "reasonable" profit. The kinked demand curve explains price inflexibility but not price itself.

The kinked demand situation described above may be decidedly unappealing to oligopolists. It is surrounded by an air of uncertainty. Although there may be a strong disposition towards price stability, the possibility always does exist that a firm may shade its price to expand its share of the market and thereby precipitate disastrous rounds of price cutting. This is particularly likely if firms have excess capacity due to, say, a general business recession; under these circumstances a firm can

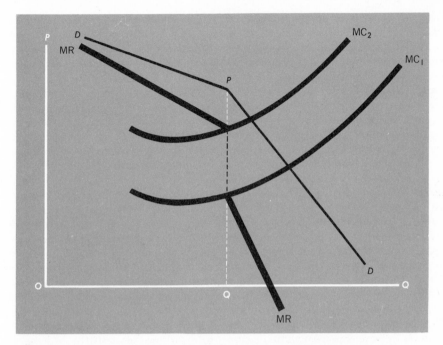

FIGURE 27-2. COST CHANGES AND PRICE STABILITY UNDER OLIGOPOLY.
The kinked demand curve *DPD* and the accompanying broken marginal revenue curve
MRMR help explain the price inflexibility which characterizes oligopoly. Because any
shift in marginal costs between MC_1 and MC_2 will cut the vertical (dotted) segment
of the marginal revenue curve, no change in either price QP or in output Q will occur.

lower unit costs by increasing its market share. Then, too, the possibility is always present that new firms may surmount barriers to entry and initiate aggressive price cutting to gain a foothold in the market. In addition, the tendency toward rigid prices may adversely affect profits if general inflationary pressures increase costs. All this is conducive to the establishment of some sort of collusive action by oligopolists as a means of avoiding disastrous price warring, on the one hand, and of achieving orderly price increases, on the other.

Formal collusion

There are many forms of collusion. At one extreme a number of oligopolistic firms may form a *cartel*. Under this arrangement firms may enter into a formal written agreement which fixes product price and divides the market, the latter possibly on a geographic basis. In the United States such an arrangement is clearly at odds with our antitrust laws and, hence, a most rare occurrence.

Somewhat less formal *gentlemen's agreements* undoubtedly enjoy greater currency in American capitalism. Such agreements arise when competing oligopolists reach a verbal agreements on product price, market shares almost invariably being left to the ingenuity of each seller as reflected in nonprice competition. Gentlemen's agreements arise at trade conventions, on the golf course, or at cocktail parties, not in a lawyer's office. Although they too collide with the antitrust laws, their *sub rosa* and intangible character make them more difficult to detect and prosecute successfully.[2]

[2] For a fascinating case study of collusive pricing read Richard Austin Smith, "The Incredible Electrical Conspiracy," *Fortune*, April and May, 1961.

What will be the economic consequences of a gentlemen's agreement? Assuming the entry of new firms is blocked, the price-output consequences of a gentlemen's agreement are likely to be very much like those of a pure monopoly. Output will be restricted in the interest of maximizing profits for the several firms, and this will mean higher prices and underutilized plants. As a matter of fact, the price-output results of collusive oligopoly may from the consumer's standpoint be inferior to those of pure monopoly for several reasons.

1. Pure monopoly in the United States is almost invariably subject to government regulation to mitigate abuses of such market power. A *sub rosa* gentleman's agreement may create an approximation of pure monopoly, yet it maintains the outward appearance of several independent and "competing" firms.

2. It is possible that the existence of several distinct oligopolistic producers will cause the industry and society to forgo some economies of scale which those firms, combined as a pure monopoly, could realize. For example, a multiplant pure monopolist can ship to customers from that plant which is closest to the buyer. But under a gentlemen's agreement on price, wasteful crosshauling may result. The oligopolist located in California ships to a customer in New Jersey, while the New York oligopolist ships to an Oregon buyer.

3. Collusive oligopolists may engage in extensive competitive advertising and sales promotion which is of little benefit to the public. This is particularly so when products are differentiated. Under pure monopoly this would be largely, if not fully, eliminated.

4. Because price agreements are difficult to negotiate, oligopolists may be inclined to maintain the existing agreed-upon price even though cost-reducing technological advances would make it profitable for the firms to lower this price. Fearing the inability to reach precise agreement on a new and lower price and a possible breakdown of the gentlemen's agreement, the firms may simply let well enough alone and accept a less-than-maximum profit. This will mean that consumers are deprived of the lower price and the greater output that

lower unit costs now justify. The pure monopolist, unhampered by the problem of price negotiation with rivals, would cut price and increase output to his own benefit and to the benefit of consumers.[3]

Informal, tacit collusion

The illegality of gentlemen's agreements has prompted many oligopolistic industries to seek still less formal means of avoiding the uncertainties of independent, noncollusive action. Many important American industries have long followed the practice of *price leadership,* that is, one firm—usually the largest in the industry—initiates price changes, and all other firms more or less automatically follow that price change. In some cases—for example, the oil and cigarette industries—the identity of the price leader may vary over time, while in other industries—the steel industry—a single firm may persistently enjoy the position of price leader. The importance of price leadership is evidenced in the fact that such industries as farm machinery, anthracite coal, cement, copper, gasoline, newsprint, tin cans, lead, sulfur, rayon, fertilizer, glass containers, and nonferrous metals are practicing or have in the recent past practiced price leadership. Because price leadership is an informal, tacit agreement involving no written or spoken commitments, it is generally accepted as a legal technique by the courts in interpreting the antitrust laws.

Why do firms follow the leader? There is no simple answer here. On the one hand, the situation clearly obligates smaller firms to do so. Followers are obliged to match a price cut, or they will loses sales to the price leader. They must match price increases or else find themselves in effect in the position of a price cutter and exposed to the unhappy prospect of provoking a price war with the price leader. An intermixture of custom and convenience also

[3] It must be acknowledged that arguments 2 and 4 are reversible; that is, the combining of several oligopolists into a pure monopoly may lead to *dis*economies of scale, and it is more certain that cost increases will cause *higher* prices and greater output restriction with pure monopoly than with oligopoly.

helps to explain price leadership. In some industries the practice has achieved the status of a deeply ingrained custom which is accepted by all participants with little or no question. Then, too, small followers may be ill-equipped to determine their present and estimate their future cost and demand situations; hence they find it convenient to follow the estimates and the judgment of the price leader on these matters. If the price set by the leader yields a reasonable profit for the followers, the latter are not likely to stray from the price leadership pattern. The belief is professed by followers in many industries that profits will be greater in the long run under price leadership than could be obtained under alternative pricing arrangements. In other words, price leadership largely avoids the uncertainties of independent pricing and, at the same time, usually results in substantial profits for both leader and followers.

A final question remains: How will the price leader determine price? If the position of the price leader is well established, chances are good that he will seek out the price he feels will maximize his own profits. If the price leader's position is less secure or he is of a benevolent nature, he may seek a price which is mutually satisfactory to price followers and therefore unlikely to upset the price leadership arrangement. And, too, the price leader may be subject to restraints similar to those facing the pure monopolist. Price must not be "too high" or new rivals will enter, or adverse public opinion and governmental interference may be induced.

Multiproduct firms and cost-plus prices

Thus far our discussion of price and output determination has proceeded on the assumption that each oligopolistic firm produces a single product. In practice, this is the exception, not the rule. Most oligopolistic manufacturers produce a variety of products. And this is not merely a matter of one major product being supplemented by a number of side-line products. To illustrate: besides producing about half the nation's passenger cars, General Motors is listed in government reports as one of the four largest companies in some twenty-three different lines of production including diesel engines, trucks, buses, railroad locomotives, bicycles, aircraft engines and propellers, household refrigerators, electric ranges, storage batteries, cast iron heating boilers, and air-conditioning equipment.[4] There are some manufacturers that produce literally hundreds and others thousands of separate products.

Motives for product proliferation. A moment's reflection reveals several good reasons for this proliferation of products by manufacturers.

1. In some cases the same productive process necessarily turns out several different products; some products are *joint products.* Meat-packing concerns necessarily produce a variety of products ranging from fillets and frankfurters to hides, glue, fertilizers, and pharmaceuticals. Gasoline and kerosene both result from the process of cracking petroleum; coke and gas are jointly created in the distillation of coal.

2. Firms seek product diversification to lessen the effects of fluctuations in demand. The local coal dealer sells ice in the summer and the furnace manufacturer produces air conditioners to lessen seasonal variations in demand. Automobile manufacturers would be more significantly affected by cyclical fluctuations in consumer spending were it not for the fact that they produce a variety of makes and models. Specifically, the demand for the low-priced models holds up better during recession than does that for luxury models.

3. The long-run quest for profits also induces product proliferation. A firm which now has a decided advantage over rivals in the production of a given product will likely find that that advantage and the accompanying profits will decline over time as competitors successfully imitate or duplicate the product. It thus behooves each firm to develop new products as a means of sustaining profits. To this it must be added that a firm is more likely to incur adverse public opinion and risk an antitrust suit by expanding its share of the market for a given

[4] Senate Committee on the Judiciary, *Administered Prices: Automobiles* (Nov. 1, 1958), pp. 25–28.

product than it will by channeling its efforts to the production of other existing products or the development of new products.[5]

4. Product diversification is also a means by which a firm can more fully utilize its plant capacity. At any point in time excess plant capacity is likely to plague oligopolistic producers as a result of the tendency of such firms to restrict output in order to realize economic profits. It is tempting for a firm thus situated to devote its excess capacity to some related product to which its capital facilities are adaptable. A television manufacturer, for example, may have excess plant capacity because fuller utilization in television set production would call for lower prices (and hence the risk of price warring) and lower profits. The firm therefore uses its excess facilities to produce radios, electric clocks, and parts for radar equipment. Incidentally, a firm's research department is in effect a part of its plant capacity. Failure to produce any promising new products which this department develops will obviously mean it is underutilized.

Complexities of multiproduct pricing. For reasons already noted, it may be difficult for a single-product firm to practice marginal-cost-equals-marginal-revenue pricing. The task is virtually impossible for the multiproduct firm. This is partially so for the obvious reason that there are so many more prices to be determined and then redetermined when cost and revenue conditions change. But complex problems also arise because it is difficult for a multiproduct firm to allocate its costs accurately among the many specific products it produces. Some costs are *separable* costs; that is, they can be associated with the production of specific products. For example, labor and materials used exclusively in the production of a specific product are separable costs. These pose no great problem. But other costs—costs which we have previously classified both as fixed and variable —are *common* costs; that is, they are costs

which are associated with the firm's many products as a group. Most fixed costs will be common costs: rental payments, salaries of management, some depreciation charges, interest charges, and insurance costs are good illustrations. And some variable costs will be common costs: the materials and labor used in the production of joint products are examples. How is the cost of a steer to be apportioned among the many meat products, the hide, the fertilizer, and the pharmaceuticals which will result from its slaughter? What about the cost of the labor employed in the rendering process? Because there is no precise way to allocate variable common costs among specific products, it is impossible to calculate the marginal costs of these many products.

Multiproduct pricing poses a second problem: product proliferation contains the seeds of price warring. Unless oligopolistic firms allocate common costs to the various products in some more or less uniform way, they will establish significantly different costs and hence different prices on their products. But under oligopoly, firms producing high-priced products will of necessity be forced to meet the lower prices of competitors. To illustrate: Firm A charges a low price on its refrigerators and a high price on its air conditioners because it has arbitrarily apportioned most of its common costs to its air conditioners. Firm B, however, has arbitrarily allocated most of its common costs to refrigerators and therefore charges a high price for refrigerators and a low price for air conditioners. This means that A will have to cut its air-conditioner price to meet B's and, conversely, B will need to slice its refrigerator prices to meet A's low prices. Price cutting and possibly price warring will result in this situation. To the benefit of consumers and the dismay of producers such aggressive price competition, caused by nonuniform allocations of common costs, may result in losses for both firms.

Cost-plus pricing. To circumvent both these problems oligopolistic multiproduct firms very frequently employ cost-plus pricing. There are two basic steps in this pricing technique.[6] First,

[5] See A. D. H. Kaplan, *Big Enterprise in a Competitive System* (Washington: Brookings Institution, 1954), pp. 187–188.

the firm simply estimates the separable costs per unit on its various products when it is producing at some average or typical rate of output, for example, two-thirds or three-fourths of capacity. The resulting figure is the "standard cost" of the product. Second, price is determined by adding some "markup," or "margin," to the standard cost figure to allow for common costs and a "fair," or "reasonable," profit. To illustrate: if the standard cost of product X is estimated to be $10 and the markup is 20 per cent, the product's price will be set at $12.

Though cost-plus pricing may be an accurate picture of how many multiproduct businesses set prices, it is not a very satisfactory theory of oligopolistic pricing, because it does not explain why the markup is 10, 15, 25, or 35 per cent. In many instances the markup is "customary"; that is, it is a figure which has been evolved through trial-and-error experimentation by the industry and which seems to yield a satisfactory profit to firms.

The simplicity of this rule-of-thumb pricing technique need hardly be elaborated. Cost-plus pricing is a workable and expedient means of price determination. However, its usefulness as a means of avoiding oligopolistic price warring is not quite so evident. If a group of oligopolists employ essentially the same productive techniques, as is often the case, the application of cost-plus pricing will provide each firm with approximately the same standard cost figure. The application of a common markup figure which is customary to the industry will then result in identical or at least very similar prices. In other words, cost-plus pricing is a means by which multiproduct oligopolists can successfully avoid price competition and price warring. When a group of firms employ standard or similar cost accounting techniques and apply

the same markup figure to the resulting standard cost estimates, they have at their disposal, in the form of cost-plus pricing, a subtle and tacit technique of price collusion.

BASIC ROLE OF NONPRICE COMPETITION

We have noted that, for several reasons, oligopolists have a notable aversion to price competition. This aversion may lead to some more or less informal type of collusion on price. In the United States, however, price collusion is usually accompanied by nonprice competition. It is typically through nonprice competition that each firm's share of the total market is determined. This emphasis upon nonprice competition has its roots in two basic facts.

1. Price cuts can be quickly and easily met by a firm's rivals. Because of this the possibility of significantly increasing one's share of the market through price competition is small; rivals will promptly cancel any potential gain in sales by matching price cuts. And, of course, the risk is always present that price competition will precipitate disastrous price warring. More positively stated, oligopolists seem to feel that more permanent advantages can be gained over rivals through nonprice competition, because product variations, improvements in productive techniques, and successful advertising gimmicks cannot be duplicated so quickly and so completely as can price reductions. And there is less likelihood of nonprice competition forcing all firms to the wall profitwise in the manner of unbridled price competition. Nonprice competition is less likely to get out of hand. It might be added that many oligopolistic producers of consumer goods apparently are of the opinion that consumers are more product- and advertising-conscious than they are price-conscious.

2. There is a more obvious reason for the tremendous emphasis which oligopolists put upon nonprice competition: manufacturing oligopolists are typically blessed with substantial financial resources with which to support advertising and product development. Hence, although nonprice competition is a basic char-

---

[6] There are many variations of and qualifications to the simple technique here explained. The interested reader is referred to Joel Dean, *Managerial Economics* (Englewood Cliffs, N.J.: Prentice-Hall, Inc., 1951), pp. 444–457, and Milton H. Spencer and Louis Siegelman, *Managerial Economics* (Homewood, Ill.: Richard D. Irwin, Inc., 1959), p. 292f.

acteristic of both monopolistically competitive and oligopolistic industries, the latter are in a financial position to indulge more fully.

We need not restate the pros and cons of advertising. The arguments stated in Chapter 26 with respect to advertising under monopolistic competition are substantially pertinent when applied to oligopoly. However, the implications of the rather prodigious outlays which manufacturing oligopolies frequently make for technological research on both product quality and productive techniques are a matter of major concern.

OLIGOPOLY AND ECONOMIC EFFICIENCY

The troublesomeness of evaluating the economic efficiency of oligopoly is matched only by the importance of such an evaluation. The root difficulty is that of deciding whether it is more realistic to look at the probable effects of oligopoly in a short-run (static) or in a long-run (dynamic) environment.

Restrictive oligopoly

The more or less traditional view holds that, because oligopoly is close to pure monopoly in structure, we should expect it to operate in a similar way. Being characterized by barriers to entry, oligopoly can be expected, according to this view, to result in a restriction of output short of the point of lowest unit costs and a corresponding market price which yields substantial, if not maximum, economic profits. These points usually rest upon an analysis similar to that shown in Figure 27-3a. Facing a *given* demand and a *given* cost situation, the oligopolist will find that it pays him to be restrictive. As indicated in Figure 27-3a, higher unit costs will soon arise if output is expanded far beyond Q_1, and the lowering of price which such an expansion requires courts the disaster of a price war. Other things being equal, the price and output results under such an oligopoly would be clearly inferior to those of pure competition. Worse yet, for reasons noted earlier, the results of oligopoly might even be inferior to those of a pure monopoly. If pure monopoly

impairs the efficient allocation of resources, so then does oligopoly.

At the level of macroeconomics we have previously noted that cost-push and structural inflation are based upon the existence of market power. Therefore, oligopoly may also be criticized as a potential source of inflationary pressure.

Progressive oligopoly

The above view of oligopoly seems at odds with the historical facts surrounding the operation of many oligopolistic manufacturing industries such as the automobile, farm equipment, electronics, home appliance, and steel industries. These industries have been characterized by falling product prices, improvements in product quality, and expanding levels of output and employment over a period of years. But caution is required here. The basic issue is whether this progress would have been even greater had these industries been organized on a purely competitive basis. And, lacking the ability to conduct controlled laboratory experiments, the economist cannot offer a clear-cut answer. It is evident, however, that there has been significant progress in some oligopolistic industries, and the possibility does exist that in the long run some oligopolistic industries may well have fostered lower unit costs, lower prices, and a greater output than the same industry would have provided if organized competitively. Graphically, the restrictive situation portrayed in Figure 27-3a may give way over time to the progressive situation reflected in Figure 27-3b wherein demand and output have been substantially increased and unit cost and price reduced as compared to Figure 27-3a.

Technological progress: the argument. Generally speaking, the reasons for this possible progressiveness lie in the fact that many oligopolistic industries focus their competitive energies upon technological competition as reflected in both the development of productive techniques and improvement of product quality. The betterment of productive techniques will have the effect of expanding the range of constant or,

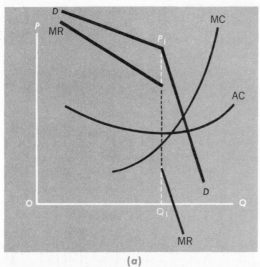

(a)

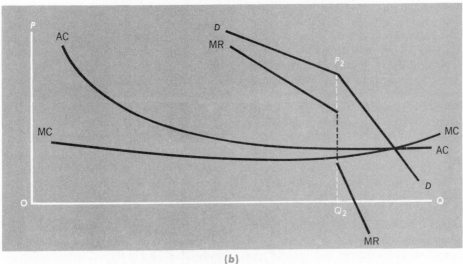

(b)

FIGURE 27-3. RESTRICTIVE AND PROGRESSIVE OLIGOPOLY.
Restrictive oligopoly (a): Faced with given demand and marginal revenue data (such
as DP_1D and MRMR) and given cost data (such as AC and MC), the oligopolist will
maximize profits by restricting output to Q_1 and charging price Q_1P_1. In expanding
output beyond Q_1 the oligopolist must accept considerable price reductions and run
the risk of starting a price war. Furthermore, by the expanding output the producer
may soon encounter rising average costs AC.

Progressive oligopoly (b): In fact many oligopolists have been progressive, achieving
lower average costs AC and marginal costs MC through technological advance. Similarly, demand DP_2D and marginal revenue MRMR have been pushed far to the right
as a result of product development and want-creating activities. As compared to the
restrictive oligopoly of (a), the net result of progressive oligopoly has frequently
been a larger output (Q_2 as compared to Q_1) and a lower price (Q_2P_2 as compared to
Q_1P_1).

517

better yet, declining unit costs. Advances in product quality, accompanied by advertising and related want-creating activities, will shift the firm's demand curve to the right. As indicated in Figure 27-3b, product price is very likely to decline with declines in unit costs.

At present there is a rather widely held presumption that modern oligopolies have both greater means and a stronger inclination for technological advance than does any other market structure. Let us summarize the arguments underlying this presumption and then test them against such statistical data as are available.

First, oligopolies typically possess the *means*—substantial profits—with which to undertake the incredibly expensive task of modern research. Technological progress, it is contended, is no longer in the domain of the back-yard Edison or the basement Whitney. Rather it is the result of highly organized and co-operative efforts of a variety of scientists and engineers housed in the elaborate research departments of such giant oligopolies as du Pont and General Electric. Purely and monopolistically competitive firms, being smaller and less prosperous, are decidedly less progressive.

Second, oligopolistic producers have a host of good *incentives* for accelerating technological advance:

1. Given their disposition to avoid price competition, technological, or cost, competition provides an obvious alternative means for enlarging total profits through an expanded product demand and lower unit costs. Like advertising and product development, the discovery of more efficient productive techniques is less certainly and less quickly matched by one's rivals than is a price cut.

2. Technological superiority is a basic means by which an oligopolist can ensure survival in the event that a price war should somehow plague the quiet life of the industry.

3. In contrast to an unrivaled, pure monopolist, the presence of several strong rivals puts the oligopolist under considerable pressure to seek maximum productive efficiency. Failure to do so may mean that his several competitors may in time drive him out of business. The

pure monopolist, being devoid of rivals, is under no competitive spur to technical progress. But the oligopolist, though with few rivals, clearly is in an environment of technological competition.

4. The existence of barriers to entry gives the progressive oligopolist some assurance that he will actually realize the profit rewards to which his research expenditures may give rise. This is in contrast to a monopolistically competitive market, wherein the rewards of a new productive technique will be shared by many competitors who will quickly copy or imitate a progressive firm without bearing any of the research and development costs. And the presence of a large number of rivals will hasten price reductions to consumers, based upon the cost reductions stemming from the advance. The presence of fewer rivals and the proclivity of oligopolists not to cut price enhance the possibility of the innovating oligopolist's realizing greater profit rewards from his technological progress. The importance of this point is evident in an economy such as American capitalism, wherein the basic drive wheel is profits.

Technological progress: the evidence.[7] Such data as are available do considerable damage to the image of the oligopolistic industry as a mainspring of research and development activity. Available statistics suggest that the research laboratories of giant corporate oligopolies are *not* the fountainhead of technological advance. A recent study[8] of 61 important inventions made since 1900 indicates that over half were the work of independent inventors, quite disassociated from the industrial research laboratories of corporate enterprise. Such substantial advances as air conditioning, power steering, cellophane, the jet engine, insulin, the helicopter, and the catalytic cracking of petroleum have

[7] This section draws heavily upon Daniel Hamberg, "Size of Firm, Monopoly, and Economic Growth," in *Employment, Growth, and Price Levels, Hearings of the Joint Economic Committee, Part 7* (Washington: Government Printing Office, 1959), pp. 2337-2352.

[8] John Jewkes, David Sawers, and Richard Stillerman, *The Sources of Invention* (New York: St Martin's Press, Inc., 1958).

this individualistic heritage. Other equally important advances have been provided by small- and medium-sized firms. According to this study, about two-thirds—40 out of 61—of the basic inventions of this century have been fathered by independent inventors or the research activities of relatively small firms. Other studies—for example, analyses of patent statistics—reinforce the conclusion that a large proportion of basic technological advances originates outside the laboratories of giant oligopolies.

This, of course, is the over-all picture and does not in any way repudiate the fact that in a number of oligopolistic industries—for example, the aircraft, chemical, petroleum, and electrical equipment industries—research activity has been pursued vigorously, fruitfully, and on an expanding scale. But even here we must amend at least two important qualifications. In the first place, there are a number of other oligopolistic industries wherein it is generally agreed that the interest in research and development activity has been modest at best; the steel, cigarette, and aluminum industries are cases in point. Secondly, a very substantial portion of the research carried on by oligopolistic industries is actually financed with public funds. For example, about 85 per cent of the research performed in the aircraft industry is government sponsored, over 60 per cent in the electrical equipment industry, 54 per cent in the communications industry, and so forth. Despite the increased interest of businesses, the Federal government remains the most important source of funds for research and development activity.

Countervailing power. There is a second consideration which brightens somewhat the traditional dim view of oligopoly. John K. Galbraith of Harvard has recently developed the notion that many oligopolies (and monopolies) tend to induce the development of oligopolies (and monopolies) on the opposite side of the market.[9] That is, the existence of a monopolistic (or oligopolistic) seller tends to stimulate the growth of a monopsonistic (or oligopsonistic) buyer and

[9] John Kenneth Galbraith, *American Capitalism,* rev. ed. (Boston: Houghton Mifflin Company, 1956), particularly chap. 9.

vice versa. More specifically, there is a tendency for "countervailing power" to evolve on the opposite side of those markets in which strong positions of "original power" have already developed. The development of countervailing power is not a matter of chance. It stems, on the one hand, from the desire of resource suppliers or customers to protect themselves from any abuses of the original-power position and, on the other hand, from the desire to share in the profits of the original-power position. Stated differently, for both defensive and offensive reasons, countervailing power is self-generating. Oligopoly begets oligopoly on the opposite side of the market. Oligopoly, in effect, generates its own antidote.

The significance of countervailing power is implicit in the concept itself. Countervailing power, or "across-the-market" competition, can be an important competitive force in those very markets in which "same-side-of-the-market" rivalry is weak. Oligopolistic sellers may be restrained by a few large buyers. The Big Four of the tire industry face the Big Three of the automobile industry; chain grocery stores and mail order houses buy in quantity from oligopolistic food processors and manufacturers. Oligopsonistic buyers may be faced with a small number of sellers. Labor unions face gigantic employers; agricultural marketing cooperatives sell to large food processors. Now, to the degree that these opposed positions of market power are successful in checking or restraining the power of one another, the successful operation of a market system characterized by oligopoly will be furthered. Buyer and seller may cancel the power and negate the potential market abuses of one another. The monopolistic seller who seeks a high monopolistic price is faced with a monopsonistic buyer who obviously is interested in a low monopsonistic price. That is, each seeks to use his market power to raise or depress price to his own advantage. The market power of each may be largely self-canceling, and the resulting compromise price close to the competitive level. Furthermore, given the compromise price, the monopolist will have no incentive to restrict his output and sales as he would be obligated to do in establishing a monopolistic price. Thus the net result of monopoly on both sides of the market may be a price and output closer to those of pure competition than if monopoly existed on only one side of the market. This is true of oligopoly as well. Countervailing power is an important regulatory force in American capitalism and makes the economy more competitive than any discussion limited to same-side-of-the-market competition would lead one to conclude.

Countervailing power, however, is not devoid of shortcomings and criticisms. One shortcoming is that it is not universally present. In the automobile industry, for example, dealers are highly dependent upon manufacturers and thus in a poor position to bargain for lower automobile prices which may benefit both themselves and consumers. In other cases—for example, the petroleum industry—manufacturers are integrated down to the consumer, thus excluding the possibility of countervailing power. Because the residential construction industry is composed of thousands of small and unorganized contractors, no countervailing power is exerted against oligopolistic suppliers of building materials.

Even where countervailing power is firmly established, it does not function with equal effectiveness under all economic conditions. In particular, during periods of inflation countervailing power does not operate effectively as a competitive force, because with excess demand buyers are no longer able to restrain sellers. When a resource buyer enjoys a seller's market for his product, he is not apt to offer stiff resistance to the demands of resource suppliers. This is best exemplified in the labor market, where unions as "sellers" of labor are in a most strategic position in bargaining with employers during inflation. Management does not want to risk a work stoppage when consumer demand is burgeoning. Why resist? Increases in wage costs (and more) can be readily passed on to the consumer through price increases with no loss of sales, and profits thereby can be maintained or even expanded. The results of this situation are anything but socially desirable.

Finally, it has been pointed out that the two power positions may both benefit at the expense of the rest of the economy by combining their forces rather than by offsetting one another. Across-the-market rivals may find mutual advantages in collusive action or outright merger rather than in expending their energies in negating the market power of one another.

Oligopoly: tentative appraisal

Having surveyed these two viewpoints, what, if anything, can we conclude about the economic efficiency of oligopolistic industries? Not much more than this: assuming *given* long-run costs of production, an oligopolistic industry will produce less, provide fewer jobs, and charge a higher product price than would the same industry organized competitively. But to the extent that oligopoly results in lower unit costs and improvements in product quality, this conclusion must be altered in a manner less condemnatory of oligopoly. That is, *if* large oligopolistic producers are in a better position than competitive firms to realize existing (known) economies of scale or are more able and willing to develop improved productive techniques and better products, then oligopoly *may* be more desirable socially than competition. However, despite plausible arguments why oligopoly may be progressive, such empirical evidence as is available suggests that giant oligopolistic corporations are not the basic source of technological advance in our society. Furthermore, there are many known instances (see footnote 2) in which oligopolists, unbridled by countervailing power, have sorely abused their market power to the detriment of society as a whole. Indeed, the picture is a mixed one: when oligopolies are good, they may be very good; when they are bad, they tend to be very bad. The examination of specific cases will reveal both restrictive and progressive oligopolies. This tentative conclusion is worth venturing: oligopolistic industries may be much more palatable over time, that is, in the long run, than they seem to be at a particular point in time.

SUMMARY

1. Oligopolistic industries are characterized by few firms, each of which has a significant fraction of the market. Firms thus situated are mutually interdependent; the behavior of any one firm directly affects and is affected by the actions of rivals. Products may be virtually uniform or significantly differentiated; entry is substantially restricted, frequently by technological considerations.

2. The wide variety of oligopolistic markets and the uncertainty which stems from mutual interdependence limit the applicability of formal economic analysis to oligopolistic markets. The factual record indicates, however, that (*a*) oligopolistic prices tend to be inflexible, or "sticky," and (*b*) the price changes which do occur are "orderly" in the sense that firms tend to change their prices together.

3. Independent (noncollusive) oligopolists in effect face a kinked demand curve. This curve and the accompanying marginal revenue curve help explain the price rigidity which characterize such markets; it does not, however, explain the level of price.

4. The uncertainties inherent in independent pricing are conducive to collusion. Gentlemen's agreements on price may entail economic consequences even less desirable to society than pure monopoly because (*a*) the oligopolists are likely to escape public regulation, (*b*) economies of scale may be sacrificed, (*c*) wasteful competitive advertising may persist, and (*d*) the resulting price rigidity may forestall price reductions which cost-reducing technological advances justify.

5. Price leadership, whereby all firms in the industry follow the price changes of a dominant firm, is a less formal and widely practiced form of price collusion.

6. Many oligopolistic producers are multiproduct firms. There are many reasons behind product proliferation: (*a*) some products are jointly produced, (*b*) product diversification provides insurance against demand fluctuations, (*c*) the initial advantage of being the sole producer of a newly developed product is conducive to high profits, and (*d*) a firm can more fully utilize its plant through product diversification.

7. In multiproduct firms some costs are separable, that is, associated exclusively with the production of specific goods, while others are common, associated with many products taken as a group. This poses two difficulties: (*a*) it is extremely difficult to calculate marginal costs for each product, and (*b*) significant price differences and price warring may result from the lack of a uniform technique in allocating common costs to different products.

8. Cost-plus pricing is used to sidestep these difficulties. By this rule-of-thumb pricing technique, per unit separable costs are calculated, or estimated, for a typical rate of output; a customary markup which includes common costs and a fair profit is then added to this standard cost figure in determining price.

9. Market shares in oligopolistic industries are usually determined on the basis of nonprice competition. Oligopolists emphasize nonprice competition because (*a*) advertising and product variations are less easy for rivals to match and (*b*) oligopolists frequently have ample financial resources to finance nonprice competition.

10. There is no clear-cut conclusion as to the social desirability of oligopoly; oligopoly may be either restrictive or progressive. Where oligopoly is restrictive, abuses of its market power may be curbed by countervailing power.

QUESTIONS AND STUDY SUGGESTIONS

1. What features distinguish oligopoly from monopolistic competition? Be specific.

2. "Fewness of rivals means mutual interdependence and mutual interdependence means uncertainty as to how those few rivals will react to a price change by any one firm." Explain. Of what significance is this for determining demand and marginal revenue? Other things being equal, would you expect mutual interdependence to vary directly or inversely with the degree of product differentiation? Explain.

3. What are the basic characteristics of oligopolistic prices? How are these characteristics best explained?

4. What assumptions concerning a rival's responses to price changes underlie the kinked demand curve? Why is there a gap in the marginal revenue curve? How does the kinked demand curve help explain oligopolistic price rigidity?

5. What is price leadership? Explain its operation.

6. Why, from society's standpoint, might the economic consequences of collusive oligopoly be inferior to those of pure monopoly?

7. What advantages might accompany product diversification?

8. Why do oligopolists prefer nonprice to price competition?

9. "If each firm knows that the price of each of its few rivals depends on its price, how can the prices be determined?" Explain.

10. What is cost-plus pricing? What might its advantages be to the oligopolist?

11. "Oligopolistic industries have both the means and the inclination for technological progress." Do you agree? Explain.

12. Under what conditions will oligopoly be economically efficient? Economically inefficient? Which set of conditions do you feel best describes oligopoly in American capitalism? Justify your answer.

13. What is countervailing power? How does it differ from ordinary competition? Why is it self-generating? What are its limitations?

SELECTED REFERENCES

Adams, Walter (ed.), *The Structure of American Industry,* 3d ed. (New York: The Macmillan Company, 1961), chaps. 5, 6, 8–10, and 12.

Bain, Joe S., *Pricing, Distribution, and Employment,* rev. ed. (New York: Holt, Rinehart and Winston, Inc., 1953), chap. 6.

Bober, M. M., *Intermediate Price and Income Theory,* rev. ed. (New York: W. W. Norton & Company, Inc., 1962), chap. 12.

Colberg, M. R., and W. C. Bradford, *Business Economics,* 3d ed. (Homewood, Ill.: Richard D. Irwin, Inc., 1962), chaps. 6–9.

Galbraith, John K., *American Capitalism,* rev. ed. (Boston: Houghton Mifflin Company, 1956), chaps. 7 and 9.

Joint Economic Committee, *Employment, Growth, and Price Levels, Hearings, Part 7, The Effects of Monopolistic and Quasi-monopolistic Practices* (Washington: Government Printing Office, 1959), papers by James S. Duesenberry, William J. Fellner, and Daniel Hamberg.

Kaplan, A. D. H., *Big Enterprise in a Competitive System* (Washington: Brookings Institution, 1954).

Spencer, Milton H., and Louis Siegelman, *Managerial Economics* (Homewood, Ill.: Richard D. Irwin, Inc., 1959), chap. 8.

Weiss, Leonard W., *Economics and American Industry* (New York: John Wiley & Sons, Inc., 1961), chaps. 7 and 8.

Chapter 28

PRODUCTION AND THE DEMAND FOR

ECONOMIC RESOURCES

THE PRECEDING FOUR CHAPTERS have been concerned with the pricing and output of goods and services under a variety of product market structures. In producing any commodity a firm must hire productive resources which, directly or indirectly, are owned and supplied by households. It is appropriate that we now turn from the pricing and production of goods to the pricing and employment of resources needed in accomplishing production. In terms of our circular flow diagram of the economy we now shift our attention from the bottom loop of the diagram, where firms supply and households demand products, to the top loop, where households supply and businesses demand resources. It is in part this reversal of roles which makes necessary a separate discussion of resource pricing.

SIGNIFICANCE OF RESOURCE PRICING

The importance of studying resource pricing is almost self-evident. The most basic fact about resource prices is that they constitute a major determinant of money incomes. The expenditures which businesses make in acquiring economic resources flow as wage, rent, interest, and profit incomes to those households which in turn supply the human and property re-

sources at their disposal. We have already discussed the factual results of resource pricing in terms of both the functional and personal distributions of income (Chapter 7); here we are concerned with explaining the resource prices which play such a crucial role in determining these distributions.

Another important aspect of resource pricing is that, just as product prices ration finished goods and services to consumers, so resource prices allocate scarce resources among various industries and firms. An understanding of the manner in which resource prices negotiate the allocation of resources is particularly significant in view of the fact that in a dynamic economy such as American capitalism the efficient allocation of resources over time calls for continuing shifts in resources among alternative uses.

A very special aspect of the resource allocation problem faces the individual firm. To the firm, resource prices are costs, and to realize maximum profits a firm must produce the profit-maximizing output with the most efficient (least costly) combination of resources. Given technology, it is resource prices which play the major role in determining how much land, labor, capital, and entrepreneurial ability are to be combined in the productive process.

Finally, aside from these objective facets of

resource pricing, there are a myriad of ethical questions and public policy issues surrounding the resource market. In particular, the amoral nature of resource prices results, as we have seen, in considerable inequality in the personal distribution of income. Too, the age-old question of the sizes of the income shares going to specific groups is still very much alive. What is the proper distribution of the national income between profits and wages? What shares should go to farmers, factory workers, white-collar employees? Indeed, the pursuit of these questions leads into a consideration of the alternative economic ideologies. Most of Part 6 of this book is concerned with endeavors—both public and private—to alter the distribution of income. Chapter 35 is concerned specifically with the ethics of income distribution.

COMPLEXITIES OF RESOURCE PRICING

Economists are in substantial agreement as to the basic principles of resource pricing. Yet there exists considerable disagreement and sometimes an element of confusion as to the variations in these general principles which must be made as they are applied to specific resources and particular markets. While economists are in general agreement that the pricing and employment of economic resources, or factors of production, are a supply and demand phenomenon, they also recognize that in particular markets resource supply and demand may assume strange and often complex dimensions. This is further complicated by the fact that the operation of supply and demand forces may be muted or even largely supplanted by the policies and practices of government, business firms, or labor unions, not to mention a host of other institutional considerations.

Our major objective in this chapter is a limited one: to explain the basic factors which underlie the demand for economic resources. We shall couch our discussion in terms of labor, recognizing that the principles outlined in our discussion are also generally applicable to land, capital, and entrepreneurial ability. In Chapter 29 we shall combine our understanding of resource demand with a discussion of labor supply in analyzing wage rates. Then in Chapter 30 we shall emphasize the supply side of the market for property resources.

DEMAND FOR A SINGLE RESOURCE

The simplest approach to resource demand is that which assumes a firm is hiring a single resource in a competitive market and in turn is selling its product in a competitive market. The simplicity of this situation lies in the fact that under competition the firm can dispose of as little or as much output as it chooses at the going market price. The firm is selling such a negligible fraction of total output that it exerts no influence whatever on product price. Similarly, in the resource market, competition means that the firm is hiring such a small fraction of the total supply of the resource that its price is unaffected by the quantity the firm purchases.

Resource demand as a derived demand

Having specified these simplified conditions, the most crucial point to note is that the demand for resources is a *derived* demand, that is, derived from the finished goods and services which resources help produce. Resources do not directly satisfy consumer wants, but do so indirectly by producing goods and services. No one wants to consume an acre of land, an International Harvester tractor, or the labor services of a farmer, but households do want to consume the various products which these resources help produce.

Marginal revenue product (MRP)

The derived nature of resource demand correctly implies that the strength of the demand for any resource will depend upon (1) the capability of the resource in producing a good and (2) the value of the good it is producing. In other words, the demand for a resource depends upon its productivity and the market price of the commodity it is producing. A resource which is highly productive in turning out a commodity highly valued by society will be in great demand. On the other hand, demand will be very weak for a relatively unproductive resource which is only capable of producing some good not in great demand by households. There will be no demand for a resource which is phenomenally efficient in the production of something which no one will buy!

The roles of productivity and product value in determining resource demand can be brought into sharper focus through Table 28-1. Here it is assumed that a firm is adding one variable resource—labor—to its fixed plant. Columns 1 through 3 remind us that the law of diminishing returns will be applicable in this situation, causing the marginal physical product (MPP) of labor to fall beyond some point. For simplicity's sake it is here assumed that diminishing marginal physical product sets in with the first worker hired. But we have already emphasized that the derived demand for a re-

source depends not only upon the productivity of that resource but also upon the price of the commodity it produces. Column 4 adds this information. Note that product price is constant at $1 because we are supposing a competitive product market. Multiplying column 2 by column 4, we get the total revenue data of column 5. From this total revenue data we can readily compute *marginal revenue product* (MRP)—*the increase in total revenue resulting from the use of each additional input of labor.* This is indicated in column 6.

Rule for employing resources

The MRP schedule—columns 1 and 6—is crucial in that it constitutes the firm's demand schedule for labor. To explain why this is so we must first discuss the rule which guides a profit-seeking firm in hiring any resource. To maximize profits a firm should hire additional units of any given resource so long as each successive unit adds more to the firm's total revenue than it does to its total costs. Economists have special terms which designate what each addi-

TABLE 28-1. THE DEMAND FOR A RESOURCE: PURE COMPETITION IN THE SALE OF THE PRODUCT

(1) Units of resource	(2) Total product	(3) Marginal physical product (MPP), or Δ(2)	(4) Product price	(5) Total revenue, or (2) × (4)	(6) Marginal revenue product (MRP), or Δ(5)
		15			$15
1	15		$1	15	
		12			12
2	27		1	27	
		9			9
3	36		1	36	
		6			6
4	42		1	42	
		3			3
5	45		1	45	
		1			1
6	46		1	46	

tional unit of a resource adds to total cost and what it adds to total revenue. We have just noted that MRP measures how much each successive worker adds to total revenue. The amount which each additional unit of a resource adds to the firm's total (resource) cost is called *marginal resource cost (MRC).* Thus we can restate our rule for hiring resources as follows: *it will be profitable for a firm to hire additional units of a resource up to the point at which that resource's MRP is equal to its MRC.* If the number of workers a firm is currently hiring is such that the MRP of the last worker exceeds his MRC, then the firm can clearly profit by hiring more workers. But if the number being hired is such that the MRC of the last worker exceeds his MRP, the firm is hiring workers who are not "paying their way," and it can thereby increase its profits by laying off some workers. The reader will recognize that this MRP = MRC rule is very similar to the MR = MC rule employed throughout our discussion of product pricing. The rationale of the two rules is the same, but the point of reference is now inputs of resources, not outputs of product.

MRP is a demand schedule

Just as product price and marginal revenue are equal in a competitive product market, so resource price and marginal resource cost are equal when a firm is hiring a resource competitively. In a competitive labor market the wage rate is set by the total, or market, supply of, and the market demand for, labor. Because it hires such a small fraction of the total supply of labor, a single firm cannot influence this wage rate. This means that total resource cost increases by exactly the amount of the going wage rate for each additional worker hired; the wage rate and MRC are equal. It follows that so long as it is hiring labor competitively, *the firm will hire workers to the point at which their wage rate (or MRC) is equal to their MRP.*

Accordingly, employing the data in column 6 of Table 28-1, we find that if the wage rate is $14.95, the firm will hire only one worker. This is so because the first worker adds $15 to

total revenue and slightly less—$14.95—to total costs. For each successive worker, however, we find that his MRC exceeds his MRP, indicating that it will not be profitable to hire him. If the wage rate is $11.95, we apply the same reasoning and discover that it will pay the firm to hire both the first and second workers. Similarly, if the wage rate is $8.95, three will be hired. If $5.95, four. If $2.95, then five. And so forth. It is evident that *the MRP schedule constitutes the firm's demand for labor,* because each point on this curve indicates the number of workers which the firm would hire at each possible wage rate which might exist. This is shown graphically in Figure 28-1.

Resource demand under imperfect competition

Our analysis of labor demand becomes slightly more complex when we assume that the firm is selling its product in an imperfectly competitive market. Pure monopoly, oligopoly, and monopolistic competition in the product market all mean that the firm's product demand curve is downsloping; that is, it must accept a lower price in order to increase its sales. Table 28-2 takes this into account. The productivity data of Table 28-1 are retained, but it is now assumed in column 4 that product price must be lowered in order to sell the marginal product of each successive worker. The MRP of the competitive seller falls for one reason: marginal physical product diminishes. But the MRP of the imperfectly competitive seller falls for two reasons: marginal product diminishes and product price falls as output increases.

It must be emphasized that the lower price which accompanies every increase in output applies in each case not only to the marginal product of each successive worker but also to all prior units which otherwise could have been sold at a higher price. To illustrate: The second worker's marginal product is 12 units. These 12 units can be sold for $1.20 each or, as a group, for $14.40. But this is not the MRP of the second worker. Why? Because in order to sell these 12 units the firm must take a 10-cent

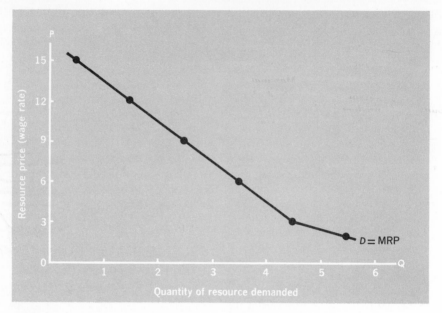

FIGURE 28-1. THE PURELY COMPETITIVE SELLER'S DEMAND
FOR A RESOURCE.
The MRP curve is the resource demand curve. The location of the curve depends
upon the marginal productivity of the resource and the price of the product. Under
pure competition product price is constant; therefore, it is solely because of diminishing marginal productivity that the resource demand curve is downsloping.

price cut on the 15 units produced by the first
worker—units which could have been sold for
$1.30 each. Thus the MRP of the second
worker is only $12.90 [$14.40 − (15 × 10
cents)]. Similarly, the third worker's MRP is
$7.20. Although the 9 units he produces are
worth $1.10 each in the market, the third
worker does not add $9.90 to the firm's total
revenue when account is taken of the 10-cent
price cut which must be taken on the 27 units
produced by the first two workers. In this case
the third worker's MRP is only $7.20 [$9.90 −
(27 × 10 cents)]. And so it is for the other
figures in column 6.

The net result is obvious: the MRP curve—
the resource demand curve—of the imperfectly
competitive producer tends to be less elastic
than that of a purely competitive producer. At
a wage rate or MRC of $11.95 both the purely
competitive and the imperfectly competitive

seller will hire two workers. But at $8.95 the
competitive firm will hire three and the imperfectly competitive firm only two. And at $5.95
the purely competitive firm will take four and
the imperfect competitor only three. This difference in elasticity can be readily visualized
by graphing the MRP data of Table 28-2 as
Figure 28-2 and comparing it with Figure 28-1.
It is not surprising that the imperfectly competitive producer is less responsive to wage cuts in
terms of workers employed than is the purely
competitive producer. The relative reluctance
of the imperfect competitor to employ more
resources and thereby produce more output
when resource prices fall is merely the resource
market reflection of the imperfect competitor's
tendency to restrict output in the product market. Other things being equal, the imperfectly
competitive seller will produce less of a product than would a purely competitive seller. In

TABLE 28-2. THE DEMAND FOR A RESOURCE: IMPERFECT COMPETITION IN THE SALE OF THE PRODUCT

(1) Units of resource	(2) Total product	(3) Marginal physical product (MPP), or Δ(2)	(4) Product price	(5) Total revenue, or (2) × (4)	(6) Marginal revenue product (MRP), or Δ(5)
		15			$19.50
1	15		$1.30	$19.50	
		12			12.90
2	27		1.20	32.40	
		9			7.20
3	36		1.10	39.60	
		6			4.50
4	42		1.05	44.10	
		3			0.90
5	45		1.00	45.00	
		1			−1.30
6	46		0.95	43.70	

producing this smaller output he will demand less resources.

But one qualification is pertinent. We noted in Chapters 25 and 27 that in some instances the market structures of oligopoly and pure monopoly might be progressive rather than restrictive. That is, they might give rise to a higher level of production, more employment, and lower prices in the long run than would a purely competitive market arrangement. This, you will recall, seems more likely in the case of oligopoly. The resource demand curve for progressive oligopoly and monopoly would not be so restricted.

Market demand for a resource

Can we now derive a market demand curve for a resource? Yes, we can. You will recall that the total, or market, demand curve for a product is developed by summing the demand curves of all individual buyers in the market. Similarly, the market demand curve for a particular resource can be derived in essentially the same fashion, that is, by summing the individual demand or MRP curves for all firms hiring that resource.[1]

CHANGES IN RESOURCE DEMAND

What will alter the demand for a resource, that is, shift the demand curve? The very derivation of resource demand immediately suggests two related factors—the resource's pro-

[1] The matter is actually not quite this simple. The resource demand, or MRP, curve *for each firm* is drawn on the assumption that product price is constant. However, if a lowering of resource price causes *all firms* in the industry to hire more of the resource and thereby expand total output, we can expect product price to decline. The result is that the resource market demand curve will not be quite identical with the sum of the individual firms' demand curves for that resource. The whole will not equal the sum of the parts. We will ignore this complication in our discussion and accept the approximation in the text. If interested, consult Neil W. Chamberlain, *Labor* (New York: McGraw-Hill Book Company, Inc., 1958), pp. 331–333.

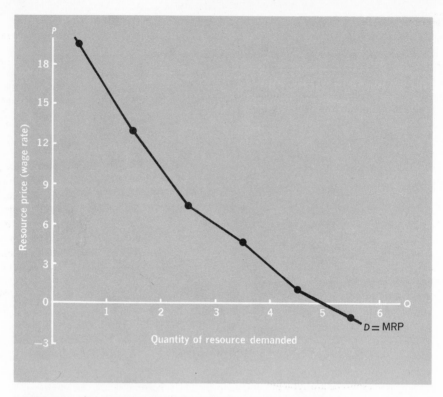

**FIGURE 28-2. THE IMPERFECTLY COMPETITIVE SELLER'S DEMAND
FOR A RESOURCE.**
An imperfectly competitive seller's resource demand curve slopes downward because
marginal product diminishes and product price falls as output increases.

ductivity and the market price of the product it is producing. And our previous analysis of changes in product demand (Chapter 4) indicates another factor—changes in the prices of other resources.

1. Because resource demand is a derived demand, it is obvious that any change in the demand for the product will affect product price and therefore the MRP of the resource. An increase in the demand for automobiles will cause the demand for the services of automobile workers to shift to the right; a decline in the demand for automobiles will shift the demand for automobile workers to the left.

2. Changes in productivity will also cause resource demand to shift. The productivity of any resource can be altered in several ways.

(a) The marginal productivity data for, say, labor will depend upon the quantities of other resources with which it is combined. The greater the amount of capital and land resources with which labor is combined, the greater will be the marginal productivity and the demand for labor. (b) Technological improvements will have the same effect. The better the quality of the capital, the greater the productivity of labor. A worker equipped with a steam shovel is very much more productive than the same worker armed with a spade. (c) Improvements in the quality of the variable resource itself—labor—will increase the marginal productivity and therefore the demand for labor.

All these considerations, incidentally, are important in explaining why the average level of (real) wages is higher in the United States than in foreign nations. American workers are generally healthier and better trained than those of foreign nations, and in most industries they work with a larger and more efficient stock of capital goods and more abundant natural resources than do the workers of most foreign nations. This spells a strong demand for labor. On the supply side of the market labor is *relatively* scarce as compared to most foreign nations. A strong demand and a relatively scarce supply result in high wage rates. This will be discussed further in Chapter 29.

3. Just as changes in the prices of other products will change the demand for a specific commodity, so changes in the prices of other resources can be expected to alter the demand for a particular resource. And just as the effect of a change in the price of product X upon the demand for product Y depends upon whether X and Y are substitute or complementary goods, so the effect of a change in the price of resource A upon the demand for resource B will depend upon their substitutability or their complementariness.

Within limits resources are typically substitutes for one another. A drop in the price of machinery may prompt a firm to substitute machinery for labor; this is the obvious adjustment to make if the firm seeks to produce any given output in the least costly fashion. At given wage rates, less labor will now be employed. The demand for labor will have fallen. But this *substitution effect* may be offset wholly or in part by an accompanying *output effect.* Because the price of machinery has fallen, the cost of producing various outputs will also have declined. And with lower costs the firm will produce and sell a larger output. This greater output will tend to increase the demand for all resources, including labor. The net effect of a decline in the price of machinery upon the demand for labor will depend upon the sizes of these two opposed effects. If the substitution effect outweighs the output effect, the demand for labor will decline. If the reverse holds true, the demand for labor will increase.

When resources are complementary or jointly demanded, the situation is a bit more clear-cut. In some situations the nature of the productive process allows little or no room for substituting resources; resources are combined in fixed proportions. Suppose, for example, that a small manufacturer of metal products uses punch presses as its basic piece of capital equipment. Each press is designed to be operated by one worker; the machine is not automated—it won't run itself—and a second or third worker would be wholly redundant. Now assume that a significant technological advance in the production of these presses substantially reduces their cost. Other things being unchanged, this reduction in the price of capital goods will induce our manufacturer to use more presses. However, because labor and capital are required in fixed proportions—one man for one machine—there will be no substitution of capital for labor. On the contrary, the purchase of more machines will increase the firm's demand for punch-press operators. The output effect will bolster this increase in labor demand. To the extent that the firm's metal products are reduced in price because of the drop in the cost of the presses, its volume of sales and therefore its demand for labor will increase.

ELASTICITY OF RESOURCE DEMAND

The considerations just discussed are responsible for shifts in the location of resource demand curves. Such changes in demand are to be carefully distinguished from a change in the quantity of a resource demanded. The latter, you will recall, does not entail a shift in the resource demand curve but rather a movement from one point to another on a stable resource demand curve, because of a change in the price of the specific resource under consideration. To illustrate: an increase in the wage rate from $5.95 to $8.95 will reduce the quantity of labor demanded from four to three workers, as can be readily seen in Table 28-1 and Figure 28-1.

This raises a question: What determines the sensitivity of producers to changes in resource prices? Or, more technically, what determines the elasticity of resource demand? Several long-standing generalizations provide some important insights in answering this question.

1. A purely technical consideration is of importance to us—the rate at which the marginal physical product of the variable resource declines. If the marginal product of labor declines slowly as it is added to a fixed amount of capital, the MRP, or demand curve for labor, will decline slowly and tend to be highly elastic. A small decline in the price of such a resource will give rise to a relatively large increase in the amount demanded. Conversely, if the marginal productivity of labor declines sharply, the MRP, or labor demand curve, will decline rapidly. This means that a relatively large decline in the wage rate will be accompanied by a very modest increase in the amount hired; resource demand will be inelastic.

2. The degree to which resources are substitutable for one another is a highly important determinant of elasticity. The larger the number of good substitute resources available, the greater will be the elasticity of demand for a particular resource. If a furniture manufacturer finds that some five or six different types of wood are equally satisfactory in making coffee tables, a rise in the price of any one type of wood may cause a very sharp drop in the amount demanded as the producer readily substitutes other woods. At the other extreme, it may be impossible to substitute: bauxite is absolutely essential in the production of aluminum ingots. This means that the demand for it tends to be very inelastic.

3. The elasticity of demand for any resource will depend upon the elasticity of demand for the product which it helps produce. The greater the elasticity of product demand, the greater the elasticity of resource demand. The derived nature of resource demand would lead us to expect this relationship. A small rise in the price of a product with great elasticity of demand will give rise to a sharp drop in output and therefore a relatively large decline in the amounts of the various resources demanded. Indeed, our comparisons of resource demand when output is being sold competitively (Table 28-1 and Figure 28-1), on the one hand, and under imperfectly competitive conditions (Table 28-2 and Figure 28-2), on the other,

have already suggested that, other things being the same, the greater the elasticity of product demand, the greater the elasticity of resource demand.

4. Finally, the larger the portion of production costs accounted for by a resource, the greater will be the elasticity of demand for that resource. The rationale here is rather evident. If labor costs account for, say, three-fourths of the total cost of a product, a given increase in wage rates will alter total cost and therefore product price by a relatively large amount, resulting in a significant increase in product price. Given the elasticity of product demand, this will cause a relatively large decline in sales and a sharp decline in the amount of labor demanded. But if labor cost is only 5 or 10 per cent of total cost, the same given increase in wage rates will have little effect upon total cost and product price. Given the same elasticity of product demand, a small decline in sales and therefore in the amount of labor demanded will result.

A FIRM'S DEMAND FOR SEVERAL RESOURCES

So much for the character of the demand for a single resource. Now we must examine resource demand from the standpoint of an individual firm that is employing several different resources for which, within limits, there are substitutes. The problem faced by the producer is much like that confronting the consumer. You will recall from Chapter 22 that the consumer seeks that combination of goods which gives him the maximum utility for his given money income. In achieving the utility-maximizing collection of goods the consumer considers both his preferences as reflected in (diminishing) marginal utility data and the prices of the various products. The producer is in a similar boat. He seeks that combination of resources which will provide the maximum output and, given product price, the maximum total revenue, for a given money outlay, or cost. The producer obviously wants to maximize his profits, just as the consumer seeks to maximize his utility. In pursuing this combination of resources the producer must consider both the productivity of the resource as reflected in (diminishing) marginal physical product data and the prices (costs) of the various resources. A firm may very well find it profitable to employ very small amounts of a highly productive resource if its price is high. Conversely, it may be sensible to hire large amounts of a relatively unproductive resource if its price is sufficiently low.

In effect two related questions face the producer in hiring resources. (1) What relative amounts, or what *proportions*, of two or more resources should be employed? (2) What *absolute amounts* of these variable resources should be hired? These questions are analogous to those faced by a painter who wants to paint a room a very light pink. He is faced, first, with the question of combining white and red paint in the correct proportions to achieve the desired shade of pink. Should quarts of white and red paint be combined on a 2 to 1, 3 to 1, or 4 to 1 basis to get the correct shade of pink? Then, secondly, he must determine what absolute amounts of white and red will provide just enough paint to complete the room. For example, the painter may find that 3 quarts of white and 1 of red provide the right shade of pink. But then he must determine what absolute amounts of white and red paint—6 of white to 2 of red, 9 white to 3 red, or 15 white to 5 red—will give just enough paint to do the room.

Resources in best proportions

Suppose a farmer is adding two resources—labor and capital—to a fixed amount of land. (Though we limit our discussion to just two variable resources to simplify the exposition, our analysis can readily be extended to any number of resources.) Assume, too, that the farmer purchases labor and capital competitively, so that the prices of these resources are given to him. The law of diminishing returns tells us that, as labor and capital are added to a fixed amount of land, their marginal physical products will diminish beyond some point.

In what proportions, or relative amounts, should the farmer hire labor and capital? The answer is this: *the producer should allocate his money outlays on labor and capital so that the last dollar spent on each adds the same amount to his total revenue.* This rule should have a familiar ring. It is simply a variation of the utility maximizing rule which is a cornerstone of the theory of consumer behavior. Note that the farmer is balancing the relative, or proportionate, contributions of labor and capital. That is, he is comparing and balancing the contributions of labor and capital in relation to, or in proportion to, their prices (what they cost). In simple algebraic terms the rule for employing labor and capital in the best proportion is

$$\frac{\text{Marginal revenue product of labor}}{\text{price of labor}}$$
$$= \frac{\text{marginal revenue product of capital}}{\text{price of capital}} \quad (1)$$

Verbally, this equation merely says that the ratio of the MRP of any resource to its price should be the same for each variable resource employed. These two ratios simply show the amounts that the last dollars spent on labor and on capital add to the farmer's total revenue. Their equation, then, indicates that the last dollar spent on labor and the last dollar spent on capital each add the same amount to the firm's total revenue.

We can verify that this rule indicates the best relative amounts of labor and capital to employ by assuming that the farmer is initially violating the best-proportion rule and discovering that he can increase his total revenue for the same total outlay, thereby increasing his profits. To illustrate: Suppose that labor costs $10 per man per day and capital costs $20 per unit per day. Suppose, too, that labor and capital are currently being employed in such relative amounts that the MRP of the last worker hired is $20 and the MRP of the last unit of capital is $60. It is obvious that our ratios are now unequal:

$$\frac{\text{Labor MRP: \$20}}{\text{Labor price: \$10}} < \frac{\text{capital MRP: \$60}}{\text{capital price: \$20}} \quad (2)$$

The last dollar spent on labor adds $2 to the farmer's total revenue, while the last dollar spent on capital adds $3. Because capital is more profitable than labor at the margin, it will pay the farmer profitwise to substitute capital for labor.

As dollars are channeled from labor to capital, the MRP of capital will fall as the result of moving down the declining MRP schedule for capital, and the MRP of labor will rise as the farmer moves up the declining MRP schedule for labor. At some new combination of more capital and less labor, the equality of the above ratios will be restored. This may be, for example, where

$$\frac{\text{Labor MRP: } \$25}{\text{Labor price: } \$10} = \frac{\text{capital MRP: } \$50}{\text{capital price: } \$20} \quad (3)$$

Here the last dollars spent on both labor and capital contribute the same amount—$2.50—to the firm's total revenue. When this point is reached, there is no further possibility of increasing total revenue with the same total outlay by substituting between the two resources. Given the farmer's money outlay, there is no possible way for the farmer to increase profits by substituting labor for capital or capital for labor.

Resources in best absolute amounts

But using labor and capital in the correct proportions does not mean that the farmer is employing these two variable resources in the right absolute amounts. Three quarts of white and one quart of red paint may provide the right shade of pink; but four quarts of paint may be too much or not enough to paint a room. If the farmer finds that he should use about three times as many units of capital as he does labor in order for the MRP of the last dollar spent on each to be equal, the question remains as to what is the best—that is, the profit maximizing—number of units of capital and labor to employ. Stated differently, what output of product, and therefore outlay of cost, will maximize the firm's profits? Note that the problem now is not simply that of apportioning a given total outlay (cost) but that of de-

termining what level of output, and therefore level of outlay on resources, will permit the firm to achieve the maximum attainable profit.

From our analysis of the product market we know that a firm will maximize its profits by supplying a product up to the point at which marginal revenue equals marginal cost. To produce less is to forgo profitable units of output; to produce more is to produce units of output which are simply not profitable. The problem is one of balancing how much an extra unit of *output* adds to the firm's total revenue and how much that unit adds to total costs. This same question can be readily reformulated in terms of *inputs* of resources. Because a product is produced with the use of several inputs, the question becomes one of how much each extra input of resource adds to total revenue and how much it adds to total cost. In looking at the profit maximizing problem from the supply side of the product market, we compare the marginal revenue and marginal cost of each additional unit of output to find what level of output should be produced. In viewing the same question from the demand side of the resource market, we contrast the marginal revenue and marginal cost of *each* of the resources used in the production of that good to find how much of each should be employed. We have already found that the marginal revenue of any resource is its MRP, and its marginal cost under competitive conditions is simply the price of the resource. (Remember: when hiring resources under pure competition, resource· price and marginal resource cost are equal.) By the rule for employing a resource, the firm will find it profitable to hire each variable resource up to the point at which its MRP equals its price. Glancing back at equation (3), we see that the firm is using the right relative amounts of labor and capital, that is, the last dollar spent on each adds the same amount to total revenue. We now know that this combination of labor and capital involves insufficient absolute amounts of both resources for the attainment of maximum profits. How do we know this? Because with the absolute amounts of labor and capital involved in equation (3), the MRP of each resource exceeds its price. The farmer can therefore increase his profits by hiring more of both labor and capital, because extra units of each will add more to his revenue than to his costs. When does the farmer stop adding the two resources? When the MRP of each resource equals its (constant) price. In other words, to use labor and capital in the right proportions *and* in the right absolute amounts, labor and capital should be hired up to the point where

$$\frac{\text{Labor MRP: \$10}}{\text{Labor price: \$10}} = \frac{\text{capital MRP: \$20}}{\text{capital price: \$20}} = 1 \,(4)$$

This is merely an application of the rule for employing resources to more than one resource.

The reader will readily recognize that changes in the productivity or price of either resource will tend to change both the relative and the absolute amounts of the resources which a firm will find it most profitable to employ.

SUMMARY

1. Resource prices are a major determinant of money incomes, and simultaneously perform the function of rationing resources to various industries and firms.

2. Though economists agree that resource pricing is a supply and demand phenomenon, they frequently disagree as to the exact characteristics of, and the operation of, supply and demand in particular resource markets.

3. The fact that the demand for any resource is derived from the product it helps produce correctly suggests that the demand for a resource will depend upon its productivity and the market value of the good it is producing.

4. The marginal revenue product schedule of any resource is the demand schedule for that resource. This follows from an application of the rule that a firm operating under competitive conditions will find it most profitable to hire a resource up to the point at which the price of the resource equals its marginal revenue product.

5. The demand curve for a resource is downsloping, because the marginal physical product of additional inputs of any resource declines in accordance with the law of diminishing returns. When a firm is selling in an imperfectly competitive market, the resource demand curve will fall, too, because product price must be reduced in order to permit the firm to sell a larger output.

6. The market demand for a resource can be derived by summing the demand curves of all firms hiring that resource.

7. The demand for a resource will change, that is, a resource demand curve will shift, as the result of (*a*) a change in the demand for, and therefore the price of, the product the resource is producing, (*b*) changes in the productivity of the resource due either to increases in the quantity or improvements in the quality of the resources with which a given resource is being combined, or improvements in the quality of the given resource itself, and (*c*) changes in the prices of other resources.

8. A decline in the price of resource A will typically give rise to a substitution effect; that is, resource A will tend to be substituted for resources B and C. But these declines in the demand for resources B and C may be partially, wholly, or more than offset by an output effect; that is, the decrease in cost which the decline in the price of resource A entails will increase output and tend to increase the demand for resources B and C. When resources are not substitutes but are complementary, a decline in the price of resource A will increase the demand for complementary resource B.

9. The elasticity of resource demand depends upon (*a*) the rate at which the marginal physical product of the resource declines, (*b*) the number of good substitute resources available, (*c*) the elasticity of demand for the product, and (*d*) the portion of total production costs attributable to the resource.

10. A firm will employ several variable resources in the best relative amounts when the last dollar spent on each resource adds the same amount to total revenue, or, algebraically, when

$$\frac{\text{MRP of resource A}}{\text{Price of A}} = \frac{\text{MRP of resource B}}{\text{price of B}}$$

$$= \frac{\text{MRP of resource N}}{\text{price of N}}$$

These several resources will also be used in the right absolute amounts (in profit maximizing amounts) when the MRP of each resource is equal to its price, that is, when the above ratios are equal to 1.

QUESTIONS AND STUDY SUGGESTIONS

1. Explain or define the following terms: (*a*) marginal physical product, (*b*) marginal revenue product, (*c*) marginal resource cost, (*d*) output effect, and (*e*) substitution effect.

2. What is the significance of resource pricing? Explain in detail how the factors determining resource demand differ from those underlying product demand.

3. Why do resource demand curves slope downward?

4. Explain the meaning and significance of the notion that the demand for a resource is a *derived* demand.

5. Complete the following labor demand table for a firm which is hiring labor competitively and selling its product in a competitive market.

Units of labor	Total product	Marginal physical product	Product price	Total revenue	Marginal revenue product
1	17		$2		
2	31		2		
3	43		2		
4	53		2		
5	60		2		
6	65		2		

a. How many workers will the firm hire if the going wage rate is $27.95? $19.95? Explain why the firm will not hire a larger or smaller number of workers at each of these wage rates.

b. Show in schedule form and graphically the labor demand curve of this firm.

c. Now redetermine the firm's demand curve for labor on the assumption that it is selling in an imperfectly competitive market and that, although it can sell 17 units at $2.20 per unit, it must lower product price by 5 cents in order to sell the marginal physical product of each successive worker. Compare this demand curve with that derived in question 5*b*. Explain any differences.

6. Distinguish between a change in resource demand and a change in the quantity of a resource demanded. What specific factors might give rise to a change in resource demand? A change in the quantity of a resource demanded?

7. Using the substitution and output effects, explain how a decline in the price of resource A *might* cause an increase in the demand for substitute resource B.

8. What factors determine the elasticity of resource demand?

9. What effect will each of the following have upon the elasticity or the location of the demand for resource C, which is being used in the production of commodity X? Where there is any uncertainty as to the outcome, specify the causes of that uncertainty.

a. An increase in the demand for product X

b. An increase in the price of substitute factor D

c. An increase in the number of resources which are substitutable for C in producing X

d. A technological improvement in the capital equipment with which resource C is combined

e. A decline in the price of complementary resource E

f. A decline in the elasticity of demand for product X due to a decline in the competitiveness of the product market

10. Assume that a manufacturer of machine tools is employing variable resources A and B in his fixed plant in such amounts that the MRP of the last units of A and B employed are $70 and $45 respectively. Resource A can be hired at $20 and B at $15 per unit. Is the firm hiring A and B in the best relative amounts? Are the two resources being employed in the absolute amounts which will provide the firm with maximum profits? In each instance explain the precise nature of any required substitutions or changes in the absolute amounts of A and B purchased.

11. Answer question 10 at the end of Chapter 5.

SELECTED REFERENCES

Bober, M. M., *Intermediate Price and Income Theory,* rev. ed. (New York: W. W. Norton & Company, Inc., 1962), chap. 13.

Due, John F., and Robert W. Clower, *Intermediate Economic Analysis,* 4th ed. (Homewood, Ill.: Richard D. Irwin, Inc., 1961), chap. 13.

Chamberlain, Neil W., *Labor* (New York: McGraw-Hill Book Company, Inc., 1958), chap. 17.

Enke, Stephen, *Intermediate Economic Theory* (Englewood Cliffs, N. J.: Prentice-Hall, Inc., 1950), chap. 26.

Hyde, Francis E., et al., *A New Prospect of Economics* (Liverpool: Liverpool University Press, 1958), chap. 7.

Chapter 29

THE PRICING AND EMPLOYMENT OF RESOURCES:

WAGE DETERMINATION

ARMED WITH SOME UNDERSTANDING of the strategic factors underlying resource demand, we must now combine this information with the supply situations which characterize the markets for labor, land, capital, and entrepreneurial ability to see how wages, rents, interest, and profits are determined. For two reasons we discuss wage rates prior to other resource prices. (1) The marginal productivity explanation of resource demand is probably more applicable to an explanation of wage rates than it is to the pricing of other resources. (2) To most households the wage rate is the most important price in the economy; it is the sole or basic source of income to most households. At least two-thirds of the national income is in the form of wages and salaries.

Our basic objectives in discussing wage determination are fourfold: (1) to understand the forces underlying the general level of wage rates in the United States; (2) to see how wage rates are determined in particular labor markets and therefore to discuss several representative labor market models; (3) to explain wage differentials; and (4) to raise a question: What effect, if any, do wage changes have upon employment? Throughout this chapter we will rely upon the marginal productivity theory of Chapter 28 as an explanation of labor demand.

MEANING OF WAGES

Wages, or wage rates, are the price paid for the use of labor. Economists often employ the term "labor" broadly to apply to the payments received by (1) workers in the narrow sense of the term, that is, blue- and white-collar workers of infinite variety, (2) professional people—physicians, lawyers, dentists, teachers, and so forth, and (3) small businessmen—barbers, plumbers, television repairmen, and a host of retailers—for the labor services they provide in operating their own businesses. This broad definition of labor, incidentally, encompasses individuals who would be considered as profit receivers in national income accounting. Hence, under this definition, wages would clearly amount to more than two-thirds of the national income.

Though in practice wages may take the form of bonuses, royalties, commissions, and monthly salaries, we shall use the term "wages" to mean wage rates per unit of time—per hour, per day, and so forth. This designation has the advantage of reminding us that the wage rate is a price paid for the use of units of labor service. It also permits us to distinguish clearly between "wages" and "earnings," the latter de-

538

pending upon wage rates and the number of hours or weeks of labor service supplied in the market. It is important, too, to distinguish between money wages and real wages. _Money wages_ simply refer to the amount of money received per hour, per day, per week, and so forth. _Real wages_, on the other hand, indicate the quantity of goods and services which one can obtain with his money wages; real wages are the "purchasing power" of money wages. Obviously one's real wages depend upon his money wages and the prices of the goods and services he buys. Note that money wages and real wages need not move together. For example, money wages may rise and real wages simultaneously decline if product prices rise more rapidly than do money wages. Unless otherwise indicated, our discussion will be couched in terms of real wage rates by making the simple assumption that the level of product prices is constant.

GENERAL LEVEL OF WAGES

Wages tend to differ among nations, among regions, among various occupations, and among individuals. Wage rates are vastly higher in the United States than in China or India; wage rates are generally higher in the North and East of the United States than in the South; plumbers are paid more than cotton pickers; physician Smith may earn three times as much as physician Jones for the same number of hours of work.

Our approach will involve moving from the general to the specific. In this section we are concerned with explaining why the general level of wages is higher in the United States than in foreign nations. This explanation will be largely applicable to regional wage differences within nations. In the following section we seek to explain wages in terms of markets for specific types of labor. In both these discussions a supply and demand approach will offer the most fruitful results.

The general level of wages, like the general level of prices, is a composite concept encompassing a wide range of different specific wage rates. This admittedly vague concept is a use-ful point of departure in making and explaining international and interregional wage comparisons. Statistical data indicate that the general level of real wages in the United States is higher than that of any other nation. The simplest explanation of this fact is that in the United States the demand for labor has been great in relation to the supply.

Let us look behind these forces of demand and supply. We know that the demand for labor—or any other resource—depends upon its productivity. The greater the productivity of labor, the greater the demand for it. And, given the total supply of labor, the stronger the demand, the greater the level of real wages. The demand for American labor has been high because American labor is highly productive. But why the high productivity? The reasons are several:

1. American workers are used in conjunction with large amounts of capital equipment. For example, the average American worker in manufacturing is assisted by some $20,000 worth of machinery and equipment.

2. Natural resources are very abundant in relation to the size of the labor force. The United States is richly endowed with arable land, basic mineral resources, and ample sources of industrial power.

3. The level of technological advance is generally higher in the United States than in foreign nations. American workers in most industries not only use more capital equipment but better, that is, technologically superior, equipment than do foreign workers. Similarly, work methods are steadily being improved through detailed scientific study and research.

4. The health, vigor, education and training, work attitudes, and adaptability of American workers to the discipline of factory production are generally superior to those of the labor of other nations. This means that, even with the same quantity and quality of natural and capital resources, American workers typically would be somewhat more efficient than their foreign brethren.

5. Less tangible yet important items underlying the high productivity of American labor are (a) the efficiency and flexibility of American

management, (b) a business, social, and political environment which puts great emphasis upon production and productivity, and (c) the vast size of the domestic market, which provides the opportunity for firms to realize mass production economies.

The reader will recall that the aforementioned factors are merely a restatement of the cornerstones of economic growth (Chapter 18). It is also notable that the productivity of labor depends to a very great degree upon consider-

ations other than the quality of labor itself. A worker's productivity is determined largely by the quantity and quality of the property resources at his disposal.

The dependence of real hourly wages upon the level of productivity is indicated in Figure 29-1. Note the close relationship in the long run between real hourly wages and output per man-hour in nonfarm private industries.

But simple supply and demand analysis suggests that, even if the demand for labor is strong

FIGURE 29-1. OUTPUT PER HOUR AND REAL AVERAGE HOURLY EARNINGS.
Over a long period of years there has been a close relationship between real hourly wages and output per man-hour in nonfarm private industries. [Joint Economic Committee, Productivity, Prices, and Incomes (Washington, D.C.: Government Printing Office, 1957), p. 48 and author's calculations.]

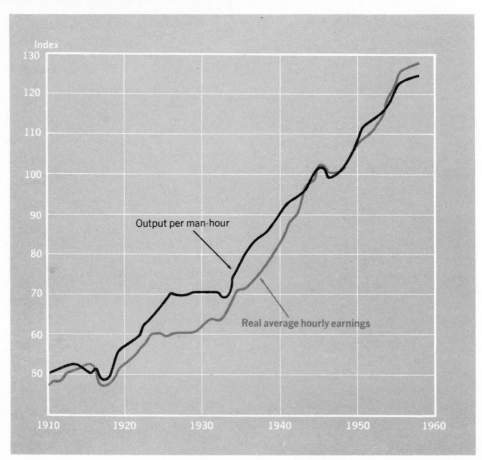

in the United States, increases in the supply of labor will cause the general level of wages to decline over time. It is certainly true that the American population and the labor force have grown significantly over the decades. However, these increases in the supply of labor have been more than offset by increases in the demand for labor stemming from the productivity-increasing factors discussed above. The result has been a long-run, or secular, increase in wage rates as suggested by Figure 29-2.

WAGES IN PARTICULAR LABOR MARKETS

We now turn from the general level of wages to the wage structure, that is, to the system of specific wage rates which comprises the general level of wages. The question now is this: What determines the wage rate received by some specific type of worker? Demand and

supply analysis again provides the most revealing approach. Our analysis covers some half-dozen basic market models.

Competitive model

Let us suppose that there are many—say, 100—firms demanding a particular type of semiskilled or skilled labor.[1] The total, or market, demand for this labor can be determined by summing the labor demand curves (the MRP curves) of the individual firms as suggested in Figure 29-3a and b. On the supply side of the picture we assume there is no union; workers compete freely for available jobs. The supply

[1] These firms need not be in the same industry; industries are defined in terms of the products they produce and not the resources they employ. Thus firms producing unupholstered furniture, window and door frames, and cabinets will all demand carpenters.

MRP curves as labor demand curve -

FIGURE 29-2. THE SECULAR TREND OF REAL WAGES IN THE UNITED STATES. The productivity of American labor has increased substantially in the long run, causing the demand for labor to increase in relation to the supply. The result has been increases in real wages.

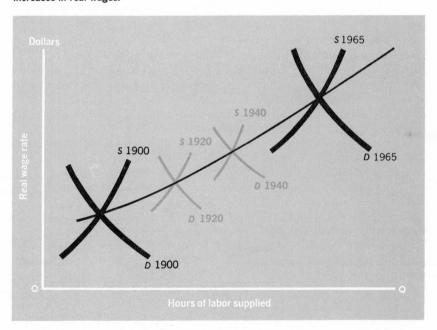

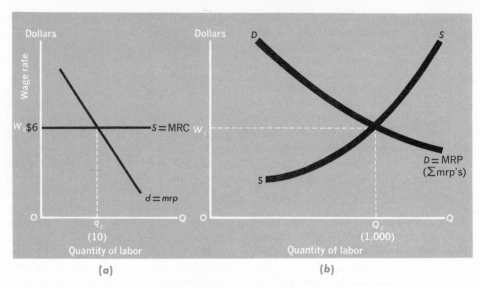

FIGURE 29-3. THE SUPPLY OF, AND DEMAND FOR, LABOR TO A SINGLE COMPETITIVE FIRM (a) AND IN A COMPETITIVE MARKET (b).

In a competitive labor market the equilibrium wage rate W_c and number of workers employed Q_c are determined by supply SS and demand DD, as shown in (b). Because this wage rate is given to the individual firm hiring in the market, its labor supply curve, $S = MRC$, is perfectly elastic as in (a). The firm finds it most profitable to hire workers up to the MRP = MRC point.

curve for a particular type of labor will be upsloping, reflecting the fact that, in the absence of unemployment, hiring firms as a group will be forced to pay higher wage rates to obtain more workers. Why? Because the firms must bid these workers away from other industries and other localities. Within limits workers have alternative job opportunities; that is, they may work in other industries in the same locality, or they may work in their present occupations in different cities or states. In a full-employment economy the group of firms in this particular labor market must pay higher and higher wage rates to attract this type of labor away from these alternative job opportunities. The reader will note that the upsloping labor supply curve is merely a manifestation of the alternative cost doctrine.

The equilibrium wage rate and the equilibrium level of employment for this type of labor is obviously determined by the intersection of the labor demand and labor supply curves. In Figure 29-3b the equilibrium wage rate is W_c ($6) and the number of workers hired is Q_c (1,000). To the individual firm the wage rate W_c is given data. Each of the many hiring firms employs such a small fraction of the total available supply of this type of labor that none can influence the wage rate. Technically, the supply of labor is perfectly elastic to the individual firm, as shown by S in Figure 29-3a. Each individual firm will find it profitable to hire workers up to the point at which the going wage rate is equal to labor's MRP. This is merely an application of the MRP = MRC rule developed in Chapter 28. As Table 29-1 indicates, if the resource price is given to the individual firm, the marginal cost of that resource (MRC) will be constant and equal to resource price. In this case the wage rate and hence the marginal cost of labor are constant to the individual firm. Each additional worker hired adds precisely his wage rate to the firm's total resource cost. The firm then will maximize its profits by hiring workers to the point at which their wage rate and therefore marginal resource cost equal their marginal revenue product. In Figure 29-3a the "typical" firm will hire q_c (10) workers.

Monopsony model

But in many labor markets workers are not hired competitively. Rather employers are monopsonists; that is, they have some monopolistic buying power. In some instances the monopsonistic power of employers is virtually complete in the sense that there is only one major employer in a labor market. For example, the economies of some towns and cities depend almost entirely upon one major firm. A silver-mining concern may be the basic source of employment in a remote Colorado town. A New England textile mill, a Wisconsin paper mill, or a farm-belt food processor may provide a large proportion of the employment in their localities. In other cases *oligopsony* may prevail; three or four firms may each hire a large portion of the supply of labor in a particular market. Our study of oligopoly correctly suggests that there is a strong tendency for oligopsonists to act in concert—much like a monopsonist—in hiring labor.

The important point is this: when a firm hires a considerable portion of the total available supply of a particular type of labor, his decision to employ more or fewer workers will affect the wage rate paid to that labor. Specifically, if a firm is large in relation to the labor market, it will have to pay a higher wage rate in order to obtain more labor. For simplicity's sake let us suppose there is only one employer of a particular type of labor in a specified geographic area. Obviously, the labor supply curve to that firm and the total supply curve for the labor market are identical. This supply curve, for reasons already made clear, is upsloping, indicating that the firm must pay a higher wage rate to attract more workers. This is shown by SS in Figure 29-4. The supply curve is in effect the average-cost-of-labor curve from the firm's point of view; each point on it indicates the wage rate (cost) per worker which must be paid to attract the corresponding number of workers.

But the higher wages involved in attracting additional workers will also have to be paid to

TABLE 29-1. THE SUPPLY OF LABOR: PURE COMPETITION IN THE HIRE OF LABOR

(1) Units of labor	(2) Wage rate	(3) Total labor cost (wage bill)	(4) Marginal labor cost
1	$6	$ 6	$6
2	6	12	6
3	6	18	6
4	6	24	6
5	6	30	6
6	6	36	6

all workers currently employed at lower wage rates. If the firm does not, labor morale will surely deteriorate, and the employer will be plagued with serious problems of labor unrest because of the wage rate differentials existing for the same job. Costwise the payment of a uniform wage to all workers will mean that the cost of an extra worker—the marginal labor cost (MLC)—will exceed the wage rate by the amount necessary to bring the wage rate of all workers currently employed up to the new wage level. Table 29-2 illustrates this point. One worker can be hired at a wage rate of $6. But the hire of a second worker forces the firm to pay a higher wage rate of $7. Marginal labor (resource) cost is $8—the $7 paid the second worker plus a $1 raise for the first worker. Similarly, the marginal labor cost of the third worker is $10—the $8 which must be paid to attract him from alternative employments plus $1 raises for the first two workers. The important point is that to the monopsonist marginal labor cost will exceed the wage rate. Graphically, the MLC curve (columns 1 and 4 in Table 29-2) will lie above the average cost, or supply, curve of labor (columns 1 and 2 in Table 29-2). This is shown graphically in Figure 29-4. How much labor will the firm hire, and what wage rate will it pay? To maximize profits the firm will equate marginal labor (resource) cost with MRP, the monopsonist's demand curve for labor. The number of workers hired by the monopsonist is indicated by Q_m, and the wage rate paid, W_m, is indicated by the corresponding point on the resource supply, or average cost of labor, curve. It is particularly important to contrast these results with those which a competitive labor market would have yielded. With competition in the hire of labor the level of employment would have been greater (Q_c), and the wage rate would have been higher (W_c). It simply does not pay the monopsonist to hire workers up to the point at which the wage rate and labor's MRP are equal. Other things being equal, he maximizes his profits by hiring a smaller number of workers and thereby paying a less-than-competitive wage rate. In the process society gets a smaller output,[2] and workers get a wage rate less by bc than their marginal revenue product. Just as a monopolistic seller finds it profitable to re-

[2] This is analogous to the monopolist's restricting output as he sets product price and output on the basis of marginal revenue, not product demand. In this instance resource price is set on the basis of marginal labor cost, not resource supply.

TABLE 29-2. THE SUPPLY OF LABOR: MONOPSONY IN THE HIRE OF LABOR

(1) Units of labor	(2) Wage rate	(3) Total labor cost (wage bill)	(4) Marginal labor cost
			$ 6
1	$ 6	$ 6	
			8
2	7	14	
			10
3	8	24	
			12
4	9	36	
			14
5	10	50	
			16
6	11	66	

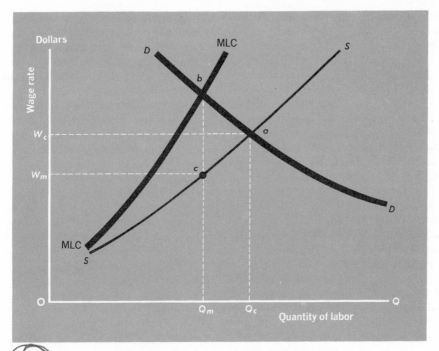

FIGURE 29-4. THE WAGE RATE AND LEVEL OF EMPLOYMENT IN A MONOPSONISTIC LABOR MARKET.
In a monopsonistic labor market the employer's marginal labor cost (MLC) curve lies above the labor supply curve (S). Equating MLC with labor demand MRP at point b, the monopsonist will hire Q_m workers (as compared to Q_c under competition) and pay the wage rate W_m (as compared to the competitive wage W_c).

strict product output to realize an above-competitive price for his goods, so the monopsonistic employer of resources finds it profitable to restrict employment so as to depress wage rates and therefore costs, that is, to realize below-competitive wage rates.

Will a monopsonistic employer also be a monopolistic seller in the product market? Not necessarily. The New England textile mill may be a monopsonistic employer yet face severe domestic and foreign competition in selling its product. In other cases—for example, the automobile and steel industries—firms have both monopsonistic and monopolistic (oligopolistic) power. How does the presence of monopoly or oligopoly power affect our analysis of a monopsonistic labor market? Through the labor demand curve. If the monopsonistic employer is

also a restrictive monopoly or oligopoly, we can expect the resource demand curve of Figure 29-4 to be depressed. The result will be a wage rate even lower than W_m and a volume of employment less than Q_m. On the other hand, a progressive monopoly or oligopoly may entail a resource demand curve to the right of that shown in Figure 29-4, with the result that the wage rate and level of employment will exceed W_m and Q_m. In short, monopoly (oligopoly) power will depress or increase labor demand, depending upon whether the monopoly is restrictive or progressive.

Some union models

Thus far we have been content to assume that workers are actively competing in the sale of their labor services. In a good many markets workers sell their labor services collectively through unions. To envision the economic impact of unions in the simplest context let us suppose a union is formed in an otherwise competitive labor market. That is, a union is now bargaining with a relatively large number of employers. Later we will consider the case where the union faces a large single employer.

Unions seek many goals. Their basic objective, however, is to raise wage rates. The union can pursue this objective in several different ways.

Increasing the demand for labor. The most desirable technique for raising wage rates from the union's point of view is to increase the demand for labor. As shown in Figure 29-5, an increase in the demand for labor will result in both higher wage rates and a larger number of jobs. The relative sizes of these increases will depend upon the elasticity of labor supply.

Classic examples are the International Ladies' Garment Workers Union and the Amalgamated Clothing Workers Union, both of which have positively assisted clothing firms to increase their productivity. The New York locals of the ILGWU have even assisted employers in financing advertising campaigns to bolster the demand for their products. And it is no accident that some unions have vigorously supported their employers in seeking to maintain protective tariffs designed to exclude competing foreign products. The American Watch Workers Union is a case in point. Some unions have sought to expand the demand for labor by forcing make-work, or "featherbedding," rules upon employers. The Railway Brotherhoods force railroads to hire train crews of a certain minimum size; diesel engines must have a fireman even though there is no fire.

But the opportunity for unions to increase the demand for labor is limited. The main

FIGURE 29-5. UNIONS AND THE DEMAND FOR LABOR.
When unions can increase the demand for labor (D_1D_1 to D_2D_2), higher wage rates (W_1 to W_2) and a larger number of jobs (Q_1 to Q_2) can be realized.

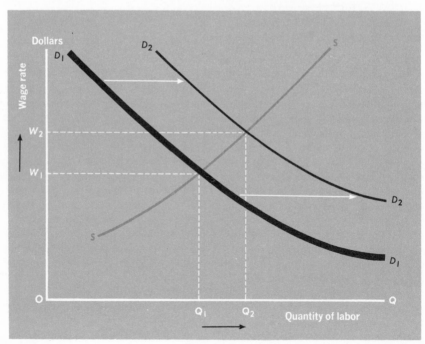

reason is obvious: as noted in our earlier discussion of the general level of wages, the basic forces underlying the productivity and therefore the demand for labor are largely outside the control of labor unions. The quantity and quality of the capital equipment with which labor is combined are the basic determinant of labor productivity in most firms, and this is a matter over which unions typically have little or no control. It should be noted, too, that, in many of the instances in which unions have pleaded for tariff protection and have practiced featherbedding, the situation has been that of a union attempting to forestall anticipated declines in the demand for labor rather than actually increasing the existing demand for a particular type of labor. This comment seems pertinent to the watchmakers and the Railway Brotherhoods, both of which find themselves in the unfortunate position of being employed in declining industries. In view of these comments it is not surprising that union efforts to increase wage rates have concentrated upon the supply side of the market.

Exclusive unionism. Unions may boost wage rates by reducing the supply of labor, that is, by shifting the supply curve of a particular type of labor to the left. Historically, the labor movement has favored policies designed to restrict the supply of labor to the economy as a whole in order to bolster the general level of wages. Labor unions have supported legislation which has (1) restricted immigration, (2) reduced child labor, (3) encouraged compulsory retirement, (4) enforced a shorter work week, and so forth.

More relevant for present purposes is the fact that specific types of workers have adopted through unions a host of techniques designed to restrict their numbers. This has been especially true of *craft unions*—that is, unions comprised of workers of a given skill, such as carpenters, bricklayers, plumbers, and printers. These unions have in many instances forced employers to agree to hire only union workers, thereby giving the union virtually complete control of the supply of labor. Then, by following restrictive membership policies—long apprenticeships, exorbitant initiation fees, the limitation or flat

prohibition of new members—the union causes an artificial restriction of the labor supply. As indicated in Figure 29-6, this results in higher wage rates. For obvious reasons this approach to achieving wage increases might be called "exclusive" unionism. Higher wages are the result of excluding workers from the union and therefore from the supply of labor.

Inclusive unionism. Most unions, however, do not attempt to limit their memberships. On the contrary, they seek to organize all available or potential workers. This is characteristic of the so-called *industrial unions*—unions such as the automobile workers and steelworkers which include all unskilled, semiskilled, and even skilled workers in a given industry. A union can afford to be exclusive when its members are skilled craftsmen for whom substitute workers are not readily available in quantity. But a union comprised largely of unskilled and semiskilled workers will undermine its own existence by limiting its membership and thereby causing numerous highly substitutable nonunion workers to be readily available for employment.

If an industrial union is successful in including virtually all workers in its membership, firms will be under great pressure to come to terms at the wage rate demanded by the union. Why? Because the union can obviously deprive the firm of its entire labor supply.

Inclusive unionism is illustrated graphically in Figure 29-7. Initially the competitive equilibrium wage rate is W_c and the level of employment is Q_c. Now an industrial union is formed, and it imposes a higher, above-equilibrium wage rate of, say, W_u. The imposition of this wage rate changes the supply curve of labor to the firms from the preunion SS curve to the post-union $W_u aS$ curve shown by the heavy line.[3] No workers will be forthcoming at

[3] Technically, the imposition of the wage rate W_u makes the labor supply curve perfectly elastic over the $W_u a$ range in Figure 29-7. In hiring any number of workers within this range, the union-imposed wage rate is effective and must be paid, or the union will supply no labor at all—the employers will be faced with a strike. If the employers want a number of workers in excess of $W_u a$ (which they never will when the union sets an above-equilibrium wage rate), they will have to bid up wages above the union's minimum.

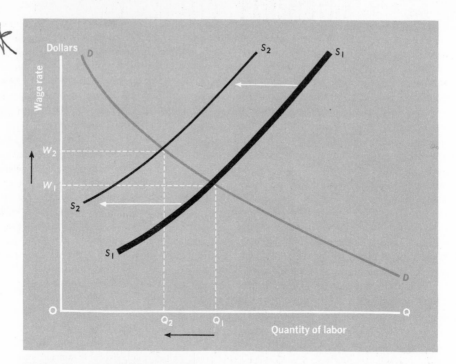

FIGURE 29-6. EXCLUSIVE UNIONISM.
By reducing the supply of labor (S_1S_1 to S_2S_2) through the use of restrictive member-ship policies, exclusive unions achieve higher wage rates (W_1 to W_2). However, the restriction of labor supply also reduces the number of workers employed (Q_1 to Q_2).

a wage rate less than that demanded by the union. If the employers decide it is better to pay this higher wage rate than to suffer a strike, they will cut back on employment from Q_c to Q_u. In other words, the above-equilibrium wage rate will cause some unemployment of union workers in this particular labor market.

Needless to say, this unemployment effect constitutes an important restraining influence upon the union in formulating its wage demands. A union cannot expect to maintain the solidarity of its members if it seeks a wage rate so high that the result will be joblessness for 20, 30, or 40 per cent of its members. The elasticity of labor demand is the basic consideration in determining the amount of unemployment which will accompany a wage hike: the more inelastic the demand for labor, the smaller will be the resulting unemployment.

You will recall from Chapter 28 that the determinants of the elasticity of labor demand include the elasticity of demand for the product, the portion of total costs for which wages account, and the substitutability of other resources for labor. It is notable that substitutability and hence elasticity vary directly with time. That is, over a short period of time—say a few weeks or months—a firm may hire about the same number of workers after a pay hike as it did before. But then, as the months pass, employers have sufficient time to substitute laborsaving capital equipment for workers. The practical significance of this is that, as substitution occurs, workers will be *gradually* unemployed and typically will drift into other jobs and other geographic areas. And with the absence of job opportunities new workers entering the labor force will be discouraged from entering this line of work. For these reasons the unemployment restraint upon union wage demands may be less pressing than it first appears to be. Even though industrial unions encourage rather than restrict membership, there is clearly a restrictive aspect to this analysis. But in contrast to exclusive unionism the restriction of employment is here done not by directly influencing labor supply but by enforcing an above-equilibrium wage rate and allowing the market to restrict the number of jobs available.

The United Mine Workers provide an excellent illustration of how an industrial union can achieve substantial wage increases, but only at the cost of a reduction in the number of jobs the industry has to offer. The UMW has clearly done an outstanding job of raising wage rates for miners. In December, 1961 the average

weekly earnings of bituminous coal workers were $119.07 as compared to $96.63 for all manufacturing industries. However, employment in December, 1961 stood at only 146,000 in bituminous coal as compared to a peak figure of almost 705,000 in 1923. There is little doubt that UMW wage pressure has been a major cause of this decline in the number of jobs. Labor costs constitute about 70 per cent of total costs in bituminous coal production. Hence, union-imposed wage increases have increased the total cost of coal sharply in relation to those of oil and gas, causing a sharp drop in coal output and in the number of jobs the industry can offer. Simultaneously, the increased cost of labor has accelerated the substitution of machinery for labor, causing further diminutions in the number of miners employed. The

FIGURE 29-7. INCLUSIVE UNIONISM.

By organizing virtually all available workers and thereby controlling the supply of labor, inclusive industrial unions may impose a wage rate, such as W_u, which is above the competitive wage W_c. The effect is to change the labor supply curve from SS to $W_u aS$. At the W_u wage rate employers will cut employment from Q_c to Q_u.

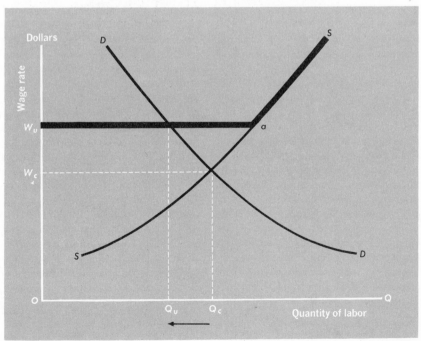

UMW has explicitly taken the position that the fattening of pay envelopes which it has brought about more than compensates for the sacrifice of jobs that these high wages have entailed.[4]

Bilateral monopoly model

Now let us suppose that a union is formed in a labor market that is not competitive but monopsonistic. Let us assume further that the union is a strong industrial union. In other words, let us combine the monopsony model with the inclusive unionism model. The result is a case of *bilateral monopoly*. The union is a monopolistic "seller" of labor, in that it can exert an influence over wage rates; it faces a monopsonistic employer (or combination of oligopsonistic employers) of labor who can also affect wages. Is this an extreme or special case? Not at all. In such important industries as steel, automobiles, meat packing, and farm machinery, "big labor"—one huge industrial union—bargains with "big business"—a few huge industrial giants.

Under these circumstances the employer(s) will seek a wage rate like that shown in the monopsony model (Figure 29-4). The union, on the other hand, will press for a wage rate similar to that indicated by the inclusive unionism model (Figure 29-7). Which of these two outcomes will result? We cannot say with any certainty. The outcome is logically indeterminate in the sense that economic theory does not explain what the resulting wage rate will be. We do know that there is an upper limit to what the employer will pay—a limit which depends primarily upon the firm's demand for labor. An employer cannot pay labor or any other resource in excess of its MRP without eventually incurring bankruptcy. The lower limit is influenced by supply considerations—in particular the willingness of workers to move to other occupations or other geographic areas or to strike. As a practical matter, minimum wage rates and the size of unemployment compensation or relief payments may establish the

lower limit. Within these broad limits it is the relative bargaining power of the union and the employer which will determine where the wage rate will be established. For example, if the union is well organized and has accumulated a sizable strike fund and prosperity prevails, the actual outcome may be reasonably close to the upper limit. On the other hand, a union which is weak both numerically and financially and is bargaining in a recession or depression environment will find itself in a disadvantageous bargaining position. The resulting wage may then be closer to the lower limit. Sheer bargaining ability also affects the outcome. In a subsequent chapter we will discuss some of the criteria which labor and management invoke in justifying their wage rate positions.

Do unions raise real wages?

Consideration of the three union models and the bilateral monopoly (union monopsony) model raises an interesting question: Do unions actually raise wages? At first the question seems naïve. Time and again we encounter newspaper articles to the effect that the UAW, the UMW, or the Teamsters has negotiated an 18-cent or 24-cent "wage package." A look at government statistics makes it clear that wages paid in organized industries generally exceed those in nonunionized industries. And our theoretical discussion of the various market models indicates that it is possible for unions to achieve wage rates above those which the market would otherwise determine. Despite these points, we must not leap to hasty conclusions.

Keep in mind, first of all, that the alternative to union-negotiated wage boosts is the wage level which the market forces of supply and demand would have determined in the absence of collective bargaining. There is a distinct possibility that market forces would have pushed wages up by as much as, or by more than, a union could through its bargaining efforts. Statistical evidence is not at all clear on this point.[5] Unions seem to gain the

---

[4] See Gordon F. Bloom and Herbert R. Northrup, *Economics of Labor Relations*, 3d ed. (Homewood, Ill.: Richard D. Irwin, Inc., 1958), pp. 389–392.

[5] Arthur D. Butler, *Labor Economics and Institutions* (New York: The Macmillan Company, 1961), chap. 17, provides a good summary of relevant statistical studies.

largest wage increases at the time a firm or industry is organized. This may be the result of wage increases granted by the company in a last-ditch effort to forestall unionization, or it might stem from overly aggressive union wage demands as the newly established union attempts to justify its existence to the workers. But once established, the union and the employer typically settle down to hard-bargain negotiations. It is not at all clear that unions are able to bargain for further increases in excess of wage hikes which the less dramatic operation of market forces would bring. As a matter of fact, a study[6] of wages in the basic steel industry in the 1945–1948 period concludes that collective bargaining by the United Steelworkers was not a significant factor in determining wage increases. It is suggested that wage increases *may* have been greater in the absence of the union! The fact that unions are extremely reluctant to accept wage cuts may make employers more unwilling to grant boosts than would be the case in an unorganized labor market. When a union is present, employers may show greater resistance to wage increases, recognizing that there is little possibility of negotiating future wage reductions which they feel a slumping market situation demands.

Furthermore, we must not attach too much weight to the fact that wages in many organized industries—for example, the steel and automobile industries—generally exceed those paid in unorganized industries. Even before they were organized these prosperous, expanding industries paid higher wages than most other industries.

Finally, looking at the slices of the total income pie, it is worth remembering that the share of the national income going to labor has been surprisingly stable over a long period of years during which unions have become more widespread and stronger. This suggests that, apart from the possibility of specific unions' raising the real wages of their own constituents, unions have not been particularly successful in enhancing the share of national income going

[6] Albert Rees, "Postwar Wage Determination in the Basic Steel Industry," *American Economic Review*, June, 1951, pp. 401–402.

to labor as a whole, that is, to both organized and unorganized workers. It should be remembered that the basic factor determining the general level of wages—productivity—depends primarily upon the quantity and quality of the capital and material resources with which labor is combined. This is a matter over which unions have very limited control. And, too, it is possible that where strong unions have actually been successful in boosting wages ahead of market forces, their gains may have come at the expense of unorganized workers and not interest, rent, and profit receivers. Why? Because unions typically raise wages by restricting the supply of labor directly (by restricting union membership) or indirectly (through above-equilibrium wage rates). This means that workers who cannot find jobs in unionized, high-wage occupations will drift into other nonunionized labor markets. As the supply of labor increases in relation to the demand for it, wages tend to fall in unorganized occupations.

All this is not to say that specific unions have not achieved wage increases in excess of what the forces of supply and demand would have established. Indeed, it would be difficult to explain the high wage rates of the mineworkers and construction workers apart from union wage policies. What these comments do suggest is that unionization does not automatically mean higher wages—for either the unionized workers or for labor as a whole—than would otherwise prevail.

WAGE DIFFERENTIALS

We have discussed the general level of wages and the role of supply and demand in a series of specific labor market situations. Yet to be explained are the wage differences which persist between different occupations and different individuals in the same occupations. Why does a corporate executive or a movie star receive $200,000 per year while garbage collectors and retail clerks get a paltry $2,000 per year? Table 29-3 indicates the substantial wage differentials which exist among certain common occupational groups. Our problem is to explain these differences.

Once again the forces of supply and demand

TABLE 29-3. AVERAGE HOURLY AND WEEKLY EARNINGS IN SELECTED
INDUSTRIES, DECEMBER, 1961

Industry	Average hourly gross earnings	Average weekly gross earnings
Contract construction	$3.29	$114.49
Bituminous coal	3.15	119.07
Petroleum refining	3.03	123.32
Motor vehicles	2.99	132.76
Printing and publishing	2.79	107.96
Chemicals	2.62	109.25
Fabricated metals	2.54	105.41
Food products	2.22	90.58
Retail trade	1.69	64.73
Apparel and finished textiles	1.67	60.12
Laundries	1.27	49.15

SOURCE: "Monthly Labor Review."

provide a general answer. If the supply of a particular type of labor is very great in relation to the demand for it, the resulting wage rate will be low. But if demand is great and the supply very small, wages will be very high. Though a good starting point, this supply and demand explanation is not particularly revealing. We want to know *why* supply and demand conditions differ in various labor markets. To do this we must probe those factors which lie behind the supply and demand of particular types of labor.

If (1) all workers were homogeneous, (2) all jobs were equally attractive to workers, and (3) labor markets were perfectly competitive, then all workers would receive precisely the same wage rate. As such, this is not a particularly startling statement. It merely suggests that, in an economy having one type of labor and in effect one type of job, competition will result in a single wage rate for all workers. The statement is important in that it does suggest the reasons why wage rates do differ in practice. (1) Workers are not homogeneous. They differ in capacities and in training and, as a result, fall into noncompeting occupational groups. (2) Jobs vary in attractiveness; the

nonmonetary aspects of various jobs are not the same. (3) Labor markets are typically characterized by imperfections.

Noncompeting groups

Workers are not homogeneous; they differ tremendously in their mental and physical capacities and in their education and training. Hence, at any point in time the labor force can be thought of as falling into a number of *noncompeting groups*, each of which may be composed of several or possibly just one occupation for which the members of this group qualify. For example, a relatively small number of workers have the ability—the capacity and the training—to be brain surgeons, concert violinists, and research chemists. Few people have the inherent capacity to enter these occupations, and even fewer have the financial means of acquiring the necessary training. The result is obviously that the supplies of these particular types of labor are very small in relation to the demand for them and the resulting wages and salaries are high. These and similar groups do not compete with each other or with other skilled or semiskilled workers. The violinist does not compete with the surgeon, nor does the garbage collector or retail clerk compete with either the violinist or the surgeon.

This is not to say that each of the thousands of specific occupations in the United States constitutes a noncompeting group of workers or that workers fall into isolated occupational compartments. A number of unskilled or semi-skilled occupations may well fall into one non-competing group. For example, gasoline station attendants, farm hands, and unskilled construction workers may all fall into the same group, because each is capable of doing the others' jobs. Yet none of the workers in this group currently offers severe competition for printers or electricians, who find themselves in other, more exclusive groups.

It should be noted, too, that the lack of competition between noncompeting groups of workers is actually a matter of degree. *Within limits* unskilled construction workers can be substituted for printers and electricians. Furthermore, this substitutability will be greater over a period of time than it will be in the short run; over time workers may move from one noncompeting group to another as they are able to develop their native capacities through education and training. The assembly-line worker who has an IQ of 140 may become an accountant or lawyer by going to night school. But here another obstacle arises: education is a costly business. Our ambitious but low income laborer does not have the same opportunity of entering the higher-paid occupational groups as do the offspring of the lawyers and accountants who are already in those groups. And, needless to say, differences in inherent capacities provide an even more permanent obstacle to occupational mobility. In short, both native capacity and the opportunity to train oneself are unequally distributed, causing the wage differentials of noncompeting groups to persist.

The concept of noncompeting groups is a flexible one; it can be applied to various subgroups and even to specific individuals in a given group. Some especially skilled surgeons are able to command wages considerably in excess of their run-of-the-mill colleagues who

perform the same operations. Mickey Mantle, Willie Mays, and a few others demand and get salaries many times that of the average major-league ballplayer. Why? Because in each instance their colleagues are only imperfect substitutes.

Equalizing differences

Now if a group of workers in a particular noncompeting group are equally capable of performing several different jobs, one might expect that the wage rate would be identical for each of these jobs. But this is not the case. A group of high school graduates may be equally capable of becoming bank clerks or unskilled construction workers. But these jobs pay different wages. In virtually all localities construction laborers receive better wages than do beginning bank clerks.

These differences can be explained on the basis of the *nonmonetary aspects* of the two jobs. The construction job involves dirty hands, a sore back, the hazard of accidents, and irregular employment both seasonally and cyclically. The banking job entails a white shirt, pleasant air-conditioned surroundings, and little fear of injury or layoff. Other things being equal, it is easy to see why workers will prefer picking up a deposit slip rather than a shovel. The result is that construction contractors must pay higher wages than banks to compensate for the unattractive nonmonetary aspects of construction jobs. These wage differentials are sometimes called *equalizing differences*, because they must be paid to compensate for the nonmonetary differences in various jobs.

Market imperfections

The notion of noncompeting groups helps explain wage differentials between different jobs for which limited numbers of workers are qualified. Equalizing differences aid in understanding wage differentials on different jobs for which workers in the same noncompeting group are equally qualified. Market imperfections in the form of various immobilities help explain wage differences paid on identical jobs. Though these immobilities are not mutually exclusive, we shall label them *geographic, artificial*, and *sociological*.

Labor is far from mobile. Workers take root geographically. They are reluctant to leave friends, relatives, and associates, to force their children to change schools, to sell their houses, and to incur the costs and inconveniences of adjusting to a new job and a new community. Geographical mobility is likely to be particularly low for older workers who have seniority rights and substantial claims to pension payments upon retirement. Then, too, workers who may be willing to move may simply be ignorant of job opportunities and wage rates in other geographic areas. As Adam Smith noted almost two centuries ago, ". . . a man is of all sorts of luggage the most difficult to be transported."

Geographic immobilities may be reinforced by artificial restrictions on mobility which are imposed by institutions. In particular, we have already noted that craft unions find it to their advantage to restrict their membership. After all, if carpenters and bricklayers become plentiful, the wages they can command will decline. Thus the low-paid nonunion carpenter of Brush, Colorado, may be willing to move to Chicago in the pursuit of higher wages. But his chances of successfully doing so are slim. He will be unable to get a union card, and no card, no job. The professions impose similar artificial restraints. For example, at most universities individuals lacking advanced degrees are simply not considered for employment as teachers. Quite apart from one's competence as a teacher and command of the subject matter, a "union card"—an M.A. or Ph.D.—is the first requisite for employment.

Finally, we must acknowledge sociological immobilities. Despite efforts of unions to the contrary, women workers frequently receive less pay than do men working at the same job. Negroes, Mexicans, Jews, and other minority groups are often forced to accept lower wages on given jobs than fellow workers receive.

A final point: it is more than likely that all three considerations—noncompeting groups, equalizing differences, and market imperfections—will play a role in the explanation of actual wage differentials. For example, the differential between the wages of a physician and a construction worker are largely explainable on the basis of noncompeting groups. Physicians fall into a noncompeting group where, because of mental and financial requisites to entry, the supply of labor is small in relation to demand and wages are therefore high. In construction work, where mental and financial prerequisites are much less significant, the supply of labor is great in relation to demand and wages low as compared to those of physicians. However, were it not for the unpleasantness of the construction worker's job and the fact that his craft union pursues restrictive membership policies, the differential would probably be even greater than it is.

EFFECT OF WAGE CHANGES ON EMPLOYMENT

Thus far we have been concerned with explaining the general level of wages, wage rates in particular labor markets, and the reasons why wage rates might differ between specific labor markets. Emphasis has been largely placed upon wage rates apart from any detailed consideration of accompanying levels of employment. We must now examine the relationship between wage rates and employment. In so doing it is crucial to distinguish between an individual firm's or industry's demand for a particular type of labor and the demand for labor of the economy as a whole.

Single firm or industry

The fact that a particular firm's demand curve for labor is downsloping correctly suggests that, *given its demand for labor*, the wage rate and the number of workers the firm employs will be inversely related. An increase in the wage rate will reduce and a decrease in the wage rate will increase the number of workers the firm will hire. This relationship was evident in our discussions of both exclusive (craft) and inclusive (industrial) unionism.

Though their techniques differ, both types of unionism will tend to reduce the number of jobs available by moving up the labor demand curve (see Figures 29-6 and 29-7).

There are several recognized exceptions to the general rule, however. Under certain circumstances higher wage rates will not cause unemployment in a specific labor market.

1. During periods of inflationary prosperity a firm faced with a union-imposed wage increase will find it opportune and relatively easy to pass the increase in wage costs on to consumers in the form of higher prices. This is particularly true of oligopolistic producers, who tend to boost prices only when some significant increase in costs has occurred which assumedly justifies higher prices. Because of the expanding money demand for goods which prosperity entails, the firm will suffer no decline in sales for its price-increasing efforts. Higher prices have the effect of increasing the demand for labor, because product price, along with productivity data, are the main components of the demand for labor. And wage boosts need not cause unemployment when the labor demand curve is shifting to the right.

2. A related possibility is that the prospect of higher wage rates will force firms to operate more efficiently, that is, to increase the productivity of their resources through greater managerial efficiency. This so-called "shock effect," by increasing the demand for labor through the productivity component, can offset the unemployment which normally accompanies higher wage rates. Labor economists, however, feel that the possibility of such productivity increases is limited.

3. Under oligopolistic conditions—particularly the kinked demand situation—significant increases in wage costs may have no effect upon product prices, the volume of output, and therefore the number of workers employed by such a firm. So long as the oligopolist's marginal cost schedule remains within the gap, or vertical segment, of its marginal revenue curve (see Figure 27-2), the firm will stand pat on price, output, and employment in seeking to avoid the potentially undesirable consequences of raising product price.

4. We have seen that where labor is being hired under monopsonistic conditions, the employer will find it profitable to restrict his employment of labor. By restricting employment the monopsonist can depress wage rates and therefore costs. This was demonstrated in Figure 29-4, where the monopsonist would hire Q_m workers at a wage rate of W_m. Now, if a union is organized and succeeds in imposing a higher wage rate upon the monopsonist —say, a wage rate in the vicinity of W_c—the result may be an *increase* in the number of workers the monopsonist will hire. By refusing to work at the monopsonistic rate of W_m, the union has eliminated the monopsonist's incentive to restrict employment. Where monopsony exists, a union can increase wages up to their marginal revenue product without causing any unemployment.[7]

These and similar exceptions do not destroy the notion that there is an inverse relationship between the price of a particular type of labor and the number of workers who will be hired. They do, however, suggest that this relationship is not a hard and fast rule, but rather a statement of a general tendency.

Economy as a whole

Reasoning in terms of an individual firm or industry, we have come to the conclusion that, with exceptions, a decline in the wage rate causes a movement down any given labor demand curve and results in more employment. But this reasoning is not applicable to the entire economy; that is, general wage cuts will not necessarily increase employment in the economy as a whole. Why? Because of the fallacy of composition: the wage rate–employment relationship which exists for an individual firm or industry is simply not relevant to the economy as a whole.

In talking about an individual firm's demand for labor it is reasonable to suppose that a decline in the wage rate paid by the firm will have little or no effect upon the demand for its

[7] The reader who seeks the graphic details of this analysis should pursue question 4 at the end of this chapter.

product and hence upon its demand for labor. After all, a firm's or industry's own workers account for a negligible portion of the total demand for its product; this is true even in the largest industries. This means in turn that it is proper to regard a firm's or industry's demand curve for labor as stable when it alters the wage rate it pays. We therefore can and do conclude that wage cuts can reduce unemployment in particular labor markets.

Businessmen have seized upon this reasoning to argue that general wage decreases are an effective means of combatting general (cyclical) unemployment. However, this reasoning loses its validity when couched in terms of general wage decreases which permeate the economy as a whole. If the wage rates of *all* workers were reduced, a significant decline in the (money) national income would result. Remember: wages account for over two-thirds of the national income. This would bring about a general decline in the demand for goods and services, which would then be mirrored in the resource market as a decline in the demand for labor. Employers might, as a result, hire no more (and possibly less) labor than originally, even though wage rates would now be lower.

In short, the individual firm can ignore the impact of lower wages upon national income and upon his product and resource demand curves, but employers as a group cannot. They must recognize that a general lowering of wages will adversely affect product and labor demand. As a matter of fact, if employers feel that a given general wage cut is indicative of further wage declines, unemployment may increase as firms postpone current production in anticipation of future cost reductions.

Labor leaders have reasoned that, if general wage *reductions* are of doubtful efficacy in reducing unemployment, the obvious solution is general wage *increases*. By putting more money into the hands of workers, they argue, total spending and the level of employment will increase. But a closer examination of this policy also reveals possible pitfalls. Will higher wages actually bring about significant increases in consumption during a recession? During a cyclical downswing, households might use wage increases to retire outstanding indebtedness, or they may hoard this extra income in anticipation of job losses or declines in product prices. And, even if higher wages do boost consumption, businessmen, faced with higher costs, may simultaneously reduce their investment spending. This could leave total spending unchanged or even diminished. The interrelationships involved here are very complex, and much depends upon the pessimism or optimism of households and businesses and the precise stage of the business cycle at which a general wage change is invoked.[8] Awaiting the time when economic theory clarifies the repercussions of general wage changes, most economists are content to accept the tentative conclusion that general wage decreases or increases are not likely to have significant or certain effects upon the general level of employment. At least the anticyclical measures described in Part 2 of this book are much more dependable means of seeking full employment.

SUMMARY

1. Wages are the price paid per unit of time for the services of labor.

2. The general level of wages in the United States is higher than in foreign nations, because the demand for labor is great in relation to the supply. The strong demand for American labor is based upon its high productivity, which in turn depends upon the quantity and quality of the capital equipment and natural resources used by labor, the quality of the labor force itself, the efficiency of management, a favorable sociopolitical environment, and the vast size of the domestic market. Over time these factors have caused the demand for labor to increase in relation to the supply, accounting for the long-run rise of real wages in the United States.

3. The determination of specific wage rates depends upon the structure of the particular

[8] The interested reader should consult Gordon F. Bloom and Herbert R. Northrup, *Economics of Labor Relations*, 4th ed. (Homewood, Ill.: Richard D. Irwin, Inc., 1961), chaps. 14 and 15.

labor market. In a competitive market the equilibrium wage rate and level of employment will be determined by the intersection of labor supply and demand.

4. Under monopsony, however, the marginal labor cost curve will lie above the labor supply curve, because the monopsonist must bid up wage rates in hiring extra workers and pay that higher wage to *all* workers. The monopsonist will hire fewer workers than under competitive conditions in order to achieve less-than-competitive wage rates (costs) and thereby greater profits.

5. A union may raise competitive wage rates by (a) increasing the derived demand for labor, (b) restricting the supply of labor through exclusive unionism, and (c) directly enforcing an above-equilibrium wage rate through inclusive unionism.

6. In many important industries the labor market takes the form of bilateral monopoly; that is, a strong union "sells" labor to a monopsonistic employer. The outcome of this labor market model is logically indeterminate. Such factors as the numerical and financial strength of the union, the phase of the cycle, and sheer bargaining ability are important in determining the actual wage rate established.

7. It is not at all clear that unions by and large have been successful in raising wage rates. (a) The unfettered forces of supply and demand may have accounted for wages as high as, or even higher than, those bargained by unions. (b) Though many unionized industries are high-wage industries, they paid relatively high wages before they were unionized. (c) The share of national income going to labor has remained relatively constant over a period of years despite the growth of organized labor.

8. Wage differentials are largely explainable in terms of (a) noncompeting groups, that is, differences in the capacities and training of different groups of workers, (b) equalizing differences, that is, wage differences which must be paid to offset nonmonetary differences in jobs, and (c) market imperfections in the form of geographic, artificial, and sociological immobilities.

9. A particular firm or industry's downsloping labor demand curve will be unaffected by a change in wage rates paid by that firm, because its workers demand a negligible portion of the good they produce. Hence, a lower wage rate will increase the number of workers employed by that firm or industry. A general lowering of wage rates, however, will reduce the national income and therefore reduce product and labor demand. As a result, no more (or even fewer) workers will be hired at lower wage rates than originally. Most economists feel that general wage changes are neither a significant nor certain means of altering the level of employment for the economy as a whole.

QUESTIONS AND STUDY SUGGESTIONS

1. Explain why the general level of wages is higher in the United States than in foreign nations. What is the most important single factor underlying the long-run increase in the average real wage rates in the United States? What, if anything, does this suggest concerning the ability of unions to raise real wages?

2a. Describe wage determination in a labor market in which workers are unorganized and many firms are actively competing for the services of labor. Show this situation graphically, using W_1 to indicate the equilibrium wage rate and Q_1 to show the number of workers hired by the firms as a group.

b. Suppose now that the formerly competing firms form an employer's association which hires labor as would a monopsonist. Describe verbally the impact upon wage rates and employment. Adjust the graph drawn for question 2a, showing the monopsonistic wage rate and employment level as W_2 and Q_2 respectively.

3. Describe the techniques which unions might employ to raise wages. Evaluate the desirability of each from the viewpoint of (a) the union and (b) society as a whole.

4. Assume a monopsonistic employer is paying a wage rate of W_m and hiring Q_m workers, as is indicated in Figure 29-4. Now suppose that an industrial union is formed and that the union forces the employer to accept a wage rate of W_c (Figure 29-4). Explain verbally and graphically why in this instance the higher wage rate will be accompanied by an *increase* in the number of workers hired. (*Hint:* a careful appraisal of the section on inclusive unionism and Figure 29-7 will help.)

5. Complete the following labor supply table for a firm hiring labor competitively.

Units of labor	Wage rate	Total labor cost (wage bill)	Marginal labor cost
1	$14		
2	14		
3	14		
4	14		
5	14		
6	14		

a. Show graphically the labor supply and marginal labor cost curves for this firm. Explain the relationships of these curves to one another.

b. Compare this data with the labor demand data of question 5 in Chapter 28. What will the equilibrium wage rate and level of employment be? Explain.

c. Now redetermine this firm's supply schedule for labor on the assumption that it is a monopsonist and that, although it can hire the first worker for $14, it must increase the wage rate by $1 to attract each successive worker. Show the new labor supply and marginal labor cost curves graphically and explain their relationships to one another. Compare these new data with those of question 5 for Chapter 28. What will be the equilibrium wage rate and the level of employment? Why does this differ from your answer to question 5b?

6. What are the basic considerations which help explain the wage differentials between particular labor markets?

7. Evaluate and explain these two statements:

a. "Wage differentials can be explained in terms of two factors: first, vertical immobilities, that is, obstacles to the movement of workers from one occupational level to another and, second, horizontal immobilities, that is, factors which prevent workers from being perfectly mobile geographically."

b. "If all workers were of equal capacity and training, all jobs equally attractive to workers, and labor markets were free of imperfections, all workers would receive the same wage rate."

8. "Wage cuts lower costs, and lower costs tend to increase output and the employment of labor. Therefore, general wage reductions will help eliminate general unemployment." Evaluate critically.

9. Evaluate and explain:

a. "Do unions raise wages? Of course, they do! Unions have been so successful in achieving such secondary goals as the union shop, seniority rights, and pension plans in the face of management opposition that it is unbelievable unions have been ineffective in achieving their major goal—compelling the payment of higher wage rates than management would otherwise offer."

b. "Craft unionism directly restricts the supply of labor; industrial unionism relies upon the market to restrict the number of jobs."

SELECTED REFERENCES

Bloom, Gordon F., and Herbert R. Northrup, *Economics of Labor Relations,* 4th ed. (Homewood, Ill.: Richard D. Irwin, Inc., 1961), chaps. 9–15.

Bober, M. M., *Intermediate Price and Income Theory,* rev. ed. (New York: W. W. Norton & Company, Inc., 1962), chap. 14.

Butler, Arthur D., *Labor Economics and Institutions* (New York: The Macmillan Company, 1961), chaps. 15–17.

Cohen, Sanford, *Labor in the United States* (New York: Charles E. Merrill Company, 1960), chaps. 11–13.

McKenna, Joseph P., *Intermediate Economic Theory* (New York: The Dryden Press, Inc., 1958), pp. 215–222.

Rothschild, K. W., *The Theory of Wages* (Oxford: Basil Blackwell & Mott, Ltd., 1956).

Chapter 30

THE PRICING AND EMPLOYMENT OF RESOURCES:

RENT, INTEREST, AND PROFITS

THE DISCUSSION in Chapter 29 of wages is rather lengthy. In contrast the discussions of the other income shares—rent, interest, and profits—found in the present chapter are relatively brief. There are two reasons for this difference in emphasis. (1) Wage incomes are clearly the major component of the national income. Statistics tell us that about two-thirds of the national income is in the form of wage and salary incomes, the remaining one-third accruing as rent, interest, and profit incomes. And because economists define wages more broadly and interest, rent, and profits more narrowly than do national income accountants, labor's share is understated in national income figures, and the size of the other three shares is overstated. (2) The economic theories of rent, interest, and profit are very unsettled; there are honest differences among authorities as to definitions, explanations, and implications where nonwage incomes are concerned. For these two reasons we shall concentrate upon the basic features of rent, interest, and profit determination and forgo the many controversial points and the often ambiguous details which are encountered in more advanced discussions of these income shares.

ECONOMIC RENT

To most people the term "rent" means the seemingly exorbitant sum one must pay for a two-bedroom apartment or a dormitory room. To the businessman "rent" is a payment made for the use of a factory building, machinery, or warehouse facilities. Closer examination finds these common-sense definitions of rent to be confusing and ambiguous. Dormitory room rent, for example, includes interest on the money capital the university has borrowed from the government or private individuals in financing the dormitory's construction, wages for custodial and maid service, and so forth. Economists therefore use the term "rent" in a narrower but less ambiguous sense: *economic rent is the price paid for the use of land and other natural resources which are completely fixed in total supply*. It is the unique supply conditions of land and other natural resources —their fixed supply—which makes rental payments distinguishable from wage, interest, and profit payments.

Let us examine this feature and some of its implications through simple supply and demand analysis. To avoid complications, assume, first, that all land is of the same grade or quality, that is, that each available acre of land is equally productive. Suppose, too, that all land has just one use, that is, that all land is capable of producing just one product—say, corn. And assume that land is being rented in a competitive market—that many corn farmers are demanding and many landowners offering land in the market.

In Figure 30-1 SS indicates the supply of arable farm land available in the economy as a whole and D_1 the demand of farmers for the use of that land. As with all economic resources, demand is a derived demand. It is downsloping because of the law of diminishing returns and the fact that, for farmers as a group, product price must be diminished to sell additional units of output.

The unique feature of our analysis is on the supply side: for all practical purposes the supply of land is perfectly inelastic, as reflected in SS. Land has no production cost; it is a "free and nonreproducible gift of nature." The economy has so much land, and that's that. It is true, of course, that within limits existing land can be made more usable by clearing, drainage, and irrigation. But these programs constitute capital improvements and not changes in the amount of land as such. Furthermore, such variations in the usability of land are a very small fraction of the total amount of land in existence and therefore do not undermine the basic argument that land and other resources are in virtually fixed supply.

The fixity of the supply of land means that demand is the only active determinant of land rent; supply is passive. And what determines the demand for land? Those factors discussed in Chapter 28—the price of the product, the productivity of land (which depends in part upon the quantity and quality of the resources with which land is combined), and the prices of those other resources which are combined with land. If in Figure 30-1 the demand for land should increase from D_1 to D_2 or decline from D_1 to D_3, land rent would change from R_1 to R_2 or R_3, but the amount of land supplied would remain unchanged at OS. In technical terms there is a large price effect and no quantity effect when the demand for land changes. If the demand for land is only D_4, land rent will be zero; that is, land will be a "free good," because it is not scarce enough in relation to the demand for it to command a price. This situation was approximated in the free-land era of American history. Changes in economic rent will have no impact upon the amount of land available; the supply of land is simply not augmentable.

Land rent is a surplus

The perfect inelasticity of the supply of land must be contrasted with the relative elasticity of such property resources as apartment build-

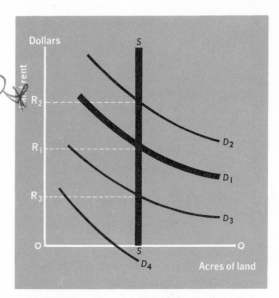

FIGURE 30-1. THE DETERMINATION OF LAND RENT.
Because the supply of land and other natural resources is perfectly inelastic (SS), demand is the sole active determinant of land rent. An increase (D_1 to D_2) or decrease (D_1 to D_3) in demand will cause considerable changes in rent (R_1 to R_2 and R_1 to R_3). If demand is very small (D_4) relative to supply, land will be a "free good."

ings, machinery, and warehouses. These resources are not fixed in total supply. A higher price will give entrepreneurs the incentive to construct and offer larger quantities of these property resources. Conversely, a decline in their prices will induce suppliers to allow existing facilities to depreciate and not be replaced. The same general reasoning applies to the total supply of labor. Within limits a higher average level of wages will induce more workers to enter the labor force, and lower wages will cause them to drop from the labor force. In other words, the supplies of nonland resources are upsloping, or, stated differently, the prices paid to such resources perform an *incentive function*. A high price provides an incentive to offer more; a low price, to offer less.

Rent could be eliminated and not affect economy—

Not so with land. Rent serves no incentive function, because the total supply of land is fixed. If rent is $10,000, $500, $1, or $0 per acre, the same amount of land will be available to society to make a contribution to production. Rent, in other words, could be eliminated without affecting the productive efficiency of the economy. For this reason economists consider rent to be a *surplus*, that is, a payment which is not necessary to ensure that land will be available to the economy as a whole.

Should rent be paid?

If land is a free gift of nature, costs nothing to produce, and would be available even in the absence of rental payments, why should rent be paid to those who by historical accident or inheritance happen to be landowners? Socialists have long argued that all land rents are unearned incomes. Therefore, they argue, land should be nationalized—owned by the state—so that any payments for its use can be utilized by the state in furthering the well-being of the entire population rather than a landowning minority. In the United States criticism of rental payments has taken the form of a *single tax movement* which gained considerable support in the late 1800s. Spearheaded by Henry George's provocative book, *Progress and Poverty* (1879), this reform movement centered upon the notion that economic rent might be taxed away completely without impairing the available supply of land or therefore the productive potential of the economy as a whole. If the relevant supply and demand conditions for land are as shown by D_1 and SS in Figure 30-1, land rent will be R_1. A land tax of that same amount—R_1 per acre—will obviously confiscate this land rent but will leave the amount of land available for productive purposes unchanged at OS. The complete inelasticity of land supply makes it impossible for the landowner to shift this tax to renters.

The simplicity and apparent justice of a single tax gained considerable support for the single tax movement. But glaring defects become apparent upon closer analysis:

1. As noted earlier, in practice most income payments combine elements of interest, rent, wages, and profits. As a practical matter, it would be virtually impossible to determine how much of any given income payment is economic rent.

2. A single tax on land rent would not be capable of financing modern government. It is estimated that only 3 or 4 per cent of the national income takes the form of economic rent. Modern governments spend in excess of 20 per cent of the national income in peacetime and much more during war. In short, it is no longer realistic to espouse a tax on land as a *single tax*.

3. The apparent justice of a single tax on land disappears once it is recognized that in the course of history virtually all pieces of land have changed hands many times. Hence, a single tax would fall not upon the original settlers or expropriators who claimed nature's free gift but rather upon recent purchasers who have bought the land at prices reflecting the capitalized rental income of the land.

4. Although rent performs no incentive function, it does perform a rationing function. In the absence of a single tax, landowners will supply land to those renters who are willing to pay the highest rent for it. And, under competitive conditions, it will be those producers for whom the marginal revenue product of land is greatest who will be able to pay the highest rent. In other words, rent will ration the available supply of land to the most productive uses. On the other hand, landowners would be completely indifferent as to which producers obtained the use of their land if government stood ready to tax away the entire rental payment. *Rationing Function*

Productivity differences and alternative uses

Our analysis thus far has proceeded upon the assumption that all units of land are of the same grade. In practice, this simply is not so. Different acres vary greatly in productivity. These productivity differences stem primarily from differences in soil fertility and such climatic factors as rainfall and temperature. It is these factors which explain why Iowa soil is excellently suited to corn production, the plains of eastern Colorado are much less so, and desert wasteland of New Mexico is incapable of corn production. These differences in productivity will be reflected in resource demand. Competitive bidding by farmers will establish a high rent for the very productive Iowa land. The less productive Colorado land will command a much lower rent, and the New Mexico land no rent at all. Location may be equally important in explaining differences in land rent. Other things being equal, renters will pay more for a unit of land which is strategically located with respect to materials, labor, and customers than for a unit of land whose location is remote from these markets.

We have also supposed thus far that land has only one use. Actually, we know that land usually has a number of alternative uses. An acre of Iowa farmland may be useful in raising not only corn, but also wheat, oats, milo, and cattle, or it may be useful as a site for a house or factory. What is the importance of this obvious point? It indicates that, although land is a free gift of nature and has no production cost from the viewpoint of society as a whole, the rental payments of individual producers are *costs*. The total supply of land will be available to society even if no rent at all is paid for its use, but, from the standpoint of individual firms and industries, land has alternative uses, and therefore payments must be made by specific firms and industries to attract that land from those other uses. According to our alternative cost doctrine, such payments by definition are costs. Once again the fallacy of composition has entered our discussion. From the standpoint of society there is no alternative but for land to be used by society. Therefore to society rents are a surplus, not a cost. But because land has alternative uses, the rental payments of corn farmers or any other individual user are a cost, because such payments are required to attract land from alternative uses.

INTEREST

Interest is the price paid for the use of money or, better yet, for the use of loanable funds. Three related aspects of this income payment are immediately notable:

1. Because it is paid in kind, interest is typically stated as a percentage of the amount of money being borrowed rather than as an absolute amount. It is less clumsy to say that one is paying 5 per cent interest than to proclaim that interest is "$50 per year per $1,000." Furthermore, stating interest as a percentage facilitates the comparison of interest paid on loans of much different absolute amounts. By expressing interest as a percentage we can immediately compare an interest payment of, say, $144 per year per $2,880 and one of $600 per year per $12,000. In this case both interest payments are 5 per cent—a fact not at all obvious from the absolute figures.

2. Money is not an economic resource. As such, money is not productive; it is incapable of producing goods and services. However, businessmen "buy" the use of money, because money can be used to acquire capital goods—factory buildings, machinery, warehouses, and so forth. And these facilities clearly do make a contribution to production. Thus in hiring the use of money capital businessmen are ultimately buying the use of real capital goods. As a matter of fact, it is the expected marginal revenue productivity of capital goods which sets an upper limit upon the rate of interest businessmen will pay to obtain the funds needed for the purchase of those capital goods.

3. Though economists find it convenient to talk as if there existed a single interest rate, it must be recognized that there are actually many different rates of interest. The Federal government currently borrows at 3 to 4 per cent on most of its securities. Corporate bonds may pay 4½ to 5½ per cent. FHA mortgage loans may entail interest rates of 5½ to 6 per cent. Bank loans to consumers for automobile or refrigerator purchases may run 10 or 14 per cent. Those whose credit standing forces them to borrow from consumer finance companies may pay extremely high rates—24 or 36 per cent is not uncommon.

Why the differences? (*a*) The varying degrees of *risk* on loans are important. The greater the chance the borrower will not repay the loan, the more interest the lender will charge to compensate for this risk. (*b*) The *length* of a loan also affects the interest rate. Other things being equal, long-term loans command higher rates of interest than do short-term loans, because the long-term lender suffers the inconvenience and possible financial sacrifice of forgoing alternative uses for his money for a greater period of time. (c) Given two loans of equal length and risk, the interest rate will be higher on the smaller of the two loans. This is so because the administrative costs of a large and a small loan are about the same absolutely. (d) Market imperfections are also important in explaining some interest rate differentials. The small-town bank which monopolizes the local money market may charge high interest rates on loans to consumers because households find it inconvenient to "shop around" at banks in somewhat distant cities. The large corporation, on the other hand, can survey rival investment houses in disposing of a new bond issue and thereby secure the lowest obtainable rate.

To circumvent the difficulties involved in discussing the whole structure of interest rates, economists talk of "the" interest rate or the "pure" rate of interest. This pure rate is best approximated by the interest paid on long-term, virtually riskless bonds such as the long-term bonds of the United States government or of American Telephone and Telegraph. This interest payment can be thought of as being made solely for the use of money over an extended time period, because the risk factor and administrative costs are negligible and the interest on such securities is not distorted by market imperfections. The pure interest rate in the spring of 1962 was about 4 per cent.

If the interest rate can be defined as the price paid for the use of loanable funds, then it is clear that to understand the determination of the rate of interest we must understand the factors which underlie the demand for, and the supply of, loanable funds.

Demand for loanable funds

Who borrows money? For what purposes? Generally speaking, businesses, households, and government are the primary demanders of loanable funds.

The great bulk of loanable funds is borrowed by *businesses* for use in the purchase of more and better capital goods. Businesses seek the use of capital goods (Chapter 3) because "roundabout production" through the use of tools and equipment increases productivity. Hence, we can draw a marginal revenue product curve—a capital demand curve—for the various specific types of capital goods. Like other resource demand curves, this MRP curve will diminish because of the law of diminishing returns. However, this resource demand curve is more complex than other resource demand curves because capital goods are durable. A lathe or drill press may have a life of ten or fifteen years. Therefore, businessmen must assess as best they can the uncertainties of the future and estimate the return above acquisition, maintenance, and operating costs which the purchase of additional units of capital will probably yield. This net *expected* return can be expressed as a percentage of the cost of the capital goods and compared with the rate of interest.

Now we found in Chapter 28 that under competition it is profitable for a firm to purchase any resource up to the point at which the price of that resource equals its marginal revenue product. In this instance the marginal revenue productivity of a capital good is measured by the expected net return on the capital good expressed as a percentage of its cost. The price of the loanable funds required to purchase the capital good is obviously the interest rate. Hence, it will pay businessmen to demand loanable funds up to the point at which the expected net rate of return on the capital good equals the rate of interest.

Households also demand loanable funds when they wish to make purchases in excess of their current incomes and cash resources. The long-run relative increase in the production of durable goods which has taken place in our economy has encouraged the growth of consumer credit. Automobiles, refrigerators, and television sets are typically purchased on credit.

At times *government* is also a major borrower. This is particularly so during periods of war or intense mobilization, when it is difficult for both political and economic reasons to finance large volumes of Federal spending from taxes on a pay-as-you-go basis.

The demand for loanable funds is clearly downsloping. Businessmen will find it profitable to purchase larger amounts of capital goods when the price of loanable funds declines. Similarly, lower interest rates may encourage some increase in consumer and governmental borrowing. Economists are in general agreement, however, that the demand for loanable funds is inelastic. The reasons for this are several. Interest costs are usually a relatively small portion of the total cost of any capital goods purchase; hence, the demand for loanable funds for investment purposes tends to be insensitive to changes in the interest rate. Consumer short-term borrowing is also interest-inelastic. Consumers are interested more in the size of their "small monthly payments" than in their interest charges. On long-term housing loans, on the other hand, interest rates undoubtedly exert a significant influence on consumer borrowing. The amount of loanable funds demanded by government is also insensitive to interest-rate fluctuations—particularly for Federal borrowing, which is usually associated with wartime emergencies. Here interest charges are a very secondary consideration. With everything taken into account, the demand for loanable funds is downsloping and in all probability interest-inelastic.

Potential supply of loanable funds

There are three basic sources of loanable funds.

1. The current saving and the past savings accumulated by households are one potential source of loanable funds. In any reasonably prosperous year households as a group will consume less than their disposable incomes, the difference being personal saving. These funds may be augmented by decreases in the liquid savings which households now hold as idle hoards; these accumulations may be drawn down and offered in the money market.

2. The current and accumulated savings of businesses are a major source of loanable funds. In each prosperous year businesses save very substantial amounts in the form of depreciation charges and undistributed corporate profits. And, as with households, current business saving may be supplemented by declines in the cash hoards or bank balances of businesses. These business sources of loanable funds are often demanded for investment purposes by the firms themselves and therefore do not enter the market for loanable funds.

3. A potential source of loanable funds is newly created money, that is, money created by commercial bank lending or by government's simply printing new money.

Actual supply of loanable funds

We have been careful to designate the current and past saving of households and businesses and commercial bank lending as the *potential* supply of loanable funds. The reason is that households, businesses, and banks may not actually be willing to make these funds available to borrowers. Money, remember, is a store of value. Households and businesses may not want to offer either their current saving or any of their accumulated savings to borrowers. On the contrary, they may choose to add a portion of their current saving to their accumulated savings balances.

Having made choices as to how to divide their incomes and receipts between spending and saving, households and businesses must then decide the specific form in which to hold their saving. The basic choice is between money in the form of either idle cash or bank accounts, on the one hand, and securities of some sort, on the other. Idle cash and bank accounts are highly liquid assets; securities acquired from borrowers are somewhat less liquid. That part of saving (current or accumulated) which households and businesses want to hold as securities flows into the money market as the supply of loanable funds. That part which households and businesses want to hold as money obviously does not. This division depends upon the *liquidity preferences* of households and businesses. More specifically, there are three main reasons why households and businesses prefer to hold money rather than securities:

1. There is a *transaction motive* for holding money rather than securities. Households and businesses both need to keep a stock of cash on hand to make the ordinary day-to-day purchases. Households, for example, receive a sizable chunk of income every two weeks or every month. Disbursements, on the other hand, occur more or less evenly over time. This means that households will have an average money balance of some size bridging the gap between paydays. And it is simply more convenient to have one's assets in their most liquid form, that is, as idle cash balances or bank accounts, than in the form of securities. Liquidity permits one to avail himself readily of any extraordinarily good buys or bargains he may chance upon. Furthermore, there are costs—brokerage fees— in transferring cash into securities and back again.

2. There is a *precautionary motive* for holding money. Households and businesses may hold cash balances to meet any rainy day contingencies which might arise. Particularly relevant are those risks which one cannot protect himself against by purchasing insurance policies—prolonged illness, unemployment, unfavorable shifts in consumer demand, and so forth.

3. There is a *speculative motive* for holding money. At any point in time there is a certain rate of interest which households and businesses as potential suppliers of loanable funds consider to be about "normal." If the rate of interest is currently low, that is, "below normal," households and businesses may withhold a part of their savings which would otherwise flow into the money market as a part of the supply of loanable funds. They hold more money and less securities than they normally would. Why? Because they expect that the current below-normal interest rate will probably rise in the future. Hence, households and businesses refrain from supplying their loanable funds now in anticipation of a higher interest return in the future. Conversely, if the current interest rate is unusually high, that is "above normal," households and businesses will choose to hold less money and more securities in order to take advantage of high current interest rates as opposed to the lower normal rate expected to prevail again in the future.

The supply of loanable funds is clearly upsloping. Though the interest rate probably does not exert a very strong influence upon the amount households and businesses save, higher and higher interest rates will induce households and businesses to be less liquid. At relatively high interest rates households and firms will prefer to hold their assets in the form of interest-bearing securities rather than as non-interest-bearing checking accounts and idle cash balances. There is little clear-cut evidence as to how sensitive or insensitive the supply of loanable funds is to changes in the interest rate.

The interaction of the upsloping supply-of-loanable-funds curve and the downsloping demand-for-loanable-funds curve determines the equilibrium rate of interest.

Interest rate: an administered price

Though we have concluded that the interest rate is determined by the demand for, and the supply of, loanable funds, few would argue that the interest rate is a free market price. The interest rate is actually an administered price —a price which is profoundly and purposely influenced by government. Government's influence is apparent on both the demand and the supply sides of the picture. As previously noted, government is an important borrower. Fiscal policies appropriate to recession and depression call for Federal deficits. During wartime government assumes the dominant role on the demand side of the market for loanable funds. Finally, the Treasury is constantly refunding portions of the public debt as outstanding government bonds mature. On the supply side, the Federal Reserve authorities influence the supply of loanable funds and therefore the interest rate through the application of tight and easy money policies (Chapter 17).

The reasons why government is interested in administering the interest rate are apparent upon examination of the ways in which the interest rate may influence the operation of the economy. Specifically, the interest rate affects both the *level* and the *composition* of investment goods production.

Interest, capital accumulation, and employment. The interest rate affects the level of investment and therefore the level of employment in the economy. Other things being equal, a lowering of the interest rate will induce businessmen to increase their purchases of investment goods. This stimulates total spending and the volume of employment. Conversely, other things being equal, an increase in the interest rate will cause businessmen to cut their expenditures for capital goods, thereby causing total spending and employment to fall.

This is not to say, however, that adjustments in the interest rate brought about by changes in either the private or public components of the demand for, and supply of, loanable funds will be sufficient to alter investment spending to the level required for achieving full employment. The interest rate is only one of many forces which have a bearing upon the investment plans of businesses. The rate of technological advance, population growth, the acquisition and operating costs of capital goods, government tax and expenditure policies, the stocks of capital goods on hand, anticipated market conditions, and business confidence are all important determinants of investment. Changes in any of or all these factors may easily offset any alterations in the interest rate which government may initiate in seeking to influence investment spending and employment. Stated differently, frequent and significant fluctuations in all those factors which affect the expected marginal revenue productivity of capital goods are considerably more important than changes in the interest rate in determining the actual level of investment spending. It is also notable that, if interest rates are initially low, as they typically are in industrially advanced nations, it simply is not possible for significant declines in the interest rate to occur. For all these reasons we must conclude that there is nothing inherent in the market for loanable funds or, more specifically, the interest rate, which gives rise to the level of investment required for achieving full employment.

Interest and the allocation of capital. Prices, you will recall, are rationing devices. The interest rate, being the price of loanable funds, is no exception. The interest rate performs the function of allocating money capital and therefore real capital to various firms and investment projects. It rations the available supply of loanable funds to those investment projects whose rate of return or expected profitability is sufficiently high to warrant payment of the going interest rate. If the expected marginal revenue productivity of additional real capital in industry X is 10 per cent and the required loanable funds can be secured at an interest rate of 6 per cent, industry X will be in a position to borrow and expand its capital facilities. On the other hand, if the marginal productivity of additional capital in industry Y is expected to be only 3 per cent, it will be unprofitable for this industry to accumulate more capital goods. In short, the interest rate allocates money and ultimately real capital to those industries in which it will be most productive and therefore most profitable. Such an allocation of capital goods is obviously in the interest of society as a whole.

But the interest rate does not perform perfectly the task of rationing capital to its most productive uses. Many firms finance their capital expansions internally and therefore are not subject to screening by the interest rate. Similarly, large oligopolistic borrowers are in a better position than competitive borrowers to pass interest costs on to consumers by virtue of their ability to administer prices. And, too, the sheer size and prestige of large industrial concerns might allow them to obtain money capital on favorable terms, while the market for loanable funds screens out less well-known firms whose profit expectations might actually be superior.

BUSINESS PROFITS AND ECONOMIC PROFITS

As is the case with rent, economists find it advantageous to define profits more narrowly than do businessmen or accountants. To most businessmen "profit" is what remains of a firm's total revenue after it has paid other individuals and firms for materials, capital, and labor supplied to the firm. To the economist this definition is too broad and therefore ambiguous. The difficulty, as the economist sees it, is that this view of profits takes into acount only *explicit* costs, that is, payments made by the firm to outsiders. It therefore ignores *implicit* costs, that is, payments to similar resources which are owned and self-employed by a firm. In other words, the businessman's concept of profits fails to allow for implicit wage, rent, and interest costs. *Economic*, or *pure*, *profits* are what remain after both explicit and implicit wage, rent, and interest costs have been subtracted from a firm's total revenue. Economic profits may be either positive or negative (losses).

An example may sharpen these comments. As the economist sees it, a farmer who owns his land and equipment and provides all his own labor is grossly overstating his economic profits if he merely subtracts his payments to outsiders for seed, fertilizer, gasoline, and so forth from his total receipts. Actually much or possibly all of what remains are the implicit rent, interest, and wage costs which the farmer forgoes in deciding to self-employ the resources he owns rather than make them available in alternative employments. Interest on the capital or wages for the labor contributed by the farmer himself are no more profits than are the payments which would be made if outsiders had supplied these resources. In short, the businessman's definition and the economist's definition of profits are compatible only if the businessman includes both explicit and implicit costs in determining total costs. Economic profits are a residual—the total revenue remaining after *all* costs are paid.

Economic profits and the entrepreneur

Generally speaking, economic profits may be regarded as a payment accruing to a very special type of human resource—*entrepreneurial ability*. As noted in Chapter 2, in a dynamic and uncertain economy labor, land, and capital resources do not automatically come together in the production of some good or service. Rather it is the entrepreneur who assumes the initiative in combining these resources and in making the nonroutine decisions which guide their use in the productive process. The entrepreneur is also an innovator. He undertakes to introduce commercially new products and new productive techniques, to try new methods of business organization, administration, marketing, to open new markets, and so forth.

In performing these two functions in the economy the entrepreneur necessarily bears risks. The continuous and unpredictable changes which characterize the economy rule out any guarantee that the entrepreneur will realize a profit for his efforts as either a combiner, or director, of resources or as an innovator. In short, we can say that profits are paid to the entrepreneur for (1) combining and directing the use of resources in an uncertain environment, and (2) being an innovator.

Sources of economic profit

Our understanding of economic profits and the entrepreneur's functions can be both deepened and widened by describing an artificial economic environment within which pure profits would be zero. Then, by noting real-world deviations from this environment, we can lay bare the sources of economic profit.

In a purely competitive, static economy pure profits would be zero. By a static economy we mean one in which all the basic data —resource supplies, technological knowledge, and consumer tastes—are constant and unchanging. A static economy is a changeless one in which all the determinants of cost and supply data, on the one hand, and demand and revenue data, on the other, are constant. Given the static nature of these data, the economic future is perfectly foreseeable; economic uncertainty is nonexistent. The outcome of price and production policies is accurately predictable. Furthermore, the static nature of such a society precludes any type of innovational change. Under pure competition any pure profits (or losses) which might have existed initially will disappear with the entry or exodus of firms in the long run. All costs—both explicit and implicit—will therefore be precisely covered in the long run, leaving no residual in the form of pure profits.

The entrepreneur clearly has no function to perform in such a society. There is no uncertainty and therefore no nonroutine decision to make in the combining and directing of economic resources. And in a static economy innovations are ruled out. Stated differently, in the absence of uncertainty and innovational changes there are no risks to be borne. The "businessman" in such an economy would be merely a highly skilled worker whose job is the rendering of routine business decisions. His income payment is a wage, not a pure profit.

The notion of zero economic profits in a static, competitive economy enhances our understanding of profits by suggesting that the presence of profits is linked to the dynamic nature of real-world capitalism and the accompanying uncertainty. Furthermore, it indicates that economic profits may arise from a source apart from the directing, innovating, risk-bearing functions of the entrepreneur. And that source is the presence of some degree of monopoly power.

Uncertainty, risk, and profits. In a dynamic economy the future is always clothed in uncertainty. This means that the businessman necessarily assumes risks. Profits can be thought of in part as a reward for assuming these risks.

In linking pure profits with uncertainty and risk bearing it is important to distinguish between risks which are insurable and those which are not. Some types of risks—for example, fires, floods, theft, and accidents to employees—are measurable in the sense that actuaries can estimate their occurrence with considerable accuracy. As a result, these risks are insurable. Firms can avoid, or at least provide for, these risks by incurring a small known cost in the form of an insurance premium. It is the bearing of uninsurable risks, then, which is a potential source of economic profits.

What are such uninsurable risks? Basically, they are uncontrollable and unpredictable changes in demand (revenue) and supply (cost) conditions facing the firm. Some of these uninsurable risks stem from unpredictable changes in the general economic environment or, more specifically, from the business cycle. Prosperity brings substantial windfall profits to most firms, while depression means widespread losses. But, in addition, changes are constantly taking place in the structure of the economy. Even in a full-employment noninflationary economy changes are always occurring in consumer tastes, resource supplies, and so forth. These changes continually alter the revenue and cost data faced by individual firms and industries leading to changes in the structure of the business population as favorably affected industries expand and adversely affected industries contract. Changes in government policies are pertinent at both levels. Appropriate fiscal and monetary policies by government may reverse a recession while a tariff may significantly alter the demand and revenue data of the protected industry.

The point is this: profits and losses can be associated with the assumption of uninsurable risks stemming from both cyclical and structural changes in the economy.

Uncertainty, innovations, and profits. The uncertainties just discussed are external to the firm; they are beyond the control of the individual firm or industry. One other extremely important dynamic feature of capitalism—innovation—occurs at the initiative of the entrepreneur. Business firms deliberately introduce new methods of production and distribution to affect their costs favorably and new products to influence their revenue favorably. The entrepreneur purposely undertakes to upset his existing cost and revenue data in a way he hopes will be profitable to him.

But once again uncertainty enters the picture. Exhaustive market surveys to the contrary, entrepreneurs do not know in advance whether consumers actually want more horsepower in their automobiles, clothing made of paper, color television sets, three-dimensional movies, and ball-point pens. Nor do they know certainly whether a new machine will actually provide the cost economies it should realize while it is still in the blueprint stage. Innovations purposely undertaken by entrepreneurs entail uncertainty, just as do those changes in the economic environment over which an individual enterprise has no control. In a sense, then, innovation as a source of profits is merely a special case of risk bearing.

Under competition and in the absence of patent laws innovational profits will be temporary. Rival firms will imitate successful (profitable) innovations, thereby competing away all economic profits. Nevertheless, innovational profits may always exist in a progressive economy as new successful innovations replace those older innovations whose associated profits have been competed away.

Monopoly profits. Thus far we have emphasized that profits are related to the uncertainties and insurable risks surrounding dynamic events which enterprises are exposed to or initiate themselves. The existence of monopoly in some form or another is a final source of economic profits. As explained previously, because of his ability to restrict entry, a monopolist may persistently enjoy economic profits provided demand is relatively strong and costs relatively low. This profit stems from the monopolist's ability to restrict output and administer product price to his own advantage.

There are both a causal relationship and a notable distinction between uncertainty, on the one hand, and monopoly, on the other, as sources of profits. The causal relationship involves the fact that an entrepreneur can reduce uncertainty, or at least manipulate its effects, by achieving monopoly power. The competitive firm is unalterably exposed to the vagaries of the market; the monopolist, however, can control the market to a degree and thereby offset or minimize potentially adverse effects of uncertainty. Furthermore, innovation is an important source of monopoly power; the short-run uncertainty associated with the introduction of new techniques or new products may be borne for the purpose of achieving a measure of monopoly power.

The notable distinction between profits stemming from uncertainty and from monopoly has to do with the social desirability of the two sources of profits. Bearing the risks inherent in a dynamic and uncertain economic environment and the undertaking of innovations are socially desirable functions. The social desirability of monopoly profits, on the other hand, is subject to very great doubt. Monopoly profits typically are founded upon output restriction, above-competitive prices, and a contrived misallocation of resources.

Functions of profits

Profit is the prime mover, or energizer, of the capitalistic economy. As such, profits influence both the level of resource utilization and the allocation of resources among alternative uses. It is profits—or better, the *expectation* of profits—which induce firms to innovate. And innovation stimulates investment, total output, and employment. Innovation is a fundamental aspect of the process of economic growth, and it is the pursuit of profit which underlies innovation. We know from our previous analysis of the determination of national income that profit expectations are highly volatile, with the result that investment, employment, and the rate of growth have been unstable. Profits have functioned imperfectly as a spur to innovation and investment.

Profits perform more effectively the task of allocating resources among alternative lines of production. Businessmen seek profits and shun losses. The occurrence of economic profits is a signal that society wants that particular industry to expand. Indeed, profit rewards are more than an inducement for an industry to expand; they also are the financial means by which firms in such industries can add to their productive capacities. Losses, on the other hand, signal society's desire for the afflicted industries to contract; losses penalize those who fail to adjust their productive efforts to those goods and services most preferred by consumers. This is not to say that profits and losses result in an allocation of resources which is now and forever attuned to consumer preferences. In particular the presence of monopoly in both product and resource markets impedes the shiftability of firms and resources, as also do the various geographic, artificial, and sociological immobilities discussed in Chapter 29.

SUMMARY

1. Economic rent is the price paid for the use of land and other natural resources whose total supplies are fixed.

2. Rent is a surplus in the sense that land would be available to the economy as a whole even in the absence of all rental payments.

3. The notion of rent as a surplus gave rise to the single tax movement of the late 1800s, which advocated a confiscatory single tax on land rent. This proposal, however, is subject to serious limitations. (*a*) It overlooks the administrative difficulties of determining what portion of specific income payments constitute economic rent. (*b*) A single tax on land will not provide enough revenue to finance modern government. (*c*) The tax would unjustly penalize those who have purchased land. (*d*) A confiscatory tax on land rent would undermine the rationing function of rent.

4. Differences in land rent are explainable in terms of differences in the fertility and climatic features of land and in its location.

5. Land rent is a surplus rather than a cost to the economy as a whole; however, because from the viewpoint of individual firms and industries land has alternative uses, rental payments of firms and industries are correctly regarded as costs.

6. Interest is the price paid for the use of loanable funds. Specific interest rates vary because of differences in the degree of risk loans

entail, the length of loans, the relative size of administrative costs associated with lending, and market imperfections.

7. Businesses, households, and government are the principal demanders of loanable funds. The current and past saving of businesses and households and commercial bank credit are the major potential sources of loanable funds. However, the actual supply of loanable funds may differ from the potential supply because of changes in the liquidity preference of households, businesses, and banks. The intersection of the supply of loanable funds and the demand for them determines the equilibrium interest rate.

8. Because of the borrowing activities of the Treasury and the Board of Governor's control over the loan-creating activities of commercial banks, the price of loanable funds is largely administered by government.

9. The interest rate influences the level of capital accumulation and helps ration capital goods to specific firms.

10. Economic, or pure, profits are the difference between a firm's total revenue and the total of its explicit and implicit wage, rent, and interest costs.

11. Profits accrue to entrepreneurs for assuming the uninsurable risks associated with the organizing and directing of economic resources and innovating. Profits also result from monopoly power.

12. Profit expectations influence the innovating and investment activities and therefore the level of employment. The basic function of profits and losses, however, is to induce that allocation of resources which is in general accord with the tastes of consumers.

QUESTIONS AND STUDY SUGGESTIONS

1. Define "economic rent." How does the economist's usage of the term "rent" differ from everyday usage?

2. "Though rent need not be paid by society to make land available, rental payments are very useful in guiding land into the most productive uses." Explain.

3. Explain why economic rent is a surplus to the economy as a whole but a cost of production from the standpoint of individual firms and industries. Explain: "Rent performs no 'incentive function' in the economy."

4. What arguments can be made for and against a single tax on land?

5. How is interest defined? What considerations account for the fact that interest rates differ greatly on various types of loans? Use these considerations to explain the relative size of the interest rates charged on (a) a long-term $1,000 government bond, (b) a $20 pawnshop loan, (c) an FHA mortgage loan on a $17,000 house, (d) a $2,000 commercial bank loan to finance the purchase of an automobile, and (e) a $100 loan from a personal finance company.

6. If money capital, as such, is not an economic resource, why is interest paid and received for its use? Answer from the standpoint of both borrower and lender, and from the borrower's standpoint distinguish between business and consumer borrowing.

7. What are the three sources of the demand for loanable funds? What are the three potential sources of the supply of loanable funds? Explain liquidity preference in terms of its underlying motives. Use this concept to explain the difference between saving and the supply of loanable funds.

8. What are the major economic functions of the interest rate? Of economic profits? How might the fact that more and more businesses are financing their investment activities internally affect the efficiency with which the interest rate performs its functions?

9. How do the concepts of business profits and economic profits differ? Why are economic profits smaller than business profits?

10. What are the three basic sources of economic profits? Classify each of the following in accordance with these sources:

a. The profits acquired by a firm from developing and patenting a ball-point pen containing a permanent ink cartridge

b. The profit of a restaurant which results from construction of the interstate highway past its door

c. The profit received by a firm benefiting from an unanticipated change in consumer tastes

11. Distinguish between insurable and noninsurable risks. Why is this distinction significant for the theory of profits?

12. Carefully evaluate: "All economic profits can be traced to either uncertainty or the desire to avoid it."

13. Explain the absence of economic profit in a purely competitive static economy. Realizing that the major function of profits is to allocate resources in accordance with consumer preferences, evaluate the allocation of resources in such an economy.

SELECTED REFERENCES

Bober, M. M., Intermediate Price and Income Theory, rev. ed. (New York: W. W. Norton & Company, Inc., 1962), chaps. 15–17.

Carter, W. Harrison, and William P. Snavely, Intermediate Economic Analysis (New York: McGraw-Hill Book Company, Inc., 1961), chaps. 17–19.

Due, John F., and Robert W. Clower, *Intermediate Economic Analysis*, 4th ed. (Homewood, Ill.: Richard D. Irwin, Inc., 1961), chaps. 16–19.

Hansen, Alvin, *A Guide to Keynes* (New York: McGraw-Hill Book Company, Inc., 1953), chaps. 6 and 7.

Meyers, Albert L., *Elements of Modern Economics*, 4th ed. (Englewood Cliffs, N.J.: Prentice-Hall, Inc., 1956), chaps. 14–16.

Stonier, Alfred W., and Douglas C. Hague, *A Textbook of Economic Theory*, 2d ed. (New York: Longmans, Green & Co., Inc., 1957), chaps. 13–15.

Chapter 31

GENERAL EQUILIBRIUM: THE PRICE SYSTEM

AND ITS OPERATION

IN AMERICAN CAPITALISM

THIS CHAPTER is a way station in our study of economics. Here we seek to gain perspective—to envision "the big picture"—in two different senses. Ⓐ It is imperative that, at the conclusion of our detailed analysis of the various categories of product and resource markets, we reemphasize that these many diverse markets are interwoven into a *price system.* Ⓐ This is a convenient juncture for an over-all evaluation of the operation of American capitalism—to ask ourselves what the major accomplishments and the basic defects of our economy are.

These two objectives are not unrelated. The dominant feature of American capitalism is that it relies primarily upon a price system in organizing its resources for production. In evaluating the operation of American capitalism we are largely evaluating the efficiency of the price system in the economy of the United States. Furthermore, we will find that only when the interrelatedness of individual markets and prices is understood can the major and secondary shortcomings of American capitalism be fully appreciated.

GENERAL EQUILIBRIUM ANALYSIS

The preceding eleven chapters have provided us with a rather detailed analysis of how prices are established in several particular types of product markets and how the prices of specific categories of resources are determined. Thus far our discussion of prices has been compartmentalized; we have examined representative product and resource prices one at a time and apart from any detailed interrelationships each may bear to the other. In the jargon of the economist, we have been concerned with *partial equilibrium analysis*—a study of equilibrium prices and outputs in the many specific markets which are the component *parts* of the price system.

Much of the value of studying individual product and resource prices would be lost if we failed to examine the interrelationships which exist between the many specific markets and prices of the economy. Hence, our vantage point in this chapter shifts from individual prices in isolation to an analysis of the price

574

system as a whole. In technical language, our discussion now shifts to *general equilibrium analysis*—an over-all big-picture view of the interrelationships among all the various prices (parts) which comprise the price *system*.

Price interrelationships

The interrelatedness of individual prices can best be grasped through an illustration.[1] Suppose initially that general equilibrium exists, that is, that all product and resource markets are "at rest." Now assume there occurs an increase in the demand for automobiles. What will be the effects?

The immediate impact is obviously an increase in automobile prices. This will in turn induce an increase in the derived demands for, and therefore the prices of, all those resources used in the production of autos. This interrelationship between product and resource prices is not new to us; it was a key point in our analysis of resource demand (Chapter 28).

But now a myriad of more subtle but nevertheless potentially important price interactions comes into the picture. On the one hand, an increase in the price of automobiles will affect the demand for, and prices of, other goods. The exact nature of these effects depends primarily upon whether the "other goods" happen to be complementary to automobiles or substitutes for them. The demand for, and prices of, such complementary products as gasoline, motor oil, and tires will increase in response to the initial increase in the demand for automobiles. The demand for, and prices of, substitute goods, on the other hand, will tend to decline. Bus lines, interurban railways, and taxis will be so affected. These changes in the prices of complementary and substitute goods will be communicated back into the resource markets relevant to all these industries. The initial change in the price of automobiles will have little or no impact upon the prices of such independent goods as, for example, po-

[1] This illustration follows the excellent example discussed in Francis E. Hyde et al., *A New Prospect of Economics* (Liverpool: Liverpool University Press, 1958), chap. 9.

tatoes, wrist watches, razor blades, and file cabinets.

But there is still another, less direct route through which an increase in the price of automobiles will alter the prices of other finished products. We have noted that an increase in the demand for automobiles will increase the derived demands and the prices of resources used in their production. Now, there will be many industries other than the automobile industry using these same resources. For example, a list of firms using steel would read like a *Who's Who* of American industry. In brief, innumerable other industries using the same types of land, labor, and capital as the automobile industry will find that their costs have increased. This will give rise to increases in the prices and declines in the sales of the products produced by these industries.

This is not all: an equally subtle series of price alterations will emanate in the resource market from the initial price increases of those resources used by the automobile industry. As the prices and employment of resources used in automobile production rise, the prices of both substitute and complementary resources will be affected. To illustrate: If the increase in the automobile industry's derived demand for steel significantly increases the price of steel, automobile manufacturers may substitute aluminum where possible for engine and body parts. All other industries using steel may make similar substitutions. As the prices of resources change, all industries and firms employing these resources will tend to shuffle the quantities of the various resources used to reachieve the least costly combination of resources. This will affect the demand for, and prices of, these resources.

Noteworthy, too, is the fact that the immediate or secondary changes in resource prices which we have sketched will affect the personal distribution of income. In our example, automobile workers will find themselves moving into higher income brackets as the result of the initial increase in the demand for automobiles. They may well react by demanding more superior, or normal, goods such as butter and steak and less of such inferior goods as oleomargarine and potatoes. Indeed, they may even decide to buy still more automobiles, prompting a whole new series of price interactions such as we have already outlined.

The reader will readily note many loose ends in our discussion. If one had the patience and inclination, these price interrelationships could be pursued almost indefinitely. But our discussion is sufficiently detailed to emphasize our major point. Individual prices are interrelated in a number of both evident and subtle ways. Any initial disturbance such as a change in demand, a change in technology, or a change in resource supply will set off a highly complex economic chain reaction.

Economic understanding

In what respect, if any, is a knowledge of general equilibrium analysis—or, more specifically, the interrelatedness of individual prices —important? Is a knowledge of the interrelationships between prices useful? Up to a point, at least, an understanding of price interrelationships is an indispensable tool in evaluating the over-all operation of the economy, in understanding specific economic problems, and in formulating economic policies. A failure to recognize price interrelationships is an important source of misunderstanding and faulty reasoning on important economic questions.

Some examples will clarify this point. In Chapter 29 we noted that the immediate effect of a general wage cut is to reduce the costs of specific firms. And, other things being equal, lower costs will cause a firm to lower prices, increase production, and hire more workers. But general equilibrium analysis tells us that this seemingly obvious conclusion is of very doubtful validity. Lower wages mean lower incomes, which are communicated into the product market as general declines in the demand for, and prices of, products. These price declines are then projected back into the resource market once again as declines in resource demand. And these declines in resource demand will mean unemployment. The immediate impact of wage cuts (more employment) which

partial equilibrium analysis suggests may be swallowed up by the secondary effects (less employment), which are discernible only by an understanding of general equilibrium analysis.

Another example: Many people favor protective tariffs levied on, say, Japanese or German toys, because the immediate and obvious effect is to increase the price of foreign toys and therefore increase the demand for American-made toys. The result is that output and employment rise in the American toy industry. But this ignores the fact that incomes in Japan and Germany will decline as a result of their inability to sell toys in the United States. And with smaller incomes they will be less able to buy from American industries exporting machine tools, chemicals, grains, and so forth. The obvious increase in employment in the protected industry may well be offset, wholly or in part, by the indirect, subtle declines in employment in American export industries. As a matter of fact, apart from any decline in domestic employment stemming from tariff-induced declines in exports, general equilibrium analysis reminds us that the extra resources which are shifted into the expanding toy industry must come from other industries. That is, in a full-employment economy the tariff-inspired expansion of the toy industry will entail a contraction in the production of other goods. A final illustration: It would not be legitimate to consider the impact of a general sales tax upon the production of one industry in isolation, thereby ignoring its simultaneous effects upon related products. In analyzing the effects of the imposition of a sales tax upon the butter industry one must not ignore the fact that oleomargarine will also be subject to the same tax.

General equilibrium analysis provides a broader perspective for analyzing the effects of given economic disturbances or policies than does partial equilibrium analysis. Partial equilibrium analysis shows merely "the big splash" of an initial disturbance; general equilibrium analysis traces the waves and ripples emanating from the big splash. In some instances the waves and ripples are relatively unimportant;

in others they may prove to be a tidal wave which changes completely conclusions one would draw from the big splash viewed in isolation. As we noted in Chapter 1, a basic task of the economist is that of ascertaining which waves and ripples are important to the analysis of a given question and which can be safely ignored. In any event an understanding of the general equilibrium point of view is essential in evaluating our economy.

AN EVALUATION OF AMERICAN CAPITALISM

Equipped with this overview of the price system, let us now turn to the task of evaluating the price system as it has operated in American capitalism. At the outset we must note that the price system of American capitalism is a far cry from the purely competitive system described earlier, which tended to allocate resources in a highly efficient manner. Rather our economy is based upon an interrelated network of imperfectly competitive markets and prices. Oligopoly and monopolistic competition, not pure competition, pervade American product and resource markets. The question then is this: How well has American capitalism—based upon an imperfectly competitive price system whose operation is modified by government—managed to reconcile the fact of resource paucity with the insatiability of human material wants?

Problems of evaluation

It is no easy task to evaluate objectively those individuals and institutions with which one is closely associated. This also holds true in attempting to evaluate the performance of our economy. As participants in American capitalism it is quite a chore for us to stand back and assess objectively its shortcomings and accomplishments. In the first place, biases are likely to plague our analysis in many subtle and almost imperceptible ways. And, too, most of us have no firsthand experience with the operation of alternative economic systems as background in attempting the evaluating proc-

ess. Another significant stumbling block lies in the fact that it is virtually impossible to determine whether a particular achievement or shortcoming of American capitalism stems from the capitalistic ideology as such (see Chapter 3) or the specific environmental setting of the United States in which it functions. Is it the quantities and characteristics of American resources or is it the particular set of assumptions and institutions constituting the capitalistic ideology which account for American capitalism's successes and failures? Obviously, any analysis of American capitalism cannot clearly distinguish between the two. The present discussion can do no more than evaluate capitalism as it has actually operated in the environment of the United States.

If we wanted to be finicky and detailed, it would be possible to sketch innumerable virtues and vices associated with American capitalism. At this juncture such hair-splitting will be avoided in favor of an over-all evaluation which concentrates upon the economy's major accomplishments and defects. Furthermore, we are not so much interested in minute facts and figures as we are in a summary "balance sheet" statement of the assets and liabilities— the pros and cons—of American capitalism as they are voiced and acknowledged by both proponents and opponents of our economy. Such an evaluation will kill two birds with one stone: it will provide us with a thumbnail evaluation of our economy and simultaneously focus attention upon some of the specific problems and issues which are to be explored in Parts 6 and 7 of this book. Our evaluation will be both a look backward and a look forward.

Accomplishments of American capitalism

Generally speaking, there is rather clear-cut agreement that American capitalism has been successful in two respects:

1. The economy has been remarkably productive, providing its citizenry with a high and rising standard of living.

2. American capitalism has provided for a high degree of individual freedom.

Expanding production and a rising standard of living. Over a century ago an intense and vitriolic man penned the greatest tribute to the productivity of capitalism that will probably ever be offered:

The bourgeoisie (capitalist class), during its rule of scarce one hundred years, has created more massive and more colossal productive forces than have all preceding generations together. Subjection of nature's forces to man, machinery, application of chemistry to industry and agriculture, steam navigation, railways, electric telegraphs, clearing of whole continents for cultivation, canalization of rivers, whole populations conjured out of the ground —what earlier century had even a presentiment that such productive forces slumbered in the lap of social labor?

The time? 1848. The writer? Karl Marx, founding father of the communist ideology. The document? The *Communist Manifesto.* And capitalism's most ardent opponents continue to admire its productive capabilities. Current propaganda emanating from the Kremlin boasts of the Soviet Union's *catching up* with the productive performance of American capitalism.

Needless to say, more sympathetic scholars are also cognizant of the affluency of our economy:[2]

Make no mistake about it, capitalism has performed exceedingly well in the United States and it holds every promise of being able to surpass its own performance . . . if the trend of the past continues into the future for another twenty years, we may within our lifetimes usher into being the first economy of universal sufficiency the world has ever seen.

These testimonials by both friend and foe can be readily fortified with a myriad of facts. Example: the real per capita national income of the United States has expanded from a meager $405 in 1850 to a creditable $833 by 1900, and subsequently to a remarkable $1,811

by 1961. Example: the aggregate real national income has tended to double every two decades (Table 18-1). Improvements in product quality and tremendous increases in the amount of leisure with which to enjoy this higher standard of living make these figures all the more impressive. International comparisons also underscore the prolificacy of the American economic machine. The living standard of the average American citizen exceeds that of any other nation of the world (Table 39-1). In terms of aggregates the population of the United States is about 6 per cent of the world's population, the land area of the United States is about 7 per cent of the world's total, yet our economy annually produces over 33 per cent of the world's goods and services and almost one-half of the world's factory-produced goods.[3]

As noted earlier, it would be impossible to prove that the opulence of American society has been caused by that particular set of institutions which comprise the capitalist ideology rather than by the fact that an abundance of natural resources is embraced by our national boundaries. On the other hand, it is equally difficult to discount the contention that these institutions have played an important role in making the United States the wealthiest nation the world has ever known. It is hard to shrug aside the argument that the capitalist ideology has been highly successful in harnessing the incentives of individuals. Nor can one readily ignore the assertion that the capitalist ideology has assisted the economy in remaining remarkably flexible over time, helping it adapt itself, for example, to varying rates of technological advance and from a situation of "fabulous exploitation of virgin resources" to a condition of "a relative paucity of undeveloped resources."[4]

A final reminder: despite this glowing commentary, we must not lose sight of the fact that a rapidly expanding level of production may

[2] Robert L. Heilbroner, *The Worldly Philosophers* (New York: Simon and Schuster, Inc., 1953), pp. 282–283.

[3] Thomas R. Carskadon and George Soule, *U.S.A. in New Dimensions* (New York: The Macmillan Company, 1957), p. 4.

[4] William N. Loucks, *Comparative Economic Systems,* 6th ed. (New York: Harper & Row, Publishers, 1961), p. 43.

entail significant economic and noneconomic costs. For example, rapid technological advance may contribute to structural unemployment and the persistence of economically distressed areas. And we have seen (Chapter 19) that the causes and characteristics of inflation in an increasingly wealthy society may change in such a manner as to call for new, and possibly less palatable, policies in order to contain the price level.

Individual freedom. The great emphasis which American capitalism puts upon individual freedom is held to be a virtue in and of itself and, at the same time, an important causal factor underlying its other successes.

One of the most creditable features of our economy is that freedom of choice has persisted largely unscathed despite the many problems which arose as the economy has matured and become increasingly complex in its structure and operation. Consumers are still free to choose that collection of goods and services which they feel best satisfy their wants. Resource suppliers are free to choose among the alternative employment opportunities available to them. Further, resource suppliers are free to become entrepreneurs, to assume the uncertainties and risks inherent in forming and operating a business. And the entrepreneur can go into whatever line of production he wishes and freely choose among various methods of production.

Freedom, of course, is a relative concept. Through both legislative action and institutional forces, freedom of choice is limited somewhat. The freedom of individuals is purposely curtailed by government when the exercise of such freedom may impair the freedom or well-being of others. For example, consumers are not free to purchase narcotics because of the great social costs involved. Institutional factors also limit freedom of choice: the required discipline of modern factory production requires that individual workers forgo the freedom to choose the precise number of hours they want to work each day. And, as we have seen, the imperfectly competitive price system puts artificial barriers upon the choices of resource suppliers and

potential entrepreneurs. Despite the increasing role of government in regulating economic affairs and the many nongovernmental deterrents to free choice which have developed in modern capitalism, free individual choice is still a dominant characteristic of our society. Democratic government, the political counterpart of this freedom, still flourishes.

To a certain extent progress—industrialization, technological advance, economic expansion, and a higher standard of living—can be forced by government. Even those who have strong emotional ties with capitalism acknowledge the rapid rate of industrialization and the startling technological advances Soviet Russia has achieved in recent years. But the human and sociopolitical costs involved have been great; coercion and the injection of government ownership and operation of industry have drastically curtailed freedom of choice. In contrast American capitalism has achieved its successes in a context of individualism and freedom of choice.

This emphasis upon individualism has undoubtedly played a causal role in accounting for the achievements of American capitalism. Individual freedom has permitted capitalism to harness very effectively the incentives of both workers and entrepreneurs. An individualistic environment is certainly an important stimulant to technological advance and innovation. Similarly, freedom of choice has been at least a permissive factor in inducing the accumulation of property resources.

Having paid our compliments to American capitalism, let us now turn to the less palatable chore of stating and discussing the United States economy's more apparent defects.

Defects of American capitalism

Two basic shortcomings of our economy are frequently cited:

1. The economy has been characterized by instability. Periods of unemployment and sieges of inflation have characterized American capitalism, giving rise to serious economic insecurity for its citizenry.

2. The growth of monopoly power in both

product and resource markets has impaired the allocative efficiency of the price system.

These are the major defects. In addition there are numerous more specific trouble spots in American capitalism.

The business cycle: unemployment, inflation, and insecurity. Capitalism's most vehement critics and its staunchest defenders generally have one point in common: both groups acknowledge that the performance of American capitalism has been characterized by frequently severe instability. Serious and prolonged unemployment, on the one hand, and troublesome inflation, on the other, have plagued our economy. In particular, the historical record makes it painfully clear that the long-run climb to higher living standards has been punctuated by periodic setbacks (Figure 11-3).

The economic costs of general unemployment are tremendous. For example, in 1929 our economy was riding the crest of prosperity; GNP was a then record-setting $85.9 billion. Unemployment in that year was extraordinarily low—429,000 workers, less than 1 per cent of the labor force. The picture was reversed a scant four years later. The economy's 1933 GNP was a meager $61.5 billion.[5] And by 1933 pay lines had changed to bread lines crowded with some 12 million workers—some 23 per cent of the labor force was out of work! Worse yet, unemployment fluctuated between 6 and 14 million workers all during the 1932–1939 period. About 10½ million workers were still looking for work during the first quarter of 1940. Total cost of the Great Depression? An estimated $650 billion worth of goods and services measured in terms of 1956 prices.

But dollars and cents are not the whole story. There is no way to measure the deterioration of morale, the loss of skills, the undermining of incentives, the loss of self-respect, and the decline in loyalty to the capitalistic ideology which accompany extended periods of unemployment. No nation—not even the wealthiest—can afford the economic and human costs of depression. The potential effects

[5] Both GNP figures are in terms of 1939 dollars and hence measure real output.

of an inflationary boom can be every bit as serious. By unevenly changing resource and product prices, inflation capriciously penalizes some income receivers and rewards others, and if severe enough, inflation can undermine the value of money to the extent that the economy is thrown into utter chaos. All this is not to say that the historical record of capitalism is a hodgepodge of inflation and unemployment. There have been remarkable periods of stability and growth. But the long pull has been punctuated by periods of severe unemployment and price instability.

Perhaps the most distressing aspect of the business cycle is the fact that some of the basic causal factors lie within the capitalistic ideology itself. Decentralized, individualistic decision making based upon profit and loss is the ultimate determinant of the level of employment in a capitalistic economy. There is no central agency continually forcing the economy to operate at the full-employment mark. Thus it is possible for millions of individual decisions, grounded on self-interest, not to coincide with society's interest in fully utilizing all its available resources. Furthermore, there are at least two tendencies within American capitalism which have increased the possibility of recurring periods of instability. On the one hand, the increasing opulence of our society has been accompanied by a marked increase in the production of durable goods for both businesses and consumers. These goods are expensive, and their replacement is typically postponable. Hence, the threat or beginning of a recession might cause investors and consumers to forgo these optional purchases, thereby contributing greatly to the economy's instability. On the other hand, in a growing economy the volume of saving is on the increase. This means that a higher and higher level of investment is required to maintain a given rate of growth. Investors must spend more and more if a constant rate of growth is to be sustained.

Yet there is a brighter side to this bleak picture. Most economists feel that in fiscal and monetary policy American capitalism has the means for correcting economic instability without scrapping the major cornerstones of the capitalist ideology. But guarded optimism is required: remember that in the booming twenties many thinking people were convinced that American capitalism was a depression-proof economy.

A last point: although the business cycle is the major source of economic insecurity in American capitalism, there are others. Rapid economic growth, we have seen, is a source of structural unemployment and therefore of economic insecurity. Indeed, the highly interdependent nature of the economy is in itself a breeding ground for insecurity. In short, the business cycle is the primary—but not the only—cause of economic insecurity in American capitalism.

The growth of monopoly power. Competition is the organizing and controlling mechanism in a purely capitalistic economy. Economic rivalry forces producers to acknowledge and obey the preferences of consumers (society). It obligates them to employ the most efficient productive techniques in meeting consumer preferences. In short, competition is conducive to an efficient allocation of resources, to full production.

But the price system of American capitalism is permeated with varying degrees of imperfect competition. Monopolistic competition, oligopoly, and sometimes pure monopoly characterize the product and resource markets. As a result of his ability to influence total output, the imperfectly competitive producer can resist the dictates of consumer sovereignty and likely finds it profitable to do so. By artificially blocking or restricting entry to both product and resource markets, imperfect competition deprives the economy of the flexibility required to achieve and maintain an efficient allocation of resources. In brief, it is argued that the imperfectly competitive price system of American capitalism impedes the attainment of full production. Imperfect competition means higher prices and economic profits for those possessing monopoly power, but artificial distortions of the composition of total output for society.

As with deviations from full employment, the causal factors underlying the development of monopoly in the economy are not unrelated to

the capitalist ideology. In the first place, although competition may be highly desirable from society's point of view, it is most irksome to the individual producer or resource supplier subject to its rigors. It is inherent in the free, individualistic environment of the capitalistic system that the profit-seeking producer will attempt to break free of the restraining force of competition in trying to better his position. Combination, conspiracy, cutthroat competition, and sheer productive efficiency are all means to the end of eliminating competition.

Technological advance has also contributed to the demise of competition in some product markets. Modern technology frequently requires (1) the use of extremely large quantities of real capital, (2) wide markets, (3) a complex, centralized, and closely integrated management, and (4) large and reliable supplies of raw materials. Such an operation implies the need for large-scale monopolistic producers. In other words, the achievement of maximum productive efficiency through the employment of the best available technology often presupposes the concentration of economic power. Technological advance has brought abundance to American capitalism, but in so doing has contributed significantly to the decline of competition.

As we have seen (Chapter 27), one of the potential redeeming features of imperfect competition may lie in the area of technological advance. Many objective observers are willing to grant that, within limits, imperfect competition has provided the incentive and the financial wherewithal to foster the relatively rapid development of new products and new productive methods. But it would be naïve to suppose that each and every case of monopoly or oligopoly can be justified in terms of technological imperatives. And it would be shortsighted to ignore the possibility that pure competition in these very same industries would have been equally or more progressive.

Another, and noneconomic, aspect of the monopoly problem merits emphasis: some competent economists feel that the most fundamental danger of monopoly power lies not in its distortion of resource allocation away from the most efficient pattern, but rather in its political implications.

Monopoly . . . is an abomination in a free society. It can come into existence only by the destruction of economic freedom; it can perpetuate itself only by the continued suppression of economic freedom. . . . But monopoly, in order to preserve itself, can do more than merely destroy the free market and restrict competition; it can, transcending the narrow confines of the market place, reach out to suppress both social and political freedom. Monopoly is not, as many assume, strictly an *economic* phenomenon, the influence of which is limited to the market. On the contrary, it is a power system—and power is a social institution, indivisible and all-pervasive. . . . And herein lies the ultimate danger of unchecked monopoly power—the prospect that it might eventually dominate the entire society and suppress all freedom.[6]

The state, it is argued, must control or be controlled by monopolies.

Chapters 32 and 34 of Part 6 are concerned with the monopoly problem. In Chapter 32 the problem is explored in terms of the product market. Chapter 34 examines the monopolistic aspects of labor unions in the resource market. In each instance emphasis is upon public policy towards monopoly.

Specific trouble spots: a look ahead. Aside from economic instability and the monopoly problem, there are several other, more specific problems areas in American capitalism which will be accorded detailed treatment in Part 6.

Agriculture. As in most nations, American agriculture has been an economic trouble spot. Ironically, the problem in American agriculture is not underproduction as in most other nations but rather overproduction. Rapid technological advance and relatively stable demand conditions have given rise to the production of voluminous amounts of products which con-

[6] Walter Adams and Horace M. Gray, *Monopoly in America* (New York: The Macmillan Company, 1955), p. 5. See also Henry C. Simons, *Economic Policy for a Free Society* (Chicago: University of Chicago Press, 1948).

sumers are not willing to purchase at existing prices. The price system—sometimes assisted and sometimes hampered by government programs—has failed to negotiate adjustments appropriate to the correction of these difficulties. This is one area wherein the price system has not provided the flexibility demanded by changing conditions. The "farm problem" will receive detailed treatment in Chapter 33.

Income inequality. Another highly controversial aspect of American capitalism centers upon the distribution of income. Some defend, while others deplore, the economy's unequal distribution of income on both economic and ethical grounds. This age-old problem has many of its roots firmly embedded in the capitalist ideology. Private property, inheritance rights, the role of self-interest as a motivating force, and the largely impersonal nature of the price system all contribute to income inequality. In Chapter 35 we shall examine the facts and sources of income inequality, the pros and cons of inequality, and finally the nature of public policy in dealing with this problem.

Social imbalance. In recent years a number of leading economists[7] have contended that the evolution of capitalism in the United States, whereby a nation of relative poverty has become one of relative abundance, has been accompanied by a serious distortion in the composition of total output. A problem of "social imbalance" has allegedly arisen: resources are inefficiently allocated as between private goods and social goods. More specifically, private goods—automobiles, television sets, and electric canopeners—abound, while public goods and services—education, police and fire protection, and other basic community services—are remarkably deficient in quantity and quality. In more general terms it is argued that the phenomenal output performance of our economy behooves society to pay somewhat less attention to *how much* we produce and more attention to *what* we produce. As Harvard's Alvin Hansen has so succinctly put it; "We

[7] See Alvin H. Hansen, *The American Economy* (New York: McGraw-Hill Book Company, Inc., 1957), chap. 8, and John K. Galbraith, *The Affluent Society* (Boston: Houghton Mifflin Company, 1958).

have learned to make a living; we have still to learn how to live." The social imbalance issue is aired pro and con in Chapter 36.

International economic problems. Domestic economic problems must share the spotlight with a host of equally important problems in the international sphere. Most evident are the many problems which are associated with international commerce and finance. Some of these problems stem from fundamental imbalances in the structures and needs of the industrially advanced nations and the underdeveloped nations; others can be readily traced to questionable international economic policies. Of increasingly grave concern is the many-sided problem of the underdeveloped nations. American capitalism affects and is affected by this problem. In these underdeveloped areas lie vast potential markets and sources of raw materials crucial to the sustaining of American economic growth. And in these areas reside people whom we are morally obligated to assist in achieving higher levels of material well-being. Finally, the economic challenge of the Soviet Union presents the most acute international problem of our times. All these international economic problems are explored in Part 7 of this book.

Two qualifying comments

Two final observations must supplement our evaluation of American capitalism:

1. The defects of American capitalism are not necessarily peculiar to economies which embrace the capitalist ideology. For example, many socialist countries are plagued by unemployment and inflation. These are real problems, for example, in the liberal socialism of Great Britain. And the authoritarian brand of socialism characteristic of the Soviet Union has failed to eradicate these problems. The Soviet economy has faced rather severe inflationary pressures, and while cyclical unemployment as such does not exist, underemployment is a serious problem. Similarly, the relative inequality with which income is distributed in other nations rivals and in some cases surpasses that in the United States. In short, the present discussion of American capitalism's defects is not meant to imply that these difficulties are the exclusive heritage of capitalism. Much the same can be said of capitalism's successes. We shall discover in a later chapter that the Soviet Union's rate of growth in recent years has exceeded that of the United States.

2. The reader will undoubtedly have noted that certain of our economy's shortcomings are related to its successes. For example, technological advance, a major driving force behind the economy's high standard of living, has undoubtedly been a contributing factor in the development of monopoly power. Further, many economists have argued that varying rates of technological advance have caused variations in investment spending and therefore in the levels of national income and employment. Certainly the problem of achieving economic stability in an expanding economy is more complex than in a static economy. Similarly, as we have already noted, capitalism's emphasis upon freedom of choice and decentralized decision making has provided an environment permissive of both the business cycle and the development of monopoly power.

It may appear that the preceding discussion has unduly manhandled our beloved capitalism. This is very possibly true, but there is reason in our bluntness. Our evaluation has purposely emphasized the weak spots in our economy, because a strong statement of the defects and shortcomings of the economy helps to drive home the point that American capitalism is by no means a perfect, or ideal, economic system. Certainly we are justified in generally praising our economy's performance, but there is plenty of room for improvement; and it is through stating and analyzing the economy's defects, not through praising its accomplishments, that improvement is brought about. Our present evaluation of American capitalism is analogous to a physical examination. The main purpose is to put the spotlight on defects and weak spots, not to dwell on strong points.

It is most dangerous to ignore or to understate American capitalism's shortcomings on the implicit assumption that they will somehow correct themselves and blow away. The improvement and strengthening of the economy demands that we emphasize the economy's failures.

SUMMARY

1. General equilibrium analysis is concerned with the operation of the entire price system and the interrelationships between different markets and prices. These interrelationships are important in that they might modify or negate the immediate effects of economic disturbances or policies which partial equilibrium analysis reveals.

2. The major accomplishments of American capitalism have been (a) its tremendous productive capacity and the high standard of living which has resulted therefrom and (b) the high degree of individual freedom which prevails in the economy.

3. The basic shortcomings of our economy are (a) its susceptibility to cyclical fluctuations and (b) the development of monopoly power in both product and resource markets.

4. More specific problem areas in the domestic economy have to do with overproduction in the agricultural segment, the inequality with which income is distributed, and social imbalance. International economic problems entail certain fundamental imbalances between the advanced and the underdeveloped nations, faulty international economic policies, the economic development of the underdeveloped nations, and the economic challenge of Soviet Russia.

QUESTIONS AND STUDY SUGGESTIONS

1. Compare the natures of partial and general equilibrium analysis. In what respect is each useful?

2. Trace through the price system the economic effects of (a) the development of a man-made fiber which never wears out, fades, or stains; (b) a permanent increase in the demand for leather; (c) a sharp decline in the size of the labor force; and (d) the development of a new production technique which cuts the cost of color television by 30 per cent.

3. Cite examples other than those given in the text which indicate the contribution general equilibrium analysis can make to the understanding of economic problems and policies.

4. What are some of the difficulties involved in attempting to evaluate objectively the operation of any economic system? Be specific. By what means, if any, can these difficulties be overcome?

5. In your opinion what is capitalism's most important success? Why? What is its most significant shortcoming? Why?

6. In what ways do the shortcomings of capitalism affect the noneconomic aspects of our society? Be specific.

7. Explain in detail how the institutions and ideology of American capitalism have played at least a permissive role in (a) causing business fluctuations and economic insecurity, (b) contributing to income inequality, and (c) abetting the growth of monopoly.

8. "The most striking successes of American capitalism bear the seeds of its most significant shortcomings." Critically evaluate. Do you agree?

9. "The elimination of inequality and instability would entail the undermining and destruction of the capitalistic ideology." Evaluate critically but fairly.

SELECTED REFERENCES

Bowen, Howard R., *Toward Social Economy* (New York: Holt, Rinehart and Winston, Inc., 1948), particularly chaps. 15 and 16.

Due, John F., and Robert W. Clower, *Intermediate Economic Analysis,* 4th ed. (Homewood, Ill.: Richard D. Irwin, Inc., 1961), chaps. 20 and 23.

Loucks, William, *Comparative Economic System,* 6th ed. (New York: Harper & Row, Publishers, 1961), chaps. 3 and 4.

Phelps-Brown, E. H., *The Framework of the Pricing System* (London: Chapman & Hall, Ltd., 1936).

Stigler, George J., *The Theory of Price,* rev. ed. (New York: The Macmillan Company, 1952), chap. 16.

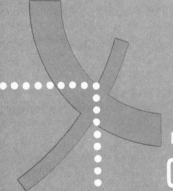

PART 6
CURRENT DOMESTIC
ECONOMIC PROBLEMS

Chapter 32

THE MONOPOLY PROBLEM: THE SOCIAL

CONTROL OF INDUSTRY

PREVIOUS CHAPTERS have made these two contrasting points: (1) Many important American industries are characterized by considerable monopoly power. Some of these industries were shown in Table 8-3. (2) It was noted in Chapter 6 that one of the basic economic functions of government is to preserve competition as a key mechanism of control in the economy.

It is the over-all objective of the present chapter to describe and evaluate governmental policies toward business monopolies. More specifically, the objectives of this chapter are three-fold: (1) to review briefly the case against, and then state the case for, business monopolies; (2) to understand and appraise government policies toward business monopolies; and (3) to explore several possible future public policy alternatives.

BIG BUSINESS AND MONOPOLY

Before considering the pros and cons of business monopoly, we must pause to define our terminology. In Chapters 20 and 25 we developed and applied a very strict definition of monopoly. A pure, or absolute, monopoly, we said, is a one-firm industry—a situation in which a unique product is produced entirely by one firm, entry to the industry being blocked by certain insurmountable barriers. When a single firm controls an entire market, pure monopoly exists.

In the present chapter we shall find it convenient to use the term "monopoly" in a broader sense. Monopoly exists whenever a small number of firms controls all or a large portion of the output of a major industry. This definition, which comes closer to the way the man in the street understands monopoly, includes many industries which we have heretofore designated as oligopolies.

What is the difference between monopoly (as we have just defined it) and big business? The term "big business" may be defined either in terms of a firm's share of the total market for its product or in terms of some absolute measure such as the volume of its assets, sales, or profits, the number of workers employed, or the number of stockholders. A firm can obviously be large in relation to the size of the total market but small in an absolute sense. The Weeping Water General Store may almost completely dominate the local market for a good many products yet be exceedingly small by any meaningful absolute standard. Conversely, a firm might be very large in the absolute sense but small in relation to the total market. For example, the Jones and Laughlin Steel Corporation is large by most absolute standards one can employ. In 1961 its total sales revenue was $736,732,000, some 37,543 employees were on its payroll, and net income after taxes totaled $32,131,000. Yet Jones and Laughlin controls less than 10 per cent of the net capital assets of the primary steel industry! In so far as the steel industry is concerned, Jones and Laughlin is a small producer. However, *in a good many instances absolute and relative bigness go hand in hand.* A firm which is large in absolute terms very frequently controls a significant portion of the market for its product. Thus, although "big business" and "monopoly" are not necessarily synonymous, they frequently do go together. The present chapter is concerned with the type of situation in which absolute and relative bigness are both present. In using the term "business monopoly" in this chapter we refer to those industries in which firms are large in absolute terms and in relation to the total market. Examples are the electric equipment industry, where General Electric and Westinghouse, large by any absolute standard, dominate the market; the automobile industry, where General Motors, Ford, and Chrysler are similarly situated; the chemical industry, dominated by du Pont, Union Carbide, and Allied Chemical; the aluminum industry, where three industrial giants—Alcoa, Reynolds, and Kaiser—reign supreme; and the cigarette industry, where the four giant firms of Reynolds, Liggett and Myers, American Tobacco, and Lorillard share the total market.[1]

MONOPOLY: CASES FOR AND AGAINST

It is not at all clear whether business monopolies are on balance advantageous or disadvantageous to the functioning of American capitalism. Note these two statements—one bitterly opposed to monopoly in any form or context and the other viewing business monopoly as an integral part of modern American capitalism:

Monopoly power must be abused. It has no use save abuse. . . . There must be an outright

[1] See George J. Stigler, "The Case Against Bigness in Business," *Fortune,* May, 1952, p. 123.

dismantling of our gigantic corporations and persistent prosecution of producers who organize, by whatever methods, for price maintenance or output limitation.

. . . Legislation must prohibit, and administration effectively prevent, the acquisition by any private firm, or group of firms, of substantial monopoly power.[2]

In our economy big business undertakes the major role of coordinating individual efforts and resources into collective achievement. This is a function that must be undertaken under modern technology, whether by private enterprise or by the state. In the United States it has been possible so to mix dispersion with centralization that the major job can be left to private competition, under government regulation. Big business has not merely been kept effectively subject to a competitive system; on the whole it has also made an essential contribution to its scope, vitality, and effectiveness.[3]

These are not propaganda blasts sponsored by antimonopoly and promonopoly pressure groups. Rather they are the well-considered arguments of respected scholars. These two assertions accurately reflect that there is ample room for serious disagreement as to the desirability of business monopolies in American capitalism. Almost endless debate on this issue has precipitated a series of rather well-defined arguments on both sides. Our immediate goal is to outline these divergent views.

Case against monopoly

The case against business monopoly was largely stated in Chapter 25 and may be summarized as follows:

1. Monopolists find it possible and profitable to restrict output and charge higher prices than would competitive producers.

2. The monopolist's profit-maximizing output entails a misallocation of economic resources.

[2] Henry C. Simons, *Economic Policy for a Free Society* (Chicago: University of Chicago Press, 1948), pp. 129, 158.

[3] A. D. H. Kaplan, *Big Enterprise in a Competitive System* (Washington: Brookings Institution, 1954), p. 248.

It is through his ability to block or retard the entry of new firms and resources into an industry that the monopolist can realize economic profits in the long run. These profits are an indication that consumers want more resources allocated to the production of the monopolized commodity. More technically, monopolists maximize profits by producing an output at which price (society's measure of product X's relative worth) exceeds marginal cost (society's measure of the worth of the alternative products which the resources used in producing an extra unit of X could otherwise have produced).

3. The persistent economic profits which monopolists realize contribute to greater inequality in the distribution of income.

4. Monopoly is conducive to a slow rate of technological advance. The sheltered position of the monopolist is conducive to inefficiency and lethargy; there is no competitive spur to productive efficiency. Furthermore, monopolists are inclined to resist or suppress technological advances which may cause the sudden obsolescence of their existing machinery and equipment.

5. Monopoly is an obstacle to the achievement of economic stability, that is, full employment with reasonable price stability. Two somewhat distinct assertions underlie this point. On the one hand, it was noted in Chapter 17 that business monopolies are in a position of relative immunity in so far as an anti-inflationary (tight) money policy is concerned. Indeed, the ability of monopolists to administer prices may cause a tight money policy to contribute indirectly to inflation as monopolists pass interest rate increases on to consumers through product price increases. On the other hand, we saw in Chapter 19 that business monopolies, in conjunction with labor monopolies, can cause cost-push inflation in the absence of full employment through the exertion of their market power. Business monopolies are allegedly active agents in an inflationary process which is not directly remedied by the demand-restricting efforts of a tight money policy or a fiscal surplus.

6. Finally, we noted in Chapter 31 that business monopoly may pose serious political dangers. The growth of monopoly, it is argued, must result in one of two possible outcomes: monopoly may come to exert undue influence upon government and therefore the formation of public policy, or government will be forced to regulate monopoly. In other words, government must control monopoly or be controlled by it. In either instance the result will be a basic alteration in the structure of our economy or the free political institutions which now characterize it.

Case for monopoly

But business monopoly is not without defense. A series of plausible arguments with which we are only partially familiar have been evolved to explain and justify the existence of the giant business enterprises which dominate various markets.

1. The presence of *workable competition* effectively regulates the operations of big businesses. It is argued that there exist certain types of competition, more subtle than the mere presence of a large number of rival producers, which in fact make so-called monopolistic industries "workably competitive." This contention suggests that any judgment of the competitiveness of an industry which rests solely on the number of existing producers is incomplete and misleading, because it overlooks other important dimensions of competition.

The general argument has several more specific facets. (a) All products are in competition for the dollars of consumers. A down payment on a house is often a good substitute for a new automobile. A new dress and accessories are sometimes in strong competition with a new vacuum cleaner for the housewife's dollars. Refrigerators compete with washing machines, television sets, and air conditioners. This argument shades into (b) interproduct competition as a factor to be considered in judging the competitiveness of an industry. The fact that only three firms are responsible for the nation's output of aluminum belies the competition which aluminum faces in specific markets from steel, copper, wood, plastics, and a variety of other products. These first two aspects of workable competition both suggest that the demand for the products of a monopolistic industry may be considerably more elastic than the number of firms in that specific industry would imply. (c) Competition in the form of counter-vailing power must not be ignored (Chapter 27). An original position of monopoly power tends to induce the growth of monopoly power on the opposite side of the market. This across-the-market competition provides effective checks, or restraints, on both the original and the countervailing power position. Counter-vailing power effectively prevents abuses of monopoly power in those very markets in which traditional same-side-of-the-market competition is weak. (d) It is argued that *potential* competition and the fear of censure can regulate the behavior of monopolists almost as effectively as does the actual presence of a large number of rivals. The possibility that new rival firms will be formed or that other industrial giants will branch out works against the monopolist's exploiting his market power. The fear of public censure, the embarrassment of an antitrust suit, or the possibility of government regulation may also contribute to the monopolist's disinclination to exert his monopoly power. (e) Of greatest importance is the competitive role of technological progress. Technological advance operates over a period of time so as to circumscribe and undermine existing monopoly positions. Innovation, in particular the development of new products, is a force which persistently destroys the market power of individual firms, making monopoly power a precarious and transitory phenomenon.

Those who emphasize the importance of workable competition feel that firms and industries should be judged not on the basis of their market structure but rather in terms of their performance. Such characteristics as the number of firms in the industry and the importance of barriers to entry should be supplanted by criteria of performance—price, efficiency of production, and rate of technological advance—in gauging the social desirability of an industry or specific firm. Defenders of business monopoly contend that many industries which fall short of the large-numbers-no-

barriers criteria nevertheless perform very well, efficiently producing a quality product at a low price.

As a matter of fact, probably the main cornerstone of the case for monopoly centers upon technology as an aspect of efficient performance. Two related arguments are made: the utilization of the most efficient technologies demands the existence of large monopolistic producers, and the rate of technological advancement is more rapid when an industry is characterized by a few large producers than would be the case if a large number of small competing firms existed.

(2) Existing mass production economies can be realized only by big businesses. Where existing technology is highly advanced, only large producers—firms which are large both absolutely and in relation to the market—can realize low unit costs and therefore sell to consumers at relatively low prices. This line of reasoning is used to counter the contention that monopoly means less output, higher prices, and an inefficient allocation of resources. Critics of monopoly, it is argued, incorrectly overlook economies of scale in their price-output comparisons of competitive and monopolistic producers.

Antimonopoly economists, while generally recognizing an element of truth in this technological defense of monopoly, offer several noteworthy counterarguments. (a) Many existing monopolies allegedly have attained a size far beyond that necessary for the realization of all existing economies of scale. It is contended, for example, that the Chevrolet, Pontiac, Oldsmobile, Buick, and Cadillac divisions of General Motors are for operating purposes independent producers. How then can their legal unification be justified on the basis of mass production economies? And how do economies of scale justify the expansion of General Motors into the appliance and locomotive fields? How can technology justify the existence of U.S. Steel, a giant business corporation composed of a number of geographically distinct plants? Furthermore, if economies of scale are so significant, how can relatively small firms successfully persist in many industries dominated by a few very large firms? (*b*) A second counterargument emphasizes that the low unit costs achieved by big producers are not so much the result of any *real* advantages over smaller firms in combining resources as they are the consequence of the larger firms exerting their superior bargaining power as large buyers to depress resource prices. The existence of business monopolies does not make for an expansion of the real output and income of the economy but rather for a redistribution of income in favor of business monopolists and at the expense of resource suppliers. (*c*) It is argued that empirical studies fail to indicate that the largest firms are the most efficient. Critics of monopoly conclude that available evidence suggests that medium-sized producers are most efficient in many industries.

3. Monopolistic industries—in particular, three or four firm oligopolies—are conducive to a high rate of technological advance. Such firms, it is contended, have both the financial resources and the incentive to undertake technological research.

. . . The modern industry of a few large firms [is] an excellent instrument for inducing technical change. It is admirably equipped for financing technical development. Its organization provides strong incentives for undertaking development and for putting it into use. . . . In the modern industry shared by a few large firms, size and the rewards accruing to market power combine to insure that resources for research and technical development will be available. The power that enables the firm to have some influence on prices insures that the resulting gains will not be passed on to the public by imitators (who have stood none of the costs of development) before the outlay for development can be recouped. In this way market power protects the incentive to technical development.[4]

4. Business monopolies exert a stabilizing influence upon the economy because of both their investment policies and their pricing policies. Concerning investment policies, it is

argued that the absolute and relative size of business monopolies permits them to gear their investment spending to long-run business prospects rather than to the short-term cyclical upswings and downswings which are so influential in determining the investment outlays of smaller, competitive firms. Thus it has been argued that a part of the stability achieved in the 1950s arose from the fact that the long-term investment programs of large monopolies were continued despite short-term changes in inventory investment and consumer spending. A more debatable assertion is that the ability of business monopolies to resist price reductions during recession (coupled with the propensity of unions to resist wage cuts) helps thwart the development of a cumulative wage-price deflationary spiral and the accompanying declines in output and employment.

5. A few economists and most business groups suggest that business leaders are blessed with a strong sense of social responsibility which will mitigate, if not eliminate entirely, abuses of monopoly power. Although industry leaders command tremendous economic power, we are assured that they have the social maturity not to wield this power in a manner detrimental to the public interest. The public-be-damned attitude of business monopolies in earlier decades is allegedly a thing of the past.

PUBLIC POLICY TOWARD MONOPOLY

In view of the sharp conflict of opinion over the relative merits of business monopoly, it is not surprising to find that government policy towards business monopolies has been something less than clear-cut and consistent. As reflected in major pieces of legislation, the Federal government's stated policy objective is the maintenance of competition. Yet the government has passed legislation and at times pursued policies which have furthered the development of monopoly power. As one scholar has aptly phrased it,[5]

[4] John Kenneth Galbraith, *American Capitalism*, rev. ed. (Boston: Houghton Mifflin Company, 1956), pp. 86–88.

[5] Fritz Machlup, *The Political Economy of Monopoly* (Baltimore: Johns Hopkins Press, 1952), p. 182.

Governments, apparently, have never been able to make up their minds as to which they dislike more, competition or monopoly. . . . Whether government activities, on the basis of the presently existing body of law, are on balance more favorable to monopoly or competition is controversial.

Government, in short, has both restrained business monopoly and promoted it.

Legislation and policies restricting monopoly

Historically, American capitalism, steeped in the philosophy of free competitive markets, has been a fertile ground for the development of a suspicious and fearful public attitude toward business monopolies. Though relatively dormant for many decades, this fundamental distrust of monopoly came into full bloom in the decades following the Civil War. The widening of local markets into national markets as transportation facilities improved, the ever-increasing mechanization of production, and the increasingly widespread adoption of the corporate form of business enterprise were important forces giving rise to the development of "trusts"—that is, business monopolies—in the 1870s and 1880s. Trusts developed in the petroleum, meat-packing, sugar, lead, coal, whiskey, and tobacco industries, among others, during this era. Not only were questionable tactics employed in monopolizing the various industries, but the resulting market power was almost invariably exerted to the detriment of all who did business with these monopolies. Farmers and small businessmen, being particularly vulnerable to the growth and tactics of the giant corporate monopolies, were among the first to censure their development. Consumers and labor unions were not far behind.

The Sherman Act of 1890. The acute public resentment of the trusts culminated in the passage of the Sherman Antitrust Act in 1890. This cornerstone of antitrust legislation is surprisingly brief and, at first glance, directly to the point. The core of the act is embodied in two major provisions:

In Section 1:

Every contract, combination in the form of a trust or otherwise, or conspiracy, in restraint of trade or commerce among the several states, or with foreign nations is hereby declared to be illegal. . . .

In Section 2:

Every person who shall monopolize, or attempt to monopolize, or combine or conspire with any person or persons, to monopolize any part of the trade or commerce among the several states, or with foreign nations, shall be deemed guilty of a misdemeanor. . . .

The act had the effect of making monopoly and "restraints of trade" criminal offenses against the Federal government. Either the government or parties injured by business monopolies could file suits under the Sherman Act. Firms found in violation of the act could be ordered dissolved by the courts, or injunctions could be issued to prohibit practices deemed unlawful under the act. Fines and imprisonment were also possible results of successful prosecution. Further, parties injured by illegal combinations and conspiracies could sue for triple the amount of damages done them. The Sherman Act seemed to provide a sound foundation for positive government action against business monopolies.

Varying interpretations of the Sherman Act. In practice, however, application of the Sherman Act has been at times weak and decidedly ineffective. Two reasons go far to explain this ineffectiveness: (1) The Federal government has varied considerably in its willingness to apply the act. Administrations "friendly" towards big business have sometimes emasculated the act by the simple process of ignoring it or by cutting the budget appropriations of enforcement agencies. (2) The courts have run hot and cold in interpreting the Sherman Act and its various amendments. At times the courts have applied the Sherman Act with great vigor, adhering closely to the spirit and objectives of the law. In other cases, the courts have interpreted the act in such ways as to render it all but completely innocuous. Let us briefly review some of the milestones in interpreting the Sherman Act.

In the Sugar Trust case of 1890 the courts distinguished between "interstate commerce" and manufacturing, ruling in effect that the Sherman Act was to be applied only to "trade" and not to manufacturing! The net effect of the courts' ruling was to exempt manufacturing from the act. Out of the Standard Oil and American Tobacco cases of 1911 the courts developed the "rule of reason," which stated in effect that not *every* contract or combination in the restraint of trade is to be deemed illegal; that is, the Sherman Act is not to be interpreted literally. Only those contracts and combinations which "unreasonably" restrain trade are to be subject to antitrust action, the courts deciding what is a reasonable and what is an unreasonable restraint of trade. It is no surprise that this interpretation of the Sherman Act inaugurated a period of uncertainty as to how it was to be applied. Then in 1920 the courts, ruling in the U.S. Steel case, took the next logical step. They attempted to distinguish between the *existence* and the *exertion* of monopoly power. It was ruled in this instance that the mere fact that a firm is large and that it possesses monopoly power is not in violation of the antitrust laws. Violation hinges upon the *use* of monopoly power.

But a quarter of a century later in the Alcoa case of 1945 the courts did a turnabout from the U.S. Steel case. The courts now reasoned that illegal price fixing is an inherent aspect of monopoly power. Therefore, the acquisition or possession of monopoly power as such is a violation of the antitrust laws. Then in 1953 in the Du Pont Cellophane case the courts mellowed once again in their interpretation of the Sherman Act by acknowledging the existence of interproduct competition, concluding in this case that, although Du Pont clearly monopolized the production of cellophane, it faced significant competition from waxed paper, metal foils, and other wrapping materials.

Two general conclusions can be drawn from this sketchy survey of major cases tried under the Sherman Act. On the one hand, it is evident that the Sherman Act can be the basis for a vigorous effort to maintain a competitive economy; on the other hand, it is equally apparent that the very general wording of the Sherman Act, as reflected in the many varying court interpretations, called for a more explicit statement of the government's antitrust sentiments.

The Clayton Act and the Federal Trade Commission Act, 1914. This needed elaboration of the Sherman Act came before the U.S. Steel case in the Clayton Antitrust Act, a 1914 amendment to the Sherman Act. The following sections of the Clayton Act were designed to strengthen and make explicit the intent of the Sherman Act:

Section 2 outlaws price discrimination between purchasers when such discrimination is not justified on the basis of cost differences.

Section 3 forbids exclusive, or "tying," contracts, whereby a producer would sell a product only on the condition that the buyer would acquire other products from the same seller and not from competitors.

Section 7 prohibits the acquisition of stocks of competing corporations when the effect is to lessen competition.

Section 8 prohibits the formation of interlocking directorates in large corporations where the effect will be to reduce competition.

Actually there was little in the Clayton Act which had not already been stated by implication in the Sherman Act. The Clayton Act merely attempted to sharpen and make clear the general provisions of the Sherman Act. Furthermore, the Clayton Act attempted to outlaw the techniques by which monopoly might develop and, in this sense, was a preventive measure. The Sherman Act, by contrast, was aimed at the punishment of existing monopolies.

The Federal Trade Commission Act was also passed in 1914. It too was based on the belief that preventive rather than mere punitive measures were needed to sustain competition. Specifically, the act was designed to prevent competition from assuming certain aggressive forms which would tend to undermine competition and bring about the development of monopoly power. The act created the Federal Trade Commission, a permanent five-man board, and charged it with the power to investigate unfair competitive practices on its own initiative or at the request of injured firms. The Commission could hold public hearings on such complaints and, if necessary, issue cease-and-desist orders where "unfair methods of competition in commerce" were discovered.

The antitrust potential of the FTC has been limited by subsequent court rulings which have restricted the investigatory powers of the Commission and made it clear that the courts, not the FTC, have the final authority in interpreting the meaning of the antitrust laws. Then in 1938 the Wheeler-Lea Act amended the Federal Trade Commission Act by prohibiting "unfair or deceptive acts or practices in commerce." As a result, a primary task of the FTC now is the prohibition of false and misleading advertising and the misrepresentation of products.

More recent antitrust legislation. More recent antitrust legislation has taken the form of amendments designed to plug loopholes in— and thereby strengthen—the Clayton Act.

The Robinson-Patman Act of 1936 amended Section 2—the price discrimination section— of the Clayton Act. The Clayton Act, you will recall, attempted to eliminate the practice by which producers charged different prices to different buyers, where the objective was to drive competing producers from business. The various trusts frequently employed such cutthroat tactics—charging extremely low prices in markets in which small competitors persisted but higher prices in markets where competition had already been eliminated—as a method of improving and strengthening their monopoly positions. The Robinson-Patman Act, or "Chain

Store Law," had a different background. It was aimed at the growing number of chain stores which, so argued independent retailers, were obtaining large and unjustified price discounts from wholesalers because of their strong bargaining positions as large buyers. By passing some of these cost savings on to consumers in the form of price reductions, the chains allegedly were driving their independent competitors to the wall. The Robinson-Patman Act outlaws quantity discounts to large buyers when such discounts are not justified on the basis of actual cost economies arising from mass buying. And, in turn, the act prohibits retailers from selling "at unreasonably low prices" when the purpose is to eliminate competitors. Many economists feel that the effect of the act has been not so much to deter the growth of monopoly but rather to stifle price competition, particularly at the retail level, and therefore to sustain inefficient retailers who would otherwise succumb to more vigorous competition.

Finally, the Celler Antimerger Act of 1950 amended Section 7 of the Clayton Act, the section which prohibits one firm from acquiring the *stock* of competitors when the effect is to reduce competition. This provision had been weakened by court decisions and had been dodged by firms who merged with competitors by acquiring their *assets* rather than their stock. The Celler Act attempted to tighten the stock acquisition ban and also prohibited the acquisition of the assets of competitors when the effect was to lessen competition.

Effectiveness of antitrust legislation. How effective has antitrust legislation been in restricting the growth of monopoly? It is hard to say. Although there is sharp and often violent disagreement on this question, the consensus seems to be that antitrust legislation has generally helped to slow the growth of business monopoly in the economy but has accomplished little or nothing by way of restoring competition. This mild endorsement is not without serious reservations. Many economists are of the opinion that stronger antitrust laws coupled with more vigorous and more discriminating enforcement could do much to make our economy even more competitive. It is felt in some quarters that faulty judicial interpretations, legal loopholes, and indifferent Federal administrations have undermined and considerably weakened antitrust policy. Most importantly, there is rather widespread agreement that many of the government's most notable legal victories in applying the antitrust laws have proven to be economic defeats. That is, the guilty firms have agreed to cease-and-desist orders or have been subject to minor penalties rather than being forced to dissolve. Indeed, even when dissolution has occurred, the economic benefits have been dubious: when it comes to price and output policies, a tight three- or four-firm oligopoly is likely to behave much like the absolute monopoly which it once comprised.

On the positive side, it must be recognized that there currently exists widespread interest in antitrust. Examples: the Kefauver Committee of the Senate has conducted detailed investigations of administered prices in the automobile, steel, and drug industries; the Department of Justice indicted the nation's principal electrical equipment producers in late 1960 for conspiracy in violation of the Sherman Act; and, finally, economists have reasserted their long-standing interest in the monopoly problem as the cost-push and structural theories of inflation have emphasized market power as a cause of rising prices.

Legislation and policies promoting monopoly

Let us now consider briefly the other side of the picture. Government has directly and indirectly promoted the growth of monopoly in several different ways. (1) In some cases government has passed legislation permanently exempting certain industries from antitrust legislation. (2) In the Great Depression and recent wartime emergencies the antitrust laws have in effect been temporarily suspended. (3) In still other instances government legislation —particularly patent and tariff laws—has directly promoted the development of monopoly. (4) Government has allegedly pursued tax, ex-penditure, and property disposal policies favorable to the concentration of economic power.

Industry exemptions to the antitrust laws. Over the years government has enacted certain laws which have either exempted certain specific industries or, alternatively, have excluded certain trade practices from antitrust prosecution. In doing so the government has tended indirectly to foster the growth of monopoly power.

In 1918 the Webb-Pomerene Act exempted American exporters from the antitrust laws by permitting them to form export trade associations. Although the act was intended to put American exporters in a stronger competitive position with international cartels, the effect has probably been to reduce competition in both international and domestic markets.

We have already noted too that the Robinson-Patman Act of 1936 had the effect of dampening price competition at the retail level. The Miller-Tydings Act of 1937, amending the Sherman Act, moved in the direction of eliminating this competition. This so-called fair trade law exempts from antitrust laws *resale price maintenance contracts* for branded and trademarked goods when such contracts are permitted by state legislation. Price maintenance contracts allow manufacturers to set the retail prices of their products by signing contracts to this effect with retailers. The Miller-Tydings Act has operated so that these agreements have applied not only to those retailers who actually enter into such contracts but also to all other "nonsigner" retailers in the state. This means that if one retailer signs a price maintenance contract, the agreement is binding on *all* other retailers in the state. The net effect has been to restrict price competition on branded products at the retail level; a monopolistic practice—price fixing—has been injected by legislation into an otherwise highly competitive segment of the economy.

It should be noted, too, that labor unions and agricultural cooperatives have been exempt, subject to limitations, from the antitrust laws. We shall see in the next chapter that Federal legislation and policy have attempted to provide some measure of monopolistic power for agriculture, feeling that this would help alleviate the farm problem. Similarly, in a subsequent chapter we shall discover that since 1930 Federal legislation on balance has generally promoted the growth of strong labor unions. This Federally sponsored growth has resulted, according to some authorities, in the development of union monopolies. This will later be discussed further.

Federal legislation has at least partially immunized exporters, retailers, farmers, and labor unions from the antitrust laws. Whether these exemptions are justified is not at all clear; indeed, the topic is one of the most controversial in the field of economic policy.

Emergency suspensions of antitrust. Despite the fact that depressions and wars entail completely different economic environments, both have given rise to the temporary abandonment of the antitrust laws.

The Great Depression of the thirties gave birth to a notable suspension of the antitrust laws. At the depth of the Depression in 1933, the Federal government passed the National Industrial Recovery Act in an attempt to pump new life into a prostrate economy. This act gave the trade associations of the various industries authority to establish "codes of fair competition." The government felt that these codes, by giving the various industries the mechanisms for eliminating price cutting, would stop the wage-price deflationary spiral and thereby set the stage for economic recovery. All resulting codes, once approved by the National Recovery Administration and the President, had the effect of law and constituted legitimate exemptions from all antitrust laws. The vast majority of the codes embodied price-fixing agreements; all of them regulated the terms of sale; some allocated markets among participating firms; others prohibited sales below cost; and still others restricted production. In short, most of the codes were highly reminiscent of the policies and practices pursued by cartels. Hence, aside from contributing little or nothing to economic recovery, the NIRA in its two years of existence

probably gave the economy a noticeable shove in the direction of increased monopoly power.

The World War II emergency brought antitrust exemptions of a different type. In this case the Chairman of the War Production Board was empowered to issue "certificates of immunity" from antitrust laws when it was felt that violations of antitrust legislations—for example, collusive action in production and pricing—would actually facilitate wartime production. Furthermore, allowance was made for the postponement of pending antitrust cases.

Public utility legislation. The Interstate Commerce Act of 1887 was the first of several Federal laws which had the effect of declaring certain aspects of the transportation, communications, and power industries to be "public utilities," or "natural monopolies."

The Interstate Commerce Act was based on the supposition that competition was unworkable in the railroad industry. Certain industry characteristics ruled out the possibility of effective competition: (1) relatively large fixed costs entailed the necessity of large-scale operations by each firm in order to achieve efficient, low-cost service; (2) the existence of several firms would entail the wasteful duplication of very costly capital facilities; and (3) the service supplied—transportation—was essential to many firms and individuals. And, as a matter of fact, "competition" had not worked well in this industry. Price competition aimed at the fuller realization of economies of scale often degenerated into cutthroat competition and losses for all participants. The results would be either the elimination of the weaker competitors and the evolution of monopoly or the establishment of a collusive price agreement of some sort by which the competitors sought to improve their lot. If monopoly resulted, the exploitation of that power through discriminatory pricing—that is, charging what the traffic would bear—was likely. If a collusive price resulted, the industry would then operate in much the same manner as a pure monopoly, at least until another round of price warring was precipitated.

In view of such circumstances the Interstate Commerce Act was passed by Congress to make railroads regulated monopolies. While their management and actual operation remained in private hands, an Interstate Commerce Commission was established to regulate the rates and the services of railroads. Similar legislation has established public utilities in the fields of air transportation, power, and radio and television and has also created appropriate regulatory commissions.

The intent of this "natural monopoly" legislation is to regulate effectively and for the benefit of the public such industries to the end that consumers might be assured quality service at reasonable rates. The rationale is this: if competition is inappropriate, *regulated* monopolies should be established to avoid possible abuses of uncontrolled monopoly power. In particular, regulation should guarantee that consumers benefit from the economies of scale —that is, the lower per unit costs—which their natural monopoly position allows public utilities to achieve. Few would quarrel with this reasoning.

But there is serious disagreement as to whether or not the government's control over the various public utility monopolies has been at all effective. Some reputable scholars feel that the various regulatory commissions have not only created, but have also protected and subsidized, the so-called natural monopolies.[6] Though willing to note that public regulation has been something less than perfect, many other economists feel that public regulation has been at least reasonably effective and that public regulation is clearly preferable to the obvious alternatives of no regulation or public ownership. A poorly regulated monopoly, it is reasoned, is superior to private monopoly and may well be more conducive to expansion and technological advance than would be public ownership. There is no simple generalization here.

Regardless of one's opinion on the effectiveness of government regulation of monopoly, it is clear that public utility legislation has created legal monopolies in certain important industries.

[6] Walter Adams and Horace M. Gray, *Monopoly in America* (New York: The Macmillan Company, 1955), p. 71.

Patent laws. Technological research is a costly and risky procedure. American patent laws— the first of which was passed in 1790—are aimed at providing sufficient monetary incentive for innovators by granting them exclusive rights to produce and sell a new product or machine for a period of 17 years. Patent grants have the effect of protecting the innovator from competitors who would otherwise quickly imitate his product and share in the profits, though not the cost and effort, of his research. Few contest the desirability of this particular aspect of our patent laws.

However, patents are a mixed blessing. The granting of a patent frequently amounts to the granting of monopoly power in the production of the patented item. Many economists feel that the length of patent protection—seventeen years—is much too long. Such an extended period of protection from competitors is likely to allow the innovator to entrench himself firmly in a monopoly position to the extent that he is able to block successfully any potential competition after his patent expires. This is particularly true if the innovating firm extends its patent rights longer than seventeen years by patenting improved models of the original innovation. By this and similar procedures innovating firms have often been able to extend their exclusive jurisdiction over a product for three or four decades!

When patents are licensed to competitors the innovating firm has the right to specify the prices which these competitors may charge for the product, the markets in which they can sell, and even the amounts which they might produce. The result is that the innovator faces no genuine competition. The worst abuses of patent rights occur when one firm accumulates by research or purchase a large number of related patents or, alternatively, several firms in an industry "pool" the patents which they own and exclude potential rivals from their use. In such situations patents can constitute a very formidable barrier to entry and thereby create and perpetuate monopoly power.

And, finally, a patent monopoly is an excellent basis for a tying agreement and the subsequent extension of monopoly power. The classic case is that of the United Shoe Machinery Corporation, which leased the machinery over which it had exclusive patents only on the condition that shoe manufacturers would purchase all their other machinery from United. This practice stripped United's competitors of their customers and firmly entrenched United as the dominant firm in the industry.

The importance of patent laws in the growth of business monopoly must not be underestimated. Such well-known firms as Du Pont, General Electric, American Telephone and Telegraph, Eastman Kodak, Alcoa, and innumerable other industrial giants have attained various measures of monopoly power in part through their ownership of certain patent rights.

Protective tariffs. Although we must postpone any detailed discussion of tariffs until a later chapter, it is most relevant at this point to recognize that tariffs and similar trade barriers have the effect of shielding American producers from foreign competition. Protective tariffs are in effect discriminatory taxes against the goods of foreign firms. These taxes make it difficult and often impossible for foreign producers to compete in domestic markets with American firms. The result? A less competitive domestic market and an environment frequently conducive to the growth of domestic business monopolies.

Tax, expenditure, and disposal policies. Some economists feel that certain aspects of Federal taxation and expenditure policies have contributed directly to the growth of business monopoly. In the area of Federal taxation it is argued that under pressure from big business government has granted certain tax concessions and immunities which have spurred the further growth of existing industrial giants. For example, generous "depletion allowances" have been granted oil and gas and other extractive industries in determining their taxable incomes. Furthermore, the wartime privilege of accelerating the rate of depreciation on defense facilities for tax purposes has been extended in a modified form into the postwar period. Both these concessions have effectuated very large

tax savings to the business community. Although smaller businesses have benefited to a degree from these tax concessions, it is felt that the lion's share of these tax benefits has clearly accrued to big businesses.

On the other side of the picture it is contended that government expenditures, particularly for military procurement, have accelerated the growth of business monopoly. Highly profitable defense contracts have gone to big businesses when evidence suggests that smaller firms could have accomplished the required production as rapidly and as efficiently. The net result is further impetus to the growth of business monopoly.

Finally, it has been charged that government has also promoted business monopoly in disposing of public property. Specifically, at the end of World War II government-owned industrial facilities were generally sold at bargain prices to corporate giants who were already dominating their respective industries. The same allegedly holds true for the disposition of tax-financed technological know-how accumulated by the government during and after the war. Most of this research information has been acquired from the government by those business monopolies which already possess technological superiority over their smaller rivals.[7]

A word of caution: The position that governmental tax, expenditure, and disposal policies have promoted business monopoly is subject to debate. As is the case with the entire question of government's role in dealing with business monopolies, there is adequate room for honest differences of opinion in assessing the impact of government policies on the development of business monopoly.

FUTURE POLICY ALTERNATIVES

Now let us look ahead. What is the most desirable path for public policy to follow in the future? There are three general positions and a host of hybrid views on this important question. There are those who are satisfied with the

[7] Walter Adams and Horace M. Gray, *Monopoly in America* (New York: The Macmillan Company, 1955), particularly chaps. 4–6.

structure and performance of American industry and therefore are generally content with the *status quo* or even advocate some relaxation of antitrust enforcement. There are those who feel that American capitalism has no choice but to move in the direction of increased governmental regulation and/or ownership of monopolized industries. There are those who believe that it is both desirable and possible to make American industry more competitive.[8] The profound nature of any choice among these sharply contrasting policy alternatives demands that we weigh each rather carefully.

Maintaining the status quo

Those who advocate maintaining the *status quo* are convinced that the presence of business monopolies and the degree of concentration of economic power which now exists are not only essential but also desirable. Supporting arguments are generally those made earlier in this chapter as the case for business monopoly.

Competition of all products for the dollars of consumers, interproduct competition, nonprice competition, countervailing power, potential competition and the fear of government regulation, and technological advance all render "workably competitive" industries which appear at first glance to be monopolistic. Then, too, it is contended that business leaders have attained levels of maturity and social responsibility far beyond those attained by their predecessors. Business leaders are trustees of economic power and can be expected not to abuse that trust.

But the most significant and the most frequently heard claim for preservation of the *status quo* is the doctrine of *technological ·determinism.* The current advanced stage of technological development, it is argued, makes it imperative that big businesses prevail. Business monopolies are necessary if the economy is to realize the productive efficiencies which

[8] The present discussion follows the general pattern outlined in Walter Adams (ed.), *The Structure of American Industry,* 3d ed. (New York: The Macmillan Company, 1961), chap. 15.

modern technology now makes available. A return to competition, in the sense of a large number of small producers, would be to forgo economies of scale. Any restoration of large-numbers competition is a step in the direction of economic *inefficiency* and the misuse of scarce resources.

The traditional arguments for fostering the *status quo* are: (1) workable competition prevails where large-numbers competition does not; (2) the social responsibility of business leaders will work against abuses of monopoly power; and (3) the realization of the effective use of productive resources which modern technology makes possible depends upon the existence of monopolistic industrial giants.

Toward public regulation and ownership

There are many observers who are less satisfied with the current structure of American industry. Public regulation or even public ownership and operation are envisioned as inevitable consequences of the need to control private monopoly power.

This position rests on three points: (1) Modern technology is assumedly such that business monopoly is here to stay if we are to achieve and maintain productive efficiency. (2) The arguments underlying the *status quo* position are discounted by those who view public regulation as the only course for future public policy. It is naïve to assume that monopolists will exercise self-restraint in using the economic power at their disposal. Workable competition is more a myth than a reality; it does not function as an effective regulatory device. Further, countervailing power is subject to many exceptions, and in many instances it functions in a very imperfect manner. (3) Present antitrust laws are deemed too weak to curb abuses of monopoly power, and if strengthened and vigorously enforced, antitrust would entail the loss of the productive efficiencies which modern technology now provides.

It is concluded that the only real alternative is the social control of business monopolies through government regulation. Only in this way can business monopoly be operated in the public interest.

Restoring vigorous competition

A final alternative seeks the restoration of "effective" competition in what now are monopolistic industries. The objective sought is not the establishment of *pure* competition; this is recognized as unrealistic and in some instances economically undesirable. Rather the goal is the establishment of markets wherein (1) the number of producers is sufficiently large so that no individual firms possess considerable market power, (2) collusion is absent, and (3) the entry to markets is relatively unrestricted.

Proponents of this policy alternative contend that the goal of effective competition is realistic, attainable, and highly desirable. They argue that the *status quo* is intolerable. Monopoly power exists, workable competition and countervailing power to the contrary, and it is being sorely abused. No effective market or moral forces exist to protect consumers from business monopolies. Hence, the restoration of competition to such industries is highly desirable.

In the second place, it is felt that in most industries the growth of big business monopolies has far exceeded that necessary for the attainment of all the economies of scale which modern technology allows. A considerable degree of competition can be reestablished in many now-monopolized markets with little or no impairment of productive efficiency.

And it is argued that past experience indicates that public regulation of monopoly has generally failed to function in the public interest. Public monopolies can abuse their power in the same way as can private monopolies.

Through what techniques is competition to be restored? On the one hand, antitrust laws should be strengthened and vigorously applied. A rear-guard defensive application of antitrust legislation to retard the rate of monopoly growth is wholly inadequate. The restoration of effective competition calls for positive action designed to *increase* the degree of competition in industries in which monopoly power is con-

siderable. And, too, it is imperative that all exceptions to the antitrust laws be eliminated. Similarly, legislation and policies which now promote the growth of monopoly—patent laws, protective tariffs, expenditures and taxation policies—must be either eliminated or modified.

SUMMARY

1. The role of business monopolies in American capitalism is a highly controversial one. The case against business monopoly centers upon the contentions that business monopoly (*a*) results in high prices and output restriction, (*b*) contributes to the misallocation of resources, (*c*) promotes income inequality, (*d*) retards the rate of technological advance, (*e*) is an obstacle to the achievement of economic stability, and (*f*) poses a threat to political democracy.

2. The defense of business monopoly is built around the following points: (*a*) "workable competition" prevails in many industries in which "large numbers" competition is absent, (*b*) the realization of mass production economies often necessitates the presence of business monopolies, (*c*) monopoly provides both the means and incentives for rapid technological advance, (*d*) the investment and price policies of monopolies tend to stabilize the economy, and (*e*) business monopolies are socially responsible.

3. Government has not followed a consistent, one-sided policy in dealing with business monopolies. It has both restrained and promoted the growth of monopoly power.

4. Government has attempted to retard the growth of monopoly through the antitrust laws. The cornerstone of antitrust policy consists in the Sherman Act of 1890 and the Clayton Act of 1914.

5. The Sherman Act specifies that "Every contract, combination . . . or conspiracy in the restraint of interstate trade . . . is . . . illegal . . ." and that any person who monopolizes or attempts to monopolize interstate trade is guilty of a misdemeanor. The general wording of the act, however, has resulted in a variety of court interpretations, many of which have served to limit the effectiveness of the act.

6. The Clayton Act was designed to bolster and make more explicit the provisions of the Sherman Act. To this end the Clayton Act declared that price discrimination, tying contracts, intercorporate stockholdings, and interlocking directorates are illegal when the effect of their use is the lessening of competition.

7. The Federal Trade Commission Act of 1914 created the Federal Trade Commission to investigate antitrust violations and to prevent the use of "unfair methods of competition." Empowered to issue cease-and-desist orders, the Commission now serves as a watchdog agency for the false and deceptive representation of products.

8. Though designed to sustain competition among retail distributors, the Robinson-Patman Act of 1936 has stifled retail price competition by prohibiting chain stores from (a) acquiring "unjustified" discounts in buying from wholesalers and (b) selling to consumers at "unreasonably" low prices.

9. The Cellar Antimerger Act of 1950 prohibits one firm from acquiring the assets of another firm where the result is a lessening of competition.

10. Government, however, has also done much to promote both directly and indirectly the concentration of economic power and the growth of monopoly. Industrial exceptions to antitrust include: (a) the exclusion of exporters by the Webb-Pomerene Act of 1918, (b) partial exclusion of retailers by the Robinson-Patman Act (1936) and the Miller-Tydings Act (1937), and (c) the exemption of unions and agricultural cooperatives.

11. Notable emergency suspensions of the antitrust laws were (a) the "codes of fair competition" developed under the short-lived National Industrial Recovery Act during 1933 and (b) the use of "certificates of immunity" during recent wartime emergencies.

12. Through public utility legislation Federal and state governments have created regulated monopolies in such industries as railway and air transportation, radio and television, telephone and telegraph, and electric power.

13. Patent laws have also served as a basis for the development of business monopoly. Similarly, high protective tariffs have shielded domestic firms from foreign competitors.

14. Some economists are of the opinion that government has adopted tax and expenditure policies conducive to the growth of business monopolies. In addition, it is alleged that the disposal of public property has often worked towards the same end.

15. Possible future policy alternatives for dealing with business monopolies include (a) maintenance of the status quo, (b) increasing public regulation and ownership of industry, and (c) the restoration of effective competition.

QUESTIONS AND STUDY SUGGESTIONS

1. "All big firms are monopolistic, but not all monopolistic firms are big." Appraise critically.

2. Suppose you are president of one of the Big Three automobile producers. Discuss critically the case against business monopoly.

3. Now suppose you are a spokesman for a farm organization and are attempting to convince a congressional committee that the presence of business monopolies is a significant factor contributing to the farm problem. Critically evaluate the case for business monopoly.

4. Distinguish between "pure," "workable," and "effective" competition.

5. Briefly identify each of the following acts, specifying the manner in which each has restrained or contributed to the development of business monopoly:

a. Webb-Pomerene Act, 1918

b. Robinson-Patman Act, 1936

c. Sherman Act, 1890

d. Miller-Tydings Act, 1937

e. Interstate Commerce Act, 1887

f. Hawley-Smoot Act, 1930

g. Clayton Act, 1914

h. Federal Trade Commission Act, 1914

i. Celler Antimerger Act, 1950

j. National Industrial Recovery Act, 1933

6. Briefly state the interpretation given the antitrust laws by the Courts in each of the following cases:

a. Sugar Trust case

b. Standard Oil and American Tobacco cases

c. U.S. Steel case

d. Alcoa case

e. Du Pont Cellophane case

7. What stake do you, as a consumer, have in the application of antitrust legislation?

8. Do you feel that antitrust legislation should be applied to labor unions? Explain.

9. Which of the three policy alternatives outlined at the end of this chapter do you feel is the most desirable? What criticisms can be made of each of the three positions? Be as specific as you can.

10. Define the concept of countervailing power. Explain its operation. How does countervailing power differ from competition as we defined it in Chapter 24? What implication, if any, does countervailing power have for the application of antitrust policy?

11. Explain the meaning and significance of each of the following:

a. Resale price maintenance contracts

b. Tying agreements

c. Interlocking directorates

d. Cease-and-desist orders

e. Certificates of immunity

12. What proposals can you make to strengthen the antitrust laws in their application to business monopolies? Be specific.

13. "The social desirability of any given business enterprise should be judged not on the basis of the structure of the industry in which it finds itself, but rather on the basis of the market performance of that firm." Analyze critically.

14. A much-discussed policy alternative in dealing with the business monopoly problem suggests that (*a*) government should establish and maintain "effectively competitive conditions in all industries where competition can function as a regulative agency . . ." and (*b*) government should gradually assume the "ownership and operation in the case of all industries where competition cannot be made to function effectively as an agency of control." [9] Evaluate these suggestions as to their social desirability and political feasibility. What practical problems do you think might be encountered in the application of these recommendations?

[9] Henry C. Simons, *Economic Policy for a Free Society* (Chicago: University of Chicago Press, 1948), p. 57.

SELECTED REFERENCES

Adams, Walter (ed.), *The Structure of American Industry*, 3d ed. (New York: The Macmillan Company, 1961), particularly chap. 15.

Adams, Walter, and Horace M. Gray, *Monopoly in America* (New York: The Macmillan Company, 1955).

Duesenberry, James S., and Lee E. Preston, *Cases and Problems in Economics* (Englewood Cliffs, N.J.: Prentice-Hall, Inc., 1960), chap. 5.

Galbraith, John Kenneth, *American Capitalism*, rev. ed. (Boston: Houghton Mifflin Company, 1956), particularly chaps. 7 and 9.

Kaplan, A. D. H., *Big Enterprise in a Competitive System* (Washington: Brookings Institution, 1954).

Simons, Henry C., *Economic Policy for a Free Society* (Chicago: University of Chicago Press, 1948), particularly chap. 2.

Stigler, George J., "The Case against Bigness in Business," *Fortune*, May, 1952.

Wilcox, Clair, *Public Policies Towards Business*, rev. ed. (Homewood, Ill.: Richard D. Irwin, Inc., 1960), particularly chaps. 3–5, 11, 12, and 18.

Chapter 33

AMERICAN AGRICULTURE:

THE FARM PROBLEM

AMERICAN AGRICULTURE is a chronic soft spot in an otherwise prosperous and expanding economy. Agriculture is a sick and, at least in relative terms, a declining industry. It is maladjusted, out of step with the rest of the economy.

The major objectives of this chapter are (1) to describe and assess the severity of the farm problem, (2) to outline the causes of the farm problem, (3) to describe government policy toward American agriculture, (4) to evaluate critically the effectiveness of public policy; and (5) to outline a positive program for American agriculture.

HISTORY OF THE FARM PROBLEM

The two decades prior to World War I were exceedingly prosperous ones for agriculture; indeed, this period has been dubbed "the golden age of American agriculture." The demand for farm products, farm prices, and farm incomes all rose. World War I intensified these good times. The foreign demand for the output of American farmers skyrocketed during, and immediately following, the war. Foreign countries, diverting resources from agriculture to war goods production, turned to American agriculture for needed food and fiber. High prices and an almost insatiable demand were the happy lot of American farmers.

These highly favorable conditions were not to last. A sharp postwar depression in 1920 was a sudden and severe shock to agriculture. In particular, the large volume of mortgage indebtedness incurred during the previous years of prosperity proved a heavy burden. The economy as a whole quickly recovered from this downturn, however, and by 1921 the booming twenties were upon us. But agriculture failed to share in this prosperity to the extent that did other segments of the economy.

The reasons for this were several. European agriculture not only recovered from the war but also began to expand rapidly under the impetus of new technological advances. Hence, foreign demand for American farm goods began to level off and decline. American foreign trade policies also contributed to this deterioration in foreign demand. High tariffs on goods imported to the United States helped undermine foreign demand for American farm products. To the extent that foreigners could not sell to us because of trade restrictions, they were unable to earn the funds they needed to buy from American producers. Furthermore, the domestic demand for farm products simply did not rise very much in the twenties. American stomachs were full, and as a result income increases were used to buy automobiles, refrigerators, and a host of new products of industry. Finally, on the supply side of the picture techno-

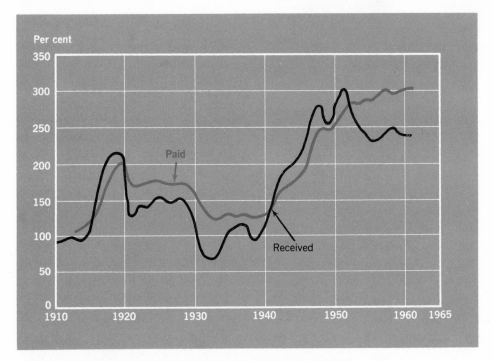

FIGURE 33-1. PRICES PAID AND RECEIVED BY FARMERS, 1910–1961.
Throughout the twenties and thirties and again since the mid-fifties, the prices re-
ceived by farmers have lagged behind the prices paid by them. [U.S. Department of
Agriculture, "Agriculture Outlook Charts," 1962 (November, 1961).]

logical advances boosted farm output markedly.
The net result of a lagging, inelastic demand
and a sharply increasing supply of farm products was low farm prices and incomes.

The Great Depression of the 1930s was a
particularly acute blow to American agriculture. The competitive nature of agriculture
makes it especially vulnerable to bad times.
Unlike sellers who possess a modicum of monopoly power, farmers are unable to administer
their prices. They are at the mercy of the market. Therefore, when market demand declines
as it did during the Depression, farm prices
and farm incomes fall sharply. Ironically, farmers buy in markets which are basically noncompetitive. Hence, while their incomes fell
by very large amounts, the prices of farmers'
purchases declined very modestly. As Figure
33-1 indicates, farmers in the 1920s and 1930s

found themselves in a harsh price-cost squeeze.

World War II provided welcome but temporary relief for the farmer. Both domestic
and foreign demand for agricultural products
boomed during the war, and prosperity returned to agriculture. Except for the 1948–
1949 slump, the middle and late forties were
peak years for American farmers. Then in the
1950s a slow but certain relapse became evident, and agriculture was once again encountering difficulty. As farm prices faltered and
declined, other prices inched upwards. The
farmer again found himself in the unenviable
position of paying more and more for what he
bought and getting less and less for what he
sold.

The relative deterioration of the economic
position of the farmer can be readily seen
through income statistics. Indeed, low incomes

TABLE 33-1. PER CAPITA INCOME OF FARM
AND NONFARM PEOPLE, SELECTED
YEARS, 1934–1961

Year	Farm people	Nonfarm people
1934	$ 165	$ 512
1937	287	666
1940	250	699
1942	484	1,034
1944	665	1,314
1946	790	1,373
1948	963	1,529
1950	884	1,618
1952	1,024	1,854
1954	999	1,889
1956	993	2,103
1957	1,066	2,166
1958	1,197	2,165
1959	1,144	2,276
1960	1,255	2,309
1961	1,373	2,345

SOURCE: U.S. Department of Agriculture,
"Farm Income Situation" (July, 1962).

are the most obvious symptom of the farm
problem. Table 33-1 provides us with a comparison of per capita farm and nonfarm incomes since the mid-thirties. Note that farm
income has been persistently less than nonfarm income over the entire period and that
the differential has been large. In the 1950s
and early 1960s the farm-nonfarm per capita
income differential has been about $1,000.

We must be careful to note that the data of
Table 33-1 are average figures. Do not jump to
the false conclusion that all farmers are poor.
This is most certainly not the case; a good
many farmers are well off by any relevant
standard. A motor trip through the corn belt
of the Middle West provides sufficient evidence to support this point. It is the "tobacco
roader" of the Deep South, the "two-cow,
twenty-chicken, 40-acre" Appalachian sharecropper, the marginal farmer of the Southwest,
and the 6-acre tobacco farmer of North Caro-

lina who cling to the bottom rung of the farm
income ladder. It is with these people that the
low income symptoms of the farm problem are
most evident.

Table 33-2 gives us a rough idea of the degree of income disparity *within* agriculture.
These figures show that in 1954, 2.8 per cent
of the farms in the United States accounted for
31.3 per cent of total farm output. At the other
extreme, cumulating the figures for the bottom
two economic classes makes it clear that 40.1
per cent of all farms sold less than $1,200
worth of farm products in 1954 and that the
output of these farms was a mere 3.4 per cent
of the total amount of farm products sold in that
year. Were we to arbitrarily label those farms
which market $2,500 worth or more of prod-
ucts each year as "efficient" and those marketing less than $2,500 worth as "inefficient," or
"marginal," it could then be concluded that
the 44 per cent of our farms which are "efficient" produce 90.8 per cent of all marketed
farm products. The 56 per cent which are
"inefficient" account for the remaining 9.2 per
cent of marketed farm output.[1] It is in this
latter group that extremely low incomes—the
main symptom of the difficulties which plague
American agriculture—are predominant.

CAUSES OF THE FARM PROBLEM

It is a bit misleading to talk of "the" farm
problem. Actually, the changes which have occurred in farm incomes suggest the presence
of both a long-run problem and a short-run
problem. The long-run problem concerns those
forces which have caused farm prices and incomes to decline over a period of years. The
short-run problem has to do with the extreme
year-to-year instability of farm incomes.

The long-run problem

Complex problems can rarely be stated accurately in brief terms. This is certainly true of
the long-run problem which plagues American

[1] *Toward a Realistic Farm Program* (New York:
Committee for Economic Development, December,
1957), pp. 12–13.

TABLE 33-2. DISTRIBUTION OF COMMERCIAL FARMS BY ECONOMIC CLASS, 1954

Value of farm products sold	Number of farms	Per cent of total farms	Dollar output, millions	Per cent of total output
$25,000 or more	134,003	2.8	$ 7,768	31.3
$10,000–$24,999	448,945	9.4	6,684	26.9
$5,000–$9,999	706,929	14.8	5,085	20.5
$2,500–$4,999	811,965	17.0	3,008	12.1
$1,200–$2,499	763,348	16.0	1,414	5.7
$250–$1,199	1,037,002*	21.7	706	2.8
Other farms †	880,829	18.4	149	0.6
Total	4,783,021	100.0	$24,814	100.0

* Slightly more than half (574,575) are part-time farms.
† Most of these are "residential farms" where the value of products sold is less than $250 per year. Also included, however, are some 2,693 institutional, experimental, and community-project farms.
SOURCE: "United States Census of Agriculture: 1954," vol. II, pp. 1132, 1216.

agriculture. Nevertheless a workable picture of the problem can be portrayed through the economic tools of demand and supply. To be more specific, the causes of the long-run farm problem are embodied in ① the *price inelasticity* of the demand for agricultural products and ② the *shifts* which have occurred over time in the demand and supply curves for farm products.

The inelastic demand for farm products. We have seen that the major determinant of elasticity of demand for any product is the number of good substitutes available. A large number of good substitutes means high elasticity; few acceptable substitutes mean an inelastic demand. The inelasticity of demand for farm products in the aggregate lies in the simple fact that there are no good substitutes for them. There are certainly no good substitutes for food. Looking at particular food products, we find that there are virtually no suitable alternatives for wheat, milk, sugar, and potatoes; the price elasticity of demand for these products is extremely low.

On the other hand, there are certain meat products that may be substitutable—lamb,

mutton, and pork can be substituted for beef. But even here statistics suggest that elasticity of demand is about unity or below. For food as a whole authoritative studies conclude that price elasticity is about 0.25. This indicates a highly inelastic demand. For all farm products, food and nonfood, price elasticity is even less, probably about 0.12.[2]

An inelastic demand for farm products means that consumers are relatively unresponsive to changes in the prices of farm products. If farm prices fall, for example, the resulting increase in sales will be very modest. Curve *DD* in Figure 33-2 represents such a demand curve.

Technological advance and rapid increases in agricultural supply. An inelastic demand for farm products is, in and of itself, innocent enough. It is the accompanying fact that the supply of agricultural products has increased in relation to the demand for them that has spelled declining farm incomes.

On the supply side of the picture a rapid

[2] The figures cited are from sources summarized in Harold G. Halcrow, *Agricultural Policy of the United States* (Englewood Cliffs, N.J.: Prentice-Hall, Inc., 1953), chap. 6.

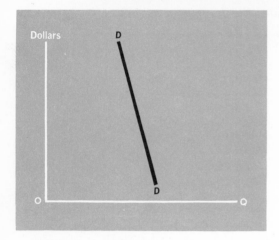

FIGURE 33-2. THE INELASTICITY OF AGRICULTURAL DEMAND.
The demand for most agricultural products tends to be highly inelastic; that is, consumers are relatively unresponsive to changes in farm prices.

rate of technological advance, particularly since World War I, has caused significant increases in the supply of agricultural products. This advance has assumed a variety of forms: widespread mechanization, improved techniques of land management and soil conservation, irrigation, the development of hybrid crops, and improved breeds of livestock.

Most spectacular among these advances has been the rapid *mechanization* of agriculture. The development and widespread use of the general-purpose tractor and a variety of specialized planting, cultivating, and harvesting machines have been the backbone of the agricultural revolution in America. The net result has been considerable increase in both the speed and efficiency of performing various farm operations. Furthermore, International Harvester and John Deere have caused the retirement of Old Dobbin to the extent that by 1948 some 63 million acres of farmland, previously required to produce animal feed, had been freed for the production of marketable farm commodities.[3]

Improved land use and *crop practices* have also been an important facet of technological advance in agriculture. The increasingly widespread application of contour plowing and crop rotation is a significant development, as is the use of cover crops. The greater use of ever-improving commercial fertilizers and insecticides has contributed significantly to agricultural production. Irrigation has changed marginal land into fertile and highly productive farmland.

Significant, too, has been the research and experimental work of agronomists and husbandmen. The development of *hybrid* crops—corn provides an outstanding illustration—has been a boon to farm productivity. Great strides have been made in the breeding and care of livestock.

How significant have these technological advances actually been? Very! The simplest index is the increasing number of people which a single farmer's output will support. Table 33-3 pictures the long-run trend. In 1820 each farm worker produced enough feed and fiber to support four persons. By 1961 each farmer produced enough to support twenty-six! There can be no question but that productivity in agriculture has risen significantly.

Two more significant points must amend this discussion of the increasing productivity in American farming: (1) Most recent technological advances have not been initiated by farmers but are rather the result of government-sponsored programs of research and education and the work of farm machinery producers. Land-grant colleges, experimental stations, county agents of the Agricultural Extension Service, the inexhaustible supply of educational pamphlets issuing from the Department of Agriculture, and the research staffs of John Deere and International Harvester are the sources of technological advance in American agriculture. (2) Technological advance has not occurred evenly throughout agriculture. Many farmers—particularly those resting on the bot-

[3] J. Frederick Dewhurst and Associates, *America's Needs and Resources* (New York: The Twentieth Century Fund, Inc., 1955), p. 851.

tom rung of the income ladder—are under-mechanized, uninformed, and startlingly inefficient.

Lagging demand for agricultural products.
Increases in the demand for agricultural commodities have failed to keep pace with technologically inspired increases in their supply. Why? The answer lies in the two major determinants of agricultural demand—incomes and population.

In underdeveloped countries consumers must devote the bulk of their meager incomes to the products of agriculture—food and clothing—to sustain themselves. But as income expands beyond the subsistence level and the problem of hunger gives way to one of obesity, consumers will increase their outlays on food and clothing at ever-declining rates. Once a consumer's stomach is filled, his thoughts turn to the amenities of life which industry, not agriculture, provides. Economic growth in the United States has boosted average per capita income far beyond the level of bare subsistence. As a result, *increases in the incomes of American consumers lead to less-than-proportionate increases in expenditures on farm products.* In brief, the demand for farm products is income-inelastic. Recent estimates indicate that a 10 per cent increase in real per capita disposable income entails at the most an increase in the consumption of farm products of only 2 per cent.[4]

Population is a somewhat different proposition. Despite the fact that, after a minimum income level is reached, each individual consumer's intake of food and fiber will become relatively fixed, more consumers will mean an increase in the demand for farm products. And it has. But population increases coupled with the relatively small increase in the purchase of farm products which occurs as incomes rise have simply not been great enough to match the concomitant increases in farm output.

[4] Joint Economic Committee, *Staff Report on Employment, Growth and Price Levels* (Washington: Government Printing Office, 1960), p. 190.

TABLE 33-3. PERSONS SUPPORTED BY PRODUCTION OF ONE FARM WORKER, SELECTED YEARS, 1820–1961

Year	Persons supported per farm worker
1820	4
1870	5
1900	7
1910	7
1920	9
1930	10
1940	11
1950	15
1952	17
1954	19
1956	22
1957	24
1961	26

SOURCE: Department of Agriculture, "Agricultural Outlook Chartbook, 1962" (November, 1961).

When coupled with the inelastic demand for agricultural products, these shifts in supply and demand have resulted in declining farm incomes. This is illustrated in Figure 33-3, where a large increase in supply is shown against a very modest increase in demand. Because of the very inelastic demand for farm products, these shifts have resulted in a sharp decline in farm prices accompanied by relatively small increases in sales. This means that farm incomes decline. Diagrammatically, income before the increase in supply occurs (measured by rectangle $OPAQ$) will exceed farm income after supply increases (OP_1BQ_1). The income "loss" of P_1PAC is not fully offset by the income "gain" of $QCBQ_1$. In summary, given an inelastic demand for farm products, an increase in the supply of farm products relative to the demand for them can result, and has resulted, in declining farm incomes.

All this is not to say that farm prices and incomes are always declining. Figure 33-1 indicates that farm prices rose sharply during the

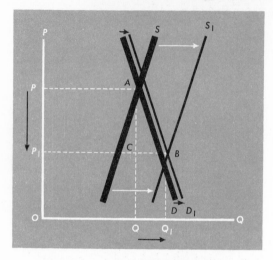

FIGURE 33-3. A GRAPHIC SUMMARY OF THE LONG-RUN FARM PROBLEM.

In the long run, increases in the demand for agricultural products (D to D_1) have not kept pace with the increases in supply (S to S_1) which technological advances have permitted. Coupled with the fact that agricultural demand is inelastic, these shifts have tended to depress farm prices (as from P to P_1) and incomes (as from OPAQ to OP_1BQ_1).

1940s, but the abnormal demand for farm products which accompanied World War II, European reconstruction, and the Korean War largely explains these increases. The price declines which farmers faced in the prosperous twenties and early fifties are indicative of the persistent tendency of farm prices to fall.

Relative immobility of farmers. Our previous discussion of the workings of the price system (Chapter 5) would certainly suggest an obvious and automatic solution to the long-run problem faced by agriculture. In a price-directed economy one would expect declining farm prices and incomes to signal an exodus of resources from agriculture. Prices and incomes which are low in relation to the rest of the economy would seemingly prompt farmers to leave their farms in favor of more lucrative

occupations. The adjustments of a competitive industry as outlined in Chapters 5 and 24 indicate that this exodus of farmers would reduce industry supply in relation to demand, thereby boosting farm prices and incomes. This reallocation of resources away from agriculture and toward industry would assumedly bring farm incomes into closer accord with those of the rest of the economy.

Many farmers have left agriculture for higher-paying jobs in industry, but this outmigration has been insufficient to solve the farm problem. Farmers have been mobile, but not mobile enough. Table 33-4 clearly reflects the long-run trend for the farm population to decline in both absolute and relative terms (see also Figure 18-3). Nevertheless—and this is the important point—the net outmigration of human resources away from agriculture has not been great enough to alleviate the low-income crisis in American agriculture. High birth rates and a relatively slow rate of outmigration of farmers have resulted in too many people trying to make a living in an industry which will not support them at an income level comparable with the rest of the economy. Statistics underscore this point. In 1910 the farm population was about 35 per cent of the total population and received about 19 per cent of the national income; by 1960 the farm population had declined to about 11 per cent of the total, but farm income was about 4 per cent of national income. It is the fact that agriculture's share of the national income has fallen at a faster rate than has the farm population which has caused low per capita incomes to persist in the agricultural segment of the economy.

In a broad sense, the relative slowness of the reallocation of farmers from agriculture to industry is the crux of the farm problem. Ironically enough, in an industry long associated with the word "surplus," we find that the biggest and most fundamental farm surplus of all is the number of farmers. Indeed, the farm problem can best be envisioned as a problem of resource misallocation. It is the fact that too many farmers are sharing agriculture's shrinking slice of the national income pie that makes income per farmer small. Later in the

TABLE 33-4. THE DECLINING FARM POPULATION, SELECTED YEARS, 1910–1961

Year	Farm population, millions	Farm population as a percentage of the total population
1910	32.1	35
1920	31.9	30
1930	30.5	25
1935	32.2	25
1940	30.5	23
1945	25.3	18
1950	25.1	17
1952	24.3	16
1954	22.1	14
1956	22.3	13
1958	21.3	12
1961	21.5	11

SOURCE: "Statistical Abstract of the United States, 1962," p. 613.

chapter this point will be discussed further.

If the relative immobility of the farm population is a major dimension of the farm problem, it is certainly legitimate to inquire why farmers have been relatively slow in moving out of agriculture. There is no simple answer. Economic considerations certainly play a role. Of greatest importance is the fact that in a less-than-full-employment economy the farmer has little or no alternative but to stay on the farm. Why move to the city when industry has no jobs to offer? And the costs of moving and retraining oneself for industrial employment may be significant, especially if the move occurs at a time when the farmer's financial plight is particularly acute. Similarly, the high fixed costs associated with farming work against any hasty decision to quit farming. Noneconomic and institutional factors are also significant: any suggested movement from the farm to a metropolitan area, and the assembly-line environment it implies, strikes fear into the hearts of most farm families.

Then, too, the Negro sharecropper of the South is restricted by his color from many of the more desirable jobs available in urban areas; minority groups are all too often the last hired and the first fired by industry. In other cases unrealistic restrictive membership practices by unions are pertinent. Or the mere lack of information about the availability of urban employment may be the vital factor.

The short-run problem

The fact that farm incomes lag behind the rest of the economy is evidence of the long-run agricultural problem. Extreme year-to-year fluctuations in farm incomes reflect a short-run problem. This short-run instability can be traced back to the inelastic demand for agricultural products. This inelastic demand contributes to the instability of farm prices and incomes in two different ways.

On the production side of the picture, the inelastic demand for farm products causes small changes in agricultural production to be magnified into relatively larger changes in farm prices and incomes. To understand this point we must first note that farmers pos-

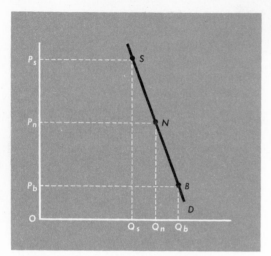

FIGURE 33-4. THE EFFECT OF OUTPUT CHANGES ON FARM PRICES AND INCOMES.

Because of the inelasticity of demand for farm products, a relatively small change in output (Q_n to Q_s or Q_b) will cause relatively large changes in farm prices (P_n to P_s or P_b) and incomes (OP_nNQ_n to OP_sSQ_s or OP_bBQ_b).

sess only limited control over their production. Floods, droughts, insect damage, and similar disasters can mean short crops. Conversely, an excellent growing season may mean bumper crops. Weather factors are beyond the control of farmers, yet they exert an important influence upon production. Furthermore, the highly competitive nature of agriculture makes it virtually impossible for farmers to form a huge combination to control their production. Agriculture is made up of millions of widely scattered and independent producers. If all should by chance plant an unusually large or abnormally small portion of their land, extra large or small outputs would result even if the growing season were normal.

Now, putting the instability of farm production together with an inelastic demand for farm products, we can readily discover why farm prices and incomes are highly unstable.

Figure 33-4 is pertinent. Even if we assume that the market demand for agricultural products is stable at D, the inelastic nature of demand will magnify small changes in output into relatively large changes in farm prices and income. For example, assume that a "normal" crop of Q_n results in a "normal" price of P_n and a "normal" farm income of OP_nNQ_n. But a bumper crop or a short crop will cause large deviations from these normal prices and incomes; these results stem from the inelasticity of demand for farm products.

If an unusually good growing season occurs, the resulting bumper crop of Q_b will cause farm incomes to *fall* from OP_nNQ_n to OP_bBQ_b. Why? Because when demand is inelastic, an increase in the quantity sold will be accompanied by a more-than-proportionate decline in price. The net result is that total receipts, that is, total farm income, will decline. Similarly, for farmers as a group a short crop caused by, say, a drought may boost farm incomes. A short crop of Q_s will raise total farm income from OP_nNQ_n to OP_sSQ_s. Why? Because a decline in output will cause a more-than-proportionate increase in price when demand is inelastic. Ironically, for farmers as a group a short crop may be a blessing and a bumper crop a hardship. Our conclusion is this: given a stable market demand for farm products, the inelasticity of that demand will turn relatively small changes in output into relatively larger changes in farm prices and incomes.

The other aspect of the short-run instability of farm incomes has to do with shifts in the demand curve for agricultural products. Let us suppose that somehow agricultural output is stabilized at the "normal" level of Q_n in Figure 33-5. Now, because of the inelasticity of the demand for farm products, short-run fluctuations in the demand for farm products will cause markedly different prices and incomes to be associated with this assumedly constant level of production. That is, a slight drop in demand from D_1D_1 to D_2D_2 will cause farm incomes to fall from OP_1aQ_n to OP_2bQ_n. A relatively small decline in demand gives farmers a drastically reduced money reward for the same amount of production. Conversely, a slight increase in demand will bring an equally sharp increase in farm incomes for the same volume of output. These large price-income changes are linked to the fact that demand is inelastic. This can be grasped by observing the much smaller price-income changes which accompany an equal shift in demand from the more elastic demand curve D_3D_3.[5] If demand drops from D_3D_3 to D_4D_4, price will fall very modestly from P_1 to P_4 and income will only fall from OP_1aQ_n to OP_4cQ_n.

It is tempting to argue that the sharp declines in farm prices which accompany a decrease in demand will cause many farmers to close down in the short run, thereby reducing total output and alleviating these price-income declines. But farm production is relatively insensitive to price changes, because the farmer's fixed costs are high as compared to his variable costs. Interest, rental, tax, and mortgage payments on buildings and equipment are the major costs faced by the farmer. These are clearly fixed charges. Furthermore, the labor supply of the farmer and his family can also be regarded as a fixed cost. So long as he stays on his farm, the farmer cannot reduce his costs by firing himself! This means that his variable costs are the small amounts of hired help he may employ plus expenditures for seed, fertilizer, and fuel. As a result of this high volume of fixed costs, the farmer is almost invariably better off by working his land than he is by sitting idle and attempting to pay his fixed costs out of pocket. The other factors, noted previously, which contribute to the relative immobility of farmers are also pertinent. In particular, if a decline in the demand for farm output is part of an overall recession, there will be no real incentive for farmers to stop production in order to seek nonexistent jobs in industry. As a matter of fact, a migration in the opposite direction— from the city to the farm—often accompanies a full-scale depression. Note in Table 33-4 the

[5] Though they may not appear so graphically, these two shifts in demand are equal in the sense that in each instance buyers want to purchase the same amount less at each possible price.

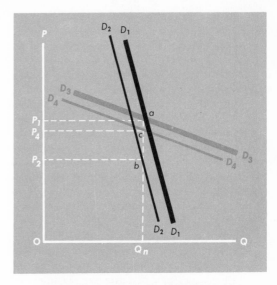

FIGURE 33-5. THE EFFECT OF DEMAND CHANGES ON FARM PRICES AND INCOMES.
Because of the highly inelastic demand for agricultural products, a small shift in demand (D_1D_1 to D_2D_2) will cause drastically different levels of farm prices (P_1 to P_2) and farm incomes (OP_1aQ_n to OP_2bQ_n) to be associated with a given level of production Q_n. Note that equal changes in a more elastic demand curve (D_3D_3 to D_4D_4) will be accompanied by much smaller price (P_1 to P_4) and income (OP_1aQ_n to OP_4cQ_n) alterations.

absolute *increase* in the farm population which occurred between 1930 and 1935. Note, too, in Figure 11-4 that between 1929 and 1933 farm prices fell by 63 per cent and farm output by a mere 6 per cent.

Let us pause at this point to bring our knowledge of the causes of the long- and short-run farm problems into sharper focus. The long-run problem centers upon a misallocation of human resources between agriculture and the rest of the economy. This misallocation is the result of three causal factors: (1) Rapid technological advance has brought significant increases in the supply of farm products. (2) Consumer demand has not increased to the extent necessary to keep farm prices and incomes from falling. (3) Human resources have not moved out of agriculture in sufficient amounts. The consequence of this set of forces is that there are too many farmers in agriculture to permit the attainment of incomes comparable with the national average. In the short run the extreme sensitivity of farm prices and incomes is based upon the inelastic demand for agricultural products which transforms small changes in farm output and demand into much larger changes in farm prices and incomes.

An alternative explanation correctly puts emphasis upon resource misallocation as the core of the long-run farm problem and couches the problem in terms of a growing economy. Of necessity primitive or underdeveloped countries have essentially agrarian economies. The total population of such a nation must devote its efforts to agricultural endeavors to provide enough food and fiber to sustain itself. But as technological advance increases productivity per farmer, the economy can maintain or even increase its consumption of food and clothing and simultaneously transfer a portion of its population into nonagricultural pursuits. This is the path which any expanding, progressive economy follows. Indeed, the shift of resources from agricultural to industrial pursuits is the earmark of a growing economy. The experience of the United States is illustrative. About 90 per cent of our population was devoted to agriculture in the eighteenth century. At present about 11 per cent of the population is in farming, the remaining 89 per cent being free to produce refrigerators, armaments, automobiles, and the thousand and one other goods and services which comprise a high standard of living. But in American capitalism the actual shift of resources to nonagricultural employments has not kept pace with the rate of reallocation which rapid technological advance permits. The economy has thereby failed to realize the increases in nonfarm output which technological progress in farming has made available. Bluntly, we need *less* than 11 per cent of our population in agriculture.

PUBLIC POLICY TOWARD AGRICULTURE

Many clouded and confused issues surround agricultural policy in the United States. Yet one basic point is clear: farmers have been highly successful in the political arena. The farm bloc has succeeded in establishing a comprehensive and many-sided program of public aid to agriculture.

Agriculture's appeal for aid

The claims to assistance voiced by individual farmers and by the major farm groups—the Farm Bureau, the Farmer's Union, and the National Grange—are many and varied. They include the following:

1. Farming, and particularly the family farm, is a fundamental American institution—a way of life which is to be nurtured and preserved for the virtues it entails. What could be more puritanical than working the soil, living close to nature, and being one's own master in an environment untainted by the evils of modern urban life?

2. Agriculture is a major cog in the American economy; prosperity for farmers is essential for prosperity in the economy as a whole.

3. Farmers face certain hazards—floods, droughts, hailstorms, and invasion by hordes of insects—to which other industries are not exposed.

4. Society as a whole, not individual farmers, should bear the cost of soil conservation, that is, of maintaining the nation's soil resources.

5. The highly competitive nature of agriculture makes it more vulnerable to changes in the market forces of demand and supply than the less competitive industries which characterize American capitalism. While selling in competitive markets, farmers must buy from monopolistic sellers.

6. A recent and ironic claim: past farm policies are alleged to have been so faulty and misguided that the government is obliged to bless the farmer with improved farm programs in the future.

Several words of caution: These arguments for public aid to agriculture are not presented on the assumption that they are correct or valid. It is up to you as a thinking individual to make such an evaluation and to decide whether the public assistance programs about to be described are justified or not. Three points are clear. (1) Most of these claims can be applied in somewhat modified forms to a host of other industries. (2) Whether our background is rural or metropolitan, as taxpayers we have a direct interest in any program of aid to agriculture or any other industry. (3) On the basis of these arguments and the disproportionately large voice which farmers have in Congress, a detailed farm program has been established. Let us consider the main elements of this program.

The farm program

"The farm program" actually refers to a whole series of more or less related government programs concerning (1) farm prices, incomes, and output, (2) soil conservation, (3) agricultural research, (4) farm credit, (5) crop insurance, and so forth. However, for the last twenty-five or thirty years the typical American farmer and the average politician have both viewed the farm problem as essentially a price-income problem. Low farm prices and the depressed farm incomes resulting therefrom are held to be the cause of the farmer's plight. As a consequence, the American farm program has become "price-centered." The major aim of agricultural policy is to raise farm incomes by raising the prices of farm products.

The enactment of the Agricultural Adjustment Act in 1933—at the depth of the Great Depression—set the pattern for American agricultural policy. This act established a framework for farm policy which has persisted down to the present time. There have been considerable differences in emphasis over time and between political parties, but these differences have concerned details. For the most part current debate concerns the manner and degree to which farm prices should be bolstered, although some critics and politicians are beginning to face the more fundamental issue of whether or not prices should be supported at all.

Briefly, the major policy goals and techniques embodied in American agricultural policy growing out of the AAA are (1) the concept of parity, (2) price supports for farm products, (3) the disposal of surplus farm output, and (4) the restriction of agricultural production.

These four aspects of farm policy are in fact closely intertwined. Application of the parity concept, we shall find, demands that government support farm prices at above-equilibrium levels. The result is surpluses of farm products and subsequent storage or disposal problems. The complexities of disposing of agricultural surpluses and the costliness of storing them lead to the establishment of programs to restrict production in the hope of preventing surpluses from arising.

The concept of parity. Established in the Agricultural Adjustment Act of 1933 as the major objective of American farm policy, the concept of parity has acquired a degree of holiness over the last quarter of a century. It is something of a symbol to American agriculture.

The simple rationale of the parity concept can be readily envisioned in both real and money terms. In real terms, parity simply says that year after year for a given output of farm products a farmer should be able to acquire a given total amount of goods and services. A given real output should always result in the same real income. "If a man could take a bushel of corn to town in 1912 and sell it and buy himself a shirt, he should be able to take a bushel of corn to town today and buy a shirt."

In money terms the parity concept alleges that it is only fair that a certain relationship be maintained between (1) the prices which farmers *receive* for the products they sell and (2) the prices which they must *pay* for the goods and services they purchase. The money income which a farmer receives from a given volume of output should have the same purchasing power over the years. This implies that if the prices of the goods farmers purchase increase, then the prices which farmers receive for their products should be increased accordingly.

Let us examine the simplest possible example to lay bare the parity principle and the manner in which parity prices are determined. Table 33-5 is relevant. Suppose a farmer produces 50

TABLE 33-5. PARITY PRICING: A SIMPLE CASE (base: year 1)

Year	Bushels of wheat	Price per bushel	Money income	Price per suit	Real income, suits
1	50	$2	$100	$25	4
2	50	4	200	50	4
3	50			65	
4	50			20	

bushels of wheat in both year 1 and year 2. If the *market price* for wheat is $2 per bushel in year 1, the farmer's money income will obviously be $100. Suppose now that the farmer spends this money income entirely on one product—say dress suits. If suits are selling at $25 each in year 1, the farmer will obviously be able to buy four of them. Using year 1 as our point of reference, or *base year*, the parity concept says that for the same output—50 bushels of wheat—the farmer should be able to acquire the same real income—four suits— in succeeding years as he did in the base year.

What if in year 2 the farmer finds that the price of suits has doubled because of inflation and now stands at $50 per suit? This means that 50 bushels of wheat selling at $2 per bushel will only provide the farmer with enough income to buy two suits. Assuming the market price for wheat remains at $2, the farmer's real income has been halved, because the prices of the goods he buys have doubled. Obviously, the concept of parity applied to year 2 would entail a $4 *parity price* for wheat. The price of the given quantity of wheat must be doubled in order for the farmer to maintain his real income in the face of a doubling in his cost of living. The reader can complete Table 33-5 by determining the parity price for wheat in years 3 and 4.

Now an important word on the mechanics of calculating parity price: Note that it is the ratio of the price of suits in the current year (year 2) to the price of suits in the base year (year 1) that determines the multiple by which the price of wheat should be changed—in-

creased in this case—to achieve parity. In our simple example, this ratio is $50/$25, or 2. Thus, multiplying the $2 base period price of wheat by 2, we get the parity price of $4. In other words, the formula for determining the parity price for wheat in this example is

Base period price of wheat

$$\times \frac{\text{current price of suits}}{\text{base year price of suits}}$$

$$= \text{parity price of wheat}$$

Substituting the figures from our illustration, we get

$$\$2 \times \frac{\$50}{\$25} = \$4$$

In practice, of course, farmers purchase a wide variety of products and services. As a result, we must substitute an *index* of prices paid for the price of suits. The formula for determining parity thus becomes

Base period price of wheat

$$\times \frac{\text{current prices paid index}}{\text{prices paid index in base year}}$$

$$= \text{parity price of wheat}$$

Let us illustrate with actual data for wheat. In the 1910–1914 base period used in determining parity prices, the average price for wheat was 88.4 cents per bushel. The 1961 index of prices paid by farmers was 301. In the 1910–1914 base period this index was, of course, 100 per cent. In effect, the prices paid by farmers had increased 3.01 times between the base period and 1961. Therefore, wheat farmers must receive 3.01 times as much per bushel of wheat in 1961 as they did in 1910–1914 to achieve 100 per cent of parity. Substituting in the above formula, it is discovered that the parity price of wheat in 1961 was $2.66:

$$88.4 \text{ cents} \times \frac{301}{100} = \$2.66$$

In many instances government has supported prices at something less than 100 per cent of parity. Legislation might give the Secretary of Agriculture the authority to establish the price of, say, wheat or corn at some level within, say, 70 to 90 per cent of parity.

Three points are vital to a complete appreciation of the parity concept:

1. Despite the seemingly "scientific" manipulations involved in establishing parity prices, parity is actually an ethical concept. Parity is a notion concerning what the economic position of farmers should, or ought to, be.

2. A bit of reflection will make clear that, in any application of the parity concept, the choice of the base year, or base period, is all-important. If the base period was one wherein the farmer's economic position was good (prices received were relatively high and prices paid relatively low), then a strict application of parity would guarantee farmers that the favorable situation would be perpetuated. Conversely, if the choice was a base period where farmers were squeezed between getting low prices and paying high prices, the application of parity would simply sustain the farmer's misery. In view of the strong political voice of agriculture it is not surprising to find that a prosperous farm era— the 1910–1914 so-called "golden age" of American agriculture—is the actual base period for determining parity.[6]

3. Also, it is notable that price parity is not income parity. For example, if price parity is rigidly maintained over a period of time wherein productivity is increasing significantly, price parity will mean rising rather than parity incomes for farmers.

Price supports. The practical importance of the notion of parity prices lies in the fact that it is

[6] Recent modifications have adjusted some parity prices from the 1910–1914 base so as to allow for more recent price trends.

the focal point for government price support programs designed to bolster farm incomes. Indeed, it is the concept of parity which provides the rationale and justification for government price supports on farm products. Embracing the notion that it is only fair that the prices received by farmers be kept on a par with the prices paid by them, Congress may enact *rigid* price supports by setting a specific figure of, say, 70, 90, or 100 per cent of parity at which the prices of wheat, corn, tobacco, cotton, rice, and other farm products are to be established. Or *flexible* supports may be put into law, establishing, say, a 70 to 90 per cent of parity price range for farm products and allowing the Secretary of Agriculture to exercise his discretion in choosing the specific support price within these limits.

In either event the fact that in the long run the actual market prices received by farmers have not kept abreast of prices paid by them means that to achieve parity or some percentage thereof the government is likely to be required to establish above-equilibrium prices on farm products. The 1920–1941 period in Figure 33-1 reflects the tendency of prices received to fall behind prices paid, as, indeed, does our simple illustration in Table 33-5. Government must take action to boost prices received above the level established by the market to prevent the real income position of the farmer from deteriorating. In short, government must support farm prices.

Effective price supports invariably result in product surpluses. Let us illustrate, using the data from Table 33-5. In this simple example the parity price for wheat in year 2 is $4 per bushel. Suppose that the market forces of supply and demand establish an equilibrium price of only $2.40 per bushel, as shown in Figure 33-6. Assuming the farmer's costs and productivity have not changed sufficiently to offset this below-parity market price, the farmer's income from the sale of a bushel of wheat will fail to keep his real income at the level of year 1. If 100 per cent of parity is the objective of public policy, then it is up to government to establish a legal, or supported, price of $4 per bushel for wheat in year 2. But it is all too evi-

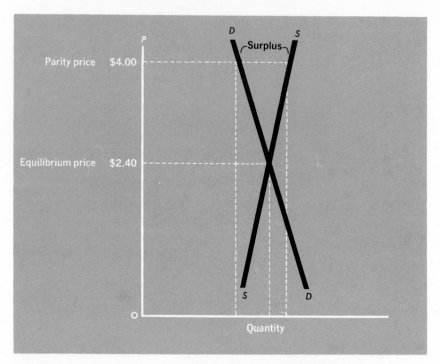

FIGURE 33-6. EFFECTIVE PRICE SUPPORTS RESULT IN FARM SURPLUSES.
Application of the parity concept obligates government to support farm prices at above-equilibrium levels. These supported prices result in persistent surpluses of farm products.

dent from Figure 33-6 that private buyers will not be willing to consume the quantity of wheat forthcoming at this supported price. There will be a market imbalance; specifically, a *surplus* of wheat will result at the supported price of $4. The competitive price mechanism will no longer perform the rationing function of automatically equating quantity demanded and quantity supplied when a higher-than-equilibrium legal price is imposed.

What happens to the surplus, that is, the quantity of wheat which private buyers will not take at the $4 price? It is the government's headache. To make the above-equilibrium supported price effective, government must buy what private purchasers will not.

In some cases government purchases surplus output directly in the market to maintain the supported price. In many cases, however, the surpluses are handled through the use of *non-recourse loans* to farmers. These loans, which are often the equivalent of the outright purchase of surpluses by the government, work something like this: The Commodity Credit Corporation (CCC), affiliated with the Department of Agriculture, has the power to make loans to farmers equal to the supported value of their wheat, corn, cotton, tobacco, and so forth. For example, if a farmer has 50 bushels of wheat and the supported price is $4, as in our prior illustration, the farmer can obtain a CCC loan of $200 (or $4 times 50), the 50 bushels of wheat serving as security on the loan. The farmer will often store the collateral —the wheat—on his own farm. Should the market price of wheat rise above $4—say, to

$5—the farmer has the right to sell his wheat and pocket the $50 difference between the revenue from his sale ($250) and the amount of his CCC loan ($200). If the market price fails to climb above the supported price, the farmer simply defaults on the loan, turning his wheat over to the CCC. In this case, the farmer in effect has sold his wheat to the CCC at $4 per bushel.

This program is clearly aimed at bolstering farmers' incomes. The plan is a "heads the farmer wins, tails the government loses" proposition. The $4 price support guarantees the farmer an income of $200 for his wheat and leaves the door open for favorable market conditions to better that figure. As the program has worked in practice, however, the farmer very typically ends up selling a considerable portion of his output to the CCC. The result? Government-owned farm surpluses.

In 1948 the CCC had $294 million tied up in inventories of surplus farm products and nonrecourse loans. By 1954 this figure had jumped to $3,688 million, and at mid-1960 it stood at a whopping $7,223 million. And had it not been for a drought and two wars, these figures would be much larger. These ever-growing surpluses of farm products are by no means a goal of public policy; rather they are a troublesome consequence of the government's attempt to bolster sagging farm incomes through the use of price supports.

Farm surpluses are undesirable on several counts. First and foremost, the very existence of these surpluses indicates a gross misallocation of the economy's resources. Government-held surpluses reflect the fact that the economy is devoting large amounts of resources to the production of commodities which, *at existing supported prices,* are simply not wanted by consumers. And, of course, surpluses are politically embarrassing. The CCC storage bins which one cannot help but encounter on a Sunday drive in the country are impeccable evidence that neither political party has made substantial progress in resolving the basic resource imbalance which lies at the heart of America's farm troubles. Furthermore, the storing of surplus products is a costly proposition which has

added to the cost of the farm program and ultimately to the consumer's tax bill. Currently storage costs on existing surpluses are about $1.5 million per day.

Disposing of surpluses. In view of these facts it is not at all surprising that Congress has attempted in a variety of ways to reduce farm surpluses. The possible courses of action are (1) to dump the surpluses on foreign markets, (2) to dump them on domestic markets, (3) to destroy the surpluses, and (4) to restrict agricultural production so as to avoid the accumulation of the surpluses in the first place.

The first alternative—selling the surpluses on foreign markets at low prices or even giving them away—is enticing. On the surface it would seem a policy destined to create international good will. But there are weighty objections. American taxpayers, docile as they are, may object to having their tax money used to subsidize foreign buyers while simultaneously having to pay above-market prices domestically for the same products. On the other hand, in practice foreign dumping is almost invariably a source of international ill will. Foreign producers violently resent the government-subsidized competition of American food and fiber. How are Argentinians to get a fair international price for their wheat or Egyptians for their cotton when they are in competition with American wheat and cotton substantially subsidized by the United States government? Therefore, instead of friendship, foreign dumping may easily breed retaliatory trade policies and the shrinking of foreign markets for American exporters. Our current Food for Peace program is an attempt to overcome these problems by distributing our farm surpluses to the hungry people of the underdeveloped countries in ways which will not depress the domestic agricultural markets of the recipient countries.

Dumping at home embraces a variety of programs. Food stamp plans have been invoked to distribute surpluses to low income families. School lunch programs and the distribution of surpluses to welfare and charitable institutions are other variations of domestic dumping. Or, after buying the surplus crops at high supported prices, the government may sell them back to farmers at low token prices as feed for livestock.[7] But these programs have done little more than make a small dent in the aggregate of farm surpluses. Domestic dumping is restricted by the fact that such programs are self-defeating in the task of reducing surpluses if they provide products to those who would otherwise obtain them through the market.

A third disposal technique is appallingly simple and at the same time destined to fan the flames of public resentment. This solution is to destroy the surpluses—burn them, dump them in the ocean, or simply let them rot. This is not an easy solution politically. The most persuasive orator will find himself incapable of explaining to the public why potatoes, grains, and dairy products are deliberately destroyed when large portions of the world's population go hungry.

Despite domestic and foreign disposal, surpluses continue to grow. Aside from CCC storage bins, such unlikely installations as liberty ships and abandoned airplane hangers bulge with farm surpluses. This suggests the need for a more positive approach to the problem of farm surpluses.

Restricting farm production. Why not create programs designed to manipulate market demand and supply so as to prevent farm surpluses from occurring in the first place? That is, by increasing demand or reducing supply the market prices of farm products can be brought up to the desired supported prices. As a result, no surpluses will appear at the supported prices. Much public and private money has been spent to uncover new uses for agricultural commodities. The results have been very modest. Most agricultural economists agree that such research ventures will result in slight

[7] The late Senator Joseph R. McCarthy of Wisconsin once received this letter from a constituent: "I have six children. My brother-in-law lives outside the town. He is raising hogs. He can buy Grade A potatoes at 25 cents a bushel to feed to his hogs. But when I go to the grocery store I have to pay 85 cents a peck for No. 2 potatoes. My question is, are his hogs more important to the nation than my children are?"

increases in demand at best and will prove a complete waste of time and effort at worst.

But on the supply side of the market public policy has long been aimed at restricting farm output in order to bolster market prices. The programs center upon taking farmland out of the production of certain basic crops.

The _soil conservation_ program provides direct income subsidies to farmers who do not plant certain soil-depleting crops. Aside from its conservation objective, this program has bolstered farm incomes and at the same time restricted farm production.

Of greater significance is the _acreage allotment_ program, which accompanies the application of price supports. In return for the privilege of getting CCC nonrecourse loans on their crops, farmers must agree to limit the number of acres planted in those crops whose prices are supported. Attempting to bring quantity supplied and quantity demanded into balance, the Department of Agriculture estimates the amount of each product which private buyers will take at the supported price. This amount is then translated into the number of acres of planting which will produce this amount. The total acreage figure is apportioned among states, counties, ultimately individual farmers.

Under the _soil bank_ program, inaugurated in 1956, the Department of Agriculture has been authorized to get farmland entirely out of production by "renting" land from farmers. Such idle land is to be planted in cover crops or in timber, not in other cash crops. This program ties together the restriction of output, soil conservation, and income subsidies to farmers in one package.

But these programs have proved to be relatively unsuccessful, as is evidenced by the continued growth of surpluses. The basic reason lies in the fact that acreage reduction invariably results in less-than-proportionate declines in production. Why? (1) Farmers retire their worst land and keep the best in production. (2) Those acres which are used are cultivated more intensively. The use of better seed, more and better fertilizer and insecticides, and more manpower will enhance output per acre. (3)

By alternating retired acreage over the years, crop rotation in effect is enforced, thereby boosting per acre yields. And, of course, (4) the fortuitous occurrence of a good growing season will mean large per acre outputs. For these and other reasons the supply of farm products may actually *increase*, although acreage is reduced. To illustrate: In 1953 some 80 million acres of corn were planted, and the resulting total output was about 3.2 billion bushels. Approximately 72 million acres of corn were planted in 1957, and output was 3.3 billion bushels. A 10 per cent *reduction* in corn acreage was accompanied by a 3 per cent *increase* in output!

It is to be emphasized that production restriction programs are in substance a government-sponsored attempt to give some measure of monopoly power to the last major industry in American capitalism which approximates pure competition. Restricting supply in relation to demand in order to increase receipts is the stock in trade of the monopolist. And this is precisely what the farm program has attempted to do in seeking to solve the surplus problem.

EVALUATING THE FARM PROGRAM

How successful has public policy been in resolving the chronic imbalances which plague American agriculture? Not very. Evidence is abundant: farm incomes continue to sag, agricultural surpluses continue to accumulate, and the costs of the farm program persist in rising. What specific criticisms can be made?

First and foremost, the farm program has failed to get at the causes of the farm problem. Public policy toward agriculture is designed to treat symptoms and not causes. The root *cause* of the farm problem is a misallocation of resources between agriculture and the rest of the economy. Crudely put, the problem is one of too many farmers. The effect or symptom of this misallocation of resources is low farm incomes. *For the most part, public policy in agriculture has been oriented toward supporting farm prices and incomes rather than alleviating the resource allocation problem, which is the fundamental cause of these sagging farm*

incomes. As a matter of fact, the income-oriented farm program which both political parties have pursued has probably deterred the migration of resources out of agriculture, thereby fostering the resource misallocation it should seek to alleviate. Price-income supports encourage people to stay in agriculture who might otherwise migrate to industry. On the other hand, were the farm program reoriented to speed the movement of resources out of agriculture, the resulting reduction in the supplies of agricultural products would boost farm prices and thereby increase the average incomes of those who remained in agriculture.

A second criticism is this: The price-income support schemes which have been the focal point of our farm program tend to benefit most those farmers who least need government assistance. Assuming the goal of our farm program is to be the bolstering of low farm incomes, it follows that any program of government aid should be aimed at farmers at the bottom of the farm income distribution. It is the "inefficient" low income farmer of Table 33-2 who desperately needs income subsidies. But such farmers get very little help from price supports. Why? Because the "inefficient" farmer simply does not produce and sell enough in the market. The "inefficient" 56 per cent of American farmers who produce only 9.2 per cent of the total marketed output cannot gain much from any income subsidy based upon the quantity produced. It is the "efficient" farmers —the 44 per cent of the farmers who supply 90.8 per cent of the marketed farm output— who reap the benefits of price supports. Individual subsidy checks running into hundreds of thousands of dollars are not easy to justify. If public policy must be designed to supplement farm incomes, then a strong case can certainly be made for making those benefits vary inversely with one's position in the income distribution. An income support program should be geared to *people*, not *commodities*. It is not too difficult to understand why the farm program entails misguided income subsidies: the poverty-stricken farmer of the Deep South and subsistence farmer of the West are rarely members of the major agricultural interest groups—

the Farm Bureau, the Farmers' Union, and the National Grange.

Another criticism is that there are certain embarrassingly evident inconsistencies within the farm program and between the farm program and other public policies. In particular, at the same time that government is making attempts to cut back on agricultural production, other government policies are aimed at boosting farm output. Specifically, acreage allotment, soil conservation, and soil bank programs work at cross purposes with government-sponsored research designed to increase farm output and Federal irrigation-reclamation programs tailored to increase the supply of arable land. There clearly exists a real dilemma here in public policy. As we have seen, in the long run technological advance in agriculture is a basic permissive force in economic growth. Furthermore, future population growth and the ever-present prospect of war demand that we develop both our land resources and our agricultural technology. Yet in the short run, given the tardy exodus of human resources from agriculture and government's commitment to a price-centered farm program, it is desirable to restrict farm production to avoid the problems and costs associated with ever-expanding surpluses.

A POSITIVE PROGRAM FOR AGRICULTURE

Many individuals and groups, including some of the major farm organizations, are convinced that fundamental difficulties, such as those just outlined, plague the present farm program. But these groups disagree sharply as to what *ought* to be done to remedy the farm problem. Let us pause to consider the challenging program suggested by the Committee for Economic Development (CED).[8] To choose this particular program for discussion is not to ear-

[8] *Toward a Realistic Farm Program* (New York: Committee for Economic Development, December, 1957). The CED is a "non-profit, non-partisan, and non-political" organization of businessmen and scholars. The brevity of the present discussion does not do justice to the CED's program. The interested student is urged to read the program in its entirety.

mark it necessarily as the best of all possible programs. This is a judgment which the reader must make for himself. However, the program does lay bare the nub of the farm problem, and it does make some thought-provoking suggestions aimed at a permanent solution to the economy's farm troubles.

The policy statement of the CED is based upon the contention that the current farm program has been grossly unsuccessful in achieving the objective of stabilizing and supporting the incomes of farmers. The government, it is pointed out, has spent over $50 billion over the last twenty-five years on programs of direct and indirect assistance to American agriculture, but farm incomes continue to decline, and agricultural surpluses to accumulate. If anything, the present farm program has perpetuated the misallocation of resources which is the core of agricultural difficulties. The positive program suggested by the CED centers around the following five points:

1. *Free markets* should be restored in agriculture by the *gradual* elimination of price and income supports. The economic position of farmers should be bettered by means which are consistent with free markets. The key to success in achieving this goal is to bring agricultural supply (ultimately the number of farmers) and demand into balance at prices which yield reasonable incomes for the farm population.

2. Implementation of this return to free agricultural markets calls for an *effective land retirement program,* aimed primarily at the least productive land and the lowest income farmers who cultivate it. This program could be achieved by reorienting the current soil bank program away from the immediate objective of subsidizing farm incomes and toward the single goal of getting agricultural resources—both land and farmers—out of agricultural production. The CED contends that any effective land retirement program should be on a "whole farm" basis. Not only is such an approach more efficient to administer, but it also avoids a fundamental difficulty inherent in current acreage allotment programs: farmers cultivate their remaining land more intensively and thereby produce a larger output per culti-

vated acre. Furthermore, past experience with such programs, according to the CED, indicates that the whole-farm approach has most appeal for the lowest income farmers; it tends to get the least productive land and at the same time the least productive farmers out of agriculture. Payments to farmers retiring their land may assume a variety of forms: annual payments extending over a period of years, "rental" payments, or even government purchases where this seems to be the most effective. The net result of the return to free markets which this land retirement program permits will be *lower* average farm prices but *higher* average farm incomes.

3. The CED thinks it most desirable that an advisory *agricultural board* be established to work with the Secretary of Agriculture. Reminiscent of the Federal Reserve Board, the agricultural board would work with the Secretary of Agriculture in formulating and implementing agricultural policy. The board would be charged

... with the tasks of protecting over-all policy against crippling exceptions and special privileges, of examining agricultural policy in the light of general economic conditions and policy, and of moving agricultural programs as rapidly as is practical toward their stated objectives.[9]

To ensure that the Secretary of Agriculture does not emasculate the board by ignoring it, the CED suggests that the Secretary be required to report to Congress the action he has taken upon the board's policy recommendations. Similarly, the Secretary should be required to explain why he has not acted in the manner suggested by the board.

4. The *instability of farm incomes* which stems from abnormal growing conditions or cyclical fluctuations is regarded by the CED as a special short-run aspect of the over-all farm problem. The CED feels that it is legitimate to use price supports to protect the farmer from these short-run fluctuations in income, but that such supports should be based upon estimated normal market prices in order to avoid the accumulation of surpluses which

[9] *Ibid.*, p. 9.

above-equilibrium supports inevitably entail. In effect these temporary price and income supports would be a kind of unemployment compensation for farmers.

5. Recognizing the particular plight of the *low-income farmer,* the CED contends that price supports do not alleviate the poverty of this group of farmers. The reason? Such farmers do not produce enough to benefit significantly from the higher prices. Arguing that we may be overestimating the alleged immobility of low-income farmers, the CED recommends special assistance programs to retrain these farmers for alternative employments and to assist them financially in making the transition to nonagricultural pursuits. These farmers are not to be starved off their land but are to be subsidized into nonagricultural employment. Government must preserve a high level of employment throughout the economy to encourage the movement of low-income farmers into industry.

SUMMARY

1. Agriculture is a maladjusted industry. The major symptom of this maladjustment is relatively low farm incomes.

2. The core of the long-run farm problem is a misallocation of resources between agriculture and the rest of the economy. Rapid technological advance coupled with a highly inelastic and relatively constant demand for agricultural output have caused low farm incomes. The price system has failed to correct the farm problem by reallocating sufficient amounts of human resources out of agriculture.

3. In the short run the highly inelastic nature of agricultural demand translates small changes in output and small shifts in demand into large fluctuations in prices and incomes.

4. The disproportionately large political voice of farmers and a number of claims for public assistance have resulted in a detailed farm program. These claims include the following: (*a*) Farming is a way of life. (*b*) Agriculture is the backbone of the economy. (*c*) Farmers face

special risks and hazards. (*d*) The community should bear the costs of soil conservation. (*e*) Farmers are in an unfavorable market position in relation to the rest of the economy. (*f*) The inadequacies of past farm programs obligate the government to establish more effective forms of public assistance in the future.

5. The farm program is price-centered and based upon the concept of parity. Parity is the notion that a given real output should always result in the same real income. Parity price can be determined by the following formula:

Base year price

$$\times \frac{\text{current prices paid index}}{\text{prices paid index in base year}}$$

$$= \text{parity price}$$

6. The application of parity prices results in farm surpluses. Attempts to dispose of these surpluses by (*a*) dumping them on foreign markets, (*b*) dumping them on domestic markets, and (*c*) destroying them have fallen far short of success. Productivity increases have reduced the effectiveness of acreage allotment programs

in restricting output. Surpluses therefore continue to accumulate.

7. Basic shortcomings of the current farm program are several. Foremost is the fact that the program treats symptoms rather than causes; public policy is designed to boost farm incomes rather than to speed the reallocation of resources away from agriculture. More specific criticisms concern (*a*) the inverse relationship between the size of income subsidies and need and (*b*) certain inconsistencies which exist between short-run and long-run aspects of farm policy.

8. The CED has offered a thought-provoking program for resolving the farm problem. It embraces (*a*) a gradual return to free markets, (*b*) an effective land retirement program, (*c*) the establishment of an advisory agricultural board, (*d*) the use of price supports which are based on expected normal prices, to insulate farmers from being victimized by short-run price fluctuations, and (*e*) special aid programs to induce "inefficient" low-income farmers to leave agriculture.

QUESTIONS AND STUDY SUGGESTIONS

1. "The whole process of economic growth is one of making agriculture less fundamental in the economic system. The fewer people the nation needs to employ in the production of food and fiber, the better off it is—and the better off farm people are." [10] Evaluate this statement.

2. The CED concludes that in American agriculture "Lower average prices can be made consistent with higher average income." Explain the assumptions which underlie this conclusion.

3. Reconcile these two statements: "The farm problem is one of overproduction." "Despite the tremendous productive capacity of American agriculture, plenty of Americans are going hungry." What assumptions about the price system are implied in your answer?

4. Briefly state and evaluate agriculture's claims for public aid. If you were a spokesman for one of the major farm groups, what priority would you put on each of these claims in presenting agriculture's case? Would you change these priorities as the economy moved from an inflationary boom into recession? Be explicit. What arguments, if any, can you add to this list?

5. "Industry complains of the higher taxes it must pay to finance subsidies to agriculture. Yet the fact that the trend of agricultural prices has been downward while industrial prices have been moving upward suggests that on balance agriculture is actually subsidizing industry." Explain and evaluate.

[10] Lauren Soth, *Farm Trouble* (Princeton, N.J.: Princeton University Press, 1957), p. 40.

6. "To reduce agricultural output by a certain percentage an even larger percentage reduction in acres planted is required." Explain.

7. "Because consumers as a whole must ultimately pay the total incomes received by farmers, it makes no real difference whether this income is paid through free farm markets or through supported prices supplemented by subsidies financed out of tax revenues." Analyze this statement very carefully.

8. "Uncle Sam should dispose of troublesome farm surpluses by selling them at special low prices to those Americans who are in the lower income brackets." Evaluate this proposal.

9. "The supply and demand for agricultural products are such that small changes in agricultural supply will result in drastic changes in prices. However, large changes in farm prices have modest effects on agricultural output." Carefully evaluate. *Hint:* a brief review of the distinction between *supply* and *quantity supplied* may be of assistance.

10. What relationship, if any, can you detect between the fact that the farmer's fixed costs of production are large and the fact that the supply of most agricultural products is generally inelastic? Be specific in your answer.

11. "The long-run demand for farm products depends more upon future growth in the size of our population than it does upon the growth which occurs in average family or per capita incomes." Do you agree? Explain.

12. Suppose you are the president of a local chapter of one of the major farm organizations. You are directed by the chapter's membership to formulate policy statements for the chapter which cover the following topics: (*a*) antitrust policy, (*b*) monetary policy, (*c*) fiscal policy, and (*d*) tariff policy. Briefly outline the policy statements which will best serve the interests of farmers. What is the rationale underlying each statement? Do you see any conflicts or inconsistencies in your policy statements?

13. Explain and evaluate the following statements:
a. "Price supports intensify rather than resolve the farm problem."
b. "The best farm program is the Employment Act of 1946."
c. "The trouble with parity prices in agriculture is that they strip the price mechanism of its ability to allocate resources."

14. The price of wheat was 88.4 cents per bushel in the 1910–1914 base period. In 1955 the prices paid index was 281. If the government decided to support the price of wheat at 90 per cent of the parity in 1955, what would the supported price be?

SELECTED REFERENCES

Committee for Economic Development, *Toward a Realistic Farm Program* (New York: Committee for Economic Development, 1957).

Iowa State University Center for Agricultural Adjustment, *Problems and Policies of American Agriculture* (Ames, Iowa: Iowa State University Press, 1959).

Joint Economic Committee, *Policy for Commercial Agriculture* (Washington: Government Printing Office, 1957).

Schickele, Rainer, *Agricultural Policy* (New York: McGraw-Hill Book Company, Inc., 1954).

Schultz, Theodore W., *The Economic Organization of Agriculture* (New York: McGraw-Hill Book Company, Inc., 1953).

Smith, Mervin G., and Carlton F. Christian (eds.), *Adjustments in Agriculture: A National Basebook* (Ames, Iowa: Iowa State University Press, 1961).

Soth, Lauren, *Farm Trouble* (Princeton, N.J.: Princeton University Press, 1957).

Chapter 34

LABOR UNIONS AND

COLLECTIVE BARGAINING

ABOUT 18 million workers—roughly one-third of the nonagricultural labor force—now belong to labor unions. Bare statistics, however, understate the importance of unions. The wage rates, hours, and working conditions of nonunionized firms and industries are influenced by those determined in organized industries. Unions are clearly permanent and powerful institutions of American capitalism.

In this chapter we seek, first, an understanding of the historical background and the present status of labor unions. Attainment of this objective necessarily involves a discussion of government policy towards organized labor, because labor legislation and union growth are intimately related. A friendly government and prolabor legislation cause unions to flourish and grow; an indifferent government and unfavorable legislation can result in stagnation and decay of the labor movement. Second, we want to analyze labor-management relations. Here our discussion will center upon the process of collective bargaining. Finally, we must examine carefully the economic impact of unions upon the operation of American capitalism—what effect do they have on economic stability and efficient resource allocation?

BRIEF HISTORY OF AMERICAN UNIONISM

The history of the labor movement in America is long, colorful, and flavored with violence.[1]

Very generally, the American labor movement has gone through three phases: repression (1790 to 1930), encouragement (1930 to 1947), and intervention (1947 to date). Though the dates are somewhat arbitrary, these three phases serve as an excellent guide for our discussion.

Repression phase: 1790 to 1930

Labor unions have existed in the United States for well over 150 years. The shoemakers, carpenters, printers, and other skilled craftsmen formed unions of some permanence in the early 1790s. As Figure 34-1 indicates, despite this early start, union growth was relatively slow and sporadic until the 1930s. Two considerations go far to account for this meager prog-

[1] The following are highly recommended: U.S. Department of Labor, *Brief History of the American Labor Movement* (1950), and Foster Rhea Dulles, *Labor in America*, 2d ed. (New York: Thomas Y. Crowell Company, 1955).

ress: (1) the hostility of the courts towards labor unions and (2) the extreme reluctance of American businessmen to recognize and bargain with unions.

Unions and the courts. It was not until the 1930s that Federal legislation spelled out the Federal government's policy towards labor unions. In the absence of a national labor policy it was up to the courts to decide upon specific union-management conflicts. And, much to the dismay of organized labor, the courts were generally hostile towards unions. This court hostility had two sources. (1) Most judges had propertied-class backgrounds. (2) The courts are inherently conservative institutions charged with the responsibility of protecting *established* rights. Unions, throughout the 1800s and the early decades of the 1900s, were in the unenviable position of seeking rights for labor at the expense of the *existing* rights of management.

The hostility of the courts was first given vent in the *criminal conspiracy doctrine*. This doctrine, "imported" by the American courts from English common law at the turn of the nineteenth century, was unbelievably narrow by modern standards. The doctrine flatly concluded that combinations of workmen to raise wages were criminal conspiracies and hence illegal. Though weakened by subsequent court rulings in the 1840s, the shadow of the conspiracy doctrine hung heavy over organized labor throughout most of the 1800s. While unions, as such, were later recognized by the courts as legal organizations, the techniques employed by unions to enforce their demands—strikes, picketing, and boycotting—were generally held to be illegal. And in the latter part of the 1800s the courts employed both antitrust laws and injunctions in such a way as to impede the labor movement significantly.

Although Congress passed the Sherman Act of 1890 for the express purpose of thwarting the growth of business monopolies, the courts interpreted the loose wording of the act to include labor unions as conspiracies in restraint of trade. As a matter of fact, until relief came in the 1930s, the Sherman Act proved more effective against unions than in its application to industrial monopolies.

A simpler and equally effective anti-union device was the *injunction*. An injunction, or restraining order, is a court order which directs that some act not be carried out, on the grounds that irreparable damage will be done to those affected by the action. The attitude of the courts toward unions was such that it was extremely simple for an employer to obtain injunctions from the courts, prohibiting unions from enforcing their demands by striking, picketing, and boycotting. Stripped of these weapons, unions were relatively powerless to obtain the status and rights they sought.

In brief, the courts employed the criminal conspiracy doctrine, the Sherman Act, and injunctions to the end that union growth was greatly retarded during the 1790–1930 period.

Anti-union techniques of management. American businessmen did not rely entirely upon the courts in their attempt to impede the growth of unions. The business community, hostile to unions from their inception, developed a group of anti-union techniques to undermine unions. A startlingly simple anti-union technique was that of ferreting out and firing pro-union workers. Too, the average employer felt it his Christian duty to inform fellow employers that the discharged workers were "troublemakers" and "labor agitators" and not fit to be hired. This combination of *discriminatory discharge* and *blacklisting* made it extremely risky for workers even to think in terms of organizing a union. One's present and future employment opportunities were at stake.

Another potent weapon in management's struggle to keep unions down was the *lockout,* management's counterpart of the strike. By closing up shop for a few weeks employers were frequently able to bring their employees to terms and to destroy any notions they might have about organizing a union. In some cases this might prove a bit costly to the employer in the short run. In other cases, when business was slack, the lockout was a good means of killing two birds with one stone—working off excess inventories and undermining worker attempts to organize. Remember: workers of the late 1800s and early 1900s were not blessed with savings accounts or multi-million-dollar strike funds to draw upon in such emergencies.

Where workers were determined to organize, pitched battles often ensued. Rocks, clubs, shotguns, and an occasional stick of dynamite were the shadowy ancestors of collective bargaining. Some of the darkest pages of American labor history concern the violent clashes between workers and company-hired *strikebreakers*. The Homestead strike of 1892, the Pullman strike of 1894, and the Ludlow Massacre of 1914 are cases in point. Less dramatic skirmishes erupt down to the present time.

But management tactics were often more subtle than a cracked skull. The *yellow-dog contract* was one of the more ingenious antiunion devices fostered by management. In such contracts workers agreed to remain nonunion as a condition of employment. Workers had little choice but to sign such contracts— no contract, no job. Violation of a yellow-dog contract exposed a worker to a lawsuit by his employer, the result of which might be a court-imposed fine or even imprisonment.

As a last resort, an employer might shower his work force with such amenities as group insurance and pension programs, stock ownership and profit-sharing schemes, and even company magazines to convince them that employers would look after the interests of the workers as effectively as would unions established by "outsiders." The next step beyond such *paternalism* was employee representation schemes or *company unions,* that is, employer-dominated "dummy" unions which it was hoped would discourage the establishment of genuine unions. Paternalism and company unions were decidedly effective in retarding union growth as late as the 1920s.[2]

[2] During a prolonged strike in the bituminous coal industry in 1902, a spokesman for the mine operators, George F. Baer, issued the classic statement of business paternalism: "The rights and interests of the laboring man will be protected and cared for—not by the labor agitators, but by the Christian men to whom God in His infinite wisdom has given the control of the property interests of this country."

Evolution of business unionism. The growth which occurred in the labor movement during the 1800s not only was modest, but it also embodied a variety of union philosophies. The mid-1800s were in effect a laboratory wherein American labor experimented with alternative forms of unionism—Marxism, utopianism, reformism, and a host of other isms.

The most important nationwide union prior to the American Federation of Labor was the Knights of Labor. Founded in 1869, this fascinating labor organization reflected most of the divergent isms with which American labor flirted. Embracing the Marxian idea that all working people had common interests, the Knights sought the establishment of "one big union" made up of farmers, skilled and unskilled workers, shopkeepers, and professional people.[3] Yet the major goal of the "Noble Order" was the utopian one of establishing producer cooperatives to be operated by both labor and management. Furthermore, the over-all program of the Knights clearly expressed the reform movement of the time: industrial health insurance, prohibition of child labor, compulsory public education, the adoption of income and inheritance taxes, government ownership of the railroads, and the 8-hour day. And, ironically enough, although the Knights allegedly sought their goals through political action, much of the organization's spectacular growth came as a result of a series of successful strikes against the railroads in 1885 and 1886. The heterogeneous membership and diverse goals of the Knights ultimately pulled the organization apart at the seams. By the close of the 1890s the Knights of Labor was largely a matter of history.

The demise of the Knights of Labor was overshadowed by the formation in 1886 of a new labor organization—the American Federation of Labor—which was to dominate the labor movement for the next fifty years. Under the leadership of Samuel Gompers, labor charted a conservative course which has been

[3] Only bankers, lawyers, professional gamblers, liquor salesmen, and Pinkerton detectives (an unlimited source of strikebreakers) were deprived of membership.

very influential down to the present date.[4] Appropriately honored as "the father of the American labor movement," Gompers preached three fundamental ideas: (1) practical business unionism, (2) political neutrality for labor, and (3) the autonomy of each trade or craft.

Gompers was firmly convinced that "safe and sane" business unionism was the only course for American labor to follow. In 1903 he declared:[5]

I want to tell you, Socialists, that I have studied your philosophy; read your works on economics . . . studied your standard works. . . . I have heard your orators and watched the work of your movement the world over. I have kept close watch upon your doctrines for thirty years; have been closely associated with many of you, and know how you think and what you propose. I know, too, what you have up your sleeve. And I want to say that I am entirely at variance with your philosophy. I declare it to you, I am not only at variance with your doctrines, but with your philosophy. Economically, you are unsound; socially, you are wrong; industrially, you are an impossibility.

Gompers flatly rejected long-run idealistic schemes entailing the overthrow of the capitalistic system. He spurned intellectuals and theorizers and emphasized that unions should be concerned with practical short-run economic objectives—higher pay, shorter hours, and improved working conditions. In the words of one scholar, Gompers felt that ". . . you must offer the American working man bread and butter in the here and now instead of pie in the sky in the sweet by and by."[6]

In addition to espousing "bread and butter" unionism, Gompers had strong opinions on labor's role in politics and the basis upon which workers should be organized. In so far as politics was concerned, Gompers was convinced that government should keep its nose out of labor-management relations and collective bargaining. Although he recognized that governmental interference on behalf of labor might be a boon to union growth, Gompers was equally certain that anti-union government policies could stifle the progress of the entire labor movement. In pursuing the idea of political neutrality, Gompers cautioned organized labor not to align itself with any political party. Preoccupation with long-run political goals, he argued, merely causes labor to lose sight of the short-run economic objectives it ought to seek. Gompers admonished organized labor to follow one simple principle in the political arena: rewarding labor's friends and punishing its enemies at the polls without regard to political affiliation.

Finally, Gompers was firmly convinced that "autonomy of the trade," that is, unions organized on the basis of specific crafts, was the only permanent foundation for the labor movement. Unions composed of many different crafts lack the cohesiveness, he argued, that is essential to strong, hard-hitting, business unionism. These craft unions should then be affiliated in a national federation. "One union to each trade, affiliated for one labor movement."

This philosophy—conservative business unionism, political "neutrality," and the craft principle of union organization—was destined to dominate the AFL and the entire labor movement for the next half century. Indeed, the AFL, operating under Gompers' leadership, met with considerable success—at least for a time. AFL membership hit a highwater mark of about four million members by the end of World War I. Then a combination of circum-

---

[4] This is not to say that all unions have followed conservative paths since Gompers first espoused the virtues of business unionism. The Industrial Workers of the World, founded in 1905, advocated a decidedly revolutionary brand of left-wing unionism. And in the late thirties and early forties Communists infiltrated a number of CIO unions. In 1949 and 1950 the CIO expelled eleven affiliated unions whose leaderships had come to be dominated by Communists.

[5] From the *Proceedings* of the 1903 AFL convention, reprinted in G. P. Shultz and John R. Coleman, *Labor Problems: Cases and Readings*, 2d ed. (New York: McGraw-Hill Book Company, Inc., 1959), pp. 16–17.

[6] Charles C. Killingsworth, "Organized Labor in a Free Enterprise Economy," in Walter Adams, *The Structure of American Industry*, 3d ed. (New York: The Macmillan Company, 1961), p. 570.

stances arose in the 1920s which forced the AFL into an eclipse (see Figure 34-1). One factor was a strong anti-union drive by employers. Spearheaded by the National Association of Manufacturers, businesses waged a last-ditch effort to stem the rising tide of organized labor. Then, too, many firms introduced employee representation plans, company unions, and a host of paternalistic schemes to convince workers that employers were better prepared to look out for their employees' interests than were labor leaders. Finally, the AFL clung tenaciously to the craft principle of union organization, thereby ignoring the ever-increasing number of unskilled workers employed by the rapidly expanding mass production industries —the automobile and steel industries in particular.

Encouragement phase: 1930 to 1947

Two significant events occurred in the 1930s which revived the labor movement and inaugurated a period of rapid growth. Most importantly, the attitude of the Federal government towards unions changed from one of indifference, not to say hostility, to one of encouragement. Also, a major structural change in the labor movement accompanied the founding of the Congress of Industrial Organizations in 1936. Both events, coupled with the wartime prosperity of the 1940s, greatly swelled the ranks of organized labor.

Prolabor legislation of the 1930s. Against the background of the depressed thirties, the Federal government enacted two decidedly prolabor acts. In part the passage of these acts reflects the violent opposition of organized labor to the previously described weapons employed by the courts and by management to suppress unions. In part they reflect a Democratic administration replacing a Republican administration. In part they echo the widely held opinion that strong unions, by achieving higher wages through collective bargaining, would increase total spending and help alleviate the Great Depression.

The Norris-La Guardia Act of 1932 did much to clear the path for union growth by outlawing two of the more effective anti-union weapons. Specifically, the act (1) made it decidedly more difficult for employers to obtain injunctions against unions and (2) declared that yellow-dog contracts were unenforceable.

Three years later, in 1935, the Federal government took more positive steps to encourage union growth. The Wagner Act (officially the National Labor Relations Act) guaranteed the "twin rights" of labor: the right of self-organization and the right to bargain collectively with employers. The act listed a number of "unfair labor practices" on the part of management. Specifically it (1) forbade employers from interfering with the right of workers to form unions, (2) outlawed company unions, (3) prohibited anti-union discrimination by employers in hiring, firing, and promoting, (4) outlawed discrimination against any worker who files charges or gives testimony under the act, and (5) obligated employers to bargain in good faith with a union duly established by their employees. The Wagner Act was clearly "labor's Magna Charta."

A National Labor Relations Board was established by the act and charged with the authority to investigate unfair labor practices occurring under the act, to issue cease-and-desist orders in the event of violations, and to conduct worker elections in deciding which specific union the workers wanted to represent them. The NLRB, you will note, is reminiscent of the Federal Trade Commission discussed in Chapter 32.

The Wagner Act was tailored to accelerate union growth. It was extremely successful in achieving this goal. The protective umbrella provided to unions by this act in conjunction with the Norris-La Guardia Act played a major role in causing the ranks of organized labor to mushroom from about 4 million in 1935 to 15 million in 1947.

Industrial unionism. We have already noted that one of the causes of stagnation in the AFL during the 1920s was its unwillingness to organize the growing masses of unskilled assem-

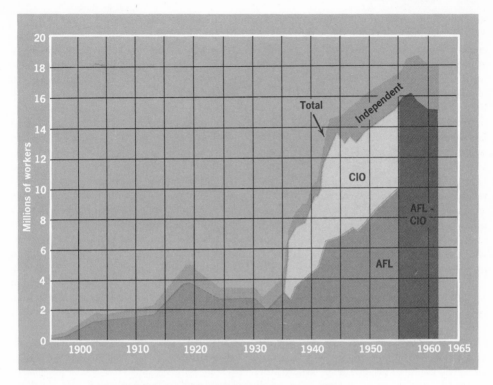

FIGURE 34-1. THE GROWTH OF UNION MEMBERSHIP, 1897–1961.
Most of the growth in organized labor has occurred in the last twenty-five years. (U.S.
Bureau of the Census and Bureau of Labor Statistics.)

bly-line workers. Though the majority of AFL leaders chose to ignore the unskilled workers, a vocal minority under the leadership of John L. Lewis contended that craft unionism would be completely ineffective as a means of organizing the hundreds of thousands of workers in the growing mass production industries. According to Lewis and his followers, the basis for organization should be shifted from *craft unionism* to *industrial unionism*, that is, away from unions which only encompass a specific type of skilled worker to unions which include all workers—both skilled and unskilled—in a given industry or group of related industries. This conflict came to a head, and in 1936 Lewis and his sympathizers withdrew their unions (and were simultaneously expelled) from the AFL.

The withdrawing unions established them-selves as the Congress of Industrial Organizations. The CIO met with rather startling success in organizing the automobile and steel industries. So great was this success that the AFL also moved in the direction of organizing on an industrial basis. By 1940 total union membership approximated 9 million workers.

Intervention phase: 1947 to date

In recent years there has been a decided increase in government regulation of, and intervention in, labor-management relations. It is important to understand the background of this governmental interference.

The prolabor legislation of the 1930s, the birth of industrial unionism, and the booming prosperity of the war years brought rapid union growth (see Figure 34-1). As unions gathered strength—both numerical and financial—it became increasingly evident that labor unions could no longer be regarded as the weak sister or underdog in their negotiations with management. Just as the growing power of business monopolies brought a clamor for public control in the 1870s and 1880s, the upsurge of union power in the 1930s and 1940s brought a similar outcry for regulation. This pressure for union control came to a head in the postwar years.

Many people felt that the wartime strike record of American labor left much to be desired. Despite no-strike pledges, work stoppages reached a new high at the height of the war effort in 1944. Equally harmful to the favorable climate of public opinion which labor enjoyed in the 1930s was the series of nationwide strikes which broke out during the reconversion period in such basic industries as steel, coal, meat packing, and railway transportation. The man in the street felt that these strikes not only slowed the reconversion process but also inaugurated the severe wage-price inflationary spiral which was to plague the immediate postwar years (see Chapter 11). Businessmen, needless to say, were happy to fan the flames of public resentment. By the mid-forties the pro-labor climate of the prior decade had done a virtual turnabout.

Taft-Hartley Act of 1947. This growing public hostility toward unions was crystallized in the Taft-Hartley Act (officially the Labor Management Relations Act) in 1947. A very detailed piece of legislation, this act mirrors the increasing complexity of labor-management relations. Generally its specific provisions fall under four headings: (1) provisions which designate and outlaw certain "unfair union practices"; (2) provisions which regulate the internal administration of unions; (3) provisions which specify collective bargaining procedures and regulate the actual contents of bargaining agreements; and (4) provisions for the handling of strikes imperiling the health and safety of the nation. 1. You will recall that the Wagner Act outlined a number of "unfair labor practices" on the part of management. A new and crucial

feature of the Taft-Hartley Act was that it introduced a number of "unfair labor practices" on the part of unions. These unfair practices, which constitute some of the most controversial sections of the act, are as follows: (a) Unions are prohibited from coercing employees to become union members. (b) *Jurisdictional strikes* (disputes between unions over the question of which has the authority to perform a specific job) are forbidden, as are *secondary boycotts* (refusing to buy or handle products produced by another union or group of workers) and certain *sympathy strikes* (strikes designed to assist some other union in gaining employer recognition or some other objective). (c) Unions are prohibited from charging excessive or discriminatory initiation fees or dues. (d) *Featherbedding,* a mild form of extortion wherein the union or its members receive payment for work not actually performed, is specifically outlawed. (e) Unions cannot refuse to bargain in good faith with management.

2. Taft-Hartley also imposes significant controls on the internal processes of labor unions: (a) Unions are obligated to make detailed financial reports to the National Labor Relations Board and to make such information available to its members. (b) Unions are prohibited from making political contributions in elections, primaries, or conventions which involve Federal offices. (c) Union officials are required to sign non-Communist affidavits.

3. Other Taft-Hartley provisions are designed to control the actual collective bargaining process and the contents of the work agreement resulting therefrom: (a) The *closed shop* (which requires that a firm hire only workers who are already union members) is specifically outlawed; that is, a closed shop arrangement cannot be written into a collective bargaining agreement. (b) The *checkoff* (whereby union dues are deducted from the workers' pay checks by the employer and turned over to the union in a lump sum) cannot be written into a bargaining agreement unless authorized in writing by individual workers. (c) Collective bargaining agreements must provide that, where they exist, welfare and pension funds are kept separate from other union funds and jointly ad-

ministered by the union and management. (d) Bargaining agreements must contain termination or *reopening clauses* whereby both labor and management must give the other party 60 days' notice of their intent to modify or terminate the existing work agreement.

4. Finally, the Taft-Hartley Act outlines a procedure for avoiding major strikes which might disrupt the entire economy and thereby imperil the health or safety of the nation. According to this procedure, the President may obtain an injunction to delay such strikes for an 80-day "cooling-off" period. Within this period the involved workers are polled by the NLRB as to the acceptability of the last offer of the employer. If the last offer is rejected, the union can then strike. The government's only recourse—one of questionable legality—is seizure of the industry.

The Taft-Hartley Act is difficult to evaluate.[7] It has been a subject of heated debate since its enactment. Unions have condemned Taft-Hartley as a "slave labor act," claiming that it has undermined the status of unions and imperiled many of organized labor's basic weapons. Most employers feel that the act is merely a step in the right direction—a long-overdue attempt to restore a better balance of power between labor and management.

This much is agreed upon: the Taft-Hartley Act represents a marked shift in public policy. This shift is essentially one from "government-sponsored" collective bargaining to "government-regulated" collective bargaining. The underlying philosophy of the Wagner Act was that a balance of bargaining power between labor and management should be established. This balance would be conducive to effective collective bargaining free of government intervention. The Taft-Hartley Act, however, envisions a need for detailed and continuous government control of collective bargaining to assure labor-management relations which are not unduly injurious to the welfare of the general public. Most objective observers feel that this shift in public policy toward labor has

[7] See "The Taft-Hartley Act after Ten Years: A Symposium," *Industrial and Labor Relations Review*, April, 1958.

been a necessary one. Disagreement is strong, however, with respect to the form these controls should take and the manner in which they should be applied.

Landrum-Griffin Act of 1959. Government regulation of the internal processes of unions has been recently extended by passage of the Landrum-Griffin Act (officially the Labor-Management Reporting and Disclosure Act) in the fall of 1959. This act places regulations upon union elections and union finances and guarantees certain rights of union members. Specifically, the act regulates union elections by requiring regularly scheduled elections of officers and the use of secret ballots; restrictions are placed upon ex-convicts and Communists in holding union offices. Furthermore, union officials are now held strictly accountable for union funds and property. Officers handling union funds must be bonded, the embezzlement of union funds is made a Federal offense, and close restrictions are placed upon union loans to its officers and members. The act is also aimed at preventing autocratic union leaders from infringing upon certain rights of their constituents. The individual worker's rights to attend and participate in union meetings, to vote in union proceedings, and to nominate officers are guaranteed. The act permits a worker to sue his union if it denies him these rights. Under the act the Secretary of Labor is given broad powers in investigating violations of the act.

Labor unity

In 1955 unity was formally reestablished in the American labor movement with the merger of the AFL and CIO. Many forces were significant in closing the breach which existed between the two for almost two decades. (1) The AFL's increased willingness to accept and practice industrial unionism lessened the original structural differences between the AFL and the CIO. (2) The political and legislative setbacks which labor has encountered since the prolabor era of the 1930s convinced labor leaders that unity in the labor movement is a necessary first step toward bolstering the political influence of organized labor. (3) Failure to achieve the desired rate of growth in the ranks of organized labor in the postwar years made evident to organized labor that a concerted, unified effort is needed to organize currently non-union firms and industries. (4) The 1949 expulsion of eleven Communist-infiltrated unions made the CIO more palatable to the AFL and, at the same time, made the CIO more interested in unification by reducing the latter's numerical and financial strength. (5) Then, too, considerable turnover in top leadership in both the AFL and CIO pushed into the background certain personality conflicts which had proved to be a significant obstacle to reunification of the labor movement at an earlier date.

At present the AFL-CIO boasts 15 million members. Independent unions, of which the four Railroad Brotherhoods, the Teamsters, and the United Mine Workers are the major ones, add another 3 million members. Hence, the ranks of organized labor now embody about 18 million workers, or one-third of the nonfarm labor force.

The labor movement remains basically conservative, and, assuming reasonably full employment, we can expect organized labor to remain concerned with the practical topics of the collective bargaining agenda rather than schemes designed to alter radically the framework of American capitalism. One point is clear: history has demonstrated that effective political action by organized labor is essential to union welfare and growth. While there is little likelihood that a labor party will evolve in the United States, the upsurge of union activity in the political arena which has occurred in recent years is likely to continue in the future.

Labor stagnation?

A number of prominent labor economists are currently talking of an "organizational plateau" and "stagnation" in the labor movement. Noting that union membership has been approximately 25 per cent of the civilian labor force in the entire post-World War II period, they predict a relative decline in the economic and

political importance of organized labor. A number of factors underlie this thinking. (1) The previously noted (Chapter 19) shift in the composition of the labor force from blue- to white-collar employment has tended to reduce the potential membership base of organized labor. (2) The remaining unorganized blue-collar workers are in smaller plants, in agriculture, in service industries, and in the South—all of which are "hard to organize" jobs and areas. (3) Legislative reversals, comprising the shift of public policy from encouragement to intervention, pose a more hostile legal environment for organized labor. (4) The evolution of public apathy or hostility towards organized labor which has resulted from (a) the corrupt and fraudulent union practices uncovered by the investigations of the Senate's McClellan Committee, (b) prolonged strikes such as the 1959 steel strike, and (c) the implication of the cost-push inflation concept that unions are inflation-causing institutions, may work against future union growth. (5) Finally, it is frequently alleged that complacency and internal squabbles in the AFL-CIO are retarding expansion of the labor movement. The labor movement and its leaders have become complacent as the result of past successes. Organized labor has "arrived" and has no place to go; the labor movement has been reduced from a "cause" to a day-to-day way of life. Furthermore, differences between various labor leaders and specific unions have diverted attention and energy away from the task of organizing the unorganized. To what extent these problems will impair future growth in the labor movement is difficult to ascertain; it is safe to conclude that in the future expansion will not be as easy to come by as it has been in the past.[8]

COLLECTIVE BARGAINING

As a result of the rapid growth of unions in recent decades, collective bargaining has become "a way of life" in labor-management re-

[8] For a contrasting view consult Irving Bernstein, "Don't Count the Unions Out," *Challenge*, November, 1961, pp. 17–19.

lations. It is estimated that over 125,000 collective bargaining agreements are now in force in the United States.

The bargaining process

To the outsider, collective bargaining is a dramatic once-a-year clash between labor and management. Chief participants are a John L. Lewis type character with baggy suit, bushy eyebrows, and calloused hands, and on the other side of the table a Daddy Warbucks with diamond stickpin and formal attire. Furthermore, one gets the impression from the newspapers that labor and management settle their differences only with strikes, picketing, and not infrequent acts of violence.

These impressions are largely inaccurate. Collective bargaining is a somewhat less colorful process than most people believe. In negotiating important contracts the union will be represented by top local and national officials, duly supplemented with lawyers and research economists. Management representatives include top policy-making executives, plant managers, personnel and labor relations specialists, lawyers, and staff economists. The union usually takes the initiative, outlining its demands. These take the form of specific adjustments in the current work agreement. The merits and demerits of these demands are then debated. Typically a compromise solution is reached and written into a new work agreement. Strikes, picketing, and violence are clearly the exception and not the rule. A rough indication of this is mirrored in the fact that 0.15 per cent—about one-seventh of 1 per cent—of all working time was lost in 1961 as a result of work stoppages resulting from labor-management disputes. *Labor and management display a marked capacity for compromise and agreement.* We must keep in mind that strikes and labor-management violence are newsworthy, while the peaceful renewal of a work agreement hardly rates a page-5 column.

The work agreement

Collective bargaining agreements assume a variety of forms. Some agreements are amazingly brief, covering two or three typewritten pages; others are highly detailed, involving two hundred or more pages of fine print. Some agreements involve only a local union and a single plant; others set wages, hours, and working conditions for entire industries. There is no such thing as an "average" or "typical" collective bargaining agreement. Nevertheless, the following skeleton agreement, based on an actual contract, provides a fairly accurate notion of the scope and content of collective bargaining.

CONTRACT AND AGREEMENT

Article I. Intent, union status, management prerogatives. Section 1. This agreement entered into June 30, 1963, between the Deep South Manufacturing Company, hereinafter referred to as the "Employer" and the International Brotherhood of Boilermakers, Iron Shipbuilders, and Helpers of America, Local No. 167, hereinafter referred to as the "Union." It is the intent and purpose of the parties hereto that this Agreement will promote and improve industrial relations between the Employer and the Union.

Section 2. The Employer recognizes the Union as the sole and exclusive bargaining agency for the purpose of determining rates of pay, hours of employment, and all other conditions of employment for all the Employer's production and maintenance employees. It is understood and agreed that Local 167 shall designate a representative who is duly authorized and will be consulted in all matters pertaining to the application of this work agreement.

Section 3. There shall be in each unit no less than one (1), nor more than two (2), Shop Stewards, these Stewards to be appointed by the Union. A unit shall be defined as any part of the Company Organization that provides for a foreman. Shop Stewards may leave their work during their regular working hours, without loss of pay, for the purpose of adjusting grievances.

Section 4. The Employer shall have the sole right of determining plant layout, the means of manufacturing and distributing products, the scheduling of production operations, and the setting of work shifts.

Section 5. Upon receipt of a written authorization by any employee the Employer shall deduct from the first pay each month and remit to the local Union such sum as the employee shall specify in said authorization.

Article II. Wages, hours of work, holidays. *Section 1.* The minimum wage rates per hour shall be as follows:

Layout man	$2.12
Welders	1.94
Tackers	1.94
Painters	1.90
Riveting machine operator	1.85
Truck drivers	1.70
Helpers	1.52

When employees are transferred to a new job, their rate of pay shall not be changed for a period of fifteen (15) working days. If they are retained on the new job after this probationary period, the job rate called for by this agreement shall then be paid to them. If such job change involves a pay raise, the new rate shall be retroactive to the date the job was assigned.

Section 2. Wage rates shall be adjusted every three (3) months in accordance with changes in the U.S. Government Department of Labor's Index of Consumer Prices. For each one (1) point change upward in the index there shall be a one (1) cent per hour raise in wages. For each one (1) point downward change in the Index, there shall be a one (1) cent per hour decrease in wages. Wages in no case shall fall by more than five (5) cents per hour in any three-month period.

Section 3. All employees shall receive a two (2) per cent longevity increase in hourly wages for each year of service. This two (2) per cent shall be based on the previous year's hourly base rates.

Section 4. Forty (40) hours shall constitute the work week, from Monday to Friday, inclusive. The established schedule of hours shall be from 8 A.M. to 12 noon and from 12:30 noon

to 4:30 P.M. The employer shall provide thirty-eight (38) weeks of employment per year.

Section 5. Time and one-half shall be paid for work performed in excess of eight hours in one day and for hours worked on Saturday. Double time shall be paid for hours worked on Sunday.

Section 6. When the following legal holidays —New Year's Day, Memorial Day, Fourth of July, Labor Day, Thanksgiving Day, and Christmas Day—occur or are celebrated during the employee's work week, he shall receive said holidays off duty with his regular straight-time pay, provided that he shall have been in the employ of the Employer at least thirty (30) calendar days. If said holiday falls on Saturday, it shall be celebrated on Friday, and if it falls on Sunday, celebration shall be on Monday. In the event an employee is required to work on one of the above-named holidays, he shall receive double time for such time worked in addition to his regular holiday pay. However, if any employee shall refuse to work on a holiday if he is requested by the Employer, he shall forfeit his holiday pay, but only if he refuses for other than a legitimate reason.

Section 7. All overtime work shall be divided among the workers according to seniority.

Section 8. All employees within the bargaining unit of the Union who shall have been in the service of the company one year and less than three years shall receive a paid vacation of five (5) days; those who have been in the services of the company three (3) years or more shall receive a paid vacation of ten (10) days.

Article III. Seniority and job opportunities. *Section 1.* Seniority is defined as the principle that if, because of lack of work, the employer deems it advisable to reduce his work force, the last man hired shall be the first man laid off, and, in rehiring, the last man laid off shall be the first man rehired, until the list of former employees is exhausted.

Section 2. Seniority shall be on the basis of job classification. If an employee is transferred to another classification, he shall carry his seniority with him.

Section 3. Seniority shall be the determining factor regarding layoff and reemployment, transfers, demotions, promotions, or other job changes where the necessary skill and ability are present to perform the work required.

Section 4. Seniority shall be lost for the following reasons: (*a*) voluntary quitting; (*b*) discharge for cause; (*c*) layoff for twelve (12) consecutive months; (*d*) if laid-off employee is notified by the Employer by registered mail sent to his last known address to return and fails to do so within five (5) days of mailing the letter, unless a reasonable excuse shall be established.

Section 5. A seniority list shall be maintained and kept up to date by the Employer and shall be available to the Union at all times.

Article IV. Grievance procedure. Section 1. In the event a grievance arises between an employee or group of employees and the Employer, such grievance shall be handled according to the following procedure.

Section 2. The employee or employees having a grievance shall report the same in a signed statement to the Shop Steward, who will in turn take up the grievance with the Foreman verbally. The Foreman will attempt to make a satisfactory settlement and will advise the Steward of his decision.

Section 3. If the Steward and employee are not satisfied with the decision of the Foreman, the Steward shall then submit the grievance to the Plant Superintendent verbally. The Superintendent shall make his decision within ten (10) days of the time the grievance is submitted to him. If the Steward or employee is not satisfied with the decision of the Superintendent, the Steward shall report the grievance to the Local Union's President, who shall submit the grievance to the management within ten (10) days and endeavor to reach an agreement.

Section 4. If no agreement is reached within ten (10) days, the grievance shall be submitted to an impartial arbitrator. The arbitrator shall be jointly selected by the Employer and the Union. The arbitrator shall be required to hand down a decision within thirty (30) days. This decision shall be a binder, so long as it does not change the terms of this Agreement in any way.

Article V. Termination. Section 1. This Agreement shall remain in full force and effect until June 30, 1964, and thereafter from year to year unless, within the ten (10) day period immediately preceding the sixty (60) days prior to the day of expiration, notice is given in writing to the other party indicating a desire to change the agreement.

Section 2. Anything in this Agreement found to be contrary to any State or National law shall be automatically voided.

- - - - - - - - - - - - - - - -

International Brotherhood of Boilermakers, Iron Shipbuilders and Helpers of America, Local 167

Deep South Manufacturing Company

This contract is representative in that it covers four basic areas: (1) the degree of recognition and status accorded the union and the prerogatives of management (Article I); (2) wages and hours (Article II); (3) seniority and job opportunities (Article III); and (4) a procedure for settling grievances (Article IV).

Union status. Unions enjoy differing degrees of recognition from management. Listed in order of the union's preference are (1) the closed shop, (2) the union shop, and (3) the open shop.

Prior to being outlawed by the Taft-Hartley Act, the *closed shop* afforded the greatest security to a union. Under a closed shop a worker must be a union member before the employer can hire him. A *union shop*, on the other hand, permits the employer to hire nonunion workers but provides that these workers must join the union in a specified period—say, thirty days—or relinquish their jobs. In the sample contract sketched above, an *open shop* exists (Article I, Section 2). Management may apparently hire union or nonunion workers. Those who are nonunion are not obligated to join the union; they may continue on their jobs indefinitely as nonunion workers. In this contract, the union is the bargaining agent for *all* the firm's production and maintenance workers. In other cases the union may bargain only for union members. Finally, we must also mention the *nonunion shop*. Here no union exists, and the employer makes a conscious effort to hire those workers who are least inclined to form or join a union.

Interesting variations of these basic types of union status have been developed. During World War II the *maintenance of membership shop* was evolved. Under this arrangement workers have the choice of joining or not joining the union. Those who join are obligated to maintain their membership in the union for the duration of the contract or sacrifice their jobs. Those who choose not to join the union can work indefinitely as nonunion employees. In some instances union or open shop status will be supplemented with *preferential hiring*. Management agrees to hire union members so long as they are available; then it can hire nonunion workers.

Finally, in an *agency shop* union and nonunion workers may be hired and continue on their jobs indefinitely as in an open shop. But in an agency shop nonunion workers must pay regular union dues and fees. These payments are in effect charges by the union for acting as the nonunion workers' agent in bargaining and enforcing a work agreement. From the union's standpoint the agency shop has the advantage of eliminating "free riders"—workers who benefit from, but do not financially support, the union.

Many businessmen fear that in time the expansion of the scope of collective bargaining may reach the point where certain fundamental management decisions will become matters to be decided jointly by management and labor. It is felt by businessmen that such an eventuality will "tie the hands" of management to the extent that efficient business operation may be jeopardized. For this reason at the insistence of management an increasing number of work agreements contain clauses which outline certain decisions which are to be made solely by management. These *managerial prerogatives* usually cover such matters as the size and loca-

tion of plants, products to be manufactured, types of equipment and materials used in production, and the scheduling of production (Article I, Section 4). Frequently the hiring, transfer, discipline, discharge, and promotion of workers are decisions made solely by management but subject to the general principle of seniority and to challenge by the union through the grievance procedure.

Wages and hours. The focal point of any bargaining agreement is wages and hours. Our skeleton agreement is representative of most contracts in that basic hourly pay rates, length of work week, overtime rates, holidays, and vacations are all specified (Article II).

Both labor and management tend to be highly pragmatic in wage bargaining. The standards, or "talking points," most frequently invoked by labor in demanding (and by management in resisting) wage boosts are (1) "what others are getting"; (2) productivity, (3) ability to pay, (4) cost of living, and (5) economic stability. If a given firm has basic pay rates below those of comparable firms, the union is likely to stress that wages should be increased to bring them into line with what workers employed by other firms are getting. Similarly, if the firm has had a banner year, the union is likely to demand high wages on the grounds that the company has ample ability to grant such increments. In recent years unions have achieved considerable success in tying wages to the cost of living. It is estimated that work agreements covering about three million workers embody some kind of "escalator clause." This is true of our sample agreement (Article II, Section 2). And, many contracts link wage rates to productivity; wages automatically increase in terms of an estimated "improvement factor." Finally, when the economy flirts with unemployment, unions argue that wage increases are the best means of bolstering purchasing power and alleviating the economic slump.

Three points should be mentioned in connection with these wage criteria. In the first place, they are clearly two-edged propositions. For example, the cost of living criterion is only invoked by the union when prices are hurrying upwards; unions conveniently ignore this criterion when prices are stable or declining. Similarly, the union only considers the ability-to-pay argument to be of importance when profits are large. The economic stability argument is conveniently forgotten when the economy is besieged by inflation rather than unemployment. Management is equally inconsistent in the evaluation it places on the various wage-bargaining standards.

It must be emphasized, too, that these wage criteria are considerably less objective than might first appear. Most people might agree that it is only just that wage rates be adjusted for increases in productivity and the cost of living. But then arises the difficult question "By how much?" What wage boost should accompany, say, a two-point increase in the Consumer's Price Index? Similarly, productivity increases are not only difficult to gauge, but, once gauged, how does one determine how much of the increase should accrue to labor and how much to capital?

Another noteworthy point: wage changes—either increases or declines—based on these criteria are not necessarily desirable on either economic or equity grounds. Many economists fear, for example, that the widespread use of the cost of living criterion will cause a wage-price inflationary spiral to be built into our economy. In like manner, indiscriminate application of the what-others-are-getting standard may push a relatively inefficient firm out of business, causing considerable hardship for affected workers.

Seniority and the control of job opportunities. The uncertainty of employment in a capitalistic economy coupled with the fear of anti-union discrimination on the part of employers have made workers and their unions decidedly "job-conscious." The explicit and detailed provisions covering job opportunities which most work agreements contain reflect this concern. The importance of seniority as the guiding principle in controlling job opportunities is apparent from Article III of our work agreement. It should be noted, however, that in many cases seniority is not rigidly applied. Strategic workers, or "key" personnel, will often be exempt

from seniority regulations. And unions are typically willing to recognize that, particularly where promotion is concerned, ability must take precedence over seniority (Article III, Section 3).

Grievance procedure. It has been quipped that a collective bargaining agreement is to labor relations what the wedding ceremony is to domestic relations—only the beginning. Despite formal agreements, it is the "living together" that counts. It is unthinkable that even the most detailed and comprehensive work agreement can anticipate all the issues and problems which might occur during its life. What if Local 167 members show up for work on a Monday morning to find that for some reason the plant is closed down? Should they be given "show-up" pay amounting to, say, two or four hours' pay? This event is not covered in the contract and would therefore be a problem which might be ironed out through the grievance machinery. Then, too, there may be some disagreement in interpreting points covered in the work agreement. For example, the abbreviated work agreement upon which our discussion is centered poses some possible questions of interpretation because of which it may be necessary to invoke the grievance procedure. What is a "legitimate reason" for refusing to work on a holiday (Article II, Section 6)? Exactly how is "necessary skill and ability" to be defined in specific cases (Article III, Section 3)? What is meant by "discharge for cause" (Article III, Section 4)?

As a result, virtually all agreements contain a more or less explicit procedure for the handling of disputes which arise during the life of an agreement. In our sample agreement a very complete four-step procedure is clearly outlined. In this instance the grievance machinery culminates in arbitration, that is, a neutral third party is designated to render a decision by which both labor and management must abide.

Guaranteed annual wage. Both cyclical and technological unemployment have made labor security-minded. This concern is mirrored in recent union pressure for the inclusion of guaranteed annual wage (GAW) plans in collective bargaining agreements. In some cases such plans guarantee a certain number of weeks or hours of work per year. The 1955 Ford and General Motors bargaining agreements with the UAW call for a "supplementary unemployment benefits" plan wherein the employers really do not guarantee employment or wages at all but simply agree to pay a few cents per hour into a fund from which unemployed automobile workers will receive payments to supplement their state unemployment compensation payments. In almost all existing plans there are significant limitations: plans are almost invariably for less than fifty-two weeks, some workers are usually excluded, or the company may even reserve the right to cancel the plan if it becomes "unworkable."

The GAW is a hotly debated issue. As labor sees it, the GAW is a justified effort by labor to shift a part of the costs of unemployment to management. This shift will have several desirable consequences. (1) Employers will be forced to rationalize their production plans, thereby ironing out unnecessary instability in employment. (2) GAW plans will constitute a significant built-in stabilizer which will bolster employment and incomes in the economy as a whole when a general economic slump is encountered. (3) Labor efficiency will rise as the security of the work force is increased and labor turnover is cut.

But management sees it differently. Labor, it is argued, has the cart before the horse. The GAW will not *cause* stability; indeed, stability must exist before employers can risk the establishment of such plans. In particular, wage guarantees are simply not workable at the present time in those industries where they are most needed. Where fluctuations in employment are severe, management is simply not capable of bearing the costs which effective GAW plans might entail. And, in addition, individual firms are *not* capable of controlling cyclically caused fluctuations in employment. Management argues, too, that the GAW might do more harm than good. By making wages a fixed cost, businessmen are likely to become increasingly conservative in expanding their operations; this dampens investment spending and causes unemployment. Similarly, the GAW may impair labor mobility and therefore the allocation of labor resources. Finally, wage guarantees are likely to undermine incentives to work. Why should an unemployed worker seek a new job when his unemployment compensation and supplementary unemployment benefits provide him with an income 65 or 70 per cent as large as that which he gets while working?

Experience with GAW plans to date does not warrant a judgment as to which view is the more valid. This much is agreed upon by independent observers: it is foolhardy to look toward the GAW as a panacea for cyclical unemployment.

Three points, implicit in our discussion of collective bargaining, merit emphasis:

1. Collective bargaining is not only concerned with wage rates but also with the security and status of workers and of the union itself. Man does not live by bread alone. Workers seek protection from arbitrary actions by management; they seek a voice in determining the conditions under which they must work; they seek a means of voicing their grievances; they seek the status and dignity which accompany membership in economically powerful institutions. These objectives are fulfilled wholly or in part by membership in unions.

2. Also worthy of emphasis is the fact that collective bargaining is a continuous process. True, the *negotiation* of an agreement is an important and often dramatic point of departure. But this is followed by the equally important and continuing tasks of *administering* and *interpreting* (through the grievance procedure) the agreement. Collective bargaining is much more than a once-a-year clash of labor and management.

3. Finally, labor-management relations occur in a dynamic climate. Technological advance, business fluctuations, population changes, changes in the legislative framework, and changes in the character of businesses and unions themselves constitute some of the obvious dynamic aspects of the environment in

which bargaining occurs. Changes such as these virtually preclude the reaching of final, once-and-for-all solutions to labor-management problems. At best collective bargaining provides short-run, temporary adjustments to labor-management conflicts—adjustments which the changing economic milieu is likely to render obsolete in a relatively short span of time. In view of this observation the previously cited paucity of work stoppages due to labor-management disputes is all the more remarkable.

ECONOMIC IMPLICATIONS OF LABOR UNIONS

We must look beyond the day-to-day dealings of a specific union and a specific firm and assume a broader perspective. What is the impact of strong unions upon the operation of American capitalism? More specifically, what implications do unions have for *full production* —that is, the efficient allocation of resources— and *full employment*—that is, economic stability and growth.

Widely divergent opinions exist on this question. To achieve the clearest picture of this controversy, let us sketch the extreme views on the question of the role of unions in modern capitalism.

The case against unions

Some economists and most businessmen take a decidedly dim view of labor unions. They envision unions as uncontrollable, socially irresponsible monopolies whose operation is inimical to efficient resource allocation and economic stability.

Character of unions. The anti-union view holds that, by either restricting the supply of labor (exclusive unionism) or imposing above-equilibrium wage rates (inclusive unionism), unions impair the operation of the price mechanism in labor markets. Unions are monopolies, it is argued, in that they rig the labor market to their own advantage and to the detriment of the rest of the economy. By achieving above-equilibrium wage rates unions restrict

employment either directly (in the case of exclusive unionism) or indirectly (in the case of inclusive unionism). Workers deprived of job opportunities by these union tactics drift into nonunionized labor markets, causing wage rates there to fall.

Unions and resource allocation. By thus distorting the wage structure, it is contended, unions alter the allocation of resources away from the ideal pattern which competitive labor markets would foster. We learned in a previous chapter that under competition the wage rates paid to labor would tend to equal labor's marginal revenue productivity. Now, assuming labor markets are competitive, labor will tend to move from low-wage, low-productivity jobs to high-wage, high productivity jobs. Labor mobility, of course, is not perfect even under pure competition; but the tendency for this shifting to occur exists, and at least in the long run it would work with reasonable efficiency. The movement of labor from low- to high-productivity jobs which competition fosters is all to the good. Such shifting entails an expansion of total output; that is, it makes for an efficient allocation of labor resources.

The anti-union view contends that both exclusive and inclusive unionism impede the movement of labor from low- to high-marginal-productivity employments and therefore interfere with the efficient allocation of labor. By making a particular type of labor scarce in relation to the demand for it, exclusive unions move back up the MRP, or labor demand, curve and in so doing achieve above-competitive wages (see Figure 29-6). These high wages are sustained by restrictive membership policies which block the reallocation of workers into this occupation from other low-wage, low-productivity employments. Inclusive unionism accomplishes the same end indirectly by imposing above-equilibrium wage rates and allowing the market to restrict the number of jobs (see Figure 29-7). In this case the reallocation of workers from low-wage, low-productivity jobs to high-wage, high-productivity jobs is impeded not by the inability to get a union card but rather by the unwillingness of employers to take on more workers at the union-imposed wage rates. The basic conclusion is that by rigging wage rates unions distort the allocation of labor away from the most efficient pattern.

But this is only half the story. The growth of union monopolies induces the further development of business monopolies. This is particularly true where union power forces business firms to band together in employer associations for purposes of collective bargaining. It is only a short step from here to industry cartelization. Furthermore, union monopolies are not to be viewed as counterpoises to business monopoly; rather they are "ominously complementary" to industrial concentration. In short, ". . . each tends to foster and to strengthen the other, fighting together to maximize joint exactions from the public while also fighting each other over division of the spoils."[9] By rigging resource prices and by contributing to the growth of business monopoly, unions contribute to an inefficient allocation of labor resources.

Unions and economic stability. The anti-union position envisions unions as having shadowy implications for economic stability. It is contended that there exist no effective internal or external restraints upon the monopoly power of unions. It is naïve, according to the anti-union view, to argue that labor unions will not use their power; unions and their leaders are not socially responsible. Similarly, there are no external restraints sufficient to contain strong unions. In particular, business firms have neither the ability nor the desire to resist the demands of aggressive union monopolies. And, if the experience of the last three decades is meaningful, government has done more to promote than to curb the monopoly power of unions.

This unrestrained union power is allegedly a major cause of unemployment and inflation. The attainment of high wages, it is argued, will restrict the demand for labor, thereby causing unemployment and a slowing down of the growth rate. Marginal firms, finding it impos-

[9] Henry C. Simons, *Economic Policy for a Free Society* (Chicago: University of Chicago Press, 1948), p. 35.

sible to operate profitably in the face of above-competitive wage rates, will cease production and dismiss their labor forces. In addition, aggressive union wage policies can be expected to affect business profit expectations adversely. As a result, the levels of investment spending, aggregate demand, and employment will be reduced.

On the other hand, if the economy manages to achieve full employment despite irresponsible union wage policies, unions will then cause inflationary pressure to arise. For example, suppose that government activates the monetary and fiscal tools at its disposal so as to sustain a full-employment level of spending. Blessed with a high level of aggregate demand businessmen will find it a relatively simple matter to pass wage boosts on to consumers through price increases. But this rise in the cost of living will prompt unions to demand and receive another round of wage hikes. The wage-price spiral will then be on its way, causing a cumulative inflation problem for the economy.

Government policy toward unions. Those who embrace the anti-union position conclude that either unemployment or inflation will eventually prove inimical to capitalism; either is held to be a sufficient cause for the demise of the free enterprise system. A variety of policy recommendations have been offered to deal with the threat posed by union monopolies. There are those who feel that the only real remedy is the outright destruction of unions. Unions simply cannot be allowed to endure. Others call for increased governmental regulation of collective bargaining. It is felt that the Taft-Hartley Act is a step in the right direction but it fails to go far enough in regulating unions. It might be helpful, it is suggested, to subject unions once again to the antitrust laws. Or three-party bargaining involving labor, management, and the public as represented by government officials may be necessary to avoid the disruptive economic effects of strong unions. Still others envision the need for wage-price controls by government if economic stability is to be maintained.

The case for unions

The anti-union view just outlined is hardly a happy one. However, there exists an equally important school of thought which paints a cautiously optimistic picture of unions as being compatible with economic efficiency, stability, and growth. Let us sketch this pro-union position.

Character of unions. The pro-union view holds that, although unions have a degree of monopoly power, there are effective internal and external restraints which guard against the abuse of that power. Internal restraints are several. It is argued that the larger unions in particular represent their constituents not only as wage earners but also as consumers and savers; hence, unions are obligated to concern themselves with the effects which their wage demands might have upon job opportunities and the cost of living. And, as collective bargaining tends to become more mature, labor leaders are acquiring a greater sense of social responsibility. In addition to these internal restraints on union power there exist significant external restraints. Because of the extreme reluctance of unions to accept wage cuts, it is felt that in periods of both high and low aggregate demand employers can and do exhibit considerable resistance to union wage demands. It must be remembered, too, that, while a businessman stands to lose only a small fraction of his market as the result of a price increase, a union risks a work stoppage and the loss of income for *all* its members when it demands a wage increase. Unions may actually be subject to greater restraints in the resource market than are business monopolies in the product market.

Unions and resource allocation. The pro-union position holds that the anti-union view rests on the faulty assumption that labor markets would be highly competitive in the absence of unions. It is contended that this is simply not the case; labor markets would be imperfect ones even in the absence of unions. In particular, large business firms would exert considerable monopsonistic power in hiring workers (Figure 29-4).

More positively, the pro-union view argues that the monopoly power of unions operates so as to offset or neutralize the monopsonistic power of large employers. Because the strongest unions have generally developed in the most highly monopolized industries, unions are felt to be a primary manifestation of countervailing power. By counterbalancing the economic power of business monopolies, unions contribute to a more efficient allocation of labor resources. In short, the presence of union monopoly power on the seller's side of the labor market may serve to cancel the monopsonistic power of large employers on the buyer's side. The result is a near-competitive wage rate accompanied by an allocation of labor resembling that which would have existed if competition had prevailed in the labor market. In terms of wage rates and resource allocation, monopoly power on both sides of the labor market is allegedly superior to the presence of such power only on the buying side.

Unions and economic stability. The pro-union view alleges that it is flatly incorrect to make unions the scapegoat for unemployment and inflation. As previously explained, unions cannot and do not seek higher wages in a manner oblivious of employment and price implications. Both internal and external forces limit the exertion of economic power by unions. The wage-price spiral is a descriptive characteristic of inflation which would exist in modern capitalism with or without unions and collective bargaining. Stated differently, it is the myriad of forces which determine the level of aggregate demand, and not simply the existence of labor unions which governs the amount of unemployment or inflation the economy experiences. Strong unions are compatible with economic stability and growth; collective bargaining is not inherently inflationary, nor is it a significant cause of unemployment. More positively, the role of unions in American capitalism may be such as to make them an integral force in the complex of balances and counterbalances which permits the relatively smooth functioning of our economy despite its many market imperfections.

Government policy toward unions. The pro-union school of thought concludes that government policy should be generally aimed at the goal of encouraging the growth of unions where they constitute positions of countervailing power. Furthermore, increasing maturity is envisioned in labor-management relations. As a result, less control over collective bargaining will be needed in the future.

Although each of the two views just sketched can be applied with little or no modification to specific unions, both represent the extremes. Hence, neither is acceptable as a general explanation of the economic impact of unions. Their value lies in the fact that the contrast they provide serves as an important point of reference for policy makers and an informed citizenry.

SUMMARY

1. The growth of labor unions was slow and irregular until the 1930s. The repression of unions by the courts and by management was an important factor in accounting for this retarded growth. The courts employed the conspiracy doctrine, injunctions, and the antitrust laws against unions. Management invoked such varied anti-union techniques as discriminatory discharge, blacklisting, lockouts, strikebreakers, yellow-dog contracts, paternalism, and company unions in slowing the development of unions.

2. The AFL dominated the American labor movement from its inception in 1886 until the CIO was formed in 1936. Its philosophy was essentially that of Samuel Gompers—business unionism, political neutrality, and craft unionism.

3. Union growth was rapid in the 1930s and 1940s. The shift toward industrial unionism triggered by the formation of the CIO in 1936 was a significant factor in this growth. Equally

important were the wartime prosperity of the 1940s and the pro-labor legislation passed by the Federal government in the 1930s.

4. The Norris-La Guardia Act of 1932 rendered yellow-dog contracts unenforceable and sharply limited the use of injunctions in labor disputes.

5. The Wagner Act of 1935—"labor's Magna Charta"—guaranteed labor the rights to organize and to bargain collectively with management. The act prohibited certain "unfair labor practices" on the part of management, thereby paving the way for unions to organize unimpeded by management.

6. The Taft-Hartley Act of 1947 entailed a shift from government-sponsored to government-regulated collective bargaining. The act (*a*) specifically outlaws certain "unfair practices" of unions; (*b*) regulates certain internal operations of unions; (*c*) controls the content of collective bargaining agreements; and (*d*) outlines a procedure for handling "national health and welfare" strikes.

7. The Landrum-Griffin Act of 1959 was designed to regulate the internal processes of unions—in particular the handling of union finances and the union's relationships with its members.

8. At the present time about 18 million workers are union members; this constitutes about one-third of the nonfarm labor force. A number of economists feel that, for a variety of reasons, future growth in the labor movement will be modest.

9. Labor and management "live together" under the terms of collective bargaining agreements. These work agreements cover four major topics: (*a*) union status and managerial prerogatives; (*b*) wages and hours; (*c*) seniority and job control; and (*d*) a grievance procedure. The guaranteed annual wage is a new and controversial issue in collective bargaining. Experience indicates that both labor and management are very willing to compromise and reach agreement short of work stoppages.

10. There is considerable disagreement as to the economic impact of strong unions. The anti-union view holds that unions are potent labor market monopolies. Exertion of their monopoly power contributes to a misallocation of resources and causes instability in the levels of employment and prices. The destruction of unions, increased public regulation of unions, three-party bargaining, and wage-price controls are possible public policy alternatives that have been suggested by various writers who embrace the anti-union position.

11. The pro-union view contends that unions are socially responsible organizations which can be expected to temper their wage demands if unemployment or inflation looms as a probable consequence. The monopoly power which unions exert serves to counterbalance the monopsonistic power of large employers. The result is that labor allocation and wage rates are likely to be closer to the competitive situation than would be the case in the absence of unions. Collective bargaining is not a basic cause of instability; rather instability stems from all those factors which influence the components of aggregate demand. The pro-union view envisions increasing maturity in collective bargaining and a decline in the need for government controls over labor-management relations.

QUESTIONS AND STUDY SUGGESTIONS

1. The first unions to develop in the United States were composed of skilled craftsmen rather than unskilled workers. Can you explain why?

2. Identify the following terms:

a. Injunction	*g.* Criminal conspiracy doctrine
b. Black-listing	*h.* Secondary boycott
c. Lockout	*i.* Sympathy strike
d. Checkoff	*j.* Discriminatory discharge
e. Featherbedding	*k.* Jurisdictional strikes
f. Company unions	*l.* Yellow-dog contract

3. Distinguish clearly between craft and industrial unionism. Which is generally associated with the AFL? The CIO?

4. Distinguish between a closed shop, a union shop, an open shop, an agency shop, and a nonunion shop.

5. "There are legislative, executive, and judicial aspects to collective bargaining." Explain.

6. What are the major provisions of the Norris-La Guardia Act? The Wagner Act? How do you account for the passage of these prolabor acts? What are the functions of the National Labor Relations Board?

7. "In the 1930s public opinion was prolabor, but by the mid-1940s the public was of an antilabor disposition." Account for this turnabout.

8. What are the major provisions of the Taft-Hartley Act? If you had the power to revise this act, what changes would you make? In what ways has the Taft-Hartley Act directly or indirectly affected the sample work agreement studied in this chapter? Be specific.

9. It has been said that the Taft-Hartley Act was passed to achieve three major goals: (*a*) to reestablish an equality of bargaining power between labor and management to maintain industrial peace; (*b*) to protect "neutrals," that is, third parties who are not directly concerned with a given labor-management dispute; (c) to protect the rights of individual workers in their relations with unions. Review the Taft-Hartley provisions as outlined in this chapter, and relate each to these three major goals.

10. Briefly indicate the nature of the Landrum-Griffin Act.

11. Suppose you are the president of a newly established local union which is about to bargain with an employer for the first time. Make a list of those points which you would want to be covered explicitly in the work agreement.

12. Suppose you are a union president bargaining for higher wages. Assuming the economic climate which exists at this moment, what wage criteria would you use in backing your demands? Explain.

13. Briefly contrast the anti-union and pro-union views of organized labor. To what degree does the anti-union view depend upon an affirmative answer to the question "Do unions raise wages?" Which of the two views do you feel is the more accurate? Outline a compromise position less extreme than either the anti-union or the pro-union view sketched in this chapter.

SELECTED REFERENCES

Bakke, E. Wight, Clark Kerr, and Charles W. Anrod (eds.), *Unions, Management, and the Public*, 2d ed. (New York: Harcourt, Brace & World, Inc., 1960).

Butler, Arthur D., *Labor Economics and Institutions* (New York: The Macmillan Company, 1961).

Chamberlin, Edward H., *The Economic Analysis of Labor Union Power* (Washington: American Enterprise Association, 1958).

Davey, Harold W., *Contemporary Collective Bargaining*, 2d ed. (Englewood Cliffs, N.J.: Prentice-Hall, Inc., 1959).

Dulles, Foster Rhea, *Labor in America*, 2d ed. (New York: Thomas Y. Crowell Company, 1955).

Morgan, Chester A., *Labor Economics* (Homewood, Ill.: The Dorsey Press, Inc., 1962).

Shultz, G. P., and John R. Coleman, *Labor Problems: Cases and Readings*, 2d ed. (New York: McGraw-Hill Book Company, Inc., 1959).

Chapter 35

THE ECONOMICS OF INEQUALITY

AND INSECURITY

HISTORICALLY, income inequality—the vivid contrast of poverty and opulence—has been a sore spot in American capitalism. Animosity between the "haves" and the "have nots" is hardly a recent phenomenon. Similarly, though much has been done to ameliorate economic insecurity, the problem remains very pertinent.

Though by no means identical, the problems of income inequality and economic insecurity are related in many ways. In particular, the causes of economic insecurity—old age, prolonged illness, industrial accidents, seasonal and cyclical unemployment—are major sources of income inequality. The majority of households at the bottom of the income distribution have been so placed by one or more of these maladies. Similarly, public policies aimed at alleviating insecurity affect the distribution of income and vice versa.

In this chapter we first review the facts of income inequality and spotlight the long-run changes which are occurring in the distribution of total money income. Then the basic cases against and for income inequality are summarized. Next governmental policies designed to reduce income inequality are surveyed. The major sources of economic insecurity are then discussed. This is followed by an outline of both private and public programs aimed at reducing economic insecurity.

INCOME INEQUALITY

The factual data on income inequality in our economy were presented in Chapter 7. Table 35-1 once again states the basic picture for us. It is evident that *income inequality is considerable.* At the low end of the scale we find that 12 per cent of all consumer units, that is, families and unattached individuals, received about 2 per cent of total personal income. A mere 10 per cent of the total income went to the 31 per cent of the consumer units receiving an annual income of less than $4,000 per year in 1961. At the top of the income pyramid we find that 17 per cent of the consumer units received incomes of $10,000 or more per year; this group got about 42 per cent of total personal income. These figures clearly point to considerable income inequality.

Causes of income inequality

The price system is an impersonal mechanism. It has no conscience, and it does not cater to any set of ethical standards concerning what is an "equitable," or "just," distribution of income. As a matter of fact, the basically individualistic environment of the capitalist economy is more than permissive of a high de-

TABLE 35-1. THE DISTRIBUTION OF PERSONAL INCOME BY CONSUMER UNITS, 1961

(1)	(2)	(3)	(4)	(5)
Personal income class	Per cent of all consumer units in this class	Per cent of total personal income received by consumers in this class	Per cent of all consumer units in this class and all lower classes	Per cent of income received by this class and all lower classes
Under $2,000	12	2	12	2
$2,000–$3,999	19	8	31	10
$4,000–$5,999	22	16	53	26
$6,000–$7,999	19	18	72	44
$8,000–$9,999	11	14	83	58
$10,000 and over	17	42	100	100
	100	100		

SOURCE: "Survey of Current Business," April, 1962.

gree of income inequality. More specifically, you will recall that the specific factors of importance in explaining income inequality are: (1) differences in the native abilities of resource suppliers, (2) differences in training and education, (3) the unequal distribution of property resources, (4) the differing abilities of resource suppliers to exert market power, and (5) the simple fact that economic misfortunes—unemployment, accidents, illnesses, and so forth—apportion themselves rather arbitrarily and unequally over the population (Chapter 7).

Has income inequality diminished?

We know from Chapter 18 that economic growth has brought increases in incomes: *absolutely* the entire distribution of income has been moving upward over time. Changes in the *relative* distribution of income are quite another thing. Incomes can move up absolutely, and the degree of inequality may or may not be affected. Table 35-2 is instructive on this point. Here we divide the total number of income receivers into five numerically equal groups, or *quintiles*, and show the percentage

of total personal income received by each. These data suggest that there has been some reduction in the degree of income inequality since 1929. For example, comparing the 1929 and 1960 data we find that for the lowest 40 per cent of the families the relative income share increased from 12.5 per cent in 1929 to 15.6 per cent in 1960. The third and fourth quintiles also show gains of 2 or 3 percentage points. These increases came primarily at the expense of the top quintile, which experienced a decrease from 54.4 to 45.5 in the per cent of total income received. Note, interestingly enough, that the income distribution has been remarkably constant in the postwar period.

The major factors underlying this long-run shift toward greater equality have been the maturation of the economy and the structural changes which maturity has entailed. First, the long-run trend has been for interest and dividends, income payments which accrue largely to those at the top of the income ladder, to decline in relative importance (see Figure 7-2). Second, long-term changes in the structure of our economy have reduced the number of low-paying unskilled jobs and have increased significantly the number of higher-paying semiskilled, skilled, technical, and professional

TABLE 35-2. PERCENTAGE OF TOTAL PERSONAL INCOME RECEIVED BY EACH
ONE-FIFTH OF THE CONSUMER UNITS, 1929, 1935–1936, 1944, 1960

Quintile	1929	1935–1936	1944	1960
Lowest	12.5	4.1	4.9	4.6
Second	12.5	9.2	10.9	11.0
Third	13.8	14.1	16.2	16.3
Fourth	19.3	20.9	22.2	22.6
Highest	54.4	51.7	45.8	45.5
Total	100.0	100.0	100.0	100.0
Top 5 per cent	30.0	26.5	20.7	20.0

SOURCE: "Survey of Current Business."

positions. Then, too, innovation has become "institutionalized"; that is, the development of new products and processes increasingly has become a corporate venture. Where successful, the resulting profit rewards flow to thousands of stockholders rather than to one or two pioneering individuals. Further, the general full employment witnessed since the early 1940s has undoubtedly aided the cause of those in the lower quintiles. One controversial point might be added: some feel that in our maturing economy there are fewer opportunities to become exceptionally wealthy than in prior decades.

A reminder: this analysis is couched in terms of personal income, that is, income *before* personal taxes. In an ensuing section on public policy we shall gauge the impact of taxes and government expenditures upon income inequality.

The case against income inequality

The desirability of income inequality is anything but a new subject for debate. Indeed the long-standing nature of the controversy has resulted in the development of a more or less standardized set of arguments that condemn and an equally traditional group of contentions that defend income inequality.

Five points constitute the case against inequality in the distribution of income: (1) Income inequality is ethically undesirable. (2) Income inequality is an obstacle to maximizing consumer satisfactions. (3) Inequality tends to impair productivity. (4) Income inequality limits the occupational opportunities of the poor. (5) Economic inequality fosters noneconomic inequalities.

1. A basic argument against income inequality is the purely ethical contention that it is highly inequitable that a portion of the population of a wealthy society should live in poverty. The persistence of pockets of extreme poverty in an opulent economy is a social disgrace.

2. It is alleged that income inequality is a large obstacle in maximizing consumer satisfaction. The underlying reasoning is this: money income is subject to the principle of diminishing marginal utility. In any time period income receivers spend the first dollars received on those products which they value most, that is, on products whose marginal utility is high. As their most pressing wants become satisfied, consumers will spend additional dollars of income on increasingly frivolous, lower marginal utility items. Suppose, for example, that $10,000 worth of annual income is unequally distributed among Brooks and Anderson—the former getting $8,000 and the latter $2,000. As a result, the last, or marginal, dollars spent by Brooks will yield him relatively small increments of satisfaction or utility. Why? Because these dollars will be spent in satisfying less urgent needs;

that is, they will be spent on frivolous products or on extra units of items already possessed in abundance. In either event the marginal utility of these dollars will be relatively low.

But, alas, poor $2,000-a-year Anderson is in a much different situation. His annual pittance is such that his marginal dollars are spent on very basic, high marginal utility products. He is able to buy such small quantities of most products that the marginal utility of added units is still relatively high. It is concluded that any transfer of money income from high income Brooks to low income Anderson will increase the satisfactions or utility of the latter by more than it will decrease those of the former. The result is a net increase in *total* consumer satisfaction. Greater income equality has moved the economy closer to the goal of maximizing aggregate satisfaction. In a somewhat altered form this argument contends that income inequality causes economic resources to be misallocated. Inequality results in inefficient resource use by drawing resources into the production of frivolous, unimportant products at the expense of more essential products that low income groups desire but are unable to afford.

This is a very persuasive argument. But there is a major loophole: the argument assumes that Brooks and Anderson have equal capacities to enjoy income. In fact, however, *interpersonal* comparisons of the subjective concept of utility cannot be scientifically made. Although the above argument against inequality rests on the supposition that Brooks and Anderson are equally capable of enjoying income, that is unlikely. The chances are at least fifty-fifty[1] that Brooks has a greater capacity to derive satisfaction from spending money income than does Anderson. Were this actually the case, an *unequal* distribution of income would be required to achieve maximum consumer satisfaction. So, although this argument for greater income

equality cannot be disproved, it also cannot be proved valid. The ability to derive satisfaction from the expenditure of money income eludes quantitative measurement.

3. It is also argued that excessive income inequality impairs productivity. In the first instance, laborers who find themselves at the base of the income pyramid may not be able to obtain that minimum of food and shelter needed to maintain their physical and mental vigor, not to mention the effects which poverty may have upon their morale. And, ironically enough, inequality may impair the productivity of those at the pinnacle of the pyramid. Leveling off the income peak might induce the "idle rich" and the "I retired at thirty-five" segment of the economy's human resources back into harness. The latter argument is obviously more pertinent than the former for our economy.

4. Income inequality means unequal opportunities for training and education. The sons of the poor are at a decided handicap in getting the education required for entering many occupations. To overstate the situation, an individual must be an M.D. in order to finance a medical education for his son. Or one must be a successful businessman to provide the money capital prerequisite to setting his son up in business. Other things being equal, the poor man's son has a much smaller chance of becoming an M.D. or an entrepreneur. The implications for resource allocation are clear: the unequal distribution of opportunities fostered by income inequality distorts the allocation of resources. Resources should be allocated in terms of ability and productivity, not by accident of birth.

5. The final pillar in the case against inequality links income inequality to political and social inequality. Money talks in politics. Theoretically, of course, the rich man and the poor man have equal voices in politics; that is, each has one vote. In practice, it is no secret that the rich man, by virtue of his wealth, is in a position to influence many other votes. How? By financing the campaigns of "right-minded" politicians, by "recommending" candidates to subordinates, by using his resources to support lobbyists, and so forth. A similar set of argu-

[1] They may be better than fifty-fifty. It is plausible to argue that the ability to enjoy income varies directly with the size of one's income. A high income provides (and presupposes!) the education prerequisite to the intelligent allocation of money income and the greater enjoyment of the goods and services thereby obtained.

ments can be offered to support the view that there is a direct relationship between wealth and social inequality.

The case for income inequality

Two time-honored arguments anchor the defense of income inequality.

1. Income inequality gives rise to sizable amounts of private savings which, when invested, provide the capital goods which are the core of economic growth. Indeed, it is primarily as a result of this expanding stock of capital which the savings of the wealthy finance that the productivity and standard of living of the entire economy are bettered. The savings of the very wealthy, it is argued, provide the means for improving the lot of the very poor.

But proponents of greater income equality are quick to point out a major loophole in this capital formation argument: the alleged relationship between inequality and capital formation is not at all clear. Norway, for example, has moved far in the direction of income equality; yet in the postwar era it achieved a high rate of capital formation. In contrast low rates of capital formation persist in those Middle Eastern nations in which income inequality is particularly great.

2. Income inequality is also defended on the grounds that it furnishes the incentives to work, produce, and innovate which are the driving forces of any economy. Monetary gain—the opportunity to better oneself financially—is alleged necessary to induce workers and entrepreneurs to rise above mediocrity. Income inequality is essential if risky ventures are to be undertaken and workers are to perform effectively and faithfully over time. An unequal distribution of income is a necessary and desirable consequence of the price system in allocating resources in terms of their productivity.

Skeptics feel that this justification of income inequality has been overdrawn. They question, in particular, whether there is any firm relationship between income and productivity. Business executives, enthralled by their work and anxious to be heralded as "top men" in their field, may put out the same effort at $20,000 per year as they will at $50,000. Nor is it clear that the unskilled assembly-line worker will be more productive after his union negotiates a $150 increase in his annual income than before.

Although the capital formation and incentive arguments constitute the basic defenses of income inequality, several other points of significance bolster the case for inequality. A most pragmatic point is this: because of the relatively small number of people at the top of the income pyramid and the extremely large number at the base, a redistribution of income from rich to poor would only raise the income of the latter by minute amounts. Defenders of inequality also claim that high-income consumers have played a crucial role in the development of new products. The rich, it is said, support new industries during their high-cost, high-price infancies. This support allows low-cost mass production to evolve, bringing the new products within the financial means of the masses of consumers. Finally, it is invariably argued that the philanthropic actions of the very wealthy devote resources to cultural and educational pursuits and to humanitarian activities—a reallocation of resources which greater income equality would not foster.

Thus go the cases for and against income inequality. Each of us must weigh the relative merits of the two positions and judge for himself which is superior.

Public policy and income inequality

Society has taken a stand in favor of greater equality and, through government, has sought to lessen existing income inequality. Specific policies aimed at this goal are many and varied. They can be grouped, however, under four general headings: (1) government taxation and expenditure programs, (2) governmental programs of direct and indirect market intervention, (3) programs to increase occupational and geographic mobility, and (4) social security and public assistance programs.

The redistributional impact of taxes and government spending. Through its taxation and expenditure policy government functions as an equalizing force in American capitalism. The American tax system is a somewhat progressive one (Table 9-6); the three levels of government take a relatively larger amount of taxes from the rich than from the poor. Because the benefits of government expenditures on social goods and services are widely disbursed throughout the economy, it is very difficult to estimate with accuracy their impact upon the distribution of income. Nevertheless, there is little doubt that many of these expenditures have an equalizing effect: free public schools, public libraries, free public medical and legal services, and so forth. It is more evident that many transfer payments—relief payments, social security benefits accruing to the aged and the unemployed, and transfers to the disabled and needy—tend to bolster the incomes of many households which would otherwise find themselves at the bottom of the income distribution. In brief, as the tax and expenditure structures now stand, government collects more taxes from high-income receivers than that group receives in benefits from social goods and services and transfer payments. The reverse holds true for those families in the low income brackets: they get more benefits from governmental expenditures and transfer payments than they pay in taxes.

A pioneering study on the redistributive impact of government provides empirical support to the conclusion that income is more equally distributed *after* taxes and government expenditures than before. Though the figures are for the immediate postwar period and are, of necessity, broad estimates, the general picture portrayed in Table 35-3 is probably of reasonable accuracy. Note that the "Under $1,000" income class had about 73 per cent more income *after* taxes and expenditures than before. This particular group paid taxes equal to 19.6 per cent of their money incomes and received benefits (social goods and services and monetary transfers) valued at about 93 per cent of their incomes. Therefore, the net impact of government on this group was to increase their incomes by 73.4 per cent. The four lowest in-

come groups shown in Table 35-3 received benefits from government, the value of which exceeded their tax payments. The $4,000–$4,999 group stood in about the same position after taxes and expenditures as it did before. The two highest income groups clearly paid taxes in excess of the value of the benefits they received from government.

Market intervention and income inequality. Supplanting free market prices by governmentally determined prices can significantly alter the distribution of income. Chapter 33 had much to say about the classic example. Price supports on agricultural products have bolstered the incomes of farmers, a segment of the population which is concentrated in the lower income classes. Minimum wage legislation is also explicitly aimed at aiding those receiving meager incomes.

Increasing occupational and geographic mobility. A variety of government policies directly and indirectly enhances occupational and geographic mobility, thereby providing opportunities for low-income receivers to better their income status.

Many specific programs and policies might be cited in this connection. Public education is a basic avenue through which the offspring of poor families may acquire the training needed to climb the income ladder. Fair employment practices legislation at the state and local level is aimed at alleviating artificial occupational restrictions upon minority groups. Governmental prohibitions upon certain restrictive policies of unions also contribute to mobility. The special programs for reallocating labor out of chronically depressed areas (Chapter 19) are particularly relevant here. And, when vigorously enforced, the antitrust acts break down barriers to entering monopolized industries. The resulting increase in entrepreneurial mobility alleviates the income inequalities based upon monopoly power.

Though obviously not its primary objective, there is little doubt that the application of full-employment policies by government encourages geographic and occupational mobility. For example, full employment is essential to real-

TABLE 35-3. GOVERNMENTAL REDISTRIBUTION OF INCOME THROUGH
FEDERAL, STATE, AND LOCAL TAXES AND EXPENDITURES, 1946–1947

Money income class	Net gain (+) or loss (−) in income as a result of government taxes and expenditures, per cent
Under $1,000	+73.4
$1,000–$1,999	+22.4
$2,000–$2,999	+11.1
$3,000–$3,999	+ 6.6
$4,000–$4,999	− 1.5
$5,000–$7,499	− 7.4
$7,500 and over	−11.4

SOURCE: John H. Adler, "The Fiscal System, the Distribution of Income and
Public Welfare," in Kenyon E. Poole (ed.), "Fiscal Policies and the American
Economy" (Englewood Cliffs, N.J.: Prentice-Hall, Inc., 1951), p. 396.

locating low-income farmers to higher-income jobs in industry. Similarly, artificial job restrictions based upon race, religion, national origin, and so forth, diminish as prosperity gives rise to labor shortages.

Social security payments. By providing income payments to the aged, the widowed, the unemployed, and the mentally and physically infirm, the various social security programs supplement the incomes of many households which find themselves near the bottom of the income distribution. It is to a discussion of economic insecurity and the role of the social security system to which we now turn.

ECONOMIC INSECURITY

Any event which entails a loss of income, added abnormal expenditures, or both, is a source of economic insecurity. A dynamic, essentially individualistic economy such as American capitalism provides ample room for economic insecurity.

Sources of insecurity

The major source of economic insecurity—*cyclical unemployment*—is macroeconomic. Cyclical unemployment imposes itself upon the economy as a whole, largely independently of the characteristics and circumstances of specific industries, firms, and individuals.

Insecurity also stems from many types of *noncyclical unemployment.* Variations in the weather, model change-overs, and consumer buying habits, for example, all contribute to *seasonal unemployment. Structural unemployment* is invariably present in a dynamic economy; such forces as automation, the development of new products, and changes in the structure of consumer demand mean that there are always declining industries (agriculture, coal, railroads) which are releasing resources, and expanding industries (electronics, plastics) absorbing them. The imperfect, time-consuming reallocations which are involved mean that at any time there will exist a certain amount of structural unemployment. Then, too, there is *frictional unemployment* resulting from labor-management disputes, bottlenecks in the supplies of essential resources, machinery breakdowns, and social incompatibility on the job. *Terminal unemployment* might be added to this list. Be it voluntary or involuntary, retirement is a source of economic insecurity. The unemployment arising from all these noncyclical sources is essentially a microeconomic phenomenon. It affects specific firms and specific types of workers.

Economic hazards are also basically of a microeconomic nature. Specific households bear the impact of prolonged illnesses, accidents, permanent disability, and loss of the family breadwinner through death. All these misfortunes couple loss of income with abnormal increases in expenditures.

Needless to say, there is an obvious and significant relationship between the issue of economic insecurity and that of income inequality. Economic insecurity accounts for the very low incomes which many households receive. Cyclical unemployment, noncyclical unemployment, and a host of economic hazards drive many families to the very base of the income pyramid.

The attack on insecurity

The defenses against economic insecurity have been every bit as varied as the causes. Figure 35-1 provides us with a general notion of the many-pronged attack which is being waged against insecurity. It is to be emphasized that some programs are private, and others public. Some are *preventive*, attempting to reduce or eliminate the cause of the insecurity, and others are *curative*, designed to alleviate the consequences of economic insecurity. Furthermore, some of the defenses against insecurity entail *formal* programs of insuring, that is, the pooling of risks and the paying of premiums to a private or public insurance agency; other defenses are highly *informal*.

Private security programs. Households and businesses protect themselves against insecurity through the purchase of life, health, accident, property, and liability insurance. Less formally they accumulate savings to meet the financial impact of economic insecurity. Through unions, individuals seek and obtain pension plans, disability and severance pay, and guaranteed annual wage plans.

Businesses, particularly the larger corporations, have been notably successful in meeting privately many of the sources of insecurity which they face. Prodigious advertising expenditures and diversification of the product line

have helped protect against adverse changes in consumer tastes. Formidable research expenditures keep many large corporations at the forefront of technological advance, guarding against the disastrous implications of new products and production methods in the hands of rival firms. Through the attainment of monopoly power, many businesses have alleviated the insecurity arising from the uncertainties associated with competitive markets.

In certain cases in which specific groups of individuals have been unable to insulate themselves from particular sources of insecurity, these groups have sought and frequently obtained the assistance of government. The great success of the farmers in achieving price supports has already been elaborated (Chapter 33). Similarly, small businessmen have achieved a degree of protection from the vagaries of competitive markets through the Robinson-Patman Act and fair trade legislation.

It is obvious that certain of these private means of reducing economic insecurity collide with other goals, in particular the basic objective of economic efficiency. While monopoly power may provide greater security for the holders of that power, it may also mean an impairment of full production for the economy as a whole. Similarly, we have previously noted that farm price supports impede the correction of the misallocation of resources which is the core of the farm problem.

Public security programs. On the public side of the ledger government attacks insecurity in two different ways. (1) Through full-employment policies designed to counter cyclical unemployment, the government attempts to deal with the major source of economic insecurity. The use of fiscal and monetary policies to maintain full employment and economic growth has already been detailed. (2) The social security system attempts to alleviate the adverse financial effects of retirement, unemployment, and destitution.

The social security system was legislated in 1935, put into operation in 1937, and has been frequently amended since that date. The system provides for (1) contributory old age and

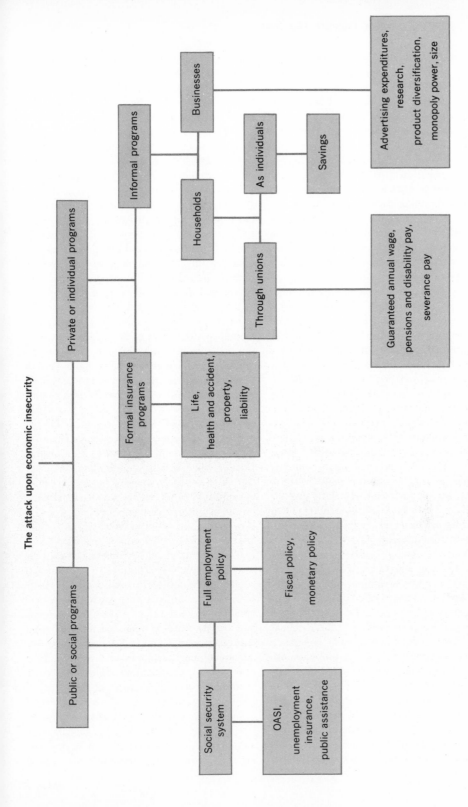

The attack upon economic insecurity

Public or social programs

Private or individual programs

Full employment policy

Social security system

Fiscal policy, monetary policy

OASI, unemployment insurance, public assistance

Formal insurance programs

Informal programs

Life, health and accident, property, liability

Businesses

Households

Through unions

As individuals

Savings

Advertising expenditures, research, product diversification, monopoly power, size

Guaranteed annual wage, pensions and disability pay, severance pay

FIGURE 35-1. THERE IS A VARIETY OF BOTH PUBLIC AND PRIVATE PROGRAMS DESIGNED TO PREVENT AND OFFSET THE EFFECTS OF ECONOMIC INSECURITY.

survivors insurance (OASI), (2) unemployment insurance, and (3) programs of public assistance to the needy.

The philosophy upon which the social security system is based focuses attention upon two fundamental points. (1) Society has an obligation and the ability to provide a minimum standard of living for those who are permanently or temporarily unable to care for themselves. Many households lack the ability to cope with the financial adversities which accompany old age, unemployment, sickness, and accidents. Some who do have the means to provide for, say, old age or prolonged illness do not have the foresight to make such provisions. (2) Certain types of insecurity—in particular, cyclical unemployment—are not amenable to private insurance. Private insurance companies can predict with reasonable accuracy the number of persons per thousand who will be hospitalized each year, the number of barns that will burn, the number of people in each age group who will die, and the number of fenders that will be dented. Hence, on the basis of such predictions they can establish premiums which will provide enough funds to pay medical, property, and life insurance benefits to all those who will encounter the stated misfortunes and permit a not inconsequential profit for the company. But unemployment—cyclical unemployment in particular—cannot be predicted with accuracy. If insurance is to be provided against unemployment, the government must therefore undertake the task.

Old age and survivors insurance (OASI) is essentially a gigantic program of compulsory savings. The program is financed by compulsory taxes (premiums) levied upon both employers and employees. In 1963 these taxes are each 3⅝ per cent upon the first $4,800 of annual income. Legislative provisions have been made which will increase the tax on both employer and employee to 4⅝ per cent by 1968. The self-employed now pay a tax of 5.4 per cent, a figure which will rise to 6.9 per cent by 1968. Benefit payments are made to those reaching the retirement age of sixty-five; if the worker dies before sixty-five, benefits accrue to his survivors. Widows can retire and collect old age benefits at age sixty-two. Currently over 90 per cent of all employed persons in the United States are covered by OASI.

The actual size of benefit payments varies according to the amount the worker has contributed to the program, the number of dependents, and so forth. At the beginning of 1962 over 16 million people were receiving OASI checks averaging about $75 per month. Benefit payments redistribute income to some degree; small contributors get relatively more in comparison with their contributions than do large contributors. On the other hand, benefit payments are not based upon the recipient's "need"; a participant's contribution gives him the right to benefits regardless of whether or not he would be otherwise financially secure.

The Social Security Act does not provide for a federally operated program of *unemployment insurance*. But it does provide the incentive for the states to establish and operate such programs;[2] all 50 states now have them. Though the same in principle, the programs of the various states differ considerably with respect to details.

The program is financed by taxes on employers; these taxes probably average about 1½ per cent of covered payrolls. Any insured worker who finds himself unemployed can, after a short waiting period (usually a week), become eligible for benefit payments. The size of the payments and the number of weeks they may be received vary considerably from state to state. In 1960 some 7 million workers received a total of $2.7 billion in benefits; the average check was about $33 per week. Of course, the number of people receiving benefits at any time will vary with the over-all health of the economy. In 1960 about 45 million people were covered by unemployment compensation. It is to be recalled that unemployment compensation benefits are one of the important built-in stabilizers of American capitalism.

Needy persons who do not qualify for OASI or unemployment compensation are assisted by

[2] The incentive: Congress levied a tax on employers, returning the tax collections only to those states willing to set up an unemployment insurance program.

a variety of special *public assistance* programs. These programs—for the needy aged and blind, the permanently and totally disabled, and dependent children—are administered by the state governments and financed out of state tax revenues and Federal grants-in-aid. In 1960 about 6.3 million persons were receiving benefits under the various assistance programs. In addition, all the states have passed legislation providing for workmen's compensation. These programs assure medical expenses and partial wages to workers who are victims of industrial accidents. Finally, local governments provide outright relief to the destitute.

Though many details of the social security system invariably entail controversy—Who shall be covered? How large should benefits be? How should the costs of the programs be allocated?—there can be no doubt as to the general popularity of the system. The persistent extensions of the various programs which both political parties have eagerly sponsored are ample evidence of popular acceptance of the American social security system.

SUMMARY

1. The distribution of personal income in American capitalism reflects considerable inequality. Though income inequality lessened between 1929 and the end of World War II, little change has occurred in the postwar period.

2. Five arguments constitute the case against income inequality. Income inequality (*a*) is ethically undesirable; (*b*) impedes the maximization of consumer satisfaction; (*c*) impairs productivity; (*d*) limits the occupational opportunities of the poor; and (*e*) fosters noneconomic inequalities.

3. Income inequality is defended as follows: (*a*) income inequality is conducive to a high rate of savings and a rapid rate of capital accumulation, and (*b*) income inequality is essential as an incentive to work and invest.

4. A variety of government policies and programs alleviate income inequality both directly and indirectly: (*a*) Taxation and expenditure programs are such that the income distribution is considerably more nearly equal after taxation and expenditures than before. (*b*) By manipulating product and resource prices government has influenced the distribution of income in the direction of greater equality. (*c*) Government has lessened a basic cause of income inequality —geographic and occupational immobility— through a variety of programs and policies. (*d*) The social security system assists many households which would otherwise receive extremely low incomes.

5. The main sources of economic insecurity are cyclical unemployment, noncyclical unemployment, and economic hazards. Households defend themselves against these sources of insecurity by saving, buying insurance, and seeking pension plans, severance pay, and guaranteed annual wage plans through unions. Businesses rely upon advertising and research expenditures, a diverse line of products, and monopoly power to insulate themselves from insecurity. At the public level, full-employment policies and the social security system spearhead the attack against insecurity. The latter is comprised of OASI, unemployment insurance, and a host of programs providing public assistance to the needy.

QUESTIONS AND STUDY SUGGESTIONS

1. What are the major causes of income inequality? The degree of inequality in the distribution of personal income, that is, income before taxes, has lessened slightly over recent decades. How do you account for this? Briefly explain the various means by which government has promoted a greater degree of income equality.

2. Outline and critically evaluate the arguments for and against income inequality. Which position do you favor? Why?

3. Explain: "To endow everyone with equal income will certainly make for very unequal enjoyment and satisfaction."

4. Are the issues of "equity" and "equality" in the distribution of income synonymous? To what degree, if any, is income inequality equitable?

5. In what way and to what degree are the problems of income inequality and economic insecurity related?

6. "The main cause of the persistence of low incomes in the United States is our failure to invest sufficiently in the development of people." Explain and discuss.

7. What are the major sources of economic insecurity? By what means have households, businesses, and government sought to reduce insecurity? Distinguish as best you can between (a) preventive and curative measures and (b) formal and informal measures.

8. Briefly sketch the main features of the OASI and unemployment insurance programs. Why don't private insurance companies sell policies which insure workers against the loss of income that accompanies unemployment?

9. Critically evaluate: "We need more private insurance and less social insurance. If workers claim they can't pay for private insurance, then how can they meet the added tax burden necessary in financing social insurance?"

10. "To eliminate insecurity is to undermine the incentives to produce and invest. These incentives are the mainspring of the capitalist economy. Hence, the specter of economic insecurity is essential to economic efficiency." Explain and critically evaluate.

11. In his *The Affluent Society*, John K. Galbraith has argued that "A high level of economic security is essential for maximum production. And a high level of production is indispensable for economic security." Explain and evaluate these statements. Carefully contrast this point of view with the statements made in question 10.

SELECTED REFERENCES

Carlson, Valdemar, *Economic Security in the United States* (New York: McGraw-Hill Book Company, Inc., 1962).

Conference on Economic Progress, *Poverty and Deprivation in the United States* (Washington: Conference on Economic Progress, 1962).

Galbraith, John Kenneth, *The Affluent Society* (Boston: Houghton Mifflin Company, 1958), particularly chaps. 7 and 8.

Grampp, William D., and Emanuel T. Weiler (eds.), *Economic Policy: Readings in Political Economy*, 3d ed. (Homewood, Ill.: Richard D. Irwin, Inc., 1961), chaps. 12–16.

Harrington, Michael, *The Other America* (New York: The Macmillan Company, 1962).

Lampman, Robert J., *The Low Income Population and Economic Growth*, for the Joint Economic Committee (Washington: Government Printing Office, 1959).

"Our Developing Social Security System: The First Twenty-five Years," *Industrial and Labor Relations Review*, October, 1960.

Wallich, Henry C., *The Cost of Freedom* (New York: Harper & Row, Publishers, 1960), chap. 4.

Chapter 36

THE SOCIAL IMBALANCE CONTROVERSY

A NUMBER of well-known economists[1] currently argue that the evolution of the United States from a nation of relative poverty to one of relative abundance has created a distortion in the composition of the economy's total output. It is asserted that the increasing affluence of American capitalism has been accompanied by a lack of social balance. That is, an inefficient allocation of resources between private goods and services, on the one hand, and social goods and services, on the other, has arisen. Television sets, automobiles, and a profligacy of gadgetry are produced in abundance, while education, police and fire protection, streets and highways, and a myriad of basic community services are slighted. In short, it is contended that the development of our economy has fostered the poverty-amidst-plenty problem in a new guise: private goods abound, but social goods are remarkably deficient.

The primary purposes of this chapter are to (1) present the arguments of those economists who feel a serious social imbalance exists in the composition of our total output; (2) outline a number of criticisms of, and counterarguments

[1] See, in particular, the works of John Kenneth Galbraith, Alvin H. Hansen, W. W. Rostow, and Francis M. Bator listed at the end of this chapter.

to, the social imbalance position; and (3) note briefly various policy means of alleviating social imbalance should it exist now or in the future.

THE NATURE OF SOCIAL IMBALANCE

It must be acknowledged at the outset that the question as to whether social imbalance actually exists is ultimately an ethical one; that is, it is a question of what the proper or optimum balance of private and social goods *ought* to be. It is impossible to compare scientifically the marginal utility of an extra dollar spent on an electric can opener or power mower with that of a marginal dollar of expenditures on education or space research. Yet it can be argued that there is substantial evidence which lends credence to the position that social imbalance now exists as a basic economic problem. Simple observation—evidence of the eye—is said to be abundant: overcrowded and ill-equipped schools, a paucity of parks and recreation areas, overcrowded streets and inadequate highways, underpaid and undermanned police forces, and so on. Simple statistical comparisons may also be invoked as evidence. In 1960 United States consumers spent $19.4 billion on recreation as compared with the $18.7 billion which all state and local

661

governments spent on education. Approximately $12 billion was spent on advertising, some $7.5 billion on tobacco products, and $16 billion on automobile purchases, as opposed to total (public and private) spending of $12.5 billion for research and development.[2]

What of more comprehensive statistical information on the question of social imbalance? Professor Bator of MIT has explored this general problem, deriving elaborate statistics on the economic role of government. Most pertinent for our discussion, he has sought to determine the trend of government purchases on social goods and services by subtracting defense expenditures from total government spending on goods and services, on the one hand, and from gross national product on the other, and comparing the two. By contrasting government's nondefense purchases of goods and services with the size of the nondefense GNP over a period of years, we can envision what share of "civilian" GNP has been in the form of social goods and services. His data show that government's nondefense spending as a percentage of nondefense GNP rose from 7.5 per cent in 1929 to 13.4 per cent in 1939, only to decline to 10.3 per cent by 1957. Professor Bator offers this conclusion:

It appears . . . that of the resources left over for private and public "civilian" consumption and capital formation—left over, that is, after military provision for survival—we have been committing in the postwar period only a slightly larger fraction to such communal uses as schools, roads, sanitation and urban renewal, etc., than we did in 1929, and a smaller share than in 1939 and 1940.[3]

Bator's per capita data are also revealing. Per capita real nondefense spending by government was approximately the same in 1957 at

[2] Data from *Economic Almanac, 1962* and *Statistical Abstract of the United States, 1961.*

[3] Francis M. Bator, *The Question of Government Spending* (New York: Harper & Row, Publishers, Inc., 1960), pp. 21–22. The National Planning Association, *National Investment for Economic Growth* (Washington: National Planning Association, 1957), has reached a similar conclusion.

$234 as in 1939, despite the fact that total real civilian output per head increased from $1,514 to $2,281 in the same period.

SOCIAL IMBALANCE AS AN ECONOMIC PROBLEM

Those who embrace the social imbalance thesis argue that it constitutes a first-rank economic problem because it embodies a misallocation of resources, constitutes a threat to economic stability and full employment, and has critical implications for the economy's rate of economic growth.

The allocation of resources

As already noted, social imbalance suggests a misallocation of economic resources and, therefore, a failure of the economic system to maximize the satisfactions of society. More specifically, private goods, because of their very superabundance, are now relatively low priority (low marginal utility) goods; the production of additional private goods is not a matter of very high urgency. In contrast, the very paucity of social goods makes them relatively high priority (high marginal utility) goods; the production of more social goods *is* a matter of relatively high urgency. It is argued, in brief, that given an initial position of social imbalance—too much private and not enough public goods—a reallocation of resources in favor of the latter is a rechanneling of resources away from low toward high marginal utility employments. This obviously accomplishes an increase in the total satisfaction (utility) of society.

Economic stability

Social imbalance is also a crucial economic problem because of the contribution it might make to economic instability and unemployment. Professor Galbraith has emphasized that a sustained demand for private consumer goods has become highly dependent upon want-creating activities (advertising) and the willingness and ability of consumers to increase their indebtedness. Now, if a point is reached at which the myriad of claims and counterclaims of advertisers renders consumers immune to the claims of all, or, if any of the innumerable uncertainties which characterize our economy should interrupt the expansion of consumer credit, then consumption spending would decline and unemployment would result. The reduction or amelioration of social imbalance would lessen the possibility of these difficulties arising.

Since public wants are not contrived, they are not subject to a failure of contrivance. Since they are not sold on the installment plan, they are not subject to curtailment by any of the factors which make people unwilling or unable to incur debt. Thus the better the social balance the more immune the economy to fluctuations in private demand.[4]

To these contentions can be added the simple fact that social balance might contribute to stability for the simple reason that the production of public goods is not motivated by profit considerations.

Economic growth

The final reason for the great significance of social imbalance as an economic problem may well be the most crucial of all. The manner in which a nation chooses to divide its *current* output between public and private goods may well have a bearing upon the size of that economy's *future* output. More specifically, the present relationship between private and social goods may be an important determinant of the nation's economic growth potential. This is so because many basic social goods—for example, education, basic scientific research, and preventive medicine—are important factors contributing to the process of economic growth. Thus a current public-private goods choice which puts heavy emphasis upon such private consumer goods as automobiles, television sets, and air conditioners and therefore slights the

---

[4] John Kenneth Galbraith, *The Affluent Society* (Boston: Houghton Mifflin Company, 1958), p. 279.

aforementioned social goods is necessarily reducing its potential rate of growth in so doing. Bluntly put, a nation which becomes overly obese with consumer goods may, by that very act, undermine its future economic health.

Some international implications

In view of the current Soviet challenge (Chapter 40) the economic, political, and military overtones of these three points cannot be minimized. The misallocation-of-resources aspect of the social imbalance problem is highly relevant with respect to the Soviet military threat. By choosing a higher ratio of public to private goods than the United States, the Soviet Union has created a military force which rivals or, in the opinion of some military experts, surpasses that of the United States. This fact is particularly disconcerting when it is acknowledged that the nuclear instruments of modern warfare bar the United States from having the time necessary to reallocate resources away from private (civilian) goods to social (war) goods. Assuming the distinction between "winners" and "losers" is meaningful in an age of nuclear rocketry, it is safer to suppose that future major wars will be won by those nations whose existing stock of military goods is quantitatively and technologically superior, rather than by those countries who can amass the greatest gross national product.

Similarly, on the politico-economic front we find the emerging and uncommitted underdeveloped nations closely observing the productive performances of American capitalism and Soviet communism in an effort to ascertain which model to pursue in structuring their own political and economic institutions. To the extent that social imbalance may actually contribute to unemployment and retard economic growth in the United States, the destiny of the free world may be impaired.

ALLEGED CAUSES OF SOCIAL IMBALANCE

How has this alleged paucity of social goods developed amidst an affluence of private goods? It would seem that mixed capitalism embodies the mechanisms necessary for obtaining a reasonably good balance between private and public output. Consumers govern the production of private goods by the dollar votes they register in the market place. Through political means—the process of political voting—consumers in effect select the amount of social goods they desire. In brief, in a democracy is not the considered judgment of the majority of the citizenry transformed through dollar and political voting into a choice as to how total output is to be divided among private and social goods? How, then, can social imbalance arise?

Economists who envision a social imbalance in current GNP argue that the matter is not as simple as that just described. True, mechanisms exist in mixed capitalism by which the citizenry can render a private-social goods decision. But it is argued that in practice certain historical, attitudinal, and politico-economic forces bear upon this decision so as to cause the production of social goods to fall seriously out of balance with the production of private goods.

What are these distorting forces? In examining the alleged causes of social imbalance we are in effect asking, "What happens to the amounts of social goods and services demanded and supplied in an expanding economy?" [5] If the amount of social goods demanded seems to increase ahead of the amount supplied, then a "disequilibrium" in the form of social imbalance will result. Let us first consider the demand for social goods; then we shall turn to supply considerations.

DEMAND FOR SOCIAL GOODS: WAGNER'S LAW

The forces underlying the growing demand for social goods and services are well known: hot and cold wars, population growth, industrialization and the subsequent urbanization and socioeconomic complexity which it entails, and so forth. Also, of course, as real incomes rise, the demand for both private and social

[5] This is loose terminology because there is no market for social goods and services in the sense in which there is a market for private goods and services.

goods can be expected to increase. There are plausible reasons to argue that as real per capita incomes rise, the pattern of consumer wants may alter in favor of relatively more social goods and relatively less private goods. This alleged alteration of wants in the growing economy is labeled *Wagner's Law*.

The rationale underlying Wagner's Law is relatively simple. The poor society, dominated by agriculture, must consume its entire real income in the form of such basic private goods as food, shelter, and clothing. After these basic wants have been largely fulfilled, the growing wealth of society permits it to turn its attention more and more to the satisfaction of somewhat less urgent but nevertheless important "new needs." Many of these new wants entail social goods—for example, education, streets and highways, police and fire protection. Economic growth is characterized by increasing industrialization and urbanization. This creates a demand for sanitation and sewage facilities, a water supply, extensive police and fire protection, and similar social goods which in a poorer and simpler agrarian society would be provided by each family for itself or simply not provided at all. Similarly, the industrialization and urbanization which characterize an expanding economy lead to increasing interdependence and greater socioeconomic complexity. Government's regulatory role may therefore be expected to expand markedly. Further, the increased leisure which is typically a component of economic growth can be expected to enhance the demand for educational facilities. And, too, the poor society spends little or nothing on national defense for the simple reason it has little wealth to protect from external aggression; opulence changes this and makes armament expenditures an important social good. All these considerations may give rise to a tendency for the demand for social goods to increase, not only absolutely, but also relative to the demand for private goods.

Those who accept the social imbalance theme may thus argue that the demand for social goods is increasing not only absolutely, but also in relative terms, as society becomes more affluent.

SUPPLY OF SOCIAL GOODS

Economists who view social imbalance as an acute issue feel there are a number of considerations which prevent the supply of social goods from keeping pace with the growing demand for them.

The mechanisms and mores of capitalism

The very nature of the capitalistic ideology and the attitudes of large numbers of Americans concerning the public sector of the economy have both fostered obstacles to an expanding volume of social goods production. A number of related points are involved here.

1. The ideology of pure capitalism embraces the concepts of consumer sovereignty, free competitive markets, and a highly restricted economic role for government. This long-obsolete portrayal of capitalism provides that virtually all resources are channeled into the production of private goods and services. Furthermore, as the economy evolves and becomes more affluent, the capitalistic ideology obviously provides both the philosophical basis and the mechanism—consumer sovereignty and the price system—to provide for ever increasing amounts of private goods. No such philosophy or mechanism exists to provide automatically for the additional social goods which a growing and more opulent nation may require. Indeed, the provision of additional social goods requires that government must somehow take positive steps to divert resources from private to public uses. In practice, government must convince the citizenry—government must "prove"— that particular social goods are needed and are clearly to be preferred to the private goods at whose expense their production must come in a full-employment economy. An individual need not justify his purchase of a new car, an automatic dishwasher, or a color television set to his community or to the nation. Yet the burden of proof is on government to justify increases in expenditures on highways, educa-

tional facilities, urban renewal, or expanded police and fire protection.

2. In fulfilling its role as a provider of social goods, government is typically viewed as an intruder upon the private sector of the economy and therefore as a threat to individual freedoms. Tax payments needed to finance social goods are compulsory as, indeed, is the consumption of certain social goods and services—education, for example. And at any point in time the provision of more social goods in a full-employment economy necessarily entails a restriction of private goods production. Implicit in these observations is the frequently voiced contention that governmental provision of social goods necessarily impinges upon individual liberties. There is little doubt but that this view of government as a freedom-limiting agency is partially a public reaction to the upsurges of governmental activity during the Great Depression and World War II.

3. The attitude of much of the business community, large parts of the citizenry, and some political leaders envisions private goods to be sacrosanct while public goods are held to be wasteful, of secondary significance, or at best a necessary evil. "The public, as a general rule . . . gets less production in return for a dollar spent by government than from a dollar spent by private enterprise."[6] The closely related notion that "economy in government" is synonymous with minimal public expenditures is also widely accepted (Chapter 6); believers are apparently oblivious of the fact that "economy" is concerned with the employment and efficient allocation of resources.

Ironically, the presumption of modern fiscal policy that public expenditure should accommodate itself to changes in the level of private spending has probably fostered such thinking indirectly and inadvertently by implying that public spending is expendable so long as the private sector is sufficiently exuberant to provide full employment. The notion that public expenditures should be of a compensatory character is an obstacle to a careful evaluation

[6] National Association of Manufacturers, *The American Individual Enterprise System* (New York: McGraw-Hill Book Company, Inc., 1946), p. 952.

of the composition of total output as between private and public goods.

4. Social imbalance may also reflect in part certain attitudes widely held in our society. Professor Hansen, for example, envisions social imbalance as a deeply rooted "frame of mind."

We are living in a tumultuous age—an age of disillusionment. The World War, the Korean conflict, the cold war. We are trying to escape from reality. We do not like to face the cold facts of the world we live in. We are caught up in a wave of escapism and comfortable complacency. [7]

Political realities

Because they are overweighted with the representatives of sparsely populated, rural areas, the Federal legislature and many state legislatures are relatively insensitive to the acute social goods needs of the heavily populated metropolitan areas. "We do not have majority rule in many of our State legislatures" with the result that rapidly expanding urban areas are denied even the traditional types of community services.[8] Similarly, the dire social needs of the Negro are clearly underrepresented in the southern states. At the level of local government, it will be noted later, heavy dependence upon property taxes works against the expansion of social goods production.

Character of social goods

The inherent characteristics of public goods, as opposed to private goods, also tend to impede their production. Private goods are sold on the basis of this-for-that transactions in the market place. The consumer knows precisely how much he pays for a private good, and the benefits he receives from such a purchase are immediate and certain; private goods entail a close link between costs and benefits. Not so with social goods and services. Here benefits are both more remote and less certain than in

[7] Alvin H. Hansen, *Economic Issues of the 1960's* (New York: McGraw-Hill Book Company, Inc., 1960), p. 82.

[8] *Ibid.*, pp. 111–112.

the case of private goods, and, with minor exceptions, the production of social goods is divorced from specific tax revenues (costs). The production of social goods is undertaken by the government and financed through taxes levied on the community or society as a whole. These differences in the characteristics of social goods and private goods tend to restrict the output of social goods in at least two ways.

1. The remoteness and uncertainty of the benefits derived from social goods prejudice the consumer (voter) against their production. In the realm of goods and services, individuals prefer the immediate and certain benefits of autos, television sets, and automatic dishwashers to the remote benefits of public education, municipal libraries, streets and highways, a boost in the budget of the local park department, or the highly uncertain benefits of aid to underdeveloped countries, space research, and a continuing arms race. It is particularly lamentable that investment in individuals (that is, in education) is slighted relative to investment in capital goods primarily because the former is in the public and the latter is in the private domain. In general, in any expression of choice between public and private goods which the electorate may render, public goods find themselves at a decided psychological disadvantage because of the remoteness and uncertainty of their benefits.

Unfortunately, there appear to be no alleviating factors or correctives in the picture. As a matter of fact, as the economy matures and becomes more affluent and complex, the benefits of additional social goods may well become increasingly remote and uncertain, further threatening their production. That is, the benefits of the highways, sanitation programs, and public schools provided by the government of a semideveloped economy are less remote and less uncertain than are the benefits of the foreign aid and space research programs undertaken by the governments of those nations which are most highly advanced economically.

It is tempting to argue that, if the tax payments which finance social goods were as vague to the citizenry as are their benefits, this would constitute a compensating factor by stimulating the flow of social goods. This is not felt to be the case, however. Relatively few taxes are really hidden taxes.[9] Income and property taxes entail explicit and often detailed consideration by the taxpayer, assuring his awareness of the cost of social goods to him. In contrast, the greatly expanded use of consumer credit in the postwar era has undoubtedly made the total cost of private durable consumer goods less immediate and less explicit to buyers, thereby increasing consumer preferences for private as opposed to social goods. In short, the remoteness and uncertainty of the benefits associated with the production of social goods coupled with the immediacy of their tax costs tends to prejudice the production of social goods.

2. Another characteristic of social goods or, more precisely, of the public sector, allegedly impedes the achievement of social balance. In the private sector of the economy each individual consumer exercises a great deal of selectivity in his purchases. He considers the marginal utility of various commodities relative to their prices and, subject to his budget restraint, achieves consumer equilibrium by freely selecting those goods and services which yield the greatest marginal utility per dollar and rejecting those yielding less (Chapter 22).

However, the individual's economic dealings with government are on a nonselective basis. The consumer cannot select and therefore contribute financially only to those programs in the public sector's budget which he favors, thereby rejecting and withholding tax payments for programs he disfavors. Thus, assuming realistically that the policy mix of the government is so complex that it will not precisely match the social goods preferences of any specific consumer, it follows that there will invariably be a number of social goods and services which he is compelled to help finance, but of which he does not approve. The practical conclusion is that each voter feels that the public budget is too high relative to the benefits he derives from it; that is, each taxpayer feels

[9] In 1961 sales taxes, which are usually thought of as "hidden," constituted only about 15 per cent of total governmental revenues.

that a cut in government spending is warranted. Government, therefore, is persistently faced with significant pressure to reduce the flow of social goods and services.

Tax obstacles

It is also asserted that a number of tax problems contribute to the difficulties of social imbalance.

Tax levels. Over a period of time the existing level of taxation tends to become acceptable—to become "proper"—to large numbers of households and businesses for the simple reason that they have had time to adjust to it. As a result, it becomes politically feasible to maintain existing levels of taxation, while at the same time it becomes extremely dangerous politically to raise tax levels. As the existing tax level acquires a measure of sanctity with the passage of time, it becomes exceedingly difficult —short of an obvious and acute military or domestic crisis—to raise the tax level in order to finance an increased flow of social goods production. No doubt the fact that added tax costs are not linked to specific social goods programs and their benefits contributes to this difficulty. Such thinking with respect to the tax level has been more or less formalized by a number of proposals seeking to limit the level of taxes and expenditures to a fixed proportion of the national income. For present purposes the important point is that allegiance to existing tax levels works against the expansion of social goods production.

Allocating tax burdens. Even where voters are in general agreement as to the desirability of having more of particular social goods and are willing to accept a higher tax level to finance them, the problem of allocating the tax costs of these goods may still impede their production. For example, a majority of the voters of a community may be convinced of the need for street improvements and repairs, but they may be deadlocked with respect to what taxes should be used to finance these repairs. Should a special tax (for example, a wheel tax) be assessed on auto and truck owners? Or should property taxes be raised? Or should a city sales tax be used? At the national level the citizenry might be convinced of the need to hasten the development of domestic natural resources or to strengthen our national defense posture. Again, these projects might be blocked by disagreement as to how the tax cost should be distributed. Most liberals are likely to favor progressive (for example, individual and corporate income) taxes, whereas conservatives plump for regressive (for example, sales and excise) taxes. Inability to reach agreement on the distribution of tax costs may cause the community and the nation to forgo sorely needed social goods and services.

Tax competition. A special tax obstacle to the increased production of social goods exists at the state level. States compete for industry on the basis of low tax rates or preferential tax structures—for example, a tax structure which omits the income tax. "States compete in niggardliness. . . . The result inevitably is that community services are starved." [10]

Advertising and emulation

Advertising and sales promotion activities, which are an integral part of the production and sale of private goods, are almost entirely absent with respect to social goods. For example, while gigantic advertising campaigns by automobile manufacturers operate to convince consumers of the virtues of being a two-car family, no similar persuasion extolls to the citizenry the need for more and better roads on which to operate the ever expanding mass of automobiles. While advertising stresses the merits of stereophonic phonographs, no similar persuasion suggests that better education may be a prerequisite to understanding the fine recorded music playable thereon. The public sector, under persistent pressure to reduce expenditures, is prohibited from the exhortative techniques which characterize the private sector. The result is a tendency for private to expand ahead of social goods.

[10] Hansen, *op. cit.*, pp. 112–113.

Like advertising, emulation also favors greater production of private goods. Families witness the new gadgetry of their neighbors—a second car, an automatic dishwasher, a food freezer, a backyard swimming pool—and feel compelled to "keep pace" by also acquiring these amenities. Emulative inducements work very weakly, if at all, between towns and between states in stimulating the output of social goods and services.

Inflation

The contribution of persistent inflation to the relative shrinkage and deterioration of public goods and services is twofold.

1. Inflation causes product and resource prices to rise in a very uneven and irregular fashion. While the incomes of most profit receivers (stockholders and proprietors) and many wage earners rise rapidly and significantly, the wages and salaries of public employees typically rise belatedly and by considerably less than the general level of prices. That is, inflation tends to reduce the real incomes of many government employees. This seems to be particularly true of the employees of state and local governments, where pay scales are highly formalized and insensitive to the over-all economic environment. Thus, as a practical matter, it is particularly difficult for governmental agencies to match the increasingly lucrative salaries offered by private industries which, in the mainstream of inflation, are generally in a good position to raise their prices and revenues in time with or ahead of the general level of prices. In brief, inflation tends to divert human resources from public services to private industry. Through this diversion, inflation discriminates in favor of private goods at the expense of public goods.

2. Inflation may contribute to social imbalance in another way. By creating inflationary pressure a burgeoning private sector tends to create strong political pressures to retrench on government spending as an anti-inflationary technique. The dogma of price-level stability is invoked to hold down government expenditures. Given the previously noted disposition to hold taxes at present levels and the question-

able effectiveness of a tight money policy, the obvious and politically least offensive means of ameliorating inflation is to restrain government purchases of social goods and services. Thus it is that, when the rate of production of private goods is very high and inflation occurs, the pressure may be greatest for the output of social goods to be constrained. The congressman who, under these circumstances, advocates greater social balance finds himself in the embarrassing position of a "friend of inflation," no matter how crucial the need for the social goods he seeks.

SOME COUNTERARGUMENTS

There are those who seriously question that social imbalance exists or, at least, that it is a pressing problem; and, even if it were to assume acute dimensions, it is argued that the suggested remedies may be both ineffective and very costly.[11]

Does social imbalance really exist?

Critics of the social imbalance thesis have raised a number of points in questioning whether or not social imbalance actually exists.

Affluence and the average consumer. Overinfatuation with the notion of an affluent society and the conception of extravagant and frivolous consumer spending do not square very well with the fact that the median family income in the United States is currently $5,720. Given the current price level, this level of income is hardly permissive of consumer overindulgence on unessential goods and trivia. It is inaccurate and misleading to classify any substantial portion of consumer spending as being devoted to low-priority goods or sheer gadgetry. Furthermore, because total spending for consumer durables is only about 13 per cent of personal consumption, one must be cautious in exaggerating the emphasis our society puts upon such

[11] The counterarguments of this section stem primarily from the writings of Henry C. Wallich cited at the end of this chapter.

goods as color television sets, heavily chromed automobiles, and electric can openers.

Growing expenditures on "the new needs." The rates of increase in spending on the allegedly neglected "new needs" of the social imbalance position—for example, education, research, health and welfare services, and so forth—have been very substantial and, in general, have exceeded the rate of growth in the GNP. Note, for example, that in the 1950–1960 decade expenditures on research increased by 336 per cent, expenditures for highway construction by 146 per cent, and state and local spending for education rose by 161 per cent, while GNP increased by only 77 per cent. Although other social needs—for example, urban renewal and the economic revitalization of depressed areas—have admittedly been neglected, the over-all conclusion must be that many of the "new needs" of the social imbalance position have not been ignored by our society at all; on the contrary, they have been accorded substantial attention.

Forces accelerating social goods production. Though the aforementioned obstacles which allegedly impede the expansion of social goods production infer the existence of social imbalance, there are important counterbiases which facilitate the growth of social goods output at the expense of private goods. (1) The apparent unrelatedness of taxation and public spending decisions has admittedly caused the citizenry to view taxes only in the negative sense, that is, as a cost which entails no observable benefits. However, this same unrelatedness has encouraged the public attitude that government spending is costless, that is, the benefits of social goods and services are relatively free. It is argued that the latter attitude has encouraged public goods production more than the former has inhibited it. (2) Assuming that taxing and public spending decisions are related by the citizenry, it is admittedly true that some citizens rebel at paying taxes whose benefits to them as individuals are uncertain. By the same token, others are very willing to vote for expenditures from which they expect to benefit, although they have not contributed. Indeed, our progressive tax structure means that most of the taxpayers who are in the lower income brackets obtain social goods at bargain prices; hence, there is every reason for them as a political majority to be inclined to favor and vote for the expansion of social goods (Table 35-3). (3) Finally, political reality is such that vocal and active minorities constantly press for and achieve increased public expenditures.

The conclusion, then, is that, considering both the obstacles which inhibit *and* the forces which accelerate social goods production, it is difficult to determine whether, on balance, the public sector is expanding too slowly or too rapidly.

Public spending: a corrective?

Assuming social imbalance actually exists, will the advocated increases in public spending resolve this imbalance? It is argued that for at least two related reasons this need not be the case. First, the complexity of the problem is such that it is misleading to pose it simply as a "public-versus-private expenditure" issue. To suggest that more public and less private spending will resolve social imbalance invokes the implicit assumption that the reallocation of resources from private to public uses will necessarily entail less "unwise" private expenditure and more "wise" public spending, given the value schema of those who insist social imbalance now exists. Is it not possible that reductions in private spending may come more at the expense of adequate housing, medical care, education, and cultural pursuits rather than at the expense of TV sets, electric can openers, and microscopic radios? Might not a disproportionate share of any increase in public expenditures on, say, education be for gymnasia and stadia as opposed to laboratories and classrooms? There is no reason to suppose that public spending is inherently "wise" (on high-priority goods) and more conducive to growth, whereas private spending is "unwise" (on low-priority goods) and not conducive to rapid growth.

Secondly, it is not at all evident that the

"new needs" of society are social goods and therefore clearly fall within the public sector. That is, education, research, providing for old age, health services, and so forth lie in the twilight zone between the public and private sectors of the economy. For example, about one-third of the nation's total research expenditures originate in private industry, and the remaining two-thirds in government. And a very substantial portion of total expenditures on education, particularly higher education, is private. Expenditures on health services are predominantly private.

For both these reasons it is allegedly a misleading oversimplification to say that our major scarcities of specific goods and services can be corrected by merely expanding the public sector at the expense of the private sector of the economy.

Social balance, growth, and international problems

It was noted earlier that those economists who envision the existence of social imbalance feel that it is detrimental to growth and may therefore impair the United States' chances of meeting the Soviet challenge. Professor Wallich is dubious, arguing, on the one hand, that military posture depends as much on the composition of gross national output as it does on the size and rate of growth of output and, on the other, that percentage growth rates are not likely to be the ultimate determinant of the ideological evolution of the underdeveloped nations.

In short, there is little to show that the issues between us and the rest of the world will be governed predominantly by our economic successes, or that we can buy survival with an additional per cent or two of economic growth.[12]

Indeed, if one accepts the previous argument that public expenditures are not necessarily more conducive to growth than private spend-

[12] Henry C. Wallich, *The Cost of Freedom* (New York: Harper & Row, Publishers, 1960), p. 158.

ing, then the production of more social and less private goods is simply not very pertinent to the issue of economic growth.

The cost of social balance

Even if social imbalance is really an acute problem, certain very substantial costs may be involved in its resolution—costs which may well be prohibitive.

1. In the first place, the provision of tax-financed public services is a crude and inefficient way of meeting consumer needs. This is so because, in contrast to the market, there is no neat this-for-that adjustment of benefits and costs. This poor adjustment means that the taxpayer is likely to get more or less of some public service than he desires. Furthermore, the apparently "free" character of social goods and services provides no incentive for the taxpayer to economize in their use.

2. Short of a military emergency the balance of interests in our society works against any marked shifts in the composition of public spending. This "balance of interests" effect causes components of the government budget to increase and decrease, not selectively, but rather on an across-the-board basis. Politicians, it is contended, have a low propensity for setting priorities on various social goods and services. If not all public expenditures are conducive to the elimination of social imbalance, the consequence is that increased spending on "desirable" public programs entails a heavy political surcharge in the form of increased spending on other "less desirable" programs. This means that the over-all cost of those public programs which are essential in rectifying a condition of social imbalance may be inordinately high. In effect, the dollar of public spending is typically subject to a discount; it only buys 75 or 80 cents worth of needed, high-priority social goods and services.

3. Of greatest significance is the argument that the expansion of the public sector advocated as a corrective for social imbalance may come at the very high cost of freedom. The cumulative effect of expanding a number of particular government programs could be a serious threat

to freedom, despite the fact that each individual program may be of merit. In drawing a line between the public and the private sectors, it must be recognized that not only economics, but also freedom, is involved. "The centralized economy puts a strain upon democracy and freedom; the free economy does not." As a practical guide, Professor Wallich suggests that, because the expansion of government impinges upon freedom and causes

the cumulative discouragement of private and local initiative . . . , it would have to be shown that the people could do something only very imperfectly, and the government very substantially better, before the government should step in.[13]

CORRECTIVES FOR SOCIAL IMBALANCE

It is not the purpose of this chapter to argue that social imbalance does or does not exist in our economy, but rather to pose the controversy for the reader's understanding and evaluation. Nevertheless, it is interesting to examine what might be done to remedy social imbalance if it now exists or arises in the future as a significant economic problem. A number of events and policies would be helpful in redressing social imbalance. Unfortunately, the simplest and most effective correctives tend to be either the least likely to occur or the least palatable politically.

Disarmament

Potentially the happiest solution to the problem of social imbalance would be an effective disarmament agreement. The presumption here is that a cessation of the arms race would set the stage for a rechanneling of government military spending to such non-military social goods and services as research, education, urban renewal, and so forth. This transfer of government expenditures from defense to non-defense categories has the virtue of imposing no direct constraints upon private goods output; a crude, direct clash between private and

[13] *Ibid.*, pp. 57 and 71.

public wants is happily avoided. In fact, in the absence of the huge backlog of consumer and business demand and the condition of over-employment which facilitated reconversion after World War II, increased spending on public goods might be imperative in sustaining full employment.

Most obviously, the main difficulty with demobilization as a remedy for social imbalance is the fact that its potential pleasantness as a corrective is greatly exceeded by its unlikeliness of occurrence. Even waiving this, there is a further possible problem. Disarmament could generate tremendous public pressures for tax cuts; tax rates which are acceptable during hot or cold wars might prove highly objectionable when peace breaks out. Our post-World War II experience suggests that it might be naïve to expect any easy transfer of resources from armaments production to the production of "civilian" social goods and services.

Growth as a palliative

It must also be noted that the extent to which the provision of more social goods collides with the production of private goods depends upon the rate of growth achieved by the economy. The correcting of social imbalance in a static economy—that is, an economy whose GNP is unchanging—obviously implies a painful retrenchment in consumer goods production both absolutely and relatively. However, if the economy continues to achieve the 3 to 4 per cent annual growth rate of past full-employment years, an annual increment of $16 billion to $21 billion in output will result, as the simple application of these percentages to the 1961 GNP of $521 billion quickly reveals. A division of this increment which favors social goods can clearly alleviate social imbalance and simultaneously provide for modest increases in total consumption. Moreover, it is of no little significance that such a distribution of the increment might contribute to an acceleration of the growth rate.

Again, this solution is not devoid of problems. Even with a favorable annual growth rate, the correcting of fairly acute social imbalance may require an absolute decline in private consumption. Then, too, the growth process itself may intensify certain aspects of a social imbalance problem. Has it not been noted earlier that the industrialization and urbanization which characterize economic growth are basic factors underlying the increasing demand for social goods and services?

Acknowledging that demobilization is a pleasant but unlikely answer and that economic growth is a palliative in correcting social imbalance, let us consider two more concrete and more immediate proposals.

Increased use of sales taxes

Some economists have strongly endorsed the greater use of sales taxation as a means of attacking social imbalance.[14] Because they are shifted to consumers, sales taxes raise the prices of consumer goods. The result is that a given total amount of consumer spending commands less private goods and automatically provides more government revenues to reabsorb the released resources through larger purchases of social goods. As private production expands, public revenues and therefore public goods increase on a pro rata basis. Furthermore, given the present high level of marginal income tax rates and the fact that sales taxes are effectuated through the price mechanism, the financing of increased public expenditures by

[14] Galbraith notes that the personal and corporate income taxes which provide about 80 per cent of Federal tax revenues are progressive and thus admirable agents of social balance. That is, an increase in the national income will result in more than proportionate increases in tax revenues for Federal use. At the same time, he emphasizes that (1) over half of Federal revenues are committed to defense expenditures and (2) social imbalance is more crucial at state and local levels. Galbraith rejects property taxes as a means to social balance because, in contrast to the sales tax, the property tax base is relatively insensitive to changes in the over-all level of economic activity. This means that property tax rates must be raised to finance additional social goods, resulting in a conflict with the aforementioned resistance to increases in tax rates. Galbraith, *op. cit.*, pp. 311–315; Hansen, *Economic Issues of the 1960's*, pp. 104–110.

sales rather than income taxation is less likely to blunt incentives. Finally, to the degree that sales taxes are hidden in prices and paid in relatively small amounts spread more or less evenly over a period of time, the cost of the social goods financed thereby is neither very explicit nor very immediate to the taxpayer. To the extent that this remoteness or vagueness of tax costs offsets the remoteness of social goods benefits, the cause of social balance may be furthered.

A new budget philosophy?

Current conceptions of fiscal policy—in particular, the cyclically balanced budget and functional finance (Chapter 14)—embrace the notion of compensatory spending by government. That is, the public sector, and especially the level of government spending, should be adjusted to compensate for the exuberance or lethargy of the private sector of the economy. This implies that social goods and services are expendable, or of a lower urgency, than private goods. Hence, if private consumption and investment spending are at high levels, it is held that government purchases of social goods can and should be sacrificed in the interest of restraining inflationary pressures. As already noted, the application of such a fiscal policy over time can contribute to social imbalance.

The most direct and most obvious assault upon a social imbalance problem would therefore seem to be the development and acceptance of a new budget philosophy whereby private and social goods would somehow be evaluated on their own merits and neither would be considered inherently inferior and therefore expendable in the pursuit of economic stability. The goal is a *socially optimum budget* wherein government spending is aligned more closely with the long-run goal of social balance and less closely with the short-run goal of alleviating cyclical variations in output, employment, and the price level. In other words, if social imbalance actually exists, there may be a need for a new budget philosophy which pays attention, not only to the full-employment, but also to the resource alloca-

tion, aspect of the economizing problem. Under this philosophy the public and private sectors would compete on a more nearly equal footing for the economy's scarce resources. Depending upon the initial presence or absence of social imbalance, this new budget philosophy may or may not call for an expansion of the public sector of the economy.

There can be no doubt that the problems involved in the acceptance and application of a socially optimum budget would be considerable in both number and severity. Two of the more obvious ones require special mention.

1. The political and administrative obstacles to the adoption and application of this new budget philosophy are obvious. Indeed, many of these are essentially the same obstacles to the production of social goods and services which we have already discussed in this chapter.

2. Would the adoption of a socially optimum budget philosophy seriously weaken the government's role in providing for full employment and reasonable price stability? Would discretionary fiscal policy as we now know it cease to be an important stabilizing force in our economy? More specifically, if government spending is fixed at a level designed to fulfill society's demands for social goods, does this not rule out the compensatory changes in government spending which current fiscal philosophies require?

Although a weakening of fiscal policy *might* be involved, a number of offsetting considerations must be noted. First, the level of government spending is not now as flexible as it might be. Previously mentioned attitudinal and political factors make increases in government spending difficult to negotiate. And the fixity and size of defense and defense-related expenditures in the Federal budget make significant reductions equally improbable. In the second place, it is possible that taxation may be strengthened as a fiscal device. In Chapter 14 it was noted that postwar discretionary fiscal policy had been criticized because of failure to invoke countercyclical tax changes. Greater flexibility in altering taxes could make up for any possible weakening of fiscal policy arising from an increase in the rigidity of government spending which a socially optimum budget might demand. Third, because of the many political problems which impede the enacting of appropriate fiscal policy (Chapter 14), a number of economists have taken the position that we would do well to strengthen our automatic or built-in stabilizers and thereby reduce our dependence upon discretionary fiscal policy. Still other economists have called for the consideration of new stabilizing techniques to supplement existing fiscal policy.[15] Such changes will tend to compensate for any potential weakening of discretionary fiscal policy which a socially optimum budget philosophy might entail. And, to the extent that future inflations are of the "new" cost-push and structural varieties, traditional fiscal policy will be inappropriate in any event. In summary, although at first glance a budget philosophy which pays greater attention to the achieving of social balance would thereby seem to be less effective in providing for economic stability, there are a number of offsetting considerations which make this something less than a clear-cut conclusion.

SUMMARY

1. Economists are currently debating whether economic growth and the affluence it has brought to our economy have created a social imbalance problem, that is, an overallocation of resources to private goods and an underallocation to social goods. In addition to having an obvious and direct bearing upon the problem of efficiently allocating resources, the social imbalance issue also has implications for economic stability and economic growth.

2. Those who feel that a social imbalance problem now exists argue that the amount of social goods and services demanded has increased ahead of the amount supplied. On the one hand, Wagner's Law asserts that as an economy becomes increasingly wealthy the demand for social goods and services increases both absolutely and relatively. On the other hand, there exist in our society a number of

[15] See question 9 at the end of Chapter 14.

obstacles which inhibit social goods production. (*a*) The ideological framework of capitalism and the attitudes fostered thereby are not conducive to an expansion of social goods production. (*b*) The growing urban population whose social goods needs are most acute is allegedly underrepresented politically. (*c*) The remoteness and uncertainty of the benefits from social goods puts them at a psychological disadvantage as compared to private goods. (*d*) A number of tax problems make it difficult to finance social goods production. (*e*) Advertising and emulation are forces which tend to pull resources toward private goods production and away from social goods production. (*f*) Inflation draws resources from the public to the private sector and simultaneously creates political pressures to cut government spending because private spending is high.

3. Equally respected economists take the opposite position, and in so doing offer a number of counterarguments. (*a*) Statistical evidence and a careful consideration of both those forces which retard and those which accelerate social goods production do not bear out the contention that social imbalance exists; they may even suggest that, in general, society's "new needs" are receiving ample attention. (*b*) Increased public spending may not correct social imbalance because, first, this falsely assumes that all private goods are low-priority goods and all social goods are high-priority goods and, second, it is not correct to suppose that all the "new needs" of society entail public, as opposed to private, goods. (*c*) It is very questionable that the implications of a social imbalance problem for American economic growth and United States–Soviet competition for the allegiance of the new emerging nations are as clear-cut or dramatic as those who embrace the social imbalance position would suggest. (*d*) The economic and political costs of correcting a social imbalance problem might be more substantial than the problem itself: the nonmarket and "free" character of social goods means that they might easily be overproduced; the tendency of public spending to increase "across the board" rather than selectively imposes a heavy surcharge on the production of high-urgency social goods; and, finally, a substantial increase in the production of social goods may seriously impair individual freedoms.

4. If social imbalance exists now or is encountered in the years ahead, disarmament and the achievement of rapid economic growth are potential means of redressing this imbalance.

More specific remedies are an increased use of sales taxation and the adoption of a socially optimum budget philosophy which removes social goods from the stigma of being "expendable." All these potential correctives entail serious questions concerning likelihood of occurrence and substantial problems of political and administrative feasibility.

QUESTIONS AND STUDY SUGGESTIONS

1. What is social imbalance? Why is it an economic problem? Why is social imbalance more likely to arise in a wealthy, growing economy than in a poor, static economy?

2. What is Wagner's Law? Do you think this law is valid? Explain how (a) the character of social goods, (b) advertising, and (c) inflation might contribute to a social imbalance problem.

3. Explain why one might argue that an increase in government spending may not resolve a social imbalance problem.

4. What are the possible economic and political costs of correcting social imbalance? How important do you estimate these costs to be? In your opinion are these costs prohibitive?

5. Carefully evaluate the following statement: "The root cause of our difficulty lies not in our income or our growth potential but in certain American habits of mind, carried over from earlier phases of our history, and in the workings of the political process, as they affect the allocation of resources. This interplay of intellectual conception and conventional politics conspires to make it difficult for Americans to increase the scale of public outlays except at moments of acute crises. Here lies a danger to the national interest as well as a threat to the quality of American society."[16]

6. Why is the greater use of sales taxes, as opposed to income or property taxes, recommended as a corrective for social imbalance? Why might disarmament and rapid economic growth help correct a social imbalance?

7. What are the basic characteristics of a socially optimum budget? How does it differ from functional finance? To what degree, if any, do you think a socially optimum budget philosophy would impair achievement of the goals of full employment and price level stability? Explain.

SELECTED REFERENCES

Bator, Francis M., *The Question of Government Spending* (New York: Harper & Row, Publishers, 1960).

Downs, Anthony, "Why the Government Budget Is Too Small in a Democracy," *World Politics*, July, 1960, pp. 541–563.

Galbraith, John Kenneth, *The Affluent Society* (Boston: Houghton Mifflin Company, 1958), particularly chaps. 18, 19, and 22.

[16] W. W. Rostow, "Summary and Policy Implications," in Joint Economic Committee, *Comparisons of the United States and Soviet Economies* (Washington: 1960), p. 601.

Hansen, Alvin H., *The American Economy* (New York: McGraw-Hill Book Company, Inc., 1957), chap. 8.

Hansen, Alvin H., *Economic Issues of the 1960's* (New York: McGraw-Hill Book Company, Inc., 1960), chaps. 7 and 8.

Rostow, W. W., *The United States in the World Arena* (New York: Harper & Row, Publishers, 1960), Book 6.

Wallich, Henry C., *The Cost of Freedom* (New York: Harper & Row, Publishers, 1960), particularly chap. 5.

Wallich, Henry C., "Private vs. Public: Could Kenneth Galbraith be Wrong?" *Harper's Magazine*, October, 1961, pp. 12–25.

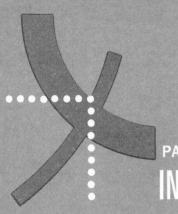

PART 7

INTERNATIONAL ECONOMICS, THE UNDERDEVELOPED COUNTRIES, AND THE SOVIET ECONOMIC CHALLENGE

Chapter 37

INTERNATIONAL TRADE AND
INTERNATIONAL EQUILIBRIUM

THUS FAR OUR ANALYSIS of American capitalism has been based upon the assumption that it is a "closed," or isolated, economy. This obviously is not true. Our economy is linked to other nations of the world through a complex network of international trade and financial relationships. It is the purpose of this and the following chapter to describe and analyze these relationships.

The specific objectives of the present chapter are fourfold: (1) to explain the bases of international trade, noting the ways in which it is similar to, and dissimilar to, domestic trade, (2) to introduce the monetary aspects of international trade, (3) to define, analyze, and interpret the international balance of payments, and (4) to discuss international disequilibrium and the mechanisms for restoring international equilibrium.

INTERNATIONAL SPECIALIZATION

The same basic rationale underlies both domestic and international trade. We recall from Chapter 3 that individuals or regions can achieve a greater real output and therefore a higher standard of living by specializing according to comparative advantage; that is, each individual or region should specialize in those goods which it can produce with the greatest relative advantage or the least relative disadvantage.[1] This results in a more efficient allocation of resources, as is evidenced in the fact that more output will result from the same volume of resources. The same reasoning extends beyond international boundaries. The world can achieve a more efficient allocation of resources and a higher real output by specializing according to comparative advantage and trading.

We must recognize, however, that there are limitations upon international specialization. Only in very rare instances is a single nation responsible for the world's production of some product. South Africa's role as the sole producer of diamonds is the exception which helps illustrate the rule. Even in the "one-crop" economies, for example, the sugar economy of Cuba and the coffee economy of Brazil, we find that many other goods are produced for both export and domestic use. In short, most products of international trade are produced by several, if not many, nations. Specialization is less than complete.

Why is this so? The first limitation upon specialization is economic and goes back to the production possibilities curve and the law of increasing costs. As a nation expands its production of any particular commodity, it must employ resources which are less and less suited to that commodity's production. To illustrate:

[1] The student should reread the examples given in Chapter 3, substituting, say, the United States for Anderson and Brazil for Brooks.

Farmers in Iowa, Illinois, and a few other Midwestern states can probably produce corn at a lower cost than can farmers in any other nation. Yet the United States does not produce the world's total supply of corn, because to do so would necessitate the use of more land in the South, New England, and the Far West for corn production. Since land and climate in these latter areas are not particularly suitable to corn, costs would be considerably higher. Therefore, some foreign farmers in, say, Canada or South America may produce corn at lower costs than it can be produced in some parts of the United States. In short, the comparative advantage of the United States in corn does not apply to *all* levels of output. This means that many nations may export the same product, and, as a matter of fact, a given nation may both export and import the same product.

Secondly, there are political limitations upon international specialization. These limitations, which often stem from the disadvantages that specialization entails (Chapter 3), usually take the form of governmentally imposed trade restrictions which limit the size of the export market for a product. In particular, the United States flatly prohibits the export of military equipment and strategic raw materials to the Soviet Union and has attempted to persuade allied nations and friendly neutrals to follow similar policies. Furthermore, the United States has placed import quotas and embargoes upon certain foreign farm products to avoid disruption of the domestic farm price support programs. Finally, political pressures exerted by domestic producers of certain goods have resulted in trade barriers which restrict the amounts foreign firms can sell in the United States and thereby limit the extent to which those nations can specialize. High tariffs on watches imported to the United States limit the degree to which the Swiss can specialize in watchmaking.

Domestic and international trade

If the basic principle of comparative advantage underlies both domestic and international trade, then why do we devote special attention to the topic of international trade? There are several reasons:

1. Though the difference is a matter of degree, the mobility of resources is considerably less between nations than it is within nations. American workers, for example, are free to move from Iowa to California or from Maine to Texas. Of course, there are sociological limits on this mobility, but otherwise there are no serious obstacles. If a worker wants to move, he can do so. Crossing international boundaries is a different story. Immigration laws, not to mention language and cultural barriers, put severe restrictions upon the migration of labor between nations. Different tax laws, different governmental regulations, different business practices, and a host of other institutional barriers limit the migration of real capital over international boundaries.

International trade is a substitute for the international mobility of resources. If human and property resources do not move readily between nations, then the movement of goods and services can serve as an effective substitute.

2. Each nation uses a different currency. This poses complications. For example, in buying a British automobile you must first buy British pounds sterling (£) and then spend these pounds on the Hillman or Austin of your choice.

3. As already noted, international trade is subject to political interferences and controls which differ markedly in degree and kind from those applying to domestic trade.

American trade

In 1961 United States exports of goods and services were slightly greater than, and its imports somewhat less than, 5 per cent of the national income. And this 5 per cent figure clearly understates the significance of international trade to the United States and, in particular, to the nations with which we deal, for several reasons:

1. The 5 per cent figure is very large in absolute terms. In 1961, for example, American exports of goods and services totaled in excess of $28 billion, and imports were about $23 billion. Though other nations may derive as

high as 30 or 40 per cent or more of their national incomes from international trade, the absolute volume of American imports and exports exceeds that of any other nation.

2. Despite the versatility of American capitalism, we are almost entirely dependent upon other nations for our supplies of specific commodities. Bananas, coffee, spices, tea, raw silk, nickel, tin, natural rubber, and diamonds are cases in point. Similarly, a host of American industries are highly dependent upon foreign markets. Almost all segments of agriculture rely heavily upon foreign markets—rice, wheat, cotton, and tobacco exports vary from one-fourth to more than one-half of total output. The petroleum, automobile, machine tool, and coal industries are only a few of many American industries which sell significant portions of their output in international markets. Table 37-1 shows the major commodity exports and imports of the United States.

3. Changes in net foreign spending, that is, in the difference between the value of a nation's exports and imports, will have multiple effects upon the level of national income in roughly the same fashion as will fluctuations in the various types of domestic spending. A small change in the volume of American imports and exports can have magnified repercussions upon the domestic levels of income, employment, and prices.

With these points in mind we need not belabor the significance of international trade for such nations as the Netherlands, Japan, Australia, and Great Britain, whose volumes of international trade range from one-fourth to over one-half their national incomes.

So much for the volume and composition of American trade. Let us now survey its financial aspects.

FOREIGN EXCHANGE

Though the particular techniques of financing international transactions are rather detailed, their general nature can be readily grasped. To simplify our discussion of international finance, we shall treat trade on a nation-to-nation basis, recognizing that in practice most trade is carried on by private businesses. Thus in talking about "United States exports" we really mean the sales of thousands of

TABLE 37-1. PRINCIPAL COMMODITY EXPORTS AND IMPORTS OF THE UNITED STATES, 1961 (in millions)

Exports	Amount	Per cent of total	Imports	Amount	Per cent of total
Machinery	$ 4,317	21	Wood and paper	$ 1,645	11
Automobiles and other vehicles	2,814	14	Petroleum and products	1,543	11
Chemicals	1,680	8	Machinery and vehicles	1,464	10
Grains and preparations	1,650	8	Coffee, cocoa, and tea	1,240	9
Iron and steel manufactures	1,291	6	Textiles	1,237	8
Unmanufactured cotton	988	5	Nonferrous metals	1,148	8
Petroleum and products	479	3	Sugar	570	4
Coal	361	2	Meat products	324	2
All other exports	6,720	33	All other imports	5,491	37
Total	$20,300	100	Total	$14,652	100

SOURCE: "Statistical Abstract of the United States, 1961," pp. 881–884.

private American businesses to foreign buyers and do not imply that American export trade has been nationalized. Furthermore, we shall couch much of the remainder of this chapter in terms of a two-nation world. Again this is to simplify; bilateral trade can be discussed more readily than can multilateral trade. Now, how are international transactions financed?

When the United States purchases goods and services from foreign nations, Americans must exchange dollars for foreign currencies in negotiating these purchases. For example, suppose an American firm wants to buy £10,000 worth of woolens from a British manufacturer. Because the British firm must pay its own obligations in pounds rather than dollars, the American firm must somehow exchange its dollars for pounds in order to make payment to the British firm. How is this accomplished? Suppose the *rate of exchange*—that is, the rate or price at which dollars can be exchanged for pounds and vice versa—is $3 for £1. The American importer can go to an American bank and purchase for $30,000 a check for £10,000. This check can then be sent to the British woolens manufacturer in payment for the desired woolens. But where does the American bank get pounds sterling? It buys pounds from a British bank for $30,000, and in so doing makes American dollars available to the British bank. Our basic conclusion is this: American import transactions simultaneously create a demand for foreign exchange (pounds in this case) and make a supply of domestic currency (dollars) available to foreigners.

American export transactions have precisely the opposite results. Suppose a British manufacturer wants to purchase $30,000 worth of American-made machinery. At a $3-for-£1 exchange rate, the British manufacturer can buy $30,000 for £10,000 at a British bank and use this $30,000 check to make payment to the American machine manufacturer. The British bank gets the needed $30,000 from an American bank by buying it for £10,000. Our conclusion: American export transactions create a foreign demand for dollars and simultaneously make a supply of foreign currency available to Americans.

We can say, then, that American exports make available a supply of foreign currencies, and American imports create a demand for those foreign monies. Similarly, British exports to the United States earn a supply of dollars and British imports create a demand for these dollars. Briefly, *any nation's exports finance, or "pay for," its imports.* By selling to foreign nations a given country earns the foreign exchange it needs in order to buy from those nations.

INTERNATIONAL BALANCE OF PAYMENTS

Nations of the world systematically record and summarize *all* the transactions which take place between their residents (including individuals, businesses, and governmental units) and the residents of all other foreign nations and present them in an annual accounting statement called the *international balance of payments.* Despite its name, this statement is more like a business firm's profit and loss statement than a balance sheet. Like a profit and loss statement, a nation's balance of payments records its sales to, and purchases from, all other nations, and it accounts for any differences between its sales (receipts) and its purchases (expenditures). A simplified balance of payments for the United States in 1961 is presented in Table 37-2. Let us analyze this accounting statement to see what it reveals about American international trade and finance.

Balance of trade

In items 1 and 2 on the United States balance of payments, it is important to note that exports and imports are defined rather broadly. There is no question about the inclusion of items 1a and b as a part of American exports. As with domestic trade, international trade involves the exchange of both goods and services. The United States exports not only machinery, automobiles, and farm products, but also sells transportation services, insurance, and brokerage services to residents of foreign nations. Note, however, that one of the very special services which foreigners get from the United

TABLE 37-2. THE UNITED STATES INTERNATIONAL BALANCE OF PAYMENTS, 1961 (in billions)

(1) United States exports		$+28.3
(1a) Goods	$+19.9	
(1b) Services	+4.7	
(1c) Income from United States investments abroad	+3.6	
(2) United States imports		−23.1
(2a) Goods	$−14.5	
(2b) Services	−7.7	
(2c) Income from foreign investments in United States	−0.9	
(3) Net balance due United States on exports and imports		+5.2
(4) Balancing transactions:		
(4a) Net unilateral transfers		−4.3
(4b) Net capital movements (short- and long-term)		−2.6
United States capital outflow	−4.9	
Capital inflow to United States	+2.3	
(4c) Net gold flow from the United States		+2.5
(4d) Errors and omissions		−0.8
		0.0

SOURCE: "Survey of Current Business," March, 1962, p. 22. Details may not add to totals because of rounding.

States consists of the services of American money capital which has been invested abroad. As item 1c indicates, the dividend and interest income received from the use of this American capital which has been invested in foreign nations is a payment for the American "export" of the services of this capital. United States imports, item 2, obviously include three analogous items. Americans import goods and services, including the services of foreign money capital which has been invested in the United States.

A comparison of items 1 and 2 reveals that United States exports of $28.3 billion exceeded United States imports of $23.1 billion by about $5.2 billion in 1961. Economists call the difference between a nation's total exports and its total imports the *balance of trade*. If a nation's exports exceed its imports, as is the case here, a nation is said to have a balance of trade *surplus*. On the other hand, if a country's imports exceed its exports, it is incurring a trade *deficit*. Note that, because United States exports are the rest of the world's imports and United States imports are the rest of the world's exports, an American trade surplus of $5.2 billion obviously appears as a trade deficit to the rest of the world in its trade with the United States.

In Table 37-2 we have designated American exports with plus signs and American imports with minus signs. You will recall from our earlier discussion of foreign exchange that American exports entail payments of dollars from foreign buyers to the United States. These transactions, which involve dollar "inpayments" to the United States, have been marked plus. Conversely, American imports require that Americans make dollars available to foreigners. Such transactions, which involve dollar "outpayments" from the United States, have been marked minus. Thus the fact that the balance-due figure is a *plus* $5.2 billion indicates the United States incurred a trade surplus, and as a result net inpayments of that amount are due the United States from the rest of the world. This $5.2 billion balance due the United States correctly suggests that the rest of the world had to enter into some additional transactions so as to get the extra dollars needed to finance its trade deficit with the United States.

Balancing transactions

These extra dollars were obtained through the three balancing transactions shown as item 4 on the balance of payments. The net result of these transactions must be to make dollars available to foreigners; that is, over-all they must be minus transactions. Item 4a, net unilateral transfers, indicates that the United States made net dollar gifts of some $4.3 billion to the rest of the world during 1961.

A small portion of the gifts were private, for example, immigrants' remittances to their families in the "old country." The bulk of these grants, however, were United States government grants made for purposes of providing military assistance to allies or aid in the economic growth of the underdeveloped nations. Item 4b indicates that the United States made net investments in, and extended net loans to, foreign nations in the amount of $2.6 billion dollars. These loans and investments were both public and private.

These two balancing transactions totaled $6.9 billion and therefore provided foreign nations with more than enough dollars to settle their balance of trade deficit with the United States. Foreign nations used the extra dollars to purchase gold bullion from the United States. Because gold bullion is readily acceptable as a medium of international exchange, we can say that foreign nations added to their international monetary (gold) reserves by receiving American grants, investments, and loans which were more than sufficient to cover their trade deficit with the United States. From the American point of view the trade surplus of the United States in 1961 was inadequate to cover the flow of American grants, loans, and investments abroad, causing the United States to lose gold reserves. We shall have more to say about this gold outflow in Chapter 38.

Though a trade imbalance—a trade deficit or surplus—may occur, the balance of payments must always balance. It must balance for the simple reason that every transaction must be settled in one way or another. If an individual or nation sells (exports) more than it purchases (imports), it must provide a net amount of its currency through gifts and lending to cover the difference. Similarly, a nation can only purchase (import) more than it sells (export) by being on the receiving end of grants and loans.

INTERNATIONAL DISEQUILIBRIUM

Though a balance of payments statement always balances, nations are not always in equilibrium in achieving that balance. Nations can and do incur balance of payments deficits and surpluses. Although international equilibrium is a rather slippery concept, we can say that *international equilibrium exists when a nation's "normal" needs for foreign exchange are met by its "normal," or "dependable," sources of supply.* International equilibrium implies a stable, or maintainable, situation. Conversely, disequilibrium means that a nation is achieving a balance in its balance of payments through some abnormal, undependable sources of foreign currencies which are of a temporary, or stopgap, nature and therefore not maintainable.

Now at first glance it might appear that international equilibrium exists only when a nation's exports (item 1) equals its imports (item 2), eliminating the need for any balancing transactions. But this is not the case, because long-term private capital flows can be regarded as a normal source of foreign currencies for certain nations. That is, private long-term loans and investments can and do flow rather persistently into some nations, providing a regular and dependable source of foreign currencies. Thus we can say that, if a nation's exports and its net long-term capital inflows equal its imports, it is in international equilibrium. A young, expanding economy in which there are many opportunities for profitable investment and lending may achieve international equilibrium in its balance of payments even though its imports are persistently greater than its exports. Indeed, the United States was in precisely this position throughout much of its early history, receiving large capital inflows from

Great Britain in particular to offset an American trade deficit.

A nation incurs a balance of *payments deficit* when its imports exceed the sum of its exports and net private capital inflows. The best evidence of such a condition is that this nation must invoke such temporary nonmaintainable measures as selling gold reserves for foreign exchange, obtaining short-term foreign credit, or receiving grants and loans from foreign governments to cover the deficit and make the balance of payments balance. These transactions are temporary and nonmaintainable, because a nation's gold stock and its ability to get credit from exporters and foreign banks will be limited. Similarly, a nation cannot depend upon the receipt of loans and grants from foreign governments. In short, such transactions are evidence that a nation is not "paying its way" internationally; that is, it is living beyond its income. An outstanding example of a balance of payments disequilibrium occurred in the immediate post-World War II period, when most nations of Europe incurred large and persistent payments deficits in their trade with the United States. Of course, such deficits appear as balance of *payments surpluses* to the United States, evidence of which took the form of American government loans and grants, the granting of short-term credit by American firms and banks, and the receipt of gold from abroad. The causes and cures of the postwar "dollar shortage" will be examined in detail in the next chapter.

RESTORING INTERNATIONAL EQUILIBRIUM

Because it is a nonmaintainable situation, some adjustments must occur to correct a balance of payments disequilibrium. There are three basic mechanisms for restoring international equilibrium: (1) freely flexible exchange rates, (2) the international gold standard, and (3) exchange control.

Freely flexible exchange rates

When foreign currencies can be freely bought and sold, the rate of exchange between any two currencies will be determined by the forces of supply and demand. Let us examine the rate, or price, at which American dollars might be exchanged for British pounds sterling. As indicated in Figure 37-1, the demand for pounds will be downsloping, and the supply of pounds will be upsloping. Why? The downsloping demand for pounds shown by D_oD_o reflects the fact that, if pounds become less expensive to Americans, British goods will become cheaper to Americans. This causes Americans to demand larger quantities of British goods and therefore larger amounts of pounds with which to buy those goods. The supply of pounds is upsloping like S_1S_1, because, as the dollar price of pounds rises, the British will be inclined to purchase more American goods. The reason, of course, is that at higher and higher dollar prices for pounds, the British can obviously get more American dollars and therefore more American goods per pound. In other words, American goods become cheaper to the British, inducing the British to buy more American goods. Such purchases, we have seen, will make larger and larger quantities of pounds available to Americans. The intersection of the supply and demand for pounds will determine the dollar price of pounds. Suppose that the equilibrium rate of exchange is $3 to £1. At this rate American-British trade is in balance; American imports from Great Britain create a demand for the precise quantity of pounds which American exports to Great Britain make available.

Now let us assume that American tastes change so that they begin to import more British goods. Americans want more Hillman automobiles, more Scotch whiskey, and more Harris tweeds. This increase in imports causes an American trade deficit, and if it is not offset by long-term private loans and investments from Britain, an American balance of payments deficit results. The immediate impact of the increase in American imports from Britain is to increase the American demand for pounds, as indicated by the shift from D_oD_o to D_1D_1 in Figure 37-1. Because of this shift, a shortage of pounds equal to AB now appears at the existing $3-for-£1 exchange rate. Since this is a free competitive market, the shortage will change the exchange rate (the dollar price of

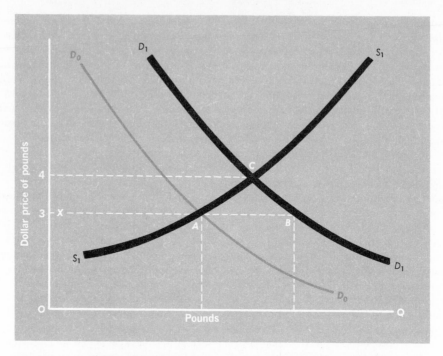

FIGURE 37-1. ADJUSTMENTS UNDER FLEXIBLE EXCHANGE RATES, THE GOLD STANDARD, AND EXCHANGE CONTROLS.
Under flexible rates an American trade deficit at the $3-for-£1 rate would be corrected by an increase in the rate to $4 for £1. Under the gold standard the deficit would cause changes in domestic prices and incomes, which would shift the demand for (D_1D_1) and the supply of (S_1S_1) pounds into equilibrium at the $3-for-£1 rate. Under exchange controls the government would ration the available supply of pounds XA among persons demanding the quantity XB.

pounds) from $3 for £1 to, say, $4 for £1. This obviously means that the value of the dollar has depreciated—it is worth less—in international trade.

This change in the exchange rate will alter the relative attractiveness of American imports and exports in such a way as to restore equilibrium in the balance of payments of the United States. From the American point of view, as the dollar price of pounds changes from $3 to $4, the Hillman automobile priced at £500, which formerly cost an American $1,500, now costs $2,000. Also other British goods will be more expensive to Americans. Hence, American imports of British goods will tend to decline.

Graphically, this is shown as a move from point B toward point C in Figure 37-1.

Conversely, from Britain's standpoint the exchange rate, that is, the pound price of dollars, has fallen. The international value of the pound has appreciated. The British previously got only $3 for £1; now they get $4 for £1. American goods are therefore cheaper to the British, and as a result American exports to Great Britain tend to rise. In Figure 37-1 this is indicated by the move from point A toward point C. These two adjustments—a decrease in American imports from Great Britain and an increase in American exports to Great Britain —are precisely what are needed to correct the

American balance of payments deficit. The reader should reason through the operation of freely fluctuating exchange rates in correcting an initial American balance of payments surplus in its trade with Great Britain.

Though freely flexible exchange rates automatically correct a balance of payments disequilibrium, they may entail several serious problems:

1. The risks associated with flexible exchange rates are likely to discourage the flow of trade. To illustrate: Suppose an American automobile dealer contracts to purchase ten Hillman cars for £5,000. At the current exchange rate of, say, $3 for £1, the American importer expects to pay $15,000 for these automobiles. But if in the two- or three-month shipping period the rate of exchange changes to $4 for £1, the £5,000 payment contracted by the American importer will now amount to $20,000. Obviously, this unheralded increase in the dollar price of pounds may easily turn the American importer's anticipated profits into substantial losses. Aware at the outset of the possibility of an adverse change in the exchange rate, the American importer may simply not be willing to assume the risks involved. He therefore confines his operations to domestic automobiles with the result that international trade does not occur on this item. Note, too, that contracting for payment in terms of dollars rather than pounds does not solve the risk problem, but merely shifts the risk to the British exporter.

2. A nation's terms of trade will tend to be worsened by a decline in the international value of its currency. For example, an increase in the dollar price of pounds will mean that the United States must export a larger volume of goods and services to finance a given level of imports from Britain.

3. Flexible exchange rates may also have some destabilizing effects upon the domestic economy as widely fluctuating exchange rates stimulate and then depress those industries producing internationally traded goods. Furthermore, if the American economy is operating at full employment and the international value of its currency depreciates as in our illustration, the subsequent rise in American exports

and decline in imports will tend to increase net foreign investment and cause domestic price inflation.

For all these reasons nations of the world have sought a means of stabilizing exchange rates. For a half century prior to World War I and again for a period in the 1920s, most of the major trading nations looked to the international gold standard for that stability.

The gold standard

A nation is on the gold standard when it fulfills two conditions: (1) It must define its monetary unit in terms of a certain quantity of gold and stand ready to convert gold into paper money and paper money into gold at the rate stipulated in its definition of the monetary unit. (2) It must allow gold to be freely exported and imported.

If each nation defines its monetary unit in terms of gold, the different currencies will have a fixed relationship to one another. For example, suppose the United States defines a dollar as being worth, say, 25 grains of gold and Britain defines its pound sterling as being worth 75 grains of gold. This means that a British pound is worth 75/25 dollars or, simply, £1 equals $3.

Now, if we momentarily ignore the costs of packing, insuring, and shipping gold between countries, under the gold standard the rate of exchange would not vary from this $3-for-£1 rate. And the reason is clear: no one in the United States would pay more than $3 for £1, because he could always buy 75 grains of gold for $3 in the United States, ship it to Britain, and sell it for £1. Nor would an Englishman pay more than £1 for $3. Why should he, when he could buy 75 grains of gold in England for £1, send it to the United States, and sell it for $3?

Of course, in practice the costs of packing, insuring, and shipping gold must be taken into account. But these costs would only amount to a few cents per 75 grains of gold. For example, if these costs were 3 cents for 75 grains of gold, Americans wanting pounds would pay up to $3.03 for a pound rather than buy and export 75 grains of gold to get that pound. Why?

Because it would cost them $3 for the 75 grains of gold plus 3 cents to send it to England to be exchanged for £1. This $3.03 exchange rate at which gold would flow out of the United States is called the *gold export point*. Conversely, the exchange rate would fall to $2.97 before gold would flow into the United States. Englishmen wanting dollars would accept as little as $2.97 in exchange for £1, because from the $3 which they could get by buying 75 grains of gold in England and reselling it in the United States 3 cents must be subtracted to pay shipping and related costs. This $2.97 exchange rate at which gold would flow into the United States is called the *gold import point*. Our basic conclusion is that under the gold standard the flow of gold between nations would result in exchange rates which for all practical purposes are fixed.

But these gold flows would do more than stabilize exchange rates. They would also cause internal adjustments within the domestic economies which would tend to restore equilibrium in the balance of payments. These adjustments involve both (1) price changes and (2) income and employment changes.

Suppose that, as in our analysis of freely fluctuating exchange rates, the United States incurs a balance of payments deficit by importing more from, than it exports to, Great Britain. The immediate result is that the dollar price of pounds will move up to the $3.03 gold export point and gold will flow from the United States to Great Britain to settle the deficit. But as gold is purchased in the United States, bank reserves and the supply of money will tend to decline. Other things being unchanged, this is conducive to a decline in total spending and a fall in the price level in the United States. The reverse occurs in Great Britain; the inflow of gold expands bank reserves and the money supply. Spending tends to increase and inflation occurs in Great Britain. Declining American prices and rising British prices will encourage American exports to, and discourage American imports from, Great Britain, thereby tending to correct the initial American payments deficit. These price level changes were envisioned by the classical economists as the only adjustment necessary under the gold

standard in restoring equilibrium in the balance of payments. The classical economists (Chapter 12) reasoned that Say's Law would provide perpetual full employment. Therefore, changes in spending would affect only prices and, through these changes, would restore international equilibrium.

Modern economists, on the other hand, know that changes in spending will cause not only price changes but also changes in the levels of employment and income. In our illustration, the decline in spending which accompanies the outflow of gold from the United States will cause incomes and employment to decline in the United States. Conversely, the increase in spending which follows the inflow of gold to Great Britain will increase incomes and employment in Great Britain. These income changes will also tend to correct the balance of payments disequilibrium. As their incomes fall, Americans import less British goods. As their incomes rise, the British buy more American exports. In reality the corrective process of the gold standard is a combination of changes in price and income levels.

Gold standard adjustments can be envisioned in terms of Figure 37-1. You will recall that under a system of freely fluctuating exchange rates an American payments deficit would be corrected by a rise in the exchange rate from $3 to $4. In the case of the gold standard, gold flows between the two nations hold the exchange rate approximately at the $3 level. But gold flows result in changes in the price, income, and employment levels of the nations receiving and losing gold. These domestic adjustments shift the demand for and supply of foreign exchange so as to achieve equilibrium at the fixed $3-for-£1 exchange rate. Specifically, given the initial American payments deficit and the resulting American pound shortage of AB at the $3 exchange rate, gold will flow from the United States to Great Britain. The contractionary impact in the United States will tend to lower the American demand for pounds, and the expansionary impact in Great Britain will tend to increase the available supply of pounds. These shifts continue until equilibrium is restored at the $3-for-£1 gold standard rate. Graphically, this means the D_1D_1 curve of Figure 37-1 will shift to the left, and the S_1S_1 curve to the right, providing a new intersection (equilibrium) point somewhere on the dotted white line between points A and B.

The gold standard entails obvious advantages: (1) The stable exchange rates which it fosters reduce the riskiness and thereby stimulate the volume of international trade. (2) The gold standard automatically corrects balance of payments disequilibria. International equilibrium under the gold standard does not require the action of governmental bodies; inevitable gold flows adjust trade deficits or surpluses to the end that a balance of payments disequilibrium will be resolved.

The basic drawback of the gold standard is apparent from our discussion of the adjustment processes it entails. Nations on the gold standard must accept domestic adjustments in such distasteful forms as deflation, unemployment, and falling incomes, on the one hand, or inflation, on the other. These adjustments may obviously collide with monetary and fiscal programs designed to foster domestic economic stability.

Exchange controls

Another means of resolving a balance of payments deficit is through government control of the exchange rate. To see how exchange controls work let us suppose the United States government has fixed the legal dollar price of pounds at $3 to £1 as in Figure 37-1. Now assume as before that American imports increase, resulting in an American trade deficit. The main symptom of this deficit is an American foreign exchange shortage of AB in Figure 37-1. Under exchange controls the government handles this problem by requiring that all foreign exchange obtained by American exporters and other recipients be sold to the government. Then, in turn, the government allocates or rations this short supply of pounds (XA) among the various American importers and other users, who demand the quantity XB. In this way government can restrict American imports to the amount of foreign exchange earned by American exports.

In effect government rationing of foreign exchange "forces" a balance of payments equilibrium by restricting imports to the value of exports. The rationing process necessarily involves government discrimination between different importers, typically denying foreign exchange for the importation of luxury, or nonessential, goods in order to make the short supply available for necessary, or essential, goods.

Exchange controls may permit nations to achieve stable exchange rates when they do not have the gold required to achieve exchange rate stability under the gold standard. But exchange controls do not free nations from internal price and income adjustments. Specifically, the restriction of imports in the control nation leads to domestic scarcities of certain goods and materials ordinarily imported. The prices of these products and resources therefore tend to rise. This is reinforced by the fact that the restricting of imports to the value of exports will increase national income in the control economy; expenditures formerly made on imported goods are now reallocated to domestically produced goods.

On the other hand, deflation tends to occur in other nations as the exchange controls tend to curtail their export markets and the production of goods normally exported begins to depress the domestic markets of these foreign nations. Furthermore, the loss of export markets which the imposition of exchange controls forces upon foreign nations will cause the incomes of those nations to decline. The decline in the net foreign investment of these nations will have a contractionary impact upon their economies.

If government has the legal power to establish exchange rates, it obviously also has the power to alter those rates. Historically, when faced with (1) persistent trade deficits or (2) domestic unemployment, individual nations have *devaluated* their currencies for the express purpose of overcoming these difficulties. For example, if the United States should find itself faced with a persistent deficit in its trade, it might increase the dollar price of pounds from $3 for £1 to $3.50 or $4 for £1. This will make

American goods cheaper to the British and British goods dearer to Americans, increasing American exports and decreasing American imports to the end that the deficit is alleviated or corrected. During the Great Depression most nations devaluated their currencies in the hope of alleviating domestic unemployment. They reasoned that the increase in exports and decline in imports which devaluation would bring would stimulate their domestic economies. That is, by increasing international sales and reducing international purchases, it was felt that domestic income and employment would be bolstered. However, most nations found that the resulting stimuli to their domestic economies were short-lived, as other nations embraced the same rationale and in turn devaluated their currencies.

SUMMARY

1. Nations can achieve a more efficient allocation of economic resources in essentially the same way as can regions and individuals by specializing in accordance with comparative advantage. The degree of international specialization is limited by the law of increasing costs and by political considerations.

2. International and domestic trade differ in that (*a*) resources are less mobile internationally than domestically; (*b*) each nation uses a different currency; and (*c*) international trade is subject to more political controls.

3. International trade is vital to the United States in several respects. (*a*) The absolute volumes of American imports and exports exceed those of any other single nation. (*b*) The United States is completely dependent upon trade for certain commodities and materials which cannot be obtained domestically. (*c*) Changes in the volume of net foreign investment can have magnified effects upon the domestic levels of output and income.

4. American imports simultaneously create a demand for foreign exchange and make a supply of dollars available to foreigners. Conversely, American exports create a foreign demand for dollars and make a supply of foreign exchange available to Americans. It follows that each nation's exports earn the foreign currencies needed to pay for its imports.

5. The balance of payments is an annual accounting statement of all of a nation's international trade and financial transactions. A nation's balance of trade is the difference between its exports and its imports. An excess of exports over imports is a trade surplus; an excess of imports over exports is a trade deficit.

6. A balance of payments equilibrium exists when a nation's normal needs for foreign exchange are met by its normal and dependable sources of supply. Generally speaking, the purchase of imports constitutes a nation's normal needs for foreign exchange, and its exports and its net long-term private capital inflows are its dependable sources of supply. Disequilibrium calls for temporary adjustments such as selling gold reserves, obtaining short-term foreign credit, and receiving aid in the form of grants and loans from foreign governments.

7. Freely flexible exchange rates, the gold standard, and exchange controls are mechanisms by which a balance of payments disequilibrium can be adjusted. Flexible exchange rates restore equilibrium primarily by affecting the relative attractiveness of internationally traded goods. The gold standard entails stable exchange rates but brings about international equilibrium through changes in the price, income, and employment levels of trading nations. Under exchange controls government forces imports into equality with exports by rationing foreign exchange.

QUESTIONS AND STUDY SUGGESTIONS

1. In what ways are domestic and foreign trade similar? In what ways do they differ? What are the limitations upon international specialization?

2. "The United States is the world's most efficient producer of primary steel. Yet other nations of the world produce and export steel." Explain.

3. What is the rate of exchange? "A rise in the dollar price of pesos necessarily means a fall in the peso price of dollars." Do you agree?

4. The United States can produce product X more efficiently than can Great Britain. Yet we import X from Great Britain. Explain.

5. Why are resources less mobile internationally than domestically? Of what significance is this for international trade?

6. "Exports pay for imports. Yet in 1961 the rest of the world imported about $5.2 billion more worth of goods and services from the United States than were exported to the United States." Resolve the apparent inconsistency in these two statements.

7. Define and compare (a) the balance of payments and the balance of trade and (b) a balance of trade deficit and a balance of payments deficit. Explain how a nation can incur a balance of trade deficit or surplus and yet achieve an equilibrium in its balance of payments.

8. Explain in detail the adjustments which must occur to resolve a balance of payments surplus under (a) the gold standard (b) flexible exchange rates and (c) exchange controls. Now trace the adjustments entailed by a payments deficit. Evaluate the virtues and shortcomings of the gold standard and flexible exchange rates.

9. "The operation of the international gold standard undermines domestic full-employment policies, and, conversely, the active pursuit of full employment domestically is inimical to the operation of the gold standard." Explain and evaluate this statement.

SELECTED REFERENCES

Enke, Stephen, and Virgil Salera, *International Economics*, 3d ed. (Englewood Cliffs, N.J.: Prentice-Hall, Inc., 1957), chaps. 1–3, 7–8.

Kindleberger, Charles P., *International Economics*, rev. ed. (Homewood, Ill.: Richard D. Irwin, Inc., 1958), chaps. 1–4.

Krause, Walter, *The International Economy* (Boston: Houghton Mifflin Company, 1955), chaps. 1–5.

Peck, H. Austin, *International Economics* (New York: Thomas Y. Crowell Company, 1957), chaps. 1–7.

Chapter 38

THE BREAKDOWN AND RECONSTRUCTION

OF INTERNATIONAL TRADE

WITH THE ELEMENTS of international trade and finance in mind we are now in a position to explore international economic problems and the economic policies which have sometimes alleviated and sometimes contributed to these problems. In particular we seek, first, to explain how depression, war, and political tensions caused world trade to disintegrate in the 1929–1946 period. Next the real, or production, aspects of world trade disintegration are explored. Third, we examine the international financial problems posed by this breakdown of world trade. In accomplishing the second and third objectives emphasis is placed upon national and international policies designed to remedy both the financial and real impediments to trade. Next, the perennial problem of protectionism versus free trade is discussed. Finally, the changing position of the United States in the world economy is outlined. The increasingly acute problems associated with the underdeveloped nations are discussed in Chapter 39.

DISINTEGRATION OF INTERNATIONAL TRADE

During most of the nineteenth century a harmonious network of international trade and finance linked the nations of the world. Some

nations—particularly those of northwestern Europe—quickly grasped the new techniques of the Industrial Revolution, while others remained almost completely unaffected. These differences formed the basis for a highly complementary pattern of trade wherein underdeveloped nations exported raw materials to the manufacturing nations. The latter in turn came to depend upon the expanding markets of the semideveloped and underdeveloped nations in selling their manufactured goods. This trade pattern was accompanied by relatively large flows of private long-term capital from the manufacturing to the raw material nations. These flows increased the production of raw materials and simultaneously strengthened overseas markets in the raw material nations. Furthermore, *laissez faire* was the dominant ideology during this golden age of international trade. Governmental interference with the composition and volume of trade was at a minimum. Each nation accepted any and all internal adjustments which inevitable changes in the structure and terms of trade demanded. The gold standard worked automatically and effectively during this period to resolve balance of payments disequilibria. The world of the last half of the nineteenth century was a closely knit economic unit wherein the volume of trade was large and generally in accord with the principle of comparative advantage. Events of the twentieth century—the Great Depression, World War II, and the cold war—brought changes that have resulted in the demise of this golden age of international trade.

World trade in the thirties

The Great Depression of the 1930s severely disrupted the volume and composition of international trade. Nations heavily dependent upon foreign trade found that the Depression caused their overseas markets to collapse, preventing them from earning the foreign monies needed to finance the importation of essential goods. Nations which imported more than they exported witnessed the disappearance of the long-term capital flows which financed this difference as the Depression undermined profit expectations. Furthermore, drastic and uneven changes in the price levels of the various nations rendered existing exchange rates unrealistic and raised serious questions about the terms of trade. It is easy to see why many nations faced severe balance of payments difficulties during the thirties.

In addition to upsetting the international flow of goods and capital and posing exchange rate problems, the Great Depression prompted a myriad of trade controls. Domestic unemployment invariably gives rise to trade barriers designed to create more employment domestically. A most obvious means of bolstering domestic employment and production is to increase exports and cut imports. Success in this endeavor expands net foreign investment, which through the multiplier effect promises a magnified expansionary effect upon the domestic economy. In seeking this trade surplus the nations of the world imposed high tariff barriers, created import quotas and export subsidies, established government controls upon foreign exchange, and devaluated their currencies. Unfortunately, because the exports of one nation are the imports of another, all nations could not succeed in stimulating their domestic economies by exporting more than they imported. But most tried. And the trade barriers which accompanied the attempts further distorted and choked off the declining flow of international trade.

World War II: disruption of trade

Following on the heels of the Great Depression, World War II completed the disintegration of world trade. The impact of war upon international trade is manifold:

1. Most obviously, the pattern of trade is altered so that it is in accord with military objectives rather than comparative advantage. At the outset of World War II Great Britain and France sought to mobilize as many resources as possible—both domestic and foreign—for war goods production. On the one hand, this means cutting exports, that is, shifting resources from export goods to war goods production. On the other hand, it means increasing imports to supplement the productive capacity of the domestic economy. The resulting excess of imports over exports poses an obvious balance of payments problem: How can a warring nation, when restricting exports, obtain enough foreign exchange to expand greatly its volume of imports?

2. War invariably means inflationary pressures, and, like depression, inflation affects different nations in differing degrees. Some encounter creeping inflation, and others are maligned with the galloping variety. Those nations which experience the greatest amount of inflation find that at existing exchange rates their goods are less attractive to foreign buyers and, unhappily, domestic consumers are attracted to foreign goods. Down go that nation's exports and up go its imports. This again contributes to a balance of payments deficit and a shortage of foreign monies.

3. World War II had dramatically different effects upon the productive capacities of nations. The capital facilities of some—particularly Great Britain, France, and Germany—were seriously reduced as the result of physical destruction through invasion, bombings, and the inability to replace depreciated capital during the wartime emergency. Those nations

whose capital facilities are seriously impaired by war will want to achieve an excess of imports over exports to supplement domestic productive capacity in the postwar reconstruction period. But how is this trade deficit to be financed?

For example, Great Britain was the unwilling victim of all these war-borne difficulties during the 1940s. The war itself called for persistent trade deficits. Inflationary pressures, though admirably contained, were strong, complicating domestic and international postwar adjustments. Finally, Great Britain faced the gigantic task of restoring its productive capacity at the cessation of hostilities. All these considerations meant long-term balance of payments deficits and posed in this instance the specific problem of a *dollar shortage*.

The cold war

The Great Depression and World War II destroyed the harmonious trade structure of earlier decades. The cold war of the postwar period has proved a hostile environment in which to rebuild world trade. This has been so for a variety of reasons:

1. The World War II victors are ideologically divided. The cessation of hostilities brought forth no common ideological basis upon which world trade could be reconstructed. On the contrary the end of the war merely ushered in the cold war and brought to the fore the ideological cleavages of the Communist bloc and the Western nations. More practically, the cold war has brought a virtual embargo upon American-Communist trade. And the nationalization of industry in both Communist nations and some nations of Western Europe injects *political* objectives into any evolving trade pattern, making it difficult to restore an *economically* desirable pattern of world trade.

2. The nationalistic emotions aroused by war are not easily abated with the end of hostilities. Mutual distrust, fear, and insecurity tend to linger on. Furthermore, the effect of the Great Depression on these nationalistic tendencies continues to operate. As a result of the chaos of the 1930s, the governments of most nations now explicitly accept responsibility to maintain domestic full employment and reasonable price stability. The pursuit of domestic stability can and frequently does collide with the goal of rebuilding international trade and finance.

3. Fired by a rising spirit of nationalism, the underdeveloped nations now seek to reduce their economic dependence upon the industrially advanced nations and to improve their domestic living standards. Industrialization and diversification of their domestic economies are held by these nations to be the best means of accomplishing these ends. Tariffs, import quotas, and similar impediments to the flow of international trade have been techniques by which industrialization and diversification have been sought.

REBUILDING THE WORLD ECONOMY

In short, at the close of World War II world trade was nearly prostrate. Old trade patterns were almost completely destroyed, the productive capacity of Europe was at a very low level, the price levels of the various nations had changed in a disjointed fashion as a result of the war, and the Depression had imposed a myriad of restrictions upon the flow of trade. The problem of rebuilding the world economy in the postwar period was clearly a formidable one.

The postwar programs and institutions concerned with reconstructing world trade sought three closely related objectives: (1) to assist in European economic recovery, (2) to provide an international monetary system capable of providing relatively stable exchange rates and the supplies of foreign exchange needed for trade, and (3) to liberalize trade by reducing artificial barriers to the flow of trade.

The most pressing postwar problem in the reconstruction of world trade was that of rebuilding the economy of Europe. The end of World War II found the nations of Europe near economic prostration. The victorious and the conquered both paid heavily in terms of foregone consumption and tremendous physical destruction to their industries. The major economic problem of the postwar period was all too clear: to rebuild European economies and facilitate their transition to peacetime production. Europe was destitute; it needed crucial goods and services but had nothing to sell in financing their importation. American capitalism, on the other hand, emerged from the holocaust more vigorous and with a greater productive capacity than when it had entered. Thus, the solution to reconstruction was almost as evident as the immediate problem: American economic aid to the needy nations. The fact that the United States had contributed some $37 billion to its allies through Lend-Lease during the war was indicative of the postwar role it was to play.

Foreign aid in postwar years

American postwar aid to foreign nations has assumed several different forms and has been extended with a number of different objectives

in mind. Table 38-1 indicates that in the 1945–1961 period some $80 billion worth of aid in the form of military grants, economic grants, and loans has been extended by the United States. The bulk of this aid has been received by Western Europe. In the immediate postwar years foreign aid was aimed at reconstructing the war-torn economies of Europe. Later, however, aid was designed to provide the military and economic strength needed by foreign nations to resist the spread of communism. Though specific aid programs are difficult to classify in terms of these varying objectives, our present discussion will focus upon immediate postwar aid for the economic revival of Europe and more recent programs of military assistance. Then in the ensuing chapter we shall survey those aid programs whose primary objective is the economic development of underdeveloped nations.

TABLE 38-1. UNITED STATES POSTWAR FOREIGN AID EXPENDITURES, 1945–1961 (millions of dollars)

Net United States military grants		$28,792
Western Europe	$14,720	
Far East and Pacific.	8,592	
Near East, Africa, and South Asia*	4,553	
Latin America.	615	
Rest of world	312	
Net United States economic grants.		$38,812
Western Europe.	$17,639	
Far East and Pacific.	10,593	
Near East, Africa, and South Asia*	6,803	
Latin America.	1,064	
Rest of world	2,713	
Net United States loans.		$12,157
Western Europe.	$ 7,114	
Far East and Pacific.	852	
Near East, Africa, and South Asia*	2,057	
Latin America.	1,752	
Rest of world	382	
Net total military and economic aid		$79,761

* Includes Greece and Turkey.
SOURCE: Department of Commerce, "Foreign Grants and Credits," December, 1961, table 1-A.

Immediate postwar aid. The immediate, basic needs of postwar Europe were met through the United Nations Relief and Rehabilitation Administration (UNRRA). The aid extended by UNRRA amounted to almost $4 billion, centering for the most part upon the provision of food, clothing, and medical services. About three-fourths of the total cost of this program was met through the contributions of the United States. Though successful in providing temporary relief, UNRRA did not provide in any significant way for the economic recovery of Europe.

Other American aid programs, however, supplemented UNRRA. (1) The United States distributed over $3.2 billion in emergency relief aid through the armed forces located in occupied countries. (2) Loans were made to specific foreign nations, the most notable of these being a $3.75 billion loan made by the United States Treasury to Great Britain in 1946 to help ease the acute dollar shortage then faced by the British. (3) Piecemeal grants of aid were made in 1947 to specific nations threatened by economic and political disorder. Austria, France, Italy, Greece, and Turkey were among the recipients of these grants.

All told the United States extended some $16.8 billion in foreign aid between the end of World War II and early 1948. This aid was almost evenly divided between outright grants and loans.

The Marshall Plan (ERP). Though substantial, it became increasingly clear that this immediate postwar aid was simply not sufficient to cope with the economic and political crises of the postwar era. On the economic front, European recovery was lagging. American inflation in the late 1940s made serious inroads on the purchasing power of American loans and grants. Trade between European nations was stifled by serious balance of payments problems. Drought, crop failures, and material and fuel shortages added to these economic woes. It was more apparent than ever that a freer and an expanding volume of international trade depended upon European recovery. On the international political front, Soviet Russia was

becoming increasingly aggressive in seeking the world-wide spread of communism. And the Russians found a potentially fertile ground for this advance in the destitute and hungry peoples of Europe. On the domestic political front, there was a growing desire to abandon piecemeal aid programs designed to meet each individual economic and political crisis in favor of a comprehensive and coordinated aid program designed to restore the economic health and the political stability of Europe once and for all.

Out of this background the United States established in 1948 the European Recovery Program (ERP), called the "Marshall Plan" for its progenitor, Secretary of State George Marshall. The fundamental objective was to restore the productive capacity of European industry and agriculture. Related objectives were domestic political stability, the establishment of sound monetary and fiscal systems in the reviving nations of Europe, and the overcoming of the serious balance of payments problems which hampered trade between the nations of Europe in particular and world trade in general. In the four years of its existence the Marshall Plan channeled well over $10 billion in American aid to Europe, virtually all of which was in the form of outright grants.

Although comprehensive aid programs such as the Marshall Plan are elusive of precise evaluation, most experts agree that ERP was highly successful both economically and politically. In 1951 the average level of industrial production in all participating nations was 55 per cent above the 1947 level. Though far from completely successful in resolving balance of payments difficulties, considerable progress was made in this area. A very rough indicator of the political success of ERP lies in the fact that after 1948 no European nations succumbed to communism. The political ties of the United States and Western Europe were strengthened immeasurably by the Marshall Plan.

Mutual Security programs. Aid to Europe did not end with the expiration of the Marshall Plan in 1951. ERP in effect has been superseded by the Mutual Security Agency, which continues through a variety of specific programs to provide large amounts of military, economic, and technical assistance to both European and non-European nations.

Several brief statements concerning the volume, objectives, and direction of American aid must be made:

1. Since the outbreak of World War II the United States has extended about $117 billion worth of foreign aid. This aid includes Lend-Lease during the war and the variety of postwar aid programs just outlined.

2. American aid has been primarily in the form of grants rather than loans.

3. While American aid in the immediate postwar years was for economic reconstruction, the volume and direction of aid has been dominated by political and military security objectives since the early 1950s.

4. With the economic revival of Europe the direction of American aid has shifted to the Near East, Africa, Asia, and Latin America in more recent years.

RESTORING THE INTERNATIONAL MONETARY SYSTEM

It was well recognized at the end of World War II that the reconstruction of world trade would depend upon some satisfactory international monetary system to encourage the flow of international trade. In particular it was felt that relatively *stable exchange rates* and *exchange convertibility* were essential monetary prerequisites to the revival of the world economy. Fluctuating exchange rates would discourage the flow of trade; inconvertibility, that is, the inability of any nation to obtain needed supplies of foreign monies, would obviously pose a serious financial obstacle to trade.

In particular, it was evident that some means of providing an adequate volume of *international monetary reserves* was essential. As suggested in Chapter 37, a nation's balance of payments is not likely to be in equilibrium year after year. A nation might occasionally or rather persistently incur significant balance of payments deficits. This is true not only during a period of economic reconstruction, such as that following World War II, but also during

more normal times. When it incurs deficits, a nation in effect has two choices. First, it may finance its payments deficit by paying out some kind of international money, or international monetary reserves, to the nations which are realizing payments surpluses at its expense. As among the free world nations, gold and two "key currencies"—American dollars and British pounds—have come to be acceptable as international money in settling payments deficits. Of course, in time a nation incurring persistent payments deficits must overcome them through internal economic adjustments, for example, by halting domestic inflation, increasing productivity and accelerating the economy's growth rate, or altering the structure of its domestic industry. Such adjustments, if they are not to be acutely painful, may be time consuming; they may take several years to accomplish. Hence, in the meantime deficits will persist and the need for international monetary reserves will continue.

The second alternative for a deficit nation is to undertake rapid, and therefore very painful, domestic readjustments or to invoke exchange controls and trade barriers which, as we have already seen, have the very undesirable effect of choking off the flow of international trade. (Remember that the increasing of trade barriers by one nation may induce retaliatory action by other nations.) This second means of adjustment, then, is clearly less desirable than the first. But—and this is the important point—the first alternative is only relevant when an adequate volume of international monetary reserves is available. Hence, the need for an adequate source of international monetary reserves was, and continues to be, an obvious prerequisite to the restoration and expansion of world trade.

The International Monetary Fund (IMF)

Against this background an international conference of Allied nations was held at Bretton Woods, New Hampshire, in 1944. Out of this conference there was created the International Monetary Fund (IMF), an organization designed to deal with problems of the type just described. More specifically, the Fund was designed to assist nations in meeting financial problems posed by both temporary and fundamental disequilibria in their balance of payments.

The IMF was empowered, in the first place, to make short-term loans to nations faced with temporary, or short run, balance of payments deficits. These loans were to be made out of currencies and gold contributed by the participating nations on the basis of size of national income, population, and volume of trade. The United States was the major contributor, providing about $2.75 billion, or roughly one-third of the total. If Great Britain or France, for example, faces a temporary shortage of dollars, it can borrow the needed dollars from the Fund by supplying its own currency as collateral. The dollars so acquired are in the form of a loan, not a grant, and must be repaid with interest in a relatively short period of time. The maximum a nation can borrow in any year is an amount equal to one-fourth of its own contribution to the Fund.

The Fund provides for the orderly alteration of exchange rates to cope with international disequilibrium stemming from long-run, or fundamental, causes. It was recognized that, if a nation's currency was overvalued in relation to other currencies, that nation would encounter severe difficulties in exporting. Hence, it would persistently be faced with a payments deficit. To cope with such situations the Fund allows each member nation to alter the value of its currency by 10 per cent without explicit permission from the Fund to correct a deeply rooted balance of payments deficit. Further exchange rate changes require the sanction of the Fund's board of directors. This procedure for changing exchange rates is more significant than first appears. By requiring approval of significant rate changes the Fund attempts to guard against arbitrary and competitive currency devaluation prompted by nations seeking a temporary stimulus to their domestic economies or the solution to a payments deficit.

As originally instituted, the IMF had neither sufficient authority nor sufficient financial resources to cope with the postwar international financial problems, which loomed more severe and prolonged than had originally been anticipated. But with the economic reconstruction of Western Europe and the rebuilding of world trade in general, the IMF has proven itself to be a very useful institution.

New proposals: Triffin Plan

There is good reason to expect that the authority, the financial resources, and therefore the role of the IMF in facilitating Free World trade will increase in the years ahead. Indeed, the need for international monetary reserves is clearly on the increase. There are a number of reasons why this is so; let us explore two of the more important ones.

1. In the postwar period the volume of world trade increased rapidly. This has been the result of both the economic reconstruction of Europe and a general reduction in artificial trade barriers such as tariffs and import quotas. Hence, because the flow of trade is greater, the likelihood that various nations will incur larger deficits in the future is also greater.

2. Payments deficits may be less temporary in the future than they have been in the past. Aside from the immediate postwar period, past deficits were typically the result of the business cycle; for example, substantial domestic inflation might make a nation's exports less attractive and its imports more attractive, thereby causing a payments deficit. The arresting of this inflation through appropriate monetary and fiscal policies could usually be accomplished in a relatively short period of time, say, one or two years. Some recent payments deficits, however, are of a more long-run character because they entail basic structural changes in the domestic economies of the trading nations. To illustrate: in the last section of this chapter we will find that the rapid economic growth of the economies of Western Europe and Japan have cut substantially into many of the United States' export markets and have been a major cause of persistent American payments deficits

in the late 1950s and early 1960s. A proper adjustment of this chronic deficit calls for policies (for example, the modernization of our productive facilities and changes in the structure of American industry) which may only prove effective over a substantial period of time. In the meantime the United States may incur more or less chronic payments deficits. In short, free nations have faced, and will encounter in the future, balance of payments deficits larger and more chronic than those originally anticipated when the IMF was created.

In view of this it is not surprising that a bevy of proposals has been offered in recent years to strengthen the international monetary system —that is, to increase the volume of international monetary reserves—by bolstering the IMF. Professor Robert Triffin of Yale has made one of the most far-reaching proposals. Skirting the many technical details, he suggests that the IMF be made an international bank which would perform the same functions for the international economy that the commercial banking system performs for a domestic economy, that is, accept deposits and make loans. Specifically, instead of holding key currencies as monetary reserves, surplus nations would be required to deposit these reserves in the IMF. On the basis of these deposits the IMF could *create* needed international monetary reserves by lending to deficit nations. In essence, the IMF's ability to provide needed monetary reserves would no longer be limited to the pools of currencies and gold received as the required subscriptions of its members. Rather, like a commercial banking system, the Fund could create credit (international monetary reserves) as required to meet payments deficits, and in so doing greatly facilitate the flow of international trade and investment.

Whether the world community of free nations is ready to accept the Triffin Plan or some similar proposal remains to be seen. The fact that in early 1962 ten leading free world nations agreed to increase the reserves of the IMF by $6 billion is indicative of current strong interest in improving the present international monetary system.

LIBERALIZING WORLD TRADE

A final aspect of the problem of rebuilding world trade has to do with the lessening or abolishing of artificial obstacles to trade. Though nations of the world retard the flow of international trade in many ways, the basic means are protective tariffs and import quotas.

Protective tariffs and import quotas

Tariffs are simply excise taxes on imported goods; they may be imposed for purposes of revenue or protection. Revenue tariffs are usually applied to products which are not produced domestically, for example, tin, coffee, and bananas in the case of the United States. Rates on revenue tariffs are typically modest. Protective tariffs, on the other hand, are designed to shield domestic producers from foreign competition. While protective tariffs are usually not high enough to prohibit the importation of foreign goods, they obviously put foreign producers at a competitive disadvantage in selling in domestic markets.

Import quotas specify the maximum amounts of specific commodities which may be imported in any period of time. Frequently import quotas are more effective in retarding international commerce than are tariffs. A given product might be imported in relatively large quantities despite high tariffs; low import quotas, on the other hand, completely prohibit imports once the quota is fulfilled.

The imposition of protective tariffs and import quotas is rooted in several different factors. (1) Throughout history, special interest groups have sought to preserve or improve their economic positions by persuading government to use tariffs and quotas to protect them from foreign competition. (2) As we have already noted, during depression nations are inclined to seek a trade surplus by imposing tariff and quota barriers upon imports. (3) Postwar international tensions have prompted nations to use tariffs and quotas to protect domestic producers of materials and goods essential to mobilization and war. (4) We have earlier called attention to the fact that underdeveloped nations have turned to tariffs and quotas in attempting to industrialize and diversify their economies.

Protectionism versus free trade

The issue of protectionism versus free trade has long been a subject of academic and political debate. Let us survey the basic cases for and against protectionism.

The case for free trade. The case for free trade rests on one potent argument: *through free trade based upon the principle of comparative advantage, the world economy can achieve a more efficient allocation of resources and a higher level of material well-being.*

A collateral benefit of free trade also should be noted: unimpeded international trade deters the establishment of domestic business monopolies. As opposed to free trade, protection from foreign competition creates a domestic economic environment more conducive to the development of monopoly and the host of restrictive practices associated therewith.

The case for protection. Though large in number, the arguments for protection vary greatly in quality. The first two arguments are of some validity under certain conditions and within certain limits. The remaining arguments vary from subtle half-truths to outright fallacies.

1. The *infant industry* argument contends that protective tariffs are needed for the purpose of allowing new domestic industries to establish themselves. Temporarily shielding young domestic firms from the severe competition afforded by more mature and therefore currently more efficient foreign firms will give the infant industries a chance to develop and become efficient producers. This argument for protection rests upon an alleged exception to the case for free trade. The exception is that all industries have not had and, in the presence of mature foreign competition, will never have the chance to make long-run adjustments in the direction of larger scale and greater effi-

ciency in production. The provision of tariff protection for infant industries will therefore correct a current misallocation of world resources now perpetuated by historically different levels of economic development between domestic and foreign industries.

Though the infant industry argument has logical validity, these qualifying points must be noted. (a) This argument is simply not pertinent to industrially advanced nations such as the United States. (b) In the underdeveloped nations it is very difficult to determine which industries are the infants capable of achieving economic maturity and therefore deserving of protection. (c) Unlike old soldiers, protective tariffs rarely fade away but rather tend to persist and increase even after industrial maturity has been realized. (d) Most economists feel that, if infant industries are to be subsidized, there are better means than tariffs for doing it. Outright subsidies, or "bounties," for example, have the advantage of making clear what industries are being aided and to what degree.

2. The *military self-sufficiency* argument contends that protective tariffs are needed to strengthen industries producing strategic goods and materials essential for war. Unlike the infant industry argument, the present argument is of a political-military nature. It very plausibly contends that in an uncertain world political-military objectives (self-sufficiency) must take precedence over economic goals (efficiency in the allocation of world resources). Unfortunately, there is no objective criterion for weighing the relative worth of the increase in national security, on the one hand, and the decrease in productive efficiency, on the other, which accompany the reallocation of resources toward strategic industries when such tariffs are imposed. The economist can only call the politician's attention to the fact that certain economic costs are involved when tariffs are levied to enhance military self-sufficiency.

This argument is also subject to abuses. Virtually every industry can directly or indirectly claim a contribution to national security. Can you name an industry which did not contribute in some small way to the execution of World War II? Aside from abuses, are there not means superior to tariffs which will provide for needed strength in strategic industries? Achieved through tariffs, self-sufficiency gives rise to costs in the form of higher domestic prices on the output of the shielded industry. Hence, the cost of enhanced military security is apportioned arbitrarily upon those consumers who buy the industry's product. Virtually all economists agree that a subsidy to strategic industries, financed out of general tax revenues, would entail a more equitable distribution of these costs.

Apart from the infant-industry and military self-sufficiency arguments, the case for restricted trade is very weak. Yet we must outline the remaining contentions in order to explore their shortcomings.

3. The *increase-domestic-employment* argument for tariffs becomes increasingly fashionable as an economy encounters a recession. The core of this argument has already been noted: A trade surplus, that is, an excess of good and service exports over imports, stimulates the domestic economy. By reducing imports protective tariffs and import quotas will give rise to such a surplus, bolstering domestic employment.

The shortcomings of this argument are several and serious. First, although the immediate effect of an export surplus is to bolster domestic employment, it is obvious that all nations cannot simultaneously succeed in this endeavor. The exports of one nation must be the imports of another. To the extent that one country is able to stimulate its economy through an export surplus, some other economy's unemployment problem is worsened by the resulting trade deficit. It is no wonder that tariff boosts and the imposition of import quotas for the purposes of achieving domestic full employment are termed "beggar my neighbor" policies.

In the second place, nations adversely affected by tariffs and quotas are likely to retaliate, causing a competitive raising of trade barriers which will choke off trade to the end that all nations are worse off. It is not surprising that the Hawley-Smoot Tariff Act of 1930, which imposed the highest tariffs ever enacted in the United States, backfired miserably. Rather than stimulate the American economy, this tariff act only induced a series of retaliatory restrictions by adversely affected nations. This caused a further contraction of international trade and tended to lower the income and employment levels of all nations.

Lastly, in the long run a trade surplus is doomed to failure as a device for stimulating domestic employment. Remember: it is through American imports that foreign nations earn dollars with which to purchase American exports. In the long run a nation must import in order to export. Hence, the long-run impact of tariffs is not to increase domestic employment but at best to reallocate workers away from export industries and toward protected domestic industries. This shift implies a less efficient allocation of resources, that is, an increase in disguised unemployment. Tariffs shift resources away from those industries in which production is so efficient as to provide a comparative advantage. There is little doubt that intelligent, well-timed monetary and fiscal policies are far superior to tariff quota adjustments as anticyclical techniques.

4. Closely related to the increase-domestic-employment argument for tariff protection is the *diversification-for-stability* argument. The point here is that highly specialized economies —for example, Brazil's coffee economy or Cuba's sugar economy—are highly dependent upon international markets for their incomes. Wars, cyclical fluctuations, and adverse changes in the structure of industry will force large and frequently painful readjustments upon such economies. It is therefore alleged that tariff and quota protection is needed in such nations to induce greater diversification and therefore less dependence upon foreign markets. This will insulate the domestic economy from wars and depressions abroad and from random fluctuations in world supply and demand for one particular commodity, thereby providing greater domestic stability.

There is undoubtedly some truth in this argument. There are also serious qualifications and shortcomings. (*a*) The argument has little or no relevance to the United States and other advanced economies. (*b*) The economic costs of diversification may be great; one-crop econo-mies are likely to be highly inefficient in manu-facturing. (c) Might it not be better to seek full employment through monetary and fiscal measures?

5. Proponents of tariff protection frequently argue that tariffs are essential to *protect high wages and the high standard of living* now en-joyed in American capitalism. Cheap foreign labor, it is contended, will cause cheap foreign goods to flow into the United States. As a re-sult, the prices of American goods and ultimately wage rates and the level of living will be driven down by this competition.

This appeal is tempting but fallacious. The argument falsely presumes that low foreign wages will necessarily mean low prices on for-eign goods and high domestic wages mean high prices on domestic goods. This is not necessarily the case. Indeed, the argument conveniently ignores the fact that wage rates and per unit production costs are related through productivity. Hourly wage rates may be high and unit costs and product price low, if produc-tivity is high. And what determines the produc-tivity of labor? Basically the quality of labor and the quality and quantity of the capital with which it is equipped. As compared to most other nations, American labor is of a high quality and is extremely well equipped. The consequence is that high wages in the United States usually are accompanied by low unit costs and low product prices. As we have al-ready discovered, wages are high in the United States for the simple reason that productivity is high!

These comments, of course, do not rule out the fact that in the production of certain arti-cles higher American productivity is more than offset by the low money wages paid foreign workers. This is particularly likely to be the case where production of a commodity requires much hand labor and little capital equipment, for example, Swiss watches or Japanese toys. Is protection warranted under these circum-stances? Certainly not on economic grounds. These nations will simply have a comparative advantage in these lines of production. Limit-ing American imports of these goods by impos-ing tariffs will also curtail American exports. The result is that American workers will be re-leased from efficient, high-productivity export industries and absorbed in relatively inefficient, low-productivity industries which can only sur-vive under an umbrella of protective tariffs. This reallocation will lower, not increase, real wages domestically and impair the domestic standard of living.

Though the arguments for protection are many and varied, they fail to overshadow the case for free trade: unimpeded international trade permits greater specialization and a more efficient allocation of world resources. Under proper conditions, the infant industry argu-ment stands as a valid exception, justifiable on economic grounds. And on political-military grounds, the self-sufficiency argument can be used to validate protection. Both arguments, however, are susceptible to severe abuses, and both neglect alternative means of fostering in-dustrial development and military self-suffi-ciency. Most other arguments are semiemotional appeals in the form of half-truths and outright fallacies. These arguments only note the imme-diate and direct consequences of protective tariffs. They ignore the simple truth that in the long run a nation must import in order to export.

American policies

Since the enactment of the first American tariff in 1789 and up to 1934, the long-run trend was in the direction of higher tariffs on American imports. This trend, however, en-compasses periods of tariff boosting and tariff cutting—the Republicans usually doing the boosting and the Democrats the cutting. In-tense foreign competition after World War I and the Great Depression led to significant tariff increases in the 1920s and 1930s. The previously noted Hawley-Smoot Tariff Act of 1930 enacted the highest tariffs ever imposed by the United States.

In view of the foregoing evaluation of the case for protection, this trend towards higher tariffs may be a bit surprising. If tariffs are economically undesirable, then why has Congress been so willing to employ them? The answer lies in the political realities of tariff making. Those interest groups who stand to benefit from protection have done an effective job of lobbying for tariffs. And in a sense the pressure for protection is cumulative. With some tariff protection domestic producers increase their economic strength. This means they have greater financial resources to plead for more protection and also more to lose if they fail in their efforts to sustain protection. Most consumers, ignorant of all the economic implications of tariffs, are impressed not only by the vigor but also the plausibility ("Cut imports and prevent domestic unemployment") and the patriotic ring ("Buy American!") of the protectionists. Alleged tariff benefits seem immediate and clear-cut to the public. The adverse effects cited by economists seem ever so obscure and widely dispersed over the economy. Then, too, the public is likely to trip on the fallacy of composition: "If a protective tariff on Swiss watches will preserve profits and employment in the American watch industry, how can it be detrimental to the economy as a whole?" Those relatively few individuals who do recognize that the benefits gained by protected industries come at the expense of the general welfare are incapable of financing lobbyists to offset the protectionists. When political logrolling is added in—"You back tariffs for industry X in my state and I'll do the same for industry Y in your state"—the sum is protective tariffs and import quotas.

In the last twenty-five years there has occurred a reversal of the trend towards higher tariffs. This turnabout in American tariff policy was inaugurated with the Reciprocal Trade Agreements Act of 1934.

Specifically aimed at tariff reduction, this act has two main features: (1) It authorizes the President to negotiate agreements with foreign nations which reduce American tariffs up to 50 per cent of the existing rates. Such negotiations occur on the assumption that the other nation will reciprocate by lowering tariffs on American exports. (2) By incorporating "most favored nation" clauses in these agreements, the resulting tariff reductions apply not only to the specific nation negotiating with the United States but would be *generalized* so as to apply to all nations.

Tariff reductions under Reciprocal Trade have been very substantial. Today the United States stands as one of the leading free-trade nations of the world. This is not to deny, of course, that substantial tariffs persist on many foreign goods. Nor is it to deny that the Reciprocal Trade Act has led a precarious existence. Congress has frequently threatened not to renew the act and has in several ways limited the tariff-cutting authority of the President. The fact remains, however, that the United States has gone far in the direction of freer trade since 1934.

American policies in establishing import quotas are also explained largely in terms of political considerations. Specifically, the United States imposes import quotas primarily upon agricultural products to avoid upsetting the operation of the domestic farm program. Supported farm prices make foreign producers eager to sell in the high-price American market. Permission to do so would only add to American surpluses which already embarrass congressmen and burden the taxpayer. On the other hand, as with tariffs, import quotas work against the most efficient allocation of world resources and at the same time, conflict with the avowed United States policy of promoting freer trade.

International policies

In the post-World War II era the United States spearheaded a drive for freer trade. This objective was to be sought through a proposed International Trade Organization (ITO). This organization was to foster international economic cooperation in general and to promote freer multilateral trade in particular. Out of much open debate by the representatives of some fifty-seven nations there evolved a charter for this proposed organization—a charter unacceptable to the United States Congress. American rejection spelled defeat for the ITO, and the organization has simply never come into being.

However, out of the negotiations which led

to the ITO charter, a General Agreement on Tariffs and Trade (GATT) was signed in 1947 by some twenty-three nations, including the United States. GATT is based upon three cardinal principles: (1) equal, nondiscriminatory treatment for all trading nations, (2) the reduction of tariffs by negotiations similar to those carried out under the Reciprocal Trade Act, and (3) the elimination of import quotas. The nations participating in GATT have increased significantly in number, and the resulting tariff and quota agreements have done much to lower artificial trade barriers. Table 38-2 provides a rough indication[1] of the extent to which tariffs have been reduced under Reciprocal Trade and GATT.

AMERICA'S CHANGING POSITION IN THE INTERNATIONAL ECONOMY

In the late 1950s and early 1960s two highly important and related developments occurred which have profound implications for American international trade and trade policies. These developments are (1) the changing of our bal-

[1] These figures understate the importance of tariffs by not accounting for the fact that some goods are *excluded* from American markets because of existing tariffs. Then, too, average figures conceal the extremely high tariffs on particular items: watches, china, hats, woolens, scissors, wine, jewelry, glassware, and so forth.

ance of payments position from a surplus to a deficit and (2) the emergence of an integrated European economy in the form of the Common Market. Let us examine these developments in the order stated.

AMERICA'S CHANGING PAYMENTS POSITION

For many years prior to 1950 the United States balance of payments was characterized by a payments surplus. This excess of exports over imports was persistently large during the 1940s, when American grants and loans during and after the war provided a means by which the rest of the world could finance it. The 1950s brought a marked change in this position. As suggested by Table 37-2, American imports have increased in relation to exports to the extent that American grants and loans to foreign nations more than cover the rest of the world's trade deficit with the United States. The result has been a significant loss of American gold reserves—a loss which reached sizable proportions in the late 1950s and early 1960s.

Causes of the changing payments position of the United States are basically twofold. (1) The productivity of the nations of Western Europe and Japan has increased rapidly in recent years. This is partly a reflection of the success of postwar economic recovery programs. The economies of Western Europe and Japan have

TABLE 38-2. AVERAGE RATES OF DUTY UNDER UNITED STATES TARIFF LAWS, 1913–1960

Year	Tariff law	Duties collected, per cent of value of dutiable imports
1913–1921	Underwood Law	27.0
1922–1929	Fordney-McCumber Law	38.5
1930–1933	Hawley-Smoot Law	52.8
1939	Reciprocal Trade Agreements Law	37.3
1947	GATT	15.3
1960	GATT	12.1

SOURCE: Walter Krause, "The International Economy" (Boston: Houghton Mifflin Company, 1955), p. 237. Data for 1960 from Department of Commerce.

been rebuilt and strengthened with new and modern productive facilities, increasing the capacities of these nations to compete successfully with the United States in world markets. In the case of the Western European nations, productivity increases have been fostered by the transformation of Western Europe from a number of small, localized markets into a single, growing mass market through the Common Market. This has permitted European producers to realize greater economies of scale and lower unit costs. (2) American trade surpluses have tended to decline because of domestic inflation. The prices of American export goods have generally risen faster in the 1950s than have those of our closest competitors for world markets. In short, inflation has priced American producers out of certain export markets.

The changing world trade position of the United States obviously poses a problem. No nation can indefinitely lose gold reserves at recent rates of $2 to $4 billion a year. Because there is little evidence to suggest that the payments difficulties of the United States will resolve themselves, some adjustments must be made in our international trade accounts to restore equilibrium. The crucial question involves the character of these adjustments. The most immediate techniques are to expand the American trade surplus by restricting American imports through the raising of tariff barriers, the tightening of import quotas, or devaluation of the dollar. Use of these techniques, however, would seem ill advised. These methods are likely to induce retaliatory actions of a similar nature by adversely affected nations. This would not only reduce the effectiveness of these techniques in solving the American payments problem but, more importantly, would tend to reverse the current trend towards a larger and freer volume of international trade.

This suggests that a more responsible program by the United States is needed. Several lines of attack are suggested by the very nature of the problem:

1. Western Europe might well assume a larger share of the costs of the mutual defense effort and of economic aid programs designed to benefit the underdeveloped nations. The balance of payments problem of the United States stems immediately from the fact that American military and economic assistance are considerably in excess of its trade surplus, causing an outflow of gold. European recovery and the resulting substantial shrinkage of the American trade surplus suggest that Europe can now share more fully in the free world's defense against communism and in the vital programs which assist the underdeveloped nations in improving their economic lot. This is not to suggest an over-all cut in mutual defense spending or in economic assistance to less fortunate nations; rather the aim is to redistribute the financial burden of these programs.

2. A second line of attack is for American producers to intensify their efforts to increase productivity as a means of making American goods more competitive in international markets. This is obviously more easily said than done. It implies the maintenance of full employment and a high level of net investment spending. It suggests increased activity in technological research by both industry and government. It demands farsightedness by labor and management in introducing automation and in eliminating obsolete work rules.

3. The effective use of monetary and fiscal policies to restrain domestic inflationary pressures may help in resolving our payments problem. Further increases in the domestic price level will cause further shrinkage in the trade surplus of the United States. Sufficient restraint by domestic labor and management in increasing wages and prices might even allow American productivity increases to be reflected in lower product prices. This, of course, would clearly tend to bolster American exports.

4. The United States might bolster its trade surplus by negotiating the reduction or elimination of discriminatory trade restrictions which still apply to some American goods. These restrictions developed during the turbulent thirties and forties. Now that most European nations have substantially overcome their "dollar shortages," the United States might well press for the relaxation of these discriminatory restrictions.

All these programs call for adjustments which are likely to be unpalatable either to our Allies or to specific groups within the domestic economy. But inconvenient and painful adjustments are an inevitable by-product of resolving balance of payments difficulties. The most important point is that such alternatives as import restrictions and devaluation of the dollar are not likely to provide an effective long-run solution to the problem and may well prove to be a major roadblock in the expansion of international trade.

ECONOMIC INTEGRATION: THE COMMON MARKET

A second development of major significance for the United States' world trade position has been the emergence of an integrated economy in Western Europe. The reconstruction of the postwar years attempted to do more than simply restore the prewar economic structure of Europe; *economic integration* of the nations of Western Europe was also sought. Economic integration entails (1) the removal of barriers to trade and to the making of payments between nations and (2) the free flow of labor and capital resources across national boundaries.

Several notable strides have been taken in the direction of economic integration in Europe. In the immediate postwar period Belgium, the Netherlands, and Luxembourg attempted to achieve a closer economic union. Their success, however, was limited to the formation of *Benelux*, a customs union which has eliminated tariffs and most import quotas among the three nations. Much more significant is the *Schuman Plan* (European Coal and Steel Community) of 1952, through which France, Germany, Italy, and the Benelux nations integrated their coal and steel industries by eliminating trade barriers on coal, iron ore, iron, and steel.

The most notable milestone in European economic integration was the establishment in 1958 of the *European Common Market* by the six Schuman Plan nations. The Common Market calls for (1) the abolishment of tariffs and import quotas on all products traded among the six participating nations over a 12- to 15-year period and (2) the establishment of a common system of tariffs applicable to all goods received from nations outside the Common Mar-

ket, and envisions (3) the eventual free movement of capital and labor within the Market and the creation of common policies with respect to monopoly and agriculture. If fully realized, the Common Market has tremendous implications. The result will be a huge free-trade market with a population of some 170 million, more than ample to remove any market limitations upon the achievement of mass production economies by European industry.

Achievements of Common Market

The Common Market nations have achieved considerable success in working towards these stated goals, particularly so with respect to the first two objectives. Member nations have actually accelerated their scheduled internal tariff reductions and will have accomplished common external tariffs by the end of 1965. Future expansion of Common Market membership is on the horizon; Great Britain has applied for membership, and such other nonmembers as Denmark, Norway, and Ireland are likely candidates.

The tangible success of the Common Market is reflected in the high levels of output and growth and the dramatic expansion of both internal and external trade which have been enjoyed.

... the Six [member nations] as a group have been growing faster than the United States ... and ... their share of world trade has been expanding.... From 1953 to 1960, the [Common Market] area's total product grew 45 percent, while that of other European countries ... expanded by 26 percent, and that of the United States by only 15 percent. In per capita terms, the contrast between the United States and the Community during the 1953–1960 period is even greater: per capita output rose by 36 percent in the community as compared with only 6 percent in the United States.... [The Common Market's] share of total world trade rose continuously throughout the 1950's. From 16 percent in 1950, it reached 26 percent in 1960, while the shares of the United States and the rest of Europe remained constant at 18 percent and 17 percent.[2]

What are the causes of this outstanding economic performance? It is impossible to determine with any degree of accuracy how much of the Common Market's economic success has been due to economic integration as such; one can plausibly argue that the gradual reconstruction of the European economy and world trade would have brought an expansion of output and trade to Europe even if the Common Market had never been formed. On the other hand, the potential benefits of economic integration in Europe are very great. Two merit explicit comment. First, economic integration generally promotes a more rational allocation of Europe's economic resources in accordance with the principle of comparative advantage. Second, integration of the national economies of Western Europe creates a large-scale mass

[2] Robert R. Bowie and Theodore Geiger, *The European Economic Community and the United States*, for the Joint Economic Committee (Washington: Government Printing Office, 1961), pp. 23–25.

market which is essential for European industries in realizing economies of large-scale production. More efficient production for a large-scale market permits European industries to realize the lower costs which small, localized markets have historically denied them. Indeed, it is this greater productive efficiency on the part of European firms that has contributed to the United States' balance of payments difficulties.

All things considered, there can be but little doubt that the Common Market as an institution has been a significant factor in the buoyancy and expansion of the economies of its member nations.

Economic potential of an Atlantic Alliance

Prior to the Common Market, the United States was the leader of a number of industrially advanced nations allied by the ties of international trade and devoted to the common causes of political and economic freedom. With the growth and success—past and anticipated

TABLE 38-3. ECONOMIC AGGREGATES FOR THE ENLARGED COMMON MARKET, CANADA, AND THE UNITED STATES, 1960

Country or area	Population, millions	Gross national product, billions	National income, billions	Per capita national income
Common Market nations............	169.2	$179.1	$130.5	$ 771
Great Britain....................	52.5	65.1	56.7	1,080
Other prospective Common Market members*..............	30.9	38.0	30.9	1,000
Subtotal....................	252.6	282.2	218.1	863
Canada.......................	18.0	37.1	28.3	1,572
United States....................	180.7	505.2	417.5	2,310
Grand total	451.3	$824.5	$663.9	$1,471

* Austria, Denmark, Ireland, Norway, Sweden, and Switzerland.
SOURCE: Robert R. Bowie and Theodore Geiger, "The European Economic Community and the United States," for the Joint Economic Committee (Washington: Government Printing Office, 1961), p. 36.

—of the Common Market, this picture is now changing to one in which two economic giants —the United States and the Common Market —are dominant in the free world. Table 38-3 summarizes several of the major economic aggregates for the present and potential Common Market membership, the United States, and Canada. There is little doubt but that these two giant organizations, with a combined GNP of about $825 billion, embrace a tremendous amount of economic power.

Assuming effective political and economic ties and reasonable unity of action between the United States and the Common Market, this new "Atlantic Alliance" could be in a very strategic position to meet the most crucial problems now faced by the free world. In particular, such a partnership could (1) provide the military strength needed to deter or meet Communist aggression, (2) afford the resources for effective aid programs to the underdeveloped countries, and (3) create the institutions and unity of policies and efforts to assure continuing prosperity and economic growth within such a partnership.

. . . the European Community . . . offers an effective means to enable the developed countries of the West to join together in discharging their common obligations and responsibilities. In tandem, the European Community and the United States can work for the creation of a more viable world order which can accommodate the needs and interests of the less developed countries as well. Together they can assure the growth of their own economies, provide their own people rising standards of life, and help the less developed nations in the gigantic effort to modernize. And finally they can concert more effectively for military defense against Communist aggression and for a common political approach designed to bring about ultimate changes in Soviet purposes and objectives.[3]

Achieving economic harmony

But it is by no means a foregone conclusion that such objectives will be achieved. Many problems exist for both the Common Market

[3] Bowie and Geiger, op. cit., p. 12.

nations and for the United States in establishing an effective Atlantic Alliance.

Comparable growth rates. It is well known that the prospects for an expanding level of mutually advantageous trade between any two nations or groups of nations are greater if both are realizing adequate rates of growth. Vigorous growth means rising incomes, new products and production techniques, rising productivity, and an environment conducive to the lowering of existing trade barriers. We have seen that the growth rates of the Common Market nations have generally exceeded those of the United States. Hence, it is important that the United States achieve both short-run economic stability and an adequate growth rate if the opportunities for increased trade and investment between the United States and the Common Market are to be fully realized.

Trade policies. The trade policies adopted by the United States toward the Common Market, and in turn the Common Market's trade policies toward the United States, will be most crucial in determining the degree of unity and harmony realized by these two economic giants. Upon these policies might also hinge the fate of the free world.

Most economists feel it is imperative that the United States seize the initiative and forge policies which will closely link our economy with that of the Common Market. The most obvious and most effective policy in establishing close economic ties would be for the United States to negotiate substantial reciprocal tariff reductions with the Common Market nations. There are a number of compelling reasons why it is felt such a policy should be pursued vigorously by the United States.

1. Given our position as the leading nation in world trade and our current policy commitment to more liberalized trade, any other policy would be detrimental to the prestige and image of the United States and might split the Free World economically and politically.

2. The basic economic argument for freer international trade is applicable: the more efficient allocation of the world's resources result-

ing from freer trade based upon comparative advantage will be mutually beneficial to the United States and the Common Market.

3. Unless substantial reciprocal tariff reductions are negotiated, the United States faces the prospect of future losses of export markets and therefore a worsening of its balance of payments position. The loss of export markets is anticipated for several reasons. First, the Common Market embodies a rapidly growing, but as yet relatively unsaturated, market for our manufactured goods. European incomes and living standards are rising, and the Common Market nations are generally entering the "high mass consumption" stage of their economic development. The lowering of European tariffs on imports from the United States would make increasingly accessible to United States manufacturers a growing mass market for consumer durables and semidurables—those very products which American firms produce with such great efficiency.

In the second place, as the Common Market reduces internal tariffs toward zero and simultaneously establishes a common external tariff, it will necessarily become more difficult for the United States and other free world nations to sell in the Common Market. For example, *before* the establishment of the Common Market, American, German, and French automobile manufacturers all faced the same tariff in selling their products to, say, Belgium. However, *after* the establishment of the Common Market, Belgian tariffs on German Volkswagens and French Renaults fall to zero, but an external tariff of, say, 25 or 30 per cent applies to all nonmember nations such as the United States. This obviously puts American firms at a serious competitive disadvantage. And, of course, to the extent that this disadvantage results in a growing mass market for European producers, they may realize greater economies of scale (lower unit costs) and find themselves increasingly able to compete with American manufacturers in the export market of nations outside the Common Market. It is obvious that such declines in our ability to export to the Common Market will intensify the United States' balance of payments difficulties.

In brief, the successful negotiation of reciprocal tariff reductions with the Common Market will (1) provide for the more rational use of Free World resources which liberalized trade generally promotes, (2) prove consistent with the United States' free trade philosophy and its role as the leading trading nation, and (3) make the Common Market more accessible to American exporters and thereby tend to alleviate American balance of payments problems. These reasons for achieving an Atlantic Alliance are all the more compelling because the only real alternative may be the United States' economic isolation from the Common Market nations and the potential political-military disunity which might very well be involved:

. . . if the challenges and opportunities immediately ahead are constructively seized for united free world action on trade, payments, and aid —the tide can indeed lead on to fortune. But if the challenges and opportunities are *not* taken, or are postponed out of calculations of tactical advantage, there is a good chance that we shall be "bound in shallows and miseries" — new recession and protectionism and isolationism at home; abroad, a fractured free world for Khrushchev to divide and conquer.[4]

Trade Expansion Act of 1962

In the fall of 1962 Congress took a major step toward the achievement of close economic ties between the United States and the Common Market by passing the Trade Expansion Act. This act provides the President with broad powers to negotiate reciprocal tariff reductions. More specifically, the act gives the President authority to (1) lower or eliminate entirely all tariffs on products where the Common Market and the United States together have 80 per cent or more of the world's trade and (2) lower tariffs up to 50 per cent on other goods over a five-year period. The reductions are to be made by reciprocal negotiations and are to embody "most-favored-nation" clauses, automatically extending the lower tariffs to all countries.

[4] Henry S. Reuss, *The Task for 1962: A Free World Community,* for the Joint Economic Committee (Washington: Government Printing Office, 1961), p. 1.

The Trade Expansion Act explicitly acknowledges that the sweeping tariff reductions required for a close alignment of the Common Market and the United States economies will entail certain costs. These costs are of two general types. On the one hand, a number of domestic industries, when relieved of tariff protection, will be faced with declining markets, falling profits, and unemployment. The act therefor provides for "trade adjustment assistance" to those who are adversely affected. Specifically, workers who lose their jobs because of increased import competition can get vocational retraining, relocation allowances, and cash payments up to $61 per week for as long as 78 weeks of unemployment. Adversely affected businessmen can get tax relief and loans and technical assistance for the modernization and reorganization of plants.

There is a second type of "cost" implicit in the act. Any close linking of the United States and Common Market economies will call for a closer harmonization of national economic policies and conditions among participating nations. As the economies of nations in an Atlantic Alliance become increasingly interdependent through expanding trade and financial relationships and through integration, the issues, problems, and policies which were once of a purely domestic character will now become of international importance. For example, the monetary and fiscal policies, agricultural policy, and antitrust policy of the United States or of any other participating nations will now necessarily become increasingly important to all other participating nations. Despite these costs, there can be little doubt as to the overriding merits of the Trade Expansion Act as a mechanism for achieving closer economic and political harmony among free world nations.

SUMMARY

1. In the 1929–1945 period the Great Depression and World War II severely disrupted the volume and pattern of world trade. The cold war has posed serious obstacles to the rebuilding of international trade.

2. Postwar reconstruction of world trade has centered upon resolving three related problems: (a) European economic recovery, (b) providing exchange rate stability and exchange convertibility, and (c) reducing trade barriers.

3. In the postwar years the United States has provided some $80 billion worth of economic and military aid to foreign nations. Much of this aid was channeled to Europe through UNRRA, the Marshall Plan, and more recently the Mutual Security Program.

4. The International Monetary Fund is designed (a) to make short-term loans to help nations meet temporary payments deficits and (b) to provide for an orderly adjustment of exchange rates to help correct fundamental payments deficits. The Triffin Plan is designed to strengthen the IMF by making it in effect an international bank, that is, by empowering it to create international monetary reserves by lending to nations with payments deficits.

5. Artificial trade barriers usually take the form of protective tariffs and import quotas. The basic argument for free trade is that it fosters a more efficient allocation of resources and a higher standard of living for the world as a whole. When applicable, the strongest arguments for protection are the infant industry and military self-sufficiency arguments. Most of the other arguments for protection are half-truths, emotional appeals, or fallacies which typically emphasize the immediate effects of trade barriers while ignoring long-run consequences.

6. The long-run trend of American tariffs to rise has been reversed by the Reciprocal Trade Agreements Act of 1934.

7. The proposed International Trade Organization sought to increase economic cooperation and to promote freer multilateral trade. In 1947 the General Agreement on Tariffs and Trade was formed (a) to encourage nondiscriminatory treatment for all trading nations, (b) to achieve tariff reductions, and (c) to eliminate import quotas.

8. In recent years the international trading positions of many foreign nations have improved to the extent that the American trade surplus has been more than offset by its loans and grants, causing sizable losses of American gold reserves. American productivity increases, restraints against inflation, the reduction of discriminatory trade barriers against American exports, and a redistribution of the costs of Western military and economic aid programs are possible remedial measures.

9. One of the remarkable international developments of the postwar period has been the move toward European economic integration in the form of the Common Market. Member nations seek the gradual elimination of internal trade barriers, the establishment of common external tariffs, and the eventual free movement of labor and capital resources within the Common Market area. The Common Market nations have achieved very substantial economic success as reflected in rapidly growing GNPs, expanding per capita outputs, and a rising share of world trade.

10. Most economists take the position that close economic and political ties between the United States and the Common Market can provide the resources for (*a*) the military strength required to deter Communist aggression, (*b*) more effective aid programs for the underdeveloped countries, and (*c*) continuing prosperity and growth of all nations participating in such an Atlantic Alliance. Reciprocal tariff reduction is the most obvious path to this alliance. In addition to providing for a more rational allocation of free world resources, tariff reduction entails a special advantage to the United States: lower tariffs will make the expanding market of Western Europe more accessible to American exporters and thereby help alleviate our balance of payments deficit. The Trade Expansion Act of 1962 is an important step toward the achievement of these objectives.

QUESTIONS AND STUDY SUGGESTIONS

1. What factors underlay the disintegration of international trade? Explain the impact of each.

2. What were the character and size of American postwar economic aid? Describe and evaluate the Marshall Plan and the Mutual Security Program. What changes have occurred in the volume, character, and direction of American foreign aid since the end of World War II?

3. What is "economic integration"? Why do many economists feel that European economic integration is an essential measure in reconstructing world trade? Identify and discuss (*a*) Benelux, (*b*) the Schuman Plan, and (*c*) the European Common Market. Use the "economies of scale" analysis of Chapter 23 to explain why the Common Market has enabled many European industries to compete more effectively in international markets.

4. Identify and discuss the International Monetary Fund, indicating the nature of its goals and its operation. What is the Triffin Plan?

5. Identify and discuss each of the following: (*a*) the Hawley-Smoot Tariff Act of 1930, (*b*) the Reciprocal Trade Agreements Act of 1934, (*c*) ITO, (*d*) GATT, and (*e*) the Trade Expansion Act of 1962.

6. Explain the existence of artificial barriers to international trade.

7. Carefully evaluate the following statements:

a. "Protective tariffs limit both the imports and the exports of the nation levying tariffs."

b. "The extensive application of protective tariffs destroys the ability of the international price system to allocate resources efficiently."

c. "Apparent unemployment can often be reduced through tariff protection, but by the same token disguised unemployment typically increases."

d. "American imports and exports since World War II are higher than they have ever been. This indicates that tariffs are not restricting the volume of trade."

8. "The most valid arguments for tariff protection are also the most easily abused." What are these arguments? Why are they susceptible to abuse?

9. Suppose the currently high American tariffs on Swiss watches are abolished. What would be the short-run economic effects upon the American and Swiss watch industries? Upon total American exports to and imports from Switzerland? What will the long-run effects of this abolishment be upon (*a*) the volume of employment, (*b*) the allocation of resources, and (*c*) the standard of living in the two nations.

10. Carefully evaluate the use of artificial trade barriers such as tariffs and import quotas as a means of achieving and maintaining full employment.

11. In view of the fact that the United States is running a trade (export) surplus, how do you explain recent American gold outflows? How should this loss of gold be corrected?

12. What economic and noneconomic advantages might accrue to the free world from an Atlantic Alliance? To the United States in particular?

SELECTED REFERENCES

Bowie, Robert R., and Theodore Geiger, *The European Economic Community and the United States,* for the Joint Economic Committee (Washington: Government Printing Office, 1961).

Ellsworth, P. T., *The International Economy,* rev. ed. (New York: The Macmillan Company, 1958), chap. 12.

Harris, Seymour E. (ed.), *The Dollar in Crisis* (New York: Harcourt, Brace & World, Inc., 1961).

Kenen, Peter B., *United States Commercial Policy: A Program for the 1960s,* for the Joint Economic Committee (Washington: Government Printing Office, 1961).

Krause, Walter, *The International Economy* (Boston: Houghton Mifflin Company, 1955), chaps. 6–8, 14, 20–22.

Reuss, Henry S., *The Task for 1962: A Free World Community,* for the Joint Economic Committee (Washington: Government Printing Office, 1961).

Schelling, Thomas C., *International Economics* (Boston: Allyn and Bacon, Inc., 1958), chap. 26.

Chapter 39

THE UNDERDEVELOPED COUNTRIES: A SPECIAL
PROBLEM IN ECONOMIC GROWTH

IT IS EXCEEDINGLY DIFFICULT for the typical American family, whose 1961 average income was $5,720, to grasp the simple fact that some two-thirds of the world's population is persistently on the brink of starvation. The typical American is too busy waging a loud but losing battle against obesity or watching his television set to acknowledge the abject poverty which characterizes much of our planet. A five-room suburban home, a new Buick, and a healthy bank account all tend to make the hunger, squalor, and disease which prevail in most nations of the world seem remote.

UNDERSTANDING THE UNDERDEVELOPED NATIONS

This ignorance and lack of concern cannot be condoned. We must (1) identify the underdeveloped nations, (2) appreciate the attitudes of the peoples of the underdeveloped nations towards their economic circumstances, and (3) understand the interest of the advanced nations in the development of these nations.

Low per capita income

The underdeveloped nations of the world bear a common brand: poverty—low per capita incomes as compared with such industrially ad-

vanced countries as the United States, Great Britain, and Canada. Table 39-1 clearly identifies most of the underdeveloped nations. Of course, where one draws the line between "developed," "semideveloped," and "underdeveloped" is an arbitrary matter. Nevertheless, in Table 39-1 we can roughly envision these three classifications. Looking at the annual average data for 1957–1959, we might tag those nations with per capita incomes of $600 or more as developed, or advanced, nations. Included here, primarily, are the United States, Canada, Australia, New Zealand, and the countries of Western Europe. Next is the semideveloped group, whose per capita incomes vary from, say, $400 to $599 per year. This heterogeneous group includes two Latin American nations, several countries of Eastern and Southern Europe, and Ireland. The rest of the world—most of Asia, Africa, Latin America, and Southeastern Europe—bear the designation "underdeveloped."

We need not belabor the pitifully low per capita annual incomes evidenced in Table 39-1. However, the implications of the poverty reflected by these figures merit emphasis.

The poverty of underdeveloped countries means that their people, on a broad average, have a life expectancy only about half that of

713

TABLE 39-1. PER CAPITA NATIONAL INCOME IN SELECTED COUNTRIES, ANNUAL AVERAGE, 1957–1959 (in dollars*)

Income range	Country	Income range	Country
$2,100–2,199	United States	$200–299	Algeria
1,500–1,599	Canada		Colombia
1,200–1,299	New Zealand		Dominican Republic
	Switzerland		Greece
1,100–1,199	Australia		Japan
	Sweden		Mexico
1,000–1,099	Luxembourg		Portugal
900–999	Belgium		Romania
	Denmark		Yugoslavia
	France	100–199	Brazil
	United Kingdom		Ceylon
800–899	Iceland		Ecuador
	Norway		Ghana
	West Germany		Guatemala
700–799	Czechoslovakia		Honduras
	Netherlands		Paraguay
600–699	Finland		Peru
	Israel		Philippines
	Soviet Union		South Korea
	Venezuela		Tunisia
500–599	Austria		Turkey
	Hungary		United Arab Republic
	Puerto Rico	Under 100	Bolivia
400–499	Argentina		Burma
	Ireland		Congo
	Italy		Ethiopia
	Poland		India
	Uruguay		Kenya
300–399	Chile		Nigeria
	Cuba		Pakistan
	Jamaica		Thailand
	Lebanon		
	Panama		
	Spain		
	Union of South Africa		

* In United States dollars of current purchasing power.
SOURCE: United Nations data.

the people of the highly developed countries. They suffer much of the time from malaria, dysentery, tuberculosis, trachoma, or other ills. ... Their food supply is about one-third less, measured in calories, than that of the developed countries, and when account is taken of the needs of the human body for the relatively expensive "protective" foods, such as milk and meat, the extent of malnutrition is found to be very great indeed. The opportunity to attend school is limited to a small minority. . . . Only one person in four or five, again on a broad average of underdeveloped countries, knows how to read or write. The supply of cloth for clothing, home furnishing, and other purposes is about one-fourth as great per person in underdeveloped as in highly developed countries. Nonhuman energy to supplement the labor of human beings in industry, agriculture, transport, and household tasks is less than one-twentieth as plentiful, measured in horsepower-hours per person. Incomes, on the average, are less than one-tenth as high.[1]

Viewpoint of underdeveloped nations

The income disparities revealed in Table 39-1 —great as they are—conceal the discontent harbored by the people of the underdeveloped nations. These people are not resigned to their fate. Far from it. Most seek and feel they have a right to a better life. As they see it, poverty is not inescapable.

Two recent developments—one economic and the other political—have fanned the desire of the underdeveloped nations for material and social betterment:

1. The per capita income gap between the economically advanced nations and the underdeveloped nations has not merely persisted, but in many instances it has widened. As between nations, the rich have been getting richer and the poor have been getting relatively poorer.[2]

This widening has intensified the discontent of the peoples of the underdeveloped countries. The equation for social unrest is no secret:

[1] Eugene Staley, *The Future of Underdeveloped Countries* (New York: Harper & Row, Publishers, for the Council on Foreign Relations, 1954), pp. 15–18.

[2] The grim jokes of the day mirror the widening economic gap between the United States and the underdeveloped nations:

Polish Communist party secretary: "Hear you've got a brother out of work in Detroit. Why don't you write him and tell him to come home?"

Warsaw automobile worker: "Sure, but who'd send us the food parcels?"

aspirations minus standard of living equal social unrest. As the living standards of the advanced nations have improved, the economic goals and aspirations of the underdeveloped nations have increased accordingly. But their actual standard of living in most instances has shown meager growth. The differential—social unrest —has clearly been on the increase. One need only review the political and military crises of the post-World War II era to validate this point.

2. In recent years many of the underdeveloped lands have achieved or are in the process of achieving political independence. Accompanying this freedom from colonial status has been a tremendous upsurge of nationalistic spirit. The underdeveloped nations seek the economic independence, the respect, and the social status which they feel are due them as independent nations.

Viewpoint of advanced nations

Like it or not, the advanced nations, the United States in particular, have a great stake in the future of the underdeveloped nations. This interest has several roots. The *humanitarian* aspect of this interest is obvious: the wealthier nations have a tremendous moral obligation to relieve the stark poverty of the less fortunate peoples. The *political-military* importance of the underdeveloped nations is also clear: the ideological conflict between the Western world and communism may well be won or lost according to the paths of development pursued by the underdeveloped countries. Then, too, for purely *economic* reasons the United States has a vital interest in these less-advanced nations: in selfish terms, these nations provide us with vital raw materials and, simultaneously, with markets for our finished goods. Through trade with these nations all participants can reap a portion of the benefits of international specialization.

Dubious lessons of history

It is disarmingly tempting for the advanced nations to offer less fortunate nations a simple formula for economic development: "Do what we did." Such a formula is glib, inaccurate, and, to the informed foreigner, downright insulting. This advice is akin to advising an undernourished, one-legged youngster that he too can bat cleanup for the Yankees if he will just follow Mickey Mantle's training schedule. The simple fact of the matter is that the now advanced nations initiated their development in an environment vastly different from that currently faced by the underdeveloped countries. Witness the favorable setting for American economic development: abundant and diverse mineral resources, opulent sources of power, navigable rivers, fertile and free farm land, a temperate climate, a small but energetic and (for the time) intelligent labor force, and, finally, the virtual absence of social and moral taboos on business and commerce. This is an environment ripe for economic growth.

Throw these characteristics into reverse and you have the typical underdeveloped nation: a niggardly resource base, a lack of power, low-quality land, a teeming and untrained population, and a host of fetishes narrowly circumscribing any existing spirit of enterprise. The spontaneous growth arising from the favorable environs of the North American continent is not likely to blossom forth in such a briar patch. In most cases growth, if and when it is to be achieved, must be forced by a degree of government planning and nurtured by the aid of the more advanced nations. This is not to imply that communism or socialism is the modern-day path to economic development, nor to say foreign aid is the primary fountainhead of economic growth. We are saying that economic growth must be actively pursued and not merely awaited. We are also saying that many underdeveloped countries cannot pull themselves up by their own bootstraps without external assistance.

BREAKING THE POVERTY BARRIER

The avenues of economic growth are essentially the same for both advanced and underdeveloped nations: (1) Existing supplies of resources must be used more efficiently. This entails not only the elimination of unemploy-

ment but also the achievement of greater efficiency on the allocation of resources. (2) The supplies of productive resources must be altered —typically, increased. By expanding the supplies of raw materials, capital equipment, effective manpower, and technological knowledge, a nation can push its production possibilities curve to the right.

Why have some nations been so successful in pursuing these avenues of growth while other countries have lagged far behind? The answer, as noted above, lies in differences in the physical and sociocultural environments of the various nations. Our plan of attack is to examine the obstacles in the underdeveloped countries to altering the quantities and improving efficiency in the use of (1) natural resources, (2) human resources, (3) capital goods, and (4) technological knowledge. Emphasis here will be upon the private sector of the economy. In addition, social and institutional impediments to growth will be illustrated. And, finally, the roles of government and foreign aid in the development process will be analyzed.

Natural resources

A nation's endowments of natural resources constitute an obvious but crucial element in its capacity for economic development. Poor nations are frequently burdened with an adverse climate, a paucity of arable land, very scarce mineral resources, and few sources of power. An inadequate resource base poses a more serious obstacle to growth than does, say, a lack of capital goods or a qualitatively inferior labor force. The reason for this lies in the fact that there is little or nothing that can be done to overcome a weak resource base. Certainly swamps can be drained and jungles cleared, but the prospects here are usually very limited and the process exceedingly slow. As a matter of fact, faulty soil conservation practices and the application of wasteful technologies in mining often cause a premature shrinkage in an underdeveloped nation's natural resources. Then, too, there is the ever-present possibility that technological improvements in the advanced nations will impair the economic value of the underdeveloped nation's natural resources. Witness the impact of synthetic rubber upon the natural rubber industries of Malaya and Indonesia.

The crucial limiting role of natural resources must be kept clearly in mind in programming the economic development of any nation. Though an inviting and pleasant mental exercise, it is flatly unrealistic for many of the underdeveloped nations to envision an economic destiny comparable to that of the United States, Canada, or the Soviet Union. Automated steel, automobile, and aluminum plants are simply not in the cards for such nations as Pakistan, Ethiopia, and Iran. This is not, of course, to rule out future development for those underdeveloped nations plagued with severe scarcities of natural resources. Switzerland, Israel, and Japan, for example, have achieved relatively high levels of living despite narrow resource bases. At the same time, other nations with more affluent natural resources— for example, Bolivia—have not done so well. In almost all underdeveloped nations, despite the lack of natural endowments, there is ample room for growth. But it must be recognized that the unaugmentable character of natural resources may set very real limits on this growth.

Employment of human resources

Three statements describe the typical underdeveloped nation's circumstances with respect to human resources: (1) It is overpopulated. (2) Disguised unemployment is widespread. (3) The quality of the labor force is exceedingly low.

Overpopulation. Ironically, many of the nations with the most meager natural and capital resources have the largest populations to support. Table 39-2 compares the population of some of these nations with that of the United States. Overpopulation in some of these nations approaches the point at which population actually presses upon the food supply to the extent that per capita food consumption is pulled down perilously close to the subsistence level. In the worst instances it is only the despicable team

of malnutrition and disease and the high death rate they provide which keeps incomes near subsistence.

It would seem at first glance that, since

Per capita standard of living

$$= \frac{\text{consumer goods (food) production}}{\text{population}}$$

the standard of living could be raised simply by boosting consumer goods—particularly food —production. But in reality the problem is much more complex than this, because any increase in consumer goods production which initially raises the standard of living is likely to induce a population increase. This increase, if sufficient in size, will dissipate the increase in living standards, and subsistence living levels will again prevail. But why does population growth tend to accompany increases in output?

First, the nation's death rate will decline with initial increases in production. This decline is the result of (1) a higher level of per capita food consumption and (2) the basic medical and sanitation programs which almost invariably accompany the initial phases of economic development. Second, the birth rate will remain high or may even increase, particularly so as the medical and sanitation programs cut the rate of infant mortality. The cliché that "the rich get richer and the poor get children" is uncomfortably accurate for many of the underdeveloped nations of the world. In short, an increase in the per capita standard of living may give rise to a population upsurge which will cease only when the standard of living has again been reduced to the level of bare subsistence.

Most authorities advocate birth control as the obvious and most effective means for breaking out of this dilemma. But the obstacles to this solution are typically great. Those nations which stand to gain most by accepting birth control as a release from this cycle of poverty are often those least willing, for religious and sociocultural reasons, and least able, for literacy reasons, to accept the practice.

Caution: Not all underdeveloped nations suffer from overpopulation, nor is it to be concluded that a large population necessarily means

TABLE 39-2. POPULATION PER SQUARE MILE OF
SELECTED COUNTRIES, 1960

Country	Population per square mile
United States	50
Cuba	153
China	181
Philippines	237
Pakistan	258
Haiti	319
India	324
El Salvador	327
Ceylon	384
Japan	653
South Korea	662
Puerto Rico	784

SOURCE: National Industrial Conference Board, "The Economic Almanac, 1962" (New York: Thomas Y. Crowell Company, 1962), pp. 24–25. The datum for China is for 1953;
the Ceylon datum is for 1959.

underdevelopment. The points to note are: (1) an initially large population may pose a special obstacle to initiating economic development, and (2) many of the underdeveloped and semideveloped nations are so burdened.

Disguised unemployment. Aside from the drag of overpopulation, the underdeveloped countries are faced with a serious unemployment problem. In contrast to the advanced nations the source of this problem is not so much cyclical fluctuations—most underdeveloped nations are simply too poor to afford a business cycle!—but rather a chronic and large-scale surplus of labor in agriculture.

How has this problem of disguised unemployment come about? The predominance of agriculture is common to virtually all the underdeveloped nations. It is very likely that two-thirds or four-fifths of an underdeveloped nation's labor force will be engaged in agricultural pursuits. Much—possibly 25 to 30 per cent—of this farm labor is underemployed, or surplus, labor,[3] that is, labor which contributes little or nothing to total agricultural output. In terms of our earlier discussion of the principle of diminishing returns, the agricultural "plant" (the fixed supply of arable land) of most underdeveloped nations is hopelessly overmanned, to the extent that the marginal product of one-fourth or one-third of the nation's agricultural labor force may be zero or even negative! This means that a large fraction of an underdeveloped nation's labor force might be reallocated from agricultural to industrial pursuits with little or no decline, and possibly an increase, in food production.

But, as a matter of fact, the shift of human resources, which we recall is the earmark of a growing economy, has simply not come to pass. Why not? The most important and most obvious reason is that there are very few industrial jobs available in these underdeveloped nations to attract surplus labor from agriculture. The people of underdeveloped nations farm because there is nothing else to do. In addition, ignorance of alternative employments plus a

[3] See Ragnar Nurkse, *Problems of Capital Formation in Underdeveloped Countries* (New York: Oxford University Press, 1953), p. 35.

host of religious and sociocultural factors may bind the worker to his land. It is apparently more pleasant to starve while busy (though unproductive) in familiar surroundings than to suffer the same fate in total idleness amidst the impersonal environment of a city. A final factor also retards any potential migration of surplus labor from agriculture to industry: the qualitative characteristics of the labor force may prohibit workers from accepting industrial employment even if it were readily available. A minimum level of training and education is necessary in operating the most simple machines; the labor forces of many underdeveloped nations have not as yet achieved that level. The result is that labor immobility is pronounced in most underdeveloped countries, and disguised unemployment persists.

Quality of the labor force. Though long on numbers, the populations of the underdeveloped nations are pitifully short on quality. Malnutrition, the absence of proper medical care, and insufficient educational facilities all contribute to populations ill equipped for economic development and industrialization. Particularly vital is the absence of a vigorous entrepreneurial class willing to bear risks, accumulate capital, and provide the organizational requisites essential to economic growth. Closely related is the dearth of labor prepared to handle the routine supervisory functions basic to any program of development.

Capital accumulation

Most economists feel that an important focal point of economic development is the accumulation of capital goods. There are several reasons for this emphasis upon capital formation:

1. All underdeveloped countries do suffer from a critical shortage of capital goods—factories, machinery and equipment, public utilities, and so forth. There can be no doubt that better-equipped labor forces would greatly enhance the productivity of the underdeveloped nations and help to boost the per capita standard of living.

2. Increasing the stock of capital goods is crucial because of the very limited possibility of increasing the supply of arable land. If there is little likelihood of offsetting the law of diminishing returns in agriculture by increasing the supply of land, the obvious alternative is to counter its operation by better equipping the available agricultural manpower or by providing industrial capital to which agricultural labor can be reallocated.

3. Once initiated, the process of capital accumulation can be cumulative. If capital accumulation can increase output ahead of population growth, a margin of saving will arise which permits further capital formation. In a sense capital accumulation can feed upon itself.

Let us first consider the prospects for underdeveloped nations to accumulate capital domestically. Then we shall examine the possibility of foreign capital flowing into them. In each case we are concerned with private capital; public investment will be considered later.

Domestic capital formation. How does an underdeveloped nation—or any nation for that matter—accumulate capital? The answer: through the processes of saving and investing. A nation must save, that is, refrain from consumption, to release resources from consumer goods production. Investment spending must then occur to absorb these released resources in the production of capital goods. But the impediments to saving and investing are much greater in an underdeveloped nation than in an advanced economy.

The savings potential. Consider first the savings side of the picture. The savings potential of the underdeveloped countries is low. Statistics indicate that the underdeveloped countries manage to save at best some 5 per cent of their national incomes, while the advanced nations save about 10 per cent. In explaining this point it is important to distinguish between (1) the masses of people, who are unable or unwilling to save, and (2) the very wealthy who can save but do not make their savings available for the accumulation of productive capital goods.

1. Saving is a luxury far beyond the reach of the masses of people in the underdeveloped

nations; most consume their entire incomes to keep body and soul intact. Incomes are simply too low to permit the masses to save.

But this is only half the picture. There is serious doubt as to whether significant increases in per capita incomes will generate much saving. Most experts agree that the propensities of underdeveloped nations to consume—that is, their willingness to spend—depends not only upon their own levels of income but also upon the relationship of their income levels to those of the advanced nations. Better communications, increased literacy, expanding hordes of American tourists, and, in some instances, the presence of foreign troops have made the peoples of the underdeveloped nations increasingly aware of the superior consumption levels of the advanced nations. This whets the appetites of the poverty-ridden and intensifies their dissatisfaction with their own standard of living. New wants and higher aspirations lead to a high propensity to consume.[4] The underdeveloped nations, in short, are most anxious to spend, not save, any forthcoming increases in their national incomes.

2. This is not to say that no one saves in an underdeveloped nation. We have noted that savings might be as high as 5 per cent of the national income. This saving stems from the highly unequal distribution of income which characterizes most of the underdeveloped nations. Ironically, both the poorest and the richest families of the world reside in the most underdeveloped countries. Those fortunate few with astronomical incomes—the tribal chieftains, the kings, and the religious leaders—do have ample capacity to save. Unfortunately, these high-income receivers frequently squander their wealth on luxury goods, trivialities, foreign travel, the hoarding of precious metals, or the purchase of existing properties in the form of land or urban real estate. The monetary saving which does occur often flows abroad for safekeeping or to take advantage of the more convenient saving outlets provided by the securities markets of the advanced nations. The important point is that those few who have the ability to save are unwilling to do so or, if they

are willing, do not make their savings available for investment in productive facilities.

The investment side. The investment side of the capital formation process abounds with equally serious obstacles. These obstacles serve to undermine the rate of capital formation even when a sufficient volume of savings is available to finance the needed investment. *The major obstacles to investment fall into two categories: the lack of investors and the lack of incentives to invest.*

Oddly enough, in some underdeveloped countries—Turkey and Pakistan, for example—the major obstacle to investment is simply the lack of businessmen who are willing to assume the risks associated with investment. This, of course, is a special case of qualitative deficiencies of the labor force previously discussed.

But even if substantial savings and a vigorous entrepreneurial class are present, an essential ingredient in capital formation—the incentive to invest—may be weak. And clearly a host of factors may combine in an underdeveloped nation to cripple investment incentives. Political and social instability—in particular, the fear of nationalization of industry—may dampen the incentive to invest. Similarly, very low incomes mean a limited domestic market for most nonagricultural goods. This factor is especially crucial when it is recognized that the chances of successfully competing with the matured industries of the advanced nations in international markets are typically nil. Then, too, the previously cited lack of trained administrative and operating personnel may be a vital factor in retarding investment. Finally, many of the underdeveloped countries simply do not have a sufficient accumulation of the *basic social capital,* that is, the public utilities, which are prerequisite to private investment of a productive nature. Poor roads, inadequate railways, little gas and electricity production, antiquated communications, unsatisfactory housing, and meager educational and public health facilities hardly provide an inviting environment for investment spending.

The absence of basic social capital presents more of a problem than one might first surmise. The dearth of social capital means that a great

[4] Nurkse, *op. cit.,* p. 584.

deal of investment spending which does not *directly* result in the production of goods and which may not be capable of bearing profits must take place prior to, and simultaneously with, productive investment in manufacturing machinery and equipment. Statistics for the advanced nations indicate that about 60 per cent of gross investment goes for housing, public works, and public utilities, leaving about 40 per cent for directly productive investment in manufacturing, agriculture, and commerce.[5] These figures probably understate the percentage of total investment which must be devoted to social capital in the underdeveloped nations. The volume of investment required to initiate economic development may be much greater than it first appears.

There is one potential bright spot in this otherwise dismal picture: the possibility of accumulating capital through *nonfinancial investment,* or investment in kind. Given the prerequisite leadership and willingness to cooperate, capital can be accumulated by simply transferring surplus agricultural labor to the improvement of agricultural facilities or to the construction of basic social capital. If each agricultural village would allocate its surplus manpower to the construction of irrigation canals, wells, schools, sanitary facilities, and roads, significant amounts of capital might be accumulated at no sacrifice of consumer goods production. Nonfinancial investment simply bypasses the problems embodied within the financial aspects of the capital accumulation process. Such investment does not require consumers to save portions of their money income, nor does it presume the presence of an entrepreneurial class anxious to invest. In short, provided the leadership and cooperative spirit are present, nonfinancial investment is a promising avenue for the accumulation of basic capital goods.

External capital formation. Can flows of private capital from the advanced to the underdeveloped nations avoid the obstacles to internal capital formation and thereby compensate for the paucity of investment spending in the underdeveloped nations? Most underdeveloped

[5] W. Arthur Lewis, *The Theory of Economic Growth* (Homewood, Ill.: Richard D. Irwin, Inc., 1955), p. 210.

nations have received considerable assistance from such capital flows. But extreme caution is required lest we regard external capital as a panacea for economic underdevelopment. The obstacles to foreign flows of private capital are serious and on the increase. Virtually all the deterrents to private domestic investment apply to foreign capital flows. In addition, there are certain unique barriers:

1. The underdeveloped countries seek to make their economies more diversified. They want to develop home markets, on the one hand, and to reduce their dependence upon the economic well-being of the advanced nations, on the other. Foreign private capital, however, seeks out those industries which are currently the most profitable, that is, the ones which are now producing for the export market. In brief, while the underdeveloped nations strive for less dependence on world markets, flows of foreign private capital tend to enhance that dependence.

2. The growing spirit of nationalism in the underdeveloped nations has made them increasingly reluctant to have their domestic economies dominated by foreign interests. Having won political independence, the typical underdeveloped nation seeks control over its own economic machinery. The result has been a maze of policies detrimental to the international flow of private capital into the underdeveloped regions. Discriminatory taxation, limits or prohibitions upon the withdrawal of profits, and cumbersome governmental regulations and red tape concerning incoming capital are some of the more common barriers. To this must be added the ever-present danger of confiscation which political instability entails. This is not to deny that considerable private foreign investment does occur. But, relatively speaking, the flow is not large, and over the years it has failed to keep pace with the rising national incomes of the advanced nations.

Technological advance

Technological advance and capital formation are frequently part of the same process. Yet there are advantages in treating technological advance, or the accumulation and application of new ideas concerning methods of producing, and capital formation, or the accumulating of capital goods, as separate processes.

This is particularly so in discussing the underdeveloped countries. We view technological advance in the industrially advanced nations as a slow, evolutionary process wherein researchers first inch forward the boundaries of technological knowledge. Then follows the financing and construction of the ever-larger amounts of complex capital equipment which the technological advance demands. But this picture is not accurate for the underdeveloped countries. The rudimentary state of their current technology puts these nations far from the frontiers of technological advance. There already exists a huge body of technological knowledge accumulated by the advanced nations which the underdeveloped countries might adopt and apply without undertaking the expensive tasks of basic research. For example, the adoption of modern crop rotation practices and the introduction of contour plowing require no additional capital equipment, but they may contribute very significantly to productivity. By raising grain storage bins a few inches above the ground, significant grain spoilage can be avoided. Such changes may sound minor to people of advanced nations. However, the resulting gains in productivity can mean the difference between subsistence and starvation in the most poverty-ridden nations.

In most instances the application of either existing or new technological knowledge entails the use of new and different capital goods. But, within limits, this capital can be obtained without an increase in the rate of capital formation. That is, if the annual flow of replacement investment is rechanneled from technologically inferior to technologically superior capital equipment, productivity can be increased out of a constant level of investment spending. As a matter of fact, some technological advances may be *capital-saving* rather than *capital-using*. A new fertilizer, better adapted to a nation's topography and climate, might be cheaper than that currently employed. A simple metal plow which will last ten years may be cheaper in the long run than a technologically inferior wooden plow which requires annual replacement.

All this is not to deny that, before a nation's development program is far along, further technological progress will call for an expanding flow of investment in capital goods. However, even here we must keep in mind that the productivity increases which the most fundamental technological advances permit may provide an increase in the standard of living sufficient to generate a part of the saving prerequisite to meeting the nation's expanding capital goods requirements. By boosting incomes basic technological advances may provide for the capital accumulation upon which still further technological progress depends. To a degree technological advance and capital formation may feed upon one another. But we must guard against overoptimism even when this mutual reinforcement of technological and capital accumulation occurs. Remember that the lack of entrepreneurs, of qualified industrial labor, or of essential natural resources can block technological progress as effectively as can a dearth of capital equipment.

Social and institutional aspects

Purely economic considerations are not sufficient to explain the occurrence or the absence of economic growth. Massive social and institutional readjustments are usually an integral part of the growth process. Economic development entails not only changes in a nation's physical environment (that is, new transportation and communications facilities, new schools, new housing, new plants and equipment) but also drastic changes in the ways in which people think, behave, and associate with one another. The emancipation from custom and tradition is frequently the fundamental prerequisite of economic development. Possibly the most crucial but least tangible ingredient in economic development is "the will to develop." Economic growth may hinge upon ". . . what individuals and social groups *want*, and *whether they want it badly enough to change their old ways of doing things* and to work hard at installing the new." [6]

Eugene Staley, chief economist of a 1950 economic survey mission to Cuba, has outlined

[6] Staley, *op. cit.*, p. 218.

an excellent case study[7] of the key role of social and institutional changes in economic growth. Cuba was found to have a relatively high growth potential based upon excellent natural resources, an abundant supply of technical and industrial personnel, sufficient investment capital, and proximity to the vast United States market. Yet Cuba's actual rate of development had been meager. The cause for this poor showing lay in social and institutional barriers to growth.

Public administration was ineffective and often corrupt. The nation received much less than full value for monies invested in public works. These lacked a coherent plan related to development needs and were often left incomplete because of a change in administration. A mass of overly rigid labor regulations, erratically and politically administered, acted as a drag on enterprise, new and old. Like many other countries, Cuba has tried to legislate modern standards of social security without building up the productivity to sustain them. Agricultural experiment and extension services, mining, and other resource surveys, vocational training, current information on economic and social trends, and other potent aids to economic expansion were inadequate and poorly supported. The tax system was cumbersome and unjust, unnecessarily discouraging constructive initiative. . . . the public school system had been weakened and demoralized by maladministration and large-scale misappropriation of funds. . . .

Commerce and manufacturing mostly followed the old pattern of high markups, low turnover, limited markets. Personnel management, with outstanding exceptions, was 25 to 50 years behind modern practice. This fact, the lack of competent and responsible trade union leadership, the sense of insecurity resulting from an unstable economy, and the lingering resentment in the ranks of labor over past abuses were largely responsible for the extremely bad labor relations which were probably the major obstacle to industrial development. . . .

Though it [Cuba] has ample resources and opportunities, it is caught in a mesh of vicious circles. It could cut its way out if somehow improvement could be brought about in the organizing factors—government, business leadership, labor leadership—and if there could be

[7] *Ibid.*, pp. 208–210.

a stronger sense of social cohesiveness and civic responsibility throughout the community. Here we are at the heart of the social problems of economic development.

Because of the predominance of farming in the underdeveloped nations, the problem of achieving that institutional environment in agriculture which is most conducive to increasing production must be a vital consideration in any growth program. More specifically, the institutional problem of *land reform* demands attention in virtually all underdeveloped nations. But the needed reform may vary tremendously as between specific nations. In some underdeveloped countries the problem assumes the form of excessive concentration of land ownership in the hands of a few wealthy families. This situation is demoralizing to the incentives of tenants to produce and is typically not conducive to capital improvements. At the other extreme is the absurd arrangement whereby each and every family owns and farms a minute fragment of land far too small for the application of modern agricultural technology. An important complication to the problem of land reform lies in the fact that political considerations often push land reform in that direction which is least defensible on economic grounds. Land reform may well be the most acute institutional problem to be resolved in initiating the process of economic development.

Crucial role of government

One of the most debated aspects of economic development concerns the role of government. What should be the size and nature of the role of an underdeveloped nation's government in the growth process? Such a complex question is not susceptible to a simple answer. Each case must be evaluated separately. The circumstances of one nation may call for vigorous, widespread, and persistent governmental action. In a neighboring nation growth may best be achieved through major reliance upon private enterprise and the price system.

This much can be said with reasonable certainty: at least during the initial stages of economic growth we can expect government to play a more important role in the underdeveloped countries than did the governments of, say, the United States and Great Britain in their initial phases of industrial development.[8] The economic development of Japan, Germany, and Soviet Russia have all entailed governmental sponsorship and/or direction of the growth process. As a matter of fact, economic development and the level of governmental participation in economic life are positively correlated.[9]

There are several closely related reasons for the expectation that government's role in the development of the underdeveloped nations is likely to be a major one. These reasons stem from the character of the obstacles facing these nations.

1. The absence of a sizable and vigorous entrepreneurial class, ready and willing to accumulate capital and initiate production, indicates that in many cases private enterprise is simply not capable of spearheading the growth process.

2. Many of the basic obstacles to economic growth center upon deficiencies of social goods and services. Sanitation and basic medical programs, education, irrigation and soil conservation projects, and the construction of highways and transportation-communication facilities are all essentially indivisible goods and services yielding widespread benefits throughout a nation. These characteristics preclude their production by private enterprise and distribution to consumers through the price system. Government is the sole institution in a position to provide these goods and services in required quantities.

3. Government action may also be required to break through the saving-investment dilemma which impedes capital formation in the underdeveloped nations. We have noted that when the ability to save does exist, the desire to emulate the consumption standards of the ad-

vanced nations may make an underdeveloped nation's citizenry unwilling to save. And, when an entrepreneurial class exists, the deficiency of domestic markets and the temptation to invest in the advanced nations may similarly slow capital formation.

It may well be that only governmental action can provide a solution by forcing the economy to accumulate capital. The alternatives here are essentially twofold. One is to force the economy to save by increasing taxes. These tax revenues can then be channeled into top-priority investment projects. The problems of honestly and efficiently administering the tax system and achieving a relatively high degree of compliance with tax laws are frequently very great.

The other alternative is to force the economy to save through inflation; that is, the government can finance capital accumulation by printing and spending new money or by selling bonds to banks and spending the proceeds. The resulting inflation, you will recall, is the equivalent of an arbitrary tax upon the economy. There are serious arguments against the advisability of saving through inflation. In the first place, inflation tends to distort the composition of investment away from productive facilities to such items as luxury housing, precious metals and jewels, or foreign securities, which provide a better hedge against rising prices. Furthermore, significant inflation may reduce voluntary saving as potential savers become less willing to accumulate depreciating money or securities payable in money of declining value. Internationally, inflation may boost the nation's imports and retard its flow of exports, creating balance-of-payments difficulties.

4. Government is obviously in the key position to deal effectively with the social-institutional obstacles to growth. Population growth —in particular the persistence of high birth rates—is a basic problem which calls for the broad approach that only government can provide. The same can be said for the particularly crucial problem of land reform and the difficulties entailed in inducing the migration of labor from agriculture to industrial pursuits. And government is in an advantageous position

---

[8] The student of history will recognize that the role of government was considerably greater in the development of the United States and Great Britain than most people recognize or care to admit.

[9] Charles P. Kindleberger, *Economic Development* (New York: McGraw-Hill Book Company, Inc., 1958), p. 139.

to stimulate the will to develop, to change a "Heaven and faith will determine the course of events" philosophy to a "God helps those who help themselves" point of view.

5. The underdeveloped nations seek *rapid* economic growth. The surging spirit of nationalism and the widening gap between the aspirations and the economic positions of the peoples of the underdeveloped nations constantly fan this passion to catch up with the advanced nations. The price system, you will remember, operates slowly, without certainty, and often with little regard for considerations of equity. It may be that government is the only mechanism through which the development process can be accelerated with certainty and with a reasonably equitable distribution of costs.

But all this must not blind us to certain potential problems and disadvantages which a governmentally directed development program may entail. If entrepreneurial talent is lacking in the private sector, can we expect men of quality to be present in the ranks of government? Is there not a real danger that government bureaucracy will prove an impediment, not a stimulus, to much-needed social and economic change? And, too, what of the tendency of centralized economic planning to favor the spectacular "showpiece" projects at the expense of less showy but more productive programs? Might not political objectives take precedence over the economic goals of a governmentally directed development program? Finally, did we not see in our brief notation of the social obstacles to growth in Cuba that maladministration, corruption, and a lack of leadership on the part of public officials were major problems?

It must also be emphasized strongly that we are not here advocating socialism or communism as the most likely paths to opulence. The point to be made is that government might well be obligated by the environmental characteristics of an underdeveloped country to provide the incentive and the means of *initially* breaking the poverty barrier. With economic growth there may evolve a price system, an entrepreneurial class, and all the institutions and attitudes prerequisite to a strong private economy. Government may then relinquish its key role, assured that the private sector of the economy is capable of sustaining the growth process. Such has been the role of government in the economic development of Turkey and Japan.

ROLE OF THE ADVANCED NATIONS

Experience suggests that economic development depends primarily upon the capacity and will to develop that are present in a nation's economy. In virtually every case of significant and sustained economic growth most of the initiative and means for development have been provided by that nation's domestic economy. Yet external aid can serve as a vital supplement to any country's development process and very frequently may be the deciding factor in the success or failure of its endeavor to grow.

As the most advanced industrial nation of the world, the United States has a very great responsibility to assist in the development of the underdeveloped countries. The United States and the Common Market nations are the only free-world sources of economic assistance sufficient to help the underdeveloped nations break the poverty barrier and initiate economic growth. And for both altruistic and selfish reasons we are obligated to provide such assistance. What are the ways in which American capitalism can assist the underdeveloped nations? And to what degree has each of these avenues of assistance been pursued?

The United States has aided the underdeveloped nations through a variety of American programs and through participation in international institutions designed to stimulate economic development.

Loans and grants

The most obvious way of assisting the underdeveloped nations is to extend credit or simply make outright grants to them. In this way the underdeveloped nations can obtain dollars without having to export; foreign aid permits the underdeveloped nations to offset their low domestic saving potential. Expenditure of foreign loans and grants on American capital goods and technical assistance permit the underdeveloped nations to expand their productive capacity without current curtailment of their domestic standard of living. This correctly implies the vital role which foreign aid can play in the early, crucial years of an underdeveloped nation's growth program. Provided foreign capital is channeled into sufficiently productive uses, loan repayment can be made out of increases which occur in the underdeveloped country's national income. As noted at the outset of this chapter, there are humanitarian, political-military, and economic reasons underlying American aid to underdeveloped areas.

It is generally recognized that there is a need for both public and private financial assistance to the underdeveloped countries; private capital cannot be expected to do the job itself. This is so for two basic reasons: (1) Many of the underdeveloped nations lack the basic social capital—irrigation and public health programs and educational, transportation, and communications systems—prerequisite to the attraction of either domestic or foreign private capital. Foreign public aid is needed to tear down this major roadblock to the flow of private capital to the underdeveloped countries. (2) In those nations in which the political-military reasons for economic aid are most compelling, the climate for private capital is likely to be least appealing. That is, those nations which are the most undecided as to their ideological allegiance will attract little or no private capital from the West. But at the same time keeping these nations in the free-world camp may well depend upon the amount of aid which they can obtain from the West.

After appraising other means by which the advanced nations have helped the underdeveloped nations, we shall discuss the quantitative aspects of American foreign aid.

Export-Import Bank and the World Bank

In 1934 the Export-Import Bank of Washington was created as an agency of the United States government to help in the financing of American exports to ease the domestic unemployment problem of the 1930s. Over the years, however, the bank's financial resources have been increased substantially and its objectives reoriented in the direction of lending to underdeveloped nations. Such loans have been extended not only to the governments of underdeveloped countries but also to private enterprises for the undertaking of specific development projects. Currently the bank has over $3 billion in loans outstanding.

The United States has also been a major participant in the International Bank for Reconstruction and Development. The World Bank, as it is often called, grew out of the same Bretton Woods Conference which gave birth to the International Monetary Fund (IMF). Though its first loans in 1947 were for postwar reconstruction, the World Bank's major objective now is to assist underdeveloped nations in achieving growth. The sixty-eight member nations have subscribed to the bank's $9 billion worth of capital stock roughly in proportion to their economic strength. The share of the United States is $3.175 billion, over one-third of the total. In a sense this $9 billion capital stock figure is misleading. Only a small fraction, 20 per cent to be exact, of the capital stock subscribed has actually been paid in, the remaining 80 per cent being on call. On the other hand, the World Bank not only lends out of its own capital funds but also (1) sells bonds and lends the proceeds and (2) guarantees and insures private loans.

Several characteristics of the World Bank merit comment. (1) The World Bank is in a sense a "last resort" lending agency; that is, its loans are limited to productive projects for which private funds are not readily available. (2) Because many World Bank loans have been for basic development projects—multipurpose dams, irrigation projects, health and sanitation programs, communications and transportation facilities—it has been hoped that the bank's activities will provide the basic social capital prerequisite to substantial flows of private capital. (3) The bank has played a significant role in providing technical assistance to underdeveloped nations by helping them discover what avenues of growth seem most appropriate for their economic development.

The World Bank has met with at least limited success in promoting economic development. Since its operation began in 1947 the World Bank has lent about $3 billion to nations which can be classified as underdeveloped or semideveloped. Yet two basic criticisms have been levied at the bank. Some economists feel that the bank has been overly conservative in its lending policies; $3 billion is a relatively small amount of lending in view of the tremendous needs of the underdeveloped nations. Furthermore, the bank has only been mildly successful in stimulating the flow of private capital to the underdeveloped nations.

The Point Four program

Underdevelopment cannot be remedied by capital formation alone; technical assistance is equally essential and in many cases more productive dollar for dollar than is the acquisition of real capital. Earlier American aid programs that provided tractors, but not knowledge of how to operate them, brought home the urgency of American exports of technological "know-how."

In his January, 1949 inaugural address President Truman laid the basis for a program designed to encourage the growth of underdeveloped nations through the extending of technical assistance by the United States.

Fourth, we must embark on a bold new program for making the benefits of our scientific advances and industrial progress available for the improvement and growth of underdeveloped areas.

The United States is pre-eminent among nations in the development of industrial and scientific techniques. The material resources which we can afford to use for the assistance of other peoples are limited. But our imponderable resources in technical knowledge are constantly growing and are inexhaustible.

I believe that we should make available to peace-loving peoples the benefits of our store of technical knowledge in order to help them realize their aspirations for a better life. . . .

Our aim should be to help the free peoples of the world, through their own efforts, to produce more food, more clothing, more materials for housing, and more mechanical power to lighten their burdens.

Point Four was put into effect in 1950. Currently some 5,000 American technicians are now scattered about the globe, increasing the stocks of knowledge in the underdeveloped nations. In general this grass-roots approach to economic development has met with considerable success; results in particular instances have been startling.

Expanding the volume of trade

Some authorities contend that the simplest and most effective means by which the United States can aid the underdeveloped nations is by lowering trade barriers. "Trade, not aid," they say, will promote economic development. The easing of American protective tariffs and the elimination of import quotas will allegedly enable foreign nations to expand their national incomes through an increased volume of trade with the United States.

Though there is undoubtedly a kernel of truth in this view, it is easily exaggerated. It is true that some nations—for example, Iraq, Saudi Arabia, and Venezuela—need only obtain large foreign markets for their raw materials to achieve some measure of growth. Other underdeveloped nations, however, clearly need trade *and* aid. Their problem is not that of obtaining markets for the utilization of existing productive capacity or the sale of relatively abundant raw materials, but rather the more fundamental one of getting the capital and technical assistance needed to produce something for export! An expansion of international trade will help most of the underdeveloped nations, but it will not prove a panacea for the problems of most of them. Ironically, while condemning the trade restrictions of the industrially advanced nations, many of the underdeveloped nations have simultaneously invoked higher tariffs, import quotas, and exchange controls to encourage the growth of their domestic industries.

American economic stability

In absolute terms the United States is the leading trading nation of the world. Like it or not, many other nations—both underdeveloped and semideveloped—find their economies closely linked to the health of American capitalism. The old quip that "When Uncle Sam gets his feet wet, the rest of the world gets pneumonia" is of some accuracy.

A recession both in the United States and in Europe, though relatively mild, will typically cause serious suffering and hardship in the underdeveloped countries. Indeed in the 1958 recession the losses sustained by the underdeveloped countries by reason of the decline in raw-material prices by far outweighed any foreign aid given over several years.[10]

The implication of these comments is clear: the maintenance of domestic full employment and relative price stability may be the greatest. contribution which American capitalism can make to the progress of the underdeveloped nations. This suggests in turn that the United States should seek full employment through domestic fiscal and monetary policies, not through the artificial manipulation of imports and exports. The inappropriate and self-defeating character of attempts to "export unemployment" was illustrated all too clearly by the Hawley-Smoot Tariff in 1930. Any American attempt to increase domestic employment by restricting imports in relation to exports will greatly intensify, not relieve, the weighty problems of economic development faced by our less fortunate neighbors.

Too little, too late?

How much economic aid is needed to provide a noticeable increase in the standard of living of the underdeveloped nations of the free world? A recent estimate indicates that a reasonable rate of growth—a 1 to 2 per cent annual increase in per capita incomes—will require from $5 to $10 billion of foreign capital per year over the next 10 or 15 years. After this time, it is hoped that the underdeveloped nations would be off dead center and growth would be self-sustaining.[11]

How much aid has the United States provided for underdeveloped nations? Though any answer to this question will depend upon the breadth of one's definition of "aid," the statistical data of Table 38-1 provide a partial answer. Although United States foreign aid totaled about $78 billion in the postwar period (1945 to 1960), only $50 billion of this was for economic assistance; the remaining $28 billion was in the form of military assistance. Furthermore, the relatively advanced nations of Europe received about $25 billion—about 50 per cent—of this $50 billion worth of American aid, much of it under the Marshall Plan. Of the remaining $25 billion, $2½ billion went to Japan, whose level of economic growth and industrialization is relatively great; another $3½ billion went to underdeveloped nations for disaster relief. This leaves $19 billion worth of aid actually available for economic development—slightly more than $1 billion each year. In relative terms this amounts to about ⅓ to ¼ per cent of the United States GNP! Of course, private capital flows and international lending agencies have helped some. But at best the annual total flow of aid for economic development is currently at about the $3 billion level, clearly short of the minimum goal noted above. One has little choice but to conclude that American economic aid to the underdeveloped nations has been anything but extravagant. And, as one authority has put it,[12]

There is practically no danger that the United States government will spend more than our national interest requires on economic aid to underdeveloped countries. The danger is all the other way. Underdeveloped countries are

[10] Alvin H. Hansen, *Economic Issues of the 1960's* (New York: McGraw-Hill Book Company, Inc., 1960), p. 136.

[11] Delbert A. Snider, *Introduction to International Economics,* rev. ed. (Homewood, Ill.: Richard D. Irwin, Inc., 1958), p. 543.

[12] Staley, *op. cit.,* p. 372.

not represented in Congress where the appropriation logs are rolled, and the compelling American interest in the advancement of the underdeveloped parts of the free world is less easy for statesmen to explain than for narrowmindedness and shortsightedness to obscure.

The implications of the relative paucity of American aid to the underdeveloped nations are many. In particular, the ideological clash between the "free world" and communism may well be won or lost on the basis of the relative rates of growth achieved by the underdeveloped nations of the free world and their communist-dominated brethren.

Soviet aid offensive [13]

Until 1953 the free world nations, and the United States in particular, were the sole source of aid to the underdeveloped nations. But in that year the Soviet Union inaugurated a competitive aid offensive. Several factors underlay the development of this program. (1) Russia's post-Stalin leadership, Malenkov and Khrushchev, were more interested in a growing international role for the U.S.S.R. than was their predecessor. (2) By 1953 the Soviet Union had recovered from the war and was achieving substantial economic growth; hence, it now had the economic capacity to extend foreign aid. (3) Finally, the Soviet aid program was designed to offset the effectiveness of American aid in thwarting the spread of communism in both the underdeveloped countries and Europe.

As is the case with Russian foreign trade, Soviet aid is motivated by both economic and political considerations. At least two facts underscore the importance of political considerations. First, Soviet aid conflicts with the tremendous emphasis which the U.S.S.R. puts upon its own domestic industrialization program. Soviet foreign aid entails the exportation of

machinery and equipment which the Soviet Union could well use at home to fulfill the ambitious targets of its Five-year Plans. Secondly, in payment for its loans the U.S.S.R. has frequently been willing to accept certain raw materials and foodstuffs which it has in ample supply domestically. The political-ideological return which the Soviet Union anticipates from its aid may take the form of a genuine political friendship with the underdeveloped nations wherein aid is followed by trade missions, educational and cultural exchanges, and the export of Soviet "technicians," or aid may lead to close economic ties and ultimately economic and political dependence upon the Soviet Union.

Although the Soviet aid program has expanded substantially since 1953, it is currently modest in comparison to the United States program. Soviet aid now amounts to something slightly in excess of $1 billion per year while our total aid averages about $4 or $5 billion per year. Nevertheless, the political-ideological and propaganda impacts of Soviet aid have been out of proportion to the volume of its aid. A number of factors explain why the propaganda and political impact of Soviet aid has been so very substantial. Consider briefly three of the more significant:

1. The Soviet aid program has attracted favorable comment because of its newness. Soviet aid is novel; United States aid is "old hat." Uncle Sam suffers from a "what have you done for us that's new?" effect in its aid competition with the U.S.S.R.

2. The Soviets have been more willing to go along with the whims and desires of the recipient nations for specific projects than have the Americans. Soviet aid has catered to the underdeveloped nations' desire for industrial development; Soviet aid has tended to emphasize the construction of facilities for heavy industry, for example, steel plants. United States aid, on the other hand, has been more concerned with the economic soundness of development projects and, therefore, has been directed toward less spectacular projects involving agricultural development, sanitation, and the providing of basic social capital.

[13] This and the following section have benefited greatly from Franklyn D. Holzman, "Moscow's Motives—Profits or Politics?" *Challenge*, April, 1961, pp. 13–17, and Walter Krause, *Economic Development* (San Francisco: Wadsworth Publishing Company, Inc., 1961), chaps. 23 and 24.

3. Soviet aid has generally taken the form of low-interest (2 per cent) "businesslike" loans, while American aid has been largely in the form of grants or, less frequently, relatively high-interest (4 to 5 per cent) loans. Soviet propaganda has managed with some success to decry our grants as a debasing form of charity which implies political, ideological, and military commitments from the recipients and, at the same time, to criticize our loans because of the "exploitative" interest rates they entail!

"Key countries" approach

This comparison of Soviet and United States aid programs is rather disheartening to the free world. Although the American brand of aid may prove superior in the long run, the short-run political-ideological impact of Soviet aid has been substantial. Furthermore, many economists who are authorities in this field admit that the American aid program has had at best a minor impact upon the recipient nations. The growth rates of most recipient countries are about the same as they were a decade ago. Assuming that humanitarian, economic, and political considerations preclude any suggestion that the United States abandon its aid program, what are the alternatives?

On the one hand, given the level of our GNP, we have ample resources with which to expand the volume of our foreign aid. But, as we have already noted, domestic political considerations make unlikely any dramatic increases in our foreign aid budget. A second alternative is to restructure and reorient the use of the available funds in an effort to increase the economic effectiveness of our aid. In particular, it has been argued that the basic flaw in the present program is that we spread a relatively modest amount of aid very thinly over some sixty-five or seventy recipient nations with the result that no significant growth is achieved anywhere. (The Russians, incidentally, concentrate their aid on only ten or twelve nations.) Hence, it is contended that the United States should redistribute the bulk of its aid in the direction of a relatively few "key countries." The key countries would be those which (1)

have the greatest economic potential for achieving growth; (2) possess the "will to develop" as reflected in their willingness to initiate land and tax reform, establish sound fiscal and monetary policies, and maintain a stable, honest, and reasonably efficient government; and (3) are strategic politically, geographically, or in terms of land and population size. Thus, for example, Brazil in South America, Turkey in the Middle East, and India in Asia might readily be labeled as key countries.

Advocates of the key country approach to American aid cite two potential merits of such a reorientation. First and foremost, this approach has a greater chance of success than our present one. Because they now will receive a substantially larger amount of aid, the key countries are in a better position to establish the conditions necessary for getting off dead center and into a process of self-sustaining economic growth. Furthermore, this approach puts the underdeveloped nations in a position in which they must display a will to develop and to make necessary institutional and policy changes in order to qualify as key countries. A second and more selfish merit is this: the key countries approach might effectively meet the Soviet aid challenge. We shall find in Chapter 40 that the Soviet Union itself is an outstanding example of rapid industrialization and economic growth achieved under a system of totalitarian central economic planning. The economic achievements of the U.S.S.R. have favorably impressed many underdeveloped nations. The free world would benefit substantially if it were able to demonstrate by example to the uncommitted nations of the world that an underdeveloped country can achieve economic progress through nontotalitarian techniques.

The main weakness of the key countries approach lies in the fact that for a time many underdeveloped countries—the non-key countries—will receive less aid than they do now. But there are possible offsets: assuming the current key countries will achieve self-sustaining growth, aid to these advancing countries could be reduced in the future and reallocated to other nations which could then be reclassified as key countries. That is, the nations which get less aid now will conceivably get a larger amount of aid in the long run. In addition, the total volume of aid coming from the free world —the United States and the Common Market nations in particular—may hopefully be expected to increase modestly in the future, thereby mitigating the declines in aid to non-key countries.

Alliance for Progress

Some of the thinking underlying the key-countries approach to foreign aid is reflected in the Alliance for Progress program. Established in 1961, the Alliance obligated the United States to provide some $20 billion worth of aid to South America over the next ten years. The program simultaneously obligates the recipient Latin American nations to undertake a number of self-help measures which are felt to be prerequisite to the effective utilization of American aid. Specifically, such institutional changes as tax reform, land reform, and the establishment of a stable and reasonably efficient political system (conditions which would be characteristic of key countries) are required of the South American nations. Although it is too early to evaluate the effectiveness and potential of the Alliance for Progress, many close observers are of the opinion that the economic and political destinies of the Latin American nations may well be intimately related to the fate of the Alliance.

SUMMARY

1. Most nations of the world are underdeveloped (low per capita income) nations. Spurred by (*a*) the widening gap between their incomes and those of the advanced nations and (*b*) the rising spirit of nationalism, the people of the underdeveloped nations are far from content with their current economic status.

2. Initial scarcities of natural resources and the limited possibility of augmenting existing supplies may impose a rigid limitation upon a nation's capacity to develop.

3. The presence of large populations in the underdeveloped countries contributes to low per capita incomes. In particular, increases in per capita incomes frequently induce rapid population growth to the end that per capita incomes again deteriorate back to near-subsistence levels.

4. Disguised unemployment in the form of surplus agricultural labor exists in most of the underdeveloped nations. This unemployment stems from the absence of alternative job opportunities, on the one hand, and the occupational and geographic immobility of agricultural labor, on the other.

5. In the underdeveloped nations both the saving and investment aspects of the capital formation process are impeded by formidable obstacles. The vast majority of households in the underdeveloped nations receive incomes too small to permit them to save. Furthermore, little saving may be forthcoming out of incomes considerably higher than those currently received by this group. A high propensity to consume accounts for this expectation. The very wealthy have considerable ability to save but prefer to spend lavishly or to invest their savings unproductively.

6. The absence of a vigorous entrepreneurial class and the weakness of investment incentives are the major obstacles to capital accumulation when money capital is readily available. Political and social instability, the lack of large domestic markets, shortages of operating and administrative personnel, and deficiencies of basic social capital all contribute to an uninviting environment for private investment. Some degree of capital accumulation can usually be achieved, however, through nonfinancial investment.

7. Discriminatory taxation, limits and prohibitions upon profit withdrawals, and a host of diverse government regulations are additional obstacles which impair the flow of private capital from the advanced to the underdeveloped nations.

8. Within limits the underdeveloped nations may achieve a degree of technological advance with little or no increase in their expenditures for research and capital accumulation. It must be acknowledged, however, that severe limitations may be imposed upon such advance by capital accumulation and the requirements of natural and human resources.

9. Appropriate alterations in the quantity and quality of a nation's economic resources will not guarantee economic growth. Appropriate social and institutional arrangements and, in particular, the presence of "the will to develop" are essential ingredients in economic development.

10. The role of government in the development of the underdeveloped nations is likely to be considerable. The nature of the obstacles to growth—the absence of an entrepreneurial class, the dearth of social capital, the saving-investment dilemma, and the presence of social-institutional obstacles to growth—and the fact that the underdeveloped nations seek rapid growth suggest the need for government action in initiating the growth process.

11. The United States can assist the underdeveloped nations in their quest for growth in several ways. (a) The United States can extend aid in the form of grants, loans, and technical assistance directly through American programs and institutions—for example, the Export-Import Bank and the Point Four program—or indirectly through participation in international institutions—for example, the World Bank. (b) By reducing its trade barriers, the United States can help the underdeveloped nations increase their national incomes through an expanding volume of international trade. (c) Finally, the United States can help provide a world environment conducive to economic development by maintaining domestic economic stability. American economic aid to the underdeveloped nations has been modest in relative terms.

12. In 1953 the Soviet Union inaugurated a competing program of aid to the underdeveloped nations which has strong political-ideological overtones. Although the volume of Soviet aid relative to United States aid has been small, the political and propaganda impact of the Soviet program has been substantial. This success has prompted a number of American experts to advocate a new "key countries" approach to our own aid program in an effort to enhance its effectiveness in promoting self-sustaining growth in the underdeveloped nations.

13. The Alliance for Progress obligates the United States to extend $20 billion in aid to Latin America over the next decade and requires the recipient nations to negotiate a number of domestic reforms.

QUESTIONS AND STUDY SUGGESTIONS

1. What are the major characteristics of an underdeveloped nation? List the major avenues of economic development available to such a nation. State and explain the obstacles which face the underdeveloped nations in breaking the poverty barrier. Now outline in detail the steps which an underdeveloped country might take to initiate economic development.

2. "The path to economic development has been clearly blazed by American capitalism. It is only for the underdeveloped nations to follow this trail." Critically evaluate.

3. "Economic inequality is conducive to saving, and saving is the prerequisite of investment. Therefore, greater inequality in the income distribution of the underdeveloped countries would be a spur to capital accumulation and growth." Critically evaluate.

4. "The spirit of nationalism sometimes aids and sometimes impedes the process of economic growth." Explain and illustrate.

5. "The underdeveloped nations are hurting themselves by seeking too quickly the living standards and the social legislation which their productive potential is now incapable of producing. They must resign themselves to 'less now' to get 'more later.'" To what degree is this position valid? What problems might its application entail?

6. "The advanced economies fear the complications which stem from oversaving; the underdeveloped countries bear the yoke of undersaving." Explain.

7. "The core of the development process involves changing human beings more than it does altering a nation's physical environment." Critically evaluate.

8. Much of the initial investment in an underdeveloped country must be devoted to basic social capital which does not directly or immediately result in a greater production of goods and services. What bearing might this have upon the degree of inflation which results as government finances capital accumulation through the printing and spending of new money? Be specific.

9. "The nature of the problems faced by the underdeveloped nations creates a bias in favor of a governmentally directed as opposed to a decentralized development process." Do you agree? Substantiate your position. If you do agree, specify the implications of your position for the foreign aid programs of the United States.

10. Contrast United States and Soviet aid programs as to characteristics of the aid. Given its modest size as compared to the United States program, why has the Soviet program yielded substantial political and propaganda returns to the U.S.S.R?

11. What is the "key countries" approach to foreign aid? What are its advantages and disadvantages? Would you recommend such a reorientation of our present aid program? Describe briefly the Alliance for Progress.

12. Explain and evaluate: "Poverty and freedom cannot persist side by side; one must triumph over the other."

SELECTED REFERENCES

Bauer, Peter T., and Basil S. Yamey, *The Economics of Underdeveloped Countries* (Chicago: University of Chicago Press, 1957).

Kindleberger, Charles P., *Economic Development* (New York: McGraw-Hill Book Company, Inc., 1958).

Krause, Walter, *Economic Development* (San Francisco: Wadsworth Publishing Company, Inc., 1961).

Mikesell, Raymond F., and Robert Loring Allen, *Economic Policies Toward Less Developed Countries,* for the Joint Economic Committee (Washington: Government Printing Office, 1961).

Millikan, Max F., and Donald L. M. Blackmer (eds.), *The Emerging Nations* (Boston: Little, Brown & Company, 1961).

Myrdal, Gunnar, *Rich Lands and Poor* (New York: Harper & Row, Publishers, 1957).

Staley, Eugene, *The Future of Underdeveloped Countries* (New York: Harper & Row, Publishers, for the Council on Foreign Relations, 1954).

Chapter 40

THE ECONOMIC CHALLENGE

OF SOVIET RUSSIA[1]

IN NOVEMBER of 1957 Nikita Khrushchev declared economic war on the United States with these rather immodest assertions:

We declare war upon you—excuse me for using such an expression—in the peaceful field of trade. We declare war. We will win over the United States. The threat to the United States is not the ICBM, but in the field of peaceful production. We are relentless in this and it will prove the superiority of our system.

While mending fences in Hungary in April of 1958, Khrushchev cited with pride the fact that Soviet production had far outdistanced the "so-called advanced capitalist countries" of Britain, France, and Germany. "Now there are only two countries that compete with one another economically, the Soviet Union and the United States of America." Khrushchev noted in

passing that this economic competition would soon find the "good people" of America in second place.

REALITY OF THE CHALLENGE

The economic challenge of Soviet Russia is not a propaganda blast nor an idle threat. It is an uncomfortable, well-acknowledged reality. Allen W. Dulles, former head of the Central Intelligence Agency, has emphasized that Soviet industrial progress is threatening to outstrip the United States and poses "the most serious challenge" that has ever been faced by the United States in peacetime.

The Soviet challenge, of course, is multidimensional—its aspects are military, political, sociocultural, and economic. But these facets clearly overlap, and it is felt by many competent observers that the economic dimension is the most vital of all. There is certainly a direct, though admittedly loose, relationship between opulence and sociocultural advance. And, even in totalitarian countries, governments may stand or fall upon the degree of economic efficiency they achieve. Similarly, as we saw in Chapter 39, the political-ideological domina-

[1] This chapter is necessarily a brief survey of a very complex economy. Space simply does not permit a detailed analysis of many important and interesting aspects of Soviet economic life. The interested reader is urged to consult the highly recommended references cited at the end of the chapter and in the pages that follow.

tion or allegiance of the underdeveloped countries is sought in good measure through economic means.

Why study the Soviet economy?

The main reason for studying the Soviet economy is obvious. We must understand this competing economy—its goals, its ideology, its institutions, and its operation—to evaluate the challenge it poses to the West and to comprehend the appeal it has to underdeveloped nations. But there are additional reasons for studying the Russian economy. Soviet Russia's economy provides the sharpest possible contrast with American capitalism. The vividness of this contrast is helpful in more clearly visualizing the ideology, institutions, and functioning of our own economy. Also, the Soviet economy is a fascinating case study in forced economic growth; the mistakes, shortcomings, and accomplishments of the Soviet economy serve as invaluable lessons.

Problems of comparing systems

Whether explicit or implicit, American capitalism will be our point of comparison in describing and evaluating the Soviet economy. It is therefore important that we be aware of certain pitfalls and dangers in comparing economic systems.

First, there is the powerful and often subtle problem of maintaining objectivity. It is undoubtedly difficult to subordinate one's emotional biases and prejudices in evaluating the Russian system. We must be particularly cautious to avoid comparing the operation of theoretical, or *ideal*, capitalism with the *actual* operation of the Soviet economy. "On paper" versus "in practice" is not a fair basis for comparison.

Next, we must keep in mind that the various economic systems do not pursue the same goals, nor do they have the same quantity and quality of resources available for the attainment of these goals. If Russia's major goal is a rapid build-up of industrial and military capacity and the United States puts greater emphasis upon consumer welfare, whose goals are we to use

in comparing the performances of the two economies? Certainly it is not fair to evaluate the Russian economy in terms of the objectives of American capitalism. You will remember, too, that "other things" are not equal between the Soviet and American economic systems. Quantities and the quality of resources vary considerably. So do climate and rainfall. There is no laboratory in which we can modify our analysis to compensate for these differences. Strictly speaking, there is no *scientific* way of comparing different economies.

In addition, Soviet statistics leave much to be desired. In relation to data for the United States, Soviet figures are less complete, less accurate, in some cases not conceptually comparable to United States figures, and sometimes slanted, if not purposely falsified.

Our approach

With these points in mind we are in a position to outline our discussion of the Soviet economic system. Our first goal is to sketch the institutional framework of the Soviet economy, explicitly employing the institutions of American capitalism as a point of reference. Next, we seek an understanding of the essentials of Soviet economic planning. How does centralized planning decide what is to be produced, how to allocate resources, and the manner in which total output is to be distributed? What degree of economic stability has Soviet planning achieved? How efficient is the planning process? Then we discuss how the GNP and the rate of growth of the Soviet Union compare with those of the United States. Finally, a brief summary statement of the strengths and weaknesses of the Soviet system is offered.

INSTITUTIONS OF THE SOVIET ECONOMY

By now you are well acquainted with the major institutions and operating mechanisms of American capitalism. We summarize these features here to provide a point of comparison with the Soviet economy: (1) American capitalism is based upon the private ownership of economic resources. (2) Economic freedom is basic. The consumer is free to dispose of his money income as his preferences dictate; the worker is free to select his occupation and to locate where he chooses; the businessman is at liberty to produce commodities of his own choice and to sell them when and where he prefers. (3) The seeking of monetary rewards is the basic motivating force in capitalism. Within a fairly competitive environment the producer is spurred on by the profit motive. Resource suppliers also make their services available largely on the basis of monetary returns. Self-interest is paramount with consumers in disposing of their money incomes. (4) The price system is the coordinating, directing mechanism of capitalism. The innumerable decisions of free-acting, profit-seeking economic units are registered and made effective through the price system. Market prices, reflecting individual decisions, play a major role (a) in determining the size and composition of total output, (b) in allocating resources needed to produce that output, and (c) in rationing that output among the various economic units. The price system in effect establishes the economic goals of capitalism and implements the attainment of those goals.

We recognize, of course, important deviations from this brief sketch. Democratic government accounts for about a fifth of total output, imposes broad legal limits upon the actions of individual economic units, and assumes ultimate responsibility for economic stability. We know, too, that imperfect competition is characteristic of both product and resource markets. However, this general picture of capitalism is reasonably accurate.

Let us sketch the main characteristics of the Soviet economy. Chapter 1 of the Soviet constitution of 1936 plainly and accurately outlines the economic framework of the Soviet Union. Omitting those articles which deal with political arrangements, let us first present this segment of the Soviet constitution and then spotlight its main features.

Article I. The Union of Soviet Socialist Republics is a socialist state of workers and peasants.

Article IV. The economic foundation of the U.S.S.R. is the socialist system of economy and the socialist ownership of the instruments and means of production, firmly established as a result of the liquidation of the capitalist system of economy, the abolition of private ownership of the instruments and means of production, and the elimination of the exploitation of man by man.

Article V. Socialist property in the U.S.S.R. exists either in the form of state property (belonging to the whole people) or in the form of cooperative and collective-farm property (property of collective farms, property of cooperative societies).

Article VI. The land, its mineral wealth, waters, forests, mills, factories, mines, rail, water and air transport, banks, communications, large state-organized agricultural enterprises (state farms, machine and tractor stations, and the like), as well as municipal enterprises and the bulk of the dwelling houses in the cities and industrial localities, are state property, that is, belong to the whole people.

Article VII. The common enterprises of collective farms and cooperative organizations, with their livestock and implements, the products of the collective farms and cooperative organizations, as well as their common buildings, constitute the common, socialist property of the collective farms and cooperative organizations.

Every household in a collective farm, in addition to its basic income from the common, collective-farm enterprise, has for its personal use a small plot of household land and, as its personal property, a subsidiary husbandry on the plot, a dwelling house, livestock, poultry, and minor agricultural implements—in accordance with the rules of the agricultural artel (collective farm).

Article VIII. The land occupied by collective farms is secured to them for their use free of charge and for an unlimited time, that is, in perpetuity.

Article IX. Alongside the socialist system of economy, which is the predominant form of economy in the U.S.S.R., the law permits the small private economy of individual peasants and handicraftsmen based on their own labor and precluding the exploitation of the labor of others.

Article X. The personal property right of citizens in their incomes and savings from work, in their dwelling houses and subsidiary home enterprises, in articles of domestic economy and use and articles of personal use and convenience, as well as the right of citizens to inherit personal property, is protected by law.

Article XI. The economic life of the U.S.S.R. is determined and directed by the state national economic plan, with the aim of increasing the public wealth, of steadily raising the material and cultural standards of the working people, and of consolidating the independence of the U.S.S.R. and strengthening its defensive capacity.

Article XII. Work in the U.S.S.R. is a duty and a matter of honor for every able-bodied citizen, in accordance with the principle "He who does not work, neither shall he eat."

The principle applied in the U.S.S.R. is that of socialism: "From each according to his ability, to each according to his work."

These articles focus upon two institutional features of the Soviet economy which contrast vividly with those of American capitalism: *public ownership* of property resources and *central economic planning.*

Public ownership of property resources

As Articles V, VI, and VII make evident, the Soviet state owns all land, natural resources, transportation and communication facilities, the banking system, and, subject to modest exceptions (Article IX), all of industry. Most retail and wholesale enterprises and most urban housing are state owned. In agriculture some farms are state owned; most, however, are gov-

ernment-organized collective farms, that is, essentially cooperatives. For the most part private property consists of clothing, household furnishings, and small tools and implements used by craftsmen. Workers in rural areas and farmers typically own their homes.

Central economic planning

Despite a highly democratic constitution, in practice the government of Soviet Russia is a strong dictatorship. The Communist party, although its membership includes only 3 or 4 per cent of the total population, stands unchallenged. Indeed, the party and the government can be regarded as virtually synonymous.

As Article XI makes clear, the Soviet government, through economic planning, sets the objectives of the economy and directs resources towards the attainment of these goals. In contrast with the decentralized, free economy of the United States, the Soviet Union has a centralized, "command" economy which functions in terms of a detailed economic plan. The economy of the Soviet Union is government-directed rather than price-directed.

This is not to say that personal freedom is nonexistent. Within the over-all limits imposed by the government plan consumers are relatively free to dispose of their money incomes as they see fit. In other words, consumers are free to select from those consumer goods for which the government plan provides. And most workers are *generally* free to provide their services where they choose. At times, however, workers have been frozen to their jobs, and particularly scarce skilled workers have been assigned to jobs by the government. In short, economic freedom exists when and where it is consistent with the objectives of government planning.

Incentives

Two important aspects of the Soviet economy are not elaborated in the Soviet constitution. One concerns the question of incentives, the other the role of the price system.

Though a detailed discussion of these points must await the ensuing analysis of the operation of Soviet economic planning, a few brief comments are essential to our preliminary view of the over-all structure of the Soviet economy.

Production in the Soviet Union is motivated by a variety of monetary, nonmonetary, and coercive techniques. These three techniques blend into one another. Wages are closely geared to productivity and skill and therefore provide substantial monetary inducements to produce and to develop one's abilities. Awards, public acclaim, and nationalistic propaganda appeals are important nonmonetary incentives to produce. A wide range of coercive techniques, ranging from the admonitions of Article XII to imprisonment are also vital motivating forces in the Soviet economy.

Role of the price system

The price system plays a secondary, implemental role in the Russian economy. In American capitalism basic decisions regarding the size and composition of total output are made by individual economic units and rendered effective by the price system. It is through prices that capitalistic society establishes its goals; and it is essentially through the price system that resources are allocated to implement or fulfill these goals.

In the Soviet Union, however, basic economic goals concerning the size, composition, and distribution of total output are determined by government planners, not by the price system. Prices are then used to implement the fulfillment of these goals. In other words, for the most part prices in Soviet Russia are governmentally determined and are used to facilitate the allocation of resources and distribution of output necessary to achieve the goals of the economic plan.

THE NATURE OF CENTRAL PLANNING

To understand economic planning as it operates in Russia we must first examine the general nature of central planning.

A centrally planned economy differs markedly from a price-directed economy. Yet the differences can be overdrawn.

To plan or not to plan

In a very broad sense all economies involve planning of one sort or another. Someone must plan, that is, make the decisions which determine the level and composition of total output. The question is "Who shall do the planning (decision making)?" The basic choice is between individualistic, decentralized "planning" through a system of free markets and centralized planning executed through government regulation of the economy.[2]

In American capitalism there exists no preconceived, governmentally composed plan which sets the goals society (and the individual economic units of which it is composed) must seek. Rather, capitalistic "planning" consists of a mass of individual decisions, based on limited amounts of pertinent technological and price data, and registered by the price system. The decentralized "planning" of capitalism rests to a large degree upon consumer sovereignty. Relative product and resource prices guide producers and resources into the most profitable lines of output and away from the unprofitable. In this way the price system, functioning both as a *directing* and *rationing* mechanism determines the size of total output, its composition, and its ultimate distribution among economic units. The price system coordinates the plans (decisions) of millions of individual economic units, balances them against one another, and forces adjustments to make them consistent with technology and total resource supplies. In practice we recognize that the price system operates in an imperfect manner in answering the Five Fundamental Questions (see Chapters 5 and 31). Government alters both the size and composition of total output in an attempt to improve upon the "planning" embodied in the

---

[2] In practice, the basic choice is not an either-or proposition. The question to be decided is actually "What mixture of the two institutions—government regulation and the market system—is best?" For an excellent discussion of this point see Robert A. Dahl and Charles E. Lindblom, *Politics, Economics, and Welfare* (New York: Harper & Row, Publishers, 1953), chap. 1.

functioning of the price system. Yet free individual decisions and the market system predominate.

There is no comprehensive set of preconceived production targets in a decentralized price-directed economy. In fact, society's economic goals for any year are not actually known until that year's production has been accomplished. The size and composition of GNP is the result of innumerable individual economic decisions. Capitalism's "plan" for any year is not known until the year's production has been completed.

Tasks of central planning

Central planning by government—planning in the narrow sense of the term—is a different proposition.[3] First, a central planning board of some sort sets society's economic objectives prior to any year's production. Consumer sovereignty is supplanted by governmentally determined goals. These objectives specify (1) the size of total output, (2) the division of total output between investment, consumption, public (social) goods, and military goods, (3) the specific composition of each of these categories of goods, and (4) the general manner in which investment and consumption goods are to be allocated among various industries and households. Next, a detailed economic plan is devised to prescribe the specific manner in which available supplies of resources must be used to achieve the predetermined production goals. The economic units of the economy are integrated by the government's plan, not by a system of markets and prices. Then the plan is put into effect and executed.

Claims for central planning

The advocates of detailed central planning contend that planning results in greater economic efficiency than can be achieved in a decentralized capitalistic economy. First and foremost, it is argued that central planning can

[3] Our comments here refer to detailed government planning of the general type employed in the Soviet Union and not to the very general planning of, say, Great Britain.

achieve and sustain the full employment of economic resources. The government, as owner and operator of all industry, makes its decisions to produce and to employ apart from profit and loss considerations. The government will simply plan a volume of production which, when executed, will necessitate the full employment of all resources. In contrast the decentralized nature of capitalism, wherein decision making is entrusted to millions of individual profit-motivated units, allegedly makes full employment an accident rather than a certainty.

Second, it is claimed that central planning is more likely to achieve an efficient allocation of resources, that is, full production, than a capitalistic system operating according to consumer sovereignty. It is argued that individual consumers in a capitalistic economy are not in the best position to judge what particular combination of goods and services is best for society. The property incomes fostered by capitalism make the "dollar voting" of consumers a very unequal procedure; the rich have many more votes than the poor. Therefore consumer sovereignty will not result in a product mix which is capable of maximizing the satisfactions of society as a whole. Government, on the other hand, is allegedly in a superior position to determine what specific collection of goods and services is best for the entire economy. The broader perspective of government avoids the capitalistic price system's bias against social goods. Similarly, government is in a strategic position to determine the proper balance between investment goods and consumer goods, that is, to achieve a sound balance between future and present consumption.

In short, it is claimed that central economic planning will do a better job of achieving full employment and full production than can capitalism. The validity of these claims is a subject of endless debate. As informed citizens, we must form our own judgments on this vital issue.

Feasibility of planning

It was emphasized in Chapter 5 that each and every economy must face the same Five Fundamental Questions: What should be produced? How should this output be produced? How should it be distributed? How is the full employment of resources to be maintained in accomplishing this production? How is flexibility to be achieved in order to ensure continued efficiency in resource use?

American capitalism is basically a decentralized, price-directed economy. That is, the decision makers who in the aggregate supply answers to the Five Fundamental Questions are relatively small economic units. Because of their size, these individual units deal only with limited amounts of proximate data; each firm deals with a relatively small number of resources and component parts. Further, the management of each firm is "on the spot," close to the economic and technological data relevant to the production of this product. The capitalistic businessman is in a highly strategic position to grasp the data essential to efficient production. Personal gain prompts him to do so. The price system meshes the decisions of millions of individual firms, and the final result is a set of answers to the Five Fundamental Questions. To be sure, these answers do not entail the highest degree of efficiency—market gluts, unemployment, inflation, production bottlenecks, and so forth are recognized defects of American capitalism. This is true despite the multidimensioned economic role of government. Yet the system is considerably efficient.

Now the significance of these comments for our immediate discussion is that with government planning decision making is obviously centralized. This means that the central planning board—the small group of officials who have the job of answering the Five Fundamental Questions—is necessarily remote from the mass of specific facts and details pertinent to the thousands of industries and millions of firms which comprise a modern complex economy. The question then is this: *In practice can the central planning board grasp the myriad of facts and figures which are essential to efficiency in the employment and allocation of scarce resources?* Stated in the terminology of Chapter 23, will diseconomies of scale prohibit a central planning board from rendering the mass of decisions prerequisite to the achievement of an efficient allocation of resources?

Let us explore this question through some specific illustrations. What problems might be encountered by a central planning board in achieving the full employment and efficient allocation of a basic material—say, steel—in its production plan for 1964? Obviously, a precise balance must be struck between the total supply and the total planned utilization of steel to attain its full employment.

On the supply side of the picture the central planning board would need the following information: How much steel is now available as inventory stocks? How much will be produced domestically in 1964? How much, if any, will be imported? The problems involved in answering these queries are many. Bluntly, in a country the size of Soviet Russia, is it possible to calculate with accuracy the total amount of steel which will be available in 1964? Counting current inventories is complex enough. But accurately forecasting the amount of steel to be produced in 1964 is even more difficult. (The answer here depends upon the anticipated available supplies of iron ore, coke, appropriate capital equipment, labor, and so forth.) And what about imports? In part this is an aspect of supply which cannot be controlled or accurately predicted by the central planning board; decisions made in other countries are basic in determining the amount of steel coming from this source.

After the supply of steel is somehow estimated, the available quantity must be apportioned among the various components of planned demand. That is, the supply of steel must be allocated among the alternative uses provided for in the production targets established by the central planning board. How much steel should be channeled to the construction of capital goods? To armaments? To diesel locomotives? Automobiles? Television sets? How much steel for exports? What size inventories are desired at the end of 1964? If the central planning board prefers armaments to automobiles, it must allocate a *relatively* larger amount of steel to the former than to the latter. But this is more difficult than it sounds. Determining the *absolute* amounts of steel needed to produce a MIG fighter, on the one hand, and an automobile on the other, demands that the central planning board know precisely the technological requirements for producing these products. This means in turn an understanding of the technological requirements for producing the thousands of component parts going into each of these items. Can the central planning board accurately allocate enough steel to fulfill exactly the production target of, say, 2,500 aircraft and 60,000 automobiles? Can the central planning board see to it that these innumerable component parts somehow are brought together in the right place and at the right time to turn out the fabricated product? And can the central planning board efficiently determine the most economic location of a new tractor or automobile plant in a country about three times the size of the continental United States? Can proper planning decisions be made to induce money flows just sufficient to implement the goals set by the central planning board?

This much is clear: Soviet planning, which attempts to allocate some 1,500 basic materials, has proved that detailed economic planning is definitely workable. Whether or not Soviet planning is workable to the extent that it rivals or surpasses the economic efficiency of American capitalism is another question.

CENTRAL PLANNING IN THE SOVIET UNION

Now let us move from this general discussion of central planning to an analysis of central planning as it is practiced in the Soviet Union. What is the origin of Soviet planning? What are its major characteristics? How does Soviet planning cope with the complex problems just discussed?

The relative newness of detailed central planning in the Soviet Union must first be emphasized. After the revolution in 1917 the Soviet Union entered a chaotic *period of War Communism*, lasting from 1917 until 1921. Civil war, foreign invasions, political uncertainty, and the rapid nationalization of industry characterized this period. Planning was attempted, but the effort was exceedingly crude. The sum of these factors was a prostrate economy.

Ironically enough, the Soviet government relaxed its controls to meet this crisis and for a time actually encouraged private enterprise to develop in light industry and in wholesaling and retailing. Heavy industry, banking, and transportation remained nationalized. This *period of the New Economic Policy* (1921 to 1927) was considerably successful in reviving the Soviet economy. As a matter of fact, the Soviet economy was strong enough so that, beginning in 1927, the Soviet government ruthlessly retracted the concessions of the NEP and the country embarked upon a *period of Socialist Reconstruction*. The objective, achieved by the mid-1930s, was complete state control of the Soviet economy. Private trade and manufacture were abolished (made criminal offenses!) in the early 1930s. The nationalization of industry was soon complete. The collectivization of agriculture proved a more difficult task. But in time alternating policies of liquidation and appeasement humbled Soviet agriculture. By 1936 the collectivization of agriculture was virtually complete, but the human and economic costs involved were unbelievably high. It was at the beginning of the period of Socialist Reconstruction that detailed central planning was launched in Soviet Russia; the first Five-year Plan was inaugurated in 1928.

The over-all character of Soviet economic planning has been succinctly described in these words:[4]

The Soviet economic plan is a gigantic, comprehensive blueprint that attempts to govern the economic activities and interrelations of all persons and institutions in the U.S.S.R., as well as the economic relations of the U.S.S.R. with other countries. To the extent that the plan actually controls the development of events, all the manifold activities of the Soviet economy are coordinated as if they were parts of one incredibly enormous enterprise directed from the central headquarters in Moscow.

Now let us see how Soviet economic planning (1) establishes the over-all economic goals

[4] Harry Schwartz, *Russia's Soviet Economy*, 2d ed. (Englewood Cliffs, N.J.: Prentice-Hall, Inc., 1954), p. 146.

for Soviet society; (2) constructs a detailed central plan designed to fulfill these goals; and (3) implements or executes this plan.

Setting the goals

The Soviet government—in reality the Communist party—sets the basic objectives for the Russian economy. These objectives have varied somewhat as succeeding Five-year Plans have been formulated, but emphasis has been upon rapid economic growth through the development of heavy industry. The attainment of a high level of military strength is a closely correlated goal. Lip service is invariably accorded the goal of a higher standard of living for consumers, but the lower priority assigned to this goal means that it is frequently sacrificed to achieve the objectives of industrial expansion and military strength.

The contrast provided with American capitalism is strikingly clear: consumer sovereignty is nonexistent in the Soviet Union. It is not the citizenry, but the government, which decides the uses toward which resources are to be directed. In Russia economic objectives are established not by society but rather by the government for society to fulfill.

Constructing the plan

Given the over-all economic objectives established by the Communist party, it is the task of the state planning commission, or Gosplan, to construct a detailed economic blueprint designed to bring about the realization of these goals. In formulating a Five-year Plan, the Gosplan collects voluminous amounts of statistical data from a host of subordinate ministries, each of which is concerned with the operation of certain industries. From this data, a tentative plan is constructed. The plan is then submitted to the various units of the Soviet administrative hierarchy for study, evaluation, and criticism. This criticism, it must be noted, concerns the specific details of the economic plan and not the over-all goals which the plan seeks.

Let us illustrate this procedure. The segment of the over-all plan which concerns, say, the production of machine tools will be handed to the *minister* in charge of that industry. In turn he will circulate the plan to those lower in the hierarchy—the *chief administrators* (subministers) who control plants located in a given geographic area or producing a specific type of machine tools. They too will evaluate the plan and in turn hand it on to the *trusts* or *combines*, that is, groups of plants which are combined for administrative purposes. Finally, *individual plants*—the ultimate production units—receive the specific plan which will govern their operations. Regional and local planning groups also analyze those segments of the plan relevant to them. At each level the plan will be evaluated, suggestions made for revisions, and these comments passed back up the hierarchy to the Gosplan. Taking into account those suggestions and criticisms which it feels are worthy, the Gosplan then draws up a final plan. When rubber-stamped by the party and the government, this becomes the Five-year Plan.

The point to be emphasized is this: by breaking the over-all plan into its component parts and subjecting these detailed segments to considerable critical examination by subministries, combines, and plants, the Gosplan is able to establish a final plan which is more realistic and workable than would otherwise be the case. Soviet planners apparently recognize their limitations in obtaining and digesting masses of detailed information. The "down-and-up" evaluation of the tentative plan by the administrative hierarchy and its subsequent revision is aimed at obtaining on-the-spot knowledge and an understanding of immediate, detailed facts and circumstances which a relatively small group of planners could not otherwise grasp.

In addition to this preliminary "testing" of the Five-year Plan, three other factors have played significant roles in coping with the complexities inherent in central economic planning. First, over the years Soviet Five-year Plans evolved from simple plans covering only a few major industries to highly detailed plans directing the operation of the economy in virtually every nook and cranny. The ill-fated plans of the period of War Communism were very limited in scope, the first being based for the most part on the development of the electric power industry. In making the plans more ambitious and more comprehensive, the Gosplan has had a chance to learn with experience and to avoid old errors as additional segments of the economy have been added to the plan.

Closely related is the fact that each new plan is in effect a modification and extension of existing and past plans. The present and past serve as invaluable benchmarks for charting the future. Each new plan builds upon, and profits from, experiences with prior plans; the Gosplan is not faced with the gigantic task of deriving each new plan "from scratch."

Finally, Soviet planning is flexible, not rigid. Each Five-year Plan is subject to constant reevaluation and revision. To this end each plan is divided and subdivided into annual and even monthly plans to facilitate the achievement of flexibility. Errors are therefore quickly corrected or adjusted for as they are discovered. This point leads us into a discussion of how Five-year Plans are actually executed.

Executing the plan

The proof of the pudding is in the eating. Setting up detailed production goals is one thing; achieving those objectives may be something else again.

Control agencies. The Soviet government is not inclined to sit back, after each industrial plant and collective farm has been assigned its production targets, and hope for favorable results. On the contrary, an abundance of control agencies supervise the carrying out of each Five-year Plan. Most obvious, of course, is the Gosplan and the network of ministries, subministries, and regional and local planning groups affiliated with it. These administrative units keep a running check on the progress of the plan. The Central Committee of the Communist party and a variety of subordinate party organizations function as watchdog agencies by uncovering, reporting, and helping to correct deviations from the plan. The brutal control functions of the infamous secret police are well known. And, too, a less formal type of control is exercised through a much-publicized program of "criticism and self-criticism," whereby the Soviet citizenry is encouraged to register complaints concerning deviations from, and violations of, the plan.

Clearly the most vital enforcement agency is the state banking system, or *Gosbank.* The Gosbank with its thousands of branches supervises the financial aspects of each plant's production activities and in this manner has a running account of each plant's performance. More precisely, this supervision—"control by the ruble"—works something like this: The government establishes prices on all resources and finished products. For a greatly simplified example, the Leningrad Machine Tool Plant may require 1,000 tons of steel and 100 workers to produce 5,000 units of output per year. If steel costs 60 rubles per ton and each worker is paid 1,000 rubles per year, the total cost of the 5,000 units of output will be 160,000 rubles. Gosplan then directs the Gosbank to make this amount of credit available to the plant over the course of the year. Now, because all the plant's financial transactions—both receipts and expenditures—must be completed through the use of checks, the Gosbank will have an accurate record (in effect, a running audit) of the plant's progress, or lack thereof, in fulfilling the production targets assigned by the Five-year Plan. Should the plant achieve its assigned output at an expense less than 160,000 rubles, it will have overfulfilled its production goal. Inefficient, wasteful production will cause the plant to exhaust its bank credit before its production goal is reached. Either eventuality will be reflected in the plant's account with the Gosbank.

How are the various economic units motivated toward fulfillment of the Five-year Plan? A combination of monetary and nonmonetary incentives, on the one hand, and coercive techniques, on the other, are employed to this end. Let us summarize these motivations (1) in industry and (2) in agriculture.

Incentives in industry. In industry the Soviet government relies heavily upon *monetary incen-*

tives to induce the maximum productive effort from labor. In particular, wages are geared to skill and productivity. The resulting wage differentials are considerable: the highest-paid workers may earn wage incomes fifty times those of the lowest-paid workers. Great emphasis is put upon piecework, more so than in the United States. Probably as much as four-fifths of the Soviet labor force works under a piecework plan of one sort or another. Elaborate systems of bonuses and premiums induce workers to exceed normal production rates. Most competent observers conclude that wage incomes in the Soviet Union are as unequally distributed as in the United States. Keep in mind, too, that Soviet income receivers, though not free to determine the portion of total output which is to take the form of consumer goods, are able to spend their incomes as they wish on the consumer goods which the Gosplan makes available to them. This means that differences in money incomes are generally reflected in real income differentials.

A variety of *nonmonetary inducements* also exist to stimulate labor to greater productivity. A rather comprehensive system of awards and decorations exists to cite exemplary workers. These are closely correlated with material rewards. For example, a "Hero of Socialist Labor" is likely to be accorded certain tax exemptions, monthly bonuses, low rental on state housing, free use of transportation facilities, government-supplied vacations at a Crimean resort, and so forth. The real standard of living of the average Soviet worker is about one-fourth that of his American counterpart, so that the value of such benefits is considerable. Much publicity accompanies these awards. A member of the "Order of Lenin" may enjoy fame and prestige comparable to that of a professional baseball player or movie star in the United States. In addition, "socialist competitions" are encouraged by the party, pitting the productive capacities of various groups of workers against one another. Since 1935 the Stakhanovite Movement—a program whereby workers are encouraged to develop and apply new and more efficient productive techniques—has been much acclaimed.[5]

The labor unions to which the vast majority of Soviet workers belong bear little or no resemblance to their American counterparts. In effect, Russian labor unions are functionaries of the state whose basic goals are to encourage a high rate of productivity among their members in carrying out the economic plan, to train new workers, and to aid in the solution of labor discipline problems. Wage rates are set by the government. Collective bargaining as we know it does not exist, and strikes simply do not occur. Soviet labor unions do, however, prevent undue exploitation of their members by plant managers eager to fulfill their assigned production quotas. They also play an active role in providing recreational and cultural programs for workers.

Monetary and nonmonetary inducements are duly supplemented by a variety of coercive techniques. Indeed, Article XII of the Soviet constitution of 1936 flatly states that "Work in the U.S.S.R. is a duty and a matter of honor for every able-bodied citizen, in accordance with the principle 'He who does not work, neither shall he eat.'" But labor discipline has at times been very poor: absenteeism, tardiness, and worker indifference are common problems. The rate of labor turnover has also been a major problem. Plant managers frequently "pirate" the personnel of one another to ensure a labor force adequate for fulfillment of their output targets. Workers seem very willing to change jobs, however slight the resulting improvement in their standard of living might be.

Soviet authorities have taken action to cope with such problems. Fines, pay reductions, dismissal, eviction from state housing, the freezing of workers to their jobs, and discriminatory treatment with respect to social insurance benefits all hang over the head of the bungling, the lazy, the indifferent, and the overly mobile worker. "Spies" and "wreckers" may be subject to the wrath of the secret police and as-

[5] In 1935 one Alexis Stakhanov, a coal miner, achieved immortality in the Soviet Union by "knocking down" in one work shift 102 tons of coal—fourteen times the then-existing norm—through the use of more efficient work methods. See Michael T. Florinsky, *Towards an Understanding of the USSR*, rev. ed. (New York: The Macmillan Company, 1953), p. 125.

signed to "correctional labor camps" in Siberia or similarly remote areas. An estimated 8 to 12 million unfortunates have met this fate. Most, however, are so situated for political rather than economic reasons.

Comparable monetary and nonmonetary inducements and compulsory techniques bear upon plant managers. High salaries, bonuses, awards, and promotion await those who fulfill their production targets. Failure exposes the plant manager to investigation and reassignment to a less palatable position. A good many plant managers are party members and therefore inspired by party doctrines.

Incentives in agriculture. Emphasis upon state compulsion in agriculture seems to exceed that in industry. Virtually all Soviet agriculture is carried on by state farms and collective farms. *State farms* are in effect government owned and operated "grain and meat factories." They account for about 10 per cent of total farm output. As in industrial plants, workers are hired by state-appointed farm managers and are paid wages geared to productivity. Furthering agricultural research and illustrating the advantages of large-scale operations to the peasantry are main goals of the state farms. About 90 per cent of Soviet agricultural production is carried on by *collective farms.* These farms are cooperatives, voluntary in theory but in practice imposed by the state. Member families pool their tools and talents, sharing the net proceeds of the farm's operations according to the quantity and quality of work they perform. In addition, each family is assigned a small plot of land and a small quantity of livestock for its own personal use.

Incentives to produce on collective farms are somewhat different from those in industry or on state farms. Through the concept of the *labor day* the income of a collective farmer is determined by the quantity, quality, and "social usefulness" of his efforts. A labor day is not simply eight hours of work, but rather an arbitrary estimate of the worth of specific jobs. For example, one labor day of work may be given for the relatively simple, nonskilled task of weeding a field of sugar beets. A tractor driver's skill may entitle him to one and one-half labor days of work for harvesting several acres of wheat. The larger the number of labor days a farmer has to his credit, the greater his share of the net proceeds of the collective farm.

The relative inefficiency of Soviet agriculture, coupled with the fact that the state appropriates large portions of the collective farms' output, make the masses of Soviet farmers poor. The result is the passive but vigorous opposition of many peasants to collectivization. This resistance takes several forms: evasion of work for the collective farm, appropriation and illegal sale or use of the crops and property of the collectives, and, most commonly, the expansion and intensive cultivation of the private plots of land assigned to each family. The Soviet government has countered this resistance with a variety of coercive techniques.

Planning and economic stability

Theoretically there is no room for the business cycle in a centrally planned economy. As we have noted, the alleged superiority of a centralized over a decentralized economy lies for the most part in the ability of the former to eliminate economic fluctuations. It is argued that decentralized decision making, based upon private profits, is conducive to cyclical fluctuations in business activity; effective central planning designed to achieve realistic production targets will supposedly overcome this inherent defect of the capitalistic economy.

But theory and practice can, and often do, differ. Has the Soviet Union eliminated the business cycle? The answer is "Yes and no."

Unemployment. It is true that since about 1930 Soviet planning seems to have virtually eliminated prolonged involuntary unemployment. Cyclical unemployment is not a characteristic of the Soviet economy. Indeed, the pressures of the ambitious Five-year Plans have resulted in "overfull" employment in the Soviet Union. Various government pressures to induce women and young people into the labor force are evidence of this condition. Many people who now have jobs in the Soviet Union would probably prefer to be unemployed!

But to say that cyclical unemployment is largely absent in the Soviet economy is not to say that all unemployment is nonexistent. *Underemployment,* stemming from planning errors, and *frictional unemployment,* due in part to high rates of labor turnover, do exist.

To the extent that production goals for specific groups of workers exceed or fall short of the actual amount those workers are capable of producing, underemployment will result. For example, if the production goal for the 100 workers at the Leningrad Machine Tool Plant is 5,000 units per year and if these workers are actually capable of producing, say, 6,000 units, the mere fulfillment of the 5,000-unit goal will result in underemployment. Specifically, these workers will be one-sixth underemployed.[6] To misplan in the other direction—that is, to set a production goal beyond the 6,000 maximum —will also cause underemployment, but in other plants. To illustrate: A production target of 7,000 cannot be fulfilled by the 100 workers, even though they are fully employed in every sense of the term. But this failure will mean that other plants whose production plans and labor forces are geared to the anticipated receipt of 7,000 units will find themselves underequipped with machine tools. The result of this equipment shortage is that some fraction of these labor forces in other plants will be underemployed.

Inflation. Although cyclical unemployment has been largely resolved by Soviet planning, the other side of the cycle—inflation—has been a knotty problem in the Soviet Union since the early 1930s. Because of its tremendous emphasis upon investment, social, and military goods, a very large part of Soviet production results in consumer incomes which are unmatched by consumer goods output. Specifically, nonconsumer goods constitute about 43 per cent of total Soviet production (see Figure 40-1). The

[6] Producing 6,000 units, exactly 1,000 more than required by the plan, will eliminate this underemployment. See Alfred R. Oxenfeldt, *Economic Systems in Action,* rev. ed. (New York: Holt, Rinehart and Winston, Inc., 1957), pp. 91–92.

production of these goods creates incomes but not goods for consumers to buy. The result is inflationary pressure.

As in a capitalistic economy, there are two basic means for alleviating this pressure. One is to induce income receivers to save; the other is to tax away inflation-causing income. The Soviet Union has used both techniques, but emphasis has clearly been upon taxation. Despite a network of savings banks and definite government encouragement to save, the actual volume of savings has been low. On the one hand, the absence of the fear of prolonged cyclical unemployment removes an important motive for saving; on the other, living standards are simply too low to permit many the luxury of saving. Hence, the emphasis on taxation.

From the equalitarian tenor of the Soviet ideology, one would expect a highly progressive income tax at the core of the Soviet Union's tax system. But this is not the case. By American standards the Soviet income tax is very mildly progressive, and the tax itself is secondary to the *turnover tax* as a revenue getter. Accounting for about 60 per cent of annual tax revenue, the turnover tax is in effect a sales tax which imposes heavy and widely different rates on various consumer goods.

Two reasons go far to explain why the Soviet government attacks inflation through the turnover tax rather than through the use of income taxes: (1) The turnover tax is "hidden" in product prices and is therefore less likely to hurt incentives to produce than an income tax tailored to collect the same amount of revenue. (2) More important, turnover taxes are more selective in their effects on the consumption of specific goods. While income taxation can force the *aggregate* of consumer spending into balance with the *aggregate* output of consumer goods, it does not guarantee a balancing of the amount demanded and the amount supplied for specific products at government-imposed prices. A balancing of *total* consumer demand and *total* consumer goods output will not avoid sharp inflationary pressures on particularly scarce products such as automobiles and television sets. The turnover tax, on the other hand, can be used not only to match total consumption spending and total consumer goods output, but also to force the pattern of consumer demand into accord with the composition of consumer goods output provided by the plan.

It works like this: High turnover taxes on particularly scarce goods greatly discourage their consumption and force the amounts demanded into accord with the skimpy quantities allowed by the plan. Lower rates on consumer staples—for example, potatoes and other vegetables—available in relative abundance encourage their consumption. The greater the relative scarcity of a product, the higher the turnover tax placed upon it. The total prices of such products will necessarily be higher and purchases discouraged. Lower tax rates on more abundant products give them lower relative prices and encourage their consumption. In this way inflation-causing income is taxed away, and the pattern of consumer spending is forced into rough accord with the planned composition of consumer goods output.

On consumer goods as a whole, turnover taxes are high, amounting to about 44 per cent of retail prices.[7] This provides a very rough indication of the severity of inflationary pressure in the Soviet Union. In the postwar era two drastic policy steps by the Soviet government have also testified to the persistence of inflation. The monetary reform of 1947 saw the Soviet government exchange new rubles for old rubles held as cash at a 1:10 rate. Savings in the form of bank accounts and government bonds were somewhat less harshly treated. Then in 1957 the government virtually repudiated its outstanding public debt.

Soviet planning has seemingly eliminated cyclical unemployment. Yet underemployment accompanies faulty planning, and frictional unemployment still persists. Forced economic growth has given rise to considerable inflation-

[7] Robert W. Campbell, *Soviet Economic Power* (Cambridge: Houghton Mifflin Company, 1960), p. 151.

ary pressure. The turnover tax has been the basic technique employed by the Soviet Union to hold this pressure in check.

Planning and the price system

At the risk of oversimplification it can be said that in a capitalistic economy consumers express their desires for particular products through the demand side of the product market. Given the ability and willingness of producers to supply various products, firms will be attracted to the manufacture of those items which are most profitable and repelled from those which entail losses. In this way producers, responding to consumer wants, guide or direct resources into those lines of production which individuals deem most urgent.

In contrast the Soviet price system, as noted earlier, does not function as a *guiding mechanism*. Rather it is a mechanism used for implementing the production objectives established by the state. *Soviet prices are government-manipulated to aid in the achievement of state-established goals; capitalistic prices are market-established and induce the fulfillment of individually determined goals.*

Actually, the function of prices in the Soviet Union differs considerably as between the production process, on the one hand, and the sale of final products to consumers, on the other. In the first instance prices are simply accounting devices which facilitate checking the efficiency with which products are manufactured. In the latter case prices are employed as rationing devices to distribute products to consumers without the use of government rationing.

In producing, say, a television set a Soviet plant will be faced with certain governmentally established prices for component parts, labor, and other needed resources. And, similarly, government will determine the price of the final product. Generally speaking, the basic principle in establishing these prices is that a plant or industry of average efficiency should realize total receipts from its production which will just cover its total costs; that is, it should break even. If production is less efficient than that deemed average by the plan, losses will result. Greater-than-average efficiency will result in unplanned profits.[8] In short, the prices of resources and components are used as accounting costs to assess the efficiency with which various plants and industries operate. Except for the fact that capitalistic prices are market determined rather than government determined, this role of the Soviet price system parallels that of its capitalistic counterpart. But here the similarity ends.

In a capitalistic economy losses call for a contraction of output and a release of resources by the affected industry; profits signal industry expansion and the absorption of resources. Not so in the Soviet Union. Expansion and contraction of industry is determined by the government, not the price system. Therefore a relatively inefficient industry which is considered vital by the state may be expanded despite losses. Similarly, a highly efficient, profit-realizing industry may be purposely contracted by state planning.

While prices in the production process are essentially accounting devices to gauge efficiency, the prices of finished goods are established to serve as rationing devices. In other words, consumer goods prices are set by the government to eliminate any persistent product shortages or surpluses. As a result, the price of television sets which is used for accounting purposes may vary considerably from the price which is charged consumers who purchase them. The difference typically takes the form of the turnover tax.

To illustrate: Suppose the accounting price of a finished television set is 1,500 rubles. This price is used by the Gosplan in judging the efficiency of the fabricating plant. But, for reasons explained in the previous section, consumer demand in the Soviet Union has persistently exceeded the available supply of consumer goods. This means that, if shortages and gov-

[8] For the most part, these profits will accrue to the government as revenue from state-owned enterprises. A part may be used to expand the industry, if such expansion is consistent with the objectives of the plan. Another portion may be shared by the plant's workers and executives as a bonus for their efficiency.

ernment rationing are to be avoided, the price charged by the state in selling television sets to consumers is very likely to be higher than the accounting price. Suppose the government estimates that the consumer price of television sets must be 3,000 rubles to bring the quantity demanded into balance with the quantity of television sets currently available. This is accomplished by adding a 100 per cent turnover tax to television sets. At this price the market will be cleared and government rationing avoided. For some items consumer prices are lower than accounting prices, to encourage the purchase of relatively abundant products. In this case the government subsidizes consumer purchases of such items.

Efficiency of Soviet planning

How efficient is Soviet economic planning? This is an extremely difficult question to answer. As best as can be ascertained, the Soviet Union has been fairly successful in achieving the main goals embodied in the various Five-year Plans. At the same time, fulfillment of the plans has been very uneven. Some industries have produced far beyond their assigned goals; others have fallen woefully short. The fact that the Soviet press periodically contains pronouncements of Soviet leaders decrying the lack of efficiency in achieving specific targets of the plan makes clear that Russian planning is far from perfect. A major shortcoming is that emphasis upon the quantity of output is often at the expense of quality, particularly in the production of consumer goods. Capital equipment is sometimes sorely overworked to fulfill or exceed production quotas. And, despite the elimination of cyclical unemployment, the presence of noncyclical unemployment and inflationary pressures partially reflect planning weaknesses. All this implies that Soviet planning is still in a rather rudimentary stage of development.

But several points must be made in defense of Soviet planning, lest we leap to the conclusion that it is highly ineffectual.

1. Remember that detailed central planning is historically new. One has no right to expect

such a profound social experiment to yield miracles in the relatively short span of three or four decades.

2. Recall that no alternative economic system is perfectly efficient. Indeed, the bulk of this book is devoted to a study of the real and potential inefficiencies of American capitalism and the policies designed to correct them.

3. There are certain aspects of the Soviet economy which by their very nature are monkey wrenches in the planning machinery. (a) The weather simply does not obey the dictates of the Communist party. Agricultural production is therefore very difficult to plan with any degree of accuracy. A short crop may, of course, have serious repercussions throughout the entire plan. (b) Foreign trade, as previously noted, is another imponderable. It cannot be controlled in the same manner as domestic production. Unforeseen shifts in sales to, and purchases from, the Soviet Union by nonsatellite nations may cause serious imperfections in the Five-year Plan. (c) Ironically, unanticipated technological breakthroughs can wreak havoc with central planning (as they also can in a private enterprise system). Sudden and significant productivity increases call for resources to be reallocated, thereby necessitating significant revisions in the plan. (d) Military considerations are another unpredictable facet of economic life. The Hungarian and Polish uprisings of 1956, for example, would entail unexpected shifts of human and property resources from nonwar to war goods production, calling for significant planning adjustments.

4. The point that speaks the most strongly for efficiency in Soviet planning is that the Soviet economy has achieved a remarkable rate of economic growth under its system of planning. Of course, it can be argued that this growth has occurred *despite*, and not *because of*, central planning. Yet the fact remains that Soviet leadership has explicitly aimed at rapid industrialization and accelerated growth. The Five-year Plans have all pointed toward these objectives. The fact remains, too, that in a short span of years Soviet Russia has been transformed from an industrially backward, economically dormant nation to its present position

as the world's second strongest economy. It is to the question of Soviet economic growth that we now turn.

SOVIET ECONOMIC GROWTH

Soviet Russia's challenge to the economic superiority of American capitalism is being closely observed by both underdeveloped and semideveloped nations. In seeking opulence, should the less-developed countries alter their institutions and ideologies in the direction of central planning of the Soviet variety or in the direction of the American vintage of decentralization? There is no simple answer to such a complex and profound question. Some light can be thrown on the issue by assessing the present economic strengths and current rates of growth of these two competing economic systems.

GNP comparisons

Authoritative estimates put the GNP of the Soviet Union at about one-half that of the United States. And, as Figure 40-1 makes clear, its composition is significantly different. The relatively greater emphasis upon investment and government spending is the result of the Soviet Union's drive toward rapid industrialization and military superiority. This has come at the expense of consumer goods production.

But this absolute comparison, favorable as it appears to the United States, should not be a cause for celebration in the West. The reasons are twofold: (1) When the production of the European satellites and Communist China are added to this picture, their combined GNPs total roughly three-fourths that of the United States. (2) Figure 40-1 presents a comparison of the economic strengths of the two competing powers at a specific point in time. This picture fails to consider relative rates of growth.

Comparing economic growth

Problems of estimating and comparing rates of economic growth are formidable; hence, there exist no definite figures which present a comparison of progress in the Soviet Union and the United States. Nevertheless, most scholars are in agreement that the annual rate of growth in the Soviet Union is two or three times as great as that now achieved in the United States. A 1957 study of the Joint Economic Committee suggests that the Soviet growth rate is about 7 per cent as compared to 3 or 4 per cent for the United States. Other studies put the Soviet growth figure at about 12 per cent.[9]

These growth estimates raise two most pertinent queries: (1) By what manner has the Soviet Union achieved this remarkable rate of growth? (2) Can the Soviet economy maintain this pace in future years?

Sources of Soviet economic growth

How can the rapid rate of Soviet growth be explained? Before we examine the specific policies which have fostered growth, it must be emphasized that the Soviet Union has both the *ability* and the *guiding mechanism* to accomplish rapid expansion. By "ability" we refer, of course, to the natural wealth of the Soviet economy. The Soviet Union has an abundant and diversified resource base upon which to develop. By "guiding mechanism" we allude to Russia's highly centralized, dictatorial government. Dedicated to rapid industrialization, it provides a ruthless but apparently highly effective mechanism for *forcing* economic growth. There is little doubt but that the Soviet government is pushing economic expansion at a rate more rapid than the Soviet citizenry might themselves choose.

We need not doubt the desire of the regime to develop the economic potential of the Soviet

[9] Joint Economic Committee, *Soviet Economic Growth: A Comparison with the United States* (Washington: 1957), pp. 135–136. The interested reader should also consult Abram Bergson (ed.), *Soviet Economic Growth* (New York: Harper & Row, Publishers, 1953), chap. 1, and A. Nove, "The Pace of Soviet Economic Development," *Lloyds Bank Review*, April, 1956.

Union as rapidly as possible, and that it will continue to push, prod, drive, cajole, and tempt the country in that direction.[10]

Given ample resources and the desires of Soviet government, what specific policies or techniques have been invoked to achieve rapid growth?

1. Government planning has emphasized high levels of investment in basic heavy industries—steel, coal, electric power—at the expense of consumer goods production (see Figure 40-1). With the exception of the exploitation of the capital of conquered nations, Russia's relatively high level of investment spending has been achieved internally. Little foreign capital has aided Soviet development. This means that the cost of industrialization and growth has been borne by the Soviet citizenry in the form of low standards of living. Even the composition of Soviet investment spending reflects this. Investment in consumer goods industries and in housing, for example, has been woefully neglected in hurrying the development of basic industry.

2. Industrialization has also been accelerated by significant increases in the size of the labor force and by tremendous shifts of human resources from agriculture to industry. In 1925, 84 per cent of the Soviet labor force was employed in agriculture; by 1959 only 46 per cent was thus employed.

3. There is no doubt that rapid expansion in Soviet production has stemmed in good measure from the adoption of the superior technological knowledge pioneered by the Western nations. Indeed, in the earlier stages of its development program the Soviet Union imported Western specialists not only to detail and construct basic capital facilities, but to train Soviet personnel in the management and operation of these industrial plants.

4. Soviet growth has undoubtedly been spurred by the government's success in achieving continuous full employment through central planning.

[10] Bergson, *op. cit.*, p. 21.

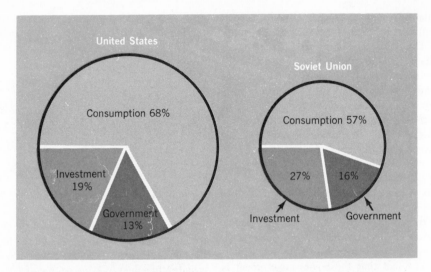

FIGURE 40-1. SIZE AND COMPOSITION OF GNP IN THE UNITED STATES AND THE SOVIET UNION, 1955.
Soviet Russia's GNP is roughly one-half the size of the United States's GNP. The composition of Russia's GNP indicates the heavier emphasis it is putting upon industrialization, military goods, and social goods. [Joint Economic Committee, "Soviet Economic Growth; A Comparison with the United States" (Washington: Government Printing Office, 1957), pp. 127–149, data for 1955.]

Sustaining Soviet growth

Authorities disagree as to whether the Soviet Union will be able to maintain its remarkable growth record.

It is not too difficult to cite a number of plausible reasons why the Soviet growth rate might decline in the future: (1) Much of the Soviet Union's past growth has stemmed from the fact that Russia has been catching up with the industrially advanced nations by borrowing and applying their superior technology. As the technological gap closes, there will simply be fewer technological windfalls to accelerate Soviet expansion. (2) As the Soviet Union's stock of real capital goods expands, an ever-increasing portion of each succeeding year's capital goods output must be used simply for the replacement of depreciated capital facilities. This means that a larger and larger output of capital goods will be required over the years to sustain

a *constant* rate of expansion in the stock of capital facilities. (3) Some experts feel that Soviet growth has now brought the best and most accessible natural resources into production. This means that further expansion of metal production, for example, will entail the use of less accessible and lower grade mineral deposits. Similarly, less and less suitable land is available for any expansion of the amount of land under cultivation (4) High casualty rates and low birth rates during World War II are currently reflected in a slowing down in the rate of growth of the Soviet labor force. This is reflected primarily in a relative shortage of industrial labor. (5) Some authorities feel that Soviet foreign aid commitments to China and to noncommunist underdeveloped nations will sap resources from investment goods production and retard future growth. Growing domestic pressures for more and better consumer goods tend to have the same effect.

But there are at least two impressive arguments which suggest a sustained or even accelerated rate of growth in Soviet Russia.

1. The Soviet Union is putting tremendous emphasis upon scientific education and technological research. Remarkable Soviet successes in space research imply that similar advances may be forthcoming in industry. As a matter of fact, it is generally conceded that the Soviet Union now has the skills and industrial capacity for the production of large quantities of modern, technologically advanced capital equipment. The importance of Soviet technological advances cannot be minimized; remember that technological advance is becoming an increasingly important ingredient in economic growth (Chapter 18). It has a habit of sweeping aside all other obstacles to growth.

2. The fact that the Soviet government is firmly committed to the objective of catching up and surpassing the economic performance of the United States also suggests sustained or accelerated growth. The past productive performance of the Soviet Union suggests that central planning has proved a highly effective means of forcing economic growth. As a matter of fact, future improvements in the over-all efficiency of Soviet planning as such can be expected to have a favorable impact upon the Soviet growth rate. Of particular relevance for United States–Soviet comparisons is the fact that Soviet planning has virtually eliminated cyclical unemployment. Therefore, central planning forces the Russian economy to realize its growth potential. In contrast the United States falls far short of its growth potential whenever a recession is encountered. For example, because of the 1958 recession, the annual realized rate of growth of the United States from 1955 to 1958 was 0.5 per cent, far short of its estimated 3 to 4 per cent growth potential. It is obvious that future American lapses from full employment, if they occur, will hasten the Soviet Union's "catching up" even if the Soviet growth rate slackens to 6 or 5 per cent in future years.

Over all, there is little room for American complacency. The Soviet economic challenge and its implications cannot be regarded lightly.

EVALUATING THE SOVIET ECONOMY

The lack of reliable information and the presence of an abundance of prejudices make the Soviet economy difficult to evaluate. And, of course, it is impossible to evaluate the Soviet economy on economic grounds alone. In any event most recent assessments embrace the points that follow.

Accomplishments

1. The Soviet Union has proved the workability of central economic planning. Despite the complexities involved, the Soviet Union has apparently achieved some degree of efficiency in economic planning. This is not to say that Soviet planning is highly efficient, that it operates smoothly without bottlenecks and blunders, or that it functions with greater efficiency than does American capitalism. Evidence suggests that, although Soviet planning is becoming more and more efficient, it is still "rough and clumsy." *But Soviet planning does work,* claims by respected economists that detailed planning is not practicable to the contrary.

2. There can be no question that the Soviet Union has achieved a high level of industrialization in a relatively short period of time and, in doing so, a remarkable rate of economic growth. Forced economic growth has made Soviet Russia a first-rate economic and military power. The fact that there is debate over the relative military strengths of the Soviet Union and the United States and increasing concern in the West as to the rate of Soviet economic development is ample evidence on this point. Whether one agrees or disagrees with Soviet goals and techniques, there is no denying that Soviet Russia ranks second only to the United States in economic strength.

3. Though circumscribed by communist doctrine, Soviet Russia has made tremendous strides in improving the educational levels of the masses of Russian peoples. Medical and health standards have been marked by similar im-

provement. Much has been done to encourage cultural pursuits, again within limits imposed by the party line.

Shortcomings

Generally speaking, the major shortcomings of the Soviet economic system are the offspring of its accomplishments. Two major points merit emphasis:

1. The Russian people have not received the benefits of a higher standard of living. The cost of rapid industrialization and economic growth has been great and, as previously noted, borne for the most part by consumers. This shortcoming is reflected not only in the quantity of goods available, but also in their quality.

A recent study of the Joint Economic Committee of the United States Congress summarizes the Russian citizen's plight:

It is apparent from the record of Soviet behavior that the goal of the system is not primarily to better the life of the consumer, but to enhance the power of the state. Consumers receive improved benefits only as the rulers believe more goods or shorter hours will increase productivity and keep unrest within manageable limits.

The Soviet level of living was little better in 1955 than it was in 1928. However, conditions were so bad in some intervening years that the progress from 1950 to 1955 was very considerable. . . .

Although it is extremely difficult to compare living levels, the real wages of Soviet workers appear at the very best to be only one-fourth to one-seventh as high on the average as those in the United States.[11]

The fact that during the first Five-year Plan Russia exported grain in order to import machinery and technological assistance, despite domestic food rationing and famine in the Ukraine, is vivid testimony to the economic cost of forced industrialization.[12]

2. The noneconomic costs of the collectivi-

---

[11] Joint Economic Committee, *op. cit.*, pp. 142–143.
[12] Schwartz, *op. cit.*, p. 138.

---

zation of industry and agriculture, the development of economic planning, and the relentless pursuit of industrialization and economic growth have undoubtedly been tremendous. The coercive and punitive tactics of the Soviet government are well known. The brutal deportation of an estimated 4 to 5 million of the more prosperous peasants (kulaks) in the drive to collective agriculture, the use of an estimated 8 to 12 million prison laborers under unbelievably harsh conditions, the many-dimensioned role of the secret police, recurring purges, and the complete absence of political democracy as we know it are some of the more evident noneconomic costs which Soviet economic successes have entailed.

Implications

Of this there is no doubt: the Soviet economic challenge injects an element of urgency to the economizing problem in American capitalism. The goals of sustained economic stability and adequate growth (Parts 2 to 4) take on new, critical dimensions in view of rapid Soviet economic expansion. In particular, a prolonged depression would seriously impair our chances of winning the economic war Soviet Russia has imposed upon us. Certainly the question of achieving efficiency in the allocation of resources through the mechanism of the price system becomes increasingly acute (Part 5). American capitalism must continuously appraise the allocative efficiency of the market mechanism and the balance between private and social goods. This obviously entails a detailed reexamination of specific problem areas and existing public policies designed to cope with those problems (Part 6). And clearly the military, political, and economic significance of the less-developed nations of the world calls for a farsightedness in our international trade policies and practices which historically has been highly elusive (Part 7).

The role of American capitalism in the political, military, and sociocultural affairs of the world can continue to be the dominant one.

An awareness of economic principles, problems, and policies can play a central role in preserving that dominance.

SUMMARY

1. The vivid contrast which the Soviet economy provides to American capitalism, the economic challenge it presents to the Western world, and the rapid economic growth achieved in Soviet Russia are important reasons for studying the Soviet economic system.

2. Virtually complete public ownership of property resources and detailed central economic planning are the outstanding institutional features of the Soviet economy. Monetary, non-monetary, and coercive techniques are all used to induce productive effort. The price system does not direct the Russian economy, but is rather a tool for implementing government directives.

3. Central planning entails (*a*) determining economic objectives—that is, establishing the desired size, composition, and distribution of total output; (*b*) evolving an economic plan which will fulfill these objectives; and (*c*) carrying out this plan so as to realize its fulfillment.

4. Proponents of central planning contend that a government-directed economy can achieve full employment and full production to a greater degree than can a decentralized, price-directed economy. However, efficient planning rests on the debatable assumption that a relatively small group of planners can collect, assimilate, and efficiently employ a mass of detailed technological and economic data.

5. As established by the Communist party, the basic objectives of the Soviet Five-year Plans have centered around rapid industrialization and military strength. In forming a final plan to implement these goals the Gosplan circulates a tentative plan down through the planning hierarchy for evaluation and criticism. Gradual expansion in the scope of Soviet planning, the ability to build new plans on the basis of old, and the fact that plans are flexible also aid in overcoming the problems that are inherent in central planning.

6. Many agencies check upon the actual execution of the Five-year Plans—the planning hierarchy, the Communist party and its numerous officials, and the secret police. The most important of these agencies is the Gosbank, which exerts "control by the ruble."

7. The problem of cyclical unemployment has apparently been resolved in the Soviet Union, but underemployment and frictional unemployment persist. Inflation, a persistent and reoccurring problem since the early 1930s, has been fought primarily through the use of the turnover tax and drastic monetary reforms.

8. In the production process, governmentally determined prices on resources and components and on finished products serve as accounting devices to evaluate the efficiency of production. In consumer goods markets, prices are adjusted through the turnover tax to ration products to consumers, that is, to balance the amount demanded with available supplies.

9. Fulfillment of the various Five-year Plans has been uneven and spotty. Indications are that Soviet planning is still a rather crude procedure; yet there is no doubt as to its over-all workability. The rapid rate of Soviet economic growth bespeaks of at least a minimum level of efficiency in Soviet planning.

10. For many reasons comparisons of the rates of growth and current outputs of the Soviet Union and the United States are necessarily hazardous. A good estimate is that the current Soviet GNP is roughly one-half that of the United States. Its composition is such that only about 57 per cent is in the form of consumer goods as compared with 68 per cent in the United States.

11. It is estimated that the current Soviet rate of economic growth is two or three times as great as that of the United States. This rapid rate of growth has been forced by the Soviet government and has been achieved by (*a*) sacrificing consumer living standards, (*b*) negotiating significant shifts of human resources from agriculture to industry, and (*c*) adopting the superior technological knowledge of the West. Soviet emphasis upon technological research and its commitment to the objective of surpassing the productive performance of the United States make it difficult to accept the view that the Soviet Union's growth rate will decline greatly in the near future.

12. The major achievements of the Soviet economy have been twofold: (a) proving the feasibility of detailed central planning and (b) achieving a substantial rate of economic growth through rapid industrialization. These accomplishments have not been without significant costs: (a) the output of consumer goods has been sacrificed, and (b) the human costs of forced economic expansion have been extremely high.

QUESTIONS AND STUDY SUGGESTIONS

1. "So long as a central planning board, as opposed to society as a whole, sets the economic goals, there can be no freedom of occupational or consumer choice. This is true despite the existence of no government restrictions whatever upon the job one chooses or the manner in which he disposes of his money income." Explain.

2. Compare the sources of insecurity which face an American and a Soviet steelworker.

3. "It has become increasingly difficult for thoughtful men to find meaningful alternatives posed in the traditional choices between socialism and capitalism, planning and the free market, regulation and laissez faire, for they find their actual choices neither simple nor so grand."[13] Explain and evaluate.

4. Compare the institutional framework of the Soviet economy with that of American capitalism. Contrast the manner in which production is motivated in these two economic systems.

5. State and carefully evaluate the claims for the superiority of a centrally directed economy over a price-directed economy.

6. How does Soviet planning attempt to cope with the Five Fundamental Questions which all economies must face? Evaluate the success of Soviet planning in answering these questions.

7. What is a state farm? A collective farm? Why is it difficult to plan accurately the production of the agricultural segment of the Soviet economy?

8. "Technological progress has made it even more difficult to keep the state out [of industrialization]. In the eighteenth and nineteenth centuries, when technology was still relatively primitive, plants were small, and initial capital investments were relatively low. In the twentieth century, industrialization means huge initial capital investments, so huge that they can be provided only by foreign investors or the state. If foreign investors are unwilling to invest, or are excluded by political regulation, the state is left as the only big investor."[14] Carefully evaluate this argument. What role, if any, has this argument played in the rapid economic development which has occurred in Soviet Russia? What implications does this statement embody for American capitalism in meeting the Soviet economic challenge?

9. Why have inflationary tendencies in the Soviet Union apparently tended to be more acute than those encountered in the United States? What measures are employed in Soviet Russia to deal with the inflationary problem? What advantages does a turnover tax have as opposed to an income tax in relieving inflation?

[13] Robert A. Dahl and Charles E. Lindblom, *Politics, Economics and Welfare* (New York: Harper & Row, Publishers, Inc., 1953), p. 1.

[14] William Ebenstein, *Today's Isms*, 2d ed. (Englewood Cliffs, N.J.: Prentice-Hall, Inc., 1958), p. 59.

10. Evaluate carefully the level of efficiency which has been achieved in Soviet economic planning.

11. Compare recent rates of economic growth for the United States and the Soviet Union. What have been the major sources of Soviet economic expansion? Do you feel that the Soviet Union will be able to sustain its past growth performance? Explain.

12. Carefully contrast the role of the price system in Soviet Russia and the United States.

13. How is the number of automobiles to be produced determined in American capitalism? In the Soviet Union? How are these decisions implemented in the two economies?

SELECTED REFERENCES

Bergson, Abram (ed.), *Soviet Economic Growth* (New York: Harper & Row, Publishers, 1953), particularly chap. 1.

Campbell, Robert W., *Soviet Economic Power* (Boston: Houghton Mifflin Company, 1960).

Holzman, Franklyn D. (ed.), *Readings on the Soviet Economy* (Chicago: Rand McNally & Company, 1962).

Joint Economic Committee, *Comparisons of the United States and Soviet Economies* (Washington: 1959), parts 1–3.

Joint Economic Committee, *Soviet Economic Growth: A Comparison with the United States* (Washington: 1957).

Loucks, William N., *Comparative Economic Systems,* 6th ed. (New York: Harper & Row, Publishers, 1961), chaps. 22–28.

Nove, Alec, *The Soviet Economy: An Introduction* (New York: Frederick A. Praeger, Inc., 1961).

Schwartz, Harry, *Russia's Soviet Economy,* 2d ed. (Englewood Cliffs, N.J.: Prentice-Hall, Inc., 1954).

Spulber, Nicolas, *The Soviet Economy: Structure, Principles, Problems* (New York: W. W. Norton & Company, Inc., 1962).

Wilcox, Clair, Willis D. Weatherford, Jr., and Holland Hunter, *Economies of the World Today* (New York: Harcourt, Brace & World, Inc., 1962).

Index

NATIONAL INCOME AND RELATED STATISTICS

NATIONAL INCOME STATISTICS*
(in billions of current dollars)

FOR SELECTED YEARS, 1929-1961

		1929	1933	1937	1939	1940	1941	1942	1943	1944	1945	1946
	The sum of:											
1	Personal Consumption Expenditures	$79.0	$46.4	$67.3	$67.6	$71.9	$81.9	$89.7	$100.5	$109.8	$121.7	$147.1
2	Gross Private Domestic Investment	16.2	1.4	11.7	9.3	13.2	18.1	9.9	5.6	7.1	10.4	28.1
3	Government Purchases of Goods and Services	8.5	8.0	11.7	13.3	14.1	24.8	59.7	88.6	96.5	82.9	30.5
4	Net Foreign Investment	.8	.2	.1	.9	1.5	1.1	−.2	−2.2	−2.1	−1.4	5.0
5	Equals: **Gross National Product**	104.4	56.0	90.8	91.1	100.6	125.8	159.1	192.5	211.4	213.6	210.7
6	Less: Capital Consumption Allowances	8.6	7.2	7.7	7.8	8.1	9.0	10.2	10.9	12.0	12.5	10.7
7	Equals: **Net National Product**	95.8	48.8	83.0	83.3	92.5	116.8	149.0	181.6	199.4	201.0	200.0
8	Less: Indirect Business Taxes	8.0	8.6	9.4	10.5	10.9	12.1	11.3	11.3	16.8	19.8	19.1
9	Equals: **National Income**	87.8	40.2	73.6	72.8	81.6	104.7	137.7	170.3	182.6	181.2	180.9
10	Less: Social Security Contributions	.2	.3	1.8	2.1	2.3	2.8	3.5	4.6	5.2	6.1	6.0
11	Corporate Income Taxes	1.4	.5	1.5	1.4	2.8	7.6	11.4	14.1	12.9	10.7	9.1
12	Undistributed Corporate Profits	2.9	−4.6	.0	.5	2.2	2.4	4.0	5.4	5.2	3.0	2.4
13	Add: Transfer Payments	2.5	3.3	3.6	4.2	4.4	4.4	4.7	5.1	6.4	9.8	15.6
14	Equals: **Personal Income**	85.8	47.2	73.9	72.9	78.7	96.3	123.5	151.4	165.7	171.2	179.3
15	Less: Personal Taxes	2.6	1.5	2.9	2.4	2.6	3.3	6.0	17.8	18.9	20.9	18.7
16	Equals: **Disposable Income**	83.1	45.7	71.0	70.4	76.1	93.0	117.5	133.6	146.8	150.3	160.6
17	Less: Personal Consumption Expenditures	79.0	46.4	67.3	67.6	71.9	81.9	89.7	100.5	109.8	121.7	147.1
18	Equals: **Personal Saving**	4.2	−.7	3.7	2.9	4.2	11.1	27.8	33.0	36.9	28.7	13.5
19	Real Gross National Product**	181.8	126.6	183.5	189.3	205.8	238.1	266.9	296.7	317.9	314.0	282.5

RELATED STATISTICS

* Details may not add to totals because of rounding
** In 1954 dollars
*** 1947-49 = 100

		1929	1933	1937	1939	1940	1941	1942	1943	1944	1945	1946
20	Consumer Price Index***	73.3	55.3	61.4	59.4	59.9	62.9	69.7	74.0	75.2	76.9	83.4
21	Index of Industrial Production***	59	37	61	58	67	87	106	127	125	107	90
22	Supply of Money (in billions)	26.4	19.8	29.6	36.2	42.2	48.6	62.8	79.6	90.4	102.4	110.0
23	Unemployment (in millions)	1.6	12.8	7.7	9.5	8.1	5.6	2.7	1.0	0.7	1.0	2.3
24	Unemployment as a % of the Civilian Labor Force	3.2	24.9	14.3	17.2	14.6	9.9	4.7	1.9	1.2	1.9	3.9
25	Total Consumer Credit Outstanding (in billions of dollars)	6.4	3.5	6.7	7.2	8.3	9.2	6.0	4.9	5.1	5.7	8.4

	1929	1933	1937	1939	1940	1941	1942	1943	1944	1945	1946